AMERICAN WOMEN'S HISTORY

DORIS WEATHERFORD

PRENTICE HALL GENERAL REFERENCE

New York   London   Toronto   Sydney   Tokyo   Singapore

PRENTICE HALL GENERAL REFERENCE
15 Columbus Circle
New York, New York 10023

PRENTICE HALL is a registered trademark and colophon is a trademark
of Prentice-Hall, Inc.

Library of Congress Cataloging-in-Publication data

Weatherford, Doris.
    American women's history : an A to Z of people, organizations,
issues, and events / Doris Weatherford.
      p.   cm.
    ISBN: 0-671-85009-1: ISBN 0-671-85028-8 (pbk)
    1. Women—United States—History—Encyclopedias.   2. Women—United
States—Social conditions—Encyclopedias.   3. Feminism—United
States—History—Encyclopedias.   I. Title.
HQ1115.W4   1994
305.4'0973—dc20   93-35513
                                                       CIP

Designed by Richard Oriolo

Manufactured in the United States of America

10 9 8 7 6 5 4 3 2 1

First Edition

Introduction

When Lucy Stone gave what would turn out to be the last of a lifetime of speeches at the 1893 Columbian Exposition, she summarized nicely a historical point that, while seemingly obvious, is somehow often ignored: "These things," she said of the achievements women had made, "did not come about by themselves."

All too often history is told as though events have indeed "come about by themselves," as if human progress were predetermined by an omniscient presence or immutable fate. While all topics are subject to this approach, it has been particularly likely in the case of women; until recently, when women's history was taught at all, it was frequently told as if milestones were simply destined—as though, for instance, the times were simply ripe for giving women the vote in 1920. The thousands of lifetimes of dedicated work for this goal are thus minimized, while the political sagacity of the women involved is scarcely acknowledged at all.

Truth lies in the details, and the aim of this work is to provide some of the substance to fill in the background of this larger picture of American history. Nonetheless, in a one-volume work that covers subjects as well as people, many significant women and ideas had to be omitted. It is the framework itself that is important, however, and the intention of this work is to expand horizons in regard to the half of the population that was female.

If, for example, one glances through the "As" in several biographical dictionaries that are still on the shelves of good libraries, there will be an entry for "Mary Anderson." The woman cited, however, is not the Mary Anderson who founded and headed the Woman's Bureau of the Department of Labor for a quarter of a century, but rather a Mary Anderson whose mediocre acting career (1875–1889) seemed noteworthy to editors accustomed to thinking of women as actresses, but not as governmental officials. A tendency to overemphasize the role of women as entertainers leads several biographical dictionaries to include, for example, singers Kate Smith and Bessie Smith while excluding Lillian Smith, author of the racially controversial *Strange Fruit,* as well as Senator Margaret Chase Smith—to say nothing (and they don't) of excluding the fact that Smith's 1960 race was the first general election between two women for the U.S. Senate.

This work thus excludes literally hundreds of entertainers, poets, and others in gender-stereotyped occupations to make room for women whose nontraditional achievements are overlooked. It similarly deemphasizes "firsts," especially in fields (such as sports) that are of little historical importance, and in cases of chance, such as the first woman to win a lottery or the first to be sworn into the Marine Corps. In general, celebrities were excluded to emphasize instead the memorable and deservedly famous—even in cases where that fame is not as well defined as it should be. Often this meant grouping anonymous or nearly anonymous women into such entries as, for example, Pilgrim Women, Frontier Women, and Revolutionary War Women to properly acknowledge their vital contributions to American history. Similarly, there is an emphasis on those who accomplished things for other women, which axiomatically limits the attention given those whose celebrity reflected more personal achievement.

Because this work focuses on the history of American women the only attention to women abroad is in the context of American experience. Likewise, the historical approach reduces the attention given to people and events during the second half of the twentieth century, which is not yet easily defined as history. Whole entries are included on some vital issues and individuals, the space allotted, for instance, to Betty Friedan and Gloria Steinem is significantly shorter than that for Susan Anthony and Elizabeth Cady Stanton. A number of contemporary women who are likely to be part of the future fabric of American history have been left out until their contributions are more nearly complete and their true importance secure. At the same time, a number of living women are included who are omitted from other feminist reference books merely because they are still alive. Oveta Culp Hobby and Daisy Bates are just two examples of living women whose achievements entitle them to a place in history, but who are too often ignored in the present by those who might honor them while the opportunity remains.

A strong effort also was made to place these historical figures and events in the context of their time, with frequent commentary on how an individual was unique or similar to her place and time. The generous use of cross-references to contemporaneous events and individuals will provide a larger framework for understanding the issues involved; the intention is that readers will follow cross-references to other entries and thereby develop a fuller view. Women are listed by the name that was most likely to be publicly known, whether or not this was their name at death. In a time when marriage almost inevitably required a name change for women, many had three or more surnames, and the last one was often irrelevant to their genuine identity. Pseudonyms similarly are used if that was the most recognizable name. The subject of pseudonyms itself merits another entry—and all of this is revelatory in the loss of women to history, for simply placing a woman's name in alphabetical order is far more complex than is the case with men.

Significant points about historical events are woven throughout the biographical entries. Most biographical dictionaries (especially of living people) are really business forms set into sentences; they invariably include the same fill-in-the-blank information for all entries, detailing such items as parents' names, the birth day as well as year, and similar data. The result is that the trivial becomes dangerously equalized with the significant in terms of space, making it difficult for the reader to sort out what the point is. One must exercise creative thoughtfulness and expand these sterile facts to truly understand a life—as, for example, the unstated but probable pregnancy that ended Mary Antin's brilliant beginning and the thirty years that Lucille Ball actually worked in show business before she became an "overnight success."

Yet even if key points lie buried between the lines of such biographies, at least these women have made it into most reference works. There are multitudes of significant women who have been almost routinely excluded seemingly because they were women, not because their achievements were not comparable to those of men who were included. (The entry on Hall of Fame is instructive in this regard.) Moreover, until recently, subjects related to women as a whole seem to have been thoughtlessly turned aside by most editors as unworthy of attention: in a twenty-three-volume set of encyclopedias new enough to include articles on space flight, there are just two entries for woman/women—"Woman's Christian Temperance Union" is separated from "women's diseases" by "wombat."

Indeed, there often seems to be an unconscious "only room for one" theory that is implemented when women are the subject matter. The result is that in cases where the achievements of two or more are quite comparable—as in Margaret Sanger/Mary Dennett and Clara Barton/Mary Ann Bickerdyke—only one is acknowledged. Similarly, the entire suffrage movement is often portrayed as almost wholly Susan Anthony's, though the leadership of a dozen others was fairly comparable to hers.

Even women (even Anthony) sometimes thoughtlessly colluded in this tendency to accept symbolic generalization instead of actuality. In the case of Anna Ella Carroll, for instance, suffragists supported Carroll's effort to get a pension from Congress, arguing that she was a symbol of women's Civil War roles—even though Carroll did not support suffrage and even though hundreds of other women were as deserving of such recognition.

For far too long, such symbolism of one woman as a substitute for all has allowed historians to excuse themselves from undertaking the research to detail individual contributions. Astonishingly capable women such as Lucy Terry Prince were forgotten, and a Molly Pitcher-like idea was accepted as homage to all. With women reduced to one homogeneous lump meriting merely a paragraph or two in most texts, students naturally came to believe that there was only one "Molly Pitcher"—and that she was not quite real.

The goal of this book is to join with others of today's feminist writers in changing that regrettable situation. I have aimed to create a book that is readable and relevant, and I hope that you will enjoy it and learn.

ABBOTT, EDITH (1876–1957) Born in Grand Island, Nebraska, a descendent of New England and QUAKER colonists, Edith Abbott and her sister GRACE ABBOTT were pioneers in the infant fields of sociology and economics.

Edith, the older, began TEACHING immediately after high school graduation, when her family suffered from the Depression of 1893. She worked for a decade while taking college courses in summers and by correspondence before moving to the UNIVERSITY OF CHICAGO in 1903. After earning a Ph.D. in economics in 1905, she studied further at the London School of Economics, where she was influenced by socialists Beatrice and Sidney Webb, as she had been by Thorstein Veblen at Chicago.

Edith Abbott taught for a year at WELLESLEY COLLEGE before returning to her beloved Midwest in 1908, where she joined Grace in living at JANE ADDAMS' Hull House. Her experience there with the settlement problems of the nation's "new immigrants" would provide her with academic material and political issues for the rest of her life.

In 1910, Abbott published *Women In Industry*, a study of the labor conditions of women so comprehensive that it could easily be considered a seminal work rather than a first publication. She followed that with *The Real Jail Problem* (1915), hundreds of articles, and two volumes written with her close friend, SOPHONISBA BRECKINRIDGE, on delinquent children. Abbott's works on immigration are classics still studied by sociologists and historians. *Immigration: Select Documents and Case Records* was published in 1924 and *Historical Aspects of the Immigration Problem: Select Documents* in 1926.

In 1924, Abbott was named dean of Chicago's School of Social Service Administration, which was an outgrowth of the educational program in social work that she and other Hull House women had founded and which they successfully brought under the auspices of the University of Chicago in 1920. The nation's first such graduate school, Abbott developed its curriculum to include the broad-based liberal arts education in medicine, political science, and economics that students needed to work for their ultimate goal of social reform. She and Breckinridge founded the school's *Social Service Review* in 1927, a journal that soon became highly respected and which, again, provided an important historical record.

Not merely an academic, Edith Abbott spoke out on many political controversies, especially on behalf of PROTECTIVE LEGISLATION for women and against immigration quotas. As a result, she was appointed to the Committee on Crime and the Foreign Born of the national Wickersham Commission in the late twenties. During the Great Depression, she worked tirelessly to educate the public on the injustices of local charities based on political patronage; her 1941 book, *Public Assistance*, is a summation of these views.

Abbott retired in 1953 and returned to Nebraska, where she died at age eighty.

ABBOTT, GRACE (1878–1939) After graduating from a Nebraska college, Grace Abbott spent eight years TEACHING in the local high school before taking wings to the wider world. Armed with some graduate work at the University of Nebraska and a summer at the UNIVERSITY OF CHICAGO, she moved to Chicago like her sister EDITH ABBOTT in 1907, where she would be a resident of Hull House for the next nine years.

By the time Grace Abbott earned her master's degree in political science from the University of Chicago in 1909, she was already deeply involved with the Immigrants' Protective League, an early legal aid organization founded by herself and other Hull House women. As the league's director, she opened an office near the city's main railway station and dealt on a daily basis with the myriad problems of the new arrivals.

In 1911, Abbott spent four months in eastern Europe, studying the origins of her clients; earlier that year, she had actively supported them in the great STRIKES in the Chicago GARMENT INDUSTRY. Her testimony before Congress in 1912 on immigration quotas resulted in a position as head of an investigation authorized by the Massachusetts legislature. That experience, in turn, resulted in her first publication, *The Immigrant in Massachusetts* (1915). It was followed two years later with a more comprehensive study, *The Immigrant and the Community*. Like her sister Edith Abbott, Grace Abbott contributed regularly to both scholarly and popular publications.

With the outbreak of WORLD WAR I and the consequent interruption of immigration, she turned her attention to the needs of children and accepted an appointment from her friend, JULIA LATHROP, head of the federal Children's Bureau, as the chief of the bureau's child labor division. Her carefully developed systems to enforce Congress' 1916 prohibitions on child labor came to a halt, however, when the Supreme Court declared the act unconstitutional in 1918. For the rest of her life, Abbott would work for a constitutional amendment to overturn that decision.

Returning to Chicago in 1919, she became director of the new Illinois State Immigrants' Commission, but that effort, too, was soon thwarted by an unsympathetic governor, and by 1921, Abbott was back in Washington, where she would serve as head of the Children's Bureau for the next thirteen years. Her chief achievement in this role was the development of administrative systems for the SHEPPARD-TOWNER ACT, the nation's first serious attempt at a social welfare program to alleviate infant mortality and maternal death. With Abbott's leadership, approximately three thousand prenatal/pediatric clinics were established, providing a valuable model for New Deal programs that were to follow in the next decade.

In addition to her noted work on behalf of immigrants and children, Abbott supported women's suffrage and was part of the effort that won the vote for Illinois women in 1913. Never bothered by charges of "communism" and other attacks, she campaigned actively for Theodore Roosevelt before she had the right to vote and attended the pacifist INTERNATIONAL CONGRESS OF WOMEN during World War I. In the twenties, she served as president of the National Conference of Social Work, and, despite U.S. failure to join the League of Nations, she was for more than a decade an unofficial member of the League's Advisory Committee on Traffic in Women and Children.

Abbott left the Children's Bureau in 1934 to return to Chicago, where she taught at her sister Edith's University of Chicago social work school, but the Roosevelt administration nonetheless continued to find uses for her talents. As a member of the Council on Economic Security (1934–35), she helped plan the administration of Social Security, and follow-

ing that, she was appointed a delegate to the International Labor Organization (1935–37). During this time she also edited the *Social Service Review* and worked on her two-volume study, *The Child and the State* (1938).

Still very active despite years of failing health, Grace Abbott died of acute anemia at age sixty. Her ashes were buried at Grand Island, Nebraska.

ABOLITION AND ABOLITIONISTS MOVEMENT The nineteenth-century effort to end slavery in America is generally credited with also beginning the women's movement in this country. The initial event usually cited is a world conference on slavery held in London in 1840, when American women attending were not allowed to be seated because of their gender. The irony of working on behalf of civil rights for black men that they themselves lacked did not escape these women, but for the next three decades, most saw the end of slavery as the greater goal.

Their work for abolition of slavery, however, provided women with the organizational skill, experience in PUBLIC SPEAKING, and political bravery that was essential when they set about seeking the vote for themselves. Even after the CIVIL WAR began, abolitionists were reviled by much of the northern public who fought the war for the Union and not to end slavery. Abolitionist women, along with their men, learned to live with public abuse and threats from the 1830s through the 1860s. Many showed great courage and ingenuity in hiding runaway slaves and in coping with riots that resulted from abolitionists' speeches.

Among the women pioneers of the abolitionist movement who were involved by the 1830s were LYDIA MARIA CHILD, MARIA WESTON CHAPMAN, PRUDENCE CRANDELL, ABBY KELLY FOSTER, ANGELINA and SARAH GRIMKE, and LUCRETIA MOTT. They would be joined by thousands of other sympathetic women by the time slavery was officially abolished in 1865.

ABORTION In medical terminology, "abortion" refers to any termination of pregnancy before the fetus is capable of life on its own, with "spontaneous abortion" used as the term for what the public generally calls "miscarriage" and "induced abortion" for the deliberate act.

Women, with and without the aid and/or coercion of men, have terminated their pregnancies since ancient times. This was accepted as an understandably private matter in some cultures, but others have proscribed it. Motivations for such bans include the desire of most societies for larger populations and the interest of male patriarchs in preventing uncontrolled sexuality among the female members of their group, as well as concern for maternal health.

Nonetheless, women historically have used a number of methods to rid themselves of unwanted pregnancies, including violent exercise and deliberate falls; drinking or eating various herbal potions; wrapping themselves tightly in abdominal tourniquets designed to expel the fetus; and inserting any number of foreign objects into the cervix that might induce labor. Knitting needles and wire coat hangers have become the symbolic representatives of such vaginal intrusions, but many other items and purgatives, including turpentine, lye, and castor oil have been used since ancient times. Need-

This 1856 drawing of a slave auction was published in London, and is illustrative of international networks between abolitionists. Many of the women who provided the leadership of the American women's rights movement learned their organizational skills in, and drew their motivation from, abolitionist activity. LIBRARY OF CONGRESS.

less to say, millions of women have died from the resulting infections.

English common law tolerated abortion in the early stages of pregnancy, and in the early years of the United States, little law spoke to the subject. The evidence is that from the colonial era through the immigrant era of the late nineteenth century, many women aborted themselves without feeling that they had done a moral or legal wrong. It was only with the growth of organized medicine that state laws against abortion began to be adopted, usually because of lobbying by physicians. While their arguments were made in terms of protecting patients, it was also true that restrictive legislation seriously disrupted the business of midwives who also worked as abortionists.

The right to medically safe abortions slowly became central to the modern women's movement, as feminists came to understand that there could be no true freedom or equality without establishing a woman's right to control her own body. Reformists' measures introduced in state legislatures during the 1950s and 1960s reflected essential political compromise by focusing on the cause of unwanted pregnancies (rape and incest) and the possibility of maternal mortality (extreme age or youth, physical disability, and, most controversial, mental health). Hospital committees usually composed of male doctors decided whether or not to grant a petitioning woman the opportunity to abort. This procedure naturally was likely to limit safe abortions primarily to wealthy women, who, even if refused local medical care, could go to clinics abroad.

Meanwhile, twentieth-century medicine had developed several methods of safe abortion, including the use of labor-inducing vaginal suppositories, the saline method of injecting a salt solution into the uterus via the abdomen, as well as the surgical technique of dilation of the cervix followed by scraping of the uterus known as D&C (dilation and curettage). Most abortion clinics today have come to rely on the suction hose method of removing the contents of the uterus.

Legal permission to use these medical advances finally became genuine when the Supreme Court ruled in *ROE VS. WADE* on January 22, 1973, that state laws prohibiting abortion were an unconstitutional invasion of privacy. Several later decisions reinforced the court's commitment to this principle, with *Planned Parenthood vs. Danforth* in 1976 striking down a Missouri law that required the consent of a woman's husband for an abortion. That principle was extended to minors in *Bellotti vs. Baird* (1979), which struck down Massachusetts' parental consent requirement.

In the 1980s, however, with the election of conservative Republican presidents, the Court began to show more ambivalence on the question of abortion. In *Harris vs. McRae* (1980) the Court upheld a ban on using Medicaid funds to pay for them, and in the last year of that decade, it issued its dramatic *Webster vs. Reproductive Health Services* ruling that made explicit the rights that states implicitly had since *Roe vs. Wade* to regulate abortion as all public health is regulated. At the same time, the Court issued other, positive decisions, including a 1983 nullification of an Akron, Ohio city ordinance that required hospitalization for first trimester abortions and the striking down of a Pennsylvania law similarly designed to discourage abortions in *Thornburgh vs. American College of Obstetricians and Gynecologists* (1986).

The result was a confused mixture of attitudes in the public, with neither side of the issue feeling secure in the protection of such an ambivalent, divided, and politicized judiciary. The Court, with more Reagan appointees, continued to chip away at the principles established in the 1970s as the 1990s began. In *Rust vs. Sullivan* (1991), the Court not only attacked the right of privacy established by *Roe vs. Wade*, but also assailed the fundamentals of free speech by ruling that health professionals in clinics receiving government funds could not answer patients' questions on abortion except to disapprove. The only woman on the Court, SANDRA DAY O'CONNOR, dissented from the 5-4 ruling.

Beyond the free speech and privacy issues, the decision also threatened to erode the principle of separation of church and state, for the continued activism of the Catholic church against liberalized abortion policies is demonstrated in the above cases attempting to overturn *Roe vs. Wade:* Missouri, Massachusetts, and Pennsylvania are all examples of areas where state legislatures responded to large Catholic populations. In 1991, Louisiana Catholics were responsible for the harshest of state laws, one that threatened physicians with sentences of ten years at hard labor for performing abortions. The Mormon Church, too, lobbied for restrictive legislation in Utah.

In practice, however, women continued to seek and obtain abortions, and clinics, often run by women, were established even in small cities throughout the United States during the seventies and eighties. Though abortion continues to be a controversial issue at all political levels, the 1973 Supreme Court decision has stood for two decades, during which time millions of women have availed themselves of the opportunity to safely end unwanted pregnancies. They have come to take this right as fundamental to their personal freedom.

ABZUG, BELLA (1920–   )

A New Yorker all her life, Bella Savitsky was born and educated there. She graduated from Hunter College in 1942 and studied during WORLD WAR II at Columbia University Law School, graduating the year the war ended. She married Martin Abzug soon after graduation, was admitted to the bar two years later, and successfully practiced law during the fifties and sixties. Specializing in labor and civil rights law, much of her work was *pro bono* defense of victims of this reactionary era.

She was a founder of Women's Strike for Peace in 1961 and became active in the anti-Vietnam War movement later in that decade. In 1970, Abzug unseated a congressional incumbent in the Democratic primary and went on to win the general election. On her first day in Congress, she defied tradition by rising to offer a resolution calling for immediate withdrawal of American troops from Southeast Asia. She published a book detailing her first days in government, *Bella! Ms. Abzug Goes to Washington*, in 1972.

The object of a great deal of media attention, both negative and positive, Abzug left her congressional seat after three terms to run for the Senate in 1976. She was defeated, and subsequently also lost elections for mayor and Congress. President Jimmy Carter appointed her to co-chair his National Advisory Committee on Women, but she served only about a year before he asked for her resignation; once again, Abzug's famously abrasive style was questioned as counterproductive. In 1982, New York Democratic party leaders similarly refused to seat her as a delegate to the national midterm conference

in Philadelphia, although a few years later, she was again serving on the Democratic National Committee.

During the 1980s, Abzug practiced law, wrote, taught, and worked as a television commentator. Always recognized as a prime leader in the women's movement, few national gatherings were held without her fiery speeches, and her famous hat was seen at the head of prochoice marches throughout the eighties. In 1991, Abzug co-chaired the Women's Environmental & Development Organization and was a featured speaker at the World Women's Congress for a Healthy Planet. Abzug's papers are on deposit at the Butler Library of Columbia University.

ACTING AND ACTRESSES

Few historical examples so clearly spell out the limitations of women's lives as the fact that from the beginnings of Greek drama through the Shakespearean plays, the roles of women, which playwrights found essential to good theater, were nonetheless acted by men.

Women began acting on English stages in the mid-1600s; the term "actress," as opposed to "actor," came into use around 1700. For most of the next two centuries, however, it was commonly assumed that such women were little better than PROSTITUTES, with Americans holding this view even longer than Europeans.

After the American Civil War, when the "legitimate theater" had established itself in America and begun to distinguish itself from vaudeville, the status of women in acting also began to rise. Many women listed in turn-of-the-century compilations of the "famous" were stage actresses whose names are unknown today, but who clearly were able to use this profession to establish independent lives and fortunes.

Although vaudeville provided an entree for American women such as Lillian Russell and the more famous foreigners Sarah Bernhardt and Lily Langtry, it was the development of the movie industry that insured monetary opportunity for actresses, as exemplified by MAE WEST, who was the first American woman to earn a million dollars for her work.

While feminists have insisted on the elimination of feminine suffixes on words such as "authoress," "poetess," etc., the usage of "actress" remains acceptable to many because acting roles are almost always defined by gender. "Actor," however, is increasingly used to refer to both men and women.

ADAMS, ABIGAIL SMITH (1744–1818)

A First Lady who deserves to be remembered in her own right, Abigail Adams is famous primarily for the voluminous correspondence she carried on throughout her life, not only with her husband John, but also with her friend MERCY OTIS WARREN and others of her contemporaries, including Thomas Jefferson. The warm, unpretentious language of her letters provides wonderful reading even today, giving us an understanding of early American life from its petty domestic details to its great philosophical innovations.

Abigail Smith was born in Weymouth, Massachusetts; both of her parents came from distinguished New England families. The fact that her father was a Congregational minister meant that she grew up in a household accustomed to classical literature, but though she read widely in English and French, Abigail was given no formal schooling. In later life, she commented frequently on the unfair treatment of girls in education, for she doubtlessly would have attended a university had she been male.

Instead, she met John Adams, a former schoolteacher and rising lawyer, when she was but fourteen and married him at nineteen. Their courtship correspondence shows her to have been a spirited and independent young woman, with enough sexual awareness to belie the stereotypes of Puritan myth. The result was that she bore five children in seven years; like many women of her era, there almost was no time during her twenties when she was not pregnant or nursing or both. Also like many mothers of her era, she suffered the death of her children, losing a daughter at age two and a daughter and son as adults.

When their youngest child was only two, John began the travels that would take him from home during most of the children's growing-up years. His work in the Continental Congresses meant that soon Abigail had the additional disruption of war; like other REVOLUTIONARY WAR WOMEN, she saw battles nearby as she educated her children and managed the family properties. Living alone much of the time, she soon developed a reputation as a sound businesswoman, buying land and animals, and managing tenants and employees. For the rest of her life, Abigail Adams was acknowledged by John and others as the partner of their marriage who provided the family income. Even when they lived abroad, it was she who wrote letters back to Massachusetts, detailing the decisions necessary for farms and dairies. The Adamses grew modestly prosperous, unlike Jefferson and others of the nation's founders who were financially ruined by their time in government.

Despite the personal difficulties it meant for her, Abigail Adams was at least as strong a supporter of the American Revolution as John. Moreover, her devotion to liberty probably exceeded his in regard to race. An early opponent of slavery, Abigail Adams also defended her right to teach a black servant to read. In letters to John, she tried to see that the new government being constituted would begin the abolition of slavery and, of course, she is noted by feminists today for her famous injunction to Congress at that time to "Remember the Ladies."

The Adamses spent five years together in Europe after the Revolution while John held several diplomatic assignments. Though Abigail tolerated prerevolutionary France better than might be expected, she preferred the time spent in England and was frankly glad to return home in 1788. When John was elected vice-president under the new Constitution the following year, she alternated her time between her Massachusetts business obligations and the capital cities of Philadelphia, New York, and finally, Washington. While she was the first First Lady to occupy the White House, the few months she spent there between November, 1800 and the end of John's term in March, 1801 were noted only for the cold and damp of the still unfinished mansion.

The remaining years of her life were spent in retirement in Massachusetts, but the mail still flowed from Abigail Adams' pen. She took a special interest in the rising political career of her son John Quincy, who would become president less than a decade after her death.

Abigail Adams died at age seventy-four; John, though nine years older than she, lived another eight years. Buried together at the First Church of Quincy, Massachusetts, theirs

Jane Addams in 1910, when she received the first honorary degree Yale University gave to a woman. Addams went on to win the Nobel Peace Prize in 1931. LIBRARY OF CONGRESS.

was an uncommon marriage of intellectual equals, as witnessed by the many volumes of their correspondence filled with mutual love and respect.

ADAMS, MAUDE (1872–1953)

Born as Maude Kiskadden to an acting family, she took her mother's maiden name and became a turn-of-the-century stage star. Several plays were written specifically for her, including *Peter Pan*, which she performed over fifteen hundred times. It was a highly successful vehicle for her wistfully charming face, as was Shakespeare's "Juliet."

Retiring from the stage at the end of WORLD WAR I, Adams returned twenty years later during the Depression to act in more mature classical roles. She taught drama into her seventies, and is considered a first lady of the American theatre.

ADDAMS, JANE (1860–1935)

Even though a New York settlement house was built independently of her Chicago Hull House, Jane Addams is lovingly remembered in almost every high school history book as the founder of the SETTLEMENT HOUSE MOVEMENT in the U.S. At the same time, what may instead be her highest achievement—America's first woman to win the Nobel Peace Prize—usually comes late in standard biographies, if at all. Such emphasis on selfless ministrations to the poor reflects traditional portrayals of womanhood, but Addams' political involvement was controversial in her lifetime and her Nobel Peace Prize remains today an achievement shared with few men.

Like others of the socially conscious women of her era, Jane Addams was descended from QUAKER colonists who had migrated to pre-Civil War Illinois. After her mother's death when she was two, Jane grew up devoted to her father and his ABOLITIONIST and public service views. Though she wanted to attend the new SMITH COLLEGE in Massachusetts, she gave in to his wishes and went to the nearby Rockford Female SEMINARY, graduating at the head of her class in 1882.

Student leadership had come easily to her, but the next decade would see young Addams foundering and depressed. Her father's death in 1881 was part of the cause, compounded by her unhappiness to discover, after a year at WOMAN'S MEDICAL COLLEGE OF PENNSYLVANIA, that she was not suited to what she thought had been her goal of becoming a physician. After recovering from spinal surgery, Addams spent a year touring Europe with her stepmother, followed by two years in Baltimore, spent primarily resisting her stepmother's entreaties that Jane marry her son.

Though she had attended some classes at JOHNS HOPKINS UNIVERSITY and done a little charity work in Baltimore, Addams was still suffering from ennui when she returned to Europe with a Rockford friend, Ellen Gates Starr, in 1887. A Madrid bullfight proved an epiphany; the long-standing guilt and boredom of her overprivileged life came spilling out in conversation with Starr. When she discovered that Starr also was interested in doing something more worthwhile, the two of them returned to London to investigate Toynbee Hall, an East End settlement begun three years before by Oxford men.

Early in 1889, Addams and Starr opened a similar social effort in an abandoned Chicago mansion that had once been the country home of the Hull family. By the late nineteenth century, the neighborhood was a teeming center of immigration from eastern Europe and the Mediterranean—poor people adrift in urban America who soon availed themselves of the aid offered by these educated young ladies and their friends.

Within a few years, Hull House was offering medical services, child care, and legal aid, as well as dozens of clubs and classes to teach English, vocational skills, music, and drama. Starr was the leader in the cultural activities, organizing even Greek drama played by Greeks, while Addams worked in the more pragmatic areas. They were soon joined by other activist women and men, including EDITH and GRACE ABBOTT, EMILY BALCH, SOPHONISBA BRECKINRIDGE, ALICE HAMILTON, FLORENCE KELLY, and JULIA LATHROP, all of whom became pioneers in the field of social work.

By 1893, when a serious depression hit the economy, Hull House was offering services to over two thousand people a week. As Addam's personal fortune could not meet the needs, she developed fund-raising skills that were necessarily also political skills, becoming a personality capable of relating to both the poorest of the urban poor and the wealthiest of Chicago's industrial powers. At the same time, Hull House's charitable efforts quite naturally developed into political ones aimed at the causes of poverty. Its women pressured Illinois into adoption of a factory inspection law and the nation's first juvenile justice system; they worked also for legislation to protect immigrants from exploitation, limit the hours of working women, mandate schooling for children, recognize labor unions, and provide for industrial safety.

All of this, of course, led them to involve themselves in the right to vote for women. Addams worked for Chicago municipal suffrage in 1907 and became first vice-president of the NATIONAL AMERICAN WOMAN SUFFRAGE ASSOCIATION in 1911; she campaigned nationwide for Theodore Roosevelt and the Progressive Party in 1912.

Her activism on behalf of women was not nearly as controversial as that on behalf of economic reform. When Chicago's harsh working conditions turned into the Haymarket Riot and other confrontations, Addams found that her pleas for worker understanding and the right of free speech for socialists resulted in both personal attacks on herself and loss of donor support for Hull House. Nonetheless, with regular lecturing and article-writing, she earned money for Hull House as well as international acclaim. Her first book was published in 1902 and others followed almost biannually. All were well received, but her 1910 summation, *Twenty Years at Hull House*, became a phenomenon of publishing sales and a classic of autobiography.

The optimism expressed in this book seemed justified by the electoral triumph of the Progressive party two years later, but soon the world and then the nation were at war. Progressive goals were shelved; immigration, with its diversification of cultures and philosophies that Addams so admired, came to a halt. She responded by organizing the WOMAN'S PEACE PARTY in 1915, becoming head of both it and the INTERNATIONAL CONGRESS OF WOMEN, which met at The Hague a few months later and made serious diplomatic attempts to stop what would become known as the Great War, and later, WORLD WAR I.

When these efforts proved fruitless and the United States entered the war in 1917, criticism of Addams rose. Among other vilification, she was expelled from the DAUGHTERS OF THE AMERICAN REVOLUTION, but her efforts for pacifist principles continued in the postwar era. Elected as the first president of the WOMEN'S INTERNATIONAL LEAGUE FOR PEACE AND FREEDOM in 1919, she continued in this position until her death. At the same time that she worked for peace, she truly worked for freedom, serving as a founder and officer of the American Civil Liberties Union. With free speech frequently repressed during both the war and the postwar eras, this position earned her even more criticism than her pacifism.

Nonetheless, Hull House's success continued. A dozen buildings were added to the original, and Addams continued to reside there when not abroad. Renewed and more serious economic depression in the thirties justified many of her earlier advocacies, and she lived to see those ideas that were not adopted during the Progressive Era become part of Franklin Roosevelt's New Deal. Honors were heaped upon her as she aged, including the Nobel Prize in 1931.

Her health began to fail that same year, though she stayed active almost until her death four years later. When she died at seventy-four, her funeral was held at Hull House; thousands of people paid their last respects before she was buried at her family home of Cedarville, Illinois.

ADKINS VS. CHILDREN'S HOSPITAL (1923)

A setback for women, the Supreme Court, by a five to three vote, ruled unconstitutional a 1918 act that established a minimum wage for women. Congress had set this timid precedent in its role as the governing power of the District of Columbia, and for five brief years Washington women and children had a theoretical right to a floor beneath which their wages could not fall. Both decisions were reflective of their times: Congress passed the act during the last year of WORLD WAR I, a time when women were proving themselves an essential part of the economy; the Court struck it down in the postwar twenties, a time of political and economic repression.

With this decision, the Court nullified minimum wage laws throughout the country, a factor that contributed to the economic collapse of the next decade. Supposedly liberal Justice Oliver Wendell Holmes—who earlier had argued that the Court was bound to give legislative acts the benefit of the doubt—nonetheless voted against this legislation for women. His statement that "the criterion of constitutionality is not whether we view the law to be for the public good" placed him among nineteenth century strict constructionists who favored law over justice.

The Court's majority even had the temerity to use women's recent enfranchisement as voters to argue that women were no longer entitled to any PROTECTIVE LEGISLATION, thus overturning a principle that had been established by *Muller vs. Oregon* in the Progressive Era. A classic cartoon illustrated the case's meaning, picturing a Supreme Court Justice handing his opinion to a woman and saying, "This decision affirms your constitutional right to starve."

AGASSIZ, ELIZABETH CARY (1822–1907)

The daughter of an educated Boston family, Elizabeth Cary married Swiss natural scientist Louis Agassiz in 1850 and cared for his three children. Soon she was also sharing his interest in nature, and together they built an island laboratory. She proved her ability with two well received publications, *Acetaea: A First Lesson in Natural History* (1859) and *Seaside Studies in Natural History* (1866). During the years of writing the books, Agassiz also founded and ran a school for girls in Cambridge.

After the Civil War, she and her husband set out on a long and difficult South American expedition, the results of which she published as *A Journey to Brazil* (1867). The death of Louis Agassiz five years later did not end her career; she published a memoir of him in 1885, but also spent the 1870s and 1880s pursuing her interest in providing educational opportunity for young women. Agassiz led the efforts to make the inadequate "Harvard Annex" into a true women's college. By serving as president of RADCLIFFE COLLEGE from 1882 to 1903, she insured the future of the institution during the first crucial decades of its existence.

ALCOTT, LOUISA MAY (1832–1888)

The fact that Louisa May Alcott was born in Germantown, Pennsylvania is all but irrelevant to a life grounded in Massachusetts. Except for two European tours, a few months in Washington, and occasional business trips to New York, Louisa May Alcott lived her entire life in the Boston area, which also provided the setting for most of her fiction.

Like many other famous women, young Louisa May was strongly influenced by her father; his presence affected her to the last moment of her life, when she died on the day of his funeral. Amos Bronson Alcott had a complex reputation among his contemporaries: while he was welcomed as an associate of America's greatest early philosophers (Emerson and the Transcendentalists), he was also seen as a consummate ne'er-do-well whose idealism and naivete led his family into one financial disaster after another. The second of his four daughters, Louisa soon came to see the family's financial needs as her own.

Doubtless this sense of responsibility was conveyed to her by her mother, Abigail (Abba), who, although a member of the old Bostonian May family, not only lived a married life of genteel poverty but also actually worked outside the home when the need was desperate. Though this would be seen by her social group as an almost unforgivable failure on the part of her husband, Abba Alcott not only did not seem to resent Bronson, but held him up to her daughters as a paragon of good.

While his radical ideas brought few paying students to the schools Bronson Alcott established, this progressive education (along with tutoring from family friend Henry Thoreau) played a significant role in developing Louisa May's writing talents. She began publishing in 1851 when just nineteen and by the end of her life had written almost three hundred works. Since many were issued under PSEUDONYMS, it is only recently that she has been credited with authorship that was previously assumed to be male.

Her first decade of work consisted of lurid short stories, adventurous plays, sentimental poems, and novelettes clearly written for the money that they would bring. Many of her sensationalist tales were distinctly masculine—aimed at an audience of boys, reflective of CIVIL WAR violence, and signed with initials that presumed a male author. Yet all of this artifice and potboiling was not enough, as during this time young Alcott also worked as a GOVERNESS, seamstress, schoolmarm, and even DOMESTIC SERVANT to help support her family. Much of this employment served as material for later writing, especially her experience as a companion on a European trip in 1865.

Though her first book, *Flower Fables*, came out in 1854, another decade passed before she published one that was deemed "successful." *Hospital Sketches* (1863), was based on Alcott's experience as a nurse in Washington during the Civil War, an adventure cut short when she succumbed to typhoid fever and nearly died. It was followed by a novel, *Moods*, in 1864. The cool reception her novel received must have been a great disappointment to the author, for during the years she ground out the potboilers, she also worked seriously on *Moods*, and yet had difficulty finding a publisher for it (though her father worked hard as its agent).

In 1867, she took her only job as an editor, supervising the publication of a girls' magazine called *Merry Museum*. Meanwhile, her publisher friend Thomas Niles renewed his requests that she write a book-length work for girls, and Alcott reluctantly began what would become her greatest achievement, unequaled by anything she would write later. *Little Women*, published in two parts in 1868 and 1869, became America's first classic of juvenile literature.

Little Women is not the denigration of women that its title may suggest to modern feminists; rather its characters, secure in themselves, live in a world almost devoid of male presence. Modeled on Bunyan's *Pilgrim's Progress* and clearly autobiographical, Alcott's women portray a struggle for virtues that may sound quaintly nineteenth century, but which are nonetheless timeless constants of personal growth. Set in the middle-class North of the Civil War, it gives an intimate picture of domestic life that readers for more than a century have found captivating.

Even though its publishers expected that there was a market for this type of book, both they and Alcott were astonished by *Little Women*'s immediate and continued popularity.

Booksellers found it hard to get enough copies to meet the demand, a phenomenon plainly showing that the reading interests of young women had been ignored. For Alcott, this might have meant financial freedom, but her sense of duty again overwhelmed her, and she responded to appeals by readers for more with almost annual publications for the next twenty years. The best are *An Old Fashioned Girl* (1870), *Little Men* (1871), *Eight Cousins* (1875), *Rose in Bloom* (1876), and *Jo's Boys* (1886). She also wrote two novels aimed at adults: *Work* (1873), the experience of a young woman forced to earn a living in the harsh employment world of the nineteenth century, and the less successful *A Modern Mephistopheles* (1877).

Alcott spent these years summering in Concord and did most of her writing in Boston during the winters. She frequented the New England Woman's Club there and lent her name to the SUFFRAGE MOVEMENT. Indeed, just three years before she died, Alcott sent a letter to the annual convention of the AMERICAN WOMAN SUFFRAGE ASSOCIATION repudiating those who said she opposed suffrage. "I should be a traitor to all I most love," she wrote, "if I did not covet a place among those who are giving their lives to the emancipation of the white slaves of America."

She had that coveted place and much other acclaim in her lifetime, but it brought her little joy. Alcott suffered Concord's tourists poorly and seemed to view her readers as an incessantly demanding audience who failed to grasp the great moral principles she intended to convey. She never outgrew the dominance of her family and her own sense of duty; she spent her professionally successful adulthood in the same way that she had spent her youth, caring for her family.

Abba Alcott died in 1873; seven years later, at age forty-eight, "Aunt Louy" adopted the infant child of her youngest sister Abbie, who died just a year after she married. The 1880s were thus devoted to tending both the young and the old, as Bronson Alcott lingered into incoherent senility. Louisa's own health declined, meanwhile, but she pressured herself into finishing *Jo's Boys* while seeking relief for her ailments from various healers, including MARY BAKER EDDY and Dr. Rhoda Lawrence. Though just fifty-five when she died, her last years were so stressful that she seemed much older. She was buried only a few days after her father, with him and her mother in Concord.

ALCOTT, ROSALIND W. (1885–1990)

A turn-of-the-century secretary at the *Wall Street Journal*, Alcott was a millionaire when she died at 105.

Though hired for an eight-dollar-a-week secretarial position, she developed a masculine telephone voice and signed her letters with initials so that her contacts would assume she was male. She invested her savings with savvy, but when she left the newspaper for banking, Alcott still had to enter via the secretarial route. By the 1920s, however, she was a full partner and personally wealthy. Her financial acumen was again demonstrated when she sold her stock portfolio a month prior to the great 1929 crash.

She married twice, but had no children. Alcott moved to Los Angeles in 1940, continued to invest wisely, and was a prominent civic donor until her death fifty years later.

ALDEN, PRISCILLA MULLINS (1602?–prior to 1687?)

Immortalized by Longfellow's sentimental poem, Priscilla Alden has become part of American folklore. Instead of being vaguely known only as the object of a romantic contest between two men, however, she should be remembered for her strength as a PILGRIM WOMAN.

Priscilla Mullins (or perhaps Molines or Mollins) emigrated from England on the *Mayflower* with her father, mother, brother, and a servant; she was the only member of this family to survive the terrible first winter of America's Pilgrims. Her father's will left her guardianship to Massachusetts Governor John Carver, but he, too, soon died.

Sometime between 1621 and 1623, when Priscilla was in her late teens or early twenties, she married John Alden. Their wedding probably was Plymouth's first between two young people; the colony's very first wedding had been held under much more somber conditions. Susanna White wed Edward Winslow in May, 1621, just eleven weeks after she had been WIDOWED in the great sickness of the first winter. She had delivered the first child born in the new land and needed a provider for her children; he too had lost his spouse only weeks before.

The Mullins/Alden wedding was a contrastingly happy occasion. It was embellished beyond any historical evidence by Longfellow's poem, "The Courtship of Miles Standish," which was written more than two hundred years later. Based on a descendent's report of family legend, the poem depicts Standish sending his subordinate, John Alden, to arrange marriage between himself and Priscilla Mullins; she, instead, rejects Captain Standish for the poorer, younger Alden, urging him to speak for himself. The "moral lesson" taught to generations of schoolchildren is spoken by Priscilla: "You must do it yourself, you must not leave it to others!"

Lost in the traditional interpretation, however, is a second possible view of the story, even if apocryphal: that Priscilla Mullins exemplified a new type of woman who thought for herself, though a young orphan. She apparently also was independent enough to reject the wealthy and powerful Standish for a more companionate husband, for Alden was her social inferior. The devout congregation of the *Mayflower* had picked him up when they departed from Southampton only because the law required that they have a cooper on board, and young Alden had this skill.

Most importantly, nowhere in this folklore is the genuine historical situation spelled out: Priscilla Mullins was one of just a handful of women to survive the trials of that first American winter. Fourteen of the eighteen mothers who arrived on the *Mayflower* died within a few months of landing, and she should be remembered as a paragon of strength.

After about a decade at Plymouth, she and John moved north to settle the town of Duxbury. Priscilla Mullins Alden bore at least eleven children before her obscure death.

ALLEN, AGNES ROGERS (1894–1986)

A VASSAR graduate and successful author, Allen was also a founding editor of Reader's Digest Condensed Books, where she worked from 1947 to retirement in the late 1960s. She followed precedents laid down there by LILA BELL ACHESON WALLACE, who, with her husband, founded *Reader's Digest* magazine in 1922.

Some of Allen's writing focused on women, including

Women Are Here to Stay (1949). She married Fredrick Lewis Allen in 1932 and co-authored several social histories with him. After his death, she worked to finance a room in the New York Public Library, named for him, which is for the use of writers. She died at her home in Bergenfield, New Jersey at age ninety-two.

ALLEN, FLORENCE ELLINWOOD (1884–1966) The holder of several "firsts" in the legal field, Florence Allen was another of the successful American women who were descended from New England colonists; Ethan Allen was among her ancestors.

Born in Salt Lake City when the West was still a frontier, Allen's parents were Utah pioneers. She was educated there and "back East" in Ohio, where her grandparents had been pioneers. Also like many other successful women, Allen had a close relationship with her father, an unusual man who combined a life of classical scholarship with service in Congress. Her mother, Corinne Tuckerman Allen, was the first student admitted to SMITH COLLEGE.

After graduating in 1904 from Western Reserve University's College for Women, she studied music in Berlin. When hopes of a concert career were negated by an injury, she wrote music criticism for the *Cleveland Plain Dealer* for three years while also working on a master's degree in political science. She then went to New York, lived at the Henry Street SETTLEMENT HOUSE, and worked for the Immigrants Protective League. After rejection by several law schools, she was able to earn her degree from New York University and passed the Ohio bar in 1914.

Then thirty years old, Allen used her position as a lawyer on behalf of the women's SUFFRAGE MOVEMENT, and that activism paid off personally. In 1919, before women had the vote, she was appointed assistant prosecutor of Cuyahoga County (Cleveland), Ohio. The next year, in the first election in which American women could vote, she was elected to a local judgeship.

With incredible confidence in herself and the voters, she ran in the very next election (1922) for the state supreme court. She filed by petition in the late summer after the primaries were over and credited women with her amazing success, saying: "The women were my organization. They simply got in touch with the women in every county who had been active in the suffrage movement. They handled my publicity, wrote letters to the newspapers, arranged my meetings, and distributed my very meager campaign literature. We had little money . . . and won by a 350,000 vote majority."

Reelected by a wide margin in 1928, she was the first woman in the world to sit on a court of last resort. Another "first" was established in 1934 when Franklin Roosevelt appointed Allen to the United States Court of Appeals, which is just beneath the Supreme Court. She stayed there until retirement in 1959, serving also as chief justice.

She published two books on law before retiring, as well as her memoirs, *To Do Justly*, in 1965. Judge Allen died at age eighty-two in Waite Hill, Ohio.

ALLEN, GRACIE (1895–1964) Born into a San Francisco show business family, Gracie Allen first performed at age five. Her formal education was scant, and by fourteen, she was doing vaudeville comedy and dance with her sisters. She worked alone after each of her three sisters left show business, at one point doing a strenuous six acts daily before she, too, gave up and entered secretarial school in New York.

Then she met a minor comic, George Burns (who had changed his name from Nathan Birnbaum), and began doing his straight lines. They soon realized, however, that she got more laughter than he even when she wasn't supposed to be funny and switched their roles. Ever after, Burns praised Allen as the natural talent of the two, crediting her for his success after many dismal years of effort.

His writing and her delivery proved a magic combination, and their vaudeville bookings became secure. They married early in 1926 before beginning a six-year contract touring the U.S. and Europe, where they were received with great enthusiasm. Their first radio performance was in 1930, and two years later, they signed with CBS for their own show, which was an instant hit. Gracie made America laugh during the Great Depression, and by its end, they had a regular audience of 45 million and were earning nine thousand dollars a week.

Despite this fantastic popularity and despite the fact that the 1930s were a golden era for women in film, Gracie Allen's movie roles were insignificant. But when television was introduced after World War II, Burns and Allen greeted their former radio audience in this new format, meeting with tremendous success from the first 1950 show. Live television was very demanding, however, and the strain began to show in the migraine headaches that Gracie Allen developed.

She retired in 1958, finally able to give up the pretense of being a dizzy dame. Although she did the final editing of her scripts and was quick to strike offensive lines, her brainless character was a difficult role for a mature, successful woman. Moreover, despite her obvious talent, Allen always claimed that she never enjoyed show business.

She focused retirement on her two adopted children and her grandchildren, but had less than a decade to enjoy before dying in Los Angeles of a heart attack. George Burns has spent his life since testifying to the undying goodness and ability of Gracie Allen; he published books on her in 1955 and 1988.

ALTRUSA CLUBS Although altruism is a virtue long associated with women, the attitudes that led to the 1917 founding of these women's clubs were nonetheless new in their time. As women became involved in support organizations for WORLD WAR I, which was then at its height, and as they saw their enfranchisement as voters in an increasing number of states, they also began to suspect that women's efforts could be effective in dealing with local civic and social welfare problems previously left to male governments and organizations.

Altrusa was thus one of many such groups that developed as part of the CLUB MOVEMENT of the late nineteenth and early twentieth centuries. These groups raised funds to build hospitals, parks and playgrounds, libraries, and all manner of other civic amenities previously ignored. Today Altrusa continues to design and implement community service projects, with a special concentration on literary improvement. With approximately eighteen thousand members who are executive and professional women, Altrusa International is headquartered in Chicago and has more than five hundred local groups. Its *International Altrusa Accent* is published quarterly.

AMERICAN ASSOCIATION OF UNIVERSITY WOMEN Originally called the Association of Collegiate Alumnae, the organization's founding date of 1881 is significant, for it was a direct outgrowth of the new women's COLLEGES that sprang up after the CIVIL WAR. In a time when millions of women did not personally know a single female college graduate, the association provided a comforting solace for those who had pioneered in higher education and gave them an opportunity to communicate with others like themselves.

For over a century, AAUW has focused on lifelong learning for its college-graduate membership with the use of annual study/action programs on topics of concern to women. Local chapters sometimes memorialize women such as ELLEN RICHARDS and ANNIE JUMP CANNON by naming themselves for a woman who might otherwise be forgotten.

The AAUW currently has a membership of approximately 150,000 in two thousand local chapters; it conducts research, lobbies, and sponsors competitions and awards. The *AAUW Outlook* is published bimonthly, and its headquarters is in Washington.

AMERICAN BIRTH CONTROL LEAGUE— *See* PLANNED PARENTHOOD

AMERICAN EQUAL RIGHTS ASSOCIATION Formed in 1866 soon after the CIVIL WAR ended, the organization was intended as a merger between feminists and ABOLITIONISTS who had to some extent gone their separate ways during and just before the war. With slavery at an end, this new organization promised to merge the Anti-Slavery Society and the Women's Rights Society into an organization to work for legal protection for both black men and all women—or at least that was the intention of SUSAN ANTHONY and ELIZABETH CADY STANTON, the prime leaders of the Women's Rights Society.

Wendell Phillips, who was president of the Anti-Slavery Society at the time, was distinctly cool to the merger, even though it was approved by a unanimous vote that included many influential men. The new organization seemed on the right track when it elected a woman president, LUCRETIA MOTT, whose abolitionist credentials were also impeccable, with Anthony as secretary and Stanton first vice-president. Nonetheless, the group's primary goal was the passage of the Fourteenth (and later, the Fifteenth) Amendment, with the implicit assumption of securing constitutional rights only for male ex-slaves.

Phillips continued to play a dominant role, and by the second anniversary of the organization, the split was apparent. Even though Stanton presided over the 1868 convention, due to Mott's recent widowhood, she and Anthony were permanently alienated by the attacks made on them for their advocacy of women. Frederick Douglass, who as a black man owed his very life to some of these women, nonetheless supported Phillips' agenda of priorities: "first Negro suffrage, then temperance, then the eight-hour movement, then woman suffrage." Clearly, in his mind, women of his own race were not included under "Negro suffrage."

Many women, notably LUCY STONE and JULIA WARD HOWE, accepted this male primacy, fearing that constitutional protections for freedmen would be lost if the newer ideas of women's rights were also included. They argued that abolition had been hotly debated and a horrible war fought over it, while feminism was still a new and largely undeveloped topic. While these women wanted the vote and other legal rights, they understood the political risks of demanding all or nothing. The friction came to a head in a January, 1869 meeting when Anthony's faction split to form the NATIONAL WOMAN SUFFRAGE ASSOCIATION for women only. The Stone side retaliated in November by organizing the AMERICAN WOMAN SUFFRAGE ASSOCIATION, and the Equal Rights Association drifted into oblivion with the ratification of the FIFTEENTH AMENDMENT a few months later.

AMERICAN RED CROSS The International Red Cross predated the American affiliation by almost twenty years. Its 1863 Swiss founders gained wide support in Europe, but American isolationists refused involvement until CLARA BARTON, famous for her CIVIL WAR activities, began a campaign in the 1870s for Senate ratification of the relevant Geneva treaty. Barton emphasized the need for an organization to deal with natural disasters, something that was a wholly new direction for the established Red Cross, but which was successful in arousing support in America.

Senate ratification came in 1882, and Barton headed the organization until 1904. Thus from the beginning, women played major roles in its leadership. Tens of thousands of women have learned skills in Red Cross work, while wartime activities have taken them to remote and dangerous places. Volunteerism in the Red Cross has given many the credentials for professional positions, and women have raised billions of dollars for the organization.

AMERICAN WOMAN SUFFRAGE ASSOCIATION (AWSA) An organization including both men and women supportive of women's right to vote, the AWSA was formed in 1869 as an outgrowth of the AMERICAN EQUAL RIGHTS ASSOCIATION. Its early members had been active in ABOLITIONISM, but with the CIVIL WAR over and slavery ended, they set about working for the enfranchisement of women as well as ex-slaves. JULIA WARD HOWE, well known as the author of the "Battle Hymn of the Republic," was the AWSA's first president. Like Howe, its most prominent members were Bostonians, including LOUISA MAY ALCOTT, HARRIET BEECHER STOWE, LUCY STONE, and MARY LIVERMORE.

For two decades, until a merger in 1890, the AWSA contrasted with the NATIONAL WOMAN SUFFRAGE ASSOCIATION; the NWSA, formed by SUSAN ANTHONY earlier in the same year, was the more radical organization, excluding men and concerned with divorce reform and other issues beyond suffrage. The AWSA, intent on the sole goal of the right to vote, was careful to avoid the more controversial areas of the women's movement and worked for suffrage on a state-by-state, rather than a national basis. AWSA leadership tended to be based in Boston and to reflect the values of New England transcendentalism, while the NWSA focused its activity in New York and Washington and was less literary and more political. The rivalry between the two groups was intense and destructive.

The AWSA's publication, WOMAN'S JOURNAL, was edited by Lucy Stone with her husband, Henry Blackwell, from 1872 until Stone's death in 1893. It was considered the leading magazine of the SUFFRAGE MOVEMENT and remained in publication under the editorship of their daughter, ALICE STONE BLACKWELL, until 1917, when the vote was near.

AMES, JESSIE DANIEL (1883–1972)
Unlike many other girls who became leaders, Jessie Daniel had no particular role models to emulate when growing up in small east Texas towns, and nothing in either of her middle-class parents would predict the future of their courageously independent daughter.

In 1905, three years after graduating from a local Methodist college, she married U.S. Army physician Roger Ames. He was stationed elsewhere during most of their short marriage, and his wife was rearing their son and daughter and was pregnant with a third child when Dr. Ames died in Guatemala in 1914. A thirty-one-year-old widow, she went into business with her mother, who also was recently widowed, and together they supported her young family. Moreover, with Mr. Daniel's negative influence removed, both women became active in the SUFFRAGE MOVEMENT and helped make Texas the first southern state to ratify the NINETEENTH AMENDMENT.

Ames acted immediately to turn the newly enfranchised women into a genuine voting bloc. She was the founding president of the Texas LEAGUE OF WOMEN VOTERS in 1919 and was active also in the AMERICAN ASSOCIATION OF UNIVERSITY WOMEN, the Democratic Party, and other organizations. But in Texas, as elsewhere, the reform that many expected to follow women's right to vote failed to materialize, and Jessie Daniel Ames found the new women's organizations disappointingly traditional.

Instead, she came to focus on a controversial area undertaken by few others. During the repressive postwar years of the 1920s—an era filled with injustices toward immigrants, labor unionists, and other minorities—Jessie Daniel Ames began a career of speaking out against mob violence, especially the lynchings of black men common in the South. Her cause soon became her full-time job. In 1924, she was named Texas director for the Commission on Interracial Cooperation, an organization based in Atlanta. After five years of work in Texas, she was promoted to direct all of the CIC's work with women and moved to Atlanta. The following year, under the aegis of the CIC, she led twenty-six other white women in founding the Association of Southern Women for the Prevention of Lynching. Eventually, the ASWPL had the endorsement of more than a dozen Protestant and Jewish groups, and their petitions had been signed by more than forty thousand women and thirteen hundred law enforcement officials.

Though IDA WELLS-BARNETT and other black women had led earlier campaigns against lynching, Ames was unique as a southern white who traveled the Depression South, speaking about the unspeakable. Lynching, she told her audiences, was not the defense of white womanhood that men implied; in fact, her studies showed that fewer than one in three lynchings resulted from even the accusation of rape, let alone actual, proven rape. In the incongruous setting of ladies' missionary society meetings in small town churches throughout the South, Jessie Daniel Ames asked women to think about a subject that respectable women were not supposed to know about; she urged them to stop their husbands and sons and brothers from abetting such violence, even by their silence. She issued press releases, argued with editors and sheriffs, and tried to convince public officials to see that prisoners got their right to a fair trial—in a time when many Southern states excluded women from JURY DUTY. Always she tried to deliver the message that such male violence was not a defense of innocent women in need of protection, but was instead fascist political control of both men and women through fear.

With particularly strong support from Methodist women, Ames and the ASWPL made a difference; the civil rights attitudes of the Roosevelt administration and the increased economic opportunities of the New Deal probably made more difference. In any case, lynchings declined throughout the thirties, and in 1940, for the first year ever, there were none. By 1942, with the world at war, the ASWPL dissolved itself.

Unfortunately at odds with New Dealers and apparently unable to share leadership, Ames was forced from her job with the Commission on Interracial Cooperation in 1944 when she was sixty-one. The author of two books, Southern Women Look at Lynching (1937) and The Changing Character of Lynching (1942), she lived in retirement in North Carolina until returning to Texas to die at eighty-eight in an Austin nursing home. Despite this sad end, Jessie Daniel Ames deserves credit for being one of the first to refute—in her life, as well as in her words—the myth of white womanhood in need of male protection.

ANABLE, GLORIA HOLLISTER (1903–1988)
A twentieth-century explorer, Anable climbed the highest mountains and plumbed the depths of the ocean. In 1931, she set the women's record for ocean descent, and in 1936, flying a light plane, she discovered forty-three previously unmapped waterfalls in British Guiana, including Kaieteur Falls, which is five times Niagara's height. A fellow of the New York Zoological Society, Anable led exploration parties throughout the world.

ANASTASI, ANNE (1908–)
A lifelong New Yorker, Anastasi was primarily educated by her Italian grandmother, while her widowed mother supported the family. The teaching these women provided the child was so exceptional that she was admitted to BARNARD COLLEGE at age fifteen, where she soon became an outstanding student in the relatively new field of psychology.

Anastasi kept her MAIDEN NAME when she married another psychologist in 1933. She stayed at Barnard until 1939, when she began the psychology department at Queen's College; in 1947, she moved on to Fordham, where she remained until retirement in 1979. Her reputation rests primarily on her writing, especially Psychological Testing (1954), which in eight editions has been used by countless students in psychology and education. Other millions have been affected by her mental testing work with the military and the College Entrance Examination Board on the development of tests free from cultural biases.

Elected president of the American Psychological Association in 1972, she was the first woman to serve in this position since MARY CALKINS pioneered in psychology a half-century earlier. Anastasi was awarded the National Medal of Science by President Ronald Reagan in 1987 and is considered by many to be the most prominent woman in American psychology.

ANDERSON, EUGENIE MOORE (1909–1990)
Born in Adair, Iowa, Anderson was the first American woman to hold ambassadorial rank. Appointed by President Truman as United States ambassador to Denmark, her signature on a 1951 commercial treaty was another first for women. From 1962–1965, she served as the American minister to Bulgaria.

ANDERSON, MARGARET CAROLYN (1886–1973)
Born in Indianapolis to a socially ambitious mother and a prosperous businessman father, nothing in Margaret Anderson's early world would seem to have inspired the daring literary and artistic life that she built for herself.

After just one year at Western College in Miami, Ohio, Anderson left for Chicago, where, despite musical intentions, she quickly developed into a major figure of the literary world. Working first as a bookstore clerk and as a writer for various publications, this amazing young woman founded her own literary magazine while still in her twenties and went on to establish herself as a daringly innovative PUBLISHER.

The *Little Review*, established in 1914 just before the outbreak of WORLD WAR I, was an artistic success from its first issue, which published Chicago poet Vachel Lindsay. During Anderson's brief but stellar editorship, *Little Review* featured works by undiscovered writers who would become literary giants, including Sherwood Anderson, Hart Crane, T.S. Eliot, Robert Frost, Ernest Hemingway, AMY LOWELL, and GERTRUDE STEIN.

Indifferent to financial success, Anderson could pay none of these writers, but nonetheless willingly lost patronage when she published anarchist EMMA GOLDMAN during the magazine's first year. She soon attracted others to her cause, including artist Jane Heap and poet Ezra Pound. In 1917, *Little Review* moved its offices to New York, where it would be at the center of the literary world.

WORLD WAR I brought an era of repression of free speech, and *Little Review*'s serialization of James Joyce's *Ulysses* again demonstrated Anderson's devotion to artistic freedom. Four issues were confiscated and burned by postal authorities, and in 1921 the editors were convicted of obscenity charges and fined. The government's action ruined the magazine's precarious financial condition; it never again appeared on a regular basis. Nonetheless, though she published it for less than a decade, Anderson provided in *Little Review* a comet that heralded the rise of twentieth-century American literature.

She moved to Paris the year after her court conviction, where she lived with singer Georgette Leblanc until Leblanc's death in 1941. She returned to the U.S. in 1942 (during the Nazi occupation of France) and remained until 1955, working on her autobiography and living with Dorothy Caruso, the widow of famed singer Enrico Caruso. After Dorothy Caruso's death, Anderson returned to France, where she died at eighty-three in Cannes.

Her autobiography was published in three volumes over a period of more than forty years: *My Thirty Years' War* was published while she lived in France in 1930; *The Fiery Fountains* was issued when she was back in the U.S. and living with Caruso in 1951, and the last, *The Strange Necessity*, came out in 1970, just three years before her death. Together, they provide an uncommon chronicle of the era's life and literature.

ANDERSON, MARIAN (1902–1993)
With her Philadelphia parents too poor to pay for lessons, Marian Anderson received her musical education through the black church. From the age of six, Union Baptist Church provided a platform for this gifted child; when, as a teenager, she could sing any part from bass to soprano, they raised the money she needed for music school.

By her late teens, she had come to the attention of internationally known musicians, and her career was assured when in 1925 she placed first among three hundred in a musical contest. The prize led to a scholarship and appearances with the Philadelphia Symphony and New York Philharmonic Orchestra, but most American music halls remained closed to Anderson because of her race.

Beginning in 1930, she used her savings and scholarships to study abroad, and like other black artists of the twenties, found success by this circuitous route; Marian Anderson was acclaimed in Europe long before she was known in her own country. After a successful debut in Berlin, she made several tours of Europe during the thirties, performing before royalty and singing at the most famous musical festivals. Jean Sibelius was so impressed by Anderson that he wrote a composition

Marian Anderson receiving the Medal of Freedom from President Lyndon Johnson at the White House in 1963.
NATIONAL ARCHIVES.

especially for her, and she was praised by music critics from Italy to Russia.

While she was briefly back in the United States in 1936, Anderson was invited by ELEANOR ROOSEVELT to sing at the White House and a lifelong friendship between the two developed that was to prove especially important in 1939, when most Americans finally heard of Anderson. Though she had performed to rave reviews earlier that year for integrated U.S. audiences, including some in the Deep South, when HOWARD UNIVERSITY tried to schedule her for a benefit concert in Washington's Constitution Hall, permission was refused by its owners, the DAUGHTERS OF THE AMERICAN REVOLUTION.

Roosevelt's subsequent resignation from the DAR and her role in rescheduling the concert at the Lincoln Memorial was widely publicized, ensuring the concert's success. Beyond Roosevelt's support, however, was that of Interior Secretary Harold Ickes, under whose jurisdiction the memorial was, as well as hundreds of other white Americans who signed on as Anderson's sponsors, including two Supreme Court justices, several Cabinet members, and prominent women such as TALLULAH BANKHEAD, KATHERINE HEPBURN, and CLAIRE BOOTH LUCE. Violinist Jascha Heifetz denounced the DAR from its stage.

The concert was a turning point for blacks seeking equality. Anderson was finally recognized by her government in the 1950s, when the State Department promoted her tours abroad and she was appointed as a delegate to the United Nations. The first black to sing with the Metropolitan Opera, she debuted there in 1955. She sang for President Kennedy's inauguration in 1961 and was the recipient of many awards and honorary degrees before making her farewell tour in 1964–1965. In 1978, Anderson was presented with a gold medal by Congress, and her eightieth birthday celebration was held at Carnegie Hall in 1982. She received a lifetime achievement Grammy award in 1991 and died at ninety-one. Famed conductor Arturo Toscanini called Anderson's voice a phenomenon of "once in a hundred years."

ANDERSON, MARY (1872–1964) By heading the Women's Bureau of the Department of Labor for the first quarter century of its existence, Mary Anderson made a tremendous contribution to the welfare of working women.

She grew up in Sweden, where her only education came from the local Lutheran school, and emigrated with her sister Anna at age seventeen. She worked at various domestic service jobs in rural Michigan before moving to Chicago in 1892, when she joined thousands of other IMMIGRANT WOMEN who worked in the garment factories there. Along with them, she suffered the era's harsh employment conditions, made worse by the Depression of 1893. These years of experience as a manual laborer who worked to support herself made Anderson exceptional when she later became a government official in charge of working women.

Her life made a fateful turn in 1899, when Anderson's sewing shop joined the International Boot and Shoe Workers Union; the following year, she became president of her local. By representing her fellow workers at Chicago Federation of Labor meetings, she began to meet other women leaders and to develop organizing skills. Yet, though she joined the WOMEN'S TRADE UNION LEAGUE (WTUL) in 1905, Anderson continued to work as a stitcher for more than a decade after her union involvement.

It was the great STRIKE in the Chicago GARMENT INDUSTRY in 1910–11 that finally changed her life; at age thirty-nine, when the working lives of most industrial women of that era were considered over, Anderson began her career as a labor leader. She was hired by the WTUL to enforce the contract won in the strike and began the daily rounds of factories, educating women on their rights and negotiating for them with management.

The skills she developed became important when the U.S. joined WORLD WAR I in 1917; AFL president Samuel Gompers appointed her to a wartime women's committee and early in 1918, she was named assistant director of a new women's branch of the Army Ordnance Department. This eventually grew into an appointment by President Wilson as director of the Women's Bureau of the Department of Labor, a new agency created by Congress in recognition of women's wartime roles. She was the first woman from organized labor to hold a responsible position in Washington.

Almost immediately thereafter, however, Republicans returned to the White House; Anderson's tenure as head of the fledgling office might well have been brief but for the intervention of Republican women who supported her. Instead, she served through the three Republican administrations of the twenties and continued under Democrat Franklin Roosevelt through the Great Depression and most of World War II.

That she was able to manage such potential political pitfalls is testimony to the exceptional job Anderson did in setting up the bureau, as well as to her pleasant personality. Despite a lingering Swedish accent, she was long known as one of Washington's most popular officials; a 1940 reporter commented that "workers everywhere feel that Mary Anderson, the former factory worker, is still one of them." Roosevelt admired her so much that he appointed her head of the U.S. delegation to the International Labor Organization in 1933, over the objections of Labor Secretary FRANCES PERKINS.

It was, sadly, Anderson's disappointment with Perkins that led to her resignation in 1944. She had looked forward early in FDR's administration to working for a woman, but had seen Perkins largely ignore the needs of women to cater instead to the traditional male heads of labor unions. When the work of the Women's Bureau was tremendously increased by the influx of millions of women into the labor market in World War II without a corresponding increase in its budget, Anderson finally decided to resign. She was, after all, seventy-two years old and had given her whole life to the cause of working women.

Anderson published her autobiography, *Woman at Work* in 1951 and was honored on her ninetieth birthday in 1962 by the Kennedy administration. She died in her Washington home.

ANGELOU, MAYA (1928–   ) Perhaps the best known of contemporary poets, Maya Angelou began life in the rural poverty of a black family in Stamps, Arkansas, during the Great Depression. Her mother's boyfriend raped her when she was seven, and when he was killed a few days after being released from prison, she believed herself responsible

and was mute for more than five years. Most thought her retarded when she refused to speak, but her grandmother had faith in her. This "tall tree of a woman" profoundly influenced Angelou's writing.

Her voice reached out to other women in her first volume of autobiography, *I Know Why the Caged Bird Sings* (1970), and Angelou has been widely read ever since. She has added several more autobiographical books as well as plays, songs, and a number of volumes of poetry. Among her books are, *Just Give Me A Cool Drink of Water Fore I Die* (1971), *And Still I Rise* (1976), *Shaker, Why Don't You Sing?* (1983), and *I Shall Not Be Moved* (1990).

Fellow Arkansan Bill Clinton honored Angelou by asking her to read for his presidential inauguration in 1993. "On the Pulse of the Morning," the poem she composed for the occasion, was reprinted in newspapers across America.

ANNE (1665–1714)

Queen Anne reigned over the American colonies from 1702–1714. Though her reign was relatively brief, it was a crucial time in the country's settlement, and a number of American place-names honor her either as queen or in her much longer role as Princess Anne.

She was a strong monarch in foreign policy, even though her health was sadly ruined by the lack of BIRTH CONTROL. Queen Anne bore seventeen children, with all but one dying at birth or in infancy. Her deliveries may well have been safer had they been assisted by MIDWIVES rather than by the nascent practice of obstetricians.

Queen Anne lost her last child when he was eleven and was succeeded by George I, a relative imported from Hanover in what is now Germany, who did not speak English. A few decades later, Americans would revolt against his grandson.

ANN LANDERS— *See* FRIEDMAN, ESTHER PAULINE.

ANONYMOUS— *See* AUTHORS and PSEUDONYMS.

ANTHONY, KATHARINE SUSAN (1877–1965)

The daughter of SUSAN ANTHONY's brother, Katharine Anthony combined interests in sociology and feminism in her writing. Her first book, *Mothers Who Must Earn* (1914) (eight years after the death of her illustrious relative), was a careful sociological study of urbanized working women who were primarily of German and Irish origin. It concentrated on these women's home-centered problems in child care and health, and through budget analysis showed that they generally were good financial managers and conscientious mothers whose poverty was due to their low wages and, often, the abandonment of male responsibility for families.

Anthony followed this with *Feminism in Germany and Scandinavia* (1915), and in 1920, returned to the themes of her first book with *The Endowment of Motherhood*. She also published a biography of MARGARET FULLER that year, and then returned to thinking about European women with books on Catherine the Great, Elizabeth I, and Marie Antoinette, as well as a study of pre-Victorian England. Focusing on American women during most of the last years of her life, she wrote biographies of LOUISA MAY ALCOTT, DOLLEY MADISON, and SUSAN ANTHONY. Her last book, on MERCY OTIS WARREN, was published in 1958 when she was eighty-one.

ANTHONY, SUSAN BROWNELL (1820–1906)

Susan Anthony is to the women's movement as George Washington is to the nation; she is generally recognized as the outstanding leader of the revolution—but in her case, the battle lasted more than half a century and she did not live to see the victory.

Like other nineteenth-century reformers, Susan Anthony was a descendent of QUAKER colonists. Born in Massachusetts, she grew up in western New York and received what formal education she had at a Quaker school in Philadelphia. She worked as a TEACHER while still in her teens, and, at age nineteen, moved away from home for a better position to help her father support the family's eight children after the Panic of 1837. When the debts were paid, she exhibited the interest in quality clothing that—despite renewed poverty and contrary images—she would retain for the rest of her life. Dropping Quaker dress codes, she bought a new wardrobe, including a $22.50 shawl—on a $125 annual salary.

Thus Anthony was busy with her teaching career when her parents and a sister attended the famous 1848 SENECA FALLS WOMEN'S RIGHTS CONVENTION while she did not. Returning to their Rochester home in 1849, however, she quickly joined their involvement in this as well as in the temperance and ABOLITIONIST movements. She soon discovered, as did other women, that their voices were not necessarily welcomed even in reformist groups.

Three separate occasions confirmed in her mind the necessity of focusing on women's rights: she was refused permission to speak because of her gender at a temperance rally in Albany in 1852; women delegates were not seated at a World's Temperance Convention in New York City in 1853; and she had to fight for the right to participate in a New York State Teachers' Association convention that same year.

It was these negative experiences with PUBLIC SPEAKING, as well as Anthony's awareness of lower pay for women teachers, that resulted in her spending the 1850s organizing the nascent women's rights movement. Working from Rochester, she concentrated on improvement of MARRIED WOMEN'S PROPERTY RIGHTS as well as the right to vote; in 1854, she began organizing women in every county in New York for local canvasses to garner signatures on petitions. She met with her first success in 1860, when the legislature granted married women the right to retain their own earnings and to file court suits.

The CIVIL WAR that began the following year displaced women's rights from the reformist agenda, however, as the abolition of slavery assumed greatest importance. Anthony joined her female colleagues in organizing the LOYAL LEAGUE and working for emancipation—but even as she worked for an end to slavery, she strongly opposed giving the vote to illiterate males ahead of educated women.

The end of the war confirmed her fears. Though she helped with the formation of the AMERICAN EQUAL RIGHTS ASSOCIATION in 1866, she soon realized that its male leadership saw women's rights as secondary to those of ex-slaves. She made her first long trip that year, TRAVELING to Kansas to work without success in an election on both issues. The trip was not a total loss, however, for she met George Francis Train, an eccentric who was willing, at least for a while, to finance a publication to further her goals.

Susan Anthony in the study of her Rochester home. The photograph nearest to her is that of her dearest friend, Elizabeth Cady Stanton. Note also the quality of Anthony's silk dress; despite her Quaker upbringing, she enjoyed fine clothing.
LIBRARY OF CONGRESS; PHOTOGRAPH BY BENJAMIN JOHNSON.

With her friend ELIZABETH CADY STANTON, Anthony began the *Revolution* in 1868. In addition to supporting women's enfranchisement, it advocated improvement in other areas of women's lives such as DIVORCE laws and employment opportunity, as well as Train's idiosyncratic ideas on subjects other than women's rights. Soon the *Revolution* was deep in debt, and in 1870 Anthony began a grueling tour aimed at paying off the ten thousand dollars owed with seventy-five dollar lectures. Despite the steady scorn of newspaper critics, women clearly identified with what she had to say, for her speeches proved so popular that the debt was paid within six years.

Meanwhile, she was sharing her ideas with thousands of women and building networks throughout the country. Early in 1869, she and Stanton organized some of those women into the NATIONAL WOMAN SUFFRAGE ASSOCIATION. With Stanton as president but Anthony as the tireless devotee, the NWSA adopted the radical position of opposing the FIFTEENTH AMEND-

MENT to the Constitution, which enfranchised ex-slaves. Anthony's belief in an educated electorate regardless of race or sex was seen as elitist by many of her abolitionist friends, who a few months later formed an alternative organization, the AMERICAN WOMAN SUFFRAGE ASSOCIATION.

After the Fifteenth Amendment was adopted despite Anthony's objections, she decided to test its language, which states: "The right of citizens of the United States to vote shall not be denied . . . on account of race . . ." When she cast a ballot in the 1872 presidential election, she found that Rochester officials were not only unwilling to count her vote, they also had her arrested. She was tried in U.S. District Court and convicted without benefit of jury by a judge who had his opinion written before the trial began. Anthony refused to pay the one hundred dollar fine he imposed, but no enforcement action was taken—thus providing no opportunity for appeal as she had hoped.

In any case, it was clear that the men in power believed

the Constitution did not mean women when it said "citizens," and Anthony continued her crusade for an unambiguous amendment assuring women's right to vote. She traveled tirelessly, working campaigns in California, Michigan, and Colorado during the 1870s and going abroad to organize the INTERNATIONAL COUNCIL OF WOMEN in the 1880s. She also spent those years recording the history of the movement, with the first volume of the HISTORY OF WOMAN SUFFRAGE being issued in 1881. A joint effort of Anthony and three other women, the last of its six volumes would appear in 1922.

The AWSA and NWSA at last resolved their differences and merged in 1890. Stanton was chosen the first president of the renamed National American Woman Suffrage Association, with Anthony becoming president in 1892 and serving until the turn of the century.

Settling down again in Rochester, she was tireless even in retirement, working especially for local educational opportunities for women. She continued to travel, going to Chicago in 1893 for the COLUMBIAN EXPOSITION and to California in 1895. She was honored on her seventy-fifth birthday that year, and spent the rest of the 1890s working on her memoirs, *Life of Susan Anthony*. Her leadership in the International Council of Women took her to London in 1899 and to Berlin in 1904; she lived to see women vote in two nations, Australia and New Zealand. Her last U.S. women's rights meeting was in Baltimore early in 1906; she died the next month in Rochester at eighty-six. Though she did not live to see the victory, her last prediction at the Baltimore meeting that "failure is impossible," would finally come true fourteen years later.

Susan B. Anthony's election to the HALL OF FAME in 1950 is a true indication of her stellar place among women, for no woman had been elected to the Hall of Fame during the previous thirty years, and no other suffragist has ever been elected. A similar honor was the coinage of the Susan B. Anthony silver dollar in 1978.

ANTHONY, SUSAN B. II (1916–1991)

Susan Anthony's namesake was born in Pennsylvania a decade after the death of her famous relative and four years before women received the vote. Gifted with the same keen logic and persuasive writing ability as her great-aunt, Susan Anthony II was a journalist and the author of eight books. She worked for two Rochester newspapers, the Associated Press, and was one of the first women hired by the *Washington Star*.

Her most important book was *Out of the Kitchen—Into the War*, published in 1943 when the nation was in the worst of WORLD WAR II. Overcoming a leftist inclination to pacifism, Anthony wrote a powerful piece on the great dangers to women if the fascists won the war. She also made many insightful observations on the conditions of contemporary women, studying everything from model childcare centers in West Coast shipyards to fatalities among women in the munitions industry.

Anthony ended her days in Florida, where she worked for the *Key West Citizen*, overcame a problem with liquor, and was certified as an alcoholism counselor. She commented in 1987 on the irony of the situation: "Here I was—an alcoholic—and did you know Aunt Susan's first public speech was a temperance lecture?" In 1975, Susan Anthony II cofounded Wayside House, a Delray Beach, Florida rehabilitation center for women alcoholics. She died of bone cancer in Boca Raton a few days short of her seventy-fifth birthday.

ANTIN, MARY (1881–1949)

Antin was born in the town of Plotzk in the Russian "pale" to which Jews were confined. Her family, like millions of other Russian Jews in the late nineteenth century, emigrated to the United States, following a common pattern of the father coming first while the mother and children maintained themselves independently. Antin's father came to Boston in 1891; three years later, at age thirteen, Mary, her mother, and three siblings joined him.

They lived the ordinary lives of impoverished immigrants, with the entire family working to eke out an inadequate income. To her parents' credit, however, they understood that Mary was exceptional and, in a rare move for their culture, placed her education above that of her brother. She quickly moved through elementary school and then was encouraged by her teachers to attend Boston's prestigious Girls Latin School.

While still a student there and only five years after emigrating, she became a published author. She translated a series of letters to an uncle that she had written in Yiddish about her immigration experience, and with the help of adults interested in her, *From Plotzk to Boston* was published in 1899, when Mary was just eighteen.

Everyone, including Mary, assumed that this brilliant young woman would move from Girls Latin to RADCLIFFE, as bright female Bostonians did. On a natural history field trip, however, she was charmed by the leader, German-American geologist Amadeus W. Gradau. Antin found herself pregnant, fated to become a mother instead of a college student. They married in October, 1901, and a daughter was born soon after. The young family moved to New York, where he established a career at Columbia University. Although she studied at Columbia's female associate, BARNARD COLLEGE, and at its Teachers College, she never earned a degree.

Yet even if she took no more courses after 1904, her mind was still at work. She began publishing in the *Atlantic Monthly* in 1911, and the next year saw the publication of her most famous work, *The Promised Land*. It was the bestselling nonfiction book of 1912, and its readership provided Mary Antin (who used her MAIDEN NAME professionally) with recognition and a platform that remained as long as immigration was an issue.

Her next book, *They Who Knock at Our Gates* (1914), was less a personal remembrance and more a political argument against efforts to restrict immigration. Antin lectured widely on the subject and, though women still lacked the vote, campaigned at Theodore Roosevelt's invitation for the Progressive Party in 1912; in 1916, she campaigned for progressive Republican presidential candidate Charles Evans Hughes.

WORLD WAR I brought not only a temporary halt to debate on immigration, but also active harassment of German-Americans. Professor Gradau's refusal to adopt a politic attitude invited trouble at Columbia, where Germanic science was currently out of vogue. Their marriage, which never resulted in the birth of any child beyond the first, quite probably was further strained by incompatibilities between their opposite ethnic origins of German Lutheran and Russian Jew, as well as Antin's positive attitudes towards Americanization, while Gradau thought many aspects of German culture were superior to the "Promised Land."

The stress brought a breakdown in Antin's health from which she never recovered. Soon after the war's end, Gradau left for China and, though they did not divorce, the marriage was over. With the passage of legislation that effectively ended immigration in the early 1920s, Antin's area of expertise faded from popularity. She spent most of her remaining years with her family in Massachusetts, where she wrote occasional essays and increasingly returned to her Jewish roots. Though she lived through the Nazi holocaust, she did not publish after 1941. She died at sixty-eight in an Albany, New York nursing home.

ANTIOCH COLLEGE Chartered in 1852 near Dayton, Ohio, Antioch was one of the first COLLEGES open to women equally with men. Its first president was Horace Mann, and the emerging school was strongly influenced by the president's wife, MARY PEABODY MANN. Indeed, the unpaid position of faculty wife was a factor in virtually all institutions of higher education well into the twentieth century, for the wives of presidents, deans, headmasters, and professors were all expected to interact with students on a daily basis—even in all-male institutions. In the new coed colleges, this availability became even more important; Mary Peabody Mann and others actually functioned as deans of women, though they drew no salary and had no title.

Nonetheless, Antioch was decades ahead of most American colleges in simply admitting women. The Manns had to move from Boston to find such a progressive community, and Antioch is another example of the greater opportunities that were available to WESTERN WOMEN. OLYMPIA BROWN was one of Antioch's early feminist graduates; ELINORE HERRICK was among later graduates of historical importance to women.

ANTI-SALOON LEAGUE OF AMERICA Begun in 1895, this organization came rather late in the PROHIBITION movement and was dominated by men. Its initial aim of passing prohibitionist legislation on a statewide basis was changed in 1913 to pushing for a constitutional amendment forbidding the sale of alcohol anywhere in the United States. This aim was achieved in 1919, before women began voting in 1920. Though women were actively involved with the Anti-Saloon League, much of their activity and virtually all of their leadership roles were reserved instead for the WOMEN'S CHRISTIAN TEMPERANCE UNION.

APGAR, VIRGINIA (1909–1974) Educated at MOUNT HOLYOKE and Columbia University's medical school, Apgar became a specialist in the relatively new field of anesthesiology in the mid-1930s. In 1949, she was the first woman among Columbia's medical faculty to be accorded a full professorship.

She is famous for development of the Apgar Score, a five point assessment of infant health to be done within one minute of birth. Her testing system was adopted worldwide soon after its 1952 presentation. Apgar became associated with the March of Dimes and its campaign to end birth defects in the 1960s. Her 1972 book, *Is My Baby All Right?*, came out three years before her death in New York City.

ARDEN, ELIZABETH (1878?/84?–1966) Born to Canadian parents and named Florence Nightingale Graham, the woman known as Elizabeth Arden obscured the year of her birth so that it is still debatable. She grew up poor, with her mother dying when she was still a child. After working at various traditional women's jobs, she joined her brother in New York and began work in a beauty salon in 1908 when she was about thirty.

After developing some expertise in facial massage, she briefly merged with an established beautician, Elizabeth Hubbard, before buying out their partnership with about one thousand dollars borrowed from her brother. In the first display of the tremendous business ability that she would develop, she redecorated the small Fifth Avenue salon to match the elegance of the clientele that she hoped to attract, and thereby came upon her name change. Understanding that business frugality must nonetheless afford an impression of success, she hired a sign painter to replace her former partner's surname with a short (and thereby low cost) name chosen from Tennyson. "Elizabeth Arden" soon replaced Florence Graham as her own name, though it was never legally changed.

Possessed of a naturally wonderful complexion that made her look much younger than she was, Arden saw the marketing opportunity to other women who wanted her look. By 1914, only six years after arriving in New York, she had set up a second salon in Washington; traveled to Paris to begin international contacts; and hired chemists to create the first cosmetics of a line that would eventually include three hundred items. The outbreak of WORLD WAR I slowed her only briefly, and when the war was over and respectable American women began emulating Parisians in the use of cosmetics, Arden was well positioned to take advantage of the "new woman" look of the Roaring Twenties.

She married banker Thomas Lewis in 1915; their relationship proved a business but not necessarily a personal success. He ran the cosmetic side of the business, which was always more profitable than the salons, for almost twenty years. They divorced in 1934 during the Great Depression, but Arden, with a clientele composed of the world's wealthiest women, suffered little from the times.

A Russian prince became her second husband, but the marriage lasted only two years during the midst of World War II. Now a multimillionaire, Arden indulged her interest in horse racing and produced the 1947 Kentucky Derby winner. Still the sole owner of her business, she had a hundred salons throughout the world and annual cosmetic sales of $60 million by the time of her death. One of the nation's first self-made businesswomen, she left her fortune to her sister, a niece, and her longtime employees.

ARENDT, HANNAH (1906–1975) Born and educated in Germany, Arendt received a Ph.D. in philosophy in 1929 from the University of Heidelberg, where she was a student of, and became lifelong friends with, the great philosophers Martin Heidegger and Karl Jaspers. She fled from the Gestapo in 1933 after a week of imprisonment; after seven years in France, she was again arrested by the occupying Nazis and interned for six weeks.

Arendt had married in 1929, but the marriage had begun

to fail by 1933 and was formally ended in 1936. In 1940, she married a German gentile, Heinrich Blucher, who had also escaped from Berlin and who was targeted by the Nazis for his leftist views. Though uneducated, Blucher's politics strongly influenced Arendt's for the rest of their lives.

They escaped together with Arendt's mother to New York in 1941. Arendt, who was then thirty-five and still without employment credentials despite her prestigious education, was faced with learning English and establishing a career in a new place. For ten years, she worked for Jewish organizations, edited for a Jewish publishing house, and wrote for leftist publications.

Her first book, *The Origins of Totalitarianism*, came out in 1951, a decade after she immigrated and the year in which she became a citizen. The first postwar study of fascism, the book received serious readership and gave Arendt recognition in the academic world. She received a Guggenheim fellowship the next year and subsequently was invited as a visiting professor to universities from Princeton to California.

Arendt further developed her philosophical and political views in *The Human Condition* (1958), *Between Past and Future* (1961), *On Revolution* (1963), *Men in Dark Times* (1968), *On Violence* (1970), and *Crises of the Republic* (1972), while a more journalistic 1963 book on the war crimes trial of Adolf Eichmann resulted in great controversy and personal pain. Her last work, *The Life of the Mind*, was edited by MARY MCCARTHY and published in 1978 after Arendt's death.

ARMWOOD, BLANCHE MAE (1890–1939)

Born in Tampa, Florida, to a relatively prosperous family of ex-slaves, Blanche Armwood showed early promise, graduating with highest honors in 1902 from St. Peter Claver Catholic School. Though only twelve years old, she passed the Florida State Teacher's Examination, but went on instead to Atlanta, where in 1906 she graduated *summa cum laude* from the "High school English-Latin course" of Spelman SEMINARY (later Spelman College). At sixteen, Armwood returned to Tampa and began TEACHING in the segregated public schools. She taught for seven years before marriage in 1913 to Tennessee attorney Daniel Webster Perkins.

The following year, she adapted public interest in the new field of HOME ECONOMICS to organize an enterprise promoting "household arts schools for cooks and housewives of the Negro race." Having gained the cooperation of Tampa's public utilities as well as the school board, she taught black women the mysteries of the era's new electrical appliances and plumbing systems; since most of these women were DOMESTIC SERVANTS, the utility companies would benefit if their employers would then install the new household equipment. Armwood also organized such projects in other Southern states, and the idea was adopted in Washington as the Federal Household Arts Training Schools.

By 1917, again single, Armwood had arrived in New Orleans, where she was employed by the U.S. Department of Agriculture as the state supervisor for home economics; she organized twenty-one Domestic Science Clubs in this role. Less than a year later, she was taking the lead in creating the Louisiana Federation of Colored Women's Clubs and then bringing that organization into the National Association of Colored Women. In 1919, she married Dr. John Calhoun

These members of the Army Nurse Corps trained in England for the invasion of the Continent during World War II. U.S. ARMY CENTER OF MILITARY HISTORY.

Beatty of Alexandria, Louisiana, but that did not stop her from political involvement when women received the vote in 1920. Republican President Warren Harding appointed her as a national campaign speaker for his party that year.

Returning to Tampa in the 1920s, Armwood organized the local Urban League and went on to become the first black superintendent of black schools; she managed to achieve her goal of an accredited high school for students of her race.

In 1931, Armwood changed careers and locales once again. She moved to Washington, D.C., married Edward Thomas Washington, and graduated from HOWARD UNIVERSITY's law school with honors in 1937. The promise of a new career was not to be, however; two years later, while visiting Medford, Massachusetts, Armwood died at age forty-nine.

ARMY NURSE CORPS

On June 10, 1861, the secretary of war appointed DOROTHEA DIX as "Superintendent of the United States Army Nurses." Though American women had worked as NURSES in past wars, this was the first formalization of a nurse corps. Unfortunately, Dix was not a successful commander and other CIVIL WAR nurses sought to keep themselves separate from her authority. The nurse corps, such as it was, ended with the war, and was not revived until the 1898 Spanish-American War. Led by Civil War veteran CLARA BARTON and her Red Cross, civilian women once again volunteered to serve the army as nurses under conditions that cried out for professionally organized effort.

At last, in 1901, Congress responded with the creation of the Army Nurse Corps to give this critical area the peacetime attention that it needed to be prepared for war. From the beginning, the assumption was that nurses were by definition female, and Dita H. Kinney was chosen as the first commander. By the time that the nation entered WORLD WAR I, the ANC was trained and equipped to render valuable service. In field hospitals in France and England, these women saved the lives of men wounded in this fiercely fought war, and they oversaw the convalescence of others on hospital ships as well as in army hospitals throughout the United States.

During the twenties and thirties, the nation was at peace and women could find exceptional opportunity in the Nurse Corps. Although women who joined the ANC—unlike male recruits—had to remain single and had to pay for their own nursing training prior to acceptance, once they were sworn in, they were treated as officers and led reasonably comfortable lives. Especially when contrasted with the conditions of other women during the Great Depression, an ANC member did well: her pay was better than that of the average civilian woman; her room, board, and laundry were taken care of; she was assured of free medical care, graduate education, and liberal retirement benefits. The opportunity to travel attracted many women, for nurses were stationed around the globe and usually could expect relative leisure and an interesting life.

WORLD WAR II changed that comfortable situation, for nurses were caught in the very first battles of the Pacific. They were bombed and starved in the Philippines, and many of them were among the five hundred British and American women who became prisoners of war with the fall of Manila. The army had begun recruitment of additional nurses in peacetime, and when war was declared, the ANC's numbers soared. The Corps had numbered a mere seven hundred in 1940, but by April of 1941—even before Pearl Harbor—that many were enlisted in a single month. Eventually, it would rise to almost sixty thousand, but even that would not be nearly enough; though nurses supervised large numbers of medical corpsmen to do unskilled tasks, most nurses worked so many hours for so many weeks and months that by the last year of the war, more than a thousand had to be hospitalized for exhaustion. This nursing shortage resulted in the BOLTON BILL and finally the NURSES SELECTIVE SERVICE ACT of 1945, which almost drafted women.

After stateside training that was toughened in response to the harsh conditions nurses endured in the Philippines, ANC members were assigned to hospitals throughout the world. Most of them remained lieutenants for the duration of the war, serving under other women who were captains and majors. They did heroic work with little recognition, for the government did not want to remind the public (and potential nurse recruits) that bombs also fell on women. Nurses were in fact killed in hospitals in Europe as well as in Asia, despite supposed Red Cross protection, and the ships on which they traveled were torpedoed—but few sought to get out of their commitment. From the new "flight nurses" aboard the planes that ferried wounded men from the mountains of Burma to the nurses who staffed the battle stations of D-Day and those who endured the desert warfare of North Africa, tens of thousands of American military nurses had the experience of their lifetimes during World War II.

They had been commanded by Julia Flikke until her retirement in 1943, when FLORENCE BLANCHFIELD took over. In 1947, during the peacetime adjustments of the military, Colonel Blanchfield became the first woman to hold a regular army commission, as the ANC and other women's units became more integral to the military and less auxiliary in their nature. This regularization meant changes in pay, rank, and other areas that brought women more nearly equal status with military men—even though Blanchfield was not promoted to general, as she should have been by usual promotion standards.

It was not until the Korean and Vietnam wars that discrimination against women began to disappear from official policy, and even then it often remained in practice. Military nurses particularly struggled with the favoritism shown to male paramedics in the Vietnam War, who were trained at taxpayer expense and who often obtained civilian salaries after discharge that were disproportionately large compared with those of better credentialed nurses.

ASSOCIATION FOR THE ADVANCEMENT OF WOMEN Convened by JANE CUNNINGHAM CROLY under the aegis of SOROSIS in 1873, the AAW's leadership included JULIA WARD HOWE with LUCY STONE and FRANCES WILLARD among its vice-presidents; MARY LIVERMORE was its first president. The organization aimed to promote the entrance of women into scholarship and the professions. Women clearly had a deep interest in this area, as evidenced by the fact that four hundred attended the group's first meeting in New York.

REVEREND AUGUSTA CHAPIN was a charter member, delivering a paper on women in the ministry at this first "Congress" of the AAW; other papers were delivered by ANTOINETTE BLACKWELL and CATHARINE BEECHER. Astronomer MARIA MITCHELL was also active in the organization, encouraging young women to study science. Among other leaders was Ednah Littlehale Cheney, who used her financial influence to create opportunities for women—a new horticultural school, the opening of NEW ENGLAND FEMALE MEDICAL COLLEGE, and the sending of Boston TEACHERS to the Reconstruction South. Many of these women were more interested in the future of their daughters and granddaughters than in seeking opportunity for themselves; the mother of geologist FLORENCE BASCOM, for example, was a charter member.

The AAW continued through the 1880s, with its annual conferences in different cities being covered by the national press. Julia Ward Howe's speeches were a particular attraction of these meetings, and a directorship for her in the new GENERAL FEDERATION OF WOMEN'S CLUBS in 1893 doubtlessly was part of the reason for the decline of the AAW. By the mid-1890s, when women's COLLEGES were well in place and many new state colleges had opened their doors to women, the AAW no longer seemed as necessary as it had been two decades earlier, and by the turn of the century, the organization had died. To a large extent, it was replaced by the similar goals and objectives of the AMERICAN ASSOCIATION OF UNIVERSITY WOMEN.

ASTOR, CAROLINE WEBSTER SCHERMERHORN (1830–1906) Being one of nine children did little to diminish Caroline Schermerhorn's view of herself as possessed of an exceptional lineage. Though her 1853 marriage to William Backhouse Astor (grandson of John Jacob Astor) gave her access to the wealth of what was then the richest family in America, she remained convinced that because of her Dutch colonial ancestry she was socially superior to her husband.

It was this belief in the primacy of family history that impelled Mrs. Astor to ordain herself as the leader of American society. She spent the first years of her marriage unremarkably enough, bearing four daughters and a son (John Jacob IV), but when CIVIL WAR parvenus threatened to erase the line between the nation's old monied families and its new, she set herself up as the arbitrator of who "belonged" and who did not.

With the help of Ward McAllister, an Astor relative who exceeded all other men in snobbery, she identified the famous "Four Hundred," a term that entered the language to define ultimate elitism. Seldom accompanied by her husband, Mrs. Astor also defined the proper lifestyle of the wealthy, with winters in New York, springs in Europe, and summers in Newport, Rhode Island. Throughout the Gilded Age of the 1880s and 1890s, aspiring businessmen as well as fortune-hunting women coveted invitations to her January balls and seven-course dinner parties, while millions of other Americans were amused by her well-publicized rivalry with her sister-in-law, Mrs. John Jacob Astor III.

Though her organizational ability and leadership skills were real, Caroline Astor (who wished to be known simply as "Mrs. Astor," to the diminishment of her sister-in-law) was fortunate to have died eight years before WORLD WAR I would put a permanent end to her privileged world.

ASTOR, NANCY (LADY) (1879–1964)

Born Nancy Witcher Langhorne, she was a Virginian whose family was impoverished from the CIVIL WAR. By her adolescence, however, their fortunes had been restored, and with her tremendous beauty, she married into more wealth. Her first marriage lasted only a decade, and in 1906, she left the United States to wed Waldorf Astor, a descendent of America's first millionaire family whose father, William Waldorf Astor, had become a British citizen in 1899.

In 1910, Nancy and Waldorf moved from London society to Plymouth where he was elected to Parliament. Nancy Astor's work in seeing to the needs of her husband's constituents was rewarded when he was elevated to the House of Lords after his father's death, and she was elected to his former seat in 1919. The first woman to be a member of Parliament, she unhesitatingly focused on issues concerning women and children. Officially a Tory, she parted company with the party often and especially displayed her American background in advocacy of temperance laws.

Lady Astor's constituency reelected her for more than two decades, and she served throughout the crises of the Great Depression and World War II. The Tory party was clearly in trouble at the end of the war, however, and rather than suffer defeat along with Churchill, she took her husband's advice and retired in 1945. Quite bitter about the situation, she withdrew almost entirely from public life, dying twelve years after Waldorf at age eighty-five.

ATHERTON, GERTRUDE FRANKLIN HORN (1857–1948)

A great-grandniece of Benjamin Franklin, Atherton was a popular writer at the turn of the century, with her career reaching its acme in 1923 when her *Black Oxen* was the bestselling book of that year.

Mrs. Atherton—as she preferred to be known—was born prior to the Civil War and lived beyond World War II, seeing the era of greatest change in human history in a place of tremendous change, California. She was born in San Francisco less than a decade after the great gold rush brought that remote area into the United States; though she lived for short periods throughout the U.S. and Europe while researching new locales for her novels, California would remain her home. Its pioneer saga was chronicled by her in more than a dozen books, the most famous of which is *The Californians* (1898).

Her parents divorced when she was three, a most unusual and scandalous thing for a child of this era to bear. Afterwards, her maternal grandfather, who edited California's first newspaper, became the strongest influence in young Gertrude's life. In 1876, rebelling against her mother, eighteen-year-old Gertrude Franklin eloped with George Atherton, who in fact had been courting her mother.

Atherton, despite his Yankee father's name, was a landowner of native Californian Spanish descent, and the bride went to live in his typically Spanish close and closed household, where she was both loved and discouraged from reading. The two children she bore in this servant-filled household were not enough to keep her mind occupied, however, and Mrs. Atherton first published anonymously in 1879, writing for periodicals.

After her husband was killed at sea in 1887, she published her first novel using a male PSEUDONYM, but soon the young WIDOW established her independence. By 1889, she was living in Paris and writing openly; she would continue to write for sixty years, publishing more than forty books. The loss of manuscripts in the 1906 San Francisco earthquake put no pause in her publication list; between 1888 and 1931, Mrs. Atherton deliberately moved her residence every other year between the United States and Europe, where her aristocratic family connections introduced her to new societal scenes that nourished her literary imagination. Indeed, European critics recognized this American writer earlier than her own compatriots.

In addition to her favorite themes of manners and morals, other fiction dealt with the supernatural. Mrs. Atherton wrote non-fiction as well, especially California history and her autobiography, *Adventures of a Novelist* (1932). In 1937, this woman who had little formal education was granted an honorary doctorate by the University of California at Berkeley, and the following year, at age eighty-one, she was elected to membership in the National Institute of Arts and Letters. She published her last book, *My San Francisco, A Wayward Biography* (1946), two years before her death at ninety.

AUNT JEMIMA

A trademark of the Quaker Oats Company, Aunt Jemima has come to symbolize black servants, especially cooks. For many years, she was drawn with a scarf wrapped around her head in the turban style commonly worn by female slaves who were household workers. The pictorial image has recently been updated to that of a modern black woman; her turban is gone and her modest pearl earrings bespeak respectability. Nonetheless, many black women see Aunt Jemima's image on pancake-related products as a vestige of servitude.

AUNT TOM

A derivative from "Uncle Tom" of HARRIET BEECHER STOWE's famous book, *Uncle Tom's Cabin*, "Aunt Tom" is a term for women who see themselves as powerful—and perhaps even are powerful—because of their sycophantic alignment with those in authority. Such women obtain their power by allying themselves with dominant men, while either ignoring or opposing the aims of feminists on behalf of all women.

Usually exceptionally intelligent and/or personally wealthy, historically "Aunt Toms" have dealt with the frustrations of limitations upon their gender by denying the existence of those limitations, rather than seeking change. With motivations that usually were based less on philosophical principle than on personal promotion, such women identified with men rather than women. Because they wished to be seen as akin to men in thought and behavior, they could not acknowledge their common status with other women and rationalized away their lack of fundamental civil rights.

Examples of such Aunt Tom personalities are ANNA ELLA CARROLL, who participated actively in pre-Civil War politics while opposing women's suffrage, and MARY ABIGAIL DODGE, a political commentator who was a ghostwriter for presidential nominee James G. Blaine, and yet argued against the enfranchisement of women.

AUSTEN, ELIZABETH (1866–1952) Without seeking public attention or establishing herself as a careerist, Austen nevertheless was an experimental photographer in the latter half of the nineteenth and early twentieth centuries. Her collection of some five thousand photographs of the upper-class, suburban New York life she led was recognized as not only a pioneer achievement but also a valuable pictorial record of that era—a time very different from the 1950s when Austen was "discovered," crippled and penniless, in a Staten Island shelter for paupers.

AUTHORS When no other occupational opportunity was open to educated women, there always was the possibility of the pen. From the time of colonials such as ANNE BRADSTREET, there have been women who took pen in hand to record their thoughts, often anonymously. Indeed, the world will never know how many talented women emulated Bradstreet, the later EMILY DICKINSON, and others who entirely hid their work from the public, whose thoughts vanished in humble hearth smoke after their deaths. Even women who ultimately met with literary recognition, such as ELLEN GLASGOW and JULIA WARD HOWE, published their first work anonymously, while other popular writers such as HANNAH WEBSTER FOSTER remained behind a veil of anonymity all of their lives. Even established authors, including PEARL BUCK and LOUISA MAY ALCOTT, sometimes thought it wise to use PSEUDONYMS, usually male.

Despite these longlasting social constraints that demanded women disguise their true identity, many emulated SUSANNA ROWSON, the author of the first American bestseller. There were in fact so many women writing so early in the nation's history that Nathaniel Hawthorne complained, "America is now wholly given over to a damned mob of scribbling women, and I should have no chance of success . . . and should be ashamed of myself if I did succeed." He specifically had in mind MARIA SUSANNA CUMMINS, whose 1854 first novel sold forty thousand copies in a few weeks, a sales feat that would be favorably noticed by publishers even among today's much larger population. A similar achievement was made by SUSAN BOGART WARNER, whose 1851 story of the adventures of an orphaned girl outsold Charles Dicken's *David Copperfield* (1850), even in England.

Yet Hawthorne's self-pitying comments were the opposite of the facts, for he was indeed succeeding in that very era: his 1850 and 1851 bestsellers were sandwiched between the 1848 work of the Bronte sisters and the 1852 success of HARRIET BEECHER STOWE. Not surprisingly, Stowe's work also met with publicly stated scorn from such literary luminaries as William Dean Howells and Mark Twain—attitudes that also may have been based in jealousy of her unprecedented sales of 2.5 million copies in *Uncle Tom's Cabin*'s first year (Twain's first bestseller did not come until seventeen years later).

A comparable record of success for women authors continued through the CIVIL WAR era: bestsellers by Charles Dickens in 1861 and Lewis Carroll in 1866 were separated from each other by Mrs. E.D.E.N. SOUTHWORTH and MARY MAPES DODGE, the bestsellers of 1863 and 1865. To believe that Southworth and Dodge merit their current obscurity is to believe that somehow the reading public totally lost its taste after *A Tale of Two Cities* and yet recovered it a mere five years later for *Alice's Adventures in Wonderland*.

Nor did the era's women authors limit themselves to fiction; already by 1855 a Philadelphia publisher issued a volume entitled *Female Prose Writers of America*. Many of them nonetheless suffered from excessive dubiousness on the part of potential publishers. FANNIE FARMER, for instance, whose first cookbook has sold upwards of 5 million copies during the century since its 1896 publication, was asked by a skeptical Little Brown & Company to assure the costs of its meager first printing. Like other publishers then and now, the company's male editors demonstrated that they had no awareness of the potential market of millions of women as buyers.

Those women who aimed at a market that included men found easier publication. George Washington was an enthusiastic reader of JUDITH SARGENT MURRAY's nonfiction, and HANNAH FARNHAM LEE also proved early in the nation's history that the public would buy books written by women. Lee's 1837 book responding to America's first economic depression was one of the country's first nonfiction bestsellers, running to thirty editions. There was a similarly receptive audience for Anne Newport Royall, a widow who began writing at fifty-four and who supported herself with ten books of TRAVEL between 1826 and 1831. Settling in Washington, she became the PUBLISHER of two newspapers; her attacks on corrupt politicians predated more famous muckrakers by half a century.

Because there clearly was an audience for their writing, women continued to "scribble." Between 1900 and 1910, for example, women held the bestseller title for five of the ten years (FLORENCE BARCLAY, MARY JOHNSTON, Frances Little, and two-time winner Mrs. Humphry Ward). Public appreciation of women authors during the next two decades is indicated by the fact that during this period, there were three women whose bestseller led the list for two consecutive years, a record unmatched by any man. (The women were Lulu Hunt Peters in 1924–1925 for her nonfiction *Diet and Health*; PEARL BUCK in 1931–1932 for *The Good Earth*; and MARGARET MITCHELL in 1936–1937 for *Gone With the Wind*.)

Yet despite the long popularity of women authors with readers, as publishers increasingly emulated other corporate entities after World War II in their promotion and advertising policies, women's names also disappeared from bestseller lists. While thirty-one women held the annual title between 1852 and 1952 (or approximately one every three years), only one woman held it during the fifties and just two in the sixties. Moreover, the bestselling work of earlier women authors was not kept in print, with the result that their names are not known today.

Critics and historians, indeed, often seem to have dismissed women's work in a double standard of literary merit. Women such as PEARL BUCK were criticized for having written too much, while the opposite position was also used to dismiss MARGARET MITCHELL as capable of only one book. The effect is to diminish the work of women as meritorious, either critically or popularly. The result is that historical figures such as GERTRUDE ATHERTON and FRANCES HODGSON BURNETT, who were bestsellers in their time, are almost wholly unacknowledged, while at the same time, Pulitzer Prize winners such as OLA E. WINSLOW and JULIA PETERKIN are also forgotten. Nor have things necessarily improved for writers working in the postfeminist era: GWENDOLYN BROOKS, for example, a contemporary Pulitzer Prize winner, receives so little publicity that she is not known by most of the public in which she lives today.

Occasionally, women have hurt themselves with the use of pseudonyms and with inhibiting restrictions on the circulation of their work, such as WILLA CATHER's injunction against the anthologizing of her fiction. Then too, stereotypes of appropriate "women's writing" has resulted in the inclusion of hundreds of insignificant female writers (especially poets) in biographical dictionaries, while more thoughtful and unconventional women such as KATE CHOPIN and ZORA NEALE HURSTON were excluded.

Yet despite all this, the positive conclusion to be drawn is that American women have been writing from the nation's earliest days, and the thoughts of tens of thousands of women are available in print.

AUXILIARIES Women's groups associated with and supportive of more powerful male American organizations have long existed. Lodges such as the Masons, which added the Eastern Star as its female counterpart in 1875, doubtlessly expected that the food served and the company enjoyed would be more interesting with the occasional participation of women. Political groups emulated social ones in creating women's auxiliaries, even before women had political rights; American men, for example, demonstrated during the Revolution that they needed the support of women organized into auxiliaries, as the DAUGHTERS OF LIBERTY functioned as ancillary to the Sons of Liberty.

Powerless women thus came to exercise whatever influence they could manage through auxiliaries, which were defined as subordinate to and supportive of a larger whole. Women's clubs in both political parties were organized prior

to full women's suffrage, but even after suffrage, these clubs continued to act in secondary roles rather than as participatory, decision-making groups. While the Women's Clubs associated with the Democratic and Republican parties today do not call themselves auxiliaries, they have historically functioned as such; no comparable men's groups exist within the parties, and the women who belong to such clubs are less likely to define themselves as feminists than women who work directly in the party. Such organizations are a half-step for ambivalent women evolving into independence; while such women willingly accept a subordinate place, they nonetheless perform functions that can be crucial to a cause.

Even in trade unionism, women's auxiliaries were recognized early on as essential to survival. In industries such as mining that were exclusively male, professional organizers were quick to form parallel women's groups to ensure that wives understood and supported the union cause. Women's auxiliaries actively participated in violent turn-of-the-century STRIKES from Pennsylvania coal mines to Colorado copper mines; some women were arrested and even killed. During the great sit-down strikes in Detroit's car factories in the 1930s, it was the United Auto Workers women's auxiliaries who defied security guards to bring food and supplies to the men occupying the factories. Even today, the women's auxiliaries of craft unions such as plumbers and electricians often meet at the same time and place as the union meeting and continue to provide support during contract negotiations and strikes.

Finally, while the usual assumption is that a female organization was derived from an earlier male group, the reverse can be true—even if seldom acknowledged. Such conservative women's organizations as the DAUGHTERS OF THE CONFEDERACY, for example, are older than the comparable male organization, showing that it was the women who provided the impetus and organizational model for founding of the men's group. Moreover, such women, who usually lack careers, are likely to value their organizations more and therefore create groups that are much larger, wealthier, and more active than the comparable male group.

The DAUGHTERS OF THE AMERICAN REVOLUTION is a good example of such a case: it has almost ten times as many members as the Sons of the American Revolution. The DAR is organized into more than three thousand local groups, compared with the Sons' fifty-four, and the women employ a staff of 150 in Washington, while the Sons manage only ten in Louisville. Clearly, these men do not share the women's level of interest and support. This observation could well be extended to other parallel organizations, for it may be true in many cases that women's auxiliary is more active than the "real" male organization. In their organizations, as in their lives, such women, for many complex reasons, historically have allowed their work and ideas to be seen as less valid than those of men and themselves as merely extensions of their men.

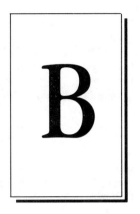

BACHE, SARAH FRANKLIN (1743–1808) Sarah Bache was the daughter of Benjamin Franklin and Deborah Read Rogers, who entered into a formal common law marriage in 1730. They could not legally wed because she was unable to DIVORCE her long-absent husband, but Philadelphia society accepted Sarah as legitimate when she was born thirteen years later. Her mother was thirty-six at the time, and she was their only child to survive infancy.

Remembered for her role in the American Revolution, Sarah Franklin Bache was herself a young mother at the time, with both her husband and father gone to war duties and her mother recently dead. Twice she had to flee Philadelphia when British armies approached—once just four days after she delivered a baby. As fiercely devoted to independence as the men in her life, she wrote her father of the damage done by British troops to his "electrical apparatus" and musical instruments. "I shall never forget nor forgive them," she wrote in February, 1777, "for turning me out of house and home in midwinter."

Moreover, Bache was determined to do more about it than women had ever done in war. Along with other REVOLUTIONARY WAR WOMEN, she volunteered as a fund-raiser for the infant American government and was a leader among the Philadelphia women who managed to raise over three hundred thousand Continental dollars to aid the soldiers of Washington's army. After a successful door-to-door canvass of Philadelphia, she undertook similar responsibility for other Pennsylvania towns. Her home was a gathering place for women, who sewed as they planned their financial strategy, and provided the army with over two thousand linen shirts.

Sarah Bache spent the post-revolutionary period as her father's hostess, maintaining friendships with Washington and other governmental leaders. The mother of eight, she died at sixty-five.

BAGLEY, SARAH (1806–?) Like many other New Hampshire natives during the 1830s, Sarah Bagley left the depressed agricultural economy of her birth, with its lack of job opportunities for women, and came down to the northern Massachusetts town of Lowell to become a TEXTILE WORKER.

Better educated than some of her co-workers, Bagley conducted night classes and wrote for the local industrial publication, but, as working conditions in the mills harshened by the 1840s, she began moving towards labor agitation. By January, 1845, she and others had formed the LOWELL FEMALE LABOR REFORM ASSOCIATION; soon there were five hundred members and Bagley was elected president. She led the women in effective organization against management demands; when one mill tried to increase the standard work load from three looms to four, for example, almost every woman in the mill signed a pledge refusing to accept the work without a commensurate increase in pay, and management dropped its plan.

She led the women into affiliation with the New England Workingman's Association, regularly wrote for that organization's publication, and served as one of its three-member editorial board. In 1846, she and two other women were elected, along with five men, as directors of the New England Labor Reform League—a demonstration of equality unmatched in most of today's labor unions.

Beginning in 1843, Bagley joined a statewide petition campaign for the ten-hour day and other labor reforms and was responsible for thousands of signatures gathered in Lowell during the next three years. So effective was this petition drive that the state legislature responded with hearings, and Bagley led the two men and six women who testified before the committee—something that was almost unheard of in legislative annals at that time. Moreover, when the committee ended up making no recommendations for legislation, she again led these voteless women in a genuine political campaign that defeated the committee's chairman as well as Lowell's legislator at the next election.

While this was a tremendous organizational victory, Bagley's personal life was shattered when the defeated committee chairman struck back with effective defamation of one of the union's men, smearing her with guilt by association. Presumably deciding that the best thing for her union would be her resignation, she made this sacrifice and left both it and the mills.

Doubtless some enterprising man had noticed Sarah Bagley's exceptional abilities, for when a telegraph station opened in Lowell late in 1846, she added business credentials to her political and labor skills—she became the nation's first woman telegraph operator.

Though Sarah Bagley's name is largely forgotten today, when the conditions of women in the 1840s are remembered, the enormity of her achievement can be seen. This was an era before women spoke in public and when the very idea of women's right to vote had not yet surfaced. Despite these serious handicaps, Bagley used her exceptional speaking, organizing, and fund-raising skills to win a political campaign that was sophisticated even by modern standards.

BAKER, ELLA JO (1903–1986)

Born in Virginia, Ella Baker grew up in North Carolina on land that her grandparents bought from their former master shortly after Emancipation. With her family's encouragement, she graduated from Shaw University in Raleigh, a black Baptist institution; in 1927, she moved to New York and began her lifelong career as a writer for black publications as well as a civil rights organizer.

Baker was named office manager for the *Negro National News* in 1932 and also worked as the national director of the Young Negroes' Cooperative League, a consumer group funded by the Depression era's WPA. She began working in a paid position for the National Association for the Advancement of Colored People (NAACP) in Florida in 1938, and by 1943, had advanced to national field director. In 1954, she was elected president of the New York City branch of the NAACP, where she concentrated on integrating that city's schools in 1957 (the same year that the Little Rock efforts of DAISY BATES captured most national headlines). This presidency was an unpaid position; much later, in response to a question on how she made a living, Baker replied, "I haven't. I have eked out an existence."

Soon after Martin Luther King's Southern Christian Leadership Conference (SCLC) began in 1957, Baker moved South to use her twenty years of experience with the NAACP to help with the integration of buses and other public facilities. While King got the attention of the media, it was Baker, as the executive secretary of the new organization, who was back at the office managing the agenda. It was largely her organizing ability, for example, that brought out thirteen thousand people in twenty-two Southern cities on Lincoln's birthday in 1958, when—on "the coldest night in 50 years"—the SCLC kicked off its program to double the number of registered black voters within the next year.

Baker was fifty-four when she joined the SCLC and had a lifetime of organizing work behind her that she felt was not fully utilized by the young male ministers who led the SCLC. When she left the conference in 1960, it was in large part for the same reasons that she had left the NAACP's employment: Baker criticized both organizations for their heavy hierarchy and their exclusion of ordinary blacks, especially women, from policy roles. As early as the 1940s, she reproached the NAACP for an excessive emphasis on a large dues-paying membership to support its national lawyers and lobbyists rather than encouraging local, grass-roots activism. Symbolic of that was, for example, her move of the New York office from a downtown office complex to a Harlem storefront.

Baker therefore was seeking a new vehicle for both women and youth when she played another founding role in 1960. She organized the Student Nonviolent Coordinating Committee (SNCC), setting up its Atlanta office. While carefully playing a behind-the-scenes role that left decision-making to the students, she supported these young people in their efforts to integrate lunch counters and other public facilities. Baker replicated the SNCC approach in 1964, when she organized the dissident Mississippi Freedom Democratic party that challenged the credentials of the whites who claimed to represent Mississippi at the Democratic party's national convention.

She worked to keep SNCC from becoming too strongly identified with any one individual, believing that it was "a handicap for oppressed peoples to depend so largely upon a leader, because . . . it usually means that the media made him, and the media may undo him. There is also the danger . . . that . . . such a person gets to the point of believing that he *is* the movement." The superiority of Baker's philosophy would be clear in 1968, when the leadership vacuum resulting from King's assassination disrupted the forward progress of the civil rights movement.

Baker also understood the critical contributions of women, something that was seldom acknowledged by either black or white leadership. "The movement of the '50s and '60s," she said, "was carried largely by women, since it came out of church groups. It was sort of second nature to women to play a supportive role . . . But it's true that the number of women who carried the movement is much larger than that of men. Black women have had to carry this role . . ."

Withstanding violence and slander in all of the challenges to the racial apartheid that then existed in America, Baker slowly saw her integrationist efforts come to fruition. She never fully retired and lived out the rest of her life in New York, where she continued to serve with various civil rights organizations, including the Puerto Rican Solidarity Committee, until her death at eighty-three. In the dedication of his 1964 book, *The New Abolitionists*, political scientist Howard Zinn called Ella Baker "the most tireless, the most modest, and the wisest activist I know."

BAKER, JOSEPHINE (1906–1975)

Born in St. Louis, Freda Josephine McDonald was the child of a black mother and a Jewish/Spanish father who deserted them. She grew up in extreme poverty and was terrorized by a 1917 race riot. Determined nonetheless to develop her talent for dancing, she ran away to join a Philadelphia-based traveling troupe. Billed at first as a comic rather than a dancer, Josephine was still a teenager when she appeared at the Cotton and Plantation clubs, which were fashionable New York entertainment spots during the Harlem renaissance of the 1920s.

In 1925, she was offered the chance to join *La Revue Negre*; she moved to Paris at age nineteen and it soon became her home. Though the show failed, she successfully auditioned for the famous *Folies Bergere* and was a hit. The French were not only receptive to the new jazz sounds and seminude dances that became Baker's trademark, but they also allowed blacks to live their daily lives without the constraints of segregation. Baker quickly became a celebrity, painted by Picasso and publicized for her exotic behavior, which included keeping a pet leopard and dancing with only a skirt of bananas.

Performing simply as "Josephine," she allowed neither the worldwide depression of the thirties nor her natural aging to deter her career; encouraged by her second husband, a French Jew, she took ballet and singing lessons in the thirties, adding more dimensions to her personal style. After more than a decade of European success, she returned to the U.S. to dance with the Ziegfeld Follies, but the shock of segregation was such that she returned to Europe and became a French citizen in 1937. A miscarriage in 1938 so disappointed her that it resulted in the end of her marriage.

When Paris was overrun by the Nazis in 1940, Baker joined the Resistance, gathering valuable information in the cafe society to which she had easy access, and traveling throughout the Middle East and North Africa entertaining troops. Her services were considered so valuable that she was later honored with three medals from the French government, including the *Croix de Guerre*.

She wrote her memoirs after the war, but that was only a sign of changed direction, not retirement. Disappointed that so little had changed for black Americans after the war, she became active in the U.S. civil rights movement, including the 1963 march on Washington. She continued to perform to earn the money to support, with the help of her third husband, the twelve children of different nationalities they adopted in the years after the war. This "rainbow tribe" and Baker's extravagant lifestyle finally meant that her estate was sold, for a fraction of its value and against her will, to pay creditors in 1968. Offered a home by Princess Grace of Monaco (GRACE KELLY), Baker continued to dance and sing, giving her last performance two days before her death at age sixty-nine.

BALCH, EMILY GREENE (1867–1961)

Born less than two years after the end of the CIVIL WAR, Emily Balch would live well beyond WORLD WAR II, a long life during the century of the greatest change in human history. The third of six girls and one boy, Emily benefited from a family history in Massachusetts that dated to 1623 and from a father who was emotionally and financially supportive of his daughters, only one of whom married.

Educated at Miss Ireland's School in Boston's fashionable Louisburg Square, Emily had met only one woman college graduate before entering BRYN MAWR in 1886, an institution founded by QUAKERS just the previous year. COLLEGE for women was an idea still so controversial that the chief reason for choosing Bryn Mawr over the closer RADCLIFFE was so that Emily could accompany a friend whose Harvard professor father, Emily wrote, "was not willing to have it known among his Cambridge friends that he was disgraced by having a daughter at college."

After a postgraduate year in Paris, she returned to Boston. In the spirit of social good that motivated many New England and Quaker women of her era, Balch cofounded a SETTLEMENT HOUSE on the model of JANE ADDAMS' Chicago Hull House, which was itself only three years old. Balch soon became the "headworker" at Denison House, busy with the poverty engendered by the 1893 depression.

The economic conditions she saw not only motivated her to join the American Federation of Labor in 1894, but also caused her to change fields. "I gradually became dissatisfied with my philanthropic efforts," Balch said of herself, and she took up the study of economics at the UNIVERSITY OF CHICAGO and the University of Berlin. Offered a TEACHING position at WELLESLEY COLLEGE upon her return to the United States, she would become a source of both pride and controversy there for the next two decades.

In 1900, Professor Balch joined a group of faculty who protested the college's acceptance of Rockefeller's "tainted money," but also that year, she was invited to begin a curriculum in sociology. Her off-campus activities during this period included becoming the first president of the Boston WOMEN'S TRADE UNION LEAGUE and chairing the Massachusetts Minimum Wage Commission. By 1913, Balch had risen to become chair of the Department of Economics and Sociology, at least in part because of her classic sociological study, *Our Slavic Fellow Citizens* (1910).

A pioneer of field work, the book reflected Balch's personal commitment of thousands of dollars spent traveling in Eastern Europe, followed by a year among Slavic settlements throughout the United States. Unaware that this work would become required reading for students of immigration throughout the twentieth century, Wellesley trustees fired its author eight years after its publication. Their reasons had nothing to do with her work, but rather her politics, for Balch had played a strong role in opposition to WORLD WAR I.

She was one of forty-two American women who, in April 1915, crossed the war-imperiled Atlantic for an international peace conference of women at The Hague. This was a radical thing to do at a time when women not only lacked the vote, but when most Americans were still provincially proud of their ignorance of European power politics. Having traveled in some of the remotest parts of Europe to study Slavs and being fluent in three foreign languages with a passable knowledge of a half-dozen others, Balch was among the first internationalists of the twentieth century.

Beginning the organization that became the WOMEN'S INTERNATIONAL LEAGUE FOR PEACE AND FREEDOM (WILPF), the women soon sent delegations urging peace to the highest European officials. Balch traveled throughout northern Europe, meeting with the prime minister of Denmark, the king of Norway, and the foreign ministers of Sweden and Russia, where the delegation's request for a meeting with the czar was denied. After her return to the United States, she spent an hour with President Wilson reporting on her trip and urging neutrality.

When the United States nonetheless entered the war, Balch was among the pacifists to suffer personally for their views, and she was "not reappointed" to her position at Wellesley in 1919. Although she was supported by most of the faculty and alumnae, in the words of a Wellesley colleague, "the hard-headed businessmen just succeeded in carrying the vote." After twenty years of teaching and at age fifty-two, she lost her pension as well as her position.

Balch's credentials as a writer now proved valuable, for in addition to her immigration classic, she had published (with Jane Addams and ALICE HAMILTON), *Women at The Hague* in 1915 and *Approaches to the Great Settlement*, a 1918 survey of peace treaty proposals. She joined the *Nation* as a contributor on international issues.

Returning to Europe in 1919 for the postwar conference that the women at The Hague had planned four years earlier, Balch became secretary/treasurer of the WILPF. She spent the next three years getting its office in Geneva underway before resigning from this paid position to instead volunteer for the league. Throughout the rest of the twenties, she moved between Europe and America, organizing women and speaking for peace.

The thirties forced her away from absolute pacifism; Balch had a deep appreciation for the complexities of internationalism and recognized fascism early for the danger that it was. Speaking out on the Japanese attack of Manchuria, Italy's aggression in Ethiopia, the Spanish Civil War, and Germany's attacks on Jews, she declared, "Neutrality in the sense of treating the aggressor and his victim alike is morally impossible."

When the controlled conflict of the thirties became WORLD WAR II in the forties, Emily Balch was seventy-five years old but far from finished. She spent the war years in the United States, speaking to the "freedom" portion of the Women's International League for Peace and Freedom and defining the differences between the two world wars. She worked for Japanese-Americans maltreated in this country, as well as for Jewish refugees, and for her lifetime of such work, she was rewarded at the war's end with the 1946 Nobel Peace Prize.

Only two other women had been so honored since the prize began in 1901. (Bertha von Suttner, an Austrian writer who urged Nobel to begin the prize, won it in 1905 and Balch's colleague, Jane Addams, in 1931.) She gave most of the Nobel money to the causes she supported, but used the renewed interest in her life for continued writing and speaking during her eighties.

Balch entered a Cambridge nursing home just before her ninetieth birthday, and though her four years of life there was sometimes "duller than ditch-water," her mind remained alert. "I am bringing my days to a close in a world still hag-ridden by the thought of war," she said in one of the last items of a life of writing, "but when I reflect on the enormous changes that I have seen myself . . . how can I fail to be of good courage?"

BALDWIN, FAITH (1893–1978) A bestselling author in the early part of the twentieth century, Baldwin grew up in a prosperous New York family. She received a FINISHING SCHOOL education and lived abroad, including residence in Germany during the first two years of WORLD WAR I.

Baldwin married in 1920, but did not use her husband's name when she published her first novel the following year. Immediately popular, she would write more than eighty-five books during the next half-century. She wrote for newspapers and magazines as well, and her stories were made into movies—four in 1936 alone. Her romance novels found a receptive audience among women; during the Great Depression, when such escapist fiction may have been necessary to the mental health of many, she earned more than a quarter-million annually. Though her career waned later, she continued to publish until just before her death, with *Adam's Eden* being published in 1977.

BALL, LUCILLE (1911–1989) Though lovingly remembered as a favorite by millions, Lucille Ball endured three decades in the entertainment business before becoming successful. She spent the twenties seeking dramatic roles in New York, finding instead only moderate success as a model with the PSEUDONYM of Diane Belmont. During the thirties she made a series of unremarkable movies, a career she continued for another decade after her 1940 marriage to Desi Arnaz, who spent the forties on the road with his band.

In 1950, they formed Desilu Productions and transformed their lives with the new medium of television. "I Love Lucy," a comedy that was based on their lives up until that time—with the exception that Lucy was portrayed as an inane housewife—was an immediate hit. Desilu made other major productions, but their financial success dissolved into personal unhappiness and they divorced in 1960. Ball replaced her husband as company president two years later and returned to television with "The Lucy Show" in 1968. She received many honors, including four Emmys and induction into the Television Hall of Fame in 1984. Her death in Los Angeles, following heart surgery, was mourned worldwide by the masses who loved Lucy.

BANKHEAD, TALLULAH BROCKMAN (1903–1968) It was her stunning blond appearance and uncommonly deep voice as well as her unusual background as the daughter of a powerful political family that propelled Bankhead into fame that her talent never quite matched. Motherless from an early age, she persuaded her Alabama father to allow her to move to New York when she was only fifteen; family money allowed her to live in style, but in six years there, the only roles she acted were undistinguished.

In 1923, Bankhead went to England, where she quickly met a different fate. Though her roles were still light, she soon became a sensation with her clever witticisms and the unconventional behavior that was fashionable among the post-Edwardian young. Enticed by a Paramount contract, she returned to the United States and made several films in the early thirties, but achieved her greatest critical success on the New York stage in 1939, starring in LILLIAN HELLMAN's *Little Foxes*. Tallulah—as she was simply known—was married during the time of the Hellman success, having wed only once and briefly, from 1937 to 1941.

A 1944 Hitchcock movie won her a film critics award, but by the fifties her career was faltering. Though she made radio, nightclub, and television appearances and wrote her autobiography, the shock value of her Roaring Twenties style was gone, and she lacked the classical training she needed to continue in stage roles that matched her age. Increasingly dependent on drugs and alcohol, she was still idolized by millions but also was increasingly parodied when she died from emphysema at age sixty-five.

BARCLAY, FLORENCE LOUISA CHARLESWORTH (1862–1921)

The author of the 1910 bestseller, *The Rosary*, Barclay was an extremely popular turn-of-the-century novelist who attracted a worldwide audience. Her books were translated into many languages and published by companies in such places as Chile, Iceland, and Romania as well as in Paris and London. *The Rosary* alone had upwards of twenty editions.

Like many other women AUTHORS, Barclay began with a PSEUDONYM, calling herself Brandon Roy for her first 1891 novel. She did not publish again for over a decade until *The Wheels of Time* in 1908, but after the 1910 success of *The Rosary*, she averaged a book a year, for a total of thirteen books in the thirteen years before she died at fifty-nine. *The Life of Florence L. Barclay* came out in 1932, and some of her novels were still being translated and published abroad as late as 1940.

BARKER, KATE "MA" (1872–1935)

Born in Springfield, Missouri, Barker was a rare female version of the Jesse James heritage. Despite marriage and motherhood, she adopted the same post-Confederacy justifications of outlawry that inspired James and other criminal gangs who operated from the Missouri-Oklahoma area.

Heading the last of these great outlaw bands and rationalized finally by the Great Depression, she was the brains behind the crimes committed by her three sons. Ma Barker held complete domination over her "boys," insisting that they attend church while also outlining plans for the kidnappings, murders, and bank robberies that netted them more than $3 million.

Her name was a household word in the thirties, epitomizing everything that women were not supposed to be, but the notoriety meant that she could not spend her millions and she lived her life in low-class accommodations on the run. Ma Barker died with her son Fred in a machine gun battle with authorities while they were hiding out in Oklawaha, Florida.

BARNARD COLLEGE

Founded as a female complement to New York City's Columbia University in 1889, Barnard was the last of the SEVEN SISTERS schools to be established. Named for the man who was president of Columbia at the time, it was integrated into the male structure sooner than any other women's COLLEGE of its type; Barnard operated as a separate entity only eleven years before being incorporated into Columbia in 1900.

It retained its own board of trustees and fund-raising foundation, in which women have always been active. Among Barnard's most distinguished students are ANNE ANASTASI, MARY ANTIN, HELEN GAHAGAN DOUGLAS, VIRGINIA GILDERSLEEVE, FREDA KIRCHWEY, ELIZABETH JANEWAY, MARGARET MEAD, and AGNES MEYER. ZORA NEALE HURSTON was the first black student at Barnard.

BARNETT, IDA WELLS— See WELLS-BARNETT, IDA BELL

BARRY, LEONORA MARIE KEARNEY (1849–1930)

Known as both "Mother Lake" and "Mrs. Barry-Lake" after her 1890 marriage, her record in union organizing was achieved under the name of Leonora Barry.

She emigrated from Ireland as a child and worked as a TEACHER until marriage. After becoming a WIDOW with a family to support, Barry worked in the GARMENT INDUSTRY, where the low wages and harsh conditions motivated her to join the Knights of Labor in 1884. Two years later, she was elected to head the national women's department of this early union coalition.

For almost four years, she traveled extensively organizing women into unions. She had virtually no models to follow, for labor activism among women had been largely limited to local or regional efforts. Through speeches, correspondence, and factory inspections when she could obtain entrance, Leonora Barry accumulated information on the conditions of women in industry and encouraged activism. She spoke to the INTERNATIONAL COUNCIL OF WOMEN in 1888 and is credited with the passage of a factory inspection law in Pennsylvania, but her achievement was limited by her personal conservatism—particularly her refusal to take visible political action.

She retired from union organizing after remarrying, but continued to be active in the SUFFRAGE MOVEMENT and was included as a speaker at the 1893 COLUMBIAN EXPOSITION. Despite her Irish Catholic affiliations, she also was involved in the largely Protestant WOMEN'S CHRISTIAN TEMPERANCE UNION and was a lively and popular lecturer. Like MOTHER JONES, another well known speaker and labor organizer of the time, "Mother Lake" was conservative on feminist issues; both believed that women's place was in the home and that a proper economic system should enable that goal.

BARRYMORE, ETHEL (1879–1959)

Born into the great theatrical families of Drew and Barrymore, Ethel Barrymore made her stage debut at fourteen with her maternal grandmother and older brother Lionel. She appeared on London and New York stages while still in her teens and had her first starring role in 1901. Performing roles from light comedy to Shakespearean tragedy, she soon was recognized as the queen of Broadway and her appearance guaranteed a show's success.

Barrymore exhibited her versatility by working in other media, too, including vaudeville, radio, movies, and finally television as each appeared during her lengthy career. In 1944, she was finally recognized by Hollywood with an Academy Award—but only for Best Supporting Actress.

Barrymore was married for just fourteen years of her life, wedding in 1909 and divorcing in 1923. Age thirty when she married, she quickly bore three children between 1911 and 1913, and, like her mother and grandmother, continued her career with little disruption. Ethel Barrymore published her memoirs in 1955 and died at age eighty.

BARS AND BARTENDING The owners of bars and saloons throughout the nineteenth and much of the twentieth centuries generally assumed that any woman who would patronize their business was a PROSTITUTE; therefore, those businesses that wanted an image of respectability often either banned women outright, or provided a separate ladies lounge.

State laws not only protected such businesses in discriminating against both customers and employees of the female gender, but often even mandated it. The changed behavior of men and women during WORLD WAR II brought millions of women into bars for the first time as women joined men in smoking and drinking. A Michigan lawyer, Anne Ruth Davidow Seeger, filed suit in 1948 to overturn legislation that prohibited women from working as bartenders unless their husbands or fathers owned the bar—and lost the case.

As late as 1975, five schoolteachers on vacation in Florida were ejected from a table in their hotel's bar and threatened with arrest on the assumption that women in bars were prostitutes. In that same era, even a state as ostensibly liberal as Massachusetts still maintained legislation that forbade women from sitting at a bar, rather than at a table. Such laws were used as arguments for the EQUAL RIGHTS AMENDMENT, which would have nullified discriminatory state decrees.

BARTLETT, MARY (?–1789)

The history of the American Revolution often has been taught in such a way that it is easy to ignore the fact that the "Founding Fathers" in their time were, of course, rebels and traitors with a price on their heads. Even less recognized are the results for their families.

Mary Bartlett, who married her cousin Joseph Bartlett in 1754, was one such example. Her husband was the first to answer the roll call in the Continental Congress when the Declaration of Independence came to a vote, and his positive response meant disaster for her. Their Kingston, New Hampshire home was burned to the ground by Tories as a demonstration that she should warn him to cease his "pernicious activity."

Like other REVOLUTIONARY WAR WOMEN, however, she had political ideas of her own, and her letters conveyed neither the Tory message nor self-pity. Instead, Mary Bartlett took her brood of homeless little children (she bore twelve, with eight living to adulthood), resettled on their farmland, and maintained the family throughout the war so that her husband was free to continue his public service.

BARTON, CLARA (CLARISSA) HARLOW (1821–1912)

Barton is one of the handful of American women famous enough to be assured of a place in every schoolbook. Most texts, however, reinforce the stereotypical traits assigned to women by emphasizing her roles as founder of the AMERICAN RED CROSS and as a CIVIL WAR nurse, while ignoring other aspects of her life, as well as the similar contributions of other women. Barton herself was quick to point out that her Civil War experience was shared by hundreds who are forgotten; some, such as MARY ANN BICKERDYKE, did far more than she.

Named Clarissa, she preferred to be called Clara. She grew up in rural Massachusetts, was informally educated, and began TEACHING while still in her teens. She had a teaching career of almost two decades before she ever embarked on the ventures that would make her famous, and, indeed, it was sexism in the teaching field that caused the change in her life. After many years in schools near Worcester, Massachusetts, she went to the Liberal Institute of Clinton, New York for a year of study in 1850 and then moved to New Jersey, where, in Bordertown, she began one of that state's first non-tuition schools. It soon grew so large that local officials decided that a male head was required—and Barton resigned in protest.

She left teaching forever and moved to Washington in 1854, where Barton also has the distinction of being one of the first (quite probably, *the* first) woman employee of the federal government. Though treated with hostility by her male coworkers in the Patent Office, Barton's organizational abilities soon became obvious to her superiors. Federal jobs at the time, however, were highly political, and despite some congressional support, Barton lost her position after the election of 1856. She spent three aimless years at home in Massachusetts before being called back to the Patent Office in 1860, when political winds were shifting and the Civil War was on the horizon.

Barton was thus in her forties when the war brought her to public attention. Like other Washingtonians, she was shocked by the Union's disastrous lack of preparation at the Battle of Bull Run and especially by the Army's apparent indifference to casualties. Entirely on her own initiative, she demonstrated the resourcefulness she had learned in establishing the New Jersey school and at the Patent Office: Barton advertised in Massachusetts newspapers for medical supplies and food that she could distribute to the troops. When they began arriving, she quit her job, converted her home to a storehouse, hired mules and wagons, and organized her friends to go with her to bring the badly needed goods to the 1862 battlegrounds of Maryland and Virginia.

Barton's genius was thus in procurement and distribution of supplies rather than in the nursing for which she is usually remembered. NURSES, instead, were organized under DOROTHEA DIX and the U.S. SANITARY COMMISSION. Moreover, because these donations of supplies depended on publicity, Barton soon learned to use both the media and her congressional contacts to bring soldiers' needs to the attention of the public.

As the army's Quartermaster Corps and the Sanitary Commission became more efficient, there was less need for Barton's intervention, and she was relatively inactive during the middle of the war. Finally, in June 1864, less than a year before the war's end, she received an official appointment as a nurse; General Benjamin Butler made her head nurse of his Army of the James. She kept that position only about eight months, however, for in February, 1865, with the war coming to an end and with Lincoln's endorsement, she opened an agency to work on missing soldiers.

Again, the Army had no experience in this sort of concern for troops and Barton once more set about building a structure to accomplish the goal. Taking advantage of the newspapers again, she drew up lists of men whose families considered them missing and then served as a clearinghouse for the responses from comrades and ex–prisoners of war. She spent the summer of 1865 under the hot Georgia sun, marking the graves of almost thirteen thousand men who died of disease and starvation in the appalling Andersonville prison camp.

Like her supply procurement, this work depended on donations, and Barton not only spent her personal funds but also took to the postwar lecture circuit to pay debts. Overcoming the timidity she claimed she felt since childhood, she made about three hundred speeches throughout the Union states. No doubt it was this tour and its resulting publicity that established her name so firmly as the premier Civil War nurse; the hundreds of other women, in both the North and South, that she acknowledged as having done work similar to hers did not mount such platforms.

In 1869, her Civil War work done, Barton went to Europe for much needed rest and stayed four years. After hearing of the International Committee of the Red Cross that had been formed in Switzerland in 1863, she went to Geneva and discovered that the American State Department refused to be involved with the Red Cross. She nonetheless worked closely with it, seeing the organization in action during the Franco-Prussian War of 1870–71. There Barton implemented still another new idea by creating a sewing shop in Strasbourg, an Alsace-Lorraine city at the center of the war, where women who were impoverished by the bombardment could earn a living.

Returning to the United States in 1873 at age fifty-one, she retired to upstate New York—but a forty-year career yet lay before her. With the outbreak of war between Russia and Turkey in 1877, the Red Cross again came to her attention, and she began her efforts to educate Americans on the goals of the international organization and to urge congressional ratification of its Geneva treaty. Most Americans, however, not only were exhausted by their own war experience but also were steadfast isolationists. Because European wars seemed so irrelevant to her audience, Barton began speaking to the need of an organization to deal with natural disasters and found a better reception.

Finally, after almost a decade of political work, the Senate ratified the Red Cross treaty in 1882. Barton, sidetracked only slightly by six months as head of a Massachusetts women's prison, set about developing the organization's funding base and state affiliates. Under her presidency, the Red Cross dealt with several late nineteenth-century natural disasters, including the Johnstown flood, and in 1898, it proved its need to exist during the Spanish American War. Barton traveled to troop staging grounds in Florida and went on to Cuba, doing her best at age seventy-seven to deal, once again, with inadequate quartermaster supplies and a Medical Corps that lost more than five times as many men to disease as battle deaths.

But, for the first time in her life, Clara Barton's role in this war received as much criticism as acclaim. Soon members of her own board were saying that her role as president meant that she should be behind a desk in Washington rather than making soup in the field. Despite her clear organizational and political skills, Barton had an abhorrence of bureaucracy, which when reinforced by her frugality, meant the Red Cross' bookkeeping and decision-making systems were informal, and therefore, likely to be controlled solely by her. By 1904, rebellion among board members to what they saw as her autocratic and outdated style reached a crisis, and Barton was forced to resign her presidency.

Still not ready to retire, she spent the remaining eight years of her life organizing the National First Aid Association, supporting the women's suffrage organizations with appearances, and keeping up the thirty-five volumes of her diaries. She still looked and behaved much younger than her ninety-one years when she died in suburban Washington. She is buried where she was born in North Oxford, Massachusetts.

BASCOM, FLORENCE (1862–1945)

The daughter of the president of the University of Wisconsin, Florence Bascom took advantage of the coeducational opportunity available in state COLLEGES TO WESTERN WOMEN, enrolling there in 1878. She soon developed an interest in the non-traditional field of geology and took additional science courses before earning her master's degree there in 1887. After TEACHING for two years, she became the first woman to earn a Ph.D. from JOHNS HOPKINS in 1893.

After two years at Ohio State, Dr. Bascom went to BRYN MAWR and taught young women there for the rest of her academic career. In 1894, she was the first woman elected to membership in the Geological Society of America, and two years later, she became the first woman credentialed by the United States Geological Survey. Thereafter, she spent her vacations exploring the geologic history of the Mid-Atlantic states and also served as an associate editor of *American Geologist*.

Dr. Bascom retired from Bryn Mawr in 1928, and two years later was the first woman to be elected a vice-president of the American Geological Society. She was further recognized with inclusion in the first edition of *Men of Science*.

BATES, DAISY GASTON (1922–   )

A rock thrown at Daisy Bates as she sat in her living room signaled the beginning of several years of living in a home that was an armed camp, with round-the-clock guards necessary to preserve her life.

As head of the Arkansas chapter of the National Association for the Advancement of Colored People (NAACP) from 1953–61, Bates demonstrated her leadership abilities when the Supreme Court ruled in 1954 that segregated schools were inherently unequal. She inspired Little Rock's blacks to avail themselves of the decision and organized the nine students (six girls and three boys) who attempted to enroll in all-white Central High School when classes began in 1957.

Neither the local NAACP nor the school board expected the violent response that continued for several years. Arkansas Governor Orval Faubus, seeing an exploitable campaign issue that could break precedent and elect him for a third term, overruled school and city governments that were trying to follow the law. He called out the National Guard to block the integration, rioting broke out, and finally President Eisenhower sent federal troops to enforce the Court decision and protect the students. Through all the controversy to follow, Daisy Bates, though a young woman still in her thirties, was a strong and successful leader for the NAACP.

She withstood arrest, threatening letters and phone calls, bombing and shooting attacks on her home, and twice being hung in effigy. The *Arkansas State Press*, the newspaper that she and her husband had published for sixteen years, was bankrupted as white corporations withdrew their advertising and black businesses were intimidated into doing the same. When they were forced out of business in 1959, both Daisy and L.C. Bates were offered jobs elsewhere, but they chose to stay in Little Rock where the next year, they witnessed the graduation of the last of the original nine students. Bates was honored with the Spingarn Medal, the highest award given by the NAACP, in 1958; two years later, the Supreme Court reversed her conviction in a lower court for refusal to reveal NAACP membership lists.

She published her memoirs, *The Long Shadow of Little Rock*, in 1962; when she returned home after delivering her manuscript to New York, she was greeted by a Ku Klux Klan cross. Given this, and especially given that when she was five, her mother was gang raped and killed by three white men who were never prosecuted, her ability to empathize with the relatively minor suffering of Little Rock's white integrationists becomes remarkable. Nonetheless, her memoirs gave full credit to several white men whom she felt indirectly gave their lives to the cause. Eventually justice prevailed, and Daisy Bates managed to make her voice heard as a PUBLISHER again. She sold her newspaper in 1988 and lives in retirement in Little Rock.

BATES, KATHERINE LEE (1859–1929)

Associated with WELLESLEY COLLEGE all of her life as first a student and then an English professor, Bates is known for her authorship of "America the Beautiful," which she wrote after climbing Pike's Peak in 1893.

"America the Beautiful" was published in its final form in 1911 and has become an unofficial national anthem, which many find preferable in both melody and message to the official anthem.

BAY, JOSEPHINE PERFECT (1900–   )

Despite the general regression of women in the 1950s, Josephine Bay became the first woman to head a member firm of the New York Stock Exchange in 1956. Already chairman of the board of American Export Lines, she had an established reputation as a businesswoman, and when her financier husband died, she made active use of her inheritance of about a third of the stock of A.M. Kidder & Company to become chairman of the board and president of this old and distinguished brokerage house.

Having stayed single until age forty-two, Bay's experience was not limited to that of a businessman's wife, but she candidly asserted the significance that role could have. Her late husband, she said, "time and time again, would discuss a business problem with me—urging me to take the opposite viewpoint to help clarify his thinking." Evidently his Wall Street colleagues similarly respected her opinion, for her election was without opposition.

A multimillionaire with homes on Park Avenue and in Palm Beach, Bay clearly could have lived a leisurely life, but instead her speeches were full of admonitions to women to avoid being "just sweet and naive things to be provided for." The result, she believed, would not only benefit women, but also the nation: "When women are . . . not in the role of mere passive coupon clippers but as active investment owners, our economy will be more vibrant and more venturesome."

BEACH, SYLVIA WOODBRIDGE (1887–1962)

Born in Baltimore, Sylvia Beach lived her teenage years in Paris where her father was minister of the American church. The family returned to the U.S. in 1906, and after spending her twenties uneventfully in Princeton, New Jersey, Beach returned to Paris in 1917, the year the United States entered WORLD WAR I.

Two years later, using her mother's savings, Beach opened Shakespeare & Co., an English-language bookstore that became a gathering place for expatriates who rejected the U.S. during the intellectually repressive postwar years. Her bookstore served as a haven and information network for Fitzgerald, Hemingway, KATHERINE ANNE PORTER, and others who would later be recognized as great American writers.

When both American and English publishers succumbed to the era's censorship, Beach undertook the publication of the complete manuscript of James Joyce's *Ulysses*, parts of which had been declared obscene by U.S. officials. After deciphering Joyce's nearly illegible handwriting and then paying a printer, Beach's bookshop became the sole source for the first one thousand copies. Although later printings earned her royalties as publisher, she lost these rights at the same time that the Great Depression nearly bankrupted her. Beach closed her store and hid its books rather than risk Nazi confiscation in 1941, but she was nonetheless imprisoned for seven months in 1943. Though she did not reopen her store after the war, she continued to be an important literary figure and published her autobiography in 1959.

Shakespeare & Co., near Notre Dame and still under American ownership, continues her tradition of welcoming Americans in Paris.

BEALS, JESSIE TARBOX (1870–1942)

Though she was born into a prosperous Ontario family, Jessie's father lost his fortune and took to drink while she was still young. Like most women of her class and era who had to make a living, she began TEACHING school in 1888; she moved south of the Canadian border to western Massachusetts and taught for almost a decade.

She never enjoyed the occupation, and after winning a camera as a magazine subscription sales premium, Miss Tarbox soon discovered that taking photographs could be more than an amusement for her students. She saved up two weeks salary (twelve dollars), bought a better camera and, during summer vacation, set up a photography studio on her front porch. Since she made more money that summer than she was paid for a school year, it was understandable that after marriage (when women no longer were allowed to teach in most communities) she turned to photography as the key to an independent and interesting future.

In 1897, Jessie Tarbox married Alfred Beals, and for the first years, their marriage seemed an ideal match between adventurous equals. When she reached thirty the same year the twentieth century dawned, Jessie persuaded Alfred to give up their Massachusetts home and see the world via itinerant photography. They went first to a fair at Brattleboro, Vermont, where, in September of 1900, Jessie Tarbox Beals became the world's first woman news photographer by taking pictures of the fair that were published in local newspapers. They spent the rest of the fall in Brattleboro, with Jessie riding her bicycle around town recruiting customers, as well as actually taking the pictures. Alfred meanwhile developed the glass plate negatives and made the prints, soon establishing a reputation for unusual speed under difficult circumstances.

That winter they went on to Florida, where Mrs. Beals, unable at first to connect with the locally prominent, took many photographs of Jacksonville blacks who were willing to spend money on pictures of their families. Although a May, 1901 fire that devastated the city provided her with material that could have been nationally syndicated, Beals was still such a business ingenue that she didn't realize how to turn the tragedy into a personal triumph.

She soon learned. After enduring some difficult months back north, including the death of an infant, Beals demonstrated such unusual determination that she was hired as a staff newspaper photographer in Buffalo. The credentials she earned there were sufficient to convince her that she could truly establish herself by covering the World's Fair held in St. Louis in 1904. Though fair officials were initially hostile, when Beals' scoop of an unauthorized photo of a Patagonian woman among the fair's visiting aborigines was nationally published, she was given a photographer's permit. Almost overnight, Jessie Tarbox Beals herself became a fair attraction, as she received credentials from several of the era's chief magazines and newspapers. During the next six months, she lugged her thirty pounds of photographic equipment around the miles of fairgrounds, not only earning the title of photographic journalist by creating stories about the exhibits, but also establishing connections with celebrity visitors, including President Theodore Roosevelt. She even floated in a balloon for aerial shots.

After the fair was over, Jessie Beals ensured her continued reputation by sending out press releases and hustling for new accounts. Alfred, meanwhile, was tiring of their busy life; originally an Amherst agriculture student, he preferred quiet leisure in the country where he studied mosses. The first serious sign of their increasing incompatibility occurred when he insisted that she turn down an expense-paid trip to the Philippines offered by secretary of war and soon-to-be president, William Howard Taft. He did permit a trip to San Antonio, where she photographed Roosevelt's reunion with his Rough Riders.

In the spring of 1905, they compromised by settling in New York, where the Greenwich Village arts community would become Jessie's true home for the rest of her life. Her appointment book soon filled, and she was one of several women photographers who exhibited in a 1906 show. With her marriage turning increasingly into a business relationship, she traveled as much as she could, taking photos from Maine to Minnesota. Her subjects were equally varied, from slum immigrants to commercial buildings to the cats of society women. She needed the income to support her expensive tastes, and she spent most of her leisure in cafe society while Alfred fretted about the bills and imposed allowances.

When Nanette Tarbox Beals was born in 1911, Alfred's fatherhood was open to serious doubt, for Jessie's private poetry clearly revealed an affair. Still they did not divorce, and

Alfred treated Nanette as his own. Age forty-one when her baby was born, Jessie had yearned for a child, yet Nanette had no memory of living with her mother until she was seventeen. Her parents separated when she was six, and after that she lived at boarding schools and with friends while her mother maintained a large studio at the New York address formerly held by Louis Tiffany.

Jessie Beals held her fiftieth birthday there with one of her renowned parties. Its 1920 date, however, reflected the widespread growth of photography, so that at the same time she encountered additional competition, age also prevented her from the audacious tactics she had used to achieve unusual photos in her youth. She handled the problem with her lifelong persistance and began specializing in garden photography during the twenties, being published in the major gardening magazines.

With increasing expenses in New York and better gardens in California, she moved there in 1928, taking Nanette along. But Wall Street crashed the following year, business was bad without the support of longtime clients, and when Nanette finished high school, they returned first to Chicago and then New York.

In her sixties during the depths of the Depression, she struggled financially, even while she continued to win awards. A 1941 trip to Florida was a complete monetary loss, and the following year, Jessie Tarbox Beals died at age seventy-one in the charity ward of Bellevue Hospital.

BEARD, MARY RITTER (1876–1958)

Mary Ritter met Charles Beard when they were undergraduates at DePauw University in Indiana. After graduation, she taught German for three years before they married in 1900; it was to be a marriage that inevitably would eclipse her individual reputation, but it also would be an uncommon example of how a couple can live intellectually and personally satisfying lives.

They went together to Oxford, where he studied and she became active with the British suffrage movement and working-class organizations. Returning to New York two years later, they both enrolled at Columbia despite the birth of a daughter, but Mary Beard's graduate work in sociology ended in 1904, with her expressing distaste for academia and a preference for self-education.

While Charles went on to a professorship at Columbia, she bore a son in 1907 and the same year, began working for the WOMEN'S TRADE UNION LEAGUE. From 1910 to 1912, she edited the *Woman Voter*, the publication of New York's Woman Suffrage Party, and then worked for the Wage Earners' League, which was the party's working class unit. She belonged to the militant wing of the SUFFRAGE MOVEMENT that was headed by ALICE PAUL, but split from that faction after suffrage passed because Beard's labor involvement convinced her of the need for PROTECTIVE LEGISLATION in the workplace, which would be lost if Paul's goal of the EQUAL RIGHTS AMENDMENT were obtained.

In 1917, when the United States entered WORLD WAR I, the Beards moved to coastal Connecticut after Charles resigned in protest of Columbia's repression of antiwar views. Undistracted by New York's organizations, Mary's life now turned to more reflective study of women's historical roles. She had already published *Woman's Work in Municipalities* (1915) and would add *A Short History of the American Labor Movement* in 1920. She and her husband spent the twenties collaborating on what would become a highly successful series of sweeping American histories, the first volume of which, *The Rise of American Civilization*, appeared in 1927.

While their coauthored books would give more attention to women than any similar texts for a long time to come, Mary Beard also, during the thirties, published three books that dealt explicitly with women: *Understanding Women* (1931), *America Through Women's Eyes* (1933) and *Laughing Their Way: Women's Humor in America* (1934). She attempted to build an international women's archive as well during this period, but fund-raising during the Great Depression proved impossible and the project was abandoned. Meanwhile, their daughter Miriam emulated her parents, publishing books on Japan and on business history during the thirties.

Though the sales of the Beards' joint books was indicative of a public desire for a broader historical view, many historians discounted their work, much in the way that the similarly popular Will and ARIEL DURANT were also disdained by academicians. Since Charles Beard had stellar academic credentials, their contempt focused particularly on Mary Beard, with reviewers crediting their joint books to him and ignoring her individual publications.

Her seminal work, *Woman as a Force in History*, appeared at the end of WORLD WAR II, when historians seemed as eager as the public to see women returned to the kitchen after what they viewed as the aberrations of war. At age seventy and after a lifetime of scholarship, Mary Beard should have been given a respectful evaluation, but her work was attacked with extremely hostile reviews. Decades later, however, it would provide a guide to those in the revived women's movement who were searching out their histories.

Charles Beard died in 1948, two years after Mary's great unacknowledged book; she continued to write, but not on American history. Turning to an aspect of women's history new for both herself and the public, she published *The Force of Women in Japanese History* in 1953. A 1955 memoir of her husband was Mary Beard's last work before dying three years later. She destroyed most of her personal papers.

BEAUX, CECELIA (1893–1942)
One of the few nineteenth-century women to achieve recognition as a painter, Cecilia Beaux was born in Philadelphia and received her initial artistic training there. She opened a studio, and in 1885, won a major prize that earned her attention in Paris. She studied there in 1888–89, returned to Philadelphia, and established herself as a portraitist. In 1895, Beaux was the first woman appointed as an instructor at the Pennsylvania Academy of Fine Arts, and the following year, a Paris exhibition brought her the honor of election to the *Societe Nationale des Beaux-Arts.* After 1900, she divided her time between New York City and a Massachusetts seaside home.

Her most famous painting probably is "The Dancing School," but it is her specialty of portrait painting that sets her apart from the more stereotypical areas of still life and landscape painting that are often associated with women. Beaux did a number of mother/daughter portraits, as well as portraits of the era's prominent men. Her work is exhibited in galleries in Boston, Chicago, and other cities, as well as in Washington's Corcoran Gallery and New York's Metropolitan Museum of Art.

Among other honors, Beaux was awarded the Gold Medal of the American Academy of Arts and Letters in 1926. She published her autobiography, *Background With Figures*, in 1930.

BEECHER, CATHARINE ESTHER (1800–1878)
The oldest of Reverend Lyman Beecher's thirteen children, Catharine assumed much of the responsibility for his household—which, with servants, other relatives, and constant visitors, often numbered two dozen for daily meals. The experience developed in her a deep appreciation of women's work that made her an early proponent of what would later be called HOME ECONOMICS.

Her father's influence on his sons was clear: all seven became Protestant ministers. Had Catharine Beecher been a boy, she doubtless would have become a famous preacher like her brothers Henry Ward and Edward. Instead she was a writer like her sister HARRIET BEECHER STOWE, and while she would never write a bestseller, she was nonetheless very influential among women.

Betrothed at twenty-two, Beecher resolved never to marry when her fiance died at sea. Instead, she and her sister Mary began a girl's school in Hartford, Connecticut—a venture that was still fairly unconventional in 1823. Even more unconventional was the curriculum that Beecher developed; though her own education had consisted almost entirely of tutoring at home, she insisted on a new TEACHING model for girls, with high academic standards as well as the introduction of calisthenics.

The latter was indicative of Beecher's belief that American women shamefully ruined their health through poor diet, lack of exercise, and dangerously constrictive clothing. Yet while she preached this message all of her life, Beecher herself suffered several nervous collapses and sought care in upwards of a dozen types of sanitariums.

It was her health, at least in part, that caused her to abandon her successful Hartford Female Seminary to accompany her father when he moved west to Cincinnati in 1831. She opened the Western Female Institute there, but the time and place were not propitious; it was bankrupted in 1837, the year of America's first major depression.

She turned to writing, joining with the famed William McGuffey on his fourth reader for schoolchildren and then issuing her own book on educational issues, *The Duty of American Women to Their Country*, in 1845. She followed up its arguments for public education with speaking tours that culminated with the formation in 1852 of the American Woman's Educational Association. Her two main goals, the establishment of educational institutions for young women and the establishment of societies to send teachers to western states to build schools, met with considerable success.

Beecher's writing, however, was doubtlessly more influential than her organizational skills. The two books on household arts that she published before the CIVIL WAR, *A Treatise on Domestic Economy* (1841) and *The Domestic Receipt Book* (1846), went through many editions and were widely read.

After the war, her popular sister Harriet joined her in updating these views with *The American Woman's Home* (1869).

Since Beecher was far too conservative to have ever contemplated the idea of women clergy, she sublimated the energies that propelled her preacher brothers into an unofficial ordination of herself as a minister to women. Her books on domesticity preached a moralistic, antimodern message, advocating pity and frugality along with hints on baby care and cooking. Portraying home and school as omnipotent societal forces, she strictly limited women's roles to these institutions, opposed SUFFRAGE, and was even unenthusiastic about the ABOLITIONIST movement that made her siblings famous. Even her advocacy of temperance did not find organizational or political expression.

Though she could be considered elderly in the 1860s and 1870s, Beecher returned to brief teaching stints in these postwar years, probably seeking both the income and an established position. She died at age seventy-eight, four years after the scandalous trial of her brother Henry for adultery in the TILTON-BEECHER AFFAIR.

BEERS, ETHEL LYNN (ETHELINDA) ELIOT (1827–1879)

Her CIVIL WAR poem, "All Quiet Along the Potomac To-night," was so popular that the phrase became part of the language and its author was frequently unattributed, even in her own lifetime.

The original poem was published by *Harper's Magazine* in 1861, the first year of the war, and was named "The Picket Guard," but its first line quickly became used as the title. Beers, whose poems appeared regularly in postwar periodicals, was superstitiously reluctant to publish her collected work, believing this would be an omen of her death. Finally relenting, *All Quiet Along The Potomac and Other Poems* was issued on October 10, 1879; she died the next day, only fifty-two years old.

BELMONT, ALVA ERSKINE SMITH VANDERBILT (1853–1933)

It is almost as though Alva Belmont lived two lives: the first as a Southern belle who married into one of the richest families in America and climbed to the top of elite international society; and then a second life as a feminist and labor activist.

Born in Alabama with a long southern lineage, Alva spent her teenage years in France, where her family lived after the CIVIL WAR devastated the South. The Smiths returned to the United States to debut their daughters into New York society, and Alva reaped rich rewards with her marriage to William K. Vanderbilt in 1875. She soon set about earning societal

Alva Belmont, left, stands with Alice Paul outside the Washington headquarters of the Woman's Party. LIBRARY OF CONGRESS.

recognition for herself and her *nouveau riche* husband in a well publicized and ultimately successful competition with CAROLINE SCHMERHORN ASTOR. To display the Vanderbilt wealth, she supervised the building of family mansions on Fifth Avenue and at Long Island and Newport.

Less than three years after the last building project was done, she stunned society by divorcing her husband. Her charge of adultery was doubtlessly true, but also was to be expected of men of Vanderbilt's class. The fact that she would bring such a charge was shocking in itself; but even greater rumors spread about Mrs. Vanderbilt's relationship with Oliver Hazard Perry Belmont, the son of a prominent banker who was younger than she and who was also seeking a DIVORCE from his socially prominent wife.

The gossips proved correct when Vanderbilt married Belmont in 1896, a year after her divorce. The civil ceremony the bride was forced to accept was evidence of the defiance of mores that divorce was at the time, and the criticism she endured for having the temerity to leave one of America's most powerful men doubtless was a factor in leading Alva Belmont to what would be, in effect, a second life.

When Oliver Belmont died just over a decade later, his widow surprised her world once again by transforming herself into an activist for not only women, but especially working women. When the great STRIKES in the GARMENT INDUSTRY broke out in 1909, Mrs. O.H.P. Belmont, as the newspapers referred to her, personally went to jails and bailed out striking women. Both unionists and feminists were initially skeptical of support from this unlikely source, but Belmont proved her staying power.

She organized meetings for the striking garment workers to speak to the wealthy women who set fashion trends, and she urged a boycott of nonunion dress manufacturers. Expanding into the SUFFRAGE MOVEMENT that same year, she paid for an entire floor of Fifth Avenue office space for the NATIONAL AMERICAN WOMAN SUFFRAGE ASSOCIATION. It was actually at Belmont's Newport home that the CONGRESSIONAL UNION conceived its strategy of holding the president's party responsible for suffrage, and when that group transformed itself into the WOMAN'S Party in 1915, Belmont was elected to the executive board.

She would make many other donations to the cause in the decade before the vote was won, including financing a speaking tour by British militant suffragist Chistabel Pankhurst and coauthoring and staging a feminist operetta. Throughout the era, her name appeared on articles in the popular magazines of the day, such as *Good Housekeeping* and *Harper's Bazaar,* where her support of suffrage positively influenced millions who would not have been impressed by arguments from women of lesser social standing. With the vote finally secured, she was rewarded with the presidency of the NATIONAL WOMAN'S PARTY in 1921.

Over sixty when her term ended, Belmont spent most of the remainder of her life in France, where she represented American women at international conferences. In addition, the interest in construction that she had displayed with the Vanderbilt mansions in the 1880s and 1890s reasserted itself in the 1920s and 1930s. Her restoration of a fifteenth-century castle, along with other projects, was sufficient to earn international recognition, and Belmont became one of the few women elected to the American Institute of Architects.

This honor alone would be sufficient reason to consider Alva Belmont notable, and it was but one relatively minor aspect of a remarkable life. She died in Paris a few days after her eightieth birthday and was buried in New York.

BENEDICT, RUTH FULTON (1887–1948) Like many

other women, Benedict was well into adulthood before she found her career.

The daughter of a widowed teacher/librarian, she was nonetheless able to go to VASSAR. After graduation in 1909, she worked as a high school TEACHER in California and then married biochemist Stanley Benedict. They returned to New York in 1914, and though Ruth Benedict published some poetry in well known magazines, she used a PSEUDONYM and was not serious about a career as a poet. Finally, in 1919, she began to study anthropology and earned her doctorate from Columbia in 1923, fourteen years after college graduation.

At age thirty-seven, Benedict launched her career with a Columbia instructorship. She spent the late twenties and early thirties researching southwestern Native American cultures, publishing two books of ethnology from this field work. It was her *Patterns of Culture* (1934), however, that brought international acclaim. Translated into more than a dozen languages and still considered a classic, Benedict put forth arguments for what would become known as cultural relativism, asserting that it was the accepted patterns of individual behavior that defined a culture: the same traits that could label a person as an outcast in one society might make him a saint in another, for there are no universal definitions of, for example, success or sin. Because combinations of human behavior are limitless, she argued, new cultures will continually evolve. The *New York Times* called the book "expertly conceived and brilliantly developed."

Benedict's husband died in 1936, but she went on teaching and writing, and her next book brought even more attention. *Race: Science and Politics* (1939) was a timely argument against the concept of racial distinctions that appeared when the Nazis were beginning to implement completely opposite ideas—with a philosophy that was grounded in the works of men who were considered respectable scholars. The originality and importance of her work can be seen in the fact that the word "racism" was coined by Benedict in this book.

Her expertise was finally acknowledged in 1943 by the Office of War Information, which employed her for advice on dealing with enemy peoples in WORLD WAR II. This experience, combined with earlier research, resulted in the 1946 publication of *The Chrysanthemum and the Sword,* a best-selling study of Japanese culture.

Benedict also edited the *Journal of American Folklore* from 1925 to 1940 and was elected president of the American Anthropological Association in 1947. When she received a grant from the Office of Naval Research in 1948 to undertake a huge study of contemporary European and Asian cultures, Benedict had finally proven herself worthy of full professorship. Though she had served as acting department chairman from 1936 to 1939, she had remained an associate professor.

Columbia's academicians granted this belated entitlement just months before her sudden death at sixty-one. Along with her former student, MARGARET MEAD, Ruth Benedict is acknowledged today as a premier anthropologist. Mead honored her with a book, *An Anthropologist at Work* (1958), published a decade after Benedict's death. Neither of these outstanding women ever received the honors they were due from their university or their profession.

BERRY, MARTHA McCHESNEY (1866–1942) The daughter of a wealthy Georgia planter, Berry went to a Baltimore FINISHING SCHOOL, but returned to the Deep South and spent the rest of her days educating the poor. She began with her own novel approach, traveling by horse and wagon in the hill country near her Rome, Georgia home to teach Bible stories to isolated children. Known as the Sunday Lady of the Mountains, her method came to be followed throughout the South. Even as late as the 1950s, there were elderly ladies traveling in the southern mountains with their feltcloth picture shows of Biblical characters.

In 1902, Berry pioneered a second educational method that was also much emulated. She built a log cabin school on her father's plantation and allowed her students to earn their tuition with work. Since publicly financed education was still a rarity in the Deep South, students quickly took advantage of

National African-American leader Mary McLeod Bethune in her office at Bethune-Cookman College in Daytona Beach in 1943. LIBRARY OF CONGRESS; OFFICE OF WAR INFORMATION; PHOTOGRAPH BY GORDON PARKS.

the opportunity. In 1926, Berry College was added to the system, and by the time she died, Mount Berry Schools had thirteen hundred students who lived, studied, and worked on thirty-five thousand acres of land. The need Berry had identified was so great that as many as five thousand applicants annually were turned down—and this was without even thinking of the needs of black students, for there was never any consideration of integration.

Though she had no formal college education herself, by the 1920s, Berry was nationally recognized as an educational leader. Her work/study combination provided a model for both private and public colleges, and until after WORLD WAR II, southern students of both sexes and races often worked on the college farm. She was honored with the Theodore Roosevelt Memorial Medal "for services to the nation" in 1925, and in 1937, Georgia made her the first woman appointed to their Board of Regents. Much better known then than now, Berry was voted one of twelve "greatest American women" in a 1931 national poll. She died at age eighty-six in Atlanta.

BETHUNE, LOUISE BLANCHARD (1856–1913) After a few years of traditional TEACHING, Jennie Louise Blanchard began drafting blueprints in a Buffalo architectural office in 1876. After a five-year apprenticeship, she and architect Robert Bethune opened their own office in 1881 shortly before their marriage.

The first American woman known to practice as an architect, she supervised the construction of many types of buildings in the Buffalo area over a thirty-year period. In 1888, still early in her career, Bethune became the first woman to be elected to the American Institute of Architects.

BETHUNE, MARY JANE MCLEOD (1875–1955) Mary McLeod was born to freed slaves just a decade after the CIVIL WAR ended. Her mother continued to work for her former master after emancipation and bought five acres for the family. "Then my parents," Mary wrote much later, "built our cabin, cutting and burning the logs with their own hands. I was the last of seventeen children . . . When I was born, the first free child in their own home, my mother exulted, 'Thank God, Mary came under our own vine and fig tree.' "

Yet Sumter County, South Carolina, was an area in which the plantation economy was so deeply embedded that the switch from slavery to sharecropping did little to improve the lives of its largely black population. Their community had only a rude one-room school built as a Presbyterian mission, and when Mary finished its basic curriculum, there was no choice but to return to the fields. She was working amid the cotton plants when a Board of Missions representative came to tell her mother that Mary would be the recipient of money donated by Mary Chrissman, a young Colorado QUAKER and TEACHER who intended to donate her earnings from dressmaking "to give an education to a colored girl, providing you can find one you know will make good." For the next fifty years, Chrissman provided financial and emotional support to Mary, though they did not meet until Bethune visited the retired teacher in Los Angeles in 1930.

With her tuition secured, twelve-year-old Mary, who had never seen a train before, took one to Scotia Seminary in

North Carolina, where she benefitted from an uncommon integrated faculty. When she graduated in 1894, another scholarship allowed her to move to Chicago, where she studied for a year at the school that later became well known as Moody Bible Institute. For the first time in her life, she had the experience of being the only black face in a crowd, something that was reinforced when she toured the Northwest with the school's gospel choir.

Mary's hopes of becoming a missionary to Africa were dashed after graduation because she could find no church willing to sponsor her. Returning South, she taught at a series of schools in Georgia and South Carolina before marrying Albertus Bethune in May, 1898; their only child, Albert Mcleod, was born in February, 1899. The young family soon moved to Palatka, in northeast Florida, where she secured a job with a Presbyterian school and also sold policies for the Afro-American Life Insurance Company. Here the marriage quickly deteriorated; though they separated rather than divorced, a husband was a factor in her life for only a few years. She kept his name, however, and obviously understood the value of the sound of "Mary McLeod Bethune"; she made lifelong objections when patronizing whites failed to address her by her surname.

In 1904, at age twenty-nine, she and her young son moved to Daytona Beach, where she began what would become her great life's work of building a superior boarding school for blacks. The Daytona Beach Literary and Industrial School for Training Negro Girls, which had a strong religious emphasis, began in an old house with wooden crates as desks for five elementary girls, who used ink she made from elderberries. Though sometimes Bethune had no food for the next meal, her ability to inspire confidence from others always resulted in needs supplied. She outfitted her students in uniforms to disguise disparities in background and set them to work on the school's maintenance and fund-raising. Because Daytona's relatively large black population had no access to free education and because many mothers were maids who went north with their white employers in summer and therefore needed boarding for their daughters, the school grew rapidly.

Bethune used all sorts of methods to finance her project, developing fund-raising skills that could net five thousand dollars from a single bazaar. The students' musical performances in Daytona's winter resorts were especially important fund-raisers, and Bethune used the contacts made at these concerts to bring together a board of trustees that included some of America's wealthiest people. Especially valuable contributions came from James Gamble of Proctor & Gamble, who was among the area's winter vacationers, as well as from sewing machine manufacturer Thomas H. White and John D. Rockefeller, Jr.

From the old house, the school moved to "hell's hole," a trash dump where Bethune led her girls in carrying out thousands of pounds of junk to clear the land. By 1941, however, she was able to write, "We have fourteen modern buildings, a beautiful campus of thirty-two acres . . . entirely unencumbered. When I walk through the campus, with its stately palms and well-kept lawns, and think back to the dump-heap foundation, I rub my eyes." Just as important as these physical achievements was the fact that the multimillionare men Bethune persuaded to join her board had come to respect the

business acumen of a black woman. Moreover, she also had withstood the racism of local men, including a night attack by the Ku Klux Klan when Bethune urged Daytona blacks to register and vote in a school election.

In 1923, with free (though segregated) schools becoming increasingly available to southern blacks, Bethune began the process of changing her school from a largely elementary curriculum to a true college. The first step was coeducation, accomplished by bringing to Daytona the male student body of the Cookman Institute in nearby Jacksonville. Renamed Bethune-Cookman College in 1929, it ended its high school role in 1936 and, with about one thousand students, issued its first college degrees in 1943. Though she remained president after the male merger, Bethune resigned the position in 1942 just as the college-level achievement was made, for her life—like that of so many Americans in the era—was changed by WORLD WAR II.

Already by WORLD WAR I, Bethune had enough friends in high places that she was called upon to make a tour urging black participation in Red Cross activities. She became politically active as soon as Florida women received the vote in 1920, registering blacks and voting despite threats. When the Roosevelt administration signaled greater receptivity to minorities than had been the case with the Republican administrations of the twenties, Bethune was there to help bring about the great political switch of blacks from the GOP—which they had seen as the party of Lincoln—to the New Deal Democrats.

Having developed a close personal friendship with ELEANOR ROOSEVELT from her work in the NATIONAL COUNCIL OF NEGRO WOMEN, Bethune became one of a handful of FDR's advisors on black affairs. He appointed her to the Office of Minority Affairs of the National Youth Administration in 1935—the first time such a high-level post had been created for a black woman. Although initially reluctant to accept the appointment, Bethune worked at it with her usual enthusiasm; in 1939, for example, she traveled thirty-five thousand miles speaking for equal educational opportunities for minority youth, including Native Americans and Mexican-Americans as well as blacks. Especially after World War II broke out, she argued strongly that the nation needed skilled young workers and the NYA must see that schools were no longer segregated. Moreover, she led the other (mostly male) members of Roosevelt's "Black Cabinet" in regular meetings that developed an agenda for joint action.

When the NYA was disbanded in 1943 after its depression-based need was gone, Bethune did not fully retire, even though she was sixty-eight. She continued to serve on the Advisory Committee to the WOMEN'S ARMY CORPS, as she had from its inception, and in 1944, she toured European installations observing the work of black WACs and arguing for fuller integration. President Truman appointed her to the founding conference of the United Nations in 1945, when she was the only woman of color with an official status. She briefly resumed the presidency of Bethune-Cookman in 1946–47, and acted as a governmental emissary to Liberia in 1952.

In what time was available during her busy life for private business ventures, Bethune developed her interests in housing programs and in insurance. She was a founding director of Central Life Insurance Company of Tampa in 1923, which for many decades provided insurance otherwise unobtainable to blacks. By 1952, all thirteen of the men who cofounded Central Life with her had died, and she became the only woman president of an insurance company in America.

Long active in many organizations, at various points Mary McLeod Bethune was also president of the NATIONAL ASSOCIATION OF COLORED WOMEN, the National Association of Teachers in Colored Schools, and the Association for the Study of Negro Life and History. The founding president of the NATIONAL COUNCIL OF NEGRO WOMEN, she served from 1935 to 1949; she was a vice-president of the NAACP when she died, having held that position since 1940; and was on the board of PLANNED PARENTHOOD and other national organizations. She nonetheless managed to find time throughout her life to write for black publications, including weekly columns for the *Pittsburgh Courier* and the *Chicago Defender*.

Though her national reputation was recognized already in 1931, when she was tenth on a journalists' list of fifty outstanding American women, Bethune received many more honors in the postwar period when the civil rights movement was strengthening—including what was probably the first honorary degree given to a black by a white southern college, when Rollins College in Orlando honored her in 1949. The United States Post Office issued a stamp in her memory in 1985.

The outstanding leader of black women from the twenties through the forties, Mary McLeod Bethune died at age eighty; she is buried on the grounds of Bethune-Cookman College. Her students still remember the way she began almost every speech with "my beautiful black boys and girls." One former student said, "That was in the '50s and we weren't ready for that word 'black.' She was way ahead of her time."

BETTY CROCKER The longtime symbol of General Mills, Betty Crocker's image first appeared in 1921. An early example of successful marketing and advertising strategies, the concept began with the Washburn-Crosby flour milling company of Minneapolis, which merged with General Mills a few years later. Its home service department, headed by Marjorie Child Husted (1892–1986), replied to consumer inquiries by using "Betty Crocker" as their common signature. After the General Mills merger, the name was expanded into a larger advertising image, with the expectation that housewives would identify with a woman who looked like themselves and therefore would trust Betty Crocker's advice on flour, cereals, and other processed foods.

Betty Crocker was thus designed to look like a contemporary woman, and the twenties were an era of revolution in women's appearance—the DRESS REFORM of the times included short skirts, bobbed hair, and new makeup. Betty Crocker, whose appearance was updated with future fashion changes, was created to symbolize this modern woman and to reassure homemakers that they could be stylish and also care about what their families ate. It was a deliberate attempt to feminize the milling business in the minds of its customers.

Though primarily the brainchild of Husted, Betty Crocker's image was drawn by Neysa McMein (1888–1949), who contracted with General Mills. McMein was a successful fashion expert and illustrator who was at the height of her career when Crocker was created; she had done covers for major

magazines prior to WORLD WAR I and would go on to draw patriotic posters for WORLD WAR II. Husted also went on to top executive positions with General Mills and later formed her own consulting firm. Their Betty Crocker would endure, with regular updates, long afterwards.

BICKERDYKE, MARY ANN BALL (1817–1901) Perhaps more than any other woman, Mary Ann Bickerdyke epitomized the NURSES of the CIVIL WAR. A widow who was older than the requisite physical strains would seem to allow, she served with the U.S. SANITARY COMMISSION through all four years of the war; the nineteen battles in which she worked were far more than most soldiers saw.

She began in Illinois in 1861, going to a Cairo hospital to deliver money from her church. Appalled at the neglect of the wounded and dying that she found, she started working aboard a Sanitary Commission hospital ship that carried patients from General Grant's Mississippi River battles. During 1862, she followed his army through field hospitals in Mississippi and Tennessee. In the cold and rain of the battles of Lookout Mountain and Missionary Ridge in late November, 1863, she was the only woman available to nurse almost two thousand Union casualties.

Called Mother Bickerdyke by her patients, she went on with Sherman's army to the battle of Atlanta in 1864 and assisted with the starving men liberated from the notorious prisoner of war camp at Andersonville, Georgia. In North Carolina when peace was declared, she joined Sherman's victorious parade into Washington a month later.

Bickerdyke not only operated in bloody surgical tents, nursed the sick, and covered the dead, but also did the essential tasks of camp cooking and laundry. Like other nurses, she often obtained supplies only by using personal ingenuity; several times she interrupted her nursing for lecture tours back north that raised the funds necessary to feed and heal the Union armies.

So respected was she that Mother Bickerdyke was the only female that General Sherman permitted in his camps. She received considerable praise in the press at the time and also was honored by Union veterans after the war, but she never held a postwar position worthy of the skills she clearly had. Always on the edge of poverty, Bickerdyke was finally granted a pension by Congress in 1886; the twenty-five dollars a month she received was not only long overdue, but also a very small amount to support her for the rest of her long life.

Despite recognition in her time, Mary Ann Bickerdyke is largely forgotten today, while others (especially CLARA BARTON) who did less as Civil War nurses are nonetheless credited for this role. Both the assignment of stereotypical virtues to Barton and the neglect of Bickerdyke are indicative of the shallow teaching of much of women's history.

BIRTH CONTROL All societies have regulated reproduction in some form or another since the evolution of humans, although often these methods are not commonly recognized as "birth control." In many societies, for example, marriage is delayed until a decade or more of a woman's reproductive capacity is past; in other cultures, marriage occurs soon after puberty, but taboos on remarriage after widowhood accomplish the same objective of dissipating reproductive years.

Some groups place taboos on sex with nursing mothers, which creates spacing between births; in others, ABORTION is frequently practiced.

Thus, from CELIBACY to infanticide, all societies have exercised techniques to distinguish humans from animals in the deliberate, though often unacknowledged, manipulation of reproductive capacity. The result is that women's reproductive lives have been regulated (again, often in unacknowledged ways) for the interests of their particular society, with attitudes dependent on whether it was in the interest of the group to have a large or a small population. Militaristic societies regulated reproduction to produce large numbers and, usually couching those bans in patriotic and religious terms, prohibited contraception and abortion. Meanwhile, societies that wished to keep their populations small enough to match the resources available created other taboos to achieve that result.

Native Americans, for example, did not encourage excessively large families; although humans had inhabited the western hemisphere for at least fifteen thousand years, their populations were sparsely settled, with a consequent preservation of the natural resources. The Europeans who migrated here, on the other hand, had a manipulative attitude towards nature, which was totally opposite that of the natives, and they set out to obey their Biblical injunction of "be fruitful and multiply."

The result was that colonial families were often so large that several mothers could be sent to an early grave in the production of a single family. Colonial diarist Cotton Mather, for example, did not consider his family of sixteen children to be unusual, for he cited cases of women who bore twenty-two and twenty-three babies, as well as men who fathered more than twenty-five children by two or more wives. Yet, as these early settlers became "natives" in the New World and more economically secure, their birth rate also decreased. They then began to decry the fecundity of the Irish and German immigration of the nineteenth century—a pattern that continues today with different ethnic groups.

In America, therefore, the idea of birth control has long been accepted in reality, if not in theory, with one frequent technique being the quiet acceptance of male extramarital sex. In the late nineteenth and early twentieth centuries, however, the women's movement began to speak openly about previously unacknowledged areas of sexuality and sought access to information that would allow women to consciously resolve reproductive questions in their own individual interests, rather than that of society.

This revolution in thought quickly resulted in the invention of new mechanical and pharmacological techniques. While evidence of both female and male devices to interfere with conception exists from ancient times, it was not until population pressures arose in the late nineteenth century that serious research began to be conducted in contraception. Ideas imported from Europe in that era quickly met with official censorship under the terms of the COMSTOCK LAW. During the WORLD WAR I era, when MARGARET SANGER was prosecuted for birth control advocacy in her magazine, the *Woman Rebel*, the American birth control movement truly began.

Throughout the twenties, Sanger and others in the cause battled officials for the right to run birth control clinics and teach sex education. That this message was getting through to the public became clear during the Great Depression of the thirties, when American birth rates plunged to their lowest level ever and then soared again during and immediately after WORLD WAR II. Obviously, millions of Americans were exercising various forms of birth control, with the most common devices of the era being male use of condoms and female use of diaphragms.

A final revolution occurred in the sixties with the development of "the pill," the first dependable pharmacological approach to contraception. Its use was challenged in the last stand of the legal prohibitionists when, in 1965, the Supreme Court in GRISWOLD VS. CONNECTICUT ruled that states could not ban the distribution of contraceptives to married people. The Court reinforced this ruling only a few years later with *Eisenstadt vs. Baird*, a 1972 Massachusetts case that extended the right to purchase contraceptives without regard to marital status. Birth control pills were quickly and widely marketed in the late sixties, and their popularity with millions soon made it clear that women understood the inseparable connection between contraception and the personal freedom they believed was their right as Americans.

BLACKWELL, ALICE STONE (1857–1950) The only child of premier suffragist LUCY STONE and her feminist husband, Henry Blackwell, Alice would live for almost a century during the era of greatest progress for women in human history.

Her childhood was somewhat lonely as a result of her parents' frequent travel, but whatever timidness she may have developed was no longer evident when she and another young woman entered an otherwise all-male class at Boston University in 1881—and Alice went on to be elected class president and to graduate Phi Beta Kappa.

She went to work immediately for her mother's *Woman's Journal*, which had been publishing from Boston since 1869, and spent the rest of her life publishuing the cause, writing and editing its pages for more than three decades. Though the *Woman's Journal* was considered the leading suffragist publication, Blackwell soon reached out to a much wider audience by developing a syndicated column that she distributed for the free use of newspapers throughout the country. Because she was a talented writer, her column was respected by some editors who disagreed with her views.

Also during the first decade after college, Blackwell worked at reconciling the long conflict between her mother's AMERICAN WOMAN SUFFRAGE ASSOCIATION and SUSAN ANTHONY's rival NATIONAL WOMAN SUFFRAGE ASSOCIATION. When the two merged in 1890, she reluctantly allowed herself to be elected corresponding secretary; she was reelected for almost twenty years.

After Lucy Stone died in 1893, her daughter, then in her mid-thirties, indulged in her only known romance. Though the young man died shortly after they met, he had a lasting effect; he was Armenian and his reports of Turkish persecution aroused her interest in the Armenians centered in Massachusetts, as well as in other oppressed minority groups. She soon was publishing the work of freedom-loving poets translated from Yiddish, Hungarian, and other languages.

After the long struggle for the NINETEENTH AMENDMENT was finally over, Blackwell was a founder of the Massachusetts LEAGUE OF WOMEN VOTERS, seeing this organization as a potential third party that would put women's interests first. Her efforts in that regard were diminished, however, by her simultaneous involvement in a plethora of causes, including TEMPERANCE, PEACE, vivisection, and others. She used her position as a Boston University trustee to protest post-WORLD WAR I repression and took a special interest in Massachusetts's particular outrage, the Sacco-Vanzetti case. She also found time during the twenties to finish her biography of her mother, a labor of four decades. *Lucy Stone* was published by Little, Brown & Co. in 1930.

An open socialist by the thirties, Blackwell suffered severe financial harm during the Great Depression and was saved from poverty only by contributions. Having long since given up the family's big Dorchester home and her summer place in Martha's Vineyard, she spent the WORLD WAR II years in a Cambridge apartment. Blind but still alert, Alice Blackwell remained ready to comment for visitors on history as well as current events. She died at ninety-three, having lived at the very center of a century of change.

BLACKWELL, ANTOINETTE LOUISA BROWN (1825–1921)

Born in western New York State where there was a long tradition of religious enthusiasm, young Antoinette was so gifted that the fathers of her Congregationalist Church, moved by her speaking ability, voted her full membership at age nine.

One of ten children, Nettie was not only exceptionally bright, but also fortunate to have supportive parents who allowed her to go to Ohio and attend the recently opened OBERLIN COLLEGE, where she completed the "literary" curriculum in 1847. They drew the line, however, when she wanted to enter Oberlin's theological department, an idea that even her college classmate, LUCY STONE, found farfetched. Despite these objections and the faculty's doubts, Brown enrolled in theology and studied for the next three years. Oberlin's professors, liberal though they were by the standards of their time, still could not bring themselves to recognize her achievement; when her course work was complete, she was not graduated nor licensed to preach.

Having nonetheless found occasional pulpits open to her during her student years, she set out to preach anywhere she could find an audience. For two years, she traveled the pre-CIVIL WAR lecture circuit, speaking on the era's burning topics of ABOLITION and TEMPERANCE, including a tour with SUSAN ANTHONY. She was, in fact, with Anthony at the 1853 World Temperance Convention in New York City; Brown was among those who attempted to break the barriers of silence imposed by the era's taboo on PUBLIC SPEAKING by women, and she found herself shouted down by male preachers.

Finally her faith seemed justified when she was invited to the pastorate of a Congregational Church in a community about fifty miles east of Rochester and just north of SENECA FALLS, the site of the first women's rights convention five years earlier. Though still not sanctioned by the Congregationalist denomination, on September 15, 1853, Antoinette Brown became the first woman minister ordained by a congregation of a recognized American denomination.

But she found her long-sought vocation less than satisfying. When she focused more on theology and less on the political issues of the lecture world, Reverend Brown realized her faith was wavering; the Calvinistic creed of Congregationalists, with its emphasis on predestination and original sin, no longer fitted her more progressive views. Less than a year after the First Congregational Church installed her, she asked to be released from its pulpit, and soon thereafter, she converted to the more optimistic Unitarian Church.

Without a job, she spent 1855 volunteering among the poor of New York City, writing up her experiences for Horace Greeley's newspaper, and being courted by Samuel Blackwell, an Ohioan who had moved to New York. They had met two years earlier when Blackwell heard about the remarkable Miss Brown from his brother Henry, who was engaged to Lucy Stone. Samuel asked to be introduced to Miss Stone's classmate, and they were married early in 1856. Like his brother Henry and his sister ELIZABETH BLACKWELL, Samuel was an early proponent of women's rights.

Though Lucy Stone had thought her friend Nettie too radical when Brown had pursued theology, now their views seemingly reversed, for Antoinette Brown did not follow Lucy Stone's example in keeping her maiden name. As Mrs. Blackwell, she devoted herself largely to motherhood for the next two decades and bore seven children (in contrast to Stone's one). Five of the seven survived infancy; all were girls, of whom three grew up to be professionals.

Yet though she stayed close to home, Blackwell kept active in her maternal years. She wrote a half-dozen books between 1869 and 1902, including a novel, a volume of poetry, and philosophical works, especially a feminist critique of Darwinism, *The Sexes Through Nature* (1875). She also returned to the lecture circuit in the late 1870s when her husband's business failed, and she was involved in the AMERICAN WOMAN SUFFRAGE ASSOCIATION formed by her sister-and brother-in-law, Stone and Blackwell. She preached occasionally and even ordained two other women preachers.

The Blackwells lived most of their married lives in New Jersey, returning to New York City five years before Samuel's death in 1901; his widow spent her remaining years there and with her daughters in suburban New Jersey. A famous FEMINIST in her old age, Reverend Brown was a feature of the 1911 suffragist parade. She published two more philosophical works in 1914 and 1915 and preached her last sermon at age ninety. Five years later, she triumphantly voted in the presidential election of 1920, a year before her death.

BLACKWELL, ELIZABETH (1821–1910)

Like many other successful women, Elizabeth Blackwell had a father whose attitudes made a tremendous difference in not only her life, but also, as it would turn out, in the lives of her sister EMILY BLACKWELL and of his two daughters-in-law, LUCY STONE and ANTOINETTE BROWN BLACKWELL, whom he did not live to meet. An English merchant, Samuel Blackwell brought up his nine surviving children, boys as well as girls, with an uncommon belief in women's rights; his four unmarried sisters who also lived in this large household doubtlessly added to its FEMINIST perspective.

Because a fire destroyed their business, the family moved to America in 1832 during an era of relatively little immigration. The third oldest, Elizabeth was eleven at the time and her mother was pregnant—a condition that was almost constant throughout most of Elizabeth's childhood. They were welcomed in New York City by friends who shared their dissenting religious views and lived in that area until further financial losses in the Panic of 1837 caused their migration to the frontier of that day, Cincinnati, Ohio.

Then true calamity struck, with Samuel's sudden death only months later leaving the family destitute. Teenage Elizabeth, along with her mother and older sisters, contributed to the family income for four years by TEACHING in a school they quickly established. Going off at age twenty-one to a teaching position in Kentucky, she realized that this traditional job with its inevitable culmination in marriage and motherhood was not for her, and she began consciously thinking about a way to avoid marriage in an era with virtually no employment opportunities for women. She settled on the idea of becoming a doctor—something that, for women, was wholly without precedent.

Reading medical books as she taught, Blackwell moved to the Deep South in 1845, where she studied privately with two Carolina physicians. Two years later, she returned north to Philadelphia, where she hoped QUAKER friends could help with admission to a proper medical school. (Medical education then had almost a hundred years of history in the U.S., with the first school founded in Philadelphia in 1765.) Blackwell applied to and was rejected by eight institutions before Geneva College in western New York—which was only a few miles from SENECA FALLS, the site of the nation's first women's rights meeting the following year—sent an acceptance. Blackwell was elated, only to find later that her admission had been viewed as a practical joke.

Surprised when she actually arrived on campus, her colleagues at first treated Blackwell with extreme hostility, while the professors excluded her from laboratory work and even participation in lectures. In an era when women had "limbs" rather than "legs" and "arms," it was hardly surprising that men found it difficult to discuss the inner workings of the body with a female student, but through perseverance, pleasantness, and hard work, she slowly won the respect of most. Elizabeth Blackwell graduated at the head of her class in 1849 and was the first woman in the modern world to earn a medical degree.

This phenomenon became clear when she went to Europe for postgraduate study and found herself, especially in Paris, relegated to the realms of MIDWIVES and NURSES. One of the benefits of the trip, in fact, would be a lifelong respect for nurses, partly because of friendships formed then with Florence Nightingale and others working to professionalize nursing. This appreciation of the value of "women's work" also made Dr. Blackwell—unlike most male physicians of her era—emphasize preventative health care and especially the importance of good hygiene. After her return to the United States, she would publicize these ideas with lectures, issuing them in 1852 as *The Laws of Life with Special Reference to the Physical Education of Girls*.

In the fall of 1851, Dr. Blackwell began to establish herself as a medical practitioner in New York, but again there was tremendous resistance, with all of the city's hospitals and clinics closed to her and anonymous letters threatening her. She could not even find anyone willing to rent rooms to her, at least in part because she was suspected of being an abortionist, since that is what the public associated with the term "female physician." Once again, it was Quaker friends who finally began to bring her patients, and in 1853 she was able to open a small clinic where she treated mostly poor women.

Four years later, joined by her younger sister Emily, who had just finished her medical training, and by another recent graduate, Dr. MARIE ZAKRZEWSKA, she opened a hospital; the New York Infirmary for Women and Children was staffed entirely by women. An able fundraiser and politician, Dr. Blackwell also managed to secure a distinguished board of trustees, including a half-dozen prominent male physicians and the indefatigable Horace Greeley, who was befriending her sister-in-law Antoinette at the same time.

With the hospital established, Dr. Emily Blackwell took over its management while her sister went to England during 1858–1859 to further the cause of medical education for women there. She returned just before the CIVIL WAR broke out, and like her ABOLITIONIST family, spent the war years supporting the Union. Under the aegis of the War Department and the Woman's Central Association of Relief, the Doctors Blackwell selected and trained nurses for wartime hospital work.

The end of hostilities meant that Elizabeth Blackwell could finally begin her long-term plans for an outstanding women's medical college. In 1868, she officially opened a college in conjunction with her hospital, which featured uncommon entrance exams, a strict curriculum of study combined with practice, and graduate examinations administered by an outside body. All of these were innovative ideas, providing her students with an education superior to that of most male medical schools.

The following year, she left her hard-won institution to her sister and returned to England permanently, despite having become an American citizen in 1849. She took with her Kitty Barry, whom she had adopted in the bleak days when she was without patients. Barry, an orphan who was seven when adopted, provided lifelong companionship for Blackwell.

She quickly built a successful London practice, and in 1875, Dr. Blackwell became a professor of gynecology at the new London School of Medicine for Women. Though she soon tired of full-time teaching, she held this post until 1907 and continued to lecture and write for the rest of her life. Living at a seaside home in Hastings with Scottish summers in later years, she helped found the National Health Society in 1871 and wrote two controversial books advocating sex education, as well as her autobiography, *Pioneer Work in Opening the Medical Profession to Women* (1895). Her final book, *Essays in Medical Sociology*, was published in 1902. Elizabeth Blackwell made her last visit to the U.S. at age eighty-six and died in Hastings three years later.

Her New York Infirmary, founded in 1857, continues to be staffed by women.

BLACKWELL, EMILY (1826–1910)

Five years younger than her sister ELIZABETH BLACKWELL, Emily must have felt that she lived much of her life in the shadow of the first Dr. Blackwell, but Emily had exceptional abilities of her own and proved herself on the same rough road to success.

Geneva Medical College, keenly aware of its practical joke gone awry, refused admission to Emily, even though Elizabeth had graduated at the head of her class. Turned down by almost a dozen other medical schools, she finally was accepted by Rush Medical College in Chicago in 1852—six years after she had made the decision to study medicine. During that time, she supported herself by TEACHING elementary school, an occupation she despised as much as Elizabeth had.

But after the expense of moving to Chicago and despite successful completion of her first year, Rush Medical College bowed to pressure from Illinois physicians and refused to accept her for the second year. Finally Western Reserve University in Cleveland admitted her, as they had her future colleague, Dr. MARIE ZAKRZEWSKA. After graduation, Emily Blackwell had two years of excellent postgraduate work abroad. Using the contacts established by her sister, she managed not only to earn experience in England and France, but also went on to internships in Germany. In 1856, she joined in her sister's struggle to establish the New York Infirmary for Women and Children.

Perhaps even more talented than Elizabeth in administration and fundraising, Dr. Emily Blackwell also did their surgery because Elizabeth's sight had suffered from an eye disease she contracted while working in Paris. Within two years, Emily was completely in charge of the clinic when her sister went abroad during 1858–1859 and Dr. Zakrzewska moved to Boston. She achieved a real political success during this time by convincing state legislators to fund their project.

With Elizabeth's return and the establishment of a medical school in 1868, Emily added teaching and educational administration to her duties. Soon she was solely in charge; Elizabeth settled permanently in England in 1869 and Emily demonstrated her independent abilities during the next thirty years. By the mid-1870s, her establishment had grown so large that she expanded into a converted mansion, with over seven thousand patients treated annually. The medical college also was improved, with expansion into a three- and then a four-year program—years ahead of many male medical institutions that were still requiring only two years of shorter months.

Dr. Emily Blackwell retired at the turn of the century, closing her college when Cornell University began to accept women medical students. More than 350 physicians had been educated there, and the associated infirmary still exists as proof of Dr. Blackwell's pioneering administration in the health care field.

In another uncommon act for a single woman, Emily and Elizabeth Blackwell each adopted a daughter. Emily Blackwell enjoyed a decade of retirement before her death at her Maine summer home, only a few months after Elizabeth Blackwell's death in England.

BLANCHFIELD, FLORENCE A. (1884–1971) Influenced

by nursing experience in her family, Florence Blanchfield graduated from a Pittsburgh nursing school in 1906. She followed this with additional education, including study at JOHNS HOPKINS, while working for a decade in various civilian nursing positions before she discovered her true life's work in the ARMY NURSE CORPS.

In her thirties when she enlisted a few months after the U.S. entered WORLD WAR I, Blanchfield served in France and saw the horrifying casualties of this extremely bloody war.

Colonel Florence Blanchfield viewed the liberation of these Army Nurse Corps members as one of her most profound responsibilities, for they had been prisoners of war in the Philippines for over a year when she took command of the ANC in 1943. The women were liberated and awarded Bronze Stars early in 1945. U.S. ARMY CENTER OF MILITARY HISTORY.

After only a few months back in civilian life at the war's end, she returned to the ANC, and, during the peaceful decades of the twenties and thirties, found broad experience in her assignments to several posts in the United States as well as China and the Philippines.

Blanchfield was thus exceptionally well qualified to serve as assistant superintendent of the corps when WORLD WAR II broke out; with the retirement of Julia Flikke, she became head of the ANC in 1943. For the duration of the war, she directed its NURSES throughout the world in hospitals and battle stations from Australia to Alaska; hundreds of her nurses in Asia and Europe saw combat and death and became prisoners of war.

A model of administrative efficiency, she also fought for equal rank and pay for the ANC. The corps' problems in this area were illustrated by its commander: though Blanchfield commanded as many as sixty thousand, she was only a colonel, which was a rank given to men who often commanded no more than five hundred. No woman was promoted to general until well after the war, though Blanchfield and others held positions that called for great creativity as well as tremendous responsibility and should have held that rank. When the ANC finally became a full part of the Army in 1947, with regularized commissions, pay, and rank, Blanchfield had the honor of receiving from five-star General Eisenhower the first regular Army commission given to a woman—but she remained a colonel.

Retiring in 1947, she had served the Army for three full decades, seen the battlefronts of two world wars, and supervised the training and work of tens of thousands of women. She soon turned to writing the history she had seen, publishing *The Army Nurse Corps in World War II* in 1948 and *Organized Nursing and the Army in Three Wars* in 1950. Florence Blanchfield lived out retirement in the Washington area, dying at eighty-seven.

BLATCH, HARRIOT EATON STANTON (1856–1940)

The daughter of ELIZABETH CADY STANTON and her ABOLITIONIST husband (a western New York State senator), Harriot grew up in fortunate circumstances, graduating from VASSAR in 1878, going to Boston for a year of study in oratory, plus living abroad for two years.

Her mother was working with SUSAN ANTHONY on their HISTORY OF WOMAN SUFFRAGE when she returned, and Harriot did these two eminent women the favor of pointing out that their work omitted any reference to their rivals in the AMERICAN WOMAN SUFFRAGE ASSOCIATION. Assigned the task of adding this information, the young Miss Stanton wrote a section of volume two of the history in 1881; her historiographical honesty later played an important part in the merger of the two organizations, ending the wasted energy and political division that had thwarted the movement throughout the post–CIVIL WAR era.

But she had met an English merchant on her European voyage and soon after the book was done, returned to marry him. For the next twenty years, Mrs. Blatch lived in an English village, bore two daughters and lost one. She was nonetheless active in local causes, earned a master's degree from Vassar by correspondence, and, influenced by British Fabians, became increasingly a socialist as well as a militant suffragist.

In 1902, the year her mother died, Harriot Blatch and her family returned to the United States. Shocked at the inactivity of the aging SUFFRAGE MOVEMENT here, she quickly introduced British-style politics: understanding the principle that political scientists now call "visibility," she organized parades, outdoor rallies, and poll watchers, with a special emphasis on reaching beyond the comfortably middle class women who had previously dominated the movement. Soon she had twenty thousand members in her Equality League of Self-Supporting Women.

Changing its name to Women's Political Union in 1910, Blatch's organization also differed from her mother's in that it concentrated on New York State, accepting the AWSA's strategy of more local goals. Blatch lobbied the New York legislature throughout the Progressive Era, and after she got pledges of support from a majority of the candidates in the election of 1912, the legislature passed a suffrage referendum. However, partly because of the accidental death of her husband and partly because of her inability to work with CARRIE CHAPMAN CATT, Blatch was not part of the campaign that finally gave New York women the vote in 1917.

After going to England to settle her husband's estate in the early days of WORLD WAR I, Blatch increasingly turned from state suffrage to international issues. Though she campaigned against President Wilson in 1916 because of his indifference to suffrage, she nonetheless worked closely with his administration once the United States entered the war. She headed the speaker's bureau of the federal Food Administration and was a director of the Woman's Land Army, writing a book, *Mobilizing Woman-Power*, (1918) that would be almost passe by the time it was on the market, but would presage the larger roles of American Women in WORLD WAR II. She quickly followed this with a *A Woman's Point of View* (1920) on the general issues of war and women's potential for peace; two years later, with her brother, she published *Elizabeth Cady Stanton, as Revealed in Her Letters, Diary and Reminiscences.*

Blatch spent the postwar years supporting the Socialists, despite differing with them by rejecting PROTECTIVE LEGISLATION. Also a member of the NATIONAL WOMAN'S PARTY, she ran for office several times; but, already in her sixties when women got the vote and far too liberal for the reactionary politics of the twenties, she never came close to developing an elective career as her father had.

An injury in 1927 essentially ended her career, though she lived on to age eighty-three. Blatch's autobiography, *Challenging Years* (1940), was written with Alma Lutz, a popular journalist of the era, and came out the same year she died.

BLOOMER, AMELIA JENKS (1818–1894)

While the term "bloomers" is strongly associated in the public mind with the woman, few realize that Amelia Bloomer not only did not invent the costume, but also, because she was a conventionally married woman, "bloomers" actually derives from a man's name.

Indeed, it was through QUAKER attorney and newspaper editor Dexter Bloomer that Amelia Jenks came to be involved in the liberalizing issues of her era. They married in 1840 when she was twenty-two, and Amelia Bloomer, who had been a TEACHER until marriage, began writing articles for her husband's newspaper, especially on TEMPERANCE—which was in fact her chief lifelong interest.

Living in the western New York State area that spawned SUSAN ANTHONY and others, she attended the 1848 SENECA FALLS women's rights meeting organized by LUCRETIA MOTT and ELIZABETH CADY STANTON, but probably was there more in the role of reporter than participant. The next year she branched out with her own paper, an idea proposed by her temperance society. Perhaps the first newspaper to be edited by a woman—certainly the first since the colonial era of women PRINTERS—it was called the *Lily* and began publication in January, 1846. While primarily devoted to temperance, it increasingly called attention to the needs of women that naturally evolved from temperance advocacy.

In contrast to the common image, Amelia Bloomer was actually rather slow to accept FEMINISM, publishing her paper for a dozen years before she made public appearances with women rights leaders, and then her speeches were devoted to the right of women to DIVORCE alcoholic husbands. Still timid on the suffrage question, she also served as Seneca Falls' deputy postmistress during this time—appointed by her husband, the postmaster.

The dress style that came to be called "bloomers" was derived from actress FANNY KEMBLE and others, and Bloomer's name became linked with it because she reported on it. In 1849, Elizabeth Smith Miller appeared in Seneca Falls wearing the new "turkish trousers"; Miller was the daughter of abolitionist Gerrit Smith, and it was he who was the most vocal advocate of the new style, arguing that women would be better accepted by men if their appearance was less strikingly different. When the town's famous feminist, Elizabeth Cady Stanton, adopted the fashion—which was sometimes also called the "American Costume"—Amelia Bloomer wrote of it in the *Lily*. The idea was picked up and repeated by newspapers all over the country; almost overnight, the *Lily*'s subscriptions doubled, presumably by readers more interested in fashion than in temperance.

Astonished by the reaction, Amelia Bloomer responded to the flood of requests for sewing instructions and, wearing the loose-fitting pants under a short skirt herself, defended its practicality. The result was that the wearing of pants by women has been irrevocably linked with her name—but within a few years, she came to agree with her friends who led the nascent women's rights movement that the ridicule they received because of bloomers was diminishing their efforts in more seriously needed areas of attention, and they returned to conventionally long skirts.

Indeed, the *Lily*'s existence after the focus on DRESS REFORM in 1851 was brief. She managed to continue it after moving with her husband to Ohio in 1853 (while also assisting him with his *Western Home Visitor*), but when they went on to frontier Iowa two years later, conditions would be too difficult for either of them to continue publishing, and she sold the *Lily* early in 1855. Her replacement editor, apparently not as able as Amelia Bloomer, allowed it to die the following year.

She lived with her husband in Council Bluffs, Iowa for the rest of her life; he made a fortune in land and was elected mayor. They adopted two children, and she sharpened her skills in gardening and gourmet cooking while continuing to advocate women's rights. She served as president of the Iowa Woman Suffrage Society in 1871; worked on MARRIED WOMEN'S PROPERTY RIGHTS in the state's legal code; and wrote, especially in volume three of her friend Stanton's HISTORY OF WOMEN SUFFRAGE, on the movement in Iowa.

Amelia Bloomer lived a much more conventional life than most believe; she not only did not invent bloomers, but wore them for only a few of her seventy-six years.

BLOOMERS— *See* BLOOMER, AMELIA JENKS

BLY, NELLIE (ELIZABETH COCHRANE SEAMAN) (1865?–1922)

Best known for taking up the fictional challenge of going "Around the World in Eighty Days," Bly was the public's favorite woman in late nineteenth-century news reporting.

Born Elizabeth Cochran, her showmanship was obvious from the beginning of her career, when—not content with merely the adoption of a PSEUDONYM—she also varied the spelling of her legal name, adding an "e" to Cochran. She chose "Nellie Bly" from a popular Stephen Foster song when she began writing for the *Pittsburgh Dispatch* in 1885. Her predilection for invention also caused her to obscure the date of her birth, but she was probably twenty at the time and had little formal education. She got the job by impressing the editor with a letter opposing his antisuffrage views.

During the next year, Nellie Bly wrote articles exposing the ills of Pittsburgh's factories and slums; in this era of tremendous exploitation of the city's immigrants, she drew attention to problems that later would be documented by scholars such as EMILY BALCH, ELIZABETH BEARDSLEY BUTLER, and MARGARET BYINGTON. Bly was no scholar, but her standard investigative methodology might have come closer to the truth of any situation, for she repeatedly disguised herself as a worker or a potential mark for a scam and then revealed her victimization in the *Dispatch*. In the winter of 1886–1887, Bly went on assignment to Mexico, where she wrote similar stories on the exploitation of the poor, with additional emphasis on the contrasting lives of the rich. The Mexican government was so outraged by her temerity that they expelled her from the country.

Recognizing that her reputation was a perfect match for the sort of journalism that Joseph Pulitzer was establishing at the *New York World*, she persuaded him to hire her by offering to pose as insane, thereby gaining admittance into the city's notorious Blackwell Island asylum. She wrote this experience into her first book, *Ten Days in a Madhouse* (1887), and it resulted in reform of the treatment of the mentally ill. The book's success inspired her to offer a retrospective of her Mexican experience, *Six Months in Mexico* (1888). Meanwhile, she continued her exposé style for the *World*, employing the incognito technique to bribe politicians and entrap would-be sexual transgressors.

On November 14, 1889, Nellie Bly undertook her most publicized journalistic effort—an exceptional venture that employed no disguises or victimization. Jules Verne's *Around the World in Eighty Days* had been an 1873 bestseller and continued to capture the imagination of a public still unfamiliar with the concept of science fiction. Bly's innovative mind was responsive to anything new, and she persuaded Pulitzer that he should sponsor her on a worldwide race to see if she could match Verne's balloonist using the transportation system then extant. She sailed for France, where she interviewed Verne, and then sped around the globe via the Middle East, India, China, and Japan. By the time she arrived in San Francisco, newspapers were selling at unprecedented rates, and she was welcomed in New York with a Broadway parade. Arriving back on January 25, she had beaten Verne's fantastic prediction by a wide margin: Pulitzer proudly announced that the trip took seventy-two days, six hours, ten minutes, and eleven seconds.

She wrote up this experience in her most popular publication, *Nellie Bly's Book: Around the World in Seventy-Two Days* (1890), and continued to write for the *World* until her marriage to a man more than forty years her senior in 1895. His wealth enabled her to live well without working, but when he died in 1904, her failure at managing the business she inherited was so complete that she retreated to Europe, where she stayed until the end of WORLD WAR I. Nellie Bly (or Elizabeth Cochrane Seaman) made an attempt at a journalistic revival upon her return in 1919 by working for the *New York Evening Journal*, but she died of pneumonia less than three years later at fifty-six.

BOARDING HOUSES

One of the few income-producing opportunities open to women throughout American history, boarding houses existed all over the country, with variations of place, time, and ethnic group.

Methods of boarding varied, but its development was especially important for the women of the massive immigration of the late nineteenth and early twentieth centuries. In the first decades of any ethnic group's migration, the chances were that dozens of men had left their families behind, and they gravitated to the one or two available women of their group who spoke their language and could cook their food in the familiar way. The result was extremely hard work—but a genuine income opportunity—for the women who ran the places where these newcomers lived.

Such a boarding house mistress usually began her day before dawn, packing lunch pails and fixing breakfast. Her boarders who worked the night shift might arrive then, ready to occupy the precious beds during the day. Another meal would have to be prepared for them, dozens of dishes washed, and the laundry begun. Clothes soiled by sweat and grime of the mine or mill had to be scrubbed by hand, and the water needed to do this had to be drawn from the well and heated under a fire. In the evening there were more meals to fix, more lunches to pack, dishes to be done again. In the midst of this, a woman often also had to care for her own children, keeping them quiet in the interest of the day sleepers. Doubtless she fell into bed exhausted, but that was providing she could find a bed, for the best were usually rented out, with the family, especially the woman, accepting the leftovers.

Indeed, it was the leftover food of boarders that some families counted on to provide their meals. Feeding methods varied in different communities; in some, boarding house women cooked to individual tastes, with each man placing his order and the woman shopping for and preparing a dozen different suppers. In others, men did their own shopping and the woman cooked, while occasionally men cooked and paid only for rent and laundry.

Earnings varied, but could be quite good. In western mining communities around 1910, a woman who boarded ten or fifteen men could earn eighty dollars monthly—as much as the average man made. Married women who did this work, however, often did not get either the money or the credit; the man of the house would be known as the "boarding boss."

Because the work was so difficult and so disruptive to family life, it was most common among young women and in the early stages of immigration. When families had earned enough to feel themselves secure, these women gave up their boarding businesses and concentrated instead on their children.

At the same time, boarding houses also existed that catered to Americans and the Americanized, and they too were usually run by women. In any frontier situation before hotels were built, there was opportunity for a woman with managerial skills sufficient to run a clean house with good food. Again, if there was a man involved, the establishment usually would be known as his, even if she was primarily responsible for its success; the history of many hotels apparently run by men can be traced instead to a woman who expanded household hospitality into a business that came to be seen as her husband's.

But boarding houses actually demanded little male help, and especially in Americanized situations, widows and other needy women found them one of the best opportunities to make a long-term living. Such unattached women were almost always highly aware of the need to maintain a spotless reputation for their establishments, and strict rules of behavior were commonly imposed—rules that often discriminated against other women for fear that a boarding house be confused with a brothel.

Not until after WORLD WAR II did the boarding house begin to disappear from American life. Though the women who ran them were often seen more as glorified housewives rather than as businesswomen, the operation of such establishments provided one of the few chances for women to earn independent income throughout most of American history.

BOLTON, BILL (1943)— *See* BOLTON, FRANCES PAYNE BINGHAM

BOLTON, FRANCES PAYNE BINGHAM (1885–1977)

Frances Bolton was a Washington wife, married to a congressman and the mother of three small sons, during WORLD WAR I. When the nation's lack of NURSES to deal with war casualties became apparent, she and other women persuaded the secretary of war to establish an Army training school for nurses, and by the war's end, the Army School of Nursing had students in camps all over the country. Bolton was so committed to the interests of nurses that she used over a million dollars of her inherited wealth to endow a school of nursing at Western Reserve University in 1929.

When the next war appeared, Bolton's life had changed drastically, for she replaced her late husband in Congress in 1940. Like her Ohio district, she was Republican, but when the party leadership did not support her efforts to be elected in her own right, she put together a campaign of women and won without them. Appointed to the House Foreign Affairs Committee, Representative Bolton was in a key position when the United States entered WORLD WAR II the following year. "One of her major contributions," in the words of ELEANOR ROOSEVELT, "was a successful effort to subdivide the committee by global geographical areas so that they could better specialize."

But her chief congressional service followed up on her interest in nursing during World War I. Aware that a second war was coming, she introduced legislation soon after entering Congress to provide $1.2 million for assistance to nursing schools. But passage of this appropriation was not enough, and by 1943, she successfully brought further attention to nurses with her "Bolton Bill," as it was called, which provided direct financial aid to students, as well as to schools, and set up a Cadet Nurse Corps that ultimately trained almost 125,000 young women in 1,225 schools throughout the nation. Aware that mature women had skills that should not be wasted, she also saw passage of incentives to bring former nurses back to the profession. With the exception of earlier legislation promoting HOME ECONOMICS, the Bolton Bill was a historic precedent for direct appropriations of federal funds to primarily aid women.

Representative Bolton served as the main proponent of both civilian and military nurses throughout the war. Strongly interested in the tens of thousands of women in the ARMY and NAVY NURSE CORPS, she paid her own way to Europe in 1944 to check on the results of her work, visiting London hospitals during bombing raids. With cooperation from General Eisenhower, she followed the troops after D-Day and was in Paris two days after its liberation. Though personally wealthy, Frances Bolton never sought a life of luxury, and her acceptance of harsh wartime living conditions was simply one more way in which she demonstrated a willingness to work hard at her job.

The courage she showed in going to war zones and her service on the Foreign Affairs Committee were the reasons

Representative Frances Bolton with President Truman and other dignitaries for the signing of the foreign aid bill in 1950. Bolton served in Congress longer than any other woman of her era and was the ranking Republican on the House Foreign Affairs Committee. NATIONAL ARCHIVES.

President Eisenhower appointed her as a representative to the United Nations during the 1950s. Frances Bolton also made history in the post-war era when she and her son, Oliver Payne Bolton, earned the distinction of being the first mother-son team in Congress. He was elected from another Ohio district, while she continued to serve a total of fourteen terms, ably representing not only her constituents, but also American women. Already middle-aged when she went to Congress, Representative Frances Payne Bolton lived to be ninety-one.

BONAPARTE, ELIZABETH PATTERSON (1785–1879)

An eighteen-year-old Baltimore belle, she married Jerome Bonaparte, the younger brother of Emperor Napoleon, on Christmas Eve, 1803, during his visit to the young United States.

Napoleon, who used his relatives' marriages to seal political alliances, refused to recognize their wedding, even though it had been conducted by a Catholic bishop. The young couple sailed to France in 1805, but found that orders had been issued forbidding Elizabeth Bonaparte to disembark any-

where on the Continent. Now pregnant, she was forced into exile alone in England, while her husband consented to end their marriage.

Despite the Pope's initial refusal to issue an annulment, Jerome was married off in an alliance with the German principality of Westphalia in 1807. Meanwhile, Elizabeth, using the twelve thousand dollar annual pension Napoleon offered as a payoff, returned to Baltimore with her son, whom she had named Jerome for his father. Young Jerome was ten when Napoleon fell in 1815, and his mother immediately took him to Europe, where, despite losing their pension with Napoleon's fall, they entered society. Using her independent wealth, Elizabeth Bonaparte (who was called Madame Patterson in Europe) remained abroad until 1834, while her son returned to the U.S., graduated from Harvard in 1829, and married an American—thus dashing his mother's hopes for the establishment of a European dynasty through marriage.

Two decades later, after Napoleon III ascended to power, Elizabeth Bonaparte's lifetime goal of having her son declared legitimate was achieved; her son and grandson went to

France and were recognized by their kinsmen. Never herself acknowledged, she also eventually lost most of her inheritance to her brothers. She lived in genteel and lonely poverty until her death at ninety-four, having seen American history from the early republic through the CIVIL WAR and its aftermath.

BONNEY, ANNE (?–1721?)

A legendary pirate, the facts on Anne Bonney are obscure, but supposedly she was born illegitimately in Ireland near the end of the seventeenth century. Her father allegedly left his wife for Anne's mother, who had been his wife's servant, and they fled the scandal to South Carolina.

Here Anne, grown into a beautiful young woman, apparently met Captain Jack Rackam, more commonly known as Calico Jack, and joined him on his pirating adventures in the South Atlantic. Their "honeymoon cruise" presumably featured an attack on a Spanish ship off the coast of what now is Fort Myers, Florida.

Bonney and her female colleague, Mary Reed, are credited with a reputation for bravery greater than that of most male pirates, but they met their doom in October, 1721, when their ship was defeated in battle with an English naval vessel sent by the governor of Jamaica to capture them. Calico Jack and the others were hung, but Anne, who was pregnant with her second child, managed to have her hanging deferred. It is not known whether the sentence was carried out.

BOOTH, EVANGELINE CORY (EVA) (1865–1950)

Born into the exceptional English family that founded and autocratically ran the Salvation Army for the first half-century of its existence, little Eva was named for the heroine of *Uncle Tom's Cabin*, still a new and radical book when she was born. Her family was also highly unusual in that it combined religiosity with FEMINISM; her mother was a preacher just like her father, and the daughters—whose husbands modified their names to include "Booth"—were expected to live the same street missionary lives as the sons.

Already as a teenager, Eva went alone into London slums to preach despite the expectation that she would be greeted with ridicule, physical abuse, and even arrest. Although she was among the youngest of her parents' eight children, Eva soon developed a reputation for uncommon maturity and ability to solve difficult problems. It was for this reason that her parents hurried her to America in 1896 to deal with her older brother and his wife, who, in proper American style, were rebelling against English rule. Following out her orders, she effectively held the American Salvation Army together until the arrival of her sister and brother-in-law, Emma and Fredrick Booth-Tucker.

Eva Booth went on to Canada, but returned to the United States less than a decade later after Emma was killed by a train. In 1904, she assumed the title of commander of the American Salvation Army, and at the same time changed her first name. Though her stated reason was that "Evangeline" was "more dignified," doubtless Booth was at least subconsciously aware of the subliminal effect of its connection with "evangelical," compared with the connotations of "Eve," the original sinner.

For the next three decades, Evangeline Booth demonstrated tremendous administrative and especially fund-raising skill, beginning a transition from her family's style of street begging to corporate donor support. She led the army through the Progressive Era with the creation of new charities, including homes for unwed mothers and for working women, and then expanded it to meet WORLD WAR I needs. She followed up the war with the organization's first national fund-raising drive, netting a hugely successful $16 million. Her fundraising was doubtlessly the reason that Booth avoided any identification with politics; she did, however, spend the twenties urging maintenance of PROHIBITION and, after becoming a citizen in 1923, quietly exercised the right to vote that she had always believed women should have, while never involving herself in the SUFFRAGE effort.

The 1920s also marked the final rebellion of the international Salvation Army against the tyranny of the English Booths, and once again, Evangeline demonstrated her problem-solving abilities by developing a smooth transition from the family heritage to the sophisticated organization that the army had become. After the deposition of her oldest brother in 1929 (who had inherited power from their father), Evangeline Booth was elected the fourth general of the Salvation Army in 1934. She moved to London, from which she directed the eighty-country organization for five years, and then allowed power to pass outside of the Booth family with her retirement in 1934. She lived the rest of her life in suburban New York.

Always physically active, Booth had joined the first women who rode bicycles in the 1880s and enjoyed horses and diving. She was also the author of several religious books published between 1908 and 1930, as well as a number of hymns.

BORDEN, LIZZIE ANDREW (1860–1927)

Throughout her life and into modern times, a great deal has been written about the few hours of Lizzie Borden's life that made her the star of the childhood rhyme, "Lizzie Borden, took an ax . . ." Most of what has been written emphasizes the miserliness of her Yankee father, who was a descendant of colonists, and especially Lizzie's hatred for her stepmother, who might inherit his frugally saved fortune. Little attention is paid to the fact that Lizzie's biological mother died when she was two and the stepmother had cared for her since she was five.

Lizzie Borden and her sister Emma, who was nine years older, grew up in the usual way for daughters of a Massachusetts merchant, except that their home was not as fashionable as presumably their father could afford; they kept only one servant and the girls complained of bad food. Lizzie graduated from high school, joined local church and temperance groups, and, at thirty-two, was apparently on her way to quiet spinsterhood until on a hot summer day in 1892, when she presumably fetched an ax, found her napping stepmother and then her father, and chopped them to their bloody deaths.

The case, with its unlikely setting, became one of the first sensationalist murder trials of modern journalism. Reporters descended upon Fall River, exploiting the division between oldtime New Englanders and the more recent Irish immigrants. Unable to envision a lady such as themselves justly imprisoned, the era's leading feminists and temperance leaders (virtually all of whom had an English heritage) proclaimed her innocence. Some attempted to pin the blame on the Bordens' Irish maid, while others accepted Lizzie's vague allegations of an unnamed intruder.

Despite strong evidence against her that in all probability would have convicted a man (or a woman of lesser economic standing), Lizzie Borden was acquitted of the murders by an all-male JURY. She stayed in Fall River for the rest of her life, although shunned by most of its residents; she moved to a new house, became estranged from her sister, was devoted to animals, and left instructions in her will that she be buried secretly at night.

Of the many books and articles written about the case, one of the best has this telling title: "She Didn't, and Even if She Did, She Couldn't Have." The men who composed the jury (no women served on juries then) chose not to believe that a young woman so like their own daughters could be capable of so heinous a crime. The acquittal revealed the blinders that many men wore when dealing with women; it was an embodiment of male refusal to see the actions of women—whether positive or negative—as somehow quite real. Discussed as it was in millions of American parlors, the murder also may be seen as a death knell for patriarchy. It signaled an end to the era of adult daughters who had no lives outside of their fathers' homes.

BOURKE-WHITE, MARGARET (1906–1971)

An early example of twentieth century FEMINISM, young Maggie, as she was called, was born in New York but grew up in Cleveland. The wanderlust that would make her famous was already apparent in her youth, for by the time that she graduated from Cornell in 1927, she had attended six COLLEGES and ended a brief marriage. That DIVORCE was the impetus for creating the new name of "Bourke-White," a combination of her mother's maiden name with hers.

She had earned money by taking photographs at Cornell, and soon established herself as an industrial photographer. This career choice, unusual for the times, was probably influenced by the examples of her parents: her father was a design engineer and amateur naturalist and her mother worked in publishing. Within two years, Bourke-White not only created a solid client list, but also was chosen in 1929 as a photographer for the new *Fortune* magazine.

Even though she was affiliated with a business magazine, Bourke-White was independent enough to make a communist country the subject of her first book. *Eyes on Russia* (1931) appealed to many Americans who were suffering from the Depression, and she followed it with two more books of photos from the Soviet Union. With a growing reputation among publishers, a Bourke-White photograph was featured on the first cover of *Life* when that magazine appeared in 1936. This honor came less than a decade after she had graduated from college.

Despite this personal success, however, the thirties deepened the exposure to leftist views Bourke-White had begun in the USSR, and she was further influenced by both the Depression and her relationship with novelist Erskine Caldwell. Traveling with him in 1936 through the Deep South to photograph the desperate lives of its poor, she began to shift from the "machine age" attitude portrayed in her industrial photography to an awareness of human suffering. Her photos

in *Have You Seen Their Faces?* (1937) not only set a new photographic standard, but also documented the poignancy of those terrible years.

She married Caldwell in 1939, and they published two more collaborative books before their divorce three years later. *Say, Is This the U.S.A.?* (1941) followed up on the American themes of their first book, but the other, *North of the Danube* (1939), returned to Bourke-White's international interests. Promptly on the European scene with the 1939 outbreak of WORLD WAR II, they were in Moscow when the Germans attacked the USSR in 1941. Bourke-White was the only foreign photographer then in the Soviet Union.

Soon after the United States entered the war, she became the first woman to be accredited by the Army as a war correspondent and quickly established a reputation equal to that of any male reporter/photographer. Covering the North African invasion in 1942, she was on a ship that was torpedoed; she lived with the soldiers through the blood and mud of the Italian front and was with Patton's troops when the German border was crossed. During all of this, Bourke-White sent home extraordinary photos to be published by *Life*—photos with tremendous personal meaning to Americans, especially women, whose knowledge of their loved ones' lives was primarily dependent on the print media.

Life's editorial board was faced with a crucial publishing decision soon after the war's end, when Bourke-White sent back graphic pictures of the Buchenwald death camp. Although in earlier warfare there had been unspoken "gentlemen's agreements" that the horrific aspects of battle would not be portrayed, the editors found her work so compelling that they defied convention and published the photos. That this unspeakable evidence of fascism became available to the world's conscience is to the everlasting credit of *Life* and Margaret Bourke-White.

She continued to roam the postwar world, taking the last photo of India's Gandhi before his assassination and covering rebellion in South Africa. On her return from assignment to the Korean War, Bourke-White felt the first signs of what would be diagnosed as Parkinson's disease. Nonetheless, she published several more books of photos and stayed on *Life*'s staff for a total of thirty-three years before formal retirement in 1969. Her autobiography, *Portrait of Myself*, was published in 1963.

BOW, CLARA GORDON (1905–1965)

A star of the silent screen who rocketed to success in the twenties, Clara Bow's film career was brief and mercurial, as befits the age of the FLAPPER. Her Brooklyn home and its resulting accent is often credited for her inability to make the transition to sound movies, but that home, and especially a dysfunctional mother, also caused emotional problems that plagued her all of her life.

Clara Bow was nonetheless a hard worker who made a dozen films within a year of her first contract in 1923. By 1933, however, her career was over, as even a comeback attempt had failed within the decade of her stardom. She lived quietly the rest of her life in Nevada and Los Angeles.

Bow is remembered not only for the expressive ability she exhibited in wordless stories, but also because she represented a new screen sex symbol: a guileless girl-next-door

Women of the Roaring Twenties getting the liberated "Clara Bow haircut." The innovative woman who owned the shop set it up in conjunction with a movie theater. COURTESY OF TAMPA-HILLSBOROUGH COUNTY PUBLIC LIBRARY SYSTEM.

type, in contrast to, for example, the sophistication of a MAE WEST. The "Clara Bow haircut" was widely copied during her era, with its short, pixie style depicting the boyish, androgynous trends of the daring twenties.

BOWEN, CATHERINE SHOBER DRINKER (1897–1973)

Growing up in a family of achievers who lived in the academic atmosphere of Pennsylvania's Haverford and Lehigh universities, Catherine Drinker nonetheless received the relatively informal education that was still often given to girls at the turn of the century. Her lack of schooling was at least in part her own decision, for much later she said that she had sworn, "Never, never to Bryn Mawr . . . to be a spinster." Instead, while her brothers stayed at school, much of Catherine's adolescence was spent TRAVELING with her mother and older sister. This wider exposure to the world, however, gave her a broad background that ultimately proved valuable.

She studied the violin in Baltimore and New York during her late teens, but gave up any thoughts of a career as a musician, when, at age twenty-two, she married Ezra Bowen, an econo-

mist at Lehigh. Nevertheless, she retained a lifelong interest in music, and not content to be solely a professor's wife, she began writing articles on music and other subjects for popular periodicals. While also bearing two children during the twenties, Bowen saw a children's book and a local history into print. Experimenting with other literary forms in the thirties, she published a novel, a book of essays on music, and finally, two studies of musicians. It was the latter that led her at last to the work that would make her reputation—biography.

Meanwhile, the Bowens had separated, they divorced in 1936. Returning to her hometown with her children, she married a surgeon in 1939, but because of both her children and her growing literary repute, she kept the Bowen name. It was in the forties and fifties (with her own age being approximately the same), that Bowen finally found her forte with the writing of biography that specialized in those men whose philosophies shaped American constitutional law.

She entered the field by degrees, seeking first to do a biography of a "worthy" man because of her disappointment with the personal characteristics of some of the musicians she had studied. Whatever the motivation, after publication of a half-dozen books, her next one became the turning point of her life. *Yankee from Olympus: Justice Holmes and His Family* (1944), reviewed by distinguished historian Henry Steele Commager, was an immediate popular and critical success. A brief ban on distribution to soldiers at its wartime publication (due to alleged political bias) may have helped make it a bestseller.

Bowen followed it up with a 1950 book on John Adams, and three years later, published *The Lion and the Throne: The Life and Times of Sir Edward Coke*, which won her a prize from the American Philosophical Society as well as a National Book Award. Firmly established by then, she wrote two more major works in the sixties, a biography of Francis Bacon and *Miracle at Philadelphia*, a study of the drafting of the Constitution that became assigned reading for history and government students at hundreds of colleges for years into the future. Bowen also published three works on the writing of biography and was at work on a biography of Benjamin Franklin when she died.

While FEMINISTS may view her pointed refusal to write a biography of a woman as painfully limited, it must be remembered that, after two decades of writing, she finally was successful during the late forties and fifties—a period during which others who wrote on women, such as historian MARY BEARD, saw their work maligned. Catherine Drinker Bowen chose a different subject area; with no formal college education, but with thorough research and an engaging style, she achieved both critical and popular success. She had shown, as Commager said of her in the Holmes' review, that "the best scholarship is art."

BOYD, BELLE (1844–1900)

A CIVIL WAR spy for the Confederacy, the change of her name from Isabelle illustrates the nature of her character, for this intelligent and daring young woman used a carefully crafted image as a Southern belle to charm Union soldiers into giving her information helpful to the South.

Early in the summer of 1861, when her Martinsburg, Virginia town was one of the first to fall to Union forces, Belle Boyd fatally shot a Union soldier, and when no consequences followed, she felt encouraged to begin a career in espionage. Courting the attentions of Union men, she sought out important military information and sent it South. Even though one of her messages was soon intercepted, Federal officers took no action beyond reprimanding what they assumed was an innocent teenager.

Confederate officers understood her true value, however, and she continued to play her dangerous game of passing messages. Arrested and detained for a week in Baltimore early in 1862, she moved on to Front Royal, Virginia, where, with her mother, she brazenly shared the same hotel as Union officers, and after scouting out a knothole in a room over their headquarters, listened until the plans of troop movements were clear. An expert rider with a fine horse named Fleeter, Belle Boyd made her most famous ride on the night of May 23, 1862, when she delivered intelligence of "immense service," as General Stonewall Jackson termed it in his thank-you note.

Though briefly arrested that night, she was not detained. Soon, however, rumors were flying about the young woman on horseback, and another woman, Annie Jones, reported Boyd to the Federals. Detectives were assigned to watch her,

and on July 29, Secretary of War Edwin Stanton issued an order for her arrest. Belle Boyd, now something of a national celebrity and still only eighteen, was escorted from Front Royal by over one hundred cavalrymen. Taken to Old Capitol Prison in Washington, she was supposed to be in solitary confinement, but again managed to get both prison guards and inmates to ignore their orders.

She was released a month later and exiled to Richmond, but was back in the northern Virginia action again the following summer. Again arrested and delivered to Washington, this time she was confined at Carroll Prison, where three other female political prisoners were also incarcerated. Imprisoned six months, she was once more banished to Richmond in December.

This time Boyd did not return North, but set sail for England with Confederate dispatches, beginning the journey on her twentieth birthday, May 9, 1864. Just off coast, however, the *Greyhound* was captured; she was taken prisoner first to New York and then to Boston, where the *Post* reported that "her deportment on shipboard is described by the officers as very lady-like" and added that she traveled with three servants. More importantly, the interview included her prediction that General Grant would be the key Union factor in ending the war. Since Grant had then commanded for only two months, her sagacity exceeded that of most military experts at the time.

Ultimately, Boyd was banished to Canada, under a sentence of death should she return. She left Quebec for England, hoping to further the Confederate cause there. Having meanwhile captivated the heart of the Union officer who had taken her ship, Belle Boyd married him in London in August, 1864, with the wedding featured in newspapers worldwide and attended by the highest ranking Confederate representatives in England. She remained there through the end of the war, while he returned to the United States, where he was arrested for his presumed role in helping her to allow the Confederate ship captain to escape. His health broken by extremely harsh prison conditions, he died soon after his release, leaving his wife with an infant daughter and in such poverty that Confederates in London took up a collection for her.

Belle Boyd published a two-volume memoir in London in May, 1865, and then took up an ACTING career that she pursued after returning to the United States late in 1866. Marrying again in 1869 to a prosperous businessman, she had four children before divorcing him in 1884. Her third marriage the following year to a young actor brought renewed poverty, and the irrepressible Boyd returned to the stage, this time telling her own Civil War story. She died suddenly at age fifty-six while on tour in Wisconsin and was buried in the Wisconsin Dells—ironically, by an honor guard of Union veterans.

Belle Boyd's life centered on the Civil War, when she was arrested for espionage six times—a record that had it been held by a male, would have surely resulted in his execution. Much like LIZZIE BORDEN's murder acquittal, because Belle Boyd was a woman, her actions were not deemed worthy of either credence or punishment.

Although her well-documented activities have been generally ignored in the teaching of history, the *Index*, a Confederate newspaper published in London, summarized her significance appropriately when it wrote late in 1864: "Probably the history of the world does not contain a parallel case. Her adventures in the midst of the American War surpass anything to be met with in the pages of fiction. . . . Her . . . attributes render her such a heroine as the world has seldom, if ever seen, in a lady only now in her twentieth year."

BRADFORD, CORNELIA SMITH (?–1755) One of the appreciable number of women PRINTERS in the colonial era, Bradford's husband founded the *American Weekly Mercury* in 1719 in Philadelphia. She worked on the paper after their 1740 marriage and then inherited it when he died two years later. Although she was sufficiently wealthy that she did not need the paper as a source of income, she not only kept it, but also did most of the editing and printing without assistance.

Like other printing establishments at the time, Bradford also sold various goods, especially books and stationery items. Even after the *Mercury* ceased publication in 1746, she continued to run her store and do bookbinding and contract printing until four years before her death. Bradford's will freed the two slaves that she had owned.

BRADFORD, DOROTHY E. (1929–1990) A Kansas City woman, Bradford corresponded with hundreds of soldiers during the Vietnam War. During the late sixties and seventies, she sent her pen pals more than ten thousand gifts and wrote as many as 250 letters weekly to service members and their families.

BRADSTREET, ANNE (1612–1672) Young Anne Dudley's life is illustrative of her era's extended families, especially in Europe, and of girls' roles in them: at sixteen, she married her foster brother (who was nine years older than she) and two years later, they accompanied her parents to America. She was part of the large party of prosperous religious dissenters called Puritans who settled in Boston in 1630.

Though the people who became known as the Pilgrims had settled south of Boston a decade earlier, living conditions in the Bay Colony were still very primitive. Accustomed to the comforts of an English estate, the eighteen-year-old Mrs. Bradstreet initially was dismayed by the wilds of America, but soon accepted her role as a pioneer mother. As the years passed, she developed a deep love for her husband, and together, they moved by degrees away from Boston, ending up in the northern Massachusetts town of Andover. From 1644, she mothered her eight children there and wrote the poetry for which she is remembered.

Clearly her poems were something she did for herself, for the only work that saw publication in her lifetime was taken to London without her knowledge by a proud brother-in-law. They appeared in 1650 with the (abbreviated) title of *The Tenth Muse Lately Sprung Up in America*. Like much of early American literature, this volume of Bradstreet's poetry was an aping of European ideas and style, for even though she wrote with no eye to publication, her poems were nonetheless stiffly inhibited. The book received what acclaim it did primarily because of public marvel that it was written by a woman—and an American woman, at that.

Despite publication, Bradstreet still hid her work. Thirty-

eight when the book appeared, she continued to write privately until her death at sixty, maturing as a poet all the while. A fire in her home when she was fifty-four doubtlessly destroyed much of her work, but what remained was enough to rank Anne Bradstreet as a genuinely creative poet. She wrote prose also, and while that was not intended for the public, either, it offered advanced thinking in the concise style of ancient proverbs, as, for example: "Diverse children have their different natures; some are like flesh which nothing but salt will keep from putrefaction; some again like tender fruits that are best preserved with sugar: those parents are wise that can fit their nurture according to their Nature."

Six years after her death, a second volume of Bradstreet's work was published in Boston, titled *Several Poems Compiled with great variety of Wit and Learning*, which had been part of the subtitle of the first book. Mostly a reprint of the London edition, it included only some of her newer works. Not until 1867, almost two centuries after her death, was a good edition of her collected poems published. By then, the reputations of many male poets who, unlike Bradstreet, published their work and publicized themselves, had begun to displace her.

Perhaps the most famous of her poems, commonly reprinted in American literature textbooks, is "To My Dear and Loving Husband," a beautifully written tribute to lifelong romance that belies the stereotype of repressed Puritanism. The first American poet of either gender, Anne Bradstreet's achievement is particularly significant given that she wrote without any formal education and with the responsibilities of serving twice as First Lady of Massachusetts, while also bearing and rearing eight children amid the privations of an unsettled land.

BRADWELL, MYRA COLBY (1831–1894) Myra Bradwell shared her husband's legal studies before his admission to the Illinois Bar, but in that pre–CIVIL WAR era, there was no thought of her actually becoming a lawyer. Like other liberal women of her time, she did charitable work and, when the war came, joined in the activities of the U.S. SANITARY COMMISSION.

Three years after the war ended, Bradwell, who had an uncommonly supportive husband, took the unusual step of beginning publication of the weekly *Chicago Legal News*, working as both editor and business manager. The following year, while also helping to organize the first meeting of Chicago suffragists, she passed the bar examination. The Illinois Supreme Court, however, refused to allow her to practice law on the grounds of her gender, and the case went all the way to the United States Supreme Court.

Bradwell vs. Illinois (1873) was a sound defeat for women. The Court essentially said that the Fourteenth Amendment did not mean what it said about equal protection under the law if the citizens involved were women, for, in the words of the majority, the Constitution was overruled by the "law of the Creator." Given the natural "timidity and delicacy" of females, states could and should bar them from practicing law. This was particularly true in the case of a married woman, who, since she could not even sign a contract without her husband's permission, obviously was incapable of carrying on a law practice. The only justice who dissented did not bother to write an opinion to explain his view.

While the case was in court, the Illinois Bar offered Myra Bradwell honorary membership; she accepted and was later elected to its vice-presidency four times. Meanwhile, she continued to publish the *Chicago Legal News*, where she editorially supported women's issues and other reforms. Through her husband, now a state representative, she succeeded in drafting and passing legislation to allow women to hold school offices and to serve as notaries as well as improvements to the laws governing MARRIED WOMEN'S PROPERTY RIGHTS and GUARDIANSHIP.

Recognizing her behind-the-scenes contributions to the legal field, the Illinois Supreme Court, acting on its own in 1890, reconsidered her 1869 application and admitted Bradwell to the bar. In 1892, two years before her death, she was admitted to practice before the United States Supreme Court. The *Chicago Legal News* was carried on by her daughter, who became a lawyer without the struggle that her mother had gone through.

BRADWELL VS. ILLINOIS (1873)— *See* BRADWELL, MYRA COLBY

BREAD AND ROSES

Written for use during the violent LAWRENCE, MASSACHUSETTS TEXTILE MILLS STRIKE of 1912, "Bread and Roses" became a popular slogan conveying the ideas of James Oppenheim's poem of the same title. Set to music by Caroline Kohlsaat, "Bread and Roses" provided a powerful marching stimulus at many labor and feminist parades.

The third of the four verses is probably the most famous: "As we come marching, marching/unnumbered women dead/Go crying through our singing their/ancient cry for bread . . . Yes, it is bread we fight for—but we fight for roses, too!"

The phrase, outside of its context, was also used later in the century. During the renewal of the women's movement in the late 1960s, a collective of Boston women called their group "Bread and Roses," and artist Ralph Fasanella has a work depicting the Lawrence strike that uses "Bread and Roses" in its title.

BREAST-FEEDING

Most women during most of American history never thought of not nursing their babies. Except in dire circumstances when the mother died or had no milk, early American women of all classes expected that they would use their breasts to feed their infants; even after the factory system developed, it was assumed that a nursing mother unfortunate enough to have to work would be given the necessary time off to nurse her baby. It was not until the accumulation of wealth and leisure in the nineteenth century that some women hired WET NURSES rather than directly nurture their offspring. It was not until the twentieth century that masses of women began to use bottle-feeding, deliberately cutting off the supply from their breasts.

Reasons for this historic switch to bottle-feeding are complex. Victorian notions that forbade knowledge of one's body may have motivated some who switched to bottle-feeding in the early twentieth century. Because the major abandonment of breast-feeding took place after the Roaring Twenties negated Victorianism, however, it would seem the young women of that era had begun to see their roles as wife/lover to be more important than their roles as mother, and stopped breast-feeding because of fears that it would damage their attractiveness to men. Probably most important of all, however, was new "scientific" advice offered to new mothers by the medical community.

Growth in availability of physicians by the twentieth century meant that doctors involved themselves with births that a century earlier would have been managed by MIDWIVES or by female friends. As the specialties of obstetrics and pediatrics grew, more and more physicians advised their patients to bottle, rather than breast, feed. Early in the century, some may have given this advice thinking it would help protect a woman's health: because physicians could not prescribe realistic birth control measures, some of their patients would be pregnant and lactating, often simultaneously, throughout young adulthood, and bottle-feeding would seem to offer a relief from this bodily drain. Mostly, however, bottle-feeding was depicted as the new (and therefore better) technology, available because of advances in refrigeration and sterilization, and axiomatically superior to the old ways. Public health nurses and social workers followed up with lessons on formula mixing, bottle cleaning, and rigid schedules for baby's hunger that banned "feeding on demand."

Most of this public health push for bottle-feeding took place around WORLD WAR I and was concentrated on the immigrant community and the poor, but bottle-feeding was also adopted by the middle class, who, taking their cues from women's magazines and advertising, delivered their babies in hospitals and had their breasts bound to cut off the milk supply. By the time of WORLD WAR II, breast-feeding was increasingly rare, and the trend of bottle-feeding continued through the fifties and sixties. The mobile young families of those decades carried with them the paraphernalia of sterilizers, bottles, and formula that had to be first refrigerated and then heated (without a microwave), all the while ignoring their grandmothers' advice on the comparative simplicity of breast-feeding.

It wasn't until the revived women's movement of the late sixties that the trend began to reverse. New research showed the importance of antibodies found in the colostrum of breast-milk that protected newborns from specific diseases; more and more people had experience with infants who were allergic to cow's milk and other substitutes for nature. Mostly, however, it was the activism of FEMINISTS and the LA LECHE LEAGUE that renewed breast-feeding by emphasizing the natural role of a woman's breasts in nurturing her offspring and rejecting the sex symbol attitudes towards breasts that had prevailed.

BRECKINRIDGE, MARY MARTIN (1905–   )

Americans listening to radio newscasts during WORLD WAR II did not expect to hear a woman's voice reporting serious news, but Mary Breckinridge broke through that media barrier in the same way that DORIS FLEESON, MARGUERITE HIGGINS, and others established themselves in the era's print media.

A member of the same Kentucky family as SOPHONISBA BRECKINRIDGE, Mary graduated from VASSAR COLLEGE in 1927 and then studied at the New School for Social Research in New York. The Great Depression hit just as she was finishing her education, and this well-prepared young woman went to work as a secretary in Washington, first for the Democratic National Committee and then for a member of Congress.

Well versed in foreign languages and an experienced European traveler, Breckinridge went abroad in 1930 to work as a freelance photographer. A London photo syndicate hired her, and when World War II broke out in 1939, she was well placed. Edward R. Murrow, CBS's famous radio broadcaster from London during the war's first bombing raids, put Breckinridge on the air to give listeners the different slant of a young, American woman, and CBS executives back in New York were so pleased with her performance that she began to broadcast regularly.

Although her first reports were in the "women's areas" of evacuation of the city's children and women firefighters, soon she was sent to Ireland to report on its tacit support of Germany. In December, 1939, Breckinridge broadcast from the Continent, first from the Netherlands and then from the German capital of Berlin, where she temporarily replaced the renowned William L. Shirer. Back at her regular post in Amsterdam, she continued to cover the news until forced to flee from the Nazi invasion. She left on the last available train to Paris, reported from there, and when Paris fell, went on to Italy.

Breckinridge gave up her CBS affiliation at that point, for she had fallen in love with an old friend who worked for the American State Department on prisoners of war. Protected by his diplomatic immunity, she returned to the dangers of Berlin; after a three-day honeymoon, she joined her husband in prison camp inspections. Even though the United States was not yet officially at war with Germany, American officials would not allow Breckinridge to broadcast while she was romantically involved with a State Department employee.

Though she lived much of the rest of her life abroad as a diplomat's wife, Breckinridge maintained her maiden name professionally and continued to publish photographs.

BRECKINRIDGE, SOPHONISBA PRESTON (1866–1948)

Born just after the Civil War to a distinguished Kentucky family that included a number of elected officials, "Nisba" became another of the successful women who were clearly influenced by their fathers. A liberal lawyer, he supported ABOLITION and the SUFFRAGE MOVEMENT and paid his daughter's tuition at WELLESLEY COLLEGE.

After graduation in 1888, however, like many educated women of her day, Breckinridge had difficulty finding a place for herself. She first was a high school mathematics TEACHER in Washington, D.C. while her father was in Congress, and then read law after they returned to Kentucky. In 1895, she became the first woman to pass the Kentucky bar examination, but she was not seriously interested in practicing law. Finally, at the invitation of a Wellesley friend, she went to the UNIVERSITY OF CHICAGO and there, in 1901, she became the first woman in the world to earn a Ph.D. in political science.

Thirteen years after college graduation, Breckinridge had found her life's work; she would stay with the University of Chicago in various teaching and administrative roles for the rest of her life. In 1907, she moved in at JANE ADDAMS' Hull House, where she became especially close to EDITH and GRACE ABBOTT. It was with Edith Abbott that she coauthored her first book, *The Delinquent Child and the Home*, in 1912.

Like Addams, Breckinridge soon became a prolific writer, publishing an average of one book every other year between 1917 and 1939. Most dealt with national and international political and social issues; two of them, *Women in the Twentieth Century* (1931) and *Marriage and the Civic Rights of Women* (1931), were explicitly on women.

In addition to influencing world opinion through her writing, she also served in women's organizations, holding national office in the AMERICAN ASSOCIATION OF UNIVERSITY WOMEN and the NATIONAL AMERICAN WOMAN SUFFRAGE ASSOCIATION. An early member of the NAACP, she also helped form the Woman's Peace Party and was part of the delegation of Americans whose pre-WORLD WAR I European meeting resulted in the WOMEN'S INTERNATIONAL LEAGUE FOR PEACE AND FREEDOM.

Dr. Breckinridge's professorship was the focus of her life, however, and by the time of the second Roosevelt administration, she had influenced hundreds of former students who became the innovators behind the New Deal. She did not move to Washington at this opportunity as some of her colleagues did; though Roosevelt honored her early in his administration with an appointment to the 1933 Pan-American Congress in Uruguay, she stayed at the University of Chicago, teaching a full load, until 1942, when she was seventy-six. More fortunate than many other female pioneers in academia, she had been granted full professorship in 1925 and was elected president of the American Association of Schools of Social Work in 1934.

BREHM, MARIE CAROLINE (1859–1926)

The Prohibitionist party's nominee for vice-president in 1924, Brehm was the first woman to be nominated for national office by a recognized political party after women had received the vote.

The 1920 presidential election took place in November after the ratification of the NINETEENTH AMENDMENT in August, so the election of 1924 was the first in which women had time to organize. The election thus could have been of great political significance, but women did not take advantage of their new power as a voting bloc and instead followed the same political patterns as men. The country was in a conservative mode after WORLD WAR I changes, and Republican Calvin Coolidge outran Democrat John W. Davis by an almost two to one margin. In addition, Brehm and Herman Faris, with whom she shared the ticket, had the disadvantage of lacking a genuine platform because PROHIBITION was currently in effect (having been passed before women were enfranchised). The votes they received were statistically insignificant.

An Ohio native, Brehm was a lifelong lecturer for the WOMEN'S CHRISTIAN TEMPERANCE UNION (WCTU). Unmarried, she spent most of her life traveling and speaking throughout the country; she held offices in temperance organizations in Illinois, Nebraska, and California. She supported the SUFFRAGE MOVEMENT and was a member of the Chicago Political Equality League during the time she lived there. In 1911, Brehm represented the United States government at the World's Congress on Alcoholism in London; she also attended other international conferences and lectured on temperance from Ireland to Germany.

She died in Long Beach, California two years after her nomination for vice-president of the United States.

BRENT, MARGARET (1600?–1671?)

Though of noble birth and a descendant of royalty, Margaret Brent was also one of thirteen children, and English inheritance law allowed relatively little for her. As her Catholic faith represented a second problem during this era of religious warfare, she emigrated with her sister Mary, two brothers, and a staff of servants to newly founded MARYLAND in 1638.

A grant from Lord Baltimore, proprietor of the colony, provided her with land, and through steady acquisition, she ultimately became one of the largest property owners in the area. Maryland, as a proprietary colony, was analogous in that era to a feudal state, and Mistress Brent's life was somewhat akin to that of the ruling monarch in a small principality. That she remained single is a testament to her independence, for men greatly outnumbered women and, being beautiful as well as wealthy, she did not lack for suitors. Perhaps she emulated the recently deceased Queen Elizabeth, who also managed to turn down men without alienating them.

In any case, Mistress Brent was a close ally of Maryland's governor, who was Lord Baltimore's brother, and she helped raise an army to support him in civil strife with Protestants. He repaid her by naming her executor of his will when he died in 1647. Though this was an uncommon display of confidence in a woman, it also proved a serious dilemma for Brent because the governor owed money to the soldiers who had put down the rebellion. Since his estate was insufficient for what was owed and since the nearly starving soldiers represented a real threat, she faced a severe political problem.

She solved it by extending her powers as executor to include the power of attorney that the governor held for his brother; under that rubric, she sold some of Lord Baltimore's cattle to satisfy the debts. Baltimore, safely in England, was outraged, but Maryland's legislative assembly answered his rebukes by praising Brent; she not only had no alternative, they declared, but also had used her feminine diplomatic skills to deal with the menacing soldiers more effectively than a man could have done in the situation. Without Mistress Brent, they wrote, "All would have gone to ruin."

Whether because of Baltimore's anger or not, Margaret Brent, along with her sister, moved to Virginia in 1651, where their brother had already settled. Never marrying, she lived prosperously there until her death sometime prior to May, 1671. Though FEMINISTS today sometimes name Margaret Brent as an early lawyer because she appeared in court and exercised powers of attorney, this activity was not in the role of a lawyer for hire, but was instead a personal appearance in the interests of her property and the Catholic state of Maryland. Not an ideological feminist, but rather a religious and financial conservative, she should be remembered instead for her exceptionally successful demonstration of women's business and political abilities.

BRICE, FANNIE (1891–1951)

Like many immigrants of both sexes who wanted to be successful in show business, Fannie Borach anglicized her name. The daughter of a saloonkeeper father and a mother who actually ran the family business, Fannie left school at thirteen with aspirations of a singing career. By sixteen, she had found a place on George M. Cohan's chorus line, but dancing was not her forte and she was fired. After going from one vaudeville house to another, she became a hit one night in 1910 when, while singing an Irving Berlin song, she made the audience laugh and discovered that her talent was as much in comedy as music.

Brice was soon featured as a *Ziegfield Follies* favorite, becoming the biggest star of those performances for more than three decades. She played the best vaudeville houses when that genre was at its height, and then moved on to make six movies as well as stage musicals. Her only theatrical failure was when she attempted the serious role of *Fanny* in 1926.

The invention of radio allowed her to reach her greatest audience; "Baby Snooks," a character that she had created many years earlier, brought laughter to radio millions from the late thirties to Brice's death. In this persona, like all of her other roles, Brice lampooned the false and pretentious; she also was careful not to join the crowd of comedians who made women and other minorities the object of jokes.

She married three times: the first was a very short fling in 1910; the second, from 1918 to 1927, brought her two children; and the third, to producer Billy Rose, lasted from 1929 to 1938. These disappointing marriages and the pain of Brice's personal life contrasted with her comic public persona, giving poignancy to her story as told first in a 1939 movie, *Rose of Washington Square*, and then, in the sixties, as the Broadway hit and award-winning movie *Funny Girl* and its sequel, *Funny Lady* (1975).

BROOKS, GWENDOLYN (1917–   )

Gwendolyn Brooks was keeping a poetry notebook already at age eleven. Published in children's and black periodicals in her teens, she studied for two years at a junior college in Chicago and worked as the publicity director for the Chicago NAACP during the 1930s. Her marriage to H.L. Blakeley in 1939 resulted in two children.

She found time to write, however, and was rewarded with four poetry prizes between 1943 and 1945 at the Midwestern Writers Conference. Her first book, *A Street in Bronzeville*, came out in 1945 when she was just twenty-eight; she was featured also that year as one of "Ten Women of the Year" in *Mademoiselle*. Critical praise won her grants from the American Academy of Arts and Letters and the Guggenheim Foundation, which resulted in her book *Annie Allen* (1949). When that book won the 1950 Pulitzer Prize in poetry, Brooks became the first black woman to be so honored.

One of the first to use black speech as art, she has gone on to publish a dozen books of poetry, as well as children's literature, a novel, and an autobiography, *Report from Part One* (1972). Proud to be a lifelong Chicagoan, she holds the newly endowed Gwendolyn Brooks Distinguished Chair of Creative Writing at Chicago State University. A leader in the effort to inculcate a positive black aesthetic, she gave up her twenty-six year association with Harper & Row to join a black publishing company, Broadside Press, in 1969.

Gwendolyn Brooks has been much honored, including election to the National Institute of Arts and Letters in 1976. She was the first black woman to be a Library of Congress consultant in poetry; she holds more than fifty honorary doctorates and was awarded a major lifetime achievement grant by the National Endowment for the Arts in 1989.

Brooks' writing continues to reflect an awareness of current events and is especially sensitive to political repression and personal suffering. Past seventy, she still considers herself to be a student, saying recently, "I was joyous at the release of Nelson Mandela. And I was just appalled by Tiananmen Square. I want to write about all of them, but I don't know how yet . . . You have to work at it."

BROWN, HELEN GURLEY (1922–   ) Born in Arkansas, Helen Gurley grew up there and in California, a common pattern among poor "Arkies" and "Okies" not only when the Gurley family moved during the Great Depression, but also for decades thereafter. Her move from the provincial mid-South to sophisticated Los Angeles was key to Gurley's development.

Between ages fifteen and twenty-five, she held eighteen different secretarial jobs, and she would continue to work for decades before becoming successful. Even though her 1942 college graduation coincided with increased employment opportunities for women during WORLD WAR II, she spent the war as a Los Angeles secretary. Finally landing a more suitable position as an advertising copywriter in 1948, she won awards for her clever prose; another decade brought promotion to advertising account executive in 1958.

She was thus forty years old and living the life of an average working woman when she published *Sex and the Single Girl* in 1962. An overnight sensation, the book's positive approach to what commonly had been negatively portrayed as "spinsterhood" was enough to make it controversial, but even more worrisome to conservatives was the author's assumption that sex was and should be a part of the life of a single "girl."

Brown, who herself had given up the single life three years earlier when, at age thirty-seven, she married a movie producer, saw her world completely transformed within five years of the book. She sold the title of *Sex and the Single Girl* to the movies; offered more lively advice in *Sex and the Office* (1964); and wrote a syndicated column aimed at single women—but her real opportunity came in 1965 when she was chosen editor of *Cosmopolitan* magazine.

In publication as a reputable family magazine since 1886, *Cosmopolitan* was suffering the circulation decline that affected many periodicals after television took away their audiences. Brown, using ideas developed jointly with her husband, completely turned around the magazine's image, transforming it into a sassy, self-assured publication aimed at the newly liberated woman and especially the single woman.

Subscriptions skyrocketed and advertising followed. Suddenly publishers realized that young women represented an untapped audience of millions who had previously found nothing of interest to them, and similar publications followed. Brown, meanwhile, wrote additional books, made television appearances, and became widely known as a celebrity who has stayed as editor in chief of *Cosmopolitan* for more than a quarter-century, while also maintaining her marriage.

Some FEMINISTS deplore the magazine's emphasis on physical attraction and what they see as its predatory "how to get a man" message, but it is nonetheless true that Helen Gurley Brown presented the world with a celebration of casual, independent womanhood like nothing ever seen before. She correctly identified a large group of potential readers whose existence had been snubbed by earlier publishers, and she may be the only American editor in history to have so completely and successfully transformed a publication that had lost its appeal.

Brown published several other books, including a cookbook, and in 1982 published an autobiographical work, *Having It All*. In 1993, she added *The Late Show: A Semiwild But Practical Survival Plan for Women Over 50*.

BROWN, OLYMPIA (1835–1926) The daughter of New Englanders who had moved to frontier Michigan just prior to her birth, young Olympia was refused admission to the University of Michigan because of her gender. Instead, she went to Massachusetts in 1854 to study at the single-sex MOUNT HOLYOKE, but left after a year in favor of Ohio's new, more liberal ANTIOCH COLLEGE. Soon becoming a leader at this coeducational school, she invited ANTOINETTE BROWN BLACKWELL to preach there and, after an inspiring sermon, decided to emulate Reverend Brown (who had not yet married) by becoming a minister. Though they were no relation, these two women named Brown led the way for other American women who wanted to study theology.

Olympia Brown found her goal far easier to obtain than had been the case with Antoinette Brown's struggle a decade earlier, and she entered the theological department of St. Lawrence University in Canton, New York in 1861. Both the time and place may have been influential in her admission: the school, only a few years old, might have been reluctant to turn down applicants in this first year of the CIVIL WAR when so many educational institutions lost their male student bodies; moreover, it was located in the SENECA FALLS area of New York State that spawned many women leaders. Whatever the cause of the propitious opportunity, she studied there for two years, and unlike Antoinette Brown, was ordained when she completed her course work.

The first woman to be thus sanctioned by a major denomination, Reverend Brown would pursue a genuine career pastoring Universalist churches, even after she was married and had children. She was called first by a congregation at Weymouth, Massachusetts in 1864; after six years there, she accepted a pastorate at Bridgeport, Connecticut. During the six years she spent at Bridgeport, she married John Henry Willis.

Like Antoinette Brown, Olympia Brown preached a loving theology and was a loving person who wanted a husband and children; unlike Antoinette Brown Blackwell, she not only kept her MAIDEN NAME, but also continued in the ministry after marriage and motherhood. She bore her first child in 1874 at age thirty-nine; when the second was born two years later, she took a short sabbatical before leading her family to Racine, Wisconsin in 1878.

The Universalist Church of the Good Shepherd had called her there, and she would serve it for nine years, retiring in 1887 after twenty-one years as a full-time pastor. Though she did interim preaching afterwards, Reverend Brown was then fifty-two years old and the mother of children going into their teenage years, and she wanted more time for other projects. Wisconsin remained her home while she expanded from church work to a second life as a businesswoman who ran her husband's publishing firm for seven years after his 1893 death—and, more importantly, as a women's rights leader.

In 1884, she was elected as a vice-president of the NATIONAL WOMAN SUFFRAGE ASSOCIATION and as president of the Wisconsin Woman Suffrage Association. She soon led the state organization into making use of legislation that allowed women to vote in school elections, and for many years she pursued a court case that would affirm an expansion to all elections. She also was a founder of the FEDERAL SUFFRAGE ASSOCIATION at an 1892 Chicago meeting and served as its president from 1903 to 1920, when the vote was won. Active in suffrage campaigns throughout the Midwest, Reverend Brown was also a fixture (especially for invocations) at women's conferences throughout the nation during the late nineteenth and early twentieth centuries. She published an autobiographical work, *Acquaintances, Old and New, Among Reformers*, in 1911.

The following year, younger women displaced her from the presidency of the Wisconsin suffrage association after she had served almost three decades in that position. Reverend Brown moved to Baltimore, where her daughter lived, in 1914 and continued her activist life, though in her eighties. Baltimore was handily close to Washington, and she campaigned in front of the White House against Woodrow Wilson's lack of support for suffrage.

She outlived the intransigent president, and unlike most other FEMINISTS of her pre-Civil War era, Reverend Brown and her mentor, Antoinette Brown Blackwell, lived to vote in 1920. Exceptionally strong, she took her first trip to Europe when she was past ninety, dying a few months after returning to Baltimore.

BROWN, VIRGINIA MAE (1924–1991)

The first woman to head an independent administrative agency of the federal government, Brown became chairman of the Interstate Commerce Commission in 1969.

She had a childhood example of an independent woman in her widowed mother, who was president of a small West Virginia bank. A college student during WORLD WAR II, Brown passed the bar in 1947 during a time when few women practiced law. The first West Virginia woman to be an assistant attorney general, she was also the first in the nation to be appointed state insurance commissioner.

Her marriage at age thirty-six to a man whose name was also Brown brought two daughters, but did not keep her from additional service as counsel to the governor and as a member of the state public utilities commission. Brown was thus exceptionally well qualified for federal appointment, but it was a surprise to her when President Lyndon Johnson used his speech

A class from Bryn Mawr's summer school for working women in 1931. NATIONAL ARCHIVES.

at a 1964 Women's National Press Club dinner to announce that he was making an effort to include more women in his administration and therefore was appointing Brown as the first woman to serve on the Interstate Commerce Commission.

Four years later, she was elected vice-chairman by her colleagues and the following year, became chairman. Since the chairmanship was as much an administrative as a policy position, Brown actually directed the agency's activities. She put particular emphasis on disproving the railroads' assertions of losses from passenger service, trying instead to maintain this public transportation option. Brown also broke old bureaucratic habits when she forbade the acceptance of free trips or other gifts by ICC employees.

Republican Richard Nixon took office in 1969 and did not reappoint Brown when her term expired later that year.

BRYN MAWR COLLEGE Founded by the Society of Friends (QUAKERS) to bring higher education to young women of the faith, Bryn Mawr was chartered by the state of Pennsylvania in 1880 and began classes in 1885. Its lovely campus near Philadelphia afforded a pleasant and safe situation for families who were still unsure that COLLEGE was advisable for young women. Among its earliest students was EMILY BALCH, who typified the idealistic young women who established Bryn Mawr's early reputation for serious graduates committed to social good.

Already in 1888, the college offered a course on "Charities and Corrections," and it soon acquired a New Jersey SETTLE-MENT HOUSE where students gained practical experience in community welfare. Bryn Mawr also led the way in expanding educational opportunity beyond the daughters of the upper class with summer schools that were open to working women, many of whom were laid off from their factory jobs during summers. Even in the 1920s, when the FLAPPER had firmly replaced the benevolent lady of the nineteenth century, Bryn Mawr resisted modern self-indulgence; instead, its summer schools did studies of working women's issues for the new WOMEN'S BUREAU OF THE DEPARTMENT OF LABOR.

Acknowledged as one of the SEVEN SISTERS schools and still single sex, Bryn Mawr opened its graduate school to men in 1937.

BUCK, PEARL COMFORT SYDENSTRICKER (1892–1973)

After her Presbyterian missionary parents awaited her birth in West Virginia, baby Pearl accompanied them back to their duty in China and spent her early childhood there. The Boxer Rebellion of 1900 was only a temporary setback in the Sydenstrickers' devotion to China; as a result, most of Pearl's education was in the setting of missionary schools and tutors. Her most conventional instruction occurred between 1910–1914, when she returned to the United States and was a superior student at Virginia's venerable Randolph-Macon Woman's College.

Soon after graduation, she went back to her family in China and worked as a TEACHER there until marrying an American agriculturist, John Lossing Buck, in 1917. They moved together to north China, where their life among the rural peasantry supplied her with the background of her greatest literary work. After the birth of a child who was mentally retarded, Buck went to the United States for, as she termed it, "certain

medical care not then to be had in China." After brief convalescence, she was back in China, where she adopted a second daughter. She and her husband both taught at the University of Nanking, but their marriage was beginning its long decline.

John Buck was unhappy in his work and took out his frustration on those around him; the distance between them grew to the point that Pearl Buck referred to him as "the man in my house." When she nursed her dying mother in 1922, she began to write to help herself clarify the tangled emotions of her life, but did not attempt to sell her work. Finally, when the family returned to the U.S. in 1925 to seek help for their retarded daughter (whose story she would tell much later in her 1950 book, *The Child Who Never Grew*) she used the quiet time of the sea voyage to write the first story she sold. Desperate for money for a winter coat, she sent it to *Asia Magazine* and was surprised when they published it.

While in the states, Buck also earned a master's degree in English at Cornell. Equipped with this additional degree, she taught at two other Chinese universities, in addition to Nanking, between 1925 and 1931. In 1927, however, she and her family had to flee from violence directed at foreigners; they were hidden by a Chinese friend, but when they returned home, the manuscript of her first novel had been destroyed along with most of their furnishings. After waiting out the revolution living in Japan and after restoring her Nanking home (Buck termed herself "an inveterate homemaker"), she managed to see her first book, *East Wind: West Wind*, into print in 1930.

Her second book, which followed the very next year, was indisputably her greatest—even though she would write over one hundred more. *The Good Earth* (1931) was an immediate success of unparalleled proportions; it not only won the Pulitzer Prize, but also was made into a play and an Academy Award–winning film. Translated into dozens of languages, it sold millions of copies and made its author instantly rich and famous. She spent the year following publication of *The Good Earth* back in the United States, enjoying her new success. She also began to fall in love with her publisher, Richard Walsh.

After returning to China, she continued to write at a furious pace, publishing *Sons* in 1932 and *The Mother* in 1934, the year that she also finally separated from John Buck. It was not only the collapse of her marriage, however, that caused her to leave China that year, for Buck was always keenly aware of world events, and she correctly foresaw the violent end of colonialism and the coming of WORLD WAR II. She traveled throughout Southeast Asia after leaving China in the spring of 1934, fearing that she would never again see that part of the world.

Retaining the now-famous name of her first husband after her Reno DIVORCE, she married Walsh in 1935 and continued to write at a seemingly frantic rate. *A House Divided* came out that year, biographies of each of her parents in the next, and a two-volume translation from Chinese, *All Men Are Brothers* in 1937. For this body of work she was awarded the Nobel Prize in 1938—just eight years after publication of her first book. Pearl Buck remains the only American woman to win the Nobel Prize in Literature, and one of just six women winners of any nationality. She spoke to that in her acceptance speech. Addressing the Swedish king and Nobel officials, she said, "You . . . cannot perhaps wholly understand what it means in many countries and even in my own, that it is a woman who stands here . . ."

Buck spent the next four decades publishing fiction and nonfiction, in both book and periodical length; she produced as many as five books annually. Millions of women read her stories in magazines such as *Ladies Home Journal*, *Redbook*, *McCall's*, and *Woman's Home Companion*, for a great deal of fiction was printed in magazines during this pre-television era. She also wrote a number of children's books, some plays, and even, eventually, a cookbook. Probably most important, though, were the nonfiction books and articles she wrote on the Far East.

As Japan took over China and French Indochina at the beginning of World War II, Americans began to focus on the importance of Asia—and many derived their information primarily from Pearl Buck. She not only spread her message of tolerance and internationalism with the written word, but also took an active organizational role. The East and West Association that she formed in 1941 sponsored cultural exchanges, and, with Walsh, she published *Asia Magazine* through the war years. An even more profound commitment was her adoption of a half-dozen children of mixed races.

Her emphasis on the evils and stupidities of racism made Buck more controversial than she had been in her earlier career, especially when China fell to the Communists after World War II. Perhaps it was not coincidental that during the time when McCarthy demagogy over "who lost China" was most shrill, she published several novels under a PSEUDONYM. By attributing authorship to "John Sedges," Buck gained freedom to see her work reviewed without prejudice against either her gender or her political views. Yet though the Sedges novels, especially *The Townsmen*, were well received, her work continued to be popular under her own name as well, selling even better overseas than in the U.S.

She gave up the Sedges experiment and put her name back on the cover of a book of personal revelation, *My Several Worlds*, in 1954 and continued to spell out opinions on subjects from illegitimacy to the new issues of the nuclear age. Though elderly when the women's movement began to revive in the sixties, Buck had long provided women with thinking material in her novels, drawing scenes that dealt with prostitution, marriage, abortion, and childbirth in Asian and American settings. Her interest in women through the decades can be seen in novels such as *Pavilion of Women* (1946), *First Wife* (1947), *Imperial Woman* (1956), *Angry Wife* (1969), and particularly the autobiographical *The Proud Heart* (1938). Buck's nonfiction work of special interest to women includes *To My Daughters, With Love* (1967) and especially *Of Men and Women* (1971). She even wrote *The Kennedy Women: A Personal Appraisal* in 1970.

Pearl Buck's stature among her peers was such that she served as president of the Authors Guild, an activist organization strongly attuned to free speech issues, for almost a decade during the tumultuous civil rights years of the late Eisenhower to early Johnson administrations. Her advocacy for the unwanted children of Asian mothers and American fathers, which continued from World War II through the Korean and Vietnam wars, was formalized in the Pearl S. Buck Foundation in 1964; she had begun an adoption program

with Welcome House—as she called the family's Pennsylvania farmhome where orphans were accepted—already back in 1949. Mental retardation was still another concern that she supported financially as well as intellectually, for she had known its personal pain since 1920.

Any one of these ventures would be enough to entitle Pearl Buck to remembrance, but it was, ironically, this very multiplicity of her interests that brought her criticism. Her literary repute likely would have been enhanced had she written less frequently and more carefully, but Buck—although aware of the damage done by her prolific pen—seemed so imbued with ideas and so eager to share them that she was incapable of slowing down. She ran out of time at eighty-one, surrounded by manuscripts.

BULL, SARAH WELLS (1693–1795)

As an eighteen-year-old orphan, Sarah Wells journeyed inland from New York City to the Orange County area that became known as "land o'goshen." It was a nameless wilderness then, and she went to settle on 100 acres of free land that had been promised to her if she would secure the claim—granted by Queen ANNE—for its owner, who had been delayed by other business in New York.

On May 27, 1712, accompanied by two native guides and a carpenter, she left to build a home in the primeval forest. Others soon joined her, but she continued to live a very independent life. She TRAVELED alone, for instance, to get grain ground at "Madam Brett's mill." The journey, which involved rowing across the Hudson, took at least two days; once she had to climb a tree to escape from wolves.

An English stone mason named John Bull joined the wilderness community several years later, and Sarah Wells married him in 1718. Together, they built a three-story stone house with walls three feet thick that still stands. Marriage did not mean an end to wilderness trials, however; the isolation was still so real that, for example, she tied her toddler to the bedpost when she had to go search for her husband, who failed to return as scheduled. She found him ten miles away, overcome with sickness. Meanwhile, the tied-up baby cried.

In 1912, fifteen thousand Americans could trace their ancestry to Sarah Wells Bull, whose courage and enterprise built a magnificent home in the wilderness. The Sarah Wells Trail commemorates her today.

BUNDLING

Practiced in some communities in colonial days, bundling was a custom brought from Britain of ancient Celtic origin. Unmarried young men and women, with societal approval, would occupy the same bed in a sort of trial marriage situation. They would remain fully clothed, and sometimes a board placed down the center of the bed would also separate the two. It was especially prevalent among the lower classes in Connecticut and western Massachusetts, and, although famed colonial preacher Jonathan Edwards railed against it, the custom was still seen as late as the Revolution. A 1777 commentator said that it was "in some measure abolished along the sea coast," but still prevailed in the more rural areas inland.

Though shocking to Victorian Americans two centuries later, bundling graphically depicts early New England attitudes towards sex and marriage. There was little opportunity in colonial times for courtship to include the fancy dress, dancing, and flirtatious manners that came later. Instead, bundling spelled out to young couples that a woman's role was to reproduce and a man's role was to make it possible for her to do so; rather than a titillating amusement, it was instead intended to make clear that the purpose of courtship was marriage and the purpose of marriage was procreation.

BUNKER, CAROL LAISE (1918–1991)

A pioneering woman in diplomacy, Carol Laise began her career with the State Department in 1948. By 1966, she had risen to become the ambassador to Nepal, where she served until 1973. During most of those years, she maintained a commuter marriage with Ellsworth Bunker, the ranking diplomat in Vietnam during the war; their 1967 marriage was the first between two American ambassadors. She adopted his name and went on to serve at the United Nations. The first woman to be an assistant secretary of state, Bunker died in Virginia.

BURNELL, ESTHER (1890–1964) and ELIZABETH (1888–1960)

Two of the first female nature guides of the National Park Service, the Burnell sisters worked in Colorado's Rocky Mountains in the days when much of the area had yet to be explored.

Esther was the first to go west from their native Ohio, filing a HOMESTEAD claim near Estes Park in 1916. After building a cabin, she lived alone through the first winter, traveling with snowshoes on those infrequent occasions when she broke the isolation of the wilderness. Elizabeth, who, as head of an Ohio college mathematics and physics department, was also an uncommon woman, joined Esther the following summer. Both women were trained as nature guides by the infant park service in 1917 and received their official "permits" the following year.

Esther eventually married the man whose speech in Ohio had motivated her move, but he died soon afterwards. She supported their child by running the inn she inherited from him, while Elizabeth went on to become a serious naturalist, writing a book on birds and running nature study programs in California as well as Colorado. An expert mountain climber, she was the first woman to lead expeditions up Colorado's Longs Peak.

BURNETT, FRANCES HODGSON (1849–1924)

When she was just five, Frances Hodgson's father died, and the family's resulting poverty caused them to emigrate from England when she was sixteen. Settling in the mountains of western Virginia in the last year of the CIVIL WAR, their impoverishment might well have continued indefinitely but for young Frances. Without any educational advantages, she somehow sold a story to GODEY'S LADY'S BOOK three years later and soon was regularly publishing in the era's popular periodicals, including *Peterson's Ladies' Magazine*.

Her marriage to Dr. Swan Burnett in 1873 did not entirely end the family's financial problems, and the young bride continued to write. Her first book was published in 1877 when she was twenty-eight, but Burnett's fame and financial freedom was made the following decade with *Little Lord Fauntleroy*, which was probably the best-selling book of 1886. Serialized the previous year in MARY MAPES DODGE's *St. Nicho-*

las magazine, it soon was made into a play popular enough that some four hundred U.S. theatrical troupes simultaneously produced it.

This popularity is an interesting demonstration of the power of mothers in domestic matters, for fathers and sons were seldom pleased with Fauntleroy's carefully curled long hair and genteel manners. The image, however, so captured the imagination of the era's women that "Little Lord Fauntleroy" developed into a lasting fashion term for costumes of black velvet with white lace. Adding to male horror was the interestingly androgynous casting of girls in the title role of dramatic versions, with Mary Pickford starring in the first movie. Yet until after the drastic post-WORLD WAR I changes in manners and mores, so many mothers attempted to model their boys' appearance and behavior after Burnett's character—and so many males lampooned the image with cartoon ridicule—that the term became synonymous with male misery among the overprivileged.

Its Master Cedric Errol, who became the little lord, was drawn from Burnett's own young son. She similarly used her English birth to great sales advantage, understanding well the predilection of her readers for things Victorian. Tremendously popular, Burnett wrote more than fifty books and was reputed to have never had a line rejected by a publisher. Her tales were rather Dickensian, featuring unfortunate young people who rose above their problems in complex plots dominated by remarkable circumstance. Yet despite this seeming triteness, Burnett's fiction was unusual for featuring poor people at all, let alone drawing the realistic portrayals of poverty that she did. Doubtless the plots did not seem excessively fantastic to a woman whose life had been so similar. Beyond that, Burnett's reputation as a romantic is also belied by her actions as a businesswoman; already in 1888, she sued in British court to secure her copyright in the dramatic productions of Fauntleroy, thus establishing an important legal precedent for all authors.

Burnett's books continued to sell long after her death, with *The Secret Garden*, originally published in 1911, displacing *Little Lord Fauntleroy* as the most popular Burnett book by the late twentieth century. Made into a 1949 movie, it was reissued as a novel in 1962, as both a book and a movie in 1987, and as a 1991 Broadway musical. Late twentieth-century girls found a heroine in this tale, set in a Yorkshire moor with an innocent girl in menacing circumstances triumphing over fear and evil to bring a happy ending. Burnett's imagination clearly continues to have great reader appeal more than a century after she began writing.

BURNS, LUCY (1879–1966)

Lucy Burns' life, more than that of most women, seems to divide naturally into three distinct and quite different stages.

Born to a "lace curtain Irish" family in Brooklyn, she began what might have been a stellar academic career. After graduation from VASSAR in 1902, she taught high school briefly and then went on to graduate studies in linguistics at Yale, the German universities of Berlin and Bonn, and Oxford.

It was while she was working on her doctorate at Oxford in 1909 that Burns began her second stage of life as a suffragist, the role for which she is deservedly famous. Having volunteered with the British militant suffragists led by the Pankhurst women, Burns soon proved so valuable an organizer that she was hired to work in Scotland from 1910 to 1912. With her fiery red hair and ready wit, she argued and charmed and moved a crowd.

While in Britain, Burns met ALICE PAUL, an American also working in the suffrage movement. They would end up a highly complementary team, with Paul's role emphasizing philosophy and strategy, while Burns specialized in organizing—much in the same way that ELIZABETH CADY STANTON thought out many of the speeches that SUSAN ANTHONY delivered. After both Burns and Paul had returned to the United States, they opened an office in Washington in January, 1913, and in no time, they turned around the American SUFFRAGE MOVEMENT.

The old NATIONAL AMERICAN WOMAN SUFFRAGE ASSOCIATION was badly in need of revitalization, and these new leaders provided the impetus to stir the suffrage issue again. Their first move was to organize a huge parade in support of suffrage, which attracted five thousand marchers after only two months of organizing. Timed for the day prior to Wilson's inauguration (inaugurations took place in March then), it was aimed at influential political visitors who would be in Washington as well as the extra journalists in town. The parade, though a terrible experience for the marchers who were attacked by mocking crowds, was nonetheless a huge media success. Readers were sympathetic to the brave marchers, and ultimately the Washington police chief lost his job in part because of his failure to maintain order.

The energized team of Paul/Burns moved on to build a new organization, the CONGRESSIONAL UNION FOR WOMAN SUFFRAGE (CU) in April. Introducing the tough techniques of the British militants, they shocked Americans with their deliberate law-breaking and zealous campaign style. Having discovered abroad the value of martyrdom as a publicity tool, Lucy Burns sought her first arrest in 1913 for defacing public property with suffragist graffiti; she was proud of her eventual record as the suffragist who served the most jail time.

Burns demonstrated her strength again during the election of 1916 when she took two dozen women across the country on a railroad car called the "Suffrage Special." Concentrating on WESTERN WOMEN in those states where women could vote, they campaigned against Democratic candidates without regard to the details of particular races, arguing that Democrats should be defeated because the White House was occupied by a Democrat. That Wilson was only the second Democratic president to hold office in more than a half-century was of little importance to Burns and her supporters; they simply wanted to send a powerful message of the depth of women's feelings.

Wilson's reelection did not diminish Burns' zeal. In 1917, with attention diverted from suffrage by the United States' entrance into WORLD WAR I, she got her issue back on the front pages by emulating the British technique of hunger striking. She led regular demonstrations against Wilson and when, in November, she was arrested and imprisoned, she went without food for almost three weeks before her jailers finally managed to force feed her. She used that against Wilson, too, organizing another railroad car in 1919, this one occupied by women who had served their time for suffrage in jail.

But when the vote was finally won in 1920, Burns behaved as though her life was over. Unlike Alice Paul, she did not go on to work for the EQUAL RIGHTS AMENDMENT or other changes in women's lives that the vote could have brought. Instead, after just a decade in the women's movement (and part of that in Britain), she entered into what seems the third phase of her life. It was a life typical of that of millions of women who shared her Irish ancestry, for the era's census figures show that Irish-American women were far more likely than most to remain single and to maintain close ties with adult siblings. She moved in with two unmarried sisters and lived the rest of her life as a conventional Catholic woman, caring for an orphaned niece. Lucy Burns never made use of the strong academic credentials she had, nor was she active in any organization other than the church.

Had she exercised her very real organizing skills during all the decades that she continued to live, it is possible that the history of American women might have taken a different course. Instead, the victory of the vote was dissipated, for the original suffragists were dead or dying—ANTOINETTE BLACKWELL in 1921, OLYMPIA BROWN in 1926—and though Alice Paul tried to carry on with the NATIONAL WOMAN'S PARTY, the retiring attitudes of most younger women meant that the movement became leaderless just at the point of its potentially greatest impact. Lucy Burns would live on through the Roaring Twenties when young women lived liberated lives while labeling FEMINISM passe; on through the Great Depression and its psychologically scarring squander of women's abilities; on through the increased opportunities of WORLD WAR II and even through the baby boom years of the fifties, but she would offer no leadership and, ultimately, few remembered her name and her very real contribution.

BURROUGHS, NANNIE HELEN (1878–1961)

Born in Virginia, Nannie grew up the only surviving child of a young, widowed ex-slave. When she was five, her mother moved to Washington, D.C., a post–CIVIL WAR mecca for blacks, and Nannie thus matured in a relatively favorable situation, with her mother able to concentrate on providing her with opportunities. Jennie Burroughs established herself as a cook, while Nannie was able to attend public (though segregated) high school, graduating with honors in 1896.

Like BLANCHE ARMWOOD, she wished to specialize in the new field of domestic science, but was unable to find a job. She worked in various unsatisfactory occupations before finding employment with the Women's Convention of the National Baptist Convention in 1900. Her maiden speech to the organization showed that the young Miss Burroughs understood gender discrimination, as well as racial prejudice, for she titled it, "How the Sisters Are Hindered from Helping." The energy with which Burroughs approached her task is clear from her report to the organization the following year. She had worked every day of the year, traveled over twenty-two thousand miles, made two hundred fifteen speeches, and written more than nine thousand letters.

Burroughs spent several more years working for that organization before she was able to persuade the Baptist women to back her with establishment of her life's dream, a school for young black women. In 1909, classes began at the National Training School for Women and Girls, situated on a six-acre campus in what was then suburban Washington. The student body quickly grew from its initial seven, and Burroughs, like MARY MCLEOD BETHUNE and other entrepreneurial educators, spent the rest of her life raising money and administering her school. Again like other similar institutions of that time, her school had a strong religious emphasis. Burroughs' philosophy was based on three *b*'s: "The Bible, the bath, the broom," for cleanliness in body and mind fit not only with oldtime Puritan ethics, but was also the gospel preached to immigrants of that era in Americanization classes. There were other areas, however, in which Burroughs' educational ideals were distinctive and new.

With the assumption that black women would be income-producers, her school's curriculum emphasized not only domestic arts, but also classes in such subjects as bookkeeping and shorthand. Even more striking were the courses that were not usually women's occupations: shoe repair, printing, gardening, etc. In addition to vocational education, there were classical academic requirements, especially grammar, and Burroughs's school was most unique in establishing a Department of Negro History. Hers was a pioneering curriculum that balanced competing values: while at the same time Burroughs sought to ease her students' entry into the labor market by standardizing their language, she also understood their need to develop pride by studying black history. This unusually strong curriculum kept her school alive through the Great Depression and the pressures of WORLD WAR II, which were especially difficult in Washington.

In addition, Burroughs found time to write for black and religious publications and to develop other community projects, always with a strong self-help philosophy. She used her writing and her knowledge of history to explain the impatience of blacks with their situation, drawing an analogy, for instance, between a Harlem riot in 1935 and the destruction of British property during the American Revolution. Moreover, she also wrote honestly of the subjugation of black women by black men. A 1933 column in a black publication, for example, demanded: "Stop making slaves and servants of our women . . . The Negro mother is doing it all. The women are carrying the burden. The main reason is that the men lack manhood and energy . . . The men ought to get down on their knees to the Negro women. They've made possible all we have . . ."

A supporter of suffrage, she organized women to register when the vote was obtained in 1920, worked with the NATIONAL ASSOCIATION OF COLORED WOMEN and the National League of Republican Colored Women, and maintained her leadership in the (black) Baptist Women's Convention for more than a half-century. It was primarily her school, however, that demonstrated what was possible for women. Using as her motto, "We specialize in the wholly impossible," Nannie Burroughs educated more than twenty-five hundred young black women. She was particularly proud of the fact that hers was the only such school funded solely by blacks.

Three years after her death, the school was renamed the Nannie Burroughs School. An elementary school now, it is at Northeast Eighteenth and Monroe in Washington.

BUSINESS AND PROFESSIONAL WOMEN

Founded in 1919, just as women got the vote, BPW was also a response to the new job openings women found during World War I. As more and more women went to college and entered into the professions, they quite naturally felt the need for an organization to promote their goals of increased opportunity in the workplace. BPW differed from the well-established AAUW (AMERICAN ASSOCIATION OF UNIVERSITY WOMEN) in that it did not require its members to be college graduates, nor did it place the emphasis on group study that AAUW did. Instead, it worked for economic self-sufficiency for women and soon developed into an effective lobbying force.

Particularly during the Roosevelt era, BPW lobbied not only for legislation to improve job opportunity, but also for appointments of women to the managerial levels of government. It maintained one of the first TALENT BANKS, and BPW leadership regularly used their connections with ELEANOR ROOSEVELT, MARY ANDERSON, and other women leaders in FDR's administration to bring attention to the abilities of these underutilized women. Its publication in that era, *Independent Woman*, clearly reveals the discontent of BPW members with their secondary place in business and government.

The group's current publication is *National Business Woman*; it has a membership of 125,000 organized into thirty-five hundred local groups and is headquartered in Washington. During the 1970s, BPW joined in coalitions with other FEMINIST organizations to pass the EQUAL RIGHTS AMENDMENT, and it continues to maintain its Congressional Lobby Corps on issues such as dependent care and other employer responsiveness needs.

BUTLER, ELIZABETH BEARDSLEY

An early government labor investigator, Elizabeth Butler actively improved the lives of working women by writing three pioneering books of sociology and economics between 1909 and 1913. Her *Women and the Trades* (1909) was especially important as part of a six-volume report by reformers on industrial conditions in Pittsburgh. Butler's study detailed the unconventional work that women were doing without acknowledgement—then or later—from middle-class America.

She found, for example, that thousands of women worked at the strenuous job of core making in Pittsburgh foundries, where they routinely lifted sixty pounds of metal. Most of these were IMMIGRANT WOMEN from the Slavic countries of eastern Europe; fewer than one in five could speak English. Women accounted for nearly a quarter of all core makers, and the metal industry was in fact the third largest employer of women in the city, exceeded only by laundries and cigar factories.

Butler also studied the latter two industries, as well as the conditions of women who worked in canneries, cracker and chocolate factories, and other occupations that demanded terribly long hours in harsh working conditions while paying almost nothing. The detailed data of exploitation that she provided helped lead to PROTECTIVE LEGISLATION, but is also important for its revelation of the many and difficult types of work that women did. At a time when most Americans believed that women did not work except occasionally as TEACHERS OR NURSES, she showed that, in one city alone, there were tens of thousands of women who did not fit the mold.

BYINGTON, MARGARET (1877–1952)

An early sociologist, Byington specialized in the Slavs who settled in the mining and mill towns of Pennsylvania. *Homestead: The*

Households of a Mill Town was published in 1910 by the same RUSSELL SAGE FOUNDATION that financed ELIZABETH BUTLER's study of Pittsburgh women. While Butler specialized in urban, working women, Byington concentrated on the lives of IMMIGRANT WOMEN, especially young mothers, in semirural settings.

She did extensive interviewing of these women, analyzed their spending priorities and studied their housework and child-rearing methods. Clearly objective in her methodology, Byington acknowledged that some of the results of her studies surprised her: among them was the relatively high status of women in making most financial decisions in these homes and the revelation that employment in American homes did not necessarily develop young women into better housekeepers.

Byington's work was well known and her views were respected by early social workers and sociologists, who bought the thirteen books she published between 1908 and 1941. Most of these were written in the activist era around WORLD WAR I, for neither the egocentric values of the twenties nor the depressed thirties was as propitious as the Progressive Era for the charity-centered minds of women such as Byington.

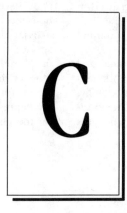

CABLE ACT Passed by Congress in 1922, an era when all immigration legislation was drastically revised, this act also reflected the fact that women had begun to vote two years earlier. It repealed previous regulations that jeopardized a woman's citizenship if she married a noncitizen. The result would be not only that American women were freer to move about the world and marry foreigners, but also that American women who remained in this country could marry immigrants without endangering their legal status.

CABRINI, FRANCES XAVIER (1850–1917) The first American citizen to be declared a saint by the Catholic Church, Maria Francesca Cabrini was born in a small town in Lombardy, near Milan in northern Italy. From a middle-class family, she was educated in convent schools and took vows as a nun in 1877.

Though still young, she soon became known as Mother Cabrini because of her work in a local orphanage. When the orphanage closed in 1880, she organized seven of its young women into what became the Missionary Sisters of the Sacred Heart of Jesus. Clearly she had struck a nerve with Italian nuns, for her order grew so rapidly that within seven years, there were seven new convents. Her dream was a mission to China, but Pope Pius XIII, after formally recognizing the order in 1888, decided that its best use would be in America.

Millions of Italians had begun streaming to the United States in the 1880s, where they found (except for the Irish immigrants of the 1840s and some small French influence from colonial days) an almost wholly Protestant society. The church was desperate for Italian-speaking workers who could keep these souls within the fold. Arriving in early 1889 with six other sisters, Cabrini's first move was the establishment of a convent, school, and orphanage in New York.

She followed this with similar complexes in New Orleans, Chicago, Denver, Seattle, and Los Angeles. A hospital in New York in 1895 was followed by hospitals in other cities, and the sisters also ministered to prisoners, especially those sentenced to death. Not content to define America as only North America, Mother Cabrini also set up institutions in Nicaragua, Argentina, Brazil, and Panama during the 1890s; with amazing rapidity, the order became truly international with turn-of-the-century establishments in four European countries. Though she was a world traveler with a global outlook, Mother Cabrini chose to become an American citizen, taking the oath in Seattle in 1909.

When she died at age sixty-seven from a relapse of malaria she had contracted in Latin America, she left over fifteen hundred daughters in sixty-seven convents throughout the world. Proceedings were begun to canonize Mother Cabrini in 1928, and she was elevated to sainthood in 1946, less than a century after her birth.

CALAMITY JANE (MARTHA JANE CANNARY BURK) (1848?–1903) Though accounts vary with the hyperbole of romanticism that surrounds FRONTIER WOMEN, there is general agreement on certain aspects of the woman known as Calamity Jane. Despite a lifetime of alcoholic haze, she fairly consistently reiterated the information, whether exaggerated or not, of the seven-page autobiography she sold late in life.

She was likely born in Princeton, Missouri a decade prior to the CIVIL WAR as Martha Jane Cannary (or Canary) and moved with her parents to Montana near the end of the war. Montana was truly a frontier then, and she learned the traditionally male survival techniques of riding and shooting—something that was especially valuable when both of her parents died soon after their wilderness move.

An orphaned teenager, she dressed in pants and spent most of her time in Virginia City saloons and other masculine habitats where she gambled, smoked cigars, and swore like a man. References to her "unholy career" during the late 1860s appear in towns from Montana through Wyoming and Utah. So masculine in appearance that strangers sometimes did not realize she was a woman, she worked with railroad construction gangs and as a mule skinner, but only long enough to earn the money "to go on a toot." Exactly when or why Martha Jane Canary came to be called Calamity Jane cannot be determined, but she introduced herself as such from 1872 on. She claimed to have scouted for General Custer's cavalry in Wyoming during that period, but though she lived in Cheyenne at the time and offered her services at Fort Laramie in the spring of 1875, the lack of confirming Army records make it doubtful she was hired as a scout.

The discovery of gold in South Dakota's Black Hills brought her and thousands of others there, and from 1876, the South Dakota town of Deadwood became as close to a home as she had. The summer of 1876, when she was presumably in her late twenties, was in fact the high point of her life, as Calamity Jane and Wild Bill Hickok developed into the twin stars of Deadwood sagas. Tales that they married have often been repeated—encouraged by Calamity, who much later was sometimes called "Jane Hickok"—but in fact, Hickok was married at the time to a circus woman to whom he appeared devoted. More significantly, he was killed on August 2, 1876, and Jane's first appearance in Deadwood was apparently in June, so their common time was only a matter of weeks.

Calamity Jane stayed in Deadwood for several years, adding to her local legend by exhibiting genuine bravery and kindness during an 1878 smallpox epidemic when she and the lone doctor tended the town's pesthouse. With Deadwood's gold panning out, she left in 1880, and lived for a time in the South Dakota town of Pierre, where for a while she was said to have dressed as a woman and to have served as a MIDWIFE for at least one baby. From there she returned to Montana and Wyoming and added to her image in the dime novels of the day, where she was labeled the "White Devil of the Yellowstone."

When probably in her forties, she married a man named Clinton Burk (or Burke). Some accounts put this in California in 1885, while others argue for Texas in 1891. In fact, she may well have never left the Montana/Wyoming/Dakota area, for newspapers there note her presence during the same time period. In any case, Burke made no difference in her life, and if indeed the marriage existed at all, it was extremely brief and may or may not have resulted in the birth of a daughter.

As the West was settled, reality and artifice blended into Wild West shows that were extremely popular in the East,

but arguably exploitive of those who were exhibited much like animals in a zoo. Calamity Jane joined such a show in 1896 at the Palace Museum in Minneapolis and then went on to Chicago, St. Louis, and Kansas City. Thousands of copies of her autobiographical pamphlet were sold to the crowds who came to see her, but, though she was a good draw, management fired her when she proved unable to stay sober.

In 1899, she returned to Deadwood with a seven-year-old girl she said was her daughter. The *Deadwood Times* editor and others organized a sellout benefit at the Opera House, and Calamity Jane took the next day's train out of town, seated in the men's smoking car. The following year, she joined the Pan-American Exposition and toured as far East as Buffalo, where she was jailed overnight for fighting with two policemen. Allegedly, she got out of the show in Chicago when Buffalo Bill found her crying in her beer and paid her way back West. Whether or not this is specifically true, it is certain that the joyful attitude characterizing Calamity Jane's early days was gone, for after the turn of the century, her way of life—always an anomaly—was increasingly seen as bizarre.

The *Daily Yellowstone* reported that when Calamity shot up a Billings, Montana bar in 1902, she responded to her jailing with indignation, for similar exhibits of her indoor marksmanship skills during the past three decades had brought admiration, not arrest. Ill and depressed, Calamity Jane was headed to Deadwood in July 1903, but made it only as far as nearby Terry, South Dakota. She died in the Calloway Hotel there, on August 2, 1903, noting beforehand that it was the twenty-seventh anniversary of Hickok's death. Deadwood added to the legend by burying her alongside Wild Bill.

CALDERONE, MARY STEICHEN (1904–)

A leader in the effort for non-judgmental sex education, she graduated from VASSAR COLLEGE and earned advanced degrees in medicine and public health. A QUAKER and the mother of three, Dr. Calderone came to public attention when she was past sixty.

She served as the medical director of PLANNED PARENTHOOD from 1953–1964 and then organized the Sex Information and Educational Council of the United States. Its purpose was to address the era's problem of changed moral standards; religious prohibitions of premarital sex were taken less seriously than in earlier times, and yet most young people lacked the necessary reproductive knowledge to practice effective BIRTH CONTROL.

Dr. Calderone wrote and lectured widely during the next decade, focusing especially on physicians, parents, and educators. Her advocacy of the inclusion of sexuality with other public health education from kindergarten to senior high school was considered radical at the time, but thirty years later, most of her ideas have been adopted in standard educational curricula. Especially for young women, possession of this knowledge made all the difference in how their lives were lived. Millions of women owe the fact that they have been able to enjoy careers other than motherhood, at least in part, to the efforts of Mary Calderone.

CALDWELL, (JANET) TAYLOR (1900–1985)

Janet Taylor Caldwell emigrated with her family from Manchester, England when she was just seven. She grew up in Buffalo, and because her father disapproved of higher education for women, she married at eighteen and bore a daughter. When the marriage failed, she spent the twenties working for various government agencies to support herself at the University of Buffalo, from which she finally graduated in 1931. She married a second time that same year and had another daughter.

Caldwell, who later estimated that her passion for writing "had destroyed two or three forests," had been writing massive tomes of fiction since childhood and finally published her first book when she was thirty-eight. She used a *nom de plume* that omitted both her feminine first name and her married surname, and reviewers assumed that she was male and had a literary background. The novel, *Dynasty of Death*, published by Scribner's in 1938, was about a munitions manufacturing family and sold extremely well; sequels came out during WORLD WAR II when weaponry and death were topics of considerable interest.

At the same time, she published a half-dozen other novels during the war years, and perhaps because many women needed books to occupy their minds during years of lonely evenings in those pre-television years, Taylor Caldwell became widely read. She published an average of almost book a year from 1938 to 1980, many of which were made into movies or television productions. Among the best known are *This Side of Innocence* (1946), *Dear and Glorious Physician* (1956), and *I Judas* (1977). *Growing Up Tough* (1971) is an autobiography.

In addition to the many books published with the self-created name by which she was known, Caldwell also wrote under two other male PSEUDONYMS, Max Reiner and Marcus Holland. Her work was considered masculine at the time, and she prided herself on her antiliberalism, especially during the political repression of the 1950s. Not a feminist, Caldwell came of age just as women ended their long struggle for the right to vote, and she was among the young women of the twenties and thirties who considered FEMINISM passe.

Though Caldwell was married four times, her second marriage was by far the most significant; she was married to Marcus Reback for almost forty years, and his work as her agent and as researcher-assistant played an important role in her success. Taylor Caldwell's last book was published in 1980, when she was eighty years old. She died five years later.

CALDWELL, SARAH (1924–   )

Growing up in Fayetteville, Arkansas, Sarah Caldwell was such a prodigy that she was giving violin lessons before she was ten. After studying at Hendrix College and the University of Arkansas, she moved to Boston, which would become her home.

Graduation from the New England Conservatory of Music brought her several offers to join symphonies, but Caldwell chose instead to work in opera. She learned the complexities of staging operas and produced her first in 1946, when she was just twenty-two. Its favorable reviews led to a position with Boston's famed summer music festival, Tanglewood, which she held for six years before becoming head of the opera workshop at Boston University.

She left the security of that position in 1957 to develop her own innovative opera company. It was not a particularly auspicious time for women and Caldwell struggled with debt for the next two decades, but also earned an outstanding

reputation as a creative impresario. Despite the inadequacies of low-budget theaters, she managed to stage such rich productions that financial success eventually came, and the Opera Company of Boston bought a sumptuous home in 1978.

More importantly, her serious scholarship led Caldwell to discover, edit, and stage unusual works overlooked by most musicians; the opportunity to premier in a previously unstaged opera attracted performers that she otherwise might not have been able to pay, including Marilyn Horne, Beverly Sills, and Joan Sutherland, as well as famous male singers.

Caldwell came to the attention of FEMINISTS in the 1970s with her effort to be recognized for her skills as a conductor as well as a producer. She triumphed by conducting the New York Philharmonic in 1975, and a few months later, became the first woman to conduct the Metropolitan Opera.

CALKINS, MARY WHITON (1863–1930)

A descendent of PRISCILLA ALDEN, Mary Calkins graduated from SMITH COLLEGE in 1885, when that institution was only a decade old. After a European tour, she began teaching Greek at WELLESLEY COLLEGE, but three years later, Calkins changed fields and found her life's work.

Studying first at Clark University and then at Harvard, she specialized in philosophy when psychology was still part of that field. Working closely with famed William James, Chairman of the Department of Philosophy and Psychology at Harvard, she completed the requirements for a Ph.D. in 1896, but the Harvard Corporation refused to grant the degree to a woman. (Calkins refused the offer of a RADCLIFFE degree, on the logical grounds that she had not studied at Radcliffe.)

Wellesley, understanding the reality of her scholarly work, granted full professorship in 1898. Calkins pioneered there with establishment in 1891 of one of the world's first experimental laboratories in psychology, where she did some of the initial research on dreams. She was the author of a dozen psychological monographs during the 1890s, and her first book, *An Introduction to Psychology*, was published by Macmillan in 1901. Though her theory of "self-psychology" emphasized a consciousness that was denied by the emerging behaviorists, Calkins received enough recognition from her male colleagues that in 1905, they elected her the first woman president of the American Psychological Association. Presumably many of them also placed orders for her 1909 *A First Book of Psychology*, for it went through four editions.

When psychology began separating itself from philosophy, however, Calkins chose to stay with that more ancient and complex field. With Harvard's Josiah Royce as her philosophical mentor, she specialized in metaphysics. Already in 1907 she had published *The Persistent Problems of Philosophy*, a work popular enough to be reprinted five times. In 1918, she wrote her first nontextbook and, indifferent to future FEMINIST semantics, titled it *The Good Man and the Good*. That same year she achieved the acme of her career with election to the presidency of the American Philosophical Association.

Remembered by her students as a happy, caring personality, Calkins was also concerned with social issues. Aligning herself with the left, she voted Socialist and paid dues to the American Civil Liberties Union and other peace and justice organizations. She retired from Wellesley in 1929, after forty years of teaching women. She died the following year.

Like her Wellesley colleague EMILY BALCH, Mary Calkins—the only woman to be president of both the American Psychological Association and the American Philosophical Association—merits more recognition than she has been given.

CAMPBELL, HELEN STUART WEEKS (1839–1918)

Born Helen Campbell Stuart, she began her writing career with children's literature during the CIVIL WAR, using her married name of Weeks. After a DIVORCE in 1871—still daring at that time—she wrote adult novels under several PSEUDONYMS, including male ones. In the late 1870s, she settled into usage of the Helen Stuart Campbell name.

She also began writing nonfiction at that point, turning her attention first to the new field of HOME ECONOMICS and then to the problems of women workers and the poor generally. The best known of her many books is *Prisoners of Poverty* (1886). Campbell was also widely read in the era's popular magazines and newspapers, where one of the chief points she made was the bald financial impossibility of women's wages actually covering their needs. She reported average earnings and analyzed budgets to show that women were virtually always paid half (or less) of what men were paid and yet were ex-

Camp follower Mary Tippee, who was a sutler with the 114th Pennsylvania regiment during the Civil War, holding a stringed instrument. Sutlers functioned as storekeepers for troops, so the musical instrument may well have been for sale. NATIONAL ARCHIVES.

pected to maintain living standards that were actually higher in terms of the housing they rented, the clothes were wore, etc. Campbell saw moral danger in this economic situation, for it meant that women inevitably were vulnerable to male lust, either as employees or as dependent family members.

Though her methodology in documenting poverty was less statistical and more emotional than would be condoned by nascent social scientists, Campbell did enough investigative work in support of her theses that she won a 1891 prize from the American Economic Association for her work on women wage-earners. Along with her concern for better wages, she also wrote of the need for occupational health and safety regulations and was far ahead of her time in pointing out the dangers to tobacco industry workers of what she called "nicotine poisoning." A supporter of Edward Bellemy's utopian ideas, Helen Campbell's writing played a significant role in the reform of nineteenth-century capitalism.

CAMP FOLLOWERS Though the term usually denotes PROSTITUTES who make themselves available to soldiers, this usage differs from the actual situation in America's earliest warfare, when women in military camps were not necessarily seen as morally loose.

Not only did Martha Washington sometimes share a camp tent with George, but so did numerous other women who accompanied their men to the battlefields of the American Revolution. In an era when there were few occupations open to women, it was difficult for a married woman to support herself if her husband went to war; especially in the case of young, childless, and propertyless couples, the most sensible alternative was for the woman, as well as the man, to follow the Army.

She could earn money by laundering and cooking for other troops to support herself and even perhaps to support her husband, when soldiers went unpaid. Some women invariably ended up in battle, as for example, MARGARET CORBIN. Indeed, women were so commonly recognized as part of military camp life that Continental Army regulations took the trouble to exclude them from rum and whiskey rations.

Despite increasing standards of female decorum by the CIVIL WAR, some women continued the patterns set in the Revolution; indeed, officers on General Grant's staff were delighted when Julia Grant was in camp with him, for her calming presence brought sobriety. Yet even though this war had hundreds of female battlefield participants, women in military camps increasingly began to be seen as inherently prostitutes. General Sherman, for example, banned all women except MARY ANN BICKERDYKE on the assumption that they distracted his troops and caused fights between men instead of against the enemy.

When Civil War soldiers could get passes from camp, however, the men of both sides found plenty of women who, quite logically, had moved to the towns nearest these masses of potential customers. Washington, which in addition to being the Union capital was also a transportation center close to battle sites, was said to have over four hundred brothels. Venereal disease naturally became rampant, with virtually all of these women eventually suffering untreatable problems. Sizable numbers of men also brought infections home to their wives, for more than 10 percent of Union troops sought the ineffectual medical care available; doubtless many more didn't bother the doctors.

By the time of WORLD WAR I, the military organized to restrain camp followers, both because of their diverting effect on the fighting spirit and the venereal disease problem. The result was the CHAMBERLAIN-KAHN ACT and its serious violations of women's civil liberties. The military's approach to sexually transmitted diseases and other problems of sexuality in WORLD WAR II was less hysterical, but the first members of the WOMEN'S AUXILIARY ARMY CORPS suffered severely from the now well-developed stereotypes about women in military camps.

As World War II lengthened, however, another usage of "camp follower" appeared, with a meaning similar to that of the Revolution. These were the young war brides who, often with babies in tow, withstood tremendous hardships of rationed travel and housing to follow their husbands to military camps in the U.S. so that they could be together for at least part of the time before the soldier was shipped overseas. Though condemned by much of the press and the military, the thousands of young women who became WIDOWS during the next few years would feel more than justified in having followed their hearts.

CANNON, ANNIE JUMP (1863–1941)

That Cannon was far better known in her lifetime than now is clear from her obituary, which included a reference to her listing in a 1929 poll of the members of the LEAGUE OF WOMEN VOTERS as one of twelve "greatest living American women."

After graduation from young WELLESLEY COLLEGE in 1884, she moved into Cambridge, where she would be an astronomer affiliated with RADCLIFFE and Harvard for the rest of her life. Though she did not receive the title of "assistant" at the Harvard Observatory until 1897, Annie Cannon did important research in classifying and cataloging stars under the mentorship of the observatory's director, Edward C. Pickering, using the model established for women there by WILLIAMINA FLEMING.

A tireless worker, her observations accumulated in staggering numbers: between 1918 and 1924, Cannon published nine volumes that included information on more than 225,000 stars. In an unfortunate move for women's place in science and history, this massive work was titled the *Henry Draper Catalog*, in honor of a physician whose interest in astronomy led him to take some of the first photographs of stars. Few users would realize that Draper (who had died in 1882, while Cannon was still an undergraduate) had his name attached to this original, scholarly work only because his WIDOW endowed the observatory's project in his name.

Cannon went on to classify almost four hundred thousand stellar bodies before her death and was influential in moving astronomy from its stargazing nineteenth-century status to its greater theoretical and philosophical roles. Oxford University honored her by making her the first woman in the world granted an honorary doctorate, and her American colleagues elected her as the first woman officer of the American Astronomical Society. Harvard finally gave her the rank of professor in 1938, after almost fifty years of work and just two years before official retirement, but Cannon continued her observatory research until she died.

CAROLINA

North and South Carolina are among the places named for Queen Caroline (1683–1737), wife of George II, who was lovingly called "Caroline the Good" by the English and her colonial subjects in America. Born as very minor royalty in a tiny Bavarian principality, she was apparently so charmingly intelligent and attractive that she turned down an offer from the King of Spain before marrying the Prince of Wales in 1705. An extremely popular queen, she actually reigned in the absence of her husband, supported artists, and set an early example of faith in scientists by having her children vaccinated.

CARAWAY, HATTIE OPHELIA WYATT (1878–1950)

The first woman to be elected as a United States senator, Hattie Caraway's place in that body was preceded only by the one-day tenure of REBECCA FELTON. Like Felton, she received what was intended as a courtesy appointment, but Caraway instead went on to a genuine political career in her own right.

Hattie Caraway had lived the traditional life of a politician's wife, mothering three sons and dividing her time between the family's Jonesboro, Arkansas home and Washington after her husband was elected to Congress in 1912. Because she had been in the capital during the most visible years of the SUFFRAGE MOVEMENT but had limited her activity to the Methodist Church, Arkansas' male politicians viewed Caraway's Senate appointment and its special election confirmation as little more than an honorary position. They assumed she would occupy her late husband's seat for the months between his November 1931 death and the Democratic primary the next summer, when she would step aside for the new nominee (the Democratic primary being tantamount to election in southern states at that time).

But on May 9, 1932, while establishing another precedent by presiding over the United States Senate, Hattie Caraway took the publicity opportunity to spring her surprise: she planned to join the seven men who had already announced for her seat. When Congress recessed in August, she and popular Louisiana Senator Huey Long launched a legendary nine-day campaign tour of Arkansas' major towns. Caraway won soundly in unprecedented heavy voting, for thousands of Arkansas women who had never before exercised their still-new right to vote came out to rid themselves of Herbert Hoover and to support this new age of politicians, including a woman so uncommonly like themselves. Given the depths of poverty in Arkansas during this nadir of the Great Depression, most of these women likely walked to the polls or rode behind mule-drawn wagons; they lived in homes without telephones or electricity and heard Hattie Caraway's campaign speeches on battery-powered radios.

Returning to Washington, Caraway continued her diligent ways, never missing a vote and, unlike many male politicians, actually reading the bills and listening at committee hearings. Though she seldom spoke in debate, her colleagues appreciated her unflappable personality and droll humor, and they respected her refusal to follow Huey Long's extremism and her quiet rejection of his pronouncements that she owed her election to him.

Senator Caraway demonstrated the astuteness of her own political abilities by winning another victory in 1938, defeating

Representative John McClellan, a politician whose tough demeanor would make him a powerful senator in the 1950s. Women played a significant role in this close election, as did organized labor and WORLD WAR I veterans, who remembered the support this woman gave them during her first year in office when Depression-poor veterans marched on Washington only to see the Hoover administration aim weapons at them.

As a legislator, Senator Caraway concentrated on supporting the programs of Roosevelt's New Deal that transformed the lives of many of her Arkansas constituents, with women particularly benefiting from communal kitchens, free garden supplies, and other projects designed to lift them from poverty. As the war replaced the Depression in congressional attention, Caraway again showed herself to be an independent thinker, for she had long rejected the isolationist views of other populists and instead proclaimed the internationalism of the last Democratic president, Woodrow Wilson.

Like all members of Congress except JEANETTE RANKIN, Hattie Caraway voted for the declaration of WORLD WAR II, and during the war years, she continued to set other precedents by becoming the first woman to chair a Senate committee and the first to be chosen as president pro tempore of the Senate, both in 1943. In that same year, she departed from her female colleagues in the House (FRANCES BOLTON, MARY NORTON, and others) to become the first woman in Congress to co-sponsor the EQUAL RIGHTS AMENDMENT.

Busy in wartime Washington, she failed to pay sufficient attention to the campaign of a one-term House member from northwest Arkansas (the most Republican district in the state). Arkansas voters surprised her by electing young, intellectual William Fulbright—just as they had surprised the nation by electing the first woman senator a dozen years earlier.

President Roosevelt quickly appointed Caraway to the Federal Employees' Compensation Commission, but at sixty-seven, her career was ending. She died in Washington five years later and was buried with her husband in Jonesboro.

Despite an unfashionable appearance and matronly manners that caused some (including even FEMINISTS) to take her less than seriously, Hattie Caraway demonstrated political skill that was little short of superlative.

CARNEGIE, HATTIE (1886?–1956)

No relation to the millionaire Andrew Carnegie, Henrietta Koningeiser took his name as a young woman because she shared his immigrant heritage and hoped to emulate his riches.

Born in Austria, she emigrated with her family as a child, attended elementary school in New York and began work at Macy's when she was thirteen. With a neighbor, Rose Roth, she opened a shop in 1909; theirs was a magic combination with Roth using her sewing skills to create the clothes, while Carnegie designed the hats and used her beauty and innate sense of style to model and sell. A decade later, when Roth retired, the business was worth more than one hundred thousand dollars.

Carnegie adapted quickly to the dramatic DRESS REFORM that occurred after WORLD WAR I, while nonetheless maintaining an image as a conservative, distinctively American designer. Her classic clothes were never trendy, and the "little Carnegie suit" was part of the fashionable woman's wardrobe for de-cades. This stability carried her through the Great Depression, though she did have to lower her prices and begin a line of mass-produced clothing for retail sale.

She was married three times; the third, which lasted almost thirty years, was an early "commuter marriage" with her husband on the West Coast while she spent most of her time in the fashion capitals of New York and Paris. Her occasional trips to Los Angeles also included her business there in designing clothing for ACTRESSES to wear in movies.

When she died, her estate was worth more than eight million dollars. Obituaries noted that she never wore a HAT, though Hattie Carnegie began and ended her career in eras when most considered hats obligatory to the status of a lady.

CARROLL, ANNA ELLA (1815–1894)

Although kin to the Carroll family that founded MARYLAND, when Anna Ella Carroll needed their support in her old age, it was not forthcoming; she had insulted the Catholic branch of the family with her rabid writings for the Know-Nothings in the 1850s and alienated the remainder of her secessionist relatives with her loyalty to the Union in the next decade. They had long since written her off as a woman of offensively strong views and excessive ego.

Nonetheless, her childhood was much like theirs, for Carroll had lived a privileged life on Maryland's Eastern Shore until the Panic of 1837 took the family's plantation. She spent the rest of her young life assuming financial responsibility for her seven younger siblings, because, much like LOUISA MAY ALCOTT, she was blessed and burdened with a father whom she adored despite his lack of business acumen. Like SUSAN ANTHONY, ELIZABETH BLACKWELL, and others whose families also suffered from the 1837 depression, Carroll's first response was to organize a school and become a TEACHER, but she too discovered teaching was not her destiny.

Unlike these women, Carroll never became a suffragist. She used the same lobbying and strategizing behavior as men did when they sought political goals, and she apparently dealt with the fact that she personally could not vote by ignoring that reality. By 1845, she had moved permanently to the Baltimore-Washington area, and for the next several decades, she wrote campaign material, lobbied for clients who wanted government jobs, and otherwise used her name, intelligence, and tremendous nerve to establish herself as a political player.

She worked hard for Millard Fillmore in the election of 1856, helping to secure his nomination by the American (Know-Nothing) party. Her first book, *The Great American Battle* (1856), and subsequent writing was promoted by the party in its attempt to refocus the campaign from the slavery issue to that of immigration. The diatribes against Catholicism that so offended Carroll's wealthy relatives were the result of this strategy of garnering votes from those Americans who worried about the era's Irish and German (Catholic) immigration. She also promulgated the doctrine of Manifest Destiny, including expansion into Central America. Her ideas were popular enough that *The Star of the West*, a long book published just a month before the election, nonetheless went to three editions.

Fillmore lost the 1856 election and with it, Carroll's hopes for direct White House patronage. Despite the loss, Carroll continued to be politically active, working successfully in

Maryland's gubernatorial races in 1857 and 1859. She was regarded well enough by the politically knowledgeable that she again played a significant insider's role in the 1860 presidential election—but not for the eventual winner, the formerly obscure westerner Abraham Lincoln.

Though it is not well known, Carroll performed what was probably the most important political service of her entire career early in 1861 for Lincoln and the Union. She strongly advised the governor of Maryland that he not call the special legislative session anti-Lincoln elements wanted; in urgent communications to him, she stressed Maryland's unique position—for if it seceded, the nation's capital would be cut off from the Northern states. The issue of maintaining the Union was so important to Carroll that she dropped the feminine artifices and apologies she had used in earlier political writing and published several legalistic, closely reasoned pieces defending Lincoln's right to respond militarily to secessionists. The administration thought enough of her argument that it distributed *The War Powers* to all members of Congress.

A man who had rendered such service to the government in that era almost certainly would have been rewarded with a job, or at the very least, a military commission, but Carroll's gender made that out of the question. Nonetheless, she was now in her forties and, despite possibilities, had chosen not to marry. Her powerful connections brought little personal profit, and Carroll's life continued to be a constant struggle for money. In this era when many war profiteers became millionaires at the taxpayers' expense, it was understandable that her interminable financial need would drive Carroll to controversial activities.

The unauthorized use of Fillmore's name for a questionable fund-raiser; a lobbying enterprise aimed at exporting freed slaves to Belize; and the solicitation of friends for one hundred thousand dollars to buy a newspaper that she said offered her its editorship are but a few examples of Carroll's deep involvement in political games. She played by the rules men established, and was not part of the reformist women who organized groups such as the AMERICAN EQUAL RIGHTS ASSOCIATION in the CIVIL WAR era. It was these women, however, who ultimately took up and publicized her cause after the war, when Carroll belatedly petitioned for payment for her war work.

She had in fact been paid approximately two thousand dollars by the War Department for writing she had done, but in Carroll's estimation, she was due as much as fifty thousand dollars. More attention-getting than that dispute, however, was her claim for compensation (as much as $250,000 at one point) for her role as the key strategist behind the Union's invasion of the South through the Tennessee and Cumberland Rivers rather than the Mississippi. Though there is no doubt Carroll urged such a strategy, the idea that it was unique to her and had not occurred to any of the thousands of others who were more familiar with both military strategy and the area's topography is almost laughable. (Indeed, at the beginning of her claims, Carroll was willing to credit the original idea to a river pilot named Scott, but by 1876, she was ungrateful enough to confront the inarticulate pilot before a congressional committee, where her superior argumentation skills won the day.)

Repeated billing of the War Department during the late 1860s brought no result. Carroll, uncharacteristically, did not seem to press her claim with President Andrew Johnson. It would have appeared worth pursuing, not only because of her commonalty with him as border state natives who stayed loyal to the Union, but also because he respected women's mental abilities, openly crediting his wife for his education. Perhaps Carroll did not lobby him because he was overwhelmed with political problems from the beginning, or perhaps it was because she feared her Tennessee River theory might have sounded less than brilliant to a native of Tennessee.

In any case, Carroll gave up on the executive branch in 1870 and turned to Congress, where she filed a compensation claim every session throughout the 1870s and on into the 1880s. Though she had letters of support from many outstanding men and met with varying degrees of success at the committee level, her bill never came close to making it through the entire legislative process. In *Anna Ella Carroll vs. The United States* (1885), she tried the judiciary and lost there, too. More than twenty years had passed since the strategy was supposedly thought out; potential witnesses were dead; and while the court agreed that she might have a moral claim, there was no legal debt.

Indeed, even her supporters argued for Carroll's claim more as a symbol of women's importance in the war than for her individual merit. Much of the organized women's movement adopted this symbolic argument also—without serious debate on the disservice done to women who really did suffer for their war roles. Carroll, who never supported suffrage, was thus included by MATILDA JOSELYN GAGE in the HISTORY OF WOMAN SUFFRAGE, and portrayed as a penniless victim of males too jealous to acknowledge her invaluable military contribution.

Carroll's death at age seventy-nine was not the end of the cause; her paralyzed and pernicious condition at the end only enhanced her martyrdom. The story was picked up and embellished upon by numerous other authors, so that, by the 1950s, Carroll was depicted in some works as the brains of the Lincoln administration, issuing orders by teletype as she sat with the president in the War Department.

Such hyperbole, of course, served only to discredit her genuine abilities as a politician. Almost alone among mid-nineteenth-century women, Anna Ella Carroll attended national party nominating conventions as a power behind the scenes; she lobbied for paying clients when most women hesitated to demand even the right to vote; and she wrote detailed analyses of national affairs with superior political awareness. Had she been a man, no doubt she would have risen to the power and fame she so strongly desired.

CARSON, RACHEL LOUISE (1907–1964) The mother of

modern environmentalism, Rachel Carson was born in a small town in the Allegheny River valley of western Pennsylvania, where Pittsburgh provided a nearby contrast to nature's intentions.

She grew up an introspective child who loved both the outdoors and books, and at age ten, published a story in MARY MAPES DODGE's magazine, *St. Nicholas*. Always intending to be a writer, Carson majored in English at Pennsylvania College for Women until a biology requirement changed her life. Switching to JOHNS HOPKINS UNIVERSITY, which offered a better scientific education, she studied genetics with distinguished male researchers. In 1929, she graduated *magna cum*

Rachel Carson at work near the edge of the sea. PHOTOGRAPHY BY ERICH HARTMANN; COURTESY OF FRAN COLLIN.

laude, and despite the onset of the Great Depression that year, received enough scholarship money that she earned her master's degree in zoology in 1932.

While teaching zoology at the University of Maryland during the next years, Carson spent her summers in the exciting atmosphere of the oceanographic institute at Woods Hole, Massachusetts. Leaving teaching in 1936, she became one of the first women to be hired by the U.S. Bureau of Fisheries as a biologist. She would spend the rest of her employed life defined as a federal bureaucrat—except that, in her private time, she wrote.

The first year after she joined the Fisheries Bureau (later the U.S. Fish and Wildlife Service), Carson published an article on the sea in *Atlantic Monthly*. Her ability to write poetically about the scientifically technical was so uncommon that she was urged to expand the topic into a book, on which she worked for the next four years. *Under the Sea-Wind*, a beautiful book, had the bad fortune to come out only weeks before Pearl Harbor; it was buried in the avalanche of more pressing topics.

So Carson spent WORLD WAR II writing publicity primarily aimed at encouraging citizens to eat fish instead of rationed meat. With the war providing employment opportunities that had been closed to women during the Depression, she was also promoted to manage the U.S. Fish and Wildlife Service's publications department, where she encouraged lively and informative governmental prose. Meanwhile, though she continued working to support her widowed mother and two orphaned nieces, Carson found the time around the edges of her life to write.

A decade after the first book's disastrous timing, she published her second. *The Sea Around Us* (1951), which was serialized in advance by the *New Yorker*, received not only the critical praise of her first book, but also popular attention and sales. It won the National Book Award as well as a *New York Times* poll for the outstanding book of the year and ultimately was translated into more than thirty languages. This global bestseller enabled Carson, at last, to leave the government and devote herself to full-time writing. Her first book was reissued and also became a bestseller, and a Guggenheim grant sponsored her research for a third work, *The Edge of the Sea.* (1955).

But it was her last book that took the sixties by storm and made Carson into an icon for the new environmental movement. *Silent Spring* (1962) required a relatively long time to write, for it broke such new and controversial ground that it needed years of research. The book had a very specific genesis: a friend who lived in the lovely colonial town of Duxbury, Massachusetts saw the birds she cherished die when the town was sprayed for mosquitoes, and she asked Carson for the intervention of some authority to stop such wanton destruction.

Realizing that there were no government agencies dedicated to the preservation of the natural environment—while Agriculture, the Corps of Engineers, and others, in fact, sponsored a multiplicity of programs designed to overcome nature—Carson came to understand that the subject called not only for a book, but also for a changed political philosophy. Much more than an attack on the DDT pesticide, *Silent Spring* pointed out the tremendous damage done to the human habitat on a global level in only a few decades, and it prophesied the appearance of a silent spring without birds and small animals unless steps were taken to curb the use of toxins.

Because of Carson's previous popularity with both the scientific community and general readers, the whole force of the multibillion dollar chemical and agricultural industries felt called upon to attack and ridicule this woman. Their attempts to discredit her, however, met with little success, for Rachel Carson was no mere nature lover issuing an emotional appeal, but a scientist who grounded her predictions in documented data. Especially after President Kennedy appointed a committee on pesticides to follow up her work, the seriousness of her alert was clear.

But by then Carson could scarcely savor the fruits of her labors, for she was so seriously ill that completing her final manuscript required tremendous determination. She died just two years after the publication of her warning of a spring without songbirds, her own prescient voice silenced by bone cancer.

CARTER, GWENDOLEN (1907–1991) One of the white founders of African Studies as an academic field, Carter was born in Ontario. She became an American citizen in the early days of WORLD WAR II, soon after beginning her academic

career teaching political science at SMITH COLLEGE, where she stayed from 1943 to 1964.

In 1948, she began to specialize in Africa, something that was unusual at the time, and in 1955, published *The Politics of Equality*, an early analysis of South African apartheid. Dr. Carter published two more books on Africa before leaving Smith in 1964 for a decade at Northwestern University, which was followed by her tenure at Indiana University from 1974 to 1984. She moved to the University of Florida in her seventies and taught there until four years before her death. Dedicated to educating Americans on Africa, she believed apartheid could be ended without excessive violence and that racism would ultimately disappear.

CARTER, MRS. LESLIE (CAROLINE LOUISE DUDLEY CARTER) (1862–1937)

Interesting primarily because of her lifelong public use of her ex-husband's name, Carter married a wealthy Chicagoan at eighteen; their scandalous 1889 DIVORCE charged her with infidelity. By 1895, she had made the difficult transition to success as a stage ACTRESS but continued to call herself Mrs. Leslie Carter. She was acclaimed for her acting during the next decade with some of her plays running for over two hundred performances, but her career plummeted when she broke from her producer to marry a young actor. The producer never forgave her and Mrs. Carter was forced into retirement in 1916. She made one movie, aptly named *The Vanishing Pioneer* when she was in her seventies, and died in Santa Monica, California.

CARY, ALICE (1820–1871) and PHOEBE (1824–1871)

Cincinnati sisters whose poetry was locally published when they were still in their teens, they moved to New York a decade before the CIVIL WAR and soon managed to establish themselves as literati. Regular contributors to such popular magazines as *Harper's* and *Atlantic Monthly*, their home became a literary salon. As a result, Alice Cary holds the distinction of being termed the first president of the first women's CLUB in America, a group that they called SOROSIS.

Nonetheless, neither was very active publicly. Though they believed in ABOLITION and women's rights, most of their influence was through the written word. Alice published a dozen books of poetry and fiction between 1851 and 1868; her stories were particularly important for their portrayal of the difficulties of FARMWOMEN's lives. Phoebe published just two books of poetry, but critics generally deem her work of better literary merit. She also served briefly as an editor of the *Revolution*, the publication of the NATIONAL WOMAN SUFFRAGE ASSOCIATION. Phoebe also spent a great deal of time nursing Alice through a long illness, and, unable to cope after Alice's death, died herself a few months later.

CARY, MARY ANN SHADD (1823–1893)

Born during the Era of Good Feelings to free blacks who lived in the Philadelphia area, Mary Shadd was educated in a QUAKER school and then taught children of her race in several area schools for the next decade. At twenty-seven, she fled with her family to Canada after the passage of the 1850 Fugitive Slave Act endangered the lives of free blacks anywhere in the United States.

Settling across the Detroit River barely inside Ontario,

Shadd opened a school to teach Underground Railroad refugees, for whom literacy could be a matter of life or death. In addition to operating the school for the next decade, she also became an important writer for blacks. She was known especially for recruiting them to Canada and the West with her pamphlet, *Notes on Canada West*, which argued that it was naive to hope for any serious change in the older parts of the U.S.

After 1853, she edited the *Provincial Freeman*, a Toronto weekly publication aimed at blacks in the Canadian provinces. She editorialized in favor of an integrationist philosophy, resisting the "back to Africa" ideas then popular. As the first black female newspaper editor, she was a target of criticism both in and out of the black community, but Frederick Douglass defended her in 1856: "This lady, with very little assistance from others, has sustained the *Provincial Freeman* for more than two years. She has had to contend with lukewarmness, false friends, open enemies, ignorance and small pecuniary means . . . We do not know her equal among the colored ladies of the United States."

Shadd risked her freedom in returning to the northern U.S. to do a series as a PUBLIC SPEAKER for ABOLITIONISTS in 1855–56. Her 1856 marriage to a barber changed her name to Cary and resulted in the birth of a girl, but she continued her editorial work throughout. She became a Canadian citizen in 1863—but when the Union appeared to be losing after Gettysburg, she secured credentials from the governor of Indiana to enlist black volunteers and traveled through several Ohio River Valley states recruiting soldiers. A WIDOW by 1869, she moved that year to Washington—a city seen as the nation's most progressive by many post–Civil War blacks—and worked as a teacher and principal in the public schools there for fifteen years.

Mary Ann Shadd Cary was also one of the few minority women to be involved with the SUFFRAGE MOVEMENT. She preceded SUSAN ANTHONY, OLYMPIA BROWN, and other women who claimed a right to vote under the FIFTEENTH AMENDMENT, when, in March, 1874, she and sixty-three other Washington women attempted to register to vote. (Ironically, their District of Columbia residence would limit that right even today). White women suffrage leaders acknowledged Cary's leadership and oratorical ability by inviting her to speak at the 1878 meeting of the NATIONAL WOMAN SUFFRAGE ASSOCIATION, and two years later, she organized the Colored Women's Progressive Franchise Association. In this role, she continued to urge her black sisters to demand equality with their men.

Meanwhile, she also studied law at HOWARD UNIVERSITY, finally receiving her degree in 1883 when she was sixty. Possibly because of her age, there is no record that she ever passed the bar or practiced law. Mary Ann Shadd Cary should be remembered, however, as the first black woman editor of a newspaper and an effective speaker for the rights of both blacks and women.

CASSATT, MARY (1844–1926)

Although usually credited as the first American woman artist to achieve genuine success, Mary Cassatt lived most of her life in France.

Born near Pittsburgh, she grew up there and in the Philadelphia area. Her family was wealthy enough to travel, and Mary decided at an early age to emulate the work she saw in art museums. She spent the CIVIL WAR years studying at the Pennsylvania Academy of Fine Arts (where CECELIA BEAUX would teach three decades later), but Cassatt was dissatisfied with the education she received there, and in 1866, persuaded her family to let her go to Paris. Except for a brief return during the Franco-Prussian War, she stayed in Europe until long after she was established as a great artist. She remained emotionally close to her family, who also lived abroad during much of her life.

After TRAVELING and painting in Italy, Spain, and Holland, Cassatt settled permanently in Paris, where Edgar Degas became her chief supporter. Considered part of the pioneering French impressionist artists, her 1876 exhibit for the Society of American Artists was the first impressionism seen in this country. Cassatt contributed to the popularity of impressionism for many years thereafter by advising American art collectors on their purchases.

After the 1880s, she stopped displaying with the impressionists; her work became more linear and she developed the mother and child theme for which she is remembered. Cassatt also began to specialize in prints, producing several new techniques in this area. A hard worker who regularly painted eight hours a day, she held a one-woman show in Paris in 1891 and another in 1893; in between, she was commissioned by BERTHA PALMER and the Board of LADY MANAGERS to paint a mural for the Woman's Building at the COLUMBIAN EXPOSITION of 1892. The mural was shipped to the United States, and Cassatt did not return to her native land until 1898; her last visit was in 1908.

Her eyesight had begun to fail when she was made a Chevalier of the Legion of Honor in 1904, and by 1914, she could no longer work. The battles of WORLD WAR I, which drove her from home, prevented access to ophthalmologists and left this artist, to whom sight was everything, nearly blind and bitterly unhappy. Cassatt died at her country home near Paris at age eighty-two and was buried in France.

CASKET GIRLS From the French, *filles a las cassette*, the term literally means girls with boxes or money cases; in English such a reference would be more clearly understood in terms of HOPE CHESTS or DOWRIES. More specifically, "casket girls" referred to the importation of young women to French colonies, where they would become brides.

Especially in early New Orleans, there was a concerted effort led by Jean Baptiste Bienville (who had acted as governor of the newly founded Louisiana colony when he was just twenty-one) to bring French women to the lonely men there. On a trip back to France in 1727, he recruited a number of "casket girls" willing to go to Louisiana under the protection of Ursuline NUNS, and there to marry and become founding mothers of New France.

CATHER, WILLA SIBERT (1873–1947) Though lovingly associated in most minds with the midwestern prairie of her *O Pioneers* and *My Antonia*, Willa Cather (who was born Wilella) actually lived a relatively short portion of her life there.

Until she was nine, "Willie" led a rather pampered life in a large brick home set in the prosperous farm country of northern Virginia. The migration of her family to frontier Nebraska, where people lived in huts with nothing but the earth

for walls and floors, was a shock from which she never quite recovered; it would make the problems of change the dominant theme of her literary life.

Willa Cather went to school for the first time in Nebraska and, after high school graduation in 1891, went on to the University of Nebraska, where her writing ability became so evident that one of her stories was sent by a teacher to a Boston magazine. Published already as a student, it was relatively easy for Cather to develop a journalistic career. She spent a year at a Lincoln newspaper before moving in 1896 to Pittsburgh, where she worked first at a magazine and then a newspaper. She would never return to the Midwest.

Bored after five years of writing arts criticism, Cather took the reverse course of most women and turned from journalism to high school teaching in 1901, but her career as a TEACHER would be relatively brief. By 1906 she was back in journalism, having been offered a position with the popular *McClure's* magazine as a result of her collection of stories written during summer vacations, *The Troll Garden* (1905). *McClure's* moved her to New York, and when two years later she was promoted to managing editor, Cather's name began to be known in literary circles. By 1912, she was sufficiently sure of herself to publish her first novel, *Alexander's Bridge*, in serialized form in *McClure's* and then retire to full-time writing.

Cather was thus forty years old when *O Pioneers* (1913) came out. It and *My Antonia* (1918) were deeply moving and important treatments of the American themes of virgin land, frontier development, and immigrant transition. Cather featured female protagonists in them and also in the book published between her two great rural sagas: *The Song of the Lark* (1915). It explored what was to become another recurring midwestern theme for Cather and others—ambivalence towards small towns, with their conflicting repression of individualistic spirit and their comforting, nostalgic security.

Like many authors, Cather did her best work before she was well known. After her WORLD WAR I book, *One of Ours* (1922), won the Pulitzer Prize, the next novel, *A Lost Lady* (1923), brought public fame and sales. She was elected to the National Institute of Arts and Letters in 1929 and received many other honors thereafter. Yet, though Cather published almost biannually between 1913 and 1935, with the exception of *Death Comes for the Archbishop* (1927), none of the rest of her novels could rival the quality of her first work. She left enough unpublished writing—essays as well as fiction—to fill more than a half-dozen posthumous volumes.

Cather's work is beautifully styled and consistently themed, a refrain in favor of the natural versus the artificial, the eternal versus the fashionable. Yet, though she wrote with sadness and disillusionment of a passing frontier and the sturdy virtues associated with it, Cather nonetheless never moved from the contrary setting of New York City. She died there at age seventy-three, leaving instructions for burial at her autumn vacation locale in New Hampshire. She probably did a considerable disservice to the reputation of women AUTHORS by forbidding the anthologizing of her literature, and perhaps as a result, increasing numbers of young people do not recognize her as the stellar novelist that she is. Cather ranks as as one of the top American writers in the age of Frost, Hemingway, and others.

CATT, CARRIE CLINTON LANE CHAPMAN (1859–1947)

The year after the CIVIL WAR ended, seven-year-old Carrie Lane moved with her family to Iowa, where they farmed in virgin prairie country. She graduated from high school, and when her father refused to fund college, Carrie taught for a year, saved her money, and then continued to work part time while attending Iowa State Agricultural College (now Iowa State University). She graduated first in her class in 1880.

After reading law for a year, Carrie Lane was offered the unusual opportunity of becoming principal of the high school in Mason City, Iowa; two years later, she was promoted to superintendent of all the Mason City schools—a recognition of feminine ability most uncommon in that era. It would give her a profound awareness of the freer status of WESTERN WOMEN, a point that later colored her association with women from the East who dominated the early SUFFRAGE MOVEMENT.

Although she gave up a potentially illustrious career in education when she married Leo Chapman in 1885, she continued to work. Their joint success in editing the local newspaper led

them to look for a larger market, and Leo went on an exploratory trip to California in 1886. Carrie, who traveled separately, arrived to find her husband dead of typhoid fever.

A WIDOW at twenty-seven, she worked for a year as a reporter for a San Francisco paper before returning to Iowa, but during the time in California, she had established a relationship with a man she knew at Iowa State and in 1890, she married him. Carrie Chapman's marriage to George Catt was unusual in that it included a notarized agreement that she would be free during two months in the fall and two months in the spring to work for the suffrage movement, which the groom supported both philosophically and financially. She moved with him to Seattle and later to New York City, and when she was widowed a second time in 1905, Carrie Chapman Catt inherited enough money that she could devote all of her time to the cause of women.

She had joined the Iowa Woman Suffrage Association in 1887, and the first national suffrage convention she attended was the historic 1890 meeting that merged rival organizations into the NATIONAL AMERICAN WOMAN SUFFRAGE ASSOCIATION. At

Carrie Chapman Catt, whose work as president of the National American Woman Suffrage Association was of tremendous importance in obtaining the vote for women, in her study. Note the copy of her book, Woman Suffrage and Politics *(1923) to the bottom left.* NATIONAL ARCHIVES.

its head was SUSAN ANTHONY, and among the thousands of women who idolized Anthony, it was Carrie Chapman Catt who caught the aging leader's attention. Catt rapidly undertook the challenges of the new organization, and, as chairman of its Organization Committee, she revived old suffrage groups gone dormant, built new ones, systematized fund-raising, and insisted on modern methods of office procedure. Within five years, she effectively had become the NAWSA's executive secretary. When Anthony retired at the turn of the century, she chose as her replacement, not DR. ANNA HOWARD SHAW as expected, but rather Carrie Chapman Catt.

Catt held the presidency, however, only from 1900 to 1904, when she resigned because of her dying husband. For the next decade, she concentrated her efforts on the new Woman Suffrage Party, the 1915 passage of state suffrage for New York, and the nascent women's movement abroad. Having helped to found the INTERNATIONAL WOMAN SUFFRAGE ALLIANCE in 1902, she presided over its biannual meetings throughout Europe until WORLD WAR I interrupted; between 1911 and 1913 she led a world tour for women and visited every continent.

Drafted for the presidency of NAWSA late in 1915, she not only found the group again in organizational disarray, but also under challenge from the more militant women led by ALICE PAUL. Catt quickly put in place a detailed and secret political strategy termed the "Winning Plan," to which NAWSA leaders pledged themselves. Basically, Catt's plan supported state as well as national suffrage campaigns and also supported those Democrats who were pledged to suffrage; Paul, in contrast, worked solely for an amendment to the national Constitution and believed that the party occupying the White House should be held accountable for women's enfranchisement—thus declaring the entire Democratic party to be the enemy. Catt instead maintained communications with those in power so effectively that when President Wilson ultimately endorsed suffrage, it was largely to her credit.

World War I brought even more internal organizational complications, as both pacifism and patriotism—from opposite directions—threatened the suffrage issue. Though Catt was a founder of the WOMAN'S PEACE PARTY, she supported the war and served on the Woman's Committee of the Council of National Defense. Her belief that suffrage would evolve from women's performance in this national emergency eventually proved correct, and she stayed busy with ratification campaigns during and immediately after the war. When the NINETEENTH AMENDMENT was finally adopted, Carrie Chapman Catt had devoted virtually all of the thirty years between 1890 and 1920 to full-time, unpaid work for women's right to vote, beginning when she was thirty-one and ending when she was sixty-one. She had built the membership of NAWSA to an amazing two million.

But her efforts for the public good were not yet over. She helped to found the LEAGUE OF WOMEN VOTERS that followed up the suffrage victory and was its honorary president for the rest of her life, yet willingly stepped aside for younger league leaders. Instead, she published *Woman Suffrage and Politics: The Inner Story of the Suffrage Movement* (1923) and renewed her interest in internationalism. In 1925, Catt founded the National Committee on the Cause and Cure of War, serving as active chairman of that group until 1932 and as honorary chairman until the outbreak of WORLD WAR II in 1939. Tireless to the end, she spent the war years helping Jewish refugees and pushing for the establishment of the postwar United Nations, as she had supported the League of Nations after World War I.

Carrie Chapman Catt's hardworking heart finally wore out at age eighty-eight. Her political sagacity, efficient administration, tireless lobbying and speechmaking were central to the success of the suffrage movement; she proved the abilities that Susan Anthony saw in her thirty years before the vote was won. Except for Anthony, Carrie Chapman Catt was the single best organizer in the women's suffrage movement, and American women owe her a debt every time they cast a ballot.

CATTLE KATE (1862–1889) The "Cattle Kate" of lurid news stories in 1889 referred to Ella Watson, who had changed her name to Kate Maxwell just prior to her national notoriety. She was a PROSTITUTE who practiced in Billings, Montana until she went west at the invitation of Jim Averill, a Casper, Wyoming saloonkeeper and part-time politician who led small ranchers in their battles with the giant land barons. Averill saw mutual profitability in Watson's presence and built a small house for her. She filed a land claim in the Sweetwater Valley in the spring of 1888, but—unlike legitimate HOMESTEADING women—her primary business was not ranching.

Men so greatly outnumbered women on the range that prostitution was not merely tolerated, but probably welcomed by the majority. Her troubles came not from this business, but from accepting stolen calves as payment from her customers, and especially in allowing her corral to be used as a shipping point for the rustlers led by Averill, whose grievances against the big landowners were so great that they regularly stole calves by shooting their mothers.

On Sunday, July 20, 1889, a band of men kidnapped first Kate and then Averill, took them to an isolated gully, and hung them from a cottonwood tree. Later, there were protestations that the hangings were accidental and that they had only intended to frighten the two into leaving the Sweetwater Valley, but the evidence was clear that there had been plenty of time to rescue them, for the amateur executioners did not do a neat job and their deaths had been slow and painful.

When the *Casper Mail* spread the story across the country the next day, there was national condemnation of this outlawry so late in the frontier era, and especially for the lynching of a woman. Nonetheless, the men arrested were never tried, for the crucial witnesses all disappeared or mysteriously died. There was at least one person who cared enough about Cattle Kate to come to her defense: her father traveled from Kansas to Wyoming, where he told reporters that his daughter was the eldest of ten children and "a fine girl . . . modest and unassuming, with not a particle of fastness." Most people in Wyoming, however, including those newspapers who published Jim Averill's angry charges against the cattle barons, clearly believed the opposite.

CELIBACY The word not only denotes a dedication to the unmarried state, but also abstinence from sexual activity of any sort. While often associated with the Roman Catholic Church, celibacy has been practiced by many other American sects, including some, such as the Shakers, founded by "Mother" ANN LEE, who believed in the equality of women and saw celibacy as a liberating condition.

Celibacy, which was not adopted by the Christian clergy until after 500 AD, was also a key factor in the Protestant revolution of the 1500s. The continued adherence of the Roman Catholic Church to this ideal was crucial in the development of North America, for even though parts of what was to become the United States ranging from California to Florida were actually settled by Spanish and French Catholics much earlier than any English Protestant presence, the Catholic settlements were dominated by single men who served as either priests or soldiers. Their exclusion of women meant that these cultures left little imprint on what was to become the United States, for they created no future generation to replicate themselves. Celibacy as an ideal understandably could not compete with the mandate of "be fruitful and multiply" that motivated the English Protestants—with the result that Americans speak English and have largely adopted English culture and government.

When significant numbers of Catholic IMMIGRANT WOMEN came centuries later, Protestant values, including high esteem for marriage and reproduction, were well in place. Moreover, most nineteenth-century Catholic immigrants themselves held conflicting ideas on celibacy; they accepted it as an ideal for the very pious, while at the same time, their general view of it was strongly negative. Indeed, many Catholic immigrants believed that abstinence caused mental and physical illness in both men and women. Young women in those cultures who did not marry were the subject of strong opprobrium, and the same was true for Jewish women in that era. Unmarried Protestant women who came into this immigrant world as social workers reported that their clients consistently argued against the single state, with men especially viewing any marriage as better than none.

Increasing numbers of American women rejected this advice, however, for as educational opportunities began to develop for women in the late nineteenth century, many seemed to believe that education and marriage were mutually exclusive, and graduates of the first women's COLLEGES who were serious about careers often lived celibate lives. Though not herself college educated, SUSAN ANTHONY was clearly among the adherents of this view, turning down several marriage proposals and many times recording her distress that ELIZABETH CADY STANTON and others were too often distracted from their political work by the pregnancies and child-rearing that resulted from sexual activity. Indeed, before BIRTH CONTROL was available to women, celibacy may have been a strong factor in achieving success.

CENTENNIAL EXHIBITION (1876)

The hundred years since Americans declared their independence was celebrated with a great centennial fair in the city of the nation's birth, Philadelphia. Almost ten million people came to see the exhibits put on by fifty countries in 180 buildings assembled at the huge fairgrounds. American women also played a role,

though the men in charge of the exhibition did virtually everything they could to discourage women's involvement.

No women were included as speakers at programs, and requests for this from both the NATIONAL WOMAN SUFFRAGE ASSOCIATION and the AMERICAN WOMAN SUFFRAGE ASSOCIATION were denied. While an exhibition request from the latter was eventually granted, the space allotted was seriously lacking in visibility. A small Women's Pavilion featured displays on new technologies in sewing, laundry, and other domestic tasks—with a number of the inventions credited to women—and the Women's Centennial Committee offered *The National Cookery Book* for two dollars. Other exhibits indicated the greater diversity of women's lives: there were pharmaceutical products prepared by students of the WOMAN'S MEDICAL COLLEGE OF PENNSYLVANIA; a display of Rocky Mountain wildlife and fossils was done by taxidermist Martha A. Maxwell and U.S. Geological Survey artist Kate F. Andrews; and an exhibit of the era's popular books by women AUTHORS, which included not only novels and poetry, but also manuals on watchmaking and marble working by Mary L. Booth and an astronomy text by Hannah Bouvier.

The NWSA women, meanwhile, rented a headquarters in Philadelphia only with difficulty—this being another of several cases in which only SUSAN ANTHONY could sign their contracts, since she was the only leader who was single and therefore not subject to laws restricting MARRIED WOMEN'S PROPERTY RIGHTS. On the Fourth of July, however, Anthony and four other women upstaged the Centennial's organizers by managing to reach the platform at the fair's Fourth of July ceremony, where they deposited their DECLARATION OF RIGHTS FOR WOMEN. They also distributed hundreds of copies to the men assembled, many of whom stood on chairs and pushed each other in their efforts to get copies. Outside the hall, the women took over an empty bandstand in Independence Square, and Anthony read the Declaration to a surprisingly receptive crowd. Instead of being jailed, as they had expected, the suffragists celebrated a day that gave them hope for the future.

Reasons for optimism were apparent even in their Declaration. Like the 1848 SENECA FALLS Declaration of Rights for Women, this statement also was modeled on the nation's Declaration of Independence that was being celebrated on the Fourth of July. The 1876 version, however, differed from the 1848 one: demands for educational opportunity and the right to speak in public, for example, were dropped since those goals were being achieved, while new demands, such as the inclusion of women on juries, were added. The overall effect was to show that the women's movement was making measurable progress, even though much remained to be done.

CHAMBERLAIN-KAHN ACT (1918)

Passed in an era of increasingly hysterical "Americanism" and censorship, the act was intended to curb sexually transmitted diseases during WORLD WAR I. However laudable this goal, the legislation seriously discriminated against women, since it provided for "mandatory examination" of any woman suspected of PROSTITUTION. Women found to be infected were to be locked in secure facilities where they could pose no threat to lustful soldiers.

Among the violations of women's civil liberties that were

imposed by local health authorities were 9:00 P.M. curfews for women in towns near military camps and requirements that women be able to demonstrate in writing the propriety of their relationship to a male escort, showing either kinship or parental permission. By the War Department's own estimate, upwards of fifteen thousand women felt the brunt of this law through incarceration, but many times that number of women were detained, questioned, and otherwise abased by officials. Meanwhile, male sexual activity was accepted as the norm.

Some women's organizations such as the YWCA cooperated with enforcement efforts, believing such PROTECTIONIST LEGISLATION to be of ultimate benefit to the women, whom they saw as needing moral instruction and rehabilitation to prevent their victimization by males. These women, however, were often frustrated in their efforts by military authorities whose primary interest was not longterm reform, but simply keeping soldiers fit for battle by keeping them away from women. Though the legislation expired in 1923, the mindset it represented continued to place the burden of sexuality on women.

CHANNING, CAROL (1923–   )

After growing up on the West Coast, Carol Channing went East to Bennington College in 1939 and then to New York City in 1941, where a successful career as an ACTRESS eluded her most of the decade until in 1949, she opened on Broadway with the play that would forever define her—*Gentlemen Prefer Blondes* by ANITA LOOS.

During the 1950s, she appeared in several musical comedies and even returned to nightclub work before her 1964 hit revival on Broadway with *Hello Dolly!* She won a Tony Award that year, and in 1967, earned the Golden Globe as best supporting actress for the movie, *Thoroughly Modern Millie.* Awards and popularity continued to follow Channing, whose humor and musical talent entertained millions of fans.

CHAPIN, AUGUSTA (1836–1905)

Augusta Chapin shares a place with ANTOINETTE BROWN BLACKWELL as an early woman minister.

A brilliant child blessed with supportive parents who had pioneered in Michigan, she went to school at three and was a TEACHER by fourteen. After the University of Michigan several times refused to admit her because of her gender, she settled for small Olivet College in Olivet, Michigan. She preached her first sermon in 1859 and for the next several years, suffered the travel hardships of a "circuit rider" who preached on an itinerant basis, while also teaching school to support herself.

Granted credentials by the Universalist Church in 1862, she was formally ordained at Lansing, Michigan in December, 1863—only six months after OLYMPIA BROWN became America's first ordained woman at Malone, New York. Reverend Chapin finally obtained her first pastorate in 1864, and from then until 1901, she had a serious career as a preacher. She was ordained by congregations in Iowa, Illinois, Nebraska, Pennsylvania, and rural New York. As was the case with other FRONTIER WOMEN, Chapin found greater opportunity in remote areas than in eastern cities.

Unlike Brown and Blackwell, Chapin never married. An active FEMINIST, she was also a charter member of the ASSOCIA-

TION FOR THE ADVANCEMENT OF WOMEN and spoke at several national suffrage conventions. In 1893, she chaired the general committee for women at the COLUMBIAN EXPOSITION, and that same year, Reverend Chapin also received the first honorary doctorate of divinity given to an American woman.

She retired to New York City at age sixty-five and, four years later, was preparing to lead a tour to Europe when she died.

CHAPMAN, MARIA WESTON (1806–1885)

One of the earliest ABOLITIONISTS, Chapman supported an end to slavery when it was dangerous to do so, even in her native Boston.

Although born in Massachusetts, Maria Weston was educated in Europe and returned as a cultured young woman in 1828. For two years, she was the "lady principal" of Young Ladies High School, but her marriage to Henry Chapman ended that position. The groom was a liberal merchant who early supported abolitionism, even though that cause was considered radical in the 1830s when they wed.

Maria Chapman soon became the leader of the Boston Female Anti-Slavery Society, of which she was a founder in 1832. For years to follow, she circulated the society's petitions and not only broke social bans on PUBLIC SPEAKING by women, but even spoke under threat of mob attack. Once in 1835, when Boston's mayor came to a meeting of the society and begged the women to disperse before they were assaulted, Mrs. Chapman calmed the situation by directing each white woman to take the hand of a black sister and walk out of the building—and then to meet the mobsters in the eye. Nor was disapproval limited to the rabble, for soon the Chapmans' upper-class friends, many of whom benefited financially from the era's slave-based economy, also ostracized them. By 1836—less than a decade after she had been the "lady principal"—Maria Chapman wrote that she was afraid to walk Boston's streets.

But fear did not keep her from activism. From 1836 to 1840, she edited the Female Anti-Slavery Society's annual report on abolitionism and, while she and William Lloyd Garrison were still in their twenties, she helped him edit the *Liberator;* he soon acknowledged Mrs. Chapman as a key assistant. She was also an effective fund-raiser, especially with the development of fairs beginning in 1834, a moneymaking technique that was copied in other states. She again demonstrated her personal courage in Philadelphia in 1838; while rioters gathered in the City of Brotherly Love, she continued to conduct the Anti-Slavery Convention of American Women. The mob later succeeded in burning the building in which the women met.

One of the first to foretell the split between advocates of women's rights and those of slaves (especially in her 1839 pamphlet, *Right and Wrong in Massachusetts*), Chapman steadfastly adhered to the primacy of abolition over the nascent women's movement. Some male abolitionist leaders, in turn, recognized her abilities: she was elected to the executive committee of the American Anti-Slavery Society in 1840, despite objections from many men in that movement to women in leadership positions. Chapman was especially visible as an editor, serving from 1839 to 1842 for the *Non-Resistant*, a New England abolitionist publication, and in cofounding and coediting the *National Anti-Slavery Standard*, a position she held throughout most of the 1840s.

As abolitionism became more acceptable and even fashionable with Bostonians, Chapman began to decrease her activism. Her husband died in 1842, and she saw it as her responsibility to take her three children to Europe for their educations in 1848. She returned to the United States in 1855 and published *How Can I Help to Abolish Slavery?*, but Chapman played a relatively minor role during the CIVIL WAR and Reconstruction.

Instead, she returned to writing. Already back in 1836, she had published *Songs of the Free* and *Hymns of Christian Freedom*, and her *Liberty Bell*, an annual giftbook featured at abolitionist fairs, had sold well. In the postwar period, she wrote a biography of her close friend, English writer Harriet Martineau. A massive, two-volume work published in 1877, it includes much of Chapman's own thought and experience, especially in letters the two women wrote to each other during the momentous Civil War that culminated in Chapman's lifelong goal, the abolition of slavery.

Maria Chapman died where she was born, in Weymouth, Massachusetts.

CHARLOTTE A number of cities, counties, and other places in the United States are thus named because the area's were settled in the latter half of the eighteenth century when Queen Charlotte (1744–1818) shared the English throne with George III. Born in the German principality of Mecklenberg, she came to England and married at seventeen. Though she was more popular with Americans than her husband was, those who admired her did so for her domestic virtues, for Charlotte showed little interest in other activities. She was the domineering mother of fifteen children; her daughters referred to their lives as "the nunnery," because they had so little freedom. Charlotte was queen of England for fifty-seven years, during which the American colonies achieved independence.

CHAUTAUQUA MOVEMENT On the shores of Lake Chautauqua, which is very near Lake Erie in southwestern New York, an 1870s Methodist Church camp spawned a movement that was to have tremendous impact on American life for the next half-century. Summer vacationers there realized the great appeal of combining intellectual stimulation with recreation for Americans who were just beginning to have time and money for leisure activity. Located near Rochester, in an area that was home to many of the original FEMINISTS, the Chautauqua movement soon attracted thousands of adherents.

In 1878, the Chautauqua Scientific and Literary Circle was set up to provide guidance to local, coeducational study groups; a few years later, a correspondence division was added. One of the first educational institutions to use the correspondence method, Chautauqua was also one of relatively few educational innovations to be uniquely American. By 1886—less than a decade after the movement began— there were upwards of fifty such groups throughout the United States.

Though some gathered in the winter for lectures and meetings, summer was the prime Chautauqua time. By the turn of the century, "traveling Chautauquas" came to small towns in rural areas all over the country, put up tents for a week or a portion thereof, where they offered drama, music, and lectures on all the topics of the day.

Chautauqua gatherings were of special importance to women for two reasons: they offered a rare gainful employment opportunity to the educated women who were featured on their platforms; and they also prompted discussions of the era's burning issues, including the SUFFRAGE MOVEMENT, TEMPERANCE, and MARRIED WOMEN'S PROPERTY RIGHTS, as well as GUARDIANSHIP, DIVORCE, and other reforms. The Chautauqua opportunity was virtually indispensable in spreading new, feminist ideas.

The development of motion pictures after the turn of the century, followed by radio and finally television, led to an end of these gatherings for the masses, but the Chautauqua movement remains today for the thoughtful. Thousands of people still come to western New York each summer to the Chautauqua Institute, and traveling Chautauqua shows still awaken memories of SUSAN ANTHONY and others who once graced its stages.

CHESNUT, MARY BOYKIN MILLER (1823–1886) Both the daughter and the wife of United States senators whose importance has faded, Mary Chesnut's name remains familiar today for her private writing, which was not published until decades after her death.

To all appearances the epitome of a Southern belle, Mary Miller was born to a distinguished South Carolina family and educated only in local FINISHING SCHOOLS—yet the diaries she kept all of her life belie the stereotypes of belles, for she had a mind so keen that her understanding of political and military strategy was equal to that of almost any Confederate leader and superior to many. Had she been male, Mary Chesnut might well be remembered along with Robert E. Lee, and indeed, the history of the South might have been different.

Her father, a former governor and U.S. House member, left the U.S. Senate and moved his family to frontier Mississippi in 1835, but twelve-year-old Mary stayed at a Charleston boarding school. She received an uncommonly good education there, learning French and German so well that even though she never visited those countries, she could converse fluently with Europeans years later. Mary Miller's mind, doubtlessly, was a large part of the attraction she held for twenty-one-year-old Princeton honors graduate James Chesnut when the two met while she was still thirteen, for the books he smuggled to her as gifts would not have charmed a giddy girl.

When Mary's father died in 1837 (the year of America's first genuine depression), Mrs. Miller suffered the same reverses experienced by many WIDOWS unfamiliar with their husbands' finances. Doubtless this was a major factor in Mary's return from the wilds of Mississippi to marry only weeks after her seventeenth birthday. She moved with James to his parents' South Carolina plantations, where, partly because she never became pregnant, life was often tediously isolated and boring to the point of depression and illness. Finally, in 1859, James' political career took him to the U.S. Senate—but the next year, South Carolina seceded from the Union and a disappointed Mary Chesnut had to leave Washington.

She understood far more than most of her compatriots the dangers of secession, and though powerless to affect policy, feared what was in fact the eventual result. Moreover, again unlike most Southerners, Mary Chesnut had recorded her opposition to the idea of slavery since school days. While she cannot be called an ABOLITIONIST (just as most Northerners in the era were not abolitionists, either), she not only shared the compassion that abolitionists felt for slaves, but also understood from personal experience the economic, political, and social evils spread by the system. Her observations from a FEMINIST view are almost unprecedented, for she frequently and vehemently argued to her diary that white women suffered along with black from the emotional pain wreaked by white males' nocturnal visits to slave cabins.

But the same blinders that were supposed to prevent white women from seeing the mulatto babies on their plantations also kept most of Southern society blind to the prospect of loss, and the war came. Mary Chesnut set out very deliberately early in 1861 to keep her diary more faithfully than she had in the past, recording details clearly intended for the benefit of future historians. She was in a key position to do so, since her husband, with the rank of general, soon became an aide to Confederate President Jefferson Davis. As the Confederate cabinet bounced around from Montgomery to Richmond and finally into exile, Mary became close to Varina Howell Davis, and the daily experience of living amid the Confederate White House gave her a rare opportunity to record the decline and fall of the government from the inside.

The events recorded in many notebooks during the busy and insecure war years were understandably cryptic. For two decades after the war was over, she experimented with writing them up in several different genres, but there was never enough time to do a satisfying job of it. The Reconstruction years instead demanded that her time be spent first in simple survival, for the war's destruction of the Southern economy meant that they were literally penniless at first. Then, because inheritance law gave no protection to childless widows, she had to make arrangements to secure her future; and finally, she left her writing to care for her husband and mother, who died within a week of each other.

Despite all this, she managed to almost finish a fairly polished book in 1884, but left its execution to others when she died two years later. Doubtless she would have been disappointed with the job that they did, for *A Diary from Dixie* was not published until 1905; a second edition came out in 1949. Both contained scholarly inadequacies that remained to be rectified with additional primary research in the 1980s. Nonetheless, the diary that was available for most of the twentieth century was still of inestimable value to students of history. Chesnut's work has been called both the best of such CIVIL WAR chronicles and the best diary by a woman in American history.

Especially when one remembers that she wrote her almost half-million words with inkwell and blotter and by candlelight, under emotional pressure and constant interruption and without the reinforcing incentive that anyone cared about her work, Mary Chesnut's words become an admirable measure of the ideas that poured from her brilliant mind during a lifetime of thought.

CHICAGO, UNIVERSITY OF Chartered in 1891, the University of Chicago was coeducational from its beginning and offered women some of the best educational and employment opportunities available at that time. Its first president accepted the position only under the condition that funding would be available to quickly make the university a first-rate research institution, and though some of the era's reformers objected to the Rockefeller endowments that made this possible, the school nonetheless quickly became a progressive leader.

It placed particular emphasis on the fields of social work and education, which included women from their earliest days. Even more significantly, ALICE FREEMAN PALMER was recruited as the University's first dean of women. She was offered an extremely rewarding situation that contrasted with her position in the East, for Palmer had been forced to resign as president of WELLESLEY COLLEGE when she married. Chicago's officials, however, did not see marriage as the inherent end of a woman's professional life and made a commuter marriage possible for her. With the aim of developing a "western Wellesley," Palmer recruited female faculty and developed a house system that provided students close contact with mentors. She also pushed for courses (especially in social science) that appealed to women students.

JANE ADDAMS' Hull House, which developed in the same era, became a virtual laboratory extension of the University, and by the turn of the century, the relationship between the two made Chicago alive with intellectual and political reformists. It provided an experience of profound significance to many future women leaders, including EDITH and GRACE ABBOTT, EMILY BALCH, SOPHONISBA BRECKINRIDGE, ALICE HAMILTON, FLORENCE KELLY, JULIA LATHROP, and others.

Almost a century before the prestigious Ivy League universities on the East Coast admitted women, Chicago demonstrated the different status of WESTERN WOMEN. Nor did it limit its women simply to the status of students; Breckinridge, for example, after becoming the first woman in the world to earn a Ph.D. in political science in 1901, remained as a faculty member for the rest of her life. When the School of Social Service Administration was formalized as a graduate program in 1924, Edith Abbott was named as the first dean, and many of her students went on to play important roles in Washington during Roosevelt's New Deal, where the educations they had received at Chicago had an impact on millions.

In 1969, the University added its first woman to the Board of Trustees with the appointment of 1938 graduate KATHARINE MEYER GRAHAM, and in 1977, Hanna Holborn Gray was named president.

CHILD, JULIA McWILLIAMS (1912–   ) A 1938 graduate of SMITH COLLEGE, Julia McWilliams was another of the many talented women who found only limited opportunity in their Depression-era youth, but whose horizons were expanded by WORLD WAR II. The wartime Office of Strategic Services sent her to Ceylon as a clerk, which introduced her to a completely different cuisine and began her lifelong interest in food.

She also met Foreign Service officer Paul Child there, married him in 1946, and went with him to Paris when he was posted there in 1948. She was thus thirty-six years old when this reassignment gave her the opportunity to attend the outstanding Cordon Bleu cooking school. The friendship she developed there with two other women students resulted in the three opening their own school in 1951, the *L'Ecole des Trois*

Gourmandes, and after a decade in business together, they published a book aimed at the American market.

Mastering the Art of French Cooking came out in 1961, the same year that the Childs returned to their native land, settling in Cambridge, Massachusetts. Julia Child did such an outstanding job promoting the book on a Boston television show that she was invited to make some pilots for a potential gourmet cooking series on educational television. "The French Chef," begun in 1963, was immediately popular in the Boston area and its programs were soon repeated all over the country. Only two years later, the show won a Peabody Award and the following year, it won an Emmy.

Not only was the subject matter popular with women, but also and more importantly, Julia Child was a role model with whom women could identify. Instead of cherishing the mysterious and temperamental image associated with male chefs, she insisted on an honest display before the television cameras of the whole process of gourmet cookery, complete with occasional failures. She showed women that they, too, could be chefs, not merely cooks.

Julia Child went on to write several more books, turning to native American as well as French styles of cuisine. She continued to make regular television appearances in the decades to follow. She writes often for *Parade* newsmagazine and remains immensely popular.

CHILD, LYDIA MARIA FRANCIS (1802–1880)

Lydia Maria Child's life can be interestingly viewed as a precursor of the lives of CATHERINE BEECHER and HARRIET BEECHER STOWE, for some of Child's early writing was devoted to the domestic advice area in which Catherine Beecher later shone, and she also published inflammatory ABOLITIONIST work years before Harriet Beecher Stowe wrote *Uncle Tom's Cabin*.

But Lydia Maria Child's interests ranged much wider than either of those. She was born to upper-class Bostonian parents, whose fears for her marriage proved correct: though she loved David Lee Child and shared with him an exemplary companionable, childless marriage, he was never able to support her in the fashion of the times, and they sometimes lived in near poverty. Much of her writing therefore was motivated by the simple need for money.

She had already begun writing as Lydia Francis, publishing in 1824 and 1825 two works of historical fiction set in early New England. They sold well, and in 1826, she began publishing the first American children's magazine, a bimonthly called *Juvenile Miscellany*. Her 1828 marriage only reinforced her career, for although David Child was a Harvard graduate, his quixotic idealism interfered with his ability to earn a living as a lawyer. Their family needs can be seen in the subject matter of the first book written by the bride only a year after her wedding: *The Frugal Housewife* (1829) was one of America's earliest domestic advice books and presaged the HOME ECONOMICS movement by a half-century. Immediately popular, it went through twenty-one editions in the first decade after publication. Child followed it with *The Mother's Book* (1831), and, the same year, continued her interest in children's literature with *The Little Girl's Own Book*—another audience identified by her far earlier than by most.

Not content to stay in the limited realm of domesticity, however, Child also wrote in 1829 *The First Settlers of New England*, which was not a history of the English colonists as its title might imply, but rather a book on the area's Native American tribes. Though this is sometimes cited as indicative of her evolution from her family's conservatism to her husband's concern for oppressed minorities, she already had revealed unusual empathy for Native Americans in her very first book—*Hobomok* (1824) was a love story that featured a colonial woman and a Native American Man.

Whatever the impetus, Lydia Maria Child's political identification was clear by 1833, when she published her most famous work, *An Appeal in Favor of That Class of Americans Called Africans*. By carefully spelling out the realities and complexities of slavery, her appeal brought many influential personalities to join the Childs' friend, William Lloyd Garrison, in abolitionism. It also created an uproar among family friends, who bankrupted Child's magazine by cutting off their children's subscriptions to *Juvenile Miscellany*. Like MARIA WESTON CHAPMAN, Lydia Maria Child found herself ostracized.

Unlike Chapman, however, she was not naturally an organizer or even a joiner. She never attempted to lead meetings or speak on abolitionism, though Child nonetheless showed courage by continuing to write on the subject throughout the 1830s, and the American Anti-Slavery Society rewarded her with election to its executive committee in 1840. Meanwhile, the sales of her work in other areas suffered from the controversy over slavery. Her attempts to return to a female audience with the biographical *Good Wives* (1833), *The History of the Condition of Women* (1835), and *The Family Nurse* (1837) were not very successful, though an 1836 romantic novel sold better.

She joined her husband during the late 1830s in an agrarian enterprise doomed to fail; like LOUISA MAY ALCOTT, whose writing supported her father's family while he experimented with utopian agronomy, Lydia Child soon needed income. In 1841, she moved to New York and edited the weekly *National Anti-Slavery Standard* for two years before internal abolitionist conflicts took their toll and she resigned. Her next publishing project was the two-volume *Letters From New York* (1843–45), a collection of correspondence columns she had written for a Boston newspaper. Her observations on the city and times proved surprisingly successful, and the work was reissued almost a dozen times during the next three decades.

For part of this era, the Childs maintained an early commuter marriage while he worked as a journalist in Washington and she in New York. They returned to Massachusetts in 1850, settling permanently in Wayland in 1852. Though she became increasingly reclusive there, her literary horizons continued to expand. Demonstrating her prescience again, she published first *Fact and Fiction; A Collection of Stories* (1846), a book that was sympathetic to women engaged in illicit sex, and followed it less than a decade later with *The Progress of Religious Ideas* (1855). In this three-volume work of comparative religion, Child rejected the common belief in revealed truth and instead viewed religions as having evolved along with human development. Meanwhile, she kept the bills paid with periodical articles, inspirational anthologies, biography, more children's literature, and abolitionist works.

During the CIVIL WAR, she edited *Incidents in the Life of a Slave Girl* (1861) for ex-slave Harriet Jacob, and at the war's end, she cared enough about the publication of other, similar people that she paid personally for *The Freedman's Book* (1865). Two years later, she published her last novel, and the following year returned to the subject of her youth with *An Appeal for the Indians* (1868).

David Child died in 1874, and his grieving WIDOW, who had increasingly isolated herself from all but him, found the energy for only one more book, *Aspirations of the World* (1878). Lydia Maria Child died at age seventy-eight, the author of more than two dozen books and countless periodical pieces. Had she written nothing else, she would be remembered for one of her enduring children's pieces: a Thanksgiving favorite, her 1844 "Over the River and Through the Woods" was sung even before Thanksgiving was an official holiday. Her reputation as one of America's first literary women was secure when two years after her death, John Greenleaf Whittier did her the honor of publishing Lydia Maria Child's biography and two volumes of her correspondence.

CHISHOLM, SHIRLEY ANITA ST. HILL (1924–   )

The daughter of Caribbean immigrants, Shirley St. Hill spent part of her childhood in Barbados before graduating from high school during WORLD WAR II. Wartime increased opportunities for women and minorities, and she graduated from Brooklyn College in 1946. Although her first job was in the traditional area of TEACHING, within three years, St. Hill had risen to director of Brooklyn's Friends Day Nursery.

Her 1949 marriage to detective Conrad Chisholm did not mean an end to work. She completed a master's degree in elementary education at Columbia in 1952, and the following year, became director of the Hamilton-Madison Child Care Center in Manhattan. After six years there, she joined the city's Bureau of Child Welfare as a day-care specialist in 1959.

As the civil rights and feminist movements gathered strength in the sixties, Chisholm was thus well positioned to push for child care and other issues of concern to women, especially poor and minority women. This, plus her Caribbean background and fluency in Spanish, paid off in 1964, when, after years of involvement in Democratic precinct politics, she was elected to the New York State Assembly. Though she had to run again the next year because of reapportionment, she proved popular enough to be re-elected twice. When the Supreme Court ruling that called for reapportionment to equalize urban and rural representation also created a new congressional district for the impoverished Bedford-Stuyvesant area in 1968, Chisholm declared her candidacy. After first defeating the Tammany Hall establishment in the Democratic primary, she went on to outrun a Republican-Liberal coalition that promoted James Farmer, a popular civil rights leader, in the general election.

Shirley Chisholm was sworn in as the nation's first black congresswoman in January, 1969. It was a time of upheaval in America, as protests against the Vietnam War also brought focus to racism and sexism, while clashes between the counterculture and the establishment brought rioting, jailings, and deaths. Through it all, Chisholm headed marches and spoke from hundreds of platforms. Soon recognized as a national leader of women as well as of racial minorities, she became a candidate for president in 1972. The first black woman to run a credible campaign for national office, Shirley Chisholm received the votes of 151 delegates to the tumultuous Democratic convention that year.

Chisholm used her campaign slogan as the title of her 1972 book, *Unbought and Unbossed*, and followed that the next year with *The Good Fight*. She received national attention with a 1970 *MaCall's* article titled "I'd Rather Be Black than Female," which asserted that in her experience of dealing with double prejudices based on color and gender, she found gender to be the more intractable problem.

She continued in Congress through the seventies, where her chief legislative accomplishment was the inclusion of domestic workers under minimum wage and Social Security coverage. She successfully fought the male power structure that originally attempted to assign this woman, who represented an urban ghetto, to the Agriculture Committee, and eventually rose to be a member of the powerful Rules Committee. After twelve years in Congress, however, Chisholm announced her plans to retire in February, 1982; like BARBARA JORDAN, she stated a preference for teaching and writing.

In retirement, Chisholm taught at MOUNT HOLYOKE COLLEGE and in 1984, organized the National Political Congress of Black Women. She earned numerous honorary degrees and awards from dozens of organizations, as well as three years of placement in the Gallup Poll's "Ten Most Admired Women in the World." In 1993, President Clinton appointed Shirley Chisholm ambassador to Jamaica.

CHOPIN, KATE O'FLAHERTY (1851–1904)

Born to a prosperous St. Louis family of Irish and Creole extraction, Kate O'Flaherty attended convent schools and married at twenty-one. She joined her husband in Reconstruction Louisiana, living in New Orleans and on the family plantation for twelve years, during which time she bore six children, until his death in 1882.

Still youthful as a WIDOW, Chopin began to write of her Louisiana experience, and eight years after returning to St. Louis, published her first novel. During the next decade, she wrote over a hundred short stories for magazines, including *Atlantic, Harper's* and *Vogue*; two collections of her stories were published in book form in 1894 and 1897.

Set in Louisiana bayou country, her tales told millions of Americans of the Cajun and Creole cultures, intimately and sympathetically describing a way of life that few understood. This literature gave Kate Chopin a prominent place as a regionalist AUTHOR, but her reputation should have exceeded that, for Chopin practiced careful craftsmanship and dealt with universal values.

She stopped writing after publication of *The Awakening* (1899), stung by the criticism she received because of its portrayal of female sexuality. Her themes of female psychology, depression, and suicide had proved her too strong an author for Victorian tastes; she was too far ahead of her literary times. Suddenly ostracized by those whom she had considered friends, Kate Chopin died just five years later.

The Missouri Historical Society has a large collection of her papers, while others are in the American Women Writers Collection at the University of Wisconsin.

CHURCHILL, JENNIE JEROME (1854–1921)

Typical of the wealthy young American women who were sought after by titled but not necessarily prosperous European men in the late nineteenth century, Jennie Jerome was remembered by all who encountered her as beautiful, witty, and a true belle.

Born in New York, she went to Paris when she was just entering her teens with her sisters and mother, who sought to escape from the scandals caused by her financier father. At twenty, she moved to England and married Lord Randolph Churchill, a son of the Duke of Marlborough. Her position in international society was secure, though her husband would follow the pattern of her father in leading a personal life that was deeply humiliating to his wife (and even life-threatening after he developed syphilis). Lady Randolph managed to find activities of her own, however, especially in the upbringing of her promising elder son Winston.

After Lord Randolph's death in 1895, she not only continued with the community work expected of nobility, but also exhibited creative ability with the publication of a carefully worded autobiography, two plays, and a collection of the articles she regularly wrote for *Pearson's Magazine*. During the same time, she assured her reputation as an enticingly beautiful free spirit by twice marrying men younger than her son. Jennie Churchill did not live to see Winston become prime minister, dying at age sixty-seven soon after WORLD WAR I put a permanent end to the lifestyle of her Gilded Age.

CIVIL WAR (1861–1865)

So strong is the link between the American Civil War and the liberation of American women that it is hard to overstate its importance. A multitude of individual women and women's organizations had their genesis in this War Between the States (as Southerners preferred to call it).

This is particularly true in the North, where ABOLITIONISM and FEMINISM were almost inseparable ideas for women from the 1830s to 1850s. It was in the anti-slavery cause that women first realized how deep was the discrimination against them and first began to counter it by learning to engage in PUBLIC SPEAKING, demanding civil rights for themselves as well as for others. Even those women who insisted on the greater importance of abolitionism over feminism, such as MARIA WESTON CHAPMAN and LYDIA MARIA CHILD, nonetheless learned from their abolitionist experience the skills of organizing, writing, and argumentation, and gained as well the courage to assert their convictions.

The organizations that they formed to advance abolition, especially the LOYAL LEAGUE, led directly to such groups as the AMERICAN EQUAL RIGHTS ASSOCIATION and the AMERICAN WOMAN SUFFRAGE ASSOCIATION. More traditional women also benefited from organizational experience during the war through such volunteer groups as the Woman's Central Association of Relief that networked through the U.S. SANITARY COMMISSION. For many women, such activity was a wholly new thing; they learned for the first time to elect officers, form committees, raise funds, and do all the other organizing necessary to accomplish a political goal. It would be wartime labor shortages, too, that would bring women their first opportunities in federal employment.

It was these changes that the writers of the 1872 Republican platform had in mind when they wrote their plank on women. While the rhetoric was doubtless intended to mollify those who demanded the vote, it nonetheless spelled out that even in the minds of these conservative males, the war had changed the status of women. The party, it said, was "mindful of its obligations to the loyal women of America for their noble devotion to the cause of freedom . . . and the honest demands of any class of citizens for equal rights should be treated with respectful consideration."

That consideration was merited in many minds especially because of the war work women undertook as battlefield NURSES and hospital organizers. CLARA BARTON, MARY ANN BICKERDYKE, DR. ELIZABETH BLACKWELL, DOROTHEA DIX, and others provided stellar examples of how capable women could be, even in a world torn asunder by men. Less well known CONFEDERATE WOMEN did the same for their troops. Hundreds of Southern women defied convention to care for bloody male bodies in makeshift hospitals; some were recognized for their abilities, such as CAPTAIN SALLY TOMPKINS, a hospital director who held a cavalry commission.

While Confederate women were less likely than Northern ones to TRAVEL to distant battlefields, they had the greater challenge of literally defending lives and homes. Even when battle was not near, for thousands of women on both sides, the war meant running farms and businesses alone, often for years. Especially on the frontier, it brought genuine hardships, isolation, and danger. It was not accidental that Minnesota Sioux mounted a revolt when troops moved south: moving quickly in 1862, they killed some 400 settlers, captured more, and struck fear into the hearts of thousands of Midwesterners. IMMIGRANT WOMEN there, new to the land and the language, had to manage alone when husbands were drafted and sent to fight a war they scarcely understood.

The war also motivated women to take on activities even more unconventional than battlefield nursing, some of them so unusual as to have been set aside by historians as not somehow quite credible. The exploits of DR. MARY WALKER, a physician on the battlefields of Tennessee who was captured and taken prisoner, have been diminished because of controversy in her postwar life. Similarly, the spy work of BELLE BOYD, PAULINE CUSHMAN, ROSE GREENHOW, and ELIZABETH VAN LEW has been treated almost more as mythology than history, but their stories, along with those of other women, are well documented. Tales of women who dressed as men to become soldiers also have been greeted with skepticism, yet MARY LIVERMORE, a respected author and lecturer who was an active participant in the war, estimated the number of women soldiers who disguised themselves as men at four hundred.

An even stronger statement comes from Frank Moore's *Women of the War* (1866), published just a year after the conflict ended, which asserted that "hundreds" of graves marked "unknown" were actually "those of women obliged by army regulations to fight in disguise." If hundreds of women died, then thousands must have participated as soldiers, and Moore identified some, both from the North and the South. MATILDA JOSLYN GAGE, a nineteenth-century feminist historian and activist, also chronicled the roles of a dozen women soldiers who dressed as men. Probably the most famous of such women on the Union side was Sarah Emma Edmonds, who, like LORETTA JANETA VELAZQUEZ on the Confederate side, later wrote about the incognito experience.

MATILDA JOSLYN GAGE, a nineteenth-century feminist historian and activist, also chronicled the roles of a dozen women soldiers who dressed as men. Volume II of the *HISTORY OF WOMAN*

A volunteer nurse sits with wounded men outside a Fredricksburg, Virginia, hospital in 1864, the last full year of the Civil War. LIBRARY OF CONGRESS.

SUFFRAGE included the report of a woman who committed suicide upon the discovery of her gender and an even more extraordinary report of a nameless woman who recaptured a Union ship taken by pirates. The *J.P. Ellicott* was a merchant marine brigantine out of Maine that was sailing in the South Atlantic when overtaken by pirates who captured its crew. The pirates kept its mate's wife, but rather than accepting her status as a prize of war, she "succeeded in getting the officers intoxicated, handcuffed them and took possession of the vessel, persuading the crew, who were mostly colored men from St. Thomas, to aid her. Having studied navigation with her husband," she reached St. Thomas, where she "placed the vessel in the hands of the United States Consul, who transferred [the offenders] as prisoners of war. Her name was not

given, but had this bold feat been accomplished by a man or boy, the country would have rung with praises of the daring deed . . ." Indeed, the reason that the woman remained nameless might well have been because she was raped—something that seldom threatened male combatants.

The visibility that focused on the activities of ANNA DICKINSON in support of the Union at the time is an interesting contrast to the silence on this naval heroism, but Dickinson too is largely forgotten today. At a time when women still could be subject to criticism for speaking in public, Dickinson's oratorical skills were so exceptional that she was offered thousands of dollars in speaking fees by the Republican Party to convert the antiwar element in the North. ANNA CARROLL was another woman whose political sagacity was of genuine value to the Lincoln administration; at a time when the majority of women did not even consider voting, Carroll's drawing room maneuvers and especially her writing promoted the Union's political cause.

Indeed, writing about the war was a major factor affecting women long after the war was over. LOUISA MAY ALCOTT's wartime setting of *Little Women* alone shaped the thought of millions of young minds. HARRIET BEECHER STOWE, of course, is often credited as a major cause of the war, as *Uncle Tom's Cabin* redirected political focus from legalistic questions such as the right of secession to the drama of ending human bondage. For dozens of other, lesser-known women, the conflict provided an impetus for putting pen to paper.

That the works of abolitionists such as Alcott and Stowe are well known is the logical result of Union victory, while Southern historians, starved for funds by state legislatures and inhibited by moonlight and magnolia myths, have done less to publicize their Civil War women. The outstanding diary of MARY CHESNUT

is a notable exception, but it was not published until the twentieth century. With the current rise of feminist scholarship, the efforts of other, similar women are coming to light.

Finally, the overwhelming importance of the Civil War to black women is self-evident. As with whites, however, attention has been focused on a very few women (especially HARRIET TUBMAN and SOJOURNER TRUTH), while many others who also overcame the double prejudices of race and sex are only now being recognized. MARY ANN SHADD CARY and FRANCES ELLEN WATKINS HARPER are but two examples of black women who deserve greater recognition for their roles in the Civil War.

CLARK, GEORGIA NEESE (1900–1989) The first woman to become treasurer of the United States, Georgia Neese was born in Kansas, graduated from college there, and returned after spending the twenties in New York seeking a career in the theater. She married her theatrical manager in

A rare photograph of a Civil War refugee family, with their belongings loaded on a mule-drawn cart, preparing to leave a combat area. Note that the standing woman has a corncob pipe in her mouth, and that they are leaving their home in the winter. NATIONAL ARCHIVES.

1929, which resulted in the surname she kept the rest of her life.

After both the nation's economy and her marriage failed, Clark returned to Kansas in 1930 to care for her ailing father. She took over his business interests throughout the Depression years, and when he died in 1937, replaced him as president of the Richland State Bank.

Like millions of Americans but relatively few bankers, she had been active in Democratic politics during the Roosevelt years. Elected to the Democratic National Committee in 1936, she worked especially hard for the candidacy of fellow Midwesterner Harry Truman in 1948. Since Truman was not expected to win that election, he was particularly grateful to those who had faith in him and rewarded her with the position of treasurer.

The nation's treasurer is a largely ceremonial post, with that of the secretary of the treasury being the true power. Nevertheless, Georgia Neese Clark's signature became the first feminine name to appear on United States currency. She served out her term in Washington, and in 1953, returned to Kansas and remarried. When the Republicans took over the presidency that year, Eisenhower was careful to appoint a woman to replace her, as all presidents have done since.

CLARK, SEPTIMA POINSETTE (1898–1987) Referred to as the "Mother of the Movement" by Martin Luther King, Jr., Septima Clark was active in civil rights before King was born, even though she lived most of her life in and near the segregationist stronghold of Charleston, South Carolina.

The daughter of ex-slaves, Septima Poinsette passed the state TEACHERS examination at age eighteen, after completing the twelfth grade. She began her lifelong career in education in 1916 at Johns Island, a community near Charleston that was home to a large black population. Here, like elsewhere in the South, few tax dollars were spent on minority needs and, despite the 1898 Supreme Court's "separate but equal" ruling in *Plessy vs. Ferguson*, black schools were anything but equal. Miss Poinsette and her assistant teacher were paid thirty-five dollars and twenty-five dollars monthly for teaching 132 students; the white teacher across the street in a better building taught three students and was paid eighty-five dollars. Encouraged by the brief post–WORLD WAR I civil rights movement, she gathered about ten thousand signatures on petitions to hire black teachers and to allow blacks to become principals, and the legislature responded positively in 1919.

Septima Poinsette married seaman Nerie Clark in 1920 and bore two children, one of whom died in infancy. When her husband died five years after they married, Mrs. Clark returned to teaching to support herself and her young son. She moved to the state capital of Columbia, South Carolina in 1929; during the two decades she lived there, she earned a B.A. at Columbia's Benedict College and an M.A. from the famous Hampton Institute in Virginia. She also used her earlier experience to lead statewide efforts for teacher salary equalization, and in 1945—after wartime needs again brought some labor equity—a federal court ruled that teachers' salaries could not be based on race.

Clark returned to Charleston in 1947 and taught there until 1956, when—at age fifty-eight and after forty years of teaching in the South Carolina schools—she was fired. The rationale used to get rid of this activist woman was a 1956 state law that forbade city and state employees from membership in civil rights organizations. Clark refused to hide her NAACP membership and was dismissed.

She turned this disaster into opportunity, however, and joined the faculty of the Highlander Folk School, a leftist institution in the mountains of Tennessee. There she worked with ELLA BAKER and ROSA PARKS to develop programs of adult literacy aimed at political action. In 1961, at age sixty-three, Clark began working eleven Deep South states under the aegis of the Southern Christian Leadership Conference (SCLC), setting up schools that taught basic literacy to blacks. In churches, beauty parlors, and even under trees, she led workshops that taught people first to write their names and then to write checks and, finally, to register to vote. She recruited teachers for these schools who were not necessarily professional educators, but who were instead the natural community leaders. She taught these volunteer teachers to use a "folk" approach that emphasized practical reading and writing as well as political involvement for their adult students.

The program she developed was recognized as so fundamental to the success of the civil rights movement that Clark was the first woman elected to the SCLC Executive Board. Like Ella Baker, however, she was open about the sexism she encountered there: "The thing that I think stands out," she said later, "was the fact that women could never be accorded their rightful place even in the Southern Christian Leadership Conference."

Yet her involvement was recognized as important enough that she was one of the delegation that accompanied Martin Luther King to Norway when he accepted the Nobel Peace Prize in 1964. The following year, Septima Poinsette Clark—who had begun as an inequitably paid teacher a half-century earlier—was elected to the Charleston School Board. The College of Charleston gave her an honorary doctorate in 1978, and the next year she was honored by President Jimmy Carter. When she died at eighty-nine, most of her integrationist goals had been achieved.

CLEVELAND, EMELINE HORTON (1829–1878) Apparently the first woman to perform major surgery, Dr. Cleveland accomplished this just three years before she died.

Like so many early FEMINISTS, Emeline Horton grew up in New York State; she followed the pattern of others by first TEACHING to earn the money to attend OBERLIN COLLEGE, graduating in 1853. Although she married Reverend Giles Cleveland in 1854, she received her M.D. from the FEMALE MEDICAL COLLEGE OF PENNSYLVANIA in 1855. Reverand Cleveland, a childhood friend and Oberlin graduate, suffered from poor health, which not only prevented their initial plan to become missionaries but also meant that her earnings would be their main source of income.

After a year of private practice, Dr. Cleveland returned to her Philadelphia alma mater and taught medicine there for the rest of her life, finally rising to become dean. After winning prizes in Paris during 1860–1861 when she studied abroad, Dr. Cleveland continued to teach and practice while also bearing a son in 1865. She eventually established an outstanding reputation among male colleagues (one of whom read a paper of hers to the Philadelphia Obstetrical Society), and was responsible for gaining acceptance of women physicians by medical societies that had vehemently opposed the entrance of women into their field.

In 1875, she was forty-six, she performed several ovariotomies, which seems to be the earliest record of a woman physician practicing as a surgeon. Dr. Cleveland died of tuberculosis at age forty-nine; her invalid husband and ten-year-old son survived her.

CLEVELAND, FRANCES FOLSOM (1864–1947) Washington gossip was seldom equaled by that caused in 1886, when President Grover Cleveland, a bachelor all his life, seemed at last to be courting. It was natural that people assumed the object of his attention was a longtime widowed friend, but instead Cleveland was courting the woman's daughter—Frances Folsom, a Wells College senior whom Cleveland had known since she was a baby.

The White House's first presidential wedding occurred on June 2, 1886, when the twenty-two-year old Folsom married Cleveland, who at forty-nine, was more than twice her age. Perhaps awareness of the age difference motivated his change of the word "obey" in her wedding vow to "keep," for Cleveland was no feminist.

Their honeymoon attracted national interest. Indeed, until Jacqueline Kennedy in the 1960s, no other First Lady saw her privacy so thoroughly invaded as she. Reporters followed the young Mrs. Cleveland's every move, creating stories if there were none, and advertisers used her image without permission. Not surprisingly, she seemed to accept this attention better than her husband did. He called her "Frank," the press called her "Frankie," and such amiability soon made her a popular Washington figure.

Nonetheless, the president's sexuality became a campaign issue when he was up for reelection two years later—as it had been in his first election. In 1884, Republicans had publicized the ILLEGITIMATE child Cleveland had fathered as a young man: "Ma, Ma, where's my Pa? Gone to Washington; ha, ha, ha" was one of the campaign's highlights in this era of only male voters. In 1888, his marriage to the much younger woman also was a popular election topic. Frances Cleveland, in fact, finally found it necessary to confront rumors that he beat her and even threw her out of the White House; the statement she issued to "the women of our country" assured them that her husband was "kind, attentive, considerate, and affectionate."

Cleveland lost that election, though he won more popular votes than his Republican opponent. He became the only U.S. president to be elected to nonconsecutive terms when he returned to the White House in 1892. This time, Democratic Party leaders dealt with the sexuality question head-on, adding Frances Cleveland's photo in campaign posters—something that no other First Lady had done. This was not, however, any indication that Cleveland welcomed women's political participation; he not only opposed suffrage but even took the trouble to write against the women's CLUB MOVEMENT of the 1890s.

Frances Cleveland retired with her husband to Princeton, New Jersey after his second term, reared their five children, and, after his 1908 death, enjoyed a second long marriage to a professor. She lived on through WORLD WAR II and was healthy enough to return to the White House for a visit during the Truman administration.

CLOTHING— *See* DRESS REFORM *and* GARMENT INDUSTRY

CLUB MOVEMENT Men formed organizations for political and social reasons almost as soon as the nation began, but the mores of that time did not accord women the same privilege; their lives centered exclusively in the home, except for church services—and even there, men ordinarily sat together, leaving women and children on the opposite side of the aisle.

With the exception of Quakers and a few other minorities, women also were banned from PUBLIC SPEAKING—and this became a large part of the reason for their failure to form clubs, for it is difficult to organize without speaking. The case of ANNE HUTCHINSON, for example, illustrates the inordinate response of colonial clergymen when women gathered to hear another woman. At the same time, TRAVEL bans reinforced women's isolation in their homes, for while men could hitch up their horses and go to meetings, women seldom went anywhere unescorted. For two centuries, women's organizations simply did not exist.

The DAUGHTERS OF LIBERTY formed by REVOLUTIONARY WAR WOMEN was a short-lived exception to this rule, but it was largely AUXILIARY to the work of men and faded after the need was gone; many decades would pass before women formed another political group. Nor were there social organizations for women: George Washington was a Mason, for example, but his wife had no comparable opportunity, for the Masons did not develop their feminine counterpart, Eastern Star, until 1875—a century after Martha Washington would have been a likely member.

When women finally began to formally associate, it was likely to be under the auspices of a benevolent society that was usually controlled by a male minister. Mainstream Protestant women in the pre-CIVIL WAR era, emulating the more direct behavior of QUAKER WOMEN, developed groups to befriend the deserving poor and, as the missionary movement grew in the nineteenth century, they educated themselves on foreign lands and raised funds to assist missions. Again under the leadership of male ministers, some churchwomen organized temperance societies, but decades passed before these evolved into the WOMEN'S CHRISTIAN TEMPERANCE UNION or similar bodies directed by women. Instead, these societies remained local and controlled by male officials. Such church-based groups—often called "Ladies Aid" or some variation thereof—were the only organizations that most women ever joined until the twentieth century.

Even the ABOLITIONISTS who joined groups such as the Boston Female Anti-Slavery Society did not see these bodies as FEMINIST, but rather as auxiliaries to the "real" organizations run by men. It was therefore not surprising that no one was willing to preside when the SENECA FALLS WOMEN'S RIGHTS CONVENTION was held in 1848, for most women had no experience even as dues-paying members of organizations, let alone as a president. The mechanics of organizing—writing by-laws, electing officers, and engaging in structured debate—were all new to them, but they quickly learned. Though that first meeting was presided over by LUCRETIA MOTT's husband, a follow-up meeting two weeks later had a female president. A crucial factor in all of this was the participation of a large number of Quaker women, for they had long conducted meetings separate from men and were accustomed to organizational procedure and group decision making.

The needs of the CIVIL WAR brought a tremendous expansion of the activity of such nascent groups, as is illustrated by women such as MARY LIVERMORE and CLARA BARTON, who initially depended on church-based societies in their hometowns to supply the materials they needed to treat wounded men. Wartime emergencies also brought an end to strictures on travel and speaking, while at the same time, increasing numbers of women entered COLLEGE. All of these factors resulted in a postwar explosion of women's groups, especially in the North.

Three years after the war ended, two important clubs arose virtually simultaneously when both the New England Women's Club and SOROSIS began in 1868. That Sorosis is often cited as the first is probably due to the fact that one of its chief founders, JANE CUNNINGHAM CROLY, wrote the *History of the Woman's Club Movement in America* (1898). Both she and JULIA WARD HOWE of the New England Club, however, lectured across the nation during the next decades on their clubs and on the importance of female association. They stressed the good that such groups could do to lessen the problems of an increasingly urbanized and needy nation, but at the same time, both Sorosis and the New England Women's Club fell squarely into the category of "study clubs."

Study clubs aimed to provide personal fulfillment and educational opportunity for their members, while de-emphasizing both the benevolent activity of the older church-based groups and the political action of suffrage organizations. A model for study clubs had existed as early as the self-created classes organized by LUCY LARCOM and other TEXTILE WORKERS, but as factory life harshened after the 1840s, these work-based clubs disappeared. Still, some pre-Civil War women who had a desire to learn managed to find each other, as ELIZABETH PEABODY and MARGARET FULLER could attest. Similarly, HARRIET BEECHER STOWE and CATHERINE BEECHER belonged to a mixed-gender reading and discussion group called the Semi-Colon Club—in Cincinnati in 1832. Recent scholarship has turned up evidences of pre-Sorosis women's study clubs in places as far west as Illinois and as early as 1800.

Most of those who joined the expanding study clubs after the Civil War were middle-aged and upper-middle-class women to whom colleges had been closed in their youth. Intent on educating themselves, their clubs had a fundamentally different goal from earlier benevolent or reform societies. Their meetings were devoted to topics of learning, not to discussion of community needs or fundraising events. To the extent that these clubs did raise money, it was for women's higher education; since many clubwomen were also active in the ASSOCIATION FOR THE ADVANCEMENT OF WOMEN, they might, for example, establish scholarships for women or buy equipment for female professors.

But these were secondary goals, for the main purpose of study clubs was self-improvement. Some clubs took on immense programs of serious study, planning their curricula with great care. They tended to emphasize literature and history (especially that of ancient Greece and Rome), and often used the presentation of papers by members as a learning method. A number of clubs, especially in cities, developed specialties that were of greatest interest to members. The Portia Club of San Francisco, for example, was composed of women interested in law and government, while Chicago's Heliades concentrated on geography and serious travel experience.

Others—even in remote areas of the country—studied science, with botany and astronomy as the most likely branches because they are less dependent on laboratory facilities. Philosophy, French, poetry, and especially music were other popular specialties; music probably proved the most enduring, with some musical organizations dating to this time still in existence today. Most study clubs obtained their materials and reading lists through libraries or bookstores and led their own classes, but a few hired professors to assist them. An Atlanta club that studied contemporary history was so devoted to their correspondence work with professors at JOHNS HOPKINS UNIVERSITY that these men said the clubwomen had the equivalent of a five-year graduate course.

Many study clubs limited their membership to about twenty-five in order to have reasonably sized classes, for discussion and public speaking experience was part of their aim. An unfortunate consequence of membership quotas, however, was that an aura of exclusivity and snobbishness soon developed around study clubs. Almost by definition, of course, women who had enough leisure to engage in such activity were affluent, and it was easy to depict them as self-indulgent and silly, for what small town housewife needed to know the history of Egypt?

While the husbands and sons of clubwomen were seldom criticized for their memberships in groups that were even more exclusive and frivolous, women's behavior was somehow expected to be democratic and practical. Unable or unwilling to join their wives' seemingly purposeless intellectual quests, most husbands saw the activity with bemused toleration. Indeed, much of the public—including an unfortunately large number of women—soon saw clubwomen as an appropriate target of cartoons.

This criticism was reinforced when a second type of club evolved from earlier roots, as women used their Civil War organizational abilities for reform movements closer to home. As women educated themselves, they naturally became more aware of civic needs (particularly libraries and schools), and the new clubs thus combined literary and civic intents. Often they were the only women's club in their towns—with the result that they were frequently named for their locality, as in the Des Moines Woman's Club or the Peoria Woman's Club.

These groups continued earlier traditions of feminine selflessness by putting community goals ahead of individual ones, but at the same time, they also assertively used political techniques to accomplish their aims. They worked to establish kindergartens, parks and playgrounds, school lunch programs, and especially libraries, and they even ventured into such male provinces as the installation of sewer systems and streetlights—without the power of the vote.

In 1890, Croly and others drew these groups together into the GENERAL FEDERATION OF WOMEN'S CLUBS (GFWC) to reinforce each other's educational efforts and work for a reformist agenda. By 1899, the GFWC had established a national model for juvenile courts, for instance, and by 1906, when it had some five thousand local clubs under its umbrella, the federation played an important role in passage of the Pure Food and Drug Act. The GFWC worked for the eight-hour day and against child labor, and in 1914, its members were finally sufficiently politicized to endorse the SUFFRAGE MOVEMENT.

Though these clubs did an immense amount of civic good at no cost to taxpayers, they were not necessarily welcomed by city fathers—some of whom took that term's gender implications seriously enough to resent the intrusion of women. Since clubwomen were often family members or lifelong friends of the propertied men who governed such towns, it was not unusual for women to lobby for their goals using their personal connections in the same way that men did. The president of a Tampa club in 1910 greeted the mayor on his first day in office with a list of the improvements she wanted: her father and brother had been mayors and she felt wholly comfortable in this political action, despite her lack of a vote. Moreover, she led clubwomen who were ostensibly opposed to suffrage in similar political behavior. Though the city had no suffrage organization, large numbers of club-women intent on playgrounds lobbied the city council meetings for weeks, vowing that "they are going to continue to be present until some definite action is taken, even if they have to put off their summer vacations." They won, and the first playground was named for the club's president—years before they had the right to vote.

Black women could not expect similar political success, but nonetheless they also developed organizations earlier than has been commonly recognized. MARIA STEWART, for example, spoke to the African-American Female Intelligence Society in Boston already in 1832, and when she moved to New York the following year, she joined a Female Literary Society—many decades before what is usually termed the era of the club movement. Black women had even more reason than white to keep a low profile on such activity, however, for their attempts at self-improvement were even more likely to be interpreted as self-important, and the consequences could be more dangerous than simply becoming the target of laughter. Like white women, they subordinated themselves to men in both church and political organizations, confining most of their activism to auxiliaries. As a class of affluent black women arose in the late nineteenth century, however, their organizational development paralleled that of white women.

The NATIONAL ASSOCIATION OF COLORED WOMEN was founded just six years after the General Federation of Women's Clubs. Its local bodies were made up of upper-middle-class black women who were the leaders of their communities, but they were less concerned with personal self-improvement than with advancement of their entire race. For many years thereafter, they were ably represented by MARY CHURCH TERRELL, who elicited almost universal admiration for her educational achievement and personal poise. African-American women's clubs under the aegis of the NACW worked on projects similar to those of the GFWC, although NACW members focused less on the aesthetic and more on the practical, especially in building aids for working women such as nursery schools. Though black women expected less from local government and were therefore less political, the NACW endorsed suffrage two years prior to the GFWC.

Despite their mutual interests and similar organizational styles, there was little exchange between these two federations or between their members at the local level. Segregation remained the rule through most of the twentieth century, with some GFWC clubs rebuffing coalition efforts from African-American clubs. When black and white women finally began interacting in the same groups, it was through such bodies as the BUSINESS AND PROFESSIONAL WOMEN'S CLUBS and the NATIONAL ORGANIZATION FOR WOMEN.

COCHRAN, JACQUELINE (1910?–1980)

The contrast between Jackie Cochran's modern, glamorous image as an adult and her almost Dickensian childhood could not be greater: an orphan, she grew up in such severe poverty that she worked in a Georgia textile mill when only eight. Cochran was reluctant to talk about her youth after she became famous, and perhaps to protect herself from age discrimination, she made a point of not disclosing the date of her birth. By thirteen, however, she was working as a beautician and by nineteen, owned her own shop. She practiced that trade in the Georgia-Alabama-Florida area around her native Pensacola until 1931.

Despite the Great Depression, she saved enough money to move to New York, where she began flying lessons in 1932. Friendship with a Navy pilot brought a move to San Diego and greater aviation skills, while at the same time she began to build her own cosmetics firm, which she managed so well that it provided her with income while she concentrated on flying. Though she retained the cosmetics company until 1963, Jackie Cochran's life was in the sky.

She began entering air races soon after learning to fly, and set several records during the thirties. Her reputation in the aviation world was already sufficiently important that Cochran retained her maiden name when she married Floyd Odlum in 1936, and when she beat a field of men to win the 1938 Bendix Transcontinental Air Race, her aviation fame was secure. By 1940, Cochran held seventeen official national and international speed records, earned at a time when aviation was still sufficiently new that many of the planes she flew were of dangerously experimental design. "In endurance, in stamina, and in flying ability," one periodical said of her, "she is the match of male aviators and she has wrested many trophies from men."

But her mind was not limited to mere air sport. More prescient than many of the era's governmental specialists, Cochran understood the implications of European fascism and already in 1939, she wrote ELEANOR ROOSEVELT in an attempt to plan a place for women pilots in the war that she foresaw. By June of 1941, she was so frustrated with American neutrality that she flew a bomber from Canada to England and signed on as a captain in the British Air Transport Authority. From there, she recruited other women pilots who flew the ATA's range of 120 types of planes, from the large and sophisticated to the small and dangerous.

After Pearl Harbor forced American involvement in WORLD WAR II, Cochran returned to the U.S. and organized the WOMEN'S AIRFORCES SERVICE PILOTS (WASPS) in 1942. Based in Texas, Cochran's WASPs were experienced fliers who performed vital services to the military in ferrying planes, training troops, and other tasks—yet, while they were subject to military regulations, they were officially civilians who received no benefits.

For Cochran, the WASP program was both a stellar achievement and a heartbreak, for the bureaucratic horrors inflicted on her WASPs ultimately forced her to seek a congressional solution. Supported by Air Corps' Chief, General Hap Arnold, she asked for full military status or disbandment—and overplayed her hand. Congress had heard from too many male pilots who wanted the women's jobs now that the war was almost over, and the WASP was disbanded in December, 1944. There may well have been an element of personal jealousy behind the votes of many congressmen, for both Hap Arnold and Jackie Cochran had celebrity images that politicians crave for themselves.

But a woman whose intelligence could be seen simply in the language she used—such as, for example, "aerial dishwashing" to describe some flying assigned to WASPs—was also talented enough to find a place in the different field of writing. Cochran spent 1945 reporting from both the Pacific and European theaters of war for *Liberty* magazine, and in that year, she also became the first woman civilian to receive the Distinguished Service Medal.

By 1948, the military had reorganized itself, separating the Air Force from the Army as well as integrating women, and Cochran became a lieutenant colonel in the Air Force Reserve—still arguably a lower rank than would be given to a man with her experience. (Cochran never was assigned a rank during her time with the WASP; she was addressed as "Miss.")

She went on to experiment with the new jet planes, becoming the first woman to break the sound barrier in 1953. During the sixties, when she was presumably over fifty, she continued to set records, including an altitude mark of over fifty-five thousand feet in 1961. Finally promoted to colonel in 1969, she retired in 1970.

Cochran won many aviation awards for women in the 1930s, and the International League of Aviators also cited her for accomplishment in that era. As late as 1959, her male aviation colleagues continued to recognize her by electing her president of the *Federation Aeronautique Internationale*, the first woman thus honored; she served until 1963. In 1954, she published an autobiographical work written with her husband, *The Stars at Noon*.

COLLEGES, WOMEN'S Single-sex institutions of the FINISHING SCHOOL type existed for young women since colonial times, but these were not colleges; their offerings were usually limited to sewing, art, music, and in the best cases, French and German. Troy Female Seminary, established in 1821 by EMMA WILLARD in Troy, New York, was the first institution to expand this standard curriculum to emulate the more rigorous courses available to young men.

Though it defies stereotypes, the first American institution of higher education for women to use the term "college" was in the Deep South. GEORGIA FEMALE COLLEGE was established at Macon in 1836, and it survives as Wesleyan College today, the nation's oldest educational institution for women.

These establishments were soon replicated. The "SEVEN SISTER" schools can trace their origins back to the pre–Civil War era, for western Massachusetts' MOUNT HOLYOKE Seminary (re-

named "college" in 1893), was founded by MARY LYON in 1837. Similar institutions appeared on the frontier almost as soon as there was settlement; CATHARINE BEECHER opened her Western Female Institute in Cincinnati already in 1831, for example, and Milwaukee Female College was in existence by the 1850s, while Mary Sharp College in Tennessee began in 1851. Educational institutions in the Midwest also opened to women several decades sooner than was the case in the urban East, indicating once again the greater opportunity available to WESTERN WOMEN.

OBERLIN COLLEGE, a private Ohio institution, set the precedent for coeducation by declaring itself open to women (and blacks) when it was chartered in 1833. Two other private Ohio institutions pioneering with female students were ANTIOCH COLLEGE, which admitted women from its 1852 beginning, and Western Reserve, an older school that distinguished itself by accepting MARIE ZAKRZEWSKA and EMILY BLACKWELL for medical studies in the early 1850s. In Virginia, Hollins College began as a coeducational school in 1842; it restricted itself to women only in 1852 and is still extant.

Several state universities in this pre-Civil War era also admitted women, including Wisconsin, Michigan and Ohio State. Nevertheless, even in these seemingly progressive coeducational schools, women students were invariably held to higher standards and, even after meeting these standards, were sometimes arbitrarily denied admission or graduation. Women were often segregated at the back of classrooms and denied the use of laboratories and other facilities. Professors refused to recognize them in class and closed courses and even entire departments to female students. Often the object of ridicule, some women found it difficult to obtain housing and meals, even though most were older than the average male student and almost all had previous work experience—usually, ironically, as TEACHERS.

After the CIVIL WAR, there was a veritable explosion of higher education opportunity for women. Bates College, a coeducational institution in Maine, became the first on the East Coast to grant degrees to women soon after the war, but it was the single-sex institutions that grew out of Matthew Vassar's 1865 brainchild that truly changed higher education for women in this era.

VASSAR COLLEGE, up the Hudson River from New York, was the first college for women to be located near a large eastern city, but it was Vassar's ambitious aims that made the new school distinctive and controversial. It aimed not merely to tolerate women students, but to actively recruit only women and to develop their academic potential with a strong curriculum offered in an atmosphere of quality. The idea—though vehemently resisted by establishment males and especially by medical doctors who argued that serious study would damage women's reproductive ability—proved so popular that the rest of the schools later to be known as the "SEVEN SISTERS" soon found plenty of students eager to pay their high tuition.

Just five years after Vassar opened, WELLESLEY COLLEGE was chartered (1870), and SMITH COLLEGE followed the very next year (1871). Despite the fact that both of these, as well as MOUNT HOLYOKE, were located in Massachusetts, they not only survived but prospered sufficiently that Harvard saw fit to formalize its "Annex" into RADCLIFFE COLLEGE in 1879. Philadelphia's BRYN MAWR COLLEGE, which had QUAKER origins, was added to the list in 1880, and BARNARD COLLEGE completed it in 1889, when Columbia emulated Harvard by adding a women's college that was geographically almost indistinct from its male counterpart. Although part of the reason that parents paid tuition to these Seven Sisters schools was to give their daughters an opportunity to mingle with the sons of the seven Ivy League Schools, it was nonetheless true that the women's colleges had high academic standards. They played a critical role in developing thousands of future community leaders, as well as in giving a superior opportunity to women faculty members.

Black women followed these same patterns of expanding opportunity, but for them the progress was much slower. Although Oberlin was open to both blacks and women already in 1833, it was not until 1862 that Mary Jane Patterson was the first to overcome the double discriminations of race and sex to become the first female black college graduate. An 1890 survey of universities accepting women found that only thirty bachelor of arts degrees had been granted to black women, and just one bachelor of science—granted that year by Cornell. Twenty years later, just 114 black women graduates were found in a study of 107 "non-Negro colleges"—and over half of those were from Oberlin.

Yet precedents of both race and sex were being set, and by the end of the nineteenth century, higher education for women was an accepted reality. As the nation moved west during the post–Civil War era, states routinely opened their colleges to women; many, like the UNIVERSITY OF CHICAGO, were coeducational from the beginning, while those premier universities that remained male preserves nonetheless often admitted women in graduate schools. Although most states maintained at least some segregation by gender through WORLD WAR II, the campuses of 1960 bore no resemblance to those of 1860. The relative speed of this century of progress can be seen by remembering that America's oldest college, Harvard, had existed for almost 250 years before the first woman was ever admitted to a class.

COLLINS, CARDISS (1931–) A black woman elected to Congress in 1973, Collins entered the House of Representatives just four years after SHIRLEY CHISHOLM became the first black Congresswoman. Collins, however, came by the more traditional route of replacing her husband, who had been killed in a plane crash a few months earlier. A graduate of Northwestern University and an auditor for the Illinois Department of Revenue, she was elected to represent a Chicago district overwhelmingly made up of black constituents.

Despite her grief and initial shyness, Collins immediately made herself a congressional leader and was appointed Democratic whip-at-large just two years after her election. She has served as chair of the Congressional Black Caucus, is a leader in sponsoring legislation to benefit women and minorities, and continues to be re-elected by huge margins.

COLLINS, MARTHA LAYNE (1936–) The first woman elected governor of Kentucky, she graduated from the University of Kentucky in 1959 and married that same year. Collins worked as a TEACHER throughout the sixties, while also mothering two children.

She became active in the state Democratic party during the

1970s, serving as a Democratic national committeemember and as secretary of the state party. In 1978, she was elected lieutenant governor, where she proved so esteemed that her colleagues in other states elected her vice-chair of the National Conference of Lieutenant Governors in 1981. She chaired this organization the following year.

Elected governor of Kentucky in 1983, Collins made educational reform her top priority and led the legislature in adopting increased academic standards. She also cut down on strip mining in the state, provided incentives for clean new industry, and set up a clearinghouse for missing and abused children. In 1984, just a year after her election, Collins presided over the national Democratic convention and was among the women considered by Walter Mondale as his presidential running mate. Limited by the state's constitution to one term, Collins left office in December, 1987. She continues to be active in the Democratic Party.

COLUMBIAN EXPOSITION (1892–1893) A celebration of the four hundredth anniversary of Columbus' voyage, the exposition was held in Chicago. Having learned from the disruptions at the CENTENNIAL EXHIBITION of 1876, this event was carefully planned to include women. The timing was also more propitious than the 1876 event because peace reigned among women's groups after the AMERICAN WOMAN SUFFRAGE ASSOCIATION and the NATIONAL WOMAN SUFFRAGE ASSOCIATION put aside their destructive competition and merged in 1890.

A presumably older and wiser SUSAN ANTHONY started working behind the scenes as early as 1889 to see that women played a role in the Columbian celebration. Expecting that radicals such as herself would be dismissed as they had been in 1876, she quietly recruited less controversial women into a committee that presented Congress with a petition early in 1890, asking for women on the Board of Managers for the event. Since the petition was signed by a hundred of Washington's finest ladies, including the wives of Cabinet members, Supreme Court justices, and their own wives and daughters, congressmen could not ignore it.

The result was the creation of a separate Board of LADY MANAGERS—which, with 115 members, probably was intended to be more ornamental than active. But anyone with such expectations did not know the woman appointed to chair the board, for BERTHA HONORE PALMER was a rare woman who combined her wealthy socialite status with active FEMINISM. A dynamo of energy and business acumen, she appointed an executive committee of twenty-five that created a highly successful presence for women at the exhibition, with a woman's hall for displays and meetings during the year-long event. She commissioned a mural by MARY CASSATT, an American artist working with pioneer impressionists in France, that was shipped for display. Exhibits from forty-seven nations proclaimed the diversity of women's lives, and there was even a chamber orchestra of women that performed works composed by women. The exposition became an important factor in the emergence of women as a social and economic group that merited political attention.

Palmer's only significant failure was not recognized as such at the time, for most Americans were as indifferent as she to including black women in the exposition. Black women nonetheless organized more than two years prior to the event and used every conceivable method in attempting to see that their culture also was included in the exhibits. Though Palmer did meet with them several times, her responses were merely politely palliative and clearly intended to avoid political criticism. Ultimately, about a dozen black women were included as speakers and a small "Afro-American" exhibit was allowed, which included a statistical compilation of "Evidences of the Advancement of the Colored Women of the United States." Male fair officials belatedly organized a "Negro Day" in response to "representatives of the civilized world." Meanwhile, IDA WELLS-BARNETT conducted an independent symposium on "The Reason Why the Colored American is not in the Columbian Exposition."

Officially opened on Columbus Day, (October 20) 1892, the fair's greatest activity was in the summer of 1893; the exhibits covered 686 acres and were seen by more than 21 million visitors. Although Anthony continued to keep a low profile out of respect to Palmer, she did attend a number of receptions that spring and summer, and when tens of thousands of people made clear their eagerness to see her, she felt that the women's movement was finally achieving success. The Exposition also was notable because LUCY STONE made the last of her famous speeches there. Her friends commissioned a bust of her from sculptor Ann Whitney that was displayed at the Expo, and Lucy Stone died only a few months later.

The most striking event of the Exposition occured in May, when the World's Congress of Representative Women convened. The first such event in human history, it gathered together women from twenty-seven nations, who were delegates from 126 organizations. So popular was this new opportunity for women that though the building in which the meeting was held could seat ten thousand, there were constantly lines waiting to get in. More than a dozen simultaneous sessions were held every day for a week, with 150,000 total attendance.

A marvel of organizational ability for its time, this gathering was of tremendous significance to women, who had little opportunity until that era even to attend meetings, let alone be in charge of them. The explosion of ideas and the personal contacts made during the Columbian Exposition had echoing effects for years, as all across America women went back to small towns and used the CLUB MOVEMENT of the 1890s to implement the ideas discussed in Chicago. The National Household Economic Association, which promoted the new field of HOME ECONOMICS, was only one of several bodies that had its roots in contacts established at this fair. Indeed, the Columbian Exhibition prompted so much discussion and so many women speakers that the published proceedings fill six interesting volumes.

COMEDY AND COMEDIANS

The dying usage of "comedienne" to denote a female comic is illustrative of the changes recently made by women in this area. Until the twentieth century, however, women may have had less performance opportunity in comedy than in any other creative field.

While female ACTRESSES became acceptable on the stage in colonial times, they were most often featured in dramatic roles, and when they appeared in comedies, women were more likely to have "straight lines" instead of those that pro-

duced the comedic effect. Women as stand-up comedians remained extremely rare, even after such turn-of-the-century women as FANNY BRICE began to prepare the public for women in active, rather than passive, comedic roles. For many years, women remained far more likely to be the object of jokes than the teller of them.

Radio began to change this in the 1930s, especially when GRACIE ALLEN demonstrated how popular women comedians could be even while limited to "dizzy dame" roles. LUCILLE BALL, adding to this befuddled woman tradition, reached great popularity on the new medium of television in the 1950s. When occasionally women were portrayed as both funny and smart, compensation was made by giving them an inherently inferior status—as in "Hazel," who both in print cartoons and on television, regularly proved to be smarter than anyone in town, and yet contentedly remained a maid.

As television matured in the 1970s, Phyllis Diller, Joan Rivers, and others broke new ground for women as stand-up comedians, while Erma Bombeck used a gentler print style to join them in a revolutionary willingness to laugh at motherhood. After that, all bets were off, as the women of "Laugh In" and "Saturday Night Live" took on any number of previous sacrosanct areas as the targets of their jokes. By the 1990s, the liberation of women in comedy was complete, as new female comedians, particularly on cable TV, rivaled men in scatology with jokes on menstruation, sexual activity, and other subjects hitherto unspoken outside of the most intimate conversation, let alone on national television.

Meanwhile, women also emerged in cartooning. Nonpolitical newspaper cartoons began with the "Mutt and Jeff" comic strip in 1907; in more sophisticated cartooning, the *New Yorker* magazine led the way in the 1920s. From the beginning, it featured women such as Rea Irvin and HELEN HOKINSON, while in the newspapers and in animation, Marge Henderson's "Little Lulu" became a success. While cartoonists remained overwhelmingly male, their images of women slowly began to change. Though the dizzy dame remained in strips such as "Blondie," those that featured women in a strongly negative way, such as "Maggie and Jiggs," faded from popularity by the 1960s. They were replaced by a wider range of female types, such as those of "Doonesbury," which, while it had a stereotypically dumb woman in Boopsie, also had a congresswoman and, even more strikingly, a woman who left her husband and children to go to law school in the 1970s. A decade later, entire FEMINIST families could be found in "Sally Forth" and "For Better or For Worse." While the vast majority of cartoonists continued to be male, Cathy Guisewite set a new standard with her "Cathy," an uproarious chronicle of the trials of single women.

Laughter is a liberating experience, and successful American revolutionaries from the "Boston Tea Party" onwards have seen the value of packaging explosive thoughts with a light touch. By this measurement, women comedians in the late twentieth century provide a solid benchmark of achievement for all women.

COMSTOCK LAW/COMSTOCK COMMISSIONS

So effective was the crusading of moralist Anthony Comstock that his name was used in the early twentieth century as a common noun denoting censorship—seizing artistic work as pornographic, for example, was called "comstocking." The effect of his movement on women was great, since he not only strengthened double standards of morality, but also significantly retarded the BIRTH CONTROL movement during the half-century between 1870 and 1930.

Comstockian promotion of double standards limiting women while excusing men can be most clearly seen in the trial of VICTORIA WOODHULL for the 1872 "crime" of telling the Victorian world of the illicit sexual activity of the era's most popular preacher in the TILTON-BEECHER AFFAIR. Indeed, it was free speech that was the true target of most Comstock activity, not necessarily changed behavior.

The most serious censorship affecting women's lives was the 1873 passage of federal legislation known as the "Comstock Law," which defined information on contraception as inherently obscene, and as such, forbade its distribution through the U.S. mail. Comstock received a special appointment as a U.S. Postal Inspector, which, with renewals, allowed him to conduct an intellectual reign of terror for the rest of his life. Under the law, mailings were seized, newspapers raided, and speakers entrapped. The result was that editors censored any article that might suggest women could control their reproductive rate, while sellers of contraceptive products produced by new rubber industry developments found that they could not advertise. Newspapers read by IMMIGRANT WOMEN that accepted advertising from abortionists and booksellers with cultural standards that differed from Comstock's found their businesses shut down, even when the controversial subject matter was in a foreign language.

Several VICE COMMISSIONS on the subjects of PROSTITUTION and other sexuality issues also were closely associated with Comstock's name. The last at which he was present was held in 1915; under the aegis of President Wilson, its official title of the International Purity Congress is especially ironic in view of the epidemic rates of sexually transmitted diseases among young men then fighting WORLD WAR I.

Possessed of so great an ego that he boasted he had driven at least fifteen people to suicide, Anthony Comstock met his maker in 1915. His legacy continued long after, however, particularly in the Post Office's attempts to halt the work of MARGARET SANGER, MARY WARE DENNETT, and others during the decade after Comstock's death.

CONFEDERATE WOMEN Despite strong evidence to the contrary, the image of the helplessly passive Southern belle has been a favorite fixture of American mythology. Even in what is probably the best-known story of this prototype, *Gone With the Wind*, readers and especially moviegoers have chosen to steadfastly ignore MARGARET MITCHELL's clear portrayal of Scarlett as an ambitious, hard-working, and clever businesswoman.

Aside from fictional assertions, however, Confederate women left a good deal of information showing their CIVIL WAR roles to have been anything but passive. They recorded comparisons of themselves to REVOLUTIONARY WAR WOMEN and saw secession from the Union as analogous to the colonies' separation from Britain. Like their grandmothers in that era, Southern women toiled as NURSES on battlegrounds and in make-shift hospitals; they raised money to fund their armies and defended their homes from marauding soldiers, while

doing without many of the necessities of life because of blockades and then because of destruction. Especially in sieges such as Vicksburg, starving women cooked rats and tree bark for their children; in Richmond and Mobile, women rioted in bread shortages.

Nor was the war limited to those in the Deep South. Indeed, its effect on women in border states often was worse, for during the four long years of the war, some saw their homes taken by one side and then recaptured by the other more than once. Yet even in such dangerous places, there were women whose activities in support of the South were so defiant that Union officers had no choice but to ignore the era's chivalric attitudes and arrest them.

Elizabeth Waring Duckett, for instance, was an eastern Maryland resident who was jailed in Washington's Old Capitol Prison for a month in 1863 because of her Southern sympathies and presumed treason. When released, she continued to help Confederates in the Washington area prisoner-of-war camps and worked for the release of her prisoner father and brother, twice personally lobbying President Lincoln on behalf of these rebels. Duckett wrote, for example, of a train trip back from Fort Delaware, where she had seen her father: "I was the only woman on the car. The men, all soldiers, had been drinking, and I was really afraid to sleep; but I had a revolver in my belt which I intended to use if necessary." Duckett's sisters showed similar resolve; one of them, Julia Waring, went South to work in the Confederate Treasury Department in Richmond, a most unconventional occupation for a woman at the time.

Duckett's experience in prison, however, was not nearly as bad as that of a Louisiana woman, an Irish-American recorded only as Mrs. William Kirby. After Federal occupation of the Baton Rouge area, Mrs. Kirby began stealing soldiers' supplies and running them through the lines to rebels. Finally caught with two cavalry rifles under her dress, she was sentenced to close confinement on Ship Island, where, depressed and weakened by poor prison food, she died.

The victor of any war inevitably writes the history of those times, and therefore, it is not surprising that women of the North are better known than women of the South. CLARA BARTON, for example, has an almost exact parallel in Ella K. Trader, for the aptly named trader had the same executive abilities in procurement in which Barton excelled. Between 1861 and 1865, she moved with the armies, establishing hospitals in Memphis, Nashville, and Chattanooga, Tennessee; Bowling Green, Kentucky; Corinth, Mississippi; and, finally, Atlanta. Sometimes she ordered an entire railroad car of goods to be bought at her own expense.

Betsy Sullivan, known as "Mother Sullivan" by the soldiers for whom she cared, was a soldier's wife, who, since she had no children, had gone with her husband to the war. Joining the First Tennessee Regiment in northern Virginia, "she marched on foot [and] slept on the frozen ground." When her husband was wounded and taken prisoner in October 1862, she went with him to a prisoner-of-war camp. The experience of a Kentucky woman, Bettie Taylor Philips, was similar; she also accompanied her husband to war and nursed at Shiloh, Donelson, and other battlefields.

As on the Union side, there were Confederate women who disguised themselves as soldiers, fought, and died; to the

South also belongs the exploits of daring women spies, especially ROSE GREENHOW and BELLE BOYD. The execution of MARY SURRATT for her presumed role in Lincoln's assassination is another clear example of limits of chivalric myths. Finally, perhaps the best tribute to the activism of Southern women was made by an enemy, when Union General Shields wrote to Secretary of War Stanton in the spring of 1862 that reinforcements were imperative: "I can retake the [Shenandoah] Valley . . . but you must send men to keep it. The women will take it if we don't."

CONGRESSIONAL UNION (CU) Seldom called by its formal name of the Congressional Union for Woman Suffrage, the group began as a loosely organized local society in the Washington, D.C. area. The CU became a transitional organization for ALICE PAUL and her supporters; it was the mechanism by which Paul separated from her initial work in the NATIONAL AMERICAN WOMAN SUFFRAGE ASSOCIATION (NAWSA) and went on to leadership of the WOMAN'S PARTY.

As head of the NAWSA's Congressional Committee, Paul and her friend LUCY BURNS led the lobbying work during the congressional session of 1913 for a suffrage amendment to the United States Constitution. But when Paul retained that chairmanship while also serving as head of the CU that she and Burns formed that same year, a power struggle was inevitable

That the summer headquarters of the Congressional Union/Woman's Party was in the fashionable resort town of Newport, Rhode Island, is indicative of the affluence of much of the leadership of this more impatient faction of the suffrage movement. Note the Suffragist *newspaper held by the woman on the far left and the map in the window, which shows the relative conservatism of the South.* LIBRARY OF CONGRESS.

between the older, more staid members of the NAWSA and its more militant CU offspring. After a tumultuous summer convention and complicated follow-up negotiations, Paul was removed from her NAWSA role and, early in 1914, the groups separated.

The CU reflected the experience Burns and Paul had in the British SUFFRAGE MOVEMENT and took a parliamentary approach; they held the political party in power responsible for women's lack of the vote, whether or not individuals in that party were supportive of women. Thus, the CU urged FEMINISTS in the twelve states where women were enfranchised to vote against all Democrats in the congressional elections of 1914, because a Democrat (Woodrow Wilson) held the White House. The result was that even those Democrats who had given women the right to vote in their own states were targeted for defeat because of the apathy of their national party, a position that NAWSA women found untenable. CU policy seemed even more irrational to NAWSA members after the election, when twenty of the forty-three Democrats targeted were defeated—all of whom had voted for suffrage.

Yet whether or not one agreed with this strategy, it was clear that the CU membership, which rose to about fifty thousand by 1916, was a political powerhouse in terms of making threats real. More technically skilled and dynamic than most suffragists, CU women were also well financed, in part due to generous support from ALVA BELMONT. Among other activities, these funds supported a weekly newspaper, the *Suffragist*. The group also was adept at introducing political visibility to the cause, utilizing parades, street theater, campaign buttons and banners, and later, militant protest that resulted in arrest.

To make its cause clear for the campaign against Wilson's reelection, at its convention in June, 1916, the CU reorganized itself as the NATIONAL WOMAN'S PARTY.

CONNELY, CORNELIA (1809–1879)
An interesting example of the subordinate positon of women in religion, Connelly was a thiry-one-year-old married woman with three children when her husband decided that he wished to become a Catholic priest. Canon law allowed only one way for him to achieve his ambition: to obtain the deed of separation that would effectively dissolve his marriage; his wife had to agree to enter a convent.

Mrs. Connelly gave up her children and entered the sisterhood in 1844, and soon was accorded such respect that she was chosen to establish a new order in England. Her husband, unable to adjust to her independence, followed her to England and tried to take over the order and when he could not, renounced his ordination and the church, sued for resumption of his conjugal rights, and spent the rest of his life defaming her character.

For her patient martyrdom, as well as her service as the mother superior of the half-dozen schools that she founded in England, France, and the United States, she was proposed for beatification in 1959.

CORBIN, MARGARET COCHRAN (1751–c.1800)
Although she is often confused with the similar historical figure known as MOLLY PITCHER, Corbin's experience in becoming the first woman to earn a disabled soldier's pension is well documented.

Margaret Cochran was orphaned at five when her father was killed and her mother captured in hostilities with natives on the Pennsylvanian frontier. Like other FRONTIER WOMEN, Mrs. Cochran never returned, and Margaret grew up with relatives. She married John Corbin at twenty-one, and when the American Revolution began four years later, they went east together to join the fight.

Margaret Corbin was thus present with other REVOLUTIONARY WAR WOMEN who were CAMP FOLLOWERS on the battlefield near Manhattan's Fort Washington on November 16, 1776, when her husband, an artillery gunner, was shot through the head by Hessian fire. Taking no time to mourn, she immediately assumed his battle station and kept up the cannon fire, and though wounded by grapeshot, she stayed in position until the post was surrendered.

Corbin's injuries were permanently disabling, and three years later, the Continental Congress granted her a pension based on her "distinguished bravery." Though she remarried in 1782, she continued to be included on regimental muster lists until the formal end of the war in 1783.

Since her second husband was listed like her as an indigent invalid, she probably lived an impoverished life before dying, apparently prior to her fiftieth birthday. In 1926, the DAUGHTERS OF THE AMERICAN REVOLUTION erected a monument to her at West Point, over what they believed to be her bones.

CORNELL, KATHERINE (1893–1974)
Supported both financially by an inheritance from her mother and intellectually by a father whose devotion to theater was so great that he gave up a medical practice for it, Cornell joined the Washington Square Players in 1916 and spent the rest of her life as an ACTRESS and producer.

Her first hit was in London in 1919 under the tutelage of a woman producer, Jessie Bonstelle. During the twenties, Cornell was featured in almost a dozen Broadway plays, most of them produced by her husband, Gutherie McClintic, whom she married in 1921. At the end of the twenties, she joined him in backstage management while continuing to act.

Showing an innovative management style, Cornell responded to the Great Depression by taking first-rate actors out on national tours, an experience she thought vital to artistic expression as well as financially rewarding. Similar creative management can be seen with Cornell's very first production in 1931, *The Barretts of Wimpole Street* (in which she played Elizabeth Barrett), for although the play had been turned down by more than two dozen other producers, it ended up earning a huge profit.

Cornell finished the thirties with publication of her autobiography, *I Wanted To Be An Actress* (1939). The forties were occupied with playing for soldiers in Europe; her first venture into movies, a war morale effort; and comforting revivals of classics on Broadway. She made the transition to television with two productions in the fifties and also made her second movie, on HELEN KELLER, which won an Academy Award in 1955. Katherine Cornell's last performance was in 1960, and her husband died the following year.

Far more than most producers, Cornell and McClintic Productions were inclusive of women. Cornell learned early on that women did not need to hide their strengths: Her first lead role was that of Jo in *Little Women*, a strong woman in a play both written and produced by women; the playwright for her Broadway debut was RACHEL CROTHERS; and her first significant acclaim as an actress was in a 1924 production of feminist George Bernard Shaw's *Candida*. As a producer herself, Cornell portrayed women in significant roles, as indicated in several Barrett revivals, as well as classics that featured powerful women such as Saint Joan, Antigone, and Cleopatra. Clearly, she understood that the public would respond warmly to female characterization as intelligent and independent.

CRABTREE, LOTTA (CHARLOTTE) (1847–1924) A nineteenth-century ACTRESS, she is remarkable for managing to create (in a time before image makers) a celebrity image that made her popular with Victorian audiences despite her beginnings as a performer in the rough male mining camps of the Far West.

Lotta, as she came to be known, was not yet in her teens when, with her mother, she toured California's frontier towns. She made her New York debut during the CIVIL WAR, when she was seventeen, and played for many years thereafter in England and the United States, enjoying tremendous popularity, especially in roles developed by Charles Dickens, who was riding a crest of popularity in the same era.

Given that a childlike style defined her, Lotta was fortunate to work until age forty-four, when she retired in 1891 as the Gay Nineties began. She died at seventy-seven in Boston, a complete contrast to her Wild West origins.

CRANDALL, PRUDENCE (1803–1890) Prudence Crandall's fame rests on just two years of her life, 1833–1834. The product of a QUAKER education, she opened a girls' school in Canterbury, Connecticut in 1831, and two years later, when she still in her twenties, found herself the subject of national controversy.

Her parents and the community had encouraged her to open the school, which was not unusual for single women of this era, especially Quakers: what caused the controversy was her acceptance of a black girl as a student. The daughter of a freedman who farmed in the area, the girl had already completed her primary education in the district school and wished to train for TEACHING other girls of her race. All of this made her so respectably middle class that Crandall, who had not intended to do anything particularly radical, was surprised by the town's rabid negativism.

Her response, however, was not to give in as her neighbors expected, but rather to strengthen her resolve; Crandall's basic Quaker belief in ABOLITION became focused, and, instead of backing down, she expanded her efforts on behalf of "young ladies and little misses of color." She wrote to abolitionist William Lloyd Garrison in January, 1833, and he responded by helping her recruit young black women from prosperous families throughout the Northeast. In April, she reopened her school as expressly a teacher-training institute for young black women, who began arriving at the school, which was a big boarding house prominently located near the town common.

Many of her neighbors did not consider themselves to be illiberal, and some were involved in efforts to end slavery and resettle blacks in Africa, which was in itself a controversial position for the early 1830s. They expressed outrage instead at what they saw as Crandall's deliberate obstinacy in accepting their financial support for opening the original school and then excluding them from its governance while completely changing its nature. She, of course, saw these objections as simply a cover for their genuine prejudice against the skin color of her students.

Canterbury's leadership organized to close down the school, first through social ostracism and exclusion from the local Congregational Church, as well as through economic boycott when local merchants refused to sell to her. After those tactics failed, the town successfully sought state legislation designed to cover the case. Passed in May, Connecticut's "black law" banned schools from teaching "any colored person . . . not an inhabitant . . . in this state" without permission of the town government. Again, the citizens demonstrated what they considered to be a more enlightened attitude than most people of their era, for the law provided education for Connecticut children of both races, and even out-of-state students might be taught with the town's permission.

But abolitionists understandably took up Crandall's side of the argument, and the cause was joined. When Miss Crandall, a Quaker schoolmarm, was arrested and jailed, newspapers throughout the country responded with alarm, providing invaluable publicity for the still-infant abolitionist movement—who milked the story for all it was worth, allowing Crandall to spend the night in jail before posting her bail.

That there was some local sympathy for her can be seen in the fact that her first trial ended with a hung jury (juries, of course, were all male in this era). The second trial convicted her, but was overturned by a higher court the next July. Meanwhile, opposition passed from town government to its rabble, and Crandall coped with emotional terrorism and property damage. Stones were thrown through windows and even at Crandall and her sister. Among other trials, the school had to bring its water from the Crandall farm two miles away because of the deliberate pollution of their well. When a mob assailed the school on a September night in 1834, Prudence Crandall's spirit was broken.

In the midst of all this chaos and danger, she had fallen in love with Reverend Calvin Philleo, an abolitionist despite his Baptist faith, and married him a month before the mob attack. They left Canterbury, and she became a mother to his three children. Although they talked of opening another school for black girls in a large city, they went west to Illinois in 1842. She joined in women's rights activities and, like many other TEACHERS on the frontier, ran a school in her home. When her husband died in 1874, she moved on to live with a brother in Kansas, where she continued to speak for the SUFFRAGE MOVEMENT and temperance.

The Connecticut legislature attempted to atone for the state's past wrongs by voting her a modest pension in 1886, four years before her death.

CROLY, JANE CUNNINGHAM (1829–1901) Croly's newspaper articles under the PSEUDONYM of "JENNIE JUNE" became so popular that she emerged as a persona in her own right, playing a crucial role in the CLUB MOVEMENT that dominated the lives of many women leaders in the late nineteenth century.

Jane Cunningham's family came to the United States from England when she was twelve. Educated at home, she worked marginally as a TEACHER until her father's death in 1854 forced her to seek more remunerative employment. She moved to New York City, freelanced as a newspaper writer and, within a few years, was regularly published in several papers; showing exceptional creativity, she also sent copies of her articles for publication in other cities. She continued to work after her 1856 marriage to David Croly and—most unconventionally—even after becoming a mother. She eventually bore five children, four of whom lived to adulthood.

From 1862 to 1872, while her husband was managing editor of the *New York World,* Croly headed its women's section, establishing important precedents for the inclusion of a broader range of subjects in daily newspapers. She also published *Jennie June's American Cookery Book* (1866) and a collection of columns, *Jennie Juneiana: Talks on Women's Topics* (1869); she contributed to magazines and was active in New York's literary society, where she made many contacts that proved valuable in the creation of the club movement.

This movement generally is dated to Croly's 1868 formation, with ALICE CARY and others, of a club called SOROSIS. Prompted by the exclusion of women from a New York Press Club function for Charles Dickens, Croly intended Sorosis to provide women with an independent network and support group (though those terms would not be used until more than a century later).

While she may have worked from choice during the decade with the *World,* Croly's husband exhibited financial irresponsibility throughout their marriage, and her income became fundamental to the family after he became unemployed and then ill during the late 1870s and 1880s. Despite these burdens, she was remembered by her contemporaries as invariably cheerful and energetically practical, and this attitude showed in her work. In 1875, she published *For Better or Worse* on marriage and in 1891, two years after her husband's death, a book of advice to working women, *Thrown on Her Own Resources*—a title that doubtless reflected the reality of her personal life.

Her husband's death probably provided Croly with the freedom to expand her activities, for also in 1891, she organized the Women's Press Club in New York and called a national meeting that resulted in the formation of the GENERAL FEDERATION OF WOMEN'S CLUBS. Though she edited several women's magazines in this era, Croly increasingly concentrated her attention on the club movement. She was, for example, the keynote speaker for a meeting that led to the formation of the Atlanta Woman's Club, but her major contribution was not so much that of an organizer but rather as a chronicler, thereby facilitating the transfer of the ideas of established clubs to new places. By 1898, she had done so much work of this sort that she was able to publish a massive *History of the Women's Club Movement in America.*

Much more liberal than many of the women who came to dominate the club movement, Croly's writing from its beginning advocated fair treatment of blacks, liberation from foolish fashion decrees, and especially equal educational and employment opportunity for women—along with equal responsibilities that necessitated more sensible attitudes than those adopted by many style-setters of this era. Though she supported suffrage in the abstract, Croly spent little of her time in the SUFFRAGE MOVEMENT, for she believed that economic and social change were more important than political change—and that the vote would follow if women were emotionally and financially independent.

CROSBY, FANNY (FRANCES JANE) (1820–1915)
Educated in a New York City institution for the blind, Crosby had an innate talent for versification and published her first poetry early in the 1840s. After graduation, she stayed at the school to TEACH, and in the 1850s, began to set her words to music. Her songs became sufficiently popular that she retained the use of her MAIDEN NAME when she married another blind teacher at the school in 1858.

During the CIVIL WAR years, she moved from light secular songs to sacred music and there truly found her life's work. Collaborating with more than twenty musicians, Crosby was the lyricist for an astonishing number of hymns: because she used more than one hundred different PSEUDONYMS, her complete body of work is difficult to measure, but she wrote more than five thousand and perhaps as many as nine thousand hymns during the latter half of the nineteenth century.

Her work was especially popular in the Methodist Church, with "Blessed Assurance," as probably the best recognized title today. In addition, she participated in CHAUTAUQUA meetings and published several books of poetry as well as two volumes of autobiography in 1903 and 1906. Blind from the age of six weeks, Frances Crosby lived to be ninety-five.

CROTHERS, RACHEL (1878–1958)
Unlike most women in the theater, Crothers spent only a limited time as an ACTRESS before going on to become the most financially successful female playwright of her era.

Beginning in 1902, she wrote, produced, and directed three decades of plays that had longer runs than the Broadway average. The author of more than three dozen scripts, Crothers' gender enabled her to create female characters that were genuine, and she promoted FEMINIST ideas with a humorous touch that found receptive audiences. Though she denied any formal feminist intentions, her plays—with titles such as *A Man's World* (1909), *He and She* (1911), and *When Ladies Meet* (1932)—consistently examined aspects of the relationships between men and women.

Her last work to be produced, *Susan and God,* was staged in 1937, but she did not retire, for during both WORLD WAR I and II, Crothers played a leadership role in producing entertainment for soldiers. She stayed on until age seventy-two as executive director of the Stage Door Canteens, which flew entertainers all over the world for American troops. An active member of the Authors League and of P.E.N., Crothers won prizes for *When Ladies Meet* and *Susan and God.*

CRUSO, THALASSA (1908–   )
Though she retains her native English accent, Cruso has lived in the Boston area since 1935. Since the late 1960s, she has educated the nation on gardening with her books and especially her television shows.

Although she also has credentials as an archaeologist and curator, it was Cruso's lifelong hobby of gardening that brought her public recognition in 1967, when WGBH, Boston's outstanding public television station, began broadcasting her highly individualistic "Making Things Grow." Cruso's practical approach to gardening, her unfailing sense of humor, and her candor in dealing with gardening failures combined to make the show so lively that it quickly spread not only throughout the educational television network but even to commercial television. Her regular appearances on Johnny Carson's "Tonight Show" made Cruso a familiar figure to millions.

Two years after the TV show began, its principles were translated into a book, *Making Things Grow* (1969). It soon became a standard with indoor gardeners, and she followed it with *Making Things Grow Outdoors* (1974), *Making Vegetables Grow* (1975), and the more reflective, philosophical *To Everything There Is A Season* (1973). Cruso's insightful references to English gardening and her strict injunctions to correlate a plant's care to its native environment have provided new views even for experienced gardeners, while her entertaining style has delighted newcomers to the field. A member of several international horticultural societies, she has won many gardening awards.

CUMMINS, MARIA SUSANNA (1827–1866)
A lifelong resident of Massachusetts, Maria Susanna Cummins was amazingly successful with her first novel, *The Lamplighter* (1854). It sold an unheard-of forty thousand copies in the first few weeks after publication and seventy thousand in its first year.

Like Charles Dickens, who became popular in the same era, Cummins' work was based on sentimental emotion and implausible plot devices. She was the specific target of Nathaniel Hawthorne's general criticism of women AUTHORS, but the equally astonishing sales of her book in French and German translations demonstrated that approval was not limited to the presumably less refined tastes of early America.

Cummins, like a number of other authors of both genders, never had another book that equaled the expectations resulting from the phenomenal success of her first. She published three more novels between 1857 and 1864, but died at age forty-one, a mere twelve years after her first publication.

CURTIS, DORIS MALKIN (1914–1991)
A geologist during an era when women seldom worked in such fields, she spent most of her career exploring for Shell Oil. Curtis also taught at Rice University in Houston and began operating her own consulting firm in 1979, after the energy crisis of the late 1970s brought attention to the need for oil exploration.

Recognized by her male colleagues as a leader in their field, Curtis was president of the seventeen thousand-member Geological Society of America when she died at seventy-seven.

CUSHMAN, CHARLOTTE (1816–1876)
One of America's earliest outstanding ACTRESSES, Charlotte Cushman had experience in opera, drama, and even as a theater manager in New Orleans, New York, and Philadelphia before her 1845 London stage debut brought her overnight acclaim.

When she performed for Queen Victoria three years later, Cushman had become a specialist in Shakespearean plays. She even acted Romeo, with her sister playing Juliet, and went on to play masculine roles dozens of times, without diminishment of her feminine popularity. She was also un-

usual in her era for the seriousness with which she approached her task, including field research into the speech and mannerisms of people similar to the characters she portrayed on the stage.

Cushman returned to the United States in 1849 and toured the country for the next three years, being received everywhere with tremendous pride in her international success—something that was still very unusual for Americans in this era. A shrewd investor of the money she earned, Cushman went into semi-retirement after 1852. She lived abroad much of the time, but returned occasionally to the stage, including benefit performances for the U.S. SANITARY COMMISSION during the CIVIL WAR.

With her close friend, Emma Stebbens, she returned to the U.S. in 1870, established homes in Boston and Newport, and lived out the rest of her life there. The level of respect in which she was held can be seen in the "Charlotte Cushman Clubs" that existed up until the middle of the twentieth century. Though criticized for overplaying roles even in this melodramatic era and also criticized for an excessive number of "farewell" appearances, Charlotte Cushman remains the most renowned actress of her time.

CUSHMAN, PAULINE (1833–1893)
Called "Laughing Breeze" by the Michigan Chippewas with whom she grew up, Pauline Cushman was skilled at riding, shooting, and canoeing when she left Grand Rapids for New York City at about eighteen. She became an ACTRESS and was on tour in Louisville when she played the genuine role in the CIVIL WAR for which she is remembered.

Though not nearly as serious a spy as the Confederacy's BELLE BOYD and ROSE GREENHOW, Pauline Cushman did enough to be recognized by the *New York Herald* as the "gallant Scout of the Cumberland who did such noble work for the Union in Tennessee." She was among several women employed by William Truesdail, chief of the army police, to use their contacts with Confederates to gather information of use to the Union. Truesdail sent her South early in 1863, after first establishing credibility for her by "evicting" her from Nashville as a secessionist sympathizer.

Ostensibly searching for her brother, Cushman spent several weeks in rebel encampments throughout the Tennessee Valley, picking up valuable information. More eager than wise, however, she also drew sketches of troop placements and stole maps, which were found in her boots a few weeks later when she was returning through the lines to Nashville. She was arrested and taken South, but managed to escape her guard in a storm. Again just eight miles from Nashville, she was arrested a second time and was escorted to the headquarters of General Braxton Bragg because the case was "a grave one."

Indeed it was, for Southern chivalry did not include female Yankee spies, and in June, Cushman was court martialed at Shelbyville, Tennessee, and actually was sentenced to death. A few days later, though, the Union attacked, the rebels retreated, and Cushman was rescued from her cell by Federals. They continued to exhibit great concern for her, with General Rosecrans issuing orders to pay for her care at a Nashville boarding house where she was to be nursed back to health after her ordeal. Both he and General Garfield visited her sickbed, and awarded her the honorary rank of major with the right to wear military regalia.

Cushman did no more spying, and instead toured the country for the next decade, wearing her uniform and delivering her Civil War "narrative." She continued to act in the Far West during the 1870s, and in the 1880s, was still called "the Major" as she successfully ran hotels in Arizona. Though she had rejected proposals from several men—including publicly horsewhipping one whose attentions were excessive—she fell hopelessly in love with a younger man, and in 1879, asked him to marry her.

From that point on, her life was a downward spiral. In a pathetic attempt to retain her husband's interest, she adopted a baby that she pretended was her own; when the truth was finally revealed after the child died six years later, she had no choice but to return to California, where her sad attempts to return to the stage proved futile. In constant pain from arthritis, Pauline Cushman ended her days working as a scrubwoman for her room and board.

When she died from an overdose of the morphine she took for her aching bones, the San Francisco newspapers belatedly revived the story of her Civil War role and saved her from a pauper's burial. She was buried with an honor guard from the Grand Army of the Republic.

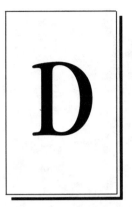

DAME SCHOOLS The term for early American schools operated by women, usually in Northern cities and towns, these schools were one of the few methods of earning a living open to women in a largely agricultural economy. Run by WIDOWS and SPINSTERS, often in their homes, such schools were supported by tuition. They were primarily intended for girls, although boys sometimes attended them for rudimentary instruction.

Their academic curriculum was limited to simple reading, writing, spelling, and arithmetic, for often the TEACHER had little formal education herself since females were excluded from COLLEGES in this era. Dame schools also taught sewing and similar feminine arts, and it was not uncommon for a girl to be enrolled at more than one simultaneously to learn a variety of skills on different days from teachers of different abilities.

Wealthy colonial families hired tutors for their sons to prepare for Harvard, Yale, and other institutions that were completely closed to young women. While tutors occasionally also taught the daughters of a household, this opportunity was limited by both the unseemliness of a man teaching an adolescent girl and the reluctance of such tutors to do the elementary teaching of younger daughters. As American wealth increased after the colonial era, young women might be sent to FINISHING SCHOOLS, and still wealthier families in the nineteenth century would employ GOVERNESSES for their daughters' elementary education. The dame school, however, was likely to be the best opportunity available to girls for most of the first two hundred years of American history.

DARE, VIRGINIA (1587–?) The mysterious and presumably brief life of Virginia Dare has long been immortalized in pageant and poem. The first recorded birth of a child to European parents in the Western Hemisphere, she came into the world on August 18, 1587. Though she was named in honor of the new country that the English called VIRGINIA, her actual birthplace was Roanoke Island, which is now part of North Carolina.

Her mother, Elenor (or Elyonor/Ellinor) White Dare, doubtless had worried about going into labor while still at sea, for she barely made it to the new land before her child was born. Clearly a woman of courage, Dare was one of just seventeen women in a party of 116 that left Plymouth on May 8, when she was probably six months pregnant. The expedition was commanded by her father, John White; Dare's husband, Ananias, was presumably her social inferior, for he was a bricklayer by trade.

Though the group intended to settle on the mainland of Virginia, they landed at their mistaken destination in July. It may well be that it was the expected arrival of his grandchild that motivated John White to set up the colony on Roanoke Island, where an earlier expedition by Sir Walter Raleigh had already failed, rather than continue explorations. At any rate, the child was presumably healthy, for she was christened on the following Sunday, August 24, and three days later, her grandfather sailed for England to make his reports and renew supplies.

When he returned three years later—after having been delayed by the famous defeat of the Spanish Armada by the

The opening session of the 1913 convention of the Daughters of the American Revolution. LIBRARY OF CONGRESS; PHOTO BY HARRIS & EWING.

naval forces of Queen Elizabeth I—his daughter, granddaughter, and the rest of the settlement had vanished. "The Lost Colony" left only the word "Croatoan" carved on a tree. Most who have studied the mystery believe this to mean that the colonists, unable to support themselves on the island in winter, had gone to join the friendly Croatoan tribe on the mainland, but others argue that the cryptic message was hurriedly written as Croatoans attacked. When the JAMESTOWN colony was established two decades later, natives told the English of white people living to the south, but no verification was ever established.

Little Virginia Dare came to symbolize belief in the future, despite adversity. Her mother, who should be remembered more than the child, certainly had shown such courage.

DAUGHTERS OF THE AMERICAN REVOLUTION, NATIONAL SOCIETY OF (DAR)

Its 1890 founding date was a year after the 1889 formation of the Sons of the American Revolution. That the Daughters became by far the better known organization is indicative of the strength of the women's CLUB MOVEMENT in that era. Moreover, the date is signifi-

cant because, of course, actual daughters, granddaughters, and other descendents of the Revolution had existed for over a hundred years without organization. The 1890 date suggests the new leisure and personal freedom available to club women in the Gilded Age, as well as increased patriotic nationalism after bitter CIVIL WAR and Reconstruction memories began to fade.

Still another factor related to the 1890 founding date is the greatly increased immigration rate of this era. Most DAR founders reacted very negatively to the Jews, Italians, and other immigrant groups from southern and eastern Europe who entered the United States by the millions in the late nineteenth century. The fear of losing their colonial heritage was a strong motivation for the DAR's formation.

The DAR quickly became known as perhaps the most exclusive women's club in America, for members had to trace their genealogy to a soldier who fought for the rebel cause in the Revolution. (A society of descendents of Loyalists was not formed until 1986.) This mandatory connection to a male soldier was just one indication of the patriarchal, conservative attitudes of the membership, for it was not only recent immigrants that the DAR wished to exclude from its membership: although many documented cases exist of black soldiers who served in the Revolution, no black women were permitted to join.

It was this racism that brought the DAR to the attention of much of the public in 1939, during the organization's fourth decade of existence. Ten years earlier, the DAR had built a magnificent Washington headquarters, Constitution Hall. Its four thousand-seat auditorium was the largest in the city, and national publicity resulted when DAR management refused to rent the hall for black artist MARIAN ANDERSON to sing there. First Lady ELEANOR ROOSEVELT resigned the honorary DAR membership she had been given, and dozens of famous Americans signed petitions objecting to the DAR's exclusionary behavior. The concert was held at the Lincoln Memorial instead, and the negative coverage seemed only to reinforce the DAR's emphasis on a nostalgic past. The organization finally accepted its first African-American member in 1977.

Nonetheless, the society deserves credit for preserving and promoting women's history—even if its focus is only on a selected type of woman. The DAR has long maintained a unique genealogical library, containing over sixty thousand books and manuscripts that predate 1830, many of which are available nowhere else. DAR publications during the last century have regularly profiled REVOLUTIONARY WAR WOMEN whose historical contributions otherwise might well have been forgotten. In cities and towns throughout the United States, it is the DAR that has paid for memorials to women, sometimes retrieving a bit of history that is in danger of being lost forever, as in the case of MARGARET CORBIN.

With over two hundred thousand members in more than three thousand chapters today, the DAR remains a powerful women's organization. Its chapters—which are often named for a local woman who figured in the Revolution—award scholarships, sponsor essay contests, and otherwise promote the study of history. With a hundred years of organizational history behind it, the DAR has reached an ironic point of evolution: with members who still list themselves by their husbands' names, they are nonetheless proud that Alex Haley used their genealogical records for his great African-American saga, *Roots*. The DAR's library and museum are open free to the public at 1776 D Street NW in Washington.

DAUGHTERS OF THE CONFEDERACY

Founded in 1894, almost thirty years after the CIVIL WAR ended, the Daughters of the Confederacy is made up of women who are descendents of Confederate soldiers. Its membership in 1990 was twenty-eight thousand organized in approximately one thousand local groups, with a headquarters and historical library located in Richmond. (The Sons of Confederate Veterans, in contrast, was organized two years later, has only 8,500 members in two hundred groups and maintains no headquarters.)

DAUGHTERS OF LIBERTY

The Daughters of Liberty may be considered the first national organization of American women, though it appeared a century prior to the CLUB MOVEMENT. It was more informally organized than the Sons of Liberty, but the Daughters nonetheless played an important role in the lives of REVOLUTIONARY WAR WOMEN. Moreover, the heartfelt participation of women was crucial to the success of rebel aims, particularly in enforcement of the boycott on tea and other English products.

Years before war was declared, these women experimented with substitutes for tea and did the political education to persuade others to use herbs, flowers, and fruit as tea bases rather than buy from English importers. It was the women, too, who returned to raising sheep and carding wool, bringing their spinning wheels down from attics and weaving patriotic homespun rather than buying cloth made in England. The Daughters of Liberty used both political argumentation and ostracism to persuade other women to boycott British goods; they joined the Sons in meetings and marches and some women physically attacked Loyalists who expressed contrary opinions.

When political action turned into actual combat, these women expanded from their Boston Tea Party roots. Known then as the "Ladies Association," Philadelphia women under the leadership of ESTHER DEBERDT REED and SARAH FRANKLIN BACHE raised funds for Washington's Army with a door-to-door canvass for contributions. Exhibiting tremendous persistence in this unconventional effort, they collected more than three hundred thousand continental dollars. Reed wanted to reward each soldier with a "hard dollar," but Washington, believing that most men would spend their money on vices, urged the women instead to invest in cloth and sew for the ragged troops. Similar groups operated in Virginia, New Jersey, and Maryland, where they raised money for medicines and food, in addition to caring for casualties. Trenton women amassed at least fifteen thousand dollars, while a comparable amount was collected in Annapolis.

These groups remained an informal network, however, and passed away with the need when the Revolution was won. In 1875, the National Council of the Sons and Daughters of Liberty was formed to commemorate this history. Based in Pennsylvania, its two thousand members are led by a woman today.

DAVIS, (DAISIE) ADELLE (1904–1974)

When nutrition became a topic of great public interest in the latter part of the twentieth century, Adelle Davis had a genuine claim as its originator, for she had successfully operated a nutrition consulting business since 1931.

An Indiana native, Davis attended Purdue University before moving to California in 1925, where she studied at Berkeley and UCLA. With additional hospital dietary experience in New York City, she was well-credentialed in HOME ECONOMICS and nutrition. These were some of the most acceptable areas for educated women during the Great Depression of the 1930s, when even ELEANOR ROOSEVELT made strong claims for the positive powers of nutritional reform. WORLD WAR II added to the popularity of the field, as rationing and mass feeding of troops brought dieticians' views to the attention of millions previously unaware.

Though the writing she did during the 1930s met only limited success, much of the reading public was ready for her message after the war. California, with its massive wartime population explosion of the young and adventurous, was the right place for her to be. Davis' 1947 *Let's Cook it Right* sold well and was followed by others in the fifties and sixties, with the best known being *Let's Eat Right to Keep Fit*. Her multimillion copy sales showed that the increasingly urbanized public was concerned about their loss of farm-fresh food, and was worried about pesticides and mass manufacturing techniques that refined nutritional values out of food.

RACHEL CARSON's popularity in the same era demonstrated the same. Carson's work, however, was not only in a less traditionally feminine field, but more importantly, was far more scientific than Davis' methodology. Despite her academic credentials, Davis quickly lost credibility with her peers. She hyperbolically linked many of society's problems to bad eating habits; wrote carelessly and was unconcerned with the hundreds of errors in her books; made exaggerated claims for the vitamins and minerals sold by "natural food" stores; and even opposed the pasteurization of milk.

Nonetheless tremendously popular with both men and women, she attracted millions to her views. Davis died of bone cancer shortly after her seventieth birthday.

DAVIS, BETTE (1908–1989)
Ruth Elizabeth Davis' birth, in the textile mill town of LOWELL, Massachusetts at the time of violent STRIKES by women there, stands in ironic contrast to the elegant image she portrayed in her long and successful career as an ACTRESS. She went to New York City to study drama while still in her teens, and by 1929, made her Broadway debut.

Davis moved to Hollywood the following year and in 1934, at age twenty-six, she received major acclaim for *Of Human Bondage*. The very next year brought her first Academy Award for *Dangerous* (1935); three years later, she won a second time for *Jezebel* (1938). Making at least a movie a year during the thirties and forties, Davis nonetheless achieved a reputation for stellar performance and versatility. Among her greatest successes in that era were *Dark Victory* (1939), and two controversial movies about sexual and racial intolerance, *The Man Who Came to Dinner* and LILLIAN HELLMAN's *The Little Foxes*, both made in 1941. *All About Eve* (1950) exhibited Davis' ability to play complex female personalities and won six Oscars.

Though she was a major box office attraction throughout WORLD WAR II, the reversed postwar attitudes on women brought a drop in the number of movies Davis made during the 1950s. Always insistent on scripts that were worthy of serious attention, she sued studios several times for better roles. She returned to Broadway in the fifties, and by the next decade, reigned once more in Hollywood. Again she made a movie a year between 1961 and 1967, the most famous of which, *Whatever Happened to Baby Jane?* (1962) and *Hush, Hush Sweet Charlotte* (1964), featured Davis' chilling depictions of macabre women.

Though a strong personality, Davis was widely popular with men as well as women. She published an autobiography, *The Lonely Life*, in 1962.

DAVIS, FANNY-FERN (1902–1989)
A botanist, Davis was working for the U.S. Golf Association when she adapted a new plant defoliant used by the military into civilian herbicide use. Living in the Washington area during WORLD WAR II, she received permission to demonstrate the weed killer's safety by using it on the White House lawn. During the same era, she worked with her husband, also a botanist, on his pioneering hydroponic growing techniques, which were aimed at increasing the fresh produce available to American troops. Davis headed the biology department at nearby George Mason College, and after retirement to Florida, compiled a statewide inventory of more than seven hundred wildflowers.

DAWIDOWICZ, LUCY S. (1915–1990)
A scholar of Jewish history, Dawidowicz specialized in Holocaust studies at Yeshiva University. She was a New York native, but studied in Poland as a young woman, leaving less than a week before the 1939 German invasion. After WORLD WAR II, she returned to Poland to work with Holocaust survivors and rebuild the library of the Vilna Scientific Institute.

The author of a number of books, Dawidowicz's best known is *The War Against the Jews* (1975), a landmark study of fascist genocide. A year before her death, her memoir of the perilous time she spent in Poland before the Nazi invasion was finally published; *From That Place and Time* (1989) won the National Jewish Book Award.

DAY, DOROTHY (1897–1980)
Almost unique in her combination of practicing Catholicism with self-described anarchism, Dorothy Day's origins were more conventional. She grew up in Brooklyn and was attracted to socialism while studying at the University of Illinois during the early days of WORLD WAR I.

When she returned to New York in 1916, her journalist father, who specialized in sports and opposed FEMINISM, told his editor friends not to hire his daughter. The socialist *Call*, indifferent to the father's commands, hired young Day. She went on the next year to the *Masses*, and, under the editorship of leftist philosopher Max Eastman, brought herself to the attention of government censors for articles opposing the war. A member of the Socialist Party and the Industrial Workers of the World ("Wobblies"), she socialized with New York's literary avant-garde. Like more conventional women, Day also worked as a NURSE in a Brooklyn hospital during the last year of the war. The experience confirmed her as a lifelong pacifist.

She wrote for radical newspapers in Chicago and New Orleans throughout the twenties, and then, in 1927, astounded most of her socialist friends by joining the Catholic Church. She also bore an ILLEGITIMATE daughter in 1927, but Catholicism attracted her largely because she saw it as the strongest institution that identified itself with the poor. In 1932, in the depths of the Great Depression, she began working with a French man on a utopian/Catholic program to develop communal farms aimed at allowing the urbanized poor to support themselves.

Programs of this sort had been tried under the aegis of the Catholic church since the 1840s, when the Irish settling in Boston and New York were encouraged by Church hierarchy to return to morally safer farming. Day's idea met with similarly limited success, though her program—which used the slogan of "green revolution"—did manage to maintain some farms, including one on Staten Island where she personally spent time.

She was often in the city, though, for her genuine success was the publication of the *Catholic Worker*. Begun in 1933, the monthly paper featured Day's brand of radical Catholicism and soon found an audience. Despite Depression problems in launching a new business, the paper had 150,000 subscribers within three years. When its circulation dropped as the Depression eased, Day's editorial stance became even more radical, and the *Catholic Worker* was one of very few publications to oppose WORLD WAR II.

During the 1950s, she continued to generate news by going to jail rather than participate in the civil defense drills that were mandatory in eastern cities during the first days of the nuclear age. During the next two decades, despite her advancing age, Day demonstrated against the Vietnam War and organized farm workers in California. Under her editorship for almost fifty years until her death at eighty-three, the *Catholic Worker* continued to sell for just a penny a copy long after a penny had little value, and it provided publication opportunity for some of the great modern leftist thinkers, especially those of the Vietnam-era counterculture. In the 1990s, it maintains a circulation of almost one hundred thousand.

Day wrote her autobiography, *The Long Loneliness*, in 1952 and selected works by her were published in 1983. Although her pacifism and socialism were widely criticized within the church, Notre Dame University honored her as an outstanding Catholic in 1972. Her ideas became increasingly acceptable throughout that decade, and when the Catholic bishops issued their 1983 pastoral letter on peace, Day was given much credit. A very different person from America's first female saint, FRANCES XAVIER CABRINI, Day's reputation as a great American Catholic leader is clearly on the ascent.

DEBO, ANGIE (1890–1988)

Angie Debo was already in her fifties when she began the career as a historian that would bring her recognition before she died four decades later. As a child, she had come to Oklahoma in a covered wagon soon after the Indian Territory was opened to white settlers; as a middle-aged woman, Debo began writing the history of her home.

Eventually the author of hundreds of articles and more than a dozen books of Oklahoma and Native American history, Debo was ultimately recognized with the John H. Dunning Prize of the American Historical Society and an Alfred A. Knopf Fellowship. Indeed, it was Knopf that disregarded Debo's lack of academic credentials and published her *Prairie City* in 1944.

Like many women AUTHORS, she suffered a decline in the 1950s, but when interest in minorities revived during the sixties, she averaged a book every other year. *And Still the Waters Run* (1966), a portrayal of the liquidation of the Five Civilized Tribes, especially is considered a classic work.

Debo's portrait was hung in the Oklahoma Capitol in 1985, and the governor presented her the American Historical Association's 1987 Award for Scholarly Distinction only a few months before her death at ninety-eight.

DECLARATION OF RIGHTS FOR WOMEN (1848 and 1876)

The 1848 declaration, which is also known as the Declaration of Sentiments, was presented to the first women's rights convention in SENECA FALLS by ELIZABETH CADY STANTON. She modeled it after the nation's Declaration of Independence, using the style that Jefferson used to speak of George III, but substituting man as the oppressor of woman and spelling out the seriousness of her charges against him. The declaration said in part:

"We hold these truths to be self-evident; that all men and women are created equal . . .

The history of mankind is a history of repeated injuries . . . toward woman . . .

He has never permitted her to exercise her inalienable right to the elective franchise.

He has compelled her to submit to laws, in the formation of which she had no voice.

He has withheld from her rights which are given to the most ignorant and degraded men—both natives and foreigners . . .

He has made her, if married, in the eye of the law, civilly dead.

He has taken from her all right in property, even to the wages she earns . . .

He has so framed the laws of divorce . . . and guardianship . . . going on the false supposition of the supremacy of man, and giving all power into his hands.

He has monopolized nearly all the profitable employments . . . He closes against her all the avenues to wealth . . . As a teacher of theology, medicine, or law, she is not known.

He has denied her the facilities for obtaining a thorough education, all colleges being closed against her.

He has created a false public sentiment by giving to the world a different code of morals for men and women . . .

The Seneca Falls Declaration was adopted by the convention, and the women set about implementing its accompanying resolutions, designed to right the wrongs cited. By 1876, some progress had been made, especially in the opening of women's COLLEGES, the entrance of a few women into professions, and improved GUARDIANSHIP and MARRIED WOMEN'S PROPERTY RIGHTS, though these gains varied with state law. SUSAN ANTHONY's updated version, sometimes called the Centennial Declaration, took cognizance of this progress.

The 1876 Declaration was written for the CENTENNIAL EXHIBITION that was held in Philadelphia to celebrate the one hundred years since American independence. The new Declaration placed less emphasis on educational and occupational opportunity, and instead demanded equal political rights, such as the inclusion of women on juries. Between the Declaration's lines, Anthony was already exhibiting concern that PROTECTIVE LEGISLATION would hurt the cause of equality, for the 1876 Declaration ended with:

We ask . . . no special favors, no special privileges, no special legislation. We ask justice, we ask equality, we ask that all the civil and political rights that belong to citizens of the United States, be guaranteed to us and our daughters forever.

DeMILLE, AGNES GEORGE (1905–   )

A member of a prominent stage and film family, DeMille became its first noted woman when she developed into Broadway's leading choreographer during the 1940s and 1950s. Her first acclaim was for Aaron Copland's *Rodeo*, which she choreographed for a Russian ballet company in 1942. The following year, she became widely known with the immensely popular *Oklahoma!* on Broadway. DeMille's most creative work may be *The Fall River Legend* (1948), which told the story of LIZZIE BORDEN.

She organized her own dance company in 1952 and toured throughout the country. DeMille continued to design the dance segments of hits on both stage and screen well into the 1960s and was recognized with many awards. She also authored a number of books on dance, as well as autobiographical works.

DENNETT, MARY COFFIN WARE (1872–1947) A

member of old Boston families, Mary Ware exhibited her independence early by studying art over their objections. It was not in art, however, that she would make her significant contribution to American history, although that background may well have influenced the crusade against censorship for which she should be remembered.

After education abroad and experience running a leather goods business in Boston, she married at twenty-eight, bore three children, and worked with her architect husband in interior design. A decade later, in her late thirties, she began the association with the women's movement that was to be her true destiny. When she was elected corresponding secretary of the NATIONAL AMERICAN WOMAN SUFFRAGE ASSOCIATION in 1910, she moved to New York, and three years later, she DIVORCED.

With the onset of WORLD WAR I in Europe, Dennett became active in pacifist as well as FEMINIST efforts. As field secretary of the American Union Against Militarism in 1916, she campaigned for Wilson's reelection—against the aims of the feminist CONGRESSIONAL UNION—because of Wilson's promises to keep the U.S. out of the war. When he asked Congress to declare war the following year, Dennett showed the strength of her principles by resigning her prestigious position with the Democratic National Committee.

With both suffrage and pacifism taking second place to the war in public attention, Dennett moved to fill a similar void in the BIRTH CONTROL movement. The National Birth Control League was in need of leadership when Dennett became involved in 1915 because its founder, MARGARET SANGER, had taken refuge in Europe from federal prosecution under the COMSTOCK LAW. Unfortunately, Sanger later saw Dennett as a rival rather than a colleague, perhaps in part because of their unusual commonalities: both were divorced from architects, both were the mothers of three children, and both experienced the death of one child.

Under Dennett, the organization was renamed the Voluntary Parenthood League in 1918. Its focus was redirected from protest tactics to sophisticated lobbying for repeal of legislation that banned contraceptive information as well as for greater attention to realistic sex education. Especially concerned with the latter, Dennett wrote a piece for her teenage sons entitled "The Sex Side of Life," and in 1918, it was published by the *Medical Review of Reviews*. The essay came to be known among doctors and enlightened parents as "the best of its kind;" during the next four years, twenty-five thousand copies were distributed under the aegis of the Birth Control League. Although the pamphlet was adopted by even

the YMCA, postal authorities deemed it obscene in 1922 and began a decade of legal difficulties for Dennett.

From 1922 to 1925 she edited the *Birth Control Herald* while battling the post office, as well as colleagues in her own field. Sanger, chagrined by Dennett's takeover of her organization and increasingly under the conservative influence of medical professionals, eventually convinced the League to endorse her new legislative position: Sanger proposed that the League compromise its lobbying position and support amendment of restrictive legislation to allow contraceptive information to be dispensed by physicians only. Dennett was outraged at this reversal of Sanger's earlier views and defended women's right to information about their bodies. When the Voluntary Parenthood League adopted Sanger's position in 1925, Dennett resigned in protest.

She spent the next year writing *Birth Control Laws* (1926), a thorough analysis of state and federal legislation on the subject. Deprived of an organization, Dennett might well have gone into eclipse at this point but for postal officials deciding to entrap and prosecute her for distribution of the "Sex Side of Life." She was indicted in 1928 and convicted the following year in a sensational trial that doubtlessly did her cause more good than harm. Newspapers throughout the country defended this woman who was trying to uphold First Amendment rights against the weight of the federal government. During the Roaring Twenties, public opinion had begun to outgrow the views embodied in the COMSTOCK LAW and, as economic need increased among urbanized people after the 1929 stock market crash, the case for birth control became obvious. People sympathized with Dennett's refusal to pay her three hundred dollar fine, and an appellate court overturned her conviction in 1930.

She celebrated her victory with the publication of a book about the case, *Who's Obscene?* (1930), and the next year, added to her literary credits with *The Sex Education of Children*. During WORLD WAR II, Dennett returned to her interest in peace, and, though entering her seventies, served as the first chairman of the World Federalists (1941–1944). She died a year after the United Nations was born.

DEPARTMENT STORES Until the second half of the nine-

teenth century, most American stores were little more than expanded trading posts that featured male clerks, as well as mostly male customers. Women did relatively little shopping compared with men; in rural areas especially, it was the man of the family who took farm goods to town to barter for necessary supplies while the woman stayed home with the children. Families raised most of the food they ate and women made most of the clothing worn, so shopping needs were few. Stores existed primarily for those items that the local economy could not produce, and while women would occasionally place an order for spices or needles, it was likely that most shopping trips would be motivated by a masculine need for hardware items (or by his desire to visit a tavern or saloon).

American manufacturing began to grow with TEXTILE MILLS and shoe factories in the 1830s, and as mass production techniques made these items cheaper to buy than to make at home, there was more reason for shopping to be added to the feminine sphere of the division of labor. Factory growth expanded tremendously with the CIVIL WAR, and by the late nineteenth century, so many items were being produced that the concept of a "department" store came to be, for the "general" store could no longer handle such a potentially large inventory.

The department store was designed to bring several types of goods under the same roof—and more importantly, with the addition of tea rooms, lunch counters, and other comforts, to make shopping pleasant. Delightful arrays of merchandise were introduced as the century lengthened, for magical new electrical appliances appeared in the cities, along with updated styles of furniture and home decoration. Trying on ready-made fashions was much more fun than tedious hours spent with a seamstress or milliner who might or might not know anything about current style—and shopping became an important part of social life, especially for urban women.

Led by Macy's in New York and Marshall Field's in Chicago, these stores took customers from their familiar neighborhoods and from the merchant who sold on credit to more anonymous cash transactions. This, plus their higher volume, meant lower prices, as well as a surplus that allowed such conveniences as the "ladies waiting room" at Macy's in the 1880s, where women could gather to talk or read. The new merchandising methods aimed at women led inevitably to the employment of more women clerks; though these jobs were almost always low-paying and seldom led to the executive suite, they were nonetheless jobs that had not been available to women in the past.

The hours spent shopping became justified in many a woman's mind as an expansion of her duties to her family. Though she was out of the home, stores created an atmosphere designed to make her feel thoroughly at home. All of these innovations, designed particularly to please women, also meant advertising to tell women about them—which in turn meant another new field of enterprise, one that would define female images in the century to come. The relationship between women and retail business would grow increasingly complex and symbiotic, for the department store presaged a feminine influence on the business world that was previously unknown.

DESERTION Often referred to as "the poor man's divorce," desertion was, for most of American history, more frequently used than DIVORCE to end unhappy marriages. Until after WORLD WAR II, divorce in most states was an excessively expensive and complicated legal process that made it an option only for the wealthy. Desertion of his family by the male was therefore the most likely method of ending a marriage. For the woman involved, however, being deserted meant not only a bitter emotional experience, but also serious legal and economic problems that were intensified by the uncertainty of her situation—for he might get tired of the single life and come back.

Indeed, many deserters left and returned repeatedly throughout the decades of a marriage, with DESERTION during pregnancy being a particularly likely phenomenon. Since there was no legal and definite end to the marriage, a male preserved his option of returning in old age or in case of illness or other need. In fact, statisticians noted that desertion was less likely to occur during economic downturns; men stayed securely with their wives and children in hard times and hit the road again when opportunities improved. Similarly, younger men were more likely to desert than older ones: the result was that women with young children were left to earn a living alone, but when the wages of teenage workers were available and when the men themselves had begun to age, they were more likely to return home. A sociologist writing in 1919 amended the adage of desertion being "a poor man's divorce" to assert instead that it was "a poor man's vacation."

Meanwhile, of course, women very rarely deserted or enjoyed any other escape from their family responsibilities. They bore the burden of supporting children in an economy that offered them few job opportunities, with those that were available consistently paying wages to women that were half as much as male pay rates. Charities and social agencies also discriminated against them, for they were less likely to aid deserted women than WIDOWS and women with disabled husbands. Their parsimony was based on the fear that precedents of assisting abandoned women would encourage more desertions. Often, too, there was a darker assumption that the deserted woman must have contributed to the breakdown of the marriage, and since she was therefore guilty along with the deserting male, she should suffer the result.

For IMMIGRANT WOMEN, desertion was likely to be a new and unpleasant Americanism. Sociologists noted that it was extremely rare in the Old World, probably because European governments, with their passports and work authorizations and military service registrations, made it much more difficult for men to disappear. In America, the lone male adventurer seemed instead to be part of a pioneer tradition that was understandably appealing to immigrant males. Moreover, European extended families and established churches worked together to force fathers to accept their responsibilities, but when men consentally separated from their wives to emigrate, they discovered a whole new world of freedom.

They saw that their women could eke out an existence without them, and having tasted the joys of renewed bachelorhood or perhaps having met new and more interesting women, they simply failed to send the promised tickets so that their families could join them. Women could and did support their families alone in Europe for decades, only hearing occasionally from husbands in America and never knowing at any given time whether their men were dead or alive, let alone know with any certainty the prospects of revived marriage. Though immigration officials seldom got involved in such situations, priests and rabbis sometimes did use their international links to track down husbands—often discovering that the men had fathered new American families.

Calls for greater regulation of the emigration of married men went unheeded, but the legislative end of massive immigration in the 1920s brought a downturn in the problem. When the Great Depression overwhelmed the country the following decade, private philanthropy increasingly gave way to government funded social work agencies and a different attitude towards desertion began to evolve. By mid-century, social agencies had moved from cruelly disallowing aid to deserted women to policies that instead were so unthinkingly and automatically supportive of the abandoned family that they unintentionally encouraged desertion. Poor families were caught in a bureaucratic situation that meant they were in fact better off financially if fathers lived apart, while middle-class couples could avoid the legal and emotional morass of desertion by ending bad marriages through easier and cheaper divorce.

DEWSON, MARY WILLIAMS (MOLLY) (1874–1962)

Part of the group that came to Washington in 1932 to revolutionize the federal government, Molly Dewson—like most other women in Franklin Roosevelt's administration—developed her reformist roots in the Progressive Era.

Though affluent enough to attend Boston's prestigious Miss Ireland's School and to graduate from WELLESLEY COLLEGE in 1897, Dewson spent her life working for those less privileged. Her first job was with the WOMEN'S EDUCATIONAL AND INDUSTRIAL UNION; under the aegis of the WEIU, she published her *Twentieth Century Expense Book* (1899), which was the first of many efforts in consumerism.

Changing fields in 1900, Dewson accepted an appointment to set up the Massachusetts Industrial School for Girls. She remained as superintendent for the next twelve years, developing innovative methods in criminology and social work. The statistical analyses she did there were part of the reason that her volunteer work on minimum wage legislation developed into her next full-time appointment, when she was named executive secretary of the Massachusetts Minimum Wage Commission. The study she directed for the Commission resulted in the nation's first minimum wage law, passed in 1912, and brought Dewson to national prominence.

Despite job offers, she took a chance on a wholly different sort of endeavor: with her close friend, Mary G. Porter, Dewson ran a dairy farm near Worcester for the next five years. She left it in 1917, when the U.S. entered WORLD WAR I; like many other women in each of America's wars, she did her duty—but not in the traditional role of a NURSE. By then in her forties and a thoroughly experienced social worker, Dewson was ideal to work with wartime refugees, and the AMERICAN RED CROSS made her chief of its Mediterranean zone.

Returning from France in 1919, she went to work for the National Consumers' League, where she specialized in its lobbying effort for minimum wages and worked closely on cases with future Supreme Court Justice Felix Frankfurter. When the Court struck down their efforts with its decision in *ADKINS VS. CHILDREN'S HOSPITAL* (1923), Dewson was so dispirited that she decided to concentrate her energies instead on New York State. As president of the New York Consumers League from 1925 to 1931, she led a successful campaign for PROTECTIVE LEGISLATION for women workers.

It was in this role that she became close friends with the Roosevelts, and it was ELEANOR ROOSEVELT who sensed Molly Dewson's innate political skills. Eight years after women had the right to vote, Dewson began her first campaign management role by organizing women in Al Smith's 1928 presidential race; two years later, she was successful in Franklin Roosevelt's campaign for governor of New York; and four years after that, the team entered the White House.

Dewson spent the 1930s employed by the Democratic Party as the first female operative of either party to be given genuine support by a president. This was the first Democratic administration since women had gotten the vote, and Dewson stressed the importance of involving women at all levels of government. She lobbied Roosevelt for the appointment of hundreds of women, the most visible of whom was FRANCES PERKINS, the first woman to sit on the Cabinet. Moreover, she pushed for power for women throughout all levels of political activity; it was largely her efforts that created the "equal division" principle of men and women as delegates to party nominating conventions and in shared chairman/vice-chairman roles. She made the Democratic Women's Clubs, which had been founded in 1922, into a vital part of the party's structure. When she developed campaign seminars for volunteers, women responded so enthusiastically that party hacks were astonished; by 1940, Dewson had over one hundred thousand trained political workers who were women.

At the same time that she did her innovative party politics, she also put her social worker experience to good use with an appointment to the President's Commission on Economic Security, which resulted in the enactment of Social Security. In 1937, she became the first woman to serve on the Social Security Board, where she had a great deal to do with the successful implementation of the law. Given the fundamental importance of Social Security in the lives of millions of older women today, this may be the most important of Dewson's many contributions.

Troubled by a bad heart and in her late sixties, she cut back on her efforts after WORLD WAR II diverted the Roosevelt administration from its original reformist agenda. Though she continued to be available to the National Democratic Committee, Dewson retired to Maine with Porter and lived there until age eighty-eight. Doubtless she remembered the prediction her Wellesley classmates had made of their senior class president: in 1897 (more than twenty years before women could vote) their class prophecy showed their awareness of Dewson's political talents and had predicted that she would be elected president of the United States.

DICKERSON, NANCY CONNERS HANSCHMAN (1927?–)

When most women's achievements regressed from their WORLD WAR II advances, Nancy Dickerson (who was known by her MAIDEN NAME until 1962) instead broke new ground. She provided one of the few female faces on serious television news, thus offering inspiration to girls in her audience—who themselves would become familiar television figures in the next decades.

She grew up in suburban Milwaukee during the war, graduated from the University of Wisconsin in 1948, and like so many other women of all eras, worked as a TEACHER until 1951. Moving east that year, she was unsuccessful in searching for work in New York and ended up in Washington in a clerical position at Georgetown University. From there, Hanschman landed a job with the Senate Foreign Relations Committee, where her authorship of a major committee report was the first to be done by a woman.

Her goal was to be on television, however, and in 1954, she began working for CBS in production. Her behind-camera activities during the next six years included the title of associate producer of "Face the Nation," and she earned a reputation as "CBS's secret weapon" during this era because her friendship with many members of Congress brought the show stories that otherwise would not have been produced.

Nonetheless, she wanted to report the news, not produce it. While competitors NBC and ABC employed women at the time as correspondents, none was on the CBS news staff. Finally, when Hanschman was in Europe in 1959 to do production on a story about the WOMEN'S ARMY CORPS, she acted on her own initiative and interviewed European political leaders about Soviet Prime Minister Khrushchev's visit to the U.S.; the stories turned out to be superior to anything male reporters had obtained. Washington insiders noticed when CBS aired her work, and six months later Hanschman managed another scoop with House Speaker Sam Rayburn, who usually turned down television interviews.

These journalistic coups made her the first woman correspondent for CBS television in February, 1960; at the same time, CBS gave Hanschman a five-minute radio show called "One Woman's Washington." Assigned to cover the civil rights bill then in Congress as well as Senate Majority Leader Lyndon Johnson, she became the first woman to sit in the anchor booth for the televised coverage of that fall's Democratic convention, when Johnson was nominated for vice-president.

Vice-presidential assignments usually are considered to be a dead-end, and so she switched to NBC when that network promised her more on-camera time. With President Kennedy's assassination a few months later, she had a key White House position because of her familiarity with Johnson. She was given her own daily news show and appeared regularly on NBC's other outstanding news editions of the era, the "Huntley-Brinkley Report" and "The Today Show." Among the top stories she covered were Kennedy's funeral, the civil rights marches on Washington, and the inaugurals of Kennedy, Johnson, and Nixon.

Meanwhile, she had married in 1962 and took her husband's name; she mothered his five children during a twenty-one-year marriage before their 1983 divorce. Meanwhile, Dickerson continued her career so successfully that she was the best-paid woman in television at the time. She stayed with NBC throughout the tumultuous news stories of the sixties, leaving in 1970 to do political commentary for two syndicated television services and to form her own production company for news documentaries. She also wrote *Among Those Present* (1976), which was an overview of the twenty-five years she had then spent in Washington. Her hour-long live interview of President Nixon for PBS was another "first," and she won awards in 1982 for her documentary on the Watergate scandal.

DICKINSON, ANNA ELIZABETH (1842–1932) KATHA-RINE ANTHONY, who was SUSAN ANTHONY's niece, called Dickinson "one of the most famous women of the Civil War era." Though she is almost forgotten now, Dickinson was indeed a phenomenon in her day.

Born in Philadelphia, she grew up the daughter of a WIDOW, and her QUAKER education was on scholarships. Imbued with the Friends' ABOLITIONIST message, she would soon abandon their quiet speech and dress, as well as their pacifism, to support instead the war that ended slavery. But first, to help support her family, Dickinson went to work at fifteen as a copyist; then she did the inevitable TEACHING done by almost every educated woman who needed to work; and finally,

with men gone to war in 1861, she got a civil service job with the U.S. Mint in Philadelphia. Though she was thus one of the first women employed by the federal government, she soon lost her position because she criticized General McClellan's handling of the first battles—a view, of course, also held by President Lincoln.

Instead of regretting the political expression that cost her job, Dickinson expanded it. She had published an article in William Lloyd Garrison's anti-slavery newspaper already at age fourteen, and, with her Quaker background that encouraged PUBLIC SPEAKING by women, LUCRETIA MOTT and others had sold more than eight hundred tickets for Dickinson's first major speech early in 1861 on "The Rights and Wrongs of Women." After losing the job at the mint, she joined Garrison's lecture network and soon developed a national reputation for the florid oratorical skills that were highly valued in this era. Only nineteen years old when she began her public speaking career, her reputation rapidly grew to the point that more than five thousand people crowded Cooper Institute for her first New York appearance. In addition to her exceptional beauty, Dickinson "could hold her audience spellbound for as much as two hours. She gave the impression of being under some magical control. . ."

The new Republican Party soon saw her potential value and hired Dickinson for speeches. They aimed to use her particularly for those tough audiences of Northerners who sympathized with the South, and so, during the draft riots of 1863, they sent this attractive young woman to speak to men with a demonstrated propensity for violence. Pennsylvania coal miners literally took shots at her. Handling hecklers became her forte, however, and Dickinson's speeches increasingly specialized in the negative. She was so successful in employing sarcasm and derision against Republican opponents that early in 1864, the party leadership showed their appreciation by inviting her to address the House of Representatives, with the president and other military and civilian leaders also in attendance. Only a few years after women began speaking in public at all, Anna Dickinson was honored by the nation's elected officials in a way that was absolutely unprecedented. She was twenty-one years old.

When the war ended, she remained on the national lecture circuit, and because lectures were a favorite social activity in this era, she continued to be well known and well paid. Her topics bordered on the sensational, such as an attack on Mormon polygamy ("Whited Sepulchers") and a more veiled discussion of venereal disease ("Between Us be Truth"). Her most popular talk featured Joan of Arc, with comparisons to herself as a natural result. She published several books as well, the most radical of which was a novel sympathetic to interracial marriage, *What Answer?* (1868).

Averaging a lecture every other day, she earned as much as twenty thousand dollars annually—a phenomenal amount of money in that time, especially for a woman. Properly invested, she could have remained financially secure all of her days, but Dickinson instead supported herself and her family in style and generously gave to others, including the SUFFRAGE MOVEMENT. Although she emphasized topics other than women's rights and never fulfilled the excessive hopes that Susan Anthony had for her when they first met in 1864, Dickinson served as a vice-president when the NATIONAL WOMAN SUF-

FRAGE ASSOCIATION was formed. She and Anthony remained warm friends for several years, with early letters using their common Quaker idioms of "thee" and "thou," and Anthony even forgoing the era's formalism in one letter to address Dickinson as "Chicky Dicky."

The political influence of both women was clear in the presidential election of 1872, when each was offered generous speaking fees by rival Republican candidates. Anthony's candidate won and Dickinson's lost, but that was only one factor in the decline of her popularity during the following decade. Partly, lectures began losing audiences to less serious entertainment, and partly, Dickinson quarreled irreparably with her business agent. More importantly, she represented little in the public mind once her Civil War speeches became irrelevant, and her continued attempts to "wave the bloody shirt" by attacking the South met with contempt.

In an effort to overcome that unhappy election year, she went to Colorado in 1873, where she built on a second reputation: Dickinson is said to have believed that "she had been on top of more of America's great mountains than any other woman alive." Because she also had scaled eastern mountains and was reputed to have climbed New Hampshire's Mount Washington almost thirty times, some believe that it was she who was responsible for the name of Colorado's Mount Lady Washington. In any case, she ascended several of Colorado's most rugged that summer and was probably the first woman at the summit of Mount Elbert, now known to be the state's highest mountain. Like JULIA ARCHIBALD HOLMES, she climbed Pike's Peak as well; unlike Holmes, she did not go on foot, but rather on horseback. Dickinson, who was thirty-one that summer, sensibly bought men's trousers—"which allow a lady to ride on both sides of a horse at once," as a local newspaper explained—and when the seams split, that too was deemed newsworthy.

A Colorado newspaper called Dickinson "the spice, the pepper and the brains of the women's movement," but it was clear that her influence back East was fading as time passed. She never recovered her wartime celebrity, and as the 1870s turned into the 1880s, she found more and more difficulty earning a living—and yet she continued to spurn offers of marriage, for she remained beautiful as she aged.

Indeed, aging was probably the most important factor of all in explaining the diminishment of her reputation. Dickinson was barely an adult when she saw the high point of her life with her speech in the U.S. Capitol, but her negative style, which was effective in youthful campaigning, did not wear well. Her emphasis on style over substance and her attention to a multiplicity of topics created a situation for her that was the exact reverse of the straightforward, single-minded Susan Anthony's. Though Anthony was reviled in her youth, she was seen as sweetly honest in old age; Dickinson—who was by far the more beautiful—could effectively use her biting tongue when young, but age made the same behavior seem bitter and mean. Indeed, the Republicans who hired her in 1888 were so embarrassed by her attacks on Democrat Grover Cleveland that she never again was sponsored for a political speech, while Anthony was welcome on most turn-of-the-century platforms.

Dickinson moved from lectures to the dramatic form in the 1880s, writing and acting in numerous plays. Few were well reviewed, however, and none was more than ephemerally successful. By 1891, she was showing such signs of paranoia that she was committed for a few days to a Pennsylvania state hospital for the insane. She filed several suits upon her release, was adjudicated sane, and recovered damages from newspapers, but the effort cost her more than three thousand dollars that she did not have.

The experience shook her self-confidence to its foundations, and despite her partial victory, she never recovered. Anna Dickinson, a genuine Civil War heroine, lived the next forty years in the household of friends, unnoticed and unwanted by the public. She died just days before her ninetieth birthday.

DICKINSON, EMILY ELIZABETH (1830–1886)

If high school students read no other work by women AUTHORS, they will almost certainly read the poetry of Emily Dickinson. Her stature as one of America's great poets—perhaps *the* greatest—is such that virtually every American knows her name. Hundreds of literary critics have written thousands of pieces on her during the century since her death. And yet, while she was alive, those talents received almost no recognition.

Nothing about her life is complex enough to merit the millions of words written on her; it was her mind that was complex. The facts of her life are so simple as to seem deprived—until one remembers her unique ability to travel in her mind, and that the distractions of a busier life could have negated the inner life essential to her creative crafting of thought.

Emily Dickinson was born and died in Amherst, Massachusetts, and only once traveled out of that state. She spent a year (1847) at MOUNT HOLYOKE, which was only a few miles from her home, but disliked the strongly Christian ambience there and did not return. It was almost a decade later (1855) that she took her sole interstate trip, traveling only as far as Washington via Philadelphia.

Other than that, she lived in her father's house with her mother and sister, who also remained single. They shared their lives with her only other sibling, a brother who lived with his family next door. Her father was the dominant factor in all of their lives, for he and his ancestors had long been powers in western Massachusetts. A Yale graduate, he was a lawyer and businessman who served as treasurer of Amherst College (an exclusively male institution), as well as in the state legislature and Congress. He expected his home to be a quiet haven from his multiplicity of interests, and expected the women in it to be as reserved as he was active.

Nonetheless, young Emily's social life was apparently as extroverted as she chose, and she retained similar—and more important—independence of mind, especially in her refusal to join her family in the affirmation of Christianity. Two young men figured strongly in her youth, but both seem to have been platonic friends with whom she exchanged ideas rather than suitors. Among the books they shared with her, she was particularly affected by Emerson and his transcendentalist philosophy, which was then in vogue with other Massachusetts women such as MARGARET FULLER. They, of course, had no idea of the existence of this young woman on the other side of the state.

In the early 1850s, Emily began to write poetry, sharing it

with only with a few special people. One of the most special in her mind—but not necessarily in his—was Reverend Charles Wadworth, a popular (and married) minister. His move to the West Coast in 1861 seems a major motivation for the increase in both quantity and quality of the poetry Dickinson wrote during the CIVIL WAR years. During 1862 alone, she produced more than 350 poems, with a resulting technical improvement of her innate talent.

Having written for a decade, she was confident enough of her ability that she replied when *Atlantic* critic Thomas Wentworth Higginson wrote of his interest in new poetry. As it turned out, he was not interested in anything as new as Dickinson provided, for her original, unconventional style was decades beyond anything then being published. In a bemused combination of admiration and disdain, Higginson's response discouraged her from publication. Nonetheless, they corresponded for the rest of her life, and his interest in her poetry was Dickinson's salvation.

She continued to write through the 1870s, while growing increasingly reclusive. Her neighbors considered her eccentric, for on those rare occasions when they glimpsed her, they saw a slim body dressed quaintly in white, with an ephemeral appearance that was as gossamer as the poetry she did not share with them. Even her friends expected the unpredictable; one recorded that Miss Dickinson had asked her to visit, but then refused to leave the bedroom when she came. Her behavior could be defined as that of an agoraphobic, but if Dickinson did show evidence of this psychological phenomenon, the effect was to give her more time to work. Probably she simply felt that she had better things to do than engage in small talk.

The death of her father in 1874 was a heavy blow that was quickly followed by her mother's paralysis the next year. In the early 1880s, however, her life took a new and happy turn, for when she was almost fifty, Dickinson seems to have fallen truly in love with a man who returned her feelings. But when first her mother and then her lover died just a few years later, she dropped into permanent, physical collapse. She died herself, at just fifty-five.

Only seven of her poems had been published in her lifetime, and those without her consent. A few were printed by a close male friend who was editor of a nearby newspaper, and the rest were published by HELEN HUNT JACKSON, who was Dickinson's best female friend and a very popular author at the time. After the funeral, Lavinia Dickinson found almost eighteen hundred poems that her sister had dated, packaged, and neatly arranged for posterity.

As late as 1889, Thomas Wentworth Higginson advised against the publication of Dickinson's work, labeling her meticulous craftsmanship "too crude in form." In 1890, however, 115 poems were published; they were received well enough that another collection was issued the next year and a third in 1896. A niece and grandniece finally saw the remainder into print with four more books between 1914 and 1945, their efforts having been delayed and complicated by Dickinson's brother's adulterous relationship with one of her literary promoters, Mabel Loomis Todd.

Had she not preceded Dickinson in death, it is possible that Helen Hunt Jackson instead would have been Dickinson's literary executor and the world would have seen her poems sooner. Even aside from this, however, the relationship between the two women is an interesting one, for Dickinson was certainly aware of the ironic contrast between her total obscurity and the fame of her friend Mrs. Jackson. While the public bought Jackson's books in bestselling numbers, Dickinson recorded her clear-eyed prescient analysis of her dear friend's work: "She has the facts, but not the phosphorescence." Not jealous nor covetously emulative of Jackson's success, Dickinson was comforted by a quiet awareness of the quality of her own efforts and was confident that time would prove her worth, for she wrote of herself: "When I die, they'll have to remember me."

DIVORCE From the earliest days of English settlement, divorce existed in America. During the brief existence of the Plymouth colony as a separate government, for instance, six divorces were granted on the grounds of adultery and DESERTION. More importantly, early New England law also allowed dissolution of marriage in cases of discovery of previously undisclosed sexual history, as well as for "criminal uncleanness," "malicious desertion," incest, and—in an area that would favor a woman, but not a man—impotence. In addition to sexuality, property rights were an important aspect of the marriage contract: the Connecticut colony, for instance, granted divorce for "fraudulent contract" and "totall neglect of duty." Case law shows this was intended as assurance of a woman's right to divorce if her husband willfully failed to provide financial support.

Nonetheless, these early governments preferred reconciliation to divorce, and, being closer to individual citizens and strongly paternalistic in attitude, they mandated specifically changed behavior in couples who were having problems. Colonial courts assumed social work functions, imposing fines and physical punishment on those who broke marital codes, and granted divorce only in cases of shocking outrage or longstanding recalcitrance. The significant point, however, is that men and women were treated alike, with both punishment and sympathy rendered on an individual rather than a legalistic basis.

But by the time that colonial governments passed into statehood after the Revolution, population had grown so that governments were less close to those governed, and divorce naturally became more legalistic and less personal. Additional damage was done by the general change in women's status during this era from pioneer settler to dependent lady. The legal status of women increasingly became that of chattel, with state laws assuming male prerogatives in marriage and its dissolution. Although some public attention was drawn to the issue in the 1820s because of the questionable marriage of President Andrew Jackson and RACHEL DONELSON JACKSON, divorce was a topic of scandalized whispers and legal mystery.

As Rachel Jackson understood, a divorce was extremely hard for a woman of this era to obtain, for the day was long gone when a woman could appeal to her local authorities and expect to be heard. Only with the support of an exceptionally powerful family could a woman afford to take the risk of seeking to nullify her marital contract, for all legal advantages of property rights and guardianship favored the male. Since women lacked even the right to sue, they were prevented from the very first step in seeking a divorce. The result was that in those rare instances when one was granted, it was more likely to be a matter of successful lobbying by the male members of a woman's family rather than justice rendered to a wife in an open court of law. Meanwhile, of course, husbands were seldom motivated to end an unhappy marriage because double standards of morality allowed them sexual freedom, while state laws guaranteed even their right to physically beat their wives, as well as their continued property rights—including the right to the earnings of their wives.

It was wholly understandable that ELIZABETH CADY STANTON considered marriage to be the female equivalent of legal slavery, and yet, even after the organized women's rights movement began in 1848, most of its leadership shied away from what they considered to be the political dynamite of the divorce issue. Though happily married herself, Stanton was largely alone in leading the divorce argument. Her advocacy began with an 1852 speech to a shocked assembly of TEMPERANCE women in which she argued that women should be allowed to divorce men who were habitual drunkards, and she continued the crusade in the newspaper that she operated with SUSAN ANTHONY in the late 1860s. Even the FEMINIST public, however, found the topic too radical, and Stanton's defense of two women accused in murder trials relating to divorce was a major factor in the financial collapse of the newspaper.

Though Anthony preferred to concentrate on suffrage, she shared Stanton's views strongly enough that she accepted great personal and political risk in an 1860 case relating to divorce. When the estranged wife of a Massachusetts senator took her daughter from the man's automatic custody and then appealed to Anthony for help, Anthony protected the woman. With all three of them in disguise, she escorted the woman and child out of the state and kept their refuge secret, despite great pressure. In one of the most striking examples of the sexism inherent even among progressives, William Lloyd Garrison and other of Anthony's male ABOLITIONIST colleagues demanded she return this fugitive wife—while at the same time they encouraged defiance of federal law on the return of fugitive slaves.

Nonetheless, Anthony joined with most feminists in giving priority to suffrage over divorce reform. The issue languished for decades, with those improvements that did occur being made instead to state laws governing GUARDIANSHIP and MARRIED WOMEN'S PROPERTY RIGHTS. The latter was especially important, for as women gained the right to sue, they slowly began to initiate more divorce suits. That it was women rather than men who were most disillusioned with marriage is clear from the fact that by 1900, two-thirds of divorce cases were brought by women.

Divorce finally became a topic of general public discussion around 1920, but attention to it was generated more by WORLD WAR I than by women's suffrage. The war, like all wars, had deleterious results for the institution of marriage, but since this was the first large-scale international war in which Americans were involved, these negative effects came as a shock to many. Divorce cases rose as men returned with a hugely increased rate of venereal disease proving their adultery, and as women found the independence of earning

their own living in a war-expanded economy. By 1920, there were 3.4 divorces per one thousand married people, up from 0.8 fifty years earlier. Rates continued to climb during the liberation of the Roaring Twenties, and then fell temporarily with the Great Depression. When prosperity returned in the forties, there was clearly a great backlog of unhappily married people who rushed to divorce as soon as they could afford the cost. With the pressures of WORLD WAR II in addition, the rate of marital breakdown skyrocketed.

Yet divorce remained a legal morass in the postwar era, comparable to no other area of contractual law. Though there were tremendous variations between states, nowhere in the U.S. at that time could a marriage be dissolved merely by mutual consent. Divorce cases continued to be adversarial civil trials, usually bitterly and expensively fought, and often in a state other than that of the couple's true residence. Many states, including New York and others with large Catholic populations, allowed divorce only for proven adultery and longstanding desertion, while one state (South Carolina) made no provision for divorce at all. Other states (primarily Nevada, but also Arkansas, Idaho, Washington, and Arizona) operated divorce mills that were profitable to local lawyers and hotels. Couples seeking divorce went there, established residence (six weeks was the minimal requirement), had their day in court and returned home with the divorce decree.

The Supreme Court in a 1945 North Carolina case insisted that the Constitution's "full faith and credit" clause meant that such "quickie" divorces must be recognized by the home state as *bona fide*. In response, state legislatures slowly began to ease the process of divorce rather than allow the travesties of justice, especially in property and guardianship, that could occur with out-of-state decrees. (In Arkansas as late as the 1960s, for instance, there were cases of people being divorced who did not realize a suit had been filed against them.) States increased the grounds for divorce, lowered costs, and smoothed the process, with California developing the nation's first "no fault" divorce law in 1969.

These changes thus were less a result of the organized women's movement than of modifications to laws proposed by lawyers and legislators. Because the new nonadversarial approach was so obviously superior to the previous situation and because the modern women's movement had other priorities, it was understandable that continued male bias in both legislation and judicial behavior often was overlooked during the sixties and seventies. By the 1980s, however, feminists were aware of many studies showing that the living standards of divorced women dropped dramatically, while those of men rose disproportionately. The needs of "displaced homemakers" and enforcement of child support orders against "deadbeat dads" then became focuses of feminist attention.

Though these problem areas remained, great personal freedom had been obtained since the days of Elizabeth Stanton's lonely crusade. Few legalists remained who would argue that the state had a right to enforce contracts that were abhorrent to the people most directly affected. American women and men, imbued from birth with ideas of freedom, would no longer live with governments that assumed a right to dictate such personal decisions as whether or not to be married.

DIX, DOROTHEA LYNDE (1802–1887) Dorothea Dix

was middle-aged before she began the innovative work with the mentally ill for which she is famous. First she had another life as a TEACHER and AUTHOR.

Born in Maine while it was still part of Massachusetts, she exhibited her independence by leaving her dysfunctional home at twelve, escaping to Boston for its greater educational opportunity and the security of her prosperous grandparents. After only two years, Dolly, as she was called, opened a school for little children in Worcester, when she herself was just fourteen. After running it successfully for three years, she returned to Boston in 1819, lived with her grandparents and studied for two years. In 1821, at age nineteen, she began a DAME SCHOOL that was an immediate enrollment success. While her pupils thought of Miss Dix as a strong disciplinarian, she also was remembered as "the most beautiful woman I had ever seen, next to my mother." Her school's curriculum was both solid and imaginative, with a special emphasis on botany through field trips.

The beginning of lifelong lung problems turned her from teaching to writing, but Dix still demonstrated remarkable energy, publishing five books between 1824 and 1829. They varied between her first, a science textbook that went through sixty reprintings during the next forty-five years, to hymns, meditations, and botany. Refreshed by an 1830 trip to St. Croix as a GOVERNESS, she felt well enough to start her third school in 1831, which she operated until 1836.

She went to England for prescribed rest then, where she met a number of progressive intellectuals whose friendship and opinions she greatly valued. Her happiness abroad contrasted with her homecoming late in 1837, for her grandmother had died and Dix was displaced from the family mansion. Still sick and increasingly depressed, she went south in the winter and north in the summer, staying with friends and living on her small inheritance. Dix seemed well on her way to lonely SPINSTERHOOD when she found her cause quite unexpectedly in 1841.

She went to a Cambridge jail to teach a Sunday school class and found among the women "criminals," most of whom were alcoholics and PROSTITUTES, a group of women guilty of no greater crime than mental illness. The day was cold, their room unheated, and the ill-fed women were kept caged in filthy conditions by a jailer who judged them incapable of feeling. Outraged, Dix bombarded local authorities with letters that she also released to the newspapers. The resulting public indignation succeeded in providing the inmates with heat and improved facilities, but also earned Dix a reputation for busybody interference in the male political world.

Undaunted, she adopted the same scientific methodology as for her botanical studies and read everything available on mental illness. Then for the next two years, in defiance of prevalent taboos against women TRAVELING alone, she rode on primitive trains throughout Massachusetts and documented conditions similar to those in Cambridge. Thus prepared, she presented her findings in writing to the Massachusetts legislature in 1843; her "memorial" was later termed "the first piece of social research ever conducted in America." She detailed the conditions of "958 insane paupers" in desperate need of care, and she invited representatives to call on her for discussion. This method of making her case was necessary because women did not yet engage in PUBLIC SPEAKING to "promiscuous" audiences that included men, although ANGELINA GRIMKE had set a precedent by testifying to a legislative committee a few years earlier.

Despite the handicap of speaking so indirectly, the Massachusetts legislature responded with hospital beds within weeks of Dix's memorial. From there, she moved on to Rhode Island, Connecticut, and New York, using the same methods of documentation and written memorials. Newspapers found her written form easy to report, and as Dix's reputation grew, she received increasing amounts of mail from people interested in her cause. Already by 1844, she was instrumental in the founding of the Medical Superintendents of American Institutions for the Insane, a landmark in the as-yet-unnamed field of psychiatry. By 1847 (a year prior to the SENECA FALLS WOMEN'S RIGHTS CONVENTION), Dix had developed enough self-confidence to break the taboo on women's public speaking and addressed the Tennessee legislature. Eventually she would travel thirty thousand miles in fifteen states and Canada, providing the impetus for thirty-two new institutions.

From 1848 to 1854, Dix spent part of each year in Washington, working for an idea that never was successful, but which nonetheless is illustrative of her political creativity: she proposed that Congress set aside a block of western land, with the income from it providing permanent funds for mental illness. With persistent lobbying, the bill passed in 1854, but was vetoed by Franklin Pierce. Since such social functions were (and still are) thought of as the responsibility of the states, not the federal government, there were not enough votes in this era of states' rights to override the veto, and even some of her New England congressional friends deserted the bill. The irony was not lost on Dix: while claiming that land grants for humanitarian purposes might be unconstitutional, the federal government had no hesitation in giving millions of acres of land to private railroads.

Dix was so disheartened by the legislative loss that she went abroad again, but this trip was combined with work overseas. She visited mental institutions from Turkey to Scotland, and even succeeded in getting the Pope to investigate conditions in Italy. Returning home in 1856, she found the country so distracted by the oncoming CIVIL WAR that progress on humanitarian issues other than ABOLITION was difficult. When the war broke out, Dix, like many other women, immediately offered her services as a NURSE. On June 10, 1861, the Secretary of War appointed Dorothea Dix as "Superintendent of the United States Army Nurses." Though American women had worked as war nurses in the past, hers was the first formal command position.

Like the experience of CLARA BARTON in the Spanish-American War, however, Dix's time as a Civil War nurse tarnished her otherwise outstanding reputation. Long past the days when she feared public speaking, her personality became increasingly imperious; moreover, she was accustomed to acting independently and had little experience in supervising a large organization. The sad result was a woman who had forgotten her own capabilities as a young woman, writing instead, "No women under thirty need apply to serve in government hospitals." She forgot, too, that she had been beautiful when she added, "All nurses are required to be plain looking women."

Given that the women to be approved were, of course, expected to do loathsome and exhausting work for little or no pay, they understandably rebelled against her arbitrary command. MARY ANN BICKERDYKE, Barton, and other nurses of sufficient age to have independent power were careful to keep themselves aloof from what they saw as Dix's petty and excessively personal management style. When the voices of military officials and male doctors were added to her critics, the War Department issued orders in 1863 that limited her authority. Dix nonetheless continued to work until well after the end of the war, refusing any compensation when she finally left the army in September, 1866.

At age sixty-four then, Dix used her remaining time to TRAVEL again the circuit of mental institutions she had helped establish, including an 1869 trip to California and visits in the Reconstruction South. After illness returned the following decade, she settled permanently in 1881 in Trenton, New Jersey, living in rooms of the first hospital she built. Although also suffering from impaired vision and hearing, she maintained her correspondence to the end. Dorothea Dix died at eighty-five at the same time that words like sociologist and psychologist were coming into use; she had been each without the title, and she had been a political activist, too, long before women could vote. She is buried in Mount Auburn Cemetery, not far from the Cambridge jail that saw the beginning of her exceptionally innovative life.

DIX, DOROTHY (ELIZABETH MERIWETHER GILMER) (1861–1951)

"Dorothy Dix" was the pen name of the nation's most popular newspaper columnist during the first half of the twentieth century.

A Southerner, Gilmer's marriage at thirty-one to a man ten years her senior was not a happy one. He eventually died in a mental institution, while, from 1895 on, she supported herself by writing. She began with an unusually candid column on women's concerns for the New Orleans *Daily Picayune*, which was owned by a woman who was Gilmer's neighbor. By the turn of the century, Gilmer had adopted the column's "Dorothy Dix" as her name.

In 1901, while continuing to write her column, she set a journalistic precedent by joining the Hearst syndicate as a crime reporter for the uncommonly high salary of five thousand dollars. Her writing gave a FEMINIST perspective to CARRY NATION, as well as to women involved in several of the era's sensational adultery/murder trials. She also published three books between 1902 and 1915, which ranged from animal fables to the homespun philosophies of southern blacks.

Switching in 1917 from Hearst to another syndicate, Dix (as she now called herself) adopted the question-and-answer format for her column. From her New Orleans base, she dealt with an average of five hundred letters daily and by the mid-1920s, her column appeared in almost three hundred newspapers. She published additional books, including a 1922 report on her trip around the world, and her *Every-day Help for the Every-day People* (1927), which went through three editions. She reinforced her column's thesis of the need for female economic independence by insisting on pay commensurate with her popularity—by the 1940s, Dix was estimated to earn one hundred thousand dollars annually.

Tulane University gave Dix an honorary degree in 1927,

but she did not take this as an indication of expected retirement. A woman of remarkable strength, she wrote her column until age eighty-eight, and died only two years later. With over a half-century of writing, the "Dorothy Dix" column was the oldest column in the world with the same AUTHOR. It was read by 30 million people on three continents when she died. The inventor of the advice columnist genre that continues to be widely popular today, Dix's willing association with the SUFFRAGE MOVEMENT also was a genuine political boon to the cause of women.

DODGE, MARY ABIGAIL (1833–1896)

Socially conventional enough to hide her true identity with PSEUDONYMS, Dodge began writing in 1858 for an ABOLITIONIST newspaper. During the CIVIL WAR era, she added to her credentials with articles in the prestigious *Atlantic Monthly*, and for two years after the war, was an assistant editor for a children's magazine. Her essay collections were considered sufficiently good to be published along with work by Hawthorne, Longfellow, and other distinguished men of the era.

She is mostly notable, however, for her writing during the 1870s when she lived in Washington with relatives, the James G. Blaine family. Senator Blaine, who also served as Speaker of the House, Secretary of State, and the 1884 Republican presidential nominee, so appreciated Dodge's writing skills that she functioned as one of the first female political ghostwriters. Indeed, the identity of the two became so mixed that while she was widely believed to have written his speeches, some also asserted that the series of columns she wrote for the *New York Herald Tribune* in 1877 were actually a cover for his opinions. She clearly collaborated in the writing of his autobiography.

Like the Republican Party with which she was associated, Dodge became increasingly conservative in the post–Civil War era. Though she remained single all her life, she opposed women's suffrage and argued in her 1874 *Woman's Worth and Worthlessness* that women's political expression should be only through male family members.

DODGE, MARY MAPES (1831–1905)

When Dodge became a WIDOW with two little children at twenty-eight, she could have easily allowed her well-connected family to support her, but instead she set about making a living by writing for children. Using her sons as critics, she published her first book in 1864 and followed it the next year with a tremendous success: *Hans Brinker; or The Silver Skates* (1865) went through more than a hundred editions in Dodge's lifetime and still is recognized as a classic of children's literature.

The book, which combined uncommon research on its setting with a secular, nonpedagogical style that was new for children, soon gave Dodge a reputation as the best in her field. Only three years after its publication, she moved to New York to join HARRIET BEECHER STOWE and others on the staff of *Hearth and Home*. After five years there, when Dodge was forty-two, she was offered the editorship of a new magazine sponsored by Scribner's. She named it *St. Nicholas* magazine, set high standards, and remained its editor from the first 1873 issue to her death in 1905.

Her personal reputation, as well as her longtime family connections, enabled Dodge to bring the foremost AUTHORS of the English-speaking world to children's literature. *St. Nicholas* published LOUISA MAY ALCOTT and FRANCES HODGSON BURNETT, as well as Longfellow, Kipling, Tennyson, Twain, Whittier, and others. Its illustrators, too, were among the nation's outstanding artists. Dodge also used the best material provided by her young subscribers and thereby gave some of the distinguished writers of the next generation, including RACHEL CARSON, their first publication.

Though she wrote a half-dozen books after *Hans Brinker*, Dodge's greatest contribution was instead her work as an editor and a promoter of high literary standards. Beginning semiretirement during the 1880s, she also wrote for adult magazines, including *Atlantic* and *Harper's*. Nonetheless, Dodge held her position at the acme of children's literature for more than three decades, influencing millions of young minds, before dying at her Catskills vacation home at age seventy-four. Distinguished historian Henry Steele Commager called her *St. Nicholas* "the best, and the best-loved, magazine for children ever published."

DOMESTIC SERVANTS Colonial households that numbered twenty or more members were not unusual, and, since it was extremely heavy work to run a home for these extended families with the primitive methods available, almost every household mistress reached out for help. Many benefited from the unpaid labor of "maiden aunts"—for female family members who did not marry very seldom set up separate households—but nonrelatives also lived in colonial homes. The line between business and home was vague in this early era, and both male and female apprentices and employees lived where they worked, in the home of their "master" and "mistress." Despite the nomenclature used, the relationships between worker and employer could be quite egalitarian.

Affluent families might have INDENTURED SERVANTS (who worked for a term of years to repay their passage to America) or slaves (even in the North), but in many early American families, there were other kinds of domestic workers who were not thought of as servants, but rather as "help." These "HIRED GIRLS" were usually the teenage daughters of neighbors who worked for a few years before marriage and who were not thought of as belonging to a serving class.

While the tradition of the "hired girl" remained strong in the farming Midwest well into the twentieth century, as agricultural traditions faded elsewhere, so did class lines rigidify. Along with industrialization came well-defined, nonegalitarian ideas on domestic workers. Men increasingly dropped out of those relatively few domestic service roles they had played, as gardeners and handymen became independent businessmen rather than household servants, while butlers and footmen disappeared altogether except in extremely wealthy estates. By 1850, as the nation urbanized and smaller families moved to townhouses from large farmhouses, women accounted for 90 percent of domestic servants. Moreover, these servants were seen as such and were not simply present as a "helping" part of an extended household.

For the next century, the demand for domestics continued to exceed the supply, for servants were a feature of any American home with aspirations of repute. Especially in the period between the CIVIL WAR and WORLD WAR I, every proper household had at least one maid. Middle-class men did not feel

that they could marry unless they could afford to provide their brides with this surrogate housekeeper, and indeed, young couples who could not maintain such a home lived in hotels rather than demean the woman's social position by expecting her to do her own housework.

While in the South, black women would fill these needs both before and after slavery, it was met elsewhere by IMMIGRANT WOMEN, especially the Irish. Beginning in the late 1840s when they fled the potato famine, practically every affluent home in the Northeast had its "Bridget", and even as late as 1920, the Irish accounted for 43 percent of all domestic servants. The second most important immigrant group in service was Scandinavian, particularly in Chicago and other Midwestern cities, and service attracted appreciable numbers of German women as well. New immigrants especially valued it for its constant availability, secure bed and board, opportunity to save, and the decent treatment they generally received, especially when contrasted with comparable work experience in Europe.

These groups continued to dominate domestic service even when massive numbers of other immigrant groups arrived in the late nineteenth century. The Jews and Italians who came in the 1880s and 1890s avoided domestic work almost entirely. What few Jews did do this work sought employment only in Jewish homes, for to enter the nonkosher kitchens of Christians was unacceptable to most. Italian women avoided it because their cultural mores did not allow females to live outside the family circle. Married Italian women might sometimes do "day's work" as laundresses or cleaning women, but for an unmarried Italian woman to "live-in," as most domestics did, was taboo. It would bring her unallowably close to male family members.

This was indeed a point of concern to many women, but the greatest complaints about domestic service focused on its demanding long hours and especially its low status. While new immigrants often reveled in its security, it did not take them long to realize that even though their bank accounts might be bigger than those of factory workers, the industrial woman was seen as free while the servant was seen as akin to slave. This was not the reason they had taken the risks of leaving home, so when they had learned the language and saved some money, most left service.

Women also left domestic work because more employment alternatives became available to them as the economy moved from an agricultural to an industrial one, and after World War I, the number of women in domestic work dropped dramatically. In 1870, when the nation was still largely a farm economy, two-thirds of employed women were domestic workers, but by 1920, their numbers had dropped to fewer than one in five. In addition to better industrial alternatives, immigration restrictions passed by Congress in the 1920s cut off the flow of willing workers. At the same time, electricity became available in an increasing number of households, which meant that appliances could do work formerly done by domestics. Finally, as families became still smaller and more nuclear, there not only was less work to be done, but also a greater desire to avoid the intrusion of an outsider. More and more housewives preferred to get by with only help from day workers.

As live-in domestics disappeared from most homes, black

women were increasingly called upon to take up the vacuum. While domestics as a percentage of all employed women dropped, the ratio of black women in the field rose, from 24 percent in 1890 to 40 percent in 1920. Black women clung to these jobs during the Great Depression, but, like whites, they left them when employment alternatives appeared with the labor shortages of WORLD WAR II. A half-million women left domestic service during the war, and with their departure, the maid as part of middle-class homes largely disappeared.

DOUGLAS, HELEN MARY GAHAGAN (1900–1980)

Remembered primarily as the victim of Richard Nixon's vicious campaign tactics, Helen Gahagan had a successful career as an ACTRESS before taking up politics.

She attended BARNARD COLLEGE and made her Broadway debut in 1922. She acted in several plays during the twenties and then, in 1928, went abroad to study opera. Back on the New York stage by 1930, she met and married film star Melvyn Douglas. She made a movie in 1935, but found she disliked that form of acting; she remained in the New York theater through 1936, when she moved to California and essentially changed careers.

Despite her personal success, the Great Depression had a profound impact on Douglas. She responded to the suffering she saw by leaving her family's Republicanism and working for New Deal reforms. In 1939, President Roosevelt rewarded her with appointment to the Works Progress Administration Advisory Committee, and in 1940, she was a delegate to the National Democratic Convention. Throughout the war years, Douglas deepened her devotion to the Democratic Party, serving as vice-chairman of California and on the national governing committee.

Thus prepared, she ran for and was elected to Congress in 1944. She held the seat for three terms, during which Roosevelt died, the war ended, and Douglas worked for the return of programs for social and economic justice that had begun with the New Deal. She supported Truman's Fair Deal, and he rewarded her with appointment as a delegate to the new United Nations General Assembly in 1946.

It was these ideas of international peace and economic security that Nixon successfully labeled "communistic" when he and Douglas ran against each other for California's vacant Senate seat in 1950. No rules of chivalry benefited Douglas in this postwar era when women were supposed to return to babies and kitchens, and he soundly defeated her. Nixon's campaign was such a classic of viciousness that women all over the country who otherwise might have emulated Douglas were intimidated from elective careers. Almost four decades passed before a Democratic woman successfully ran for the United States Senate.

Moreover, the era in which Douglas campaigned was particularly difficult, for the gains made by women in politics and journalism during WORLD WAR II largely vanished with the war. One reporter assigned to cover her wrote honestly, "At press conferences she kept to the main issues, in spite of the typical insistence of certain male reporters in asking about her clothes and her measurements when she was talking about foreign policy"—and then went on to give her height and dress size.

Douglas wrote The ELEANOR ROOSEVELT We Remember (1963), and her memoirs, A Full Life, were published posthumously in 1982. She served in appointive positions under President Johnson and worked for the WOMEN'S INTERNATIONAL LEAGUE FOR PEACE AND FREEDOM, the Democratic Party and other causes until her death at seventy-nine.

DOUGLAS, MARJORY STONEMAN (1890–   )

Known worldwide for seventy years of leadership in environmentalism, Douglas is especially recognized for her early understanding of the fragility of Florida's unique Everglades. While land developers and the Army Corps of Engineers attempted to drain Florida's swamps as late as the 1970s, Douglas had been arguing since Miami's boom days in the 1920s that survival of the earth's ecosystem was dependent on increased respect for nature.

A Massachusetts native, she graduated from WELLESLEY COLLEGE in 1912 and married shortly thereafter, but soon realized the marriage was a mistake. In 1915, she moved to Miami—then a virtual frontier town—following her father, who had established the newspaper that would become the Miami Herald. Though the marriage was an extremely brief part of her long life, Douglas retained her ex-husband's name.

Like other young women of her background, she went overseas during WORLD WAR I, but was unusual in two respects: she was not a NURSE, as most women were, and instead used her writing skills; and though she was one of the first women sworn into the U.S. Navy, she resigned when she was underutilized there and instead wrote publicity for the RED CROSS. Douglas returned to Miami in 1919, worked for the Herald, and organized charities in the growing city. In 1927, she served on the committee to bring the Everglades into the national park system and devoted herself increasingly to writing about this unique two-foot deep, fifty-mile wide river with so much grass that it looks like a prairie.

Douglas left journalism in 1924 to concentrate on delivering her message through fiction, and she soon was published in the Saturday Evening Post along with Fitzgerald, Hemingway, and other giants of the twenties. Although her early tales had European and other settings, it was clear that the Florida stories were most popular with the public. South Florida piqued national curiosity, since it was unique as largely unsettled territory on the East Coast. With plots involving hurricanes, Seminoles, and smugglers, she drew themes of destruction that emphasized the ultimate futility of working against nature rather than with it. During the 1930s and 1940s, Douglas wrote a play and over three dozen short stories, but it was her 1947 nonfiction work, The Everglades: River of Grass, that became a classic. She added to her literary store during the next decades with three novels, a history, and other work, including poetry. In her eighties, she headed the University of Miami Press, and in her nineties, wrote her autobiography. At one hundred, Douglas still wrote.

As her form varied, so did her ideas, for she was not limited to the strictly environmental. Her theme was a humanistic one intended to reveal a vision of long-term harmony based on respect for differing peoples, as well as for nature. She wrote of deaths caused by provincial prejudices, with tales pillorizing the profit-minded and exploitive who thought that violence and power could resolve conflicts. As such, her work was almost axiomatically FEMINIST, but she also used fiction to point out those areas where women's habits were wrong. Her stories made clear, for example, the horror of killing tropical birds for feathers to adorn the era's fashionable HATS that even feminists wore.

Perhaps both because her interests were more local than global and because she was connected with the state's most powerful newspaper, Douglas did not suffer the vicious attacks that were made on RACHEL CARSON. Both women appealed to much of the public that understood what the technocrats refused to accept, and as the twentieth century draws to an end, there is general appreciation for the ecological principles these women fought to establish. Douglas founded Friends of the Everglades in her nineties to campaign for environmentalist candidates.

MS magazine chose Douglas as a woman of the year for 1988, and she was honored on her one hundredth birthday in ceremonies in the Florida Senate. Marjory Stoneman Douglas spoke to the packed audience from her wheelchair, her voice and her mind still strong.

DOWRIES AND DOWER RIGHTS

An important aspect of most premarital agreements in the Old World, the role of dowries became less significant in America. While early colonial families bestowed land upon adult sons and gave their daughters dowries at marriage, by the mid-eighteenth century, land shortages in New England meant that young men went west to seek independent fortunes, while young women were free to plan marriage with less regard to expectations from the potential groom's family that property would come along with his bride. In time, Americans came to see dowries as demeaning to women, akin to declaring a woman so burdensome that no man would accept her without reimbursement.

Immigrants, however, especially those from southern and eastern Europe, would keep the idea alive. Not only was the lack of a dowry an important motivation for the young IMMIGRANT WOMEN of these cultures to leave home, but also, contracted marriages—complete with matchmakers and dowries—continued to exist for at least a generation after settlement in America. Occasionally there were women whose immigration was intended as a temporary measure based on the need for a dowry; a number of Italian women in the WORLD WAR I era, for example, told interviewers that their aim was to earn enough money for a dowry that would enable them to marry well when they returned home.

These women assumed that the money they brought to their nuptial contract insured a stronger position for them as marriage partners and especially greater security as WIDOWS. The English common law that was followed in America on dower rights entitled widows to at least one-third of their husbands' estates, partly on the assumption that a woman was entitled to a return on the investment of her dowry.

With variants between states, dower rights remained long after dowries disappeared as a common practice. Dower rights were based on minimalistic ideas, however, with the inheritance right of a son assumed to be of greater significance than that of a wife. FEMINISTS worked to change such state legislation over the years, and while dower rights were still part of the debate on the EQUAL RIGHTS AMENDMENT in the 1970s, most inheritance law

has come to be based on contributions made to the estate rather than on the gender of the recipient.

DRESS REFORM

Distinctive dress based on gender was, of course, long human habit in almost all cultures eons before American history began. Like many other aspects of life, however, it too became more pronounced and rigid as Americans accumulated wealth during the nineteenth century.

From the beginning of their organization, FEMINISTS understood that the restricting clothing they wore was both a cause and an effect of their larger societal limitations. Yet the mid-century experiment with BLOOMERS was so disastrous that the leadership of the women's rights movement agreed that the issue of dress should be subordinated. It was parenthetical to their more serious legal and economic arguments; further attention to this superficiality, they believed, would only distract from their serious points by making their appearance the object of attention and ridicule. Their political platform alone was radical enough.

Thus fashion created even more artifice during the era after the CIVIL WAR. The female members of America's newly rich families became walking symbols of the fortunes amassed by their men, as the bonnet of earlier eras was dropped for the *de rigueur* HAT, while hoop skirts and bustles contrasted impossible hips with tiny corseted waists. Medical doctors railed against these fashions and fretted over potential harm to internal organs compressed into unnatural shapes, but their fears focused on female reproductive functions, not on personal comfort.

Though there was little direct correlation, as the women's movement gathered strength in the early twentieth century, some of the artifices of the Gay Nineties were dropped. Artistic women such as ISADORA DUNCAN provided models of both liberated dress and liberated lifestyle that appealed to many during the Progressive Era, even while they joined in appearing scandalized and confused by these bohemians. As women's place in society became freer during the WORLD WAR I era, so did her dress, and almost simultaneously with the passage of the NINETEENTH AMENDMENT that assured women of the right to vote came genuine, grass-roots changes in style. Dress was no more a matter of reform, but rather a revolution—during the one decade of the 1920s, centuries of tradition reversed. The era's FLAPPERS shortened their sleeves and especially their skirts, "bobbed" their long hair into short, comfortable styles, traded high-top shoes for sandals, and threw out petticoats and whaleboned corsets altogether. It was a declaration of independence as important as any document.

Indeed, it verified the thoughts of one of the signers of the nation's Declaration of Independence, Dr. Benjamin Rush, who had written in 1787: "I . . . ascribe the invention of ridiculous and expensive fashions in female dress entirely to the gentlemen, in order to divert the ladies from improving their minds . . . to secure more arbitrary and unlimited authority over them."

DREXEL, MARY KATHARINE (1858–1955)

Katherine Drexel was a Philadelphia heiress to millions when, at age thirty-one, she entered the Roman Catholic sisterhood. After serving her novitiate, she became the head of the Sisters of the Blessed Sacrament for Indians and Colored People, a new order created by Pope Leo XIII at her request.

She established a motherhouse in Pennsylvania in 1892,

from which women were sent to serve missions for Native Americans in the West and to work with blacks in the Deep South and in Northern cities. Among her projects were over sixty schools, as well as the founding of Xavier University in New Orleans, which in 1925 became the Catholic Church's only American college for blacks. A leader in race relations, Mother Drexel was also an able administrator who attracted more than five hundred women to her order before her death at ninety-six. Steps toward her canonization began in 1964.

DREIER, MARY ELIZABETH (1875–1963)

Financially supported by her prosperous and philanthropic German-American family, Dreier spent her entire life in reform movements. Beginning with work in a Brooklyn SETTLEMENT HOUSE in 1899, she became deeply involved in labor issues. A charter member of the WOMEN'S TRADE UNION LEAGUE in 1903, she was its president from 1906 to 1914, during the most significant years of the Progressive Era.

She used her position as WTUL president to effectively speak for women workers during two great crises, the 1909 STRIKE of the INTERNATIONAL LADIES GARMENT WORKERS UNION and the TRIANGLE FIRE of 1911. During the strike, Dreier was mistaken for a worker, beaten by police, and arrested. She was taken to the station, but "when the sergeant recognized her . . . , he at once discharged her case, reprimanded the officer, and assured Miss Dreier that she would never have been arrested if they have known who she was." Dreier's speeches to her society friends in support of a boycott of the GARMENT INDUSTRY were also highly effective in educating upper-class women about unionism and the lives of working women.

The tragic fire in the Triangle factory two years later resulted in Dreier being named to the New York State Factory Investigating Commission, which attempted to prevent further industrial catastrophies. Despite the fact that virtually all of those killed were women, Dreier was the only woman appointed to this Commission. She worked on it four years and was partially responsible for the drafting of pioneer legislation in not only safety code enforcements, but also labor law in hours, wages, and other areas that helped end sweatshop conditions exploiting women, especially the Jewish women who dominated the garment industry.

The Commission's work complete, Dreier turned her attention to the SUFFRAGE MOVEMENT. Her motivation differed somewhat from that of most longtime suffragists as a result of her involvement in trade unionism. This experience made her aware that working women, even more than the usual middle-class suffragist, needed political power to improve their economic condition. It also sensitized her to the depths of male prejudice across class lines, for men consistently controlled the top labor positions, even when, as in the garment workers, the majority of a union's members were women. Dreier implemented her beliefs by chairing the Woman Suffrage Party in New York City.

From 1920, when the NINETEENTH AMENDMENT passed and Franklin Roosevelt first ran for vice-president, Dreier was active in the Democratic Party. She involved ELEANOR ROOSEVELT in the WTUL and supported her old fire commission colleague, Al Smith, when he ran for president in 1928. During the thirties, she saw many of her ideas come to pass with the New Deal's reform legislation. The depth of her commitment

to labor ideals was clear even in old age, when she split with the Democrats after Roosevelt's death to work for Henry Wallace's quixotic Progressive candidacy in 1948 rather than support President Truman, who had intervened against labor in postwar strikes.

Dreier published a biography of her activist sister, MARGARET DREIER ROBINS, in 1950. She died thirteen years later, at age eighty-eight.

DUNCAN, ISADORA (1878–1927)

A San Francisco native, Duncan spent most of her adult life abroad while scandalizing Americans of her era. Nonetheless, she was an important influence in liberating American women from their restrictive ways, as well as a creative presence in shaping modern dance.

Duncan's mother was an equally free spirit whose unconventional, if impoverished lifestyle gave her children range to roam. She moved with her daughter to Chicago, New York, and finally London. There Isadora, who was known by her first name in an era when surnames were used by all but the most intimate friends, established herself as a dancer. She made her debut in 1900, when she was twenty-two, drawing artistic attention for her highly individualistic style of dancing in bare feet while draped in flowing, ephemeral dress. She went on to Paris and was well received in 1902, setting a precedent for JOSEPHINE BAKER, another rejected American dancer who would be a Parisian hit two decades later.

She created the first of many dance schools in Germany during this era, performed in Hungary and Russia, and—defying conventions of marriage—bore an ILLEGITIMATE child in 1905. An American tour in 1908 was a failure, and Duncan returned to Paris, where her 1909 performances were widely acclaimed in artistic circles. She had a second child, fathered by a member of the Singer sewing machine family, in 1910, and for a time, she lived grandly, enjoying wealth and professional triumph. In 1913, however, her children were killed in an accident, and the baby Duncan bore to ease her grief died in infancy.

When WORLD WAR I broke out soon after, Duncan fled to the U.S., where she tried in vain to establish a dancing school in New York. After touring South America in 1916, she reached the acme of her American success with performances at New York's Metropolitan Opera House and in San Francisco in 1917. She returned to Europe when the war was over, where she ran insolvent dancing schools in Paris and Athens.

It was understandable that she would be glad to accept an offer of sponsorship from the new communist government in Moscow in 1921, for Russia had a long history of dedication to dance and she had been well received there on earlier tours. It seemed that at last her dream was coming true, and moreover, Duncan fell sufficiently in love to marry for the first time in 1922, when she was forty-four years old. But the dreams soon turned to nightmares, for the Soviet government, distracted with fighting counter-revolutionaries, did not provide the anticipated support, and her romantic young poet husband turned out to be mentally ill. She added to her miseries with an ill-timed tour of the U.S., which was then at the height of the "red scare" that followed the Bolshevik revolution.

Hurt and embittered by the rejection of her native land, Duncan said farewell and returned to Europe, but her personal life continued to be tragic, for just three years after their wedding, her mad Russian killed himself. As though to write a sweeping final chapter to her life, Isadora Duncan, nearing fifty, gave an outstanding performance in Paris in 1927; published her autobiography, *My Life*, that same year; and, while riding in an open-air vehicle on a September day, caught her long, windswept scarf in the car's wheel and broke her neck.

DUNIWAY, ABIGAIL SCOTT (1834–1915)

A pioneer in the Oregon Territory as well as in the SUFFRAGE MOVEMENT, Scott's family was part of the earliest covered wagon trains to the Northwest in 1852. The suffering and death of her mother along the way made a profound impression on the teenage girl; she would ever after insist that women must demand greater control of their fate.

Like many of her era, Miss Scott worked as a TEACHER until her 1853 marriage, and then bore six children during the next fifteen years. A decade after her emigration to Oregon, when the hard work she did (including the making and selling of thousands of pounds of butter annually) should have been beginning to pay off, her husband lost their farm because of bank notes that he cosigned for a friend without her knowledge—as he could when states made no provision for MARRIED WOMEN'S PROPERTY RIGHTS. When he also became disabled, their financial difficulties fell completely on her.

Duniway took up two of the relatively few occupations open to women in that place and time, running a BOARDING HOUSE and a millinery shop to support the young family during the next eight years. The experience was enough to cause her to found the Oregon Equal Rights Society in 1870, a year after the birth of her last child. The following year she managed SUSAN ANTHONY's first visit to the West; supported philosophically by her husband and yet mindful of the need to financially support her family, Duniway arranged Anthony's lecture tour for "one-half the gross proceeds."

The family also moved to the larger opportunities of Portland in 1871, where Duniway became the PUBLISHER of a weekly newspaper. Though her *New Northwest* competed with the paper her brother edited, which opposed women's suffrage, it was an immediate success. For the next sixteen years, assisted by a sister and later by her children, Duniway not only earned a living but also influenced the thinking of many people who flocked to settle the West after the CIVIL WAR. That the newspaper's success was dependent on her keen editorial and managerial skills is clear from the fact that it failed soon after she sold it in 1887.

Able at last to cut back on her work schedule, Duniway edited two other papers during part of the 1890s while she also remained active in the suffrage movement. She was included among the speakers at the COLUMBIAN EXPOSITION of 1893 and also served in this era as president of the Portland Woman's Club and the Oregon association of the GENERAL FEDERATION OF WOMEN'S CLUBS.

Though she had been a vice-president of the NATIONAL AMERICAN WOMAN SUFFRAGE ASSOCIATION, she left that organization in 1906—the year of Susan Anthony's death—when conflict with eastern suffragists reached a personal breaking point. WESTERN WOMEN had long differed from eastern, especially over the latter's tendency to combine the PROHIBITION and suffrage causes. After the 1906 loss of a state suffrage referendum that Duniway felt was caused by the association of women's enfranchisement with prohibition, she broke with NAWSA leadership and again took up an independent Oregon organization, as she had in 1870. Though there were two more electoral losses in 1908 and 1910, when Duniway led the 1912 effort from her wheelchair, Oregon men finally passed legislation allowing women to vote—eight years before national passage.

Duniway published her autobiography, *Path Breaking*, two years after the suffrage victory and one year before her death.

DYER, MARY BARRETT (?–1660)

Emigrating from England with her husband, Mary Dyer settled in Boston in 1635. Though the Massachusetts Bay Colony was only a few years old, the power of its theocratic government was strong. When, in 1638, ANNE HUTCHINSON was excommunicated and banished from the colony because her religious views differed from those of John Winthrop, who was both pastor and governor, Mary Dyer was the only person in the church to exit with Hutchinson. She then was also excommunicated and banished, and the Dyers, like the Hutchinsons, fled to the freedom of Rhode Island, which had been founded two years earlier when Roger Williams was expelled from Massachusetts.

They lived in Newport, where Dyer bore at least five sons. In 1652, she and her husband returned to England with Williams and other Rhode Island leaders; Dyer stayed there five years, during which she converted to the religious ideas of the Society of Friends, commonly called Quakers. QUAKER WOMEN were exceptional in the equality afforded them in both the theory and practice of religion, and when Dyer returned to America in 1657, she set about exercising her church's unusual use of women as missionaries for the humane new faith.

The Massachusetts and Connecticut colonies, meanwhile, had enacted laws banning Quakers, and Dyer was exiled from Boston in 1657 and from New Haven in 1658. When she returned to Boston in 1659 to visit two male friends from England who were imprisoned for expression of their Quaker beliefs, she herself was jailed. She was banished to Rhode Island in September, but returned a few weeks later. Her two friends were hung in October for their defiance of the ban, but Dyer—who had been marched to the gallows and bound for hanging—was granted a reprieve. She spent the following winter in Rhode Island and Long Island (where Hutchinson had also lived until her violent death in 1643).

Dyer's family, who did not share her religious ideas, used those months attempting to dissuade her from what they saw as her determined martyrdom. It had been her son who arranged the reprieve, but he could not convince Dyer to stay away from the harsh theocrats who ran Boston, for she was resolved to speak. Her husband—like multitudes of women throughout history who tried and failed to deter their men from courting danger—accompanied his wife to Boston in the spring. He pleaded for her life, but her last speech was a plea for religious freedom. Mary Dyer was hanged on the first day of June in 1660.

It did not take long for this martyrdom of a woman to sink in on the people of the Bay Colony, and her death was an important factor in lessening the powers of the church.

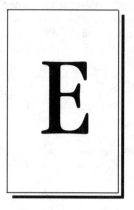

EARHART, AMELIA MARY (1897–1937) One of the most adventurous and best-loved public figures of the twentieth century, Earhart was a child of the Midwest—born in Kansas, she lived in Iowa and Minnesota before high school graduation in Illinois. She did a semester of work at a small college in Pennsylvania and then went to Canada to work as a NURSE in a military hospital during WORLD WAR I. It was there that she met aviators and developed her lifelong love of flying.

Yet Earhart's peripatetic ways continued, for it was not easy for a young woman of that era to see herself as an aviator, let alone understand how to systematically accomplish that goal. She spent a year on the fringes of SMITH COLLEGE, where her sister studied, and then enrolled at Columbia University, but soon was across the nation at the University of Southern California. It was this move to Los Angeles that turned out to be salient to her life, for it brought her first airplane ride. Earhart immediately set about learning to fly and soloed for the first time in June, 1921.

With money she earned by working as a TELEPHONE OPERA-TOR, she bought a plane for her twenty-fifth birthday. A crash only a few months later did not diminish her enthusiasm for flying, but nonetheless, family finances meant that Earhart had to revert to traditional women's work. She moved back to her sister in Massachusetts, worked as a TEACHER of English to immigrants and lived at the Denison House—a long-established SETTLEMENT HOUSE that was an important influence with IMMIGRANT WOMEN and especially the WOMEN'S EDUCA-TIONAL AND INDUSTRIAL UNION.

But Earhart was not a teacher or social worker, either by training or by inclination. She was instead again trying to force herself into the stereotyped molds available to women, and that this effort did not prevail was due in large part to chance and happenstance. The Putnam publishing firm, seeking an opportunity to expand on the public enthusiasm for Charles Lindbergh's transcontinental flight a year earlier and looking for a woman to make a second flight distinctive, settled on Earhart after she was mentioned by Bostonians who knew of her interest. Thus, on June 17, 1928, Earhart—as passenger, log-keeper, and standby pilot—set off from Newfoundland with two men, a pilot and mechanic.

When they landed in Wales, the world's attention focused on this "Lady Lindy," and almost overnight she went from settlement house worker to celebrated pilot. Earhart quickly became a public darling whose reputation far exceeded those of other women who did dangerous "barnstorming" in the era's popular flying exhibitions. A propensity for understatement and humor, added to her cute blond curls, made Earhart a public relations dream; the era's FLAPPERS saw her as the epitome of the liberated woman, while their parents pointed to her Midwestern modesty, common sense, and traditional manners.

The resulting popularity meant that her flying could be increasingly financed by those with a product to promote, while the transatlantic voyage's link with Putnam's not only brought the publication of her book about the flight (*20 Hrs. 40 Min.*), but also a position as aviation editor of *Cosmopolitan* (then a reputable family magazine). The vice-presidency of new Ludington Airlines was icing on the cake. At age thirty-one, Earhart was a national phenomenon.

The stock market collapse the following year did little to slow her down, as the nation, seeking escape during the Depression, seemed only to fall deeper in love with their Amelia. Though she did not win it, Earhart was the focus of the first Women's Air Derby in 1929 and she was elected the first president of the NINETY-NINES CLUB, an organization for women pilots also founded that year. Always willing to share with other women, she was also an active member of ZONTA INTERNATIONAL.

Aware that her initial fame was to a large extent the creation of her publicists, Earhart was determined to earn the recognition she received. She set several records for speed and distance with flights in the forerunner of a helicopter in 1931, and the following year, she became the first woman to solo across the Atlantic, setting a speed record for pilots of either gender. This flight was recognized by Congress with the Distinguished Flying Cross, by the French with their Legion of Honor, and by other esteemed groups.

She married her publishing associate, George Putnam, in 1931, but retained her MAIDEN NAME. Her second book, *The Fun of It*, came out in 1932, but more important to Earhart were additional aviation achievements. She won the ten thousand dollar prize for a flight from Hawaii to the mainland in 1935 and also received accolades for a nonstop solo from Mexico City to New York. She became affiliated with Purdue University in that same year, when its officials determined to use her as a role model for women students and supported that decision by buying her a Lockheed plane with state-of-the-art equipment.

It was in this "flying laboratory" that Earhart set out for an around-the-world trip intended not for speed, but for scientific research. With a three-man crew, she set off from California to Hawaii, but when they discovered the plane needed repairs, it was shipped back to the mainland. She began a second time from the East Coast with only one man to assist; they left Miami on June 1, 1937. Radio contact and regular landings went off as scheduled for a month, but on July 2, while they flew a dangerous twenty-five hundred mile mid-Pacific leg between New Guinea and a tiny island where Earhart planned to land on a barely visible air strip, radio contact ceased. No plane was ever found, despite well-publicized searches that have gone on for decades.

George Putnam published his wife's posthumous autobiography, *Last Flight*, in 1937. A commemorative stamp was issued in her honor in 1963, and Earhart is one of the half-dozen women selected along with over one hundred men for the National Aviation Hall of Fame. Though she was a licensed pilot for a mere sixteen years and was famous for less than a decade, Amelia Earhart made a very significant contribution to the history of American women. Presumably dying a few days short of her fortieth birthday, she had exhibited genuine courage, resourceful intelligence, and leadership ability that commanded worldwide respect. She gave millions of women suffering through the Great Depression a reason to be proud.

EATON, MARGARET O'NEALE TIMBERLAKE (1799–1879)

Although she has often been portrayed as an Irish serving wench of questionable background, Peggy O'Neale was actually the daughter of the proprietor of the Franklin House, a hotel that was home to many of the most respectable representatives in Washington during the early American republic. She received an outstanding education for a girl in her era at FINISHING SCHOOLS in both Washington and New York. As hostess for her father's business, she was not at all the tavern slut of later caricatures.

At seventeen, she married a Navy man, John Timberlake, and bore three children by him. A failure at business on land, he was often at sea and drank excessively when home, so it was not surprising that his young wife developed a special friendship in 1818 with a new Franklin House resident, John Eaton. A recent widower and protege of Andrew Jackson, Eaton's first wife had been Jackson's ward; this connection and his own ability gave him an appointment to fill Tennessee's vacancy in the U.S. Senate, even though, at twenty-eight, he did not meet the constitutional age requirement for senators. When Jackson came to Washington five years later, he too moved into the Franklin House; he saw that Eaton was especially close to the host family, but Jackson did not find anything objectionable about the relationship. Washington insiders, however, saw it differently; when Eaton obtained naval commissions for Timberlake, they whispered that this was not generosity, but instead an attempt to keep the husband out of town.

Timberlake died in the Mediterranean in 1828, a decade after Eaton moved into the Franklin House. Though the cause of death probably was chronic tuberculosis, rumors flew that it was a suicide prompted by an unhappy marriage. The gossips felt confirmed when Peggy Timberlake and John Eaton married less than a year later—at the urging of Jackson, who was soon to be inaugurated as president. He wanted Eaton to be his Secretary of War and thought a wedding would assuage the gossip.

Jackson should have known, however, that this would not be the case, for his own wife, RACHEL DONELSON JACKSON (who died just prior to the inauguration), had suffered from similar societal ostracism. Indeed, the social chasm between the Western frontier that Jackson's election represented and the Eastern establishment that had controlled America from its beginning was far too great to allow such a convenient symbol as Peggy Eaton to escape unharmed. She, like Jackson, represented the new and unconventional, and those who clung to power through their social preeminence would not permit her acceptance as a peer.

Since Jackson was a widower, Florida Calhoun, wife of Vice-President John C. Calhoun, saw herself as surrogate First Lady, and she led Cabinet wives in snubbing Peggy Eaton. While many men would have ignored this "petticoat war," Jackson, both out of loyalty to his old friends and to his late wife, took up the challenge. The new president spent much of his first year in office defending the Eatons, hunting down and trying to stop the flow of belated rumors, and even devoting Cabinet meetings to warning his men to control their wives. That the government was so long distracted by what historians have trivialized as "petticoat politics" was, in fact, because the president believed it to be not a trivial matter, but rather a symbol of un-American class distinctions. Moreover, he felt strongly that it was both socially and politically important to defeat Calhoun (represented by his wife), for

Calhoun was an aspiring presidential candidate who epitomized the Old South.

When the ostracism and resulting quarrels nonetheless continued more than a year after the inaugural, Eaton decided that the public interest would be served by his resignation. Jackson demanded the resignations of the Calhoun supporters in turn and, when reelection time came around, removed Calhoun from the vice-presidency in favor of widower Martin Van Buren, who was Peggy Eaton's sole Cabinet defender. Eaton was appointed territorial governor of Florida, and Peggy Eaton went happily to live in Tallahassee rather than Washington. She was popular on his next diplomatic assignment in Spain and eventually saw her Timberlake daughters marry into international society. The Eatons later returned to Washington and lived uneventfully there and in Tennessee.

John Eaton left Peggy a wealthy widow in 1856, but she was to scandalize Washington once more. Three years after his death and at age sixty, she married a nineteen-year-old Italian who taught dance to her grandchildren. She lived with him in Washington and New York for almost a decade, but after an 1868 DIVORCE, her husband married her granddaughter. Peggy Eaton spent her seventies writing her autobiography, which was not published until 1932. She died a few weeks prior to her eightieth birthday.

The fact that she was able to divorce in 1868, however, is significant, for the controversy that swirled around her in 1828 was slow to result in divorce reform. ELIZABETH CADY STANTON, for example, for years after the 1848 SENECA FALLS WOMEN'S RIGHTS CONVENTION tried to rally her supporters to the problems of unhappily married women, but even these advanced thinkers found the subject too controversial. It would be many years before women in general would exhibit the public sympathy for women victimized by bad marriages that Andrew Jackson showed so early in the nation's history.

EBERLE, MARY ABASTENIA ST. LEGER (1878–1942)

Determined to work as a sculptor from her teens, Abastenia Eberle moved from the Midwest to New York in 1899. She studied at the Art Students' League in winter and joined her prosperous family for summers in Puerto Rico, where her work was influenced by native primitivism. By 1904, at age twenty-six, she was sufficiently accomplished that she won a prize at the giant world's fair in St. Louis. Along with JESSIE TARBOX BEAL, she used the fair to bring national attention to women in the depictive arts.

Though she also studied in Europe, Eberle's work was distinctly American and was particularly influenced by New York's teeming immigrant neighborhoods of that era. Her next major prize came in 1910 for a sculpture of an IMMIGRANT WOMAN sweeping her doorstep, and her most famous work, produced in 1913, was also reflective of her era: *White Slavery*, a somewhat salacious piece, exhibited the genuine concern of the era's women about PROSTITUTION, then often referred to as WHITE SLAVERY.

Eberle won a medal in 1915 at the Panama-Pacific Exposition, and in 1921, she was elected to the National Academy of Design. This recognition came two years after poor health curtailed her work, and with the art déco changes of the twenties, Eberle was never again a major artistic voice, though she lived for another two decades. Her unconventional ideas

were a strong influence on American art in the Progressive Era, however, and she continues to hold a leading place among the relatively few women sculptors.

EDDY, MARY BAKER (1821–1910)

Mary Baker Eddy is well known as the only woman to found a major religion, but "Eddy" was not part of her name until she was fifty-six. It was the last of her three married names; she lived with a fourth man and came close to marrying a fifth. Moreover, though she sometimes signed her name "Mother Mary," she paid little attention to the only child she bore—and yet adopted a forty-one-year-old man as her son. Latent sexuality may indeed be one key to understanding this complex woman, who, despite a life of false starts and internal contradictions, nonetheless became one of the most influential religious leaders in American history.

Her DAME SCHOOL education in southern New Hampshire, supplemented by tutoring from her Dartmouth brother, was better than average for a girl of that time, though it was marred by chronic absences for illness. The youngest in a family of six and born unexpectedly late in her mother's life, Mary may well have used her position as the family "baby" to enlarge upon her illnesses, for contemporaries remembered her as a quick-tempered and stubborn child who nonetheless was capable of exceptional charm and charisma.

The leadership ability that seemed inherent, however, was given no expression in this era of limited opportunities for girls, and Mary was wed at twenty-two to a family friend, George Glover. She went with him to the Carolinas on business, but six months later, he was dead of the fevers that afflicted the early South in summer. The pregnant widow was sent North to her family in a state of collapse.

The birth of her son in September, 1844, did nothing to restore her. The baby, put out of the home for WET NURSING, continued to live with a foster family—perhaps in part because of his mother's hysterical response to noise, for she had regressed to infantilism so serious that she spent days rocking in a specially-built cradle. Mary Glover was treated with morphine and other addictive medications, while her son lived out his childhood with the foster family, moving to Minnesota with them at age twelve.

She recovered sufficiently during this decade to be able to work as a TEACHER and to do some writing, but again, perhaps because these limited avenues were less than fulfilling, she suffered relapses that were complicated by the death of her mother and the remarriage of her father. Three years after he married, she entered into her second union, marrying Daniel Patterson in 1853 in a ceremony marred by the fact that the groom had to carry the morphine-laden bride from her sickbed. A handsome dentist, Dr. Patterson began early to absent himself from their home, while Mrs. Patterson adopted the lonely lifestyle of an invalid. The CIVIL WAR may well have come as a personal relief to both of them, for he became a prisoner of war, while her family rescued her from the financial mess he left behind.

His disappearance from her life—and with him, her dependent wifely role—may have given her the motivation to seek a positive cure for her troubles. The era's popular "water cure" was ineffective, but a psychic treatment in Portland, Maine changed her life. Though in such prostrated condition that her brother had to carry her into the clinic, she was almost immediately strong enough to climb the city tower. The transformation was due to the charismatic technique of "Dr." Phineas Quimby, a mesmerist who believed both the cause and cure of disease to be mentally based. Like most nineteenth-century thinkers, he added a religious element to his ideas, proclaiming sickness to be "false belief."

His philosophy had great appeal to the discontented Mary Patterson, and when her husband returned to take her back into their unhappy marriage, she slowly discovered that there were alternatives to regressive invalidism and began to build an independent life. The death of Quimby in 1866 only increased her resolve, as she began to see herself as a missionary to expand his healing methods. She separated from Patterson that year and DIVORCED him seven years later on the grounds of DESERTION. The memory of their twenty years of legal union was a source of such pain that she would dismiss it with two sentences in her 1891 autobiography.

Lacking any monetary resources and devoted only to thinking through her new philosophy, Patterson wandered unwanted between the households of friends during most of the next decade. Finally, in 1871 and at age fifty, she developed a relationship with a second man who called himself "doctor." They shared rented quarters in Lynn, Massachusetts, where he practiced "manipulative" medicine, while she—in an amazingly assertive move—taught her healing philosophy for three hundred dollars tuition. Although their partnership soon broke up, that she was able to attract students at such a remarkable fee undoubtedly convinced her that her message had genuine appeal.

With her divorce final in 1873, she dropped Patterson's name and reverted to Glover, and then spent most of the next two years working on the book that she believed to be divinely inspired: *Science and Health*, despite its modern name, was combined with the Protestant Bible as the basis for her new religion. Although she was far ahead of her time in understanding that a great deal of nineteenth-century illness—especially among women—was actually depression, she was not so far ahead that she could articulate this idea without religious support. Instead, she saw her mental healing as akin to the spiritualistic healing the Bible reported of Jesus.

In 1875, she at last began to implement her ideas in rented quarters in Lynn called the "Christian Scientists' home." A publishing house was soon part of the home, as the first edition of *Science and Health* was printed a few months later. Though initial sales were disappointing, the book ultimately would prove a classic of profitability. Almost a half-million copies would be sold by 1910 to those intent on following the nearly four hundred revised editions issued during the author's lifetime.

Meanwhile, she transformed her personality from the repressed and lonely invalidism that had characterized the first half of her life; so magnetic was her teaching style that the home soon filled with captivated students. Presumably the elementary teaching that she had done out of financial need as a young widow had not been sufficiently inspiring to draw out this latent talent; perhaps also the times had changed enough during the three decades between these teaching experiences to account for the difference—her pre–Civil War teaching was prior to even the first organization of women's

rights advocates, while the SUFFRAGE MOVEMENT was well in place by the time she began to develop Christian Science.

Two years after the home's establishment, she married a student who gave her the name by which she is known. Asa Eddy was a stolid supporter whose business background was beneficial to his wife, but his influence upon her was necessarily limited when he died a mere five years after their 1877 wedding. While he lived, however, she took several significant steps: In 1879, Mary Baker Eddy formally founded the Church of Christ (Scientist), as she termed it; in 1881, she obtained a state charter with degree-granting power for her Massachusetts Metaphysical College; and the following year, shortly before her husband died, she moved the headquarters to Boston.

His death gave her only slight pause. The following year, she began a monthly publication, the *Christian Science Journal*, which had ten thousand subscribers in less than a decade. At the same time, the original congregation grew to over a hundred churches and societies throughout the nation, and at least 250 of her former students were now "practitioners" who considered their practice of mental healing to be as valid (or more so) as that of medical practitioners. In time, Eddy would bring her followers under tightly centralized control by replacing the church's "pastors" with mere "readers" and by limiting those readers to certain texts and short terms of service.

The amazing organizational ability that made all this possible culminated in an equally surprising decision in 1887: at age sixty-six and less than two decades after she began her mission, Eddy went into seclusion. She refused to appear publicly except on the rarest of occasions, a move that proved tremendously clever, for absence effectively mystified and empowered her. Eddy was the final authority on both church doctrine and business decisions, issuing orders as though from on high.

With her needs tended to by others of the succession of younger men in her life, the days when she was forced to accept bed and board from those who pitied her poverty were long over. She lived instead in a Boston mansion and "Pleasant Hills," her New Hampshire retreat. Though she had been evicted from rented rooms as a middle-aged woman, when she died at eighty-nine, Eddy left an estate worth over two million dollars.

Yet it was not as idyllic an old age as it would appear, for Christian Scientists had been plagued from the beginning by lawsuits from adherents and nonadherents alike, including one by her son and other relatives in 1907. The negative publicity from these suits and additional scandals was a motivation for the founding of the *Christian Science Monitor* in 1908. Although it began only two years prior to Eddy's death, the newspaper would become one of her most significant contributions to American intellectual life, for she intended it to be what it has become: a news medium respected by many with no belief in her church.

This happy result, of course, was not known to her, and the final years of Eddy's life instead were plagued with pain. She reverted to the morphine habit of earlier years, with half-hearted doctrinal justifications of this apparent departure from the principles of mind over matter that she taught. Worse than her physical pain, though, was the psychic. Her childhood temper tantrums returned, but more than that, Eddy's last days were marked by fear. Her belief in parapsychology was so strong that she had long ago developed a theory of "Malicious Animal Magnetism" (MAM), and her old age was plagued by the belief that negative telepathic messages from old enemies were aimed in her direction.

The complexity of her personality can be seen in the way she literally gathered her believers around her sickbed to ward off these evil spirits, like a witch doctor of a primitive society—and yet at the same time, Eddy continued to be an astonishingly effective organizer and businesswoman and an early feminist in fact, if not necessarily in theory. In addition to sexually liberated behavior for her era, she wielded absolute power over the men of her church. She also asserted a superior place for women in religion in other ways, as, for example, her revision of the Lord's Prayer to begin with "Our Father-Mother God."

Not surprisingly, Eddy attracted disproportionately more women than men to her cause. Most of those women were better educated and more affluent than average, and they were understandably rebellious about the confinement of female life in the Victorian age—a time when poor health seemed almost essential to the definition of a lady. Despite all the internal contradictions and erroneous asides in her philosophy, Mary Baker Eddy understood a fundamental truth that affected women's lives far more than men's: well ahead of Freud and modern psychology, she understood the reality of psychosomatic illness.

EDERLE, GERTRUDE CAROLINE (1906–   ) Ederle

drew worldwide attention to the changes in women's roles that marked the 1920s, for along with the passage of the NINETEENTH AMENDMENT that ensured women's right to vote, there were major changes in DRESS REFORM and in acceptable female activities such as driving cars, flying planes and participating in sports. Ederle was perhaps the most prominent focus of those interested in sports.

At a time when most women did not know how to swim, and bathing costumes were considered risque, she began breaking swimming records at fifteen. During the four years between 1921 and 1925, she set twenty-nine national and international records, once breaking seven records in one day. She was a member of a Gold Medal Olympic team in 1924, and the following year, she set out to swim the English Channel. Her first attempt did not work out, and those who argued that a swim of this distance was impossible for a woman felt themselves verified. Ederle did not give up, though, in 1926, she not only crossed the Channel against currents that forced her to swim thirty-five miles instead of the minimal twenty-one, but she also set a record for speed, swimming the distance almost two hours faster than any man had yet done. She was just twenty years old.

Americans rejoiced in her achievement, organizing a parade down New York's Fifth Avenue in her honor and retelling the story in magazines and movie reels. She held her celebrity status throughout the twenties and toured the country in swimming exhibitions. A back injury in 1933 kept her in a cast until 1937; two years later, at age thirty-one, she gave a final triumphal performance at the World's Fair in New York.

When physical fitness became an issue after the introduc-tion of television in the 1950s, President Eisenhower appointed Ederle to his Youth Fitness Committee. The fiftieth anniversary of her achievement was celebrated in New York in 1976.

EDWARDS, INDIA (1895–1990) A former reporter for

the *Chicago Tribune*, India Edwards was almost fifty before she became active in the Democratic Party, motivated by the death of her son in WORLD WAR II. Her strong support of Harry Truman in 1948, when he was widely predicted to lose the presidency, gave her access to the White House—which she used to promote women in appointive offices.

"Sometimes I felt like a ghoul," she said. "I'd read the orbits, and as soon as a man had died, I'd rush over to the White House and suggest a woman to replace him." Among others, Edwards' influence was important in the appointments of GEORGIA NEESE CLARK, the first woman treasurer of the U.S., and EUGENIA ANDERSON, the first woman ambassador.

After serving as head of the Women's Division, she became the party's vice-chairman when the Women's Division was integrated into the governing National Committee. Edwards turned down Truman's offer of the chairmanship in 1951, unwilling to do the combat with disgruntled males that she expected would result.

She attended her last national convention at age eighty-nine and died in California at ninety-four.

ELDER, RUTH (1904–1977) A student pilot who per-

sonified the liberated spirit of the 1920s, Floridian Ruth Elder intended to be the first airplane passenger to cross the Atlantic. She and a male pilot set out from Tampa in a plane called *American Girl* in September, 1927, soon after Lindbergh's famous solo flight in May. They ran into peril, however, when 250 miles short of the coast of Spain, an oil leak caused engine trouble and they were forced to deliberately crash in the ocean near a Dutch ship that rescued them.

The public was impressed with Elder's daring, and after royal treatment in Paris, she was invited to the White House. Called "the Miss America of Aviation," she was soon upstaged by AMELIA EARHART, who not only landed successfully in a June, 1928 transatlantic flight, but who also had genuine credentials as an aviator (or "aviatrix," in the terminology of the times).

Elder went on to make movies and marry six times; she died in San Francisco, a half-century after her briefly famous flight.

ELECTION OF 1876 The same year as the Philadelphia

CENTENNIAL EXHIBITION, 1876 was also the year of the most controversial presidential election in American history. Democrat Samuel Tilden of Massachusetts won both the popular and electoral vote, but nevertheless was prevented from taking office by supporters of Republican Rutherford Hayes. The election's corruption of democratic values provoked little outcry from the SUFFRAGE MOVEMENT, partly because most also considered themselves to be Republicans, dating back to their CIVIL WAR association with the party's ABOLITIONISTS, and partly because they hoped (in vain, as it turned out) for Hayes' presidency, since Lucy Hayes was a suffragist.

Serious predictions of a second Civil War also acted as a

restraint, and Hayes was reluctantly accepted by Democrats only because their compromise meant removal of federal troops from the occupied South. The result was an end to Reconstruction liberalism that granted opportunity to ex-slaves, including an end to much of the work on their behalf done by women TEACHERS who had traveled South to establish schools.

ELIZABETH I— *See* VIRGINIA

ELLISVILLE, ILLINOIS

In 1961, the women of this small town organized a write-in ballot election campaign that they kept secret from the men of the town, and they elected women to all the city council seats and the mayor's office. Though their election drew national attention, the women were not out to create a FEMINIST conspiracy, but rather saw themselves as more likely to deal with the town's longstanding problems in water and sewer delivery, roads, and other capital projects that had been ignored by the traditionally male government. The women governed throughout the sixties, leaving at the end of two terms with their goals accomplished in 1969—ironically, at the same time that the NATIONAL ORGANIZATION FOR WOMEN and other aspects of the modern women's movement were just beginning.

EQUAL PAY ACT (1963)

Though Wyoming passed a law assuring equal pay in government employment in 1869—the same year that these WESTERN WOMEN gained the vote—the idea remained an impossible notion to most Americans for another century. Well beyond the mid-point of the twentieth century, it was axiomatic that women would be paid less than men in most employment, even for identical tasks. It was almost two decades after the end of WORLD WAR II before the concept of equal pay for equal work was sufficiently acceptable to be enacted into federal law.

When wartime labor shortages forced the hiring of women for non-traditional jobs, women routinely had to accept lower pay. A Labor Department evaluation of munitions plants, for example, was wholly typical when it reported in 1942: "Time and time again the maximum rate paid to women was lower than the minimum rate paid to men working on the same machine and the same part." This had been the case throughout the history of industrialized America, for the common situation in all time periods was that women were paid half of what men earned.

Women accepted this disparity partly because they had little choice, but also because they, like most of the public, tended to see job vacancies as akin to charity that should be meted out according to need. The corollary of this maxim was that men, as the presumed heads of households, were axiomatically entitled not only to the job, but to better pay—even when women were also heads of households and were working at the same job.

In fact, however, job descriptions were seldom identical, for men and women historically had been segregated from each other in both blue and white collar work. This division of labor by gender rather than by job category was so fundamental to the thinking of personnel officials that, for instance, many World War II defense plants interviewed men in the morning and women in the afternoon on the assumption that even though they might work together, they would be treated differently—especially in pay. Well into the 1970s, newspapers commonly separated advertising by gender rather than by occupation, so that headlines read "Help Wanted—Men" and "Help Wanted—Women."

The result was that the Equal Pay Act was very difficult to enforce, for slight distinctions in job descriptions rendered the principle of "equal pay for equal work" useless because employers would argue that the work was not exactly equal. The Women's Bureau of the Department of Labor had long experience to predict that this would be the case, but it had difficulty enough in getting Congress to approve this small step, for equal pay bills introduced earlier had gone down to defeat.

A decade after the Equal Pay Act, FEMINISTS began introducing the concept of "comparable worth" as a more likely way to accomplish the principle of equal pay. They have fought for personnel studies to determine abstractly the worth of a particular job. The greatest (though still very limited) success thus far has been among employees of state and local government, in which the diversity of job categories makes it easier to see that it is gender discrimination rather than ability that is responsible for pay scales in which, for example, a garbage collector is paid more than a NURSE.

EQUAL RIGHTS AMENDMENT

Like the ABOLITIONISTS of the nineteenth century, who soon saw that the THIRTEENTH Amendment's end to slavery was insufficient to ensure the civil rights of ex-slaves and therefore added the FOURTEENTH and FIFTEENTH AMENDMENTS, so also was passage of the NINETEENTH AMENDMENT that gave women the right to vote soon thought to be inadequate by many FEMINISTS. They proposed an Equal Rights Amendment (ERA) to the Constitution to deal with the many forms of gender discrimination beyond the vote that remained in legal codes.

Drafted primarily by ALICE PAUL, the ERA was first introduced in Congress in 1923—three years after the last necessary state had ratified the Nineteenth Amendment. The chief clause of the ERA proclaimed, "Equality of rights under the law shall not be denied or abridged by the United States or by any State on account of sex." Its purpose was to negate legislation and practices that treated women and men differently. Because, however, federal and especially state laws were (and still are) replete with such distinctions, the ERA languished in Congress for decades.

Partly, it was ignored because the leadership of the NATIONAL AMERICAN WOMAN SUFFRAGE ASSOCIATION was either dead or aging; many of the women who had put their entire lives into passage of the right to vote were simply too tired to take up another and more complex cause. The membership of the NATIONAL WOMAN'S PARTY was younger, but Alice Paul and her chief associate, LUCY BURNS, had never developed a strong corp of organizational leadership committed to a longtime cause. Burns indeed typified most suffragists by bowing out of activism after the 1920 success.

Still more important in the failure of the ERA during the first decades after its proposal was the fact that many feminists opposed it. Women who had spent years during the Progressive Era working for PROTECTIVE LEGISLATION to ease the harsh employment conditions of women in the labor force were shocked by the prospect that ERA would negate, for example, the minimum wage and maximum hours laws for which these women had labored a lifetime. Since many of them (FRANCES PERKINS, MARY ANDERSON, MOLLY DEWSON, and ELEANOR ROOSEVELT, as examples) would become the powerful women in government during the 1930s and 1940s, there was almost no political chance that Alice Paul's idea would come to fruition.

Indeed, the opposition of female elected officials—who presumably represented the mainstream thought of women— was so strong that no woman in Congress was a cosponsor of ERA until 1943, when HATTIE CARAWAY—who was not a feminist—signed on. Nor did the genuine wartime needs of working women convert many to the cause of ERA, and a slight modification of the wording in 1944 brought little public support. Though both political parties included the ERA in their platforms during the forties and fifties, organizations such as the Business and Professional Womens Clubs—which represented the leadership of women's political action in the era—continued to be either ambivalent about or opposed to ERA, believing it to be a thoughtlessly simplistic answer to complex problems.

Finally, in the late 1960s, the ERA was revived as a goal for the NATIONAL ORGANIZATION FOR WOMEN and other newly-formed feminist groups, for, though it had languished neglected for decades, the counterculture turmoil of the era made this piece of legislation look mild in comparison to other civil rights acts. The necessary two-thirds of both Houses of Congress passed it in March, 1972; Hawaii ratified almost immediately, and thirty other states followed by the end of 1973.

To fulfill the constitutional requirement of ratification by three-fourths of the states, a total of thirty-eight state legislatures were needed, but after the first wave of enthusiasm, opposition began to develop. Probably the most damaging argument used against ERA was the fear that it would make women equally susceptible with men to the military draft, for even most feminists did not know enough of their history to understand that Congress had assumed with the NURSES SELECTIVE SERVICE BILL of 1945 that it already had a right to draft women.

The negation of protective legislation also remained a strong argument against ERA, even though major labor unions supported it. In addition, some women legitimately feared that ERA would add to judicial tendencies already apparent because of DIVORCE REFORM rulings against women in the division of marital property. When abortion rights also entered into the debate after the ROE VS. WADE decision in 1973, feminists found it increasingly hard to focus attention on these and other complex legal issues, and much of the ERA debate degenerated into derisive hyperbole. On the positive side, state governments repealed much of their blatantly discriminatory legislation and the federal government began enforcing laws such as Title IX of the 1964 Civil Rights Act, which thus negated some of the need for a broad constitutional mandate.

Meanwhile, conservatives saw ERA as an effective rallying tool to build their political organizations, especially since the unratified states were primarily in the Deep South and in western states dominated by the Mormon Church. Conservative groups, including business political action funds and right-wing churches, poured money into defeating candidates who supported ERA. Besides bringing ratifications in the remaining legislatures to a halt, they also managed to persuade some states that had ratified earlier to rescind their approval. In 1980, the Republican Party, despite the support of many of its most prominent women, repealed ERA as part of its platform.

Feminists, of course, rallied also. ERAmerica, an organization devoted strictly to passage, was formed in 1976. Coalitions of women from labor, churches, and other groups brought new membership into it and other feminist organizations, as the symbolism of ERA proved an organizing tool comparable to nothing seen before. In some states that had already ratified ERA, these coalitions managed to pass Equal Rights Amendments to state constitutions—but in other states, such elections were lost. Indeed, the failures were sufficient to bring Congress to extend the time period allowed for ratification from March, 1979 to June, 1982, but even that was not enough to gain the necessary three states. Indiana, which ratified the ERA in 1977, was the thirty-fifth and last state to approve it.

With the election of Ronald Reagan in 1980, the country declared itself on a conservative course and the presidential support for ERA that had extended back to Eisenhower was withdrawn. Taking their cue from this, legislatures in Nevada, Oklahoma, Georgia, Missouri, and North Carolina voted down the ERA during the extended time period. Even Illinois—an area traditionally supportive of women—did not manage the extraordinary majority their state constitution required. In many states, the House approved ratification while the Senate blocked it; this was the case in Florida, which was the last state to vote. Eight days before the extension expired, the Florida Senate voted against the ERA by twenty-one to nineteen, with one senator deserting the feminists who had campaigned for him because of his promise to ratify.

Although the ERA itself failed, most of the legislative changes it would have required came to pass anyway, and the decade of its debate brought about tremendous attitudinal transformation. Like the Child Labor Amendment that also languished in state legislatures for decades and was never passed, one factor in the defeat of ERA was the strength of the argument that it was no longer needed.

EQUAL RIGHTS ASSOCIATION— *See* AMERICAN EQUAL RIGHTS ASSOCIATION

EQUAL RIGHTS PARTY— *See* WOODHULL, VICTORIA

EQUAL SUFFRAGE LEAGUE A latecomer to the network of organizations in the SUFFRAGE MOVEMENT, the Equal Suffrage League was based in women's COLLEGES. SUSAN ANTHONY had already been dead for two years when it was founded in 1908, though it had existed in nascent form earlier with student activism by MAUD WOOD PARK. The League's first president, however, was not a student, but rather M. CAREY THOMAS, who was president of BRYN MAWR. The fact that the League existed during only the last twelve years of the decades-long struggle for the right to vote is indicative of the tepid support given by academics to the middle-class housewives who were the backbone of suffrage activism.

EVANGELINE RESIDENCES Created early in the twentieth century by the Salvation Army's EVANGELINE BOOTH, these were homes for working women that were similar to the better-known dormitories established by the YOUNG WOMEN'S CHRISTIAN ASSOCIATION (YWCA). The assumption behind such housing was that working women would not be paid enough to maintain their own homes and could live better communally. The second reason for their existence—more important to the sponsoring organizations—was that these homes provided a place where young women could live under close supervision in moral respectability. Rural parents could allow unmarried daughters to go to cities in search of employment that they otherwise would not find, assured that the young women would be safe from the city's temptations.

EVANS, ALICE CATHERINE (1881–1975) A microbiologist who worked for the Department of Agriculture, Evans played a major role in furthering acceptance of the pasteurization of milk.

Though she had degrees from Cornell and the University of Wisconsin, her lack of a doctorate made it difficult for her to gain credence in the scientific community during the pre–WORLD WAR I era in which she worked. Eventually, however, Evans was able to demonstrate that raw milk, even if clean, could transmit a disease-bearing organism. Using carefully done research, she demonstrated that two very similar bacillus had a common origin that caused disease in both cattle and humans; she therefore campaigned for the pasteurization of all milk—even if apparently sanitary—to destroy the possibility of disease.

It was not an easy task for a woman in her times to convert the farmers, veterinarians, physicians, and public health officials whose support was needed to undertake the transformation of the dairy industry, but Alice Evans's work saved lives that otherwise would have been lost to unexplained disease.

"FANNY FERN" (SARA PAYSON WILLIS ELDREDGE FARRINGTON PARTON, (1811–1872) A popular nineteenth-century literary figure, "Fanny Fern" was not only one of the first women to be regularly featured in a mainstream newspaper, but she also was one of the best-paid columnists of her era.

Like many other women, she probably would never have risen to this position except for financial need. Though both her father and two of her brothers were well-established journalists, there was no intention of a career for her: after graduation from CATHARINE BEECHER'S Female Seminary in Hartford, Sara Willis married and bore three children. WIDOWED less than a decade later, she remarried in 1849 and DIVORCED three years later. Scandalized by the divorce, her family was miserly about assisting her, and when she was unable to keep her family together on a TEACHER's salary, she began to write.

The pieces she published in Boston magazines were popular, and just two years later, they were collected as *Fern Leaves from Fanny's Port-Folio* (1853). The PSEUDONYM of "Fanny Fern" thus emerged from this title and its two follow-up books the next year, which soon sold almost two hundred thousand copies. Virtually overnight, Sara Farrington had gone from disgraced poverty to wealth and fame—and the best was yet to come. As "Fanny Fern," she joined the *New York Ledger* in 1855, where she was paid a fabulous one hundred dollars a week for her once-a-week column. She remained with that newspaper for the rest of her life, attracting a half-million readers with each issue.

The year after moving to New York, she married a man appreciably younger than herself. Thereafter known as Sara Parton, she published another half-dozen books while continuing her newspaper piece. All of her writing was aimed at broadening the minds of her audience while nonetheless avoiding controversy. Seemingly concentrated on domesticity, she gently prodded readers to think about the injustices inherent in the era's rigidly structured lifestyle and about the time and talent devoured by families that were unnecessarily large in an urbanized world. Because she knew the difficulties of divorce and widowhood, she wrote emphatically of women's practical needs. While economic goals were her primary target, Parton also supported suffrage and, like her friend JANE CUNNINGHAM CROLY, was a founding member of SOROSIS.

The fact that she and Croly were friends is indicative of her generous nature, for a less secure person might have resented the pen name of "Jennie June" that Croly adopted more than a decade after "Fanny Fern" was well known. Croly, however, would go on to be recognized by her name as well as by her pseudonym, for she lived later and longer and developed a public image separate from her pen name. "Fanny Fern," in contrast, died at just sixty-one, after years of battling cancer—but she never missed a column deadline. Four years after her death, her husband married her daughter.

FARMER, FANNIE MERRITT (1857–1915) Fannie Farmer probably would be much perplexed by the current association of her name with candy stores, for she thought of her most important work as being in the pioneer field of dietetics and health. On the other hand, she would be more pleasantly chagrined by the sales of more than 4 million copies of her cookbooks—for when Little, Brown & Company of her hometown city of Boston published her first, they were so dubious about the potential of a women's market that they insisted she assure the cost of the meager three thousand copies printed.

Afflicted with lameness in one leg since her teenage years, Fannie Farmer developed her own educational program in the kitchen of a friend where she worked as a "mother's helper." Her talent for cuisine was so obvious that her employer encouraged her to enroll in the relatively new Boston Cooking School, which, as part of the HOME ECONOMICS movement, had been founded by the Woman's Educational Association in 1879. When Farmer graduated at age thirty-two, the school was so impressed with her that she stayed on as assistant principal. She rose to principal in 1894, and in 1902, became an entrepreneur with Miss Farmer's School of Cookery.

Her business showed uncommon awareness of the differing roles of women, for her weekly cooking demonstrations were held in the morning for homemakers and in the evening for professional cooks. Moreover, her lecture technique soon proved so popular that a Boston newspaper's weekly reports were syndicated in other newspapers. Thus Fannie Farmer already had the beginnings of a national reputation when she issued the *Boston Cooking School Cookbook* in 1896. With its name changed to *The Fannie Farmer Cookbook* and with regular revisions, it became a perennial bestseller for the next century.

Though she published a half-dozen other books and wrote a column for WOMAN'S HOME COMPANION with her sister, Farmer believed that her most important work was *Food and Cookery for the Sick and Convalescent* (1904). Its emphasis on the importance of diet to health was still a fairly new message that showed the creativity of her mind, for despite her lack of educational credentials, Farmer's reputation was sufficient to allow her to lecture at Harvard and other medical schools. This, plus her cookbooks' scientific approach to measurement rather than the ill-defined "heaping cup" or "scant teaspoon" directions commonly provided by earlier authors, became the basis of Fannie Farmer's importance as a nutritional and culinary pioneer.

She continued to lecture even after losing the ability to walk, dying at age fifty-eight. Her school continued until 1944, when it ended during the pressures of WORLD WAR II food rationing and labor shortages—but by then, the dietary principles that Farmer preached were accepted even by the military as fundamental to human health and productivity.

FARM WOMEN Though the word "farmer" connotes a male image, women have farmed since the dawn of time—indeed, primitive women doubtless preceded men as tillers of the soil, while males continued to hunt for food rather than grow it. From the beginnings of the United States, too, women have worked on farms.

Early English colonists included women in several aspects of agriculture, especially dairy and poultry production. From colonial times on, countless women worked as milkmaids; it was they who tended and milked billions of cows, strained the milk and separated it from the cream, churned the butter, and made the cheese. It was women who hatched most chicks, fed and raised them, and then either gathered and sold their eggs or butchered and cooked the roosters. For much of American history, the "butter and egg" income of farms was commonly dismissed as the "pin money" of women—but for millions of families, it was often the only cash income available.

In the Southern plantation economy, black women worked in the fields along with black men, doing all the exhausting labor of planting, cultivating, and harvesting. Even after emancipation, the farm work done by black women saw little change, as an essentially feudal system continued with sharecropping, and the agricultural labor of women as well as men was essential to support families. While white Southern women were less often seen in the fields, they too chopped and picked cotton, and handled as well the work of henhouse and pig pen. Moreover, agricultural knowledge was assumed even among wealthy women, for they often acted as farm managers; the men who ranked as military and political leaders were as likely to be absent as not, and many women emulated Martha Washington, for example, in directing the agricultural systems that they called home.

When the great waves of immigration came before and after the CIVIL WAR, other types of farm women also appeared. Especially among the Slavs of eastern Europe, women commonly toiled in the fields at planting and harvesting grain; some had histories as virtual beasts of burden in plowing and other laborious work. Women from Scandinavia and northwestern Europe did less heavy tasks, but they too were accustomed to farm work. Soon, however, IMMIGRANT WOMEN realized that white American women of this era were more closely confined to gardens and farmyards, and a sure sign of the assimilation of a prairie immigrant family was when its women no longer worked in the fields.

Nevertheless, women and especially girls were called upon for harvesting corn and other emergency field work until mechanization diminished the labor necessary to large-scale farming. Meanwhile, women from southern Europe developed truck farming traditions in America; on small farms near large cities, Italians especially specialized in the production of labor-intensive crops from artichokes to zucchini. Yet while women grew and even peddled these crops to American housewives, "farmer" remained a term that somehow was exclusively male. That was the case, too, on the large farms out on the prairie, even though land claims clearly record that HOMESTEADING WOMEN were not terribly unusual.

Farming remained an enterprise best accomplished by a couple whose divisions of labor came to be seen as natural, and almost every farmer sought a wife. She would be expected to work in and out of the farmhouse from before dawn until after dark, with no money to count as her own until the reform of MARRIED WOMEN'S PROPERTY RIGHTS. Even in the twentieth century, women worked all their lives on farms without any assurance of ownership in those states that favored the inheritance rights of sons over the DOWER rights of WIDOWS.

Yet many widows and other women who found themselves in possession of land without male partnership nonetheless found that they could successfully farm, for it was the work that they knew best. These women seldom sought recognition in their own right, however, and even the labor emergencies of WORLD WAR II that brought the WOMEN'S LAND ARMY and millions of other women into agriculture did little to diminish the idea that farmers were inherently male. Not until very recently have women farmers and ranchers finally begun to organize themselves.

FARRAND, BEATRIX JONES (1872–1959)

A niece of EDITH WHARTON, Beatrix Jones grew up in the privileged world of New York society in the Gilded Age, with frequent travel abroad and summer homes that gave her early familiarity with outstanding gardens and natural beauty. Nonetheless, it was something of a leap for a woman of this background to actually work as a landscape architect; she is to be credited for calling herself a professional and working for money in a era when women of her status did not have careers.

After studying with the man who founded Boston's famous Arnold Arboretum, Jones developed a client list and began taking gardening commissions in 1897. Soon she was responsible for the planning and management of gardens owned by such wealthy Americans as J.P. Morgan and Abby Rockefeller; by 1916, she had branched out from private gardens to the landscaping of public institutions, especially college campuses. Eventually, she received commissions at Princeton, Yale, and VASSAR, as well as at midwestern colleges such as OBERLIN and the UNIVERSITY OF CHICAGO. The best surviving example of her work is at Dumbarton Oaks in Washington D.C., where, in 1944, the first plans for the United Nations were made in the serenity of her setting.

Along with America's giant of landscaping and city planning, Fredrick Law Olmstead, Jones was a cofounder of the American Society of Landscape Architects in 1899. Her 1913 marriage to Yale historian Max Farrand changed her name, but little else, for she continued to travel between her projects. Even after he accepted a position with the University of California, they lived primarily on the East Coast, where most of her work was.

An advocate of the American architectural principles publicized by Frank Lloyd Wright and others, Farrand worked with nature rather than against it; she used native plants long before others and fit her designs to natural contours rather than arbitrarily changing the land. Among her honors was the Garden Club of America Medal of Achievement, awarded in 1947 when she was seventy-five and had spent more than a half-century developing the natural beauty of America.

FAUSET, CRYSTAL BIRD (1893–1965)

The first black woman to be elected to a state legislature, Fauset became a member of the Pennsylvania House of Representatives in 1938.

Born in eastern Maryland, Crystal Bird was the youngest of nine children; her mother had been born in Virginia just after slavery ended and her father was born free in Pennsylvania a decade before the CIVIL WAR. That some of her biological ancestors had been white men who raped the women they owned was clear from the baby's light color.

Crystal Bird was orphaned at age seven, but the tragedy created an important turn in her life, for it took her from a largely segregated Southern society to an aunt in Boston, where she attended integrated schools and graduated from TEACHER training in 1914. She taught for three years and then went to work for the YOUNG WOMEN'S CHRISTIAN ASSOCIATION (YWCA), developing programs for black women throughout the nation. After almost a decade in this position, Fauset was hired by the American Friends Service Committee, a QUAKER organization, and again she traveled widely, speaking to the aspirations of young black women.

In 1931, when she was thirty-eight, Fauset not only graduated from Teachers College of Columbia University, but also married a Philadelphia educator. However—like the marriages of BLANCHE ARMWOOD, MARY MCLEOD BETHUNE, and other enterprising black women of the era—her marriage ultimately changed little other than her name, for the couple soon separated, finally divorcing in 1944. It did, however, cause her to give up her traveling job and to make Philadelphia her home, which soon became of great political significance.

Her Quaker connection was helpful in creating an Institute of Race Relations at Swarthmore College, where she worked until 1935, when she joined the staff of Franklin Roosevelt's Works Progress Administration (WPA) in Philadelphia. This naturally led her into Democratic politics, and a mere three years later, Crystal Bird Fauset would be rewarded with election to the state House, the first black woman in the U.S. to achieve such a goal.

In an urban district that was overwhelmingly Democratic, the primary fight was close and bitter, but the women supporting her organized a telephone campaign—then a novel idea—and won the election, despite the fact that two-thirds of the voters were white. Immediately an object of national attention, Fauset unfortunately did not long retain the spotlight or accomplish much in this rare opportunity, for she chose instead to resign after only a year in office. She returned to the Pennsylvania WPA as assistant director of its Education and Recreation Program.

Her WPA position, as well as her uniqueness in being the first black woman elected to a state legislature, brought Fauset to the personal attention of Franklin and ELEANOR ROOSEVELT, and she became one of their advisers on minority affairs. As a result, when the WPA's work was displaced by WORLD WAR II, the Roosevelt administration saw that Fauset was appointed as a special assistant to the Office of Civilian Defense, where she stayed until January, 1944, when she joined the staff of the National Democratic Committee.

In that fall's election, however, Fauset made an irreparable political mistake. Though she had won her election with the help of Democratic women, had been employed by a Democratic administration for over a decade, and was currently working for the party itself, she endorsed the Republican candidate for president. She was motivated by the belief that party leadership was not as devoted to the issues of black women as it had been in the past, but there was no evidence that a Republican administration led by a man who made his reputation as a prosecutor would have a greater commitment to black women. When Roosevelt defeated Thomas Dewey two months after her endorsement, Fauset was left without a political home.

The Republican Party did nothing to reward her for the tremendous risk she took, even after they regained the White House in the 1950s, when Fauset sought an African diplomatic post in vain. She never received another political appointment nor ran in another election; when she went to the founding conference of the United Nations, for example, it was as an observer, while Democrat Mary McLeod Bethune was the only woman of color in the entire world to have official status. Fauset spent most of the remainder of her years in international travel, speaking on race relations. Her experience in India, the Middle East, and Africa should have given her the credentials for a State Department position, but the Eisenhower administration was indifferent to her telegrams, and Fauset died in Philadelphia at age seventy-two.

FEDERAL SUFFRAGE ASSOCIATION

Another in the variety of organizations within the SUFFRAGE MOVEMENT, this group was founded in Chicago in 1892. The meeting was called by REVEREND OLYMPIA BROWN, who was dissatisfied with the emphasis that the NATIONAL AMERICAN WOMAN SUFFRAGE ASSOCIATION (NAWSA) seemed to be putting on campaigns to ratify state suffrage amendments. Brown and her supporters argued instead that greater efforts should be made for a federal amendment that would be applicable to all states. The idea was probably more prescient than even they understood, for the NINETEENTH AMENDMENT ultimately would not be ratified by any Deep South state; Southern women might well have gone voteless for many decades without the federal approach.

The Federal Suffrage Association changed its name in 1902 to the Federal Equality Association, but later readopted the original name. Brown served as its president from 1903 until the federal amendment was ratified in 1920, but the organization never developed a strong membership base. Instead, it coalesced with the group founded by ALICE PAUL and LUCY BURNS in 1913 that became the NATIONAL WOMAN'S PARTY.

FELTON, REBECCA ANN LATIMER (1835–1930)

The first woman to be a United States Senator, Felton was eighty-seven years old at the time and served only a day, but those facts do little to diminish the significance of this remarkable woman from rural Georgia.

Born to a privileged family, she had a supportive father who encouraged her education at Madison Female College in central Georgia, which, along with GEORGIA FEMALE COLLEGE, predated the ultimately more famous women's COLLEGES in the North. She graduated in 1852, and the following year married a physician, but his expertise would be of no help to her as a mother; only one of the five children she bore lived to adulthood.

This tragedy was complicated by that of the CIVIL WAR, for the Feltons, who lived north of Atlanta, were in the path of Sherman's march through Georgia. His maundering army, stung by the horrific battles in the mountains of southern Tennessee and north Georgia, pursued a policy of attack on civilians as it passed through Atlanta and continued south. The Feltons, unfortunately, fled to Macon, and thus continued to be directly on Sherman's route as he moved on to Savannah. Indeed, wartime deprivations may well have been factors in the loss of two of Rebecca Felton's children during the last two years of the war.

Unlike many whites who were Sherman's victims, the Feltons remained essentially populists, with their views influenced more by the small farmers of their north Georgia mountains than by the aristocrats who controlled the plantation economy in most of the state. While they rebuilt their Carterville farm that had been razed after they fled the Union Army, they also began to be involved in Reconstruction politics. Dr. and Mrs. Felton were respected by their neighbors and unencumbered by association with the rebel government, and, despite a tough race, he was elected to Congress in 1874. She acted as his campaign manager and strategist, wrote his speeches and handled his news releases.

Even after Union armies left the South in 1877 and Reconstruction was declared over, Dr. Felton was one of relatively few incumbents in the South to retain his congressional seat. By 1880, however, conservative Democrats had firmed up the "Solid South" sufficiently to defeat this mountain maverick and his wife—whom newspaper headlines credited as being a greater power than he. They did not give up their political goals, however, and under her campaign management, Dr. Felton was elected to the Georgia legislature in 1884. While continuing to edit the newspaper they owned, she also wrote his speeches and drafted legislation.

With her testimony before legislative committees and statewide speeches, she soon became the preeminent woman leader in the state. Though herself a graduate of a private school, Felton advocated free public education, which was then woefully lacking in the South, and argued especially for the admission of women to the state's universities as well as for female vocational education. A member of the WOMEN'S CHRISTIAN TEMPERANCE UNION, she also supported women's suffrage even though she knew it stood almost no chance of passage in the South. She even took on the cause of prisoners, arguing against chain gangs and especially against the housing of women and juvenile offenders with men; eventually she met with some legislative success on these issues after her husband retired from politics in 1894. Three decades of activism had made Rebecca Felton better known than he, and she continued to lobby for her legislative priorities. Her national reputation was strong enough that she was included on the Board of LADY MANAGERS for the giant COLUMBIAN EXPOSITION.

As she aged, Felton became more conservative, just as the society in which she lived also became more rigid. She nonetheless expanded her journalism career at age seventy-four, writing a column for the *Atlanta Journal* that would continue until her death twenty years later. Her views were feminist in that she understood the damage to women's lives done by men and especially by men's wars; the Civil War, in fact, was never far from her mind and was a strong factor in her determined success as a businesswoman. Much like the fictional Scarlet O'Hara, she was resolute about never being poor again, and these economic views led to her conservatism, especially in regard to labor and racial issues.

To associate herself with the Republican Party that represented business interests, however, was unthinkable in a state that had suffered from Republican policies during the Civil War and Reconstruction; at the same time, she was too much of a populist to be part of the "Bourbon Democrats" who dominated the South. It was therefore natural that she would associate herself with the Progressive Party, and she was a delegate to its national convention when Theodore Roosevelt was nominated in 1912. Though this presidential election did not succeed, Felton remained active on through her 70s and 80s, opposing WORLD WAR I and working for the election of populist friends who shared her isolationist and increasingly racist views.

It was in 1922, a decade after the Progressive election, that Felton achieved her ultimate lifetime honor. The NINETEENTH AMENDMENT ensuring women's right to vote had passed two years earlier, and when one of Georgia's U.S. senators, for whom she had campaigned, died in office, the governor appointed her to replace him. Since it was September and Congress was adjourned for the fall elections, her appointment was clearly a gesture aimed at acknowledging not only Felton, but also the newly enfranchised women.

Felton surprised the nation after the election, however, by traveling to Washington. The man who was elected had agreed to take his seat a day late, and, on November 21, 1922, Rebecca Felton, age eighty-seven, was sworn in as the first female U.S. senator. The next day she made a short speech and resigned. She returned to Georgia, wrote her column for another eight years, and died in Atlanta at ninety-four. Felton wrote three autobiographical works of her fascinating life, published in 1911, 1921, and 1930.

FEMALE MEDICAL COLLEGE OF PENNSYLVANIA— *See* WOMAN'S MEDICAL COLLEGE OF PENNSYLVANIA

FEMINISTS AND FEMINISM
The common contemporary word for the multi-faceted and long-term struggle for gender equity, "feminism" (or "feminist" as an adjective or as a noun referring to a person) is a relatively recent addition to the American vocabulary. Based on the French *femme*, it was used abroad prior to being adopted into the national nomenclature around the beginning of the twentieth century. KATHERINE ANTHONY, for instance, used the term in the title of her 1915 book, *Feminism in Germany and Scandinavia*, but the usage met with slow acceptance from linguists. As late as 1971, for instance, the curt definition offered in the massive *Oxford English Dictionary* for "feminism" was merely "the qualities of females."

The nineteenth century's great expansion of ideas in this area was usually referred to as "women's rights" or (even more likely) as "woman's rights." The names of organizations such as the AMERICAN WOMAN SUFFRAGE ASSOCIATION and the NATIONAL WOMAN SUFFRAGE ASSOCIATION reflected this preference for the singular form of the key word; it was emulative of the language's use of "man" to mean "mankind" or "human".

At the same time, "woman suffrage" alone was not an adequate term, for it referred narrowly to the right to vote, while the movement covered a range of issues, including DIVORCE, GUARDIANSHIP, MARRIED WOMEN'S PROPERTY RIGHTS, and other questions. That WOMEN'S RIGHTS CONVENTIONS were titled such reflects the broader, more amorphous nature of their agendas, for some of those who supported "women's rights" did not support suffrage.

These questions were likely to be matters of law that could be addressed through legislation and/or court decisions.

When national suffrage was obtained in 1920, another term was needed, for even after laws were adjusted to remove official discriminations against women, many areas of daily life continued to merit attention. "Feminism" came to be the accepted twentieth-century term for this broader range of intellectual ideas, and the word developed connotations far beyond the reach of law. It has come to mean a spirit of equity between men and women that can incorporate questions from the fair distribution of housework for married couples to the use of feminine pronouns in references to God.

Ironically, "feminism" has come to have a meaning that is almost diametrically opposed to "feminine." While the latter, older word emphasizes modesty, daintiness, and other "womanly" traits, "feminism" is associated with emotional strength and assertiveness based on self-respect.

FENWICK, MILLICENT HAMMOND (1910–1992)
An inspired choice for the congressional district she represented for many years, Fenwick's liberal Republicanism matched well the upper-class community centered in Princeton, New Jersey that she represented. The daughter of a privileged family, she attended an exclusive Virginia girls school and later studied at Columbia and the New School for Social Research in New York City.

The divorced mother of two, Fenwick was associated with *Vogue* magazine and Conde Naste Publications from 1938 through 1952, where she exemplified the stylish career woman, complete with a pipe-smoking habit. Her position as a publishing executive allowed her not only to develop credentials as a businesswoman, but also provided a continuing perspective on the changing roles of women through the Depression, the war, and on into the baby boom years.

Elected to local offices during the forties and fifties, she became a member of the New Jersey State Assembly in 1970. She was thus well experienced when, at sixty-four, she ran for Congress in 1974. Like much of the nation, Fenwick reacted negatively to the Vietnam War and to the Watergate scandal of the Nixon/Ford years; the incumbent Republican in her district was so closely associated with these events that he chose to retire. She was a perfect choice to replace him, for her brand of Republicanism was a careful blend of economic conservatism with social liberalism, plus a strong emphasis on ethical behavior. It was this emphasis on ethics that represented Fenwick's important contribution to the House, and she became the model for the fictional Representative Lacey Davenport of the popular comic strip, *Doonesbury*.

Reelected by overwhelming margins throughout the 1970s, Fenwick had a safe congressional position until she attempted to represent the whole of New Jersey in the United States Senate. Though she received the Republican nomination in 1982, she was defeated by Democrat Frank Lautenberg in a very close race. Appointed as an ambassador to the United Nations' Food and Agriculture Agencies the following year, Fenwick continued to be politically active beyond her eightieth year. She is included in the Oral History Collection of Butler Library at Columbia University.

FERRARO, GERALDINE A. (1935–   )
Born on August 26, on the day that women celebrated the fifteenth anniversary of their right to vote, Geraldine Ferraro holds a

firm place in the history of American women as the first to be nominated for vice-president of the United States by a major political party. (MARIE BREHM was the first by a minor party in 1924.)

The daughter of Antoinetta Corrieri and Italian immigrant Dominick Ferraro, she was born in Newburgh, a midsize town fifty miles up the Hudson from New York City, and graduated from Marymount College, a nearby Catholic women's school, in 1956. Unlike most women in the fifties, Ferraro went on to law school while also TEACHING in the New York public schools, receiving her law degree from Fordham University in 1960. When she married John Zaccaro that same year, she even more unconventionally retained her MAIDEN NAME. While she bore and raised three children, Ferraro engaged in the private practice of law. In 1974, she became chief of the Special Victims Bureau and Confidential Unit of the New York District Attorney's office, where she established a strong reputation as a prosecutor of urban crime.

In 1978, she ran a well-organized campaign for Congress, winning a firm majority in a three-person Democratic primary and a sound victory over the Republican Party's handpicked Italian male candidate. Her election from New York's Ninth Congressional District was an example of the depth of feminist success in the 1970s, for the Queens area that she represented was not chic, sophisticated Manhattan, but rather was home to the sort of New Yorker portrayed in television's "All in the Family." In replacing a man who held the congressional seat for more than thirty years, Ferraro was indeed a new kind of representative.

She aligned herself with women's issues in Congress, and just two years later, she was chosen to chair the Platform Committee of the 1980 Democratic convention. At the next Democratic convention—and a mere six years after first running for elective office—she would be the Democratic nominee for vice-president of the United States. She was chosen by presidential nominee Walter Mondale, himself a former vice-president, after he also considered two other women as running mates, Kentucky governor MARTHA LAYNE COLLINS and San Francisco mayor Diane Feinstein.

Women all over the United States held spontaneous parties when Geraldine Ferraro was nominated for vice-president on July 12, 1984. With her keenly intelligent face in every newspaper and her sharp, witty comments on daily television, she quickly became a focus of the campaign. FEMINISTS were particularly pleased when, despite her Roman Catholic heritage, she defied Archbishop John O'Connor's admonitions and continued to support the right of women to choose ABORTIONS, though this alienated some of the votes she otherwise might have received from Italians and other ethnic groups. More serious damage was done to the campaign, however, when two weeks after her nomination, over fifty charges were filed with the House Ethics Committee accusing her of failing to disclose her husband's finances. Ultimately, the Mondale/Ferraro ticket could not defeat an incumbent president with whom the majority of the populace was satisfied.

Ferraro published an autobiography, *My Story*, in 1985, for which she received a million dollar advance. In 1987, she presided at the Eleanor Roosevelt International Caucus of Women Political Leaders, a San Francisco meeting of women from more than forty nations. Her political life continued to be plagued with problems from her personal life, however, as her husband was tried and acquitted of extortion in 1987 and her son was convicted of drug charges in 1988. In 1992, Ferraro lost a bid for the U.S. Senate.

FERBER, EDNA (1885–1968)

Much influenced by a Jewish storekeeper mother (who expected her to be a boy to be named Edward), from her youth Edna Ferber admired and emulated strong women. Though her family did not actively practice Judaism, she was aware of being a minority in the upper Midwestern towns where they lived, and this perception of isolation played a part in developing the sensitivity and powers of observation that are crucial to the fiction she would write.

Unable to afford COLLEGE after her 1902 high school graduation in Appleton, Wisconsin, she went to work as the first female reporter for the local newspaper—another experience that not only taught her to write, but also provided her with future thematic material. Her journalistic ability was clear in that she began with a salary of just three dollars weekly, and two years later, at age nineteen, joined the *Milwaukee Journal* at fifteen dollars a week.

In 1909, Ferber moved with her mother and sister to Chicago after the death of her blind father. Meanwhile, she also began to write fiction. Her first short story was published by *Everybody's*, then a popular magazine, in 1910, and her first novel, *Dawn O'Hara*, appeared the following year. From that point, Ferber would be regularly and successfully published in several genres, including numerous short story collections, more than a dozen novels, and eight plays.

The Roaring Twenties with their new images of liberated women were particularly good for Ferber's fiction, which featured strong female protagonists. Her first bestseller, *So Big*, appeared in 1924; the story of a FARM WOMAN and her worthless son, it won the Pulitzer Prize. Two years later, she had the greatest of her hits as a playwright with *Show Boat* (1926), and Ferber was soon at the top of the bestseller list again with *Cimmarron* (1930), a novel set in the Southwest that, like the later *Giant*, would emphasize a sense of that place.

Her fame saw something of a decline during the depressed thirties and wartime forties, though she continued to publish both novels and plays. In one of these lesser known works, *Come and Get It* (1935), Ferber returned to her Wisconsin roots, documenting three generations of destruction of native forests. The same idea of change in land and family was behind her best-known success, for, in 1952, at age 67, Ferber made a strong revival with *Giant*, a novel that became a hit movie with ELIZABETH TAYLOR. Beginning in old Virginia and ending in oil-rich Texas, it was illustrative of her ability to write sweeping sagas that moved through time and place to develop a variety of American themes. *Ice Palace* (1958) followed up this success with a story that traced the emergence of America's last frontier, Alaska.

Immense popularity with the public (particularly with *Showboat*, which has been produced for more than a half-century), made Ferber one of the wealthiest of women AUTHORS—which may account for the disdain in which she was held by some literary critics. Never marrying, she spent a great deal of her money on the pursuit of domesticity via a lavish Connecticut country home, and left her estate to her sister and nieces when she died at eighty-two.

Ferber wrote an autobiographical novel of her youth, *Fanny Herself*, in 1917. Her major autobiography, *A Peculiar Treasure*, came out in 1939, with an update, *A Kind of Magic*, in 1963. Though most of her writing was so "American" in nature that few of her readers thought of her as Jewish, the depth of Ferber's feelings on the subject was revealed in an unused dedication she wrote for the 1939 autobiography: "To Adolf Hitler, who has made of me a better Jew and a more understanding and tolerant human being . . . this book is dedicated in loathing and contempt."

FERGUSON, MIRIAM AMANDA WALLACE ("MA") (1875–1961)
After attending Baylor Female College, Miriam Wallace married Jim Ferguson on the last day of the nineteenth century. December 31, 1899 was a propitious wedding date, for her life would change as dramatically as the century.

Ferguson quickly established himself as a lawyer and businessman and was elected governor of Texas in 1914. The First Lady performed her official functions and reared their two children, but they were devastated when he was impeached for financial corruption in 1917. The Texas Constitution provided that a person thus removed from office could not again be elected, and though he spent the next seven years appealing this, the courts upheld the state's position on his ineligibility for further office.

Meanwhile—despite Governor Ferguson's opposition—the NINETEENTH AMENDMENT to the U.S. Constitution granted women throughout the nation the right to vote (and hold office) on the same basis as men. With his court case lost, the Fergusons decided in 1924 that Miriam Ferguson would run for governor, thus clearing her husband's name with the electorate, if not with the judiciary. They campaigned together, but she clearly was personally effective on the platform, for she came in second in a nine-person Democratic primary and went on to win the runoff. In the Texas of that time, this was tantamount to victory, for Republican candidates in the general election were merely tokens.

It was during this campaign that newspaper reporters gave her the appellation of "MA," which combined the initials of first and middle names. Though she found the usage distasteful, she was smart enough to see that it was politically effective in causing voters to identify with her, and the forty-nine-year-old incoming governor would be "Ma" for the rest of her days.

She took the oath of office fifteen days after Wyoming Governor NELLIE TAYLOE ROSS, and thus was labeled as the nation's second female governor. While her campaign had been largely based on a personal need to right what she saw as the wrongs of the past, Ferguson proved a moderately progressive governor who was handicapped by a recalcitrant legislature. Her efforts to improve educational and transportation systems were not funded, but she did manage to secure passage of legislation intended to limit the Ku Klux Klan. Indeed, though the Fergusons are often portrayed as corrupt and ig-

norant, both were more enlightened than most of their time and place in their tolerance for Jews, Catholics, and other minorities. Further, while Ma Ferguson is almost always typecast as the tool of her husband, she was willing to pursue her own agenda when she felt strongly on an issue; her advocacy of temperance legislation was one area in which she differed from him.

She nevertheless continued to be hounded by charges of corruption, especially in her generous grants of pardons and paroles—which she saw as both humanitarian and as a savings of tax dollars, but which could be easily cast as the result of payoffs. The state's two-year term of office scarcely allowed her to establish an independent reputation before she was up for reelection, which she lost. She stayed out of the 1928 race and lost again in 1930, but in 1932, with the nation in the depths of Great Depression and Roosevelt progressiveness sweeping the nation, Miriam Ferguson defeated the incumbent and was again governor of Texas. (The same strain of economic revolt also elected HATTIE CARAWAY of nearby Arkansas as the nation's first female U.S. Senator that year.) The incumbent governor raised the familiar anti-Ferguson charges of electoral corruption, but the state supreme court upheld her victory.

Her own greater experience plus the backing of New Deal Democrats who took over the legislature in 1932 gave her a more successful second term. She oversaw a new congressional redistricting law; issued orders for a bank holiday before Roosevelt did; and used federal public works programs to help Texans suffering from the Depression. Continuing her populist approach of taxing the rich to aid the poor, she led the legislature in passing a tax on oil and advocated both a corporate income tax and a sales tax to benefit schools. Presumably feeling that her term had been a success, she did not seek reelection.

This was essentially the end of Miriam Ferguson's career, though she ran a half-hearted race for governor in 1940. Her husband died four years later, and she lived out the rest of her life in Austin, dispensing advice to aspiring politicians and growing increasingly liberal with age. She died at eighty-six, soon after the inauguration of Vice-President Lyndon Johnson—a Texan much in her model, with the same relative liberalism and the same difficulties with accusations of corruption. Like him, she had never been fully credited for her progressive agenda.

FIFTEENTH AMENDMENT
Ratified on March 30, 1870, the constitutional amendment that enfranchised ex-slaves reads: "The right of citizens of the United States to vote shall not be denied . . . on account of race . . ." Despite its gender-neutral language, however, the assumption of its sponsors was that the amendment would enfranchise only black males.

The proposed amendment was a major factor in the split of the SUFFRAGE MOVEMENT that occurred after the CIVIL WAR, for early in 1869, SUSAN ANTHONY and ELIZABETH CADY STANTON organized the NATIONAL WOMAN SUFFRAGE ASSOCIATION and adopted the position of opposing the Fifteenth Amendment. Anthony's belief in an educated electorate regardless of race or sex was seen as elitist by many of her ABOLITIONIST friends, who felt that she had betrayed her original cause. A few months later, they formed an alternative organization, the

Victoria Woodhull giving her famous congressional testimony in 1871. She argued for the eligibility of women to vote under the language of the Constitution's Fifteenth Amendment; many other women appeared before Congress as similar advocates before the Nineteenth Amendment finally assured women the vote half a century later. LIBRARY OF CONGRESS; WOOD ENGRAVING FROM *LESLIE'S ILLUSTRATED NEWSPAPER*.

AMERICAN WOMAN SUFFRAGE ASSOCIATION, and for the next twenty years, the two groups operated as rivals.

After the Fifteenth Amendment was adopted despite suffragists' objections, a number of women tested its language. Some 170 women, including four blacks, had already attempted to vote in 1868 in New Jersey, and in the following elections of 1870 and 1872, approximately 150 women tried to cast ballots in almost a dozen different jurisdictions. In 1871 in Washington, D.C.—where no state government existed to contradict the language of the federal amendment—women "marched in solid phalanx some seventy strong to the registrar's office, but were repulsed. They tried afterward to vote, but were refused . . ."

In the presidential election of 1872—the one in which VICTORIA WOODHULL made her quixotic campaign for president and the first after the 1870 ratification of the amendment—Susan Anthony led the women who attempted to vote in her hometown of Rochester, New York, and national attention focused on her. As expected, the local officials were not only unwilling to count her vote, but also had her arrested. She was tried in U.S. federal court and convicted without benefit of jury by a judge who had his opinion written before the trial began. Anthony refused to pay the one hundred dollar fine he imposed, but no enforcement action was taken—thus providing no opportunity for appeal, as she had hoped.

Meanwhile, the lawsuit of Missourian VIRGINIA MINOR was also making its way to the Supreme Court. When that decision came down in 1874, it was clear that the men in power believed the Constitution did not mean women when it said "citizens," and that suffragists would have to continue their crusade for an unambiguous amendment that guaranteed women's right to vote.

FINISHING SCHOOLS These boarding schools for teenage girls supplied the "finishing" touches to the elementary education girls received in DAME SCHOOLS or from tutors. Exclusive to wealthy families, finishing schools especially flourished in the nineteenth century, after upper-class Americans had accumulated sufficient fortunes to look for some schooling for their daughters, but prior to the growth of high schools or colleges. For many women, the residential life of the finishing school represented the only time in their lives that they lived outside of a home headed by either a father or a husband.

Their curriculum was distinctively feminine and much less mentally taxing than that offered by either the prep schools that sons of such families attended or by the COLLEGES for women that developed in the late nineteenth century. Typically, young women in finishing schools learned French and possibly German; the other major area of concentration was in the arts, especially music, painting, and needle crafts. Very little was taught in the sciences or math, for the chief objective of these institutions was to inculcate the social graces that defined a young woman as a "lady."

The operation of such institutions was, of course, one of the few business opportunities open to women of education and culture who nonetheless needed to support themselves. The mistresses of these institutions were almost always SPINSTERS or WIDOWS, and the schools were usually named for the owner, as in "Miss Ireland's School" or "Madame Talvande's School," to cite two famous ones in Boston and Charleston.

"FINISHING" WORK— *See* HOME CONTRACT WORK

FISHER, DOROTHY CANFIELD (1879-1958) Although

not nearly as well known today as her close friends WILLA CATHER and PEARL BUCK, Dorothy Canfield Fisher was a widely read author in her day. Like Buck, she wrote voluminously on many subjects, using "Canfield" for her fiction and "Canfield Fisher" for nonfiction.

Well schooled by her academic Midwestern family, Canfield received a doctorate in French from Columbia University in 1904. She began writing soon thereafter and published her first novel, based on a trip to Norway, in 1907, the year she also married. She and her husband moved to a Vermont farm her family owned, where she mothered two children while becoming a more successful author than her husband, although he also wrote.

Fisher is particularly noted as an early advocate of the educational methodology promoted in Europe by Maria Montessori; the first of her books on the subject appeared in 1912, and she was later recognized by Vermont with the first appointment of a woman to the state board of education. During WORLD WAR I, both she and her husband volunteered for war work in Europe, an experience that provided thematic material for several books.

She was the author of more than a dozen books and numerous magazine stories and articles by 1926, when she was chosen to be a judge for selections of the new Book-of-the-Month Club. Interestingly, although Fisher was the only woman on a five-person board, the club's first offering was by a woman, Sylvia Townsend Warner. Fisher held this position until 1951, the only woman on the group's editorial board for twenty-five years.

Like EDNA FERBER and other women AUTHORS, Fisher's greatest success came in the twenties, with her productivity declining after the thirties. She was an activist for displaced children during WORLD WAR II and wrote insightfully of the need to end patriarchal attitudes to achieve lasting peace. The combat death of her son in 1945 virtually ended her ability to write fiction, however, and her only significant nonfiction after that point was a 1953 autobiography. She died in Vermont at seventy-nine, with her husband dying soon after.

FISHER, M.F.K. (MARY FRANCES KENNEDY) (1908–1992) Fisher, who always signed her work with the initials "M.F.K.," was the author of many books dealing with food. Her unique writing style gave her books a reputation as classics of American cookery.

Indeed, recipes were almost incidental in her cookbooks, which are filled with travel descriptions, histories of foods, and odd bits of information on all manner of things. Her *How To Cook A Wolf* (1942), for example, was a compendium of thoughtful ways to keep the proverbial wolf from the door during WORLD WAR II food shortages. She herself was proudest of her translation of Brillat-Savarin's 1825 classic, *The Physiology of Taste* (1949). Beginning her career with *Serve It Forth* (1937), Fisher published magazine articles and more than two dozen books. A Californian who also lived in Europe, she was married three times and had two daughters.

Public interest in her writing flagged until a revival in the 1980s, and she was better known just before her death than she had been earlier in her career. A provider of nourishment for the soul as well as the body, W. H. Auden once called M.F.K. Fisher "the best prose writer in America."

FITZGERALD, ELLA (1918–   ) Despite the difficulties of growing up in a New York orphanage for blacks, Fitzgerald's singing talent was obvious already at age sixteen, when she performed at Harlem's famous Apollo Theater. She began traveling with a nightclub band and made her first record the following year. From 1938 on, Ella Fitzgerald became a household name, universally recognized as the major female jazz singer.

In the integrated world of music, she sang works by white songwriters such as George Gershwin and Irving Berlin, while recording with black talents such as Louis Armstrong and Duke Ellington. In 1943, Fitzgerald became the youngest person ever admitted to the American Society of Composers, Authors, and Publishers. She married in 1947, and, retaining her MAIDEN NAME, adopted a child.

Fitzgerald's ability to improvise, rewriting the material she sang, made her a decades-long favorite with jazz aficionados. The winner of countless awards, she was honored at the White House in 1987 with the National Medal of the Arts. In 1989, the Society of Singers presented Fitzgerald its first Lifetime Achievement Award; named "Ella" it will be awarded in the same manner as the "Oscar" and other arts awards.

Given the segregated society that America was when Ella Fitzgerald was young and given also that jazz was new and controversial, she brought new prestige to black women while also making a major contribution to the music that is most uniquely American.

FLAPPERS The term for women in the 1920s who, by changes in dress and lifestyle, transformed forever the image of women in the Western world. Motivated in part by their disillusioning and yet confidence-building experiences during WORLD WAR I, "flappers" in both Britain and America were especially known for "bobbing" the long hair that women had historically worn piled heavily on their heads, cutting it instead into a short, straight style that required little care. They also adopted skirts that rose first above the ankle and then above the knee, with shocking abandon of the virtues of modesty that had kept skirts to female feet for centuries.

Petticoats, HATS, high-top shoes, and especially corsets were rejected. Sleeves were cut, too, for the key to flappers' apparel was casual maintenance and ease of athletics, as women adopted sports, especially swimming, that previously had been male preserves. In addition to changes in dress, flappers prided themselves on the adoption of male habits in alcohol

This pre–World War I ensemble exhibits simpler lines than the bustle fashion of an earlier decade, but it still reaches below the ankle and is dominated by the obligatory hat. Within a few years after the war's end, women's clothing changed forever. LIBRARY OF CONGRESS.

This costume from 1921 reveals both legs and arms. The woman has not only discarded her hat but also has cut her hair. The quick but tremendous change in clothing style that took place after the war overthrew centuries of cumbersome limitations and allowed women to pursue a far more liberated lifestyle. LIBRARY OF CONGRESS; PHOTOGRAPH BY UNDERWOOD & UNDERWOOD.

and cigarette use; they drove cars, danced newly suggestive dances to revolutionary jazz music, and frequented the new moving picture houses.

While associated in many minds with the flapping movements of the era's dances, especially the Charleston, "flapper" was earlier used in Britain to denote a fledgling young woman. It developed disparaging connotations in the twenties, as the British withheld the vote from women younger than thirty. Both there and in America, however, no other generation of young women has made such major change in such a short time with such dramatic implications for the history of women as did the "flapper."

FLEESON, DORIS (1901–1970)

One of the few women in the top ranks of journalism during the fifties and sixties, Doris Fleeson had by then developed a reputation for keen intelligence and sharp reporting that brought her fear and respect from the Washington politicians she covered. At the same time, she was exceptional in her open FEMINISM and especially in her willingness to help young women who were getting their start as reporters in those regressive years.

A graduate of the University of Kansas, Fleeson worked for two midwestern newspapers before moving to New York, where in 1927, after a year with a small Long Island paper, she finally won the reporting job she coveted with the *New York Daily News*. Three years later, she married a colleague, and in 1932, bore a daughter that she named for herself. The next year, the *News* assigned the couple to Washington, where they co-wrote a political column.

Since their political views were fundamentally different, however, with Fleeson being a strong supporter of Roosevelt's New Deal, while her husband was not, the thirties were a difficult time for both their work and their marriage. When they DIVORCED in 1942, at the beginning of American involvement in World War II, Fleeson briefly returned to New York where she wrote radio news before being hired by *Woman's Home Companion* as their correspondent for WORLD WAR II.

Woman's Home Companion was no mere household hint collection in the forties; it editorialized for women doctors in the military, for example, and sponsored a woman reporter in an exhaustive investigation of rationing fraud. The magazine introduced Fleeson proudly to their audience, and she covered the armies in Europe from the Italian invasion through D-Day, writing stories with titles such as "Within Sound of the Guns" that brought the war home to the women whose husbands and sons were fighting it. Ever concerned with women, she also wrote dramatically of the hundreds of unsung members of the ARMY NURSE CORPS and the WOMEN'S ARMY CORPS.

Perhaps emboldened by her war experience, Fleeson independently began to develop herself as a syndicated columnist. With commitments from only two newspapers at the beginning, she soon was carried in more than one hundred. Ultimately writing five days a week under the aegis of United Features Syndicate, she was the first woman to be recognized as a serious national political commentator. She covered the Truman, Eisenhower, Kennedy, and Johnson administrations, finally falling ill on the 1964 campaign trail.

Meanwhile, she had remarried in 1958 to a former secretary of the Navy. Finding late in life the domestic happiness that had not been hers in youth, she died a day-and-a-half after her husband's death.

FLEMING, WILLIAMINA PATON STEVENS (1857–1911) A

Scot, Mina Stevens had worked as a TEACHER from age fourteen before marrying James Fleming and emigrating to Boston at twenty-one. A year later, pregnant and DESERTED by her husband, she was forced to go into DOMESTIC SERVICE. She found work as a maid in the home of the director of the Harvard Observatory—and her misfortune became the key to her successful life thereafter.

Her employer, unhappy with the performance of male observatory workers, declared that his maid could do a better job, and in 1881, hired Fleming to do clerical work and mathematical calculations. It soon became obvious that her mind was capable of scientific thought, as well as of detailed methodology. During the next nine years, Fleming would observe and classify more than ten thousand celestial bodies with such success that her name was adopted for the system used.

During her three decades at Harvard, her administrative duties expanded so that ultimately she supervised dozens of young women who—following the precedent she set—did the requisite mathematics that today is done by computers. This work detracted from Fleming's independent scientific research, so that the astronomical classifications credited to her were later vastly exceeded by those of ANNIE JUMP CANNON. Nonetheless, Fleming edited all of the publications that the observatory issued, and the professionalism of her work was sufficiently valuable that the Harvard Corporation rewarded her with the first official appointment given to a woman, making her curator of astronomical photographs in 1898.

Despite her many other assignments, Fleming continued her independent scientific research—and, moreover, did so at a level that makes others in her profession seem almost obtuse. When, in 1907, she published a study of the 222 variable stars she had discovered, a British astronomer noted: "Many astronomers are deservedly proud to have discovered one . . . the discovery of 222 . . . is an achievement bordering on the marvellous." Especially when it is remembered that Fleming had absolutely no higher education, the scientific ability that she demonstrated is nothing short of astonishing.

A cofounder with her male colleagues of the Astronomical and Astrophysical Society, she also supported the SUFFRAGE MOVEMENT. Feminists were glad to have her involvement, for Fleming was internationally recognized in her time. She received major honors in France and Mexico, and, in 1906, she was the first American woman to be elected to the Royal Astronomical Society. Her life amid the stars should not be forgotten.

FLETCHER, ALICE CUNNINGHAM (1838–1923) A

founding officer of the ASSOCIATION FOR THE ADVANCEMENT OF WOMEN, Alice Fletcher was a TEACHER and lecturer who, in 1878 and at age forty, began field research under the aegis of the Peabody Museum at Harvard on the shell mounds left by Native Americans in Florida and Massachusetts. The following year, she attended the lecture tour of Bright Eyes, a leader of the Omaha tribe whose Christian name was Susette LaFlesche. This brought Fletcher into contact with Midwestern Native Americans, and her attention turned from scholarly research on the past to political activism for the still extant but dispossessed tribes of her own time.

After living with the Omahas in 1881, she moved to Washington to work on their behalf, drafting legislation that divided the tribe's common lands into individual holdings—a strategy that she hoped would lessen the power of the Bureau of Indian Affairs, while providing economic incentives to individuals. Even though this was forty years before women could vote, Fletcher not only managed to lobby her bill through Congress, but also succeeded in getting President Arthur to appoint her as its executor.

She returned to Nebraska and carried out the project with such capability that she earned the respect of both the Omahas and Washington officials. She authored an exhaustive report for the Senate in 1885 titled *Indian Education and Civilization*, and the following year, went to Alaska to report on those natives at the request of the secretary of the interior. Her work was influential in the 1887 passage of the Dawes Act—legislation that, although criticized by social scientists today for the destruction of tribal life, was seen as humanitarian by most at the time. Fletcher spent the next five years overseeing its enactment with the Winnebagos of Nebraska and the Nez Perces of Idaho, encountering much hostility with the latter tribe but working to overcome it with careful appropriation to natives of the best possible lands.

Meanwhile, she also continued her scholarly work, accessing artifacts for the Peabody Museum, which granted her a life fellowship in 1891, and taking a special interest in the preservation of native songs. Recognized by her colleagues, Fletcher was elected vice-president of the American Association for the Advancement of Science in 1896; was a founder of the American Anthropological Association in 1902; and was named president of the American Folk-Lore Society in 1905. From her earliest days with the Omahas, she had informally adopted Bright Eyes' younger brother, and he was with her when she died at eighty-five.

FLORENCE CRITTENTON HOMES Known as refuges for

unwed mothers, the Florence Crittenton Homes were begun by Charles N. Crittenton, an evangelical missionary. He had a colorful past as a patent medicine salesman that included

Williamina Fleming, center, directs a group of "computers," while her mentor, E.C. Pickering, is to the left. The women with magnifying glasses are examining glass plates of astronomical phenomena, while those with the notebooks record their observations. HARVARD COLLEGE OBSERVATORY.

friendship with LYDIA PINKHAM. In 1883, he formed a society to aid "fallen women" and opened a mission in New York. With the era's emphasis on the dangers of PROSTITUTION and WHITE SLAVERY, the cause was an instant success: by 1897, there were fifty-three Florence Crittenton Homes throughout the nation. With support from FRANCES WILLARD and the WCTU, the initial Crittenton Homes aided alcoholic women, functioned as spouse abuse shelters, and taught skills so that women could earn an honest living.

As time passed, however, they increasingly emphasized unwed mothers, and many of the middle-class women who supported the homes were at least as interested in adopting a baby as in helping the baby's mother. By the mid-twentieth century, their chief purpose was to serve as shelters for teenagers who hid their pregnancies, gave up their babies, and returned to school with stories of visits to relatives. Crittenton Homes have closed as the stigma of ILLEGITIMACY has faded— ironically, during the same era that centers for displaced homemakers and refuges for spouse abuse victims are being built.

FLYNN, ELIZABETH GURLEY (1890–1964) Growing up in poor New England TEXTILE MILL towns and in the blue-collar Bronx, Flynn came to socialism early and easily via her parents' beliefs. Her innate speaking ability was so great that she drew crowds already by her teenage years; at sixteen, she left high school to begin what would become her lifelong career of political organizing.

Under the aegis of the Industrial Workers of the World, she spoke to miners in the iron range of Minnesota in 1907 and went on from there through Montana to Spokane, where her incendiary speeches twice brought arrest and jail—as well as national publicity for her cause. Returning to the East Coast in 1910, she played major roles in the 1912 LAWRENCE MASSA-CHUSETTS TEXTILE STRIKE and a strike in the Paterson, New Jersey silk mills the following year. Both of these involved large numbers of IMMIGRANT WOMEN; Flynn's FEMINISM was important in giving them the courage to strike and the organizing skills to make themselves heard.

Again arrested during WORLD WAR I for alleged violation of the Espionage Act, Flynn turned her attention to building long-term legal defense mechanisms after the charges against her were dropped. She was a founding member of the American Civil Liberties Union in 1920 and from 1927–1930, she chaired the International Labor Defense; the famous failed Sacco-Vanzetti defense occupied her during much of the twenties.

Like many leftists during the Great Depression, Flynn joined the Communist Party in 1937, but her support for democracy and the Allies during WORLD WAR II was unquestioned. Again, she took a special interest in women, urging them not only to get defense industry jobs, but also to become involved in their unions and to lobby for child care and for enforcement of PROTECTIVE LEGISLATION. In a booklet entitled "Women Have a Date With Destiny," Flynn abandoned even the pretense of endorsing Communist candidates, instead urging women not to desert Roosevelt and the Democratic Party during the crucial election of 1944.

With the repression of the 1950s, however, free speech was again under attack and she was again arrested. This time her impassioned pleas to the jury did not work, and after a nine-month federal trial, she was convicted of violating the Smith Act (a 1940 law that banned the advocacy of the overthrow of the government by force). She could have accepted deportation to the Soviet Union rather than prison, but her object was to improve her native land, not to flee it, and Flynn spent her sixty-fifth and sixty-sixth birthdays behind bars at Alderson, West Virginia. Her autobiography, *I Speak My Own Piece*, and a memoir of prison life, *Alderson Story*, were both published in 1955 while she was incarcerated.

She resumed her activities upon release and, in 1960, after winning a ruling from the Supreme Court that she could not be denied a passport because of her political beliefs, she took her first trip to the Soviet Union and the communist countries of Eastern Europe. In 1961, at age seventy-one, Flynn was elected chairman of the Communist Party USA; the first woman thus chosen, she was still in office when she died three years later while visiting Moscow. She was honored with a state funeral in Red Square, leaving behind only the legacy of her work, for her one child, who was the product of a brief youthful marriage and whose surname was also Flynn, had predeceased her.

FOSTER, ABBY KELLY (1810–1887)

Born in rural Massachusetts and educated as a QUAKER, Abby Kelly worked as a TEACHER during the 1830s, while she read the works of William Lloyd Garrison and became one of the first visible ABOLITIONIST women.

Her work as secretary for the Lynn, Massachusetts Female Anti-Slavery Society in 1835–1837 took her on door-to-door canvasses of political education, petition collection, and fundraising. She attended the first national convention of women abolitionists in 1837 and 1838, and in the latter year, she joined Garrison in founding the New England Non-Resistant Society. She also made her first public speech that year, a thing still so unusual for women that it would have brought her a great deal of attention (most of it negative) even without the fact that the Philadelphia hall in which she spoke was attacked and burned by a mob the following day.

Men as well as women in the abolitionist cause recognized her potential as a PUBLIC SPEAKER and urged her to become a full-time lecturer. After six months of soul-searching, in May, 1839, Kelly left teaching and set out on a precarious career of earning a living through lecture fees. She was controversial not only because of her gender, but also because of her subject, for most Americans in this era, even in the North, considered slavery to be divinely ordained. Kelly was attacked and slandered while she suffered the discomforts of traveling as far as the Michigan frontier; she was refused hotel rooms and, of course, struggled endlessly to cover her expenses.

Yet, despite all of this personal sacrifice, she became the target of controversy within the abolitionist movement when, at the 1840 convention of the American Anti-Slavery Society, her appointment to the business committee was viewed with such anger and disdain by male delegates that almost half of them broke permanently with the organization and founded a rival group.

Soon thereafter, however, some of the burden she carried was lifted when she met and fell in love with a former Dartmouth student, Stephen Symonds Foster, an abolitionist lecturer who was even more radical than she. Their 1845 marriage did a good deal to abate the gossip about a single woman who TRAVELED alone, and the Fosters were careful not to allow their marriage to mean the end of her career. Even though she bore a daughter in 1847 (when she was thirty-seven), Abby Kelly Foster continued to tour for at least part of each lecture season, while her husband tended their child and cared for their Massachusetts farm.

As the abolitionist message became more acceptable during the 1850s, Abby Foster and her husband moved still further left in their political philosophy. She even broke with Garrison, arguing that abolitionists should declare themselves as a third party to counter the rising Republicans, whom she distrusted. After the Civil War accomplished the abolitionist goal, she still continued her speaking and fund-raising on behalf of the newly emancipated, despite age and illness.

The controversy of her public speaking, of course, defined her from her earliest days as a FEMINIST, and her defiance of conventional standards for female behavior proved a model to many younger women, including LUCY STONE, who had been a student at OBERLIN COLLEGE when the Fosters spoke there in 1846, and SUSAN ANTHONY, who met them when they toured Rochester the same year, prior to Anthony's involvement in either abolitionism or feminism.

Moreover, the Fosters demonstrated their devotion to feminist ideals even in their old age when, in three incidents during the 1870s, they refused to pay their property taxes on the grounds that Abby Foster was being taxed in violation of the American principle of no taxation without representation. On each occasion, their farm was sold at auction for the unpaid taxes, bought by friends, and returned to them.

At age seventy, Abby Kelly Foster gave the last of her powerful speeches on the thirtieth anniversary of the first women's rights convention at her hometown of Worcester, Massachusetts. A rebel until death, she died six years following her husband.

FOSTER, HANNAH WEBSTER (1758–1840)

The anonymous author of one of the first popular works of American fiction, Hannah Foster was the mother of six young children when she published *The Coquette* in 1797. Like other women

AUTHORS who have felt it necessary to hide their work behind PSEUDONYMS, she signed herself simply as "A Lady of Massachusetts." Her name did not appear on the book until 1866, when she had been dead for more than a quarter-century.

Based on a true case, *The Coquette* featured a heroine who rejected conventional standards of female behavior. The book enjoyed long appeal, with more than a dozen editions during Foster's life and reprintings issued for decades thereafter. That it sold well for so long—during an era when the reading of fiction of any sort was controversial—is indicative of the dissatisfaction that many literate women felt with the limitations of their lives. Along with SUSANNA ROWSON in the same era, Foster set an important precedent with the reading public—several decades before America's more famous early novelists.

FREDRICK, PAULINE (1906–1990)

A pioneer for women in television journalism, Fredrick began her career with conventional assignments to "women's" stories. She broke into political and international reporting after she succeeded in an emergency assignment, moving from radio to television when the medium was new.

Like other women, Frederick found career opportunity during WORLD WAR II, but unlike many others, she managed to retain good assignments when male colleagues returned after the war was over. She covered the Nuremberg trials of Nazi officials, the "Big Four" conferences in Paris and New York, and other major postwar stories. During the 1950s, she reported on the Korean War as well as revolutions in Africa and the Middle East, and followed that with coverage of the Cuban missile crisis in 1962.

Though she worked for both of its rivals, Fredrick ultimately became a star for NBC. The first women to regularly report serious television news, she served as NBC's United Nations correspondent for twenty-one years during an era when NBC was the premier newscaster. After retiring from NBC in 1974, she broadcast for National Public Radio as a foreign affairs commentator. During the election of 1976, Pauline Fredrick was the first woman to moderate a presidential debate.

She retained her MAIDEN NAME after a later marriage and lived out her retirement in Sarasota, Florida.

FREMONT, JESSIE ANN BENTON (1824–1902)

Jessie Benton Fremont doubtlessly would have been the nineteenth century's most activist First Lady had her husband been elected to the presidency for which he was nominated in 1856. Indeed, many things might have been different had he won that election, including a stronger possibility that women would have gained the vote when black men did.

Jessie Benton was the exceptionally bright daughter of a United States senator from Missouri; she grew up in Washington and St. Louis, where her father introduced her from her earliest days to the inner circles of power. Had she been a boy, she would have been educated at one of the nation's best COLLEGES and then gone on to a political career; as it was, she read in the Library of Congress, learned French and Spanish from tutors, and rebelled against the domesticity fostered at Miss English's FINISHING SCHOOL.

True to her spirited self, she eloped at age seventeen with John Charles Fremont, a talented but poor Army officer who was beginning to build a reputation for himself as an explorer of the still unmapped western territories. Senator Benton soon reconciled himself to his son-in-law, and Fremont, with the aid of his wife, began building a political and military career that eventually would lead him to become the first presidential nominee of the Republican Party.

Jessie Fremont's sense of drama was evident in the reports to the Senate she wrote with her husband of his expeditions in 1842 and 1846—documents that were so full of excitement about the new discoveries that they sold widely. Moreover, she played a role in promoting her husband's career that went far beyond the era's bounds of conventional wifely behavior. When still nineteen, she withheld orders from the War Department that could have slowed his career; she furthered his ends with information she gained from translating confidential letters from Mexico for the secretary of state; and she lobbied presidents when she felt his interests were at stake. Naturally, she was criticized by many—including some FEMINISTS—for excessive ambition.

The mother of five children, of whom three survived infancy, she made her first, difficult trip west in 1849 and began making California the family home. The discovery of gold on their vast estate brought personal wealth, and political success followed. When her husband was nominated for president in 1856, Jessie Fremont was still only thirty-two. She may have been the first such woman to gain a substantial number of votes for her husband, as her smiling face appeared on campaign posters. After his electoral loss, they sojourned in Europe, but returned to the U. S. to fight for the Union when the CIVIL WAR broke out.

He was appointed to command the armies of the West, but lost that position when, true to the ABOLITIONIST principles they both held, he emancipated the slaves owned by Missourians who supported the Confederacy—two years ahead of Lincoln's similar Emancipation Proclamation. She traveled to Washington to argue his cause, and when that failed, she continued in the East the work she had begun in the West with the LOYAL LEAGUE. SUSAN ANTHONY was among those who cited the value of Jessie Fremont's personal donations to the war work of women.

Having lost their family fortune by 1873, Jessie Fremont sharpened the literary skills she had developed in writing her husband's geographic reports decades earlier. Throughout the rest of the century, she turned out a multitude of articles for popular magazines; between 1878 and 1891, these articles were published as four books.

The Fremonts returned to the Far West when John was appointed territorial governor of Arizona in 1878; she died in Los Angeles just after the turn of the century.

FRIEDAN, BETTY NAOMI GOLDSTEIN (1921–   )

A 1942 psychology graduate of SMITH COLLEGE, Betty Goldstein went on to the University of California for a year of graduate work in psychology before settling in New York. Even though job opportunities were at an unprecedented high during this WORLD WAR II era and even though the Navy's new WAVES trained at Smith the year after her graduation, Goldstein—at least in part because she was young, female, and Jewish—found no serious career opportunities in the jobs she worked until 1947, when she followed societal expectations, married and became a mother.

When her Smith class celebrated the fifteeneth anniversary of its graduation, she found in the responses that her friends made to the college questionnaire the same disillusionment that she felt, for most of these bright, educated women were nonetheless housewives who were spending their lives as little more than glorified servants to husbands and children. For the next several years, she used her psychological background to develop and implement valid measurements of these feelings, and then, backed by her extensive surveys and interviews, she published *The Feminine Mystique* in 1963.

The book's thoughtful message of women's unhappy state was also explosive, and Friedan suddenly went from obscure suburban housewife to controversial AUTHOR whose book was a worldwide bestseller. Her media appearances brought thousands of affirming responses from women, and in 1966, three years after being published, she moved from thinker to activist by founding the NATIONAL ORGANIZATION FOR WOMEN.

With the organization secure four years later, Friedan stepped down from the presidency in 1970, but remained active in NOW as well as other FEMINIST organizations. She wrote regularly for a number of magazines and chronicled the women's movement up through 1976 in *It Changed My Life*. Her 1981 book, *The Second Stage*, was more controversial, with Friedan being criticized this time not from the right that had panned her first book, but rather from the left, as some saw the new book as a desertion of her feminist roots. Nonetheless, Friedan is the acknowledged mother of the modern women's movement, and she continues to write, lecture and provide political leadership in a range of feminist causes.

FRIEDMAN, ESTHER PAULINE and PAULINE ESTHER (1918–   )

The identical twin sisters the world knows as "Ann Landers" and "Dear Abby" or "Abigail Van Buren" were born and raised in a mid-size town of America's heartland, Sioux City, Iowa. After graduation from a local college, they shared a double wedding ceremony.

Marriage brought separate but similar lives as each lived in Midwestern cities and volunteered in charities and local Democratic politics. It was Esther Friedman Lederer, however, who first became an advice columnist, adopting the PSEUDONYM Ann Landers when she began working for the Chicago *Sun-Times* in 1955. At thirty-seven, she was the only nonprofessional writer to contest for the job, but she quickly became as popular as the recently deceased DOROTHY DIX.

Only a month after Lederer began writing in Chicago, her sister, Pauline Friedman Phillips, offered a similar column to the *San Francisco Chronicle* and also soon achieved wide readership. The relationship of Ann Landers and Abigail van Buren remained hidden to most readers until years thereafter, but both rose to be among the most popular writers offered by features syndicates.

Millions of people depended on their practical, motherly advice and enjoyed their witty comments. Both changed their mores with the times, something that became especially apparent when Lederer divorced. Now in their seventies, the sisters show no signs of stepping down from the leadership positions they hold in molding the world's opinions.

FRONTIER WOMEN

Although often associated with the vast settlement of the Great Plains and the Far West in the decades just before and after the CIVIL WAR, in fact, of course, women were active on frontiers from the earliest days of eastern exploration. A few exceptional women were among the Spanish-speaking colonists who arrived as early as 1541, but the first women to make a lasting impact on American history were Virginia's JAMESTOWN WOMEN, the first of whom arrived in 1608; they were followed by the better known PILGRIM WOMEN of Massachusetts in 1620. These women set a pattern followed for nearly three centuries, for as long as an American frontier remained, women worked alongside men in its exploration and settlement.

The tribulations of some who arrived when the Atlantic shore was the frontier were so great that it is remarkable their feats are so largely ignored in history textbooks today. Penelope Van Princes, for example, was the only person in her Dutch party to survive their 1635 attempt to disembark near what is now Monmouth, New Jersey, for all of her family and friends were killed by ambushing natives. Left for dead with her intestines spilling out, she hid in a hollow tree, and three days later, was fortunate enough to be rescued. A native woman nursed her back to health and then sold her to the Dutch at New Amsterdam.

Even when settlements were made, life was by no means safe. MARY ROWLANDSON, a captive during King Phillip's War in 1676, saw her daughter die during their forced march from home, and another Massachusetts woman, Hannah Dustin of Haverhill, is said to have killed and scalped ten Indians in revenge for her 1697 capture. Military protections meant little: the women of Deerfield, Massachusetts, for example, lived either in or close to a stockade in 1704, but that did not prevent an attack by 200 French soldiers and 150 Maine natives of the Abenaki tribe on a cold December night. The majority of the town's 268 residents were either immediately killed or taken captive—though in one house, where "the women, as well as the men, stood with guns behind windows," ten defenders successfully repelled several assaults by the vastly larger attacking party.

Most, however, met fates similar to that of Eunice Williams, who, like other mothers, saw her babies murdered before her eyes. (The method of infanticide common to most tribes was to slam the child's head against an object until the skull broke). Williams, who had given birth to one of her eleven children only weeks before, was taken captive. When she fell while wading the cold, swift Green River a few days later, a hatchet blow dispatched her into drowning, for it was the policy of those in power to rid themselves of any who slowed their three-hundred-mile march to Canada. Surviving men cryptically wrote of the deaths of nameless women such as one who, "being near the time of her travail was wearied with her journey," was therefore slain. Another woman was recorded as ready to meet her fate: "By my falls on the ice yesterday," she said, "I injured myself, causing a miscarriage this night, so that I am not able to travel far; I know they will kill me today."

During the next two years, those who survived to reach Montreal were ransomed and returned—except for Eunice Williams' seven-year-old daughter and namesake, of whom some Macquas became so fond that they "would not give her

A frontier woman with her family of sons in the Pacific Northwest. PHOTOGRAPH BY DARIUS KINSEY; COURTESY OF RALPH W. ANDRES.

up at any price." She lived the rest of her life with them, adopting native ways and marrying within the tribe. When much later, she visited a brother, her choice of cultures was clear: she would not stay in his house, but set up a wigwam nearby and refused invitations to dress in anything other than blankets. MARY JEMISON was another woman who adopted the native culture.

Frontier conditions remained the same decades later. During the French and Indian Wars, Mary Draper Ingles was but one example of women kidnapped by warring natives. She had settled with her family in what now is West Virginia in 1747 and was days away from giving birth when she was captured in a 1755 raid, along with her sister-in-law, Betty Draper, and her two little sons. She bore a daughter at night in a forest, and when she was permitted to ride the following day, the horse's height allowed Mary Ingles to become the first white woman to see the Ohio River. When they arrived at the Shawnese village, her two toddlers were taken from her and sent north to Detroit, while her sister-in-law also was

given to other natives. She and her infant were taken further downriver to what is now Kentucky.

Ingles determined that she must escape before her postpartum period was deemed over, and she made the painful decision to leave her infant with the squaws, which she believed would be safer for both the child and herself. Along with an old Dutch woman who had been captured in Pennsylvania earlier, she slipped away from camp, and with a tomahawk, knife, and blanket, began the seven hundred-mile journey back home. The women ate what they could garner from the land, and almost emaciated, swam creeks and steered logs to float across rivers. After several precarious experiences, the Dutch woman began to show signs of insanity, and Ingles at last had to flee her, making the last part of her journey alone. Eventually she and her husband, who had survived the attack, were able to ransom their eldest son and learned that the younger had died soon after being separated from his mother. Of the baby, nothing was ever discovered.

As the American frontier moved west, similar dangers remained, and again, women faced them along with men. The Donelson party that made a perilous 1779 expedition on the Tennessee and Cumberland rivers, for example, included a number of women. When they were attacked by natives, the women had no choice except to join in the combat: A Mrs. Peyton is recorded as jumping into the icy water to free their boat from a rock, while a Mrs. Jennings tossed precious possessions into the water to lighten the load and Charlotte Robertson used her oar to beat the assailants into the river as they leapt from their canoes. The natives continued to track them along the shores, and eventually the women endured near-starvation, as during much of their four-month journey, no one could go ashore for game.

Moreover, even after these women settled in what would become Nashville, they continued to face dangers that were typical of other frontiers at different times and places: Charlotte Robertson, for example, was not unusual in that she spent a great deal of time alone while her husband pursued his military and political career. Once she awakened to see a large panther moving stealthily through her cabin and was brave enough to remain perfectly still when the panther jumped on her bed. Perhaps many frontier women, after experiences such as that, emulated Linka Preus, who, decades later on the Wisconsin frontier, sat in her rocking chair all night, her gun nearby.

Occasionally one of these dauntless but nonetheless forgotten frontier women even rose to positions of authority. Louisa St. Clair, daughter of General Arthur St. Clair, was so respected by natives for her wilderness skills that in 1792, she rode alone to negotiate a treaty with Ohio natives who trusted only her. Her understanding and respect for another culture has been largely forgotten, while natives such as POCAHONTAS and SACAJAWEA, who moved in the opposite direction, are remembered.

More typical than these, of course, are women who (like most men) stayed firmly within their cultural roots. Nonetheless, it is seldom clearly acknowledged that women suffered equally with men in the expansion of the American frontier. There was little chivalry on either side of the conflict with the natives, and typically women were killed just as men were. If they were spared in initial attacks, their fate could be worse than those quickly killed in battle—as was the case late in frontier history with Minnesota women who were burned alive by Sioux—or who were kept as slaves or hostages. Nor was there chivalry on the other side, as American soldiers shot native women and children at Wounded Knee. For as long as there was a frontier and as long as there was battle with natives, women on both of the conflicting sides fought, suffered, and died just as men did.

FULD, CARRIE BAMBERGER FRANK (1864–1944)

Working with the men of her second-generation German Jewish family, Fuld played a significant role in building a Newark-based department store chain that was so successful the stores were bought by Macy's for $25 million just before the great economic collapse of 1929. Undaunted by the Depression, Fuld and her brother (the only family members still alive) then developed and endowed an imaginative project, the Institute for Advanced Study, which opened in Princeton, New Jersey in 1933.

The Institute was one of the few signs of hope and rationality in the thirties, and its promise of support for serious thinkers attracted such intellectuals as Albert Einstein. Eventually, Fuld, who had no children in her two marriages, and her brother, who never married, gave more than $18 million to the Institute. She endowed other causes as well, and was active in the Jewish community that was suffering from the Holocaust when she died.

FULLER, MARGARET (1810–1850)

The first professional literary critic in America, Fuller's genius was well recognized by her contemporaries, some of whom considered her the most accomplished American up to her time—despite the handicaps of being female and dying young. Even so eminent a thinker as Ralph Waldo Emerson said that he "never saw her without surprise at her new powers."

Born in Cambridge, Massachusetts to a Harvard-educated father who was disappointed that she was not a boy, Margaret Fuller was reading the classics in Latin at an age when other children begin the alphabet. Although there were no COLLEGES open to women during her youth and her formal education was limited to a Groton, Connecticut FINISHING SCHOOL, she knew a number of ancient and modern languages and was thoroughly acquainted with the literature of several cultures. Like other single women of her era, she lived at home until she was in her mid-twenties, when she was hired by Bronson Alcott, the father of LOUISA MAY ALCOTT, to TEACH in his progressive school. The following year she moved to Providence, Rhode Island for a handsome increase in salary and taught there two years.

She was far too gifted too be a schoolmarm, however, even in the most liberated of educational systems, and in 1839, she returned to suburban Boston. For the next several years, she earned a living in a most creative way: Fuller held "conversations" in her home with topics so appealing that Boston's most illustrious women—and later, men—paid to participate in these seminars. Though she carefully disguised her lectures as something else, this was perhaps the first violation of societal bans on paid PUBLIC SPEAKING by women.

In 1840, at the invitation of Emerson, Thoreau, and others of the era's philosophical and literary giants, she became editor of the *Dial*, a quarterly publication of Transcendentalist philosophy that is generally recognized as the nation's first literary journal. Fuller not only worked as the *Dial*'s editor, but also contributed writing in several genres that set important precedents for the future of American literature.

Soon after the 1844 publication of her first book, *Summer on the Lakes*, Fuller moved to New York at the invitation of Horace Greeley, joined the staff of his *New York Tribune*, and became the first professional book review editor in America. The *New York Times* did not yet exist, and Greeley's paper had a national audience. Fuller's presence on his pages, therefore, had a tremendous effect in awakening the nation to its own nascent literature—for until the emergence of Hawthorne and others of Fuller's friends in this era, Americans largely had looked to London for their reading material. It was Fuller who took the lead in arguing against "books which imitate or represent the thoughts and life of Europe" and who looked for "fresh currents of life" from the new nation.

While working as a wholly new kind of editor, Fuller was

also formulating her feminist philosophies into book form. Her *Woman in the Nineteenth Century* (1845) was a factor in bringing about the SENECA FALLS WOMEN'S RIGHTS CONVENTION three years later, and for decades, it was the chief classic of American feminist thought. It was especially ahead of its time in Fuller's frank emphasis on sexuality, including the antimarriage view then known as "free love."

The year after its publication, some of Fuller's literary criticism for the *Tribune* was collected and published as *Papers on Literature and Art* (1846). Also that year, Margaret Fuller achieved her lifelong goal of traveling abroad. Greeley named her a foreign correspondent, and she sent back stories of life in London and Paris, where her reputation as America's finest literary light opened doors to many famous artists and writers.

By 1847, she settled in Rome, where her life dramatically changed. She fell in love with the Marchese d'Ossoli, who, despite his noble rank, was deeply involved in revolutionary activities. Ten years older than he, Fuller bore his child in 1848, when she was thirty-eight. They married the following year, but no staid family life was in store for them, as they were forced to flee when the Roman republic was overthrown.

After almost a year of living in Florence, where she worked on a history of the revolution, they sailed for America in May, 1850. Almost home, off the coast of New York's Fire Island, their ship ran aground in a storm and all were drowned. Though her son's body washed ashore, those of Fuller and her husband were never found, despite searches made by Thoreau and others of her friends. Friends also published her memoirs and other work posthumously. Too often remembered today merely for her unconventional sexuality and her friendship with Transcendentalist philosophers, Margaret Fuller should instead be remembered as the editor of the first book review pages in the nation's newspapers and, indeed, as the midwife who brought American literature to life.

FULTON, SARAH BRADLEE (1741–1835)

Sometimes called "The Mother of the Boston Tea Party," Sarah Fulton was militant in her support of the American Revolution. She and her sister-in-law, Mrs. Nathaniel Bradlee, arranged the clothing and makeup worn by the men who disguised themselves as Mohawks when they attacked the British ships that held the tea to be taxed. Fulton managed to allay the suspicions of a Tory neighbor who watched while she heated water for the quick removal of facial disguises upon the revolutionaries' return.

She was also present a year and a half later at the Battle of Bunker Hill. Fulton led her female friends in the rapid establishment of a field hospital and was a NURSE to the wounded who remained when the battle was over. Still later in the war, she became a local legend for her confrontation with a British officer; she dared him to shoot her when she claimed ownership of a load of wood that the British had confiscated—and he surrendered it to her. Fulton also served as a courier, since she was more capable than male revolutionaries of eluding the suspicions of British sentries. She walked alone after midnight from her Medford home to Boston; Washington later personally thanked her for this courageous effort.

Obviously a strong woman, Fulton died a month short of her ninety-fifth birthday. A monument is dedicated to her in Medford.

FURMAN, BESS (1894–1969)

The first woman to report on the House of Representatives for a news syndicate, Bess Furman covered Washington stories for the Associated Press from 1929 to 1936.

She literally had grown up with journalism, for her father ran a small-town newspaper from their Nebraska home. Openings for women in journalism were rare when she graduated from college, however, and like so many women, Furman worked as a TEACHER for almost a decade before finding a job with a Nebraska paper. Her coverage of the 1928 presidential campaign in Omaha brought her to the attention of AP, and she was fortunate to land a Washington job with them just months before the stock market crash of 1929. The fact that she hung on to the job throughout the Depression probably had a great deal to do with the fact that she also developed a close friendship with ELEANOR ROOSEVELT, who furthered the careers of many women.

Furman married a reporter almost a decade younger than herself in 1932, but kept her MAIDEN NAME and continued to work until she bore twins at age forty-one. She returned to Nebraska then and freelanced for several years before joining the Office of War Information in the early days of WORLD WAR II. The war brought many job opportunities that had been denied women during the Depression, and the *New York Times* hired Furman in 1943. She remained with their Washington Bureau for almost twenty years, retiring in 1961.

Although then sixty-five, Furman was not yet ready for genuine retirement, and she worked during the 1960s as an executive in press relations for the new Department of Health, Education, and Welfare. She was the author of two books: an autobiography, *Washington By-Line* (1949) and *White House Profile* (1951).

G

GAGE, MATILDA JOSELYN (1826–1898) Usually a footnote to the more familiar names in the SUFFRAGE MOVEMENT, Gage arguably was intellectually superior to almost all in understanding the wide range of sociological, economic, and especially historical aspects of women's issues, while most suffragists concerned themselves primarily with the immediately political.

The daughter of a cultured mother and a physician father with liberal views that included FEMINISM, Matilda Joselyn was given an education well beyond that usually afforded women in her era. Nonetheless, after her schooling at Clinton Liberal Institute in upstate New York, she married at eighteen and went on to bear five children to her merchant husband. Despite these home obligations and shyness so severe that few heard her initial speech, Gage participated in her first women's rights convention when she was only twenty-six.

Two years later, in 1854, she was vacationing at a fashionable hotel in Saratoga, New York, when SUSAN ANTHONY appeared in the resort town. Things were not going well for Anthony, who was attempting to take advantage of Saratoga's crowds for a meeting on women's rights; she had hired a hall, but had no speakers lined up, had lost her purse to a thief, and was in debt for the advertisements she was distributing. To Anthony's great joy, Gage agreed to overcome her terror of PUBLIC SPEAKING; at least in part because of the addition of the stylish Mrs. Gage to the agenda, the meeting turned out to be a rousing success. From then on, Gage was involved in almost every women's rights effort.

She was a founder of the NATIONAL WOMAN SUFFRAGE ASSOCIATION in 1869, as well as of the New York State Woman Suffrage Association, and served in various offices in each, including the presidency. She not only cast a ballot in 1872, but was the sole woman to join the speaking campaign that Anthony organized in response to her arrest for testing the FIFTEENTH AMENDMENT—despite Gage's distaste for oratory, she made sixteen speeches in less than a month. In 1875, she testified before congressional committees on behalf of suffrage, and in 1880, she attended the national conventions of the Democratic, Republican, and Greenback Parties to lobby the male delegates to include suffrage in their platforms.

It was in her writing, however, that Gage exercised the most influence. She was a contributor to the NWSA's *Revolution* from its 1869 beginning, and she soon developed a special expertise in women's history. Her early works included *Woman as Inventor* (1870) and *Woman's Rights Catechism* (1871), and in 1876, she was a principal author of the DECLARATION OF THE RIGHTS OF WOMEN that was read at the centennial celebration of American independence. Two years later, she undertook a new monthly publication for the NWSA called *National Citizen and Ballot Box*; she remained its editor during the three years of its existence.

Expanding her historical interests in 1880, Gage published a defense of CIVIL WAR figure ANNA ELLA CARROLL, and the following year, she began working with Anthony and IDA HUSTED HARPER on what would eventually be published as the first three volumes of the *History of Woman Suffrage*. Finally, in 1890, she issued her own declaration of independence, even from her friends in the women's movement, with *The Dangers of the Hour*. A summary of the views she had developed in four decades of work for women, Gage made it clear that she had advanced far beyond most in radical feminist thought.

She did not mellow with age, as Anthony had. Her major work, written when she was sixty-seven, was *Woman, Church and State* (1893). A militant book even by today's standards, it was an attack on Christianity as one of the chief sources of female oppression. She developed her tenets historically, moving from the matriarchal societies of primitive peoples to the limited roles alloted to women in nineteenth-century Christian culture. Because the church blamed original sin on Eve and taught that women were to submit themselves to men, she argued, its history inexorably evolved to give power to men and to take it from women. As could be expected, Gage's book—which was widely read—shocked the thousands of suffragists who were also active in the WOMEN'S CHRISTIAN TEMPERANCE UNION. The sad result was that she was almost entirely dropped by the leadership of the women's movement—even by ELIZABETH CADY STANTON, whose *Woman's Bible*, published two years later, promulgated many of the same views.

Gage had formed her own Woman's National Liberal Union in 1890, when the NWSA merged with the more conservative AMERICAN WOMAN SUFFRAGE ASSOCIATION over her objections. She retained the Union's presidency until her death eight years later, but it never grew beyond a minimal membership. Though she was pessimistic about the condition of women as the Gay Nineties brought increasing artificiality and the women's movement stalled into annual meetings marked more by nostalgia than political action, Matilda Joselyn Gage never gave up her efforts. She wrote a speech for the fiftieth anniversary of the first women's rights convention even as she lay dying.

GARDNER, JULIA ANNA (1882–1960)

A generation younger than geologist FLORENCE BASCOM, Gardner studied under Bascom at BRYN MAWR and earned a Ph.D. in geology at JOHNS HOPKINS UNIVERSITY in 1911. Except for volunteering as a NURSE during WORLD WAR I, she spent her career with the U.S. Geological Survey. The most remarkable of Gardner's achievements in this nontraditional field was her work during WORLD WAR II, when she studied the sand used as ballast in Japanese incendiary balloons to determine what beach in Japan was their origin.

GARMENT INDUSTRY

More than any other occupation, the making of clothing was a field relegated to women. From pre-colonial times through the modern era, hundreds of thousands of women earned a living—albeit usually a meager one—by making garments.

Before industrialization, women who worked as seamstresses usually went to the homes of clients for cutting and fitting, and then sewed the entire garment by hand. Talented ones who developed a reputation for style in their communities set up dressmaking shops and, by employing young women as apprentices, could sometimes earn good incomes. More often, however, seamstresses in the pre-industrial era merely eked out an existence for their undervalued work. New York seamstresses in 1845, for instance, earned $1.25 to $1.50 a week for days that averaged fourteen to sixteen hours.

Even after the factory system began to evolve, women continued to sew at home under the system of HOME CONTRACT WORK. In this methodology, entire families of women, children, and sometimes men spent their days doing one or two aspects of making a garment. Occasionally they cut cloth from patterns, but more often, they did the "finishing" work of hemming, sewing on buttons, cutting and trimming buttonholes, and so forth. IMMIGRANT WOMEN, bound to their homes by children and their lack of language skills, were particularly likely to do this "piecework" for pennies in pay.

Nor did factories necessarily afford working conditions that were much better in the beginning. Especially in immigrant communities, factories were likely to be operated by other immigrants who themselves were only on the edge of business security and who therefore predicated their profit margins on worker exploitation. Women in these sweatshops, as they came to be known, worked from dawn to dark in crowded, badly-lit, tuberculosis-breeding rooms, and yet earned only enough to barely survive.

Even when factories unionized and working conditions improved, women's work in the garment industry was rigidly defined as inherently inferior to that of men. Males were accorded the title of "tailor," and even when the work they did was the same as a woman's, they were paid more. Usually, though, jobs were assigned by gender and those done by males were considered of greater worth. Cutting the fabric and pressing the finished garment were jobs commonly done by men, and each was defined as "skilled," whereas the actual sewing—either by machine or by hand—that was done by women was considered "unskilled."

Employees in garment factories could actually work all week and earn nothing, for they were fined for fabric that was mistakenly sewed or otherwise ruined. In some factories, women had to buy supplies such as needles and scissors, and some even paid for the electricity required to run the machines they also were forced to buy. Few Americans were willing to put up with such despotism, and garment workers continued to be overwhelmingly immigrants. They were especially likely to be Jewish, with lesser numbers of Italians in New York, while German, Scandinavian, and Polish women worked in the factories of Chicago and other inland cities.

After the great STRIKES of 1909, these immigrant women, with the help of some natives involved in the WOMEN'S TRADE UNION LEAGUE, were able to organize most shops to bargain collectively. Nonetheless, despite much greater numbers of women than men in the garment industry, the INTERNATIONAL LADIES' GARMENT WORKERS' UNION continued to be dominated by men.

GENERAL FEDERATION OF WOMEN'S CLUBS

Founded in 1890, the General Federation was both a cause and a result of the changes in women's roles that created the CLUB MOVEMENT of the late nineteenth century. The federation, led by JUNE CUNNINGHAM CROLY, combined the many newly established women's clubs throughout the country, most of which were aimed at literary self-improvement and local civic improvement.

These organizations were a reflection of a deep need among women to do something more with their lives than

Women working at sewing machines in a badly built and highly flammable garment factory in 1937. Unemployment during the Great Depression forced workers to accept such conditions. NATIONAL ARCHIVES; WOMEN'S BUREAU OF THE DEPARTMENT OF LABOR.

the era's model of virtuous womanhood had allowed. Even women who could not bring themselves to support the SUFFRAGE MOVEMENT could join a club that had as its goal, for example, the study of Dickens or the creation of playgrounds and street lighting. The federation pulled these groups together so the women in the leadership positions could learn from and mutually support each other.

While the clubs concentrated on local needs and were generally apolitical, the federation did take stands on issues at national conventions and led the way on a number of progressive changes. By 1899, for example, the GFWC had established a national model for juvenile courts; in 1906, the federation was crucial in passage of the Pure Food and Drug Act; it worked for the eight-hour day and against child labor.

By 1915, there were so many women willing to get involved in these kinds of activities that the General Federation had more than 2 million members. At their convention the previous year, GFWC members had endorsed a suffrage plank in their platform, for they finally saw that they could better advance their civic agenda if they could vote. That their opin-

ions were those of mainstream American women is clear from the fact that a national suffrage amendment finally passed six years after their endorsement—and more than seventy years from its first proposal.

Membership has fallen to 350,000 today, but the organization continues to link the efforts of some 8,500 local groups. GFWC prides itself on being "responsible for the establishment of 75 percent of America's public libraries" and calls itself "the largest and oldest nondenominational, nonpartisan, volunteer service organization in the world." In addition to its concentration on local volunteerism, it has established a Women's History and Resource Center to document these volunteer achievements. Areas of educational emphasis include the arts, conservation, home life, and public affairs. Its headquarters, staffed with twenty-five employees and an annual budget of over a million dollars, is in a historic building at 1734 N Street NW in Washington.

GEORGIA FEMALE COLLEGE Established at Macon in 1836, the development of Georgia Female College was slowed by the financial panic of the next year, but classes began in 1839 on a four-acre campus with one large building that included a chapel, dining room, and classrooms, as well as sleeping space for the young women. Its curriculum emulated that of the extant male four-year colleges, with a year of preparatory work available to those women whose background was not sufficient for entrance. Standard courses included mathematics and science, as well as Latin and French.

The college granted its first degree in 1840, "the very first traditional A.B. degree to women." In 1843, its name was changed to Wesleyan Female College to emphasize the support that it received from Methodist Churches. By then it had approximately two hundred students, who studied, of course, under male professors. In 1859, enough graduates had been produced to form the world's first alumnae organization.

"A radical new experiment that flowered in the conservative South," the institution's open liberalism meant a continual struggle for financial support. Nonetheless, it managed to survive the hardships of the CIVIL WAR, closing only for two weeks when Sherman's troops neared Macon. Enrollment dropped to 150 during Reconstruction and the curriculum eased, with the Latin requirement dropped and the era's emphasis on physical education added. A $125,000 donation in 1880 enabled remodeling of the original building into a grander Victorian structure. The depression of 1893 brought another setback, but nonetheless, the women's enrollment of 250 was approximately the same as that of the men at the University of Georgia.

Wesleyan's endowment improved steadily during the Progressive Era, with the school headed by its first secular (but still male) president. Among its students during this time were the three Soong sisters who went on to important roles in Chinese history: especially Ch'ing-ling, a 1913 graduate who married Sun Yet-sen and played a part in the overthrow of the Manchu dynasty; and Mei-ling, who studied at Wesleyan before graduating from WELLESLEY, and who, as Madame Chiang, was a formidable influence on world history through the 1950s.

By the end of WORLD WAR I, the college was no longer merely surviving, but was expanding. "Female" was dropped from the name in 1919 and it was formally accredited as a four-year liberal arts college for women. In 1928, most programs were moved to a large, beautifully built suburban campus—and the following year was the great Wall Street crash. In a repetition of its experience almost a century earlier, the college once again struggled to stay alive through the Great Depression, with enrollment plunging from the six hundred projected for the new campus to three hundred. The million dollar mortgage for the new construction could not be paid and the college went through bankruptcy and reorganization.

By 1950, however, all debts had been paid and enrollment reached seven hundred. A 1963 fire destroyed the old downtown campus, and student population fell when women's colleges lost popularity during the post–WORLD WAR II era. Enrollment rose again in the 1980s, however, and today Wesleyan College continues to provide liberal education in a conservative state, priding itself on being the nation's oldest educational institution for women.

GIBSON, ALTHEA (1927–   ) The first black American to play tennis on England's famed Wimbledon courts, Gibson brought recognition to black women in an area of achievement that was new for them. Born in South Carolina, Gibson grew up in Harlem, where she had a rebellious youth that turned turned around when she discovered tennis through the Police Athletic League. Within a year, she won the state championship.

She held the national Negro women's championship from 1948–1958, during which time she also graduated from Florida Agricultural and Mechanical University. After winning the American Tennis Association's women's championship and the U.S. national singles title, she was named Woman Athlete of the Year by the Associated Press in 1957–58.

The State Department sponsored her on a goodwill tour in 1956 that was designed to demonstrate to the rest of the world that Americans were overcoming the prejudices against blacks from which Gibson had earlier suffered. Welcomed home from her 1957 Wimbledon championship with a parade in New York City, she published her autobiography the next year, *I Always Wanted to be Somebody* (1958). In 1960, she won the World Professional Tennis Championship.

Fifteen years later, in 1973, Gibson surprised the sports world by announcing her intention to return to professional tennis at age forty-five. Soon thereafter she became one of the relatively few women inducted into the Black Sports Hall of Fame.

GIBSON GIRL The creation of illustrator Charles Dana Gibson, the "Gibson Girl" presaged the advertising industry's development of fashionable images of women. From the Gay Nineties to WORLD WAR I, the Gibson Girl made her high-paid appearances in all of the era's most popular magazines. In a time when magazines were still illustrated with drawings rather than photographs, the Gibson Girl set fashions in hair, clothing, and—more importantly—lifestyle.

Her image was particularly important in validating a more animated way of life for women, for she was usually portrayed out-of-doors, where she engaged in leisure activities that were newly in vogue, including golf, croquet, bicycling, and sailing. The Gibson Girl represented fashion's first "American" look, with pictures of an athletic, confident young woman; she preferred shirtwaist dresses, flared skirts and boyish collars, and—while she still wore HATS—they were usually unadorned, straw sailors. Her simplified style, with its lack of ruffles and lace, bespoke a preference for action over appearance. The Gibson Girl thus gave important encouragement to young women to move away from the bustles and embellishments that forced Victorian ladyship into a staid and artificial routine, opting instead for greater freedom.

Moreover, the simpler style was a boon to the GARMENT INDUSTRY, which until then had concentrated on the manufacture of men's ready-to-wear clothing, while most women's clothing was still hand sewn. The result was not only a lower cost for women's clothing, but also a multitude of new, relatively unskilled job openings in shirtwaist factories.

The "Gibson Girl" personified youthful American womanhood at the turn of the century; her relatively liberated style of dress promoted athletics and healthy outdoor recreation.
UNIVERSITY OF SOUTH FLORIDA SPECIAL COLLECTIONS; DRAWING BY CHARLES DANA GIBSON, 1899.

GILDERSLEEVE, VIRGINIA (1877–1965) A New Yorker
all of her life, Gildersleeve graduated from BARNARD COLLEGE and received a doctorate from its Columbia University affiliate in 1908. She was appointed dean of Barnard a mere three years later, a position she held for almost four decades. A champion for both women faculty and students, Gildersleeve improved educational opportunity for thousands of women.

She reached beyond academia during WORLD WAR II to chair the advisory committee of the Navy's new female unit, the WAVES, which was headed by her fellow academic MILDRED MCAFEE. With the end of the war in sight, President Roosevelt appointed Gildersleeve as the only woman in the delegation that represented the United States at the founding conference of the United Nations.

In this pinnacle of her career, she worked on the UN's charter and especially advocated its emphasis on human rights. After victory over Japan, she went there and restructured the Japanese educational system, retiring upon her return in 1947. These international achievements earned her the French Legion of Honor. Gildersleeve's autobiography, *Many a Good Crusade*, was published in 1954 when she was seventy-seven; she died at eighty-eight.

GILMAN, CHARLOTTE PERKINS (1860–1935) While
the fame of most women of achievement diminishes with time, the reputation of Charlotte Perkins Gilman has had the good fortune of the opposite fate. Gilman has become an icon of the modern women's movement, with especially her fiction more widely read today than when she wrote a century ago.

The emphasis that both her fiction and nonfiction placed on economic independence for women doubtless was an outgrowth of the embarrassing poverty she endured in childhood. Though her father was a member of the prominent Beecher family, he DESERTED his family for long periods of time during which they had to depend on the charity of relatives. His daughter Charlotte, however, inherited the intellectual curiosity and literary skills of her great-aunts, HARRIET BEECHER STOWE and CATHARINE BEECHER, and, with the help from her stalwart mother, she overcame the limitations of intermittent education.

Perkins exhibited artistic talent before developing the literary talent for which she would be known; she attended the Rhode Island School of Design and worked as a commercial artist and art teacher before marrying artist Walter Stetson at twenty-four. Their daughter was born nine months after the wedding, and the young mother did not recover from serious postpartum depression. Much later, she wrote in her autobiography of this time, when she had "a loving and devoted husband, an exquisite baby . . . a wholly satisfying servant—and I lay all day on the lounge and cried." Stetson was overprotective (an approach opposite of that of her father), and, backed by a physician, he restricted his wife from virtually all activity—which resulted in a total breakdown.

But when Charlotte Stetson went on a therapeutic trip to California a few months later, she functioned much better. Her depression recurred when she returned to the Northeast, and she decided to accept the amicable separation her husband had offered earlier. In 1888, four years after their marriage, she left him permanently, although they did not DIVORCE until 1894. When he later married her close friend, author Grace Ellery Channing, she sent her nine-year-old daughter to live with them. The divorce and especially the perceived abandonment of her daughter scadalized her friends on both coasts.

Meanwhile, Stetson, refusing any aid from her husband, returned to California and began struggling to support herself (and, at first, her daughter and mother) by lecturing and writing. One of the first pieces published later became her most famous story: "The Yellow Wallpaper," a fictionalization of her mental breakdown, appeared in 1892. It not only contained a radically FEMINIST thesis, but also was written with a candor uncommon to the era. Its surrealistic portrayal of a mind proceeding inexorably to collapse was decades ahead of literary style.

In 1895, she left California to live for a time at Chicago's Hull House, where she was influenced by JANE ADDAMS, EDITH and GRACE ABBOTT, and others with progressive views. The interest in economics that she developed there was reinforced the following year, when Stetson attended the International Socialist and Labor Congress in London. She made important contacts there with Beatrice and Sidney Webb, George Bernard Shaw, and other writers.

Upon her return home and while still using Stetson as her name, she published *Women and Economics* (1898). As with her fiction, this first nonfiction work would be her best. The book's arguments for female economic independence held great appeal to dependent women in this late Victorian era, and her case for communal solutions for the individual needs that kept women tied to domesticity made sense to many. Translated into seven languages, *Women and Economics* brought her international acclaim, and, at last, enough profit to ease her financial worries, for she had always refused help from her ex-husband.

Two years after its publication, she married a younger cousin who was also a member of the Beecher family, took his name, and dropped Stetson. Known thereafter as Charlotte Perkins Gilman, she lived primarily in New York, where she continued to write books and, between 1909 and 1916, published a largely self-funded magazine, aptly named the *Forerunner*. Its most famous feature was the utopian "Herland" she developed as a futuristic prototype of the peaceful, cooperative society she believed could result from full inclusion of women.

Other books expanded upon the themes of her first, running from philosophical discourses on the differing natures of men and women to proposals for communal nurseries, kitchens, and other changes in family life that would ease the burden on women. When some of these changes finally developed many decades later in the form of child care centers and take-out restaurants, the transformation would be so different in appearance from what she advocated that few would make the correlation—but Gilman had in many ways predicted and planned a future in which women's lives could revolve around careers other than domesticity.

When Progressivism lost its edge with WORLD WAR I, Gilman lost much of her audience. Though of course she had supported the SUFFRAGE MOVEMENT, its passage was another factor in leading many to believe that feminist topics had become passé for the new woman of the Roaring Twenties. Moreover, Gilman appeared to be out of touch with that new woman, for she argued that the era's freer mores meant not liberation, but was instead another way of emphasizing female sexuality that would inevitably continue economic dependency.

Indeed, the Great Depression confirmed the subordinate position of women to such a degree that few dared risk any sort of independence. Meanwhile, Gilman's personal life took a tragic turn with the discovery of breast cancer and her husband's death in 1934. She published her autobiography, *The Living of Charlotte Perkins Gilman* (1935), and when the cancer was deemed incurable, she demonstrated the pragmatism that was the basis of all of her philosophical arguments, and took her own life.

GLASGOW, ELLEN ANDERSON GHOLSON (1873–1945)

Except for five years in New York City, Ellen Glasgow lived in Virginia, where most of her novels were set. Her large family had deep roots amid both its aristocratic Tidewater society and its rebellious mountaineers. Though Glasgow's life was lived in the Richmond society of the former, she showed important elements of the latter from age seventeen, when she refused to debut.

Uninterested in the FINISHING SCHOOL education afforded to women of her class, Glasgow educated herself by reading widely and unconventionally. Her family, apparently unaware of the life of her mind, gave her no encouragement, but she nonetheless wrote her first novel at seventeen and was published ANONYMOUSLY in 1897, when she was twenty-four. She followed up the next year with a second novel that included her name on the cover; the third, in 1900, began her concentration on Virginia. *The Battle-Ground* (1902), a tale set in the CIVIL WAR, is considered an outstanding example of the new realism then entering American literature.

Thereafter, Glasgow published almost biannually, skillfully exploring the many ironic aspects of her ambivalent feelings on the death of the Southern way of life. She wrote in the same era as EDITH WHARTON, who examined the lives of New York's aristocracy, and WILLA CATHER, who wrote of those on the farms and in the small towns of the Midwest. Like them, Glasgow aimed to avoid being labeled a "regional" writer through the universal quality of her work.

By the twenties, she was well established as an AUTHOR who was popular with both the public and (somewhat later) with critics, particularly for *Barren Ground* (1925). With an irony that was appropriate to her style, the years of the Great Depression were especially good to Glasgow, as she published *Vein of Iron* (1935) to much acclaim and was awarded several honorary degrees during the worst of the nation's economic suffering. She climaxed her career with election to the American Academy of Arts and Letters in 1940 and the Pulitzer Prize the following year.

Yet, like LOUISA MAY ALCOTT, Glasgow seems to have taken little joy in what she saw as belated success. An essential loneliness enveloped her from the time her mother died when she was twenty; increasing deafness added to her isolation. The men she loved did not reciprocate, and after WORLD WAR I, she became one of those disillusioned and disaffected intellectuals who focused on a bittersweet yearning for an agrarian society they knew was irretrievably lost, while holding the crassness of twentieth century America in contempt.

The "New South" was a particularly apt symbol of the change such writers deplored, and Glasgow personally held out against it as long as she could, continuing to live in the family mansion even as Richmond's industrialization surrounded her. She filled the five years after her first heart attack with work, publishing her only nonfiction, *A Certain Measure*, in 1943 and valiantly toiling at the two books that would be issued posthumously. Her autobiographical volume, *The Woman Within*, finally came out in 1954, while her last novel appeared in 1966—more than two decades after her death and in a world totally transformed from that in which she had been born.

GODEY'S LADY'S BOOK The most popular women's magazine in the nineteenth century, *Godey's* was begun as the *Ladies Magazine* in 1828 under the editorship of SARAH JOSEPHINA BUELL HALE. It was purchased in 1837 by Louis A. Godey, who added his name to the title, set the standards for what he considered proper reading for ladies, and brought Hale from Boston to Philadelphia, apparently understanding that her editorship was the key to the magazine's success.

Within two decades, over 150,000 American women held subscriptions to *Godey's*. They found in its pages the basic format that mass magazines aimed at women would use for more than a century: fashions, imported from France and including illustrations for reproduction; recipes and household hints; light poems and stories; and articles on subjects that carefully balanced progressivism with avoidance of controversy. Its editorials supported educational opportunities for women, the entrance of women into the medical profession, and DRESS REFORM to liberate women from handicapping clothing.

Godey's pages offered a first opportunity to many American writers in an era when the young nation still looked to London for its literature, and it particularly promoted the work of women AUTHORS. It also was a fundamental factor in the creation of national standards of etiquette, artistic taste, and social forms; especially during the Reconstruction Era, it offered important advice to those whose money gave them entrance into a society whose manners they did not know.

The formula worked well, and the magazine continued to be popular after Hale's 1879 retirement. In 1898, however, with its founders dead and increasing competition from *Vogue* and *Ladies Home Journal*, it was sold to Munsey Publications. They merged it with another, more obscure magazine and gave up *Godey's* name. Perhaps they foresaw that, important as it was to its time, the twentieth century was opening and the magazine's era was over—for *Godey's* was the very soul of the Victorian age.

GOLDMAN, EMMA (1869–1940)
Neither Emma Goldman's birth nor death occurred in America, but she holds a deserved place in the history of American women, for her fascinating life affected millions who did not acknowledge (or even consciously know of) her influence.

Born to Lithuanian Jews in the Russian empire, Goldman emigrated at sixteen rather than comply with the accepted custom of arranged marriage. Like many IMMIGRANT WOMEN— especially Jews from czarist Russia—she was shocked and disappointed by the gap between American promise and the rampant capitalism of the Gilded Age. After working in the GARMENT INDUSTRY in Rochester for four unsatisfying years, during which she was briefly and unhappily married, she moved to New York City in 1889. There she not only found the intellectual stimulus she craved, but also began a lifelong relationship with anarchist Alexander Berkman.

She helped Berkman with his unsuccessful plans to assassinate steel mill owners during the great Homestead steel STRIKE in 1892, for which he was imprisoned. A year later she also was behind bars—but much less justifiably, for her only offense was to exercise free speech in arguing that those unemployed in the severe depression of 1893 had a right to food. When the arrest presumably demonstrated that her oratorical skills were powerful enough to arouse official fear, Goldman took to the lecture circuit. For the rest of her life, she supported herself and earned money for her causes by speaking. She had become a naturalized citizen through the failed marriage, and thus had a passport to TRAVEL between continents. She lectured in Europe in 1895 and returned there again in 1899, for she was gifted in languages as well as in dramatic technique.

Goldman not only spoke on anarchism, but also promoted BIRTH CONTROL and the "free love" made possible by birth control. These were not merely theoretical positions; instead, she visited immigrant slums and observed the pain of early maternal death. Resisting the social worker response that motivated many other empathetic women in this era, she made political action her priority. Nor was suffrage a major part of that political agenda, for Goldman's response to the SUFFRAGE MOVEMENT was somewhat scornful; she worked instead for fundamental change of the entire political, and especially economic, structure. Her attitudes on sexuality likewise were not simply theoretical; decades ahead of her time in separating the idea of emotional commitment from that of legal marriage, she lived with Berkman without marrying him after his release from prison.

Together, they began publishing a radical monthly that Goldman named *Mother Earth* to signify her personal commitment in nurturing a better world. Although two years later, in 1908, the Justice Department stripped her of her citizenship in a despicably manipulative manner, she continued to speak and write. She published *Anarchism and Other Essays* in 1910, and four years later demonstrated the breath of her intellectual ability with *The Social Significance of Modern Drama* (1914), for she had long been devoted to the political ideas put forth in literary form by Henrik Ibsen, George Bernard Shaw, and others of the era.

Her 1916 jailing for advocacy of birth control was brief, but when the nation entered WORLD WAR I the following year, the attorney general severely cracked down on dissidents. Although Goldman had managed to edit *Mother Earth* for over a decade, the government finally succeeded in shutting it down under wartime censorship. For her arguments against the military draft as an unconstitutional violation of a man's liberty, she was sentenced to two years in prison. Goldman was deported upon release, never again to live in the United States—although she was allowed to visit in 1934, when, during the Great Depression, there were more Americans who emigrated than immigrants seeking to enter.

Exiled from the democracy that she loved enough to try to improve, "Red Emma," as she was called, found that there was no free speech in the Soviet Union, either. Foreseeing the unhappy future of the communist revolution much sooner than most, Goldman published *My Disillusionment in Russia* in 1923. She married a Welsh miner to obtain British citizenship in 1925, but when she was not on the lecture circuit, she spent most of her time in France at work on her autobiography, *Living My life* (1931).

When the Spanish Civil War gave the world a preview of fascist intentions for WORLD WAR II, Goldman was on the scene. She spent her last years helping those who resisted dictatorship, and by May, 1940, when the German Nazis were subduing the peaceful peoples of Scandinavia and the Low Countries, Goldman was in Canada raising funds to fight back. Over seventy and handicapped by the loss of her U.S. citizenship, she was doing her best to preserve the free speech that she cherished when she died.

GOLDRING, WINIFRED (1888–1971)
The official state paleontologist of New York from 1939 to 1954, Goldring graduated from WELLESLEY COLLEGE in 1909 and did further work at Columbia and JOHNS HOPKINS UNIVERSITY. In a field that women rarely entered, she was candid about the fact that her

pay was less and her opportunities were limited because of her gender. Her male colleagues nonetheless elected her president of the Paleontological Society in 1949 and vice-president of the Geological Society in 1950, twenty years after FLORENCE BASCOM held that position. The year following her retirement, Goldring was included the ninth edition of *Men of Science*.

GOLD STAR MOTHERS

During WORLD WAR II, women who had lost children (almost always, sons) in the war were known as Gold Star Mothers. They formed groups to help each other bear the burden of their loss, some of which still met regularly forty years after the war was over.

Families with soldiers or sailors on active duty displayed Blue Stars in the front windows of homes, and when a family member died as a result of war, the star was changed to gold. Some women had both blue and gold stars, and one Iowa woman sadly acquired five gold stars when all of her sons died in a Navy battle.

GOVERNESSES

A feature of wealthy families especially during the nineteenth century, the position of governess was one of the few occupations open to educated women. The infants and very young children of such families were usually tended by a woman who was referred to as a NURSE, and the governess came into a child's life at about the time that children today begin school.

The governess was considered to be a TEACHER as well as a care-giver, and she usually taught both the boys and girls of a family until the boys were at or near adolescence. Then they were turned over to a male tutor or sent to boarding schools, and the governess' main responsibility became the education of the girls of the family. While she taught the basics of reading, writing, arithmetic, and history when the children were young, a governess was expected to teach languages (especially French), art, music, and needlework to adolescent girls.

Relatively few governesses actually stayed with a family through all of the years that children grew up, for the work was usually seen as a stopgap prior to the marriage of an accomplished young woman, or—if she did not marry—prior to a career in another field. The job was considered to be by definition for young women, often only a few years older than their charges, for an essential part of it was a willingness to play with the children. LOUISA MAY ALCOTT and DOROTHEA DIX, for example, both worked as governesses while they were young and spent much of this time in outdoor activity.

One of the reasons for moving on to other occupations was that governesses were poorly paid and their employment was insecure. Often they were simply friends of a family who moved in with the understanding that they would be there only a few years, or even months. Because of their educational and, often, their social status, governesses were treated differently from other servants. They joined adults for dinner, for example, and helped to entertain guests by playing cards or singing. Sometimes young women sought this work primarily because of the opportunities such occasions gave them to meet eligible men.

The job was one that appealed to educated women from northern Europe throughout the immigrant era. A woman who was a native speaker of French or German, for example, could easily find work in cultured homes provided that her English was acceptable. Many of the *nouveau riche* of the late nineteenth century in fact preferred a foreign governess to an American woman, giving these young women an opportunity to emigrate with greater assurance of security upon arrival than was the case for most IMMIGRANT WOMEN.

GRAHAM, KATHARINE MEYER (1917–)

After study at VASSAR and graduation from the UNIVERSITY OF CHICAGO in 1938, Katherine Meyer worked for a year as a reporter in San Francisco before joining the *Washington Post*. Her family had bought the *Post* six years earlier in the depths of the Great Depression, and her mother, AGNES ERNST MEYER, was frequently published in its pages.

When Katherine Meyer married attorney Phil Graham in 1940, she repeated her mother's early history in spending the first portion of life primarily on conventional motherhood, while her husband joined her father's business. Phil Graham gradually took over his father-in-law's position at the *Post*, expanding its operations to include electronic media as well as *Newsweek* magazine. His success did not overcome his long-term struggle with depression, however, and in 1963, he committed suicide.

Katharine Graham thus became president of the Washington Post Company and, unlike many wealthy WIDOWS, began actively to lead the corporation she controlled. The sixties were an era of epic news stories, and Graham became an innovative PUBLISHER who recognized the possibilities for her paper—and for the deeper issues of freedom of the press and democratic government.

She expanded her news and editorial staff, encouraged investigative reporters, and stood behind them through the litigation nightmares that followed when the *Post* published the classified "Pentagon Papers" and the story of the Watergate burglary and coverup. Though vilified by national leaders, especially by Vice-President Agnew, Katharine Graham eventually won the nation's respect for her courage in seeking out the truth that forced both Agnew's and President Nixon's resignations.

Her colleagues recognized her by electing her the first woman to preside over the American Newspaper Publishers Association; she was also the first woman to serve on the board of Associated Press and as a trustee for the University of Chicago. Called "Kay" by her friends, Graham has been an active supporter of other women, and her donation helped to establish *Ms.* magazine. Her son is now publisher of the *Post*, but she remains influential as chairman of the board.

GRAHAM, MARTHA (1894?–1991)

During an active performance career that spanned the half-century between 1920 to 1970, Graham developed a reputation as the nation's outstanding choreographer.

She built her own dance company during the difficult years of the Great Depression, when, despite the hard economic times, her unusual choices of music and interpretative theme attracted audiences. She made her early reputation with dances that reflected the cultures of Native Americans in the Southwest and Mexico, and went on to feature a number of works inspired by women. Her *Letter to the World* was based on Emily Dickinson, for example, and she also did productions on Emily Bronte and female characters of ancient Greece, including Medea and Clytemnestra. After retirement from the stage in 1970, Graham continued to work as director of the Martha Graham Center of Contemporary Dance. She was a prime force behind what has become known as modern dance.

GRASS WIDOW

The term applied to a woman whose man had abandoned her. Usually the implication was that of a woman who bore an ILLEGITIMATE child, but it could also be used for a discarded mistress or common-law wife. The meaning was large enough to also encompass a woman who was legitimately married, but whose husband had deserted.

The origin is obscure, but it may have developed as a reference to female natives of the Americas who cohabited with Europeans. By the eighteenth century, it was generally used to denote a woman who pretended to have been married but had not been, while in the nineteenth century, the usage was expanded to include legitimately (and even happily) married couples who were living apart due to circumstances other than their relationship. Men were called grass widowers.

GREEN, CONSTANCE MCLAUGHLIN (1897–1975)

Much like MARY BEARD, Constance McLaughlin Green was a historian who combined scholarship with the life of a conventional wife and mother and who worked outside of the usual academic channels. Also like Beard, she had a greater impact on historiography than was recognized by most of her male contemporaries.

Since her father was a historian, Connie McLaughlin came naturally to the field and studied first at the UNIVERSITY OF CHICAGO where her father taught. She transferred to SMITH COLLEGE in 1916, and after graduation and marriage, earned a Master's at MOUNT HOLYOKE in 1925. More than a decade later and while bringing up three children during the Depression, she was awarded her doctorate from Yale in 1937.

Her thesis became her first and perhaps still her best-known book. A pioneer of urban history, it was a carefully documented and yet highly readable history of Holyoke, Massachusetts and its transformation from an agrarian, Protestant town into an industrial center filled with a motley mix of immigrants.

Green spent WORLD WAR II as a research director at Smith while also working as a historian for the local branch of the Army Ordnance Department. When her businessman husband died in 1946, she moved to Washington, with its greater opportunities for historians, and worked first for the RED CROSS, then as chief historian for the Army Ordnance Corps, and finally, from 1951 to 1954—in the era when women were presumed to have returned to the kitchen—she wrote a history of World War II for the Department of Defense.

GREEN, HETTY (HENRIETTA HOWLAND ROBINSON GREEN) (1835–1916)

Probably the richest woman in America during the pre–WORLD WAR I days that featured the most conspicuous displays of wealth of any American era, Green was singularly different from other women of her class and time. She inherited approximately $10 million from her Massachusetts family in 1865, and when she married two years later, she defied the era's legal presumptions and kept her finances separate from those of her husband.

A true financier, she spent her days studying the stock and bond markets and making shrewd investments. Much feared on Wall Street, she not only invested there, but also in real estate and other properties, especially in Chicago. As she grew older, Green became more and more reclusive and miserly. After the death of her husband in 1902, she lived with her son and daughter in a small apartment in the industrial town of Hoboken, New Jersey, where the gossip sheets reported that she deprived them of the necessities of life. Hetty Green died at eighty-one, three years after the nation adopted an income tax. She left an estate worth upwards of $100 million.

GREENHOW, ROSE O'NEAL (1815?–1864)

Well established in Washington society since her 1835 marriage, Rose Greenhow was a WIDOW in her forties when she rose to fame as the leader of a spy ring made up of CONFEDERATE WOMEN and the men with whom they allied themselves.

She rendered her most important service to the rebel cause early in the CIVIL WAR, when at the First Battle of Manassas (called Bull Run by the Union), she hid coded information in the hairdo of a young associate and sent her to Confederate commander McDowell. The code was prearranged and the message expected, but none knew how valuable it would turn out to be: Greenhow not only told McDowell to expect

Confederate spy ring leader Rose Greenhow with her daughter in the courtyard of Old Capitol Prison in 1862. The strain of imprisonment diminishes her legendary beauty. LIBRARY OF CONGRESS; PHOTO BY MATTHEW BRADY.

fifty-five thousand Union troops, but also detailed the route that they would march. Her predictions were accurate; the Rebels were prepared, and when Union troops fled back to Washington, it looked as though the South would soon win the war.

Greenhow followed up on her intelligence coup during the next panic-stricken days when the Capitol was expected to be attacked at any moment. From her home, which was "within rifle range of the White House," she continued to send south the military secrets that she garnered from her constant flow of late night, mostly male visitors. A woman of storied beauty and captivating manner, she had many admirers who—especially in the early days of the war before military secrecy was well developed—were easily flattered into answering her seemingly innocent questions.

The disastrous Union defeat occurred on July 21, 1861; by August 11, Greenhow had assembled copious information on the fortifications that were intended to hold the capital if the South attacked. Several pages that were captured later detailed each fort surrounding Washington, including the number and caliber of weapons, the morale of the troops, the experience of the officers, the condition of wagons and mules, and more.

She gathered much of this information simply by going on carriage rides with her female friends and studying the defenses that were being built. Moreover, although it cannot be proven, it is possible that she obtained maps and other data that was later found in her possession from a would-be lover who chaired the Senate Military Affairs Committee. Records also make it clear that she had conspirators in the Department of the Navy as well as in the Army, and her network included up to fifty women in five states who had their own contacts.

It didn't take the government long to trace the source of the information flow to her home, and soon Greenhow and several of her associates, both male and female, found themselves shadowed by Pinkerton detectives. With a naturally regal manner, she simply turned and faced these men, demanded to know what sort of impudent behavior this was, and watched as they skulked away, embarrassed by their breach of nineteenth-century manners in regard to ladies. Frustrated by his agents' failure, Pinkerton placed Greenhow under house arrest on August 24, and during the next days, his men conducted a thorough search. Dozens of love letters and other implicating documents were found, some of them pieced together from the ashes of the kitchen stove.

She was confined to her room, and her eight-year-old daughter, also named Rose, was forbidden outdoor play. As time passed, the home became a prison for other women who were Confederate sympathizers—and, despite constant surveillance—somehow the network continued. By December, even the secretary of war acknowledged that Greenhow was somehow still in "correspondence with the commanding general of the army besieging the capitol."

In January, they moved her (and little Rose) to Old Capitol Prison, a filthy, vermin-infested place where BELLE BOYD and other female political prisoners were also confined during the war. She refused to cooperate with investigators, however, and because a number of highly placed men continued to clamor for her release (quite possibly because they feared she would reveal their treason), Greenhow was released six months later. She was escorted to exile in the South, where in Richmond on June 4, 1862, President Davis led the city in welcoming her.

Soon she was ready to move on and, two months later, she set sail for Europe, eluding the Union blockades around Wilmington, North Carolina. She spent the next year abroad. After placing Rose in a French school, she met with Napoleon III and Queen Victoria as an unofficial emissary from the Confederacy and published her account of 1861–1862, entitled *My Imprisonment and the First Year of Abolition Rule at Washington* (1863).

Exactly what she planned next will never be known. She sailed from Scotland in mid-September for home, but when the ship encountered both a furious storm and a Federal gunboat off the North Carolina coast, its captain sailed up the Cape Fear River at such speed that in the dark of night, he crashed against an earlier shipwreck. Greenhow, valiant to the end, insisted upon a rowboat and the captain finally gave in to her demands. Several British and Confederate men joined her, but rowing was impossible in the storm and they capsized.

The men swam ashore, but Greenhow drowned. Like most women of her era, she did not know how to swim, and she was also weighed down by both the heaviness of female garments and the two thousand dollars in gold coins she had concealed on her body. Unlike MARGARET FULLER, who also drowned during a shipwreck within sight of land, Greenhow's body was recovered. On October 1, 1864, she was given as close to a state funeral as could be managed by the besieged rebels and was buried in Wilmington.

Honor, though, was reserved for the South, for in the North, she was a traitor. Indeed, the government had enough evidence against Rose Greenhow almost from the beginning of her spy work that, had she been a man, she would have been hung for treason. Nonetheless—despite their awareness that she continued to betray them—throughout the long months of her house arrest, her jailers continued to supply her with paper and ink. As with Belle Boyd, LIZZIE BORDEN, and other women clearly guilty of crimes, the code of chivalry and presumption of female passivity remained so strong in nineteenth-century men that they could not quite permit themselves to believe what they knew to be true.

GRIFFITHS, MARTHA (1912–   ) Martha Griffiths'
first job after graduating from law school was identical to her husband's—except that she earned less. It was something that she pointed out for the rest of a life that defied the stereotypes of women in the post–WORLD WAR II era.

A model for those who were discontented with the status of women in the regressive 1950s, Griffiths was a member of the Michigan legislature from 1949 to 1952, when she became a judge. After two years on the bench, she was elected to Congress in 1954 and was subsequently reelected for twenty years. The first woman to be a member of the prestigious Ways and Means Committee, she also was a sponsor of the EQUAL RIGHTS AMENDMENT.

It was primarily Griffiths who got the ERA out of the Judiciary Committee, where it had been ignored for two decades, and moved it through the House in 1973. Though the EQUAL PAY ACT then was ten years old, she led hearings that showed women, in fact, were not receiving equal pay for equal work and that they also routinely encountered discrimination in credit, insurance, education, and virtually every aspect of life. Among other bills, Griffiths sponsored legislation to establish equity for women in Social Security payments and (less successfully) an adequate system of health care.

After a few years out of public life, she returned to government in 1983 at age seventy-one, when she became lieutenant governor of Michigan.

GRIMKE, SARAH MOORE (1792–1873) and ANGELINA EMILY GRIMKE WELD (1805–1879)

Angelina Grimke was the last of fourteen children; her sister Sarah was more than a decade older than she, but they were kindred souls who defied the powerful traditions of their aristocratic Charleston, South Carolina heritage.

Even in her youth, Sarah rebelled against the confines of Southern ladyhood, using her obligatory role as a Sunday school TEACHER, for example, to disdain laws against teaching slaves to read. When at age twenty-six she went north for the first time, her feelings against slavery were strengthened as she saw that other white people, notably QUAKERS, reacted as she did. Two years later she moved permanently to Philadelphia, and in 1829, her twenty-four-year-old sister Angelina joined her. Neither was ever to return South, even for a visit, for soon their names were anathema in their homeland.

They read William Lloyd Garrison's newspaper, and in 1829 he published a letter to the editor from Angelina that changed their lives. ABOLITIONISTS immediately sought to include the sisters, for the antislavery cause was strengthened immeasurably by these two women who could personally testify to its cruel realities. Though women did not yet engage in PUBLIC SPEAKING, the Grimkes (especially Angelina, who was the more fearless of the two) represented too great an asset for the male abolitionist leadership to ignore. Since no white southern man ever emulated the Grimkes, male abolitionists had no choice but to encourage their participation.

Ironically, in Quaker gatherings where women traditionally did speak, there nevertheless was controversy, for abolitionism was seen as too divisive to be an acceptable topic for pacifists. When Sarah Grimke attempted to address slavery in the 1836 annual meeting of Friends, she was publicly rebuked. Just like she left South Carolina, she then left Philadelphia to join Angelina's work for the Anti-Slavery Society in New York. The situation there was little better, and the sisters continued to be condemned for their "unnatural" behavior in speaking publicly: an 1837 pastoral letter by Massachusetts Congregationalist clergy insisting that "the power of woman is in her dependence" was aimed at them. Nonetheless, they expanded their discussions from gatherings of women in private homes to large halls, and people came to hear them. By 1838—less than three years after the pivotal letter to Garrison—the Grimkes attracted thousands of men and women to their Boston lecture series.

Perhaps even more effective than lectures, however, were their writings. Angelina's first effort, published by the Anti-Slavery Society in 1836, was hopefully titled *An Appeal to the Christian Women of the South* (1836). The appeal was not only on behalf of blacks, she asserted, but also on behalf of white women. She argued (as MARY CHESNUT would much later) that slavery also harmed white women by condoning male sexuality outside of marriage, for the faces of many black children bore silent testimony to their white fathers. Readers in and out of the South were shocked by her candor: for a woman to say in print what could be seen, but what was never said, naturally caused an uproar. Postmasters in slave states confiscated and destroyed the *Appeal*, while in the North, the mildly salacious thoughts it provoked brought new attention to the Society's publications.

Later that year, Sarah Grimke targeted the consciences of another group with her *Epistle to the Clergy of the Southern States* (1836). The following year Angelina continued her pleas to southern women with *Appeal to the Women of the Nominally Free States* (1837), while Sarah spelled out the connection between the enslavement of blacks and the less obvious oppression of women with her *Letters on the Equality of the Sexes and the Condition of Women* (1838). Angelina also set a precedent for women by testifying to a committee of the Massachusetts legislature in 1838, five years prior to DOROTHEA DIX's better known "memorial."

Soon afterwards, Angelina married abolitionist Theodore Weld in a wedding ceremony that included black guests. Philadelphians angry about this integration rioted two days later, burning down the new office of the anti-slavery society and setting fire to the Shelter for Colored Orphans. Perhaps shock at this disproportionate response to their private lives was a factor in lowering their visibility, for the sisters' level of action diminished dramatically.

Sarah joined the Weld household, and while all three retained their beliefs, the marriage nonetheless changed everything. Angelina, who turned thirty-three shortly after her wedding, bore three children in the next six years, with negative effects on her health. Her husband and sister jointly published *American Slavery as It Is: Testimony of a Thousand Witnesses* (1839)—a remarkable collection of newspaper stories on the actualities of slavery that Southern editors had thoughtlessly printed—but the following year, the three adults and infant son moved to a farm and effectively retired from public life.

Though all three did some teaching and lecturing during the 1840s and 1850s, these activities were motivated by financial need as much by idealism. As abolitionism moved on to be identified with the Republican Party and the CIVIL WAR, they stayed in the background. Yet the depth of their personal commitment was clear when, three years after the war, the sisters took in two mulatto students whom they discovered were their nephews. (These boys, who used the Grimke name, went on to become respected professionals and civil rights leaders; the wife of one of them, Charlotte Forten Grimke, was a noted educator and author.) Nor did the sisters entirely abandon their FEMINISM, for in 1870, when Sarah was approaching eighty, she and Angelina were among the Massachusetts women who tested the FIFTEENETH AMENDMENT by attempting to vote.

The focus of their lives, though, was the decade between Angelina's 1829 letter to the *Liberator* and Sarah's 1839 documentary book. Although this public life was relatively brief, the sisters had a tremendously powerful effect in being so early to join the abolitionist cause and, more importantly, in standing virtually alone as Southerners whose consciences compelled them to endure hatred and ostracism rather than accept a system that offered them lives of luxury.

GRISWOLD VS. CONNECTICUT (1965)

The Supreme Court ruled in this case that states could not ban the distribution of BIRTH CONTROL materials to married couples. Connecticut, a state with a large proportion of Catholics, many of them IMMIGRANT WOMEN or their descendents, had a law, originally passed in 1879, that banned contraceptives. In ruling that the statute was a violation of several sections of the Constitution's Bill of Rights, the Court upheld the primacy of individual rights over states' rights—something that was consistent with state laws on racial segregation that were also struck down in this era.

GRUNDY, MRS.

"What would Mrs. Grundy say?" is a phrase used in American life since 1798, when Mrs. Grundy was an offstage presence in a play called *Speed the Plough*. Mrs. Grundy, who was discussed by others but who never actually appeared, became a symbol of gossiping neighbors whose standards for upright living were impossibly high. "What would Mrs. Grundy say?" became a lighthearted reference to ethics based on fear of scandal.

GUARDIANSHIP

That fathers, not mothers, were the natural guardians of children was an established tenet of the American legal system until the latter part of the nineteenth century. This assumption had its roots in European inheritance law, which took greater cognizance of land and estate than of children and their individual welfare—children, as potential heirs, were another form of property in this mindset. Early American law reflected these English ideas on patriarchy, making legitimacy of birth and paternal lineage of tremendous legal significance. Since it was the father whose name and estate mattered, it was the father who held virtually absolute power in regard to his children's discipline, career and marital decisions, and every other aspect of their lives.

Thus, in those rare cases of DIVORCE, the presumption was that children went with their father; the correctness of this principle was so absolute that colonial courts in Virginia even gave custody to fathers who were religious dissenters rather than to mothers who were members of the established church. This favoritism to fathers was a powerful tool to keep mothers bound in unhappy marriages, for women understood that to file for divorce or separation meant that they might never see their children again.

SUSAN ANTHONY's understanding of the GUARDIANSHIP problem was developed through personal experience in 1860, when she assisted the wife and daughter of a Massachusetts state senator in their flight from abuse. The legal system offered women so little protection that this man was able to commit his wife to an insane asylum after she confronted him with evidence of his mistress; he, of course, retained guardianship of their daughter. After the asylum released the clearly sane woman, she sought out Anthony and pleaded for help. In disguise, Anthony lead them to a secure home.

For over a year, Anthony withstood arrest threats from the senator's lawyers. At the same time, she also had to stand up to male ABOLITIONISTS who thought the case damaged their cause. Even William Lloyd Garrison could not see the parallel between laws restricting women's freedom and the Fugitive Slave Law; though he devoted his life to breaking laws on slavery, he thought Anthony should obey this law. In the end, the senator prevailed despite Anthony's courage; the girl was kidnapped from Sunday School and returned to him.

Cases such as this developed public awareness of the need to reform guardianship law. As states revised their codes on MARRIED WOMEN'S PROPERTY RIGHTS, guardianship also was reviewed—but well into the twentieth century, courts continued to grant custody to fathers because of their superior earning power rather than imposing child support payments. By the end of the century, however, the Victorian cult of domesticity and its veneration of motherhood was so strong that arguments in favor of automatic preference to fathers could not be sustained.

Moreover, as women also gained the right to file suit and therefore went to court in search of divorce, it became clear that most husbands had little interest in actually caring for children without the aid of their wives. Before the next century was over, custodial presumptions in divorce would be exactly the opposite of what they had been for most of the nation's history: the assumption then would be that the mother was the guardian unless the father could actively prove her unfit.

H

HADASSAH Jewish women in New York City were sufficiently well organized to merge their various groups into the Federation of Jewish Women's Organizations already in 1896, but it was Hadassah, founded in 1912 by Zionist Henrietta Szold, that went on to become the largest and most visible organization for Jewish women. The word "Hadassah" is not only the Hebrew name for the ancient Queen Esther, but also refers to the fragrance of the myrtle flower.

Especially after WORLD WAR II, Hadassah demonstrated the stellar organizational and fund-raising abilities of women with countless projects to benefit the new state of Israel. Its women have built and continue to operate a number of facilities in Israel, including hospitals, clinics, and technological colleges, as well as day-care and counseling centers. Hadassah also sponsors people wishing to live and work in Israel and helps with the resettlement of immigrants. In addition to its projects in Israel, the nearly four hundred thousand women of Hadassah also provide many services in their American communities.

Hadassah is affiliated with the GENERAL FEDERATION OF WOMEN'S CLUBS and has been part of coalitions for the EQUAL RIGHTS AMENDMENT and other legislative goals for women. Its headquarters is in New York at 50 West Fifty-eighth Street, where it also maintains a research library.

HAGER, BETSY (ELIZABETH HAGER PRATT) (1750–1843)
Betsy Hager's parents both died when she was nine, leaving her to become a "bound girl"—a traditional arrangement in which Boston's city fathers contracted for the care of orphans with families that could benefit from child labor, thereby freeing the city of charity costs. Much like an INDENTURED SERVANT, Betsy was thus apprenticed on a nearby farm, where she learned both indoor and outdoor skills. An expert at weaving, "Handy Betty" had mechanical aptitude as well as a talent for spatial relations, and it was said of her that she could "make almost anything out of iron or wood."

When the American Revolution began, Betsy Hager had served out her apprenticeship and was employed by Boston blacksmith Samuel Leverett. Both were ardent revolutionists, and working together in a secret room, they refitted old weapons that dated back to Queen ANNE's War in the early 1700s. In a time before mass production, when each weapon—and its replacement parts—was individually crafted, they retooled dozens of deteriorated muskets and matchlocks to usefulness for the rebels.

Like other REVOLUTIONARY WAR WOMEN, Betsy Hager was at the Battle of Concord to work as a NURSE, but when the British retreated and left six damaged cannon behind, it was she who realized their value. She and Leverett hid them, and during the next six weeks, they rebuilt the cannon and then turned them against the British. Hager spent the rest of the war making ammunition, and even after her marriage to John Pratt at the war's end, she continued to speak her political opinions. She supported Washington during Shays' Rebellion, and sent her husband off soldiering in 1786–1787 while she, like other FARM WOMEN, managed alone.

Her strength remained all of her life; in 1816, when she

was sixty-six, the Pratts left Massachusetts to pioneer in the wilderness of northern Pennsylvania. She had added medical lore to her skills by then and was known locally as a doctor—with that reputation enhanced by the fact that she lived to age ninety-three.

HALE, SARAH JOSEPHA BUELL (1788–1879)

Sarah Hale bore five children during nine years of marriage before she was left a WIDOW in 1822. Desperate for a method of supporting her little children in New Hampshire at a time when few occupations were open to women, she sold some poems to local newspapers under a PSEUDONYM and then, only a year after being widowed, published a collection of poetry. Her first novel in 1827 attracted enough attention that she was offered a job in Boston as editor of the infant *LADIES' MAGAZINE* the following year.

Because the entire field of magazine publishing was new—and periodicals for a female audience virtually unprecedented—Hale was in a position to exercise far more influence than she knew at the time. Indeed, it is questionable whether this woman who had no formal education would have had the temerity to take on such an overwhelming task had she not been driven by dire financial need—or had she realized how many millions of women would eventually look to her as their monthly guide to life.

In the beginning, the title of "editor" meant far more than editing, for Hale was also the author of almost everything that appeared in *Ladies'*. She wrote fiction and nonfiction, biography and poetry, book reviews and editorials, and even had enough energy left over to bring out a second book of verse. *Poems for Our Children* (1830) included one that became a part of the national folklore, known to millions who do not know its author: "Mary Had a Little Lamb" was published two years after Hale's editorial career began.

Her influence increased greatly after *Ladies Magazine* became *GODEY'S LADY'S BOOK* in 1837. Hale moved to Philadelphia with the magazine, and under her leadership, it became the single most important periodical for women in the nineteenth century. She used its pages to crusade editorially for those educational opportunities that had not been available to her, and she was a direct influence for the development of women's COLLEGES in mid-century. (She even was astute enough to understand linguistic gender bias 150 years before such ideas were promulgated, for she argued against using feminine terms in naming these colleges, since no extant college included any male identification.) She supported women TEACHERS at a time when even little children were taught by school*masters*, and she served as a vice-president of an organization to improve the quality and image of women teachers.

With less success, Hale also argued for women in medicine, and led a number of other causes less directly related to women, including the completion of the Bunker Hill Monument, the observance of Thanksgiving and the Seaman's Aid Society. An innovative editor willing to give unknown writers a chance, she also holds an important place in journalistic history for defining the basic format of magazines.

By the 1850s, her children were grown and she could find time to write books as well as to edit *Godey's*. The author of many volumes on lighter subjects, including cookbooks,

Hale's most serious accomplishment was a series of books on American women called *Woman's Record, or Sketches of Distinguished Women* (1853, 1869, and 1876), which alone would merit a place in women's history. Indeed, it is hard to exaggerate the influence she had during a half-century of writing, much of which was read monthly by almost every female community leader in America. Though she never allied herself with the SUFFRAGE MOVEMENT and though she is deservedly criticized for expanding Victorian ideas on domesticity, Hale nonetheless was as progressive as her business situation allowed her to be. A rare model of a self-made nineteenth-century woman, Sarah Buell Hale continued to work almost until death, enjoying only two years of retirement before dying at ninety.

HALL OF FAME

Formally known as the Hall of Fame for Great Americans, the memorial is literally a hall of statues and plaques, which was built in 1899 on the campus of New York University, overlooking the Hudson River. It was opened in 1900 with the election of such historical figures as George Washington and Abraham Lincoln. The next election, in 1905, added the first women. By 1955, there were eighty-nine members of the Hall of Fame, only eight of whom were women.

Given that the selection committee had 100 members who were nationally based, the standards for election seemed rigorously objective. Nevertheless, such obscure men as James Kent and John Motley have been chosen, while even such a paragon of American womanhood as, for example, CLARA BARTON, was excluded until 1976.

The women elected to the Hall of Fame during the first half of the twentieth century were: MARY LYON, EMMA WILLARD, and MARIA MITCHELL in 1905; HARRIET BEECHER STOWE and FRANCES WILLARD in 1910; CHARLOTTE CUSHMAN in 1915; ALICE FREEMAN PALMER in 1920; and SUSAN B. ANTHONY in 1950. That seven of the eight were chosen in the period prior to women's right to vote is indicative of the damage done by the apathy that followed the end of the SUFFRAGE MOVEMENT, for no women were elected during the thirty years between 1920 and 1950. Instead, some of those honored during this era (along with more justly famous men) were James Buchanan Eads, William Thomas Green Morton, Augustus Saint-Gauden, Matthew Fontaine Maury, and Simon Newcomb.

Another fifteen years passed after Anthony's selection before women were again elected. JANE ADDAMS was added in 1965; LILLIAN WALD in 1970; and Clara Barton in 1976. Not surprisingly, as the women's movement gathered strength in the second half of the twentieth century, a separate WOMEN'S HALL OF FAME was established.

HAMER, FANNIE LOU TOWNSEND (1917–1977)

The twentieth child in her family, Fannie Lou remembered when her mother lost her sight: "she was clearing up a new ground . . . for $1.25 a day. She was using an axe, just like a man, and something flew up and hit her in her eye." Fannie Lou herself picked cotton from age six and received only the rudiments of education in a segregated school, where the terms were limited to the few months of Mississippi winter when no farm work could be done.

Fannie Lou Hamer testifying before the Credentials Committee at the Democratic National Convention in 1964. Hamer's leadership of the Mississippi Freedom Democratic Party helped make voting a reality for millions of African Americans. LIBRARY OF CONGRESS; U.S. NEWS & WORLD REPORT.

She married in 1942, adopted two children, and at age forty-five, was working as a timekeeper on the plantation where she also sharecropped when she attended her first civil rights meeting. In August of 1962, when this meeting was organized partly through the efforts of ELLA BAKER, the civil rights movement was beginning to feel courageous enough to take on such bastions of segregation as Mississippi. With at least some support from President Kennedy and the U.S. Justice Department, voter registration drives were organized. All sides were aware that the consequences could be tremendous, for blacks were the majority in many southern counties and if they could vote, an end to the vestiges of slavery must necessarily follow.

Inspired by what she heard at the meeting, Hamar led seventeen people to the Sunflower County Courthouse to register to vote. They spent all day there, while shocked local officials thought up new obstacles to registering them. When the day was finally over and they left for home, their bus was stopped by police and the driver arrested for "driving a bus of the wrong color." Hamer and the others were eventually informed that they had failed the literacy and constitutional interpretation tests for voting.

When her boss heard of Hamer's activism, she was fired—which also meant eviction from her home on the plan-

tation. Her husband and daughter were arrested on trumped-up charges, and she received a nine thousand dollar waterbill for a house that did not have running water. But the harassment did not stop with such comic opera techniques, and much worse was to come. Like DAISY BATES, Hamer's home became a target for racists; she was shot at and threatened with drowning in the Mississippi River, which she knew held the bodies of others who had resisted the powerful in the past. In the fascist state that Mississippi was at the time, authorities refused to respond when she called for help, but instead searched her home without a warrant.

Yet threats did not stop Hamer, nor did actual brutality. When she and civil rights activist Annelle Ponder were jailed and beaten for their defiance of local norms in running a citizenship school, the U.S. Justice Department did file charges against five local law enforcement officials—but when the case came to trial in December, 1963, the judge made it clear to the jurors that they should decide in favor of the police. Later, Hamer lost the nerves in her arm from a brutal beating she received when she tried to integrate a bus station, and when she went to South Carolina to participate in the sit-down strikes that integrated food counters, she was also arrested and jailed. There two black male prisoners were ordered at gunpoint to beat her, inflicting severe kidney damage.

None of this broke her, and, in the spring of 1964, Hamer audaciously qualified to run for Congress. As expected, she was defeated in the Democratic primary—though, because two different vote counts were offered by officials, she never knew exactly by what margin. The congressional district in which she ran was 68 percent black, but Hamer estimated that only 6 percent or 8 percent had managed to overcome the obstacles to registration, adding that "it was easier for me to qualify to run than it was for me to pass the literacy test to be a registered voter."

The primary was in June, and in August, Fannie Lou Hamer made her most widely recognized contribution to freedom by leading a delegation of black dissenters who organized themselves as the Mississippi Freedom Democratic party (MFDP) to the Democratic National Convention in Atlantic City. There they challenged the credentials of the whites-only delegation that had always dominated the state party—while it also openly rejected the platform of the national party, especially regarding the 1964 Civil Rights Act and similar Democratic-sponsored bills. The MFDP argued that these recalcitrants had no right to call themselves Democrats and should not be seated by the convention.

Hamer was the designated speaker for the MFDP, and, in testimony to the Credentials Committee on the first day of the convention, she made a moving speech. She recounted the murders of civil rights workers in Mississippi as well as her own personal suffering and appealed to the committee to seat the MFDP and to reject the "regulars." Party leadership responded with a compromise that did not appease either group. When all but three of the "regulars" walked out of the convention, the MFDP, using credentials provided by delegates who supported their ideals, went onto the convention floor and attempted to seat themselves in Mississippi's empty area—but guards forcibly removed them. The credentials compromise had satisfied no one, and the problem would remain until the truly violent 1968 convention.

Hamer went to Africa later the next month, where, she said, "We were greeted by the Government of Guinea, which is *Black People* . . . You don't know what that meant to me." Though the trip was the dream of a lifetime for her, Southern segregationists saw it as evidence of their contention that integration was a Communist conspiracy, arguing Hamer deliberately embarrassed the United States with Third World nations.

In January 1965, she and the MFDP challenged the electoral validity of Mississippi's representatives in Congress. They lost after a nine-month effort, but Hamer continued as vice-chairman of the MFDP. Eventually, both internal organizational dissension and health problems contributed to a decline in her visibility, and Fannie Lou Hamer died prematurely of cancer at fifty-nine. Hamer received several honorary degrees from black colleges before her death, and is remembered for saying, "I'm sick and tired of being sick and tired."

HAMILTON, ALICE (1869–1970)

In over one-hundred years of life, Alice Hamilton pioneered a field that is still considered new, for industrial toxicology—in which she began specializing at the turn of the century—remains a controversial subject.

She grew up in Indiana, where she was tutored at home under the GOVERNESS system, followed by two years at the exclusive Miss Porter's, a Connecticut FINISHING SCHOOL. She had decided by then to seek a medical education, something that remained difficult for women, despite the precedents of ELIZABETH BLACKWELL forty years earlier. She also had an educational role model in her older sister EDITH HAMILTON, who was then a student at BRYN MAWR, but neither Bryn Mawr nor any other of the new women's COLLEGES in the Northeast offered the study of medicine.

After enrolling at what she described as a "little third-rate medical school" in Fort Wayne, she was admitted to the University of Michigan's coeducational medical school and received her M.D. in 1893. Dr. Hamilton did internships in Minneapolis and Boston, and then, with her sister Edith, went to Germany in 1895–1896 to study bacteriology in Munich and Leipzig; though those universities did not admit women, she was allowed to attend lectures provided that she made herself "inconspicuous." Upon her return, she did further research at JOHNS HOPKINS UNIVERSITY in Baltimore, where Edith was beginning her career. From there the sisters' lives diverged, and, apparently intent on establishing their separate identities and credentials, they seldom referred to each other in interviews later in life.

Thus well prepared, Alice Hamilton was appointed as a professor at the Woman's Medical School of Northwestern University in Chicago in 1897. She chose to live at JANE ADDAMS' Hull House, where she not only met many of the era's progressive thinkers, but also saw firsthand the needs of Hull House's clients. She soon discovered that many of the irreversible health problems of the immigrant poor were due to the noxious chemicals and unsafe conditions that they were exposed to in the course of their industrial work. Since there was no workers' compensation or health insurance at the time, many employers considered workers to be an expendable item to be used as long as profitable and then replaced by new labor fresh from Europe.

Hamilton began studying the problem, and when the governor of Illinois appointed an Occupational Disease Commission in 1910, (the first such body in the world), Dr. Hamilton became its director. The Commission's investigations resulted in passage of a state workers' compensation law (then called workmen's compensation), and the precedent was set that employees were entitled to monetary recompense when health was injured as a result of their jobs.

After Hamilton gave her report on workers' compensation to an international meeting in Brussels, the U.S. commissioner of labor asked her to replicate her research on a national level—without pay. She remained in this nonsalaried position from 1911 to 1921, when business-oriented Republicans regained control of the White House and even her unpaid efforts were cancelled. Meanwhile, she spent the first years of WORLD WAR I working for peace; along with Addams, EMILY BALCH, and others, she was part of the delegation that traveled throughout Europe trying to negotiate an end to the war, which eventually became the WOMEN'S INTERNATIONAL LEAGUE FOR PEACE AND FREEDOM. Upon her return, she and Addams coauthored *Women at The Hague* (1915) about these unprecedented efforts in international diplomacy.

When the U. S. entered the war despite the women's endeavors, Hamilton witnessed the ironically liberating effect that war has had for American women: she was finally paid for a research project undertaken for the federal government. Her investigation of the munitions industry resulted in toxic identification of a number of substances to which these workers—often women—were routinely exposed. The war's new emphasis on the need for credentialed women in employment also was partially responsible for the fact that she finally secured a postwar position equal to her abilities, but more than that, war gave visibility to her unique status as an expert on industrial toxicology: Dr. Hamilton became the first woman on the staff of Harvard Medical School in 1919, the year the war ended. She believed she was hired in this "stronghold of masculinity" because "I was the only candidate available." All of her students were male, for Harvard Medical School did not admit women until it was forced to by the needs of WORLD WAR II.

Hamilton moved to Boston, giving up the Hull House home that had been her primary residence for more than twenty years. She continued to conduct industrial research while at Harvard, publishing her classic *Industrial Poisons in the United States* in 1925 and *Industrial Toxicology* in 1934. As the only woman to serve on the League of Nations Health Committee, she investigated industrial health conditions in several countries during her 1924–1930 tenure. When the Democrats returned to the White House in 1932, she did further field investigations in the U. S. at the request of Labor Secretary FRANCES PERKINS, including studies of the new artificial fabrics industry and of the silicosis that afflicted miners.

Retirement from Harvard in 1935 did not end Hamilton's involvement. She was the Labor Department's representative to a conference on industrial accidents and disease in 1938 that was held in Germany, and her observations of the Nazi government reactivated her internationalism. Like her friend Emily Balch, she saw a distinction between the two world wars and did not oppose American involvement in the second.

At the war's end, she again sought to move a progressive domestic agenda, serving as the president of the National Consumers League and testifying to Congress on behalf of a system of national health insurance that has not yet been achieved. At the same time, she opposed the EQUAL RIGHTS AMENDMENT, as did most of her progressive friends, because of its potential for nullifying the PROTECTIONIST LEGISLATION they had worked so hard to pass.

As Hamilton had always gone beyond scholarly research to the political action necessary to benefit public health, so also did her writing expand beyond scholarly monographs to the mass media. The author of a multitude of articles, she published in everything from the *Journal of Public Health* to *LADIES HOME JOURNAL*. Her autobiography, though burdened with the title of *Exploring the Dangerous Trades* (1943), was said by one reviewer to be "more exciting than fiction."

She received several honorary degrees and other awards late in life, including a belated listing in *Men of Science* in 1944—nearly a decade after she had retired from Harvard. Alice Hamilton enjoyed her last years with gardening and painting in small-town Connecticut, dying six months after her one hundredth birthday.

HAMILTON, EDITH (1867–1963)

Edith Hamilton did not write her first book until she was sixty-three, but she went on to establish a stellar reputation for successfully translating esoteric scholarship on the ancient world into books that remain popular today with millions of lay readers.

Born two years after the CIVIL WAR ended, she grew up in Indiana, where her father began teaching her Latin at age seven, with Greek, French and German soon following. Like her sister ALICE HAMILTON, she went to Miss Porter's FINISHING SCHOOL in Connecticut, where both chose to ignore Miss Porter's hesitations about further education for women. Edith Hamilton went on to BRYN MAWR, which was then only a few years old, and graduated with an M.A. degree in 1894.

The following year she and Alice went to Europe, where each succeeded in studying her field at the universities of Munich and Leipzig, despite the fact that no woman had ever done so. While Alice was admonished to make herself "inconspicuous," Edith seems to have been displayed: "I had to take notes at a little desk on the platform," she said. "The head of the university used to stare at me, then shake his head . . ."

When Hamilton returned to the U.S., she was hired as the headmistress of the Bryn Mawr Preparatory School in Baltimore, where she directed the educations of approximately four hundred girls annually for twenty-two years. She retired in 1922, and after writing several scholarly articles on Greek drama during the twenties, she published *The Greek Way* in 1930. As was the case for a number of other AUTHORS, her first book became her most acclaimed. An unusual examination of the contrasts and parallels between life in the modern world and ancient Greece, it was widely read and discussed by a nation looking for eternal truths during the dark days after the Wall Street crash.

Two years later, she wrote *The Roman Way* (1932), with a similar structure. Her books sold well despite the Depression, and in 1936, she added a third theme with *The Prophets of Israel*, an interpretation of the Old Testament ideas. She issued other books on these themes during the war years and then, with boundless energy at age eighty-two, examined a fourth and final factor in the shaping of American thought with her fresh look at the New Testament, *Witness to the Truth: Christ and His Interpreters* (1949). Hamilton took almost a decade off before returning to her original theme and published her last work, *The Echo of Greece* (1957), when she was ninety.

That same year, she traveled to Greece to be made an honorary citizen of Athens and to see one of her translations of Greek plays performed in front of the Acropolis. In this country, she received several honorary degrees and awards, including election to the American Academy of Arts and Letters. Edith Hamilton lived her last years with winters in Washington and summers in Maine. She died at ninety-six, acclaimed as a woman "who would be unusual in any period; in ours, she is unique."

HARDING, FLORENCE KING DEWOLFE (1860–1924)

The nation's First Lady from 1921–1923 has long been suspected of poisoning her husband.

When Warren G. Harding married Florence DeWolfe in 1891, it was over his father's objections, for her ambitious personality did not match his passive one. Moreover, though she portrayed herself as a widow, she was in fact DIVORCED from a man who had recently died and also seemingly had abandoned her son to her parents. That the Harding marriage took place over these objections foreshadowed her strong role in her husband's future career. Her nickname of "The Duchess" made clear the power that she assumed.

Although aware of her husband's affairs with other women, she nurtured the Ohio newspaperman's career all the way to the presidency. When the Republican convention of 1920 was deadlocked over its nomination, Florence Harding—a former journalist—sought out reporters and discussed politics in detail, even calling herself a suffragist. After the NINETEENTH AMENDMENT was ratified the next month and the election became the first in which women could vote, she actively sought women's votes for her handsome husband—at a time when ELEANOR ROOSEVELT thought it improper to campaign for her husband, the Democratic vice-presidential nominee. Harding even went so far as to physically eject one of her husband's mistresses from a potentially damaging campaign situation.

The model of the nation's First Lady changed with women's vote and with Harding's assertiveness. She was the first to associate herself with a specific cause (WORLD WAR I veterans) and she edited her husband's speeches for substance as well as for style. Despite all of her efforts, however, Florence Harding never succeeded in doing anything more than masking Warren's true preferences for playing poker and entertaining women of dubious standards. His cronies made his administration the most obviously corrupt up until that time, and she was embarrassed and apprehensive about the scandals that were yet to break. More than that, Harding's current mistress was widely rumored to be a regular occupant of White House beds.

When the president died suddenly while alone with his wife on a trip to Alaska, many speculated that she had poisoned him. His death was attributed to eating some bad salmon, but no one else was similarly sickened. He was buried without an autopsy and with what some saw as unseemly haste and "odd comments" on the part of the widow. Upon returning to Washington, she took bundles of his papers from the White House and burned many that she thought might be "misconstrued." While some historians argue that Harding's death was "of natural causes," no exact cause has ever been established. Florence Harding herself died soon after.

HARPER, FRANCES ELLEN WATKINS (1825–1911)

During a long life that saw great changes, Frances Watkins Harper became the most celebrated black poet of her era.

Born free in Baltimore but orphaned at age three, she was educated by her uncle. She began supporting herself at fourteen by doing DOMESTIC WORK, using her free time to read and write. By twenty, Watkins had a collection of work she called *Forest Leaves*. Like MARY ANN SHADD CARY and other free blacks, she was forced to move further north after the passage of the Fugitive Slave Act in 1850. She lived in Ohio, where she taught sewing, and then in Pennsylvania before giving her first speech in Massachusetts in 1854.

It was so effective that Watkins lectured for the Maine Anti-Slavery Society for the next two years. With a speaking style that was described as "dignified" and "never theatrical," she went on to share platforms with well-known ABOLITIONISTS of both races, such as SOJOURNER TRUTH and LUCY STONE. She was sufficiently popular to support herself by lecturing throughout the Northeast from 1856 through 1860, and her poetry collection, *Poems on Miscellaneous Subjects* (1854), added another dimension to her oratorical reputation.

Late in 1860, after Lincoln was elected and the CIVIL WAR loomed, Watkins married Fenton Harper. They used her savings to buy an Ohio farm and had one child before he died four years after the wedding. At age forty and in need of income, she took her daughter and returned to the lecture circuit. When the war ended, Harper moved South and continued to travel widely, speaking primarily on the educational needs of freed slaves. In the next four years, she lectured in thirteen Southern states.

Based in Philadelphia during the 1870s, she began to write more than lecture, publishing several volumes of heartfelt poetry that emphasized the burdens of black women and their need for liberation. Harper's poetry used frequent biblical allusions and employed both standard English and black dialect; the voice of "Aunt Chloe" was especially popular for the latter. Turning to the novel form late in life, she published *Iola Leroy; or Shadows Uplifted* in 1892.

From 1883 to 1890, Harper was employed by the WOMAN'S CHRISTIAN TEMPERANCE UNION for organizational work among African-Americans. Active in the AMERICAN WOMAN SUFFRAGE ASSOCIATION as well, she also helped to found the NATIONAL ASSOCIATION OF COLORED WOMEN. Harper's reknown as an orator was sufficient that she spoke to the largely white audiences at the INTERNATIONAL COUNCIL OF WOMEN in 1888 and the COLUMBIAN EXPOSITION in 1893.

Frances Watkins Harper's last collection of poetry came out in 1894, when she was almost seventy; she died at eighty-five. She is sometimes cited as the first black woman to publish in the short story genre, for a tale titled "The Two Offers," which was included in an 1859 edition of *Anglo-African Magazine*.

HARPER, IDA HUSTED (1851–1931)

Chosen by SUSAN ANTHONY to be her official biographer, Ida Husted Harper is most closely associated with the writing of the multivolume *HISTORY OF WOMAN SUFFRAGE*.

Soon after her marriage at twenty, Harper began publishing in a local newspaper under a male PSEUDONYM. She continued to write professionally, although her husband—who was himself a labor lawyer and leftist politician—objected to her activism. This contradiction was doubtless a factor in her joining the new Indiana suffrage society in 1887 and in her DIVORCE after nineteen years of marriage.

She moved to Indianapolis with her only child in 1890 and worked for the *Indianapolis News*, and she continued to act as a correspondent for that paper when she moved on to California a few years later. When Susan Anthony campaigned for a state suffrage amendment to California's Constitution in 1896, she was so impressed by the job Harper did on publicity that she asked Harper to move back to Rochester with her and begin compiling her papers. Working in Anthony's attic, Harper went through the primary sources Anthony had saved and, in 1898, she published a detailed two-volume work, *Life and Work of Susan B. Anthony.* (In 1908, after Anthony's death, Harper would add a third volume to this work.)

The year following publication, Harper went with Anthony to London for the INTERNATIONAL COUNCIL OF WOMEN; she handled press relations there and, with other delegates, saw Queen Victoria. Upon her return, she assisted Anthony with the publication of the fourth volume of the *History*, which was published in 1902, and also began writing pieces that were eventually syndicated by a number of newspapers. By 1909, she was so popular a columnist that she had a regular page in the widely read *Harper's Bazaar.*

Meanwhile, she continued her leadership role in the SUFFRAGE MOVEMENT, going with Anthony to the White House to lobby Theodore Roosevelt in the last years of Anthony's life and writing the obituaries and biographies that were issued at Anthony's death. When CARRIE CHAPMAN CATT resumed the presidency of the NATIONAL AMERICAN WOMAN SUFFRAGE ASSOCIATION, she put Harper in charge of publicity for her 1916 "Winning Plan" to finally enact the suffrage amendment. Using public relations techniques that were remarkably modern, Harper sent out hundreds of pieces from the national headquarters in Washington that were republished in newspapers throughout the nation. The influence she thus exercised on national opinion is immeasurable.

When the NINETEENTH AMENDMENT was passed, Harper returned to the *History*, writing the fifth and sixth volumes and seeing them into print late in 1922. At seventy-one, she finally allowed herself some rest, although she remained active in the AMERICAN ASSOCIATION OF UNIVERSITY WOMEN. Ida Husted Harper died at eighty in Washington.

HARRIMAN, "DAISY" (FLORENCE JAFFRAY HURST) (1870–1967)
Born into elite New York society, Daisy Hurst had a FINISHING SCHOOL education, debuted at eighteen and was married at nineteen to banker J. Borden Harriman. By the turn of the century, however, she had begun to live a life that would make her far more than a socialite.

Daisy Harriman supported the SUFFRAGE MOVEMENT, and in 1904, was a founder of the Colony Club, the first private club for wealthy New York women comparable to the clubs that had long been available to their men. Two years later, she took a far more democratic approach to advancing women's interests: she accepted an appointment as manager of the New York State Reformatory for Women at Bedford and stuck with that inglorious position for twelve long years. During the great STRIKES in the GARMENT INDUSTRY in 1909, Harriman was one of the wealthy women who boycotted non-union clothing manufacturers and donated to the WOMEN'S TRADE UNION LEAGUE.

Meanwhile, she also began to work for the Democratic Party, campaigning for Wilson in 1912 before women had the right to vote. When he became president, Wilson appointed her to the Federal Industrial Relations Commission, where she served as the only woman from 1913 to 1916. She used this position to follow up on the interest she had already shown in labor unions and strikes, and she traveled the nation investigating the causes of worker discontent. The Commission was a factor in her move to Washington after her husband's death in 1914.

When the U. S. entered WORLD WAR I, she not only chaired the government's Committee on Women in Industry, but also helped to create the RED CROSS Motor Corps and then went to France in 1918 to supervise its five hundred ambulance drivers. Soon after she returned, the NINETEENTH AMENDMENT that enfranchised women was ratified, but the Republicans also took the White House, and Harriman's abilities were not utilized. She concentrated instead on organizing the new women voters into the Democratic Party; her role in this was so strong that ELEANOR ROOSEVELT referred to Daisy Harriman as *the* founder of what are now known as the Democratic Women's Clubs. She was the national president from 1922–1930 and was also a leader in the National Consumers League. Harriman continued to be a popular Washington hostess despite the fact that her party lost three elections in the twenties, and invitations to her Sunday night salons were sought after by conservatives and liberals alike.

She made the only real political mistake of her career by not signing on with Franklin Roosevelt early in 1932; as a delegate to the national convention, she supported Newton D. Baker, a former secretary of war who had no chance of winning the nomination. Roosevelt was too astute to hold this against her, however, and she was an ardent FDR campaigner thereafter. In 1937, he appointed her minister to Norway, making her only the second woman to hold such a position.

It was in Norway that Daisy Harriman truly demonstrated her courage and strength. Although the Norwegians were initially reluctant to accept a woman envoy, she won them over at least in part because of her athletic ability—they admired the way this lady in her late sixties swam their fjords and skied their mountains. It was when the Nazis made their surprise attack in the spring of 1940, however, that Harriman showed her mettle; she stayed on through several air raids and then helped others to flee with her to neutral Sweden. She spent her seventieth birthday there, trying to see that all Americans were out of occupied Norway.

She returned to the U. S. in September with the Norwegian crown princess and wrote the story of their escape in *Mission to the North* (1941). Daisy Harriman lived out her retirement in Washington, where she continued to be an active influence in the Democratic Party. In 1963, John F. Kennedy presented her with a Citation of Merit for Distinguished Service; she died four years later at ninety-seven. The first decades of her activism were summarized in an autobiography, *From Pinafores to Politics*, that she published in 1923.

HART, PEARL (c. 1875–c. 1924)
The last of the female desperadoes of the Far West, young Pearl had eloped from her Ontario home with a man named Hart early in the 1890s. She left him behind at the 1893 COLUMBIAN EXPOSITION in Chicago, and drifted southwest; during the next few years, she bore two babies that she sent back to be cared for by her mother. Though she clearly did not meet the moral standards of the day, Hart was not a PROSTITUTE nor a criminal, and she worked at menial jobs until 1899, when word reached her that her mother was ill and desperately in need of money.

With a man known as Joe Boot, she robbed a stagecoach in the Arizona desert, netting $431 from the four men aboard. The stage was one of the few still operating that late in the century, and highway robbery was crime that was supposed to be long since over. When the sheriff at Florence, Arizona recovered from his surprise and dispatched a posse, the two amateur robbers were caught asleep at their campfire. They were quickly identified by their victims, whom they had allowed to escape unharmed.

Public response to this anachronistic crime was a curious mix of astonishment, admiration, and nostalgia for the Old West, with only mild approbation. National reporters flocked to Hart's jail cell, and she used the occasion to deliver a feminist message. The *Arizona Star* even did her the favor of amplifying her views, editorializing: "There is much to her declaration. Why should a woman be indicted, put on trial, convicted, and sentenced under a law she or her sex had no part in making . . ."

Indeed, the jury apparently was so impressed with this reasoning that—much like the experiences of LIZZIE BORDEN, BELLE BOYD, and other female lawbreakers—they acquitted her despite the undisputed evidence, while sentencing her male accomplice to thirty years. The outraged judge, however, assembled another jury, had the prosecutor refile slightly different charges, and tried the case again, making it clear to the jury that they were to bring in a verdict of guilty.

Hart proved a difficult prisoner who was far too popular with both other inmates and the press. After an escape and recapture, she was sent to a more secure prison at Yuma in November, 1899, but in December, 1902, she was pardoned by the governor "on the grounds of the lack of accommodations for women prisoners."

She left the same day for Kansas City, where she planned to live with her sister, a playwright who intended to make her the star of *Arizona Bandit*. The play seems never to have been produced, however, and Hart apparently ended her days running a Kansas City cigar store.

HATS
The most important part of a woman's ensemble in the late nineteenth and early twentieth centuries was her hat. The hat marked one as respectable, and a woman who wished to be treated as a lady never appeared in public without one. Often this nonutilitarian, much-decorated item was symbolic of similar characteristics in its owner.

For IMMIGRANT WOMEN, there was even more symbolic importance attached to the hat. In Europe, only women of social status wore them, so for immigrants, wearing a hat meant moving beyond the peasantry and the serving class. Sociologist EMILY BALCH, for example, wrote of her interview in Slovenia with a woman whose servant had gone to America: "Tell me," she said, "It can't be true, can it? She writes that she wears a hat. Of course, even in America that is impossible."

It was immigrant girls and young women who were most eager to adopt hats, while their elders often saw this as a dangerous denial of their origins; more than one clergyman and immigrant newspaper editor criticized the servant girls of his ethnic group for buying them. Meanwhile, Americans saw the wearing of a hat as so serious a sign of assimilation that some employers refused to interview women who wore shawls instead—even for jobs that were unskilled.

The making of hats, then, became an industry that reached far beyond milliners to provide employment opportunities for women in supplying the fabric and other materials used in their creation. Tens of thousands of women, often immigrants and often working on HOME CONTRACT, worked in the production of artificial fruits and flowers to adorn summer hats and in feather production for winter ones. Indeed, the popularity of feathers for winter hats was so universal that tremendous numbers of birds were killed so that women could wear their finery. MARJORY STONEMAN DOUGLAS was among those who educated the public on fashion's extinction of tropical birds.

But it was the FLAPPER of the 1920s who began the downfall of the hat. While it remained an essential part of the wardrobe of the serious career women through the fifties, WORLD WAR II also played a role in its diminishment. Ultimately, the obligatory wearing of a hat came to be seen by most women as an interference with freedom of action, rather than the symbol of improved status that it had meant to millions a century earlier.

HAYES, HELEN (1900–1993)
A native of Washington, D.C. whose birth name was Helen Hayes Brown, she was encouraged by both her mother and grandmother to pursue the acting skills that she had "almost from the day she was born." She made her stage debut at five and performed on Broadway before high school graduation. From 1917 on, she was an acclaimed stage actress, playing both popular and classical roles.

Maxwell Anderson wrote *Mary of Scotland* especially for Hayes, and she portrayed other women of historical importance, including Cleopatra and HARRIET BEECHER STOWE; her most famous performance is perhaps that of *Victoria Regina*, a technically difficult work in which, as Queen Victoria, she aged eighty years in two hours. Hayes starred in plays and movies by the era's great writers, including Shaw, Hemingway, and Tennessee Williams, as well as ANITA LOOS.

Nor did she limit herself to visual performances, for she acted on radio throughout the Depression years, and when television appeared, she performed in that medium also. Though she made it clear that her first love was performing for live audiences on the stage, Hayes was voted radio's best actress in a 1940 poll and won Academy Awards in 1932 and 1970.

A New York theatre was renamed in her honor in 1955 to celebrate her half-century on Broadway. She served on the National Arts Council during her sixties and published her autobiography, *A Gift of Joy*, in 1965. Married to writer Charles MacArthur in 1928, she bore a daughter in 1930 and later adopted a son. Despite her international fame that increased as she aged, Helen Hayes managed a close family life in a Vermont home.

HELLMAN, LILLIAN (1905–1984)
Born a Jew in New Orleans, Lillian Hellman attended public schools there and in New York City, where she spent most of her youth. She studied at NYU and Columbia, and her marriage at twenty to an author took her into the literary world.

She wrote book reviews for the *Herald Tribune* and reviewed scripts for producers in New York and, beginning in 1930, in Hollywood. Divorcing there, Hellman returned to New York, and in 1934 saw her first play, *The Children's Hour*, become a tremendous success. Chosen for the annual Drama Critics Circle Award only three weeks after opening, the play ran for almost 700 Broadway appearances. Much reproduced since, it was also made into a film titled *Dark Angel*.

It was Hellman's daring choices of subject material that made her reputation. The *Children's Hour*, based on an actual case, showed how the lives of two Scottish schoolteachers were destroyed by a student's insinuations of LESBIANISM. Her second topical choice was less successful, and her 1936 play about strikebreakers closed in a week. She went abroad following this disappointment, where she visited the Soviet Union, witnessed the growing forces of fascism in Western Europe, and was actually under bombardment in the Spanish Civil War.

Hellman's third play, *Little Foxes* (1939) returned her to success. Starring TALLULAH BANKHEAD, its featured Southern family continued the playwright's emphasis on truth, hypocrisy, and fundamental values. *Watch on the Rhine* (1941), developed her experiences in Europe and was a powerful indictment of fascism—but her strongest political statement of the wrongs of her world at that time would not appear until much later, when *Julia* reawakened interest in the women of the WORLD WAR II Resistance movement three decades after that war was over. Instead, Hellman spent the war years living with author Dashiell Hammett on Martha'a Vineyard and writing several minor plays and screenplays; meanwhile, Hammett wrote the movie version of *Watch on the Rhine*, an award-winning film that was timely when it appeared in 1943 during the middle of the war.

When the victory came in 1945, Hellman visited the Soviet Union on a goodwill tour that featured an American plane with a Russian crew, and almost died in Siberia when a translator confused the medication needed after she fell on the ice. Even though the Soviet Union was a crucial ally of the U. S. at that time, this trip would be much criticized during the repressive McCarthy Era a few years later. Indeed, the House Un-American Activities Committee's investigation of her in 1952 temporarily destroyed her career; she went from a high income and low expenses during her Depression success years to near-poverty in the fifties.

Hellman scrambled for income during this era, doing several adaptations of other writers' work for stage and screen; she even did a book for a musical version of Voltaire's *Candide* in 1956. At fifty-five, Hellman again found acclaim for *Toys in the Attic* (1960), which won her second Drama Critics award. Her triumph was complete when she was awarded a gold medal for drama by the National Institute of Arts and Letters and the American Academy of Arts and Letters in 1964.

She began writing autobiographical works with *An Unfinished Woman* (1969), which was the story of her experiences in the Soviet Union and a National Book Award winner. *Pentimento* (1974) was a strong anti-Nazi retrospective that was interwoven with the tale of her personal life with Hammett; it was made into the award-winning film *Julia* in 1977. Her last work was *Scoundrel Time* (1976), another autobiographical piece featuring her persecution by right-wingers during the 1950s.

Lillian Hellman lived alone on Martha's Vineyard in her last years, engaged in feuds with critics, and died ten days after her seventy-nineth birthday.

HEPBURN, KATHARINE (1909–   ) A 1928 graduate
of BRYN MAWR, Katherine Hepburn debuted on Broadway that same year. After four years on the stage, she went to Hollywood in 1932 and earned her first Academy Award the following year. She made at least a film a year during the

Depression years, several of which featured famous women. Among others, Hepburn played Jo of LOUISA MAY ALCOTT's *Little Women* in 1933; starred in the film version of *Mary of Scotland*, which had been written for HELEN HAYES, in 1936; and returned to the stage to do *Jane Eyre* in 1938. In *A Woman Rebels* (1936), she portrayed a Victorian girl's growth into the English women's rights movement.

She won the New York Film Critics Award in 1940 for *The Philadelphia Story*, but spent the remainder of the forties doing a very popular series of movies with her longtime friend and lover, Spencer Tracy. After *Woman of the Year* was a success in 1942, Hepburn and Tracy went on to make several more films that featured strong, smart women. A logical result of the new images women developed with opportunities of WORLD WAR II, the idea continued to be popular long after the war was over: *Adam's Rib* (1949), in which she and Tracy opposed each other as lawyers in a murder case, and the *Desk Set* (1957), when Hepburn's brain repeatedly outwitted Tracy's new computer, are probably the best examples of her clear FEMINIST message.

The busy Hepburn continued to appear on the stage and to make films that did not feature Tracy, including PEARL BUCK's *Dragon Seed* (1944); the much acclaimed *African Queen* (1952); Tennessee Williams' *Suddenly Last Summer* (1959); and *Long Day's Journey Into Night* (1962), which won her a Cannes Film Festival award. *Guess Who's Coming to Dinner* (1967) dealt with interracial marriage and won her second Oscar; it was her last film with Tracy, who died later that year.

The naturally aristocratic style that was key to her image from her earliest years was an excellent vehicle to carry Hepburn as she aged, and at fifty-nine, she became the first woman to earn three Academy Awards for Best Actress, winning in 1968 for *The Lion in Winter*, in which she played the English queen Eleanor of Aquitaine. Articles about her at that time gave Hepburn such accolades as "the unchallenged first lady of American cinema."

She continued her stage appearances as well, adding the musical genre to her proven abilities in comedy and drama with *Coco* (1969), the story of French designer Coco Chanel. The seventies offered fewer opportunities for serious ACTRESSES, but Hepburn nonetheless continued to receive both popular and critical praise, especially for the television production of *The Corn is Green* (1979). Two years later, the world's attention focused on seventy-two-year-old Hepburn's much heralded return to the movie theatres with *On Golden Pond*. It won her fourth Academy Award; she had been nominated for nine others during her fifty-year career.

Married for six years early in her career, Katharine Hepburn has asserted that "marriage is not a natural institution—otherwise why sign a contract for it?" She sincerely mourned Tracy, who stayed in his marriage throughout their long relationship, but has lived alone in Connecticut for many years. She supported dissident Democrat Eugene McCarthy in the 1968 presidential election and maintained her health with tennis, swimming, and hiking. Katharine Hepburn published an autobiography, *Me*, in 1991.

HERRICK, ELINORE MOREHOUSE (1895–1964) Another of the high ranking women among the New Deal Democrats, Elinore Herrick was similar to MARY ANDERSON in that

she came to her specialty of labor relations slowly and through personal experience.

Her future looked promising in 1913, when she began working part-time for the *New York World* while studying economics at BARNARD COLLEGE and its Columbia affiliate (where she met MARY BEARD). She left without graduating, however, married in 1916, bore two children, and DIVORCED in 1921.

Forced to support her family without any particular skills, Herrick ended up in a series of menial jobs, including working in a paper box factory—one of the era's lowest paying industries. Finally, she went to Buffalo, where she worked with DuPont's new rayon fabric and began her ascent from pieceworker to production manager. This was possible in part because of her innate mechanical aptitude, for Herrick invented several labor-saving and safety devices on the job, the first of which was motivated by injuries she received from a defective machine.

DuPont joined other textile factories that moved production south during the twenties to take advantage of the area's lower taxes and nonunion labor. In 1923, Herrick was named production manager of a new factory near Nashville, where she was responsible for the training and output of eighteen hundred workers on three shifts. Though she soon brought the production of these new employees up to the level of established plants, DuPont made it clear that she could expect no further promotions, and so in 1927, Herrick left to resume her academic education.

She supported her family by running a BOARDING HOUSE and working part-time on campus as well, and in two years, she earned her economics degree from ANTIOCH COLLEGE. Age thirty-four at graduation, she returned to New York and worked as executive secretary of the New York Consumers League. The League was interested in the welfare of workers as well as consumers, and in this capacity, Herrick undertook studies that resulted in the publication of *Women in Canneries* (1932) and *Cut Rate Wages* (1933).

Soon after the victory of the New Deal Democrats in 1932, she joined the labor relations staff that was established by the National Recovery Act. Her abilities were so obvious that she moved quickly through the ranks, and in 1935 was appointed as the only woman to head a regional office of the National Labor Relations Board. The seven thousand dollar annual salary of this position was tremendously good for a woman during the Depression—but Herrick measurably was worth more than the men who were paid the same, for her New York division handled a vastly disproportionate number of cases. During the seven years that she held this position, she administered six thousand labor disputes involving more than a million workers.

When the nation entered WORLD WAR II, Herrick's sons joined the military and she moved back into private enterprise as the personnel director of Todd Shipyards, which employed over 140,000 workers in ten port cities. Keeping the armed forces supplied with ships during the war's naval battles was essential to victory, and Herrick's chief challenge was to integrate the necessary labor of women and racial minorities into the ancient male preserve of shipbuilding. Though approaching fifty, she routinely worked sixteen hours a day to cover portions of three shifts that ran seven days a week.

She also found time to write articles recruiting women into the defense industry. When the war was over, she followed up on this with her work at the *New York Herald Tribune*, where she not only headed the personnel department, but also wrote on labor issues. Her editorials were balanced, for—even though Herrick's basic sympathy was with labor—she had been criticized during her years as a mediator by many of the men who dominated unions, and she sometimes criticized them as well, especially when they ignored her prescient advice to end the racial and gender discrimination that excluded many potential members. Always an advocate of democratic procedures and individual rights, she editorially defended State Department employees under attack from right-wingers as postwar repression gathered strength.

H.L. Mencken, who was dainful of liberals in general and women liberals in particular, found Herrick "a really amusing old gal." Her good humor held when her physical health failed; Elinore Herrick retired in 1954 and died a decade later in North Carolina.

HERRICK, GENEVIEVE FORBES (1894–1962)
One of the most widely recognized women reporters on the front pages of newspapers during the twenties and thirties, Genevieve Forbes joined the powerful and widely syndicated *Chicago Tribune* in 1918. She developed a national reputation only three years later with a series of articles about her incognito experience with IMMIGRANT WOMEN who traveled in steerage; her resulting testimony to Congress led to an investigation of Ellis Island.

Though she had degrees from Northwestern and the UNIVERSITY OF CHICAGO and had been a TEACHER, Forbes was assigned to the rather lowlife crime beat in the twenties—but turned this into an opportunity, with her scoops including an Al Capone interview. She met her husband when both were reporters assigned to the notorious Leopold-Loeb trial in 1924, but though she took his name, she continued to work as a journalist. Assigned to Washington during the Depression, her political coverage included ELEANOR ROOSEVELT's women-only press conferences. Her esteem for New Deal Democrats, however, did not match the *Tribune's* virulent anti-Roosevelt editorial stance, and Herrick was forced into resignation in 1934.

She never held a comparably good job, in part because of disabilities from an accident the following year. However, Herrick continued to write for other newspapers and for many magazines through the Depression years. During WORLD WAR II, she did publicity for three different government agencies, and finally rose to head the magazine and book division of the Office of War Information. With her husband, she retired to New Mexico in 1951 and died there.

HEYWARD, DOROTHY HARTZELL KUHNS (1890–1961)
The coauthor of the innovative musical *Porgy and Bess*, Dorothy Kuhns met DuBose Heyward at a New Hampshire artists' colony and married him in 1923. She encouraged him to quit the insurance business the following year and supported him while he wrote. The result just a year later was the book *Porgy*, a sympathetic interpretation of the lives of coastal South Carolina blacks written by a native white. Dorothy Heyward then reworked her husband's tale into a stage version in 1927. In 1935, the Heywards collaborated on the libretto,

while George Gershwin wrote the music, for *Porgy and Bess*, a uniquely American folk opera.

HICKOK, LORENA A. (1893–1968)

Best known for her close friendship with ELEANOR ROOSEVELT, Hickok withstood an abusive father and a lonely, self-supporting adolescence. She managed to graduate from high school, however, and in 1913 began her career as a journalist, moving from Battle Creek, Michigan, to Milwaukee to the *Minneapolis Tribune* in 1917, where a supportive boss gave her the scope to become a front page reporter and then promoted her to Sunday editor. Hickok stayed with the Minneapolis paper until the onset of diabetes in 1926.

AAfter convalescence in San Francisco, she went to New York and served a year with the *Daily Mirror* before landing her most important journalistic job with the Associated Press. As in Minneapolis, her beat was a diverse mixture of sports, crime, and politics. Hickok retrospectively explained her journalistic success by spelling out her career strategy: "When I first went into the newspaper business I had to get a job as a society editor—the only opening available to women in most offices. Then I'd build myself up solidly with the city editor by volunteering for night assignments, get into trouble with some dowager who would demand that I be fired, and finally land on the straight reportial staff, which was where I had wanted to be."

When she began to concentrate on politics for AP in the election of 1932, the assignment had more than a touch of the society editor stereotype, for she covered Eleanor Roosevelt. Hickok soon realized, however, that Roosevelt did not fit the mold of traditional First Ladies. Perhaps more than any other reporter or press agent, it was she who created the public perception of Eleanor Roosevelt as the caringly powerful friend of down-and-out Americans; at the same time, she advised Eleanor Roosevelt on press strategy to expand the New Deal message. The two quickly became confidantes, with their friendship becoming so apparent by the inauguration that Hickok felt constrained to drop the pretense of objectivity and left the Associated Press.

She continued to use her reporter's skills, however, as she spent the years between 1933–1936 working as a confidential investigator of the success of programs being delivered by the Federal Emergency Relief Administration. Nearly eighty of her "reports"—in the form of personal letters to Harry Hopkins, the agency's director—were published as *One Third of a Nation: Lorena Hickok Reports on the Great Depression* in 1981, long after she was dead. Because these reports were not intended for anything except confidential use, they offer an exceptionally candid view of the Great Depression, including the mendacity of those who took advantage of the nation's economic pain. In a battered old car, she drove from Maine to California and Georgia to North Dakota, spelling out to the government how its citizens were suffering, with special attention to professionals who were educated and eager to work, and who were abashed to find themselves indigent.

In 1937, with the worst of the Depression over, Hickok settled in New York for three years, where she worked as a publicist for the World's Fair. She then returned to Washington, lived at the White House, and replaced MOLLY DEWSON as Executive Director of the Women's Division of the Democratic Party from 1940–1945. When Franklin Roosevelt died, she moved back to New York to be near Eleanor's primary residence at Hyde Park. She worked for the Democratic Party of that state for another five years before her diabetes forced retirement from a public career—but Hickok continued to work, despite continued diminishment of her eyesight.

Between 1954 and 1962, she published six books of biography and history, including *Ladies of Courage* (1954), a valuable survey of the era's outstanding women that she coauthored with Roosevelt. Hickok was at work on other manuscripts, including an unfinished autobiography, when she died four years after the death of her beloved Eleanor.

HIGGINS, MARGUERITE (1920–1966)

Educated at the University of California at Berkeley and Columbia University's School of Journalism, Maggie Higgins not only had excellent credentials but also entered the labor market at a propitious time, when new opportunities were opening to women because of WORLD WAR II. She began reporting for the *New York Herald Tribune* in 1942, the nation's first full year of war. Her marriage to a philosopher that same year did not lessen Higgins's ambition, and just two years later, she persuaded the paper's female PUBLISHER to overrule male editors and send her to cover 1944's major invasion of Europe.

Based first in London, she went on to Paris—where the language skills her native French mother gave her proved helpful—and then, in 1945, entered Berlin with the Allied victory over the Nazis. At age twenty-five, Maggie Higgins held front page stories all over the nation with her reports on Hitler's demise; like MARGARET BOURKE-WHITE, she focused public attention on the horrors of the concentration camps and on the resulting Nuremberg trials. For this, she won the New York Newspaper Women's Award for the best foreign correspondent in 1945 and two years later, she was promoted to bureau chief. In 1948, Higgins declared her six-year attempt at an early commuter marriage to be over.

She moved halfway around the world when she was named bureau chief for the Far East in 1950. Based in Toyoko, Higgins did not stay in the office and direct others; instead, she was on the first plane to Korea when war broke out there. She saw the death of the first American soldier in that war, and, sharing the dangers and harsh living conditions of the troops, was present when Seoul fell. International controversy fixed on her when Army officials ordered Higgins out of the country solely because of her gender, but General MacArthur eventually overturned the ruling. The incident was only one case in a lifetime of experiencing the biases that both men and women held about attractive blondes; Higgins repeatedly had to defend the worth of her work against intimations that her good looks were the key to her success. She was candid enough to add that any feminine wiles she could use would only "even the score" in the newspaper and military worlds that were created for males.

Instead of being sent home from Korea, Higgins went on to share the 1951 Pulitzer Prize with five men; hers was the first Pulitzer given to a woman foreign correspondent. The experience became her first book, *War in Korea: The Report of a Woman War Correspondent* (1951), which saw magazine serialization and bestselling status. She returned to the U. S. amid wide acclaim, accepted speaking invitations from dozens of prestigious groups, and according to her own records, received upwards of fifty awards.

Four years after divorcing, she married the former head of military intelligence in Berlin, but neither the marriage nor the loss of a premature child the following year put an end to her peripatetic ways. The *Herald-Tribune* sent Higgins to Moscow to open an office there, but postwar relations with the Soviet Union quickly deteriorated to the point that it had to be closed. Again, she used the material for a book; *Red Plush and Black Bread* (1955) described her 13,500 mile exploration of Russia. In the same year, she published *News Is a Singular Thing*, a retrospective of her career.

Thereafter, Higgins was based in Washington, though she continued to travel worldwide. At the same time, she began to build a personal life for herself with the birth of two children in 1958 and 1959, when she was approaching forty. In addition to maintaining her newspaper work, she used the next years to coauthor a book on the foreign service and to write a children's volume on JESSIE BENTON FREMONT; she also continued to write occasionally for magazines, as she had since 1940, especially for women's magazines. After twenty-one years with the *Herald-Tribune*, Higgins joined the new Long Island *Newsday* in 1963, syndicating her column three times a week in ninety papers.

When American involvement in the war in Southeast Asia began to expand in the early sixties, she spent increasing amounts of time there. The title of *Our Vietnam Nightmare* (1965) had a greater meaning than she could know, for Higgins came down with a tropical disease and died before most of the nation was truly aware of that war. It would be interesting to know how her views would have evolved had she been able to see the Vietnam tragedy to its end, for her book was a complex mixture of hawkish opinion that even advocated the use of the atomic bomb, while at the same time, she presciently understood the credibility problems that the government was creating for itself with its covert activities and inaccurate press releases.

A quarter-century after her death, a male journalist acknowledged, "I was one of those who argued that a woman should not be assigned to Vietnam . . . [because] I . . . saw a woman colleague killed . . . To say now that I was wrong sounds rather weak. My own admission, and that of thousands of other reformed chauvinists who used to dominate the newsrooms, is appropriately ignored. Women are too busy doing their jobs to notice."

Maggie Higgins prepared the way for the women who now win Pulitzers. Her death from the infection contracted in Vietnam was painfully slow; her children were just seven and eight when she died.

HILL, BLANCHE WILBUR (1902–1987) A businesswoman and aviation pioneer, Blanche Hill was just twenty-five when she founded Avion Corporation with John K. Northrup in 1927. Their company built the first all-metal aircraft, an important transformation from the Wright Brothers' types of wooden structures. In 1933, Hill became the founding president of Northill, an aviation development company that combined her name with Northrup's; seven years later, just as WORLD WAR II began, they merged with Garrett Corporation.

Hill also was the founding president of Aeronautical Industry Technical Institute, one of the first schools to train workers in the aircraft industry. She died in Pasadena, California at eighty-five.

HILL, PATTY SMITH (1868–1946) and MILDRED J. (1859-1916) The authors of "Happy Birthday," the Hill sisters were natives of Kentucky who lived in New York City when they wrote their famous song in 1893. Patty Smith Hill went on to make a reputation for herself as a proponent of the kindergarten movement of this era and was on the faculty of TEACHERS College of Columbia University from 1906 to 1935. Mildred J. Hill was a musician, and their celebrated song was originally written as "Good Morning All" for publication in *Song Stories for the Kindergarten* (1893).

"HIRED GIRL" Primarily a midwestern term used especially in the late nineteenth and twentieth centuries, "hired girl" described a young woman or teenage girl employed in DOMESTIC SERVICE, usually in farm households. Its use implied a more egalitarian relationship than would be the case with "servant" or "serving girl," which more commonly described a person who did the same kind of domestic work in older areas of the country. Indeed, the phrase's egalitarian origin of using the word "hired" can be seen in that "hired servant" was an antebellum phrase that distinguished free domestic workers from household slaves, who also were euphemistically referred to as "servants" in the South.

Though the work might be the same, another term was necessary on the more democratic frontier to imply a higher status than that associated with "servant." A hired girl might well be a relative or the daughter of family friends, and thus was entitled to more respectful treatment than would otherwise be the case; a hired girl, for example, expected that she would eat with the family at meals. FARM WOMEN were especially likely to look for a hired girl in the summer when they needed additional help to feed and care for extra field workers, as well as to keep up with their gardening and canning tasks. Though a hired girl might tend poultry or sometimes milk cows, she was not thought of as a farm worker and rarely worked in the fields.

Moreover, working as a hired girl did not mark one as a member of a serving class, for the employment seldom was thought of as a permanent job, but rather a stopgap before marriage or a career. For millions of women in agricultural areas, this work provided the only possible source of income—but the limitations that defined the job were inherent in the name, for a woman of whatever age was called a "hired girl," while the analogous term for a male, even though he might be a boy, was "hired man."

HISTORY OF WOMAN SUFFRAGE By 1880, ELIZABETH CADY STANTON and SUSAN ANTHONY had spent three decades working for women's rights. Because they understood that, to a large extent, their personal history was the nation's history regarding women, they began a determined effort to write that record. Working at Stanton's home, which was then in New Jersey, they began compiling decades worth of letters and other memorabilia in the late 1870s. MATILDA JOSELYN GAGE joined them in putting these disparate sources into book form,

and indeed, the prose that flows most smoothly as an intellectual work was often written by Gage. In 1881, the first volume of the *History of Woman Suffrage* appeared, with its printing—like those to follow—privately financed by donations.

Volume I began with the World Anti-Slavery Convention that led to the 1848 SENECA FALLS WOMEN'S RIGHTS CONVENTION, and it ended at 1860 with the beginning of the CIVIL WAR. The title pages featured a drawing of FRANCES WRIGHT, whom these pioneers recognized as an even earlier pioneer, and the dedication also was for predecessors, with the English Mary Wollstonecraft, author of VINDICATION OF THE RIGHTS OF WOMEN, at the head of the list. Candidly acknowledging that the book was "written from a subjective point of view," the authors thanked those who had contributed to the effort and upbraided others who missed the opportunity "through ill-timed humility."

Gage's introductory chapters reveal particularly thoughtful feminist theory, and the volume's last chapter, also written by her, presaged the later uproar over her writings on women and the church. Other chapters in the first volume, however, set the style for something of a scrapbook approach to history, for items in this and later volumes ranged from arcane to vital. One theme that ran throughout the volume, however, was that women's legal status was analogous to that of slaves. Its pages, therefore, are almost as much a history of ABOLITIONISM as of FEMINISM, for the two causes were inextricably linked in this era. The names of famous male abolitionists are frequently included, for a large number of men attended these early meetings and their words are recorded along with those of women; among the most notable were Parker Pillsbury, Samuel May, James Mott, and the ubiquitous William Lloyd Garrison and Frederick Douglass.

The separation of abolition and women's rights thus became an important theme of Volume II, which covered the Civil War and Reconstruction years of 1861 to 1876. Released in April of 1882, it featured a frontispiece portrait of war celebrity ANNA DICKINSON. Gage used its first chapters to great effect with detailed information on women's wartime roles, profiling not only individual women, but also institutions such as the SANITARY COMMISSION and the LOYAL LEAGUE. Postwar coverage included the passage and testing of the FIFTEENTH AMENDMENT and the split of the AMERICAN EQUAL RIGHTS ASSOCIATION into the NATIONAL WOMAN SUFFRAGE ASSOCIATION (NWSA) and the AMERICAN WOMAN SUFFRAGE ASSOCIATION (AWSA) in 1869.

The volume's treatment of NWSA's formation confirms the association's semi-secret origins; in contrast to voluminous detail on other subjects, most of the relevant information on this was obscured in a long footnote, with Anthony's name buried deep in the list of officers. When Stanton's daughter, HARRIET STANTON BLATCH, pointed out the exclusion of the AWSA from what purported to be a history of woman suffrage, she was authorized to write an addendum on that. Her chapter on this important aspect of the SUFFRAGE MOVEMENT was primarily based on published material, especially the WOMAN'S JOURNAL.

The need for a third volume was clear by the time the second was published, for the authors wrote in the preface to Volume II: "Many new questions in regard to Citizenship . . . grew out of the civil war. [They] have combined to swell these pages . . . with much valuable material that can not be condensed nor ignored." The authors also responded to criticism of their title, noting that some said "you can not write the 'History of Woman Suffrage' until the fact is accomplished." This argument gave them no pause; in the very next sentence, readers were confidently reassured that "already enough has been achieved to make the final victory certain." The prognostication was overly optimistic, for none of these authors would come close to living long enough to see the final victory—but this made their preservationist efforts all the more important, for without these documents, much of women's history would have been lost.

The third volume came out in 1886 and covered the decade from 1876 to the publication date. The authors, still hoping for (but less confident of) the eminent passage of suffrage, said firmly that this would be their last volume. They expressed a vague intention of publishing small annual updates "until the final victory shall be achieved," but they were convinced that their personal "earthly endeavors must end in the near future." Anthony, however, would live more than two decades into a future that was increasingly international, and Volume III reflected the global spread of feminism with information on women from Portugal to "The Orient." More than previous volumes, this one set the tone for organization by geography, with most of its pages used for states' reports on the legal status of women and the progress of suffrage efforts. In addition, it covered such events as the CENTENNIAL EXHIBITION of 1876 and the INTERNATIONAL COUNCIL OF WOMEN.

These first three volumes, of approximately a thousand pages each, listed Anthony, Stanton, and Gage as authors. Anthony used a bequest to purchase the rights of the other two women after the publication of the third volume, for she wished to donate copies without concerns about royalties. More than 1,200 copies of the three volumes were distributed to libraries in the United States and Europe. Only a few years after the publication of Volume III, however, Gage split from Anthony and Stanton; more radical than they at this point in their lives, she disapproved of the formation of the NATIONAL AMERICAN WOMAN SUFFRAGE ASSOCIATION, which she saw as excessively conservative. Gage died in 1898 and Stanton in 1902, which was the same year that the fourth volume appeared.

It bore Anthony's name along with that of IDA HUSTED HARPER, and it covered the remainder of the nineteenth century. Despite earlier resolve to sponsor no more tomes, Anthony again raised the money for publication and hired Harper, who worked out of Anthony's attic from primary sources that Anthony had continued to carefully preserve. Harper had the advantages of typewriter and telephone as well as a strong background in journalism, and her approach was more methodical and less of a "grab bag" than the earlier volumes. In reporter style, she retraced much of the earlier history in the first two chapters and then detailed each of the annual conventions of the NWSA.

Though Harper prided herself on journalistic accuracy, her loyalty to Anthony was such that she also showed little compunction about excluding the AWSA from "the history of woman suffrage." The NWSA's activities were chronicled, while those of the AWSA were largely ignored. When the two united in 1890, the merger merited one paragraph placed a half-dozen pages into that year's report, and the women who had been associated with the AWSA seem less prominently featured than those of the NWSA in the chronology that followed. With titles of annual convention reports reflecting only a one-word change, chronology set the format through 1900. Alphabetical reports from each state ended the volume.

Anthony died four years after the publication of Volume IV, and Harper's name stood alone as the author of Volumes V and VI. Both were published in 1922, and they covered the years from 1900 to the ratification of the NINETEENTH AMENDMENT in 1920. Harper organized a greater mass of material in these two volumes far more systematically than was the case in any of the earlier tomes. Because the suffrage movement grew tremendously in the years prior to final victory, there was a huge amount of information available, and Harper determined from the beginning that two volumes were necessary.

At the same time, she repeated her earlier historiographical habit and wrote from the point of view of those who financed publication: these volumes made little attempt to tell the full story of the passage of the Nineteenth Amendment, but rather was the history of the NAWSA and its affiliates. Except for "objections to [ALICE PAUL's] Congressional Union" that were necessary to the report of the 1913 convention, the important part played by Paul and the WOMAN'S PARTY was largely ignored.

Volume V began with the 1901 NAWSA convention, and a separate chapter methodically reported on each convention that followed until 1920. Additional chapters included a summation of the long struggle for a federal amendment, a history of political party platform initiatives, a report on the NAWSA's role in WORLD WAR I, and the formation of the LEAGUE OF WOMEN VOTERS. Another chapter recognized other suffrage organizations, but attention focused on the NAWSA's affiliated bodies (men, college students, and other distinctive groups), while the Woman's Party was covered in four pages and the contributions of African-American women were excluded entirely. Two pages were addressed to organizations that opposed suffrage.

ANNA HOWARD SHAW, who was NASWA president during the early portion of the twentieth century, was featured at the front of Volume V; CARRIE CHAPMAN CATT, the president who brought suffrage to completion, merited that honor in Volume VI. More than seven hundred of its pages were taken up with reports of states from Alabama through Wyoming; these were followed by territorial reports from Alaska, Hawaii, the Philippines, and "Porto Rico." The status of women in over thirty nations was addressed next, and the last chapters detail the meetings of the INTERNATIONAL SUFFRAGE ALLIANCE.

The publication of the final volumes was financed by a generous bequest from MIRIAM LESLIE. As was the case earlier, suffragists attempted widespread distribution, but because the cause quickly became considered passé, few students were exposed to this valuable documentation of America's past. With the revitalization of the women's movement in the latter part of the century, all six volumes were reprinted by a profitmaking corporation in 1969.

HOBBY, OVETA CULP (1905–   ) Hobby holds at

least three separate places in the history of American women: she organized and commanded the Women's Army Auxiliary Corps in 1942, for which she became the first woman to win the Army's Distinguished Service Medal; she was the first secretary of the Department of Health, Education, and Welfare when it was created in 1953 and, as such, was the second woman to sit on the Cabinet; and finally, as a PUBLISHER, for she was recognized by her journalism colleagues as Publisher of the Year in 1960.

Born in Killeen, Texas and supported by her lawyer father, Oveta Culp was a prodigy who "steamed through" the University of Texas, and at age twenty was not only serving as an assistant city attorney in Houston but also as parliamentarian of the Texas legislature, a post she held from 1926–1931. In addition, she wrote a textbook on parliamentary procedure, *Mr. Chairman*, and, at age twenty-one, codified the Texas banking laws. At twenty-six, she married William Hobby, the publisher of the *Houston Post* and a former governor, and bore two children while also carving out a place for herself at the newspaper. She moved up the ranks from research editor to executive vice-president by 1938.

With WORLD WAR II looming, Hobby took one of the one-dollar-a-year jobs that Roosevelt offered his policymakers, and, six months before Pearl Harbor, became head of the Women's Interest Division of the Army's Public Relations Bureau. From there, it was a natural for her to head the WOMEN'S AUXILIARY ARMY CORPS (WAAC) when it was created in 1942. The WAAC (and its later incarnation, the WOMEN'S ARMY CORPS or WAC) was a historic breakthrough of women into a totally male preserve, and as such was greeted with much skepticism. Its director also encountered opposition, especially from those who believed that, at thirty-seven, she was too young, as well as from those who were certain that no Southerner could be fair to black recruits.

Hobby was therefore careful to include a proportionate number of black women in the first class of officer trainees and worked throughout the rest of the war to dispel charges that blacks were assigned more menial jobs. (Meanwhile, the Navy's WAVES, headed by a woman from the North, did not accept black recruits at all until the last year of the war.) Indeed, the avoidance of menial assignments for all women, regardless of race or background, was perhaps Hobby's most important achievement, for there were many who would have made a cook or secretary of every woman who signed up. Hobby instead insisted that the talents of these exceptional women be used appropriately, and by the end of the war, WACs served in hundreds of military occupational specialties.

Another genuine achievement—and an interminable headache for Hobby—was the establishment of proper codes of conduct to assure that her soldiers would not be treated as CAMP FOLLOWERS. In fact, WACs had a venereal disease rate that was appreciably lower than that of the civilian female population, and they presented so few disciplinary problems that a planned military police unit for them was never formed—and yet Hobby and other officers had to spend inordinate amounts of time defending the reputation and building the morale of the troops.

Time was in fact her greatest need, for especially in the early days of the organization when every decision meant setting policy, Hobby routinely worked fourteen hours a day, seven days a week; often she had just two or three hours of sleep a night. By 1944, she was hospitalized several times for exhaustion, but she kept these problems from her troops—and thus encountered media criticism when she resigned in July, 1945, after the war in Europe was over but before the end of the Pacific war.

Few pointed out how little incentive the military had offered her to stay on, for the case of Oveta Culp Hobby is a powerful example of institutional sexism. Charged with creating a military unit comparable to nothing extant and with no models other than the brief British experience, she had managed in three years to recruit, train, and supervise almost one hundred thousand women assigned to posts all over the globe. For this, she received no rank at all until 1943, when she was made a colonel—a status given to men who sometimes command no more than five hundred. Though there was discussion in Congress of making her a general, this seemingly routine move was never made.

Hobby was gracious, never pointing out the unfairness, and saying simply that "my mission . . . has been completed," when she returned to Houston at age forty. Her career was not over, but instead was moving in new directions. She went into the new field of electronic communication, becoming station director for KPRC AM-TV in 1945 and later acquiring other television stations; in addition, Hobby was named co-editor and publisher of the *Houston Post* in 1952 and became its publisher in 1964 when her husband died. An active businesswoman throughout the postwar era, Hobby also served on the boards of General Foods Corporation and Mutual Insurance Company of New York, as well as in leadership capacities for a number of philanthropic causes, including the Corporation for Public Broadcasting.

Having established a good working relationship with General Eisenhower when she was with the WAC, she campaigned for his presidential candidacy in 1952. He recalled her to Washington when he won, where she headed the Federal Security Agency until its legislative transformation into the Department of Health, Education and Welfare (HEW). Eisenhower knew from his wartime experience that Hobby had the ability to successfully build a new organization from scratch, and thus chose her to be the first woman appointed to the Cabinet since FRANCES PERKINS's 1933 appointment.

Despite her proven credentials, Hobby's tenure was bound to be controversial, for there were many who were still opposed to the involvement of the federal government in social services or education, since these were traditionally areas that belonged to the states. In this era of increasing right-wing dominance, Hobby added ammunition to her opponents' fires with her appointment of Jane M. Spaulding, an officer in the NATIONAL ASSOCIATION OF COLORED WOMEN, as her chief assistant. The new department had a budget of $5.4 billion and a staff of thirty-five thousand—appreciably fewer personnel than Hobby had commanded in the WAC. As in the WAC, she took an organization from conceptional beginning to established operation, and made a long-term success of it, although that would not have been the consensus of opinion in 1955.

At the time, the nation was experiencing polio epidemics every summer, with thousands of cases of death and paralysis that affected primarily children. When Dr. Jonas Salk, working under the aegis of the March of Dimes Foundation, promised a vaccine in an HEW news conference with Hobby in April, 1955, the nation was hopeful but also anxious. The firestorm of controversy that occurred during the next few months centered around two questions: was the vaccine safe and would it be fairly distributed?

The answer to the former became clouded when a California laboratory manufactured considerable quantities of contaminated vaccine that resulted in several deaths. Although Hobby assembled an inspection team within two days, shut down the laboratory's operation, and instituted a "tedious batch-by-batch review of all vaccine," the resulting damage to public trust in the vaccine was real, and she received more than her share of the unfocused blame.

On the question of distribution, Hobby could more fairly be criticized, but she took her cues from the president and his Republican Party. Eisenhower (reflecting the confusion that might be expected of a man who had a lifetime of free medical care in the military) promised that every child would be vaccinated without regard to cost, and at the same time, also reassured his physician and pharmaceutical friends that there would be no federal control of a privately manufactured vaccine. Hobby was perhaps even more responsive to the arguments made by the American Medical Association that a publicly sponsored vaccine distribution was the first foothold of socialized medicine, and her conveyance of this free enterprise message in congressional testimony outraged many.

In the end, questions of safety forced governmental control of the vaccine, and the controversy was thus well on its way to resolution when Hobby resigned on July 13, 1955. Although her ostensible reason was that her husband was critically ill, most believed that the polio vaccine quandary was the real cause, even though there was no evidence that Eisenhower asked for her resignation. She probably could have ridden out the political storm, and one possible interpretation of her resignation is that she made the sacrifice of giving up her post to clear the controversy, for it is true that her departure lessened the debate and allowed the nation to get on with vaccinating its children.

She returned to Texas at age fifty, a decade after her retirement from the WAC, and would never again serve in a governmental position. Hobby concentrated instead on her businesses, and by 1983, *Texas Business* listed her as the only woman among "the twenty most powerful Texans." She sold the *Post* that year for approximately $100 million; the family worth had been estimated at between $100 million and $200 million the previous year. Hobby retains her television network and remains supportive of several cultural and educational bodies, including the ELEANOR ROOSEVELT Memorial Foundation. She has earned more than a dozen honorary degrees and many other awards, and is gratefully remembered by tens of thousands of women who served under her during the dangerous days of World War II.

HOKINSON, HELEN ELNA (1893–1949)

A pioneer as a successful female cartoonist, Hokinson was an Illinois native who studied at the Chicago Academy of Fine Arts from 1913–1918. Especially gifted in drawing, she soon began to make her living from commercial art with advertising sketches for DEPARTMENT STORES, including Marshall Field's. At twenty-seven, she moved to New York, where she lived at the SMITH

COLLEGE Club and drew sketches for Lord & Taylor, B. Altman, and other fashionable stores.

In 1925, she submitted some cartoons to the *New Yorker*, which began publication that year. Her work was soon popular, and thus from the beginning, Hokinson was associated with the magazine that became known as the nation's most chic. The cartoons that she published there for more than two decades featured women, usually middle-aged and upper middle class.

Her amusingly confused characters were frustrated by the trials of their everyday lives, but their entertaining befuddlement nonetheless gently pointed out the exclusion of many women from a more sophisticated world. Hokinson's "Madam Chairman" pieces may have satirized clubwomen, but they also pointed out the desperate attempts of such women to make themselves relevant. Her cartoons on rationing and the servant shortage during WORLD WAR II poked fun at the deprivations of the affluent, but also acknowledged real societal changes that affected the lives of women more than men.

Hokinson's work was so well received that she earned as much as forty thousand dollars a year when that was at least five times the average family income. She began publishing her collected cartoons in 1931 with *So You're Going to Buy a Book!*, but the Depression interfered and it was another decade before she published her second, *My Best Girls* (1941). The third, *When Were You Built?* (1948), appeared the year prior to her death in a plane crash at Washington's National Airport, where she had gone to deliver a speech for charity. Helen Hokinson's friends published three more collections of her work posthumously.

HOLIDAY, BILLIE (1915?–1959)

With a nativity so unheralded that she did not know her birthday, the woman who would become Billie Holiday was born ILLEGITIMATELY to a black teenager in Baltimore. Named Eleanora, she gained the surname of Holiday at age three, when her father married her mother; with few women of her own race who seemed worthy of the adulation of a young girl, she chose "Billie" from Billie Dove, a white female movie star of the twenties.

She grew up poor and lonely, for her father soon abandoned the family and her mother, a DOMESTIC SERVANT, moved with her work to New York. Other relatives sporadically looked out for Billie, but she earned much of her own living from age ten, when among other employment, she ran errands for a local brothel owner who, in return, allowed her to listen to jazz records, including some by BESSIE SMITH. Billie's education ended at the fifth grade, when she moved with her mother to New York in 1927. She worked briefly as a maid, but the Wall Street crash soon made even that poor employment problematic for one as young and untrained as she.

In 1931, she was a teenager working to support her sickly mother by dancing in a Harlem nightclub. When she was asked to sing, the response of the audience to her unique voice was instantaneous. From then on, Billie Holiday attracted followers as she moved from club to club, still singing largely for tips, but building her own technique without benefit of musical education. Two years later, she was an unacknowledged part of a Benny Goodman record, and two years after that, in 1935, she was the vocalist on a second record made by a male band. Her debut at Harlem's famed Apollo

Theater that same year established Billie Holiday's reputation, and she made her first starring record in 1936.

Welcomed by both black and white musicians who respected her talent and dignified style, "Lady Day" toured with Count Basie's and Artie Shaw's bands in 1937 and 1938. Throughout the rest of the Depression and into WORLD WAR II, she appeared in New York nightclubs and continued to build an inventory of jazz recordings. No success was sufficient to completely overcome the racial discrimination that faced such performers on tour, however, and Billie Holiday experienced the same exclusion from hotel rooms and concert halls that had distressed JOSEPHINE BAKER and MARIAN ANDERSON.

She escaped from this pain with alcohol and drugs, moving from teenage marijuana use to opium and heroin. The loss of her mother in 1945 and the unhappiness induced by a series of managers/lovers who exploited and then abandoned her added to her addictions. Even a Hollywood stint as an ACTRESS in 1946 did not ease her anguish, for this gifted musical artist was assigned the role of a maid. Though she tried several times to break her drug habits, the reality of life outside the sanitarium brought Holiday back to the needle. Yet her talent was so significant that a nine-month prison term in 1947–1948 for narcotics violations did not matter to her admirers, who packed Carnegie Hall to hear her sing upon release. Her felony status meant, however, that she could not be licensed to perform in New York, and Holiday was limited to clubs in lesser locations.

Two more arrests in 1949 and 1956 did not diminish either her popularity or her addiction, as she toured with major jazz performers in both Europe and the United States. Again like Anderson and Baker, she found greater acclaim and easier accommodation in Europe than in her native land. Working with a coauthor, she wrote her autobiography, *Lady Sings the Blues*, in 1956. Though clearly debilitated from alcoholism and narcotics use by the fifties, Holiday nevertheless performed until she was hospitalized in New York in the spring of 1959. A final indignity was an arrest for drug possession as she lay in her hospital bed.

Said by some to be the most important female jazz artist of all time, Billie Holiday won the Esquire Jazz Critics Poll in 1944 and was honored with the Metronome Vocalist of the Year Award in 1946. Her life was portrayed in a 1972 film with the same title as her autobiography.

HOLMES, JULIA ARCHIBALD (1838–1887)

The first woman to climb Pike's Peak, Julia Archibald came from a family so committed to ABOLITION that they moved from Massachusetts to Kansas in 1848 to help make that territory into a free state. Her home was a stop on the Underground Railroad, and her family supported women's rights. Marriage to abolitionist James Holmes in 1857 did not diminish her spirit of independence.

It was this willingness to risk that made the couple move further west in 1858. Julia Holmes walked most of the distance from Kansas to New Mexico; the party included one other woman, but she was disdainful of Julia's adventurism and stayed sequestered in a covered wagon. When they reached Colorado, Holmes made the Pike's Peak climb.

Wearing BLOOMERS, moccasins, and the inevitable HAT, she

A mother and her children shelling pecans on home contract for a candy factory in 1911. Note the man standing in the background; fathers rarely helped with such work. LIBRARY OF CONGRESS; PHOTOGRAPH BY UNDERWOOD & UNDERWOOD.

carried a seventeen-pound pack of supplies to accompany her husband and two other men on a six-day exploration of the mountain, while the others stayed in camp. Though it was July, they encountered several snow storms in their ascent of more than fourteen thousand feet. Her feeling of achievement was clear when she wrote: "I feel amply repaid for all my toil and fatigue. Nearly every one tried to discourage me . . . and now, here I am . . . the first woman who has ever stood upon the summit of this mountain and gazed upon this wondrous scene."

Settling in Taos, New Mexico, Holmes used her fluency in Spanish to work as a news correspondent for the *New York Tribune*, while also bearing four children and losing two. After returning East in 1870, she took advantage of new DIVORCE laws, and, as a single woman, became active in the SUFFRAGE MOVEMENT in Washington, D.C., where she also achieved some note for her poetry. She earned her living by working for the federal government and was one of the first women to be promoted in the civil service system, for she was chief of the Division of Spanish Correspondence in the Bureau of Education before her death at forty-eight.

HOME COMPANION Begun in 1873, *Home Companion* was intended to emulate the success of GODEY'S LADY'S BOOK,

which—with more than three decades of sales—had made it clear that a market existed for periodicals aimed at women. Even though *Home Companion* competed with the exceptional SARAH HALE at Godey's and later with the tremendously influential *LADIES HOME JOURNAL*, it was sufficiently popular to survive. Its name was altered to *Woman's Home Companion* in 1897, and it has now been published for almost 120 years.

HOME CONTRACT WORK From the beginning of industrialization, there were women who worked on home contract: women took an unfinished factory product and completed it at home, thus easing the manufacturer's space needs and alleviating his commitment to full-time employees—as well as providing the worker with a flexible schedule that did not require child care. Indeed, the labor of children usually was expected to be an important part of the task assigned.

In the garment industry, for example, entire families of women, children, and sometimes men spent their days doing an aspect or two of making a garment—the "finishing" work of hemming, sewing on buttons, cutting and trimming buttonholes, and so forth. In the earliest days of industrialization, when the women who did this home work were more likely to be rural FARM WOMEN, a manufacturer's representative was apt to deliver the work and then, days or weeks later, pick it up and pay for the labor while delivering a new batch. As urbanization developed and more labor was available in manufacturing centers, the workers were apt to do the pickup and delivery; women were to be seen walking through the streets of New York carrying the huge bundles of goods.

IMMIGRANT WOMEN, bound to their homes both by children and their lack of language skills, were particularly likely to do this "piecework" for pennies in pay. Women with better than average needlework skills did other kinds of handwork: they embroidered and tatted lace on home contract; they sewed sequins and beads in delicate patterns; they knitted caps, mittens, and scarves, and crocheted doilies. In the days when men wore stiff collars that were separate from their shirts, thousands of women worked as collar makers.

The creation of flowers and feathers alone employed multitudes of women during the late nineteenth and early twentieth centuries. In addition to adorning women's HATS, artificial flowers were popular home decorations and essential for funeral wreaths, and millions were employed on home contract in their manufacture. Italian women were especially likely to be flower makers, for their culture was reluctant to allow women to work outside the home, and flower making was seen as particularly feminine work. They spent their days folding and gluing little pieces of silk and wire together, shaping flowers as quickly as possible, for the low pay demanded dozens. A 1913 study, for example, found the pay to be a dime a gross—144 flowers for just ten cents. Families of four or more people worked twelve-hour days to make a dozen gross; at $1.20 a day, each worker averaged thirty cents.

Cigar making, like flower making, was sometimes done in factories and sometimes done at home—but only the most skilled workers could expect home contract work in this field. Women immigrants from Bohemia who were skilled cigar rollers established themselves in this industry soon after the Civil War; a decade later, more than half of New York's cigar makers were female. Cigar making was far more financially remunerative than any other home contract work, but as time passed, the industry became more mechanized and less of a craft. When women had to go to the factories rather than work at home, they were apt to be assigned to the less skilled preparation of tobacco leaves for male rollers.

Garment finishing, flower making, and cigar rolling were the major home contract industries, but there were dozens of other home jobs available, depending on the needs of nearby factories: women and children picked nuts from their shells for candy companies; they threaded wires through sales tags for many products; they made brooms and brushes and weaved baskets; they sorted and wrapped and packed any number of items.

There were advantages to this work methodology: there were savings in carfare and lunches and child care; there was freedom and flexibility. Nevertheless, the disadvantages were also real: women were especially likely to be exploited in this isolated work situation that offered no unionization or the benefits of PROTECTIVE LEGISLATION; and, in addition to the low pay, many manufacturers seem to have routinely cheated their workers by refusing to pay the agreed upon price after the work was done. Women were charged when products were allegedly ruined or substandard, and it was not uncommon to end up with a loss after working all week. Families worked fourteen and sixteen hours a day merely to eke out an existence on home contract labor, for manufacturers portrayed it as supplemental income for the supposedly lesser needs of women and children. They intended it to be pin money, even though it required more than full-time work from women.

Ultimately, reformers in public health and education combined with unions to demand an end to this work methodology. Unions were interested in ending exploitation of workers, as well as abolishing this source of competition with factory workers, who could more readily be organized and protected. Public health interests pointed out the unsanitary nature of home working conditions, and especially gained support for their views when contagious diseases were traced to clothing manufactured by sick workers. Educators sought to end this easy escape from child labor laws, arguing that children should be in school rather than forced to spend their days picking nuts or threading tags. States began to require licenses for home occupations, and by the twenties, industrialized states had child labor laws that cut into the profitability of home contract work. The essential closing of immigration in that era, too, curtailed the supply of women willing to accept the exploitation that was inherent to the system.

HOME DEMONSTRATION CLUBS Under the aegis of the Cooperative Extension Service, which includes the HOME ECONOMICS function of the Department of Agriculture, home economists began early in the century to educate homemakers via the era's CLUB MOVEMENT. Variously known as Home Extension Clubs, Home Demonstration Clubs, or, most often, simply HD Clubs, they featured a monthly demonstration by a professional home economist on some improved method of housework.

Food preservation demonstrations were especially likely to draw women to these clubs during the twenties and thirties, as more and more American homes converted to electricity and women wanted to learn how to can (and later, freeze) the produce from their vegetable gardens and fruit orchards. Home economists demonstrated the techniques necessary to preserve food safely, and in some communities, HD Clubs established clubhouses with communal kitchens that could be used by those who did not own canning equipment or whose homes lacked electricity and plumbing. Particularly as the Great Depression worsened, HD Clubs provided women with helpful information that assisted them in withstanding economic stress, and in the following decade, they helped women cope with the demands of wartime rationing.

Especially in the rural South and Midwest, these clubs provided the only social outlet many women had. Because HD Clubs were subsidized by the federal government through the SMITH LEVER ACT of 1914, membership in them cost little or nothing. Therefore, they were largely composed of poor women who most likely would not be either welcome or comfortable in those clubs with civic improvement aims that functioned under the umbrella of the GENERAL FEDERATION WOMEN'S CLUBS. A woman whose husband would object if she joined an GFWC club (with their aims of telling city fathers what needed to be

Cooking schools such as this one, which was conducted by Blanche Armwood, taught the use of new gas and electrical appliances in the early twentieth century. SPECIAL COLLECTIONS, UNIVERSITY OF SOUTH FLORIDA.

done) or a temperance club (with their goal of outlawing traditional male behavior) could almost always join an HD Club, where she could assure her husband that he would be the beneficiary of new recipes and household economizing.

Clubs usually met monthly, which enabled the professional home economist associated with them to serve many clubs in different geographic communities. Each club elected officers and scheduled activities, which also was important to women who otherwise had little opportunity to exercise leadership abilities. As late as the mid-sixties, approximately 1.5 million women belonged to Senior Home Demonstration Clubs, while about 6 million other women benefited from other programs of Cooperative Extension Service. With funding from both the federal government and from the agricultural departments of state universities, these clubs continue to be an uncommon instance of women's organizations being subsidized with tax dollars.

HOME ECONOMICS The late nineteenth century saw a surge of the academic sciences, as the national mindset, under the influence of Darwin, Spencer, and others, began to formalize scientific methods and attitudes. This was especially evident in the growth of social sciences, where entirely new fields developed during the last decades of this century. Home economics strove to be part of this movement.

The idea of homemakers helping each other with useful information was not new; women had taught the intricacies of their work to the next generation for eons. What was new was the attempt to codify that knowledge and to expand it in laboratories and classrooms, rather than in kitchens and bedrooms. Home economics, ironically, took its practitioners out of the home.

Its academic roots were laid with the advice and "household hint" books that existed in America since its colonial days. In the pre–Civil War period, CATHARINE BEECHER exerted great influence with her books on household management, though her overt religiosity limited the possibility of her work being considered science. As educational opportunities for girls increased, attention was paid to the seemingly natural subjects girls needed to know, and home arts became an informal part of the curricula in more and more schools. Especially in FINISHING SCHOOLS, girls were taught fancy needlework, home decoration, etiquette, and other subjects that later became part of standard home economics courses.

The most significant adoption of home lore by professional educators came after the CIVIL WAR, with implementation of the Morrill Act of 1868 that created land-grant COLLEGES, especially in the Midwest. These institutions—unlike older, eastern colleges—were often designed for both male and female students. Moreover, their emphasis was on practical, rather than classical, education, and state school officials assumed that most men would study agriculture and most women would study home economics. Variously called domestic economy, domestic science, or household arts, their curricula emphasized cooking and sewing, with lesser attention to more subtle aspects of cultured homemaking.

Meanwhile, in the cities, specialized private schools opened that were aimed not so much at the homemaker as at her DOMESTIC SERVANTS. With growing national wealth and increased travel that gave Americans exposure to a trained serving class abroad, a market developed for teaching inexperienced immigrants and ex-slaves the finer points of running an affluent home. Women formed associations to promote such activity, as, for example, the Women's Educational Association in Boston, which opened a cooking school to teach imported gourmet techniques to both professional cooks and housewives. It was in one of these schools that FANNIE FARMER got her start; her widely read turn-of-the-century cookbooks, with their strong emphasis on precise measurement and nutritional worth, gave home economics a definite scientific image.

Indeed, as biologists and physiologists discovered vitamins and developed concepts such as caloric values, it became increasingly more difficult to deny the scientific aspects of life in the kitchen. When the U.S. Department of Agriculture authorized nutritional research in 1894, home economics came of age. The American Home Economics Association was formed in 1908, after a series of educational conferences begun in 1899 by ELLEN H. RICHARDS; her credentials as the first woman admitted to the Massachusetts Institute of Technology gave additional credence. Federal programs on the subject were expanded into the Bureau of Home Economics in 1923, and home economics remains under the aegis of the Agriculture Department today.

Other turn-of-the-century advances expanded the field. The invention of electrical appliances and plumbing systems, for example, demanded increased knowledge on the part of domestic workers who otherwise could ruin expensive purchases. By the outbreak of WORLD WAR I, there were Federal Household Arts Training Schools, especially in the South, where black women such as BLANCHE ARMWOOD raised the educational level of other black women in scientifically designed home economics laboratories. Meanwhile, utility companies and other private businesses began to employ home economists who could teach customers the best use of new equipment. Women with degrees in home economics were widely sought in the food and fabric industries as thousands of new products would be designed and tested in the decades

ahead. WORLD WAR I played a role in promoting the field as well, for the military began to seek out trained dieticians; that example created a model for tens of thousands of institutional positions that were designed to be held by women.

School boards throughout the nation added home economics to high school curricula, often requiring it for girls. Congress put its stamp of approval on the movement, passing various bills between 1914 and 1937 that appropriated funds to support home economics for women in the same way that agricultural programs were supported for men. This gender-based educational approach stood largely unquestioned until the revived women's movement of the 1970s, when FEMINISTS sought to break down home economics stereotypes—seldom noting that the field was considered an overdue innovation a century earlier and was eagerly promoted by progressive women.

HOMESTEADING The Homestead Act of 1862 was one of the most important innovations of economic democracy ever passed by any legislative body. A plank of the new Republican Party when its membership was composed of ABOLITIONISTS and other radicals, the idea of giving free land to those who settled on it was aimed at attracting western voters to the new party. The act's passage early in Lincoln's administration might not have been politically possible at any other time, for powerful landowners, especially in the South, opposed this governmental largess; The Homestead Act, in its time, was as radical an idea as is the communal distribution of large estates in Third World countries today.

As in the FIFTEENTH AMENDMENT, Congress did not take care to make its language gender-based, but unlike the Fifteenth Amendment and women's right to vote, the benefits of the Homestead Act were exercised by women from the beginning with little objection. While by far the majority of homesteads were "proved up" by a family with the land title recorded in the name of the male head, there were also many cases of single women who filed claims, met the act's requirements of five years of residence and cultivation, and gained title to their own 160 acres of free land.

The act required that land be cleared and crops planted, although residence through the fierce months of winter was not essential. Single homesteaders of both genders, and even some families, commonly lived on their claims and farmed in summer, and then moved to town for the winter; this was especially likely on the relatively poor land of states like Montana and North Dakota. Educated women from the East who had moved west to homestead often used this arrangement to combine their farming with TEACHING; they earned extra income during winter by serving a school term at the same time that their students were also free from farm labor. After railroads were well established, other women homesteaders went back to midwestern cities to work through the winter, returning to the primitive living conditions and isolation of their claims in summer.

Exact figures on the numbers of women who homesteaded without male assistance are still being established, for traditional historians largely disregarded this aspect of western settlement. One recent study, however, showed that almost 12 percent of Colorado homestead claims between 1887 and

1908 were established by women. Another Colorado study demonstrates that as late as WORLD WAR I, there were women in remote areas of the state who filed for homesteads on mountainous land that was still open to those with a sense of adventure and perseverance.

A number of women left records of their homesteading experience, some of which have only recently been published. One example is Elinore Pruitt Stewart's *Letters of a Woman Homesteader*, which is set in Wyoming in the early twentieth century. Her writing describes not only the privations but also the unexpected joys. She had been worried, for instance, about depriving her daughter of books and toys, but discovered that the girl coped: "She has a block of wood which she calls her 'dear baby.' A spoke out of a wagon wheel is 'little Margaret' . . ."

HOOVER, LOU HENRY (1874–1944)

A more progressive woman than might be assumed by her position as First Lady to President Herbert Hoover, among Lou Henry's earliest distinctions was that of being one of the first women to earn a degree in geology, when she graduated from Stanford University in 1898.

In what became a lifelong pattern of blending traditional roles with unusual ones, however, she never used the degree for employment in her own right. On the other hand, she did actively participate in the business of her mining engineer husband, traveling with him (and later, their two young sons) to Egypt, India, Russia, Burma, Australia, and China, where she upset superstitious native males by descending into mines and was involved in the Boxer Rebellion of 1900. She studied at the London School of Mines in 1902 and published several technical articles in collaboration with her husband. The Hoovers spent five years translating a complex sixteenth-century mining textbook, and for that achievement received the Gold Medal of the Mining and Metallurgical Society.

Lou Henry Hoover's transformation into a public figure likewise followed that change for her husband. A largely accidental occurrence compared with the career paths of most presidents, the Hoovers developed into recognized leaders when they happened to be in London at the outbreak of WORLD WAR I and came to the aid of stranded Americans. Lou Hoover organized a committee of women that, by the end of the war, operated field hospitals on the Continent as well as in Britain. In recognition of their organizational abilities, the American ambassador recommended to President Wilson that Herbert Hoover head war relief efforts.

The Hoovers' paths began to diverge at this point, when he remained in Europe at the U.S. entrance in the war, while she returned to the U.S. to make speeches on food conservation and to organize the Food Administration Women's Club. When her husband became active in Republican politics after the war, Lou Hoover concentrated primarily on the development of two organizations devoted to increased activity for girls and young women. She helped form the Women's Division of the National Amateur Athletic Federation and also served from 1917 to 1944 on the national board of the Girls Scouts, seeing that organization grow from ten thousand to over a million. Lou Hoover exhibited outstanding organizational ability in these efforts, as well as a willingness to donate and raise substantial amounts of money.

Because scouting highlighted her genuine love of the outdoors and perhaps because she had no daughters, Lou Hoover became a leader that girls "adored." Yet at the same time that she made speeches telling them that "girls can do anything," her personal life and political philosophy in some respects contradicted that credo. She opposed involvement of women in the Olympic games, for example, arguing against competition for women. Nor was she a leader in the burning question of her day on votes for women, retroactively objecting to the methods the SUFFRAGE MOVEMENT used to obtain that goal—while at the same time she urged recently enfranchised young women in the 1920s to "realize the importance of political affairs." She spent her White House years heading the conservative Women's Committee for Law Enforcement that supported PROHIBITION, but nevertheless also dealt courageously with a tremendous public uproar when she invited of the wife of a black congressman to tea.

The overwhelming electoral defeat of her husband in 1932 and the deepening of the Great Depression that much of the public believed was caused by Hoover's indifference to the poor meant a greatly diminished national platform for her during the 1930s. She died unexpectedly in 1944.

HOPE CHESTS

Somewhat akin to a DOWRY, hope chests were kept by young women in anticipation of marriage. Throughout girlhood, items would be accumulated in a storage chest, usually made of cedar, with the intention of use in one's own home after marriage. Teenage girls, especially of the upper middle class, spent much of their leisure embellishing linens with crocheting or embroidery, for example, and then packed them in hope chests with preserving herbs. Most common in the era after the CIVIL WAR, Southern girls kept hope chests well into the twentieth century.

HOPE, LAURA LEE

An uncommon usage of a female PSEUDONYM for a male writer, Laura Lee Hope was the pen name used by Edward Stratemeyer for his series about the *Bobbsey Twins*. Although the characters featured in these juvenile books are trite by today's standards, the Bobbsey twins were very popular through the mid-twentieth century, especially with girls, who bought millions of copies.

Stratemeyer's work was so well received by the buying public that he employed a team of writers who used approximately a dozen pseudonyms—at least four of which were women's names—for hundreds of books written around his outlines. Millions of girls through several generations grew up admiring these fictitious women, especially Laura Lee Hope.

HOPPER, GRACE (1907–1992)

"Amazing Grace" was the nation's oldest military officer on active duty when she retired at seventy-nine. Her exceptional value to the Navy had been recognized with annual extensions beyond normal military retirement at sixty-two, for Grace Hopper is considered to be the mother of computer systems that are now essential to American life.

With a degree from Yale, Dr. Hopper was teaching mathematics at VASSAR COLLEGE when WORLD WAR II began. Like many other childless wives, she joined the military when her husband did, entering the Navy's WAVES in 1943. She trained at SMITH COLLEGE, where the WAVES conducted classes for officers, and then continued to be in an academic environment, for among the things that WAVES did for the Navy was to calculate ordnance ranges, and Hopper figured targets for weapons in the D-day invasion of Europe from a basement at Harvard University. There she programed the nation's first large-scale digital computer.

When she became a war WIDOW, Hopper remained in computers and with the Navy. As the electronic processing of information became more and more a part of military operations, she was the author of many programs, including the widely used computer language COBOL. Known as the "Grand Old Lady of Software" by retirement, Hopper also had a reputation for candor, even when dealing with superior officers. "She's challenged at every turn the dictates of mindless bureaucracy," said the secretary of the Navy at her retirement, with Hopper adding, "I always tell young people, 'Go ahead and do it. You can apologize later.'"

When she retired in 1986, Rear Admiral Grace Hopper had served the Navy forty-three years—more than twice as long as a standard military career. Her retirement honored her as the nation's oldest military officer with ceremonies conducted on the nation's oldest ship, Boston harbor's "Old Ironsides." Admiral Hopper was presented with the Distinguished Service Medal, the Defense Department's highest honor.

HORNEY, KAREN DANIELSEN (1885–1952)
The first psychiatrist to seriously challenge Freudian assumptions about women, Karen Danielsen was educated over the objections of her father by a supportive mother. She received her medical degree from the University of Berlin in 1911, after marrying and bearing three children while still a student, and practiced psychiatry in Berlin for almost two decades. She came to the U.S. in 1932, and after separating from the Chicago Institute for Psychoanalysis two years later because of growing intellectual differences, she chose not to return to Germany. Although neither Jewish nor active in politics, Dr. Horney saw the rise of Nazism as dangerous to the still-new field of psychiatry, as well as to individual freedom; moreover, she wanted to live in a society that seemed to offer greater opportunity to women.

Horney moved to New York in 1934, divorced in 1937 (after more than a decade of separation) and published her first book that same year. *The Neurotic Personality of Our Time* (1937) spelled out her belief that cultural practices were the basis of many psychiatric problems. Two years later, she added *New Ways in Psychoanalysis* (1939), in which she debated Freudian ideas, especially those that defined women as derivative of men. With additional books in the forties and fifties as well as in widely attended lectures, Dr. Horney insisted that female psychology be seen as positive; she argued that female functions such as PREGNANCY and BREASTFEEDING offered such genuine psychological fulfillment that Freudians might indeed question whether males were afflicted with "womb envy" instead of merely reiterating old dogma on female "penis envy."

Naturally, many saw her challenges to psychiatry's founder as heretical, and in 1941, Dr. Horney was disqualified as a training analyst by the New York Psychoanalytic Institute. No official reason was given, and almost half of the membership present refrained from voting. In response, she and several

colleagues of both genders formed a new professional group, the Association for the Advancement of Psychoanalysis. She served as the dean of its affiliated school, the American Institute for Psychoanalysis, and edited its journal until her unexpected death just over a decade later.

Only sixty-seven when she died, Dr. Horney had been treated with considerable hostility by most of her male colleagues throughout her career and did not live to receive the honors she merited. Nevertheless, her work was recognized even in her time as the first "restatement of Freudian theory that is . . . in line with sociological and anthropological" advances, and her long-term influence, especially in the psychology of women, has been tremendous.

HOWARD UNIVERSITY
Although associated in the public mind with college education for blacks, Howard University in Washington, D.C. has been open to both races and sexes from its beginning. Founded by an act of Congress in 1867 and named for the head of the Freedman's Bureau, it was a federally funded post–CIVIL WAR effort to make higher education available to those who likely would be denied admission to most colleges because of their race. Because women, too, were likely to be excluded from COLLEGES on the basis of their status at birth, a number of white women joined blacks as students at Howard.

The law school did reject BELVA LOCKWOOD's 1868 application on the grounds that this white forty-year-old schoolmarm would be distracting to young men, but they soon reversed this reasoning and admitted CHARLOTTE RAY—a young, black, and presumably more distracting woman. After Ray's 1872 graduation, women of both races were admitted, and white women soon outnumbered blacks in the law school. The 1883 class, for example, was composed of three white women, one black woman, and one black man.

Nevertheless, it was black men who primarily benefited from Howard and similar collegiate opportunities; an 1890 study found just thirty black women in the entire nation who had received college degrees—only slightly more than one for each of the twenty-five years since slavery ended. Significant numbers of black women began graduating soon after that study was done, however, and by 1910, Howard and Fiske University, the two leading black colleges, had graduated more than five hundred women.

In addition to offering educational opportunity, Howard University has also served as an important organizational base. Sororities founded there such as Alpha Kappa Alpha and Zeta Phi Beta have played an important part in the lives of black women throughout the twentieth century, and it was a concert to benefit Howard that caused the MARIAN ANDERSON controversy.

Among the historically significant women who studied at Howard are BLANCHE ARMWOOD, MARY ANN SHADD CARY, ZORA NEALE HURSTON, and CHARLOTTE E. RAY.

HOWE, JULIA WARD (1819–1910)
Despite the death of her mother when she was five, young Julia enjoyed a happy childhood at a time when affluent but pious families such as hers lived on New York's Broadway. Educated by GOVERNESSES and at FINISHING SCHOOLS, she was naturally brilliant enough that even though she was excluded from all

COLLEGE education like other women of her era, she nonetheless published articles in serious literary journals while still very young; she would go on to study Latin, Greek, and the arcane philosophy of Immanuel Kant solely out of personal motivation. Had she been male, Julia Ward doubtless would have become an accomplished professional, but as it was, she married at twenty-three.

Her husband, Boston physician Samuel Gridley Howe, would become a historical figure in his own right. A leader in progressive education and an ardent supporter of reformer DOROTHEA DIX, his liberal credentials included so great a dedication to ABOLITION that he had to flee to Canada to escape the fury that accompanied John Brown's slave revolt. Nonetheless, though he appeared committed to the same enlightened agenda that motivated early feminist leaders, Howe in fact resented not only his wife's literary talent but also her inheritance and her lack of domestic skills. Though he accepted her help with a short-lived effort at editing a progressive newspaper and though they had six children together, their marriage was not happy; he later admitted to affairs, and they discussed the possibility of DIVORCE in the 1850s, when the subject was still almost a complete taboo.

All of this was kept secret, however, and Julia Ward Howe eventually developed a contrastingly ironic image as the SUFFRAGE MOVEMENT's personification of conservative family values. This came about largely because she was identified in the public mind with her strongly Christian "Battle Hymn of the Republic," but Howe's literary body of work was far more complex than that little poem. With modesty common to many women AUTHORS, she issued her first book of poetry, Passion-flowers (1854) anonymously. When she did attach her name to two plays written in 1857, the response of her proper Bostonian friends was bewilderment; they did not understand these dark tales of obsession and violence any more than they understood the complexities of their seemingly innocuous author. Her husband, who understood the source of her thoughts on murder and suicide, was embarrassed and angry.

When the CIVIL WAR broke out, she was past forty and unknown outside of Boston. She was working with her Union friends for the humble goals of the SANITARY COMMISSION when, in February 1862, the publication of the "Battle Hymn of the Republic" in Atlantic changed her life. Set to the tune of "John Brown's Body," the song would be sung in virtually every Northern church and school, becoming a standard of American life. Its biblical allusions suited Lincoln's language well, and he soon asked to meet her. As was the case with HARRIET BEECHER STOWE, Howe's work struck a personal chord with the president; he led the nation in recognizing the artistic value of these women.

By the end of the war, Julia Ward Howe was a household name that the nascent SUFFRAGE MOVEMENT was delighted to use. When the AMERICAN WOMAN SUFFRAGE ASSOCIATION (AWSA) was formed in 1869 with LUCY STONE as its most influential backer, Howe accepted its first presidency. She was a founder of the AWSA's publication, Woman's Journal, in 1870, and though it was under the general editorship of Stone and her husband, Henry Blackwell, from 1872 until Stone's death in 1893, Howe sometimes edited and frequently contributed to the Journal. Doubtless her literary ability was a strong factor in making it the most influential of the era's suffrage publications.

Her popularity was apparent, too, in her 1871 election as president of the New England Women's Club, one of the first of the era's new CLUB MOVEMENT. Though clubwomen generally would become the object of scorn from the literati, even Emerson praised the scholarly papers he heard Howe deliver to the New England Women's Club. In 1873, again in association with Stone, Howe founded the ASSOCIATION FOR THE ADVANCEMENT OF WOMEN to promote the entrance of women into scholarship and the professions, and her speeches at the organization's annual meetings were widely covered by the nation's press. Finally, in 1893, she was chosen to be the first president of the Massachusetts Federation of Women's Clubs and a director of the new national GENERAL FEDERATION OF WOMEN'S CLUBS, where she served until eighty.

Meanwhile, she continued to write, for she needed the income as she aged and the pages of virtually every periodical were open to her. In addition to many articles, Howe wrote a number of significant books, including Sex and Education (1874), which advocated coeducation; Modern Society (1881), a critique of nouveau riche values in post–Civil War society; a biography of MARGARET FULLER in 1883 and her own Reminiscences in 1899.

She traveled not only the financially rewarding lecture circuit, but also for her own enlightenment: Howe visited such unconventional places as Cuba and the Middle East as well as Europe. Her internationalism was evident already in the 1870s, when she organized a Woman's Peace Congress in London, and it remained important to her as late as 1894, when at seventy-five, she was elected the first president of the United Friends of Armenia.

Despite her apparent commitment to the same causes, Howe nonetheless was the target of appreciable criticism from other suffragist leaders. Even though she had stressed in her initial speech for the AAW that care should be taken "to draw the circle so that it shall not strengthen the divisions of society . . . sundering rich from poor, fashionable from unfashionable, learned from simple," it was nonetheless true that some seemed to find her literary and cultural refinement to be axiomatic evidence of unacceptable elitism. Those in the NATIONAL WOMAN SUFFRAGE ASSOCIATION that rivaled Stone's AWSA certainly included Julia Ward Howe when they spoke negatively of "the Boston clique," and SUSAN ANTHONY was among those who appeared to resent what they saw as her painless path to public acclaim. By the time that both were old, however, Anthony and Howe had moved beyond the bitterness of the 1869 split in the suffrage movement and both participated in the 1890 merger of the two groups.

Though ill, both were honored at the suffrage association's 1906 convention; Anthony died a few months later at eighty-six. Howe, who was a year older, lived on, and two years later became the first woman voted membership in the American Academy of Arts and Letters. Though Julia Ward Howe had often preached from Unitarian pulpits, when she died at ninety-one, her memorial service was held at Boston's Symphony Hall. Even it could not contain the crowd that overflowed to hear a four-thousand-voice choir sing, "Mine Eyes Have Seen the Glory . . ."

HURST, FANNIE (1889–1968)

Reportedly the highest-paid writer in America in 1940, Fannie Hurst's stories and novels portrayed the lives of society's misfits. Her work especially featured women, and she was so avowed a FEMINIST that she not only kept her MAIDEN NAME when she married in 1915, but also lived apart from her husband for the first five years of what became a lifelong marriage.

Though critics panned her as saccharine, the public gladly bought her work from her first short story collection in 1914. She wrote in many genres of both fiction and nonfiction, ultimately publishing seventeen novels as well as plays, screenplays, short stories, and essays. Perhaps her most popular title was *Imitation of Life*, which was produced by Hollywood in 1934 and again in 1959. The latter version of this story, which focused on the relationship of a young mulatto woman who passed for white with her black mother, was accepted by even some of the critics who generally sneered at Hurst's work as "soapy."

Hurst's commitment to blacks was firm enough, however, that she befriended ZORA NEALE HURSTON in the 1920s. Also close to ELEANOR ROOSEVELT and other Democratic women involved in the New Deal, Hurst was especially active in Jewish causes during WORLD WAR II and its aftermath; she left a million dollars to Brandeis, a postwar university built largely by Jews, and donated generously to other causes. Though she was Jewish, her St. Louis family had largely abandoned its heritage; Fannie Hurst's concern for society's outcasts, exhibited already in her youth, was a personal crusade.

HURSTON, ZORA NEALE (1901?–1960)

Born into the all-black community of Eatonville, Florida, Zora Neale Hurston wrote literature of lasting merit in the publishing center of New York—and yet ended her days back in small-town Florida as a pauper.

Though her mother died when she was still a child, Hurston was able to attend HOWARD UNIVERSITY in Washington, where her first story was published in the school's literary magazine. Armed with this success, she won a scholarship to BARNARD COLLEGE, becoming the first black student at that prestigious women's school. Its New York City location led her to literary connections with both blacks and whites, and its anthropology department developed her lifelong interest in recording folklore. Encouraged by famed anthropologist Franz Boas, Hurston would eventually seek the folk stories of minorities in the American South, the Caribbean, and Honduras; she even used the new technology of film to record black life.

Among her literary mentors were novelist FANNIE HURST, who employed Hurston as a companion and secretary, and Langston Hughes, who collaborated with Hurston on a 1931 play, *Mule Bone: A Comedy of Negro Life*. She followed this in 1934 with *Jonah's Gourd Vine*, the story of a black preacher probably modeled on her father, and *Mules and Men* (1935), a tale that melded African folklore and rural black life in the 1920s. Her 1937 work, *Their Eyes Were Watching God*, is considered Hurston's most significant achievement and focuses directly on black women, whereas *Moses, Man of the Mountain*, which came out two years later, is less recognized. Hurston published her autobiography, *Dust Tracks on the Road*, in 1942 at the height of her success.

That she published most of her work during the thirties indicates an accumulation of experience derived from the new opportunity opened to Hurston and other African-Americans during the Roaring Twenties and the Harlem Renaissance. She sought and received the patronage of prosperous whites in this era when some found it fashionable to have black friends. Critics (including her friend Langston Hughes) thought that she softened the hard edges of her experiential writing to appease these patrons, and she also has been criticized for using black language patterns that some see as negatively stereotyped. Hurston, however, saw herself as honestly recording what her anthropologist's ear heard, using the language she knew her fictional creations would have used. Moreover, she probably believed what she once wrote: "I am not tragically colored. There is no great sorrow dammed up in my soul."

Yet the Depression of the 1930s meant that her royalties were never adequate to her needs, nor did she benefit much from the improved economy of the wartime forties. Two marriages, one early in the Depression era and the other late, were also emotional and economic disappointments. Finally, through friendship with fellow Floridian MARJORIE KINNAN RAWLINGS, she was able to acquire the great editor Maxwell Perkins at Scribner's in 1947—but he died before her first project with him was finished. He did secure money for her to go to Honduras, where she traveled into unexplored territory whose natives were feared by coastal peoples, and she worked there on *Seraph on the Suwanee* (1948). She returned to New York early that year for finalization of the manuscript, and the book was scheduled for publication on October 11. Tragically, on September 13, Hurston was arrested on a morals charge.

The ten-year-old son of her former landlady charged her (and two others) with sexual abuse, apparently in revenge for Hurston's advice to his mother urging psychiatric help for the boy. Though the case was dismissed when Hurston was able to prove that she was in Honduras during the time the alleged offenses occurred, the damage had been done. Harlem newspapers headlined the story and spread it throughout the nation, with even respected black publications embellishing the facts and compounding the lies.

It was cold comfort that white newspapers did not consider her troubles to be newsworthy. Hurston was so crushed by this betrayal by her own—for it also had been a black court employee who leaked the story—that she retreated from public life. Pointing out to a friend that this "vilest . . . thing was not done in the South, but in the so-called liberal North," she went back to Florida. Though she sold a story to the *Saturday Evening Post* in 1949 and continued to publish minor pieces, nonetheless she spent the rest of her life working at jobs that were below her ability: clerking in a library, substitute teaching in segregated schools, and even working as a maid–until the *Miami Herald* broke that story.

She had to pawn her typewriter for grocery money and eventually accept welfare assistance, but she did not give up thinking and working. She published a number of articles reflective of the era's general conservatism (including one for the *American Legion Magazine*) and was at work on a book about the biblical King Herod when a stroke struck her down.

Zora Neale Hurston died in a home operated by the St. Lucie County Welfare Agency and avoided a pauper's burial only through the fund-raising efforts of the local black community.

She came back into literary popularity in the eighties, after the 1977 publication of Robert Hemenway's biography. Several other books on her have been issued since; her plays have been revived in New York; and the 1990 reprint of her autobiography sold two hundred thousand copies in less than a year. Eatonville, Florida now proudly conducts an annual Hurston festival.

HUTCHINSON, ANNE MARBURY (1591–1643)

Like almost all white women in North America at that time, Anne Hutchinson had been born in England during the reign of Elizabeth I. The daughter of a dissident minister, she grew up in the village of Alford in Lincolnshire, moved to London as a teenager, and returned to Alford when she married at twenty-one. Anne Marbury wed William Hutchinson, a merchant and member of a prominent family, in 1612.

From then until her menopausal years, Hutchinson was almost constantly pregnant or lactating or both, for her status as an upper-class woman did not mean access to BIRTH CONTROL. In the seventeen years between 1613 and 1630, she gave birth to twelve babies, losing three to INFANT MORTALITY. This heavy physical and emotional load did not lessen her intellectual life, however, for even though—like all women of her era—she had no access to formal education, Anne Hutchinson was a natural reader and thinker.

Intellectual activity in her place and time largely meant theology, and Hutchinson was particularly taken with the views of Reverend John Cotton, vicar at the nearby Lincolnshire parish of Boston. She soon expanded upon his beliefs, and ultimately would place herself at the center of one of the raging controversies of the next century: the argument within Protestant circles of the relative merits of faith versus works in salvation. After Cotton felt constrained to flee Anglican authorities and join the religious dissidents who were settling in North America, Hutchinson and her family also joined the thousands who migrated to the Massachusetts Bay Colony in the 1630s.

Anne Hutchinson was forty-three years old when she arrived in Boston in 1634. She had established a strong relationship with her husband, who, like the husband of MARY DYER, respected and supported his wife's religious activism, even though he did not choose that path for himself. That their feelings for each other were still physical is clear from the fact that their last child was born in Boston in 1636. The Bay Colony itself was still in its infancy, for its first settlers arrived in 1630, just a decade after the PILGRIM WOMEN began populating Plymouth to the south.

Hutchinson's experience and relative education made her a natural MIDWIFE and NURSE, and therefore a leader in this youthful community. The time she spent with women in the throes of possible death also led naturally to conversations on spiritual matters. Her views that emphasized the primacy of inner faith over outward piety understandably were appealing to both men and women, and she soon was attracting large numbers to religious meetings in her home. Such gatherings were not uncommon in the Bay Colony—what instead disturbed its authoritarian clergy was Hutchinson's extreme popularity, particularly outside of the usual circles of women. Her innate charisma not only brought admiration from men, but worse, from prominent men, including affluent young civil officials.

The ministers—who were the true authority in the theocracy that the Bay Colony was—seemed unable to believe that men could be interested merely in a woman's mind. When Hutchinson was brought before a church trial in 1638, even her former mentor Reverend Cotton had joined that obtuse view. He charged his former friend with "that filthy sin of the community of women, and all promiscuous and filthy coming together of men and women ... Though I have not heard ... you have been unfaithful to your husband in his marriage covenant, yet that will follow ..."

Hutchinson's attraction indeed was so great that it became a genuine threat to the ability of the clergy to govern; this was especially clear when some of her male supporters refused to join the militia in pursuit of Pequot natives. The authorities, led by Reverend John Winthrop (who was also the colony's governor), first attacked her indirectly by banishing her brother-in-law, a minister who shared her views. Hutchinson herself was summoned to trial late in 1637 and also banished, but allowed to remain under house arrest until the end of winter. In March, 1638, she was again brought before the court and formally excommunicated; she and her children soon joined her faithful husband, who had prepared a home for them in the new colony of Rhode Island, which had been founded less than two years earlier by other dissidents exiled from Massachusetts.

At nearly forty-seven, Anne Hutchinson was once again pregnant and so severely ill that her physical condition had interfered with her ability to defend herself on trial. Her medical problem probably was a gross tumor of the placenta that had killed the fetus she delivered in late summer, but Puritan leadership—who saw all events in theological terms—deemed this "monstrous birth" to have been the judgment of God.

Hutchinson nonetheless survived this painful experience and lived peaceably on Narragansett Bay until her husband's death six years later. In 1642, at age fifty-one, she took her brood of six still-young children to the Dutch colony that now is New York, where mercantile attitudes ranked higher than the fine points of theology. The New Netherlands colony was attracting other New Englanders who wished to be free of religious orthodoxy, but Hutchinson did not settle in the city, opting instead for a remote farming area on Long Island Sound between the modern Bronx and New Rochelle. This isolation was a fatal mistake, for though she believed the Dutch had paid the natives for the land they sold her, a year later, disgruntled Algonquians attacked her home, killing all but the youngest child. Today a river and a highway in that area bear the Hutchinson name.

Anne Hutchinson had lived in America just nine years when she died, but her legacy would be timeless. In daring to think differently from the colonial autocrats who would brook no disagreement, she took an early place of prominence in the development of American intellectual life and its basic tenet of free speech. The fact that she argued merely for her own version of revealed truth does not diminish the courage that it took to do so.

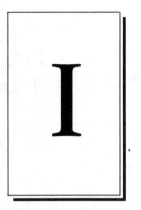

ILLEGITIMACY Both the European mores that early settlers brought with them and the English common law that was adopted into American legal codes harbored strong injunctions against premarital and extramarital sex. A child born out of wedlock and that child's mother could expect community censure and legal handicap. These standards differed from the easier sexuality and communal child-rearing patterns of natives, but European settlers took no account of native ideas, for even if they noticed and considered the differing standards, those of the natives were rejected as un-Christian, barbarian, and axiomatically unacceptable.

Yet recent research has shown that a surprising number of eighteenth-century brides—perhaps as many as one-third—were nonetheless pregnant on their wedding day. Generally this has been interpreted as the probable result of relatively harmless BUNDLING by couples who were already betrothed; sometimes it was clearly the effort of a young couple to force parental consent for marriage. Weddings of pregnant brides also are indicative of the small communities in which early settlers lived, and the social pressure that could easily be applied on the offending male to marry and legitimatize his child.

At the same time, colonial records, especially outside of New England, also indicate a fair number of men who were unwilling or unable to marry. In seaport towns, for example, pauper rolls often listed the "bastards" of women who had been impregnated by sailors long gone. Courts also regularly recorded paternity suits brought by maids against masters and against fellow servants for their offspring. Although the courts did respond to such support pleas, they also meted out pun-ishment to the unwed mother; even women whose claims of rape were likely to be true nonetheless were sentenced to be whipped and/or were fined for the crime of bearing an illegitimate child.

Despite such punishments, cases of unwed mothers who bore their babies alone because of abandonment or because the father was already married remained a familiar part of every community's experience, as indicated by the fact one of the nation's first novels dealt with that very subject. As portrayed in Hawthorne's *Scarlett Letter*, the women thus victimized were generally ostracized for years. If they stayed in a community, raised their child circumspectly, and did not succumb to the temptation to utilize their negative reputation for economic gain, they might eventually be forgiven, marry, bear other children, and live reasonably normal lives.

While they were never lax, sexual standards stiffened even more as the nation aged and wealth accumulated; there was thus more pressure on brides to be spotlessly virginal at marriage, for no patriarch wished to chance the inheritance of his property by a bastard. Bundling disappeared and there was less evidence of premarital experimentation, for the line between marriageable women and professional sellers of sex rigidified in the nineteenth century. Evidence of even one case of "compromise" condemned a woman to a lifetime outside the fold of respectability.

Meanwhile, standards for black women were exactly the opposite, for births, whether legitimate or not, were welcomed in the slave economy. Indeed, there is much evidence that many masters and their sons accounted for these births by forcing themselves upon slave women. The illegitimate

179

child thus born was never considered eligible even for freedom, let alone inheritance, regardless of how greatly the child might resemble the father. In that sense, the black sub-culture was forced into the patterns of a matrilineal society.

After emancipation, therefore, blacks were thus far less likely than whites to cruelly condemn the child born out of wedlock, and after emancipation, they continued to be more tolerant of illegitimacy. Indeed, as the twentieth century evolved, the rate of illegitimate birth among blacks rose from 17 percent in 1940 to 27 percent in 1968 to more than 50 percent as the century neared its end. Meanwhile, whites began to emulate that model, and the 1990 census showed that one-quarter of all births were to unwed mothers. More than two-thirds of these children were born to teenagers, with a 90 percent illegitimacy rate among black teenagers.

The stigma against illegitimacy in both races had declined to the point that women no longer hid their pregnancies in homes for unwed mothers, many of which lost so many clients that they closed. Indeed, so dramatic was the change in attitude that by the end of the century, there were substantial numbers of women who deliberately sought single motherhood through artificial insemination or simple refusal to wed. The former disgrace of illegitimacy was almost completely gone, and one of the most severe limitations on female freedom in America had been eliminated without any significant organized effort or political action. At the same time, more and more men felt themselves excused from any responsibility for their children.

IMMIGRANT WOMEN Although, of course, all Americans except for those natives known as Indians were at one time immigrants, historians have generally referred to those who came prior to the Revolution as "colonists," while those who came later were termed "immigrants."

Because of the French Revolution and other factors, there was relatively little immigration in the early years of the new nation. The first major wave came in the 1840s as a result of famine in Ireland; it included large numbers of women, and Irish women would continue to be a major portion of immigration throughout the nineteenth century. More than any other ethnic group, Irish women came alone, remained single, and worked to support parents and siblings. Their most common employment was DOMESTIC SERVICE, and in time, almost every affluent home in the Northeast had its faithful "Bridget" as cook or maid. Even as late as 1920, Irish women accounted for 43 percent of all domestic servants in the nation.

Political revolts on the Continent in 1848 brought relatively smaller numbers of immigrants, most of them from the principalities that later became Germany. The women of this emigration almost always moved in family groups, as did those who began emigration from Scandinavia in the pre–Civil War era. These immigrants were most likely to settle on farms or in Midwestern cities. Partly because FARM WOMEN had their assigned work roles and partly because they were more prosperous than the Irish, these Nordic women were less likely to be identifiable in the labor market.

Immigration steadily increased after the CIVIL WAR, and by the time the era ended with the passage of restrictive legislation in 1924, some 35 million Europeans had come to America; more than one in every three of them were women. In addition to

Immigrant women on a ship deck. Though they were less likely to suffer seasickness in the fresh air, it was not unusual for sea captains to keep steerage passengers below decks for the convenience of the crew and full-fare passengers. NATIONAL PARK SERVICE, STATUE OF LIBERTY MONUMENT.

larger numbers of Germans and Scandinavians, post–Civil War immigrants began coming from southern and eastern Europe. By the end of nineteenth century, millions of Jews from Russia, Poland, and other eastern European countries were joining Jews who had emigrated earlier from Germany. Jewish women, like the Irish, often emigrated without male accompaniment and worked in the large cities of the Northeast; unlike the Irish, Jewish women seldom were servants, but instead worked in business, especially the GARMENT INDUSTRY, and in retail trade.

At the same time, large numbers of Italian women began arriving in the 1880s and 1890s, almost always in family groups. Italian cultural mores were much more restrictive of women than had been the case with any previous immigrant group, but nonetheless unmarried Italian women often joined the labor force because of the economic need of their families. They were most likely to be found in the manufacture of artificial flowers and feathers for HATS and in other industries, such as candy and paper box factories, that employed few or no male co-workers. Italian women rarely worked as servants or in any other occupation that would bring them in contact with men, although married Italian women did sometimes work as street peddlers in their own communities.

The same era also brought millions of non-Jewish immigrants from eastern Europe; except for Bohemians, these women were likely to travel with their families and to settle according to male patterns of employment. Yet even in such industrial areas as Pittsburgh, which was the destination of many of these Slavic immigrants, women were to be found in the labor force soon after arrival. Hungarians, Poles, and other Slavic women were more likely than any other ethnic group to work in heavy industry; indeed, the metal industry was the third-largest employer of Pittsburgh women, exceeded only by laundries and cigar making. A 1909 investigation, for example, found forty-five hundred women working at core making in foundries, a job that could require lifting sixty pounds; fewer than one-fifth of them could speak English.

Inability to speak the language as well as cultural limitations on married women kept many immigrants restricted to work done on HOME CONTRACT. Married Jewish and Italian women often worked at finishing garments and making flowers at home, while women from Bohemia held a distinctive place in the home manufacture of cigars. Cigar making both at home and in factories was a common job for immigrant women; factories in Florida, which used tobacco from Cuba, employed almost no natives, but instead hired Cubans, Italians, and smaller numbers of women from Spain. Again, little English was spoken in these factories.

A common language meant contrastingly easy assimilation for English and Scottish women who, like the Irish, accounted for a relatively large portion of immigration throughout the era. These women quickly dispersed into many segments of the economy throughout the nation, whereas other ethnic groups gravitated to those places where they knew work would be available and their language spoken.

With the exception of some settlements in Louisiana, Texas, and Arkansas that were usually related to initial travel up the Mississippi, few immigrants settled in the South. In addition to the lack of industrial opportunity, they also wished to avoid competing with blacks who were accustomed to even lower wages than immigrants normally accepted. In the Far West, there were pockets of European immigration wherever mining existed. Scandinavians also sometimes took their seafaring and lumbering backgrounds to the Pacific Coast, but the women of these western settlements found few employment opportunities beyond running BOARDING HOUSES.

The West Coast also contained virtually all of the era's Asian immigrants. However, the Chinese Exclusion Act of 1882 and similar restrictions on the Japanese beginning in 1907 meant that Asian immigration throughout the entire era did not reach even a million, whereas that many Europeans arrived in a single year at the height of the immigrant era. Moreover, Asian communities contained many more men than women, and their employment opportunities were so limited that Asian men took even the domestic service jobs that were almost always held by women elsewhere in the country.

Natives were most blatant in their prejudice against Asians, but all immigrant groups suffered to some extent from racial and religious bias, as well as from the language barrier. One of the results was that few immigrant women were included in the SUFFRAGE MOVEMENT. Most were in fact too busy earning a living and rearing their (relatively larger) families to be concerned with political action, but other factors also excluded them. Nearly all suffragists were Protestants, often with strong ties to PROHIBITION, while many immigrants of this era were Catholic or Jewish and alcohol was a part of family and religious tradition.

At the same time, immigrant women generally held views on most aspects of sexuality that were more conservative than those held by suffragists. While there were some Scandinavian and German women and many more Jewish women who were active in the women's rights cause, the former were few in number and the latter were more likely to concentrate on economic reform via UNIONS than on the more strictly political suffrage movement. The suffrage organizations remained almost wholly native, and indeed, one of the most common arguments these native women made for suffrage was that they should be equal to recently arrived males whose knowledge of America was minimal. It was not an argument likely to appeal to immigrant women, nor did it indicate any awareness of the genuine value of those women.

The role of immigrant women thus was ignored by historians even more than that of women in general, for most immigrant women did not even come close to standard definitions of historical importance that are based on political and military achievement. Instead, what they gave the nation must be measured in their (often uncounted) contributions to the booming economy of the era between the Civil War and WORLD WAR I, as well as in the social change they quietly created in millions of American homes. From the addition to our menus of dozens of culinary items to deeper changes in cultural and religious values, American life today is far richer because of the contributions of immigrant women.

INDENTURED SERVANTS From the beginning of European settlement in North America, there were people who wished to emigrate but could not afford the ship's cost. Arrangements soon developed whereby they sold their labor for a period of years to wealthier emigrants who advanced the fare, or—as became more common—made the trip and then allowed the ship's captain to sell them into servitude upon arrival, for the demand for labor in America was so great that captains had no fear of passages going unpaid. The usual term of commitment was between five and seven years, though there were agreements for as few as two years and as many as ten. Those who thus sold themselves as indentured servants also were known as "redemptioners" or "bondsmen bondswomen."

In early VIRGINIA, approximately one of every three arrivals was a woman, and the majority of them were so "bound." (Indeed, even the first blacks—women and men—to arrive in America came to JAMESTOWN in 1619 not as slaves, but rather as indentured servants; chattel slavery was not codified into Virginia's law until after 1650.) Also common in New England, the practice was not limited to the English colonies, for Dutch women in the area that became New York also indentured themselves.

Often such women were members of the lowest class of European society, including PROSTITUTES and convicts. Although usually they were voluntarily escaping from their current troubles into what they hoped would be a better life, sometimes such bound women emigrated against their will. They were deported by local officials wishing to rid themselves of habitual felons, while others were deceived into servitude by ship captains or even kidnapped by brokers who profited from selling their indenture contract, for the usual arrangement involved a definite legal contract and not merely verbal agreement.

Contracts spelled out the expected labor and its reward, which often included a small amount of land or a payment at the end of the term, as well as the ship's fare. They might detail conditions of employment, such as the clothing to be provided or the opportunity to learn to read and write. Virtually all contracts (or colonial law) forbade indentured servants from marrying; in the case of a woman who became pregnant without marriage, the pregnancy extended the years of her service—often vastly disproportionately to the time lost to maternity and sometimes even when the ILLEGITIMATE child was fathered by the master. On the other hand, though conditions of servitude could be harsh and the work that such women were expected to do was the household's most burdensome, their lives were not necessarily worse than that of women of the same class in Europe.

Many of these women worked as dairy maids, herding, milking, and otherwise caring for cows. The prevalence of outdoor work gave them opportunities to run away and some did, but a future in the wilderness without cash or supplies intimidated most. Moreover, servants who escaped or otherwise misbehaved were whipped and even branded. Servants who were exceptionally ill-treated could and did appeal to the community's officials and sometimes saw their wrongs righted by the courts. Finally, indentured women who wished to end their servitude could do that more easily than bound men, for the ratio of the sexes was such that an appealing woman might well find a man willing to buy out her contract so that they could wed.

In addition to those who indentured themselves for ship passage, young women who had been born in America also indentured themselves as apprentices, either to learn a skill or to provide themselves with a home when they had been orphaned. While apprentices were more likely to be boys than girls, it nonetheless was common for a girl to be apprenticed to a seamstress or milliner or MIDWIFE to learn those businesses. Such young women usually were under the technical guardianship of the male head of the household, even though they actually worked for his wife; but at the same time, there were young women who worked directly for a man and even did traditionally masculine jobs, such as BETSY HAGER, who learned smithing as a "bound girl." Especially in the southern colonies, needy girls were able to choose their own "masters"; in New England, the usual practice was that the court assigned guardians.

But it was emigration passage that created most indentured servants; indeed, the system was so important to early settlement that some historians estimate between half and two-thirds of all initial colonists were indentured. The practice had begun to disappear by the Revolution and virtually ended after it. Its demise was caused in part by the criminal histories of many thus exported, for Americans declined to buy such contracts at the same time that their individual experience with Europeans also eliminated personal contact as a source of potential labor. Another factor was the system's inherent competition with slaves from Africa, for contracting with a white person whose rights had to be respected was not nearly as profitable as owning a laborer completely and permanently. Finally, as the 1800s began, the native needy who had previously been bound out were increasingly provided with almshouses or were cared for in their homes by the charities that began to be organized, usually under the aegis of women.

INFANT MORTALITY Until well into the twentieth century, American mothers could expect to lose at least one child, for health standards were such that even affluent families were not protected from the death of their most vulnerable. Indeed, physicians arguably caused some deaths among those who could afford their care; Queen ANNE, for example, who reigned over the American colonies from 1702–1714, bore seventeen children, none of whom lived beyond age eleven.

Infant mortality remained highly probable as the nation developed. The records of a Wisconsin church at mid-nineteenth century, for example, show that of 194 deaths, ninety-four were children under five. Time and urbanization did little to improve the situation among the poor, for a 1890 study of an impoverished section of New York City saw the same percentage of death, with sixty-one of the 138 children who were born in a three-year period dying. A decade later, in the immigrant city of Lawrence, Massachusetts, infants accounted for 44 percent of all deaths, and a study by KATHARINE ANTHONY just before WORLD WAR I found that among 370 working mothers there were 437 infant deaths—or more than one per woman.

Women reacted to this situation by psychologically steeling themselves, with the result that accounts of the deaths of their children can appear almost indifferent. To maintain their sanity, women whose lives saw so much grief had to adopt a stoical approach, which reinforced the fundamental fatalism that governed many of their lives. While these views were especially likely among poor IMMIGRANT WOMEN, even educated women in the nineteenth century seldom sought a genuine medical explanation of their children's deaths and instead simply resigned themselves to "God's will." The result often was still more death, as the threats to children's health remained, especially with unsanitary milk, (though this improved somewhat with the advent of MILK STATIONS) unventilated housing, and other preventable causes of death.

Infant mortality rates remained unacceptably high well into the twentieth century. A 1925 study of the industrialized area around Pittsburgh, for example, found one of every three babies born still died young. While that area was home to many who were first- and second-generation immigrants, the rate of infant death was similar in the Deep South, where virtually all mothers were women of long American descent. Nor was the cause simply the higher poverty rates of Southern blacks, for until public health programs were instituted during the Great Depression, most white families also had experience with the early death of children. Often these deaths were from typhoid and other fevers that were directly related to the lack of sanitary toilet facilities and clean drinking water.

The situation improved throughout the thirties and forties as both the New Deal and WORLD WAR II heightened the expectations of the poor, who insisted on better housing and health care delivery. As the century lengthened, however, American infant mortality rates seriously worsened in comparison with other nations. Several factors are involved, including the high rate of teenage, ILLEGITIMATE births; a much greater number of mothers addicted to drugs, tobacco, and alcohol; and especially the high cost of prenatal care and proper nutrition. Infant mortality—and what it says of female health—remains one of the intractable problems of American women.

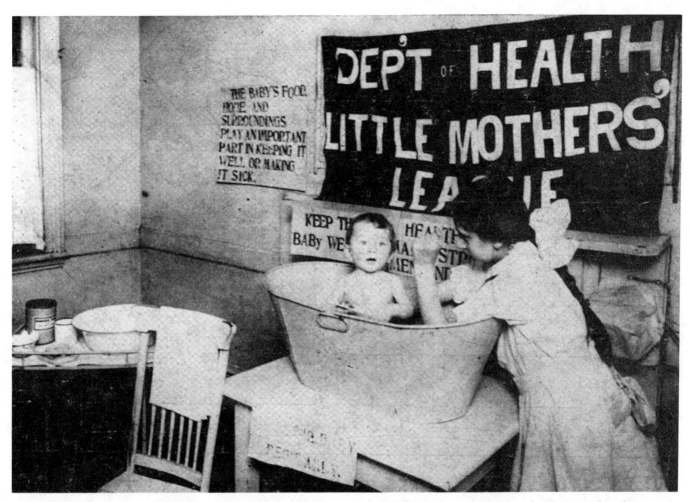

Classes such as this were designed to lower infant mortality rates by teaching proper hygiene and nutrition. This class took place prior to World War I, but for most of American history, even educated, affluent mothers could expect to lose at least one child in infancy. NEW YORK PUBLIC LIBRARY, IMMIGRANT LIFE COLLECTION.

INTERNATIONAL CONGRESS OF WOMEN (1915) Led by JANE ADDAMS, forty-two American women crossed the war-imperiled sea for a meeting at the Hague in April, 1915. The conflict that became WORLD WAR I was less than a year old; Americans were not yet involved; and these indomitable women aimed not only to keep their nation out, but also to end the war.

Addams presided over the Congress, and at its end, sent the delegates out to work for peace. EMILY BALCH, for example, traveled from the Hague to Denmark, Norway, Sweden, and Russia, where she met with foreign ministers and other officials, and she briefed President Wilson upon returning to the U.S. At a time when no national government had granted women the right to vote, the audaciousness and commitment of these women was little short of astounding.

Addams, Balch, and ALICE HAMILTON jointly published a report of the meeting and its extraordinary mission entitled *Women at The Hague* (1915). The Congress led to the post-war formation of the WOMEN'S INTERNATIONAL LEAGUE FOR PEACE AND FREEDOM and was a strong factor in the Nobel Peace Prizes that Addams and Balch each won much later.

INTERNATIONAL COUNCIL OF WOMEN A worldwide federation of women's organizations, the Council's first meeting was called largely by SUSAN ANTHONY. It met in Washington in 1888 with representatives of forty-nine nations and fifty-three American organizations. ELIZABETH CADY STANTON delivered the opening and closing speeches. The Council made itself permanent at that convocation, resolving to hold national assemblies every three years and international ones every five; FRANCES WILLARD was elected president of the American council. Its platform included many aims on behalf of women, but stopped short of demanding suffrage, which was still too radical for delegates from many foreign countries.

Future meetings not only attracted the leadership of the nascent global women's movement, but more importantly, were widely reported by the international press. Coverage was particularly extensive for the Council's 1899 convocation in London, when SUSAN ANTHONY—the aged symbol of all things new and radical—met Queen Victoria, who—close to the end of her sixty-three-year reign—was the epitome of domesticity and the status quo. The Queen asked to meet Anthony, however, and Anthony was entertained by other nobility as well, for even though many of them were dubious about suffrage, they honored her for her other accomplishments on behalf of women. The Council was chaired by the Countess of Aberdeen, and its favorable publicity did a great deal to further the cause, both in Britain and elsewhere.

Though eighty-four, Anthony also made the trip to Berlin for the 1904 convocation, when the German authorities rivaled the earlier London meeting in royally entertaining the delegates. Indeed, KATHARINE ANTHONY believed that the number of garden parties and receptions may have been intended to distract women from their work, thus leading to the formation of the INTERNATIONAL SUFFRAGE ALLIANCE by those who were more serious about accomplishing political change. Nevertheless, the 1904 meeting provided at least one remarkable opportunity for women to showcase their abilities, when MARY CHURCH TERRELL, a black American, addressed the audience in German and French as well as in English.

Competition between the English and German delegates at this meeting presaged the coming of WORLD WAR I, which, together with the formation of the new Suffrage Alliance, effectively ended the International Council of Women.

INTERNATIONAL SUFFRAGE ALLIANCE An international suffrage organization was discussed by SUSAN ANTHONY and others already by 1883, but it was not finally begun until 1892, after the merger of the rival American suffrage associations. Even then, the Alliance was appreciably less than "international," for the American SUFFRAGE MOVEMENT remained organizationally and politically ahead of other nations until the British movement began to grow at the turn of the century.

Also known as the International Woman Suffrage Alliance, the organization was formalized in Berlin in 1904 during a convocation of the INTERNATIONAL COUNCIL OF WOMEN. It included women from eight northern European countries, and to a large extent was the same body as the older Council—except that suffrage was endorsed. CARRIE CHAPMAN CATT was elected president and other officers came from Germany, Britain and the Netherlands. The "Declaration of Principles" that was adopted included an affirmation of the equality of men and women, a list of grievances of women under national laws, and a call for the ballot.

At the 1906 meeting in Copenhagen, additional delegates came from Australia, Iceland, Canada, Hungary, Italy, and Russia; the fifty-five pages of minutes show the seriousness with which these women approached their work. The 1908 conference in Amsterdam saw twenty nations represented, with Norway, Finland, and Australia's flags receiving special honor because women in those countries had suffrage rights. The new militant strategy of the British suffrage movement was debated at this convocation; the resultant resolution voiced the women's objection to any government that imprisoned women as "common law breakers instead of political offenders."

Catt presided over the Alliance's biannual meetings in London, Stockholm, and Budapest until WORLD WAR I interrupted; between 1911 and 1913 she led a global tour for women and visited every continent. WORLD WAR I, however, effectively dissolved FEMINIST international action, and German women especially lost the organizational gains they had made.

INTERNATIONAL LADIES' GARMENT WORKERS' UNION
As a careful reading of the name reveals, the ILGWU was organized as a union of those who worked on garments for ladies. The membership from the beginning was made up of men as well as women, and the leadership was (and remains) predominantly male, even though women historically far outnumbered men in the GARMENT INDUSTRY.

There was informal unionization of garment workers during the nineteenth century, and these skeleton groups were combined to form the International Ladies' Garment Workers' Union in June, 1900. They issued a report publicizing the fact that women sewing on HOME CONTRACT made less than thirty cents a day, and the union became the prime leader in efforts to end this system of labor. Not surprisingly, the membership of this early union was overwhelmingly male, made up of the men who had the preferred GARMENT INDUSTRY jobs of cutting and pressing. To the extent that women were organized at all, they were encouraged to participate in the WOMEN'S TRADE UNION LEAGUE (WTUL), which was a fundamentally different kind of organization. LEONORA O'REILLY represented the ILGWU at a 1903 meeting of the American Federation of Labor, out of which the WTUL was born.

Women came into the ILGWU by the tens of thousands, however, during the first weeks of the great industry-wide STRIKES in 1909–1910. The strikes were centered in New York, where by far the majority of garment workers were IMMIGRANT WOMEN. Largely Jewish, their culture encouraged political action by women, and Jewish women soon made up the majority of union membership. One of them, Pauline Newman, joined the union during the 1909 strike and remained on its staff the rest of her life, becoming the ILGWU's most visible woman. Lesser numbers of women from other ethnic groups were also active in ILGWU locals, and both in Philadelphia and New York, there were black women who joined the union and participated in the strike—even though some owners sought out black women as strikebreakers, offering them jobs they had never held before.

The ILGWU emerged from the strike a mature organization and was furthered strengthened by the tragic TRIANGLE FIRE the next year. In 1913, its membership was approximately ninety thousand, and despite internal battles with the more conservative United Garment Workers, the ILGWU won a fourteen-week strike in 1916. Working conditions improved dramatically; the economy was booming because of WORLD WAR I; and the ILGWU was strong enough to set a precedent with union-sponsored health centers, as well as other benefits.

After the war, however, the nation turned far more conservative through the 1920s, and with the Great Depression of the thirties, neither it nor any other union did well. Roosevelt's New Deal and the prosperity brought by WORLD WAR II enhanced the status of unions, but by then, most Jewish women had moved up and out of the garment trade, and immigrants from cultures in which women did not assert themselves predominated in the garment industry. Thus, even though the ILGWU became a long-term labor success, women were not well represented in their union. In the late 1970s, when women made up approximately 75 percent of ILGWU membership, there were just two on its eighteen-member executive board.

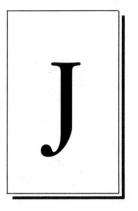

JACKSON, HELEN MARIA HUNT FISKE (1830–1885)

Like her lifelong friend EMILY DICKINSON, Helen Fiske grew up in Massachusetts, where both girls had fathers associated with Amherst College. Also like Dickinson, she rejected the Calvinist views of her family even before she was orphaned as a teenager.

Marriage at age twenty to Army officer Edward Hunt brought her a traveling life that offered new scenes, as well as freedom from community commitments, and encouraged the solitary craft of writing. During the next decade, however, Helen Hunt's literary work was increasingly motivated by both therapeutic and financial needs, as she endured the death of her entire family—her husband and her two children—between 1854 and 1865.

In a conscious effort to retain her sanity as well as to improve her skills, Hunt began a literary internship with Thomas Wentworth Higginson, a critic who also figured in Dickinson's career. Within a few years, Hunt was widely known and well respected; her work appeared in most national magazines and Emerson even acclaimed her poetry as the best by an American woman. Nevertheless, like many other female AUTHORS, she retained the modesty that she deemed proper to a lady and deliberately limited her reputation with the use of several PSEUDONYMS, some of them male, and with publication of unattributed essays and even novels.

Hunt visited Colorado for her health in 1873 (the same year that ANNA DICKINSON climbed mountains there), where she met and later married businessman William Jackson. After twelve years as a widow, she was finally relieved of the need to write merely for a living, while at the same time, her new western home introduced her to what would become her greatest claim to fame: the plight of Native Americans.

Century of Dishonor (1881) was the first widely read book to call the nation's attention to the mistreatment of its natives. A passionately written yet carefully researched work, it charged the Bureau of Indian Affairs with betrayal of treaties, gross corruption, and disregard of humane duty. Her book led to the formation of the Indian Rights Association, and it received enough attention in Washington that she was commissioned by the Interior Department to report on the condition of California's natives.

That project, in turn, provided the thematic material for Jackson's most significant fictional work, *Ramona* (1884). She intended *Ramona* to be a catalyst for action on behalf of Native Americans just as HARRIET BEECHER STOWE's novel had been for slaves, and she consciously emulated Stowe's style, even to the point of saying, as Stowe did, that a higher force controlled her pen. Three decades had passed since *Uncle Tom's Cabin* moved the nation's conscience, however, and the sentimental style that worked in a more innocent time was less effective after the war; moreover, the historical experience of whites with natives differed markedly from their experience with blacks. Nevertheless, though *Ramona* never achieved the fame of *Uncle Tom's Cabin*, it was a very popular book that has gone through more than three hundred printings. It (and its thematic problem) was sufficiently enduring that several movies have been based on Jackson's novel.

She did not live to enjoy her celebrity, however, much less to see any political results of her efforts on behalf of the natives. She broke a leg shortly after the publication of *Ra-*

185

mona and never recovered, dying less than a year later. Jackson was fifty-four when she died, and it is important to remember that her most significant works were published within four years of her death. She had just begun to discover the subject that moved her, and had she lived longer, both her reputation and the condition of Native America might well have been enhanced.

Famous in her lifetime as a poet, Helen Hunt Jackson instead should be remembered as the person who probably did more to prick the national conscience on behalf of its natives than any other white individual.

JACKSON, MAHALIA (1911–1972) The granddaughter
of slaves and a New Orleans native, Mahalia Jackson was orphaned at five. Her move to Chicago at sixteen was part of a pattern of black migration from the South after WORLD WAR I. She sang in a church choir there, where her deep, strong voice and talent for musical improvisation soon brought her offers as a soloist for black congregations.

Her local reputation grew to the point that Jackson made her first recording of gospel music in 1934 when she was just twenty-three. Immediately popular, it laid the foundation for a long career. Despite her youth and her undoubted ability to sing more lucrative jazz, Jackson limited herself to sacred music from the beginning. She made herself a model of proper behavior, even to the point of refusing to sing where liquor was served, but nonetheless overcame the obstacles of the Great Depression to establish a worldwide audience. She eventually made eight gospel records that sold more than a million copies each.

Twice married, Jackson kept her MAIDEN NAME and had no children. She was increasingly acclaimed by white audiences after the invention of television and participated in actions for racial harmony. Her annual concerts at Carnegie Hall regularly sold out, and she was popular in northern Europe, especially for her Christmas carols. Mahalia Jackson sang for the inauguration of President Kennedy in 1961, and her autobiography, *Movin' On Up*, was published in 1966.

JACKSON, RACHEL DONELSON ROBARDS (1767–1828)
Like other FRONTIER WOMEN, Rachel Donelson, at age twelve, made the perilous journey from Virginia to the wilderness that would become Nashville, Tennessee. The American Revolution was not yet over and it was far from clear to whom this new land would belong, but her family was continuing a pioneer tradition that made them relatively prominent people in old Virginia, where her father had been friends with George Washington. Rachel thus grew up blending the genuine hardships and dangers of frontier exploration with the genteel traditions of Southern life.

She wed Lewis Robards when she was eighteen, but her husband turned out to be paranoid and violent. Since DIVORCE or even separation was almost impossible in this era, she endured five years of unhappy marriage before his brutality drove her to the BOARDING HOUSE operated by her recently WIDOWED mother. There she was befriended by Andrew Jackson, a lawyer new to Nashville who was exactly her age. Robards continued his threats, however, and in December of 1790, she decided to flee far from him by joining a group

headed to Natchez, Mississippi, where some of her family had already pioneered.

Jackson was part of the expedition, and he fell in love with her on the trip. When word reached them that Robards had divorced her, they married in Natchez in August of 1791. They believed that Robards (who was from a politically connected family) had won a legislative bill of divorce, but it turned out that he had only obtained an act that permitted him to sue for a divorce in court, and—since he had not filed the suit—his wife was technically guilty of bigamy. When he finally did begin divorce proceedings in 1793, he charged her with adultery.

Legally helpless throughout all of this turmoil, Rachel Robards was finally able to remarry Andrew Jackson in January, 1794, but she would never outlive the gossip that surrounded her early twenties. That sorrow was magnified by her apparent inability to have children, for children were a strong legitimizing factor in a nineteenth-century woman's existence. Nonetheless, her husband adored her, and they filled their home with nephews, nieces, and the orphaned children of friends, legally adopting a nephew named Andrew Jackson, Jr.

They made their home near Nashville, aptly naming it The Hermitage, for Rachel Jackson stayed determinedly alone to manage the plantation while Andrew pursued his military and political ventures. She made just one exception and spent four months of 1821 in Pensacola, Florida, where Jackson served as the territorial governor. Since he had been extremely poor as a boy, the fact that they prospered enough to build a grand mansion in 1819 must be at least partially attributable to her capable agrarian management, for she worked without him most of the time. Indeed, much later Rachel would summarize their separate lives: "In the thirty years of our wedded life, he has not spent one-fourth his days under his own roof."

Jackson led the popular vote for the presidency in 1824, but in complex proceedings, lost the election anyway; he won soundly in the 1828 campaign. Throughout both races, however, Rachel Jackson was the object of much lurid attention from the era's all-male voters. Though her husband had defended her honor with a duel already in 1803 and even killed a man in another duel caused partly by aspersions cast on Rachel, the taint of their early relationship never ceased to be a source of gossip. In addition to her presumed immorality, she was also caricatured as an illiterate addicted to tobacco.

In fact, she not only was a faithful wife whose marriage was three decades long by the time of his election, but also lived a circumspect life, especially after adopting Presbyterianism in 1812. If the urbanites who scorned her had actually met her (and even more, had they visited her graceful Hermitage), such rumors would have been much harder to sustain—but, given her personal pain and the fact that she did not share her husband's political interests, her reclusiveness was understandable.

Rachel Jackson therefore took no joy in becoming the nation's First Lady. Although she was buying clothes and preparing to move to Washington, she feared being treated as a national pariah. Anxiety at this prospect might well have been a factor in the heart attack she suffered on December 17, 1828; she died three days before Christmas.

Had she lived to see her husband inaugurated in March and then faced down her slanderers from the strength of her position as First Lady, Rachel Jackson might have curtailed the cult of vacuous ladyhood that began to gather strength in this era, for she would have been a contrasting model of the more realistic values of frontier women.

Instead, she was buried at the Hermitage. Andrew Jackson wrote her epitaph, a paean of more than a hundred words praising her as "amiable" and "kind," a paragon of "piety" and "virtue." For himself, he specified a spare tombstone limited to his name. His grief colored the rest of his life, and particularly affected his presidency in the case of PEGGY O'NEALE EATON.

JACOBI, MARY CORRINA PUTNAM (1842–1906) A
member of the Putnam publishing family, young Mary was offered far better educational opportunities than those usually accorded women in her era. She published her first essay at age seventeen and would continue to write throughout her scientific career.

The CIVIL WAR that began when she was eighteen created opportunities for women to move into areas that had been exclusively male preserves; medicine was one of these, and Mary Putnam earned her medical degree from FEMALE MEDICAL COLLEGE OF PENNSYLVANIA in 1863, during the midst of the war. Nonetheless, the war did far more to create acceptability for women NURSES than for women physicians: Even the BLACKWELL sisters, who were relatively well established as physicians in this era, were limited in what they were allowed to contribute. Putnam similarly found little acceptance despite the wartime needs, and the work that she did in New York, Louisiana, and South Carolina was volunteer and largely connected to her family.

At the war's end, Dr. Putnam went to France in search of more advanced medical training. She remained there five years, for it took two years of persistent effort to enter the *Ecole de Medecine*. Finally admitted as the first woman of any nationality, she proved a brilliant student. Despite the original objections of the faculty to the presence of a woman, she not only graduated with high honors but also won an award for her thesis.

When she returned to the U.S. in 1871, Dr. Putnam was thus better educated than most physicians of either gender. Her family connections helped in developing a strong private practice, and one by one, she gained admittance to the most prestigious medical organizations. Meanwhile, she also continued her research, eventually publishing over one hundred scientific papers. She was one of the first to recognize environmental effects on health, a field later expanded by ALICE HAMILTON.

Two years after establishing herself in New York and at age thirty-one, she married pediatrician Abraham Jacobi, a European radical exiled after the 1848 revolutions. She took his name and bore three children by him, but did not give up her work—a successful combination of career and family that was extremely unusual in the post–Civil War era. Moreover, during the next three decades of increasing success, she also encouraged other women to achieve their potential.

Jacobi organized the Association for the Advancement of the Medical Education of Women in 1874 and served as its president for most of her life. She was a board member of the New York Consumers' League, a group whose goals included minimum wages for women, and she was also active in the SUFFRAGE MOVEMENT. Indeed, her *"Common Sense" Applied to Woman Suffrage* became a classic for suffragists in their ongoing debates with physicians about women's physical capacity for politics.

When Mary Jacobi died at sixty-three from an untreatable tumor, she exhibited the same scientific attitudes that had characterized her life and dispassionately documented her disease. She was widely recognized as the preeminent physician of her gender in the late nineteenth century.

JAMESTOWN WOMEN The women who settled the Jamestown colony were not the first European women in North America, for there were women among the Spanish-speaking colonists several decades before English-speaking women arrived. The Jamestown women also were preceded by seventeen women who were part of the mysterious 1587 Roanoke expedition that has been immortalized by the story of VIRGINIA DARE.

After the Roanoke colony vanished, the English made no serious attempt at settlement for two decades until Jamestown was established at the mouth of the James River in Virginia in 1607. The first women arrived the following year: Anne Forrest, a married woman, and her thirteen-year-old maid, Anne Buras, have the distinction of being the first women to settle in the first permanent English-speaking colony in America.

They were overwhelmingly outnumbered by approximately four hundred young men who had been recruited for the colony—men who, as the records of Captain John Smith made clear, did not work well as bachelors. The colony's management therefore sought to add young women to the settlement to assuage the men's complaints and to motivate them to work. In 1609, two years after the colony began, over a hundred English women arrived.

The lives of these first white women in America, however, were short and brutish, as most of them lived less than a year. The colony was so badly planned and ill-equipped and the survival skills of former Londoners in the swamps of Virginia were so poor that during the first winter after their arrival, famine became their destiny. Approximately 450 of the 500 colonists died during what became known as the "starving time" of 1609–1610. Women died of hunger along with men, and the statistical probability is that no more than a dozen of the hundred female settlers lived through that first terrible winter.

One poor woman was even cannibalized by the husband who had chosen her only a few months earlier. John Smith recorded that a man "did kill his wife, powdered [salted] her, and had eaten part of her before it was known; for which he was executed, as he well deserved." Nevertheless, Smith could not resist trivialization of the woman's fate, adding, "Whether she was better roasted, boiled, or carbonadoed [broiled], I know not; but of such a dish as powdered wife I never heard."

The Virginia Company resupplied the survivors and continued to send ships of women. While at first women were enticed to emigrate with the promise of free land, the company soon abolished that policy when it became apparent that women who were landowners preferred making their own living to marriage, and since the Company's object was to provide the men with brides, the free land policy was ended. Instead, they recruited women whose lives were so desperate that they were willing to marry strangers in the strange new land.

Young English women arrived to a scene much like that of the later sale of African slaves: Men lined up to see the women who disembarked, made their choices, and paid the ship's captain in tobacco worth approximately eighty dollars for their brides' fares. Though women probably were pressured to accept these hasty arrangements, they apparently were not forced to, and could work for the Company until an acceptable man appeared. That they would marry soon, however, was implicit in their emigration, for the Jamestown women were candidly valued for their sexual and reproductive ability.

JANEWAY, ELIZABETH HALL (1913–   ) A BARNARD

student who took a year off and wrote advertising copy to earn enough money to graduate during the Depression, Elizabeth Hall married Eliot Janeway, an editor with *Time* and *Fortune* magazines, soon after graduation. Their second child was born at the same time that she published her first novel, a 1943 psychological study of sisters that was extremely well reviewed. One critic favorably compared her to Jane Austen.

Janeway developed her skills to include the magazine format as well as books, and she added nonfiction to her established credentials as a novelist. While she sometimes addressed other subjects, she concentrated on women and ventured into areas that others did not touch. "Meet A War Widow," for example, written for *Ladies Home Journal* in the last year of WORLD WAR II, was a thoughtful discussion of the dilemmas faced by the nation's fifty thousand young WIDOWS—a subject that few other writers were willing to explore.

She continued to publish through the fifties and sixties, but it was with the revived women's movement of the seventies that an audience developed for Janeway's thoughtful analyses of women's lives. *Man's World; Woman's Place* (1971), *Women; Their Changing Roles* (1973) and *Between Myth and Morning; Women's Awakening* (1974) were all important to the growth of American FEMINISM. Her follow-up work includes *Powers of the Weak* (1980), *Cross Sections From a Decade of Change* (1982), and *Improper Behavior* (1987).

Janeway has long been active in the Authors Guild, selflessly promoting unified efforts to benefit AUTHORS less successful than she.

JANS, ANNETJE (1605?–1663) The property left by this

early Dutch settler became the subject of two centuries of litigation, for its Manhattan location made it extremely valuable.

When the New Netherlands colony was only a few years old in 1630, Annetje Jans emigrated there along with her husband, Roeloef Janssen, and three daughters (who, in the Dutch manner, took their father's first name as their surname).

Her widowed mother, Tryntje Jonas, and an unmarried sister traveled on the same ship; Jonas, a credentialed MIDWIFE and NURSE, was the first woman to practice medicine in what would become New York.

While her mother settled in New Amsterdam, Jans and her family went up the Hudson to Fort Orange (Albany), where they worked on a farm for five years and she bore two boys. The family returned to the farming village of New Amsterdam in 1635, acquiring sixty-two acres of land that ran irregularly along Broadway from Fulton to Canal Streets. Her husband died soon after, leaving Annetje Jans to make a living for her five children on a farm that was mostly still woods.

But she came from a tradition that encouraged independent women, for women in the Netherlands had long engaged in business and had a number of property rights that other European women lacked. Jans demonstrated these attitudes when she remarried in 1638 and drew up a prenuptial agreement to guarantee her financial independence. Her second husband, Dominie Bogardus, was a minister who was favored by the colony with one of its best houses. This property, too, Jans would inherit when Bogardus perished at sea in 1642—after she bore four sons in the four years of their marriage.

With six sons much younger than her three daughters and with help from her talented mother, the family was a female-dominated one, and the women continued to demonstrate exceptional capabilities. Again, the Dutch traditionally provided boys and girls with educations that were more nearly equal than that in much of Europe. Sara Roeloef, Jans' oldest daughter, was so accomplished a linguist that in addition to Dutch and English, she spoke the Algonquin language, and like some other FRONTIER WOMEN, she was employed as an interpreter with the natives. Moreover, Jans took care that her daughters received the benefit of her labors, drawing up a prenuptial marriage agreement assuring her daughter's inheritance, even though Sara married a physician.

During the two decades after her second widowhood, she not only managed to bring up the little boys alone, but acquired sufficient property to leave an impressive estate when she died in 1663. Jans' will (which referred to her married daughters by their MAIDEN NAMES) was carefully written to fairly divide her property among sons and daughters as well as grandchildren. There was no dispute over it until seventy-five years after her death, when the descendents of one of her Bogardus sons began a series of lawsuits that—despite losing verdicts—they nonetheless continued to pursue into the twentieth century.

The case of Annetje Jans thus became something of a cause celebre in eighteenth- and nineteenth-century New York, and perhaps as a result, the memory of this capable early settler was preserved. Meanwhile, the names of her contemporaries whose lives were similar have been forgotten, while the exceptionally capable Dutch women whose commercial activity was clear in early New York have been largely ignored by historians.

JEMISON, MARY (1743–1833) Mary Jemison serves as

a prototype for many FRONTIER WOMEN who settled early America and whose experience has been forgotten or minimized in the common lore.

She grew up on the Pennsylvania frontier and was fourteen

when, during the French and Indian Wars, she was captured by Shawnees who killed most of her family. They turned her over to Senecas who lived on the Ohio River; two years later, at sixteen, she was married to a Delaware man. Despite the trauma of having seen the scalps of family members being tanned, she adopted native ways, bore two children, and when she became a widow at eighteen, did not leave the new culture.

She married a Seneca leader in 1765 and lived the rest of her life in western New York state, where she became known as the "White Woman of the Genese." She bore six children by her second husband, and all of her offspring used "Jemison" in the matrilineal style of Native Americans. She so thoroughly assumed her husband's culture that he was not hindered by his marriage, and he led his tribe against American colonists when the Senecas (like most Native Americans) allied themselves with the British during the American Revolution. After the Americans won and Jemison could have returned to her original heritage, she refused to do so.

As the frontier moved west, most Senecas went towards Canada, but Mary Jemison stayed in the Genese valley, where her appreciable land rights were confirmed when she renewed what should have been her natural U.S. citizenship in 1817. As other whites settled nearby, she developed into a mediator who shared friendships with both races. She died at ninety, shortly after selling her property and moving to a reservation near Buffalo. *A Narrative of the Life of Mrs. Mary Jemison* (1824) was popular throughout the nineteenth century.

"JENNIE JUNE"

This was the pen name of JANE CUNNINGHAM CROLY, who was the first woman reporter to work for a major newspaper at a desk—as opposed to the "correspondent" style of working from home that was current in the nineteenth century.

Nonetheless, Croly was associated with what was called the "society pages" of newspapers rather than with "hard news." Like many other early women writers, she wrote because she had to earn a living and hid her true self with a PSEUDONYM. The nature of her assignments, however, made it necessary to use a female name and "Jennie June" was adopted. The first article she wrote under that name was accepted by the *New York Tribune* in 1854, and—despite marriage two years later—she continued to write for forty years. "Jennie June" was so popular that Jane C. Croly herself became a primary force in the CLUB MOVEMENT so vital to the history of women in the late nineteenth century.

JEWETT, SARAH ORNE (1849–1909)

Like many girls of her era, Sarah Jewett educated herself through wide reading and careful observation of her surroundings. She published her first story at nineteen, using—like a number of women AUTHORS—a PSEUDONYM.

She was less ambivalent about the nature of her work than about her name, however, and from the beginning, she adopted the stories of the farms and seaports of her Maine home as her literary theme. Throughout the 1870s and 1880s, she wrote fiction, poetry, and sketches for the most prestigious national magazines; these works were published as collections, the most recognized of which is *Deephaven* (1877).

In the 1890s, she expanded to the book form; *The Country of the Pointed Firs* (1896) has been called "one of the unquestioned classics of American prose writing." A constant theme of her work was the declining economy of upper New England, the consequent depression and isolation of its people, and the black humor that dealt best with such situations.

Like KATE CHOPIN much to the southwest of her, Jewett was thus an important influence in the "local color" school of literature that emerged in the late nineteenth century, which in turn was a factor in the creation of American realism. Indeed, one critic credited Jewett with "inventing" the "static" novel in which plot took a subordinate position to scene and characterization.

She encouraged WILLA CATHER when that young woman wrote her in 1908, and Cather's work indeed shows a clear influence from Jewett. Though she traveled widely and was part of Boston's literary life, Jewett lived in the same house in South Berwick, Maine all of her life. Bowdoin College, an all-male institution, gave her their first honorary degree granted to a woman in 1901. The American Women Writers Collection at the University of Wisconsin includes holdings on Sarah Orne Jewett.

JOHNS HOPKINS UNIVERSITY

Though this private Baltimore institution excluded women from its undergraduate COLLEGE, it became a turn-of-the century leader in providing educational opportunities to women at the graduate level, especially in the sciences.

Though neither was allowed to enroll, M. CAREY THOMAS (in 1877–1878) and JANE ADDAMS (in 1886–1887) attended classes there. Geologist FLORENCE BASCOM earned the first Ph.D. Johns Hopkins granted to a woman in 1893, and Bascom's protégé, JULIA ANN GARDNER, earned a Ph.D. in geology in 1911. Among other notable women who studied in its graduate schools were Dr. ALICE HAMILTON, who did postgraduate work in the medical school in 1896–1897; FLORENCE BLANCHFIELD, later head of the ARMY NURSE CORPS, who studied there in 1907–1908; and RACHEL CARSON, famed environmentalist who was granted scholarships for her 1932 master's degree in zoology. Even *avant garde artiste* GERTRUDE STEIN studied medicine there at the turn of the century.

Male professors did not disdain from working with the women's study clubs that sprang up as part of the late nineteenth-century CLUB MOVEMENT; two Johns Hopkins consultants, for example, drew up a study plan for a group of Atlanta women, and later congratulated the women upon their completion of "what amounted to a five-year graduate course." Johns Hopkins also innovated extension courses that allowed women to study at home.

JOHNSON, ELEANOR (1892–1987)

Most Americans were influenced as schoolchildren by Eleanor Johnson, for she founded *My Weekly Reader* in 1928. Her idea of a newspaper aimed at children was such a good one that it prospered despite the immediate onset of the Great Depression. The weekly paper, which was four to eight pages long, quickly became a favorite tool for TEACHERS who wished to improve reading skills while also developing responsible citizenship through knowledge of global events.

Born in Maryland and a 1925 honors graduate of the UNI-

VERSITY OF CHICAGO, Johnson taught in Oklahoma. She was working as a Pennsylvania administrator for elementary curriculum when the idea of a newspaper for children occurred to her—at least in part because she felt that children's literature concentrated too much on fantasy and fairy tales. She took the concept to American Education Publications, where she was deeply involved in developing the paper's style and content, even though she did not join them as a full-time PUBLISHER until 1935.

The first issue featured the election of 1928 from a child's point of view, and within the first year, one hundred thousand schoolchildren read the paper. Johnson scheduled its arrival so that *My Weekly Reader* was used on Friday afternoons, which provided an ideal distraction for teachers and restless students. It became so popular that two-thirds of today's adults read *My Weekly Reader* in elementary school. In addition, Johnson also supervised the publication of *Current Events* and other school-based newspapers for American Educational Press, and she served as a consultant to Xerox Educational Publications after her 1965 retirement.

Johnson had earned a master's degree from Columbia University in 1932, and she was the author of dozens of other educational texts. She served as a visiting professor to several prestigious universities and received a number of honors before her death at ninety-four.

JOHNSON, ELIZA McCARDLE (1810–1876)

Eliza Johnson was a highly unusual First Lady in that she served as an elementary TEACHER to her husband. Andrew Johnson never attended school and was basically illiterate when he married in 1827; his wife taught him to write and expanded his embryonic reading skills. In an interesting reversal of traditional roles, she read aloud while he worked as a tailor. He remained forever grateful for this education and was not embarrassed to acknowledge the debt he owed her.

When her husband began his political career a few years later, Eliza Johnson, like many political wives, lived alone for long periods of time. She bore five children, with the last arriving eighteen years after the others, when she was forty-two. Perhaps as a result, her health was not sufficiently good to serve as White House hostess, and a daughter performed those functions while Johnson continued to concentrate on reading for her husband. Her daily summaries of newspapers indicated how much confidence he continued to place in his wife's mental abilities.

JOHNSTON, MARY (1870–1936)

Known for *To Have and to Hold*, the bestselling book of 1900, Johnston was like PEARL BUCK, MARGARET MITCHELL, CARSON MCCULLERS, and other writers in that her earliest work was her best. Mitchell, in fact, consciously emulated her and felt that *Gone With the Wind* did not meet Johnston's standard.

Of the twenty-three historical novels she published between 1898 and 1927, *To Have and to Hold* was Johnston's second and her most popular. This story of the JAMESTOWN WOMEN has long endured; with sales of more than a half million copies, it was later made into movies.

Mary Johnston was a native of Virginia and most of her novels were based there in carefully researched settings. Like her friend ELLEN GLASGOW, Johnston never married and wrote at least in part because of her family's declining fortunes after the CIVIL WAR. The two authors joined in founding the Virginia Equal Suffrage League in 1909, and Johnston went on to considerable activism, especially motivated by WORLD WAR I and the WOMEN'S INTERNATIONAL LEAGUE FOR PEACE AND FREEDOM.

She lost part of her audience because of her leftist politics and more of it because of experimental styling in her later works. Nonetheless, Johnston was well known in her lifetime and is similar to her contemporary GRACE ATHERTON, whose historical novels of California were bestsellers, in that both are neglected today.

JONES, "MOTHER" MARY HARRIS (1830–1930)

The most famous female labor leader of the nineteenth century, Mary Harris emigrated from Ireland with her family at age five—a decade prior to the potato famine and its waves of Irish immigrants. She first worked as a TEACHER in a Catholic school in Michigan and then as a seamstress in Chicago. She moved to Memphis for another teaching job, and in 1861, married an ironworker named Jones (whose first name she omitted from her 1925 autobiography) and learned from him about the nascent American labor movement.

Like millions of other Irish Catholics, Mary Jones married later than the average woman, and yet she bore four children in six years before tragedy struck. Memphis, like other southern cities near water, attracted fatal mosquitoes, and Mary Jones' entire family died in the 1867 yellow fever epidemic. She dressed in black for the rest of her life.

She left the tragic city behind and returned to Chicago, again sewing for a meager living. Sorrow stalked her, however, and she lost everything she owned in the great Chicago fire of 1871. She found solace at Knights of Labor meetings, and after 1877, single-mindedly dedicated herself to improving life for working people. As the nation moved from an agrarian to an industrial economy, more and more Americans found themselves poor, for the rampant capitalism of the late nineteenth century was based on low wages and long hours—when work was to be had. Unemployment was a certainty; the economy swung wildly and workers had no pensions, health care, or other insurance. It was to these people that Mary Jones appealed, and their love and admiration for her is apparent in the appellation of "Mother Jones" by which she became known.

She first displayed her oratorical and organizing abilities in Pittsburgh during the great railroad STRIKE of 1877; she was part of the strikes that led to the Haymarket riot in Chicago in 1886; and she even worked the TEXTILE MILLS of the Deep South, leading a Birmingham strike in 1894. She paused briefly to publish *The New Right* in 1899 and a two-volume *Letters of Love and Labor* in 1900 and 1901.

From that point, she concentrated most of her efforts on miners, organizing in the coal fields of West Virginia and Pennsylvania. In her late forties when she began her union cause, she lived mostly with supporters and eked out a pass-the-hat existence, but for a few years at the turn of the century (when she also turned seventy), she was actually employed by the United Mine Workers. In 1903, however, she split from UMW when the national leadership disavowed a wildcat strike in the Colorado coal fields. Mother Jones stayed in the West for a decade, working copper mines in Idaho and Arizona, and then returned to West Virginia, where she was jailed in 1913 and—at the unlikely age of eighty-three—was sentenced to twenty years in prison.

When the governor pardoned her, she returned to Colorado and was present for the LUDLOW MASSACRE the following year. She made a national crusade of that tragedy, even lobbying President Wilson. Back on the East Coast, she participated in several industrial strikes between 1915 and 1919 that related to WORLD WAR I. Even in the postwar era, when she was in her 90s, she was still actively organizing coal miners.

Yet, despite her radicalism, Mother Jones was no feminist. She did not support the SUFFRAGE MOVEMENT, arguing that "you don't need a vote to raise hell." Though she was correct when she pointed out that the women of Colorado had the vote and failed to use it to prevent the appalling conditions that led to labor violence, this should not have negated women's inherent right to a voice in government from one who also frequently quoted the Declaration of Independence. Indeed, Mother Jones even argued that suffragists were naive women who unwittingly acted as duplicitous agents of class warfare; she wrote in 1925 (after national suffrage had been achieved) that "the plutocrats have organized their women. They keep them busy with suffrage and prohibition and charity."

More significantly, Mother Jones organized working class women only in AUXILIARY status and adamantly maintained that—except when the union called—a woman's place was in the home. Her ideals reflected her Catholic heritage, for she believed that working men should be paid well enough so that women could devote themselves exclusively to motherhood. It is not surprising, therefore, that Mother Jones was conspicuously absent from the leadership of the great strikes that involved large numbers of women, for example, the 1909 GARMENT INDUSTRY strike and the LAWRENCE TEXTILE STRIKE of 1912.

She lived another five years after publishing her *Autobiography of Mother Jones* (1925), spending her last days with friends in Silver Spring, Maryland and dying six months after a splendid celebration of her one hundredth birthday. After a ceremonious Catholic requiem, she was buried with other mine workers.

JORDAN, BARBARA (1936–) The holder of a number of "firsts" for black women, Barbara Jordan was born to a poor Houston family and has remained closely associated with Texas. After graduation from segregated Texas Southern University, she followed the practice of many Southern blacks who could obtain graduate education only in the North. After earning her law degree from Boston University in 1959, Jordan returned to Houston and initially practiced law from her parents' dining room table.

She worked hard to turn out black voters for John Kennedy and his vice-presidential running mate, Texan Lyndon Johnson—and Johnson was so impressed with the quality of her mind that he began promoting her career, in an era when it took courage for a Southern politician to mentor a young, black woman. Jordan's 1962 and 1964 campaigns for the state legislature were unsuccessful, but she built a base that succeeded in electing her to the Texas Senate in 1966—when she was just thirty.

The only woman and the only African-American in the body, she quickly won the respect of other senators. She not only was appointed acting governor, but also was invited to Washington to advise President Johnson on the 1968 Civil Rights Act. Among Jordan's chief victories in the Texas Senate was the extension of minimum wage protection to laundry workers and DOMESTIC SERVANTS, most of whom were women.

During her 1966–1972 legislative tenure, she developed enough influence to design a congressional district for herself during the reapportionment year of 1972. She easily won the seat, defeating three men in the primary with an amazing 80 percent of the vote. Barbara Jordan thus became the first black woman elected to Congress from the Deep South—just four years after New York's SHIRLEY CHISHOLM had become the first in the nation.

Jordan again sponsored minimum wage increases, as well as the extension of Social Security to housewives. It was her legal credentials that secured her appointment to the Judiciary Committee, however, and that assignment brought her to the attention of the nation when the House held impeachment hearings on President Richard Nixon. The freshman legislator from Texas immediately became a celebrity, for her authoritative voice and oratorical skill made her unique in the televised hearings. Barbara Jordan quickly moved up on the list of those with a bright political future. In 1976, the Democratic Party recognized her by choosing her as the keynote speaker for the national convention, the first woman and the first black to be so honored.

Only two years after her stirring style received thunderous applause at the Democratic convention, Representative Jordan surprised political observers by leaving Congress. She taught at the University of Texas and published *Barbara Jordan: A Self Portrait* (1979). Although suffering from multiple sclerosis, Jordan continues to take an active role in civil rights and FEMINIST issues, and she advises Texas Governor ANN RICHARDS on legal and ethical questions. Jordan has received countless honors, including at least twenty honorary degrees.

JUDSON, NANCY ANN HASSELTINE (1789–1826) The first American woman to act as a foreign missionary, Judson was not herself ordained, but nonetheless endured the same difficulties as her husband.

Called "Ann" rather than her baptismal name of "Nancy," Hasseltine was a twenty-three-year-old Massachusetts TEACHER who was also interested in theology when she married Adoniram Judson, a student at Andover Theological Seminary. Her willingness to wed was at least in part because of his plans to be a foreign missionary—and because he wished her to accompany him, something for which there was no precedent. Despite the disapproval of many, she left with him for Asia early in 1812.

By the time they arrived in Calcutta, the young U.S. was at war with the British who governed the colonies where Reverend Judson planned to preach. They evaded a deportation order by heading to Rangoon in Burma, and lived there quietly ministering for most of the next decade, during which Ann Judson bore and lost two children. She learned the local language along with her husband, taught classes to women, and wrote Christian materials in Burmese. While she made the difficult voyage back to the U.S. in 1821 for medical attention, she worked on the story of her experience, which was published in 1823 as *A Particular Relation of the American Baptist Mission to the Burman Empire.*

Her return to Burma in 1823 was ironically akin to her initial arrival, for again her life was disrupted by war. When the Burmese revolted against the British in 1824, Reverend Judson was imprisoned by the Burmese as a spy and threatened with execution. Although thirty-five and again pregnant, Ann Judson pleaded his case with every influential contact she could make; after the baby was born, she provided her husband with food, though she suffered herself from famine and disease.

He was released late in 1825 when the British re-established their military authority, but Ann Judson died less than a year later and her child soon after that. Her physical deprivation and emotional strain had been so great that she was credited with giving her life for his, and Ann Judson became something of a martyr to Christians in Burma and America. As the nineteenth-century missionary movement grew, her story was immortalized in prose and poem.

JURY DUTY For most of American history, women who found themselves in court were not judged by a jury of their peers, for jurors traditionally have been chosen from the lists of registered voters, and women in most states were not allowed to vote until the passage of the NINETEENTH AMENDMENT in 1920.

Even then, many states did not move to include women as potential jurors. As late as 1961, there were three states (all in the Deep South) that still barred women from jury duty, as well as eighteen others that automatically excluded women from jury duty unless the woman took the initiative and volunteered to serve. When the Supreme Court upheld such a law in a Florida case that year, the disparity became still another argument for passage of the EQUAL RIGHTS AMENDMENT.

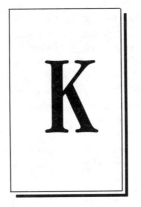

K

KAHN, FLORENCE PRAG (1866–1948) One of the earliest political beneficiaries of the NINETEENTH AMENDMENT, Kahn was elected to Congress just five years after women were assured the right to vote. Like several other women of her era, she was preceded by a husband who died in office—but the fact that she not only won the 1925 special election to replace him, but also went on to win five more races, shows that she established her separate political identity.

A San Francisco Jewish Republican, Kahn exemplified the independent and relatively liberal WESTERN WOMEN. Her first campaign centered around her opposition to PROHIBITION, which was then in effect and which was supported by most Republicans as well as by most of the longtime members of the SUFFRAGE MOVEMENT. Though fifty-nine when she was elected to Congress, Kahn was more typical of the younger women of the twenties, for she was not only candidly "wet," but also became known for an earthy sense of humor and a lively social life.

Though her initial committee assignments were trivial, her colleagues soon judged her worthy of appointments to prestigious committees, including Military Affairs and Appropriations. She used this to build California, especially San Francisco, into the vital area that it was by the time of WORLD WAR II. She brought home appropriations for naval installations and new air bases, and her popularity was great enough that she stayed in office through most of the Great Depression despite her Republican affiliation. She finally lost to the Roosevelt coalition in the Democratic landslide of 1936, when she was seventy.

An 1887 graduate of the University of California at Berkeley, Kahn had been a TEACHER in her early life and worked in Congress for pensions that would allow teachers dignified retirement. She was also active in HADASSAH and the AMERICAN ASSOCIATION OF UNIVERSITY WOMEN.

KASSEBAUM, NANCY LANDON (1932–) The daughter of 1936 Republican presidential nominee Alf Landon, Nancy Kassebaum is the first woman elected to the U.S. Senate who did not have a congressional husband precede her.

She graduated from the University of Kansas in 1954 and earned a master's degree from the University of Michigan in 1956. After working in radio in Wichita and mothering four children, she joined the staff of a Kansas senator in 1975. When he retired in 1978, the recently divorced Kassebaum ran for his seat. Her mother encouraged her to make the race, while her famous father was dubious about the public's willingness to elect a woman. To his surprise, Nancy Kassebaum—whose previous political experience was limited to a small town school board—defeated eight men in the Republican primary and carried 56 percent of the vote in the general election.

The only woman in the U.S. Senate at the time, she was appointed to major committees including Budget, Banking, and Commerce. She supported the EQUAL RIGHTS AMENDMENT and introduced legislation in 1980 that would have revised Selective Service to include women. After Republican gains in the 1980 election, Kassebaum moved up to even more influential committees, including Foreign Relations.

She was reelected in 1984 and 1990, with the latter being

especially notable because eight women held their party's nominations for the Senate in 1990, but Kassebaum was the only winner. In 1991, she was appointed to a committee drafting new ethical standards for the Senate, but disappointed FEMINISTS later in the year by voting with her party to confirm controversial Supreme Court nominee Clarence Thomas. Kassebaum is pro-choice.

KEENE, LAURA (1820?–1873) America's first female theatrical manager, Keene came to this country from England to make her New York debut as an ACTRESS in 1852. The next year, she opened a theater in Baltimore and a few months later, moved on to San Francisco and the management of another theater season. With incredible freedom of movement in this era when sail was still the only means of international travel, she took a fling in Australia—but was back in New York by 1855.

A mere four years after her initial emigration, Laura Keene opened a theater named for herself in New York City. She not only managed the theater but also produced the shows and played the leading roles. She was best known for *Our American Cousin*, the play whose Washington production Abraham Lincoln was watching when he was assassinated. She was in the audience at the time and recognized actor/assassin John Wilkes Booth.

Like many women in entertainment, middle age brought declining fortunes to Keene, and she lived in strained circumstances before dying relatively young.

KELLER, HELEN ADAMS (1880–1968) Struck both deaf and blind at nineteen months by a raging brain fever, Helen Keller might have been consigned to an anonymous life in an asylum but for her own native intelligence and a resourceful mother, who had her examined by Alexander Graham Bell and other experts. They sent Anne Sullivan, a graduate of Perkins School for the Blind, to Keller's Alabama home to act as GOVERNESS for seven-year-old Helen. Ever after called "Teacher," Sullivan would remain with Keller for the rest of her life.

She began calming the child's wild behavior and then set about developing communication methods with this girl who—because she could neither hear nor see—also did not speak. Touch was the significant sense that remained, and Sullivan expanded that to its fullest capacity with a manipulative alphabet. Bright as she was, Helen began to comprehend the system within two weeks, and the door to understanding her world was opened.

The following year, Sullivan took Helen to Boston and the Perkins School, which publicized this remarkable child. Boston newspapers chronicled her achievements as she learned not only to read Braille but also to write with a specially made typewriter, and Helen Keller thus became well known while she was still very young. At fourteen, she went to New York for two years where she improved upon her speaking ability and again made a major publicity impact, and then returned to Massachusetts to enroll in mainstream education at the Cambridge School for Young Ladies.

Two years of intensive tutoring followed that experience, for Helen wished to go to COLLEGE, and—since educational backgrounds were inconsistent in this era, especially among women—colleges routinely required rigorous entrance examinations. With Sullivan's persistent tutoring, Keller passed her tests and was admitted RADCLIFFE COLLEGE at age twenty. Sullivan accompanied her to classes to interpret, and Keller completed her work within the normal four years, graduating *cum laude* in 1904.

She had published her first books, *The Story of My Life* (1902) and *Optimism* (1903), prior to graduation, and afterwards she embarked upon a career of writing, lecturing, and opinion-making. Eventually the author of a dozen books and numerous articles in major magazines, she was especially effective in urging treatment of newborns to prevent the blindness that is caused by a mother's venereal disease. Her candid stance on this subject, beginning already in 1906, gave millions of women the permission they needed to speak of what had long been a forbidden topic.

Sullivan's relatively brief marriage changed her name to Macy, but made little other change in the strong bond between the two women—except that John Macy seems to have been responsible for making Keller politically aware. From that time, Keller not only supported the SUFFRAGE MOVEMENT, but also called herself a Socialist and wrote of that cause—despite accepting an annual stipend from industrialist Andrew Carnegie.

With her appearance at the 1915 San Francisco Exposition, Keller added to her credentials as a national figure and continued to use that platform for liberal political causes, especially during WORLD WAR I. Her celebrity was recognized by the infant movie business, which featured the story of her life, *Deliverance*, in the last year of the war. The postwar years slowly brought a moderation of her political views, especially after she became affiliated with the new American Foundation for the Blind in 1924. She eventually raised a two million dollar endowment for that organization.

"Teacher" died in 1936, but Keller, with the support of other aides, continued the international travel that resulted in her invariable listings as one of the world's most-admired women. Supported by the Foundation, she lobbied for the blind and worked on the development of talking books. Though over sixty during WORLD WAR II, she toured military hospitals and provided hope to soldiers whose misfortunes paled compared with being both deaf and blind.

A second film on her life, made with backing from KATHERINE CORNELL, won the Academy Award in 1955; *The Miracle Worker*, which centered on Sullivan, won the 1960 Pulitzer Prize as a play and was made into a movie two years later. Keller's voice continued to be heard into her eighties, and she was honored with the Presidential Medal of Freedom in 1964. When she died in Connecticut at eighty-eight, Helen Keller was known throughout the world as a model of courage and capability.

Her birthplace at Tuscumbia, Alabama is now a museum, while other material on Keller is preserved at both Perkins School for the Blind in Watertown, Massachusetts and at the American Foundation for the Blind in New York.

KELLEY, FLORENCE (1859–1932) Part of the group of women associated with JANE ADDAMS' Hull House, Kelley was a wealthy but socially concerned Philadelphian who had an uncommon education, having graduated from Cornell in 1882 and studied further at the University of Zurich. She not only became a Socialist while in Europe, but also translated Fredrick Engels' work and maintained a correspondence friendship with that founder of socialism.

She married a Russian in 1884 while still in Europe and bore three children before an 1891 DIVORCE; she met the Hull House women when she went to Illinois to take advantage of that state's divorce law. Resuming her MAIDEN NAME, she worked from then on for the labor reforms of the Progressive Era, especially those for women and children.

Kelley's reports on the conditions of factories that she investigated were instrumental in the passage of state PROTECTIVE LEGISLATION that prohibited child labor, established maximum hours for women, and ended exploitation in Chicago sweatshops. Appointed by the governor as the state's first chief factory inspector from 1893 to 1897, she created an innovative office that incurred the wrath of capitalists accustomed to doing business without state interference. Meanwhile, she added to her credentials with a law degree from Northwestern in 1894.

When the next governor was not supportive of reform, Kelley moved back to the East Coast in 1899 to head the newly founded National Consumers League, with which she would be identified for the rest of her life. During the next two decades, she organized some sixty chapters all over the country made up of liberals, for the Consumers League pursued the goals of workers as intently as those of customers. She lived at LILLIAN WALD'S SETTLEMENT HOUSE, and along with League officers such as Dr. MARY PUTNAM JACOBI, Kelley sought to replicate nationally the sort of legislation that she had passed in Illinois.

She was a strong part of the legal team that won the 1908 *MULLER VS. OREGON* case on maximum hours; she worked for the creation of the federal Children's Bureau, which was first headed by her friend JULIA LATHROP; she lobbied for factory inspection and minimum wage laws that were passed by several states in this era. At the same time, Kelley also served as vice-president of the NATIONAL WOMAN SUFFRAGE LEAGUE and volunteered in suffrage campaigns from California to Georgia. In an 1898 speech to the national convention, she argued that working women needed the ballot more than any other class of people.

A lifelong contributor to magazines, especially the *Survey* and other sociological periodicals, she published *Some Ethical Gains through Legislation* (1905) and *Modern Industry* (1913). She was a founding member of both the NAACP and the WOMEN'S INTERNATIONAL LEAGUE FOR PEACE AND FREEDOM, opposed WORLD WAR I and deplored the regression of the postwar era that saw much of her hard-fought legislation struck down by the courts or ignored by governors.

Her last career victory came in 1921 with passage of the SHEPPARD-TOWNER ACT, which benefitted infants and their mothers. After that, Kelley had to deal with increasingly conservative governments. At the same time, she also felt constrained to oppose her former suffragist friends who supported the EQUAL RIGHTS AMENDMENT because it would have nullified the PROTECTIVE LEGISLATION for women that constituted her life's work.

Florence Kelley died the same year that her friends—Lathrop, MOLLY DEWSON, FRANCES PERKINS, and others—took

power with the election of Franklin Roosevelt; eventually they would implement her ideas into even stronger legislation.

KELLOR, FRANCES ALICE (1873–1952)

The daughter of a poor widow, Kellor was one of the exceptional women who actually benefited from the lack of accepted educational standards among nineteenth-century women, for her 1894 entrance examination scores at Cornell Law School were good enough that she was admitted without any higher education—or even a high school diploma. She earned her law degree in 1897 and then, in the reverse of the usual order, enrolled in the UNIVERSITY OF CHICAGO to study sociology.

Combining these two fields into a study of women criminals and the causes of crime, she wrote a series of articles on her investigations in 1901. Soon she was associated with the women of JANE ADDAMS' Hull House, and in 1905, moved with MARY DRIER to New York, where, with support from Drier's wealthy family, the two would work for the rest of their lives to ameliorate the causes of poverty, crime, and violence. Kellor, more than most of the Hull House women, also concerned herself with the problems of black women who migrated to the urban North from the agricultural South in this era.

The ideas behind her formation of the National League for the Protection of Colored Women in 1906 soon expanded into similar efforts on behalf of immigrants, and by 1908, Kellor was secretary of the New York State Immigration Commission. From that point, immigration became her sociological specialty, and Frances Kellor was a key factor in the development of immigration policy and programs during the years just before WORLD WAR I—when the nation saw its biggest waves of immigrants and its strongest "Americanization" programs.

Although she was sympathetic to immigrant needs and helped end much previous exploitation, Kellor's attitudes towards IMMIGRANT WOMEN nonetheless were arguably overprotective. Like other women of her mindset who worked for PROTECTIVE LEGISLATION, she saw most women as helpless, and immigrants as especially vulnerable to WHITE SLAVERY, while ignoring the strength and sophistication that many immigrant women had. She took pride, for example, in practices such as the detention of women who immigrated alone until they were called for by someone who accepted responsibility for them. Kellor, like other social workers of the time, devoted her life to protecting women rather than liberating them.

After World War I and its subsequent immigration quotas virtually ended the stream of newcomers, Kellor took up another field, and at age fifty-three, she cofounded and then became chief of the American Arbitration Association. In this capacity, she wrote an ethical code for arbitrators and tirelessly educated the public on the superiority of arbitration as a settlement procedure for disputes from the labor/management level to wars between nations.

Active politically before women could vote, she campaigned for Theodore Roosevelt in 1912, and—although she worked for Woodrow Wilson's opponent in 1916—she argued Wilson's agenda on behalf of the League of Nations and international justice systems after the war. Kellor wrote avidly on her causes, authoring and coauthoring more than a dozen books and countless articles, especially in the popular magazines of the Progressive Era. She published her last book on arbitration in 1948 and died at seventy-eight.

KELLY, FLORENCE FINCH (1858–1939)

Known primarily for her leading position with the *New York Times* book review section, Kelly's pursuit of a journalism career was long and earnest.

Like many other women of her era, Florence Finch worked as a TEACHER to earn the money for college. She graduated from the University of Kansas in 1881, and after traveling to San Francisco and Chicago in search of a decent job, she moved to Boston, where she worked without much reward for the *Globe* and other newspapers.

Unlike most women of her time, she continued to work after her 1884 marriage to journalist Allen P. Kelly, and together they explored newspaper opportunities in the Far West, including the *Los Angeles Times* and the *San Francisco Examiner.* The situation of women in journalism was clear, however, in that her work was published either anonymously or under PSEUDONYMS—even when her husband was the managing editor. She bore two children during this era, losing one at age four, and also wrote three novels during the 1890s.

Almost forty-eight when she became a WIDOW, Kelly returned to New York with her ten-year-old son. Despite her "quarter century of varied and successful work," she knew that "a forthright application . . . from any woman held a very slight chance of success" at the *Times.* She cagily wrote two letters-to-the-editor that met with favorable judgement, and then went in and identified herself to the editor. She walked away with four books to review.

The book review section, begun in 1896, was still the object of some hostility from conservatives who, as Kelly said, "wanted to keep literature as a sort of Sacred Cow feeding only in the well-fenced pastures of the learned." A strong supporter of publisher Adolph Ochs' attempt to "democratize" literature, Kelly annually read and reviewed hundreds of books. Most of them were nonfiction, and in holding the job between 1905 and 1936, she doubtless became one of the best-informed women in America. In addition to writing a regular column in the book review pages, Kelly also published a half-dozen books of both fiction and nonfiction and wrote articles other than book reviews for the *Times.* Nor was she merely a bookworm; Kelly campaigned for President Woodrow Wilson in Kansas, where women had the vote, in the election of 1916. She retired at seventy-eight, dying shortly after completion of her autobiography, *Flowing Stream* (1938). She wrote in its preface that "as far as I know, I had spent more years in newspaper offices than any other woman . . ."

KELLY, GRACE (1929–1982)

Grace Kelly's fairy tale life epitomized the dreams of most girls in the 1950s, for she found early fame as a film ACTRESS and then married a prince. A beautiful young woman whose bearing suited her name, she came to public attention in 1952 with *High Noon*, an acclaimed western. She won the Academy Award only two years later; made three chilling Hitchcock mysteries during 1954–1955; and then showed the diversity of her talent with a musical, *High Society* (1956).

Only four years after stardom, Kelly married Prince Rainier III of Monaco and went to live in that tiny but wealthy Mediterranean principality. Although she never again acted, she remained an international celebrity. She bore three children, one of whom survived the car crash that took the life of Princess Grace.

KEMBLE, FRANCES ANNE ("FANNY") (1809–1893)

Perhaps the first ACTRESS to gain a national following, Kemble was a London native who began acting in her father's Covent Gardens theater in 1829. An immediate success as Shakespeare's Juliet, she toured the U.S. with her father from 1832 to 1834. Kemble met and married a wealthy Southerner in 1834, by whom she bore two children. Never entirely happy with him and his conservative family, she wrote poetry, publishing a volume in 1844, and kept diaries. The one she kept during 1838–1839 became influential when she published it decades later to aid ABOLITION: *Journal of a Residence on a Georgian Plantation* (1863) was the sort of direct-experience information on slavery that was most helpful, especially in influencing British opinion. Her independent attitudes and especially her opposition to slavery was a factor in when Kemble left her husband in 1846. He obtained a DIVORCE three years later on the grounds of desertion and kept the GUARDIANSHIP of their children, as was customary at the time.

She supported herself thereafter with Shakespearean readings that proved continually popular and the writing of a dozen volumes of poems, essays and plays. Reunited with her children after their father's 1867 death, Kemble moved easily across the Atlantic, with homes in London and in Massachusetts. She published her autobiography in three volumes from 1879 to 1891.

One of the first women to achieve celebrity in both the U.S. and Europe, Kemble is important to FEMINISTS not only for her independent lifestyle but also for her early role in DRESS REFORM; it was AMELIA BLOOMER's 1849 defense of Kemble's fashion innovation that drew attention to the new garment.

KEYS, MARTHA ELIZABETH LUDWIG (1930–   )

The first woman in Congress to marry a colleague, Keys' political career began as the Kansas coordinator for the 1972 campaign of presidential nominee George McGovern. With that base, she was elected to Congress from the Topeka area in 1974. While serving on the powerful Ways and Means Committee, Keys became acquainted with Andrew Jacobs, a congressman from Indiana, and married him in 1975. In the first commuter marriage of congressional coequals, they habitually flew together to Indianapolis on weekends and then she took the plane on to Kansas City.

Her marriage seemed to be accepted by her constituents and she was reelected in 1976. In 1978, however, she was unable to overcome the well-funded negative campaign of the Republican man who targeted her. With Keys carrying the urban portions of her district while her opponent took the rural areas, it was one of the closest and most bitter elections of that year and presaged the Reagan landslide of the next election.

Keys served briefly as Assistant Secretary of Education until the Reagan election and now works as a consultant.

KIRCHWEY, FREDA (1893–1976)

As PUBLISHER and editor of *The Nation* from 1937 to 1955, Kirchwey molded the views of the nation's opinionmakers.

Born in New York, she graduated from BARNARD COLLEGE in 1915 and worked for two periodicals before joining the *Nation* in 1919. She rose steadily there, going from a job that she described as "clipping, but not reading the news" to international news editor and finally managing editor in 1922. As the country turned to the right after WORLD WAR I, *The Nation* intensified its leftist stance, ultimately becoming the most influential liberal weekly. The magazine also noted the liberating social changes that accompanied the reactionary political changes of the Roaring Twenties, and managing editor Kirchwey even published a series of anonymous articles by women about their personal sexual experiences. The series was published as a book, *Our Changing Morality* (1925).

The 1932 election of Franklin Roosevelt meant adoption of many of the reforms *The Nation* had urged a decade earlier, which brought the magazine even more influence among the country's leading intellectuals and policymakers. Kirchwey supported the New Deal during the thirties, but again also crusaded for a futuristic view, arguing that *The Nation* "will continue to be anti-isolationist as long as it continues under my management." Clearly retaining her initial interests as international editor, Kirchwey editorials predicted the problems that would result from the unchecked growth of fascism throughout Europe and Asia.

When *The Nation's* longtime owner and editor in chief, Oswald Garrison Villard, retired in 1935, he sold the magazine to a New York banker. Within two years, however, the new owner was so distraught by the magazine's editorial views that Kirchwey was able to buy him out. In 1937, she thus became the only woman PUBLISHER of a national magazine.

H.L. Mencken referred to Kirchwey as "another wild woman," but it was her editorial vision that became reality as the U.S. retained the liberal reforms of the New Deal and fought off fascism during the next decade. Despite the sagacity of her editorial predictions, however, her position as one of the country's most visible liberals meant that Kirchwey could expect trouble from the right-wingers who dominated the Senate during the McCarthy era, but she survived the crisis and did not retire until it had passed.

Though Freda Kirchwey kept her personal life quite separate from her public persona, she had married a few months after graduation in 1915. She retained her MAIDEN NAME, while also bearing three children and losing two in childhood deaths. Her remaining son left Harvard to volunteer as an ambulance driver for the British before America entered WORLD WAR II.

Kirchwey retired in 1955 and lived in Switzerland before dying at eighty-two in a Florida nursing home.

KITT, EARTHA (1928–) An entertainer who became popular in the 1950s, Eartha Kitt's name is forever linked with one political incident in 1968.

Like JOSEPHINE BAKER and other black women, Kitt's talents were first recognized in Europe. She was born in extreme poverty in South Carolina; when she was abandoned by her parents at eight, an aunt brought her to Harlem. She dropped out of school there at fourteen to sew Army uniforms in a WORLD WAR II factory, and used her savings for music lessons. A dancing scholarship brought a job with a traveling troupe, and Kitt toured Latin America in the first year after the war

ended. In 1948, she went to Europe with the troupe, and there Kitt found stardom.

In both London and Paris, her individualistic singing style made her a nightclub favorite. Nor were her talents limited to the musical; in 1952, Orson Welles recruited her on two days notice to play Helen of Troy—and the performance in Paris was well reviewed. Gifted in languages, Kitt had picked up Spanish from her Puerto Rican neighbors in Harlem, and in Europe, she added French and German.

Returning to the U.S. in 1952, Kitt's initial debut was not successful, but she soon turned that around. She signed a record contract with RCA and by 1954, was earning as much as ten thousand dollars a week in Las Vegas. At the time, she was largely apolitical, describing herself as a "conservative Democrat." By the sixties, however, that had changed, as Kitt became active with low-income youth in Washington, D.C., initially teaching them dance and then moving on to political action.

In 1967, she testified to Congress on juvenile delinquency, seeking funds for recreational activities for her "Rebels with a Cause." In response, President Johnson named her to a Citizens Advisory Committee on Youth Opportunity, and shortly thereafter, she was invited to a January 18, 1968 "Women Doers' Luncheon" at the White House.

Kitt clearly believed that she had been invited for genuine discussion of the views of black youth. When, however, she stood to denounce the Vietnam War as a factor in creating anger among young people, the ladies at the luncheon were scandalized at her candor. For days, publicity focused on what was portrayed as Kitt's breach of good manners with the president and First Lady. In the turmoil of the times, Eartha Kitt became controversial far beyond any actual offense committed.

The debate was renewed in 1975, when it was revealed that the CIA had kept Kitt under surveillance since 1956. The dossier also included information from the FBI, Secret Service, and National Security Agencies, all of whom had forwarded their files to the White House after Kitt's speech. Kitt believed that her career was seriously damaged by the innuendo and baseless slander that resulted from what she saw as bureaucratic paranoia about a successful black woman—and it is true that she seldom performed thereafter. In 1992, however, she attempted a well-publicized comeback in New York.

Kitt has written two autobiographies, *Thursday's Child* (1956) and *Alone With Me* (1976).

KLOCK, FRANCES (1844–1908) One of the three first women elected to any legislative body in the United States, Klock won election to the Colorado House of Representatives in 1894—twenty-six years before most American women got the vote. Colorado passed a state SUFFRAGE referendum in 1893, and both the Republican and Populist parties organized women's divisions for the first election in which women could vote; Democratic women, in the minority, organized themselves into twelve clubs, even though "there was no chance of electing their ticket."

Like many WESTERN WOMEN, Klock was a liberal Republican. In addition to her two colleagues in the legislature, another Republican woman was elected as superintendent of public instruction. Two years later, Colorado women built on their success, electing three more women to the legislature, all of them from minor parties.

KNIGHT, SARAH KEMBLE (1666–1727)

Like other FRONTIER WOMEN, Sarah Knight exhibited bravery and resourcefulness that is not commonly attributed to women. In the still-primitive TRAVEL conditions of the early eighteenth Century, she undertook a journey that would have been deemed too difficult for women a century later—after transportation systems had improved, but also after definitions of appropriate female behavior had rigidified.

Knight was thirty-eight and the mother of a teenage daughter when she rode a horse from Boston to New York and back during the fall and winter of 1704–1705. She made the trip primarily to settle the estate of a relative, but there is little in her diary that explains why the business was so imperative that she undertook traveling alone with winter coming. She apparently was eager to travel, and though the trip was dangerous, her journal gives no indication that her "aged and tender mother" or anyone else objected. Presumably they were accustomed to her independent behavior, for Knight's husband was an agent for a London business and lived primarily there, while she "kept a shop," worked as a TEACHER, and ran a small BOARDING HOUSE.

Her diary contains almost no mention of her husband or other family; instead, it is a travel record replete with fording icy rivers, searching in gathering darkness for shelter, and sometimes being met with inhospitable attitudes and bad food. Nonetheless, Knight's journal is marked by good humor, as, for example, her inability to get potential guides to move from a tavern: "they, being tyed by the Lipps to a pewter engine . . ."

She mocked everything from bedbugs to the strange speech of non-Bostonians, for American colonies were then almost as alien to each other as European countries could be. She wrote, for example, "wee . . . come to New Rochell a french town." She was entertained by the local elite in several towns, but Knight did not limit herself to mere observation of societal mannerisms; she carefully recorded information about business and the economy and even the architectural details of construction. Transportation systems were spelled out, too, as, for example, between New York and New Haven when snow covered the ground and she saw "50 or 60 slays . . . so furious that they'le turn out of the path for none except a Loaden Cart."

Though she was gone from October to March, the welcome she received upon returning seemed more friendly than anxious. Presumably her contemporaries understood that women were capable of more than would be considered appropriate later on, when SUSAN ANTHONY, DOROTHEA DIX, and the few other women who dared to travel alone by stagecoach or railroad found themselves not only reproached by their peers, but questioned by innkeepers who assumed that any woman without an escort was of dubious virtue.

A WIDOW after about 1706, Sarah Knight moved with her daughter and son-in-law to Connecticut in 1714. She was a shopkeeper there also and invested in land, leaving a valuable estate when she died. Her daughter (who by then was a childless widow) died less than a decade later, and Knight's diary was forgotten until almost a century after her death. *The Journal of Madam Knight* was published in 1825 and has been reissued many times since.

KNOPF, BLANCHE WOLF (1894–1966)

The daughter of a prosperous Jewish family in New York, Blanche Wolf had a privileged upbringing with GOVERNESSES who gave her easy facility in foreign languages. Her cultural background did not encourage COLLEGE for women, however, and she was married in 1916 to Alfred Knopf, a family friend whose background was similar to her own.

Together they built the Knopf publishing enterprises—though the firm's name was Alfred A. Knopf. Blanche Knopf bore one child, who was cared for by a NURSE, while she devoted herself full time to business. With the title of vice-president from 1921, she aggressively pursued building a book list by authors whose work would appeal to the new literary tastes and changed values of the post–WORLD WAR I era.

An uncommonly active PUBLISHER, she traveled extensively to meet with her AUTHORS, entertaining them lavishly to assure their loyalty to Knopf. H.L. Mencken's diaries, for example, are replete with mentions of weekends at the Knopf country estate and of pleasant lunches with Blanche (and sometimes, though less often, with Alfred). Much more prescient than others about world trends, she said in July, 1936, "there is not a German writer left in Germany who is worth thinking about." The gifted writers and enterprising publishers, she predicted, would not be able to live with fascism. Her uncommon perceptions about the future led to such profitable acquisitions as, for example, William L. Shirer's *Berlin Diary*, which Knopf published early in 1941. The book earned the publishing house $1.5 million in that single year.

When WORLD WAR II cut off her ability to work with Europeans, Blanche Knopf creatively sought Latin American writers. Though the majority of her authors were men (including Freud, Camus, Sartre, and Kahlil Gibran), she also recruited women such as WILLA CATHER, ANNE O'HARE MCCORMICK, and FANNIE HURST in this country and Nobel winners Sigrid Undset and Simone de Beauvior abroad. The latter illustrates Knopf's understanding of the importance of diversification and her willingness to work with many sorts of personalities, for de Beauvior held leftist political views, while Mencken, for a contrary example, was a right-winger.

The Knopf firm also set publishing standards in design quality, advertising, and promotion, and Blanche Knopf paid close attention to her authors' views of potential markets. It was her uncanny ability to foresee trends, however, that was the key to Knopf's success. The result was that the company enjoyed multimillion dollar annual sales, with several bestsellers of over a million copies as well as a dozen Nobel Prize winners.

Meanwhile, their marriage deteriorated to the point that they were barely civil to each other. Doubtless Blanche Knopf resented the way that the "Alfred A. Knopf" corporate name obscured her genuine role. In addition, the business end of publishing historically has been slow to adapt to changes in other areas of life, and part of that pattern was Blanche Knopf's exclusion from professional organizations and social clubs that her husband was invited to join. She once expressed her bitterness about these gender limitations by refusing an invitation to speak at a women's college on the future of women in publishing; there as "no future worth mentioning" she said in reply.

In 1957, Alfred Knopf assumed the title of chairman of the board, while she became corporate president. Presumably tired of the competition between his parents, their son left Knopf to found another firm in 1959. Shocked, his parents sold their company to Random House the following year, and Blanche Knopf died in her sleep six years later.

She not only succeeded at the top of a world in which discrimination against women was an accepted part of business relationships, but she also discovered and introduced to the American public some of the world's most important literature. For this, Blanche Knopf was recognized with the French Legion of Honor, while the government of Brazil expressed its appreciation for her unusual interest in Latin American writers by awarding her the National Order of the Southern Cross.

KNOX, ROSE MARKWARD (1857–1950) A woman of exceptional business acumen, Rose Knox founded the Knox Gelatine Company with her husband, but the company was under her management for more than a half-century.

Rose Markward was employed in the GARMENT INDUSTRY sewing gloves when she met glove salesman Charles Knox. They married in 1883, and seven years later, used their joint savings to establish the Knox Gelatine Company in Johnstown, New York.

Gelatine was not part of standard American diets when they began their company in 1890. Diaries and cookbooks of that and earlier times make it clear that "jellies" were considered more nearly a medicinal offering to convalescents than a food to be enjoyed by healthy people. Rose Knox popularized the increased use of gelatine by testing recipes and publishing a cookbook, *Dainty Desserts*, in 1896.

Friends advised her to sell out when, in 1908, she became a WIDOW with two sons still in school. Her decision to "take over" perhaps was not as momentous as it seemed to her advisers, who probably were unaware of how strong a role she already played in a business that they assumed belonged to her husband. In less than a decade, Rose Knox demonstrated her independent ability by tripling the corporate income. Much like MIRIAM LESLIE, she cut off less profitable enterprises that had interested her husband (a racehorse named Gelatine, for example) and concentrated on quality manufacturing of one product.

She redirected the approach of her advertising agents, too, running ads that emphasized sanitation, cost efficiency, and nutritious recipes under the banner of "Mrs. Knox Says." During WORLD WAR I, when food conservation was a timely topic, she issued another promotional book, *Food Economy* (1917). Both it and *Dainty Desserts* had distribution figures of more than a million copies by mid-century. A model of enlightened management, Knox invested heavily in research, and by 1950, 40 percent of Knox gelatine was utilized in nonfood products of an industrial or medicinal nature.

Perhaps most importantly, Knox treated her employees unusually well. When she took over, she ordered the factory's rear entrance closed, saying to her employees, "We are all ladies and gentlemen working together here, and we'll all

come in through the front door." She offered paid vacations, sick leave, pensions, and a five-day week decades before those benefits became standard. The result was not only uncommon loyalty to the company (*Time* reported in 1937 that 85 percent of Knox employees had been there for twenty-five years), but also prosperity so solid that Knox was one of the few American companies that did not lay off a single employee during the Great Depression.

In 1929, Knox became the first woman elected to the board of directors of the Grocery Manufacturers' Association. She personally supervised the company until age eighty-eight, turning over the presidency to her son at ninety. Even then, he said of her in 1949, "She still runs things . . . She comes up with more bright ideas in a day than the rest of us produce in a month." Rose Knox was a life member of the BUSINESS AND PROFESSIONAL WOMEN'S CLUBS and died at ninety-three.

KOONTZ, ELIZABETH DUNCAN (1919–1989) The first African-American to become president of the National Education Association, Elizabeth Duncan grew up as the child of North Carolina TEACHERS. A product of segregated schools, she began teaching in 1938. Her assignment of special education classes brought daily challenge in attempting to teach the most difficult students in the most underfunded of settings.

In 1940, Duncan was fired from a North Carolina school for protesting the high rent that teachers were charged in a boardinghouse where the school required them to live. Armed with a master's degree earned in Atlanta the following year, she returned to North Carolina and an increasingly successful teaching career. She did graduate work outside of the South and married a colleague, Harry Koontz, in 1947.

When black teachers were permitted to join the North Carolina affiliate of the National Education Association in 1952, Koontz soon became active in her local chapter. Her colleagues were so impressed with her warm personality and her devotion to students that she moved steadily up the ranks of the teachers' association during the fifties and sixties. In 1967, she was elected president at the NEA's 106th national convention.

It was a historic change, not only because of her race and gender, but also because Koontz represented a change in NEA's power structure. After a century of domination by (usually male) administrators, the classroom teachers within the organization revolted. With a million members, the NEA was the "largest professional organization of any kind in the world," and some observers deemed Koontz's election as indicative of a "sharp turn toward liberal activism." She confirmed this when she took office the following year and called for "teacher power" in educational policymaking as well as for better salaries. When teachers in almost four hundred localities threatened to strike in 1968, Koontz not only supported them, but added, "We should have spoken out sooner."

She cut short her NEA presidency in 1969, when President Richard Nixon offered Koontz the first appointment he gave an African-American. She headed the Women's Bureau of the Department of Labor (a position first held by MARY ANDERSON) until 1973, the year that Nixon resigned. Afterwards, Koontz held high-level educational positions in North Carolina and was a delegate to the United Nations Commission on the

Status of Women. She received honorary degrees from approximately thirty colleges as well as numerous other awards. Libby Koontz died at sixty-nine.

KUHN, MARGARET "MAGGIE" (1905–) The

founder of the Gray Panthers, Maggie Kuhn spent a lifetime in social work for the YOUNG WOMEN'S CHRISTIAN ASSOCIATION and other organizations devoted to social needs, especially those of women. Both this and her editorship of *Social Progress* magazine equipped her well for the role she developed late in life as a leader in the movement to improve the status of older people.

She began that career after mandatory retirement from the United Presbyterian Church, which had employed her until age seventy. The following year, she spoke at the White House Conference on Aging, where the term "Gray Panthers" was applied to senior activists whose politics resembled that of the era's African-Americans who called themselves the Black Panthers. The first objective of the Gray Panthers was passage of legislation to improve conditions in nursing homes.

Kuhn's books, *Get Out There and Do Something About Injustice* (1972) and *Maggie Kuhn on Aging* (1977) became rallying cries for senior citizen activism. Like RUTH BENEDICT's invention of the word "racism," Kuhn coined "ageism" to denote discrimination based on age. Still active beyond her eighty-fifth year, she published an autobiography, *No Stone Unturned*, in 1991.

KUNIN, MADELINE MAY (1933–) A Jew born in

the haven of Switzerland in the era that saw the rise of Nazism, Madeline May rose to be a governor.

She escaped to the U.S. at age six with her WIDOWED mother just before Europe erupted into WORLD WAR II. Like other IMMIGRANT WOMEN, Mrs. May worked in the GARMENT INDUSTRY and taught French to support her two children. They moved to Massachusetts when Madeline was a teenager, and she worked her way through the University of Massachusetts at Amherst. After earning a master's degree at the Columbia University School of Journalism in 1957, she married physician Arthur Kunin in 1959 and mothered four children while remaining involved with public issues through the LEAGUE OF WOMEN VOTERS.

In 1972, Madeline Kunin was elected to the Vermont legislature and rose there quickly, chairing the powerful Appropriations Committee by 1976. She became lieutenant governor in a close race two years later, winning by 50.6 percent, and then made an unsuccessful bid for the governorship in 1982. She ran again two years later and defeated the male Republican, who had been attorney general, by a tiny margin—only sixty votes over the legal minimum. Polls showed that it was Republican women who provided that margin, for although Vermont had elected occasional Democrats in the sixties and seventies, it is a traditionally Republican area, and Kunin, an active Democrat, also had to overcome the popular coattails of Ronald Reagan in this 1984 election. She was the first woman and first Jew elected governor of the state.

In her first two-year term, Kunin managed to erase the state's $35 million deficit, increase the education budget by 25 percent, and pass strong environmental legislation. Nonetheless, she had a tough reelection fight in 1986 because a Socialist candidate diverted Democratic votes. She chaired the New England Governors Conference in 1987 and won a third term in 1988. She retired from the governorship in 1990, after achieving legislation on social and environmental issues.

KUSHNER, ROSE (1930–1990) A psychologist and

medical writer, Rose Kushner changed medical practices for women after she became ill with breast cancer. *Why Me? What Every Woman Should Know About Breast Cancer to Save Her Life* (1975) was about her personal fight against this illness. During the fifteen years of her life that remained, she continued to work for more thoughtful treatment of the disease.

Though her book was initially scorned by physicians, they were adopting her approach within a decade. Kushner played a major role in reducing the number of radical mastectomies, instead emphasizing chemotherapy and radiation, as well as developing public awareness of the disease.

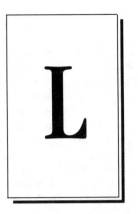

LADIES HOME JOURNAL One of the most successful magazines in the history of American publishing, *LHJ* began in 1883 under the ownership of Cyrus Curtis. His wife, Louisa Knapp Curtis, had edited the women's supplement of a farm magazine, and when it became clear that the supplement was more popular than the parent magazine, they developed *Ladies Home Journal*. She continued as editor while he worked the business side of the magazine, and they soon demonstrated that there was a large potential market for a magazine that differed from the long-time *GODEY'S LADIES BOOK*.

Readers responded to their efforts to recruit the era's popular women AUTHORS; women such as Marion Harland, a bestseller in her day who is forgotten now, attracted more than 270,000 subscribers within three years. Curtis also courted well-known women authors, as for example, when he got LOUISA MAY ALCOTT to join *LHJ's* "List of Famous Contributors" by making a donation to her favorite charity. Even though the magazine's fifty-cent annual subscription price was considered high, women judged the quality of its articles and fiction to be so good that they began paying one dollar a year in 1889, and the circulation of four hundred thousand continued to climb.

Louisa Knapp Curtis retired that same year to spend more time with her children, and *LHJ* thereafter would be linked with the editorship of Edward Bok. A Dutch immigrant, Bok's feeling for women was largely limited to his mother, with the result that the magazine thereafter presented a more idealized view of women. Even after his marriage to a daughter of founding editor Louisa Knapp Curtis, Bok continued to be an object of ridicule among other journalists, who saw him as self-righteous and egocentric. Nonetheless, he had sufficient feeling for what women wanted to read that *LHJ* would win the competition with *Godey's* and become the major publication read monthly by American women.

The magazine had regular columns written by women, as well as features by some of the most famous writers of the era. Even Mark Twain was published in the pages of *Ladies Home Journal*—albeit after careful editing. Other Bok innovations included a refusal to accept certain kinds of advertising and the publication of music, architectural drawings, and other nonverbal information. By 1903, *LHJ* had passed the million-subscriber goal that Curtis/Knapp had set at its beginning two decades earlier.

The secret to its success seemed to be balance, for many kinds of women could find appealing articles in its pages. A 1900 article advised women to stay away from office work, for example, with the warning that women lacked the stamina to deal with the nervous strain of business—but only a few years later, the same magazine published HELEN KELLER's first article, a pioneering piece on neonatal blindness. This was an important taboo-breaker, for this birth defect usually was due to parental venereal disease. Indeed, Bok lost thousands of subscribers for publishing this and other articles advocating sex education. At the same time, women viewed the magazine as so personal a part of their lives that by WORLD WAR I, *LHJ* editors received almost a million letters annually from readers.

Many in the publication industry considered *LHJ* to be the "most valuable magazine property in the world" when Bok resigned in 1919—just as the Roaring Twenties brought tremendous changes in women's lives. Probably as a result, circulation declined until the middle of the Great Depression, when a second husband/wife team of PUBLISHERS replicated the early success of Curtis and Knapp. Beatrice Gould and her husband Bruce succeeded in turning around the magazine's declining fortunes—much as MIRIAM LESLIE had done when faced with a similar situation. By running articles that reflected women's concerns outside of the domestic world, they brought readers back.

Especially during WORLD WAR II, *LHJ* published more articles that reflected women's changed roles than the era's "liberal" magazines. It included topics that other magazines ignored, as for example, ELIZABETH JANEWAY's piece on war WIDOWS. At the same time, balance was the key: the magazine's resident conservative in this era, a physician and retired naval officer, published his monthly column a few pages away from the brilliantly FEMINIST observations of *LHJ* editor DOROTHY THOMPSON.

In the 1950s, *LHJ*, like most other magazines, concentrated on the home and family issues that absorbed the postwar world—and again, circulation dropped. In 1968, with *LHJ*'s profitability falling under male editorship, Curtis Publishing sold its eighty-five-year-old erstwhile star. The new editors continued to back off from the kind of article that Dorothy Thompson would have published until, in 1970, a group of feminist employees staged a rebellion at *LHJ*. After they laid seige to offices, the publishers agreed to a special section written by feminists. The staffs of other magazines emulated these women with similar in-house revolts, and the result was a changed tone throughout the print media by the end of that decade.

LADIES MAGAZINE— *See GODEY'S LADY'S BOOK*

"LADY MANAGERS, BOARDS OF" As the nation's hospitals developed during the mid-nineteenth century, they were often run by a "Board of Lady Managers" or other similarly-titled group.

Medical care—such as it was—took place in the home during the first century or two of American settlement. The first hospital was not founded until 1751, and even then, many communities took decades to follow this precedent of Philadelphia QUAKERS. Instead, most health care was provided by informally trained women at home, with this NURSING supplemented in dire cases by physicians (also often barely trained) who came to the patient's home. Even when they developed, hospitals were frequently seen as hopeless asylums where dying indigents were callously practiced upon by medical students. Especially among immigrants, this view remained until the twentieth century.

The CIVIL WAR gave many Americans their first experience with hospitals, and similar emergencies provided the motivation for others. Epidemics demonstrated the practicality of combining patients who could more easily be cared for by those brave nurses (and the relatively fewer physicians) who did not flee. The sick would be housed in the largest available home—and continuation as a hospital after the epidemic was over was a natural result. In the South, for example, many of today's hospitals can trace their roots to yellow fever.

The women who nursed communities through such epidemics and those who donated bedding, food, and other supplies for the quarantine quite naturally assumed the management of these small hospitals. As they grew, however, they tended to repeat a pattern of disputes between the era's practitioners of holistic, osteopathic, and other variations of medicine and the "regular" physicians, who were graduates of newly standardized medical schools. Beyond that, there were the expected disagreements between the male physicians and the "lady managers" who actually owned the hospital's facilities. In Tampa, for example, the physicians ended up organizing their wives as a rival Board of Lady Managers that ultimately voted out the women who had been the hospital's original founders.

What is important to remember, however, is that in an era when health care was seen as a charity rather than a business, it was often women who cared enough to build many of the nation's hospitals. As these institutions became successful, physicians and other profit-minded males tended to take them over, pushing aside the "lady managers" who had overcome the obstacles to found the institutions.

LA LECHE LEAGUE An international organization devoted to the promotion of breast-feeding, La Leche is a Spanish phrase referring to mother's milk. The league was founded in 1956 at about the same time as the LAMAZE MOVEMENT. Both aimed at reasserting the natural aspects of mothering and returning to women some of the control that physicians had assumed over female patients and their babies.

Until the late nineteenth century, BREAST-FEEDING was routine; if a mother was unable or unwilling to nurse her baby, a WET NURSE was brought in. When pasteurization and refrigeration made it possible to safely feed infants forms of milk other than mother's milk, many women were encouraged by their physicians to adopt bottle-feeding as "more scientific." By the 1920s, increasing numbers of mothers had their breasts bound after delivery to dry up their milk, and adopted the bottle-feeding method. Especially in the urban areas, bottle-feeding was routine by the forties, and by the sixties, almost all women had abandoned breast-feeding.

The La Leche League intended to reverse this trend, and especially after the revitalization of the women's movement in the 1970s, was very successful at doing so—despite heavy discouragement from baby supply companies and others with a financial investment in the past methodology. La Leche was especially important in informing women about new research showing the beneficial effects of breast-feeding for mothers in prevention of breast cancer, and that it benefited infants with natural immunizations and other health-promoting substances that could not be replicated in artificial products.

With woman-to-woman organizing, La Leche overcame resistance from those who saw breasts as the sex symbol that they had become since the movie industry and DRESS REFORM changes of the 1920s, as well as from physicians and others whose mindset saw bottle-feeding as a scientific advancement. As more and more contrary evidence developed, La Leche's message found increasing acceptance.

With forty thousand members from forty-eight countries headquartered in suburban Chicago and a budget of $2 million, La Leche now places its emphasis on Third World countries, where it works to discourage the bottle-feeding that is promoted by multinational corporations.

LAMAZE MOVEMENT A method of childbirth that concentrates on relaxation techniques rather than painkilling drugs, the Lamaze movement began in France and was imported to the U.S. in the 1950s. The Childbirth Without Pain Education Association was headquartered in Detroit by 1958, and by the time that the women's movement revived in the early 1970s, Lamaze classes were developed in almost every urban center. Initially, patients trained in the technique were often treated with hostility by physicians and other medical personnel, and women had to seek out cooperative doctors and hospitals. Gaining acceptance required that both pregnant women and medical personnel understand the history of childbirth in America.

Until after WORLD WAR I, most babies were born at home and most mothers went through labor with little or no medication, often with only a female friend or a MIDWIFE to assist. Hospitalization for childbirth became more common during the 1920s before dropping off again as the economic pressures of the Depression and then WORLD WAR II excluded women from hospitals. With the postwar baby boom, however, physicians increasingly treated childbirth as a surgical procedure rather than a natural event, hospitalizing mothers for a week and giving them general anesthetics during labor that left the woman unconscious and unable to participate in or experience her baby's birth. Moreover, the infants themselves were born sedated, sometimes at appreciable risk to their lives.

The Lamaze method is aimed at reasserting women's active role in childbirth by educating them as to what will occur during the various stages of labor and delivery. Expectant mothers are taught relaxation methods that divert attention from pain, with a special emphasis on breathing techniques. In addition to training the patient, Lamaze classes teach a "coach" or "monitrice" who assists the expectant mother through childbirth. So many women found the method effective that they told others, and Lamaze classes quickly spread throughout the nation. With a staff of about a dozen and a frugal budget, the headquarters remains in Detroit, where it makes available films, books, and lecturers who teach both lay and medical groups.

LANDERS, ANN— *See* FRIEDMAN, ESTHER PAULINE

LANDES, BERTHA ETHEL KNIGHT (1868–1949) The first woman mayor of a major U.S. city, Landes serves as an example of the exceptional achievements of WESTERN WOMEN.

Bertha Landes was a professor's wife who was active in the CLUB MOVEMENT during the WORLD WAR I era. She moved from the presidency of the Seattle Woman's Century Club to its city council in 1921, the year after passage of the NINETEENTH AMENDMENT. Her council candidacy was strongly supported by her club, and the effectiveness of these women in their new political venture was clear when she won by the greatest number of votes ever cast.

She quickly rose to become president of the city council, which made her the acting mayor in 1924 when the mayor went out of town. Landes took advantage of his absence to fire the (probably corrupt) police chief, thus drawing the voters' attention to the need to clean up city government and close down illegal gambling and other vice that police ignored in return for payoffs. With those issues as her platform, she won the 1926 election and became mayor of Seattle.

Landes was a Republican who was supportive of the PROHIBITION laws that were in effect during the twenties under Republican presidents, but Prohibition and other restraints on personal freedom were unpopular in the frontier traditions of the Far West. Although her two-year term was marked by honest and efficient government that produced increased city revenue, her moral crusade was not what Seattle voters truly wanted, and women's experience in politics was still so new that Landes had not yet learned the political skills needed to justify her cause and maintain her position. Though she was endorsed by labor as well as by the city's newspapers, she lost the 1928 election.

Landes turned sixty the year that she was defeated and did not try again. She remained active, however, and served a term as president of the state LEAGUE OF WOMEN VOTERS before dying at seventy-five.

LANGDON, GRACE (1889–?) With years of experience in preschool education, Dr. Grace Langdon became the first head of a federal agency designed for the care of children of working mothers. As child care director of the Works Projects Administration from its beginning in 1933, she served the needs of very poor women during the Great Depression.

Organized child care itself was still somewhat novel at the time, and the idea of *publicly provided* care for preschool children is not entirely accepted even today. Thus, Langdon's establishment of some two thousand WPA child care nurseries (with at least one in every state) was an accomplishment of extraordinary bureaucratic skill. These nurseries not only gave mothers a better opportunity to compete in the limited labor market of the era, but also provided employment for other women.

When WORLD WAR II began, the need for child care was obvious to employers, who—in a reverse of the previous decade's situation—were competing for the labor of women to staff the huge industrial complex that developed to build the materiel to win the war. Langdon's WPA network, however, was seen as a vestige of times better forgotten and was abolished in 1943. When other agencies were established to address the need, Dr. Langdon was passed over for inexperienced young men who headed these better-funded programs. Susan B. Anthony II wrote at the time, "I don't want to sound immoderately feminist . . . but Dr. Langdon . . . was the *only* qualified person for the job in the entire Federal Government. Failure to appoint her was clear-cut discrimination."

Dr. Langdon nonetheless continued with the federal government, working on child care when that was a critical wartime need. She retired in 1946, a year after the war ended, and resumed her academic career. Langdon wrote a number of books on children during the fifties and sixties, and after 1948, syndicated a newspaper column. Her doctorate was from the prestigious Teachers College of Columbia University, and she retained her MAIDEN NAME when she married in 1936.

LANE, ROSE WILDER (1886–1968)

The daughter of LAURA INGALLS WILDER, Rose Wilder Lane achieved recognition as an AUTHOR before her more famous mother did.

Rose Wilder was born in the Dakota prairie that her mother later beautifully depicted, but grew up in the Missouri Ozarks. A pioneer like her parents and grandparents, she moved on to California, where she married in 1909. She DIVORCED her unambitious husband less than a decade later, but retained his name—an ambiguity that is key to her personality, for Lane's work would celebrate domesticity, even though she never remarried nor became a mother.

She found considerable success in real estate, but it was writing that Lane wanted to do. She published her first novel in 1923, while establishing herself as a nationally known writer for the *San Francisco Bulletin* and later at *Sunset* magazine. She was thus in a position to act as editor and literary agent for her mother when Wilder's first book, *Little House on the Prairie*, appeared in 1932. Indeed, some have charged that Lane went well beyond editorial suggestions to "substantially rewrite" her mother's work.

If so, she never claimed any credit while her mother's reputation eclipsed her own, nor was it apparent in Lane's independent career. She continued to write for magazines, especially *Women's Day*, for the rest of her life. She TRAVELED widely, living several years in Albania during the 1920s and going to Vietnam as a reporter when she was seventy-nine. She also wrote from her parents' Missouri home, and it was there that she produced her best-known book, *Let the Hurricane Roar* (1933), a story of pioneer life in the tradition of her mother. Her final home was in Danbury, Connecticut, where she died at eighty-one.

Despite this relatively long life, she outlived her mother by only a little more than a decade. Indeed, Lane arguably belonged to her mother's era, for she was an ardent advocate of the individualistic, risk-taking values of WESTERN WOMEN and, as the interdependency of the twentieth century grew, her opinions sounded increasingly dated. The result is that her views—from opposition to the New Deal to support of the Vietnam War—are easily dismissed as excessively conservative, but her words were belied by her liberated life.

LANGE, DOROTHEA (1895–1965)

Famous for her photographs of the Great Depression, Lange had known from childhood that she intended to be a photographer.

Brought up by her librarian mother after her attorney father deserted the family, Lange was crippled in one leg from polio suffered at age seven. Though trained as a TEACHER, she had no interest in that profession, and in 1918, after briefly studying photography at Columbia, she escaped her native New York City area for San Francisco. She married there two years later, but kept her MAIDEN NAME; during the next decade, Lange not only bore two children but also established herself so well as a portrait photographer that she provided the major share of the family income.

When the Roaring Twenties were over, she was sufficiently well connected that her clientele continued despite the Great Depression. Like MARGARET BOURKE-WHITE, however, Lange's personal success did not make her indifferent to the sufferings of others during this difficult time. Her sensitivity in capturing the emotions of the unemployed—especially of the white-

Although not as well known as "Migrant Mother," this 1937 Texas photograph by Dorothea Lange demonstrates her ability to capture the feelings of women who were psychologically scarred by the Great Depression.
LIBRARY OF CONGRESS; FARM SECURITY ADMINISTRATION, PHOTOGRAPH BY DOROTHEA LANGE.

collar men to whom unemployment was a shock—resulted in a 1934 exhibition. This led to her employment by the New Deal's Farm Security Administration to record the lives of farm workers on film. Along with John Steinbeck, she introduced Americans to the unhappy condition of the women, men, and children who produced the food that nurtured the nation.

She collaborated in this work with economist Paul Taylor, and in 1935, they DIVORCED their respective spouses and married. Lange retained her name, and Taylor never overwhelmed her individual reputation. They did several projects together, the best known of which is *American Exodus: A Record of Human Erosion* (1939). Lange's exceptional photos were acclaimed by both critics and the public, and her work was widely reproduced in books and magazines.

In 1941, Lange became the first woman to receive a Guggenheim Fellowship. After the nation entered WORLD WAR II at the end of that year, she moved on to document another oppressed group. Under the aegis of the War Relocation Authority, she recorded the forced resettlement of Japanese-Americans into camps where they were interned for the duration of the war. At least in part because her photographs showed the point of view of the people, rather than that of the Authority, Lange left that agency in 1943 for the Office of War Information.

In the postwar era, she did assignments for *Life* when it

was the nation's most popular magazine and was known especially for its photos. She devoted the last efforts of her life to planning the first exhibit given to a woman at New York's Museum of Modern Art, and Lange's retrospective was shown there soon after she died of cancer. Several collections of her work have been published as books, and thousands of her photographs of the Depression and war years are on file at the Library of Congress, the National Archives and other important locations. In 1960, Dorothy Lange's *Migrant Mother* was selected as one of the fifty best photographs of the century.

LANGER, SUSANNE KATHERINA KNAUTH (1895–1985)

One of the outstanding women in twentieth-century philosophy, Susanne Knauth was born to a cultured German-American family in New York City. She learned music and languages from her parents and went on to RADCLIFFE COLLEGE after the death of her father, who objected to such "masculine" behavior.

After graduation in 1920, she married a historian, went with him to study at the University of Vienna, and then, returning to Cambridge, earned her Ph.D. in philosophy in 1926. Yet even with these eminent credentials and with recommendations from such outstanding philosophers as Alfred North Whitehead, Langer's titles would remain "lecturer" or "assistant" or "visiting" professor for much of her long, uninterrupted teaching career. She mothered two children while also teaching at Radcliffe, WELLESLEY, and SMITH COLLEGES until her 1942 divorce. After then leaving the Boston area, she held temporary positions at nearly a dozen coed institutions, almost all of which were far beneath her qualifications.

Nonetheless, Langer was an accomplished philosopher who became widely recognized as a result of several books she published, the most famous of which is *Philosophy in A New Key* (1942). Popular enough to be reissued in new editions several times, it is a multidisciplinary work in aesthetics, linguistics, and art forms, especially music, that is still widely used. Primarily an aesthetician, Langer was concerned with explication of various forms of artistic communication and with symbolism in language. She was capable of expressing extremely abstract thought in terms that interested those outside of her field, with the result that she was interviewed and her books were reviewed by such magazines as the *New Yorker* and *Saturday Review*.

Langer was elected to the American Academy of Arts and Sciences in 1960. She died twenty-five years later, in her ninetieth year.

LARCOM, LUCY (1824–1893)

Though Lucy Larcom thought of herself as a poet—and was indeed widely published in the era's most popular magazines—she would not be noteworthy today except for the reminiscences she wrote of her more humble life as a TEXTILE WORKER.

In 1835, Lucy's mother, a recent WIDOW and the mother of eight, moved to Lowell, Massachusetts, where she ran a BOARDING HOUSE that was occupied by "mill girls" who were recruited from New England farms for work in the new textile factories. The boarders paid $1.25 a week under the standard agreement between the company and the women who ran the boarding houses, but because this amount was not suffi-

cient for their household needs, Lucy's older sisters worked in the mills. She soon joined them, beginning her working life at age eleven.

Her sisters were leaders in the mill community and founders of the *Operative Magazine* in which Lucy published her first work. Like other young women in this unique setting of industrial life, Larcom attended evening classes and lectures "got up" by the "girls" themselves; she joined a language class conducted by a German "professor" who also taught them music. She read the essays she wrote to an "improvement circle" of friends and joined a botany class formed "by a literary lady who was preparing a text-book." Yet work was still the central fact of life, and Larcom's disappointment at missing Charles Dickens when he visited Lowell was still clear when she recorded years later, "We did not leave our work even to gaze at distinguished strangers . . ."

She stayed in the mills until she was twenty-two, leaving after a decade to move West with her sister Emilie. After three years as a TEACHER in Illinois, she saved enough to go to Monticello Seminary, a women's COLLEGE, and graduated in 1852. This formal setting not only systematized her years of self-education, but also gave her the credentials to teach at similar institutions of higher education for women when she returned East later that year.

After winning a poetry prize in 1854, Larcom continued to write poems that were published in *Atlantic Monthly* and other magazines. She also edited a children's magazine and, as a close friend of John Greenleaf Whittier, ANONYMOUSLY edited three volumes published under his name. Four collections of Larcom's poems were published in her lifetime, but her most important work for posterity was her prose. In 1881, she published an article in *Atlantic Monthly* describing her life in the mills decades earlier, and in 1889, she enlarged upon that and added other details of small town life in *A New England Girlhood*. The latter became a classic that is still reissued.

Written at sixty-five, Larcom's reminiscences understandably emphasized the positive aspects of mill life. Not only was her story sifted through the veils of time, but also the nature of industrial work changed dramatically shortly after she left the mills, when major waves of immigration permanently altered the status of American factory workers. Larcom was not sympathetic to the genuine needs of these later workers—nor had she been supportive of SARAH BAGLEY and other labor leaders who had begun to organize while she still worked in the mills. A conservative who identified with the agrarian values of an earlier time, she also opposed the SUFFRAGE MOVEMENT. Nonetheless, her nostalgic record of mill life offered an idyll of industrial life as it might have been.

LATHROP, JULIA CLIFFORD (1858–1932)

A member of JANE ADDAMS' Hull House group, Julia Lathrop was the first woman to head a federal bureau that required appointment by the president and confirmation by Congress. She received this honor in 1912, before most women could vote.

Lathrop was an 1880 graduate of VASSAR COLLEGE and lived at Hull House for twenty years. Her first significant social work experience occurred during the severe Depression of 1893, when many people, especially newly arrived immigrants, would have starved but for the charitable efforts of people like Lathrop. When she was appointed to the Illinois Board of Charities, Lathrop developed a particular interest in the needs of the mentally ill; like DORTHEA DIX, she traveled the state, investigating over one hundred institutions that housed the mentally ill along with the merely indigent. The result was a model psychopathic clinic that she built in conjunction with Hull House.

From 1903, she was associated with EDITH ABBOTT and others who built the nation's first graduate school in social work at the UNIVERSITY OF CHICAGO. The respect that her students and colleagues had for her would be clear when she was elected president of the National Conference of Social Work in 1918. Throughout her lifetime, Lathrop contributed many articles on social needs to both scholarly journals and popular magazines.

She left Chicago for Washington in 1912, when President Taft appointed her chief of the Children's Bureau that Congress had mandated that year. After Taft was defeated for reelection a few months later, she was reappointed by President Wilson, thus establishing an excellent record of recognition by both parties; Lathrop would be appointed to other national positions by Republicans in the 1920s.

A chief focus of the Children's Bureau under her direction was the crusade against child labor, but in addition, Lathrop directed several programs of direct benefit to women, including work on maternal death, ILLEGITIMACY, and mothers' pensions. The clearest legislative culmination of her efforts was the passage of the SHEPPARD-TOWNER ACT in 1921.

Lathrop retired that year, secure in the belief that her work would continue with her successor, GRACE ABBOTT. She remained active in retirement, serving as Illinois president for the newly formed LEAGUE OF WOMEN VOTERS, as well as on a commission to investigate conditions that affected IMMIGRANT WOMEN at Ellis Island. Her service on international bodies resulted in honors from Poland and Czechoslovakia for her work in resettling orphans displaced by WORLD WAR I, and despite America's failure to join the League of Nations, she served on its Child Welfare Committee. Julia Lathrop died at seventy-three, in the same year that Franklin Roosevelt's election signaled the true beginning of many of the programmatic ideas to which she had devoted her life.

LAWRENCE, MASSACHUSETTS TEXTILE MILLS STRIKE (1912)

The mills of Lawrence had almost a century of experience in employing women as TEXTILE WORKERS when this violent strike occurred. By 1912, the town had become a Dickensian scene of appalling poverty in which entire families worked from dawn to dark to eke out a meager existence. Overworked and undernourished IMMIGRANT WOMEN died young from the lint in their lungs, and they lost their babies at so great a rate that life expectancy in Lawrence at the turn of the century was a mere fifteen years.

Yet even though the era was one of general prosperity, Lawrence mill owners reduced wages in January, 1912. Approximately twenty thousand workers—women, children, and men—walked away from the mills in response. Management doubtlessly believed that it would be difficult for the workers to achieve enough organizational solidarity to win the STRIKE, not only because unions were virtually nonexistent but also because Lawrence's workers spoke more than forty different languages and dialects.

Nonetheless, the strike quickly shut down the mills. Organizers from the nascent International Workers of the World came to town and led the workers in picketing and parading. Militia and reporters followed, and the strike became the first successful use of nonviolent techniques to garner public support for unions. The government, of course, used its offices to support management, and when an Italian woman named Annie LoPizzo was shot in a demonstration—probably by the police—the town's officials jailed two strike leaders and charged them with responsibility for her death, despite the acknowledged fact that the men were miles away when the riot occurred.

Women workers were firm in their support of the strike, even though they were largely unrepresented in the strike's leadership and even though many husbands refused to allow their wives to participate in union meetings. Hundreds of mothers showed so great a commitment that when they could no longer feed their families, they sent their children on trains to be cared for by out-of-state supporters. MARGARET SANGER, then working as a NURSE, supervised the first trainload of hungry, ill-clothed children to leave the Massachusetts winter, and twenty-one-year-old labor organizer ELIZABETH GURLEY FLYNN also came to work in the strike.

It was in this strike that "BREAD AND ROSES" became a popular rallying cry, but Lawrence women did not merely sing and march; they endured blatant, unprovoked brutality from the town's police. A reporter for the mainstream Collier's magazine, for example, wrote of an early morning incident when police mounted on horses attacked a quiet group of women: "I saw the patrolmen surround the twenty-five women who had huddled and flattened, frightened . . . I saw the night sticks driven hard against the women's ribs. I heard their low cries. I saw who passed me. 'Listen,' she called to a friend. 'I go home, I nurse the little one. I be back yet.'"

It was only one of many attacks on women. Several were arrested in late night raids and two obviously pregnant women were beaten so badly that they miscarried. On February 24, police attacked women who were boarding their children onto a train; they clubbed the 150 children along with their mothers, and then arrested thirty-five of the distraught women for "child neglect." Writing in 1973, Flynn called this "a day without parallel in American labor history . . . which literally shook America."

The public was so incensed at the outrageous behavior of the police that a congressional inquiry began. More than fifty strikers went to Washington to tell their stories, and by mid-March, management had relented. Not only was the wage cut revoked, but additional benefits were won. Mills in other towns soon had to follow suit, and almost two hundred thousand workers thus benefited from the courageous action of the Lawrence women, for national labor leaders acknowledged that it was the women who won the strike.

LAZARUS, EMMA (1849–1887)

A tiny ethnic minority among a minority people, Emma Lazarus was a descendent of Sephardic Jews. Even though her family had come to the New World from Portugal in the 1600s, she was Jewish and thus would never quite belong to the nineteenth-century

American society that was so completely dominated by Protestants.

She lived her entire life in New York in an affluent family that, while it allowed her no formal schooling, nonetheless provided a rich cultural education, especially in languages. Verbally gifted, Lazarus published her first poetry while still in her teens and counted Emerson and James among her literary correspondents. During the 1870s and 1880s, she earned both critical and popular acclaim not only for her poetry, but also for a novel, a play, and other prose.

When massive waves of Jewish immigrants began arriving in the 1880s, Lazarus found herself reasserting a Jewish heritage that she had not thought particularly important until that point. She explained the sufferings of Jews during the era's pogroms in Russia and eastern Europe and defended Jewish immigrants from attacks in the nation's Christian press. Her feelings are particularly well portrayed in a poetry collection, *Songs of a Semite* (1882), and a play focused on the sufferings of medieval Jews, *The Dance of Death* (1882).

The most famous of her works, however, was a poem written about all immigrants to benefit the fund for construction of the Statue of Liberty. Lazarus' poem was so instantly popular that it was inscribed at the base of the statue. Though its title of "The New Colossus" is forgotten, every American is familiar with its closing lines: "Give me your tired, your poor/ Your huddled masses yearning to breathe free/The wretched refuse of your teeming shore/Send these, the homeless, tempest-tost, to me/I lift my lamp beside the golden door!"

Emma Lazarus died at thirty-eight of Hodgkin's disease, a form of cancer that strikes young adults. Her role as the literary celebrant of immigrants would be taken up two decades later by MARY ANTIN, another Jew and an IMMIGRANT WOMAN.

LEAGUE OF WOMEN VOTERS Formed in 1919 when the passage of the NINETEENTH AMENDMENT was in sight, the League of Women Voters was a direct transformation from the last convention of the NATIONAL AMERICAN WOMAN SUFFRAGE ASSOCIATION (NAWSA). With suffrage at last won, many of the women who belonged to the NAWSA reconstituted themselves into the League of Women Voters (LWV). CARRIE CHAPMAN CATT, who brought the suffrage amendment to political success, was named honorary president of the LWV for the rest of her life, while MAUD WOOD PARK held the actual presidency from 1919–1924.

Many suffragists, however, did not see the LWV as necessary in the way that NAWSA had been, and membership dropped precipitously—as few as one in ten NAWSA members chose to join the LWV. In conjunction with other women's groups, the League initially promoted some thirty-eight legislative items, but only two (the SHEPPARD-TOWNER ACT and the CABLE ACT) came to recognizable fruition during the politically conservative twenties.

As the years went by, the League increasingly lost touch with its FEMINIST roots and, instead of becoming a political base from which women could assume genuine governmental power, the LWV fell into a pattern of reporting, rather than leading. Throughout the twenties, for example, it issued reports on the numbers of women elected to office—reports that showed numbers that were declining rather than growing. Those few women who did have the courage to run for office found themselves increasingly ostracized by the League as "too political."

When women felt themselves endangered by the economic reverses that culminated in the Great Depression, the organization became even more dominated by women who avoided controversy and who instead immersed the League in the non-political study of issues unrelated to women's rights. Disagreement about the EQUAL RIGHTS AMENDMENT was another factor that worked against continued League involvement with women's issues, for many feminists of this era vigorously opposed the ERA, and this, too, split the original suffragists.

The result was that in the twenties and thirties, the League moved away from feminist aims and instead adopted the CLUB MOVEMENT model of civic goals. The LWV especially concerned itself with technical improvement in voter participation and honest government—but it did not take on controversial needs in this area, such as the registration of black voters. By WORLD WAR II, the League had moved so far from feminism that their publications showed almost no acknowledgement of the massive changes in the status of women that the war brought about.

Instead, the LWV limited itself to taking stands only on issues, stressing its neutrality in political parties and candidate races. While the nonpartisan stand continued the suffragist tradition of accepting support from any party, the underlying feminism that was the vital reason for the suffragists' nonpartisanship was ignored. League members increasingly forgot their foremothers' experience in endorsing and opposing candidates, for the vote was won by women who actively involved themselves in campaigns—even though they could not vote.

The LWV, in contrast, wished to be seen as so far removed from the political scene that its leadership was required to abstain from any candidate-related activity. League work was in fact so gender neutral that it was a natural move when the LWV extended membership to men in 1974, as new feminist organizations were gathering strength. Its current membership of approximately 120,000 includes about five thousand men.

By then the League had achieved recognition in most communities throughout the nation as the best informed and most technically adept source of information about government. Moreover, in the 1970s, the LWV proved its great effectiveness as a training ground for women who were moving through the process of becoming involved in government. Many women—perhaps most—who are successful in politics today obtained their original governmental background in the LWV. In some cities during the 1970s and 1980s, League presidency was almost mandatory before a woman moved on to elective office—but at the same time, many local Leagues discouraged this trend as excessively political.

The twelve hundred current League chapters primarily concern themselves with issue studies, neutral information on candidates, voter registration, and the process of fair elections. The League's headquarters is in Washington and its budget is approximately $3.5 million. It has commanded special attention in recent years for its sponsorship of presidential debates, while large numbers of local male politicians have developed immense respect for the well informed, selfless devotion to honest government that is uniquely personified by the League of Women Voters.

LEASE, MARY ELIZABETH CLYENS (1850–1933)

Lease is famous for the maxim that farmers should "raise less corn and more hell." Some attribute the origin of this phrase to an unfriendly reporter, but if so, Lease was bright enough to adopt her critic's clever slogan and make it her own.

Like other Northeastern TEACHERS in the post–CIVIL WAR era, Mary Clyens moved west in 1870. Of Irish Catholic heritage, she married three years later and became the mother of four while struggling against poverty on farms in Kansas and Texas. Farmers, especially in the Midwest, had serious problems in the late nineteenth century; railroad and grain market monopolies took an unfair percentage of their income, while extremely cold winters in the 1880s plus the 1893 Depression drove them to seek protection from the era's laissez-faire capitalism. The Populist (People's) Party that resulted from these woes was a genuine grassroots movement, and Lease was one of its most visible leaders.

Despite her legal middle name, she was called "Mary Ellen," and opponents who wished to disparage her excellent oratorical skills sometimes turned this into "Mary Yellin." She was reputed to have been admitted to the Kansas bar, but though she did not practice law, she did practice politics, especially oratory, and after 1883, was well known as a speaker for the Populist cause. In addition, she edited labor newspapers and was elected a "master workman" of the Kansas Knights of Labor in 1891. The following year, she seconded the nomination of Populist presidential candidate James B. Weaver.

Kansas women voted several decades prior to the NINETEENTH AMENDMENT, and Lease was one of the first female candidates for major office when she ran for the United States Senate in 1893. Although her campaign was unsuccessful, she had genuine political credentials: she had made over 150 speeches on behalf of the Populist Party during the previous years, and her reputation was sufficient that she was chosen as the orator for Kansas Day at the 1893 COLUMBIAN EXPOSITION in Chicago. She also received a gubernatorial appointment as president of the State Board of Charity.

Lease's causes included not only the range of Populist, PROHIBITION, and SUFFRAGE issues, but also international themes, especially Irish nationalism, for which she raised funds even before adopting the farm cause. Nor were her skills limited to speaking; she wrote *The Problem of Civilization Solved* in 1895 and was hired as a political writer for the *New York World* the following year.

Lease spent the rest of her life in the New York area, DIVORCING her husband after a long separation in 1902. Though she never achieved the recognition in the East that she had in Kansas, she served as president of the National Society for BIRTH CONTROL and, in 1912, campaigned for Theodore Roosevelt and the Progressive Party. She lived to see the final success of the SUFFRAGE MOVEMENT, dying at eighty.

Much like MOTHER JONES of the same era, Lease was controversial, even within her own causes. Not a team player or a thoughtful strategist, she was capable of departing so far from her natural alliances that she even supported McKinley over Bryan in the election of 1896. Nonetheless, her lively speaking ability was much admired by men and women, and she demonstrated the possibilities for women in politics far earlier than most.

LEDERER, ESTHER FRIEDMAN— *See* FRIEDMAN, ESTHER PAULINE

LEE, "MOTHER" ANN (1736–1784)

Though Ann Lee lived in America only a decade, she merits recognition as the founder of the American religious community commonly called Shakers.

She spent most of her life in the grimy industrial city of Manchester, England, where she toiled in the exploitive textile mills. Reluctantly marrying at twenty-five, she bore four children and lost all of them to INFANT MORTALITY. Her own physical and mental health broken, she collapsed, recovering only after a mystical experience. Thereafter, she believed that she had been called to establish a new religion marking a millennium that would accentuate the feminine side of the dual nature of God, just as Christ has emphasized a masculine incarnation.

After about 1770, Ann Lee—who was known by her MAIDEN NAME—came to be seen as a saint and prophet by a group of Manchester believers who, in the same style as the QUAKERS of that time, took to the streets to convert others. They were called "Shakers" because of their highly emotional services that featured dancing, singing, speaking in tongues, and other manifestations of psychological release. Arrested for disturbing the peace and persecuted by the governmentally established Church of England, Ann Lee was imprisoned in 1772 and 1773. The following year, she and eight disciples—mostly male—left for America.

Within two years, Mother Lee and her supporters formed a settlement near Albany, New York—a colony influenced by Dutch tolerance that had given shelter to earlier religious dissenters, including ANNE HUTCHINSON and MARY DYER. The Shakers lived fairly quietly through the American Revolution, although Lee was imprisoned in 1780 by patriots who confused her pacifism with support of the British. After that, she became more visible as a preacher and successfully toured New England during 1781–1783. Baptist congregations were especially likely to convert under the spell of her powerful personality, and when she died in 1794, several thousand Americans espoused her beliefs.

Shakers took seriously the biblical admonition that in heaven, "there is neither male nor female," and thus developed an extremely democratic and FEMINIST religion. The most radical idea advanced in their creed, however, was CELIBACY. Mother Lee believed that all sexual activity was innately sinful, a view that is understandable in light of her personal experience with pregnancy. Moreover, her husband—who accompanied her to America only to resort to alcoholism and DESERTION—give her reason to devalue even marriage without sex. Presumably thousands of others shared similar experiences, for the sect continued to attract adherents.

Like the Quakers, they not only gave women equal status with men in religion, but also were generally antiauthoritarian; both religions also stressed pacifism, with the result that their resistance to government was quietly nonviolent. Members of both sects developed reputations as seriously principled, hard-working people who were devoted to charity. Shakers opposed slavery earlier than most Quakers, but the major difference between the two sects was the celibate, communal lifestyle of the Shakers. The Shakers provided a model for other utopian societies that developed in the nineteenth century; they lived on farms where the work and the profits were mutually shared—a system that was almost mandatory in a lifestyle that would have no children.

After Lee's death, her supporters organized themselves as the United Society of Believers in Christ's Second Coming, or the Millennial Church. The idea of genderless, communal life continued to have amazing appeal, and by 1826, there were eighteen Shaker colonies in eight states as far west as Ohio and Kentucky. Shakers reached their highest point in the 1850s, when they had some six thousand adherents who farmed in the summer, while in the winter, they specialized in broom and furniture making. Shaker furniture is still considered an acme of American craftsmanship. A few elderly Shakers lived on into the 1960s, and museums reflecting their lifestyle can be found today in several states.

ANN LEE, along with MARY BAKER EDDY, deserves recognition as the founder of a church with adherents who revered her as divinely inspired. In a time when most women did not even think of PUBLIC SPEAKING, she had the charisma not only to persuade thousands of extremely radical ideas, but also to convince followers to drastically alter their lives. Her individual reputation probably was diminished by the triviality that attaches to the word "Shaker," but a thoughtful analysis of the times makes it clear that she was a woman of rare power.

LEE, HANNAH FARNHAM (1780–1865) Like a number of other women AUTHORS in her era, Lee was widely read by an audience eager for American books. Moreover, her biggest success was on a serious topic well timed to current events: her *Three Experiments in Living* discussed living under, within, and beyond one's means, and it came out in 1837 when Americans experienced their first serious economic depression. The book was an immense success, with thirty editions in the U.S. and Britain. Its sales clearly demonstrated that people were not merely willing to read books written by a woman, but also took seriously a woman's advice on money.

The book's popularity was so great that her Boston publishers followed it with three similar titles, all issued in 1837. They were *Fourth Experiment in Living: Living Without Means*, which went through at least thirteen editions; *Rich Enough; A Tale of the Times*, which was issued by New York and Philadelphia publishers as well as by Lee's original house; and *Living on Other People's Means*. Doubtless Lee's personal experience was a factor in understanding financial need, for she had been WIDOWED five years prior to the 1837 crash. The mother of three, she wrote because she needed the money.

She had published novels in 1830 and 1835, and when her popularity soared in 1837, her publishers added three more of her fictional manuscripts. They were *The Harcourts; Illustrating the Benefit of Retrenchment and Reform, by a Lady*, which ran to five editions; *The Contrast: Or Modes of Education*; and *Elinor Fulton*, all of which came out in 1837. In 1839, she added another novel, *Rosanna*, with *Tales* (1842) completing her fictional works. Having established an audience, Lee turned to more direct inculcation of the principles she believed in with *The World Before You* (1844) and *Sketches and Stories for the Young* (1850). Moreover, she developed a sufficiently strong reputation that she was able to

turn away from stereotypical "women's writing" to nonfiction work in serious subjects, publishing it exclusively late in life. Specializing in history and the arts, her first work in this genre was *Historical Sketches of Old Painters* (1838), which was reissued at least four times by different publishers in Boston, Philadelphia, and England between 1839 and 1854. To this she added several other histories that sold well: *The Life and Times of Thomas Cranmer* (1841), *The Huguenots in France and America* (1852), *The Life and Times of Martin Luther* (1852), *Familiar Sketches of Sculpture and Sculptors* (1854) and *Memoir of Pierre Toussaint* (1854). The esteem in which Lee was held by the reading public was so great that even her works on Cranmer (a sixteenth-century Archbishop of Canterbury) and Toussaint (an ex-slave who liberated Haiti from colonialism) each had three editions.

Despite the obvious influence that Hannah Farmer Lee thus exerted in national thought during the formative period when American literature became distinct from British literature, she is largely forgotten today.

LESBIANS AND LESBIANISM The term for female homosexuality, the name derives from the island of Lesbos in Greek mythology. This was the legendary home of Sappho, the goddess of love between women.

Throughout American history, virtually every community had its examples of women who lived together in long-term partnerships—often with one woman assuming the role of provider, while the other was primarily the housekeeper. Until well into the twentieth century, few thought of these as lesbian relationships. Most people—men and women—believed that most women were essentially uninterested in (or even repulsed by) sex, and images of women were so dominated by ideas of purity and chastity that the asexual nature of relationships among women was commonly assumed.

When COLLEGES, SETTLEMENT HOUSES, and other residential institutions for women developed during the nineteenth century, some leaders considered the possibility of criticism for encouraging "the loves of women for each other," in the words of EMMA WILLARD. Even so, Willard's comments on the subject are so obscure that it is difficult to say with certainty that she intended to speak of physical, rather than emotional, relationships. That the possibility of slander seemed remote is clear from the openly loving behavior of women towards other women in this era: women frequently walked hand in hand, addressed loving words to each other in multitudes of letters, and sat for pictures in poses that today would be deemed evidence of physical intimacy.

Dozens of highly visible women—the most prominent of whom was JANE ADDAMS—lived with other women for years and even decades in a variety of institutional residences, and the public gave little or no thought to the sexuality of these households of women. Indeed, the voluminous correspondence and other records still extant about the relationships between these women gives abundant evidence of their intellectual regard for each other and the personal devotion of their friendships, but offers little evidence of physical relationships. Such women were assumed to have adopted CELIBACY and to have sublimated any personal desires, for in a time when women had so many other barriers to overcome, a serious career axiomatically entailed single-minded devotion to one's work.

Indeed, so reluctant were Americans to consider the possibility of homosexual relations between women that a widely used dictionary of Greek antiquities published in the 1950s alloted only a half-sentence of a lengthy definition of Sappho to obliquely refer to the "unwarrantably immoral interpretation" of her erotic poetry addressed to women. Denial prevailed until the late 1960s, when lesbians began organizing as subsections of the NATIONAL ORGANIZATION FOR WOMEN and other FEMINIST groups. The Daughters of Sappho, the Red Stockings, and other lesbian groups joined male homosexuals in what became known as the gay rights movement during the 1970s and 1980s.

They became increasingly visible in political demonstrations, lawsuits, and other methods of drawing public attention to their needs, and by the 1990s, were winning significant victories. Led by San Francisco, cities throughout the nation added sexual orientation clauses to human rights ordinances that outlawed discrimination in housing, employment, and other fundamentals of daily life. Gay couples also worked to be included in religious life, forming branches of the Metropolitan Church and other sects. While some mainstream religions continued to oppose the lifestyle as innately sinful, others reached out and began performing marriage rites to celebrate the validity of homosexual unions.

As had been the case with the black civil rights movement of the sixties, judicial response to these minority needs was greater than legislative. In a highly publicized Minnesota case, for example, a lesbian won the right to care for her disabled lover over the objections of the woman's family, while in a New York case, a woman won the right of GUARDIANSHIP for the child her partner bore through artificial insemination. Thus, from the scientifically technical to the profoundly spiritual, tremendous changes in the late twentieth century liberated the lives of lesbian women.

LESLIE, MRS. FRANK (MIRIAM FLORENCE FOLLINE) (1836–1914)

A fascinating woman, "Mrs. Frank Leslie" belied the image that is created by the use of her seemingly conservative name. Far from conservative, she was a sophisticate who understood the male world when still young. At seventeen, she manipulated an older man into marriage by threatening to sue; she went through two DIVORCES and obvious affairs while also working as an ACTRESS.

Frank Leslie, her third husband, was a well-known publisher when they married in 1872. He had invented a method of quickly producing the engravings that were used to illustrate newspapers before photography, and as a self-promoting entrepreneur, had attached his name to several mass circulation publications under his control, including a weekly newspaper founded in 1855 that was one of the first to print pictures and to seek national circulation. Miriam Leslie worked for his magazines during the decade prior to their marriage, serving as editor of Leslie's Ladies Magazine when it began in 1863 and rising to edit two other magazines in 1865 and 1871. After both managed to divorce their respective spouses and wed, she devoted herself throughout the 1870s to lavish display of his highly mortgaged wealth.

When he died in 1880, however, she showed that she was capable of far more than was expected of society WIDOWS. Legally changing her name to his, she soon became one of the most powerful PUBLISHERS of her time. She borrowed to pay off his debts, streamlined the publications from twelve to six, and concentrated on high circulation of the two lowest-priced items, Frank Leslie's Popular Monthly and Frank Leslie's Illustrated Newspaper. She soon put the business into sound condition and remained the active supervisor of her four hundred employees through the 1880s, when she was termed "the empress of journalism."

At the same time, she continued her highly publicized international social and romantic life, marrying for a fourth time in 1891 and divorcing soon after. Her retirement in 1895 was short-lived; she returned after three years to rebuild the circulation that new managers had failed to maintain. Clearly, Leslie was a multitalented woman with genuine abilities in writing and editing as well as in predicting reading trends; her acumen in management resulted in profitable production in an era of highly competitive yellow journalism. Somehow she also found time to also author several books of travel and personal observations between 1877 and 1899.

During the last decade of her career, Leslie had given contributions of a hundred dollars or less when asked by the NATIONAL AMERICAN WOMAN SUFFRAGE ASSOCIATION (NAWSA). It was therefore a surprise when, after she died at seventy-eight, her will provided almost $2 million for CARRIE CHAPMAN CATT to use in obtaining the vote for women. Though the bequest was tied up in litigation for more than a decade, knowing that the potential was there was a tremendous boon to Catt, and ultimately the NAWSA received around $1 million. The money, administered by a group that came to be known as "the Leslie Suffrage Commission," was vital for the INTERNATIONAL WOMAN SUFFRAGE ALLIANCE and in three successful 1918 state suffrage campaigns, which helped bring passage of the NINETEENTH AMENDMENT the following year. Thus, in both her life and her financial legacy, Mrs. Frank Leslie was a true liberator of women.

LINDBERGH, ANNE MORROW (1906–   )

Although closely associated with her aviator husband, Charles Lindbergh, who was already famous when they married in 1929, Anne Lindbergh merits recognition in her own right. A 1928 graduate of SMITH COLLEGE (where her mother would be acting president in 1930–1931), she published a poem in Scribner's at twenty-three and her first book, North to the Orient (1935), was a bestseller.

Public attention was focused on the Lindberghs at the time because of the kidnapping and death of their firstborn in 1932; the trial and execution of the presumed killer was also highly publicized. It was to escape from these troubles that Anne Lindbergh accompanied her husband on a six-month trip that took them over the North Pole to Asia. This experience not only resulted in the book, but also in several awards for her piloting and navigational skills, including the National Geographic Society's Gold Medal in 1934.

They lived abroad until WORLD WAR II in an attempt to escape the excessive attention given them by the American press, and Lindbergh mothered five children while publishing regularly. Her works are in several genres, including novels, poetry, and magazine articles. Among them are several volumes of diaries and letters explicating her life, especially the years in Europe prior to WORLD WAR II when Charles Lindbergh urged peaceful acceptance of the Nazis.

The author of almost a dozen nonfiction books, she is best known for *Gift From the Sea*, a 1955 bestseller that continues to be read. Though by no means a FEMINIST tract, it presaged the developments of the following decade with its troubled discussion of the roles assigned to women. Lindbergh wrote, for example, that she could "understand why the saints were rarely married women."

Anne Morrow Lindbergh has seldom made public appearances, but she has accepted honorary degrees from Smith, Amherst, and the University of Rochester.

LIUZZO, VIOLA GREGG (1925–1965) A white woman

who gave her life in the black civil rights movement, Viola Liuzzo was shot to death in Alabama on March 25, 1965. A Michigan resident, she went South to join Martin Luther King's five-day march from Selma to the capitol at Montgomery. The march was over, its twenty-five thousand participants had dispersed, and Liuzzo was preparing to drive back to Selma when she was shot by men who followed her car.

A state court failed to convict anyone of her murder, but when a trial was held in an Alabama federal court in December, three Ku Klux Klansmen were found guilty and sentenced to prison. Viola Liuzzo had grown up in Tennessee and was enrolled at Detroit's Wayne State University when she died at 39. Her husband, an official with a Teamster's local, had tried to dissuade her from making the trip, but she felt a personal commitment to the cause of integration. The publicly expressed response of many male politicians to the death of this "nigger lover," in the terminology of the times, was that she should have been home tending to her kids.

LIVERMORE, MARY ASHTON RICE (1820–1905) Mary

Livermore's name should be remembered far better than it is, for the role she played in the CIVIL WAR was very similar to that of CLARA BARTON; she was a coequal in the SUFFRAGE MOVEMENT with JULIA WARD HOWE and LUCY STONE; and, finally, she was an early PROHIBITION advocate along with FRANCES WILLARD. Her popularity in her lifetime is clear from the uncommonly high income she earned from lectures and book royalties.

A native of the Boston area, she worked as a TEACHER, including three years as a GOVERNESS on a Virginia plantation, before her 1845 marriage to a Unitarian minister. The experience in the South made her an early member of the ABOLITIONIST movement, and while she mothered three children during the 1840s and 1850s, she wrote for that and the temperance cause. The family moved to Chicago in 1857, and it was from here that Mary Livermore did her important Civil War work.

Dedicated abolitionist that she was, Livermore volunteered to do full-time war work soon after fighting began. By early 1862, she was head of the Army's SANITARY COMMISSION in the Midwest and was responsible for military hospitals in Illinois, Kentucky, and Missouri. Like Barton in the East, she discovered appalling needs, and also like Barton, her genius was in supply procurement rather than in the more stereotypical NURSING role that is usually assigned to Civil War women.

Livermore TRAVELED the Midwest, educating the public and

forming more than three thousand local units to provide soldiers with food, medicine, surgical dressings, and other essentials that the military had not yet organized for itself. Her fund-raising abilities were so great that seventy thousand dollars was netted in a single 1863 event that she organized in Chicago, and this model for Sanitary Commission fairs was emulated all over the North. Women volunteers, led by Livermore, literally saved the lives of thousands of men who would have died without the vital supplies they bought and sent South. Somehow in the midst of all this, Livermore found time to publish her first book, *Pen Pictures*, in 1863.

When the war was over, she and other abolitionist women were eager to extend to themselves the civil rights that they helped win for black men, whose legal status was spelled out in the Thirteenth, Fourteenth, and especially FIFTEENTH AMENDMENTS. In 1868, Livermore became the founding president of the Illinois Suffrage Association, and in conjunction with this, published a newspaper called the *Agitator*. She joined Howe and Stone in the 1869 formation of the AMERICAN WOMAN SUFFRAGE ASSOCIATION (AWSA), serving as a vice-president, and when she and her family moved back to Massachusetts the following year, she undertook editing the AWSA's publication, the *WOMAN'S JOURNAL*. She held that position for two years, while also launching what would become a very successful career as a lecturer.

Livermore's fund-raising speeches during the war had already shown her ability to move audiences, and she soon became a prime attraction on the lyceum circuit that provided one of the few sources of entertainment and education available in most American towns. She toured every year for more than two decades, giving thousands of speeches. Large numbers of people were thus influenced by her opinions, and they bought tickets to hear her again years later. Her topics included a range of issues, but the case for women was central to her speeches.

Not willing to merely earn a comfortable living from speaking about women's needs, Livermore also continued as an active member of several organizations. She served as the first president of the ASSOCIATION FOR THE ADVANCEMENT OF WOMEN when it was founded in 1873; she was the founding president of the WOMEN'S CHRISTIAN TEMPERANCE UNION (WCTU) in Massachusetts, continuing in that job from 1875–1885; she volunteered as the national president of the AWSA from 1875–1878; and she was a delegate to the INTERNATIONAL COUNCIL OF WOMEN in 1888. She played a conciliatory role when the AWSA merged with the rival NATIONAL WOMEN'S SUFFRAGE ASSOCIATION in 1890 and, also that year, was a leader in the formation of the GENERAL FEDERATION OF WOMEN'S CLUBS.

Meanwhile, she continued to write, publishing her lectures and other essays in several of the nation's best magazines. Her most popular lecture, *What Shall We Do with Our Daughters?* was issued in book form in 1883, and four years later she had a bestseller with her Civil War memoirs, *My Story of the War*, (1887). Along with FRANCES WILLARD, she edited *A Woman of the Century* (1893), a collection of biographical sketches of the women of her era that functioned much as *Who's Who* does today.

She finally retired from lecturing at seventy-five, the same year that the Livermores celebrated their fiftieth wedding anniversary with "a great throng of distinguished guests." Indefatigable still, she helped found the WOMEN'S EDUCATIONAL AND INDUSTRIAL UNION; received a honorary doctorate of law from Tufts University in 1896; and published the *Story of My Life* (1897). Her husband and lifelong supporter died in 1899; she lived on another six years, dying at eighty-five in Melrose, Massachusetts.

LOCKWOOD, BELVA ANN BENNETT McNALL (1830–1917)

The woman who set the precedent for female attorneys to practice law before the Supreme Court, Lockwood's achievement did not come easily.

Like many other women, she worked as a TEACHER before her 1848 marriage and again when her husband was killed, leaving her a WIDOW with a child to support. Nonetheless, she managed to graduate from Genesee College in 1857—when COLLEGE graduation was still a rare credential for women—and afterwards, was elected superintendent of her town's school. This position put her into contact with SUSAN ANTHONY, another teacher who lived in the same western New York State area.

When the CIVIL WAR was over, Belva McNall moved with her teenage daughter to Washington, D.C., looking for a less parochial life. It was an inspired choice, for living in the nation's capital ultimately would prove crucial to her success. She continued in education at first, however, opening her own school in 1867. It was coeducational, something that also was relatively rare at the time, especially for private schools run by women. The next year she married again, taking the name of Lockwood, and in 1871, she participated in the process of choosing Washington's delegate to Congress. This privilege, which was granted the city in 1871 and repealed in post-Reconstruction repression, resulted in "meetings . . . in which a number of women took part. Mrs. Lockwood . . . on one occasion lacked only one vote of election to the general convention."

Her marriage gave Lockwood the freedom to move away from education and into law. The barriers that she had to overcome to achieve her goal began with admission to a law school: Lockwood was rejected by every Washington area school, including HOWARD UNIVERSITY, on the grounds that a woman would be distracting to young men—even though she was then over forty, an experienced schoolmarm, and twice married. Finally she was accepted by National University Law School, a new institution that needed students.

When she finished her coursework in 1873, however, the school refused to grant her degree. Lockwood overcame this second barrier by appealing to President Ulysses S. Grant, who was an honorary official of the school. Grant—an honest admirer of women who was openly dependent on his wife, and grateful for the Civil War work of women NURSES and others who supplied his troops—used his influence on Lockwood's behalf.

Even after she was admitted to the bar, though, there were still more obstacles to surmount. Lockwood discovered that the federal courts (essential to practicing law in Washington, which lacks a state government) would not allow her to argue before them. She appealed to the Supreme Court, which backed the lower court decision. When Lockwood's husband died in 1877, her goal became even more important, for once again she was a widow who needed to earn a living. Turning

to political action to achieve judicial fairness, she lobbied various friends in Congress, and in 1879—a decade after beginning her quest—saw the passage of bills that required the federal courts to allow women to practice. Doing all of this a half-century before the vote was won required incredible persistance, self-confidence, and faith in democratic ideals.

While waiting for this victory, Lockwood worked on other issues. The first year after she moved to Washington, while still in education, she helped found the local unit of the SUFFRAGE MOVEMENT. Throughout the 1870s, while going to law school and trying to establish a practice, she also lobbied for the NATIONAL WOMAN SUFFRAGE ASSOCIATION (NWSA) and helped with passage of an 1872 bill intended to equalize the pay of women in federal employment. Later, she worked for the hiring of female guards in women's jails and represented women journalists' case for equitable access to news space.

Also during the 1870s, she joined the lecture circuit as a speaker on women's rights. This gave her national exposure as well as income, especially in 1872 when Lockwood took a fling at supporting VICTORIA WOODHULL's quixotic presidential campaign. While the NWSA was grateful for Lockwood's assistance with their congressional efforts in the 1870s, they were less happy with her in the next decade; for in 1884, Lockwood decided to emulate Woodhull and run for president.

She was nominated by a small group of supporters (mostly in the West, far removed from her Washington scene) who called themselves the National Equal Rights Party. Anthony and other suffragists felt that such unrealistic aims distracted from the seriousness of their efforts to win the vote for less egocentric women, and moreover, they suspected that Lockwood's campaign was in fact more nearly an exercise in what today would be called name recognition. Indeed, Lockwood used the lecture circuit not only to earn money—in competition with Anthony and other suffragists who supported themselves this way—but also exploited the national tours as a highly profitable way to unearth business for her growing law firm.

Her presidential campaign resulted in some four thousand votes in six states among the ten million cast that year. Far from seeing this as an ignominious defeat, Lockwood moved on from national to international issues. She spent most of the 1890s working for arbitration as a method of settling conflicts, as well as on the larger issue of peace. Among other things, the State Department named her a delegate to an 1896 Geneva convention on charities, and she participated in three peace conferences between 1889 and 1911. She also served on one of the first committees making nominations for the Nobel Prize.

Throughout her professional life, Lockwood consistently fought for the rights of minorities as well as women. She helped blacks and immigrants, and in 1906, won a major lawsuit for Cherokees. The tribal remnants that lived in western North Carolina and eastern Tennessee won $5 million as a result of the effective arguments she made before the Supreme Court—at age seventy-six. Tireless to the end, she campaigned for Woodrow Wilson in 1916—to the chagrin of ALICE PAUL and her NATIONAL WOMAN'S PARTY, who bitterly opposed Wilson in this election. Lockwood did not share their political strategy, however, nor did the NAWSA. Ultimately, the judgment of the older women proved sagacious, for Wilson actively urged state legislatures to ratify the federal suffrage amendment in his second term.

Belva Lockwood, who had overcome so many barriers, did not live to see this victory. The profits from her once-prosperous law practice had disappeared, and she was near poverty when she died at eighty-seven. Her papers are preserved in the National Museum of American History in Washington's Smithsonian Institution.

LOOS, ANITA (1893–1981)

The AUTHOR of the perennially popular *Gentlemen Prefer Blondes* (1926), Anita Loos was a pioneer writer for the movie industry. By 1919, she had written scripts for about two hundred silent movies—a feat that required tremendous creativity, for until sound production was invented, a writer had to be highly skilled to move a plot without benefit of actors' voices. As a result, Loos was one of the best-paid people in her field during the 1920s and 1930s. She was sufficiently sought after on Broadway and in Hollywood that she earned as much as twenty-five hundred dollars a week, even during the Great Depression.

Loos kept her MAIDEN NAME when she married a colleague in 1919; together they published two nonfiction books on film production. They also wrote and produced four films together before Loos again struck out on her own, writing plays that were staged in 1923 and 1925 before the smash hit of *Gentlemen Prefer Blondes*. The story was serialized in *Harper's Bazaar* in 1925 and published in book form the following year, when it was also produced on Broadway and quickly became internationally acclaimed.

Loos' light, cleverly written comedies managed to be funny without being hostile, and even so severe a critic as H. L. Mencken admired her way with words. Mencken, indeed, was alleged to have been the inspiration for her success when he and a male friend ignored the bright and good looking Loos—who was a brunette—to focus on a silly, but blonde, woman.

Despite the witty demeanor Loos exhibited in her work and in her personal life, she bore a serious burden in her husband, who was declared incurably insane in the forties. For the next three decades, she continued to write both comedy and drama in many different formats. Among her adaptations for Hollywood were *The Women,* a play by CLARE BOOTH LUCE, and *Susan and God*, a RACHEL CROTHERS play. In the late forties, *Gentlemen Prefer Blondes* was revived with Carol Channing, and in 1953, it was made into a movie starring Marilyn Monroe. A prolific writer, Loos also published three volumes of memoirs and autobiography before her death at eighty-eight.

LONGWORTH, ALICE LEE ROOSEVELT (1884–1980)

The daughter of President Theodore Roosevelt, Alice was so famously independent even as a teenager that her father once said that he could either govern the country or govern Alice, but he couldn't do both. Her unconventional behavior—frequenting racetracks with disreputable escorts, for example, and waving her winnings at photographers—was such that Roosevelt's supporters actually feared she might cause them to lose reelection in 1904.

Alice Lee was named for her mother; in a tragic coincidence, both her mother and her paternal grandmother died the day after she was born. Her father was devastated, and left his child to the care of others for years while he escaped to the Far West. The result was a spoiled but fascinatingly assertive girl with a propensity for seeking attention.

Called "The Princess" by Roosevelt opponents, her White House wedding in 1906 to Congressmember Nicholas Longworth helped secure her position as a woman of tremendous behind-the-scenes influence—but it was Alice Longworth's own personality that made her powerful. Politically sagacious with a bitingly witty tongue, her power lasted for decades after her husband's demise. She showed her independence from him soon after their marriage, when the Republican Party split in the election of 1912. She supported her father, who ran independently with the "Bull Moose" Party, while her husband worked for the maintstream Republicans.

Neither won, as Democrat Woodrow Wilson took the White House. When Republicans returned to power in the twenties, Nicholas rose to be Speaker of the House and Alice, at age forty-one, bore a daughter. Washington was filled with rumors that the child could not possibly belong to him, but the Speaker nonetheless adored his little Paulina. However, she would have little memory of him, for he died six years later at sixty-two.

His death in 1931 was a year prior to the Great Depression election when the Republicans lost virtually everything. The president elected then—despite the fact that Alice campaigned against him—was her distant Democratic cousin, Franklin Roosevelt. Alice and ELEANOR ROOSEVELT, however, were first cousins, and Alice had been jealous of the attention her father gave his niece when they were still children.

Moreover, Eleanor had been a painfully shy and awkward child, while Alice always sought the limelight; when their positions were reversed with Eleanor's elevation to First Lady, Alice found the secondary place hard to bear. In addition, their political philosophies were markedly different, for Alice was an elitist Republican, while Eleanor was by far the most activist liberal of First Ladies. Alice was particularly vituperative on internationalism; unlike her father, she was an isolationist who opposed all international efforts from the time of the League of Nations onward. The result was a decline in her public popularity during WORLD WAR II.

Yet Eleanor Roosevelt's liberalism was political and not necessarily personal. During PROHIBITION, for example, while Alice let it be known that she kept a distillery in her basement, Eleanor (whose father was an alcoholic) was reluctant to see alcohol again legalized. In an era still marked by reticence on sexual matters, Alice clearly enjoyed making staid people the target of her original and well-publicized risque jokes. Eleanor, in contrast, was uncomfortable with matters of sexuality. Eleanor bore six children during her first decade of marriage, but Alice did not let her life be burdened by either excessive pregnancies or by maternal behavior. Indeed, she was largely estranged from Paulina, who did volunteer work in Catholic charities until her sudden death at thirty-one.

Longworth became more politically liberal as she aged and voted for Democrat Lyndon Johnson in 1964. She lived on through Jimmy Carter's administration, furthering and hindering political careers and providing newspapers with inside stories when she chose. Her colorful quotes were popular for decades and could fill a volume of enlightening history by themselves. She died at ninety-six, having published her memoirs, *Crowded Hours* (1934), almost a half-century earlier. By her independent style, if not by her politics, Alice Roosevelt Longworth was a liberating influence for women.

LOW, JULIETTE MAGILL KINZIE GORDON (1860–1927)

The founder of the Girl Scouts was called "Daisy" by her Savannah family. Partly because they had Northern connections, the Gordons suffered little during the post–CIVIL WAR period of her youth, and she attended FINISHING SCHOOLS in the South as well as in New York City. Daisy made frequent trips to Europe as a young woman, and after her 1886 marriage to a wealthy Georgian, lived as much abroad as in the U.S.

Nonetheless, there were troubles in her life. She grew increasingly deaf from early ear problems; she had no children, which defined her as an oddity in her time; and her husband's interest in another woman as so great that he attempted to DIVORCE her. When he died after eighteen years of marriage, he left his estate to his lover, and Low was only able to secure her financial future after long legal battles.

Her life in Britain made her aware of the "Boy Scouts" and "Girl Guides" that were becoming popular there after the turn of the century. After leading a troop in Scotland, Low imported the idea to the U.S. and formed the first American Guide troops in Savannah on March 12, 1912. At fifty-two then, she would devote the rest of her life to organizing on behalf of girls. She began a national headquarters in Washington in 1913 (later moved to New York), and by the following year, there were troops from New England to Georgia and as far west as Chicago.

The Camp Fire Girls were already in existence, and merger talks were conducted between the two; although the union never took place, Low used the name that was proposed for the joint group, and in 1915, formalized her Guides into the Girl Scouts of America. WORLD WAR I cut off her ability to work with her mentors in Britain, but she continued to organize throughout the U.S. and at the war's end, American girls participated in an international meeting in London in 1919.

Her model for independent, sturdy girlhood proved extremely popular as Americans moved out of the Victorian era, and the GSA built camps throughout the country where girls learned survival skills as well as appreciation of nature. At the same time, domesticity was stressed, with early merit badges being awarded in such categories as parlourmaid, dairy maid, laundress, and cook. Girl Scouts began selling their famous cookies in the early 1920s, shortly before Juliette Low's death.

Her organizational ability and the popularity of her idea is even more impressive in view of the fact that the fundamentals of the Girl Scouts were established in just a decade—the portion of Low's life between her early fifties and early sixties. Doubtless the fact that she had no children motivated her to adopt not only the hundreds of thousands of girls who joined troops during her lifetime, but also the young women who acted as their leaders.

Low continued to expand the GSA even after being diagnosed with cancer in her early sixties. Her genius for organizing was such that Scout membership soon exceeded the older Camp Fire Girls, and by her death, there were troops in every state of the nation. Juliette Gordon Low's October 31st birthday is still celebrated by millions of girls and women who have passed through the ranks of the Girl Scouts, and her Savannah home is a museum now open to the public.

LOWELL, AMY (1874–1925)

Descended from the Lowell and Lawrence families whose names are synonymous with TEXTILE MILL towns, Amy Lowell's male relatives were not only financially powerful, but also highly respected as men of letters and science. One of her brothers, for example, was president of Harvard during the first quarter of the twentieth century.

Family expectations of girls, of course, were much lower, and Amy did not even begin formal schooling until age ten. Like other young women of wealth in her era, she devoted herself to charitable society and traveled widely, including not only the usual tours of Europe, but also Egypt and California. Clearly unhappy with this vacuous life as she moved into adulthood, Lowell's negative self-image was confirmed by her obesity. Nonetheless, she lived a life dominated by the seasons of Boston society until she was nearly forty.

Finally, in 1910, she published a sonnet in the *Atlantic*, and in 1912, a play that she translated from French was produced in a Beacon Hill community theater. These events held promise for a literary life, and from then on, Lowell devoted herself to the era's new "imagist" poetry. Further publication followed, and late in 1912—the same year as the great LAWRENCE MASSACHUSETTS TEXTILE MILLS STRIKE—she published her first book of poems. Her family connections made it possible for her to move easily into the world of Henry James, D. H. Lawrence, and others, and in 1913, she toured Europe with a letter of introduction from Ezra Pound.

Between 1915–1917, she edited three volumes of poetry from the imagist school while continuing to publish her own poems in the era's best magazines. Having at last found herself, Amy Lowell wrote prolifically throughout the WORLD WAR I era, publishing five volumes of poetry between 1914 and 1921, as well as two books of criticism. Her poems were unabashedly female in subject and tone, often carrying antireligious and candidly sexual connotations. In her lifestyle during the postwar period, too, Lowell was part of the disillusioned generation that delighted in shocking those whose manners remained Victorian. She became something of a cult figure at literary gatherings, a self-styled celebrity who obviously enjoyed her renown.

The acme of her career, however, was also quite brief. Lowell's last works included a translation of Chinese poetry in 1921; a 1922 cleverly versified work of contemporary criticism modeled after a similar piece by her ancestor, James Russell Lowell; and a biography of Keats published in 1925. The last came out just months before her sudden death from a cerebral hemorrhage, and Lowell thus witnessed only the beginnings of controversy over her unconventional biographical style. Like her poetry, the Keats biography departed from the standards of Victorian paeans to a more modern critical and psychological examination of the origins of genius.

Not only was this a new biographical methodology, but since biography itself was a new genre for Lowell, it is possible that had she lived longer, she might be remembered for areas beyond poetry. Nevertheless, Amy Lowell's rank as a poet was so well developed in her fifteen-year career that she is included in almost any anthology of American poetry. Three more volumes of her work were published posthumously; her most famous single poem is "Patterns," which is a piece clearly written by a woman. One authority calls Lowell "the leading exponent of the modernist movement in poetry in the United States."

LOWELL FEMALE LABOR REFORM ASSOCIATION

One of the first labor unions created by American women, the association flourished long before industrial unionism was seriously developed, especially among women workers.

It grew out of an early organization called the Factory Girls Association, which had been active in the TEXTILE MILLS of Lowell, Massachusetts during the mid-1830s. The loss of a STRIKE and the financial Panic of 1837 destroyed this nascent union, but a decade later, women met more success with the Lowell Female Labor Reform Association. Formally begun in 1845 with SARAH BAGLEY as its first president, the association soon had five hundred members. The women had already demonstrated their ability by then, having participated in the collection of thousands of signatures on petitions for a ten-hour day during 1842–1844.

Before DOROTHEA DIX and other well-known women timorously began PUBLIC SPEAKING, these exceptional Lowell women testified before a committee of the Massachusetts legislature in 1845. They spoke of the low wages, long hours, bad air, and other unsafe conditions in their workplace, and the legislature responded with the nation's first governmental inspection of industry. Moreover, seventy-five years prior to women's right to vote, these women campaigned against Lowell's legislator, who had opposed their efforts, and—amazingly—they won. Though disenfranchised themselves, they persuaded enough men of the justice of their cause that the legislator was defeated.

A slight name change in 1847 added "mutual aid society" to the group's goals. Like male unions, the Reform Association collected initiation fees and weekly dues that provided sick leave and other benefits then ignored by employers. The association also bought the press equipment of the male *Voice of Industry* and turned the publication's pages to women's interests; through meetings, classes, and even entertainment, the association supported the self-education that was so important a part of the era's mill life, as seen in the reminiscences of LUCY LARCOM and others.

The model of the Lowell association was adopted by women in the mills of other Massachusetts and New Hampshire towns. The constitutions drawn up by these groups reflect the era's Jacksonian democracy, for these women assumed their right to organize and to strike against New England's owning class. The Lowell women harkened back to their foremothers in a more agrarian time, clearly seeing their industrial freedom as analogous to the political freedom sought by REVOLUTIONARY WAR WOMEN.

Despite their early success, however, these unions went into precipitous decline at the end of the decade, largely because they could not compete with the lower standards accepted by the IMMIGRANT WOMEN and men who began replacing natives in the mills in the late 1840s. Most of the women who constituted the Lowell Female Labor Reform Association left the mills at that time for TEACHING or for marriage; thousands of them went west to take advantage of the opening frontier. The immigrant women who replaced them would be too docile to unionize until after the CIVIL WAR, when again the industry would be convulsed by strikes conducted by women.

LOYAL LEAGUE

An organization of Northern women in the CIVIL WAR, its name conveyed loyalty to the Union—an idea opposite that of these women's grandmothers' time; for in 1776, the Loyalists were those who supported the Crown, while the Patriots were those who rebelled against the established government.

Members of the Loyal League who had rebellious ancestors did not draw the analogy to Southern Rebels, however, for the philosophical principle that overruled the apparent contradiction was ABOLITION. Women active in the Loyal League worked because of their opposition to slavery, and their belief that the independence of people was more important than that of the independence of nations.

The Loyal League was formed in New York in May of 1863. The war was already half over by then, but few precedents existed for the organized participation of women in any great effort. Women were only beginning to engage in PUBLIC SPEAKING, and few women had organizational experience—they had never elected officers, written by-laws, or planned any of the ordinary actions required to formalize relationships. The DAUGHTERS OF LIBERTY that had supported the Revolution was only a relatively small and loosely-linked network that left little in the way of precedent for organizational action.

Instead of being modeled on earlier wartime organizations, the Loyal League was a direct outgrowth of the SENECA FALLS WOMEN'S RIGHTS CONVENTION of 1848, for the women's rights advocates had cancelled their annual meetings during the previous three years because of the war. Hundreds of women responded to the call for a May 14 meeting from ELIZABETH CADY STANTON and SUSAN ANTHONY, whose association with the abolitionist movement predated that of women's rights. Stanton was elected president of the new group, with Anthony as secretary; others on the platform included LUCY STONE, ANGELINA GRIMKE WELD, and ANTOINETTE BROWN BLACKWELL.

The League passed several resolutions, the most significant of which was to petition Congress for the immediate emancipation of all slaves in the Union—thus pointing out the political cynicism of Lincoln's Emancipation Proclamation, which "freed" only those slaves in areas controlled by the Confederate military. Between May of 1863 and August of 1864, the five thousand members of the Loyal League collected almost four hundred thousand petition signatures. Moreover, they charged a penny per signature, thus painstakingly collecting enough money to maintain a New York headquarters from which Anthony worked. All of this was important training for postwar action on behalf of women's own rights. The Loyal League was thus more a political organization than the more acceptable—but nevertheless new—voluntary association of women who worked as NURSES and fund-raisers in the wartime SANITARY COMMISSION.

LUCE, CLARE BOOTHE (1903–1987)

A celebrity from the thirties through the fifties, Clare Boothe Luce was both a writer and a public official. While she had genuine abilities, many suspected that the widespread recognition she received was enhanced because of her marriage to Time-Life publishing tycoon Henry B. Luce.

A native New Yorker, Anne Clare Boothe's formal education was of the FINISHING SCHOOL sort offered to privileged young women in the late days of the Edwardian era. Talented enough to do some acting as a child, she later served as social secretary for ALVA VANDERBILT BELMONT. She married a millionaire in 1923, bore a daughter the following year, and obtained a DIVORCE from her alcoholic husband in 1929.

Returning to her MAIDEN NAME, Boothe worked for Conde Nast publications in top editorial positions with both *Vogue* and *Vanity Fair*. These sophisticated magazines and her first book, *Stuffed Shirts*, (1931) were indicative of her well developed sense of fashion, as well as her literary *savior faire*. In 1935, she married Henry Luce and devoted herself to a career as a playwright.

Her second play, *The Women* (1936), offered candidly FEMINIST views that critics accepted better than Depression era audiences. Indeed, Luce's views were so advanced that the play has held up uncommonly well, and since its 1973 revival, it has been regularly produced. Other plays followed, including the hit *Kiss the Boys Goodbye* in 1938, as well as a second book in 1940 on Europe as it headed into WORLD WAR II. Then and later, Clare Boothe Luce was both the subject of and the author of scores of magazine articles, especially in those publications owned by the Luce corporation.

With U.S. entrance into the war, she successfully ran for the House of Representatives in 1942; her district was an affluent suburban Connecticut area that was previously represented by her stepfather. Quickly recognized and promoted by her party, she was assigned to the important Military Affairs Committee and gave the keynote address at the Republican convention in 1944. She chose not to run for re-election in 1946, primarily because of the accidental death of her daughter two years earlier. While four years in an era dominated by the Democratic Party was not sufficient time to establish herself, Luce did join with MARY NORTON, EDITH NOURSE ROGERS, and other more powerful (if less well-known) congresswomen in urging the appointment of women to federal policymaking positions.

Though she continued to write, Luce retired from politics until 1952, when Republicans returned to the White House. In the first appointment of a woman with ambassadorial rank to a major nation, Dwight Eisenhower named her ambassador to Italy in 1953. She served in that position for three years, retiring in 1956. Eisenhower appointed her ambassador to Brazil in 1959, but Luce resigned from the position only a month after winning a bitter senatorial fight for confirmation.

The Senate was reluctant to confirm her because Luce, who had always represented upper-class Republican interests, grew even more conservative as she aged. Especially after converting to Catholicism in 1946, the early feminist views she had displayed were replaced with right-wing dogma that was objectionable to many in the Senate and in women's organizations. After this rejection, Luce moved from the New York City area to the Far West, eventually settling in Hawaii.

Her increasingly rabid anti-Communism included opposition to a range of progressive achievements, and so it was natural that she seconded the nomination of conservative Barry Goldwater at the Republican convention in 1964. When he was soundly defeated, she essentially retired from politics for the next decade. During the seventies, Luce served on the editorial board of the *Encyclopedia Britannica* and wrote "a feminist play," *Slam the Door Softly* (1971), which was staged in Los Angeles. Two years later, *The Women* saw a Broadway revival. She also served on Nelson Rockefeller's Commission for Critical Choices.

Luce returned to Washington with the election of Ronald Reagan in 1980. He appointed her to his Foreign Intelligence Advisory Board and further honored her with the Presidential Medal of Freedom in 1983. The recipient of several honorary degrees and journalism awards, Luce died in Washington at eighty-four.

LUCY, AUTHERINE JUANITA (1930–   ) Too often

overlooked in the history of the modern civil rights movement, Autherine Lucy was the first black to attempt to integrate the University of Alabama—in February of 1956, which was less than two years after the Supreme Court decision ordering school integration and more than a year prior to the great crisis in Little Rock led by DAISY BATES.

Three years after beginning her attempts to study library science at the tax-supported university, Lucy won a federal lawsuit that required the university to admit her. She enrolled on February 3, but violence broke out in response to her admission, with a thousand rioters attempting to storm the car in which she rode to class with the dean of women. When the campus president's home was attacked, the administration suspended Lucy just three days after admitting her.

Despite threats on her life, Lucy went back to court and again her right to enroll was upheld. The NAACP lawyer who took over her case was Thurgood Marshall, later the first black justice of the U.S. Supreme Court. In March, however, the university's administration trumped up a technical violation of school rules and expelled her. Neither Marshall nor the NAACP pursued this obvious miscarriage of justice, allowing Lucy's case to quietly die.

Autherine Lucy's almost single-handed effort to integrate a major higher education institution in the Deep South took tremendous courage. Nonetheless, her name is not well known, while attention often focuses instead on later integration efforts by men.

LUDLOW MASSACRE (1914) Coal brought settlers to the

Colorado Rocky Mountain mining town of Ludlow at the turn of the century, including large numbers of IMMIGRANT WOMEN whose husbands worked in the dirty and dangerous mines. When the men went on STRIKE for better pay and safer conditions in 1913, the women actively demonstrated their support of the strike.

Since the state officials saw the women as committed to the union cause, they made no attempt to protect them when violence broke out on April 20, 1914. "The machine guns began spraying the flimsy tent colony," said one account of the pitched battle that day. "All day long the firing continued. Men fell dead . . . women dropped. The little Snyder boy was shot through the head, trying to save his kitten. A child carrying water to his dying mother was killed." Those alive and uninjured found themselves homeless, for the militia set fire to their rude homes. The bodies of eleven children and two women were burned beyond recognition.

When the story broke, the nation responded with outrage similar to that of the LAWRENCE MASSACHUSETTS TEXTILE MILL STRIKE two years earlier. Some of those who witnessed the incident went to Washington and successfully lobbied President Wilson to intervene. The Rockefeller interests that controlled the mines did not relent, however, even after Wilson sent federal troops to supersede the state militia and restore order. The industrial stalemate continued until early 1915, when a public relations pioneer persuaded John D. Rockefeller, Jr. to go to Colorado, where he met with MOTHER MARY JONES and other labor leaders. Jones dismissed him as "a nice young man" who "could not possibly understand the aspirations of the working class."

The Ludlow Massacre thus is often cited as the beginning of the public relations industry, but for the women involved who lost lives, homes, husbands, and children, it was instead a harsh betrayal of the American dream.

"LYING IN" A term used from colonial times to refer to childbirth, the accepted intent was that a woman should "lie in," or rest, for a month to six weeks after delivery. Only wealthy women or young mothers with supportive families nearby were likely to be able to observe this ideal, however, for most women had responsibility for a brood of older children as well as for farms, gardens, and family businesses.

Though "lying in" was originally done at home, after hospitals were established in the nineteenth century, the term was commonly included in the names of establishments that specialized in maternity. The phrase was used until quite recently; the UNIVERSITY OF CHICAGO, for example, had a lying-in clinic associated with its medical school in the late 1940s.

The Boston Lying-In Hospital, founded in 1832, was the nation's first obstetric hospital and also, in 1847, became the first to use anesthesia to ease the pain of childbirth. It retained the "lying-in" phrase in its name until 1966, when it merged with the Free Hospital for Women (founded in 1875) to become today the Brigham and Women's Hospital.

LYON, MARY MASON (1797–1849) Few Americans have single-handedly done so much to advance the cause of women as Mary Lyon did when she founded MOUNT HOLYOKE.

The daughter of a WIDOW, Lyon began working as a TEACHER at age seventeen. Like so many nineteenth-century women who taught, she had little other occupational choice—but unlike many others, Lyon was a natural teacher who would devote the rest of her life to giving women the backgrounds they needed to be truly well educated and, especially, to improve the quality of their teaching. She alternately taught and studied for most of the decade after 1817; her thirst for knowledge was so great that she even gained permission to attend lectures at all-male Amherst College, while also studying at four other institutions not qualified to call themselves COLLEGES—for no women were yet admitted to the nation's genuine colleges.

In 1824, Lyon opened the first school under her own direction, a girls' school at Buckland, Massachusetts. Beginning with twenty-five students, it quickly grew to four times that size because of Lyon's commitment to affordable tuition. In

the summers, she joined her friend Zilpah (Polly) Grant at Adams Academy in New Hampshire, where the two of them established a precedent by issuing diplomas to young women. Determined to raise standards for female education, they eliminated the usual decorative subjects that were taught in FINISHING SCHOOLS, and when the academy's male trustees insisted that they teach "music and dancing," Lyon returned to Buckland. Grant moved on to Ipswich, Massachusetts, and in 1830, Lyon joined Grant's Ipswich Female Seminary. Again the two of them battled the odds against maintaining a school that was run by women who took feminine minds seriously.

In the summer of 1833, Mary Lyon went outside of New England for the first time. She saw Philadelphia; visited western New York, where she met EMMA WILLARD; and even went on to frontier Detroit. All the time, she was observing schools and formulating a plan. Back in Massachusetts early in 1834, she set about fund-raising to implement her radical vision of a new kind of educational environment for women.

Her aim was to offer a curriculum more rigorous than any available to women anywhere in the world at that time; its varied courses would qualify students for more than the limited employment opportunities then open to women. Moreover, Lyon resolved to establish a solid financial base that not only would outlast the whims of trustees, but also would be sufficient to enable young women of any economic circumstances to enroll if they could meet the academic standards for admission.

First, she established the usual male advisory board, for Lyon understood as completely as any modern public relations expert the need to massage the egos of the powerful. "The plan," she wrote Grant, "should not seem to originate with *us*, but with benevolent *gentlemen*." Otherwise, she predicted, the men would "fear the effect on society of so much female influence." While Lyon accepted the need to give men titles, she also knew that women nevertheless would have to do the work—and endure criticism while doing it. Despite disapproval, she broke the era's mores in TRAVELING and in PUBLIC SPEAKING, albeit to audiences limited to women. As she gathered courage in this unconventional behavior, she even went door-to-door, canvassing for money. "I am doing a great work," she said to those who criticized; "I cannot come down."

Her public responded, especially the women. Lyon's goal was a thirty thousand dollar endowment—a huge amount for the times. Within two years, however, she had raised half of it, with eight thousand dollars from the town of South Hadley, Massachusetts, which thereby won the school's site, and the remainder in donations as small as six cents. With the intent of making her Mount Holyoke Female Seminary more than a local school, Lyon canvassed sixty towns and thousands of farms between them. She asked the men with whom she spoke to "cut off one little corner of their estates, and give it to their wives to invest . . . for the daughters of the common people."

Lyon's vision for these daughters of the common people was reflected in the word "SEMINARY." Although she never entertained so revolutionary a notion as the possibility of ordination for women, she clearly did intend her female seminary as a parallel to the original aim of New England's male colleges, which were built explicitly to educate ministers. Lyon saw her female students as teachers of Christian faith and morals, not only in this country but also abroad as wives of missionaries—a visionary intent with little precedent at the time.

Undeterred by the Panic of 1837 and the economic depression that followed it, Lyon opened Mount Holyoke for classes on November 8, 1837. The eighty students were required to be seventeen or older and had to pass examinations for admission. Moreover, they also were required to assist with the school's chores to keep costs low, an innovation of Lyon's that was resisted by many who found this departure from the finishing school environment particularly unbecoming to young ladies. Nonetheless, genteel manners were dropped and domestic skills learned as the students lived and studied in a five-story red-brick building whose last nails were driven as classes began. It was soon obvious that the prescient Lyon had judged the status of women correctly, for young women (and their mothers) were so hungry for educational opportunity that some four hundred were turned away for lack of space the next year.

Though Lyon did not have the temerity to call her institution a college, the curriculum met the standards of even modern colleges. The three years of required work emphasized the physical sciences, including botany, physiology, chemistry, and geology, as well as algebra, history, politics, and several areas of philosophy and theology. French was studied, and Latin was considered so vital that it was required for admission a decade later.

Far from finding these standards intimidating, women responded enthusiastically. Within a few years, the seminary was sufficiently settled on its course that Lyon could take time to travel and write, publishing her only book, *A Missionary Offering*, in 1843. Her influence became widespread as other women's schools emulated Mount Holyoke in dropping the decorous for the serious. Even such "mill girls" as those in the LOWELL FEMALE LABOR REFORM ASSOCIATION honored her with their raised aspirations, joining study clubs and saving their money so that they could avail themselves of educational opportunity that previously was beyond their financial hope.

Despite her success, Lyon continued to drive herself. She not only served as the school's principal, but also filled several other occupational positions, including teacher, counselor, and even housekeeping supervisor. Not surprisingly, she suffered increasingly from headaches during the next six years. Traumatized by her nephew's suicide, Lyon went into physical decline and did not recover; she died in her Mount Holyoke apartment at just fifty-two. Like MARY MCLEOD BETHUNE much later, she was buried on the grounds of the school to which she devoted her life.

So obviously intelligent was Mary Lyon that strangers reported the immediate perception of being in the presence of someone extraordinary. More than intelligent, however, she was also a visionary of rare commitment. In 1905, she was elected to the national HALL OF FAME, one of the first three women thus honored.

M

MADISON, DOLLEY PAYNE TODD (1768–1849)

Dolley Madison was the first First Lady to create a persona around herself and the White House; she fashioned images that set lasting standards for social and diplomatic exchange.

These precedents remained to be set even though James Madison was the nation's fourth president: the White House did not exist under Washington and was still under construction during the Adams administration, while the third president, Jefferson, was a widower. Though Madison was by no means the intellectual equivalent of her predecessor, ABIGAIL ADAMS, it thus remained for her to create a social scene that would not embarrass the new nation with its European rivals.

Brought up as a Philadelphia QUAKER, she lost her young husband and a child to an epidemic in 1793. When she married Madison the following year, his reputation as the architect of the Constitution was already established. She began to serve as the nation's hostess in 1801, when her husband was the top-ranking Cabinet member under the widowed Jefferson. Despite the fact that she smoked tobacco and played cards, her charming personality soon made Dolley Madison an American legend.

She is also remembered for her personal bravery, for she rescued state documents and important art acquisitions when the British set fire to the capital during the War of 1812. James Madison had gone with the retreating U.S. Army and the presidential home was badly burned, but Dolley Madison exhibited cool judgment in choosing what was most important to save while she was under seige.

MAHONEY, MARY ELIZABETH (1845–1926)

Known as the first black professional NURSE, Mary Mahoney graduated from MARIE ZAKRZEWSKA's school of nursing in 1879.

Born free in Boston, Mahoney worked as a cook and maid at New England Hospital for Women and Children, which was Dr. Zakrzewska's progressive institution; at age thirty-three, she was admitted as a student. After graduation, Mahoney worked as a private nurse all over the Eastern seaboard.

Though she was a member of the American Nurses Association, she also cofounded the National Association of Colored Graduate Nurses in 1908. Single all of her life, Mahoney ended her career by running a Long Island orphanage. She retired in Massachusetts in 1912, where she supported the SUFFRAGE MOVEMENT. She died at eighty and has since been honored by nursing organizations.

MAIDEN NAME

Some of the nation's earliest settlers came from European cultures in which women retained at least a form of their maiden name at marriage, as in the case of early New Yorker ANNETJE JANS and her family. When the English overtook the Dutch, Spanish, and Swedish, however, English usage became the rule. Although an occasional female celebrity such as eighteenth-century ANN LEE might continue to use her familiar name after marriage, by the middle of the nineteenth century when the FEMINIST movement began to organize, a separate surname for a married woman was considered ludicrous. When LUCY STONE introduced the idea in 1855, it became so closely associated with her that for a long time thereafter, women who used their maiden names were known as "Lucy Stoners." Her innovation nevertheless was tempered by the era's insistence on an honorific, so that almost all contemporary documents—even those written by feminists—refer to her as "Mrs." Stone.

Other women of Stone's era who wished to ensure that they would still be recognized after marriage simply added their husbands' names to their own, as in the cases of ELIZABETH CADY STANTON, JULIA WARD HOWE, CARRIE CHAPMAN CATT, and many more. Indeed, the frequency with which nineteenth-century feminists used two surnames would almost seem to indicate that they wore their married state as a badge of honor. Stone's decision becomes even more revolutionary in light of this practice: she not only accepted the expected criticism, but also gave up the benefits of association with her husband's distinguished Blackwell family. Furthermore, the common use of two names among other feminists indicates that Stone's decision to opt for her maiden name was not an attempt to protect her fledgling reputation as much as it was a statement for singularity and lifelong identity.

Only months later, DR. MARY WALKER made a point of retaining her name at marriage, and in 1858, songwriter FANNY CROSBY did the same. In general, however, emulation of the idea came very slowly. There was much public scorn for it, and the notion became a favorite target of cartoonists and jokesters. Husbands who agreed to it were invariably portrayed as emasculated, with the result that even committed feminists were reluctant to ask their lovers to accept this uncomfortable and seemingly unnecessary unconventionality. There were a few exceptions, including Reverend OLYMPIA BROWN, but most of the era's feminists viewed maiden names as they viewed DRESS REFORM: they simply felt other priorities were more important.

IMMIGRANT WOMEN from places such as Scandinavia where women maintained an identity separate from that of their husbands came to the U.S. during this era, but most quickly adapted to the American usage. They might continue to use their individual names in letters home, but immigration authorities automatically entered a married woman's name as the same as her husband's, and within a generation, there was no evidence that the nation's many Petersons and Olsons had once been Petersdatter and Olesdatter.

Most of the maiden name usage that did occur in the late nineteenth and early twentieth centuries was with women who had an important public image prior to marriage that they wished to preserve. AUTHORS were therefore among the most likely to retain maiden names—or to retain the married name of their public persona if they later married again. SARA TEASDALE and MARY ANTIN are early twentieth-century examples of the former category; PEARL BUCK is a famous example of the latter. Occasionally a woman made use of the possibilities to create a virtual PSEUDONYM, as in the case of DOROTHY CANFIELD FISHER, who used her maiden name for fiction and her married name for nonfiction.

In other cases, women used maiden names because they aimed to carefully separate their professional and personal lives. FRANCES PERKINS, for example, understood long before she was nationally famous how important it was to establish this principle; she conducted a running battle with the MOUNT HOLYOKE alumni office that for years tried to "correct" her listing into "Mrs. Paul Wilson." In her case as in others, a maiden name not only served to ensure family privacy, but it also was important to professional achievement. Until the latter part of the twentieth century, the mostly male press was so accustomed to seeing women only in relation to men that women like Perkins believed the only way to focus attention on valid issues was to allow absolutely nothing personal that could distract.

The use of maiden names was well accepted in the entertainment field, and especially for ACTRESSES who DIVORCED at a greater rate than most women and who needed to retain their name recognition. In the minds of many, however, their status was inherently different from that of most women, and ordinary women had to fight for the right to maintain their maiden names until quite recently. Lawsuits were filed in several states during the 1970s when local officials denied women the use of maiden names on marriage licenses and other documents. It thus became another argument for the EQUAL RIGHTS AMENDMENT, but like many other legalistic arguments, the problem has been largely solved through common usage.

Finally, the use of married names doubtless is a factor in the loss of women to the historical record. Most systems of tracing people have no mechanisms to take account of name changes, and thus it becomes bureaucratically difficult to follow, for example, women who served in the military on to their later status as veterans. In cases of women such as RUTH BRYAN OWEN and others with multiple marriages, historical research becomes frustratingly complex compared with work on a man whose name remains the same. Even relatively modern reference works may alphabetize women according to the name of their most recent husband, so that historians have to check three or four places to determine whether or not an entry for the person exists—something that is seldom necessary for research on a man. That difficulty alone may dissuade researchers and thus be still another factor in accounting for the absence of women from historical works.

MALONE, ANNIE TURBO (1869–1957)

The parallels between the lives of Annie Turbo Malone and MADAME C.J. WALKER begin with the fact that both were orphans who grew up poor. Aided by her older sister, however, Annie Turbo soon learned the cosmetics business, and by the turn of the century, had developed several products designed explicitly for the hair of African-American women. Some go further to credit her with the invention of heated hair appliances.

Originally from Illinois, Turbo moved to St. Louis in 1902, where she sold her products and recruited other women to use and sell them. The 1904 World's Fair in St. Louis brought her national sales opportunities, and two years later, she copyrighted her business under the name of Poro, an African term for physical achievement. By 1910, she was doing well enough to expand Poro's headquarters.

Thus, Annie Turbo Malone's reputation was established under her MAIDEN NAME; her first marriage in 1903 was brief enough that her name was unaffected, and she did not add Malone until 1914, when she married again. It would be during her thirteen-year marriage to Aaron Malone that the business would truly take off, but the years coincided with considerable upward mobility for blacks during WORLD WAR I and with the free-spending years of the Roaring Twenties. In 1917, Poro established a million dollar complex with a beauty school and manufacturing plant, as well as hospitality facilities that soon became very popular for socializing in the segregated city. The complex employed some 175 people, and by 1926, as many as seventy-five thousand women worked as Poro agents in this nation and abroad.

The Malones soon became national celebrities among blacks, as they were wealthy enough to be known as the best of the era's donors. They made major contributions to HOWARD UNIVERSITY and other colleges, as well as to women's projects such as the YWCA, and Annie Malone was particularly noted for lavish gifts, including diamonds, to her employees. Remembering her own past, she endowed an orphanage and served on its board, and she was active in other organizations, including the Republican Party, which she did not leave during the Depression and war years when most blacks did.

Eventually, however, all of this collapsed. Her husband caused her much pain, for while Aaron Malone's business ability was doubtless partially responsible for Poro's success, his claims of credit reached far beyond what she thought was owed. They were DIVORCED amid much acrimony in 1927, with prominent African-Americans throughout the country taking sides; she ultimately bought him out for two hundred thousand dollars. Three years later, Annie Malone moved Poro to Chicago. It was a disastrous decision, for she would find herself without business connections during the oncoming Great Depression.

Worse, she was the defendant in two major civil suits during this era. Nor were the legal fees that ate up her declining profits limited to these problems, for the Malones had never been careful about paying taxes. When the federal government searched for overlooked sources of revenue during WORLD WAR II, Annie Malone was hit with a one hundred thousand dollar tax bill, and the government took Poro into receivership in 1951. Meanwhile, Malone's failure to pay local taxes meant the loss of most of her property.

Annie Turbo Malone, who never had children, died at eighty-seven in Chicago. Most of her papers are on deposit with the Chicago Historical Society, while others are in St. Louis.

"MAMMIES" Black women in the pre–CIVIL WAR South who held the top housekeeping position were frequently known as "mammies." Often they were the same age as the mistress they served, for a "mammy" usually joined a household when the children were young. Sometimes her original function was that of WET NURSE, but always she provided the majority of child care.

Indeed, many Southern whites saw their biological mothers as distant, while it was their mammy who brought them through the daily difficulties of childhood. This closeness can be seen in the language, for the word was often prefaced with "black"—a Southerner speaking of a "black mammy" used that modifier to distinguish their black mother from their white one.

Mammies performed all the functions of motherhood, including discipline and the teaching of manners, and as children grew into adults, she usually remained a powerful authority figure in their lives. A woman this important to family sentiment was rarely sold, and usually her children were exempt from sale, too, for they were often the playmates of the plantation's white children. Her husband was likely to be employed as a butler or carriage driver if he lived on the plantation, but mammies were often married to men who worked on other plantations and only occasionally visited.

As the mistress and her longtime associate aged together, child care naturally absorbed less time, and the mammy came to know as much about other functions of the household as the mistress did. Sometimes mistresses defied the laws and taught their chief assistant the fundamentals of reading and arithmetic, but always a mammy could be expected to replace the cook, parlormaid, or any other specialized servant when there was a need. Her child-care role almost always gave her experience as a NURSE, and it was to her that the household looked when there was sickness. Indeed, some black women in this role had local reputations for their nursing skills and would travel to other plantations to assist with illness.

Because of these important personal bonds, most mammies were treated with respect by whites, and even visitors were expected to treat her as they would a treasured aunt. Though her personal identity had been so completely absorbed by her job that no one referred to her as anything but "Mammy," the loss of her name probably was a small price to pay in exchange for her privileged position. Her own daughters, in turn, were likely to follow in her footsteps and go to live with daughters of the family at marriage. Indeed, so complete was the bonding that it was not unusual for these black women to speak of "our family" when they meant, in fact, the family that legally owned them.

It was a reality often denied in the minds of those involved, and indeed, when the less privileged field hands of plantations fled in droves during the Civil War, many—perhaps most—of those termed "Mammy" stayed with the white family. Thus, the word had connotations of betrayal to many blacks, who saw these women as unsympathetic to their own race and willing to abandon principles of justice for short-term personal gain.

It was therefore not surprising that when the DAUGHTERS OF THE CONFEDERACY proposed to build a monument to the nation's black mammies in the U.S. Capital in 1923, there was widespread opposition from African-Americans to this "honor." Even as politically powerless as black people were in the twenties, they managed to convey their views well enough that Congress killed the bill. Instead of this sentimentality, they argued, they would prefer an end to lynchings and legalized discrimination.

MANN ACT Passed by the Congress in 1910, the Mann Act prohibited taking women across state or national boundaries for "immoral purposes." Aimed at the era's obsession with WHITE SLAVERY, it made PROSTITUTION a federal as well as a state crime if any interstate transportation—even mail—was involved. The act was vigorously enforced by several agencies, including the Post Office, which was particularly likely to read mail to and from France for tips on "the trade."

Together with the COMSTOCK ACT that restricted speech, the Mann Act had the effect of restricting women's freedom of movement. Nonetheless, well-intentioned women lobbied for it, arguing that there was a genuine need to protect innocent farm girls and naive IMMIGRANT WOMEN from preying pimps.

MARINETTES Disguised as a man, Lucy Brewer is said to have served on the *Constitution* in the War of 1812, which would make her the first female Marine. There is no doubt, however, that the first woman officially sworn into the Marine Corps was Opha Johnson, who took the oath on August 13, 1918 during WORLD WAR I. This war brought tremendous technological change, and the typewriter seemed a vital weapon to headquarters' commands. Because women had proven themselves more adept at this particular machinery than men, the Navy researched enlistment law and found that there were no barriers to recruiting women. Thus, the Navy created its YEOMEN (F), while its correlated branch, the Marines, militarized women who became popularly—though unofficially—known as "Marinettes."

The Marine Corps was less excited about this venture than the Navy, and the Marines eventually accepted just 305 women, compared with the Navy's approximately thirteen thousand. Women, however, demonstrated their eagerness to serve in the Marines; some two thousand hopefuls lined up in New York for interviews to select just five. Not surprisingly, one Marine official later would call them "his '100 percent girls,' because of the unusually high speed and accuracy requirements placed on them."

Mostly assigned to headquarters in Washington, these women had to find their own housing and meals in the overcrowded and expensive city, but the spirit of volunteerism was so complete in women that some expressed surprise when their first paycheck arrived. While the Corps left the recruits to find their own food and housing, Marine women were expected to wear their green wool and summer brown khaki uniforms with great discipline, and they also were expected to march and drill. Indeed, the women probably did more parade duty than most male Marines, partly because of the Washington location of most, and partly because one of their most valuable uses, from a male point of view, was as an unusual recruiting gimmick.

None became officers, and all were mustered out as the war wound down in 1919. As veterans, they fared far better than the one thousand civilian women who joined the American Expeditionary Force to work as telephone operators and translators overseas. The Marine women received valuable benefits, including government insurance, a discharge bonus, civil service examination points, and even the right to a military burial at Arlington Cemetery. Although the use of women as Marines officially ended with the war, a number of these women continued to work in Marine offices as civilians; many spent their entire careers doing work similar to what they had done in the war.

MARINES, WOMEN Despite its experience with women during WORLD WAR I, the Marine Corps was the greatest laggard in WORLD WAR II. It did not enlist women until more than a year after Pearl Harbor, but then it offered a typically Marine no-nonsense attitude: the women's unit, the Corps announced, would not be called MARINETTES or "Wams" or any other diminutive, but "simply Marines."

As of January 28, 1943, all branches of the U.S. military finally included women, with the Marines under the direction of Major Ruth Cheney Streeter. Some twenty thousand women enlisted during the war, despite a "tougher training course" than that of the other services. Women Marines (who were dubbed WM on paperwork) trained at the infamous boot camp of Camp LeJeune, North Carolina, where they were introduced to "all phases of marine combat training;" including firing antiaircraft guns and dropping from parachute towers. By the war's end, they worked in 225 military specialties and made up eighty-five percent of the enlisted personnel at Marine Corps headquarters.

The latter figure makes it clear that most of their actual duty was clerical; moreover, Women Marines were not permitted to go overseas as the Army's women did. When the war ended, there were no initial plans to keep women in the Corps, but commanders soon found that the world had changed to the point that they could not do without the services of women. The ultimate result was the WOMEN'S ARMED SERVICES INTEGRATION ACT of 1948.

Restructuring and new recruitment finally brought racial integration to the Women Marines, with the first black women being enlisted in 1949 under the leadership of Colonel Katherine A. Towle, who was the first director after regularization. The Korean War brought mobilization of thirteen platoons of Women Marine Reserves; in June, 1950, "for the first time in American history, women were called involuntarily to military service along with men." Though they still did not go overseas, WMs served at such famous Marine installations as Parris Island and Quantico. The need for them was so great that enlistment standards were lowered to be more similar to male standards; younger and less educated women were allowed to join.

The following decade saw another return to the status quo, but when the Vietnam War heated up, women again surmounted still more barriers. The seventies brought women out of the offices and into new occupations such as electronic technicians, military police, and mechanics. Barracks life was integrated by gender, and the first women were allowed to continue on duty through pregnancy in 1971; a 1977 study would show that "even with time off for maternity leave . . . servicewomen lost much less time than men because of their lower incidence of absence without leave, desertion, and drug-and-alcohol-related problems."

In 1973, Colonel Mary E. Bane of Camp Pendleton became the first woman to command a nearly all-male battalion—to "astonishing furor" in and out of the military. Other barriers fell in 1977, when the first joint basic training classes of men and women were conducted and the first women were assigned to the elite Fleet Marine Force. Though the technical ban on women in combat still remains, women in today's Marine Corps serve as fully as men.

MARRIED WOMEN'S PROPERTY RIGHTS Under the laws of most states when the nation began, a married woman literally did not own the clothes on her back. Though she probably sewed them herself, most states entitled her husband to legal possession of everything a woman earned, whether that was cash income or an item of value as intimate as her clothing.

These attitudes were the result of an English judicial system grounded in the axiom that the marriage contract turned two individuals into one, "and that one is the man." At marriage, a woman became *feme covert*; literally, a female hidden within the male. The distribution of land in the first New England settlements reflected the legal absorption of women by men: a man received additional land if he had a wife and/or daughters, but far from owning that property, the females were viewed by the law as a form of property themselves.

Though the European system of DOWER RIGHTS was supposed to ensure the economic status a woman brought to a marriage, in fact there was no protection if a husband chose to drink or gamble away his wife's possessions. Remnants of this old English philosophy are seen today in such aspects of law as the special treatment of a spouse's testimony in criminal cases, while in tax and inheritance law, an individual's marital state remains key.

The FEMINIST movement that emerged from the 1848 SENECA FALLS WOMEN'S RIGHTS CONVENTION enjoyed its first important successes in the revision of these laws. Though the vote would take more than seventy years to obtain, significant changes in these laws began as early as 1854, when Massachusetts passed a Married Women's Property Bill. It was largely the result of an unsung hero, Mary Upton Ferrin, who collected signatures on a legislative petition for six years after she discovered that her husband owned the property she held prior to marriage, as well as all of the results of her labor.

New York had actually passed a Married Woman's Property Act in 1848, the year of the Seneca Falls convention, but it was sponsored by wealthy men interested in very narrow application to their daughters' inheritance rights. Throughout the 1850s, SUSAN ANTHONY led efforts for an expanded bill, and in 1860, ELIZABETH CADY STANTON set a PUBLIC SPEAKING precedent by addressing a joint session of the state assembly on the subject. The bill that passed after Stanton's speech not only allowed married women to own property, but also to collect the wages they earned and to have the right to sue in court, to enter into contracts, and "to carry on any trade or perform any services of her own account."

Despite this victory, the very nature of property rights inevitably linked it closely with the controversial topic of the marital contract and the right to DIVORCE—and indeed, the New York legislature quickly repealed a provision of its progressive act that granted women joint GUARDIANSHIP rights to their children. Thus, the incremental, state-by-state changes of laws took decades, while these legal disabilities had daily ramifications for married women. They could not sign contracts or obtain merchandise on credit, which made the smallest sort of business enterprise problematic. Extra technicalities made any activity outside of the home more difficult: the feminist movement, for example, was forever seeking out single women who could sign the contracts necessary to rent office space or purchase goods. Affluent MARY LIVERMORE discovered that even her checks for CIVIL WAR charity were not acceptable because she was a married woman.

Indeed, discrimination against married women was ironically class-based, with upper-class women arguably suffering more from such laws than poor women. There seems to have been no question, for example, that the women who worked in the nation's earliest TEXTILE MILLS had the right to collect the wages they earned—but decades later, when the first middle-class women were employed by the federal government for genteel copying in the Patent Office, the paychecks of married women were made out to their husbands.

Similarly, there was a general assumption that WESTERN WOMEN were entitled to land they had homesteaded, even if their husbands died or disappeared, while property in older states, especially in the South, was more likely to be inherited by a son than by the widow who had poured her life into an estate. A childless WIDOW could find her home and possessions reverting to her husband's family, despite her lifelong contribution to what she saw as mutual prosperity with her husband; South Carolinian MARY CHESNUT is an example of an once-affluent woman who suffered from such legally imposed deprivation in her old age.

When such laws did ultimately change, it was perhaps not as much because of lobbying by feminists as it was because of fathers interested in protecting family property willed to daughters, particularly in cases of men without sons. Thomas Jefferson, for example, artfully arranged for his inheritance to bypass his son-in-law while providing for his daughter; ultimately, less talented attorneys would simplify their work by passing laws allowing women to control their inheritance.

Even more change probably occurred through usage than through actual legislation. Especially as the nation moved west, American pragmatism would prevail: the multitudes of women who—like Mary Upton Ferrin—were unaware of their state's laws would simply go about conducting their personal business. Well into the twentieth century, there was a great deal of contradiction between what outmoded law books said and what women, especially in the South, actually did. Though some of these legal relics were resurrected in the debate over the EQUAL RIGHTS AMENDMENT in the 1970s, people took them no more seriously than unrepealed laws that limit the speeds of horseless carriages.

MARTHA'S VINEYARD The Massachusetts island off the coast of Cape Cod was named for Martha Gosnold, who died in infancy. She was the oldest child of Bartholomew Gosnold, who first explored the island for England in 1602. His wife, like other women, ran the family estate while her husband roamed the New World; that Gosnold manor still stands in the English village of Otley is testament to her managerial ability.

Gosnold would go on to head the 1607 voyage to Virginia that led to the settlement of JAMESTOWN WOMEN, and eighteen years after Martha's Vineyard was named, the area to the north would be settled by PILGRIM WOMEN.

MARYLAND Unlike most of the colonies that later became the United States, the colony of Maryland was settled by Catholics. Begun in 1634—almost three decades after the JAMESTOWN colony had been the first permanent English settlement—there are various explanations for its name.

When Charles I granted its charter, the name was explained as being in honor of his wife, Queen Henrietta Maria. The colonists, however, named their first settlement St. Mary's—a clear reference to the biblical mother of Jesus. It may also be possible that, despite the king's dicta, the Catholic settlers were honoring Queen Mary I (1516–1558), whose tragic life and five-year reign was scarred by her devotion to Catholicism. Catholics had lost property and lives during the reign of Mary's father, Henry VIII, and when Protestant populists began building power in the seventeenth century, wealthy Catholics were willing to flee England for the wilderness of the New World.

The proprietary colony was governed by Lord Baltimore and, in his absence, was briefly governed by MARGARET BRENT.

MARY SHARP COLLEGE Though GEORGIA FEMALE COLLEGE claims to have been the first COLLEGE for women, some argue that the distinction belongs to Mary Sharp College in Winchester, Tennessee, which began in 1851. Its founding date was clearly later than Georgia's 1836, so the debate centers around the value of Georgia's curriculum and whether or not the earlier institution merited the designation of "college." Since Mary Sharp required both Latin and Greek, it clearly belongs in that category.

The noteworthy point, however, is that both of these institutions set standards that exceed those of most colleges today, particularly in the area of languages. Moreover, it is important to realize that—in defiance of all stereotypes about Southern women—both of these institutions existed in the South, and both were built long before the post–CIVIL WAR era finally brought higher education for women to Northern states.

MATILDA The PSEUDONYM used by a black woman who wrote in the ABOLITIONIST *Freedom's Journal*, Matilda was far ahead of her time in expressing the dangers of prejudice based on gender as well as on race. More than two decades before the SENECA FALLS WOMEN'S RIGHTS CONVENTION, her pen poured forth progressive thought.

An 1827 letter to the editor read in part: "I don't know that . . . you have said sufficient upon the education of females. I hope you are not to be classed with those who think that our mathematical knowledge should be limited to 'fathoming the dish-kettle . . .' We possess not the advantages with those of our sex whose skins are not colored like our own, but we can improve what little we have . . ."

MCAFEE, MILDRED (1906–   ) The head of the Navy's women's unit in WORLD WAR II, Mildred McAfee commanded the WAVES from its 1942 inception through the end of the war.

Educated at VASSAR and OBERLIN, she came to this position from the presidency of WELLESLEY COLLEGE. McAfee was similar to her Army equivalent, OVETA CULP HOBBY, in that both were relatively young for the responsibility they assumed. Only thirty-six when she was sworn in, McAfee would build a large, unprecedented, and yet relatively problem-free organization within two years.

Her academic background showed in the somewhat cerebral image that the WAVES soon established. McAfee's familarity with COLLEGE systems was no doubt the reason that the WAVES first unit was located at SMITH COLLEGE; eventually WAVES received their basic training at almost a dozen colleges. It was not a pattern emulated by any other military unit, but it typified McAfee's common sense approach, for

naval bases were tremendously short of space, while the nation's colleges were underenrolled.

Her style differed from that of other commanders, too, in that she fought for relative comfort for her women. While others were eager to prove that women could stand the ordeals of marching and other military maneuvers, McAfee again preferred a low key approach that simply got the job done without bowing to superfluous male traditions. She gave her WAVES a comparatively large amount of personal freedom, saw that they were assigned to occupational slots commensurate with their abilities, and treated them with respect and congeniality.

At the same time, she did not insist upon the rank that she should have had, and thus allowed a precedent to be set that did not fully recognize the work of women commanders. Though McAfee commanded almost one hundred thousand, she never rose above captain—a rank the Navy assigned to men who commanded as few as five hundred. When she retired in December, 1945, she returned to academia, but did not use this opportunity to build bridges between women veterans and women's colleges. In both this and her failure to recruit black WAVES, McAfee demonstrated an elitism that was the dominant attitude of the SEVEN SISTER COLLEGES during this era.

Called "Miss Mac" for most of her military career, McAfee married late in the war and conventionally took her husband's name of Horton. The fact that her marriage did not become an object of gossip demonstrates her exceptional ability to manage the press—an area in which she clearly excelled the Army's Hobby (who was, ironically, in the PUBLISHING business). McAfee was possessed of a clever sense of humor and overwhelming pragmatism, both of which were keys to her success.

MCCARTHY, MARY THERESE (1912–1989) One of the most respected novelists of the twentieth century, Mary McCarthy grew up in the cold environment of a Minnesota orphan. The harshness of her upbringing was an important influence on her work, especially in *Memories of a Catholic Girlhood* (1957).

After graduating from VASSAR COLLEGE in 1933, she overcame the difficult employment conditions of the thirties to establish a career as a drama and literary critic for several of the nation's most respected magazines. Her first story was published in 1939 and her first novel, *The Company She Keeps*, in 1942.

Between 1938 and 1946, McCarthy was married to Edmund Wilson, who towered over literary criticism for much of the twentieth century, but she retained her MAIDEN NAME and went on to her most important achievement after the marriage—during which he allegedly abused her—ended in divorce. McCarthy finally found a supportive husband in her fourth marriage, which lasted until her death twenty-eight years later.

Working in both fiction and nonfiction, she came to be best known for two novels: *The Group* (1966), which is the story of the postgraduation experience of a group of Vassar women that was made into a popular movie, and *The Birds of America* (1970), which dealt with Americans abroad and changing societal values.

The autobiographical basis of that tale comes from McCarthy's life in Paris during the sixties. Her discerning comments about America from an outsider's point of view, her criticism of the nation's plastic commercialism and especially her opposition to the Vietnam War made McCarthy the target of right-wingers, but this did little to diminish her popularity with both critics and the public.

McCAULEY, MARY LUDWIG HAYS— *See* MOLLY PITCHER

McCLINTOCK, BARBARA (1902–1992)
The winner of the 1983 Nobel Prize, Barbara McClintock was a pioneer geneticist. Hers was only the third unshared Nobel in science given to a woman.

She received this honor for her research on "jumping genes," or the discovery that genes are capable of moving within a chromosome. This revelation made it possible for molecular biologists to locate and study genes in greater detail. When she died at ninety, some of her colleagues termed her one of the top three researchers in the history of genetics and comparable in importance to Gregor Mendel, the founder of the science.

During most of her career, however, McClintock had to struggle against the odds of being a female in science. She earned her doctorate from Cornell in 1927, just before the Great Depression. Though her early work was impressive enough to earn her a Guggenheim Fellowship and publication by the National Academy of Science, she could not get a job. Like MARGARET MEAD and others negatively affected by the Depression, Dr. McClintock struggled through the thirties on part-time pay—including a stint in Germany, where she watched the rise of fascism with trepidation. Finally, in 1936—a decade after her distinguished Ph.D., she secured an assistant professorship in Missouri.

WORLD WAR II brought her to Cold Spring Harbor Laboratory on Long Island, a Carnegie Foundation institution that became her lifelong research home. The war years also brought enough openness that she was elected president of the Genetics Society of America in 1944. Nonetheless, her initial publication of the "jumping gene" thesis met with scorn from most scientists, and McClintock had to demonstrate its correctness. "They thought I was crazy . . . absolutely mad," she recalled of her colleagues' attitudes towards her work in the forties and fifties.

When she was in her seventies and eighties, Dr. McClintock finally received the recognition she was due, including the National Medal of Science in 1970. She cared little for honors, however, and spent most of her time alone. Learning was her lifetime challenge. "I loved to know things," she said.

McCORMICK, ANNE ELIZABETH O'HARE (1880–1954)
A longtime correspondent for the *New York Times*, Anne O'Hare McCormick obtained that position during the twenties when it was rare for a female journalist to write on anything other than women's issues in prestigious newspapers.

Anne O'Hare had grown up with writing skills, for her mother, a victim of DESERTION, struggled to make a living by writing for Catholic publications and, pitifully, by even peddling her poetry door-to-door. Marriage at age thirty freed O'Hare from these limitations, and more importantly, gave her the opportunity to travel with her husband. However,

instead of merely enjoying the leisure of a long, companionate, childless marriage, McCormick uncovered story after story in Europe and wrote so well that the *Times* gave her a permanent column after 1925.

Her unusual status as a woman doubtless gave McCormick an edge in obtaining important interviews with the era's European giants, and she did famous profiles on Hitler, Stalin, Mussolini, and Churchill. Passionately devoted to the ideals of democracy and freedom, she understood earlier than most the dangers of fascism, and it was this prescience that led the *Times* to make her the first woman on their editorial board in 1936. Her colleagues recognized her the following year, when she became the first female correspondent to win the Pulitzer Prize.

WORLD WAR II brought McCormick wide readership, as formerly isolationist Americans undertook to educate themselves in foreign affairs. The government, too, recognized her expertise and she served on a secret advisory committee to President Roosevelt charged with formulating postwar policy. This led naturally to her appointment as a delegate to United Nations formative meetings.

McCormick's wartime writings bear much resemblance to those of her friend, DOROTHY THOMPSON, whose journalistic achievements, especially in the prewar era, where similar to McCormick's. Both women were widely acclaimed in their time, and both have been neglected by modern feminists. Two volumes of McCormick's newspaper columns were published as books after her death, and her papers are on deposit with the New York Public Library.

McCORMICK, RUTH HANNA (1880–1944)
The daughter of Republican boss Mark Hanna, Ruth Hanna's early life paralleled that of RUTH BRYAN OWEN. After graduating from Miss Porter's School, Ruth Hanna joined her father, who managed the 1896 presidential campaign for the Republicans, and thus, at age sixteen, she opposed Ruth Bryan, whose father was the Democratic nominee. Three decades later, both of these young women would be elected to Congress in the same year.

Hanna assisted her father until her marriage in 1903. Her husband was a member of the McCormick family that owned the *Chicago Tribune*, which was one of the most conservative of the nation's large newspapers. When they were newlyweds, however, the McCormicks lived for a while in a SETTLEMENT HOUSE, and Ruth McCormick was active in several progressive organizations, including the WOMEN'S TRADE UNION LEAGUE. In 1912, they split from their families to be leaders in the Progressive Party that broke from the Republicans, but when that party disappeared with WORLD WAR I, they returned to the Republican fold to great reward. With help from his wife, Medill McCormick was elected to the U.S. Senate in 1918.

Meanwhile, Ruth McCormick worked for her own right to vote. She held office in the NATIONAL AMERICAN WOMAN SUFFRAGE ASSOCIATION, lobbied in Illinois as well as in Washington, and helped write the SHAFROTH-PALMER AMENDMENT in 1914. After finally obtaining the vote in 1920, however, McCormick grew increasingly conservative. Disassociating herself from her former friends in the peace movement, she opposed the League of Nations; moreover, she urged women to abandon their efforts for equal rights and to adopt male political priorities. Four years after women had the vote, she had risen to membership in the party's national executive committee.

Her husband died in 1925, leaving McCormick with three children, the youngest of whom was only four. She soon set about replacing him in Congress, however, and pulled in all of her chits to lead the party's ticket in Illinois for the 1928 election. Her victory was a validation of women's political success, even though she disavowed her feminist roots in the campaign.

Rather than using this rare opportunity to represent women in Congress, however, McCormick filed no significant legislation and instead announced her candidacy for the U.S. Senate when she had been in the House only two months. Soon thereafter, the stock market crashed and the Republican landslides of the Roaring Twenties disappeared in the misery of the Great Depression. Though McCormick handily won her party's nomination in 1930, she lost by a large margin in the general election.

Americans soon became devoted to Roosevelt's New Deal, and though the *Chicago Tribune* regularly predicted Democratic demise, Republicans would be shut out of power for the remainder of McCormick's life. She became the PUBLISHER of smaller newspapers, owned a radio station and other businesses, and remarried, but though she remained politically active, Ruth Hanna McCormick had wasted her opportunity in Congress.

McCULLERS, CARSON SMITH (1917–1967) Best

known as the AUTHOR of *The Heart is a Lonely Hunter* (1940) and *Reflections in a Golden Eye* (1941), Carson McCullers was educated in New York and lived there most of her adult life, but her Columbus, Georgia home provided important background for her fiction.

Dropping her first name of "Lulu" early in life, Carson Smith was seen as an emotional cripple from her teenage years, but the loneliness and alienation that marks her work was reinforced by rheumatic fever and its recurring effects, which at times confined her to a wheelchair. She married a fellow Georgian and writer, Reeves McCullers, in 1937; they struggled through the end of the Great Depression in the South, returned to New York in 1940 and lived in Paris after her success. The relationship, however, would prove incessantly tumultuous: they DIVORCED in 1941, remarried in 1945, and endured other separations and reunions prior to Reeve's suicide in 1953. Their arguments over literary reputations and money were accentuated by bisexuality and promiscuous behavior in both.

The publication of her first novel, when she was just twenty-three, brought almost instant fame. When she followed it with a second solid achievement the very next year, Carson McCullers became, in Gore Vidal's words, "*the* young writer" of the 1940s.

Not limited to the novel genre, McCullers won an O. Henry short story award for "A Tree. A Rock. A Cloud." in 1942; "The Ballad of the Sad Cafe" was honored two years later.

Member of the Wedding (1946) is considered by critics to be McCullers' best work, and it was the most popular in her lifetime. A stage version of it that she wrote won the Drama Critics Circle Award in 1950, but it has been superseded in public popularity by the earlier novels, which were made into movies that were released soon after McCullers' death. The recipient of grants from prestigious institutions such as the Guggenheim Foundation and the American Academy of Arts and Letters, McCullers wrote several other novels, plays, and short stories, and movies based on her work still run regularly. Her reputation nonetheless diminished after WORLD WAR II, as her health also declined. She attempted suicide in 1948, but lived on to be honored with election to the National Institute of Arts and Letters in 1952.

Despite the clear understanding of rejection and reclusiveness that marks her work, McCullers was not limited by any sense of inferiority: she said, for example, "I have *more* to say than Hemingway, and God knows, I say it *better* than Faulkner." Fellow Southerner Tennessee Williams was particularly appreciative of McCuller's work, while famed critic Louis Untermeyer called *Reflections in a Golden Eye* "one of the most compelling . . . stories ever written in America."

Carson McCullers' always fragile health grew increasingly worse with complications from other diseases, and she died in New York at fifty.

McPHERSON, AIMEE SEMPLE (1890–1944) Born

Aimee Elizabeth Kennedy in rural Ontario, the future evangelist was strongly influenced by her mother, who brought her up in the traditions of EVANGELINE BOOTH and the Salvation Army. At seventeen, she married an uneducated preacher, and they traveled from revival to revival in the upper Midwest. In Chicago the following year, Aimee Semple—not yet out of her teens—was ordained by the Full Gospel Assembly.

With her husband, she traveled to China as a missionary in 1910. Shortly after they arrived in Hong Kong, however, her husband died, leaving Semple a pregnant WIDOW of twenty. A few months after the birth of a daughter, she was on her way back home. She joined her mother in New York City, where both of them labored for the Salvation Army through 1911. The following year, she married again; it would be as Aimee Semple McPherson that she would become famous, but Harold McPherson and Providence, where they made their home, were factors in her life only briefly.

She suffered from a long illness after the birth of a son in 1913, an illness probably brought on by postpartum depression that was reinforced by her unsuitability for traditional maternity. When the opportunity arose to lead an Ontario revival in 1915, she leaped at the chance; she took her children, who stayed with her father, but left her husband behind. He later joined her, converted in a dramatic scene, and then halfheartedly assisted in her mission, to which she added faith healing at this time.

Robed in white from head to toe, McPherson preached at revivals from Maine to Florida between 1916–1918, but her marriage was soon a casualty of her calling. Few men of that era could play a secondary role to a woman in such an unconventional profession; when the additional factors of their young children and her itinerant lifestyle were added, it was not surprising that they separated permanently in 1918. He secured a DIVORCE in Rhode Island in 1921, but by then Aimee Semple McPherson was firmly established in a place seemingly made to order for her—the newly settled towns of southern California.

Joined by her mother, who acted as agent and business manager, she initially went west for her daughter's health, and in the first years after WORLD WAR I, she continued to tour widely. Her "gospel auto" made trip after trip back east, with frequent preaching engagements all across the continent and even a 1922 Australian tour. Sister Aimee's popularity reached astonishing proportions very quickly: within six years of beginning her career, she was selling out the largest available buildings even in seemingly unreceptive cities such as Denver and San Francisco.

McPherson had used the written word since 1917, when she began her interestingly titled *Bridal Call* magazine series, but the fundamentalist audience to which she appealed responded well to the new medium of radio, and she set the precedent for later televangelists when she built a five hundred-watt station in Los Angeles. As the radio and movie industries brought thousands of forward-looking people to Los Angeles in the twenties, McPherson provided another sort of tourist attraction with the hugely extravagant Angelus Temple she began building in 1921.

The five thousand seats of this "Church of the Foursquare Gospel" were filled nearly every night and three times on Sundays. A fifty-piece band backed up larger choirs, and Sister Aimee made it clear with each angelic entrance to the stage that she understood drama better than most theatre professionals. The Bible College she built with the Temple enrolled thousands of students aimed at the mission field, while the Church of the Foursquare Gospel grew to hundreds of congregations in the U.S. and abroad. Telephone counseling and other innovations demonstrated not only her originality, but also her genuine concern for the often lonely, displaced newcomers who settled Los Angeles in the 1920s.

Aimee Semple McPherson was thus thirty-six years old and at the height of her popularity when—like England's Agatha Christy—she disappeared in a mystery that has never been solved. She surfaced in Mexico a month after vanishing from a California beach, claiming that she had been kidnapped. No evidence of the alleged criminals could be found, however, and after six months of investigation and national publicity, Los Angeles officials charged her with filing a false report. A grand jury inquiry added charges of suborning perjury, but just before the case was to be heard, the prosecution dropped the charges.

There was scarcely a day in the second half of 1926 when her name was not in the news, and the publicity convinced much of the public that McPherson was not only a charlatan, but also a liar. While her fundamentalist faithful supported her and she did a European tour in 1928, she never returned to the commitment and popularity of the early twenties. She quarreled disastrously and permanently with her mother, and a nervous breakdown in 1930 was followed by another marriage and her second divorce. Her public credibility problems mounted with several lawsuits in which she was charged with cheating and lying by former associates. Many also saw the contradiction between the politically conservative views she espoused and her liberated personal life, especially as a twice-divorced woman.

Nonetheless, the sincerity of her simple religious faith was not questioned, and her church continued to grow through the thirties and into wartime. Those depressed years, however, were fundamentally different from the glamorous twenties, and McPherson lost some of her following as her working-class audience moved its priorities from social conservatism to economic liberalism during the New Deal. Her personal life was further darkened by estrangement from her daughter; only her son remained involved in her mission.

He would inherit the church's presidency when she died from an overdose of sleeping pills a few weeks short of her fifty-fourth birthday. The coroner ruled the death accidental, and Aimee Semple McPherson was buried with other celebrities at Forest Lawn Cemetery in Glendale, California. She is credited with the authorship of several books, all featuring her experiences as an evangelist and her religious views. *The Story of My Life* (1951) was published posthumously.

MEAD, MARGARET (1901–1978)

The best-known anthropologist of the twentieth century, Margaret Mead had a tremendous effect on modern thought. Perhaps more than any other academician, she shaped public opinion on such fundamentally important areas as attitudes towards children and families and the relative merits of competition and cooperation.

Mead's life is strikingly parallel to that of her mentor, RUTH BENEDICT, in that both were widely acclaimed by the public and both held highly respectable academic credentials, but neither ever achieved the academic rank that a man with a similar résumé could expect. Mead, in fact, studied under Benedict and other pioneer anthropologists at Columbia; she received her undergraduate degree—which was technically from BARNARD COLLEGE—in 1923 and earned a master's in psychology the following year.

In 1925, she made the first of many trips to the South Pacific, and upon her return in 1926, Mead became assistant curator of ethnology at the American Museum of Natural History, an affiliation that she would retain the rest of her career. Meanwhile, she continued her graduate studies at Columbia, and, at the same time, wrote her most famous book. *Coming of Age in Samoa* (1928) was published before Mead earned her Ph.D. in 1929.

Thus, Margaret Mead held a terminal degree from the most prestigious university in her field and had published an original book to wide acclaim when she was only twenty-eight. She should have faced a remarkable future—but the year was 1929, and she was one of many women during the Great Depression who did not receive the reward they merited. The Natural History Museum did not promote her to associate curator until 1942—when the economy had moved beyond the Depression and into WORLD WAR II prosperity—and she would not be given full curator status until 1964, when she was old enough to retire. Moreover, when Columbia finally hired this most distinguished graduate to teach in 1964, it was as an adjunct professor.

But when *Coming of Age* came out in 1928, the world lay before her. She returned to the field that year to study the role of children in the tribal societies of the western Pacific, which was published as *Growing Up in New Guinea* (1930). She spent the rest of the thirties studying more South Pacific island peoples, publishing another book in 1935 and a unified version of the first three, *From the South Seas*, in 1939. At the same time, she also published on Native American tribes and pioneered the use of photography, especially moving pictures, in field research.

All of this presented Americans with appealing lifestyle alternatives, for Mead seemed to have documented the reality of Rousseau's visionary noble savage. Mead explicated to the "civilized" world the societies that they considered "heathen," and she effectively pointed out how much more humane and sensible were these peaceful and communal approaches to daily life. Women in the societies she studied were not viewed as male property, and these matrilineal cultures provided women and children with more freedom and greater self-respect.

Her work would prove a long-term blow to both imperialism and zealous missionary activity, for it caused many to question whether or not Western ways were axiomatically better. At the same time, she provided important new models for child-rearing, demonstrating that the proprietary attitudes and disciplinary harshness common to the West were not the only ways to bring up children. The communal sense of responsibility for the young exhibited by these cultures struck many as not only more humane, but also more effective for producing cooperative adults capable of living less egocentric lives. Perhaps the most important of all her contributions was the demonstration that gender roles were not innate, and that men and women in different societies differed markedly in personality and behavior.

Mead caught these tribal societies at the last possible moment in time, for the introduction of violent, competitive values in WORLD WAR II irreparably disrupted their cultures. Her own life, however, was too little affected by the war, for Margaret Mead may be that era's most egregious example of governmental underutilization of female skills. This remarkably talented woman—who probably knew more than any other westerner about the indigenous peoples of Southeast Asia where wartime intelligence gathering was vital—worked for the Office of War Information, where she wrote materials on British and American relations.

She published *And Keep Your Powder Dry* (1942), a study of her own country's cultural patterns, and at the end of the war decade, issued what may be her most significant book. A synthesis of all her thought, *Male and Female: A Study of the Sexes in a Changing World* (1949) was an important precursor to today's feminist theory. Mead continued to pour forth ideas throughout the fifties and sixties, with a half-dozen books ranging from attitudes towards authority in the Soviet Union to more studies of childhood. In 1968, Fordham University at last recognized her true stature in anthropology and invited her to chair their social science division.

A popular personality in the media, Margaret Mead also frequently appeared on radio and television and lectured widely, including at prestigious universities. She was politically active as well, especially during the cultural conflict of the Vietnam era, and earlier had helped establish UNESCO and other agencies to end hunger. Though her New York institutions were slow to promote her and though she was never elected to an important office within anthropological or sociological societies, she was belatedly chosen for the National Academy of Science in 1973. Mead published her autobiography, *Blackberry Winter*, in 1972 and added a final

work that commented on her times, *Culture and Commitment; A Study of the Generation Gap*, in 1978. Busy to the end, she died that same year at seventy-seven.

Twice married and divorced in her youth, Mead's 1936 marriage to another anthropologist produced several cowritten books. Their daughter, Mary Catherine Bateson, who is also an anthropologist and a linguist, wrote a memoir of her parents, *With a Daughter's Eye* (1984). Recently acclaimed for *Composing a Life* (1989), Bateson continues to amplify her mother's pioneering themes of peace and freedom.

MEYER, AGNES ELIZABETH ERNST (1887–1970) The

mother of PUBLISHER KATHERINE MEYER GRAHAM, Agnes Ernst was of a German Lutheran immigrant heritage and found no family support when she wanted to go to COLLEGE. She financed her own way through BARNARD, graduating in 1907, and then obtained one of the first jobs the *New York Sun* gave to a female reporter.

In 1910, she married financier Eugene Meyer. The birth of four children did little to diminish her intellectual life, and in 1923, she published the first of several books. When the Meyers bought the *Washington Post* a decade later, she began to write in earnest. Agnes Meyer contributed regularly to the *Post*, and her opinions grew increasingly liberal as she aged. H. L. Mencken labeled her an "uplifter," intending to deride Meyers' concern with improved public education and equality of opportunity; Lyndon Johnson, however, was so impressed that he viewed her as one of the chief sources for his War on Poverty ideas. Though she had been active in Republican politics in the twenties, she campaigned for Democratic liberal Adlai Stevenson during the fifties.

Agnes Meyer received over a dozen honorary degrees, as well as awards from organizations ranging from the NAACP to the National Press Club. Her autobiography is *Out of These Roots* (1953).

MIDWIVES For the first two centuries of America's existence,

the delivery of the next generation was almost exclusively the business of women. It was not until the development of organized medicine in the nineteenth century that male physicians began to displace female midwives in the birthing of babies.

In the urbanized areas of colonial America, professional, European-trained midwives were among the earliest settlers; women such as ANNETJE JANS's Dutch mother were a vital part of communities such as New Amsterdam. Massachusetts legislation in 1649 ranked midwives along with physicians and surgeons, while New York City recognized midwives by licensing them as early as 1716. That some women developed their reputations into solid businesses is indicated by the 1746–1753 records of a Newport, Rhode Island, midwife who delivered 2,498 babies in less than a decade—or almost a delivery a day.

Most of the nation remained rural, however, and most midwives practiced more informally. For a very long time, many births were unattended by any professional, as expectant mothers relied on female family and friends whose knowledge was based on their own personal experience. Since virtually no early American settlers practiced any sort of BIRTH CONTROL, every community had women who had delivered a dozen or more times, and there was no lack of collective experience. Childbirth frequently was a social event, with women gathering to attend to the new mother and her family and staying for days.

Because experience was so important, midwives almost always were middle-aged or older and usually had given birth a number of times themselves. Though younger European women were sometimes credentialed by government-supported schools of midwifery, nothing similar existed in America. Instead, American women learned the trade through personal experience and apprenticeship to older women who had accumulated experience. Martha Moore Ballard, who practiced in rural Maine from 1778 to 1812 and whose diary was later published, is typical in that she began her career at forty-three and was still practicing when she died at seventy-seven.

The availability of forceps in the mid-1700s brought increasing numbers of men into delivery rooms, especially in Europe, but most midwives both in America and abroad resisted the use of this instrument, which could damage both mother and child. The eventual—but unpublicized—result was many sets of statistics in various places and times that demonstrated midwives to have fewer maternal deaths than physicians. This was partly due to the midwives' greater willingness to wait for the natural course of childbirth rather than using invasive techniques, but also because midwives usually limited their practice to healthy women—whereas physicians demonstrably spread puerperal fever by going from cadavers to wombs without properly washing their hands. The most famous of studies determining this was conducted in Vienna in 1846, when a maternity ward attended to by male medical students (who also did autopsies) had a death rate that was 437 percent higher than that of the midwives' ward.

But that study and its American proponent, Dr. Oliver Wendell Holmes, met with ridicule for many decades. Meanwhile, men had access to medical schools in America for almost a century prior to the admission of the first woman, ELIZABETH BLACKWELL, and thus they could argue that they understood anatomy and physiology better than uneducated midwives. The lack of educational opportunity was not the only handicap that midwives faced, for in this era prior to the CLUB MOVEMENT, women had no organizational experience, and, of course, they also lacked the vote and resultant political power. When the use of anesthesia was added to the advantages available to physicians, midwives increasingly found themselves isolated, maligned, and displaced. One of the few factors that worked in their favor, ironically, was the modesty of this Victorian age; institutions such as the NEW ENGLAND FEMALE MEDICAL COLLEGE were established solely because it was deemed immodest for a man to assist a woman in the intimate situation of childbirth.

Those mores were more likely to attach themselves to the upper class, however, and midwives continued to practice among the poor—especially the immigrant poor, who held these women in higher regard because of European credentialism. Because of the high rate of immigration at the turn of the century and because of the greater number of births in the average immigrant family compared with the average native family, at least half of all deliveries in 1900 were still done by midwives. Cost was an important factor: in 1917, for instance, the standard midwife fee for a home delivery was seven to ten dollars, and she visited daily for at least five days; the physician came once, and charged ten to thirty dollars.

Moreover, many midwives were demonstrably better health professionals than physicians; one study done in this era showed that midwives were far more likely than physicians to use the nitrate of silver that was prescribed to prevent blindness in infants born to mothers infected with venereal disease. No less a personage than the president of the American Medical Association concluded, "According to these reports . . . the doctors should be replaced by midwives."

The opposite happened. As organized medicine became more powerful, state laws were passed that limited the ability of midwives to practice. Twentieth-century physicians managed to portray these women as dangerously ignorant, often using racist assumptions based on the fact that midwives more often practiced among poor minorities and that proportionately more of them were older women and black women. They also succeeded in exploiting suspicions that some midwives performed ABORTIONS; that some physicians performed abortions too was left unacknowledged.

Female physicians and midwives did enjoy brief governmental support with the SHEPPARD-TOWNER ACT of the 1920s, but that innovation lasted less than a decade. As births declined and physicians lowered their fees in response to the Great Depression, midwifery, especially among whites, virtually ended. Women lost other professional gains during the Depression, but the loss in this field was particularly regrettable, for it was the end of a long occupational history of and by women.

The baby boom that erupted in response to WORLD WAR II did not bring midwifery back, for a profession made up of older women quickly dies. At the same time, the health care field was revolutionized by both New Deal philosophies and wartime experience, and, though there was some pressure on women to deliver at home to alleviate crowded hospitals during the war, these home births would be attended by physicians, not midwives. After the war, the assumption among almost all but the poorest Americans was that babies were delivered in hospitals by male physicians using anesthesia.

With the revitalization of FEMINISM in the 1960s and 1970s came an increased desire on the part of women to reassert control of their bodies, and the "natural childbirth" of the LAMAZE MOVEMENT was part of this. At the same time, nurses who also had credentials as midwives organized and began to lobby for the right to practice. Partly in response to rising health care costs, state laws on midwifery were modified during the 1970s and 1980s. Today, increasing numbers of midwives practice in clinics and in hospitals, often as government employees.

The American College of Nurse-Midwives, which was founded in 1955 and is headquartered in Washington, has more than 3,000 members who have completed postgraduate education in midwifery and passed a national certification exam. The small Midwives Alliance of North America, founded in 1982 and based in Bristol, Virginia, seeks to expand communication and support among midwives.

MILK STATIONS A great deal of the INFANT MORTALITY suffered by grieving American mothers was due to spoiled milk. Prior to refrigeration and pasteurization, the summer months invariably brought a dramatic rise in the number of children who died, and much of that death was directly traceable to contaminated milk.

The situation grew worse as the nation urbanized in the late nineteenth century, and former FARM WOMEN and IMMIGRANT WOMEN found themselves in situations where there was no deep well or nearby spring where milk bottles could be water-cooled. Moreover, prior to the passage of the Pure Food and Drug Act in 1906, it was not uncommon for sellers to dilute milk with water or even more contaminating fluids that increased profitability.

Milk also seemed unreasonably expensive in the cities, and new arrivals refused to buy it for their children or themselves—even when they were pregnant, as many of these women were during most of their young adulthood. As one tubercular woman said when she refused to drink the milk her doctor prescribed: "The milk comes in a bottle. In my country, I get it from the goat . . . I do not know what else is in the bottle; there must be something besides milk, to make it cost so much." Confused by the many transitions needed to adjust to American life, some immigrant women even tried to maintain their babies on a diet of coffee and beer simply because those were the beverages most common among adults.

As a result, the activist women who made up the era's CLUB and SETTLEMENT HOUSE MOVEMENTS began milk stations. These were simply ice-laden wagons that kept milk cool and delivered a safe product at an acceptable cost to the neighborhoods that needed it. These middle-class volunteers also used this opportunity to instruct mothers on the importance of sanitation and other good health practices; milk stations often weighed babies, for example, and introduced women to other opportunities open to them at settlement houses. Perhaps because of enforcement of the Pure Food and Drug Act and perhaps because they could not meet this charity-based competition, dairies improved their product and delivery standards. Especially after the widespread introduction of electricity and refrigeration, milk stations were among the nineteenth-century aspects of life that faded away in the twentieth.

MILLAY, EDNA ST. VINCENT (1892–1950)

The 1923 Pulitzer–Prize winner for poetry and a native of Maine, Millay's education at VASSAR COLLEGE was financed by a patron. Like a number of other AUTHORS, her first poem was printed by *St. Nicholas Magazine* when she was fourteen.

Her early promise quickly proved itself, for she published her first book of poetry in 1917, the same year that she graduated. She added a second book of poems three years later and published three plays soon after that; Millay also acted with the era's famed Provincetown Players and was a serious musician. Called "Vincent" by her family and close friends, she published short stories under the PSEUDONYM of Nancy Boyd to support herself during her first years in New York and also wrote travel articles for *Vanity Fair*.

The Pulitzer, won when she was just thirty-one, was for her third volume, *The Harp-Weaver and Other Poems*. Millay's poetry was that of a young woman living in the decade of American history that is symbolized by a young woman—the FLAPPER of the 1920s. Millay's voice fit well with the era, for she spoke of youthful, female liberation, and her poetry reflected the adventurous (and occasionally flippant) attitude of the era's social revolutionaries, many of whom seemed unaware of the profound changes their generation wrought.

Millay married the year of the Pulitzer, but retained her MAIDEN NAME. Her husband was supportive of her work, made her financially secure, and even improved her previously precarious health. She published a highly acclaimed opera in 1927, and throughout the thirties and forties, continued to write, issuing a half-dozen volumes of poetry between 1928 and 1942. Politically active as well, Millay was arrested in 1927 when she demonstrated against the executions of anarchists Sacco and Venzetti in Boston.

WORLD WAR II brought emotional and financial strain to her Dutch husband, and Millay's poetry developed a greater political message that critics found distasteful. She suffered a mental breakdown at their Berkshires farm in 1944, and died there a few years later, soon after her husband's death.

Her last book, *Mine the Harvest,* was published posthumously in 1954. Edna St. Vincent Millay's death at a relatively young fifty-eight and even her burial on her farm were particularly ironic in light of what is perhaps her most famous poem, "Dirge Without Music," which begins, "I am not resigned to the shutting away of loving hearts in the hard ground."

The Millay Colony for the Arts now graces her farm, while Westbrook College in Portland, Maine holds some of her papers.

MINOR VS. HAPPERSETT (1874)

In this Supreme Court case, Virginia Minor, president of the Missouri Woman Suffrage Association in 1872, sued a St. Louis official named Happersett for refusing to register her to vote. With the help of her attorney husband, Francis Minor, she filed a suit arguing that women were already empowered to vote under the language of the Constitution, and that especially after the addition of the FIFTEENTH AMENDMENT, they needed no further permission from state government.

The case, and the support of the Minors' SUFFRAGE MOVEMENT friends, was indicative of the assertiveness of WESTERN WOMEN. The Missouri Constitution, however, had a clause defining voters as male, and the court—not surprisingly—disagreed with the plaintiff's argument that states had no right to define their eligible voters. When the U.S. Supreme Court upheld the ruling two years later, it was clear that women would not be enfranchised by judicial interpretation of the Constitution, but rather would have to face the long political battle that absorbed the next half-century.

Virginia Minor continued to work for suffrage for the rest of her life. She served as a full-time speaker during the 1881 Nebraska campaign, testified before a number of legislative committees and, in an unusually innovative approach, worked for suffrage among Catholics, converting at least one priest. In 1890, she served on the committee that merged the rival suffrage organizations, and the new NATIONAL AMERICAN WOMAN SUFFRAGE ASSOCIATION honored Francis Minor, after his death in 1893 for his work on behalf of women. Virginia Minor died the following year, leaving one thousand dollars to SUSAN ANTHONY for continuation of the cause.

MITCHELL, MARGARET (1900–1949)

Except for a year at SMITH COLLEGE, Margaret Mitchell spent her entire life in

Atlanta, which was the setting for her famous *Gone With The Wind* (1936). Indeed, the historical novel was highly autobiographical in its details, for Mitchell, like her protagonist Scarlett O'Hara, was a petite redhead with an Irish Catholic heritage whose family had lived the Southern plantation life for generations.

Like a dutiful daughter, she returned home to be with her father after her mother died in the flu epidemic following WORLD WAR I. She got a job with the *Atlanta Journal* in 1922, married that same year and DIVORCED two years later. A second marriage in 1925 would prove lasting. Meanwhile, she wrote of her immediate world in a novel set in World War I Atlanta; she later destroyed the manuscript and began working on a historical setting, consciously writing the stories she had heard all her life from relatives who remembered the CIVIL WAR.

Mitchell, who retained her MAIDEN NAME when she married Robert Marsh, was a typical young wife of her era, and she enjoyed a wide social life in the largest urban area in the South during the Jazz Age. She largely gave up journalism after a 1926 ankle injury forced her to keep off her feet, and she viewed her novel as something intended for herself and not for publication. Childless and accustomed to servants, Peggy Mitchell kept her mind active by writing literally thousands of pages that were not in any particular chronological or plot order.

When she met a Macmillan editor in 1935, she refused his initial request to see the manuscript, but later—with Scarlett-like impetuosity—delivered the tall stack of handwritten paper. The fact that it lacked both a title and a first chapter says a good deal about Mitchell's timidity. Parts of the manuscript were nine years old when she presented it, and much of it was filled with corrections. When the editor arrived at his New Orleans hotel, there was a telegram from Mitchell reading, "Send manuscript back. I've changed my mind." He, however, had read enough on the train to know that he did not want to surrender the absorbing text.

Though parts of it had been rewritten dozens of times before it was set in print, *Gone With the Wind* came out the following year. More than a thousand pages long, it quickly caught the imagination of a Depression-weary public eager for an escapist saga. The movie three years later brought even more attention, and its Atlanta premier still stands as the most extravagant movie opening of all time.

The book has set a number of important records, including the most copies (fifty thousand) sold in a single day. Mitchell won the Pulitzer Prize for fiction in 1937 and was quickly transformed into an international celebrity as the novel was translated into more than two dozen languages. By the time Mitchell died, 8 million copies had been sold, and the movie, which won several Academy Awards, was destined to become Hollywood's all-time most valuable property. Just one 1974 television showing brought $5 million in profits.

She had sold the film rights for fifty thousand dollars, which was the highest amount ever paid at the time, but which soon proved to be less than a fair share of the tremendous proceeds made from her idea. The result was that Mitchell became more aware of intellectual property rights than most AUTHORS. Like Scarlett, she fought back against other inequities that writers commonly accepted, and she set important precedents in copyright and tax law because she was willing to pursue the cases in court.

At the same time, Margaret Mitchell did not think of herself as particularly talented, and she did not join the era's literati in New York or Paris. Nor did she attempt another novel, doubtless understanding that it would be impossible to replicate her first amazing success. She filled her days with correspondence, charitable duties, and socializing, and in 1946, stepped in front of a speeding car. She died from irreparable brain damage at forty-eight.

Unlike the myth too often associated with her, Margaret Mitchell's Scarlett was a defiant individualist with an astute sense of business. Mitchell specifically rejected the ideal of helpless femininity, and she tried to portray the plantation woman as the personnel manager that she truly was. Millions of readers have found the strength and courage to overcome hardships in her pages, and indeed, the book has proven particularly popular in postwar Germany—perhaps because the Nazis banned it, evidently hoping to eliminate ideals of independent women and clever blacks.

Only two Pulitzer-winning novels have also won Academy Awards for the movie versions; Margaret Mitchell shares this honor with Robert Penn Warren. Mitchell also remains the only female author to hold the top place for best-selling fiction for two consecutive years.

MITCHELL, MARIA (1818–1889)

Probably the most famous female American scientist of the nineteenth century, Maria Mitchell was a pioneer astronomer. She was so obviously gifted as a girl that her father encouraged her studies, but no COLLEGES were yet open to women, and Mitchell did not leave her Nantucket home for Harvard, as she doubtlessly would have done had she been male. Instead, she taught briefly and then worked as a librarian for two decades, where she educated herself by reading widely.

Meanwhile, she studied the skies. Though it was unconventional enough for a young woman to spend her nights on the roof of the local bank, this behavior was less eccentric on her island home, where everyone was concerned with everything relating to sailing, than it would have been elsewhere. Her father and other men continued to encourage her, and the observatory they built had ties to both the Harvard Observatory and the U.S. Coastal Survey, which gave her specific tasks to accomplish and, after 1849, an annual salary of three hundred dollars. Much of the work she did involved computing distances, and Mitchell and others who did this work were known as "computers."

In 1847, when she was just twenty-nine, Maria Mitchell discovered a new comet. After overcoming a challenge from an Italian man based on who had seen it first, she received an international prize offered by the king of Denmark. Moreover, in the year of the SENECA FALLS WOMEN'S RIGHTS CONVENTION, this young woman also became the first woman elected to the American Academy of Arts and Sciences—a position she would hold for almost a century before a second woman was added.

The accolades continued, as did her work. Louis Agassiz, famous naturalist and husband of ELIZABETH AGASSIZ, nominated Mitchell for membership in the American Association for the Advancement of Science, and she also was elected to the American Philosophical Society by her male colleagues in 1869. With an improved telescope given to her by women organized by the energetic ELIZABETH PEABODY, Mitchell continued her largely home-based life until the opening of VASSAR COLLEGE in 1865.

Though initially reluctant to accept Vassar's invitation because of her lack of formal schooling, she was lured by the prospect of new observatory equipment. The only woman in the initial faculty, Mitchell eventually used this innovative position to exert a tremendous influence on the evolution of higher education. She took her students seriously and refused to enforce the petty rules common to educational bureaucracies (especially those for young women). Several of her students became noted astronomers.

Mitchell also continued her own research, thus setting another model for faculty. She led the way in photographing stars, predating the work of WILLIAMINA FLEMING and ANNIE JUMP CANNON, and she specialized in the surface features of Jupiter and Saturn. A founder of the ASSOCIATION FOR THE ADVANCEMENT OF WOMEN (AAW), she served as its president and, in 1873, was elected vice-president of the mixed-gender American Social Science Association. Becoming more openly FEMINIST and antireligious as she aged, Mitchell also served as president of the Women's Congress in Philadelphia during the CENTENNIAL EXHIBITION of 1876.

Maria Mitchell enjoyed only a brief retirement before her death at seventy in Lynn, Massachusetts, the same town where LYDIA PINKHAM had died a few years earlier and where MARY BAKER EDDY built Christian Science. All were women who were exceptionally interested in science, even though they came from radically different approaches and only Mitchell was acceptable to the mainstream.

In 1905, Maria Mitchell was one of the first three women chosen for the HALL OF FAME. The comet she discovered is named for her, and her Nantucket home is open to visitors today.

MITCHELL, MARTHA ELIZABETH BEALL (1918–1976) A native of Pine Bluff, Arkansas, Martha Mitchell was an upperclass, middle-aged, conservative woman who was married to the attorney general of the U.S. when she made her contribution to history by supplying pieces of the Watergate puzzle that resulted in the resignation of the president and the imprisonment of her husband.

A colorful, brassy blonde, she was a graduate of the University of Miami and a divorced socialite prior to her marriage to Mitchell. She gained wide notoriety in the 1970s for her late night telephone calls to reporters; her favorite was Helen Thomas of UPI. After she began leaking information, she alleged that she was under constant surveillance and even physically attacked for her truth telling.

In June, 1972—months before the scandal was taken seriously by any but the most vigilant—she explained to Thomas that the phone had gone dead during their last conversation because five men (one of whom later headed security for the Committee to Reelect the President) had entered her California motel room and ripped it out. Afterward, they had drugged and beaten her; "I'm black and blue," she said, "I'm a political prisoner." In later months, she would tell reporters

that she was phoning from a bathroom, balcony, or other unlikely place.

Though Mitchell succeeded in forcing her husband's resignation as Richard Nixon's campaign manager in 1972, most politicians and journalists considered her stories to be the hyperbole of alcoholism. Women were more likely to believe her, but the women's movement was new and Mitchell neither identified with it nor asked for support. As the full story of Watergate laid itself out during 1973, however, she garnered some chagrined respect from those who had dismissed her, for much of what she had said was proven true.

Nevertheless, Martha Mitchell stories in the press continued to be reported with condescension and incredulity. Most newspapers stressed her husband's protests of his love for her, even as his behavior demonstrated that he treated her as an errant child.

At age fifty-seven, Martha Mitchell died rather suddenly of cancer. John Mitchell began serving prison time the following year, after the U.S. Supreme Court refused his appeal.

"MOLLY MAGUIRES" A radical group of miners in western Pennsylvania and West Virginia, they took their name from an earlier antilandlord group in Ireland. From 1862 onwards, they used sabotage and even murder to emphasize their unhappiness with the harsh life of coal miners; by 1880, nineteen of them had been executed for "terroristic" activities. Pioneer security agent Allan Pinkerton publicized them with a popular book, *The Molly Maguires and the Detectives*, in 1877. Despite their feminine name, the Molly Maguires had almost no connection with women—except as the mothers, daughters, and WIDOWS of those executed because labor unions were considered illegal.

"MOLLY PITCHER" (MARY LUDWIG HAYS MCCAULEY) (1754–1832) Mary Hays became famous as "Molly Pitcher" during the Battle of Monmouth in 1778. Like MARGARET CORBIN and other REVOLUTIONARY WAR WOMEN, she was on the battlefield when the British and American armies clashed.

The daughter of a German immigrant, she had done farm work until her marriage at about fifteen. When her husband joined a Pennsylvania company, she accompanied him in the tradition of many respectable women who were CAMP FOLLOWERS. Thus, when the battle near Monmouth, New Jersey took place on June 28, she had been marching with the army for more than two years. She was already known as "Moll of the Pitcher" for her voluntary but dangerous work in carrying water to soldiers during the heat of battle.

Her husband, a sergeant in charge of an artillery gun, was wounded almost as soon as the Monmouth conflict began. Since she understood the gun's operation as well as he did, she made him comfortable and then took over the gun. She held her position during the long afternoon and thus helped contribute to the British retreat that night. General Washington personally thanked her for her bravery, and he forwarded to Congress a recommendation, which they accepted, that she be commissioned as a sergeant and granted half-pay for the rest of her life. The state of Pennsylvania also honored her with an annuity.

She needed this income, for her husband died from complications of his battle wounds near the war's end. "Molly

Pitcher" later married a man named McCauley and lived to eighty-five. She is buried in Carlisle, Pennsylvania, where an elaborate tombstone was installed in her honor during the nation's first centennial in 1876. John Greenleaf Whittier helped establish her reputation with his book, *Moll Pitcher* (1832).

MONK, MARIA (1816–1849)

Though her moment of fame was personally fleeting, Maria Monk nonetheless wielded a tremendously negative influence during the nineteenth century. Her *Awful Disclosures* (1836) was a longtime bestseller that did great harm to the image of Catholicism in a nation already prejudiced against that religion.

Born a French Canadian, Monk had a troubled adolescence. She spent time as a teenager in a rehabilitation center for PROSTITUTES that was run by Montreal NUNS, which gave her a working knowledge of the convent that later made her *Disclosures* more credible. When she became pregnant in 1834, she left for New York with a traveling evangelist who introduced her to his anti-Catholic friends.

One of the darker aspects of the era's Jacksonian democracy was a rise in the number of conspiracy theorists, and Catholicism would be the target of increasing attacks throughout the antebellum period. The year prior to Monk's arrival in New York, for example, Massachusetts Protestants had attacked a Charlestown convent, and the occupants had barely escaped with their lives.

Eager for attention and in need of financial support, Maria Monk was glad to supply "details" of her convent experience to the staff of the *American Protestant Vindicator*. With embellishment on her part and outright lies on the part of the male editors, her story was serialized late in 1835 to avid readership—which, in turn, resulted in increased hyperbole and salaciousness.

The following year, the story was published as *Awful Disclosures of Maria Monk, As Exhibited in a Narrative of Her Sufferings during a Residence of Five Years as a Novice and Two Years as a Black Nun, in the Hotel Dieu Nunnery at Montreal*. Even Monk's own mother testified that her daughter had not spent seven years in the convent and was never a practicing Catholic, but a gullible public nevertheless chose to believe that the book's lurid tales were true. In an era when almost nothing of a sexual nature was published, Monk's book came as close to pornography as many would ever read. She—or more accurately, the men who actually wrote her story—averred that nuns were regularly forced to submit to lascivious priests, and that those who were unwilling were murdered, along with routine infanticide of the resultant pregnancies.

Though a number of respectable Protestants dismissed this salacious material and though many French Canadians testified to the good done by Hotel Dieu nuns, especially in their hospital, the slander continued without much abatement throughout the rest of the century. A second book, *Further Disclosures by Maria Monk* (1837), kept the controversy alive while disclosing, in fact, no new information. The first book became a bestseller, however, and copies were reprinted for decades.

But the "author" never saw any of the profits. In 1838, she bore another ILLEGITIMATE child, and in 1849, was again imprisoned for prostitution. Maria Monk died soon afterwards in the notorious Blackwell Island poorhouse. She was only thirty-three.

MONTEZ, LOLA (1818–1861)

This British dancer is noteworthy to American history only because of her libertine lifestyle here during the conservative 1850s. Not particularly talented but extremely beautiful, Montez (whose true name was Delores Gilbert) lived most of her life abroad. After growing up in India, she performed throughout northern Europe, including Poland and Russia, and then became the mistress of the king of Bavaria.

The political revolutions of 1848 forced her to flee to America, where her third marriage soon ended in a DIVORCE— in a time when other women with far better cases rarely were granted one. After touring Australia, she lived out the rest of her life in the U.S., where she gained a considerable reputation for helping other women whose lives did not meet the era's moral standards. Her *Art of Beauty* (1858) was doubtless read by many of those who nonetheless denounced her unconventional freedom.

MOORE, MARIANNE CRAIG (1887–1972)

One of the twentieth century's most distinguished poets, Marianne Moore was the daughter of a Missouri WIDOW who supported her children by working as a TEACHER in Pennsylvania. Marianne graduated from BRYN MAWR in 1909, and then emulated her mother by teaching business courses at a Pennsylvania school for Native Americans. With her mother and brother, she moved to New York during WORLD WAR I and remained there the rest of her life, working first as a librarian and then as an editor to supplement her writing income.

Personally popular among the literati who settled in Greenwich Village in this era, she published her first poems in periodicals in 1915. Her freshly original work was praised by Ezra Pound and William Carlos Williams, while other literary men invited her to join the editorial staff of *The Dial*, a revival of the magazine that had been so important to MARGARET FULLER almost a century earlier. Moore won a two thousand dollar prize from the magazine in 1924, and the following year, became its chief editor.

Much influenced by her mother, who lived with her until death, Moore continued to teach Sunday school while she began establishing herself as an avant garde poet. She published two volumes of poetry in each of the three decades between 1921 and 1951, when her seventh book brought her the Pulitzer Prize. Titled *Collected Poems* (1951), it was dedicated to her recently deceased mother. Moore worked in other genres as well; she was a noted essayist and spent ten years on a translation of French literature.

Much recognized late in life, her honors included selection to the National Institute of Arts and Letters in 1947 and its Gold Medal in 1953, the National Book Award in 1952, and election to the prestigious American Academy of Arts and Letters in 1955. Moore remained extremely modest, however, and ruthlessly eliminated works from publication that she judged beneath her standards.

She continued polishing her words until her death at eighty-four. T. S. Eliot called Marianne Moore "one of the few who have done the language some service in my lifetime."

Grandma Moses viewing a televised exhibition of her paintings in 1948. The NBC microphone to the right allowed her to interact with the commentators. NATIONAL ARCHIVES.

MORRIS, ESTHER HOBART McQUIGG SLACK (1814–1902)

The first American woman to hold an official governmental position, Esther Morris was a justice of the peace in Wyoming Territory in 1870. The territorial legislature had granted women the right to vote the previous year, and with that came other accoutrements of full citizenship, including the right to hold office.

Born in the western New York state area near SENECA FALLS that produced so many FEMINISTS, Morris had gone west to Illinois as a young WIDOW with a child in 1845. She remarried, bore three more sons and moved further west in 1869, where she quickly made herself a Wyoming leader. She had been part of the emerging SUFFRAGE MOVEMENT in Illinois after hearing SUSAN ANTHONY speak, and upon arrival in Wyoming, Morris invited territorial leaders to her home and induced them to pass a suffrage bill.

Her quick success not only typifies the extraordinary status of WESTERN WOMEN, but also the relative ease of accomplishing new ideas in new institutions, for the legislature was small enough to be easily amenable to personal influence.

The governor rose above pleas to veto the bill, and the first elections in which women voted were marked by a solemnity and respect for the process that had been missing in earlier elections that were routinely disrupted by the all-male electorate.

In February of 1870, the governor appointed Morris justice of the peace for South Pass City, a gold mining boom town then the largest in the territory and a challenge to any law enforcement officer. Her six foot stature doubtlessly was helpful in making her an effective authority figure, and she drew national attention, including articles in publications associated with MIRIAM LESLIE. Morris handled as many as seventy cases without a reversal by higher courts, but after issuing a warrant against her husband for assault in June, 1871, she moved on to Laramie. She was nominated for the state legislature on the slate of a nascent women's party two years later, but turned down the nomination to concentrate on her personal life after separating from her husband.

Morris' son, the editor of a Cheyenne newspaper, was largely responsible for preserving her history. When Wyoming was finally admitted to the Union in 1890 with woman suffrage as part of its constitution—over the objections of many in Congress—Esther Morris was honored in Cheyenne by the new state's governor. She also participated in the ceremonies surrounding the DECLARATION OF RIGHTS FOR WOMEN at the Philadelphia CENTENNIAL EXHIBITION in 1876, and Judge Esther Morris was part of a tour by Susan Anthony in 1893 when Colorado women received the vote.

A true pioneer, Esther Morris died at eighty-seven. She was commemorated with a statue in the nation's Capitol in 1960.

MOSES, GRANDMA (ANNA MARY ROBERTSON MOSES) (1860–1961)

A FARM WOMAN who worked hard all of her life, Anna Robertson Moses took up painting at seventy-seven and almost immediately became an artistic phenomenon.

Her education had been limited to a few months in a country school in New York State near the Vermont border during the post–Civil War era. She married at twenty-seven and moved with her farmer husband to Virginia, where she bore ten children and lost five to INFANT MORTALITY. After several decades in Virginia, the family returned to rural New York, where her husband died in 1927. A decade later, when arthritis made needlework too difficult, "Grandma Moses" began painting. With a lifelong habit of frugality, she used old boards rather than canvas; after painting the wood white, she developed her theme on the surface—and the white background became a signature of her work.

Like others in her area during the Depression years of the thirties, she sold homemade products at a Woman's Exchange, and it was there that an art collector saw her work in 1938. He sought out the artist, bought several paintings, and included them in a 1939 exhibit at the Museum of Modern Art. They proved popular, and the following year, Grandma Moses was featured in a one-woman show. At eighty, she received national attention and artistic acclaim.

Demand for her work grew with the prosperity of WORLD WAR II, a time that also was appreciative of her nostalgic subjects. Her depiction of apple-picking, Christmas tree cutting, and happy scenes of more peaceful times had great appeal during the strained wartime years, and Grandma Moses soon had many emulators in the school of "primitivism." During the two decades that remained in her exceptionally long life, she painted as many as fifteen hundred works.

Among the survivors when she died at 101 was a granddaughter who has recently opened a San Francisco art gallery dedicated to her memory. "None of the relatives really took her seriously," said the granddaughter in 1991. "They'd look at her paintings and say, 'Oh, for heaven's sake.'" Her family's feelings aside, today Anna Robertson Moses' paintings remain valuable and are included in such prestigious collections as that of the Metropolitan Museum of Art.

MOTHER'S DAY

The first Mother's Day was celebrated in a Philadelphia church in 1907; with energetic organizing by Anna Jarvis, the "tradition" was observed in every state within four years. Mother's Day centered in the church for many decades thereafter, with Southerners especially likely to honor living

Leadership of the Woman's Party commemorating the 135th anniversary of the birth of Lucretia Mott on January 3, 1928, in the U.S. Capitol. Mott is featured at the statue's right, while Susan Anthony is in the middle and Elizabeth Cady Stanton is at the left. Sculptor Adelaide Johnson stands nearest the wreath. LIBRARY OF CONGRESS; PHOTOGRAPH BY UNDERWOOD & UNDERWOOD.

mothers by wearing red roses to church, while white roses indicated that one's mother was dead. Meanwhile, Father's Day was first celebrated in Spokane, Washington in 1910.

Congress formally established the second Sunday in May as a day to honor mothers in 1914, with President Wilson leading the way. Many of the era's suffragists under the leadership of ALICE PAUL were already resentful of Wilson, and they objected to this sentimental response to women's economic and legal problems. Controversy has continued to surround the event every year, as its church-based origin has been replaced by advertisers and retailers promoting the purchase of billions of dollars worth of gifts.

MOTT, LUCRETIA COFFIN (1793–1880)

One of the most important of nineteenth-century women, Lucretia Mott was first a leader in the ABOLITIONIST movement.

Like her longtime friend SUSAN ANTHONY, Mott came out of the tradition of activist QUAKER WOMEN. Her independent thought was further influenced by her childhood home in Nantucket, a sailing center where women spent a great deal of time alone and the island that later produced MARIA MITCHELL. After attending school in Boston and Poughkeepsie, she worked as a virtually unpaid TEACHER—an experience that heightened her awareness of the world's view of women's worth. In 1811, Lucretia Coffin married James Mott, a liberal Quaker and former teacher like herself. The two would become Philadelphia leaders who enjoyed one of the most modern marriages of their time, for he was uncommonly supportive of her work.

Following the traditions of the Society of Friends, Lucretia Mott engaged in PUBLIC SPEAKING and preached both in and out of the meetinghouse, while also bearing six children. She was named as an official minister of the Society of Friends in 1821, and during that decade, she developed an unusually early awareness of the evils of slavery. Within a few years, she was boycotting all products of the South—which meant finding alternatives for cotton, sugar, rice, and other staples of life. Black leader Robert Purvis credited Mott with predating famous abolitionist William Lloyd Garrison and reported that she spoke in "colored churches as early as 1829."

Mott was a founder of the American Anti-Slavery Society in 1833, when abolitionism was controversial even among liberal Quakers, and she served as president of the Philadelphia Anti-Slavery Society decades before most women even considered joining organizations. She demonstrated her quiet courage repeatedly, including leading women from the building burned after MARIA WESTON CHAPMAN's speech in 1838. When the Fugitive Slave Law was passed in 1850, Mott placed her conscience ahead of the law, which she defied by opening her home to fleeing slaves. Dressed in Quaker plainness and careful to observe its gentle mannerisms, she often presented radical views on this and other subjects without alienating those who disagreed.

Mott attended the 1840 World Anti-Slavery Convention in London, which would lead to the SENECA FALLS WOMEN'S RIGHTS CONVENTION in 1848. She met ELIZABETH CADY STANTON at the anti-slavery convention. Years later, Stanton would recall learning of Mott's reputation in England: "I was amazed," Stanton said, "to hear Mrs. Mott spoken of as a most dangerous woman . . . a heretic, a disturber, who had . . . thrown a firebrand into the World's Convention." But when young Stanton spent time with Mott, the older woman "seemed like a being from some larger planet . . . I felt at once a new-born sense of dignity and freedom; it was like suddenly coming into the rays of the noon-day sun, after . . . the caves of the earth." Others felt the same, and Mott "was frequently chosen the presiding officer" of the early women's rights conventions.

When abolitionism finally resulted in the CIVIL WAR, Mott—like many in the Society of Friends—found her pacifist principles in conflict with her desire to end slavery. She rededicated herself by serving as vice-president of the Pennsylvania Peace Society, while offering encouragement to younger women such as ANNA DICKINSON. She raised money for the education of the newly free and for Swarthmore College, a co-educational institution founded by Quakers in 1864. After the war was won, she was elected the first president of the AMERICAN EQUAL RIGHTS ASSOCIATION when that group organized in 1866 to secure civil rights for ex-slaves and—as some believed—for women.

Lucretia Mott saw women's issues more broadly than most in the growing SUFFRAGE MOVEMENT, and she never gave particular primacy to the vote. Perhaps because her own domestic life was uncommonly happy and because she remained deeply religious, she was also slow to accept the DIVORCE issue. When the AMERICAN WOMAN SUFFRAGE ASSOCIATION had their bitter 1869 split and almost all activists divided sharply, Mott stood virtually alone in attempting to work with both sides and urging the compromise that she did not live to see. All of her life, she saw herself as essentially a missionary; she took "many long journeys both North and South to carry the glad tidings of justice, liberty, and equality."

Personally frugal and publicly generous, Mott was a philanthropist who was remembered for leaving five dollars "for the trouble I've made" every time that she dropped in for tea at the women's headquarters during the CENTENNIAL EXHIBITION of 1876—at a time when five dollars was a week's wages for most women. She was a WIDOW by then, for James had died in 1868; their fifty-seven-year marriage was applauded by many contemporaries. Lucretia Mott lived on to eighty-seven, actively seeking to improve her world. A faithful Quaker to the end, her last speech was to the annual meeting of the Society of Friends.

MOUNT HOLYOKE The oldest of the SEVEN SISTERS schools began as Mount Holyoke Female Seminary under the leadership of visionary MARY LYON in 1837.

It was located in South Hadley, Massachusetts because that town offered eight thousand dollars towards the idea of higher education for young women, which was a revolutionary notion at a time when COLLEGES were available exclusively to males. Moreover, Mount Holyoke evolved a work/study program that also was unprecedented; unlike the male institutions, Mount Holyoke was designed to encourage poorer students whose labor would provide part of their tuition costs. Despite this innovative economic opportunity, however, the school was slow to drop racial barriers; by 1910, it had only two African-American graduates.

With a curriculum that included sciences and languages comparable to male colleges, Mount Holyoke quickly became a financial success and a demonstration of women's desire to learn. So firm was its foundation that when Lyon died in 1849—only twelve years after the school began—Mount Holyoke continued without significant pause. The majority of its graduates became TEACHERS and many entered the mission field by marrying ordained ministers (especially from nearby Amherst and Yale) and thus fulfilled the founders' intent of a "female seminary."

Mount Holyoke, though still not calling itself a college, moved its three-year curriculum to four in 1861—several years before VASSAR began its conscious emulation of the structure of male colleges. In 1888, it was rechartered as Mount Holyoke Seminary and College; the final name change, dropping the outdated "seminary" usage, came in 1893. One of its earliest students was also one of its most important: LUCY STONE enrolled in Mount Holyoke when it was only two years old. Among other outstanding students are VIRGINIA APGAR, OLYMPIA BROWN, EMILY DICKINSON, CONSTANCE MCLAUGHLIN GREEN, and FRANCES PERKINS. SHIRLEY CHISHOLM has taught there recently.

MULLER VS. OREGON In this 1908 case, the U.S. Supreme Court upheld an Oregon law establishing a maximum ten-hour day for women employed in laundries. The state's action was still another example of the higher status of WESTERN WOMEN, but more importantly, the Supreme Court's refusal to strike down the law as unconstitutional reversed a similar case just three years earlier and was a victory for the concept of PROTECTIVE LEGISLATION. Even though the battle over whether or not states could limit the "freedom" of women to work themselves into exhaustion would still go on for another decade or two, the case set an important precedent that encouraged other governmental bodies to write similar legislation.

Muller vs. Oregon also created history because of the massive set of data on women's employment conditions that was assembled by FLORENCE KELLEY for attorney Louis Brandeis (later the first Jewish Supreme Court Justice). The Court set a precedent by giving consideration to Kelley's sociological approach over the strictly legalistic argumentation of the law's opponents. It was a victory of contemporary statistical evidence over outmoded case history, and a triumph of feminine real-world experience over masculine legalistic dogma.

MURRAY, JUDITH SARGENT STEVENS (1751–1820) A

thinker who merits greater attention than she receives, Judith Sargent Murray was a feminist theorist in eighteenth-century New England. In 1790—two years prior to English Mary Wollstonecraft's famous *VINDICATION OF THE RIGHTS OF WOMEN*—this American shared her advanced thought in the *Massachusetts Magazine,* saying in part:

"Suffer me to ask; in what the minds of females are so notoriously deficient . . . Invention is perhaps the most arduous effort of the mind . . . and we have been time out of mind invested with that creative facility . . . Will it be said that the judgment of a male of two years old is more sage than that of a female's of the same age? I believe the reverse is generally observed to be true. But from that period what partiality! How is the one exalted and the other depressed . . . The one is taught to aspire, and the other is early confined and limited . . ."

When she wrote those words, her name was Judith Sargent Stevens and she was almost forty. She had been married at eighteen, her education limited to what she could learn from her brother's books for Harvard. Her husband was a sea captain and they had no children, and her days in the comfort of a Gloucester mansion nonetheless must have seemed endlessly empty until she started to write. By 1779, Stevens was composing essays with a feminist tone, and in 1784, she adopted the PSEUDONYM of "Constantia" and began publishing.

Her husband died in the West Indies two years later. She married John Murray in 1788, who had built the first Unitarian Church in America on land donated by her family. Despite her age, she bore children in 1789 and 1791, losing one to INFANT MORTALITY. She continued to write, however, publishing poems that she sometimes signed with variations of "Honora," and after 1793, even writing plays. In fact, some credit her with the first production by an American playwright.

In need of income late in life, Murray published the tremendous number of essays she had written under a subscription plan that, headed by George Washington, guaranteed her sales. Issued in three volumes in 1798, her work was favorably compared with that of Noah Webster. In 1812, she published three more volumes based on her husband's sermons, and added his biography in 1816.

After living her entire life in the cultural center of Boston, Murray went as a WIDOW to the wilderness of Mississippi, where her daughter had married and moved. Probably frustrated in this remote and primitive setting, she died less than four years later at sixty-nine. Yet her ideas may have had more effect than is recognized, for EMMA WILLARD began her important New York school for young women in the year following Murray's death.

Judith Sargent Murray, an unacknowledged mental giant of colonial days, lies buried on a bluff overlooking the mighty river near Natchez.

NATION, CARRY AMELIA MOORE GLOYD (1846–1911)

One of the most caricaturized of American women, Carry Nation merits more serious attention than she is often given. Her obstreperous PROHIBITIONIST activity—while indeed amusingly different from the methodologies adopted by most reformers—was a very serious matter in the context of her life. Given the lack of MARRIED WOMEN'S PROPERTY RIGHTS that left wives of alcoholics totally at the mercy of husbands, the surprising thing is that more women didn't emulate her behavior.

Carry Moore had an unhappy childhood; while her father moved the family from state to state in the antebellum mid-South, her mother moved in a world of her own. Mrs. Moore was seriously deranged, and her family made extraordinary accommodations to pacify her belief that they were royalty. Eventually she was institutionalized, but "the Queen" was a dominant factor in Carry's young life.

After a two-year courtship hotly pursued by the would-be groom over the objections of her mother, Carry was married at twenty to Dr. Charles Gloyd, a teacher who claimed to be a physician, but who never established a practice. Truly in love, she did not realize until after the wedding that he was profoundly addicted to alcohol. In a pattern that was not unusual at the time, he spent his evenings with his male friends and was home only long enough to impregnate his bride. She clearly resented the changed behavior he exhibited as soon as the wedding vows were said: "There is no society or business," she would write later, "that calls men from their homes at night that produces any good result." His male bonding centered on liquor, and Gloyd's alcoholism proved to be so serious that he died a few months after their baby was born.

A WIDOW at twenty-one, Gloyd worked as a TEACHER for four years while her mother-in-law cared for her child. Their comfortable matriarchy was broken up when a school board official found an excuse to fire Gloyd so that his niece could be hired. Lacking any employment opportunity in their small Missouri town, she felt she had no choice but to accept the proposal of marriage offered by David Nation. Nineteen years older than she, Nation was a contentious lawyer/editor/businessman/preacher who—much like her father—would move his family throughout the South in search of his next personal battle. In Texas, Carry contributed the most stable part of their income by running a BOARDING hotel, but just as the establishment was prospering, David's political feuds became so threatening that he moved the family to Kansas.

It was there, in the town of Medicine Lodge, that in 1892 Carry Nation formed a local chapter of the WOMAN'S CHRISTIAN TEMPERANCE UNION (WCTU). Kansas was a likely place to draw such a response from women; psychiatrist Karl Menninger, who later founded his famous clinic there, said of that time and place: "The state was full of psychopaths and unstable characters who had failed in the East . . . It was tough going out here and the temptation to get drunk and forget it was pretty widespread . . . [Alcoholism] caused a lot of damage to life and property." Other men agreed, and the Prohibitionist movement had a great deal of male support, especially from men in religion and business. Indeed, it is important to remember that when the Prohibition Amendment was added to the Constitution, women still lacked the vote in most states.

Nation thus was not a pioneer in the movement, for the WCTU was almost twenty years old by the time she joined. She led her group in the quiet, conventional way for almost a decade before she decided more drastic measures were needed. Adopting the strategy of the Midwestern women who had pioneered the WCTU, she began praying in front of saloons. In 1899, she held her first, still-peaceful demonstrations: she closed the local saloons by singing, praying, and embarrassing the operators—who, after all, were in violation of the law, since the all-male legislature of Kansas had officially declared the state "dry."

Emboldened by this success, Nation's WCTU women moved on to other towns, where the same tactics were successful. It was the following summer that she added physical force to prayer. In Kiowa, Kansas, in May of 1900, Carry Nation took aim at a saloon where she had warned the owner the previous year. Armed with rocks and bricks, she entered and broke bottles, and when her supply of ammunition ran out, she used a hatchet to break up the furniture. She moved down the street to the next saloon, and the hatchet would be linked with her ever after.

The spectacle of a woman engaging in the wanton destruction of property was so incredible that witnesses at first seemed paralyzed into nonresistance. Men could not quite credit a woman with such violent behavior, and Nation initially wrecked "joints" almost at will. When she went to Wichita that December, however, she expected to encounter genuine resistance. While the first proprietor she attacked had addressed her as "Mother Nation" and cowered in a corner while she wrecked his business, she expected no such quarter in Wichita. It was a city with a reputation for quick and accurate gunmen, and it took no small amount of courage for this rural housewife to take advantage of her husband's absence and board the train two days after Christmas in 1900.

She chose the Hotel Carey not because of its homophonous connection to her name, but because it had a national reputation; destroying it made her a national figure. Done in marble and onyx, it was a grand place, but Nation's fury focused—when she entered the bar and saw it—on a huge nude overlooking the fifty-foot cherrywood bar. When the BARTENDER informed her that he didn't serve ladies, she smashed a bottle but held her temper until she could prepare for a full-scale assault. The next morning, she returned armed with hundreds of rocks in special pockets sewn on her garments. In a matter of minutes, she did thousands of dollars worth of damage to antique mirrors and crystal chandeliers as well as to the offending artwork—and then tried to bash the skull of the policeman who came to quell her.

Finally incarcerated, she found that the hotel had powerful customers, some of whom were not amused by the political problem she posed in pointing out the contradictions between the laws they passed and the lives they led. Jailed for two weeks, Nation attracted large groups of women who sang and prayed outside her cell—while business at the damaged bar boomed with the curious. After that incident, Nation's reputation preceded her and saloon operators were quick to resist. She would be arrested, mobbed, and threatened with hanging many times in the future, but nothing slowed her campaign.

One of her strongest points was, of course, that she was enforcing the law. A month after she destroyed the hotel bar, she was honored at a state temperance convention. While she was in the capital—in January of 1901, as the twentieth century dawned—she called on the governor and demanded that he use his legitimate powers to enforce the duly passed law so that she would not have to. When nothing happened, she returned to her crusade and once again was jailed while the saloon operators continued business as usual.

Her marriage broke up shortly afterwards. David Nation filed for DIVORCE on the grounds of desertion in July, 1901, when Carry Nation left on a national lecture tour. She did so because she needed the money that her infamy would bring on tour: faced with numerous fines and lacking any source of income, she was dependent on the small amounts that her WCTU friends could garner from their husbands' pockets. She needed funds, too, for the prohibition publications that she would try to issue, as well as for the Kansas City shelter for families of alcoholics that she established about this same time—one of the first models for today's spouse abuse shelters.

Nation was so desperate for money for these projects that she seriously damaged her credibility with the national WCTU—which was already apprehensive about the property destruction issue—with appearances such as a 1903 Coney Island sideshow. She responded to criticism by saying that she would prefer to make her appeals in churches, but that few would allow her to speak. Moreover, she reasoned, if she were to save souls from drink, she needed to be where the drunkards were.

The following year, she published an autobiography, *The Use and Need of Carry Nation* (1904), which not only provided income but also a portable platform. As the title implies, it was an apologia explaining why she felt "needed" by women whose lives were ruined by the alcoholism of their men. The autobiography provided money not only for her travel expenses and other needs, but also for the care of Nation's daughter, Charlien.

Afflicted in her youth with disease in her cheek and jaw, Charlien also inherited her father's propensity for alcohol and a tendency to mental illness from her grandmother. In 1904—a year after David Nation died in the midst of her mother's crusade—Charlien Gloyd McNabb was admitted to the Texas State Lunatic Asylum. Still a devoted mother, Nation hurried to Austin and cared for her; for the rest of Carry Nation's life, Charlien would be a financial and emotional drain.

Like the autobiography, sales of souvenir hatchets inscribed "Carry Nation, Joint Smasher" served a dual purpose: they not only supported the work that she saw as imperative, but the hatchets also symbolized empowerment of women. In her inchoate way, Nation was trying to convince women that they could be as powerful as she—even though they might lack her physical strength. At a time when the entire concept of psychology was unfamiliar to most, she understood the importance of assertiveness training for women.

One of Nation's important assets, in fact, was that she was the physical equal of most men. Even though past mid-life, she was nearly six feet tall, weighed about 180 pounds, and remained strong from a lifetime of hard work. Male witnesses acknowledged that she threw heavy cash registers and ripped off steel doors in her "demonic" demolition crusades. Nor was she tempered by the politeness usually associated with women: she ripped cigars from smokers' lips and addressed judges as "Your Dishonor." She invaded two state legislatures to offer unwelcome speeches and was ejected from the U.S. Senate gallery after shouting at senators.

She moved throughout the country during the first decade of the twentieth century, creating her own platforms from Maine to California and from Texas to Wyoming. Even though the WCTU had largely disowned her, she nonetheless managed fund-raising that exhibited considerable organizational ability. She sometimes ran newspaper advertisements addressed to women, for example, asking them to meet her at a specific place and time. "Bring your hatchets with you," read one. "I will pay the railroad fares of those not able." That she did not see herself as destructive is clear in her closing line: "This appeal is made to the gentle, loving, brave Christian women whose hearts are breaking with sympathy for the oppressed."

In addition to her size, Nation's age was a liberating factor, for she was in her mid-fifties when she became active. Hers was the freedom of a woman aware that her life was almost over and eager to make meaningful whatever time she had left. There are some who believe she had syphilis; if so, this, too, would be a powerful motivating factor, for countless American women were like her in their naive sexuality and acceptance of double standards that literally killed them with venereal disease.

In any case, the time devoted to her crusade was a relatively small part of an otherwise ordinary life: Carry Nation did her first saloon demonstration in 1899 and her last a few days into 1910. Ironically, she was put out of action by another woman; when Nation attacked a Montana saloon in January, 1910, the female owner beat her so badly that she was permanently affected. Almost exactly a year later, she fainted during an Arkansas appearance and died six months later back in Kansas. Her reputation would be forever tinged by accusations of mental illness that were reinforced by the institutionalization of both her mother and her daughter—but again, the eminent psychiatrist Menninger felt that such assumptions were wrong. "What I have always admired about Carry Nation," he said, "was the fact that she couldn't stomach hypocrisy . . . I wish that there were more people today who feel the same way."

NATIONAL AMERICAN WOMAN SUFFRAGE ASSOCIATION (NAWSA)

The largest of the SUFFRAGE MOVEMENT organizations, it was formed in 1890 when the NATIONAL WOMAN SUFFRAGE ASSOCIATION (NWSA), led by SUSAN ANTHONY and ELIZABETH CADY STANTON, merged with its rival, the AMERICAN WOMAN SUFFRAGE ASSOCIATION (AWSA), which was primarily associated with LUCY STONE and JULIA WARD HOWE. The merger took place after more than two decades of disharmony, and the NAWSA would become the preeminent suffrage body

until the passage of the NINETEENTH AMENDMENT that unequivocally gave women the right to vote.

ALICE STONE BLACKWELL and HARRIOT STANTON BLATCH were major factors in encouraging the merger, which occurred shortly before the death of their mothers, Lucy Stone and Elizabeth Cady Stanton. Amongst other minutia of the nineteenth meeting of the AWSA in Philadelphia in the fall of 1887, Blackwell recorded these historic words: "*Resolved, That Mrs. Lucy Stone be appointed a committee of one from the American W.S.A. to confer with Miss Susan Anthony, of the National W.S.A., and if on conference it seems desirable, that she be authorized and empowered to appoint a committee of this association to meet a similar committee appointed by the National W.S.A. to consider a satisfactory basis of union . . .*"

When the merged organization met three years later, Stanton became the NAWSA's first president; Anthony assumed the presidency in 1892. Following the patterns laid down by the earlier two groups, the NAWSA held annual national conventions and conducted dozens of state suffrage campaigns during the 1890s and early 1900s. After Anthony's death in 1906, however, it lost energy, and its leadership was challenged by the younger, more militant ALICE PAUL, LUCY BURNS, and others in the new CONGRESSIONAL UNION FOR WOMAN SUFFRAGE and its later incarnation, the WOMAN'S PARTY. WORLD WAR I added other policy complications, as suffragists disagreed on whether or not to support the war. CARRIE CHAPMAN CATT was amazingly effective in revitalizing the NAWSA during these war years, and it had over 2 million members by the time that suffrage became a reality in 1920.

But the NAWSA was a single-purpose organization, and when suffrage passed, many of its members turned to issues other than FEMINISM—something that would be reflected in the goals of the LEAGUE OF WOMEN VOTERS, which was a direct outgrowth of the NAWSA's ultimate success. The official history of the NAWSA can be found in volumes four through six of the massive HISTORY OF WOMAN SUFFRAGE.

NATIONAL ASSOCIATION OF COLORED WOMEN

Formally organized in Washington, D.C. on July 21, 1896, the National Association of Colored Women (NACW) grew out of a Boston meeting the previous year, when leaders in the National Colored Women's League and the National Federation of Afro-American Women discussed a merger. Margaret Murray Washington, wife of Booker T. Washington, assumed the temporary chairmanship; MARY CHURCH TERRELL was elected president when the NACW officially began. Delegates from twenty-five states represented about five thousand members at that first meeting.

Though few would realize it, the NACW's goals predated those of white FEMINISTS many decades later, for they centered around employment issues. Because "so many families are supported entirely by our women," as Terrell candidly explained in 1900, the NACW would focus on job opportunity and training, "equality of pay" and "care for the children of absentee mothers." The NACW itself was made up of mostly middle-class black women—many of whom were wealthy enough to be employers rather than employees—but their primary concern was the welfare of those of their gender and race who were less economically fortunate. They made real the principles espoused in their motto, "Lifting as We Climb."

As with all organizations, there were initial internal problems. Rivalry between the two original groups, with memberships based largely in Washington and Boston, continued for a while, and the 1899 meeting in Chicago saw conflict over delegate credentials. More serious problems were raised by the desire of the Chicago members to exclude IDA WELLS-BARNETT. President Terrell handled these difficulties with political astuteness; she got the NACW underway with a well-run convention that was favorably reviewed by white newspapers, while JANE ADDAMS was induced to host a reception.

Conventions were held biannually after 1900, and by 1904, the NACW had fifteen thousand members in thirty-one states. The organization had twelve departments, including some devoted to art, literature, and other academic interests that reflected the influence of the era's CLUB MOVEMENT. Both membership and numbers of departments had grown still more by the 1908 convention in Brooklyn, and in that year members also tackled their own internal color barriers. NACW leadership to that point had been light-skinned, and in 1908, there was a candid movement to elect darker women to office. "We prefer a woman who is altogether negro," one delegate explained, because the abilities of the previous officers "is attributed to their white blood. We want to demonstrate that the African is as talented."

From their earliest meetings, NACW members also spoke out against transportation systems that excluded blacks, no matter how wealthy or respectable, from first-class accommodations. NACW conventions at various times called for boycotts of businesses that discriminated and asked members not to travel in segregated states. Delegates called for race pride, and Mary Church Terrell early advocated classes on "African Ancestors." The NACW also campaigned against lynching and protested against convict leasing systems in the South that came dangerously close to recreating slavery.

While most NACW members would not have called themselves feminists, their issues made them so. In one of her founding speeches, for example, Mary Church Terrell urged members to speak out against the "slanders circulated against us . . . both in the press and by the direct descendents of those who in years past were responsible for the degradation of their female slaves." She went on to defend young black women who, though they were excluded from the "safeguards usually thrown around maidenly youth," strove against the odds to live sexually responsible lives. Terrell cited "statistics compiled by men not inclined to falsify in favor of my race" that showed IMMIGRANT WOMEN from certain countries were more likely than blacks to be engaged in PROSTITUTION. (Other studies done at the same time showed that immigrant women, in turn, were less often involved in the sale of sex than were native whites.)

While the NACW forged links with the WOMEN'S CHRISTIAN TEMPERANCE UNION, the GENERAL FEDERATION OF WOMEN'S CLUBS, and the YOUNG WOMEN'S CHRISTIAN ASSOCIATION, it was not a major player in the SUFFRAGE MOVEMENT. Although Terrell personally was active for the cause, she recognized that "it required a great deal of courage for a woman publicly to acknowledge before an audience that she believed in suffrage

for her sex when she knew the majority did not." Much of her membership echoed the conservatism of their husbands and regularly subordinated their feminist interests to their racial ones.

In addition, NACW members were reluctant to take on the suffrage cause because many white suffragists were less than welcoming. Terrell, who spoke at several suffrage conventions, candidly admonished white suffragists in 1904 when she said, "I want you to stand up not only for children and animals but even for Negroes. You will never get suffrage till you . . . give fair play to the colored race."

Terrell's suffrage advocacy was supported by Ida Wells-Barnett, who argued against conservatives such as Mrs. Booker T. Washington—a woman capable of dismissing suffrage by saying the issue "has never kept me awake at night." Wells-Barnett instead pointed out that women's votes could help black legislative causes and offered statistics demonstrating that lynchings declined in those states where women voted. The women's suffrage amendment finally received a full endorsement from the NACW convention of 1912—eight years before passage.

Most NACW members, however, were simply less interested in abstract philosophical issues such as suffrage than they were in concrete local activity that visibly benefited black women. Already by the second convention in 1900, the organization could report the construction of "a sanitarium with a training school for NURSES," while from Alabama to Chicago other projects were underway. Most early projects were concentrated in the Deep South, but over the years, the NACW would support dozens of facilities from New York to California.

The first nursery school in the South was an NACW Atlanta project, and it supported vocational schools for black girls in Virginia, Alabama, Mississippi, Arkansas, Florida, and Texas in an era when taxpayers in those states did not fund such operations. Summer camps and homes for delinquent children—especially girls—were other fund-raising focuses. Northern chapters sometimes adopted a particular Southern venture, but they also worked in their own states with projects such as a clubhouse for black women at the University of Iowa and a nursery school in Chicago.

By the middle of the twentieth century, virtually every state NACW branch owned property and maintained a substantial budget. For example, in Kansas—a state without a major black population—the NACW in 1954 owned a thirty-five thousand dollar PHYLLIS WHEATLEY Home in Wichita, a twenty-four thousand dollar home for UNWED MOTHERS in Topeka, as well as an eighteen thousand five hundred dollar clubhouse. A national scholarship fund for the COLLEGE education of black women was begun in 1912 with initial contributions of fifty thousand dollars.

The organization also kept the history of black women alive in the names of their efforts: Los Angeles, for example, had NACW buildings named for SOJOURNER TRUTH and MADAME C. J. WALKER. It was the NACW, too, that built a monument to HARRIET TUBMAN in Albany. The eighth president of the NACW was MARY MCLEOD BETHUNE; under her leadership the organization bought a Washington headquarters building.

Mary Church Terrell had given her first address as president when the NACW met in Nashville in 1897. She laid out an ambitious program of work, pointing out that in the three decades since the end of slavery when they were "penniless as a race," considerable progress had been made. "We challenge any other race," she said, "to present a record more credible . . . than that made by the ex-slaves of the United States . . . in the face of prejudice, proscription, and persecution." She asked her audience not to gasp when she proposed that they run free kindergartens, and she went on to suggest "Mother congresses in every community in which our women can be counseled."

She was much in advance of others: her idea for counseling services is only recently coming to fruition. Similarly, she spoke in 1900 of "infants [who] are locked alone in a room from the time the mother leaves in the morning until she returns at night"—and the problem of child care for low-income women remains unsolved. In these, as in other areas, the National Association of Colored Women led the way for white feminists.

NATIONAL COUNCIL OF NEGRO WOMEN On December 5, 1935, a meeting called by MARY MCLEOD BETHUNE resulted in the merger of a number of organizations into the National Council of Negro Women (NCNW). The leadership of these organizations was in Washington, where Bethune lived during her days with the Roosevelt administration; for weeks, these women assembled at Bethune's apartment to work on the details of the new federation. With her usual finesse at getting support from wealthy white men, Bethune persuaded department store magnate Marshall Field to finance their headquarters.

Their chief initial aim was employment opportunity for black women during the Great Depression, and WORLD WAR II simply rechanneled that purpose. The NCNW played a particularly strong role in ensuring equal opportunity in the WOMEN'S ARMY CORPS (WAC); Bethune herself served on an advisory committee for WAC policy. After the war, the NCNW worked for the constitutional amendment that banned poll taxes and for legislation to end lynchings, as well as for the establishment of a permanent Fair Employment Practices Commission.

Bethune held the presidency from its 1935 beginning to 1949. When she retired, the NCNW had eight hundred thousand members and a strong record of achievement. Today it maintains the Bethune Museum and Archives for Black Women, as well as a Washington office where more than fifty staff members serve 240 local groups. The NCNW also conducts programs in Africa and publishes *Black Women's Voice* and *Sisters Magazine*.

NATIONAL EQUAL RIGHTS PARTY— *See* LOCKWOOD, BELVA

NATIONAL ORGANIZATION FOR WOMEN The preeminent organization of the revitalized women's movement in the late twentieth century, NOW was formed in October, 1966. BETTY FRIEDAN—whose book, *The Feminine Mystique* (1963), had played a large role in reawakening FEMINIST consciousness—convened the original meeting and served as NOW's president until 1970.

When she stepped down, NOW had about six thousand members. Among their goals were ending the gender-based job descriptions that newspapers commonly ran in their classified advertisements; the establishment of childcare centers that would be seen as a public service like schools or libraries; and the reform of state laws that banned abortion. The promotion of a one-day strike by women on August 26, 1970 (the fiftieth anniversary of the passage of the NINETEENTH AMENDMENT) resulted in a great deal of press attention to NOW.

Membership grew quickly. Under the leadership of Wilma Scott-Heide, NOW's fifth national convention saw more than 750 delegates from 180 chapters representing fifteen thousand people. Ratification of the EQUAL RIGHTS AMENDMENT absorbed much of the organization's energy during the seventies, but local chapters also devoted a great deal of time to reforming the educational system, especially in changing textbooks to reflect women's roles and in expanding girls' sports.

Eleanor Smeal, elected president in 1977, was the first salaried NOW officer; she would go on to found the Fund for a Feminist Majority after her NOW presidency. This followed precedents laid down earlier in the decade, for many of the women who were founding members of NOW were also founders of Women's Political Caucus in 1971, which was created for the more specific goal of involving women in politics. As feminist awareness grew, other organizations developed that were variations on NOW's theme of true equality for women.

With headquarters in Washington, NOW has approximately a half-million members organized into more than one thousand chapters. Attorney Patricia Ireland, who was an airline "stewardess" when the movement began, became president in 1991. The organization continues to work for its original goal of "full equality for women in truly equal partnership with men."

NATIONAL WAR SERVICE ACT A subject of intense debate during WORLD WAR II, the National War Service Act was proposed to grant "the government power to direct any able-bodied citizen, man or woman, to work where needed." Its advocates pointed to the example of Britain, where compulsory registration of women for war work had already proven itself. Almost two-thirds of Britain's women were in factories, civilian defense, or the military itself, many of them assigned to jobs that were not particularly their choice.

Some felt that American women should be equally patriotic, and a lively public debate of compulsory war work for women began. Dramatic headlines appeared in 1942: "Draft for Women," declared *Business Week*; "Shall We Draft Women?" proposed the *Nation*; even *Woman's Home Companion* frightened its audience with "Should Women Be Drafted?" In most of these gripping titles, "draft" actually meant only compulsory civilian work, but even that suggestion was enough to stir a good deal of controversy.

Attention centered on Senate Bill 666, which came to be known as the Austin-Wadsworth Bill or the National War Service Act. Sponsored by Senator Warren Austin, Republican of Vermont, it called for compulsory registration of women eighteen to fifty (men eighteen to sixty-five already being registered under Selective Service) but more importantly, it would have required both sexes to serve in whatever industrial or agricultural job they were assigned. It was true that pregnant women and those with children under eighteen or with incapacitated dependents were exempt, but nevertheless the proposal was a significant one. For the first time in American history, it was being seriously proposed that women, like men, could be drafted against their will for the service of their government.

Seven similar bills were introduced on the subject, all of them—ironically—sponsored by congressmen who were Republicans or conservative Southern Democrats. Perhaps because of their antipathy to Roosevelt in pre–Pearl Harbor days, they were anxious to out-do him; perhaps their concept of compulsory labor was actually a union-busting subterfuge. But for whatever reason, support for the notion of drafting women came, oddly enough, from conservatives. A Citizens Committee for a National War Service Act was formed, led by a man from Alabama and vice-chaired by Republican icon Henry D. Cabot. The American Legion actively supported the legislation.

Equally surprising is the fact that there was very little debate in Congress of the usual emotional sort on issues pertaining to women. The arguments instead centered on such points as whether it was consistent with democratic principles to draft any civilian; whether this was best accomplished by legislation or executive order; what was the proper method of carrying out such a labor transfer; and most importantly, whether or not the legislation was needed at this time. Other than perfunctory assurances that the sanctity of the home was being protected, there was no particular attention paid to the issue of drafting *women*.

Though Secretary of War Stimson gave his support to the bill, other administration officials continued to believe the need was not yet real and warned that premature action could do more harm than good. Thelma McKelvey, women's representative on the War Production Board, sagely pointed out that it would be "unwise to raise the enthusiasm of women and then see that enthusiasm turn to skepticism because a sufficient number of outlets for their productive energies have not yet developed." The Selective Service issued a report favorable to the British and Soviet systems of compulsory allocation of female labor and concluded that the drafting of women would present no problem for them administratively, but questioning the value of a nationwide, compulsory system until the U.S. situation was as grave as that of its allies.

Throughout the war, administration officials continued to warn that if workers did not meet the demand "they bring closer the day when a National Service Act may be passed and an Employment Service agent may appear at their door, registration blank in hand." These officials were certainly not opposed to the concept of registering and drafting women, but they saw the question as more complex than did congressional proponents. It was a question of timing and especially a question of *local* need. It was not a problem that could best be solved by requiring every woman from Maine to Oregon to sign up for a potential draft.

Nonetheless, the public consistently told poll-takers that they were willing to be called for an industrial draft if the government so decided. Just a month after the war began, Gallup inquired: "Would you be in favor of starting now to draft single women between the ages of twenty-one and thirty-

five to train them for wartime jobs?" A firm 68 percent said "Yes," with more women than men supporting the idea (73 percent to 63 percent). When the question was asked of those most likely to be drafted themselves, support was still higher, with a remarkable 91 percent of potential draftees agreeing that "the government should draft persons to fill war jobs." Finally, it was the South, the home of the stereotypical Southern belle, that was most strongly supportive of industrial conscription.

Yet opposition remained. *Catholic World*, far from supporting a draft, believed "we might ponder whether there should even be such a thing as women in industry." Magazines in general took a cautious approach; although most of them enthusiastically ran articles designed to attract women to the factories, few were willing to advocate compulsion. They preferred, instead, to accent the positive.

This was also the approach taken by the White House. Roosevelt, who so often was accused of regimentation, preferred to avoid compulsion in this area, while his rivals in the legislature advocated it. For reasons that probably have more to do with party politics and labor unions than with the "proper role" of women, the National War Service Act never came to a vote.

Public opinion polls supporting a draft showed a comforting reservoir of good will and a potential for future needs. Unless the war became worse, however, it was the natural inclination of true democrats that coercion be avoided—but no constitutional authority argued that Congress lacked the right to draft women, and the public supported this unprecedented action by a wide margin. It was, unfortunately, a precedent seldom discussed in later debates on the EQUAL RIGHTS AMENDMENT.

NATIONAL WOMAN'S PARTY— *See* WOMAN'S PARTY

NATIONAL WOMAN SUFFRAGE ASSOCIATION (NWSA)

An outgrowth of the AMERICAN EQUAL RIGHTS ASSOCIATION, the NATIONAL WOMAN SUFFRAGE ASSOCIATION (NWSA) formed in early 1869, when SUSAN ANTHONY led other women in a revolt against the male leadership of the Equal Rights Association. The men had made it clear that they saw women's rights as secondary to those of ex-slaves, and Anthony rebelled.

Under her leadership, the NWSA adopted the radical position of opposing the FIFTEENTH AMENDMENT to the Constitution, which was intended to enfranchise male ex-slaves but not women. Anthony's belief in an educated electorate—regardless of race or gender—was seen as elitist by many of her ABOLITIONIST friends, who a few months later formed the AMERICAN WOMAN SUFFRAGE ASSOCIATION, with JULIA WARD HOWE as president.

ELIZABETH CADY STANTON was NWSA's president through most of its twenty-one-year existence, but Anthony was its true leader. Under the banner of the NWSA, they published the *Revolution*, a radical newspaper actually begun the previous year. Indeed, objections to the paper from the more cautious members of the earlier organization had been still another reason for the split, for in addition to supporting women's enfranchisement, the *Revolution*—most of which was written by Stanton—advocated DIVORCE legislation and publicized other extremist ideas. Soon the paper was deep in debt, and paying those debts absorbed much of Anthony's energies in the 1870s. The effort was even more difficult because the NWSA's publication never gained the prestige of the WOMAN'S JOURNAL, the AWSA's publication.

The rivalry between the two groups continued through the 1870s and 1880s and was reinforced by conflict over VICTORIA WOODHULL, the TILTON-BEECHER AFFAIR, and other burning controversies. Finally, as the leadership of both organizations aged, they merged in 1890 into the NATIONAL AMERICAN WOMAN SUFFRAGE ASSOCIATION (NAWSA). The fact that "National" preceded "American" in the new name and—more importantly—that Stanton also became the first president of the merged group shows that the NWSA can be presumed to have "won" the contest.

By 1890, its positions were not considered as radical as they had been twenty years earlier and separate operations were costly to both organizations. At the same time, the NAWSA during the 1890s and early 1900s did not demonstrate the same level of energy that had existed earlier—until it was challenged by another rival. Thus, it is possible that the seemingly harmful competition between the NWSA and the AWSA actually functioned instead as a spur to the SUFFRAGE MOVEMENT.

NATIONAL WOMEN'S HALL OF FAME— *See* WOMEN'S HALL OF FAME

NAVY NURSE CORPS (NNC) Founded seven years after the official creation of the ARMY NURSE CORPS, the Navy would follow many of the precedents laid down by the Army for NURSES. It would differ, however, in one especially significant way: the small numbers of Navy nurses on ships with men generally gave them greater status than nurses had in land-based situations.

Esther Voorhees Hanson was the first director of the Navy Nurse Corps when it officially began on May 13, 1908. Like the Army's nurses, NNC members were not officially commissioned into the military, but they were nonetheless treated as officers in daily life. With the exception of WORLD WAR I, when Navy nurses were busy with casualties, the NNC provided a fairly pleasant life.

A military nurse's pay was better than that of the average civilian woman; her room, board, and laundry were taken care of for her; she had free medical care and opportunity for travel and graduate education as well as liberal retirement benefits. Nurses worked eight-hour shifts except in emergencies, and because women were greatly outnumbered by men, their status rose in social relationships.

Thus through the twenties and thirties, the NNC was a cohesive unit of professional colleagues who provided care to the relatively small number of men in the peacetime Navy. WORLD WAR II, however, greatly expanded the Corps' numbers while also narrowing and professionalizing the nature of its work. The Navy nurse became quite different from her colleagues in the Army, for she was a teacher and administrator as well as a nurse. This was because she was not allowed to serve on combat ships, but rather remained far behind the fighting line on hospital ships; therefore, most emergency medical treatment was rendered by male medics—who were

taught by Navy nurses. "The instruction of hospital corpsmen . . . is probably the most important single duty of the Navy nurse," said a War Department official.

Yet even behind the lines on hospital ships, there were dangers: nurses were issued ID tags made of nonmeltable material, in the event that the ship burned; they were forbidden to own cameras or keep diaries, to prevent information from falling into enemy hands; radios could not be played because submarines might spot their waves; most mirrors were banned, because they would shatter if bombed. Each nurse was issued a gas mask and a steel helmet.

On most ships, there were only a handful of women and several hundred or even thousands of men. Behavior had to be circumspect, and nurses could invite only officers to their quarters—and then only in a group. On the other hand, this same shortage of women meant that corpsmen on hospital ships did most of the dull routine, while nurses supervised and handled paperwork. More than any other nursing organization, the NNC allowed women the opportunity to ignore the bedpans and be truly professionals.

On the other hand, the Navy was rigid in its demands that nurses fit the stereotype of being not only female, but also white, young, and single. Despite such need that Congress almost drafted nurses with the NURSES SELECTIVE SERVICE BILL, qualified male nurses were not automatically commissioned as women were; black nurses were not accepted by the Navy until 1945; and women over forty-five were officially excluded, while many over thirty reported that they were unofficially excluded.

Moreover, the Navy was absurdly dedicated to the single state of its nurses. Although married women were accepted into both the Army Nurse Corps and the Navy's nonnursing women's corps, the WAVES, it was not until 1944—when 80 percent of all women leaving the NNC had been forced into resignation by the regulations on marriage—that the Navy finally permitted its nurses to wed. Still the victory was an incomplete one, for only nurses already in the NNC were allowed to marry; the applications of married women who wanted to join were rejected. Congress showed more human understanding in this area and fought for greater use of married women.

The end of the war, of course, brought a dramatic reduction in size, but also recognition of the outstanding work Navy nurses had done. Captain Sue Dauser, who headed the NNC during the war, was honored with the Distinguished Service Medal late in 1945, and there was little debate when nurses were regularized into the Navy with full rank and status in 1947. A final milestone came in 1972, when Alene Duerk became the first NNC director to achieve the rank of admiral.

NEURASTHENIA A medical term connoting unexplained fatigue or other physical ailments resulting from depression, this diagnosis was frequently assigned to nineteenth-century women by physicians unable to arrive at any other explanation for their patients' maladies.

A number of women who later became active leaders had been diagnosed earlier in life as neurasthenic. CHARLOTTE PERKINS GILMAN is one of the best-known cases of a young woman who repressed her natural vitality and her anger at women's limited options to the point of illness; it was only when she disregarded her physician's advice that she recovered. Many other similar examples can be cited, ranging from the ennui of young JANE ADDAMS and DOROTHEA DIX to the full disability suffered by MARY BAKER EDDY.

Neurasthenia was almost always assigned to women wealthy enough that their roles in life were confined to that of consumer; it was not an illness of the servant class. It was usually ascribed to young, childless, often unmarried women or to women whose children were grown; it attached itself to these outsiders in a society that thought any function other than motherhood to be inherently unnatural and physically damaging to women. Despite the obvious prescription of productive activity as a preventative, assumptions of poor health remained part of the definition of womanhood for a surprisingly long time. Even modern biographies of nineteenth-century women unquestioningly accept statements about "ill health"—even in cases where the women went on to live active lives until extreme old age.

NEW ENGLAND FEMALE MEDICAL COLLEGE

The 1848 founding date of this institution would seem to indicate that medical education was in fact available to women when ELIZABETH and EMILY BLACKWELL so desperately sought it during the late 1840s and early 1850s. The explanation of this apparent puzzle is that "female medical college" was a misnomer.

Instead, the New England Medical College was a training school for MIDWIVES. Its founder, Samuel Gregory, thought that the presence of men at delivery was indecent, and he established the school to rid the world of what he saw as a contradiction in terms—the "man-midwife." Just as he thought maternity cases to be exclusively female, however, he was equally willing to see all other aspects of medicine as inherently male. He seemed to believe that appending "female" to "medical college" automatically cancelled out the customary meaning of the latter words.

Medical education was still evolving in this era, and Gregory's standards were not significantly lower than those of many other institutions—but his views were certainly not advanced and, moreover, an institution aimed solely at maternity axiomatically limited itself to second-class status. When Gregory hired MARIE ZAKRZEWSKA in 1859, she introduced higher standards and an expanded scientific curriculum that quite naturally challenged Gregory's ego.

During her three-year tenure with the school, however, she not only built its first hospital but also gained the confidence of its "Board of LADY MANAGERS." When the inevitable split came, most of these women accompanied Zakrzewska in building the New England Hospital for Women and Children, while Gregory closed the hospital associated with his school.

NINETEENTH AMENDMENT

The Nineteenth Amendment to the U.S. Constitution reads:

"The right of citizens of the United States to vote shall not be denied or abridged by the United States or by any State on account of sex.

The Congress shall have power, by appropriate legislation, to enforce the provisions of this article."

The Amendment was approved by the requisite two-thirds of the House on May 21, 1919 and by two-thirds of the Senate on June 4, 1919. Slightly more than a year later, the requirement for ratification by three-quarters of the state legislatures would be met, and the long struggle for the right of women to vote was at last over. It had been a very long labor, with at least two generations of active campaigning, plus some efforts prior to the visible SUFFRAGE MOVEMENT. Only one woman who attended the 1848 SENECA FALLS WOMEN'S RIGHTS CONVENTION lived to vote in a national election: Charlotte Woodward was nineteen in 1848 and voted at ninety-three, after devoting her long life to the suffrage movement.

The Nineteenth Amendment was the final victory of that movement, and its overriding importance was in the fact that it forbade states to disallow the vote to women. The precedent for this national approach had been set with the FIFTEENTH AMENDMENT, which was passed in 1870. That amendment was passed because the Reconstruction Congress was aware that if states continued to define who was allowed to vote, ex-slaves in the South would never be enfranchised, and the national amendment thus mandated that states allow them to vote. Women should have been included in the language of the Fifteenth Amendment, for it reads: "The right of citizens of the United States to vote shall not be denied . . . on account of race . . ." Arguing that it said *citizens*, not male citizens, a number of women in different areas tried to vote in the 1870s, but local officials consistently denied the ballot to them.

There seemed little choice except to amend the Constitution to say explicitly that women should be allowed to vote, and SUSAN ANTHONY and others introduced the first suffrage amendment to Congress in 1868. The NATIONAL WOMAN SUFFRAGE ASSOCIATION that she formed the following year continued to concentrate on Washington and an amendment of national applicability; in 1878, NWSA introduced the words that were ultimately adopted long after its authors were dead. NWSA lobbied for this amendment in each Congress that convened after every two-year election period until 1918; it presented literally millions of signatures on petitions during this long period.

Meanwhile, the AMERICAN WOMAN SUFFRAGE ASSOCIATION focused on gaining the vote in the more liberal states, believing that this goal could be more readily reached and that it would create models easing the way for national change. Though seemingly a rational strategy, the AWSA met with no measurable success: only three states adopted state suffrage during the AWSA's existence, and none of them were directly influenced by the organization. After the NWSA and AWSA merged in 1890, literally hundreds of campaigns for state suffrage would be conducted, for in many states, the question went before the all-male electorate several times in different formats and at different elections.

For many years, all of the victories in these state campaigns were in the Far West. The first to grant women equal voting rights was the territory of Wyoming, which passed this historic provision in 1869. Utah women actually cast the first votes when their election took place early in the next year of 1870. Kansas women—many of whom were ABOLITIONISTS who moved to "Bleeding Kansas" when it was a territory

The headquarters of the National Woman's Party in Nashville in the summer of 1920, which was the focus of the final campaign for ratification of the Nineteenth Amendment assuring all American women the right to vote. LIBRARY OF CONGRESS.

explicitly because of their devotion to democratic ideals— voted in school elections in 1861 and had full suffrage by 1885. Colorado included women in November, 1893, and soon thereafter elected three women to its state legislature— the first female legislators in the nation.

When the twentieth century dawned, these four states remained the only ones giving women full franchise. When WORLD WAR I began in Europe in 1914, the number had increased to nine—all in the West. The following year, four hard-fought campaigns in eastern states went down to defeat, as the men of Massachusetts, New Jersey, Pennsylvania, and New York all denied the vote to women. The war's demonstration of women's effectiveness as full citizens increased support, however, and New York reversed itself in 1916 to become the first eastern state to enfranchise women.

When Congress finally passed the suffrage amendment early in 1919, women had full voting rights in twelve states—eleven of which were in the West—with restricted rights in others. Partial suffrage was a compromise used both in this country and

abroad; Norwegian and Danish women, for instance, obtained limited voting rights after 1906. Partial enfranchisement was especially likely in school elections, for many men saw children and education as the natural domain of women. Already in 1838, for example, Kentucky allowed WIDOWS with no children currently in school to vote in school elections. After the CIVIL WAR, other states followed this model and by 1890, variations existed in nineteen states. In addition to school elections, women (especially single women who owned property) might be allowed to vote in municipal elections or on tax referenda— but since all of this was confusing, arbitrary, and decidedly second-class citizenship, partial solutions satisfied few.

Illinois created a different halfway measure in 1913, when it granted women the right to vote for president—but not other offices. The eastern states of Rhode Island, Ohio, and Indiana emulated this semisuffrage, while the Midwestern states of North Dakota and Nebraska also adopted the model.

Still another partial suffrage scheme was aimed specifically at the South, when CARRIE CHAPMAN CATT prioritized primaries over general elections. It was a sensible strategy because the South was so solidly Democratic that primaries were the only elections that mattered. Beyond that, Catt doubtless chose this strategy because it eliminated Southern legislators' objections to suffrage that focused on black women: the few blacks who dared to vote in the South were invariably Republicans ("the party of Lincoln"), and primaries therefore were so thoroughly dominated by whites that some elderly black Southerners still refer to these past elections as "white primaries." Catt's sophisticated strategy nonetheless met with only one success. Arkansas—the same state that would elect HATTIE CARAWAY as the first female U.S. senator—granted women the primary vote in 1917.

At the same time, three Midwestern states—South Dakota, Oklahoma, and Michigan—added women as presidential voters in 1918, the year that the war ended. With the voteless women concentrated in the smaller states of the northeast and the low-population South, women would make a significant bloc in the next presidential election, to be held in 1920, when they would be eligible to vote in twenty states. The leadership of the 1918–1919 Congress could not afford to be indifferent to the point, nor could a president who cared about his party's future.

Suffrage leadership deserves much credit for reading history well enough to understand that a period of political conservatism follows most wars; they moved quickly to take advantage of the immediate postwar generosity. The House gave the necessary two-thirds majority, but the outgoing Senate, in February, 1919, defeated it by just one vote—with several senators ignoring resolutions from their state legislatures urging them to vote affirmatively. When the new Congress was seated the following month, they were greeted by massive petitions and by lobbying from President Wilson. Opponents managed to delay the inevitable until summer, but on June 4, the Senate finally gave its two-thirds consent.

Winning the congressional vote is the easier part of passing a constitutional amendment, however, and suffragists then faced the massive campaign required by the Constitution's mandate for ratification by three-fourths of the states—or thirty-six of the forty-eight states then in existence. These women had long experience with state campaigns, however, as well as the goodwill of those states that had already granted women the right to vote or whose legislatures had petitioned Congress for a national amendment.

The Midwest lead the way, with Illinois and Wisconsin racing each other to be first to ratify. The states in the Far West that had pioneered women's vote a generation earlier also ratified, but at an unenthusiastic rate that foreshadowed the conservative influences that would kill the ratification campaign of the EQUAL RIGHTS AMENDMENT fifty years later. By early 1920, all of the expected states had ratified, with West Virginia and Washington providing the thirty-fourth and thirty-fifth votes. The final vote had to come from the South or New England.

When Connecticut, Vermont, and Delaware failed to ratify in the spring of 1920, attention focused on the border state of Tennessee, whose technical requirements for ratification had been recently ruled unconstitutional by the Supreme Court. In June, President Wilson led countless others, including Democratic Party officials, in urging its Democratic governor to bring the legislature into session. He somewhat

reluctantly called it for August 9, and lobbyists on both sides of the issue poured into Nashville.

The Tennessee Senate promptly voted the amendment through by a wide margin. The House, however, pandered to the mostly male lobbyists opposed to suffrage, who used everything from liquor to threats of kidnapping to change votes and to delay action. Suffragists were far from sanguine when the House vote was finally cast, for their tallies showed the issue two votes short. To their surprise, a party plea that a negative vote would hurt Democrats in the presidential election resulted in a tie. The deciding vote came from a young legislator who had promised his mother that he would vote for suffrage only in the case of a tie.

After the amendment passed, Carrie Chapman Catt summed up the effort it represented: she counted 480 campaigns in state legislatures; fifty-six referenda to male voters, forty-seven attempts to add suffrage planks during revisions of state constitutions; 277 campaigns at state party conventions and thirty at national conventions; and nineteen biannual campaigns with nineteen different Congresses. It was an immense labor, to which thousands of women literally devoted all of their lives. Moreover, it was achieved through sophisticated political strategy for which these pioneers were never given enough credit.

The amendment was officially ratified on August 26, 1920, and approximately 8 million women cast their first ballots the following November. Some of them doubtless were among the majority of women who had been silent during the campaign or who had joined men in criticizing the suffragists as excessively radical. Virtually none of them understood that it was a Democratic president and a Southern Democratic legislature that finally had made the margin of difference, and the Democratic presidential nominee in 1920 went down to crashing defeat. The winner was Warren G. Harding, a man who not only failed to support suffrage, but who was so shameless in his philandering that some suspect FLORENCE HARDING murdered him.

But that was the short-term, and in the long-term, the Nineteenth Amendment was probably the most important of milestones on the path to full equality for women. Without the power of the vote, there is no real power.

NINETY-NINES CLUB An international organization of women pilots, the club began in 1929 and was named for its ninety-nine charter members. AMELIA EARHART was its first president, and its founding took place at Curtiss Air Field on Long Island. Its most famous activity became the sponsorship of the Powder Puff Derby, a cross-country race between female aviators in the early days of such events.

Today the organization also conducts some three hundred educational programs in aviation and sponsors more than 75 percent of the Federal Aviation Authority's pilot safety programs. Members transport hospital patients and perform other charitable aviation services. With a particular emphasis on preserving history, these pilots give an annual award named for Katherine B. Wright, the sister of Orville and Wilbur Wright. The Ninety-Nines, Inc. also maintains an impressive archive on women in aviation with its headquarters at the Will Rogers Airport in Oklahoma City.

NORRIS, KATHLEEN THOMPSON (1880–1960)

An early twentieth-century novelist, Norris' first novel, *Mother*, made her instantly famous. She would go on to live a long life in which she published more than eighty books that sold 10 million copies. Her popularity with the public meant nothing to literary critics, however, and like many other women AUTHORS whose fictional ideas shaped popular thought in their times, she has been ignored by historians.

A Californian like GERTRUDE ATHERTON, she wrote in the same era and received similar recognition from the public and similar disdain from the literati. The similarities end there, however, for unlike Atherton but like women such as LOUISA MAY ALCOTT and PEARL BUCK, she initially wrote because she needed the money. When both of her parents died in the year that she was nineteen, Thompson took on the responsibility of her family. She honed her writing skills by working for San Francisco newspapers and selling freelance work.

It was not until a decade later, when her siblings were grown and she married, that she had the freedom to write a novel. Like most of her later work, *Mother* (1911) was based on Norris' Irish-American heritage. Though traditional in her portrayals of family life, her books nonetheless show insight into the lives of these IMMIGRANT WOMEN and carefully record the intimate details of an important segment of American history. It was this reflection of their personal realities that made her so enduringly popular with her many readers, for she summed up a way of life that was ending.

During the twenties, the popular *Collier's* magazine took pride in presenting Kathleen Norris' fiction alongside that of others of the era's outstanding writers, including WILLA CATHER. A lifelong Catholic, Norris also was active in the SUFFRAGE MOVEMENT and later supported radical political causes (including opposition to both capital punishment and WORLD WAR II) over the objections of her husband, who understood the adverse effects these positions would have with her readers.

A writer himself, Charles Norris was the brother of author/-reformer Frank Norris, who had died in 1902. Perhaps the experience of having a famous brother played a role in his willingness to acknowledge his wife's superior ability, for he acted as her agent, shielded her from interruptions, and in other ways functioned much like a traditional wife during their forty-year marriage. Kathleen Norris bore a son in 1910 and lost twin daughters to INFANT MORTALITY in 1912. The Norrises later adopted four other children, including the orphans of writer William Rose Benet, who had married her sister.

Kathleen Norris wrote two autobiographies, *Noon* (1925) and *Family Gathering* (1959). She wrote until eighty and died at eighty-six.

NORTON, MARY TERESA HOPKINS (1875–1951)

One of the first women elected to Congress after the passage of the NNINETEENTH AMENDMENT, Mary Norton was elected from New Jersey in 1924. She was the first congresswomen from an eastern state and the first Democratic woman not to be preceded by her husband. The House leadership assigned her to the Labor Committee, for in the politically reactionary twenties, Labor was not considered to be an important committee. Two years later, however, the stock market crashed; as the Great Depression worsened and especially after the election of Franklin Roosevelt in 1932, the committee became increasingly important.

The seniority system used by the House meant that Norton chaired the committee after 1937, since her ten years of service made her the senior member. When the United States entered WORLD WAR II in 1941, Chairman Norton was thus in an extremely influential position, for a sufficient supply of competent and willing workers was crucial to the war. Experts both then and later agreed that World War II was a battle of production: the key to victory was simply building more planes, ships, and weapons than the other side, and Norton's position was important in producing that result.

It was a position that she had not envisioned for herself twenty years earlier, and without pushing from a helpful male mentor, she probably would not have accomplished what she did. A married woman whose only child was a victim of INFANT MORTALITY in 1910, Mary Norton's political career began unintentionally during WORLD WAR I, when she went to Jersey City politico Frank Hague for help in obtaining scarce coal for a child nursery run by her Catholic church. Hague followed up on this favor three years later when women obtained the vote, surprising her by announcing that "he had a big mass meeting for the newly enfranchised women all arranged and that, as head of the Democratic women of Jersey City, she would be expected to preside."

CARRIE CHAPMAN CATT spoke at the meeting, and it was Catt who convinced Norton—who had neither opposed nor supported suffrage—to become involved. She soon organized a Democratic women's committee in every county in the state, and at the next election, Hague urged her to run for freeholder (New Jersey's equivalent of county commissioner). "You'll like it," Hague promised her, "You can run the poor farm and the orphans' home." Thus, in 1923, a mere three years after New Jersey women voted, she was elected to office. Already the following year, Hague was encouraging her to run for Congress. He met her objection that she didn't "know anything about Congress" by replying, "Neither do most congressmen."

"You'll learn," he assured her, and she did. In addition to representing her New Jersey constituency and her invaluable labor work, Norton also chaired the District of Columbia Committee from 1932 to 1937. This was another bottom-of-the-basement assignment that is still given to congressional outsiders, but instead of spending her energies to get off the committee, Norton championed equality for D.C. voters with such vigor that she became known as the "first woman mayor of Washington."

Like ELEANOR ROOSEVELT and many other progressive women of this era, Mary Norton opposed the EQUAL RIGHTS AMENDMENT, fearing its nullification of PROTECTIVE LEGISLATION. Instead, she worked hard for an equal pay law and, especially during and immediately after the war, for government-funded child care. Most important, however, was the major national change she made in the passage of progressive labor law. During her tenure as chairman of the House Labor Committee, most of the legislation that protects workers today was enacted: working with Secretary of Labor FRANCES PERKINS, Congress passed the Social Security Act, minimum wage and maximum hour laws, and many other fundamental economic policy changes. All of this was not only vital to preventing strikes and other labor disruptions during the war, but it also produced long-term results in an acknowledged role for unions and in revolutionizing managerial behavior.

Representative Mary T. Norton lacked a college education because her father had not believed in educating women. She did go to secretarial school and had supported herself in New York until she married at thirty-four. A WIDOW after 1934, Norton's husband stayed so far in the background during her first decade in Congress that many believed she was a widow when elected. After serving a quarter-century, she announced her retirement in the election of 1950, when she was seventy-five and when Congress was increasingly coming under the control of Republicans who threatened her power and priorities. She received many honors, but found no publisher for the autobiography she wrote in retirement. Norton died at eighty-four, and her papers are on deposit at New Jersey's Rutgers University. She merits far more recognition than she gets from today's working women, for Mary T. Norton was a vital part of some of the most important changes in the twentieth century. The legislation that she led moved the economy from Depression era intimidation of employees to the creation of a modern labor force, in which workers are assured decent pay, health and safety protections, retirement benefits, and economic opportunity.

NUNS Catholic priests who were included in the sixteenth-century voyages of exploration sent by the Spanish and French are well known, but the history of the sisters of the church is more obscure. Isabel de Flores y del Oliva, a Dominican, was the New World's first saint: she was born in Peru to Spanish parents in 1586 and was canonized as St. Rose of Lima in 1671. Today, she is considered the originator of social service in Latin America.

The first North American order of nuns seems to be the Ursulines, who were operating in Quebec by 1639 and in New Orleans by 1727. In Louisiana, they not only ran a hospital, orphanage, and school (where they taught blacks and Native Americans as well as French colonists), but they also "took charge of women and girls of ill-repute." Some believe that the women of this order were the "first professional elementary school TEACHERS to arrive in America."

The first convent in the area that became the early United States was not established until after the Revolution. Four Sacred Heart nuns who had been educated in Europe established the first one in Carroll County, Maryland in 1790. It moved to Baltimore in 1831, and many other convents throughout the U.S. grew from its roots. This was followed by a second Maryland establishment, the Sisters of Charity, founded in 1809 by MOTHER ELIZABETH SETON.

Other orders that were well established in Europe took much longer to export members to America. The Passionist Nuns, for example, were instituted in Europe in 1771, but did not establish themselves in the U.S. until 1924, when a community began in Providence, Rhode Island. This pattern was particularly likely among orders that emphasized a secluded, contemplative life, as opposed to the active service of more mission-oriented orders.

American society remained overwhelmingly Protestant until the late nineteenth century, and it was not until then that large numbers of nuns appeared. But even before the big waves of Catholic immigration, it was not uncommon for upper-class Protestant families to send their daughters to be educated by nuns. This was especially likely in the South, where a convent education marked a young woman as particularly innocent and refined. Even less wealthy people took advantage of Catholic schools when the public ones were decidedly inferior. Two Sisters of the Holy Names, for example, arrived in Tampa in 1881, and, after walking "all the way from the dock through the deep sand," set about building a school the very next day with "money from a collection made among the soldiers." Even though the town was largely Protestant, the school was an immediate success, for no other institution could offer comparable education. By 1897, the sisters were operating four schools, with one dedicated to black children.

Indeed, the education of blacks was a focus of nuns long before any other group attended to this need. Moreover, they made colleagues of African-Americans, and eventually three orders were formed for black sisters. The first was the Oblate Sisters of Providence, founded in Baltimore in 1829. They operated a school for girls that attracted students from Philadelphia and other cities; after the CIVIL WAR, their work dramatically expanded with orphanages for black children as far away as Kansas.

The largest order for black nuns was the Sisters of the Holy Family, founded in New Orleans in 1842 to operate a hospice for the sick and needy. Again, the Civil War provided impetus for expansion, and the order eventually operated almost fifty schools. Indeed, the cancellation of laws prohibiting the teaching of blacks gave Catholic education a tremendous boost: the number of American schools soared from about 200 before the war to 1,341 in 1870. After Reconstruction ended, however, these dedicated women faced increasing hostility in the South; in fact, the third black order, the Franciscan Handmaidens of Mary, encountered such resistance after its 1916 founding in Savannah that the sisters moved to Harlem in 1922.

Like the Civil War, the Spanish-American War also expanded service opportunities for nuns, and many American men first encountered these women in military camps. Tampa's Sisters of the Holy Names, for example, turned their schools into facilities for soldiers disembarking to Cuba, rising early every morning to cook for the inadequately supplied troops. Such interaction helped make nuns less mysterious to the Protestant majority, and they were less often the target of slander.

Thousands of nuns came along with the millions of immigrants at the turn of the century, and they spread themselves throughout the nation's schools and hospitals—for like women generally, the occupations most often assigned to them were TEACHING and NURSING. By the middle of the twentieth century, however, their numbers began to decline, and the financial situation of most orders today is dire.

In the New York City area, for example, the number of sisters is half of what it was just thirty years ago, for many younger women have left their orders, and novitiates are few—in 1991, for example, 160 orders saw only twenty-one new entrants. In some cities, the median age of nuns is upwards of sixty-five, and retirement funds are millions of dollars short; while "American dioceses have always had pension plans for their priests, [they) have only recently begun special fund drives for retired nuns."

These problems are clearly the result of an unthinking expectation that women's sacrifices could be taken for granted. As the secular world changed so that women no longer had to look to convents for intellectual and professional opportunity, fewer women were willing to devote a lifetime to an inherently inferior position. That their discontent was linked to women's limited role in the church seems clear again from the Archdiocese of New York statistics: while the number of priests declined only slightly between 1961 and 1991, from 3,729 and 3,468, the number of nuns plummeted from 12,653 to 6,382.

At least part of the cause may be a general lack of appreciation from both the Catholic and non-Catholic public for the historic roles of these women. Almost invariably, they endured hostility from the ignorant and paranoid, including calumny such as that surrounding the MARIA MONK episode. From city slums to western mining towns, they went bravely into places where they were not welcome to assist the oppressed, and almost every American epidemic saw nuns put their lives on the line to nurse the helpless. They educated millions of schoolchildren, many of whom spoke obscure languages, and for many of their female students, they offered the only possible alternative for a life other than that of marriage and motherhood.

NURSES AND NURSING The words' roots derive from a Latin verb meaning "to nourish"; women, as the nourishers of infants, have historically been seen as innately nurses, long before the profession as such developed. Indeed, for almost two centuries after European exploration of the New World, all nursing was home nursing. Even when the first hospital was built in Philadelphia in 1751, it was thought of primarily as an asylum or poorhouse; another century or more would pass before the public viewed hospitals as reputable and safe.

The CIVIL WAR gave enormous impetus to the building of hospitals and the development of nursing as a profession. Initial volunteers were often seen by the public as not essentially different from CAMP FOLLOWERS, for it was an era when some (especially in the South) preferred to allow

Carver Hospital near Washington during the Civil War. Note the nurses midway down the row of neatly made beds and the decorations (especially the unusual star flag) that made the building less bleak. NATIONAL ARCHIVES; PHOTOGRAPH BY MATTHEW BRADY.

men to die rather than subject women to the sight of male bodies. The work of MARY ANN BICKERDYKE, CAPT. SALLY TOMPKINS, and others was of tremendous value in creating a favorable image for nurses. They made the important beginnings that allowed CLARA BARTON and others to follow up with the formation of the AMERICAN RED CROSS and other systems that not only took nursing out of the home, but also created standards of education and experience. Even though it took almost three decades, in 1892 Congress recognized the value of Civil War nurses with a bill providing pensions to those still alive.

One result of this improved image for nurses was an explosion of nursing schools in the latter half of the nineteenth century. These schools were usually built in conjunction with hospitals, and even graduate nurses lived and worked at the hospital. Often called "sisters" (as British nurses still are), their lives were indeed similar to those of Catholic NUNS: early nurses were invariably single women who were cloistered in "nurses homes" on hospital grounds, where discipline in all aspects of life was strictly enforced and pay was extremely low.

Student nurses were not paid at all, and were even more sternly governed in dress and behavior. Because many hospitals valued their free labor over educational standards, student nurses spent much of their time performing menial tasks such as mopping floors and doing laundry. As time passed, however, there was pressure to improve curricula. The distinctive caps that nurses wore played a significant part in raising standards, for the cap instantly associated the nurse with the school from which she had graduated.

Like most other educational institutions, these schools did not admit black students, and informally educated nurses such as SUSIE KING TAYLOR remained the norm in AFRICAN-AMERICAN communities. MARY MAHONEY became the first known black professional when she graduated from nursing school in 1879, but her experience of integrated education remained unusual. Blacks began their own nursing schools in the 1890s, usually in conjunction with their private COLLEGES. The most outstanding probably were those of Tuskegee, Hampton, Howard, and Dillard Universities, as well as the state-supported Florida A&M.

Their graduates still found it difficult to obtain decent jobs, however, and even in the emergency of WORLD WAR II, black nurses had to fight for admission to the ARMY AND NAVY NURSE CORPS. An article published in a black magazine the same month that the war ended, for example, reported cheerfully "there are 50 schools that accept Negro students" and there are "approximately 2,000 Negro girls enrolled in schools of nursing"—but the total nursing school population at the time was 61,471, which meant that blacks made up a mere 3 percent. The fight to integrate the military's nursing corps and later, the American Nurses Association, was led by MABEL K. STAUPERS.

Nonetheless, World War II marked a milestone as significant to nursing as the Civil War had been. The long years of the Great Depression had dragged down the slight gains made during WORLD WAR I, so that during the thirties, "nursing was looked down upon by some middle-class mothers as not quite a nice sort of job, and . . . as being on the career level of glorified domestic service." Wartime needs quickly changed this demeaning view: by 1942, the National Nursing Council for War Service aimed to locate the one hundred thousand women who had graduated from nursing schools but had abandoned the profession, while the Office of Civilian Defense pleaded for another one hundred thousand volunteers to become aides in their local hospitals. The result was the BOLTON BILL, which financed nursing education and set an important precedent as federal funding that benefited primarily women.

Like all wars, World War II accelerated the breakdown of class structure, and nursing reflected this change. Earlier nursing schools had "emphasized the individual care of the patient . . . to the exclusion of a great uncared for public;" routine medical care had not been a part of life for most Americans prior to the war and treatment was sought by most only in emergencies. Nurses, therefore, were trained to deal with their most likely clientele—the wealthy—who expected a nurse to be something of a servant with properly subservient attitudes rather than a professional with independent judgment.

As soldiers and their families began to assume their right to decent health care, the sheer quantitative increase in patient load focused attention on nursing and gave the profession an importance it never had in the past. When the wartime government was willing to put money where its mouth was and educate thousands of young women at public expense, nursing reached a level of status never before achieved by any occupation dominated by women. No longer willing to accept bed and board as payment, postwar nurses liberated themselves from hospital-owned nurses' homes. The married nurse—a rarity before the war—became commonplace.

At the same time, the war also revived the art of home nursing, with thousands of professional nurses employed by the Red Cross to teach this area to women who, it was assumed, could care for their families and thus alleviate overcrowding in hospitals. The Red Cross also set up courses for volunteer nurses' aides, as hospitals all over the country used the war as a reason to expect women to donate their labor. The result was a continuation of the view that nursing was something less than a profession and a devaluation of women's work and time.

This spirit of self-sacrifice, which historically had attached itself to nursing in a way that was never the case with physicians, profoundly slowed the professionalization of nurses, and they have yet to make the progress at collective bargaining that TEACHERS made in the latter half of the twentieth century. Even the American Nurse Association, the largest and most powerful nursing organization, admits that in many states, only about 10 percent of all licensed nurses pay dues—a percentage far lower, for example, than is the case for physicians' American Medical Association or teachers' National Education Association. A particularly sad statistic that reflects a strong residue of discontent is the fact that, in the 1990s, the women least likely to enter the nursing profession are the daughters of nurses.

Indeed, few women are entering the field as options have opened in the last decades of the twentieth century beyond the traditional nurse/teacher/secretary choices. Many nursing schools—especially the ones associated with hospitals that were particularly exploitive of student labor—have been forced to close because of low enrollment. Salaries and working conditions are improving, both as a result of the nursing shortage and because of hospitals' fears of unionization after such demonstrations of discontent as a great STRIKE of Minnesota nurses in 1984.

What seems to be resulting is a breakup of the profession as such, as "medical technicians" of both genders replace traditional "nurses" for increasing numbers of health care tasks. Specialization and credentialism doubtless will assure a future far different from the past, when nurses were expected to do everything from assisting in surgery to keeping coal in the hospital stove.

NURSES SELECTIVE SERVICE BILL OF 1945
The ARMY NURSE CORPS in 1940 consisted of a mere seven hundred women; by April of 1941, even before American involvement in WORLD WAR II began, the Corps was enlisting nearly that many in a single month. Meanwhile, the nation had ten thousand civilian hospital vacancies for NURSES.

This shortage of nurses continued to worsen throughout the war. The Public Health Service wanted fifty-five thousand new nursing students in 1942; the next year, the quota was raised to sixty-five thousand. By 1944, the U.S. needed sixty-six thousand nurses for the military and almost three hundred thousand for civilian duty—one hundred thousand more than were available. Therefore, because "the need is too pressing to await the outcome of further efforts at recruiting," President Roosevelt in his State of the Union speech on January 6, 1945, called for amendment of the Selective Service Act to "provide for the induction of nurses into the Armed Forces."

The public approved of his proposal, for a follow-up Gallup poll revealed that 78 percent believed there was indeed a shortage of nurses in the armed forces, and an overwhelming seventy-three percent approved of drafting them. Representative Andrew May of Kentucky introduced HR 2277 on March 5, 1945 and his bill received prompt but thorough consideration, with committee hearings during a two-week period and House debate for a good portion of three days.

Debate generally centered on technicalities; that women would have to be drafted was accepted by most, and the object of attention was exactly how this conscription should be implemented. Beginning date, geographical quotas, appeal procedures, and commissions were the topics discussed, while little attention was given to the tremendous change this legislation was in the historical status of women.

There was almost no mention of home and family and none of the expected platitudes; most congressmen stated their regret that a draft had to be resorted to, but their regret centered upon the fact that the draftees were *nurses* more than that they were *women*. The American Nurse Association and the National Nursing Council reinforced this view, since their position was to "approve, in principle, federal Selective Service legislation," while also urging passage of a NATIONAL SERVICE ACT to cover all women so that nurses would not be singled out to appear as less than patriotic.

Those who opposed the legislation gave reasons other than the fact that it was women who were being considered for the draft. There were Republican charges that it was a power-grab by Roosevelt; there were fears that drafting nurses would discourage young women from entering the profession. There were vehement (and justifiable) attacks on the War Department for mismanagement of recruiting and underutilization of black and male nurses.

Although votes on amendments were close, the final draft of the Nurses Selective Service Act was approved 347–42. The bill was passed by the House in early March; in early April, it was reported out favorably by the Senate Military Affairs Committee, their only important amendment being to strike the exemption the House had given to married women. In early May, however, the Army entered Berlin and the war in Europe was over.

With that victory, the Nurses Selective Service Act became one of many war contingency plans that was no longer needed. Nonetheless, a significant precedent had been set, for the House passed the bill by a large majority; the Senate committee reported it favorably; the president certainly would have signed it. All indications are that if the European war had lasted another month or two, women would have been drafted. The legislation showed that, contrary to the arguments of opponents to the EQUAL RIGHTS AMENDMENT in the 1970s, there is no clear constitutional protection of women from conscription, for both Congress and the president assumed that they had the authority to draft citizens without regard to gender.

OAKLEY, ANNIE (1860–1926) Born Phoebe Ann Moses (or Mozee) in Ohio, she lived part of her childhood unhappily in an orphanage when her mother, a WIDOW who worked as a NURSE, was unable to support eight children. Phoebe ran away from a foster home, but after her mother remarried, she was able to spend her days happily hunting and selling the game she shot.

Though she remained under five feet tall and weighed less than a hundred pounds, she had innately extraordinary shooting skill based on keen eyesight and a steady hand. At fifteen, she won a championship in Cincinnati and defeated showman Frank Butler, who was so impressed that he married her. It was to be an unusual marriage in which Butler took the publicly subordinate position, while the two of them enjoyed lifelong companionship in private.

She took the name of Annie Oakley at marriage (she had hated Phoebe and especially her surname), and they traveled together in a shooting exposition called Butler and Oakley for several years. In 1885, Oakley joined Buffalo Bill Cody's Wild West Show, and Butler began devoting himself to the management of his wife's career. So expert that she could hit a moving target while standing on a galloping horse, she soon became an international celebrity. Other Oakley feats included shooting dimes tossed in the air and even hitting a cigarette held in her husband's lips.

Annie Oakley traveled and shot for sixteen years, including lengthy tours of Europe when she was presented to Queen Victoria and the crown prince of Germany, who insisted on participating in the cigarette trick. Except for Buffalo Bill's personal jealousy—which caused Oakley to briefly leave the show two years after joining it—her career was a happy one. She was particularly popular with Sioux Chief Sitting Bull, who joined the show the same year that she did.

Oakley was forty-one when her career came to a sudden close. The Wild West's train wrecked in the mountains of Virginia, and she was badly injured. Largely retired after this 1901 accident, she returned to entertain soldiers in WORLD WAR I. In 1922, however, she was paralyzed in a car accident in Florida. After several years there, Oakley returned to her Ohio birthplace, where she died of anemia at sixty-one. Frank Butler, apparently unable to go on without his lifelong friend, died three weeks later.

The Remington Gun Museum in Ilion, New York preserves her rifle, while the National Cowgirl Hall of Fame in Hereford, Texas and her birthplace of Greenville, Ohio have more extensive collections of artifacts. In demonstrating natural skill in an arena where few women ventured, Annie Oakley made the Victorian world aware of the untapped capabilities of women.

OBERLIN COLLEGE One of the most extraordinary of American institutions of higher education, Oberlin College was particularly influential for women.

Its origins lay in the suppression of ABOLITIONIST activity at Cincinnati's Lane Theology Seminary; much of Lane's male student body withdrew in 1834 and, under the leadership of student Theodore Weld (who later married ANGELINA GRIMKE), relocated to a new college at Oberlin, Ohio. It was these extremely liberal students who were responsible for the fact that Oberlin became the first COLLEGE to admit blacks and women in a coeducational atmosphere, a policy that began when Oberlin was chartered in 1833. Harvard, the nation's oldest college, was celebrating its two hundredth birthday at the time; it and most of America's other colleges would remain exclusive to white males for many decades into the future.

Its location in the frontier town of Oberlin, Ohio was not coincidental, for it was illustrative of the greater opportunity often available to WESTERN WOMEN. At the same time, however, even Oberlin initially restricted women to their own sphere with a "Ladies Course," and women did not read essays at graduation until 1874. Though a woman graduated from the "full course" already in 1841—when the school had been in existence less than a decade—each milestone had to be aggressively conquered, and most women pliantly remained in the "Female Department," which emphasized educated motherhood, not careers. By 1857, 299 female students had opted for the "Ladies" or Literary Course, while only 20 earned the genuine college degree. The very term "bachelor" in degree nomenclature may have been intimidating to these pioneers in female education, and further explanation lies in women's awareness that even those brave twenty would find few career opportunities to use their degrees.

The bias against women's education remained so strong that when sexism combined with racism, it meant that even progressive Oberlin was in existence for almost thirty years before it produced its first black, female graduate—MARY JANE PATTERSON, who graduated in 1862. Of the approximately 140 black women who studied at Oberlin between 1835–1865, by far the most were enrolled in the preparatory program; 56 went on to the literary course, but not until Patterson did a black woman earn a genuine college degree.

Yet, while educational achievement for black women was painfully slow, Oberlin made a far greater contribution than any other college. Even though its black population never exceeded 5 percent, its willingness to educate blacks at all made many think that it was "an institution for . . . people of color." As late as 1910, half of the African-American women who graduated from integrated colleges were products of Oberlin.

Black women were thus a small but vital part of life at Oberlin. They were probably more diverse than their white counterparts, for as many black women came from the South as from the North, while almost all white Oberlin students were Northerners. Most were light-skinned, and a few were the acknowledged daughters of slaveowners. Even before the CIVIL WAR, many of the black students had been born free, and most came from strong families financially able to send their daughters to college. Some, such as MARY CHURCH TERRELL, were extremely wealthy, and the average black Oberlin student was probably more affluent than the average white student. Contrary to what might be assumed, few antebellum Oberlin students were supported by abolitionists.

Among the college's most outstanding black women was Anna Julia Cooper, who, after a lifetime as a high school principal in Washington, earned a doctorate from the Sorbonne. Other important early students include theologian ANTOINETTE BROWN BLACKWELL, physician EMELINE HORTON

CLEVELAND, famous FEMINIST LUCY STONE, and Mary Willard, when she was the young mother of FRANCES WILLARD. A continual source of feminist leadership, Oberlin provided a platform already in 1846 for ABBY KELLY FOSTER. Such PUBLIC SPEAKERS were considered radical at the time, but as the nineteenth century passed, even conventional women who never studied at Oberlin came to identify with it: reports from Ohio in the fourth volume of the HISTORY OF WOMAN SUFFRAGE, for example, mention the college's historic role for women with pride.

Though no longer at the forefront of national activism, Oberlin College is still a progressive institution. It maintains a women's history collection in its library, as well as extensive records of its graduates.

O'CONNOR, SANDRA DAY (1930–) The first woman appointed to the U.S. Supreme Court, O'Connor joined the Court in September, 1981. When she became a justice, 101 men had served during the Court's 191-year history. Public impatience to at last have a woman's participation on the highest bench and in its secret chamber conferences was clear in the 99–0 confirmation vote that O'Connor received in the Senate. Some right-wingers mounted a brief attack on the politically moderate record she had established as a state judge, but hers was the last largely noncontroversial Supreme Court appointment of the Reagan-Bush presidencies.

Sandra Day grew up on an Arizona ranch and graduated from high school in El Paso, Texas at sixteen. She attended California's Stanford University, where she completed both college and law school in five years. Graduating in the top 10 percent of her class, she married John O'Connor, who was still a law school student, in 1952. After working briefly, she accompanied her husband during his Army service and bore three children.

In 1965, O'Connor returned to the full-time practice of law and became active in Republican politics, which resulted in an appointment to the Arizona Senate, where she replaced another woman, in 1969. Reelected in 1970 and 1972, she rose to a majority leader in just five years—she was the first female senate majority leader in any state legislature.

Though she clearly had the respect of her Senate colleagues, O'Connor left the legislature for the judiciary in 1974. After five years of service as an elected judge, she was appointed to the State Court of Appeals in 1979, and a mere two years later, she rose to the U.S. Supreme Court. Though there were women with stronger credentials, her moderate record and Republican affiliation made Sandra Day O'Connor an acceptable choice to both sides of the political spectrum.

Age fifty-one when appointed, she was young by the standards of Supreme Court justices, but old enough to remember when she, like many qualified female attorneys, was instead offered work as a legal secretary. That kind of life experience—unshared by the Court's men—has doubtless been a factor in moving O'Connor from the conservative intentions of those who appointed her to her current status as "swing vote" on the Court.

O'KEEFFE, GEORGIA TOTTO (1887–1986)

Perhaps America's most famous female artist, Georgia O'Keeffe painted hundreds of exquisite works that hang in many important galleries today. Among her earliest works to become national favorites were huge, highly colored flowers—especially red poppies—while her later work was strongly influenced by the spare landscape of New Mexico.

Born in Wisconsin, O'Keeffe's unusual middle name came from her Hungarian grandfather. After study at the Art Institute of Chicago and at the Art Students' League in New York City, she lived in several cities and supported herself in advertising and by TEACHING until 1916, when her work was first exhibited. The New York show was arranged in part by photographer Alfred Stieglitz; though he was nearly three decades older than she, they would share an open marriage after 1924. Both engaged in numerous affairs, including bisexual ones by O'Keeffe, while the aging Stieglitz had a penchant for women still younger than his wife. He particularly pained her with an exhibit of photographs of his young lover displayed next to those of an aging O'Keeffe. An intensely private person, she suffered a mental breakdown.

O'Keeffe began visiting the Southwest in 1929 and moved permanently to the mountains of northern New Mexico when Stieglitz died in 1946. Ever after, her work was distinctively southwestern, with pinks, purples, and reds forming rocks and deserts that contrasted with the bleached white of animal skulls and big, sunburned skies. Though she had painted both precise landscapes and abstractions in New York, it was the West that was natural to her brush: she dismissed the Adirondacks where she summered with Stieglitz as "such little, pretty scenery."

She mounted several major expositions at the nation's most outstanding galleries between 1946 and 1971 and received many honors, including election to the American Academy of Arts and Letters in 1969 and the Medal of Freedom, which was awarded by President Carter in 1977. O'Keeffe was nonetheless increasingly reclusive during the second half of her life. Even a home in the tiny town of Abiquiu north of Santa Fe was not far enough away; she had a second home called Ghost Ranch hidden deep in the mountains. She continued to paint into her nineties and died at ninety-eight.

FEMINIST in her lifestyle as well as her philosophy, Georgia O'Keeffe was adamant that her art be seen as undefined by gender. While she accepted the appellation of "American" artist, she abhorred references to "woman" artist, for much of the point of art was to liberate oneself from such presumptions. "When I was still a little girl," she once said, "I used to think that since I couldn't . . . do what I wanted to . . . at least I could paint as I wanted to and say what I wanted to when I painted . . ."

"OLIVIA"

Emily Edson Briggs (1830–1910) hid behind this PSEUDONYM when—long before the subject was considered appropriate for women—she wrote about national politics.

Briggs came to Washington during the first year of the CIVIL WAR with her husband, who was an employee of the House of Representatives. She caught the attention of the PUBLISHER of the *Washington Chronicle* with an 1861 letter to the editor defending the right of women to hold civil service jobs. The letter was so well written and its arguments so closely rea-

soned that she was offered a daily column. For the next twenty years, the views of "Olivia" were regularly published in both the *Chronicle* and its co-owned newspaper, the *Philadelphia Press*.

Briggs thus became the first woman to report from the White House. She assertively used that opportunity to develop personal friendships with the Lincoln family, which resulted in more incisive comment than that of many of her male colleagues. In the guise of "Olivia," Briggs also was one of the first women admitted to the congressional press gallery. Not surprisingly, she was elected the first president of the Woman's National Press Association when that body began in 1882.

A collection of her work, *The Olivia Letters*, was published in 1906, and she died in Washington four years later at seventy-nine. It was the same year that SUSAN ANTHONY died; each of these women had exercised strong personal influence in national politics, but neither lived to cast a ballot.

O'NEALE, PEGGY—

See EATON, MARGARET O'NEALE TIMBERLAKE

O'REILLY, LEONORA (1870–1927)

Like her Irish mother and grandmother, Leonora O'Reilly worked in the GARMENT INDUSTRY during a poverty-stricken childhood. Her WIDOWED mother became a union supporter, and Leonora joined the newly organized Knights of Labor in 1886. A natural orator and organizer, she founded the New York Working Women's Society that same year—at age sixteen. From there, O'Reilly moved on to organize a local of the United Garment Workers in 1897. Its affiliation with the American Federation of Labor (AFL) brought her to the AFL meeting where the WOMEN'S TRADE UNION LEAGUE (WTUL) was formed in 1903. She was a member of its first executive board, and the WTUL became the center of her life thereafter.

LILLIAN WALD provided her with a network of progressive women of independent wealth, and it was O'Reilly who was primarily responsible for bringing MARY ELIZABETH DREIER and MARGARET DREIER ROBINS into the WTUL. In fact, Mary Dreier counted Leonora O'Reilly's volunteer work as so valuable that she created a lifetime annuity in 1909 that allowed O'Reilly to at last quit her ten-hour factory days and devote herself full time to organizing women into labor unions.

She thus was deeply involved in the 1909–1910 STRIKE in New York's garment factories, and in 1911, she headed a committee to improve safety standards after the TRIANGLE FIRE. O'Reilly traveled nationally as well, organizing women throughout the country and especially in Chicago.

A Socialist after 1911, she also supported the SUFFRAGE MOVEMENT; she was one of the relatively few working women to counter the middle-class image of suffragists. O'Reilly spoke for the "8 million of us . . . who must . . . earn our daily bread," and cited her experience with legislators who felt safe in ignoring working women's needs because they knew that women could not retaliate at the polls.

Her activism even extended to the NAACP; she called for its founding and served on its first governing committee. Finally, O'Reilly was also an advocate of vocational education—something that stemmed from her experience as a sewing TEACHER in the early part of her working life—and testified before Congress on behalf of beginning federal aid to vocational education.

Her history as a child laborer may have been a factor in the ill health that forced O'Reilly into semiretirement at age forty-four. She managed nonetheless to be a delegate to the INTERNATIONAL CONGRESS OF WOMEN, but her postwar years were limited by caring for her mother and by her own defective heart. She died at fifty-seven, remembered by her friends for encouraging women who earned their "daily bread" to seek "not only the cake, but the ice cream as well."

Always class-conscious, O'Reilly was indifferent to honors and refused to be listed in *Who's Who*. Her papers are at the Schlesinger Library of RADCLIFFE COLLEGE.

O'SULLIVAN, MARY KENNY (1864–1943)

The first woman to be hired as an organizer for the American Federation of Labor (AFL), Mary Kenny worked from childhood. After apprenticing in a dressmaking shop where she worked for two years without pay, she entered the bookbinding trade at age fourteen.

Like other IMMIGRANT WOMEN of her Irish heritage, she earned her own living from that early age, moving with available jobs from her native Missouri to Iowa and then to Chicago, where she organized her colleagues into Woman's Bookbinding Union #1 in the 1880s. The AFL, impressed with her abilities, hired her to organize women in 1891. The labor federation itself was still new, however, and her job proved short-lived.

She lived in Chicago at JANE ADDAMS' Hull House, and—in a highly unusual situation—continued this SETTLEMENT HOUSE lifestyle after her 1894 marriage. Her husband was a Boston labor activist, and even after they had three children, they lived at Boston's Denison House, where she organized women workers for the WOMEN'S EDUCATIONAL AND INDUSTRIAL UNION. When her husband was killed by a train just eight years after they married, O'Sullivan returned to full-time union work. As a WIDOW with three young children to support, she was living testimony of the need for women workers to organize.

In 1903, she played a crucial role in founding the WOMEN'S TRADE UNION LEAGUE. Though other women were elected as WTUL officers, it was O'Sullivan who secured the AFL's permission for the convening meeting in Boston's famous Faneuil Hall. She was not blindly loyal to the AFL, however, and split from it and even from the WTUL to support the LAWRENCE MASSACHUSETTS TEXTILE MILL STRIKE in 1912. Two years later, she finally obtained steady work at decent wages in her chosen field when she became an inspector for the Massachusetts Board of Labor. She stayed with this until age seventy, setting precedents for worker welfare for more than three decades.

O'Sullivan retired in 1934, just after the New Deal revolution brought many of her reformist friends to power in Washington. Active in the SUFFRAGE MOVEMENT and in the WOMEN'S INTERNATIONAL LEAGUE FOR PEACE AND FREEDOM, she died at seventy-nine. An unpublished autobiography is in the archives of Schlesinger Library at RADCLIFFE COLLEGE.

Ruth Bryan Owen, the first woman elected to Congress from the South, stands with her aides in 1929. She garnered a great deal of attention by driving her own car to campaign in the 500-mile Florida district. FLORIDA STATE ARCHIVES.

OWEN, RUTH BRYAN (1885–1954)

The first woman elected to Congress from the South, Ruth Bryan exhibited political skill from an early age. She was uncommonly fortunate to have her father as a mentor, for she was the daughter of famed orator and Democratic presidential nominee William Jennings Bryan.

A less obvious but probably more important source of inspiration was her mother, who played a vital if unacknowledged part in Bryan's political career—long before women could vote. Mary Baird Bryan not only attended COLLEGE in an era when few women did, but also studied law and was admitted to the Nebraska bar in 1888. An extremely unusual achievement for a married woman with a child, it serves as another evidence of the greater independence of WESTERN WOMEN.

Ruth was three when her mother passed the bar; at eleven, she was handling some of her father's political correspondence. She entered the University of Nebraska in 1901, but left two years later to marry an artist on the day after her eighteenth birthday. She bore two children in quick succession, but after five years, DIVORCED her husband to marry Reginald Owen, an English military officer whom she had met in Germany. They lived in Jamaica and had a child in England in 1913.

Soon thereafter, Reginald was critically wounded during conflict in the Middle East. As WORLD WAR I began, Owen found herself essentially the head of her household; she spent the war working as a surgical NURSE in Cairo, Egypt. Pregnant with her fourth child and facing the prospect of supporting her permanently disabled husband, she settled her family with her retired parents in Florida. Thus it was in the twentieth-century frontier of south Florida that Ruth Bryan Owen would develop a political career of her own.

She began by exploiting her discovery that she, like her father, had the oratorical power to move audiences. Emulating the many nineteenth-century FEMINISTS who supported themselves on the lecture circuit, Owen traveled the country delivering speeches on her experience abroad. She also taught speech at the new University of Miami. Naturally she soon became active in politics. In 1926—just six years after women got the vote—she ran for Congress. She was encouraged by her mother, who had gone to Tallahassee in 1917 to lobby with the SUFFRAGE MOVEMENT.

The district was huge, stretching more than five hundred miles down the East Coast from the Georgia line to Key West. With her mother plotting strategy, Owen campaigned accompanied by women. Florida had not ratified the NINETEENTH AMENDMENT, however, and its women were political novices. Since her father had died the previous year, the male establishment of the Democratic Party felt free to oppose her—and in Florida at that time, the Democratic nomination was tantamount to election. Yet despite all of these obstacles, she lost by a mere eight hundred votes.

Her husband died the following year, but 1928 found Owen energetically back on the campaign trail. She drove her own car—which in itself was an attention-getter—and all of the work she had done in the previous race paid off in a solid victory. At last Mary Baird Bryan Brown could rejoice in a victory that she had organized, for after seeing her husband lose three presidential races and after losing the campaign for women's enfranchisement in Florida, she had lived to elect her daughter to Congress.

The defeated man, however, could not accept his loss and challenged the election. In a bizarre legal brief, he argued that Owen was not eligible to run for Congress because, as a woman, she had automatically forfeited her citizenship when she married a noncitizen. Even though her English husband was dead and even though this particular injustice against women had been rectified with the passage of the CABLE ACT in 1922, he creatively claimed that the seven years necessary to return her citizenship eligibility were not over when she filed to run.

The fact that the state had accepted her filing fee and placed her on the ballot seemingly did not matter to him; nor did the voters' democratic decision. In a clear indication that men retained party power in this pre-Roosevelt era, his challenge was accepted by the Elections Committee of the House. Though not an attorney (or even a college graduate), Owen argued the case herself. She turned his challenge into an impassioned feminist plea for fair treatment and democratic due process. Amidst national publicity, she was seated in Congress.

The incident may have made Owen more feminist than she otherwise would have been. She not only passed legislation to correct the technical problems women faced when they married foreigners, but also sponsored legislation to create a Department of Home and Child that would have Cabinet status. Insistent upon using her international experience, she fought to become a member of the prestigious Foreign Affairs Committee and thus became the first congresswoman to serve on a major committee. Working with environmentalist MARJORY STONEMAN DOUGLAS—a friend of her mother's since suffrage days—she wrote legislation to create Everglades National Park.

Her father's reputation forever shadowed her, however, and it was not always beneficial. William Jennings Bryan had been a strong voice for PROHIBITION, and even though his daughter was far more worldly and sophisticated than he, it was easy for her opponents to convince voters that defeating her was a part of repealing the Prohibition Amendment then in effect. The issue was a hot one in Florida in 1932, when the election of Franklin Roosevelt was a forgone conclusion and Democrats had the luxury of focusing on other internal issues, such as prohibition. After four years in Congress, Ruth Bryan Owen lost the 1932 election over alcohol—the same issue that was inextricably tangled with so much of feminist history.

Roosevelt understood how valuable she could be to the nation, however, and soon after his inauguration, he made Owen minister to Denmark. Appointed in April, 1933, she was the first American woman to hold a major diplomatic assignment. Tackling the job with her characteristic energy, Owen learned Danish and soon established a good image for the U.S. during these trying days of the Great Depression. Once again, however, romance and discriminatory legal precedents were her downfall.

After almost a decade as a WIDOW, she married Borge Rohde, a Danish noble, in 1936. Her husband was a governmental insider and their wedding took place at the Roosevelt's New York estate with ELEANOR ROOSEVELT as hostess—but despite all of these connections, no one pointed out until after the wedding that their marriage would nullify her diplomatic status. Under Danish law, she automatically became a Danish citizen at marriage and thus could no longer serve as minister.

Forced to resign, she returned to the lecture platform and wrote. Owen had published *The Elements of Public Speaking* (1931) while in Congress and a travelogue, *Leaves from a Greenland Diary* (1935), while in Denmark. She continued in this genre with three books in the late thirties on Scandinavia and its folklore and added a fourth on the Caribbean in 1949. In between, she wrote the book that most reflected her public activity during the forties: *Look Forward, Warrior* (1942) was a plea for global harmony that was published in the first year of American involvement in WORLD WAR II.

As the war wound down to its end, President Roosevelt assigned Owen to the State Department to work on the drafting of the United Nations Charter, and after Roosevelt's death,

President Truman appointed her as an alternate delegate to the United Nations General Assembly. She served the UN creditably and, beginning in 1948, chaired a research committee.

She died of a heart attack at sixty-eight in Copenhagen. She had gone there to receive the Order of Merit from the Danish king, who may have been embarrassed at the discrimination practiced by his predecessor. One of several awards, it was in recognition of her contributions to international understanding. As a congresswoman, a diplomat, an author, and an architect of the United Nations, Ruth Bryan Owen deserves such recognition.

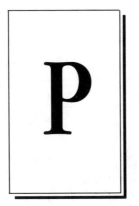

PALMER, ALICE FREEMAN (1855–1902)

Elected to the HALL OF FAME in 1920, Alice Freeman Palmer was far more famous early in the century than she is now. The second president of WELLESLEY COLLEGE, she obtained that position at just twenty-seven; she also played an important role in the founding of the UNIVERSITY OF CHICAGO.

Alice Freeman grew up in the area of New York State near SENECA FALLS that produced so many female leaders. A precocious child who read by age three, her position as the eldest of a large family almost cost her the opportunity to attend COLLEGE. She promised her parents, who were dubious about educating a girl, that she would stay single and work to provide opportunities for her younger siblings.

In 1872, she took advantage of the greater opportunity available to WESTERN WOMEN and went out to the University of Michigan. Though New York's VASSAR COLLEGE was then three years old, she needed the lower cost and preferred the coeducational experience of this public institution. Though she was later associated with private, single-sex higher education, she remained a lifelong proponent of coeducation. The primary purpose of women's colleges, she felt, was to serve women whose parents insisted on a more restricted environment.

Freeman graduated from Michigan in 1876 and was one of the first two female speakers at commencement—despite taking a semester off to serve as principal of an Illinois school because her family needed the money. Her family's needs kept her in the Midwest after graduation, for—like CARRIE CHAPMAN CATT—she found Midwesterners more open to female educators. Specifically, she could earn more in public high schools in the Midwest than was paid to female professors in Eastern women's colleges: Freeman twice turned down professorships from Wellesley because of the superior pay she earned as a principal in Saginaw, Michigan. Meanwhile, she continued her graduate education in history.

By 1879, family pressures had eased and Freeman accepted a position as head of Wellesley's history department. Two years later, the college's founder died and his handpicked president—who had been president in name only—resigned. After a year as acting president, Freeman was appointed to the position in 1882; the University of Michigan awarded her an honorary Ph.D. the same year. She used her presidency to improve curricula and especially to establish a network of preparatory schools that allowed women applicants the same advantageous secondary education young men received. By 1887, Wellesley had fifteen prep schools associated with it.

After only five years as president, however, Freeman resigned to marry Harvard philosopher George Herbert Palmer at the end of 1887. Neither they nor any of the academic community at the time seemed to consider the possibility of a married woman as a college president; her resignation was perceived as axiomatic and was duly rendered. The University of Chicago, however, showed more enlightenment four years later when Palmer was recruited to be dean of women at this new institution; she was offered extremely liberal terms that committed her to no more than twelve weeks in residence each year.

Her commitment to Chicago could not be measured by this slim requirement, however, for Palmer and her assistant, Marion Talbot, worked hard to create an equal place for women at the new university. With the aim of developing a "Western Wellesley," they established a house system that provided close contact with faculty, insisted on the hiring of women faculty, and introduced curricula, especially in social science, that appealed to women students. She held this position for three crucial founding years before resigning in 1895 to allow the university to hire a full-time dean.

Back in Boston, Palmer maintained an active involvement in education as a volunteer. A founder of the predecessor to the AMERICAN ASSOCIATION OF UNIVERSITY WOMEN, she served as its president in 1885–1886 and 1889–1890. In both Boston and Chicago, she was a featured speaker at the study clubs that formed as part of the era's CLUB MOVEMENT. A Wellesley trustee from 1888, Palmer also was appointed to the Massachusetts State Board of Education in 1889; she supported ELIZABETH CARY AGASSIZ in the founding of RADCLIFFE COLLEGE and was part of women's efforts in the 1893 COLUMBIAN EXPOSITION. An advocate of suffrage and temperance, she was not especially active in either movement, but was a strong Protestant who served as president of the Women's Home Missionary Association.

Palmer died in Paris at age forty-seven after emergency intestinal surgery. Her husband wrote her biography, *The Life of Alice Freeman Palmer* (1908) and published a collection of her poems, *A Marriage Cycle* (1915). His efforts on behalf of her memory may well have been responsible for her early selection to the Hall of Fame. Both of their ashes are buried in Wellesley's chapel.

PALMER, BERTHA HONORE (1849–1918)

The women who fill the society sections of newspapers are seldom the names that live on in the pages of history, but millionaire Bertha Palmer was one of the rare women who successfully combined the two types of lives. More commonly known as Mrs. Potter Palmer, she was of tremendous influence in her era.

From an old family with roots in Catholic Maryland, she was married at twenty-one to a man more than two decades older—a fact that defines her unusual personality, for despite this particularly unequal setting, she participated from the beginning in business decisions. The famous Chicago fire occurred the year following their wedding, and that tragedy gave the two of them exceptional opportunity in the city's rebirth. They eventually owned much Chicago real estate, with the empire crowned by the Palmer House hotel. In the tradition of women who ran BOARDING HOUSES and hotels from colonial times, Bertha Palmer shepherded her part-time home into one of the nation's great hotels. The birth of two sons did not hinder her civic involvement, and when her husband died in 1902, she was worth $8 million—which she would again double prior to her own death sixteen years later.

Despite this wealth, Palmer remained a political liberal and was actually on the stage of the 1896 Democratic convention when William Jennings Bryan gave his famed "Cross of Gold" speech. She participated in the WOMEN'S TTRADE UNION LEAGUE, supported JANE ADDAMS' Hull House, patronized MARY CASSATT and other of the era's new artists, and was active in the CLUB MOVEMENT as a member of the Chicago Woman's Club and of a well-known study club named Fortnightly.

The most important of her achievements, however, was in

Bertha Honore Palmer, a suffragist who chaired the women's activities for the Columbian Exposition in 1893, was a real estate developer who also experimented with cattle breeding. LELAND HAWES AND THE *TAMPA TRIBUNE.*

her role as chairman of the Board of LADY MANAGERS at the COLUMBIAN EXPOSITION of 1893. The exposition was a powerful factor in focusing global attention on the status of women, and SUSAN ANTHONY recorded that Palmer's opening speech "was very fine, covering full equality for women." Though some FEMINISTS objected to Palmer's appointment to this position, Anthony defended her and "lent no support to . . . [those] who thought there should have been more recognition of those who had been pioneer workers." It was Palmer's successful management of this extravaganza, with its complex melding of divergent groups, that caused President McKinley to appoint her as the only woman commissioner from the U.S. for the Paris Exposition of 1900. Again, the aging Anthony played a strong role in securing the appointment, for McKinley intended to send an all-male delegation until Anthony paid a personal visit to him.

In 1910, Palmer added a home near Sarasota, Florida to the ones she owned in London and Paris, and eventually she bought some ninety thousand acres of largely frontier land in southwest Florida. At The Oaks, she supervised the building of extensive gardens, ponds, and guest houses, as well as her own electrical and water systems. But unlike ALVA BELMONT and other socialites who built resort homes, Palmer actually worked her land. She studied cattle breeding and disease prevention, and when this animal husbandry research necessitated the fencing of thirty thousand acres, she stood up to angry cattlemen accustomed to open range. She raised hogs at another location, and by 1916, also held large tracts of land in and near Tampa, some of which she maintained as a "well-stocked hunting preserve."

Despite a mastectomy, Bertha Palmer died of breast cancer "on the eve of her sixty-ninth birthday." From her deathbed at The Oaks, she still "sought details on her business enterprises."

PARK, MAUD WOOD (1875–1955)

The first president of the LEAGUE OF WOMEN VOTERS (LWV), Maud Wood Park became a suffragist while a student at RADCLIFFE COLLEGE, from which she graduated in 1898. Two years later, she was the youngest delegate at the convention of the NATIONAL AMERICAN WOMAN SUFFRAGE ASSOCIATION (NAWSA); after that she would be ceaselessly involved with the organization until the passage of the NINETEENTH AMENDMENT.

By 1901, she replaced ALICE STONE BLACKWELL as chairman of the board for the Massachusetts Woman Suffrage Association. The infusion of younger members was particularly needed in the turn-of-the-century SUFFRAGE MOVEMENT, which sometimes seemed almost resigned to an endless task. Park focused on recruiting young women through the EQUAL SUFFRAGE LEAGUE aimed at women's COLLEGES, and for several years she TRAVELED throughout the country building new chapters on campuses. The League's object, she said in a 1906 speech, "is to bring the question of equal suffrage to college women and to help them realize their debt to the women who have worked so hard for them . . ."

In 1908, the League was officially proclaimed a part of the NAWSA, and soon thereafter, Park left on a long global voyage; when she returned, she lectured on the condition of women abroad, especially in Asia. From 1917, she lobbied full time in Washington on behalf of the suffrage amendment. Known as an astute lobbyist closely acquainted with congressmen, she played a particularly strong role in passing a 1918 bill that allowed the Territory of Hawaii to grant women the right to vote—something that the territorial legislature did not use.

Park served as president of the League of Women Voters for five years, from its 1919 founding date to 1924. Under her presidency, the organization adopted a long list of FEMINIST aims, but as the political conservatism of the postwar era hardened, she met with few successes. Her strongest efforts were on behalf of a constitutional amendment forbidding child labor, which never passed, and children were also the center of more successful legislative aims such as the SHEPARD-TOWNER ACT. In these cases, it is clear that she was beginning the LWV's abandonment of feminist issues to substitute the selfless tradition of benefiting children and others.

Maud Wood Park never had children of her own, though she married twice. She was WIDOWED in 1904 after only seven years of marriage; her second marriage in 1908 was an extremely modern arrangement, and she neither lived with her husband nor took his name. In her youth, Park also worked on behalf of IMMIGRANT WOMEN, especially via Boston's Denison House, and she was involved in forming the Parent Teacher Association in Boston. She wrote a play, *Lucy Stone* (1936) and coauthored *Victory, How Women Won It: A Centennial Symposium, 1840–1940.* That effort led her to accumulate some of the first papers placed on deposit for the unequaled collection of women's history in Radcliffe's Schlesinger Library. Finally, Park's story of the passage of the suffrage amendment was published after her death as *Front Door Lobbying* (1960).

PARKER, DOROTHY ROTHSCHILD (1893–1967)

Forever associated with the *New Yorker* and with the literati of the Algonquin Round Table, Parker epitomized the bright, sophisticated young woman of the Roaring Twenties.

Despite her Jewish origins, she was educated by NUNS and then went on to FINISHING SCHOOL. After brief employment with *Vogue*, she joined *Vanity Fair* in 1917; marriage that same year changed her name to Parker. Though the marriage never truly survived her husband's experience in WORLD WAR I and they DIVORCED in 1928, she retained her husband's name and simply appended "Miss" to it. Five years later, she married again, but did not take her husband's name—though this tumultuous relationship would last most of thirty years. Indeed, she spent much of those three decades in California because she and her husband both worked as screenwriters—but Parker nevertheless retained an image as the quintessential New Yorker.

The early twenties were hard for her. Her first marriage was dying and her professional life was difficult, for she was fired from *Vanity Fair* for writing a drama review displeasing to advertisers. Though she was published by *Life* and the *Saturday Evening Post*, her income was unreliable. After an ABORTION in 1923, she tried to commit suicide; the next year, a play that she coauthored failed, and 1925 brought another suicide attempt. Ernest Hemingway was among those who made heavy-handed bids at humor based on Parker's unhappiness.

Her first book, *Enough Rope* (1926), was a bestselling volume of witty verse that surprised the public with its cynicism, for that was a viewpoint seldom attributed to women AUTHORS. In 1927, she joined the *New Yorker* as a regular columnist, and this most elitist of magazines would provide the long-term platform for her amusingly caustic lampoons. She soon became an acknowledged leader—and the only woman—of the group of modern writers who lunched at the Algonquin Hotel; though several of the men associated with the group also were humorists, it was Parker who was best known for witticisms.

Yet, despite her reputation for sharp words, LILLIAN HELLMAN said of Parker: "I have never heard her hit mean except where it was, in some sense, justified." Hellman doubtlessly understood that a new voice was needed for women—a voice that not only would forego the sentimentality usually associated with women, but also one that could summarize the injustices women routinely encounter with a clever phrase that cut to the heart of the matter.

Best known as a drama critic, Parker wrote in several genres. Some of her poem titles became so well known that they entered the language as phrases. This was especially the case with "Men Seldom Make Passes at Girls Who Wear

Glasses," a phrase that tellingly spoke of her many unhappily resolved love affairs with intellectually inferior men. Versatile and prolific, other examples of her work include the collections *Death and Taxes* (1931) and *Not So Deep As a Well* (1936).

Though this talent for versification was a large part of her reputation, critics offer their highest praise for her short stories. "Big Blonde" (1929) won the O. Henry Prize; the tale of a suicidal alcoholic excessively needful of male approval, it came close to being autobiographical. Her revealingly titled short story collections include *Laments for the Living* (1930) and *Here Lies* (1939). She was not proud of the twenty-plus films on which she worked, even though they included the screenplay of *A Star is Born* (1937) and Hellman's *Little Foxes* (1941).

Always a political progressive, her activism in forming the Screenwriters Guild during the Depression would handsomely reward other (mostly male) writers in the future, but in Parker's lifetime, this union association became still another negative for her during postwar conservatism. Indeed, Parker published little after WORLD WAR II began, and during the fifties, she was among many artists and writers who were ostracized for their presumed leftism. She did publish a play, *Ladies of the Corridor* (1953), but its honest portrayal of women's situation was not appealing in this time when sentimentality, not satire, was the dominant mode for women.

Self-deprecation marked Parker's work and a will to fail sometimes appears to characterize her life; she made a number of comments in her last years to indicate that she saw herself as a failure. It was true that the blacklisting of her work made this appear to be a realistic assessment at the time, but, in contrast, a recently published literary reference work unequivocally calls Dorothy Parker "the sharpest wit of our century."

In 1992, the U.S. Post Office issued a stamp in her honor as part of a Literary Art Series.

PARKS, ROSA McCAULEY (1913–) .Sometimes called the "Mother of the Civil Rights Movement", Parks earned that designation because her action began the Montgomery, Alabama bus boycott that was the first success of Southern blacks in overthrowing segregation.

Born in Tuskegee, Rosa grew up without the presence of her father, but was strongly influenced by her maternal grandfather. He had been born in slavery, the son of his master, and was in fact so fair-skinned that he would be ejected from a 1923 Back-to-Africa meeting by blacks who believed he was white. Rosa's mother, Leona Edwards McCauley, was a TEACHER, but was so poorly paid that Rosa grew up in poverty. She did farm and domestic work, and as an adolescent, attended a school run by a white woman from Massachusetts; Alabama whites were so hostile to this woman, however, that she abandoned the project about 1927. Though Rosa attended what she called "Alabama State high school," she left before graduating.

In 1932, she married Raymond Parks, who had been involved with the "Scottsboro Boys" (a notorious 1931 case involving black men unjustly accused of raping a white woman), but he dropped out of activism during the rest of the Depression decade. Rosa Parks, however, read widely

enough to be aware of the changing roles of blacks during WORLD WAR II. A trip to Detroit, where her mother found wartime work, brought additional awareness of the possibility of change, and when NAACP activists began to penetrate the heart of segregation in Alabama after the war, she became an early member. Indeed, Parks was elected secretary of the state NAACP at the first meeting she attended, and in 1945, she courageously registered to vote.

For the next decade, she grew slowly in movement philosophy and skills, and in July of 1955, Parks attended the Highlander School where ELLA BAKER, SEPTIMA CLARK, and others taught political action techniques. Yet, though she thus had the credentials to be considered an activist, Rosa Parks did not plan the incident that propelled her to national prominence.

When she got on the bus on December 1, 1955, "I had a full weekend planned. It was the busy time of the year [at the clothing store where she sewed], and I was preparing for the weekend workshop for the Youth Council." In fact, Parks was in such a hurry that she failed to notice the bus driver was one whom she had deliberately avoided ever since he had humiliated her back in 1943. In that incident, she had been ejected from the bus when she tried to go down the aisle after paying her fare; blacks were instead expected to deposit their fare and then exit the bus to walk around and enter from the rear—and in this process, drivers sometimes left them behind.

When a white man entered the bus in the evening rush hour of that December day and found all the seats occupied, the driver ordered blacks to vacate for him not just one seat, but also all of the surrounding seats. The anger she felt twelve years earlier boiled up in Parks, and she refused to move. "I had enough," she explained simply. "I wanted to be treated like a human being."

As others quietly slipped off the bus, she remained firm. The driver called the police, who jailed her, and during the next days, Rosa Parks' arrest became the catalyst for the birth of the civil rights movement. *Jet* magazine appeared the next day to try to interview her, but her life was so anonymously humble that it took the local news media several days to track down Parks. Meanwhile, Martin Luther King began using her example to build the successful boycott of Montgomery buses, and for more than a year, black people—who made up more than 70 percent of the customers—walked instead of riding. Since almost none of these people owned cars, the local economy ground to a halt; thousands of workers who did the city's most menial but essential tasks quit their jobs rather than take the bus to work. It was the first successful massive resistance to American segregation.

Rosa Parks would share platforms with King and other leaders during the next decades, but she was not employed by the civil rights movement and continued to work in low-paying jobs. The bombing of a Birmingham church that killed four little girls in 1957 made more threatening the sinister telephone calls that the Parks household regularly received, and Raymond Parks—who had resisted Rosa's longtime desire to move North—decided their lives would be better in Detroit.

They have lived there ever since. Rosa Parks held places of honor at civil rights marches in Detroit and Washington; she was awarded the Martin Luther King Non-Violent Peace

Prize in Atlanta in 1980 and the Wonder Woman Foundation Award in 1984. She has spent much of her life working with children, though she had none of her own, and in 1987, the Rosa and Raymond Parks Institute for Self Development was established for children. Among other aims, this foundation sponsors an annual Reverse Freedom Tour, during which young people ride buses south and retrace the steps taken by their brave benefactors, including Rosa Parks.

PARSONS, ELSIE WORTHINGTON CLEWS (1875–1941)

Later honored by her male colleagues with the national presidencies of three professional associations, Elsie Clews enrolled at BARNARD COLLEGE when that school was only three years old. She graduated in 1896 and went on to earn her Ph.D. in history from the associated Columbia in 1899. With a concentration on the history of education and the family, she naturally moved into the emerging fields of sociology and anthropology, where her reputation ultimately was made.

Marriage the following year did not significantly hinder her separate life—a situation that is especially impressive given that her husband was an active politician who served three terms in Congress and that Parsons bore six children between 1901 and 1911. Like historian MARY BEARD, Parsons enjoyed a long marriage with a man who supported her individualism, despite suffering the political consequences of her unconventional views.

Though she was awarded only the academic rank of lecturer, Parsons began teaching at Columbia in 1902, the year after her first child was born. A course on the family developed into *The Family* (1906), and thereafter writing replaced teaching in her busy schedule. Though scholarly in its intent, the book was widely read by FEMINISTS and was one of the first arguments against artificial distinctions in the rearing of boys and girls; her comments on toys and games are points still being made to parents and educators by today's feminists. She went on to write several more popular books on the changing role of women; a 1913 book on sexual behavior she saw as so potentially explosive that she used the PSEUDONYM of "John Main."

A committed pacifist during WORLD WAR I, Parsons was so controversial that she probably could not have found a professorship in most colleges; though she lectured at the New School for Social Research when it was truly new (with RUTH BENEDICT as one of her students), she was fortunate to be affluent enough that she did not have to teach for a living. After the war, she increasingly concentrated on field research among the natives of the American Southwest, publishing several detailed books and over a hundred scholarly articles on these and other minority groups. It was this research into cultures that were fast disappearing that brought her the presidency of the American Folklore Society (1918–1920), the American Ethnological Association (1923–1925), and the American Anthropological Association (1940–1941).

Parsons was serving as president of the prestigious anthropological association when she died after routine surgery at sixty-six. Her death came only weeks after the American declaration of WORLD WAR II, something that she had opposed in the previous year's election when she supported the Socialist candidate.

PATTERSON, ALICIA (1906–1963)

The founder of Long Island's *Newsday*, Alicia Patterson has the rare distinction of creating a successful major metropolitan newspaper during the second half of the twentieth century. At a time when many newspapers were going out of business, she began an entirely new publication, brought it to profitability within six years and guided its future for the twenty-four years that remained of her too-brief life.

The daughter and granddaughter of the PUBLISHERS of the *Chicago Tribune* and the *New York Daily News*, she was educated in FINISHING SCHOOLS in this country and abroad. Patterson debuted in 1925, married and DIVORCED twice in the next decade, and appeared to be headed towards the life of a society matron—but in 1939, she took an independent route. Emulating her aunt, CISSY PATTERSON, who owned Washington's *Times-Herald*, she bought the equipment of a defunct Long Island newspaper and began issuing *Newsday* in 1940—a decade after her aunt began publishing. Though Patterson's third husband, Harry Guggenheim, supported the venture, the rest of her family was generally opposed and her father specifically advised against the unconventional format that she nonetheless used—and which soon won awards.

What Alicia Patterson understood was that suburbia would replace the cities as the dominant economic force in the postwar era. She overcame the paper and labor shortages that plagued publishing during WORLD WAR II, and by its end, was showing a profit on the $750,000 initial investment. By 1954, when the paper was fifteen years old, it had a circulation of over two hundred thousand. Its profitability was further enhanced by an exceptionally large number of advertisers, who sought out the paper because of its audience among suburban housewives.

Patterson was unique in recognizing this new market; despite the growth of suburbia throughout the country during the fifties, no other publisher demonstrated similar ingenuity in targeting these new national demographics with a newspaper specifically aimed at young, affluent, suburban readers. Moreover, she also was independent in creating a new editorial voice; much more internationalist than her relatives, she endorsed candidates of both parties and took on established political kingmakers. By 1954, *Newsday* was winning Pulitzer Prizes for exposing corruption.

Her success nonetheless was bought at a physical price, and Alicia Patterson died at fifty-six of bleeding ulcers. Less than seven years after her death, Harry Guggenheim sold *Newsday* to the publishers of the *Los Angeles Times*. Despite her demonstrable success, she was not honored by any major journalistic or business organizations. Had Patterson lived a decade longer until the revitalization of the women's movement in the 1970s, she doubtless would have received more of the recognition that she deserves.

PATTERSON, ELEANOR MEDILL "CISSY" (1881–1948)

Known by her nickname all her life, Cissy Patterson was called "the most powerful woman in America" during the WORLD WAR II era when she was the PUBLISHER of news that dominated the nation's capital.

Though she was from a powerful family whose male members included the owners of the *Chicago Tribune* and the *New York Daily News*, Patterson spent the next fifty years of her life pursuing the transitory pleasures assigned to wealthy women. Educated in FINISHING SCHOOLS, including the famous Miss Porter's School, she married a Polish noble in 1904 and bore a child the following year. His mistreatment of her and especially his kidnapping of their daughter caused international gossip, but she was unable to obtain a DIVORCE until 1917—the year that nobility in the Russian empire collapsed in revolution.

She published two largely autobiographical novels, *Glass Houses* (1923) and *Fall Flight* (1928), and, after the death of her second husband, began again to use her MAIDEN NAME. Finally, in 1930, she took over the *Washington Herald*, a low-circulation newspaper that appeared moribund during this first year of the Great Depression.

To the surprise of almost everyone, Patterson turned the paper around—at least in part because she employed female reporters and assigned topics that women found interesting. Moreover, she reported herself, including one famous series when this former international socialist disguised herself as needy to write on life among the destitute in the nation's capital. She pursued an editorial policy more liberal in both domestic and foreign affairs than that of her anti-Roosevelt relatives' newspapers—and she made money. By 1939, she had taken over the competing Heart newspapers in Washington, and by 1943, her *Times-Herald* boasted the largest audience in this most news-wise of cities.

When Patterson died in 1948, she had increased the wealth that she inherited from less than a million to more than $16 million. Long estranged from her only child, she left her estate to favored employees, but within a few years, these men had managed to put the paper back into debt. Just six years after Cissy Patterson's death, it was taken over by the *Washington Post*—where another female owner, KATHERINE GRAHAM, would similarly surprise the publishing world with managerial ability that also seemed innate. In both cases, a large part of their success can abe attributed to an enlarged definition of news that included women as readers.

PATTERSON, MARY JANE (1840–1894) The first African-American woman to graduate from COLLEGE, Mary Jane Patterson graduated from OBERLIN COLLEGE in 1862, during the first full year of the CIVIL WAR.

She had been born near Raleigh, North Carolina; her father managed to bring his family out of slavery after his own escape. Even free blacks fled the South after the 1850 passage of the Fugitive Slave Act endangered them by encouraging kidnapping and sale into slavery, and Mary Jane's parents, Henry and Emeline Patterson, were part of the exodus north. They settled in the college town of Oberlin, Ohio about 1854, where Henry Patterson did well at masonry work: his property was valued at seventeen hundred dollars in the 1860 census. The family became prosperous enough that only the oldest son followed him into semiskilled labor; the younger four Patterson children all graduated from Oberlin, with Mary Jane leading the way.

In giving Mary Jane and her sisters an education, the Pattersons would set a pattern often followed by black families in the future: well into the twentieth century, black families differed from whites in that they were as likely to educate

daughters as sons. Presumably they saw the traditional female professions of TEACHING and NURSING as steady employment opportunities that provided decent income—but these were occupations requiring credentials. Because males were always paid more than females in every area from the most unskilled labor to the professions, family funds were better invested in a female member, for she needed educational credentials to bring her pay expectations up to his.

Mary Jane Patterson completed Oberlin's fairly rigorous four-year course in 1862 and moved to Philadelphia to teach sometime thereafter. In 1869, both she and her younger sister, Channie A. Patterson, were appointed to the black school system of Washington, D.C. Washington became a mecca for blacks during and after the Civil War, and its segregated schools were the best available to black students throughout the nineteenth century. Both Patterson and her sister remained single and devoted their lives to educating the children of ex-slaves. They were later joined by their parents, brother, and another teacher sister, Emma.

In 1871, six years after the end of the war, the thirty-one-year-old Patterson was appointed principal of what was known in Washington's black community simply as the "Preparatory School." Created well before the Civil War, the school had moved from its beginnings in the basement of a Presbyterian church to an impressive three-story stone structure at the corner of Seventeenth and Church Streets. Supported by the New England Friends Mission, the school's first principal had been a white woman from New Hampshire; Mary Jane Patterson was the first black accorded such an honor.

She served the 1871–1872 term and then was replaced by Harvard University's first black graduate (who was, of course, male, for not even Harvard's feminine counterpart of RADCLIFFE COLLEGE yet existed). He was apparently unwilling to assume a longtime commitment, however, and Patterson was reappointed principal in 1873. Under her leadership, the growing school moved to Seventeenth and M Streets, where it would become informally known as "the M Street School," though its diplomas said "Washington Colored High School." In any case, it was the city's only high school for black students and its standards were high, as both students and teachers put scholastics first in attempting to prove to white society that there were no innate intellectual differences between the races.

Though it was a public institution after the war, the school emulated prep school standards—except that, unlike white prep schools, it was coeducational and accepted students regardless of their economic status. Its teaching staff was mostly female, all of whom were single, for married women were banned from teaching in Washington until 1923. Like the staffs of elitist white preparatory schools, this faculty centered their lives around their students. Among the outstanding women who taught there was MARY CHURCH TERRELL.

As the school developed an excellent reputation, however, Patterson became the victim of her own success. Like all too many women, she found that when her hard work paid off and enrollment grew, 'it was deemed advisable to place a male in charge." Her term as principal ended in 1884, though she stayed on the faculty for the rest of her life. Much later, with the school renamed Dunbar High School in 1914, it would have another outstanding black female principal in Anna J. Cooper.

Mary Jane Patterson was still teaching when she died at fifty-four. Just months before her death, she joined her friend Mary Church Terrell in drawing up incorporation papers for the Colored Women's League of Washington, D.C., which was a forerunner to the NATIONAL ASSOCIATION OF COLORED WOMEN. Had she lived, she may well have become a more recognized leader, but from her birth in the slave society of North Carolina to building the best school for young blacks in the nation's most progressive city, Mary Jane Patterson's life was one of tremendous change for the better.

PAUL, ALICE (1885–1977) While SUSAN ANTHONY and many other suffragists grew more powerful and esteemed with age, Alice Paul became largely irrelevant during the fifty-seven years of her life that remained after women won the right to vote. Yet more than any other single person, Alice Paul was responsible for revitalizing the SUFFRAGE MOVEMENT

that languished after Anthony's death, and she deserves the recognition she receives for her less successful effort as the author of the EQUAL RIGHTS AMENDMENT (ERA).

Born to affluent, progressive QUAKER parents in New Jersey, Paul graduated from Swarthmore College in 1905. She received her master's degree from the University of Pennsylvania in 1907, and after graduate work in New York and abroad, she was awarded a Ph.D. from Penn in 1912; later in life, she would earn three law degrees. It was her experience as a graduate student in England that changed Paul's life, however, for she became active in the much more militant suffrage movement there. From Englishwomen, she learned the political techniques of marching, demonstrating, and even inflicting property damage on those politicians who opposed women's rights. She was arrested on numerous occasions, but joined in the movement's hunger strikes that publicized their jailing. Several times she endured the pain of having a tube jammed down her throat to be forcibly fed.

She returned to the U.S. in 1910 and completed her Ph.D.

Under the leadership of Alice Paul, the Woman's Party implemented a number of visibility techniques to raise public awareness of the suffrage issue. This street theater on the steps of the U.S. Treasury was designed to demonstrate that these young women would be expected to pay taxes, yet could not vote. LIBRARY OF CONGRESS.

at the University of Pennsylvania in 1912. She soon became active in the National American Woman's Suffrage Association (NAWSA), where her overseas experience was rewarded with an appointment as chair of NAWSA's Congressional Committee. In this role, she organized the parade that greeted Woodrow Wilson on the day before his inauguration; it attracted more than some eight thousand women and was soon emulated as an organizing technique, for public sympathy was won over when the white-clad women were attacked by ruffians. Washington's police chief eventually lost his job because of his men's failure to ensure the women's safety.

Paul also led the lobbying work for a suffrage amendment to the U.S. Constitution during the congressional session of 1913. Along with LUCY BURNS, and others, however, she soon became disenchanted with the NAWSA's relatively staid methods. During the next months and under Paul's leadership, the CONGRESSIONAL UNION (CU) evolved as a separate organization that adopted the more militant style of British suffragists. After bitter internal disagreements, Paul was displaced from her NAWSA affiliation early in 1914.

When the CU played an active role in the congressional elections of that year, its membership soared. The NAWSA, which had held a virtual monopoly on the suffrage movement since 1890, responded to the challenge with new dynamism in the form of CARRIE CHAPMAN CATT, who was elected its president in 1915. Paul, in turn, reorganized her group as the WOMAN'S PARTY in 1916 and prepared for that year's presidential campaign. The effect of this competition was generally positive, for far more energy was devoted to the issue of suffrage, and Paul deserves credit for being the overdue catalyst to a movement in danger of becoming accustomed to failure.

She spent the 1916 campaign dogging the heels of President Wilson—but even after his conversion to suffrage, Paul continued to adhere to the parliamentary model that holds the party in power accountable for everything. Thus, she opposed all Democrats—even those who supported suffrage—because the Democratic Party held the White House. This somewhat simplistic strategy was understandably upsetting to Catt and other political sophisticates, but at the same time, the candor of Paul's rage attracted many women who were less interested in subtleties than in simply getting attention for their cause. The debate over the relative importance of Catt and her NAWSA or Paul and her Woman's Party in the final passage of the NINETEENTH AMENDMENT is impossible to resolve, but it is entirely possible that neither methodology would have worked without the other.

When the amendment was finally ratified in August of 1920, Paul remained active in the Woman's Party, though she stepped down from the chairmanship in 1921. The Party did little to develop a separate voting bloc of women, however, and most newly enfranchised voters joined neither the Woman's Party nor the NAWSA's successor, the LEAGUE OF WOMEN VOTERS. Instead, most women voted as the men of their families did, and the relatively few women who ran for office found no viable organizational support from Paul—who spent the twenties going to law schools—nor from the Woman's Party.

Rather than concentrating on candidacies in the usual way of political parties, Paul and the Woman's Party instead adopted a new single-purpose goal: once the suffrage amendment was ratified, they turned to passage of the Equal Rights Amendment as a *raison d'être*. The ERA, however, was a far more complex and difficult issue, and despite her excellent education, Paul would not be able to overcome the arguments against it from most of the era's most prominent women. Indeed, powerful women such as ELEANOR ROOSEVELT, FRANCES PERKINS, MARY NORTON, and MARY ANDERSON saw Paul's ERA as evidence of her seemingly irrational opposition to Democrats and their programs and, worse, as a dangerously quixotic ideal that would nullify the PROTECTIVE LEGISLATION to which they had dedicated their lives.

The ERA thus languished in Congress for decades, even though Paul reworked it when she again assumed the chair of the Woman's Party in 1942. Finally, at age eighty-seven, she lived to see the ERA pass out of Congress, but death spared her the pain of seeing its extended ratification period expire while state legislatures rejected it. Instead, she enjoyed acclaim by the NATIONAL ORGANIZATION FOR WOMEN shortly before her death at ninety-two.

When her efforts to include an equal rights statement in the U.S. proved futile, Paul worked instead for a similar international commitment. After 1930, she spent much of her time on the international scene, working first with the League of Nations and then the United Nations. Indeed, Alice Paul's greatest achievement may in fact be in this relatively unrecognized area, for she was a major factor in the specific inclusion of women in the preamble of the United Nations' charter.

As a lawyer, she understood that the earlier DECLARATIONS OF RIGHTS FOR WOMEN were necessary because women had discovered that men were insincere when they said women were covered by phrases such as "all men are created equal." Alice Paul is fittingly memorialized by the UN's charter, which affirms "the dignity and worth of the human person [and] the equal rights of men and women."

PAWTUCKET, RHODE ISLAND WEAVERS STRIKE (1824)

The first recorded strike by women in American industry occurred when the nation's infant industries were still very young. While Pawtucket's mills dated back to 1793, the widespread employment of women in TEXTILE MILLS was only about a decade old when female weavers organized themselves and went on STRIKE for higher wages and improved conditions in 1824.

This action came long before the emergence of formal labor unions in the U.S., which did not occur until after the CIVIL WAR. Women's history would again be ignored, as throughout the nineteenth and twentieth centuries, union organizers repeatedly argued that women were unwilling to do what Rhode Island women in fact had done decades earlier.

The history of the women and children who worked in these early mills is exhibited in the Slater Hill Historic Site at Pawtucket.

PEABODY SISTERS—ELIZABETH PALMER PEABODY, MARY PEABODY MANN, AND SOPHIA PEABODY HAWTHORNE

All three of these daughters of pre-CIVIL WAR Boston played a role in the nation's cultural development. The most individually famous of the sisters was Elizabeth Palmer Peabody (1804–1894), for the other two would find their personal opportunities eclipsed by their husbands—Horace Mann and Nathaniel Hawthorne.

Born to well-educated parents, they were taught by both their mother and father. TEACHING would continue to define the futures of Elizabeth and Mary, as both worked as GOVERNESSES and conducted DAME SCHOOLS. After her 1843 marriage, Mary Peabody Mann (1806–1887) played a major role in the development of ANTIOCH COLLEGE during the 1850s. After Horace Mann's death, she joined her sister Elizabeth in working with the kindergarten movement and also published several works, including a novel and a three-volume biography of her husband.

Sophia, who was considered a semi-invalid, had traveled with Mary in the Caribbean on a restorative trip prior to her 1842 marriage to Hawthorne. In fact, biographers have said that it was his desire to marry Sophia Peabody that caused Hawthorne to become serious about publishing—and it was his future sister-in-law, Elizabeth Peabody, who published his first children's literature. Sophia demonstrated her mental independence by persuading Nathaniel to live with her at a Transcendentalist utopian farm prior to their marriage—something that was very difficult for this painfully reticent young man—but, after marriage, they lived a quiet life that centered on his work. Her involvement in Boston's intellectual life was limited to participation in the gatherings that predated the women's study CLUB MOVEMENT.

The most accomplished, Elizabeth was the oldest and remained single. Already in 1827—a time when women still did not engage in PUBLIC SPEAKING—she modestly delivered her lectures on American history in homes, but nonetheless earned significant fees for them. During the next decade, she produced a three-volume question-and-answer series designed to teach history; her intended audience for this work and for her lectures was primarily women. In 1837, Peabody joined MARGARET FULLER as a charter member of the Transendentalist Club; they were the only women among Emerson, Thoreau, Channing, and other leaders of this early American intellect ferment. At the same time, she worked with Bronson Alcott (father of LOUISA MAY ALCOTT) in implementing progressive educational theories.

All of these contacts allowed her to open in 1840 what became a famous business enterprise—Peabody turned the parlor of her Boston home into what has been termed the nation's first important bookstore. She sought out reading material available nowhere else, and her establishment also functioned as a leading library, educational center, and publishing house for *avant garde* works. Among others items, Elizabeth Peabody was the PUBLISHER of Transcendentalist philosophical works, of daring ABOLITIONIST materials, and of Thoreau's "Civil Disobedience"—a controversial essay during this time of the Fugitive Slave Act, as well as a foundation for nonviolent resistance in the twentieth century.

After a decade of intellectual but not necessarily financial success, Peabody closed her bookstore in 1850. Thereafter, she concentrated on lecturing and writing, with her most important message being the advocacy of Germany's new kindergartens. In speeches such as the one she made at the founding meeting of the AMERICAN ASSOCIATION OF UNIVERSITY WOMEN in 1873, Peabody had tremendous influence in the eventual adoption of ideas stressing early childhood educa-

tion. The author of ten books and dozens of articles, Elizabeth Peabody also took on the cause of Native Americans prior to her death at ninety.

PERKINS, FRANCES (1880–1965) The first woman to serve on the Cabinet, Frances Perkins will remain one of the most significant cabinet members of all time. Revolutionary changes took place during her tenure as secretary of labor, including the introduction of such economic fundamentals as Social Security.

A Bostonian by birth, she graduated from MOUNT HOLYOKE COLLEGE in 1902; it was while TEACHING high school science in suburban Chicago that she began volunteering at SETTLEMENT HOUSES, including JANE ADDAMS' Hull House. Increasingly interested in economics and the problem of labor, she returned east and earned a master's degree in sociology and economics from Columbia University in 1910.

Perkins volunteered for the SUFFRAGE MOVEMENT and later said that its parades and speechmaking campaigns "did more to make me truly at ease . . . than anything else I ever did." Her first paid job in her new field was with the Consumers' League, a very active organization that pursued the goals of workers as intently as those of customers. Strongly influenced by FLORENCE KELLEY, Perkins worked between 1910–1912 for passage of the League's progressive agenda, especially a maximum hours law to protect workers from dangerously long days.

Though the TRIANGLE FIRE acted as an impetus for change with many, it affected Perkins more than most because she personally witnessed its horrifying deaths; she had been drinking tea with a friend who lived nearby when the alarm sounded. In the aftermath, she became a salaried employee of the mostly-male committee that investigated similar industrial abuses, and, along with MARY DREIER, she spurred action to see that such a tragedy would never be repeated. This investigative work, along with other field research as a graduate student, gave Perkins a profound insider's view of worker exploitation.

Her decade of learning came to fruition when Al Smith was elected governor of New York in 1918. He appointed Perkins to the New York State Industrial Commission, where she became the highest paid female state employee in the nation. Equally important, she had Smith's support for genuine labor reform; in addition to implementing rigorous factory inspections, she intervened in strikes and supervised negotiations. In 1926, she rose to the Commission's chairmanship, and when Franklin Roosevelt became governor two years later, he confirmed her in that position. While workers in most of the nation lost ground during the twenties, Perkins was part of the New York leadership that passed progressive legislation, such as a reduction in the standard work week from fifty-six hours to forty-eight.

When the fragile state of the nation's economy became clear and the stock market crashed in 1929, her work load increased as unemployment soared. Perkins tirelessly sought solutions, even going to Britain to learn the mechanics of unemployment compensation programs already in place abroad. Also during this time, she became friends with Franklin and ELEANOR ROOSEVELT as well as with MOLLY DEWSON and others who would form the backbone of the New Deal when

Roosevelt was elected president in 1932. These women, especially Dewson, thought so much of Perkins that they pushed Roosevelt to make her the first woman on the Cabinet—and not only that, but in the key position of secretary of labor during the depths of the Great Depression.

The Women's Division of the Democratic Party had played a significant role in Roosevelt's election, and he responded. It would have been easy for him to have rejected the idea, for even though Roosevelt understood that Frances Perkins' qualifications were as legitimate as those of any man, organized labor had never been inclusive of women workers and it was unlikely that they would welcome a woman in what they viewed as their top position. It is to Roosevelt's great credit that he made the appointment, even in the face of attitudes such as that of the CIO (Congress of Industrial Organizations) president who once called Perkins "woozy in the head."

At age fifty-two, Frances Perkins was sworn in on the same day that Roosevelt himself was inaugurated. She would return the loyalty by becoming one of just two Cabinet members to serve throughout his presidency—the other one being a Jewish man. That she was sworn in on the earliest possible day shows the urgency with which she and other New Dealers viewed the Great Depression. Perkins went immediately to work, overseeing the congressional authorization and the implementation of dozens of ideas to revive and stabilize the economy.

The Civilian Conservation Corps began in March of 1933, just weeks after the inauguration; May saw the passage of the $500 million dollar Federal Emergency Relief Act; June brought the beginning of the U.S. Employment Service, as well as passage of the multiprogram National Recovery Act; which included the creation of the powerful National Labor Relations Board—and Frances Perkins had accomplished more in her first few months of office than most Cabinet members do in a decade. The following year, she brought the U.S. into the League of Nation's International Labor Organization. With the implementation of Social Security in 1935 and the Fair Labor Standards Act of 1937, which banned child labor and established minimum wages and maximum hours, Frances Perkins achieved a series of changes that are basic to today's economy.

With the outbreak of WORLD WAR II, she faced a different set of problems. Labor was a key factor for military victory because millions of extra workers were needed to produce weapons and supplies. The result was the largest recruitment of minorities and women in the nation's history, and again, Perkins headed up the effort. At the same time, her moderate, politically pragmatic policy led her to take stands that appear antifeminist in retrospect. Like the majority of Roosevelt officials, she saw no immediate need for the NATIONAL WAR SERVICE ACT, and she was satisfied to let private employers undertake child care needs rather than supporting governmentally funded programs. Nor did she exert much pressure on unions to welcome women workers to their ranks.

The result is that Perkins has been criticized by some modern feminists as uninterested in women's causes. Her early career, however, was aimed at women, with the follow up of the Triangle Fire especially focused on industries that employed large numbers of women. It was this experience that convinced her of the need for PROTECTIVE LEGISLATION, and, like Eleanor Roosevelt and others who spent their lives working for laws that specifically aimed at righting wrongs done to women, she opposed the EQUAL RIGHTS AMENDMENT.

Modern FEMINISTS also have complained that she was too accommodating of the men who controlled organized labor, with the result that—especially early in her administration during the Depression—she tended to assume that the needs of working men were more important than those of working women. Though Perkins was herself a working woman who was the sole provider for her family and though she wrote many articles in women's magazines that are empathetic, even original supporters such as MARY ANDERSON became disillusioned with her lack of leadership on behalf of women during the war. In Perkins' view, however, political reality required that she work amicably with men; very much aware that she was the only female Cabinet member in the nation's history, she believed that she had to be pragmatic and keep her seat to benefit workers of both genders.

Part of the reason for Perkins' long list of accomplishments was that she served during the two great crises of the depression and the war, but in addition, she may have thrown herself into her work more than others would have because her personal life was a troubled one. She had retained her MAIDEN NAME when she married Paul Wilson, a fellow economist, in 1913; for the first five years of their marriage, her work was largely volunteer while she bore two daughters, losing one to INFANT MORTALITY. By 1918, however, it was clear that Perkins would have to provide the major income for the family.

Despite her husband's financial background, he lost most of their savings by gambling on the gold market, and after that, he increasingly displayed the behavior of a manic depressive. Only occasionally employed in the twenties, he spent much of his time after 1930 in mental sanitariums. He refused to move to Washington when she was appointed in 1933, so Perkins faithfully returned to New York every weekend and paid the expensive bills for his care. One of the results was that she had little time for motherhood, and her relationship with her daughter was less than satisfactory until late in life.

Secretary Perkins remained in the Cabinet only a few months after Roosevelt's death and the war's end. She had served more than twelve years as secretary of labor during two terribly crucial but very different periods of the nation's labor history, but even though she was sixty-five, President Truman did not allow her to rest long. He appointed her to the Civil Service Commission, where she remained until the Democrats lost the 1952 election. Somehow she also found time to write *The Roosevelt I Knew* (1946), a loving memoir published the year following the president's death, and to begin a biography of her first male mentor, Al Smith. She closed out her "retirement" by returning to her original occupation of teaching; she was working in a Cornell University labor studies program when she died at eighty-five.

Though she was recognized by President Kennedy at a dinner celebrating the Labor Department's fiftieth anniversary in 1963, Perkins was excessively modest and did not receive the honors that she was due. The innovator of unemployment insurance, minimum wages, maximum hours, Social Security, and other programs, Frances Perkins implemented so many vital ideas that working people should thank her everytime they cash a paycheck.

PETERKIN, JULIA (1880–1961)

A Pulitzer Prize winner in 1929, Peterkin was a South Carolina novelist. No less a personage than H.L. Mencken took credit for "bringing her out" when he encouraged Alfred A. Knopf publishing to accept her first novel, *Green Thursday* (1924). It was her third book, *Scarlet Sister Mary* (1929) that won the Pulitzer and brought her commercial success.

A fourth book proved less popular; Mencken felt her insufficiently grateful for the help she received from the publishing establishment, and Peterkin—like many other women AUTHORS—never recovered from a lack of promotion during the Great Depression.

PETERSON'S LADIES' MAGAZINE

The most successful of the emulators of GODEY'S LADY'S BOOK, *Peterson's* was named for its male publisher, an editor with the *Saturday Evening Post*. Seeing *Godey's* success with a female market, he founded the new magazine in Philadelphia in 1842 and hired Ann S. Stephens as its editor. Stephens' background was in fiction writing, and this accounted for much of the magazine's success: in the pre-electronic era, escapist entertainment came from the written page, and the magazine format—shorter and cheaper than books—readily lent itself to fiction. The result was that, while *Godey's* became the most prestigious and influential women's magazine of the nineteenth century, *Peterson's* actually exceeded it in circulation.

Many women's lives were so bleak that a magazine filled with fiction held great appeal, and by concentrating on stories written by women for women, including such AUTHORS as FRANCES BURNETT, it soon developed a reliable customer base. Even though both Godey and Peterson were vain enough to use their own names rather than developing more marketable titles, hundreds of thousands of women were so desperate for something to read that they spent precious money for these magazines. *Peterson's* was profitable almost from the beginning, and the meaning of this success was that male entrepreneurs had overlooked a great untapped market.

Enough others learned this lesson by the end of the century that competition and new styles brought *Peterson's* end. It was still outselling the more famous *Godey's*, however, when both were absorbed into a new publishing enterprise in 1898. For more than a half-century, its pages—mostly written by women—carried its readers out of their drab daily existence and into a world beyond.

PICKFORD, MARY (1893–1979)

Perhaps the most famous of early movie stars, Mary Gladys Smith was on the stage at age five; she took the name of Mary Pickford at thirteen. Under the direction of the famed D.W. Griffith, she acted in her first movie at fifteen, and after 1913, she worked entirely on film.

Called "America's Sweetheart" by the WORLD WAR I era, she was also a competent businesswoman and was one of the four original founders of United Artists Company. Marriage to star Fredrick Douglas in 1920 only increased the aura of glamour about her; she made hit after hit in the twenties and won the Academy Award in 1929.

She and Douglas DIVORCED in 1936, and Pickford remarried the following year. Largely retired after 1932, she had spent more than three decades in acting—and yet had more than forty years of retirement before her death at eighty-six. Mary Pickford's autobiography is *Sunshine and Shadow* (1955).

PILGRIM WOMEN

All Americans are aware in a general way of the hardships endured by the *Mayflower* settlers, but few understand that the women's sacrifices were vastly disproportionate to those of the Pilgrim men.

One birth and one death occurred during their nine-week voyage, so that the ship's register listed 104 passengers upon departure and arrival. Of these, seventy-seven were male; twenty-seven were female. During their terrible first winter, half of the Pilgrims died—but for the women, that horrifying statistic was much worse. Of the eighteen adult women on board, fourteen would die within the first few months of landing in America—for a seventy-eight percent mortality rate. No combat unit sustains a greater rate of death.

In contrast, only six of the thirty-seven children died, for a 16 percent death rate that is especially small in an era when INFANT MORTALITY was routine. The adult male fatalities fell between these extremes at 40 percent. There seems little doubt that women starved themselves so that their children, and even their men, could live.

These women were weakened, too, by a lack of BIRTH CONTROL that meant they were unable to plan the voyage for a time when they would not be pregnant or nursing or both. Like the mother of VIRGINIA DARE in the 1587 expedition that was the first English attempt to colonize the New World, some of these Pilgrims had no choice except to begin their perilous journey in the late stages of pregnancy. This was the case for at least three of the eighteen *Mayflower* women: Elizabeth Hopkins bore a son at sea, whom she named Oceanus, and Susanna White delivered a boy, Peregrine, while the ship lay at anchor in Cape Cod Bay. Mary Norris Allerton's child was born dead in dark December before they landed; she herself would die in February.

These unique physical strains for women were in addition to those suffered by all of the sojourners. They were closely confined during weeks of sailing, for the *Mayflower* was less than one hundred feet long, and it carried more than one hundred passengers plus the crew. Worse, they spent much of the time packed into the dankness below decks while North Atlantic gales blew above. In fact, one young man was swept overboard by a swelling wave when he tried to emerge from the hold.

Cold and often wet from leaking water, they were constantly seasick; with no facilities for washing away their vomit, they exchanged germs and made each other sicker. For the women, there was no release from confinement even after land was sighted. They stayed on board while male scouting parties cautiously explored; finally, on Monday, November 24, 1620, the first Pilgrim women set foot on land—to do the laundry. The first death occurred on December 7, when they were still living on ship. Dorothy May Bradford, the wife of the future governor, went overboard into the icy water and drowned. Some have speculated that her fall was not accidental.

The exploration of Cape Cod continued until they dropped anchor in the harbor they named Plymouth; Mary Chilton was the first woman to set foot on Plymouth Rock. The *Mayflower* arrived there on December 25, but the date was not significant, for the Pilgrims disapproved of England's Christmas celebrations. Indeed, there would be no rejoicing for their arrival in the new land, for by then they were all so sick that construction did not begin until January 27. Their first building was a twenty-foot square communal structure even smaller than the ship, and it was "as full of beds as they could lie one by another." In the bitter cold of that Massachusetts winter, their food supply ran out and death came almost daily in February and March. Funerals were held quickly and furtively under cover of darkness, lest spying natives see the diminishment of their numbers.

The adjustment to these horrifying conditions was a tremendous one, for many of the Pilgrim women were from fairly affluent families and were accustomed to the medical care available in Leiden and London, as well as to comfortable homes with servants. Their wedding vows of obedience had been made in exchange for male vows to provide and protect, but the marital contract seemed to have betrayed them, for they were in severe hardship and danger because of poor planning by the men who led the expedition. Women were not included in decision-making in this patriarchal society, but when they left the safety of Europe in the fall and arrived in a frozen northland in December, they and their children suffered the consequences of this thoughtless adventurism.

Only four adult women and eleven girls remained alive at the end of that terrible winter. They were, of course, greatly outnumbered by males eager for girls such as PRISCILLA ALDEN to reach "marriageable age." Susannah White, with a five-year-old son plus the baby born offshore, was a bride again after eleven weeks as a WIDOW. Fertility dominated their lives, and in the spring, this tiny remnant of females "went willingly into the fields and took their little ones with them to set corn."

PINCKNEY, ELIZABETH (ELIZA) LUCAS (1722–1793)

Perhaps the nation's first important agriculturist, Eliza Lucas ran three South Carolina plantations at sixteen.

Born in the West Indies, she assumed responsibility for her siblings at an early age because her mother died soon after the family moved to the farming area near Charleston. When her father, an officer in the British military, had to return to the Caribbean, Eliza was left in charge. She had the advantages of FINISHING SCHOOL in England, however, and though that education had stressed French, music, and other traditionally feminine subjects, she was particularly interested in botany.

From 1739, she worked annually on improving seeds of the indigo plant, for an appreciation of world markets made her aware that the growing TEXTILE INDUSTRY would reward the cultivation of new dyes—and indigo had the greatest potential for a clear blue. By 1744, she had hybridized an ideal strain and began profitably selling its seeds.

Her achievement made an astonishing difference in the colonial southern economy: in 1745–1746, a mere 5,000 pounds of indigo was exported, but two years later, more than 130,000 pounds sailed out of Charleston. The crop was second only to rice exports, for cotton did not develop its importance until later.

Although it is indigo for which she is remembered, Eliza Lucas experimented with other plants. She wrote, for example, when she was young enough that her mother was still alive, "I have planted a large fig orchard with design to dry and export them." Aware of how the world would perceive such scientific enterprise from a mere girl, she added that she knew some thought that she had "a fertile brain for scheming," but, she explained with traditionally feminine apology and dismissiveness, "I love the vegetable world extremely."

Marriage at twenty-two diminished Pinckney's initiative only slightly, for her husband was an active politician who frequently traveled and who also appreciated his wife's unique abilities. She bore four children in five years, and again demonstrated her scientific bent by going beyond the TEACHING that all mothers did in the colonial era to also study the "tabula rosa" theories of John Locke: more than a century before ELIZABETH PEABODY and other progressive educators, she experimented with very early childhood education. Moreover, as a teenager, she had defied convention by teaching black children.

Eliza Pinckney lived the most cosmopolitan part of her life in England during the 1750s, but after her husband's death in 1758, she took over the operation of their seven plantations and actively ran them until her death. Like other REVOLUTIONARY WAR WOMEN, she managed alone during the war, writing in 1780 that the crops would be small because "stock, boats, carts, etc. [were] taken or destroyed" and because of the "desertion of the Negroes in planting and hoeing time."

Meanwhile, the exceptional educations she had given her sons paid off, as they went on to play major roles in the American Revolution and the establishment of a new government. Doubtless Pinckney herself would have pursued such a career had she not been limited by gender, for her "fertile brain" had demonstrated an early legalistic inclination: as a teenager, she had written wills and served as a trustee for the estate of a friend.

Her contemporaries held Eliza Pinckney in such esteem that George Washington—the nation's president at the time—served as one of her pallbearers.

PINKHAM, LYDIA ESTES (1819–1883)

Lydia Pinkham was the first woman to become a household name through advertising. Her famous photograph, taken in 1879 when she was sixty, was the first to enhance a major project. She became a literal model for multitudes of other women who saw her face in millions of the nation's medicine cabinets during most of the last century. Much more importantly, she was an inventor, innovative businesswoman, and progressive thinker. Except for her premature death, hers was a true rags-to-riches story.

Born into a family of free-thinking QUAKERS, at age sixteen Lydia Estes became a charter member of the Lynn, Massachusetts Female Anti-Slavery Society, along with ABO-LITIONISTS LYDIA MARIA CHILD and ABBY KELLY FOSTER. Following the patterns of so many women, she worked as a TEACHER, married in 1843 and bore five children, losing one to INFANT MORTALITY. She came from an affluent family, but her husband proved to have a talent for losing money, and the Pinkhams teetered on the edge of respectability until their finances collapsed with the Depression of 1873. Like countless other women, Lydia Pinkham then found in this family disaster the permission to use the business acumen she clearly possessed.

Pinkham had for years experimented with herbal mixtures designed to improve health. She was not unusual in this, for women of her era were axiomatically deemed NURSES and many developed their own preferred medications. Lydia Pinkham's vegetable compound, however, proved exceptionally popular among her friends, who credited it with easing the "female complaints" that they were embarrassed to explain to physicians. In the tradition of womanly helpfulness, Pinkham had given her compound to those who requested it, but when the family was reduced to poverty in 1875, she began to sell it.

Turning her home into the factory, Pinkham ran production from her cellar. Her daughter, then a teenage teacher, and her oldest son worked to provide the necessary capital for the purchase of herbs, bottles, and so forth, while her two other sons undertook sales. Her husband, traumatized after his arrest for debt, took to his sickbed and soon was irrelevant to the family and its business.

At first, the Pinkham sons struggled with sales in Boston and New York. A turning point came in 1876 when they discovered that newspaper advertising reached more people faster than the traditional direct-sales methods of traveling patent medicine salesmen. The great transformation came three years later, when Lydia Pinkham posed for a photograph to be used in their advertisements. It proved absolutely priceless, allaying suspicions common to snake-oil salesmen who invented mythical originators along with their elixirs, and it showed Lydia Pinkham to be a veritable picture of mature health. The image made an astonishing difference: less than a year later, the Pinkhams rejected a one hundred thousand dollar offer for their trademark.

Like ROSE KNOX, MADAME C.J. WALKER, and other entrepreneurs, Pinkham found that the key to success was twofold: an innovative product in which the seller passionately believed, and a creative approach to advertising it. In each of these cases, success was based on a trusting relationship between the customer and the seller that developed through personalized sales. Lydia Pinkham's special touch was newspaper advertising that cut to the heart of women's lives, with understanding references to the physical and psychic drain of the limited options for women in a world without BIRTH CONTROL.

She was unusually frank about gynecological problems, even to the point that initial sales were lost because women refused to read sales brochures when they saw words like "uterine." Her grandmotherly photograph softened this candor, however, and Pinkham became adept at writing appealing ad copy. She offered women a challenge to move out of their daily drudgery through good health, and the Department of Advice that she developed demonstrated her personal concern for their individual welfare. Pinkham was soon responding to hundreds of poignant letters.

Exceptionally tall at five-feet-ten-inches and visibly strong, Pinkham believed in more than her medicine: she also prescribed cleanliness, balanced diet, rest, and other basics of modern health. These principles were not necessarily practiced in the nineteenth century; moreover, the era's physicians had a predilection for harsh chemicals and rough surgery under septic conditions, and many sensible people avoided them. Pinkham, in contrast, followed the ancient principle of "First, do no harm."

Her compound was based on five innocuous but relatively rare herbs and roots—which were preserved in a solution of 19 percent alcohol. This made it stronger than wine or beer, but that contradiction with Lydia Pinkham's PROHIBITIONIST beliefs did not bother her or the members of the WOMEN'S CHRISTIAN TEMPERANCE UNION, some of whom appeared in endorsements. Taken in the prescribed quantities, of course, the tonic could not cause drunkenness, and Pinkham never seemed to consider the possibility of abuse. Doubtless there actually were, as physicians charged, women who hid their addiction to alcohol behind this and other medications.

While her belief in the efficacy of her compound was firm, Pinkham never held that it was a cure-all. Indeed, her notebooks were filled with other remedies for other problems, and she applied all of her botanical knowledge when both of her salesmen sons came down with tuberculosis just as their efforts were beginning to pay off. The cause and cure of TB would not be known for many more decades, however, and with great sorrow and anxiety, she watched them weaken. Both died in the fall of 1881.

Pinkham had lost three of her five children, and she did not recover emotionally. Though the business continued to grow, she declined, and almost exactly a year after the death of her sons, she was paralyzed by a stroke. She died the following spring—less than four years after her famously healthy photo. Ironically, Pinkham's ghost-like husband survived her by many years.

Lydia Pinkham's Compound became the source of a number of jokes and songs even in her lifetime, which she seems to have accepted with good humor. In fact, the sophomoric males who promoted them thus added to the product's name recognition, and its sales increased each decade, reaching a peak of $3 million in 1925. Unfortunately, Pinkham's surviving son and daughter eventually quarreled, with negative effects on the business.

Finally, it is important to note that Pinkham lived her entire life in the industrial town of Lynn, which, with its shoe factories and TEXTILE MILLS, would not seem a likely candidate as a center of new ideologies. Nevertheless, Lynn was a cradle for abolitionism and other ideas—including those of MARY BAKER EDDY, who lived there during the 1870s when she developed her mental healing philosophy. Though there is no evidence that Pinkham and Baker ever met, there probably was an unconscious intellectual exchange between their ideas: at the same place and time, these two women both promulgated philosophies of health that were scorned by organized medicine, but which were adopted by millions of others—especially women—whose thinking was more holistic.

PINS AND NEEDLES A stage production of the INTERNATIONAL LADIES' GARMENT WORKERS' UNION, this musical comedy became sensationally successful during the Great Depression, especially in New York. One of its tunes that became popular in the late thirties was, "Sing Me A Song of Social Significance."

PITCHER, MOLLY— See MOLLY PITCHER

PLANNED PARENTHOOD Planned Parenthood began in 1921, having evolved from the earlier Voluntary Parenthood League and the more candidly named National Birth Control League. In addition to MARGARET SANGER, the organization owes a great historical debt to MARY WARE DENNETT, whose vital and more FEMINIST work has been far less publicized than Sanger's. MARY STEICHEN CALDERONE replaced Sanger as perhaps the most visible spokeswoman for Planned Parenthood during the second half of the twentieth century.

Today Planned Parenthood has some 750 operations throughout the U.S., where contraceptive information and materials are provided. Some also perform abortions and sterilizations, but—at the end of the twentieth century, as well as at its beginning—Planned Parenthood has had to go to court repeatedly to fight for the right to enable women to understand and control their bodies. The organization maintains the Katherine Dexter McCormick Library in New York of materials related to BIRTH CONTROL.

PLATH, SYLVIA (1932–1963) Perhaps the foremost poet of the modern women's movement, Sylvia Plath's life and work remains controversial, even as her literary fame seems secure.

The facts of her short life revolve around her father's death when she was eight; though he was absent most of her life, he was ever present in her poetry. She published her first poem soon after this trauma and was intent on a literary career throughout her school years. Plath suffered her first serious bout with depression while a student at SMITH COLLEGE, when she underwent electric shock treatment after a suicide attempt.

After graduating with highest honors in 1955, she went to England on a Fulbright Fellowship, where she met and married Ted Hughes, a poet whose reputation eclipsed hers—in part because she typed, edited, and promoted his work. Plath did retain her MAIDEN NAME, and after she received her Cambridge degree, they lived briefly in the U.S. while she taught at Smith. Her first book, *The Colossus*, was published in 1960, the same year that they returned to England and their first child was born.

Ensconced in a Devonshire manorhouse, Plath worked on *The Bell Jar*, which would be published under a PSEUDONYM in England after her death; an autobiographical novel, it was based on her earlier mental collapse. At the same time, she

nursed her daughter and bore a son after recovering from a miscarriage. Plath's dreams of mothering both many children and many words broke down, however, when she discovered her husband's affair with a married woman in the summer of 1962. He moved out and she filed for DIVORCE.

The separation liberated her as a poet, and she composed almost all of her literary treasures during the last year of her life. Although incredibly productive, neither a sense of achievement nor the presence of her little children kept Plath from depression. She moved from Devon to London in December of an extremely cold winter, and early in February, she turned on the gas and put her head in the oven.

Ariel, a collection of her last, best poems came out two years later. Three publications in 1971—*Winter Trees* and *Crossing the Water*, as well as the American edition of *The Bell Jar*—coincided with the rebirth of the FEMINIST movement, and Plath soon became a cult figure. Much has been written about her and her work since then, and Ted Hughes, who was accused of refusing to publish things that reflected negatively on him, remains a controversial literary heir.

POCAHONTAS (1595?–1617) A romantic haze usually surrounds the story of the intervention of Pocahontas in saving the life of Captain John Smith, but the tale was never doubted in his lifetime, even though he had many enemies who cast aspersions on his truthfulness in other areas. Moreover, Pocahontas' well-documented life should be credited for more than the Smith incident, for her marriage to an Englishman established her as a genuine mediator between the natives and the newcomers in early VIRGINIA and in London.

"Pocahontas" was actually a nickname, but its meaning was very similar to that of her real name, Matoaka. Both meant playful, and she lived up to that reputation with activities that today would be described as those of a tomboy. The daughter of the chief of the Powhatan confederacy in coastal Virginia, she was naturally privileged within her society, and, by logical analogy, the English deemed her a princess.

She saw her first Englishman when she was about twelve. John Smith was twenty-seven and a leader of the new JAMESTOWN colony when he was taken prisoner by Powhatan warriors in the last days of 1607. According to Smith's histories of Virginia, Pocahontas protested "at the minute of my execution," and the chief granted his daughter's request. A few days later, Smith was "safely conducted to Jamestowne" under the protection of twelve warriors. From that time on, she served as a communicator between Powhatan and the settlers.

In May of 1608, Pocahontas went to Jamestown as her father's representative on behalf of some natives taken prisoner, and—though she was merely "a little girl of a dozen winters"—these warriors were released to her in recognition of what she had done for Smith earlier. Relations between the men worsened, however, and in January of 1609—only months before most of the JAMESTOWN WOMEN arrived—Pocahontas again tried to prevent war by warning Smith of a planned attack. "In that darke night," we are told, she came "through irksome woods, and told our Captaine . . . if we would live, shee wished us presently to be gone."

Smith departed for England in 1609, and Pocahontas would not see him again until she was in London almost a decade later. Contrary to myth, their relationship was similar to that of an uncle and a niece, and he never regarded her as anything other than an extraordinary child. Her relationship with John Rolfe, on the other hand, was much more than that. Pocahontas met Rolfe in 1613, after she had spent several months with the colonists under circumstances that her father and the Englishman viewed as hostage-taking, but that she herself may well have seen as an interesting opportunity.

Clearly a curious, open personality who was eager to learn, she appears to have willingly explored the alternative lifestyle and, indeed, she adopted so much of it that she learned English and the Christian faith, was baptized, and took the name of Rebecca (or Rebekah). Rolfe, who seems to have fallen in love with her immediately, overcame the racism that initially caused him to reject her as one "whose education hath been rude, her manners barbarous." He poured out his heart in a tortured letter to the colony's governor, ending with a request to marry. Both the governor and Powhatan sanctioned the marriage, and they wed in April of 1614. Powhatan granted them land, which they named Varina. The birth of a child served to strengthen the ties between the natives and the newcomers; the anglicization of Pocahontas—or Rebecca Rolfe—was so complete that her son was named Thomas. Through him, thousands of Americans have claimed descent from Pocahontas.

Two years after their wedding, they went to England for a visit of nearly a year. Pocahontas not only met her husband's family in Norfolk, but also became a celebrity visitor in London. In fact, the Virginia Company seems to have viewed this as a public relations trip with corporate sponsorship, for Pocahontas received four pounds weekly for her expenses. The family lodged near Kew Gardens, and Pocahontas went to balls and had her portrait painted. She wore English clothing, although a male emissary of her father's who traveled with her dressed in native garb.

The high point of the trip came when she was presented to King James I and the court. The presentation may well have occurred without his intervention, but John Smith urged the meeting by writing to Queen ANNE of his trials in the New World and of the "relief . . . brought us by this Lady Pocahontas." The queen in fact was so pleased with Pocahontas that she invited the Rolfes to share the royal box at the theatre.

They were prepared to return to America when Pocahontas became ill, perhaps as a result of the "bad air" of London's coal-warmed winter. She was taken off the ship, which was already headed down the Thames, and died soon after. Pocahontas was buried on March 21, 1617 at St. George's Church in the parish of Gravesend.

Probably she was no more than twenty-two, and the course of relations between American natives and newcomers may well have been different had this remarkable peacemaker lived a longer life. When Powhatan—the grandfather of Thomas Rolfe—died also the following year, all hope for peaceful coexistence was gone.

PORTER, KATHERINE ANNE (1890–1980) Best known as the AUTHOR of *Ship of Fools* (1962), Porter was seventy-two years old when that bestselling novel was published.

A descendent of Daniel Boone and a distant relative of short story writer O. Henry, Porter was born in Texas and worked as a reporter in Denver prior to marriage. She published her first story in 1923 and seven years later issued her first collection of stories, *Flowering Judas* (1930). Though hailed by critics, the book did not become widely known, and the *New Republic* includes it on a list of "Good Books That Almost Nobody Has Read." *Pale Horse, Pale Rider* (1936), a collection of three novellas, brought more critical recognition, but nonetheless, the profoundly negative effects of the Great Depression on talented young women meant that Porter had to make a living by TEACHING and writing shorter works.

Thus, *Ship of Fools*, her only full-length novel, waited over two decades for publication. Porter began it as a result of a trip to Nazi Germany in the thirties and copyrighted it in 1945, but it was more than twenty years from the idea to the completed manuscript. She summed up this time by saying, "Most people don't realize that writing is a craft. You have to take your apprenticeship in it like anything else."

Though recognition may have come late, Porter lived to see honors heaped upon her. Her expertise with the short story form ultimately brought awards and membership in the National Institute of Arts and Sciences, and in 1965, after *Ship of Fools*, she was selected to the even more prestigious American Academy of Arts and Letters. The following year, her collected stories won both the Pulitzer Prize and the National Book Award. *Saturday Review* summarized her career by placing her "in the illustrious company headed by Hawthorne, Flaubert, and Henry James."

Twice divorced, Porter published her last book—a nonfiction work on the Sacco-Vanzetti case of the twenties—three years before her death at ninety.

PORTER, SYLVIA (1914–1991) A famous woman in the non-traditional area of finance, Sylvia Porter's syndicated columns on money matters were followed by 40 million newspaper readers at the height of her popularity.

She began writing in the depths of the Depression, when the *New York Post* hired her to do an occasional column on personal finances. With her gender disguised under the PSEUDONYM of S.F. Porter, she soon proved so popular that she was assigned a regular column. When her reputation seemed established after the publication of her second book, she began using her first name. For more than a half-century thereafter, her column was titled simply "Sylvia Porter."

Though she continued to live on the East Coast, the *Los Angeles Times* syndicated her three-days-weekly column for the business pages of as many as 450 newspapers. She was translated throughout the world, as there was international approbation of her clear writing style and her sensible, up-to-date advice on taxes and investments for the middle class.

Eventually the AUTHOR of more than thirty books, her most famous was *Sylvia Porter's Money Book* (1975), which sold more than a million copies. Porter kept her MAIDEN NAME after becoming a wife and mother, and she continued to write until her death at seventy-seven.

POST, EMILY PRICE (1872–1960) More than any other person, Emily Post defined the standards of social correctness

for much of the twentieth century. Though today her name conjures up visions of Victorian stuffiness, in fact Emily Post was something of a public relations magician, for she managed to sensitively address the changing roles of women while still maintaining an image of absolute propriety.

Nowhere was this more clear than in her personal life: she was DIVORCED in 1905, when that still meant ostracism for most women, and she earned a living as a single mother when that, too, was not considered socially acceptable. Her ability to overcome these social taboos and go on to become *the* foremost authority on proper behavior speaks volumes about Post's personal power, as well as about the depth of change in acceptable standards for female behavior during the early twentieth century.

Born to wealth, educated by GOVERNESSES and in FINISHING SCHOOLS, Emily Price debuted in New York society and married in 1892. Like others of her class in this era of immense fortunes, she traveled in Europe and enjoyed fashionable vacation homes while mothering two sons. Her husband, meanwhile, involved himself with other women, and it was her embarrassment and resentment of his affairs that caused their divorce. Most women of her status simply pretended not to notice their husband's foibles, but Post presumably preferred her self-respect to comfortable affluence.

Accepting the fact that divorce would mean financial loss, she began her independent life at age thirty-three by emulating other genteel women who supported themselves as AUTHORS and published widely for almost two decades before the famous book on manners. Her early writing included both magazine stories and novels set in upper class society, as well as works on travel and home decoration. It was her *Etiquette* (1922), however, that became the nonfiction bestseller of an era when millions of American women were changing their standards of behavior during the Roaring Twenties.

With varying titles and revisions, Emily Post updated the book to address changes wrought by the Great Depression and WORLD WAR II, when homes became servantless, formality declined, and the definitions of acceptable behavior for ladies and gentlemen became less rigid. Post managed to weave a fine line maintaining her high status among privileged conservatives, while also allowing for enough change to accommodate the realities of life amid her mass audience. In addition to her books, she also influenced opinion through a daily column that was published by about two hundred newspapers after its 1932 beginning, and she spoke regularly on radio after 1931.

When Emily Post died at eighty-eight, her name was synonymous with politeness. Her famous book lives on: by 1980, *Etiquette* had gone through more than a hundred printings.

PRINCE, LUCY TERRY (c. 1730–after 1797) Kidnapped in Africa and sold into slavery as a child, Lucy Terry grew up in Deerfield, Massachusetts.

In 1704, Deerfield had been the site of a famous attack by natives against the FRONTIER WOMEN and men who had settled there. Most of the town's inhabitants were killed or captured, and Lucy Terry, pondering this sad history in 1746, wrote a twenty-eight-line poem commemorating the tragedy. She thus is said by some to have been the first black poet in America,

for this work predated that of PHILLIS WHEATLEY, whose first poem was published in 1767.

Lucy Terry probably was sixteen when she wrote her poem; how she had become literate is not known. Presumably her freedom was purchased by her husband, a free black man named Abijah Prince, whom she married in 1756. She moved with him to Sunderland, Vermont, where they farmed and became quite affluent. Their color remained a barrier, however, and Lucy Prince was not successful in getting her son admitted to college, even though she personally presented his case in a long meeting with the trustees of newly founded Williams College in Massachusetts.

Though they were not persuaded, the trustees acknowledged that her powers of argumentation were excellent, and this was again true when Lucy Prince appeared before the Supreme Court in 1797. It was the culmination of a long lawsuit between Prince and a neighbor over property boundaries, and Prince had appealed the case to the nation's highest court. In those days, plaintiffs could personally appear before the court, and Lucy Prince successfully argued her case. Justice Samuel Chase is said to have commented that she did a better job than any Vermont lawyer could have.

PRINTERS— *See* PUBLISHERS AND PRINTERS

PROHIBITION From the beginning of American history, alcohol was an important factor in daily life and in the economy; as every student learns, rum was one of three crucial items of colonial trade. Ale was a standard part of diet, including that of children, and records indicate staggering liquor consumption. In 1784, for example, twenty-four Connecticut pastors gathering for an ordination drank "3 bitters, 15 boles [bowls] punch, 11 bottles wine, 5 mugs flip, 3 boles toddy, 3 boles smash." In 1829, the nineteen hundred residents of Dudley, Massachusetts consumed ten thousand gallons of rum alone, while in the Southern colonies, it was customary to down mint-flavored whiskey upon awakening.

Crying babies were regularly hushed with sweetened liquor, and alcohol in its various forms was the most common of medicines administered to the sick and injured. Throughout the nineteenth century, the inclusion of liquor in military rations makes it clear that it was considered a vital part of life. The result was that large numbers of Americans, women as well as men, were addicted. As the nation's manners became more refined, women hid their alcohol consumption in such ladylike forms as "elixirs," "tonics," and patent medicines such as LYDIA PINKHAM's compound.

Alcoholism among men, however, was a far more serious problem to the functioning of families simply because legal codes gave almost no recognition to MARRIED WOMEN'S PROPERTY RIGHTS. In virtually all states during the nineteenth century, men controlled not only the "communal" family property, but also the inheritance and even the wages of their wives. Thus, a woman had no legal recourse if a drunken husband beat her, took her earned income, and gambled it away. DIVORCE was almost impossible and, moreover, males were favored in GUARDIANSHIP of children.

Therefore, it was not surprising that from the first SENECA FALLS convention in 1848, the issue of alcohol was inextricably tied to women's rights. Thousands of women were active on both fronts, and indeed, most in that era considered women's rights and temperance/prohibition to be one and the same. Some of the best-known early suffragists came to that issue only after initial activity in the temperance cause, including SUSAN ANTHONY, AMELIA BLOOMER, and others.

These women were almost invariably joined—and usually officially led—by men, for many businessmen and ministers saw economic and societal peril in excessive drinking. The saloon remained central to frontier towns as the line of settlement moved west, and it was understandable that male community leaders reached out to FRONTIER WOMEN for help in dealing with towns that featured several saloons for every church or school.

For almost all of these women, the temperance club was their first organizational experience. Many such church-based societies predated the formation of the WOMAN'S CHRISTIAN TEMPERANCE UNION (WCTU) in 1874. The WCTU retained its Protestant roots and simply added political activity to its religious assumptions. Members demonstrated in front of saloons and the more radical destroyed saloon property. Throughout the nation, WCTU women worked in local elections to turn communities from "wet" to "dry"—without regard to whether or not they personally could vote. The movement grew quickly in the latter half of the nineteenth century, as women developed organizational skills and increasingly asserted themselves in local debates over the use of alcohol.

Although "temperance" was part of the WCTU's name, as the movement strengthened, it became clear that the actual aim of most members was legal bans on alcohol, not merely its temperate use. One factor in this evolution doubtless was the arrival of millions of immigrants during the late nineteenth century whose use of alcohol was in fact moderate and temperate, though daily. Most of these immigrants were from southern and eastern Europe and were either Catholic or Jewish. As the men of these ethnic groups became citizens and were allowed to vote, native women—who were almost always better educated and who were certainly more knowledgeable of the history and governance of their nation—found these men casting ballots in elections when they could not. The lines between the conflicting cultures hardened, and "temperance" increasingly meant "prohibition."

In places such as Tampa, Florida, for example, where Italian and Spanish immigrants flocked to cigar factories, the native women of the WCTU were extremely active in an 1887 election, even though none proclaimed herself a suffragist. On the day of the election: "The women went to work early, pinning 'dry' badges on the coats of the prohibition voters. . . . Prepared to brave any amount of indignity. . . . , the ladies served cool drinks and a bountiful free dinner." They lost the election by a mere twenty-five votes—with ballots from the immigrant wards overwhelmingly opposed to Prohibition, while men from the other areas split their vote.

With the creation of the Prohibition Party in 1882, male voters systematized their antiliquor efforts. As the party gained influence in future elections, the liquor industry became increasingly fearful that female enfranchisement would swell its numbers, and that interest—along with tobacco, racing, and other male-oriented industries—spent more and more money to defeat the SUFFRAGE MOVEMENT. These interests financed much of the opposition to the NINETEENTH AMENDMENT, and some lobbyists who ostensibly were devoted to preserving women's traditional place instead were merely fronts for the alcohol industry.

At the same time, there were women who recognized the damaging political effect of the link between suffrage and prohibition. This was especially true in the Far West, where libertarian attitudes had long allowed for both the free flow of alcohol and votes for women. As the century turned, increasing numbers of suffragists joined WESTERN WOMEN such as ABIGAIL SCOTT DUNIWAY in trying to divest feminists' interests from those of prohibitionists. CARRIE CHAPMAN CATT, ALICE PAUL, and other major leaders of the suffrage movement in the WORLD WAR I era had few or no ties to prohibitionists.

Thus the liquor industry that so feared women's vote found itself defeated by men, for it was not women who were responsible for Prohibition: the constitutional amendment intended to ban the sale of alcohol throughout the nation was passed before the amendment that gave women the right to vote nationally. It is a fact still obscured by those who would blame women for the "Great Experiment," but the Eighteenth Amendment on prohibition went into effect in January of 1920, while the Nineteenth Amendment on women's vote did not come until August of that year—and yet the liquor industry lobbied hard to prevent its final passage.

In fact, the two movements that once were inextricably linked had drifted so far apart that when the Prohibitionist Party nominated MARIE C. BREHM for vice-president of the U.S. in 1924, few FEMINISTS took notice. Though this was the first presidential election in which women had the opportunity to campaign as a bloc, Brehm's candidacy did not become a rallying point—as it might well have been two decades earlier when the temperance movement and the suffrage movement worked hand in hand. Instead, the issue of prohibition was so passé that the Party did not garner even 1 percent of the vote.

During the era that Prohibition was the law of the land, women joined men in disobeying it. From elderly IMMIGRANT WOMEN who made wine in their bathtubs to the FLAPPERS of the speakeasies, women flaunted the law. Neither did the women of the Roosevelt administration oppose the amendment that overturned Prohibition in 1933. Though ELEANOR ROOSEVELT, FRANCES PERKINS, and other New Deal women were in many ways strait-laced, they understood the mistake that had been made when temperance became Prohibition. They understood that instead of laws banning the sale of alcohol, women needed laws to enable them to more easily divorce alcoholic husbands and laws that assured them of equal property rights. Instead of forcing behavioral changes in men, women needed opportunities to live their own independent lives.

PROPERTY RIGHTS— *See* MARRIED WOMEN'S PROPERTY RIGHTS

PROSTITUTION In the theocracies of early New England settlements, a woman who engaged in selling sex risked severe punishment and even death. In the less religious Southern colonies, however, prostitution doubtless was present from the beginning, for many of the original settlers had spent time in English jails, and prostitution would have been the most likely female offense. Like Boston, Philadelphia originally was settled by the pious, but streetwalkers had become so common by Ben Franklin's day that he joked about their disproportionate use of shoeleather.

There are numerous accounts of prostitution during the American Revolution with little mention of governmental action to close down such activity. Instead, both British and American troops were grateful for their comforts, and there were even claims from prostitutes for monetary damages suffered during the war that openly stated their business; British officers testified to the truthfulness of at least one claim.

As the new nation grew, prostitution grew with it. The minimal estimate in New York in the early nineteenth century was twelve hundred prostitutes, and there easily could have been five times that number. A more scientific survey immediately prior to the CIVIL WAR estimated there was one prostitute for every sixty-four adult males in the city; it added that women lived only an average of four years after they began to support themselves by selling their bodies. The occupation indeed was hazardous, for in a time prior to effective BIRTH CONTROL and sanitary ABORTIONS, pregnant women died; others were in fact brutalized by pimps and madams who starved and beat them.

Yet the era's economy offered few other employment opportunities to women, and none so remunerative. Thousands of women saw no alternative because, as one student of the subject later said, "It is a known fact that men's wages cannot fall below a limit upon which they can exist, but women's wages have no limit, since the paths of shame are always open to her." Moreover, the standards of the time were such that women were easily "compromised," and sexual behavior that today would be considered quite innocent was then enough to brand a woman as fallen—whereupon she had little choice except to turn to prostitution.

When married, middle class women began to form the first timorous church-based societies to foster the welfare of women in the pre–Civil War era, reform of "the social evil" was among the agenda items that slowly took root. Under the guise of "social purity" and similar terms, respectable women began to acknowledge the existence of "fallen women," whom they almost invariably saw as an object of pity in need of assistance from the more virtuous. These attitudes are clear in the euphemism of WHITE SLAVERY, a term for prostitution that came increasingly into use after the Civil War.

In this view, prostitutes were the unhappy victims of vile male sexuality: only rarely in the massive literature that would develop on "moral reform" is there any suggestion that women might deliberately choose the illicit life. Equally rare is any indication that reformers viewed prostitutes as personal threats: although venereal disease was frequently cited as a nonmoral reason for control of prostitution, there is little indication that women reformers feared contagion via the men in their own lives. The issue was abstract, not personal, and therefore capable of increasing attention at feminist gatherings.

Nonetheless, discussions remained furtively coded even as reformers actually set about creating alternatives for prostitutes. In city after city during the late decades of the nineteenth century, missions with names such as Door of Hope were built to rehabilitate women who wished to leave "the life." The FLORENCE CRITTENDEN HOMES, for example, built over fifty institutions between 1883 and 1897; they featured signs offering "A Helping Hand" to any woman who would "Come Just as She Is." These refuges did in fact provide food and shelter along with protection from pimps and violent exploiters, but a great deal of religiosity and discipline was expected in return—and many of these experienced, sophisticated women were not satisfied to remain long in their staid environment.

The role of IMMIGRANT WOMEN in prostitution was the subject of much scrutiny throughout the era. Nativists assumed that immigrants were disproportionately numerous in the business, but careful studies showed that was true only for French women (and even in this case, the percentages represented few women because immigration from France was always low). Reformist women nevertheless did a great deal to prevent newly arrived women from accidentally falling into the hands of pimps. They set up programs for chaperons to meet ships and trains so that women would never be alone—and in doing so, they seriously infringed on the freedom of movement of intelligent adult women. Though their intentions were good, feminist fear of white slavery was disproportionate to its danger, and the effect of the PROTECTIVE LEGISLATION they sponsored was to make women more dependent on men, for these laws meant obstacles to enterprising women who were capable of TRAVEL without an escort.

Rather than immigrants, the chief source of recruits into prostitution seems to have been native women from rural areas who chose to come to city brothels where they could earn big money without hard work. The wages of sin were undoubtedly more attractive than that of other occupations open to women: A 1906 study, for example, showed that while the average factory girl earned five dollars weekly, streetwalkers could expect five times that much, while those in a well-run brothel might make as much as four hundred dollars—though the house kept a large portion of the women's earnings.

The outbreak of WORLD WAR I brought renewed attention to the issue, for the mobilization of men in war always brings women seeking to turn a profit on their presence. Venereal disease soared, especially in Europe, and Congress responded with the CHAMBERLAIN-KAHN ACT. Once again, the good intentions of the social purists had the effect of seriously violating civil liberties, and women—unlike men—were subject to arrests based on their appearance.

The history of prostitution continued in much the same manner through most of the twentieth century: the issue would be ignored until the exigencies of war or politics brought it briefly to the forefront. After the liberating social changes of the 1920s, however, fewer middle-class women were drawn to rehabilitation efforts, and indeed, mission doors largely closed after the Great Depression struck—when prostitutes probably were better off financially than most American women. WORLD WAR II brought a more mature attitude on the part of the military than had been the case a generation earlier, although the first women in nontraditional wartime jobs (such as taxi drivers) were often accused of using those jobs as fronts for illicit sex.

With the development of BIRTH CONTROL in the sixties, prostitution became less financially rewarding, as professionals encountered competition from amateurs no longer fearful of pregnancy. FEMINISTS in the seventies brought some visibility to decriminalization of prostitution, but as increasing numbers of prostitutes were in the business because of their addiction to drugs, interest in the issue again has seemed to fade. Though progress has been made in arresting men as well as women on solicitation charges, prostitution continues to account for an overwhelming number of arrests of women.

PROTECTIVE LEGISLATION

As nineteenth-century women began to assert themselves in the new field of social work and in newly refined organizational philanthropy, a class of reformist women grew whose lifelong interest was the welfare of lower-class people. JANE ADDAMS was probably the most visible of these, but thousands of women joined such leaders as GRACE and EDITH ABBOTT, SOPHONISBA BRECKINRIDGE, MARY VAN KLEECK, LILLIAN WALD, and others to work for laws protecting people—especially women—from exploitation.

Such laws generally fell into two main categories: those aimed at preventing the sexual exploitation of women and those that improved working conditions for women. Both types of legislation were grounded in the belief that women were a special case inherently different from men, and it was this view of women as essentially helpless and needy that ultimately called this body of law into question. It took many decades for these objections to arise, however, and for most of the relevant years, FEMINISTS unquestioningly supported the passage of laws designed to protect women from those who would mistreat them.

Laws protecting women from sexual exploitation were, of course, easier to pass than those that attempted to improve working conditions. Particularly as women began to TRAVEL without escorts in the latter half of the nineteenth century, reformers found it relatively easy to create rules aimed at protecting women from the era's perceived peril of WHITE SLAVERY. Usually, however, it was women rather than men who bore the onus of this protection, for these regulations created their safety net by inhibiting the free movement of women.

After 1904, for example, young IMMIGRANT WOMEN were not free to leave Ellis Island unaccompanied. One protectionist wrote proudly of her achievements in placing restraints on these arrivals: "Unprotected women and children are detained until their friends or family are telegraphed for. On no occasion is a woman or child allowed to enter New York alone . . . If she cannot guarantee the observance of all the proprieties, she is married at Ellis Island. There is hardly a day without a wedding." One ironic result was that there were cases of women who unwillingly and/or unknowingly went through a marriage ceremony simply so that they could move on with their intention of immigration.

Thus the protectionists' mindset not only did the disservice of equating women with children, but also reflected a thoughtless superiority that was actually more naive and less aware of the world's true dangers than was the case for the women who were the objects of protection. Nonetheless, well-intentioned people continued to work for such social protectionist goals through laws like the MANN ACT and the CHAMBERLAIN-KAHN ACT, as well as adjustments to immigration law. Despite the previous immigration of millions of young single women (especially the Irish), single women in the pre–World War I era of massive influx had to prove to investigators that their intended abodes were morally and physically safe. Women found themselves at risk of deportation over such things as the presence of beer bottles in their lodgings—problems that were never faced by male immigrants.

While immigrant women may have suffered from the good intentions of reformists in this area of law, almost all of them were grateful for protectionist intervention in labor law. From the earliest days of American industry—while most workers were still natives—there were attempts by both women workers and their more politically powerful nonworking sisters to pass state laws aimed at improving working conditions for women. Since the notion of EQUAL PAY remained radical for many decades, these efforts primarily focused on maximum hours of work and easier conditions at work.

To obtain passage of such laws, reformers assembled massive documentation of the exploitation of women in the work force, with the result that we have detailed information on women in dozens of industries and thousands of locations in this era. When the courts threw out such laws as unfair burdens upon employers in cases such as *Lochner vs. the United States* (1905), feminists simply kept at the cause, lobbying for new laws that corrected technical problems and amassing data for more persuasive court argumentation.

FLORENCE KELLY's hard work in preparing a brief for argumentation by future Supreme Court Justice Louis Brandeis brought an important victory in *MULLER VS. OREGON* in 1908. Reverses remained after that, such as *ADKINS VS. CHILDREN'S HOSPITAL* (1923) on minimum wages, but the Progressive Era brought a strong upswing in the passage and enforcement of laws on hours and conditions. During the two decades between 1900 and 1920, almost all states limited the hours women could work to between eight and ten daily, with the limitation of six days a week.

Often, of course, the rhetoric used to achieve these laws stressed the second job that women held at home. Many states forbade night work for women—though of course there were always sufficient exemptions to allow for those jobs that were naturally "women's work," such as nurses and telephone operators who worked at night. Moreover, while most industrial women indeed were relieved to have legal protection from managers who would work them to exhaustion in busy seasons, other women might want the extra hours of pay; laws, however, assumed that the lives of all women were the same and inherently different from those of men.

Therefore, the effect of protectionist labor law could be ironically negative. The women whom ELIZABETH BEARDSLEY BUTLER discovered working in Pittsburgh's steel mills, for example, would be "protected" out of those jobs in the future, as many states passed laws limiting the number of pounds women could lift and other restrictions that arbitrarily applied to a woman, regardless of her individual size and strength. Women who routinely held a thirty-pound child in one arm and ten pounds of groceries in the other found themselves forbidden to lift forty pounds at work—and management had a legally justifiable excuse for not hiring them.

Management found similar excuses in laws that required them to provide seating for women; other states completely forbade the employment of women in certain places, such as mines or poolrooms. Male-dominated labor unions that lobbied for the passage of such laws portrayed themselves as working for the best interests of women, when in fact their action served to eliminate competition for their members. Some feminists, of course, saw this male duplicity for what it was; moreover, they pointed out that exemptions to these laws in the emergency of WORLD WAR I demonstrated that their proponents did not truly have women's interests at heart.

The EQUAL RIGHTS AMENDMENT (ERA) that was introduced by ALICE PAUL and other leaders of the WOMAN'S PARTY in the 1920s necessarily attacked the concept of protective legislation, for the ERA would nullify such laws by demanding that men and women be treated equally in all aspects of state and federal law. The more liberated women who supported ERA disdained what they saw as the maternal basis for these laws, which gave women special protection because of their roles as reproducers of the race. Women like Paul whose lives were not family-based and who had spent little or no time among working-class women did not understand that some women did in fact care a great deal whether or not the law insisted that they be able to sit at work or that their week be limited to sixty hours.

The result was a great split over the issue of protective legislation—a split that may be more important in the history of post suffrage feminism than has been recognized. Roosevelt's New Deal would dominate the 1930s and 1940s and the women associated with it—FRANCES PERKINS, MOLLY DEWSON, and MARY ANDERSON, to name only a few—viewed these labor laws as their crowning lifetime achievements. They were not about to allow the ERA to nullify the state laws for which they had worked so hard, and because they held the positions of power, Paul and her supporters quickly became an almost invisible minority.

When the ERA was revived in the 1970s, the protectionist issue was not nearly so great a factor. Union activism and enlightened managerial changes during WORLD WAR II served to defend workers—men and women—from abuses of the past industrial system, and there was far less need for special legislation to protect women. ERA supporters argued that state laws could simply extend any valid protections to men, thereby meeting the requirements of the ERA.

It was, of course, an argument that could have been made all along—but recognizing the validity of the argument does not mean that reformers were wrong to have settled for the half-loaf that was obtainable for women, but not for men, decades earlier. Millions of working women greatly appreciated the fact that they were legally assured of Sundays off, for example, and they viewed the practical effect of protection to be much more important in their daily lives than a vague principle of equality.

PSEUDONYMS The history of women AUTHORS is replete with those who felt compelled to hide their identity under a pseudonym, often one implying that they were male.

Many did this to find an initial publisher, but pseudonyms were sometimes used by women writers after they were well known. PEARL BUCK found a male pseudonym helpful even after she won the Nobel Prize; this disguise was the only way she could see her work reviewed on its own merits, without the filter of prejudice from literary and political critics. JANET TAYLOR CALDWELL was known as Taylor Caldwell all of her life; many believed she was a man. Even famed HARRIET BEECHER STOWE wrote under the name of Christopher Crowfield.

A pseudonym could disguise work that was incongruous with an author's public persona, as, for example, in the case of LOUISA MAY ALCOTT, who has only recently been credited with many of the bloodthirsty tales she wrote for boys and signed with initials. A similar but less well known case of assuming a male persona because of an intended male audience is that of Bertha M. Bower (1871–1940), who authored fifty-seven westerns and saw many of them made into movies. Gene Stratton-Porter (1863–1924) also developed a 1922 film company because she was unhappy with the treatment given her prescient ecologically-oriented novels—but neither her seemingly male name nor sales of more than a million copies of her first novel was enough to impress critics. Though her turn-of-the-century readership was comparable to that of Charles Dickens, she is almost totally forgotten.

Some of the earliest women writers, however, seem to have been too timorous even to borrow a male identity; they allowed their femininity to show while remaining ANONYMOUS. HANNAH WEBSTER FOSTER was one such; a very popular writer at the end of the eighteenth century, she signed herself "A Lady of Massachusetts," and her name was not known until long after her death. Others who later became famous, including ELLEN GLASGOW and JULIA WARD HOWE, published their first work anonymously. Many women probably promoted the careers of men because they sought no acknowledgement of their work: LUCY LARCOM, for example, edited the poetry of John Greenleaf Whittier and MARY ABIGAIL DODGE ghosted the political writings of presidential nominee James G. Blaine. Doubtless there were others who remain anonymous.

Other women used female pseudonyms that acknowledged their gender while hiding their true identity. In some cases, as in GERTRUDE ATHERTON and HELEN HUNT JACKSON, they did this because working as a writer interfered with the social position they held. Some used pseudonyms to disguise what they knew would be seen as excessive productivity; songwriter FANNY CROSBY, for example, was so prolific that she hid her work under at last one hundred different names. The use of so many varied names ironically allowed for greater retention of one's true self, but the continued use of just one false name could completely overwhelm an identity: JENNIE JUNE is a nineteenth-century example of this phenomenon, while ABIGAIL VAN BUREN and ANN LANDERS are modern ones.

A number of journalists, including IDA HARPER HUSTED and FLORENCE FINCH KELLY, began their careers under pseudonyms. Others who initially published under male identities because their subjects were unconventional for women include SYLVIA PORTER, ELSIE CLEWS PARSONS, and political commentator Emily Edson Briggs, who wrote under the signature of "OLIVIA" and who never publicly asserted her personal identity in this nontraditional field.

A number of women found deception to be the wiser course: Mary L. Booth, for instance, published an 1869 watchmaking manual under her own name, but when she issued a book on marble work in 1876, she obscured herself with "M.L. Booth." Much later, Ruth Baldwin Cowan was a successful political writer covering the Texas legislature in the late 1920s—until an Associated Press official went to her office to praise her work, discovered that R. Baldwin Cowan was female, and fired her.

Sometimes a woman used a pseudonym for the same valid reasons that a male author would, as, for example, MERCY OTIS WARREN's political work prior to the Revolution. Male writers, too, occasionally used female pseudonyms, especially for formula-written books aimed at girls or for potboiler romances that they believed would sell better under a woman's name. Those who subscribed to this mindset believed that women wrote the trivial and the sentimental, while serious literature was done by men. It doubtless was this tradition that a 1951 reviewer had in mind when he wrote of RACHEL CARSON's work on marine science: "I assume from the author's knowledge that he must be a man."

PUBLIC SPEAKING

Although it seems almost incomprehensible today, American women did not begin to join organizations or hold meetings—much less make public speeches—until well after the turn of the nineteenth century. In other words, it has been less than two centuries since society commonly objected to any speaking by a woman outside of the context of her home.

Doubtless this was largely based in the traditions of the Christian Church, which was almost inseparable from secular life for most early Americans. The church's male-only speech tradition, in turn, was based on St. Paul's words in First Corinthians: "Women should keep silence in the churches . . . If there is anything they desire to know, let them ask their husbands at home. For it is shameful for a woman to speak in church."

The result was to reinforce female lack of self-confidence, for women never had—nor ever expected to have—the opportunity of addressing a group of people in a formal way. A few women whose minds were so brilliant that they could not avoid revealing themselves through their speech found that they were severely punished: in the cases of ANNE HUTCHINSON and MARY DYER, for example, it is difficult to determine whether the cause of banishment and death was truly doctrinal differences, or whether instead the clergy was simply outraged by competition from women. It is entirely possible that a charismatic speaker such as Hutchinson would have become a leading cleric, rather than an outcast, had she been male.

In any case, proscriptions against speaking by women had become rigid by the end of the eighteen century. ELIZABETH PEABODY and MARGARET FULLER demonstrated this when they began to share their intellectual attainments in the 1830s: both initially addressed audiences of women only; they remained seated, instead of standing to speak; and they used euphemisms such as Fuller's "conversations" for what were actually paid lectures.

Other women in this era skirted the speaking taboo with similar strategies: EMMA WILLARD and DOROTHEA DIX used written "memorials" to legislators when societal bans kept them from speaking to a "promiscuous" audience, which was the common term for a group containing men and women. Dix also invited powerful men to visit her hotel rooms, where—in a curious reversal of modern taboos—she could acceptably speak to them.

There was a class-based bias in this taboo, for factory women in the LOWELL FEMALE LABOR REFORM ASSOCIATION did not hesitate to speak before Massachusetts legislators in their 1840 unionization efforts, and the irrepressible, affluent FANNY WRIGHT cared so little for her reputation that she lectured as early as 1829. Industrial workers and committed radicals were a tiny fraction of women, however, and the ban on speaking was genuine for middle-class women. It was, in fact, a prime reason for SUSAN ANTHONY's FEMINIST awakening: on three separate occasions at TEMPERANCE and TEACHER gatherings in 1852 and 1853, she found that her gender meant that presiding officers automatically refused to recognize her. Anthony's experience at one of these meetings was shared by ANTOINETTE BROWN BLACKWELL, for whom it served to reinforce her desire to preach.

Their experience was predated by that of LUCRETIA MOTT and ELIZABETH CADY STANTON, whose treatment at the 1840 World Anti-Slavery Convention was even more egregious. Along with five other American women, they traveled to London for this convention, only to find that the male delegates not only disallowed the women's right to speak, but actually went so far as to hide them from view. It was this issue of women's exclusion from participation in meetings that provided the incentive for Mott and Stanton to call for the 1848 SENECA FALLS WOMEN'S RIGHTS CONVENTION.

These women were following in the footsteps of ABOLITIONIST women, who had begun breaking speaking taboos in the 1830s. For MARIA WESTON CHAPMAN, ABBY KELLY FOSTER, the GRIMKE sisters, and others, making speeches not only meant overcoming the fear that affected every woman who spoke for the first time, but also summoning the physical courage to resist hostile mobs that shouted insults and attacked abolitionists with rotten eggs, rocks, and even fire.

Abolitionism, in fact, was the key to women's assertion of the right to speak, for the fervency of their belief in the right of black people to be free became women's justification for public speaking. Most of these early speakers were QUAKER WOMEN who came from a different tradition from that of other Christians, for the Quaker priority of silence meant that speech, when it came in their communal church services, was considered divinely influenced. For Anthony and many other Quakers, being shouted down by males when they attempted to address secular meetings was a new and unwelcome experience; they had been reared to believe that God was as likely to speak through women as through men.

It was this willingness to believe that people were an instrument for God's words that probably is responsible for the fact that there was less public disapproval when black women broke the speaking taboo than when white women did. Many apparently found it easy to believe that women such as MARY ANN SHADD CARY, MARIA STEWART, and especially SOJOURNER TRUTH were divinely inspired, and therefore not personally responsible for the words that came out of their mouths. In cases of women such as Fuller and Peabody, however, a contrasting style of secular intellectual attainment made their personal assertiveness clear—and objectionable.

The speaking success of the early abolitionists, however, went almost unnoticed. As more and more women found the courage to stand on a platform and speak their minds on slavery, the taboo against what they were *doing* was lost in the controversy over what they were *saying*. They had managed to divert male attention from female appearance/behavior to focus instead on the controversial content of her mind. The importance of this achievement is hard to overstate, for without the right to speak, there can be no rights.

In comparison with its importance, the barrier was crossed within a very short time. By the CIVIL WAR, public speaking by women was sufficiently acceptable that ANNA DICKINSON, for example, drew huge crowds. The taboo, in fact, had so permanently evaporated that many of the era's most important feminists would find their major source of income in the making of speeches.

PUBLISHERS AND PRINTERS The distinction between the printing business and the publishing business was much less rigidly defined for most of the nation's history than it is today, and moreover, women were far better represented in it than has been commonly recognized.

While every schoolchild knows the freedom-of-press case that revolved around Peter Zenger in 1735, few know that Anna Zenger published the newspaper during the year that he was in prison; after his death in 1746, she again edited and printed it. If the roles of women in such well-known cases and in cities as large as Zenger's New York have been overlooked, then doubtlessly there were dozens of women in smaller towns who did the same.

Anne Catherine Hoff Green (c. 1720–1775), for example, was the official printer for the colony of Maryland. A WIDOW who had borne fourteen children, she inherited both the governmental contract and the *Maryland Gazette* when her husband died in 1767. The legislature was so pleased with her ability that she was paid at the same rate that her husband had been, and Green also issued other documents relating to Maryland's colonial history. Moreover, she showed courage in risking her state business to publish stories in the *Gazette* on the Boston Tea Party, John Dickinson's anti-British *Letters*, and other items that indicated her support of the Revolution in its early days. Green did not live to see her views become successful, for she died the year prior to the Declaration of Independence.

In similar circumstances, Elizabeth Hunter Holt (c. 1727–1788) was named the official printer of the new state of New York after her printer husband died in 1784. She also took over the publication of the *Independent Gazette*, running it for more than a year before turning it over to her daughter, also named Elizabeth, and her son-in-law, Eleazar Oswald. Elizabeth Oswald repeated her mother's history and continued in the newspaper business after she, too, became a widow. Similarly, Ann Smith Franklin, a sister-in-law to Benjamin Franklin, ran the *Rhode Island Almanack* for twenty-three years after her husband died.

Another widow, Sarah Updike Goddard (c. 1700–1770) provided the financing for Rhode Island's *Providence Gazette* in 1762. Her son William was the ostensible editor, but he traveled much of the time and it was Goddard and her daughter, Katherine Mary Goddard (1738–1816), who truly built the newspaper. The women ran local and foreign news, but also added popular entertainment items and had built the newspaper into a profitable business when William persuaded them to move to Phildelphia in 1768. There they published the *Pennsylvania Chronicle*, and Katherine inherited her mother's role when Sarah died two years after the move.

Katherine Goddard ran the Philadelphia paper alone until 1774, when she joined William in Baltimore. She would spend the rest of her career with the *Maryland Journal*, where she was listed with her brother as editor and publisher. In January 1777, Katherine Goddard made a place for herself in publishing history by issuing the first copy of the Declaration of Independence that included the signer's names. Katherine Goddard remained single and earned an independent living even after William displaced her from the newspaper in 1784.

Not all of these colonial women publishers supported the Revolution; Margaret Green Draper (1727–c.1804) was the last Loyalist to run a newspaper in the hotbed of rebellious Boston. Again, she had inherited the newspaper along with her husband's contract as printer for the colony of Massachusetts when he died in June, 1774. Under Margaret Draper's editorship, the *Boston News-Letter* became ever more vocal in its opposition to the rebellion that was brewing—but there seems to have been a considerable audience for this viewpoint, for she soon drove six competitors out of business. She had the only newspaper operating in Boston when the British evacuated in 1776, but Draper then had to flee with the British. She took refuge in England, where her death was so obscure that the date is not known.

A number of other occupations were naturally linked to the wordsmith business during the colonial era, and women who were printers and publishers were also likely to operate bookstores, stationery stores, and post offices. Ann Smith Franklin was the first female postal employee in the nation; she became Boston's postmistress in 1753. Combining the post office with a town's print shop was not unusual, for printers were often the most literate and well-informed people in their community, and it made sense for them to also run the post office—without regard to gender. Katherine Goddard was postmistress of Baltimore from 1775 to 1789; when she was replaced by a man, there was widespread objection from residents pleased with her performance. Goddard ran a bookstore in "retirement," and other women printers also ran stores, typically specializing in paper goods and imported items.

These traditions were continued in the early nineteenth century by ELIZABETH PEABODY, who not only ran one of the nation's best bookstores, but also published controversial Transcendental philosophical works and ABOLITIONIST materials, including Thoreau's "Civil Disobedience." During the same decade that Peabody was publishing, AMELIA BLOOMER set the standard for publications that were not only *by* but also *for* women, with her *Lily*, a temperance newspaper that began in 1846. Once again, Bloomer's husband was a publisher, and she worked with him in the mainstream newspaper business while continuing to publish her own paper even after they moved to Ohio in 1853.

Similarly, ABIGAIL SCOTT DUNIWAY supported her disabled husband and their large family by publishing the *New Northwest*, which she established in Portland, Oregon in 1871. Her paper became a financial success despite competition from her brother, who ran another paper that editorially opposed Duniway's progressive views on women's rights. Like a number of other women, however, Duniway is remembered almost solely as a suffragist, while her role as a publisher goes unacknowledged. Doubtless there were many other women—especially in small, frontier towns—whose work as printers and publishers has been forgotten.

As the nation's economy became more complex in the nineteenth century, publishing—like other businesses—was increasingly dominated by men with investment capital. Women were largely excluded from the title of publisher, though a number of them, such as SARAH JOSEPHA BUELL HALE, carved out significant roles as editors, especially in the new women's magazines. Late in the same era, MIRIAM LESLIE stands as an unparalleled publishing phenomenon who turned the magazine business that she inherited from bankruptcy to major success. Though she is less known, Ellen Browning Scripps (1836–1932) both wrote well and invested wisely; her original income multiplied more than 40 times during the building of the newspaper chain that retains her family name today.

Thus, individual women continued to be important to the publishing world, even though women as a group were largely unacknowledged. In the early twentieth century, for example, MARGARET ANDERSON accepted financial hardship and the threat of arrest to publish such writers as EMMA GOLDMAN and James Joyce. BLANCHE KNOPF endured no financial loss, but she exhibited the same enterprise as Anderson in looking for new, untested AUTHORS and in recognizing the market power of women readers.

In the magazine field during the same era, LILA BELL ACHESON WALLACE cofounded *Reader's Digest* and FREDA KIRCHWEY owned and published the *Nation*, while JESSE VANN carved out a place for herself in the specialized field of newspapers aimed at blacks. At the same time that these women were playing major roles in the most visible publishing world, women publishers continued unheralded, but nonetheless successful, in fields relating to women and children. ELEANOR JOHNSON, for example, founder of the perennially popular *Weekly Reader*, should be far better recognized as a successful publisher than she is. Similarly, two women editors who were married to the more visible male publishers were key to the long success of *LADIES HOME JOURNAL*.

Without regard to these separate publishing areas, however, there have been a number of important women in mainstream publishing in the latter half of the twentieth century. Active publishers of major metropolitan newspapers include ALICIA PATTERSON of *Newsday* and CISSY PATTERSON of the *Washington Times-Herald*, OVETA CULP HOBBY of the *Houston Post*, KATHERINE GRAHAM of the *Washington Post*, DOROTHY SCHIFF of the *New York Post*, I.O. SULZBERGER of the *New York Times*, and JESSE VANN of the PITTSBURGH COURIER.

Colonial Anne Catherine Green and modern Katherine Graham are examples of similarly important female historical figures, for Graham's courage in publishing the Pentagon papers during the Vietnam War is akin to that of Green in publishing news sources that were antigovernment during the American Revolution. All through the nation's history, there have been women with the courage and the ability to influence opinion through the printed word that they published. They deserve more attention from historians than they have received.

QUAKERS AND QUAKER WOMEN Women who belonged to the Society of Friends, more commonly known as Quakers, were tremendously influential in shaping the nation's history. The lives of all American women would be much poorer without the efforts of these early exponents of democracy, gender equality, and nonviolence.

The religion began in England at the same time that the first English colonies were developing in America. Because their new ideas subjected them to persecution from the authorities who represented both church and state in England, Quakers began coming to the New World in the 1650s. They found persecution in some of the colonies, too, and four Quakers, including MARY DYER, were hung in Boston between 1659 and 1661. The colony most open to religious tolerance was Pennsylvania, founded by religious dissident William Penn in 1682, and Quaker settlements expanded from there into other northeastern colonies. Philadelphia, however, would remain in the heart of Quaker presence.

Too often portrayed with cliches that emphasized their somber dress and quaint speech instead of their revolutionary ideas, Quaker women's avoidance of fashion was an expression of their rejection of superficiality. They did indeed dress in plain styles and muted colors; they used biblical speech patterns such as "thee" and "thou"; and their lives centered on the family and the meetinghouse. The result was that many Americans came to think of Quakers as "puritanical" and therefore akin to the Puritans. In fact, there were important theological differences between the two, beginning with the issue of religious tolerance and expanding to freedom in many other areas.

For women, the most significant of these was the willingness of the Society of Friends to grant women equal status as religious leaders. Quaker meetinghouses were architecturally and organizationally much different from churches, for there was no authoritarian (and male) figure in a pulpit as in other variations of Christianity. Instead, each believer silently meditated and spoke when the spirit called. Women were considered to have an "inner light" of divinity like men, and therefore could PUBLICLY SPEAK in devotional meetings. Business meetings were separated by gender, with those for women being run by women—something that both men and women thought facilitated church discipline and societal solidarity.

This was especially important when young women were ready to wed, for the sisters of the meeting took a serious responsibility in approving or disapproving the prospective groom. Though Quakers accepted the biblical injunction that wives should be submissive, their family structure naturally encouraged egalitarianism, not only because of the power of women in the church but also because of their belief in nonviolence.

A male member of the Society of Friends could not threaten his wife and children with physical force as other religions allowed. Moreover, a committee from the women's meeting investigated when there were serious marital conflicts, and the man who did not wish to be "read out of the meeting" had to accept its discipline when he was judged at fault. The result was that male Friends were more FEMINIST than most of the era's women; it was AMELIA BLOOMER's Quaker husband, for example, who introduced her to liberated ideas.

Families thus strove for a nonviolent harmony that emphasized generosity to the less fortunate. Unlike the Shakers founded by MOTHER ANN LEE, Quakers did not live communally nor share profits, but, like the Shakers, they developed reputations as hard-working and exceptionally skilled. Some of them became quite wealthy as a result, and the sect had no objections to wealth as long as the possessor also demonstrated charitable attitudes towards those in need. The women's meetings became the usual source of communal charity, and Quaker women thus developed organizational experience in fund-raising and philanthropic administration. From humble woman-to-woman beginnings that took special note of WIDOWS, these modest but devoted Philadelphia-based women led the way in founding America's hospitals and other havens for the needy.

Friends were also more likely than others to see that their daughters were educated, for meeting membership required literacy and elemental math. Because of these unusual advantages, Quaker women moved more easily than most women into areas that were ordinarily closed. For example, Philadelphian Quaker Margaret Hill Morris learned medical skills from her physician father and practiced medicine after being widowed in 1766, and it was sympathetic Friends who helped ELIZABETH BLACKWELL become a physician. It was Quakers, too, who built the first schools for black girls and women; PRUDENCE CRANDELL, for example, was a Friend. MARY ANN SHADD CARY was among the antebellum blacks educated in Quaker schools; much later, black leaders such as MARY MCLEOD BETHUNE and CRYSTAL BIRD FAUSET would achieve their aspirations with help from Quaker women.

Moreover, because women were preachers and missionaries in the Society of Friends, they could TRAVEL without escort—an ability that was crucial to SUSAN ANTHONY's work on behalf of women. Anthony's Quaker heritage provided her with precedents like that of JEMIMA WILKINSON, a Quaker woman who traveled widely to preach and whose charismatic personality attracted large numbers of female disciples.

Quaker women demonstrated their assertiveness as early as the American Revolution, when they resisted popular opinion on the issue of war. Pacifism had been one of the original reasons for governmental persecution of Quakers, and though men suffered more directly for refusing military service, the sect's dedication to peace required serious commitment from women, too. Sally Fisher, for example, was a Philadelphia Quaker whose husband was imprisoned for refusing to fight in 1777; she bore a child alone and noted months later that she had gained financial experience in his absence.

While unwilling to fight for the political freedom so meaningful to colonial rebels, Friends were likely to care deeply about personal freedom for people of color—something that left most other American consciences untroubled. Quakers refused to join the warfare conducted against natives in the French and Indian Wars and they did not keep slaves, even when household slaves were common in Northern colonies. Indeed, Quaker meetings issued public statements of protest against the institution of slavery as early as 1652, and in 1775 (before the Revolution began), it was primarily Philadelphia Quakers who formed the Society for the Relief of Free Negroes Unlawfully Held in Bondage.

The legalistically conservative title given to this basically liberal group presaged the turmoil of the next century, when quakers sought to reconcile their seemingly contradictory beliefs in freedom and peace as the CIVIL WAR approached. While they wanted to end slavery, many Friends could not approve of doing that by military force, and hundreds of anguished meetings were held as these principled people tried to decide whether or not to object to a war that promised liberation. Some Friends, especially the wealthy, spoke out strongly against ABOLITION, believing it to be an excessively radical idea that would engender violence.

Nonetheless, Quaker women joined the abolitionist movement in numbers vastly disproportionate to any other group and long before abolitionism gained respectability. SARAH and ANGELINA GRIMKE converted to the Society of Friends when they moved to Philadelphia in the late 1820s because of the antislavery views they found there. Among other Quaker women courageous enough to lead the way were LUCRETIA MOTT, a founder of the Philadelphia Anti-Slavery Society in 1833, and ABBY KELLY FOSTER, who joined abolitionist pioneer William Lloyd Garrison in founding Massachusetts' antislavery movement.

Quaker women defied the laws of property for what they saw as the greater rights of people, and SOJOURNER TRUTH was but one example of a slave taken in by a Quaker family when she ran away from her New York owner in 1826. After the passage of the fugitive slave law in 1850, many Quaker women hid those traveling the Underground Railroad to freedom in Canada. When the war came, Quaker women served as NURSES and sent food and clothing to comfort the wounded. The oratorical ability that ANNA DICKINSON used so effectively for the Union was due to the encouragement her Quaker background gave to public speaking by women, and the courageous resistance to slavery exhibited by Virginian ELIZABETH VAN LEW doubtless was influenced by her youth among Quakers.

After the war, Quaker women were involved in the establishment of BRYN MAWR, and they were among those who attempted to vote under the FIFTEENTH AMENDMENT. They provided much of the leadership for the WOMEN'S INTERNATIONAL LEAGUE FOR PEACE AND FREEDOM after the turn of the century and were disproportionately represented in the WOMAN'S PARTY when women got the vote.

More recent women who were either members of the Society of Friends or who were greatly influenced by that tradition include GRACE AND EDITH ABBOTT, ALICE PAUL, LYDIA PINKHAM, M. CAREY THOMAS, and Nobel Peace Prize winners JANE ADDAMS and EMILY BALCH; MARY CALDERONE is among modern women who maintain the traditions of the Society of Friends.

QUEEN BEE A pejorative term used by modern FEMINISTS, a "queen bee" is a woman who expects to receive top positions, financial rewards, and other recognition for herself, even though she spurns the efforts of other women to achieve. It derives from the way a hive of bees (male and female) devotes its collective efforts to the queen bee; human "queen bees" expect similar devotion—without reference to either their personal merit or the needs of others.

QUILTS AND QUILTING BEES Both women and men in early American communities often combined work with socializing, for there was so much work to be done that purely leisure time was rare. For women, one of the most common blends of work with visiting was the quilting bee.

Like time, cloth also was precious, especially when it was woven from wool that a woman had carded herself or linen that she spun from flax. After garments had been worn and cut down and remade—often several times—women still saved scraps from the worn-out cloth and cut these scraps into pieces for quilt tops. Individual women worked alone at accumulating material and cutting the quilt pieces; usually women did the "piecing" alone, too, sewing each small part of a planned pattern to another to form a "quilt block" and then "blocking" those larger pieces together with still more stitches. Women took pride in making their stitches so small that they could scarcely be seen.

Finally, when enough of this work had been done to make a bed-sized quilt top, a woman's friends would gather to do the actual quilting. Plain-woven cloth formed the bottom of the quilt; batting was put in the middle for warmth; and then the newly sewn quilt top was placed on top. All of this was held at a comfortable working height by a quilting frame, which was simply four pieces of wood nailed together in an rectangle large enough to hold the quilt. The materials were temporarily fastened to the sides of the frame, and then women began the actual quilting.

Working from all sides of the frame, they sewed with stitching patterns that combined the practical necessity of joining the three layers together while also again creating an aesthetically pleasing pattern of stitches. Depending on the intricacy of the pattern and the number of women working (most likely no more than a dozen women, with three to the four sides of the frame), a quilting could be expected to take all day. Meanwhile, the women would talk—and interrupt their work to nurse babies and tend to older children.

Teatime and meals were always a festive part of a quilting. In frontier communities where people lived so far apart that they seldom gathered, a quilting could go on for days. The men would busy themselves with barn work while the women sewed and the children played, and everyone would bed down on the floor at night. Often these gatherings ended with a dance, with the music usually provided by a fiddle.

Quilting bees therefore were held in the largest homes possible, with the most important factor being the availability of a room big enough to accommodate the quilting frame. Serious quilters permanently suspended their frames from the ceiling, pulling them up when the work was over and lowering them when it was time to begin again. Even after the midpoint of the twentieth century, it as not uncommon to see quilting frames on the ceilings of Southern living rooms.

In time, the arrangement of cloth scraps into elaborate quilt patterns became one of the ways that American women rose above the banality of their lives to express personal creativity. The folk art of quilts is being rediscovered today as a valid artistic form, which had significant variants between ethnic and geographical groups. The women artisans are largely nameless, though their creations are remembered by name: "Rose of Sharon" and "Star of David," for example, were among the most popular patterns. Despite their lack of recognition, hundreds of women made aesthetic contributions to American culture through their skill with scissors and needle. Given almost nothing in the way of resources, they used their imaginations to create beauty while also providing their families needed warmth.

QUIMBY, EDITH HINKLEY (1891–1982) A physicist, Edith Quimby was a research scientist who developed safe, standardized measures for radiation dosages in the treatment of cancer and related disease. Prior to her fifty articles on the subject in medical journals, each doctor treating cancer patients decided what dosage to use.

She earned her master's degree in physics from the University of California in 1916 and came East with her husband, who was also a physicist. She did her primary radiation studies under the aegis of the New York City Memorial Hospital for Cancer, and through the twenties and thirties, she was the "only woman in America engaged in medical physical research." As was the case for many women, WORLD WAR II broadened Quimby's opportunities; she worked on the Manhattan Project that built the atomic bomb while also teaching at Cornell and Columbia.

In the first year after the war, Quimby spoke to the state medical society on the futuristic use of atomic energy. In addition to her new research project on medical applications of radioactive isotopes, she investigated and publicized methods of treatment that would not be injurious to medical personnel.

Edith Quimby was given an award in 1940 from the American Radium Society, the first woman to be so honored. The Gold Medal that she received from the Radiological Society of North America the following year was only the second awarded a woman, with the first having gone to the famous French discoverer of radium, Marie Curie.

A member of the LEAGUE OF WOMEN VOTERS and a Democrat, Quimby retired in 1960. Though she had spent a lifetime in potentially dangerous experimentation, she lived to ninety-one.

QUIMBY, HARRIET (1875?–1912) The first American woman to receive a license to pilot an airplane, Harriet Quimby's career as an aviator was daring and brief.

She obscured her birth date and place, but Quimby lived most of her life in California, where she worked as a journalist. She wrote for two of San Francisco's most distinguished newspapers, the *Call* and the *Chronicle*, and moved to New York in 1903 to write for *Leslie's Weekly*, which was part of MIRIAM LESLIE's publishing empire. Quimby's position as the publication's drama critic not only gave her the flexibility to fly, but presumably also reflected the sense of the dramatic that she demonstrated in her aerobatic exhibitions.

Only five years after the Wright brothers patented their "flying machine," Quimby was issued a license by the Aero Club of America, which was the official licensing agency operating under the authority of the *Federation Aeronautique Internationale*. She passed her examination, which required landing within one hundred feet of the point of takeoff, after thirty-three lessons at a Long Island aviation school. On Au-

Harriet Quimby, the first American woman licensed to pilot a plane, was killed when she crashed into Boston Harbor in 1912. RESOURCE CENTER OF THE NINETY-NINES, INC.

gust 1, 1911, Quimby thus joined the thirty-five men and one woman (a French baroness) who were licensed to fly.

She flew days later in a Staten Island meet that drew a crowd of twenty thousand, most of whom were seeing their first airplane. In the same month, Quimby won six hundred dollars in a cross-country race and then sailed for Europe. After careful preparations in Dover, on April 16, 1912, Harriet Quimby became the first woman to pilot a plane across the English Channel. Weather prediction and air navigation were still largely unknown, and Quimby soon found herself surrounded by clouds that threw her off of her planned course. She nonetheless landed safely in a French village twenty-five miles from her destination of Calais, where the residents were astounded to see her descend from the sky.

She was celebrated in Paris and London and returned to the U.S. in May. In late June, she went to Boston to prepare for an aviation meet. On July 1, Quimby was practicing flying around a lighthouse on Dorchester Bay with a passenger who was a large man. Her aircraft—like those of the early Wright brothers—was little more than a box kite capable of holding two people, and the passenger was warned not to shift his weight and upset the balance of the plane. While coming in for landing, however, that apparently happened, and both Quimby and her passenger were thrown out of the plane and into the water. Both were killed, while the plane itself glided in to land with little damage.

Harriet Quimby's death occurred decades before the much better known death of AMELIA EARHART, and her daring was demonstrated long before the lesser accomplishments of other well-publicized women such as RUTH ELDER and ANNE MORROW LINDBERGH. Quimby is memorialized in the NINETY-NINES'S library based at the Will Rogers Airport in Oklahoma City and is included in the women in aviation collection at California's Claremont College.

R

RADCLIFFE COLLEGE Initially known as "Harvard Annex," Radcliffe is centered less than a mile from Harvard Yard. This location gave it a closer proximity to its affiliated male institution than was the case for most women's COLLEGES, but Harvard and Radcliffe nonetheless maintained strikingly separate identities during the century following Radcliffe's founding.

The fourth of the SEVEN SISTER schools, the "Annex" was established in 1879; in 1882, it was incorporated as the Society for the Collegiate Instruction of Women. Formalized into Radcliffe College in 1894, it was named for colonial philanthropist Ann Radcliffe. She had begun the first scholarship fund at Harvard College in 1643—an endowment that, like all others, remained exclusively available to male students for more than two centuries.

FANNY GARRISON VILLARD and ALICE FREEMAN PALMER were among those who were vital to Radcliffe's beginning; like other women of their era who managed to educate themselves, they were motivated by an awareness of the disabilities women suffered when denied college admission. Discrimination against women was still so real that, for example, EMILY BALCH went to BRYN MAWR in 1886 instead of the closer Radcliffe because she accompanied a friend whose Harvard professor father "was not willing to have it known among his Cambridge friends that he was disgraced by having a daughter at college."

No one was more important to Radcliffe's beginning, however, than ELIZABETH CARY AGASSIZ, who transformed the inadequate "Harvard Annex" into a true college. She served as Radcliffe's president from 1893 to 1903 and thus set a precedent for long tenure. The college has had only seven presidents during its century-plus existence, with most serving about two decades.

Coeducational classes were introduced in 1943, when WORLD WAR II diminished the number of male students and led to greater opportunity for women throughout the nation's colleges. Progress was slow, however, and women did not receive Harvard degrees until 1963—even though students such as ANNIE JUMP CANNON had a legitimate claim to these degrees many decades earlier. True coeducation began in the 1970s, when all Harvard libraries were finally opened to women, joint commencements were held, and quotas limiting the number of women admitted were abolished. Today Radcliffe maintains a separate corporate status for its property, endowments, and the special programs it conducts for women.

HELEN KELLER may be the most unique student to have ever studied at Radcliffe; among other outstanding alumnae are suffragist MAUD WOOD PARK, philosopher SUSANNE LANGER, and literary giant GERTRUDE STEIN. Radcliffe's most important contribution, however, may be in its Arthur and Elizabeth Schlesinger Library on the History of Women in America, which is an unparalleled resource for students of women's history. A second priceless contribution is Radcliffe's sponsorship of the incomparable biographical dictionary, *Notable American Women*, which was published in three volumes in 1971 and updated with a fourth volume in 1980. Finally, through the Murray Research Center, the Mary Ingraham Bunting Institute and other programs, Radcliffe leads in research on contemporary women's issues.

RANKIN, JEANETTE PICKERING (1880–1973) The
first woman in Congress, Jeanette Rankin was elected before most American women could vote. She is also exceptional in congressional history because she was the only legislator to vote against both WORLD WAR I and WORLD WAR II.

Born in Montana, she benefitted from the greater opportunities available to WESTERN WOMEN; four of the six girls in her family went on to notable professional careers. Like these sisters, Rankin remained single and graduated from the University of Montana in 1902. She worked briefly as a TEACHER and after further study in New York in 1908, she went west as a social worker in Seattle. It was as a graduate student at the University of Washington that she came into contact with the SUFFRAGE MOVEMENT, and from 1910, Rankin campaigned in western states for women's enfranchisement. After four years of full-time work for the cause, she was elected legislative secretary for the NATIONAL AMERICAN WOMAN SUFFRAGE ASSOCIATION in 1914.

Rankin's efforts were partially responsible for the fact that Montana enfranchised women in 1914, and just two years later, she built upon that success by running for Congress. Her 1916 election was the equivalent of a race for senator or governor because Montana's population was so small that it held only one seat in the House of Representatives. For Rankin, it meant hundreds of miles of TRAVEL to reach sparsely settled voters—plus persuading women to exercise their franchise for the first time and to vote for a woman.

Like most Western women and many of the era's suffragists, Rankin was a Republican. In Congress, she argued for Montana copper miners in their fight with the era's powerful capitalists, but most of her attention was devoted to women. She was the ranking minority member on the special committee charged with drafting a constitutional amendment enfranchising women, and she worked for the maternal health legislation that passed after her tenure as the SHEPPARD-TOWNER BILL.

"Deeply conscious" of her "responsibility as the first woman to sit in Congress," Rankin was faced with voting on President Wilson's request for U.S. entry into WORLD WAR I only days after taking office. As was the case with a number of suffragists, she was also a pacifist. Moreover, she had been elected just months before on a platform to keep the nation out of war—as had Wilson himself. CARRIE CHAPMAN CATT and other suffragists urged Rankin to support Wilson because of the political damage to women if she reinforced stereotypes by voting against war; at the same time ALICE PAUL and her faction of the movement pulled Rankin in the anti-Wilson direction. She would be caught between these two wings of the women's movement throughout her term in office.

Representative Rankin, however, placed her pacifism and campaign promises above either FEMINIST argument and opted to join more than fifty men in Congress who also voted against this controversial war. As Catt predicted, the vote cost Rankin the next election, when the recently ended war was at the height of its popularity. She tried for the U.S. Senate in 1918 and lost first the Republican primary and then a second bid as a third party nominee in the general election.

After her congressional loss and the victory of the NINETEENTH AMENDMENT just two years later, Rankin's life became a metaphor for the suffrage movement. Like many of her friends, she retreated into relative obscurity when political issues were displaced first by the social changes of the Roaring Twenties and then by the economic needs of the Great Depression. She spent those decades as an activist in the WOMEN'S INTERNATIONAL LEAGUE FOR PEACE AND FREEDOM and other pacifist groups, while FLORENCE KELLEY arranged a job for her with the Consumers League. Rankin worked primarily on PROTECTIVE LEGISLATION in the South and established a long-term winter home in Georgia, where her community activism would extend as late as a 1968 shelter for women.

She maintained her Montana base, however, and with Europe again at war in 1940, she ran for Congress on a pacifist platform. Isolationist sentiment was strong in the Great Plains states, and Rankin was again elected to Congress. When the war exploded in 1941, Representative Rankin held steadfast to her campaign promises and was the only member of Congress to vote against the declaration of war on the day following Pearl Harbor. The furor over her vote was immediate, and understanding the unpopularity of this position, she did not bother to try for reelection in 1942.

The next decades were difficult ones for her, as she received little public acclaim and no political reward from the Republican Party—but her affiliation with that party may have saved her from persecution in the McCarthy era of the 1950s when many pacifists came under fire. Instead, Rankin traveled extensively in Third World countries, criticized American foreign policy, and was particularly involved in Gandhi's nonviolent revolt in India. By holding on to age ninety-three, she lived to see the revitalized women's movement, and in 1968, led the Jeannette Rankin Brigade of some five thousand women in a Capitol Hill protest against the Vietnam War.

Active to the end, Jeanette Rankin died of a heart attack in Carmel, California. The ashes of this woman who gave up so much for pacifism were thus appropriately scattered on the Pacific. Her papers are in the Schlesinger Library at RADCLIFFE COLLEGE.

RAWLINGS, MARJORIE KINNAN (1896–1953) Firmly
associated in the public mind with the rural Florida about which she wrote, Marjorie Kinnan actually grew up in the incongruous setting of Washington, D.C. After her father's death in 1913, her WIDOWED mother moved the family to Wisconsin, where Marjorie graduated from the University of Wisconsin in 1918.

Determined from childhood to be a writer, she went to New York and worked briefly as a publicist for the YOUNG WOMEN'S CHRISTIAN ASSOCIATION before her 1919 marriage took her away from the city. Marjorie and Charles Rawlings moved restlessly through writing jobs across the country during the twenties before finally settling in 1928 at Cross Creek, Florida. On a small farm about twenty-five miles from the university town of Gainesville, she developed a simple life that gave her the peace to write.

In 1930, she sold a collection of stories to *Scribner's Magazine* that were based on careful listening to her neighbors' tales about this still-primitive part of Florida. After a decade of struggle, the series brought Rawlings national success and support from incomparable Scribner's editor Maxwell Perkins, who published Hemingway and others of the era's great writers. A *Harper's* story earned Rawlings the O. Henry Short Story Prize in 1932, and Scribner's issued her first novel, *South Moon Under,* in 1933.

In the ironic setting of the Great Depression, things also went well for Charles Rawlings: he sold a story on Florida fishing to the *Saturday Evening Post* for a significant amount of money at the same time that Marjorie Rawling's novel became a Book-of-the-Month success. The result was marital disaster. "Almost instantaneously," recalled a Cross Creek friend, "the two of them became very popular. And each one thought they were The Genius . . ." Marjorie Rawlings escaped to a leisurely trip up the St. John's River, where she and her female friend supplied themselves by fishing and shooting ducks, but her marital problems could not be resolved and the Rawlings divorced.

Another get-away trip to England resulted in her second novel, which served primarily to demonstrate the importance of Rawlings' affinity for Florida: the book was badly received and she returned to tales based on her rural neighbors. Five years after her first novel, Rawlings published her classic short novel, *The Yearling* (1938). Again drawn from reality, this powerfully written story of a boy's love for a deer became an immediate success. The book won the Pulitzer Prize, and its status as the 1938 bestseller at last brought Rawlings financial security. The 1946 movie, with its starring cast and Academy Awards, also became a classic, while the book has been assigned reading for millions of students. Rawlings was later awarded several honorary degrees and elected to the National Institute of Arts and Letters.

After 1941, she moved about one hundred miles to the nation's oldest city of St. Augustine, Florida, where her second husband lived. Remarriage did not diminish her writing, and Rawlings published *Cross Creek* (1942), the story of her life in the woods, to high acclaim. She won a second O. Henry Award for a 1945 short story and, venturing into new fields, published a "conversational cookbook" in 1942 and researched a biography of Southern writer ELLEN GLASGOW. Her final novel, published in the year of her death, also differed in its setting of upstate New York, where she summered after post–WORLD WAR II prosperity allowed that luxury.

But Rawlings had long been a heavy drinker. Her maid of ten years, a black woman who was also a friend, recalled that she hid Rawlings' keys to keep her from driving drunk, but that Rawlings wrecked her car several times anyway. Her alcoholism, use of profanity, and bohemian lifestyle were also responsible for the low opinion in which some Floridians held her, and this resulted in protracted legal troubles from a libel suit filed by a neighbor after the publication of *Cross Creek.* The case dragged on through the forties, and Rawlings ultimately lost her state supreme court appeal. Her unconventional behavior was a factor against her, and the court probably found her truth-telling less acceptable than that of a male writer.

These stresses caused increasingly poor health that led to her death at fifty-seven from a stroke in St. Augustine. Fittingly, Marjorie Kinnan Rawlings is buried at Cross Creek. Her home there is open to visitors, while her papers are at the University of Florida.

RAY, CHARLOTTE E. (1850–1911)
Born free a decade prior to the CIVIL WAR, Charlotte Ray became the first black female attorney in America.

She was the daughter of educated ABOLITIONISTS in New York City and was described as lightskinned with straight hair. By age nineteen, she was working as a TEACHER in the prep school affiliated with HOWARD UNIVERSITY, where she also studied law. Ray graduated from Howard's law school only five years after the university began and less than a decade after the Emancipation Proclamation. She was admitted to the bar in Washington, D.C. on April 23, 1872.

An alert ELIZABETH CADY STANTON praised Ray's graduation, writing in May of that year, "In the city of Washington, where a few years ago colored women were bought and sold . . . a woman of African descent has been admitted to the . . . bar." Indeed, Ray's ascent seemed meteoric compared with the barriers that BELVA LOCKWOOD and MYRA BRADWELL encountered in their efforts to become attorneys during the same time period.

Unfortunately, this may well have been because the legal profession did not take Ray seriously enough to oppose her; in contrast to Bradwell and Lockwood, Ray was young, black and without business connections—and she soon was forced to abandon the profession for lack of clients. By 1879, she had returned to New York and to teaching. She remained active on a minor level, with attendance at the 1876 meeting of the NATIONAL WOMAN SUFFRAGE ASSOCIATION and membership in the NATIONAL ASSOCIATION OF COLORED WOMEN during the late 1890s. Charlotte Ray, who doubtlessly possessed a fine mind that was wasted, died obscurely in Brooklyn at sixty.

RAY, DIXY LEE (1914–   )
The governor of Washington from 1976 to 1980, Dixy Lee Ray worked as a science TEACHER before taking advantage of the greater opportunities for women during WORLD WAR II to earn a Ph.D. from Stanford in 1945. She then taught at the University of Washington, where she earned a number of honors that brought her national attention. President Nixon appointed Dr. Ray to a task force on oceanography in 1969, and he followed that with an appointment to the powerful Atomic Energy Commission in 1972, which she chaired the following year. An advocate of nuclear power, she was often under attack from environmentalists, but she was warmly received by many FEMINISTS because she freely credited women for her appointment.

Ray resigned in 1975 to begin campaigning for governor. As a Democrat in a traditionally Republican area and in a time when there were few female candidates for statewide office, this apolitical college professor was not expected to do well—but she won by a surprisingly large margin. Her tenure in office, however, was marked by significant controversy, and Governor Ray lost the Democratic primary in 1980. Since then she has lectured and written on science and public policy, including a 1990 book titled *Trashing the Planet.*

RED CROSS— *See* AMERICAN RED CROSS

REED, ESTHER DeBERDT (1746–1780) Born and reared in London, Esther Reed came to the English colony of Pennsylvania after her 1770 marriage. Despite this heritage, she was soon to be a leader of REVOLUTIONARY WAR WOMEN.

Her husband, Joseph Reed, was a native of the area who was a member of the Continental Congress. Despite almost annual pregnancies that made her the mother of three by early 1775, Esther Reed was politically aware and soon befriended Washington, Adams, and others who came to Philadelphia to organize the new government. Like thousands of other women, she found herself managing alone when the war began, for Joseph Reed served as an aide to General Washington. She encouraged him to give up his law practice to do so, writing that she would not have him "act so cowardly as to fly when his country needed his assistance."

Her frequent pregnancies continued as the war moved from Boston to the Philadelphia area, and Esther Reed bore three more children during the Revolution. Three times she had to flee from attacking British armies, taking along not only her infants but also her aged mother. Nor was Reed comforted by great affluence, for both her father and husband suffered serious financial losses because of the Revolution. Yet neither this nor a smallpox epidemic that seriously sickened her and killed one of her children was sufficient to keep Reed from actively supporting the new nation.

As the head of the Ladies Association that evolved from the DAUGHTERS OF LIBERTY, she undertook a massive fund-raising campaign in 1780—an action that was wholly new for women at the time. To explicate her ideas and inspire those who worked with her, Reed wrote *The Sentiments of An American Woman,* which not only recalled women who made important contributions to world history, but also argued for the right of women to participate in public affairs. Approximately forty women conducted a door-to-door canvass of other Philadelphia women; those who donated ranged from the Marchioness de La Fayette (one hundred dollars in gold) to a "coloured woman" named Phillis (seven shillings, six pence). The women collected three hundred thousand continental (paper) dollars, or approximately seventy-five hundred dollars in specie (precious-metal coin).

Reed's aim was to give this money as a morale booster to the discouraged troops in the form of a "hard" dollar to each man. Washington, however, disapproved her plan, insisting that the women instead use it to purchase cloth and sew clothing, since the Army had no funds to supply uniforms. Reed initially objected, arguing that the women's efforts had been intended as a "bounty" for the troops and was "not to hold the place of the things which they ought to receive from the Congress . . ." Eventually Washington's views prevailed, however, and by the end of 1780, Reed's women had delivered two thousand linen shirts.

But she was not to enjoy the fruits of her labors. Esther Reed had borne six children during her ten years in America, and she left these little ones motherless when dysentery killed her at thirty-three. Among others, SARAH FRANKLIN BACHE carried on her work.

As an Englishwoman who quickly transferred her loyalty to America and who raised significant funds despite the disabilities of pregnancy and disease, Esther Reed should be remembered as a founding mother of the new nation.

REMOND, SARAH PARKER (1826–1894) By publicizing the issue of slavery in the British Isles during the CIVIL WAR, Sarah Remond did a great deal of unrecognized good: her efforts were doubtless a factor in rallying British ABOLITIONISTS to keep their nation from joining the Confederacy's cause against the Union. Many British manufacturers were sympathetic to pleas from the American South—which supplied the cotton needed to run their mills—and if Britain had joined the rebels, Lincoln would have encountered much more political and military difficulty. Those such as Remond who prevented this alliance rendered a crucial service to the nation.

Of Caribbean-African descent, Sarah Remond was born in Salem, Massachusetts, where her family had lived free for several decades. She attended public elementary school, and after she was refused admission to Salem's new girls' academy in 1835, she went to Newport, Rhode Island, where she graduated from a private secondary school for blacks. By all accounts a "refined" person, Remond returned to Salem and joined the Female Anti-Slavery Society.

About the same time, Remond's older brother Charles attended the World Anti-Slavery Conference in London, from which ELIZABETH CADY STANTON and LUCRETIA MOTT were ejected. This incident may have raised his awareness of the potential for women in the abolitionist movement, for just two years later sixteen-year-old Sarah joined him on the lecture platform. She continued to learn political organizing techniques during the next decade and drew national attention among reformers in 1853, when she tried to integrate the seating of a Boston opera audience and fell down stairs after a policeman pushed her. Like the earlier LUCY TERRY PRINCE, Remond courageously went to court, sued the officer for damages and found justice. She won a five hundred dollar judgment, as well as an important legal precedent.

Three years later, she was hired as a lecturer for the American Anti-Slavery Society. She enjoyed considerable success as a PUBLIC SPEAKER, especially in the West, where prejudice was less ingrained and where the interminable problem of hotel accommodations for black and female TRAVELERS was less severe. The lecture circuit brought Remond into contact with SUSAN ANTHONY, ABBY KELLEY FOSTER, and other FEMINISTS, and she sat on the platform of the annual Women's Rights Convention in 1858. It would turn out to be her last opportunity to do so, for Remond spent almost all of the rest of her life abroad.

She arrived in Liverpool in January of 1859 as a lecturer for the Anti-Slavery Society. Remond drew uncommonly large crowds in Ireland, Scotland, and England, for she was the first black woman that many Europeans ever encountered. She took this responsibility very seriously, and her lectures were favorably reviewed in a number of contemporary news outlets. A good deal of publicity also followed her 1859 request for a passport to France, which was denied by the American embassy in London. Declared a noncitizen because of her color, she finally went to the Continent on a British passport.

Remond continued to lecture in Britain during the CIVIL WAR and wrote a thirty-page report on "The Negroes as Freedmen and Soldiers." She also began to develop a private life by studying at the women's college of the University of

London. An 1867 return to America was disappointing, and after losing an attempt to remove the words "white" and "male" from the New York Constitution, Remond moved permanently to Europe.

Apparently soon thereafter, she went on to Italy, where she would remain for the rest of her life. She probably studied medicine at a Florence hospital, and after 1873, she is said to have become a physician, with one reputable source saying that she built a "large medical practice." At age fifty, she married an Italian named Pinto, and two sisters joined her household after 1885. Frederick Douglass visited them in 1887, when these elderly exiles doubtless reminisced about the dangerous lives they led decades earlier. Sarah Remond is buried in the Protestant Cemetery in Rome.

REVOLUTIONARY WAR WOMEN

Many Americans would find it difficult to name any woman associated with the American Revolution other than a stereotyped seamstress known as BETSY ROSS, but there were in fact many women whose contributions to independence were of far greater importance. Indeed, the best assessment of the importance of women's roles may have come from an enemy, a British officer who reported to Lord Cornwallis: "We may destroy all the men in America and we shall still have all we can do to defeat the women." It was Cornwallis who finally surrendered the army of what was then considered the world's most powerful nation.

Women were in a position to make a significant difference because when the Revolutionary War began in 1776, the lives of women and men differed from each other much less than they would a century later. As many as 90 percent of Americans lived on farms, where labor was shared and where women lived busy managerial lives similar to that of ABIGAIL ADAMS. Urban women also were often partners with their men in family businesses, and some even engaged in business ventures that are unusual by today's standards: almost a century prior to the Revolution, for example, a group of thirty Boston women were authorized by town officials to saw lumber and manufacture potash. In the same decade of the 1690s, New England women were engaged in butchering and flour milling, while many others practiced more conventional trades in the dairy and poultry businesses. The result was women who were relatively independent personally, and therefore likely to think of themselves as politically independent as well.

Women's support for the War of Independence thus came from the same motivations that the men of their era held. Some, such as JUDITH SARGENT MURRAY and MERCY OTIS WARREN, went further, making it clear that their love of liberty included a profound resentment of the unfree status of those born female. Women could take some cold comfort in the fact that many men of their era also were excluded from political participation, for the vote was restricted by both religious affiliation and property ownership. Like these unenfranchised men, women held political opinions and actively participated in the Revolution.

Years before war was declared, the DAUGHTERS OF LIBERTY organized to enforce the boycott of British goods; they used both creative home manufacturing alternatives and physical threats against those who bought imported items. After the conflict started, women such as SARAH FRANKLIN BACHE and ESTHER DEBERDT REED assumed leadership in providing funding and supplies for the army. The war was very disruptive, with the cities of Boston, New York, and Philadelphia occupied for long periods, and women either became exiled refugees or else found themselves under long siege. Families fled and many were permanently displaced.

A fairly large number of black women took advantage of this societal instability to escape from slavery, especially in the Southern colonies. The British encouraged slaves belonging to rebels to join British camps, just as they encouraged American Indians to fight with them against the white settlers. In both cases, the oppressed group used this opportunity, and a minimum of three thousand slaves joined the British. More than 40 percent of them were female, many of whom fled alone or with only their children. When the Americans won the war, however, some were returned to slavery; nor did the British ever offer protection to slaves known to belong to Loyalists.

The chance that a Loyalist was also a slaveowner was good, for those who supported the Crown were likely to be of the propertied class. This was also true for working women who had a vested interest in the status quo, such as colonial PUBLISHER Margaret Green Draper and Charleston shopkeeper Elizabeth Thompson, who spied on Americans for the British. Ultimately however, Loyalist women suffered from the war more than those who termed themselves Patriots, and many fled to Canada or England when the British surrendered. Over 450 Loyalist women eventually submitted claims for the wartime loss of their homes, and some endured far greater terror: one New York woman active for the British was "stripped naked and exposed" to a rebel mob.

There were more instances, however, of British and Hessian soldiers abusing American women. Cases of rape were particularly prevalent in the New York-New Jersey-Pennsylvania area where the war stalemated so long. A series of gang rapes there in 1776 was notably deliberate and cruel—something that was likely when a British commander characterized the resulting court martials as "most entertaining." Even when women escaped this worst sort of molestation, there were daily unpleasantries in a situation when soldiers were housed in the unwilling homes of civilians. Women could be forced for months on end to cook and clean for men whose principles they might oppose and whose presence they certainly did not welcome. Americans viewed this intrusion on family privacy so seriously that a clause forbidding the quartering of troops in homes was included in the postwar Constitution.

While it was urban women who were most likely to endure the presence of troops, multitudes of FARM WOMEN suffered the burdens of working alone when their men went to war. Mary Gill Mills "headed a band of eleven women in South Carolina, who went from farm to farm where the head of the family was in the army and helped to gather the crops." Many women saw their year's effort disappear, as crops were plundered or confiscated: this was the case for ELIZA PINCKNEY, while Catherine Van Rensselaer, the wife of an American general and mother of fourteen, destroyed her own grain rather than allow the enemy to capture it.

Similarly, South Carolinian Rebecca Motte set fire to her own plantation mansion, driving the British occupiers from it and into the ranks of attacking Americans. Young farmer Anne Kennedy of South Carolina hurriedly harvested her crops before the British came, and then fought with the troops who destroyed them and tried to burn her home. For the rest of her life, she carried the scar of a burn suffered during this fight—but she managed to throw a soldier down a staircase and save her home. Catherine Sherrill was besieged by Cherokees allied with the British in 1780; she was one of many FRONTIER WOMEN who left their homes to live in stockades during the Revolution.

Women whose husbands were in high political or military positions found themselves in great danger, for they were targeted as treasonous. In New Hampshire, a mob burned MARY BARTLETT's home because of her husband's role in the Continental Congress, while the home of wealthy New Yorker Catherine Beeker was looted and "every article of furniture" stolen. Deborah Hart, wife of New Jersey Congressman Richard Hart, died alone with the knowledge that her home was in ruins and her husband in hiding from Tories who hunted him "like a criminal." North Carolinian Margaret Gaston saw her husband, a physician for the rebels, shot to death by Tories who ignored her pleas. Another general's wife, Annis Stockton, bravely retrieved and hid the seditious papers of Princeton rebels when the British attacked that town.

Women such as MARGARET CORBIN, BETSY HAGER, DEBORAH SAMPSON, and the more famous "MOLLY PITCHER" were among those who actually participated in combat, while other daring women such as SARAH BRADLEE FULTON engaged in what was, in effect, guerilla warfare. Philadelphian Lydia Darrah, who practiced as a mortician, is another unheralded hero: she overcame both fear and the qualms of her QUAKER conscience to warn Washington of General Howe's attack plans, which she had learned by eavesdropping on troops quartered in her home.

Similarly, New Yorker Mary Lindley Murray helped retreating Americans by deceptively inviting a British general and his staff for a leisurely breakfast, which allowed the rebels time to get away. Georgian Nancy Morgan Hart placidly fixed a meal for demanding Tories—and then drew a gun on them as they began to eat and held them captive for hanging. Young Emily Geiger rode horseback for two days across a British-occupied South Carolina wilderness to deliver a message from General Greene to General Sumter; briefly taken prisoner, she managed to bluff her way out and continued the ride.

The Revolution also brought the nation's first tentative industrialization, and women were there at the beginning: about twelve hundred women and children became TEXTILE WORKERS in a new Boston factory created to support the boycott of British goods, while another four hundred were employed in Philadelphia. Meanwhile, Martha Washington, Lucy Knox, and other wives of the top military leadership accompanied their men to camp, where they slept in tents and tended to soldiers' needs. Countless women worked as NURSES, while New Jersey physician Margaret Vliet Warne "rode through the country ministering to . . . soldiers and their families without price." Finally, the era's CAMP FOLLOWERS were not necessarily women of dubious moral standards, but rather

included a sizeable number who went to war because they believed in the cause just as men did.

Records for many other similar female heroes exist. Even though their history includes an unfortunate element of racism, the DAUGHTERS OF THE AMERICAN REVOLUTION should be credited with doing a great deal to preserve the annals of this era's capable women. Much could be done to extend this knowledge instead of perpetuating false stereotypes about flag sewing.

RICHARDS, DOROTHY ANN WILLIS (1933–) The

current governor of Texas, Ann Richards reared four children before being elected county commissioner of Travis County (Austin) in 1976. Chosen state treasurer in 1982, she was the first woman elected to that position.

She moved to the governorship in a tough 1990 election. Her opponent, a conservative millionaire, did much to help her with his sexist gaffes, but Richards nonetheless had to withstand painful controversy about her status as a recovered alcoholic. Richards made a very popular speech at the Democratic National Convention in 1988, and in 1992, she chaired the convention.

RICHARDS, ELLEN HENRIETTA SWALLOW (1842–1911)

The first woman admitted to the Massachusetts Institute of Technology (MIT), Ellen Richards pioneered in the fields of chemistry and HOME ECONOMICS.

She worked unhappily as an elementary TEACHER until entering VASSAR in 1868, when the COLLEGE was less than a decade old. Age twenty-five when she began, she did so well that she graduated in two years. She was especially adept at science, and MARIA MITCHELL was among those who encouraged her to pursue a career in chemistry.

Her admission to MIT (which was initially tentative and contingent on the whim of trustees) doubtlessly was because the school was new. It had been founded at the end of the CIVIL WAR when there was an explosion in COLLEGE education, especially for women; in contrast to Boston's Harvard, then in existence for more than two hundred years, MIT was just five years old when Ellen Swallow was admitted. She earned her second bachelor's degree from MIT, as well as a master's from VASSAR, in 1873—but the MIT doctorate that she went on to earn was never awarded. Much later, her husband, an MIT professor, would write that the degree was not granted because the chemistry department refused to give its first Ph.D. to a woman. A second professor, who had opposed the admission of women, agreed that she was his best assistant in an 1872 water analysis project.

She wed Professor Robert Richards in 1875, and they would enjoy a long companionate marriage. She assisted him in his metallurgical research, but soon developed an exceptional professional life of her own—often defining the scientific field as she worked. Ellen Richards, for example, was an environmentalist long before that term was used; among other research projects, she tested home furnishings and foods for toxic contaminants, investigated water pollution, and developed safe sewage systems. A true systems thinker prior to the existence of that term, her work ranged from lead poisoning in plumbing systems to the development of nutrition education and the school lunch system.

She did much of her research via private consulting contracts and performed her early work in the Woman's Laboratory, which she set up in 1876 at MIT with donations from Boston women interested in promoting scientific education for women. After 1884, MIT finally rewarded Richards with a faculty appointment (she had taught without pay earlier), and after 1890, she joined its newly established public sanitation engineering department, where her pioneer work on air and water pollution set standards.

Richards remained on the MIT faculty for almost thirty years doing multidisciplinary research. A chemist by training, much of her work was actually engineering; at the same time, she introduced biology to MIT's curriculum and was a founder of the oceanographic institute that is known as Woods Hole. She was also accomplished in her husband's field of metallurgy; one mining expert called her "the best [ore] analyst in the United States." Nonetheless, it probably was because of her husband's connections that she was the first woman elected to the American Institute of Mining and Metallurgical Engineers.

Richards did a great deal of voluntary work on behalf of women and often financed the implementation of new ideas. She was a founder in Boston of the group that became the AMERICAN ASSOCIATION OF UNIVERSITY WOMEN; she headed some of the work of the WOMAN'S EDUCATIONAL AND INDUSTRIAL UNION; and she was active in other efforts to promote scientific education and good health. In addition, she wrote more than a dozen books and many articles, ranging from *The Chemistry of Cooking* (1882) to *Euthenics: The Science of the Controllable Environment* (1912).

Her seemingly boundless energy was also expended in the practical application of principles to her own home: she plumbed in a water system prior to the delivery of city water lines and created her own central heating system when that was "a radical innovation." In the course of this work, she and her husband developed a number of ideas that could have been patented, but with characteristic generosity, they shared their inventions.

Richards is best remembered, however, as the mother of the field of home economics. This came about because of the annual summer seminars she conducted after 1899 for those who were interested in the new ideas resulting from the era's momentous change. Ahead of sociologists and historians, she led thinking women to understand the tremendous impact of industrialization and urbanization on their lives. Skills that had been passed on for centuries via family networks were being replaced with other skills, and much of the knowledge lost in this process was related to domesticity. Just as factories taught employees the skills they needed to know, Richards and her colleagues argued, new mechanisms had to be developed to teach the skills needed in the home, for grandmother's knowledge was no longer applicable. The result was the formation of the American Home Economics Association in 1908. Ever generous and scientific in her intent, Richards underwrote its *Journal of Home Economics*.

Ellen Richards' work at MIT touched on so many scientific areas that she taught many of those who became the leaders of public health, sanitation and other new fields. The result was, as one of her male admirers has said, that "if these were the 'fathers' of their individual fields, she was the 'mother' of

them all." Awarded an honorary doctorate from SMITH COLLEGE in 1910, Ellen Richards was at work on a speech for MIT's fiftieth anniversary when she died at sixty-eight.

RIDE, SALLY (1951–   )
The first woman to fly in outer space, Sally Ride spent six days on the *Challenger* during June of 1983.

A Californian, she earned 1973 degrees from Stanford University in physics and English literature; the incongruity of subjects shows the ambivalent position of women at the time, for science was not yet a realistic major for most women. In 1977, Ride was one of 208 finalists among the eight thousand applicants for astronaut openings, and in 1978, she was chosen as one of six women among thirty-five astronauts in the Space Shuttle program.

Sally Ride continues with NASA and served on the presidential commission that investigated the 1986 *Challenger* rocket explosion that killed seven passengers, including astronaut Judith Resnik and science teacher Christa McAuliffe.

ROBESON, ESLANDA CARDOZA GOODE (1896–1965)
A coauthor with PEARL BUCK, Eslanda Cardoza Goode's name reflected her unusual heritage: Her father had been a slave, while her mother, a free woman of considerable affluence, was descended from a Spanish Jew who had a long-term relationship with a mulatto on his South Carolina plantation.

Called Essie, Goode worked as a medical technician after her 1920 graduation from Columbia University and was active in Harlem's political and literary scene. She married Paul Robeson the following year, and while he went on to major success as both an entertainer and a politically active attorney, she established her own identity as a writer after bearing a child in 1927.

Her first book was a 1930 biography of her husband, but Robeson's work was noteworthy because of the candor with which she discussed both sexuality and racial prejudice. After studying anthropology at the University of London in the 1930s, she did field research in Africa that formed the basis of her *African Journey* (1945). Following WORLD WAR II, Robeson was a delegate from the Council on African Affairs to meetings of the nascent United Nations, but she and her husband were increasingly criticized in the postwar era because of their statements in support of the Soviet Union. Both were compelled to testify before the House Un-American Activities Committee, and the State Department revoked their passports.

It is therefore much to the credit of Nobel Prize winner Pearl Buck that she coauthored a book with the controversial Robeson. *An American Argument* (1949) was a dialogue on racism published at a time when few were willing to acknowledge the problem. After Robeson's passport was returned, she was honored by the government of East Germany. She participated to some degree in the civil rights movement of the late fifties, but again lived abroad before dying of cancer in New York.

ROBINS, MARGARET DREIER (1868–1945)
Like her sister, MARY ELIZABETH DREIER, Margaret was born wealthy, but devoted her life to the poor. Called Gretchen, she grew up in affluence in Brooklyn, but already by nineteen was volun-

teering as a NURSE. It would be political action, however, that was her lifetime career, as by the turn of the century, she belonged to a number of reform organizations in New York.

In 1905, she married Raymond Robins, an activist who shared her political views—though he was "hypersensitive" about living on her wealth and invented a background for himself as a successful Alaskan gold prospector. They lived in Chicago and joined the circle of people headed by JANE ADDAMS. Within two years, Margaret Robins was president of the WOMEN'S TRADE UNION LEAGUE (WTUL), and that organization would become the chief life's work of Robins and her sister. Both women exhibited outstanding leadership in the great STRIKE of GARMENT WORKERS in 1909–1911. They were uncommonly adept at uniting the women who sewed clothing with those who bought it, working comfortably with poor seamstresses and society belles.

Robins lectured on labor issues, edited *Life and Labor,* donated funds to make the work of the WTUL possible, and, after 1914, operated a leadership training school for working women. Its year-long course in union organizing gave undereducated women skills that transferred to other areas of life, and MARY ANDERSON was among those grateful for this unusual opportunity. At the same time, unlike a number of women who lived similar lives, Robins also earned exceptional respect from men in blue-collar unions. She served from 1906–1917 on the executive committee of the Chicago branch of the AFL—an exceptional achievement for a woman even today, and almost unheard of for a nonemployed woman.

More devoted to the cause of labor than to the SUFFRAGE MOVEMENT, Robins nonetheless spoke at meetings of the NATIONAL AMERICAN WOMAN SUFFRAGE ASSOCIATION, where she stressed the needs of working women. She campaigned for Theodore Roosevelt's Progressives in 1912, but when that wing of the Republican Party disbanded, she remained a Republican long after the party ceased to represent progressive views—perhaps because she and her husband shared the PROHIBITIONIST opinions of most Chicago Republicans. The result was a loss of status in the AFL, while Robins and her husband received party appointments during the twenties.

She resigned the WTUL presidency in 1922, and two years later, they retired to their winter home north of Tampa. She was less active in Florida, but did support a number of progressive organizations. The Robinses finally transferred their loyalty to the Democratic Party after the New Deal implemented many of the ideas for which they had worked in their youth.

Margaret Dreier Robins's papers are at the University of Florida, while her home, Chinsegut Hill, belongs to the University of South Florida.

ROE VS. WADE (1973)

ROE VS. WADE (1973) The Supreme Court ruling that legalized ABORTION throughout the U.S. was actually one of two appeals on which the Court ruled simultaneously: *Roe vs. Wade,* a Texas case, and *Doe vs. Bolton,* a Georgia case. In each, women who sought abortions used anonymous identities to bring suit against state law enforcement officials.

Georgia's law allowed abortion only in cases of rape, severe fetal defect, or the endangerment of maternal life. The Court ruled against several portions of the law, striking down provisions that limited abortions to Georgia citizens, that re-

quired all abortions to be performed in hospitals, and that set up complex procedures for committees of physicians to whom a woman seeking an abortion had to appeal. In doing so, the Court brought the legal situation into alignment with modern medicine and allowed women to take advantage of safe, simple, and inexpensive treatment.

Doe vs. Bolton was probably overshadowed in the public mind by *Roe vs. Wade* because the Texas law was more severe, and in overturning it, the Court made a stronger statement. Texas prohibited all abortions and made the performance of one a felony, except when medical professionals agreed that the procedure was necessary to save the mother's life. In striking down both states' laws, the Court said clearly that women have a constitutional right under the personal liberty clauses of the Ninth and Fourteenth Amendments to decide whether or not to continue a pregnancy, and that government may not interfere with this decision.

There has never been a Court ruling of greater importance to women than this one, for it overthrew centuries of assumptions about the right of government to limit the freedom of women. It was a liberalization of law beyond the expectations of most FEMINISTS, for at the time, only four states (Alaska, Hawaii, Washington, and New York) had statutes that met the Court's standards. The ruling, in effect, declared the laws of forty-six states to be unconstitutional and in need of revision.

The decision was announced on January 22, 1973, after hearings during the previous year. The Court's internal vote was seven to two, which was a strong enough majority to give the decision credence with the legal profession. Justice Harry Blackmun wrote the majority opinion; he doubtless was influenced by his earlier experience as a Minnesota attorney with physicians who wished to practice medicine without fear of criminal charges.

The majority opinion held that the right to an abortion in the first trimester of pregnancy was inviolable. Arguments that laws against abortion existed to protect women were set aside as unreasonable, since the procedure was demonstrably safer than carrying a pregnancy to term. After the first thirteen weeks, state laws could regulate abortion to ensure maternal health, but the option could not be prohibited until the last ten weeks of pregnancy—and even then, "the life and health of the mother" had primacy.

Reaction to the decision was dramatic. The male leadership of the Catholic church pronounced it "horrifying" and "unspeakable," while feminists and population control groups praised the Court. Throughout the rest of the century, hundreds of legislative bills and legal cases would continue to refine the meaning of *Roe vs. Wade,* but the fundamental truth of the decision—that a woman has a right to control her own body—still stands.

ROGERS, EDITH NOURSE (1881–1960)

ROGERS, EDITH NOURSE (1881–1960) The mother of the WOMEN'S ARMY CORPS, Edith Nourse Rogers set a record for female longevity in Congress, serving a total of forty-five years.

Her career would not have been predictable from her privileged upbringing, for Edith Nourse went to FINISHING SCHOOL in Europe and then married Harvard-educated attorney John Jacob Rogers in 1907. They settled in Lowell, Massachusetts, where John was elected to Congress from this district of TEX-TILE WORKERS—in 1912, the year of the giant STRIKE of the Lawrence mills. Many workers and all Massachusetts women did not vote, however, and both the Nourses and Rogers were Republicans allied with the managerial class.

Edith Nourse Rogers moved to Washington and lived the life of a society hostess until WORLD WAR I, when the horrors of war showed her the need for involvement. She worked as a Red Cross NURSE, putting in far more hours than the average volunteer, and went overseas to inspect field hospitals for the Women's Overseas Service League. Ever after, soldiers and their needs would be Rogers' prime motivation. She joined the American Legion's AUXILIARY for women after the war ended, and the Republican presidents of the twenties rewarded her with several appointments on veterans' issues.

Though she had not been active in the SUFFRAGE MOVEMENT, Rogers served as a member of the Electoral College in the presidential election of 1924. That alone would make her an interesting historical footnote: she was chosen secretary, and thus was the first woman to announce a final, official vote for president. Nonetheless, Rogers was not particularly political at this point in her life and initially had no intention of building a career when her husband died. Viewed by the Republican Party as a caretaker until the next election, she did not have to campaign to win the special election in June, 1925.

At forty-four and childless, Rogers understandably found that she enjoyed serving in Congress, and she went on to win the next seventeen elections. Her honesty, concern for her constituents, and selflessness made her extremely popular, and even after unions and the Democratic Party were strengthened in her blue-collar district during Roosevelt's New Deal, Representative Rogers continued to win reelection comfortably. She served on Veterans Affairs from the beginning of the committee's existence, and after her devotion to this cause was highlighted during WORLD WAR II, she faced no election opponents at all during the war years.

After the war, Representative Rogers was influential in drafting the historic GI Bill, and, as the most senior member of Veterans Affairs, she chaired the committee when the Republicans held the House during the Eightieth and Eighty-third Congresses. Following the precedent set by RUTH BRYAN OWEN, she also won appointment to the prestigious Foreign Affairs Committee and served there fourteen years; like FLOR-ENCE KAHN, she assiduously used her seniority to bring multi-million dollar defense contracts to her industrial and seacoast district. This specialty meant that Rogers worked closely with male lobbyists—for not only defense contractors but also veterans organizations were almost exclusively male—but this powerful woman generated little hostility and was almost invariably treated respectfully in the press.

Of greater importance to women was the attention that Rogers gave to professionalizing women's formerly voluntary wartime roles. A women's army corps, she said "would make available . . . the work of many women who cannot afford to give their services without compensation . . . From the hundreds of letters I have received since introducing the bill, it is clearly evident to me that the women of America are eager and anxious to do their part." Rogers first introduced her bill on the subject in May of 1941, but it was "tossed aside" until Pearl Harbor.

The second bill passed "only after acrid debate," including criticism by one congressman who branded it "the silliest piece of legislation that has ever come before" the House. As chief sponsor, Rogers exhibited great parliamentary skill in passing this potentially explosive legislation, even in its drafting stages when she carefully manuevered recalcitrant men in the War Department. The bill marked a great historic change in the status of women, and the 249-86 margin by which it finally passed was also a mark of the esteem that Rogers' colleagues held for her.

She continued to follow military women's issues closely, and it was she who also pushed through the 1943 bill that dropped the auxiliary status of the corps. She showed considerable candor in standing up for military women when they were accused of LESBIANISM and ILLEGITIMACY; Rogers conducted an extensive investigation of stories of widespread pregnancies among unmarried WACs, and when the rumors proved false, she demanded that news outlets right the record.

Her willingness to engage these issues of sexuality stood her in good stead a few years later, when Rogers was named a party in a 1949 divorce suit. She enjoyed such a close relationship with her campaign manager that his wife was profoundly jealous and unsuccessfully attempted to include Rogers in the court proceedings. Rogers continued to maintain her relationship with the man, and though they never married, she left her Maine vacation home to him when she died.

Her death came suddenly at seventy-nine—in the midst of still another reelection campaign. Edith Nourse Rogers received a number of honorary degrees and many awards, especially from veterans organizations and the military. Among the facilities named for her is the major museum dedicated to the Women's Army Corps at Ft. McClellan, Alabama. Her papers are at RADCLIFFE COLLEGE.

ROOSEVELT, ANNA ELEANOR (1884–1962) It is difficult to overstate the importance of Eleanor Roosevelt to the history of twentieth-century women—not only in America, but also the world. Polls of historians consistently rank her as by far the most significant First Lady, and in a recent poll, the public named her the most influential American woman of the century.

Anna Eleanor Roosevelt was born with that name; when she married her cousin Franklin, her name remained Roosevelt. She was born into a wealthy but dysfunctional family and had a painful childhood. Her mother, Anna Hall Roosevelt, died young; her alcoholic father, whom she adored, died a few years later; and her maternal grandmother made the lonely child's life miserable with attacks on her self-esteem. Timid and awkward, she believed that she compared badly with other girls, especially her brilliant and beautiful cousin, the future ALICE ROOSEVELT LONGWORTH. Her happiest days were vacations with her father's family, and she was particularly fond of her Uncle Teddy—Alice's father and a future president.

There was alcoholism in the Hall family, too, and young Eleanor lived in fear of embarrassment from uncles who shared the family's New York City mansion. Like other girls of old wealth in her era, she was educated at home by GOV-ERNESSES. Her three years at a London FINISHING SCHOOL were happier, and the politically liberal French woman who headed her school became one of her few positive role models. Still, she returned home ready for her debut and a conventional life; although she taught dance and exercise classes at a SETTLEMENT HOUSE, she had no thought of any career beyond motherhood.

Despite her conviction that she was unattractive, photos of the era show her to be a tall, pleasant-looking young woman with a lithe figure. She had beaux, and her marriage to her distant cousin was not arranged by anyone other than the couple themselves. Since he was handsome, socially-skilled, and Harvard-educated, his choice of her seems only to be explained by genuine feeling. They wed in 1905, during his first year of law school at Columbia, with President Theodore Roosevelt giving away the bride.

After an extended European honeymoon, they settled in New York City. While Franklin established his career, Eleanor bore their children—an average of one every other year for the first decade of their marriage. The first, born in 1906, was their only daughter; she was called Anna, for the first name that Eleanor had and did not use. Five sons followed, with the third lost to INFANT MORTALITY; the last was born in 1916, after the Roosevelts had moved to Washington.

Burdened with an insensitive grandmother in her youth, Eleanor Roosevelt suffered from a tyrannical mother-in-law for many of her adult years. The pattern was easily established, because Eleanor was almost constantly pregnant or in postpartum recovery and because her mother-in-law, Sara Delano Roosevelt, was a dominant personality who used her control of Franklin's money to establish herself as matriarch. She treated Eleanor like a child, belittling her in front of the children and servants and overruling her decisions. Their grandmother spoiled the children inexcusably, buying them expensive presents and undoing their parents' attempts at discipline. A political and social conservative, Sara Roosevelt spent her life trying to return her family to the days of nineteenth century upper-class privilege, and she particularly objected to Eleanor's slight involvement with settlement house and other charitable work.

Franklin, however, went his own way as a reformist Democrat—and Sara Roosevelt was as indulgent with him as she was with her grandsons. When he was elected to the New York Senate in 1910, it was fitting that a dutiful wife accompany him to political events, but Eleanor viewed politics as a cross she had to bear, opposed the SUFFRAGE MOVEMENT, and remained shy. When Democrat Woodrow Wilson was elected in 1912, Franklin was able to exercise the interest in marine activity that he shared with his uncle; he became assistant secretary of the Navy and the family moved to Washington. This new locale, which was unfamiliar territory to Sara Roosevelt, and the outbreak of WORLD WAR I that followed their move, began to change Eleanor's life.

Like other women liberated by this war, she found personal identity in wartime activity outside the home that was nonetheless respectable volunteerism. She worked long hours at hospitals, where she did tangible good for soldiers, and the experience boosted her self-esteem and developed her administrative abilities. Still, she remained so politically unsophisticated that when a newspaper interviewed her about the difficulties of coping with wartime food shortages, she naively replied that her ten servants were managing just fine.

Franklin Roosevelt made a huge career leap in 1920, when he moved from an assistant secretaryship to vice-presidential nominee. The Democrats were in retreat that year, however, and the ticket was easily defeated. Though it was the first year that women voted after passage of the NINETEENTH AMENDMENT, there was little recognition of women as a bloc. As the mother of a four-year old, Eleanor Roosevelt was excused from most campaigning and did not enjoy the little that she did. In contrast, the wife of the Republican nominee, FLORENCE HARDING, was deeply involved—although her methods were not overt.

The following year, polio struck Franklin Roosevelt. To Sara, this meant a retreat from the crass publicity of national politics to the tight family life she had always envisioned. Once it was clear that his body would survive, Sara and Eleanor, in effect, struggled over Franklin's soul and their futures. Eleanor received crucial assistance from Louis Howe, Franklin's campaign advisor, and as her husband recovered, Howe mentored her in politics so that she could provide the assistance Howe needed to revive the carefully nurtured political career. Throughout the twenties, as they moved from the family home at Hyde Park, New York, to Warm Springs, Georgia, in winter and New Brunswick's Campobello in summer, Louis Howe and Eleanor Roosevelt worked to reestablish Franklin Roosevelt as a viable national leader.

Given that his highest credential to this time was as a Cabinet assistant, this took tremendous faith—and that it actually happened took tremendous political acumen. One of the conduits that Eleanor used to achieve her long-term goal was working with women's organizations. She reactivated her membership (which Sara Roosevelt had disapproved of) in FLORENCE KELLEY's Consumer's League; she not only joined the LEAGUE OF WOMEN VOTERS, but also helped establish the legislative program of this new organization; and she made lifelong friends with radicals such as MARY ELIZABETH DREIER of the WOMEN'S TRADE UNION LEAGUE. A similar mutually beneficial relationship with MOLLY DEWSON of the Democratic Women's Clubs eventually led to contacts all over the nation, while in New York, she came to know almost every activist woman. She even worked as an English TEACHER in a progressive school run by a female friend.

She had grown into an independent woman from the timorous person she had been just four years earlier (when her husband held a much higher title), and, in the election of 1924, she earned her first detailed political experience. Beginning with her own county, she methodically organized the state's women for Al Smith—against her cousin, Republican nominee Theodore Roosevelt, Jr. Smith had earlier demonstrated his willingness to appoint women such as FRANCES PERKINS to significant offices, and in working for his election, Eleanor Roosevelt showed that her political values had moved beyond promotion of her husband's career to a solidarity with other women.

Four years later, Franklin Roosevelt replaced Smith as governor when Smith became the unsuccessful presidential nominee. That Eleanor Roosevelt had become a respected political scientist in her own right can be seen in this election of 1928, for she headed the Democrats' national campaign among women during the same time that her husband was a candidate for governor.

The Roosevelts moved into the Governor's Mansion in Albany shortly before Wall Street crashed and the Great Depression began. Responding with greater speed than other governors, FDR was clearly influenced by the extensive contacts his wife had among social workers—many of them women—who were more aware than most professionals of the effects of the ruined economy on individual lives. This progressive record stood the Roosevelt team in good stead for the presidential election of 1932.

Polio had rendered Franklin Roosevelt's legs almost useless, and because it was difficult for him to travel, Eleanor became his "legs and ears." In 1932, she began the peripatetic patterns she would follow the rest of her life, for even as a WIDOW, she traveled tens of thousands of miles annually, keenly noting the political and economic ramifications of what she observed. No wife of a previous presidential candidate was even remotely analogous to her; in just a decade, she had moved from politically unaware to one of the nation's best informed and most astute strategy setters. The Roosevelt ticket won the election by the widest margin ever, and 1936 would bring an even greater mandate, when they lost just eight of 531 electoral votes. One key to this success was the establishment of "equal division" within the Democratic Party, which gave women parity with men even on the crucial platform committee—another idea Eleanor Roosevelt promoted.

While the administration set out to solve the nation's ills on a broad front, she developed a niche as the protector of those most likely to be left out—especially women, blacks, and children. Because many Depression Era jobs projects aimed at construction of public works, men received a far higher proportion of jobs than women. Eleanor Roosevelt was not so far ahead of her time that she would argue for women in these traditionally male job slots, but she did argue for an executive order assuring that a percentage of New Deal programs be directed at women. Her office was in daily contact with Ellen Woodward, who headed the Women's Work Division of the Federal Emergency Relief Administration. She also took particular interest in the National Youth Administration, an agency that was better balanced by gender and race than most. As her reputation grew, she received unprecedented amounts of mail, and she responded to literally thousands of letters with small personal checks or help in job searches. Even hate mail received a polite response in the hope of changing minds.

The assistance she rendered to African-Americans was one of the greatest causes of hate mail and other controversy that swirled around her. Much later, the fictional Archie Bunker would say on television that America didn't have any blacks until Eleanor Roosevelt discovered them, and his comment was not far from the truthful view of many whites. She repeatedly publicized their plight during the Great Depression, and though her motives were empathetic, not political, she was largely responsible for turning this voting bloc from the party of Lincoln to that of Roosevelt.

She continued this focus despite vitriolic objections from white Southern Democrats, cheerfully accepting their outrage when she did things such as inviting the young black women of NANNIE BURROUGHS' school to the White House. She stepped up such activity after German Nazis demonstrated the dangers of racism, and in March of 1941—before America entered the WORLD WAR II—she helped dispel stereotypes by flying with black (male) pilots whose ability was questioned by Army officials. Ten days after she informed Franklin of these flights at a Tuskegee, Alabama air base, their program was funded; these men went on to shoot down some four hundred Nazi planes.

Though opportunities for female pilots of either race were more limited, the First Lady involved herself with other expansion of possibilities for black women. The best known case was the controversy over MARIAN ANDERSON's 1936 concert, in which Roosevelt dramatically resigned her membership in the DAUGHTERS OF THE AMERICAN REVOLUTION. Her friendship with MARY McLEOD BETHUNE also was widely known and was crucial to Bethune's rise as the most important black woman of her era, but Roosevelt involved herself with others who were more obscure; CRYSTAL BIRD FAUSET and MABEL STAUPERS were two examples. In one much publicized incident in Birmingham, she sat in the middle of an aisle rather than choose sides of the segregated hall.

She also exhibited concern for poor whites, especially in Appalachia and in her own rural New York, and she helped establish handicraft industries in both places. This interest in craftsmanship predated the Depression and reflected her lifelong dedication to the ideals of sturdy simplicity and permanence. The fact that these cottage industries could not compete with modern manufacturing in profitability did not bother her; she saw the ideal as more important than the bottom line.

In this, she was similar to affluent reformers who preceded her, and indeed, she counted LILLIAN WALD, JANE ADDAMS, and others as friends long before FDR became governor or president. Working-class women such as ROSE SCHNEIDERMAN and MARY ANDERSON also enjoyed her friendship, and as the years passed, many came to see her as the best possible help for their goals. In the thirties, for instance, JACKIE COCHRAN wrote her on the coming war and its potential for women pilots. Roosevelt intervened with the postmaster general when LILLIAN SMITH's work was censored, and she aided female journalists with women-only press conferences; among those to whom she gave access to important news were BESS FURMAN and GENEVIEVE HERRICK.

She selflessly encouraged the governmental careers of many women, including DAISY HARRIMAN, LORENA HICKOK, RUTH BRYAN OWEN, ANNA ROSENBERG, and the incomparable Frances Perkins, and had supportive friendships with female elected officials, including FRANCES BOLTON, MARY NORTON, MARGARET CHASE SMITH, and HELEN GAHAGAN DOUGLAS, who wrote a book on Roosevelt. Clearly, Eleanor Roosevelt understood the importance of "networking" long before that term became common. She enjoyed the company of bright women and spent a lifetime introducing them to each other, [and it is important to remember this context when evaluating her close relationship with LORENA HICKOK.]

To have been of such genuine assistance to the careers of so many, it was necessary that she cultivate her own. Though she never consciously promoted herself, she understood the potential of the position of First Lady and used it to reach beyond the confines of the White House in a way that no predecessor even contemplated. Early in the administration, she held the first press conference given by a First Lady. She began her syndicated newspaper column, "My Day," at least partly in response to the conservative commentary of her cousin Alice, and wrote regularly for LADIES HOME JOURNAL and McCall's, with occasional pieces for Vogue and other women's magazines, including that of the BUSINESS AND PROFESSIONAL WOMEN'S CLUBS. She became a union member, joining the American Newspaper Guild, and despite unkind remarks about her voice, conducted a radio show.

In all of these news outlets, she urged women to become involved and to run for office; only two years into FDR's presidency, she accepted criticism for returning to New York to campaign for Carolyn O'Day's legislative candidacy. Her issue agenda was decidedly FEMINIST, with advocacy of programs that are not yet reality such as child care subsidies and national health care. To put these ideas in writing and to speak them on radio demonstrated exceptional courage and commitment: she understood that these methods meant that she was surrendering the politician's usual shelter in a storm of controversy, for she could not claim to have been misquoted.

This directness made her critics gleeful—and critics she had. Such an assertive woman challenged the foundation of the conservative world, for not only were her political and economic views radically modern, so was her professional life. Endless commentators—usually male—scorned the First Lady in print and on radio, ridiculing not only her ideas, but especially her stout figure, toothy smile, dowdy dress, arrogant children, and negligence of social standards. When, with innovative symbolism, the White House served hot dogs to the British king and queen during the Depression, these critics were apopletic. The First Lady and her causes were regularly labeled "communistic," and ultimately the charges were so unfair that even most Republicans were embarrassed by her worst maligner, columnist Westbrook Pegler.

Some of this hostility softened as the science of polling developed and results showed high public approval rates. This was reinforced by election returns in 1940, when Eleanor Roosevelt exhibited skill at the Democratic convention by settling a serious split over the vice-presidential nominee. The 1944 election again demonstrated approval of the Roosevelt team, as unprecedented third and fourth terms confirmed the nation's choice of tested leadership when facing war.

Like the world, Eleanor Roosevelt's focus shifted from the Depression to World War II, but more than most, she blended the two eras: she remembered domestic need after the war began and yet had issued prescient warnings on fascism a decade earlier. Her internationalist roots dated to her League of Women Voters' support of peace initiatives in the twenties, and early in the presidency, she invited ANNE O'HARE MCCORMICK to the White House to raise the president's consciousness of foreign affairs. During the fascist takeover of Spain, she drew the president's attention to a protest signed by Albert Einstein and DOROTHY THOMPSON, and far earlier than most, she cried out against the situation of Jews in Europe.

FDR had appointed Jewish men to the Supreme Court and the Cabinet, but he and the State Department exhibited long-term denial of the emerging Holocaust. The public failed to appreciate Eleanor Roosevelt's point on this, too, but she received more support for the attention she gave to soldiers after the war began. As he had with the Depression, FDR

encouraged her to make personal reports; code-named "Rover" for security purposes, she traveled to all wartime fronts. Countless White House briefings began with the president saying, "My Missus says . . ."

Nonetheless, he did not quote her on everything; as is obvious in the case of Jewish refugees, he sometimes ignored important points of advice. In contrast to her straightforward earnestness, he was a political pragmatist who was capable of evading hard choices and implementing contradictory policies. On the other hand, she had one significant failing that he recognized: Eleanor Roosevelt paid little heed to budgets, or, in FDR's words, "My Missus has no sense about money." Over their decades together, each had come to understand the other's strengths and weaknesses, and especially during the thirties and forties, their relationship evolved into one that was as much professional as personal.

The war killed FDR as much as it killed combatants. The strain of years filled with long days of endless problems is clear in his last photos, where he appears gaunt and exhausted. His opportunities to get away from White House worries were limited by both his lack of mobility and the need for wartime security. Because he needed relaxation and because he had always been a more social creature than Eleanor, he sought companionship during her frequent absences with a number of women who socialized at the White House. Thus, late in the war, he resumed an earlier friendship with Lucy Mercer Rutherford.

Lucy Mercer had been Eleanor Roosevelt's social secretary when the family first moved to Washington in 1913. Some historians believe that she and Franklin had a serious affair at this time, while others think it was little more than the "hero-worship" of a guileless young woman for a handsome man whose wife was absorbed with pregnancies and babies. In any case, Eleanor became sufficiently concerned about their relationship that Lucy Mercer was dismissed; she went on to marry a man named Rutherford and did not see the Roosevelts for many years. When her husband died in 1944, Franklin Roosevelt offered his condolences in person, stopping by her New Jersey home between Washington and Hyde Park. They saw each other only a few other times, and more than one eminent historian has termed these meetings "innocent"—but the president kept them secret from his wife.

Thus, Eleanor Roosevelt was devastated to discover that her old nemesis had been present when her husband died of a cerebral hemorrhage in Warm Springs on April 12, 1945. It is possible that this was merest happenstance, for Rutherford's ostensible reason for going to Georgia was to accompany a friend who was painting the president's portrait. The circumstances looked suspicious, however, and Roosevelt was especially hurt that her daughter Anna, who often acted as FDR's social secretary, had issued the White House invitation to Rutherford. The pain that Eleanor Roosevelt felt at losing her companion of more than forty years was greatly amplified by what she saw as deceit on the part of her loved ones.

But the nation was in mourning, too. A sense of duty was always Roosevelt's strongest motivation, so she hid her hurt and accompanied the funeral train. All along the tracks from Georgia to Washington and beyond to Hyde Park, tens of thousands of people gathered, even in the middle of the night, to pay their respects to the only president that many had ever known. At the same time, they also sought a glimpse of Eleanor, for she was truly "mother to a generation." When it was over, she quickly packed her White House things and returned to the little house in the woods at Hyde Park, which she had built long ago as a refuge from the mansion. She intended to be "a nobody" and told reporters that "the story is over."

President Harry Truman had different ideas, however. Despite FDR's declining health, he did not prepare Truman for the presidency, and Truman earnestly solicited Eleanor Roosevelt's advice. She rejected proposals that she run for office, but accepted Truman's appointment as a delegate to the new United Nations—at least in part because she was disappointed that he had not appointed any women to his Cabinet. She spent New Year's Eve of 1945 on her way to London for the first meeting of this unprecedented organization.

She was the only female delegate, and the State Department's old guard doubted her diplomatic ability, but in the end, even her worst foes retracted their previous criticism after working with her. For two years during tedious meetings in Geneva, Paris, and New York, she chaired the Human Rights Commission. This was not, as some might have originally thought, an uncontroversial body, for there were endless quarrels over important issues, including approximately a million refugees from Eastern Europe whom the Soviets sought to repatriate against their will. Sometimes using her fluent French, she faced down Communists who regularly insulted her country—but not her—and ultimately brought forth a document enshrining the rights of individuals, not of states. She received a standing ovation when the Universal Declaration of Human Rights was adopted on December 10, 1948.

Serving in the UN reinforced Roosevelt's feminism. She regretted the small number of women in international delegations and the obtuse behavior of many of the men, writing for example, "I notice that men always feel very passionately about rules." When work was delayed because of a Paris excursion, she added, "the boys, no matter, what their age, can't resist a good time." After she came to understand that "all men are created equal" would be taken literally in many nations, she assisted the women's caucus in drafting gender-neutral language. She even began to have second thoughts on the EQUAL RIGHTS AMENDMENT, after a lifetime of reasoned opposition to it.

Her UN service came to an end with Eisenhower's election, but Roosevelt remained active throughout the fifties. She supported the new state of Israel, spoke out against McCarthyism, and campaigned for her close friend Adlai Stevenson in 1952 and 1956. She had rejected conventional widowhood when she resumed her newspaper column the week following her husband's funeral, and she continued to write. At seventy-five, she began teaching at the new Brandeis University; she faithfully met her classes, while carrying out other obligations on weekends. After she realized that she could charge large fees that she could then donate to charity, she began television appearances. She even found time to write on how she maintained this energy level.

These years were saddened by quarrels between her sons over their father's bequests and their political careers. Moreover, for the first time in her life, she had financial concerns. Even though she earned as much as one hundred thousand dollars annually from writing and speaking, her inheritance was not large and she felt obliged to donate much of her income to projects to which she was committed. Children were her greatest joy, and she gave frequent parties for them.

Soon after he took office, President Kennedy reappointed her to the UN, and the next year, she chaired his Commission on the Status of Women. In this last official duty of her life, she worked for the EQUAL PAY ACT that was passed the following year, but by the summer of 1962, she was increasingly ill. Her pain and fever was misdiagnosed for several months, while she grew restive and impatient. Finally hospitalized for a rare form of tuberculosis, she did not want her life prolonged; she tried to avoid medication and barred virtually all visitors, for she did not wish to be seen as anything except the activist that she was. She celebrated her seventy-eighth birthday with a party for children only, and died in her New York City apartment a few weeks later.

Among the books she left are: *This Is My Story* (1937), *My Days* (1938), *The Moral Basis of Democracy* (1940), *This I Remember* (1949), *On My Own* (1948), *India and the Awakening East* (1953), *You Learn By Living* (1960), and *Autobiography* (1961). *The Wisdom of Eleanor Roosevelt* is a compilation of her columns for *McCall's*, while *Ladies of Courage* (1954), which she co-wrote with Lorena Hickok, may be her most useful book for feminists.

President Kennedy nominated Eleanor Roosevelt for the Nobel Peace Prize because of the crucial role she played as chairman of the committee that drafted the Universal Declaration of Human Rights. Though she was never awarded the prize, she received countless other honors. None of them seemed to matter very much to her, however; instead of accumulating lists of awards, she expended some of her last energy on lists of people to whom she intended to send presents. The soul of generosity, she is buried at Hyde Park, where her papers are also preserved.

ROSE, ERNESTINE LOUISE (1810–1892)

Though the U.S. was neither the land of her birth nor her death, Ernestine Rose deserves a place in the history of American women because of her early dedication to the cause. Indeed, SUSAN ANTHONY placed Rose third in chronology, after only FRANCES WRIGHT and Mary Wollstonecraft, the author of VINDICATION OF THE RIGHTS OF WOMEN. Rose is also unusual in that she was one of the few Jewish women active in the almost wholly Protestant SUFFRAGE MOVEMENT.

Reputedly very beautiful, she was called the "Queen of the Platform" not only for her exceptional style, but also for the clarity and strength of her speech—another demonstration of Rose's abilities, for English was not her native language. She showed argumentation skills as a teenager, when she went to court in Poland in 1826 to argue against limitations on her inheritance from her mother and especially against the DOWRY and arranged marriage that her father planned. Victorious, she left for Berlin in 1828 and later moved on to Paris and London. During part of this time, she supported herself by inventing and marketing a very modern idea—a room deodorizer.

At some point after learning English, she adopted "Ernestine Louise" as her name, leaving behind her original name of Siismund Potowski. This was part of the assimilation process of many IMMIGRANT WOMEN, and in her case, it was particularly likely because she had early rebelled against the theology of Judaism. When she married London jeweler William Rose in 1836, her name was finalized.

Only months after their immigration to New York, Ernestine Rose followed up on the ideas of her teenage court case by working for MARRIED WOMEN'S PROPERTY RIGHTS. She wrote later that in 1836, "I sent the first petition to the New York Legislature to give a married woman the right to hold real estate in her own name . . . After a good deal of trouble, I obtained five signatures." When the SENECA FALLS WOMEN'S RIGHTS CONVENTION occurred in 1848, Rose had already addressed the legislature five times. Meanwhile she also involved herself with utopianism and regularly shared her antireligious views in a radical Boston newspaper, a practice that she maintained for decades.

That Rose remained in high positions within the women's movement despite her objections to religiosity is testament to the strength of her personality and diplomatic ability. As early as the 1851 women's rights convention, for example, she argued against a resolution offered by REVEREND ANTOINETTE BROWN (later BLACKWELL), which stated that "the Bible recognizes the rights . . . of women." Rose's argument that "we require no written authority from Moses or Paul" carried the day, and Brown's resolution was not adopted. Both Rose's Jewish heritage and her married state probably were important factors that allowed her to make controversial points and yet maintain her popularity.

She embarked on a PUBLIC SPEAKING career almost as soon as she arrived in America, and as early as 1844, Rose lectured "in the backwoods of Ohio." The following year found her lobbying the legislature of frontier Michigan, and in 1850, she attended the first national women's rights meeting that followed up the Seneca Falls Convention. In 1854, she accompanied Anthony and others to Washington, speaking at meetings along the way in Philadelphia and Baltimore; when they returned, Anthony overcame "objections that she [Rose] is an atheist," to see Rose elected president of the National Women's Rights Convention. She and Antoinette Brown Blackwell clashed again at the 1860 convention over a DIVORCE resolution.

The emergence of the CIVIL WAR made Jews acceptable even in the South. Despite Rose's obvious preference for feminist issues over those of ABOLITIONISTS, she was welcomed in the LOYAL LEAGUE and in the postwar AMERICAN EQUAL RIGHTS ASSOCIATION. When some women in the latter organization "insisted that they did not want political rights," Rose was among those who made "powerful" speeches in rebuttal. By the end of her career, she had lectured in at least twenty-three states and was a particularly valued ally of ELIZABETH CADY STANTON, who shared her opinion on religion.

But in 1869—the year that Anthony and Stanton left the American Equal Rights Association and the women's movement divided—the Roses moved permanently to England. Anthony honored her departure by "securing a handsome sum of money and a number of presents for her." Rose returned for an 1873 meeting of the NATIONAL WOMAN SUFFRAGE ASSOCIATION, but she turned down Anthony's offer to write a segment of the *HISTORY OF WOMAN SUFFRAGE* in an 1877 letter, saying that as she "did not intend to publish anything about myself,"

Rose had kept no records. At the time that she was active, she added, "The press was not sufficiently educated in the rights of women . . . to report speeches as it does now." In 1883, Anthony visited her in England, where she found Rose "vastly more isolated . . . than fifty years ago with us." She and Stanton then made sure that Ernestine Rose was accorded her proper historical place after Rose died at eighty-two in Brighton.

ROSENBERG, ANNA MARIE LEDERER (1902–1983)

The only woman to have served at the rank of assistant secretary of defense, Anna Rosenberg won that appointment from President Truman in a supposedly regressive era for women. She was appointed in 1950 at the special request of Defense Secretary George C. Marshall, who had observed her work during WORLD WAR II. "Feminine and frilly as she is," said ELEANOR ROOSEVELT, "with the Army, Air Force, and Marine Corps and the nation's top industrialists and labor leaders to choose from, he wanted her."

A highly paid labor relations expert prior to the war, Rosenberg exhibited a special talent for negotiation and diplomacy, enabling her to "stop fights before they started." Though Roosevelt traveled tens of thousands of miles herself during the war, she credited Rosenberg with "knowing more Army privates than anyone else." This was because FDR, who liked to send incognito staff to check on his administrators, authorized Rosenberg to report on morale in the European theater of war. She ate GI rations, slept on the ground, and after returning, made some four hundred telephone calls at her own expense to the families of troops. In October, 1945, Anna Rosenberg was rewarded with the Medal of Freedom—the first woman to receive this award to civilians who perform meritorious service.

Prior to the war, Rosenberg had been a regional director of the New Deal's National Recovery Administration. Roosevelt had further demonstrated his confidence in her with appointments to the board that set policy for the administration of Social Security when that program was new, and her labor relations background also was responsible for her seat on the War Manpower Commission.

Among other things, Rosenberg used her position in the Defense Department to ensure the inclusion of almost fifty women on an advisory committee that followed up the WOMEN'S ARMED SERVICES INTEGRATION ACT. Unfortunately, her tenure at the Pentagon coincided with increased anti-Semitism in the U.S., and the similarity of her name with that of ETHEL ROSENBERG was doubtlessly a factor in her disappearance from public life. When the Eisenhower administration began in 1953, she returned to New York and died there at eighty-one.

ROSENBERG, ETHEL GREENGLASS (1915–1953)

The only woman in American history to be executed for espionage, Ethel Rosenberg and her husband Julius were sentenced to death on April 5, 1951.

The era was one of deepest paranoia about communism, and the Rosenbergs were convicted of giving secret information on atomic weaponry to the Soviet Union. It was also a time when there was fairly open anti-Semitism—some of it ironically based on resentment of the Holocaust victims of WORLD WAR II.

Ethel Greenglass grew up amid the Jewish poor on New York's Lower East Side, where the majority of the population held leftist political views during the Great Depression. While her opinions may have been termed radical, her life was conventional: after high school, she worked at clerical jobs and lived at home. Though she was a talented semiprofessional entertainer, she married Julius Rosenberg in 1939 and continued to work as a stenographer while putting him through college.

After graduating in 1941, he worked as a civilian engineer for the Army Signal Corps. Ethel Rosenberg continued to live an unexceptional life throughout WORLD WAR II, becoming a mother in 1943—the same year that her brother, David Greenglass, was assigned to the ultrasecret Los Alamos, New Mexico laboratory that finalized the atomic bomb's components. Both he and Julius Rosenberg held low-level positions that were unlikely to give them access to highly classified material, and Rosenberg's job performance was good enough to merit several promotions—until the war's end, when he was fired, apparently because of union activism, in 1945.

He was not successful in finding a steady job, and Ethel was ill much of this time. When a second boy was born to them in 1947, she had little energy for anything beyond her family and was increasingly depressed and anxious, which alienated her from family and friends. Suddenly in the summer of 1950, her brother and then her husband were arrested for stealing atomic secrets and passing them on to the Soviets. Ethel Rosenberg's arrest followed a few weeks later, and though both she and her husband continued to insist on their innocence, they were indicted.

She was confined to a women's prison in New York for eight months, even though no specific evidence was offered to support the charge of "conspiracy to commit espionage." Finally, in February of 1951, she was accused of typing secret information for her brother—by her sister-in-law, Ruth Greenglass, who was never indicted. Ethel's brother pled guilty to reduced charges and received a light sentence; with the Greenglasses as the primary witnesses against them, the Rosenbergs were tried and convicted.

The judge's sentence of death came as a shock to civil libertarians throughout the world, for it was far more severe than the prison term initially recommended even by infamous FBI director J. Edgar Hoover. The case was viewed as a gross miscarriage of justice by many, but they rallied to the cause in vain. While Ethel Rosenberg spent the next two years in solitary confinement as the only woman in New York's notorious Sing Sing prison, President Truman refused a 1952 appeal for clemency, as did Eisenhower in 1953. Liberal Supreme Court Justice William Douglas stayed the execution on June 17, 1953, but his colleagues reversed that two days later.

The decision was a tragic aberration in American history; the Rosenbergs were not only the first civilians ever executed for espionage, they were also the first people of either military or civilian status to be executed for spying during peacetime. Worse, the charge against Ethel Rosenberg was not treason, but merely "conspiracy to commit . . ." and moreover, the U.S. and the Soviet Union were allies during World War II and technically remained so. When Ethel Rosenberg's presumed actions are compared with the overt behavior of BELLE BOYD, ROSE GREENHOW, and others during the CIVIL WAR, it seems that she was executed more because of her Jewish heritage and her leftist political views than for genuinely treasonous action.

Ethel Rosenberg, along with her husband, died in the electric chair at Sing Sing on June 19, 1953—the day following their fourteenth wedding anniversary. The actuality of their deaths may have shocked the nation into ending the era's reign of intellectual terror, and the chief leader, Senator Joseph McCarthy, was formally condemned by his colleagues the following year. Ethel Rosenberg, however, was dead at thirty-seven, leaving two sons under eleven. They have tried to avenge their parents' lives since reaching adulthood.

ROSS, BETSY (ELIZABETH GRISCOM ROSS ASHBURN CLAYPOOL) (1752–1836)

Like many other colonial women, Betsy Ross was a businesswoman throughout her long life, during which time she was WIDOWED twice and married three times. Nor was her primary occupation the seamstress work that might be expected; Ross (who is known by her first husband's name, though that was the briefest of her three marriages) ran a thriving upholstering business in Philadelphia, at a time when that was the nation's largest city.

She married late in 1773; in January 1776, her husband died in an accidental gunpowder explosion while on guard duty for the Patriots. George Washington is said to have commissioned Ross to make an American flag six months later, in June of 1776. The job presumably was offered to her because an uncle of her late husband's was a signer of the Declaration and a friend of Washington's. Soon after the presumed event, Betsy Ross remarried and lost her second husband to the Revolution as well: naval officer Joseph Ashburn died in a British prison in 1782.

Her place in American history rests solely on the flag making episode, yet it is possible that this event—the only glimpse of women's history in many older textbooks—never occurred. That there was no contemporaneous record of it is not surprising, for the independence that would be declared in Philadelphia the following month was, of course, treason to the prevailing government. It would be understandable therefore if Washington and Ross conspired secretly—but if the event was of the historical importance that has been attached to it, what is surprising is that Washington later offered no substantiation of the tale.

Washington was assiduous about honoring women whose aid was valuable. He found time in the crisis year of 1776, for example, to thank African-American PHILLIS WHEATLEY for her poems on independence; while president, he served as a pallbearer for ELIZA PINCKNEY; later, he praised and promoted the work of JUDITH SARGENT MURRAY. Clearly, Washington was not reluctant to applaud women, and the omission of any mention of Ross from his records—as well as those of other contemporaries, including historian MERCY OTIS WARREN—is the strongest evidence that Ross' services, if any, were not considered greatly significant.

In fact, numerous flags were used during the Revolution by various military units. In all probability, Betsy Ross did create at least one, for there is a record of payment to her for "ship's colours, etc." in May of 1777 (a month prior to her marriage to the naval officer), but the payment was from the state of Pennsylvania, not from Washington's Continental

Congress. In June, Congress adopted a flag of "thirteen stripes in alternate red and white . . . and thirteen stars, white in a field of blue." There was no mention of Ross in connection with this flag. Moreover, Washington, camped in Cambridge, had recorded: "we hoisted the union flag in compliment to the United States"—on January 4, 1776, or a year-and-a-half prior to the adoption of the flag associated with Ross in Philadelphia. Since Washington already had a flag, he was not likely to have been the driving force behind the creation of another one.

Most telling of all is that the first written account of the Betsy Ross tale did not occur until almost a hundred years after the event presumably took place. Betsy Ross' grandson presented this family oral history in 1870 to a local historical society meeting. By then, no one was alive who could confirm or deny it, and, encouraged by the growing cult of femininity in the late nineteenth century, the story soon took root in American culture. *Harper's* reprinted it in 1873, and within the next decade, it appeared in schoolbooks as factual history. A painting of the presumed event that was exhibited at the 1893 COLUMBIAN EXPOSITION lent further credence to Betsy Ross as the designer of the American flag.

She may indeed have played a role in the evolution of the flag, for she clearly did manufacture "colours." The point that is lost in her legend, however, is that many other women doubtless were involved in the sewing of most of the era's several flags. The embellishment of the Ross story beyond all merit thus unfairly diminishes the far more valuable services of REVOLUTIONARY WAR WOMEN such as BETSY HAGER, SARAH BRADLEE FULTON, DEBORAH SAMPSON, and others.

Like CLARA BARTON and other female historical figures, Betsy Ross has been remembered for something that she might not have done at all rather than for her actual accomplishments. She bore seven children by two husbands, twice was widowed because of the Revolution, ran a profitable enterprise, and invested in land. When she died at eighty-four, Betsy Ross left a valuable estate and a successful business—which was run by a daughter.

ROSS, NELLIE TAYLOE (1876?–1977)

Known as the first woman governor of a state, Wyoming's Nellie Tayloe Ross was actually elected on the same day as MIRIAM "MA" FERGUSON in Texas, but Ross was inaugurated two weeks earlier and thus is recognized as the first. Both were elected in 1924, which was the first presidential election year in which women had enough lead time to campaign after the passage of the NINETEENTH AMENDMENT in 1920. Ross, however, theoretically could have been elected much earlier, for Wyoming women had the vote since 1869.

Born in St. Joseph, Missouri, which was a longtime "jumping off" place for wagon trains, Ross benefited from the strong heritage of WESTERN WOMEN. She accompanied her attorney husband to Cheyenne as a bride in 1902 and lived a conventional life until his death in 1924. He was then in the middle of a term as governor, and she was elected to fill the two years remaining until the next regularly scheduled gubernatorial election. On January 5, 1925, the nation had its first female governor.

A Democrat, she served until January of 1927, having lost the 1926 election. She did not give up on a political career, however, and was elected to the state legislature. After leading women in the losing presidential campaign of Democratic nominee Al Smith in 1928, Ross achieved national success in 1932. Franklin Roosevelt—who appointed many women, including FRANCES PERKINS and RUTH BRYAN OWEN—was quick to reward Ross for her loyalty to the Democratic Party and appointed her director of the U.S. Mint less than two months after he took office.

The first woman to serve in this position, she found a demoralized staff and a meager budget, but went on to skillfully administer the office. After overcoming the problems of the Great Depression, she dealt with those of WORLD WAR II, including a severe paper shortage. Like Perkins, Ross was one of the few early Roosevelt appointees to serve during his entire time in office; moreover, she stayed through the Truman administration. Ross retired, after twenty years as director of the Mint, in 1953 when Republican Dwight Eisenhower became president.

She was the first American woman to have her image struck on a medal made by the Mint and is also honored on the cornerstone of the famous Fort Knox gold depository, which was built under her leadership. Though she is usually remembered for her governorship of Wyoming, Nellie Tayloe Ross actually spent much of her life in Washington. She retired there and lived on to 101. Seemingly a living anachronism, her death in the same year as Elvis Presley's was little noted.

ROWLANDSON, MARY WHITE (c.1635– after 1678)

The AUTHOR of one of the earliest and most enduring pieces of literature based on the American experience, Mary Rowlandson wrote of the three months that she spent as a captive during the Massachusetts conflict with natives that is known as King Phillip's War.

She had emigrated from England as a child and grew up in the New England town of Salem, moving further west shortly before her marriage to Reverend Joseph Rowlandson in 1656. Mary Rowlandson bore four children, lost one to INFANT MORTALITY, and like other FRONTIER WOMEN, spent a good deal of time alone while her husband traveled his circuit of churches. She was alone with the three children when Wampanoags attacked her village of Lancaster on February 10, 1676.

Twelve settlers were killed; "there was one," Rowlandson wrote later, "who was chopped into the head with a hatchet, and stripped naked, and yet was crawling up and down." Twenty-four were taken prisoner, including Mary Rowlandson and her children. The older two were taken from her, while she and her youngest both bore bullet wounds as they force-marched with the fleeing Wampanoags. The first night Rowlandson sat "in the snow, by a little fire . . . with my sick Child in my lap, and calling much for water, being now fallen into a violent fever." They pressed on for a week in this terrible condition before her daughter died.

Rowlandson recovered from her wounds to spend the rest of the winter and early spring in anxiety and privation, while migrating several hundred miles. At the same time, she exhibited great resourcefulness in bartering amenities for herself and in arranging her own ransom. Both her courage and her needlework skills evidently impressed some of the natives, and they seemed fond of her by the time that she was released on May 2. She then had to wait several weeks for her children, who had been separated from each other far away.

Reverend Rowlandson died the following spring, and his WIDOW may or may not have still been alive when her account of the ordeal was published in Boston in 1682. Mary Rowlandson clearly had a talent for writing, and her dramatic tale has been re-read for three centuries. The oldest copy of *The Soveraignty and Goodness of God . . . A Narrative of the Captivity and Restauration of Mrs. Mary Rowlandson* (1682) belongs to the Boston Public Library. It has been reissued in at least thirty editions.

ROWSON, SUSANNA HASWELL (c.1762–1824) Known

as an AUTHOR and educator, Susanna Rowson also incorporated several other occupations into her fascinating life.

Her father was a governmental official in colonial Massachusetts and, like other Loyalists among REVOLUTIONARY WAR WOMEN, she suffered an impoverished youth. Even after the family's return to England, their need for income required her to work as a GOVERNESS. This experience gave her the opportunity to travel and provided ideas for fiction, and she published her first novel, *Victoria,* in 1786.

She wed the following year, and the difficulties of this marriage became the basis for the novel for which Rowson is best known, *Charlotte Temple: A Tale of Truth* (1791). Again, the need for income impelled her to write and even to act at a time when ACTRESSES were socially unacceptable—especially in America, where the Rowsons moved in 1793. She both acted in and wrote plays that were performed in Philadelphia and Baltimore, as well as in her home city of Boston. At least two of her plays had feminist connotations, and Rowson also played the trumpet—an unusual instrument for women—in public performances. Her genuinely cultured background and friendships with British nobility allowed her to overcome the stigma that otherwise may have attached to these unconventionalities.

In 1797, Rowson showed further enterprise by opening an academy for "young ladies" in Medford, Massachusetts, thus becoming one of the first women to establish an institute for girls that went beyond the elementary teaching of DAME SCHOOLS. At the time, little education was offered to young women—and most of what was available was operated by men. Rowson's academy proved tremendously popular after a later move to Boston, and it provided her with income until retirement in 1822. A model for the nineteenth century's FINISHING SCHOOLS, its curriculum differed from most in that it encouraged PUBLIC SPEAKING.

Rowson wrote textbooks for her students and other nonfiction, as well as songs and poetry. She also is entitled to a place in the history of American journalism as the editor of the *Boston Weekly Magazine* from 1802–1805. She published several other novels, including a sequel to *Charlotte Temple,* but never duplicated its success. Issued in America in 1794, it is considered the nation's first bestseller and was reprinted two hundred times during its first one hundred years. It is important to remember, however, that despite the obvious popularity of her work, Rowson still found it necessary to seek the more traditional occupation of TEACHING to support herself.

Susanna Rowson probably was upwards of eighty-five when she died in Boston. Her *Charlotte Temple,* with its criticism of double standards and foreshadowing of FEMINIST themes, is still taught as a beginning point in the development of the American novel.

RUSSELL SAGE FOUNDATION Endowed by Margaret Slo-

cum Sage in remembrance of her husband, financier Russell Sage, the foundation was of particular importance to the history of American women both because it funded women's organizations and because the foundation's sociological records provide us with massive documentation on the lives of needy women.

While Sage's political and social opinions were not especially enlightened, she had graduated from EMMA WILLARD's Troy Female SEMINARY in 1847—a time when few women sought any advanced education. Firm in her duty to others, she was far more generous than her husband; she gave approximately $80 million to charitable, educational, and artistic causes after becoming a childless WIDOW in 1906.

Among the beneficiaries were the YOUNG WOMEN'S CHRISTIAN ASSOCIATION, the New York Woman's Hospital and the Emma Willard School. Sage added a vocational college for women to its campus in 1916, which she named for her late husband, and she bought the island estate of SUSAN and ANNA WARNER, which she donated to West Point Academy. The total amount of her contributions makes Margaret Sage the equivalent of Andrew Carnegie and other more famous philanthropists.

She set up her foundation in 1907, at a time when the new field of sociology was attempting to formulate principles of "scientific charity." The Russell Sage Foundation thus became a leading record keeper of the behavior of poor families, as sociologists endowed by the foundation (often women) recorded the minutia of household income and expenses (almost always managed by women) to justify charitable grants. Much of this research was published, and the result is that detailed information is available to historians on many aspects of early twentieth-century households, especially among IMMIGRANT WOMEN. Examples of these publications include KATHERINE ANTHONY, *Mothers Who Must Earn;* SOPHONISBA BRECKINRIDGE and EDITH ABBOTT, *The Delinquent Child and the Home;* ELIZABETH BEARDSLEY BUTLER, *Women and the Trades;* and MARY VAN KLEECK, *Artificial Flower Makers* and *Working Girls in Evening Schools*—all of which were issued with foundation support between 1909 and 1917.

Margaret Sage died in 1918, but the Russell Sage Foundation continued its efforts to improve American life throughout the rest of the century. With projects including educational innovation, city planning, penology, and folk arts, it served as a model for other planned giving. Sage's will provided that only the interest income from the original endowment could be spent, and the foundation thus remains headquartered in New York.

S

SACAJAWEA (c.1786–1812) Along with POCAHONTAS, Sacajawea is the best known of Native American women; the fact that both are remembered for the assistance that they rendered to white men is an aspect of national history that deserves more thoughtful attention that it has received.

Clearly a bright and resourceful person, Sacajawea was a member of the Shoshoni (Snake) tribe that centered itself in modern Idaho. She first encountered whites when she was separated from her people by warfare with an enemy tribe, the Hidatsa; taken captive about 1800, her fate became tied to that of a French Canadian, Toussaint Charbonneau, who lived among the natives. By 1804, she was pregnant with Charbonneau's child.

Sacajawea (which has been variously spelled, including Sakakawea, Sacagawea, and others) met the men of the Lewis & Clark Expedition when both the natives and the newcomers camped along the Missouri River in what is now North Dakota during the winter of 1804–1805. Meriwether Lewis and William Clark sought out the white Charbonneau, and the link to Sacajawea naturally followed. They were pleased to have a native escort them into the unknown; she doubtless was grateful for the opportunity to return to her family.

Thus Sacajawea, Charbonneau, and their infant Jean Baptiste accompanied Lewis & Clark when they set off in April of 1805. Departing when her postpartum period was barely over, Sacajawea was alone amid the party of men. While breastfeeding her child, she not only acted as a guide into the unmapped wilderness, but also interpreted the languages of other tribes, crafted moccasins and other items from animal skins, and introduced the men to native plants for food and medicine. The pitfalls that she helped them avoid were eased by the presence of her baby, which indicated to natives that these white men considered themselves peaceful scientists, not an invading army.

The group saw their first Shoshoni on August 17, after traveling hundreds of miles over the prairies and into the Rockies. During Sacajawea's long exile, her brother had become chief of the Lemhi band of the Shoshonis; this proved of tremendous assistance, for Lemhis then escorted the whites over the treacherous Continental Divide. Sacajawea spent the winter of 1805–1806 with her people, while more experienced scouts helped the Lewis & Clark party accomplish its aim of reaching the Pacific. When the expedition returned in the spring of 1806, she traveled with them again, showing them through the Big Hole and Bozeman Passes of the Bitterroot Mountain Range, where elevations top seven thousand feet. A portion of southwestern Montana near the Idaho border is now named the Sacajawea Historical Area.

Clearly affected by her experience with the whites, Sacajawea settled with Charbonneau in St. Louis in 1810, where she adopted the dress of white women. Presumably this urban situation did not prove as satisfactory as either had hoped, and Sacajawea was described as "sickly" when they returned to the Dakota country the next year. Most historians believe that she was "Charbonneau's Snake Squaw" who is recorded as dying at the Army's encampment of Fort Manuel Lisa near modern Omaha on December 20, 1812.

Some give credence to a Wyoming woman who claimed that she was Sacajawea and who died on the Snake reservation of Wind River in 1884. A 1978 book based on this version proved very popular; the eight months it spent on bestseller lists—despite its nearly thirteen hundred pages—is a keen indication of continuing interest in this remarkable woman. The claims of the Wind River woman seem unlikely, however, partly because of the extreme age she would have been in 1884 if she also had been old enough to bear a child in 1804. More important is the fact that Jean Baptiste Charbonneau's well-documented life provides no indication of a long-lived mother.

In either case, however, Sacajawea indisputably was less than thirty when she made her immense contribution to the first exploration of much of modern America. Without her assistance, Lewis & Clark might well have failed to survive their perilous journey, and the pattern of western settlement probably would have slowed. William Clark showed his respect for Sacajawea by educating her son, and the records of the Lewis & Clark Expedition—which are subject to no debates on authenticity—testify to the esteem that the explorers had for her.

There probably are more monuments honoring Sacajawea than any other American woman, with the 1905 centennial of the Lewis & Clark exploration doing a great deal to preserve her memory. The NATIONAL AMERICAN WOMAN SUFFRAGE ASSOCIATION recognized the centennial by holding its annual convention in Oregon, where SUSAN ANTHONY, ANNA HOWARD SHAW, and others "paid a glowing tribute to this Indian woman." IDA HUSTED HARPER added that the unveiling of a statue of Sacajawea was "very significant of the changing sentiment toward women . . ."

SALEM WITCH TRIALS (1692)

That some women chose death over dishonesty is the great lesson of the Salem witch trials. They probably could have saved themselves with false confession, for no one who "admitted" to witchcraft was executed. Presumably each woman who died preferred to preserve her good opinion of herself, as well as to maintain an honest relationship with a personal God unfamiliar to the clergy who ruled Massachusetts.

Seventeenth-century New England was a theocracy in which church officials held power comparable to that of modern state officials. Crimes of thought were treated with a severity at least as great as that rendered to common crime. In the minds of most, witches (female) and wizards (male) held real and criminal powers, and the devil walked the New England landscape as well as God. Because women were deemed both intellectually and morally inferior to men, they were thought more culpable to Satan, and witchcraft was thus a far greater threat than wizardry. These were firm facts to most colonists, for their cultural heritage came directly from medieval Europe. Nor was this heritage remote, for the second generation of settlers had just come of age when the famous trials were held, and moreover, witches had been executed throughout New England's brief history.

The records of one minister reflect an almost casual acceptance of that tragic fact—until his own wife was accused. The first witch executed, he wrote, "was a woman of Charleston" who had been put to death in "1647 or 1648." She had been "suspected partly because that after some angry words passing between her and her Neighbors, some mischief befell such Neighbors . . . or the like." Similarly vague explanations

were sufficient for him to justify the deaths of women in Dorchester, Boston, "and two or three in Springfield . . . and another at Hartford. I have also heard of a Girl at New Haven or Stratford . . ."

With such trivialization of the deaths of women by a community leader, it was hardly surprising that people who wished to draw attention to themselves or to retaliate at enemies felt little compunction about bringing charges of witchcraft. The causes of the Salem hysteria have been long debated, with theories ranging from political power struggles to fungus in the local grain, but the era's women are always at the center of discussion, for both the victims and their accusers were primarily female. In general, it was young women and girls who brought the charges against older women, while the officials hearing the cases and issuing the orders were all male. These men listened respectfully to the testimony of girls—often in the form of frenzied screaming—while they exhibited extreme prejudice against the reasoned responses of women who were more nearly their age.

This was the case, for example, in the execution of Martha Corey. A "respectable" woman, Corey presumably paid little attention to the February 29 arrests of two white women of lesser note and of Tituba, a slave who belonged to the minister of Salem Village Church. Tituba came from the Caribbean, and it was her voodoo tales that are thought to have begun the hysteria among the town's girls. On March 20, however, "Goodwife Corey was present in the Meetinghouse [when Abigail Williams] called out, 'Look where Goodwife Corey sits on the Beam suckling her Yellow Bird!' "

On this and similarly slender evidence, the magistrates questioned Corey the next day: "The worshipful Mr. Hathorne asked her, Why she afflicted those Children? She said she did not Afflict them. He asked her, who did then? She said I do not know. How should I know?" The interrogation continued, with the woman rationally and even sympathetically responding to the seemingly endlessly gullible men. The girls, Corey said, "were poor, distracted children" to whom "no heed" should be paid, but "Mr. Hathorne and Mr. Noyes replied, it was the judgement of all that were present, they were Bewitched, and only she, the Accused Person said, they were Distracted . . ."

Like dozens of women to come, Martha Corey was imprisoned; their Puritan modesty was violated there by repeated bodily searches for the telltale marks of Satan. The arrests continued through the spring, and on June 10, Bridget Bishop was the first to be hung. Eventually 141 residents of modern Salem and Danvers were charged with witchcraft. Of those, fifty-eight were indicted and twenty-nine convicted. Six escaped the gallows by "confessing"—as had many of those whose cases did not result in convictions. Of the remaining twenty-three, nineteen were hanged, three died in jail, and one was pressed to death with rocks. The latter was Martha Corey's husband, who at first stupidly witnessed against her; he was one of the four men executed.

Among the women hanged was Rebecca Nurse, the English-born wife of a wealthy landowner and mother of eight. She had a spotless reputation, was upwards of seventy and deaf, but even though some forty prominent Salem citizens courageously signed a petition on her behalf, the lieutenant governor who presided over the trial virtually ordered a finding of guilt. She was executed in a mass hanging on July 19; one of her sisters died in the second one on September 22. It was the Nurse family that made the strongest efforts to end the reign of terror, and later, to force amends for the stigma of execution.

The autumn hangings seemed to sober the town, and in late October, the special court conducting the trials was terminated. With dozens of Salem families personally affected, the governor pardoned those who remained in jail the following spring. The Salem trials, piled upon the history of ANNE HUTCHINSON and MARY DYER, proved the beginning of the end of violence against women in the name of religion. As the enormity of their excess began to sink in on those responsible, reverse confessions took place. One of the ten trial judges admitted his guilt within five years of the hangings (perhaps not coincidentally, this man owed his place in society to his wife's fortune). The Nurse family saw that the clergyman who owned Tituba and who led the trials resigned from the ministry. Martha Corey's church restored her membership in 1707 after the confession of Ann Putnam, who—as a twelve-year-old—had been a leading accuser.

The town of Salem finally erected a monument on Gallows Hill for the three hundredth anniversary of the hangings in 1992. The name of each victim is listed along with the date and method of execution. At the same time, the trivialization of the tragedy continues, as the town's vehicles feature witches on broomsticks.

SAMPSON, DEBORAH (1760–1827)

Like a number of other REVOLUTIONARY WAR WOMEN, Deborah Sampson actually engaged in combat. Pride in this achievement, however, should be tempered with the notation that she did not join the military until the war was virtually over.

A descendent of PRISCILLA MULLINS ALDEN and other original colonists, Sampson grew up in the towns of Massachusetts' South Shore. Despite this illustrious ancestry, her father did such a poor job of supporting his family that Deborah became an INDENTURED SERVANT at about ten. Her conditions were not severe, however, and she attended school in winter when there was less farm work to be done; in the summer, she not only helped with the housework, but also plowed and planted like a man. Above average in height, she grew strong through hard labor.

When her servitude ended in 1779, Sampson had gained enough education that she was hired as a TEACHER in the Middleborough public schools; she was still there in November, 1780, but exactly how long she taught after that is unclear. On May 23, 1782, when she was twenty-one, Deborah Sampson was mustered into the Fourth Massachusetts Regiment at Worcester. She used the PSEUDONYM of Robert Shurtleff, which has also been spelled Shirtliff or Shirtlieff. Though she obviously kept her gender secret, rumors circulated back home, and in the fall of that year, her Middleborough church ex-communicated Sampson for "dressing in men's clothes, and enlisting as a soldier in the Army." By then, however, Sampson's regiment was gone from Massachusetts.

The English surrender at Yorktown in October of 1781 (seven months prior to Sampson's enlistment) had resulted in Parliament's vote that warfare cease. While peace negotiations were conducted in Paris throughout 1782, military units in America nevertheless remained on alert. Sampson's regiment was sent to West Point, where she apparently participated in several engagements in that area of New York, including one at Tarrytown in which she was wounded.

Her gender was finally discovered when she was hospitalized in Philadelphia for fever, but her physician is said to have kept this secret. Deborah Sampson, posing as Robert Shurtleff, was discharged from the service by General Henry Knox (later the first secretary of war) at West Point on October 25, 1783, about six weeks after the final peace treaty was signed.

Afterwards, she returned to conventional dress, married a farmer named Gannett, and bore three children. She was rewarded with a pension from the state of Massachusetts less than a decade after the war was over; a lump payment in 1792, it bore interest accumulated since her discharge in 1783. The authenticity of her service was further attested to by Paul Revere, when his 1804 letter to Congress on her behalf resulted in payment of a U.S. pension the next year. More strikingly, her husband also sought pension rights when he became a widower upon her death at sixty-six. He died the year prior to a congressional act in 1838 that granted their children a retroactive pension payment based on their mother's military service.

Gannett's claim included testimony of nursing his wife for wounds dating to her war service. Nonetheless, Deborah Sampson Gannett had been sufficiently mobile that she delivered speeches about her wartime experience; during 1802, she traveled throughout New England and New York on the lecture circuit. The tour was arranged as a follow-up on *The Female Review* (1797), a book written by a man. The embellishing and romantic touches that he and later male authors chose to put on her venture ultimately did her a disservice, for their hyperbole cast doubt on her actual accomplishments.

Not drawn by any lover or by other fanciful attraction, Deborah Sampson presumably joined the military at a time that was right for her and for the same reasons that men did: she wanted the opportunity to see something other than her home area, while also earning a living and accumulating pension rights. Preferring this to teaching in the staid environment of small towns, like men, she answered the liberating call of a new nation.

SANGER, MARGARET LOUISE HIGGINS (1879–1966)

The best known of the leaders of the BIRTH CONTROL movement, Margaret Sanger was the catalyst of momentous change for not only American women, but also throughout the world. More than any other single person, she originated the mindset that allowed for rational control of human population, after millions of others throughout the millennia of history chose to ignore fundamental issues of reproduction.

She was much influenced in this by her childhood in upstate New York. The death of her Irish Catholic mother at forty-nine was officially due to tuberculosis, but doubtless it was hastened by interminable pregnancies that resulted in eleven live births. Moreover, Margaret's mother bore most of the responsibilities for this brood alone, for her father was a loveable but impractical political activist whose family lived in poverty. From her youth, she resolved that she would not repeat her mother's sad history.

This determination became a crusade with another epiphany much later when she was working as a NURSE. First, however, Margaret Higgins completed her education with three years at a small college in the Catskills, where she worked for her room and board while her older sisters paid the tuition. After graduation, she turned to the only work open to most educated women and became a TEACHER; like many others, she discovered that not all women belong in that occupation. She turned to the second profession common to the era's women and completed two years of training as a practical nurse in 1902. This brought her to New York City, where William Sanger, an architect/artist, pressured her for marriage.

At twenty-three, she was past the usual age to wed and Sanger, who shared her yearnings for a sophisticated life, seemed an ideal husband. Within months, however, she was repeating her mother's history: tubercular and pregnant, she almost died with the birth of her first baby. Her husband was a more cosmopolitan man than her father had been, however, and there was no second pregnancy for five years. Even while her physical health recovered, however, Sanger denied her deteriorating mental health to pour herself into her husband's career. The house they built in affluent Hastings-on-the-Hudson not only absorbed her energies, but also served as a symbol of the financial security she had not known as a child. With the birth of a second son in 1908 and a daughter in 1910, Margaret Sanger seemed headed towards the life of a stereotypical suburban housewife.

And then the house burned. Sanger wrote vividly in her autobiography of this: as she watched the destruction of a specially-designed stained glass window of a rose, she suddenly understood the futility of investing energy in ephemeral things. Liberated by her loss, she determined that she would return to the more significant life that she had intended to live. The Sangers went back to New York City, where they lived among the Progressive Era's activists, and she began working as a visiting nurse among the poor of the Lower East Side.

Most of these were IMMIGRANT WOMEN, and it was in this setting that Sanger's final epiphany occurred with the death of one of her patients, Sadie Sacks. Like other Jewish women, Sacks' religion taught her no prohibition of contraception or ABORTION, but in practical fact, she could not get the information she needed to safely prevent pregnancy. After her physician spurned Sacks' request for help in limiting her family, she tried to induce an abortion and paid with her life for her state-imposed ignorance. The experience redoubled Sanger's resolve.

When the great LAWRENCE TEXTILE STRIKE erupted in 1912, she joined ELIZABETH GURLEY FLYNN and other Socialists who went to Massachusetts. She nursed the sick, accompanied the children who were taken to New York, and then demonstrated the same activist principles with STRIKES in New Jersey and Pennsylvania the following year. Late in 1912, she also began writing for the *Call,* a radical publication that prompted much of the Progressive agenda. Sanger, however, was unique in her perspective, for she saw—in a way that was like almost none of the writers of her time—how problems of poverty were directly related to the status of women.

One of the problems that literally destroyed the lives of women and their families was venereal disease, but this was ignored even by radicals. When Sanger wrote about syphilis for the *Call* of February 9, 1913, the post office refused to deliver the magazine and threatened arrest under the COMSTOCK LAW. Thus it was actually venereal disease, not birth control, that initiated Sanger's battles with authority. Court cases that were fundamental to constitutional issues of freedom of expression would continue through the rest of her life, as Sanger struggled to tell women what they needed to know about their bodies.

At the time, virtually all Americans associated the use of any birth control technique with PROSTITUTION, and the very notion of a respectable woman seeking to become an expert on this subject was beyond public credulity. Sanger's trip to Scotland and France late in 1913 thus was motivated by a desire to seek information that could not be imported for reading in the U.S. Returning from Europe better informed, she began publishing the *Woman Rebel* in March, 1914. Postal inspectors were watching her, however, and even though the journal included no specific contraceptive information, its FEMINISM was too overt for Comstockians. She was arrested and indicted by an all-male grand jury. Despite the outbreak of WORLD WAR I in August, Sanger fled to Europe in October.

She would remain there until October of the next year, while MARY WARE DENNETT took over the leadership of the National Birth Control League that Sanger had begun in 1914. Sanger meanwhile put her time in Europe to good use. Mentored by MIDWIVES in Dutch clinics, she learned to use the diaphragm invented by a female physician and studied the methods of their birth control counselors for replication in this country. She not only learned from famous psychologist Havelock Ellis, but also began a long affair with him. Meanwhile, William Sanger, to whom she was still married although they were increasingly estranged, was arrested for distributing *Family Limitation,* a pamphlet that she had written before departure. Their troubles compounded when the Sangers' only daughter, named for her mother but called Peggy, died of pneumonia at age five.

Margaret Sanger's profound grief and guilt at her absence from the child was only slightly assuaged when the government dropped its charges soon after the death of Anthony Comstock. Within a year, however, Sanger found the strength to carry on her plan. Inspired by the memory of her daughter, she continued her birth control crusade, for her aim was not merely to liberate mothers, but also to improve the physical and psychological lives of children. The strength of her belief in the importance of families capable of nurturing their offspring was well expressed in the phrase that she coined: "Every child a wanted child."

With her sister, Ethel Byrne, Sanger opened a clinic in a blue-collar area of Brooklyn in October, 1916. The demand for their services and for the diaphragms they smuggled in from Europe was clear: almost five hundred women visited the clinic in the ten days it operated before police closed it down. Charged with creating a public nuisance, both Sanger and Byrne were imprisoned for thirty days. As was the case with the jailing of SUFFRAGE MOVEMENT women during the same era, however, the government's strategy may have won the battle but lost the war. Many newspapers wrote sympathetically of these well-intended, middle-class women imprisoned for sharing their professional knowledge with needy women who freely sought it. Though the trial jury returned a verdict of guilty, they won a partial victory on appeal in 1918.

Although the appellate court ruled against Sanger's claims relating directly to women's reproductive rights, it did allow that physicians could give advice on the prevention of venereal disease. Thus, Sanger belatedly won a decision relevant to her 1913 article on syphilis—but it was still only a fraction of the victory she originally sought, for advice could be dispensed only by physicians and, moreover, any materials used were allowable only for the prevention of disease and not for contraception. For decades thereafter, condoms and similar items were labeled "for the prevention of disease only"— while millions of Americans, mostly male, actually bought them for pregnancy prevention.

The court decision seems key to Sanger's changed approach thereafter. Much more cautious as she aged, she accepted the "doctors only" limitations with far more willingness than did Mary Dennett. While the authorities directed more attention to Dennett in the postwar era, Sanger increasingly developed for herself a persona of scientific researcher rather than feminist agitator. Instead of the sort of articles she wrote for the *Call* (which had been republished as *What Every Girl Should Know* in 1916 and *What Every Mother Should Know* in 1917), Sanger's first major book exhibited a changed tone.

Woman and the New Race (1920) not only was respectful of physicians, but also of eugenicists, even those who argued for "racial purity." She followed it up with *The Pivot of Civilization* (1922), which argued that reproductive rights and population control were pivotal to human progress. The global sweep of this reasoning marked a significant change in Sanger's style: after WORLD WAR I, her approach would emphasize concerns of population and eugenics, with less attention to the needs and rights of individual women.

In accordance with the mores of the Roaring Twenties, her emphasis was on the social rather than the political, and her writing aimed at encouraging female sexuality and romantic marriage. Leaving behind the radicalism of her past, Sanger issued five major books during the twenties that were aimed at a broader, more affluent audience. This was also the case with her periodicals: *Birth Control Review*, which she began editing in 1917, featured a far less feminist title than *Woman Rebel*. Later periodicals under her editorship were scientifically titled *Journal of Contraception* and *Human Fertility*.

Sanger also saw money as more important after World War I than had been the case earlier. In the same year that *Woman and the New Race* was published, she finally DIVORCED William Sanger, and less than two years later, married a wealthy businessman. Their premarital agreement was predicated on both her sexual freedom and access to his funds, but despite this seemingly mercenary approach, the relationship seemed happy. Retaining the Sanger name, she stayed married to John Slee until his death twenty-one years later.

Having organized the American Birth Control League in 1921, (while Dennett went her separate way with the Voluntary Birth Control League), Sanger used funds from her 1922 marriage to open the Birth Control Clinical Research Bureau in Manhattan in 1923. While she concentrated on fund-raising and public relations, Dr. Hannah Stone and a staff of mostly female physicians fulfilled the court's order. Unlike the earlier clinic, this one stayed in business and accumulated a valuable data base of patient records. Sanger used this information to demonstrate the safety of birth control in an era when many still believed that such interference with "God's will" would cause mental and physical illness.

Perhaps more important, professionals sponsored by Sanger spread her message throughout the nation. While many of the clinics they established could not maintain themselves, these agents were more successful in persuading private doctors to educate themselves on contraception and to issue diaphragms to their patients. The education of physicians and the importation of diaphragms also was a cause of long litigation, but Sanger's court crusades were victorious with a 1936 decision that ruled, in effect, that birth control and obscenity were not synonymous terms and bans on obscenity did not imply bans on pregnancy prevention. After that decision, physicians were able to import contraceptive materials and prescribe their use.

Meanwhile, millions of Americans were obviously following Sanger's lead, regardless of whether or not they acknowledged that. The nation's birth rate dropped sharply during the Great Depression, even though the court's liberating decision did not come until the Depression was largely over. Military leaders joined with physicians in developing policies on sexuality during WORLD WAR II that were more rational than those of the first war, with a resulting decline in venereal rates. At least partly in response to these changes, Sanger's Birth Control League changed its name during the first year of the war to PLANNED PARENTHOOD ASSOCIATION. As the name implies, its emphasis was on attraction of middle-class support, while the needs of poor women were relegated to second place and the feminist and socialist rhetoric of the past was purged.

Despite the adoption of such conventionality, Sanger personally remained a sexually liberated woman who had numerous lovers, though she was married for virtually all of her adult life. This unorthodox behavior doubtless had a negative effect on the acceptance of her ideas, but Sanger insisted that sexual freedom was an important empowerment for women. She argued that sensuality was a key to personal happiness— without which, she thought, women could not be effective at motherhood or anything else. Sanger thus introduced ideas in the twenties that were not widely accepted until the "sexual revolution" of the sixties and seventies.

Not surprisingly, this part of her message made her anathema to the aging leaders of the SUFFRAGE MOVEMENT. Sanger, who supported suffrage but was not active in its passage, had hoped that after this victory was won in 1920, its leadership would see the struggle for reproductive rights as the next logical step for the women's movement. If this hope was responsible for the quieter rhetoric she adopted after World War I, however, she was to be disappointed. CARRIE CHAPMAN CATT rebuffed Sanger's 1920 approach, saying that Sanger not only inflated the importance of her cause, but also that Sanger's ideas on sexual liberation of women could easily become sexual exploitation instead. Catt believed that instead of adopting male standards, women should force men to accept the more ideal female morality. Sanger met similar responses with overtures to JANE ADDAMS, CHARLOTTE PERKINS GILMAN, and others. Except for Dennett—with whom she quarreled—

Margaret Sanger stood alone as the visible leader of the birth control movement for more than half a century.

Sanger and her husband moved to Arizona in 1937, but she never fully retired. The growth of fascism during this era kept her busy separating her principle of women's liberation through birth control from the Nazi's search for a superior race through birth control. After the war, she took advantage of the public's broadened horizons to serve as a founder of International Planned Parenthood in 1952. She traveled throughout Asia promoting the cause, especially in Japan and India. Equally important, Sanger continued to raise money to finance research on a birth control pill. The first pills went on the market in 1960; when she died a mere six years later, millions of American women were taking them.

Having more than achieved her early goal of living a longer and more satisfying life than her mother's, Sanger died in Tucson just days before her eighty-seventh birthday. She left two autobiographies, *My Fight for Birth Control* (1931) and *Margaret Sanger: An Autobiography* (1938). Despite their author's lack of literary ambition, they still provide vibrant reading—but it is for more fundamental areas of human life that Margaret Sanger will be remembered.

She straightforwardly and consistently emphasized the goal of reproductive rights and was never diverted from that cause. Unlike the popularization of Freudian psychology that also flourished in her era, she was living testament that biology is not destiny. After decades of speaking out, Sanger was an important factor in the growing public awareness that women were more than their bodies and were capable of a multiplicity of lives beyond the rigid choice of either sanctified motherhood or crass prostitution. More than any other feminist of her time, Sanger understood that the right to control one's self is fundamental to any freedom, and she managed to explicate the benefit of that particular individual freedom to the entire earth. The future will recognize Margaret Sanger as one of the most globally significant people of the twentieth century.

SANITARY COMMISSION The U.S. Sanitary Commission was a quasi-military body during the CIVIL WAR that was responsible for much of the hospital duty that seemingly should have been done by the Army's Medical Corps. Until the nineteenth century, however, soldiers' lives were apt to be considered expendable. With the entrance of women—symbolized by Florence Nightingale in Europe and CLARA BARTON in America—fundamental attitudes on both military casualties and civilian public health began to change. As a result, not only the ARMY NURSE CORPS but also many municipal hospitals can trace their historical roots to a group of unrecognized women in the Sanitary Commission.

The Commission was headed by men, but it was soon apparent that their political and financial expertise was not up to the task of actually delivering care to the thousands of daily casualties this war produced. In city after city, it was women who went to the battlefields as volunteer NURSES, and after finding dying men in unattended squalor, took it upon themselves to rectify conditions. Annie Wittenmyer, who later used the organizational skills she learned in the war to found the WOMAN'S CHRISTIAN TEMPERANCE UNION, is one example.

In April of 1861, when the war was just underway, she discovered the need when visiting troops camped near her Mississippi River home in Iowa. Predating Clara Barton's similar activity by several months, Wittenmyer did the common sense thing that women do: she sent word back home to organize the local women's aid societies to provide relief. Soon named the formal relief director for Iowa, she no longer had to accept a voluntary role; as the military men came to understand how much they needed women's abilities, she and several other women became paid "State Sanitary Agents."

Traveling down the Mississippi on hospital ships, she was under fire at Vicksburg and other battlegrounds. Combat was not as great a problem for her, however, as bureaucratic warfare. Wittenmyer worked with the Western Sanitary Commission based in St. Louis, but in 1864, rivals in the all-male Iowa Sanitary Commission introduced a bill to repeal the law that authorized the women's appointments. Legislators supporting her disproved their charge that she wasted supplies and the bill failed, but Wittenmyer—disgusted by the waste of time and energy to defend herself—resigned anyway.

Instead, she developed alternate, private support and continued to do the work that needed to be done. In Nashville and other occupied Southern cities, she set up kitchens that offered troops an alternative to the rotten, wormy food frequently supplied by corrupt Army contractors, and her dietary plan became a model adopted by the Quartermaster Corps. Nor did Wittenmyer conclude her work with the war's end; thirty years later, she was largely responsible for lobbying efforts that finally resulted in pensions for Civil War nurses.

The experience of MARY LIVERMORE was similar. Becoming head of the Sanitary Commission in the Midwest early in 1862, she eventually formed some three thousand local units to provide soldiers with food, medicine, surgical dressings and other essentials that the military had not arranged for itself. While responsible for hospitals in Illinois, Kentucky, and Missouri, she also raised tens of thousands of dollars in cash to supplement in-kind contributions. Like Wittenmyer, Livermore used the skills she developed in postwar activity for suffrage and other causes.

MARY ANN BICKERDYKE was another stellar woman who operated under the aegis of the Sanitary Commission. Beginning in Illinois in 1861, she stayed with the Army through all four years of the war; the nineteen major battles in which she was present were far more than the average soldier sees. While the work of most women was more localized than Bickerdyke's, she serves as an example of the tens of thousands of women who eventually formed the membership of some seven thousand local units of the Sanitary Commission.

They organized emergency hospitals in homes and public facilities—for few communities at the time had hospitals—and they held massive fund-raisers to buy the rations and equipment that the Army failed to supply. By the war's end, Sanitary Commission women had raised and spent approximately $30 million. Moreover, they had proven their administrative abilities in successfully competing with men for military contracts. Often more innovative than men in the fulfillment of these contracts, Sanitary Commission women, for example, doubled the good their money did by hiring soldiers' wives to sew uniforms.

Nor did their work end with the battle; women of the Sani-

Women standing with soldiers at the quarters for the U.S. Sanitary Commission at Brandy Station, Virginia, in 1863.
NATIONAL ARCHIVES; PHOTOGRAPH BY MATTHEW BRADY.

tary Commission took responsibility for wounded veterans and for families disrupted by the war. They nursed the sick and saw the dead buried and took on chaplain's duties, too, in notifying families of the status of their loved ones and in searching for prisoners of war and the missing. The "sanitary" in the commission's name is noteworthy also, for at a time prior to germ theory, it was primarily the volunteer women, not the military's physicians, who intuitively understood that men do not recover when they are treated in filth.

Southern women, such as the exceptional SALLY TOMPKINS, worked without the support of any similarly inclusive agency because their culture opted for female romanticism over efficiency. It proved a fatal mistake for the Confederacy, while for Northern women, the Sanitary Commission meant an opportunity to develop self-confidence, organizational skills and a national network. These then became a catalyst for their leadership in the postwar demand for the vote and other civil rights. Work in the Sanitary Commission not only demonstrated that women could survive the heat of battle, but also that the typical female experience gave women important expertise in areas in which men were lacking.

Volume II of the *HISTORY OF WOMAN SUFFRAGE* offers more detail on the commission's work, and its authors concluded: "Nothing connected with the war so astonished foreign nations as the work of the Sanitary Commission. Indeed, American women—who were far less familiar with the phenomenon of war than Europeans—led the way to the establishment of global conventions governing the humane treatment of war casualties and prisoners.

SCHIFF, DOROTHY (1903–1989)

One of the twentieth century's female PUBLISHERS of major newspapers, Dorothy Schiff was the daughter of publisher Jacob Schiff. She attended BRYN MAWR and became the major shareholder of the *New York Post* in 1939. Known in professional circles by her MAIDEN NAME, she was married four times and had three children, while maintaining her business independence.

Although H.L. Mencken referred to Schiff—along with FREDA KIRCHWEY—as "another wild woman," the newspaper was successful under her guidance for many decades. A number of the city's papers went bankrupt in the fifties and sixties as television displaced readership, but Schiff stayed afloat, and the *Post* emerged from the 1962–1963 strike as Manhattan's only afternoon paper. From then until its 1976 sale, she not only was publisher, but also editor in chief. A "crusading liberal" in editorial policy, she argued for "honest unionism, social reform and humane government."

Schiff was a member of the LEAGUE OF WOMEN VOTERS and served on the board of the WOMEN'S TRADE UNION LEAGUE. She also invested in radio, and the *Post* was known for publishing an unusual number of columnists, including DORIS FLEESON, SYLVIA PORTER, and ELEANOR ROOSEVELT.

Called Dolly by her friends, Schiff pursued and won several legal cases on freedom of the press. She retired in 1976, leaving intact the *Post's* record of continuous publication since Alexander Hamilton founded it in 1801.

SCHNEIDERMAN, ROSE (1882–1972)

In a life strikingly parallel to that of MARY ANDERSON, Rose Schneiderman was one of the twentieth century's most influential women in the labor movement.

Born Jewish in Polish Russia, she came to New York City at age eight and changed her name from Rahel to Ruth to Rose. Her pregnant mother became a WIDOW soon after their arrival, and Rose and her brothers had no choice except to live part of their youth in an orphanage. Even though this place was run by the Hebrew Sheltering Society, Rose thought the matrons "were very cruel"—the impoverished mothers were not even allowed to freely visit their children. Rose's mother struggled desperately to keep her family together by keeping BOARDERS and doing HOME CONTRACT WORK, and Rose never forgot these early lessons in the era's harsh injustices to women.

Very much a companion to her mother in supporting her younger siblings, Rose entered the labor force at thirteen. After a few years in ill-paid retail work, she became a cap maker in 1898. Like other GARMENT INDUSTRY women, she had to purchase her own sewing machine; when the factory burned, the women had to bear this loss alone—though management had insurance coverage. Not surprisingly, she reversed her earlier view of strikebreakers "as heroic figures because they wanted to work" and organized a union local. Though she stood only four-foot-six-inches tall, her massive crown of red hair symbolized a fiery personality that commanded respect, and in 1905, she led a victorious STRIKE.

After 1907, Schneiderman, who remained single all of her life, devoted most of her efforts to the WOMEN'S TRADE UNION LEAGUE (WTUL). It was in this organization that she rose to the top of female union leadership in the massive garment workers' strikes of 1909–1910. Under the aegis of the WTUL, she helped organize several hundred thousand women into the INTERNATIONAL LADIES' GARMENT WORKERS' UNION (ILGWU) by the outbreak of WORLD WAR I. A member of the ILGWU's Executive Committee, Schneiderman was not only an effective organizer, but also an inspiring orator. Her speech in response to the TRIANGLE FIRE is particularly famous, and an Ohio WTUL member avowed that "no one ever touched the hearts of the masses like Miss Rose Schneiderman . . . Strong men sat with the tears rolling down their cheeks."

Like other IMMIGRANT WOMEN, she lived a life torn between two cultures, and like other female union organizers, she also dealt with a lifelong tug-of-war between her labor interests and her feminist interests. Despite the disapproval of some male colleagues, she also worked as an organizer for the NATIONAL AMERICAN WOMAN SUFFRAGE ASSOCIATION in several state campaigns. A pacifist after the war, she attended international peace meetings and helped found the BRYN MAWR summer school for working women.

When the involvement of MARY DREIER and MARGARET DREIER ROBINS in the WTUL declined during the twenties, Schneiderman emerged as its most visible leader. She became national president in 1926 and remained in that position for the rest of the organization's existence. She used the position to work for minimum wage and maximum hour laws; like her progressive friends Mary Anderson, FRANCES PERKINS, ELEANOR ROOSEVELT, and others, Schneiderman opposed the EQUAL RIGHTS AMENDMENT because of its nullification of PROTECTIVE LEGISLATION. The WTUL seemed increasingly passé after the passage of New Deal legislation, and with the ascension of rightists both in and out of labor circles after WORLD WAR II, it formally disbanded in 1950.

President Roosevelt appointed Schneiderman as the only woman commissioner of the National Recovery Administration during the Great Depression, and in 1937, she was appointed New York's secretary of labor, where she remained until 1943. She retired in New York City and published her autobiography, *All For One,* in 1967.

She outlived most of her friends, with the result that her death at ninety was less noted than it might have been if, for example, Eleanor Roosevelt had not predeceased her. With an end much different from its beginning, Rose Schneiderman's life of dedication to women workers was a noble success.

SEIBERT, FLORENCE BARBARA (1898–1991)

As a biochemist who developed the skin test to identify tuberculosis, Seibert made one of the most significant contributions to public health of the twentieth century. Tuberculosis had become a massive killer after the urbanization and industrialization of the late nineteenth century, and Seibert's development was crucial to its demise. Moreover, like ELLEN RICHARDS and other female scientists, Seibert did not seek to profit from human misery and never patented her discovery.

Florence Seibert not only had to overcome the handicaps of gender that every woman of her era encountered, but also prevailed over the effects of polio when she was four. "Because I was disabled," she said, "I stuck to things harder" and because she "couldn't go out to dance and play," she studied. Wearing braces and using a cane, she entered Goucher College, a women's institution in Baltimore. After graduation during WORLD WAR I, she worked as a chemist for a paper mill and then went on to Yale University for graduate study. Yale, like other prestigious universities, had opened graduate programs to women while keeping its undergraduate college assiduously closed.

With a picture of Marie Curie on her desk to help her cope with hostility from Yale men, Seibert achieved scientific distinction while still a doctoral student in the 1920s. She developed a method of eliminating contaminants from distilled water, which was a necessary step in the invention of intravenous therapy. The UNIVERSITY OF CHICAGO rewarded her with a position and she began her tuberculosis research there.

After nine years, she moved on to the University of Pennsylvania, which specialized in tuberculosis.

While teaching mostly male medical students, Dr. Seibert also continued her research and became recognized as a worldwide authority on the bacillus that causes tuberculosis. A 1937–1938 fellowship to Sweden allowed her to work with a future Nobel winner, and it was this joint effort that led to the development of a skin test for what is usually a lung-based disease. With the assistance of her sister Mabel, she had the test ready for use by 1941. The medical establishment, however, was reluctant to use it, and WORLD WAR II brought further delays. Finally, in 1952, Florence Seibert testified before a condescending committee of the World Health Organization: "They thought that if they didn't have a big man there arguing for the test," she said, "they could push [out] this method." Seibert's arguments were persuasive, however, and her test became standard.

Dr. Seibert received numerous awards prior to moving to Florida in 1958. Even there, she and her sister both did cancer research on a volunteer basis until 1976, when at seventy-eight, Florence Seibert retired a second time. She lived to see her induction into the WOMEN'S HALL OF FAME in 1990 and maintained her interest in medical journals until her death at ninety-three.

SEMINARY Though this word denotes a theological teaching institution today, a century ago it was commonly used to mean a secondary school for young women.

The word had a much earlier definition as a place of incubation, and its meaning as a school had evolved by the colonial era when the first COLLEGES were established explicitly for the purpose of educating clergy for the new land. The women's educational institutions that began to flourish as "seminaries" during the first half of the nineteenth century harkened back to these ideas.

Not confident enough to declare their schools to be "colleges," the educators involved also used "seminary" to indicate an intent more serious and less secular than that suggested by "FINISHING SCHOOL." At the same time, this usage in no way implied a theological education that could culminate in ordination. Instead, the women of these schools modestly used "seminary" to mark the moral purpose of their mission.

At the beginning of the CIVIL WAR, there were approximately two hundred female seminaries scattered throughout the nation, many of them in the South and Midwest. Their numbers declined afterwards, partly due to wartime disruptions but mostly because of increased coeducation in the Midwest and the advent of prestigious women's colleges in the East.

SENECA FALLS WOMEN'S RIGHTS CONVENTION (1848)
The birth of the women's rights movement in not only America, but also the world, is commonly acknowledged to have occurred in the small town of SENECA FALLS, NEW YORK during a two-day meeting on July nineteenth and twentieth, 1848.

The time and place is directly related to the fact that Seneca Falls was home to ELIZABETH CADY STANTON, who with LUCRETIA MOTT, had been ejected from the 1840 World Anti-Slavery Convention in London. The experience had been a traumatic one for young Stanton; she wrote much later of its demonstration to her "that it is almost impossible for the most liberal of men to understand what liberty means for women." Shocked at the obtuse way her male ABOLITIONIST friends failed to understand the true meaning of their words, she wrote: "Would there have been no unpleasant feelings had [black men] been refused their seats and had *they* listened one entire day to . . . their peculiar fitness for plantation life and unfitness for the forum . . ."

Mott and Stanton had talked then of a follow-up meeting in America, but eight years went by before Philadelphian Mott and her husband visited central New York State. During this visit, the two of them, along with three other QUAKER WOMEN friends, decided to call a "convention" to discuss the issues that troubled them. Inexperienced in parliamentary procedure and unsure of themselves, the leaders readily agreed that Lucretia Mott's husband, James Mott, should preside over the gathering.

On July fourteenth, the *Seneca County Courier* ran a three-sentence announcement of a meeting to discuss "the social, civil, and religious rights of women." Women were "earnestly invited to attend," and because of presumed female timidity, they were assured that the first day's session would be "held exclusively for women," while the second day's proceedings were to be open to "the public generally." Though the announcement ran only once, the response proved amazing. Women throughout this agricultural area left their summertime chores, persuaded their husbands to hitch up the horses, and drove as far as fifty miles for the ten o'clock meeting at the Wesleyan Chapel. Some three hundred people appeared, including so many men that the leaders overcame their trepidation and allowed them to join the women.

The audience, which included AMELIA BLOOMER, heard a number of speakers. They were impressed by Lucretia Mott, who was the only attraction featured in the advertisement, but Stanton, who was younger and inexperienced at PUBLIC SPEAKING, also gave a carefully researched address. In addition, several liberal men spoke, especially on aspects of law that needed revision, while black ABOLITIONIST Fredrick Douglas was another highlight. The DECLARATION OF RIGHTS FOR WOMEN that the convention debated was drafted primarily by Stanton. Using the style of Thomas Jefferson in the nation's Declaration of Independence, it detailed the injustices women suffered and thus set the group's long-term goals. The only area of intense disagreement was over the right to vote, and even that passed by a close margin.

Plans were made for a follow-up meeting in Rochester two weeks later, where a woman, Abigail Bush, presided. SUSAN ANTHONY's family came into contact with the nascent network at that meeting. An increasingly interstate movement thereafter, by 1850, there were Women's Rights Conventions in Salem, Ohio and Worcester, Massachusetts. The Worcester meeting, held in October, 1850, is known as the first National Woman's Rights Convention and attracted LUCY STONE. At the 1851 gathering in Akron, Ohio, SOJOURNER TRUTH made her famous "Ain't I a Woman" speech, while ERNESTINE ROSE conflicted with ANTOINETTE BROWN BLACKWELL over the role of religion.

The movement was thus four years old when Susan Anthony attended her first convention in Syracuse in September, 1852. This meeting, known as the Third National Woman's Rights Convention, was attended by women from eight states and Canada. Each convention, of course, met with derision from the local press, but women nonetheless continued to gather. National Women's Rights Conventions were held annually until the CIVIL WAR interfered. The Boston convention of 1856 included speeches from Ralph Waldo Emerson and other cultural leaders, while the 1858 gathering in New York presented an unfortunate contrast with repeated disruptions from gangs of jeering males. No meetings were held during the five war years between the 1860 and 1866 gatherings, and then there was only a three-year period before philosophical differences over the FIFTEENTH AMENDMENT brought the division into the AMERICAN WOMAN SUFFRAGE ASSOCIATION and the NATIONAL WOMAN SUFFRAGE ASSOCIATION in 1869.

Each organization held annual conventions, however, and the reunification of 1890 continued this tradition. A sense of history pervaded these meetings. The thirtieth anniversary of the Seneca Falls convention, for example, featured pioneer FEMINIST ABBY KELLY FOSTER in her hometown of Worcester, Massachusetts. A speech by African-American MARY CHURCH TERRELL on the sixtieth anniversary in 1908 served as a vivid reminder that the first convention was held long before slavery ended. So long was

the history of these conventions that only one woman who attended the Seneca Falls Convention lived to vote in a national election: Charlotte Woodward Pierce, who was nineteen in 1848, voted in the presidential election of 1920.

SENECA FALLS, NEW YORK

Beginning with JEMIMA WILKINSON, who settled on the western shores of Seneca Lake in 1788 when it was a wilderness, this geographic area became home to an unusual number of outstanding American women. Located less than fifty miles south of Lake Ontario, Seneca Falls is approximately midway between Rochester to the west and Syracuse to the east.

Doubtless a large part of the activity generated there was due to the fertile brain of ELIZABETH CADY STANTON, who along with SUSAN ANTHONY, was the prime leader of the nineteenth-century women's rights movement. Stanton began her work for women even earlier than Anthony, and because she was a married woman who would bear a large family, Anthony and other leaders tended to come to Seneca Falls, where the busy young mother was often confined by pregnancies. AMELIA BLOOMER added to the town's reputation in the 1840s with the publication of the nation's first newspaper aimed at a female audience; in addition to publicizing the pants style for which she is known, Bloomer also served as Seneca Falls' deputy postmaster.

This cartoon ridiculing an 1859 women's rights convention was typical of many. Since galleries were almost always used by women in this era, the male presence there was considered amusing. The men in the meeting, however, are representative of those who allied themselves with the women's rights cause throughout the era. Note also the woman on the left who is wearing pants. LIBRARY OF CONGRESS; WOOD ENGRAVING FROM *HARPER'S WEEKLY.*

The spirit of protest that seemed pervasive in the area had its roots in Protestantism, and thus it is not surprising that ANTOINETTE BROWN BLACKWELL held the first female pastorate of a mainstream denomination in a town just a few miles from Seneca Falls. REVEREND OLYMPIA BROWN set other precedents as a theological student in this same geographic area, while ELIZABETH BLACKWELL, the first female medical student in America, enrolled at nearby Geneva College. The town of Auburn, just across the lake from Seneca Falls, became home to HARRIET TUBMAN; confident that her neighbors would not betray her, she built a refuge for escaped slaves there.

Nearby Rochester was home to a number of early FEMINISTS, the most prominent of whom was Susan Anthony, while DR. MARY WALKER lived in and near Syracuse. FRANCES WILLARD taught in the area as a young woman, while others with formative roots nearby include DR. EMELINE CLEVELAND, BELVA LOCKWOOD, ESTHER MORRIS, ALICE FREEMAN PALMER, and LILLIAN WALD.

In 1969, the women of Seneca Falls honored their unique heritage with the creation of the WOMEN'S HALL OF FAME. In 1977, a torch carried by more than one thousand runners began at Seneca Falls and went on to Houston, where the International Women's Year symposia took place. Among other items on women, the museum operated by the Seneca Falls Historical Society has a display of QUILTS, and the town also features a Women's Rights Historical Park.

SETON, MOTHER ELIZABETH ANN (1774–1821) The

first American-born person of either gender to be declared a saint, Mother Elizabeth Ann Seton was a WIDOW and mother of five when she converted to Catholicism and founded the first American community of NUNS.

Born Elizabeth Ann Bayley, she was a FINISHING SCHOOL graduate and, like most Americans of her era, grew up Protestant. She was introduced to Catholicism during an 1804 visit to Italy, where her husband died. Her conversion back in New York the following year met with much hostility from family and friends, while at the same time, Seton was faced with supporting her children. She barely provided for them by operating a BOARDING HOUSE; the DAME SCHOOL she attempted was a financial loss. The security of a TEACHING job for Catholic girls brought her to Baltimore in 1808. The school that she began there is sometimes credited as the beginning of parochial school education in the U.S.

Seton took her vows as a nun in 1809, and joined by two of her sisters-in-law, she began her community on donated land in Emmitsburg, which is near the Maryland border just south of Gettysburg, Pennsylvania. The property was unimproved and the women endured some genuine privations, but the idea of a community of women apparently had great appeal, for the Sisters of Charity of St. Joseph grew quickly. Under the direction of Mother Seton, they NURSED and assisted the poor in addition to the teaching that was the main financial support of the initial enterprise.

The Sisters expanded to Philadelphia in 1814. A New York convent was added three years later, and eventually as many as twenty other convents evolved from this beginning. While administering all this, Seton also mothered her children, who grew up in the community. She did not live to enjoy many of the fruits of her labors, however, for Mother Seton died at

forty-six of tuberculosis. Seton Hall College was named for her in 1856 and steps towards canonization began in 1907. She was preceded in this honor by MOTHER FRANCES XAVIER CABRINI—an American citizen born in Italy—but on September 14, 1975, Mother Elizabeth Ann Seton became the first American-born saint.

SETTLEMENT HOUSES It is difficult to understand the history of American women in the late nineteenth and twentieth centuries without reference to the settlement house movement, for many of those who led the way for women's rights were also involved in this effort. "Settlement" referred to the assimilation of the millions of immigrants who came during this era. Settlement houses assisted these newcomers with Americanization through job placement and training, citizenship classes, legal aid, health services, and many other helpful programs. "House" was also an appropriate part of the term, for the staff lived at these homes—often for years—and thus truly became part of the neighborhoods that they served. These settlements were not government-sponsored, but operated solely because of the individual enterprise of charitable people—usually women.

The idea came from London, where novice social workers (before that field truly existed) created centers designed to assist the urban poor, many of whom were recently displaced from agricultural work. JANE ADDAMS's Hull House was the first such institution in America, begun in Chicago in 1889. New York's Henry Street Settlement was independently begun by LILLIAN WALD in 1893. Boston's Denison House opened that same year with assistance from women associated with WELLESLEY COLLEGE, including EMILY BALCH. Guided for twenty years by Wellesley's Vida Scudder, Denison House became home to the WOMEN'S EDUCATIONAL AND INDUSTRIAL UNION. BRYN MAWR ran a settlement house in a blue-collar area of nearby New Jersey, where its sociology students could gain practical experience while doing good; the UNIVERSITY OF CHICAGO ran a similar program under Mary McDowell.

Other colleges and institutions, including some Protestant churches, emulated the idea and by 1900, there were some one hundred settlement houses under the aegis of a variety of sponsors. While these establishments were of tremendous value to those who used their free services, they were also important to the personal growth of the affluent, educated women who ran them. At a time when most women passed from their father's house to their husband's, the settlement house offered them a rare opportunity to live in respectable independence while developing skills in fund-raising and administration. The friendships formed there also provided vital networking contacts for later careers.

Among other influential American women who lived at least part of their lives in settlement houses are: EDITH and GRACE ABBOTT, FLORENCE ALLEN, SOPHONISBA BRECKINRIDGE, MARY ELIZABETH DREIER, AMELIA EARHART, ALICE HAMILTON, FLORENCE KELLEY, JULIA LATHROP, and FRANCES PERKINS. Although the majority of the staff of settlement houses was female, most usually included a few idealistic young men among their residents: both RUTH HANNA MCCORMICK and MARY KENNY O'SULLIVAN, for instance, lived in settlement houses with their husbands. MARY ANDERSON and ANZIA YEZIERSKA were among many IMMIGRANT WOMEN who credited settlement houses for their success in America.

That these institutions tended to die in the 1920s was probably due to the passage of immigration quota laws, as well as the fact that many progressive women found other outlets for their energies—especially within government—after the right to vote was achieved. After the Depression began, some of the affluent women who had previously funded these places could no longer afford to do so, and the federal government's New Deal programs assumed more responsibility for the needy.

In earlier decades, however, the settlement house movement was personally important to millions of American newcomers of both genders, for often it provided their best buffer against the complex difficulties of an unfamiliar society. The forerunners of today's shelters for abuse victims and the displaced, the settlement house movement was an early demonstration of the power of women working together.

SEVEN SISTERS COLLEGES

These women's COLLEGES, all of which are between Philadelphia and Boston, became known as the Seven Sisters because of their correlation to the seven male colleges of the Ivy League.

The first, MOUNT HOLYOKE, began long before football and sorority life produced the "Seven Sisters" appellation; Mount Holyoke began in 1837, though its name was not finalized as a "college" until 1893. VASSAR COLLEGE, founded in 1865, often is named as the first because it was self-consciously a college from the beginning. WELLESLEY COLLEGE, chartered in 1870, came next, while SMITH COLLEGE quickly followed in 1871. "Harvard Annex" was transformed into RADCLIFFE COLLEGE in 1879, while Philadelphia's BRYN MAWR, with backing from QUAKER WOMEN, began the next year. BARNARD COLLEGE, associated with Columbia University In New York, was the last in 1889.

Despite the fact that four of the seven are in Massachusetts, each was informally associated with a male counterpart, and men from Dartmouth in New Hampshire and Princeton in New Jersey went to the women's campuses for dances, while chaperoned women returned the favor by attending football weekends. Especially during the first half of the twentieth century—after college education for women was no longer seen as threatening and before the democratization of colleges that occurred with WORLD WAR II—this Ivy League association often made for an elitist atmosphere in which a proper marriage was the goal of many students and parents. Nonetheless, the Seven Sisters colleges had high academic standards; they developed countless community leaders; and, for many female faculty, they served as the most comfortable academic home possible during the first century of higher education for women.

SEXTON, ANNE GRAY (1928–1974)

In a life with many parallels to that of SYLVIA PLATH, Anne Sexton was also an award-winning poet who committed suicide. In both cases, the modern women's movement may have come slightly too late to have offered the support they needed.

Though she came from an affluent family in suburban Boston and her mother had studied at WELLESLEY, she eloped at nineteen. The first five years of her married life were childless, but Sexton presumably was so determined to be a conventional wife that she neither went to college nor developed a career during this period. Soon after the birth of her second child in 1955, she suffered a severe mental breakdown, but by 1960, she had recovered sufficiently to publish her first book of poetry, *To Bedlam, Part Way and Back*.

Like this title, most of Sexton's work explored themes of depression and mental illness. Her life seemingly was upward bound, as she received academic support at Harvard and RADCLIFFE and published a 1963 collection that was nominated for the National Book Award. Further books and more honors followed, including the Pulitzer Prize in 1967, but the recognition presumably was not enough. Hospitalized several times, Anne Sexton divorced in 1973 and killed herself the following fall.

SHADD, MARY ANN— *See* CARY, MARY ANN SHADD

SHAFROTH-PALMER AMENDMENT (1914)

The idea of RUTH HANNA MCCORMICK while she chaired the congressional lobbying committee of the NATIONAL AMERICAN WOMAN SUFFRAGE ASSOCIATION (NAWSA), this was a proposed amendment to the federal Constitution. Unlike the NINETEENTH AMENDMENT that passed six years later, however, the Shafroth-Palmer proposal was only a timid step towards the goal of female enfranchisement: it merely required states to hold referenda on women's suffrage if 8 percent of the voters in the previous election signed a petition calling for such.

Introduced in the Senate on March 2, 1914, it was designed to counter the arguments of congressmen who said that they favored women's right to vote, but would not vote for a federal amendment because of their reverence for states' rights. Since such arguments might well be specious in the first place and since the suffragists lost five of the seven referenda held in 1914, McCormick's idea gained little support. It not only proved distracting to the larger goal, but also had a negative effect within the SUFFRAGE MOVEMENT as it further divided the NAWSA from the rival WOMAN'S PARTY. It was not reintroduced when another Congress convened after the 1914 elections.

The proposed amendment was named for its sponsors, who were well-intended men assisting McCormick. After his term in Congress, Senator Thomas Palmer cofounded a Men's State League for Woman Suffrage in Michigan, while Senator John Shafroth of Colorado (whose female constituents had voted since 1893) was a constant FEMINIST friend. Shafroth also introduced a 1917 suffrage bill for the Territory of Hawaii that passed both Houses and was signed by President Wilson.

SHAW, ANNA HOWARD (1847–1919)

One of the stars of the SUFFRAGE MOVEMENT at the turn of the century, Reverend Dr. Shaw was the longtime protege of SUSAN ANTHONY. Many expected that she would replace the aging Anthony as the person who would bring suffrage to fruition, but that fell instead to CARRIE CHAPMAN CATT.

Born in England, she emigrated with her family in 1851. They lived in Lawrence, Massachusetts, where her parents—who came from a heritage of religious dissidence—supported ABOLITION. When she was twelve, however, they went on to Michigan, where her mother endured the privations of many FRONTIER WOMEN in caring for the family alone while her father fought in the CIVIL WAR. Anna largely educated herself through reading, and like many women of her era, began working as a TEACHER at fifteen.

Inspired by a female preacher who spoke in Big Rapids, Michigan, Shaw studied PUBLIC SPEAKING and preached her first sermon in 1870. She was licensed as a Methodist preacher the following year and, despite the disapproval of her parents, enrolled in a Methodist COLLEGE, Michigan's Albion, in 1873. After two years there, she transferred to the divinity department of Boston University. Shaw not only endured the hostilities that any woman following such an unconventional path could expect, but also suffered severe hardships, including hunger, in her struggle to study theology. She credited the women of a Boston missionary society with literally saving her life.

After her 1878 graduation, Reverend Shaw pastored two churches on Cape Cod—one Methodist and one Congregational. Despite her previous experience with Methodists, the New England Conference refused to ordain a woman and, after protracted hearings, Shaw transferred to a different Methodist synod and was ordained in 1880—seventeen years after the precedent was set by OLYMPIA BROWN. A few years into these pastorates, she began spending part of the week in the city, studying medicine at Boston University. She earned her medical degree in 1886 and thereafter usually was addressed as "Reverend Dr. Shaw."

She did not practice medicine, however, for meanwhile she had discovered the Boston-based AMERICAN WOMAN SUFFRAGE ASSOCIATION (AWSA). Shaw resigned from the churches she had pastored for seven years to begin working for suffrage in 1885, and after 1887, she became a career lecturer under the partial aegis of the WOMAN'S CHRISTIAN TEMPERANCE ASSOCIATION. It was a speech to the INTERNATIONAL COUNCIL OF WOMEN in 1888 that introduced Shaw to Anthony. Shaw's oratorical ability, plus her friendships with LUCY STONE and others of the AWSA, made her a natural consensus leader when Anthony's and Stone's associations merged in 1890.

She served as a vice-president of the NATIONAL AMERICAN WOMAN SUFFRAGE ASSOCIATION (NAWSA) from 1892 to 1904. It is to Shaw's credit that she remained vice-president in 1900, for she was crushed when Anthony retired and chose to pass the presidency to Carrie Chapman Catt instead of Shaw. When Catt resigned because of her ailing husband in 1904, Shaw became president—and Anthony's prescience was demonstrated. Despite her pleasant personality and her capacity as a speaker, Reverend Dr. Shaw lacked both the administrative and political skills that were necessary to move the suffrage issue forward. Her failings became evident with the disaffection of ALICE PAUL and other younger women, and after eleven years as president, Shaw wisely chose to again step aside for Catt in 1915.

Meanwhile, she had chaired a Suffrage and Rights of Citizenship Committee for the International Council of Women and followed that with leadership positions in the INTERNATIONAL WOMAN SUFFRAGE ALLIANCE. According to IDA HUSTED HARPER, at "nearly all" of these gatherings in Europe, "Dr. Anna Howard Shaw made the closing speech, for if she was not on the program, the audience called for her." A tireless TRAVELER, Shaw eventually spoke in every state as well as many countries abroad. Her most famous sermon was

preached in Sweden in 1911 at "the ancient State church of Gusta Vasa," where she was supported by a women's choir and a female organist/composer with the church "crowded to the last inch."

Shaw had a winter home in Florida and assisted suffrage efforts in that state between 1915 and 1919. Both there and at the Pennsylvania home she built in 1903, she was assisted by one of Susan Anthony's nieces, Lucy Anthony, who functioned as Shaw's companion and secretary for three decades. In 1915, Shaw's autobiography, *The Story of a Pioneer,* was published, but this was not the sign of retirement that it appeared to be, for she accomplished much after seventy.

She chaired the women's committee of the National Defense Council during WORLD WAR I, and after the armistice, President Wilson invited her to join him and other national leaders on a 1919 speaking tour to promote the League of Nations. As would prove to be the case with Wilson himself, the tour exhausted Shaw. She developed pneumonia in Illinois and died at her Pennsylvania home a few weeks later.

Only a month before her collapse, Shaw was honored with the Distinguished Service Medal—the highest military honor given to civilians—for her wartime work. After a lifetime dedicated to women, she did live to see the NINETEENTH AMENDMENT on its way to ratification; it passed out of Congress on June fourth and she died July second. The memory of Reverend Dr. Anna Howard Shaw was honored at the International Woman Suffrage Alliance convention in Geneva in 1920.

SHEPPARD-TOWNER ACT (1921) A pioneering piece of congressional legislation on behalf of women and children, the Sheppard-Towner Act was widely criticized under the guise of interference with "states' rights," even though whether or not a state took advantage of the funds offered was voluntary.

Passed for the "welfare and hygiene of maternity and infancy," the bill allowed the appropriation of up to a million dollars annually for states that provided matching funds to build clinics aimed at lowering INFANT MORTALITY rates. It was considered a huge victory for the SUFFRAGE MOVEMENT, for its passage in the year after women gained the right to vote nationwide was not coincidental. Among others who lobbied hard for the act was FLORENCE KELLEY, who considered it a culmination of forty years of work on behalf of women.

The clinics developed under the act were largely staffed by women, who not only provided free checkups for babies, but also taught good health practices to their mothers—many of whom were IMMIGRANT WOMEN. The free services offered thus were often rendered in an atmosphere of class superiority, and the primacy of children over women was also evident. Far more concerned with infant than maternal health, the clinics—in the words of a critical MARGARET SANGER—"taught a poor woman how to have her seventh child, when what she wants to know is how to avoid . . . her eighth."

Despite these criticisms, the act did a good deal to improve health during the 1920s, while it also provided employment for a growing number of female physicians. By 1929, however, conservatives in the medical profession took advantage of the collapse of the organized women's movement to repeal the act. Worried about this competition with their private practices, physicians labeled the program as "Bolshevik" and particularly slandered Kelley. At the same time, Sheppard-Towner supporters also had to endure complaints from within feminist ranks, for ALICE PAUL and her WOMAN'S PARTY included it with the PROTECTIVE LEGISLATION to which they objected.

Not surprisingly, the authorizing legislation collapsed with the onset of the Great Depression. Thus, throughout most of the twentieth century, the Sheppard-Towner experience stood as the nation's only experience with preventative health care—a priority that was assumed by the governments of almost all other developed nations during this time.

SIDNEY, MARGARET (LOTHROP, HARRIET MULFORD STONE) (1844–1924)

Margaret Sidney was a PSEUDONYM adopted by Harriet Stone when she wrote the first of the "Little Pepper" series of children's books, and she would be publicly known by that name throughout her long career. Her first book, *The Five Little Peppers and How They Grew* (1880), was so popular that it appears as the 1880 bestseller—followed by *Ben-Hur* and *Madame Bovary*.

Between 1880 and 1916, she published a dozen volumes of books about the fictional Pepper family. Two million copies were sold in less than a decade, and the sagas continued to be reprinted throughout the twentieth century. A series of "Little Pepper" movies in the 1950s also proved very popular with children, despite the fact that the stories were then more than fifty years old.

Sidney married her publisher in 1881, and they lived thereafter in a Concord, Massachusetts house, Wayside, that was previously occupied by both the family of LOUISA MAY ALCOTT and Nathaniel Hawthorne and SOPHIA PEABODY. WIDOWED a decade later, Sidney managed the PUBLISHING company she inherited, while continuing her own work and rearing a child. She wrote more than forty books before her death at eighty, when she was honored with burial among Concord's other famous AUTHORS.

SMEDLEY, AGNES (c.1892–1950)

That AUTHOR and journalist Agnes Smedley is more famous in China than in her native land speaks volumes about both the failure to recognize women's work and about international politics.

Though her childhood in various western states was disadvantaged and her schooling was erratic, Agnes Smedley nonetheless was TEACHING in her teens. Briefly married, she worked at several jobs and studied intermittently at colleges in Arizona and California before moving east during WORLD WAR I, where she enrolled at New York University. She was soon caught up in the protest surrounding that war, and an unjust arrest in 1918 further radicalized her. When the war ended, Smedley went to Europe, where her primary cause was independence for India.

She lived with an Indian man, taught English at the University of Berlin and worked for social change, including BIRTH CONTROL. After a decade in Germany, Smedley published an autobiographical novel and departed for China as a correspondent for a German newspaper. Although that position did not last, China would remain central to her life after 1929. Roaming that huge country during its cataclysmic modern history, she published several books and numerous articles on the emergence of Chinese communism during the thirties and forties.

Linguistically gifted, Smedley interviewed many of the young Chinese who would become internationally powerful in decades to come. She shared the sufferings of the "Long March" and gave favorable coverage to Mao Tse Tung, Chou En-lai, and others of its leaders. When the Asian portion of WORLD WAR II began in 1937, she dressed in army camouflage and traveled with the Red Army that confronted the Japanese. While most Americans remained indifferent to these ominous events, Smedley sent back a manuscript for publication in New York entitled *China Fights Back: An American Woman with the . . . Army* (1938). As the war worsened, she worked for the Chinese Red Cross and as a correspondent for England's famous *Manchester Guardian,* but also continued the traditions of American women in wartime as she located supplies and volunteered in hospitals.

Desperately ill by 1940, she returned to the U.S. in 1941; except for a brief, unsuccessful job search in 1934–1935, she had been gone since 1919. She was initially well received, as the historical American preference for the Chinese over the Japanese was reinforced by Pearl Harbor. Smedley's 1943 book, *Battle Hymn Over China,* briefly brought her a taste of the success that surrounded PEARL BUCK. She would not retain that fame, however, for Smedley's views were far to the left of Buck.

As her reading of the situation in postwar China proved correct and the Communists clearly had more popular support than the American-supported Nationalists, the public came to resent the accuracy of Smedley's predictions. She escaped McCarthyism by moving to England, where the remarkable Agnes Smedley died in Oxford. As she had planned, her ashes were returned to China, where the government buried them with honors for this "Friend of the Chinese Revolution." No other foreigner was similarly esteemed.

Though she had little systematic education, Smedley did far better than experienced diplomats and intelligence agents at predicting the course of the world's largest nation. The *New Republic* listed Smedley's *Woman of the Earth* as one of its "Good Books That Almost Nobody Has Read."

SMITH, BESSIE (1894–1937)

Recognized today as perhaps the best pioneer singer of the uniquely American musical form known as blues, Bessie Smith's career was nonetheless relatively brief and often painful.

Born into extreme poverty in Chattanooga, she received little schooling. Smith began singing as a young teenager, touring segregated entertainment spots in Southern cities, many of which bordered on disreputability. Her talent was genuine, however, and after honing her vocal skills for a decade, she moved to Philadelphia in 1920. Smith made her recording debut in 1923 with Columbia Records—and sold an amazing two million copies of her first album. She married that same year, but had no children and the marriage dissolved by the end of the decade.

The Roaring Twenties, which was also known as the Jazz Age and the era of the Harlem Renaissance, saw the zenith of Bessie Smith's career. Like dancer JOSEPHINE BAKER abroad, she was recognized by avant garde musicians as a black American who was creating a new art form. Even after the stock market crash and the beginning of the Great Depression, some of her records sold as many as 100,000 copies a week. Though her audiences were still segregated, she played at the best black nightclubs in the metropolitan centers of the North.

But both the Depression and Smith's alcoholism caught up with her, and—after more than 150 recordings—Columbia did not renew her contract in 1931. The rest of the thirties were hard for her, and like many Americans of both races, she found that the money that came so easily in the twenties had evaporated into bankruptcy a decade later.

There were hopeful signs of a comeback by 1937, when the Depression had eased, but Smith died in a car accident in Tennessee that September. Though a legend grew up that she bled to death because she was refused admission to a white hospital, recent scholars agree that the care she received was prompt and adequate, but that the injuries were too serious to be overcome by the technology then available.

Bessie Smith was buried in Philadelphia, while jazz newcomers BILLIE HOLIDAY and ELLA FITZGERALD were beginning careers influenced by hers. Gospel singer MAHALIA JACKSON was another who emulated Smith's deep, powerful voice, while assiduously avoiding her lifestyle. A number of men in her field, including white Benny Goodman and black Louis Armstrong, also acknowledged the important influence that Bessie Smith had on them and on American jazz.

SMITH COLLEGE

The first of the women's COLLEGES to be endowed by a woman, Smith College owes its beginning to Sophia Smith, an aging heiress who donated almost four hundred thousand dollars for the cause at the recommendation of her Protestant minister. Chartered in 1871 with classes beginning in 1875, Smith College was sited in Northampton, which placed it near the older western Massachusetts institutions of MOUNT HOLYOKE and (male) Amherst. Its birth in the decade after the CIVIL WAR was yet another manifestation of the transformation that the war made in the roles of American women.

Like the other new, determinedly prestigious women's colleges of that era, Smith insisted that its applicants meet the same preparatory requirements as men's colleges, and its initial class therefore had just fourteen members. Despite these high standards, the assumption was that most students were not preparing for professional careers, but rather for educated motherhood. The very first student admitted, Corinne Tuckerman Allen, confirmed this in a classic way: she became the mother of FLORENCE ALLEN, the first female appellate judge in America.

The Smith Alumnae Association began already in 1881. In addition to raising funds for the school, the association also provided a model for the alumnae of other colleges, who emulated Smith women in forming clubs throughout the nation—some of them residential—that provided important networking contacts, especially for young graduates. During WORLD WAR II, Smith College innovatively offered its campus as a major training ground for officers of the Navy's WAVES.

GWENDOLYN CARTER is prominent among Smith's historically important faculty members. Among students associated with Smith are MARY CALKINS, JULIA CHILD, AMELIA EARHART, CONSTANCE MCLAUGHLIN GREEN, MARGARET MITCHELL, SYLVIA

PLATH, MARY VAN KLEECK, ANNE MORROW LINDBERGH (whose mother served as the college's acting president), and modern FEMINISTS BETTY FREIDAN and GLORIA STEINEM. Freidan's 1957 survey of Smith alumnae was an important motivation for her in building the modern women's movement.

Like the Schlesinger Library of RADCLIFFE COLLEGE, the Sophia Smith Collection at Smith has become a leading repository for material relating to women, and letters from most of the suffrage leaders are to be found in Smith's archives. Joined by the public University of Massachusetts and the innovative Hampshire College, Smith is part of a coeducational five-college system in the Northampton-Amherst-Holyoke area.

SMITH-HUGHES ACT (1917) and SMITH-LEVER ACT (1914)

Passed at the height of political power for the Progressive agenda, these bills encouraged vocational education by providing federal funds to match those of states. Congress was particularly concerned with aiding farmers by teaching agricultural science, but the legislation also took cognizance of the farmer's wife—and of women generally—by encouraging the new field of HOME ECONOMICS.

Eventually the acts resulted in a host of home economics agents who worked alongside agricultural agents in thousands of field offices located in the county seats of rural areas. The agents formed HOME DEMONSTRATION CLUBS that taught women—usually FARM WOMEN—the new household skills needed after the invention of electrical appliances and other twentieth century changes. Especially in the South, the Federal Household Arts Schools that developed under the act taught skills to black women whose employment opportunities were usually limited to DOMESTIC WORK—but who could command higher wages if they could demonstrate professional training as cooks or laundresses.

These acts and the funding they provided were adjusted many times during the century, but the gender-based division of funding was seldom questioned. When tax dollars were spent on programs that benefited primarily women, it was most likely that these monies were aimed at domesticity.

SMITH, LILLIAN (1897–1966)

AUTHOR of the 1944 bestseller, *Strange Fruit,* Lillian Smith endured tremendous controversy over her work. It was banned in Boston, with the Massachusetts Supreme Court agreeing that her novel was a "menace to youth," and federal censorship lifted only after ELEANOR ROOSEVELT met with the postmaster general. What these northern men found so disturbing was a story of interracial love—written by a middle-aged white woman from the Deep South.

Like her fellow Georgian, MARGARET MITCHELL, Smith's first book was her most important. Unlike Mitchell, however, she continued to write, publishing both fiction and nonfiction almost up until her death two decades later. Smith's constant theme was the destructiveness of racism, and these words rang even more true when twice her home and manuscripts were the targets of arsonists.

Except for a few years in China in the 1920s—when she was music director for an American mission—Lillian Smith lived her entire life in the small towns of north Florida and south Georgia. Somehow she overcame the provinciality that was expected of her, and with the Asian experience further strengthening her views on the injustice of racism, she found her voice and spent the rest of her life leading her society out of its blindness. Nor was writing the only tool she used: Smith was an officer in the Congress of Racial Equality (CORE) and befriended Martin Luther King and other young African-Americans who rose to leadership on her shoulders.

Like PEARL BUCK and RUTH BENEDICT, who also wrote of the wrongness of American racial attitudes during this WORLD WAR II era, Lillian Smith understood the irony of losing millions of lives to racism abroad while permitting it at home. Moreover, like JESSIE DANIEL AMES, Smith put her life on the line every day as she continued to live among people who detested her message. These white women were pioneers in the 1940s of the civil rights battles that came to fruition in the 1960s, and they deserve more credit than they get.

Lillian Smith died of cancer less than two years before the death of Martin Luther King. Those of her papers that escaped burning are on deposit at the Universities of Georgia and Florida.

SMITH, MARGARET MADELINE CHASE (1897–)

The first woman to be elected to both the House and the Senate, Margaret Chase Smith served over three decades in Congress. A woman of unquestioned integrity, she was a Republican who voted with the Democratic Party more often than many Democrats. It was this personal independence and thoughtfulness that made her a source of pride for women throughout the nation. In the words of ELEANOR ROOSEVELT, Margaret Chase Smith was "the country's top woman politician" at mid-century.

A native of Maine, Margaret Chase worked as a TEACHER and TELEPHONE OPERATOR until her marriage at thirty-three. Her husband was elected to Congress in 1936, and after he died in the tenth year of their marriage, she was easily chosen to replace him. When she took office in June, 1940, the hot issue was American neutrality in WORLD WAR II, which was underway in Europe. Smith's votes backed President Roosevelt's interventionist policies rather than the isolationists of her own party, and when Pearl Harbor occurred during her first term, her prescience was justified.

Like EDITH NOURSE ROGERS, another childless WIDOW, Smith enjoyed being in Congress and ran for election in her own right in 1942—and until her career ended in 1972, she never lost an election. Also like Rogers, she represented a maritime area, and she obtained a position on the House Naval Affairs Committee in 1943. This led to her role as "The Mother of the WAVES," as Representative Smith sponsored legislation creating the women's unit of the Navy. She made inspections of naval bases in the South Pacific during the war and worked to solve the programs of naval personnel, especially women. After the war, she cosponsored the WOMEN'S ARMED SERVICES INTEGRATION ACT.

In 1948, Smith moved up to the Senate. The incumbent was retiring, and both Maine's current governor and a former governor wanted the position. Eleanor Roosevelt—who understood political skills—explained the respect that Smith was due for coming out the victor: "She had run against her party organization, most of the money in the state . . . and had won the primary with more votes than all three of her masculine competitors put together." Though Smith's initial Senate appointments were poor, she eventually rose to sit on the prestigious committees of Rules, Appropriations, and Armed Services.

Moreover, she earned the respect of civil libertarians throughout the world when on June 1, 1950, she again took on the powers in her party and denounced the tyrannical practices of fellow Republican Senator Joseph McCarthy. Her speech, "A Declaration of Conscience," remains an important historical document. It was a strong factor in turning the political tide back to moderation and tolerance, but of more importance to politicians was the demonstration she gave of the popularity of her views in the next election: Senator Smith trounced her primary opponent—who was endorsed by McCarthy—with an astonishing 82 percent of the vote. "As Maine goes, so goes the nation" proved true, and McCarthy went.

Her 1960 reelection race marked an historic milestone, as it was the first U.S. Senate race in which two women opposed each other. Smith defeated the Democratic nominee, Maine legislator Lucia M. Cormier, with relative ease. Smith's later career featured support for the National Institute of Health, and she again refused to follow the party line with her objections to Defense Department spending bills for experimental missile and supersonic systems. She also cast negative votes on two of President Nixon's controversial Supreme Court nominees.

In 1964, Senator Smith declared herself a candidate for the presidency and ran in Republican primaries in several states. She received twenty-seven votes on the first ballot of the convention that nominated Barry Goldwater—who went on to lose the general election by the greatest number of votes of any candidate up to his time.

Smith should have retired when her inclinations told her to in 1972, but she was offended by the ageist attacks of her opponent and undertook a fifth Senate race. She was seventy-four, however, and would be eighty by the time her term ended. That, plus the political stupidity of failing to maintain an office in Maine, led voters to look on her Democratic opponent favorably. She lost her first race, after thirty-two years of winning. Her defeat left the U.S. Senate all-male for the first time since the four-year period between HATTIE CARAWAY's 1944 defeat and Smith's 1948 election.

Margaret Chase Smith is associated in the minds of many with the rose, and a great deal of ink was expended during the long debate she had with Republican leader Everett Dirksen over the national flower. Smith's rose finally won over his favorite, the marigold, and in a 1987 congressional act, the rose became the national flower. It would be a shame, however, if Margaret Chase Smith is remembered primarily for the rose that bears her name, for she did far more of greater importance.

A Skowhegan, Maine library was dedicated to Senator Smith in 1986, and her papers were deposited there.

SOROSIS Often termed the first of the women's study clubs, Sorosis began in New York City in 1868. Its formation three years after the end of the CIVIL WAR is another indication of the expanded roles women assumed after that war.

The direct cause of its origin was the exclusion of journalist JANE CUNNINGHAM CROLY from a New York Press Club function. This proved a revelatory experience for Croly, and, with ALICE

CARY and others, she formed Sorosis. The organization thus had a clearly defined intent that differed from previous women's organizations, which had been largely limited to AUXILIARIES and the charitable roles of "relief" and missionary societies—though a few literary societies among WESTERN WOMEN preceded Sorosis, with the Bloomington, Indiana club dating to 1841. Sorosis, however, aimed at the emerging career woman, and not only was led by and limited to women, it consciously omitted philanthropic activity from its agenda of personal and professional growth.

Though the connotations of sisterhood in the name later would be used for "sororities" when these formed in the development of COLLEGES for women, the New York women who carefully chose "Sorosis" apparently did not intend this allusion. Instead, they were thinking of a botanical definition: the beginning flower that results in fruit. Their intention was to give themselves an opportunity to grow into their fullest human potential.

Since college education for women was still rare in 1868 (especially in eastern cities), Sorosis' sophisticated members had educated themselves. Because they were individually experienced with designing their own curricula, it was relatively easy for them to organize outlines of study and use the club as a group discussion class. The idea proved successful, and eighty-three women joined by the end of the first year.

Scholarly excellence alone, however, was not sufficient for Sorosis membership: it required some economic elitism as well, for the five dollar annual dues were equivalent to a week's wages for most women and the biweekly meetings were held at famed Delmonico's restaurant. At the same time, female presence in restaurants without male escort was in itself a statement of the group's FEMINIST aims. Many men responded to this unconventionality with scorn, and Sorosis—like clubs to follow—came in for more than its share of demeaning cartoons.

Especially because of Croly's activism, Sorosis became a direct point of origin for the CLUB movement, particularly the ASSOCIATION FOR THE ADVANCEMENT OF WOMEN and the GENERAL FEDERATION OF WOMEN'S CLUBS. Indeed, the New England Women's Club—an almost identical personal growth group that was important to JULIA WARD HOWE, LUCY STONE, MARY LIVERMORE, and others—began in Boston in the same year that Sorosis began in New York.

SOUTHWORTH, MRS. E.D.E.N. (EMMA DOROTHY ELIZA NEVITTE SOUTHWORTH) (1819–1899) AUTHOR

of what was probably the bestseller of 1863, *The Fatal Marriage*, "Mrs. E.D.E.N. Southworth" was an extremely popular writer. So singular was her reputation that book covers sometimes omitted the awkward first name she chose; "Mrs. Southworth" alone was enough to ensure sales. Eventually she published some sixty novels with titles such as *The Bride's Ordeal* and *Loves' Bitterest Cup*.

In the context of the time, however, writing in this genre was a sign of liberation, for even reading novels was considered improper behavior by many—women instead were supposed to limit themselves to the Bible and church publications. Southworth's books were the kind that women hid under their voluminous skirts when someone came into the parlor, while they quickly returned to the needlework that society deemed proper.

Like many other women authors, Southworth wrote for income, and her tales of unrequited love doubtless were based on her brief and unhappy wedded life. After her marriage broke up in 1844, she supported her two children by TEACHING before she discovered that far more money could be earned by fulfilling nascent female fantasies. It was a market largely untapped, and from her first 1849 publication, Southworth exploited it to earn a surprisingly good income—especially for a woman in this era of copyright pirating.

Many of her stories were serialized in such magazines as *Saturday Evening Post*, where fiction served to persuade millions of readers who otherwise would not have thought about the issues that affected her heroines. Influential like her friend HARRIET BEECHER STOWE, Southworth's plots helped change mindsets on such causes as DIVORCE and MARRIED WOMEN'S PROPERTY RIGHTS. She made her home in Washington, and that city's SUFFRAGE MOVEMENT included her on lists of their most prominent associates.

It was also Southworth who suggested to John Greenleaf Whittier the poem memorized by generations of school children that begins, "Who touches a hair on yon gray head . . ." She was more famous than Whittier at the time, and he sent his thanks, saying, "Thee deserves all the credit."

SPARS

The smallest of the women's military units in WORLD WAR II, the Coast Guard's SPARS came into existence on November 22, 1942. Like the Navy's WAVES, the acronym was of prime importance and the reasoning behind it secondary: SPARS stood for the Coast Guard's motto, "*Semper Paratus—Always Ready*." The SPARS enactment was precedent setting, for this was the first time women served in the Coast Guard, whereas both the Navy and the Marines had women's units in WORLD WAR I.

By the time the SPARS were created, the military was beginning to experience some difficulty recruiting women, and its enlistment standards were lower than for the WAVES; only high school or equivalent business experience was required. Like the Coast Guard itself, the SPARS remained much smaller than the Navy's WAVES or the Army's WAC; fewer than ten thousand women were recruited. Black women were not accepted until late in 1944, when the war was nearly over.

Officer candidates in the SPARS set an important precedent when they trained "along with Coast Guard cadets at the U.S. Coast Guard Academy, New London, Connecticut." Enlisted SPARS had no similarly unusual opportunity; their boot camp was in a semi-civilian setting at Plam Beach, Florida. All SPARS went on to specialty schools where they often learned non-traditional skills, but they were prohibited from overseas duty for most of the war.

Commanded by Captain Dorothy Stratton, SPARS used "Sir" even when the officer was female. Like the other women's military units, the organization's postwar existence was in jeopardy until the WOMEN'S ARMED SERVICES INTEGRATION ACT of 1948.

SPINSTERS

Considered a pejorative term by most FEMINISTS, "spinster" denotes an unmarried woman who is past the traditional age for marriage. It was, however, a more sensitive term than the commonly used alternative of "old maid," for it was based on occupation and earning capacity: a spinster worked the spinning wheel to spin thread for weaving cloth. In contrast, "bachelor" evolved from meanings related to youth and subordinate status, and referred only to marital state, not occupation.

In use by the 1360s, "spinster" originally could apply not only to a married woman performing this work, but also to a man who did. One early example of this usage was particularly complimentary: "Their women are excellent spinsters, and are saide to gaine more than the men of the towne." By the seventeenth century, "spinster" began to evolve into a legalism defining an unmarried woman, but occupational status remained more important than virginity, for even a WIDOW could be referred to as a spinster.

"Distaff"—another word referring to women that has fallen into disfavor—also has its origins in TEXTILE WORK. The "distaff" was a mechnism that held wool or flax to be spun. Perhaps because its function as a source of supply was similar to women's reproductive function, the word came to be associated with women.

STANTON, ELIZABETH CADY (1815–1902) If SUSAN ANTHONY was the chief organizer of the nineteenth-century women's

movement, then ELIZABETH CADY STANTON was its chief thinker. Moreover, Stanton led the movement for several years prior to Anthony's involvement: as the prime author of the DECLARATION OF THE RIGHTS OF WOMEN, she already had made a major contribution to women's history before Anthony ever appeared on the scene.

Elizabeth Cady was born in western New York State, where her family had long been locally influential. Like so many girls of her era, it was only because of her personal ambition that she was educated; she studied Greek and Latin in books bought for her brother, and she took advantage of the only superior secondary school available when she went to EMMA WILLARD's Troy Female SEMINARY in 1832—decades before COLLEGES opened to women. Stanton later spoke many times of Willard's influence and of the importance of such educational opportunities to young women.

After returning home—as young women of her social standing did in her era, for there was no thought of a career—Elizabeth Cady became involved with ABOLITIONIST members of her extended family, though her immediate family found this issue excessively radical. Through this, she met abolitionist Henry Stanton, a liberal journalist ten years older than she. Her family's

Elizabeth Cady Stanton speaking to a Senate committee in January, 1878. Her closely reasoned, legalistic testimony takes more than a dozen pages of fine print in the History of Woman Suffrage, *but among the best lines of this speech was: "Individual rights and individual conscience are our great American ideals. Men may as well attempt to . . . represent us at the throne of grace as at the ballot box."* LIBRARY OF CONGRESS; WOOD ENGRAVING FROM *NEW YORK DAILY GRAPHIC.*

acceptance of the abolitionist groom doubtless was not unrelated to the fact that Elizabeth was twenty-four and growing past the usual age for marriage. What few knew was that she had spent her courting years emotionally involved with her unhappily married brother-in-law—an experience that doubtless was influential in her later advocacy of DIVORCE law reform.

Henry Stanton lifted all that emotional baggage, however, and the two of them would enjoy an uncommonly egalitarian marriage. He indicated from the first his ability to be supportive of an unconventional wife, when he agreed that their 1840 wedding ceremony would omit "obey" from the bride's vows. Elizabeth Cady Stanton thus became something of a legend already in her youth, as this FEMINIST statement, along with LUCY STONE's later innovations in her 1855 wedding, became milestones of women's history.

The Stantons spent their honeymoon traveling to London for the World Anti-Slavery Convention—where another milestone occurred when Elizabeth Cady Stanton, along with LUCRETIA MOTT and other women, were banished from the convention because of their gender. This proved a learning experience for the bride in more ways than one, for instead of listening to speeches by men in the meeting, she spent her days in London parks walking with the older QUAKER leader. From Mott, Stanton learned that a life dedicated to revolutionary change could also include personal happiness. During those days in England, James and Lucretia Mott provided Henry and Elizabeth Stanton with a stellar model for their new lives.

The two women resolved that they would follow up on their discussions when they returned to America, but eight years passed before this happened. Meanwhile, the Stantons toured Europe and began their family. In the seventeen years between 1842 and 1859, Elizabeth Cady Stanton would bear seven children—or an average of one every two-and-a-half years. This colored everything that she did, for she was either pregnant or nursing or both during the formative years of the women's movement. One result was that she learned to use her pen instead of her presence and developed into a fine writer. A second result was that Susan Anthony spent so much time at the Stantons' home that the children called her "Aunt Susan."

After Henry Stanton passed the bar, they lived briefly in Boston before settling permanently at SENECA FALLS, NEW YORK. The Boston period, however, proved invaluable, for it gave Stanton the opportunity to meet more abolitionist women. Brave pioneers such as LYDIA MARIA CHILD and MARIA WESTON CHAPMAN served as further mentors, and when they moved to Seneca Falls, Stanton found reinforcement from such women as AMELIA BLOOMER. Indeed, part of Stanton's genius was her ability to stimulate thinking in others and to form networks that put bright women in contact with each other. From her home in a small town near the Canadian border, she would move the national mindset.

The beginning point for all of this was, of course, the SENECA FALLS WOMEN'S RIGHTS CONVENTION that Stanton and Mott led in 1848. Not only did Stanton draft the Declaration of Rights that was adopted at that meeting, but she also included in it a call for female enfranchisement—over the objections of Mott and others. When the resolution passed after sharp debate, Stanton could lay claim to having been the very first voice of the SUFFRAGE MOVEMENT. Her success would also shape the strategic approach she used the rest of her life, for Stanton consistently pushed just a little beyond what others thought public opinion would permit.

It was the letter-to-the-editor format that provided her initial opportunity, as Stanton responded to editorial criticism of the Seneca Falls Convention. So carefully reasoned were her views that liberal editor (and later presidential candidate) Horace Greeley was particularly likely to publish Stanton in the pages of his New York Tribune. She continued to attend abolitionist and women's rights conventions, where she soon met Susan Anthony.

Five years older than Anthony, Stanton proved the initial mentor; she educated Anthony—who at the time was more concerned with temperance than any other cause—on the imperative nature of the women's rights movement and especially the importance of suffrage. With greater freedom to TRAVEL, Anthony soon moved beyond Stanton in the organizing work of the movement, but year after year, she would return to Seneca Falls to sit by Stanton's fireplace while the two plotted strategy. In the oft repeated words of the HISTORY OF WOMAN SUFFRAGE, Stanton made the thunderbolts and Anthony threw them.

Partly out of deference to Anthony's temperance work and partly because she understood the legal helplessness of women married to alcoholics, Stanton co-founded with Anthony the Woman's State Temperance Society—after the existing temperance society made it clear that female members would not be treated equally with male ones. It was at an 1852 meeting of this women's society that Stanton made her next controversial push: she advocated the right to divorce drunken husbands. The response was outrage, for the very idea of divorce was scandalous at the time, and even these relatively advanced women feared that Stanton's radicalism would jeopardize their cause.

The chief reason for the miserable state of wives of alcoholics was, of course, the lack of MARRIED WOMEN'S PROPERTY RIGHTS. Stanton made her first major address to the New York legislature in 1854 on behalf of a bill on this subject, and for the rest of her life, she would maintain a reputation for eloquence in the spoken, as well as the written, word. Thereafter, she wrote most of Anthony's speeches as well as her own. The legislature passed a bill giving married women rights to their own wages and GUARDIANSHIP of their children in 1860, just before the CIVIL WAR erupted.

The Stantons moved to the New York City area during the war and would remain there for the rest of their lives. This gave her greater access to the public at the same time that, ironically, activity for any cause other than war-related ones was limited. Again, the Anthony/Stanton team came up with a successful strategy: they headed the LOYAL LEAGUE and collected hundreds of thousands of petitions for a constitutional amendment ending slavery. A secondary benefit was that the league again reinforced women's networks and fundraising abilities.

When the war ended, Stanton engaged in what was the most quixotic of her many forward leaps: in a test of the Constitution's gender-neutral wording on candidate eligibility, she ran for Congress in 1866. Of some 12,000 men who cast ballots, just 24 were audacious enough to vote for her. The following year, she made her first major speaking tour; with her children growing up, she accompanied Anthony to Kansas for a referendum on the enfranchisement of both ex-slaves and women.

They lost the election, but won other support, including financing that allowed them to begin publishing the *Revolution* in January, 1868. Again, Stanton did most of the writing on women's issues for the newspaper; she published editorials on JURY DUTY and PROSTITUTION as well as her standard topics before the paper collapsed in bankruptcy in 1869. That the publication could not meet its costs was not wholly due to its feminism, for the male financier included a number of eccentric topics unrelated to women's rights. Nonetheless, it was Anthony who took the debts seriously and increased her lecture load until they were paid.

Meanwhile, activists concentrated their attention on the FIFTEENTH AMENDMENT, and when it became clear that women would be omitted from any constitutional assurance of the vote for black men, Stanton and Anthony separated from their longtime associates in the women's rights movement over this issue. While the AMERICAN WOMAN SUFFRAGE ASSOCIATION (AWSA) accepted "the Negro's hour" with its implicit assumption of exclusion of women, Stanton and Anthony formed the NATIONAL WOMAN SUFFRAGE ASSOCIATION (NWSA) in 1869. Stanton would be the NWSA's president through most of its twenty-one-year existence; Anthony was vice-president.

In that same year, Stanton emulated Anthony's career as a lecturer. Not only did the adolescent Stantons benefit from the income their mother earned, but also she more effectively spread her message by traveling. By 1871, she had gone all the way to California, where WESTERN WOMEN found her suffrage advocacy less shocking. In addition to suffrage, Stanton's chief lecture point was educational opportunity for girls. The CENTENNIAL EXPOSITION brought her to Philadelphia in 1876, and Stanton also made regular trips to Washington to speak on behalf of the federal suffrage amendment.

Aware of the future importance of their cause, Stanton spent much of the 1880s working on *The History of Woman Suffrage*. After the 1887 death of her husband, she spent increasing amounts of time in England with her daughter, HARRIOT STANTON BLATCH. This, in turn, helped spark her interest in the INTERNATIONAL COUNCIL OF WOMEN that formed in 1888; Stanton's speech there celebrated the fortieth anniversary of the Seneca Falls Convention. In that same year, she also attempted to cast a ballot in a case similar to other unsuccessful tests of the Fifteenth Amendment. Two years later, the suffrage associations reunited, and Stanton served as president of the NATIONAL AMERICAN WOMAN SUFFRAGE ASSOCIATION from 1890–1892.

Though she never attended another suffrage convention after stepping down from the presidency, Stanton's days of radical leadership were not over. As the suffrage movement grew increasingly conservative and ineffective, Stanton again turned to the pen rather than the platform. In her eightieth year, she shocked even feminists with the publication of *The Woman's Bible* (1895), a carefully researched argument against women's subordinate position in religion that—like the *Revolution*—was more reasonable than its inflammatory title implied. Reverend ANNA HOWARD SHAW and others moved a resolution in the 1896 NAWSA convention disassociating

the organization from the book, and despite Anthony's impassioned plea, the motion passed. This hailstorm of outrage gave Stanton no pause, however, and in 1898, she added a second volume.

In the same year, she published her autobiography, *Eighty Years and More* (1898), and she continued to write on broad topics for newspapers and magazines. While Anthony and the NAWSA concentrated with increasing exclusivity on suffrage, Stanton remembered that the original movement had included far more than suffrage—and that it was she who had to fight for the addition of suffrage to the agenda. As she aged, her writing focused less on what she termed "sing[ling] suffrage evermore" and instead stressed issues more directly concerned with women's personal lives, particularly DRESS REFORM, divorce, and the damaging influence of religious and educational systems on the female psyche.

If Stanton had been appreciably younger and had lived into the 1920s, her leadership might well have made all the difference in keeping the movement alive after the passage of suffrage. She alone seemed to understand the importance of social—as well as political—change, and her voice could have been powerfully effective when the inchoate FLAPPERS of the post-vote era adopted liberating social changes without any awareness of the relevant political and economic connections. Had Stanton been there when women stopped wearing hats and cut their hair; had she been able to speak to them when they shortened their heavy skirts, started smoking cigarettes, and stopped joining the WCTU, she could have helped women make sense of all this and put it into the theoretical context that was needed for long-term effectiveness.

Instead, Elizabeth Cady Stanton died quietly at eighty-three. Anthony had spent a week with her in June of 1902, finding her almost blind but still alert and caring, and Anthony was one of the few guests that Stanton's family invited to the deliberately private funeral. Multitudes of eulogies followed, however, for Stanton tempered her lifelong radicalism with humor and kindness, and she remained extremely popular. More of a maternal symbol than Anthony in both appearance and personal life, she was beloved by many who never met her.

She was motivated by an unusually profound ability to empathize and by resolution that reached back to childhood: Stanton traced her activism to the female clients of her attorney father, whose lives were ruined by the law's failure to treat them equally. At the same time, Stanton's father was not supportive of her activism and once disinherited her; a judge later in life, he was more than a little judgmental. Their disagreements left her doubly depressed, for the problem was complicated by his grief for his only son, who had died young. Her insistence that she be addressed as Elizabeth *Cady* Stanton may have had partial motivation in proving to her father that a daughter could be as worthwhile as a son.

At least two of her children shared her views, however, and they published her diary and other works in 1922; others of Stanton's papers can be found in several important archives, including the Library of Congress and collections at VASSAR, RADCLIFFE, and SMITH Colleges. Elizabeth Cady Stanton's restored home is open to visitors in Seneca Falls.

Mabel K. Staupers was largely responsible for the entrance of African-American women into the Army Nurse Corps. These ANC members are disembarking in Scotland during World War II, shortly after the Corps began to accept black nurses. U.S. ARMY CENTER OF MILITARY HISTORY.

STAUPERS, MABEL KEATON (1890–1989) Born in Barbados, and a 1917 graduate of HOWARD UNIVERSITY's nursing college, Mabel Staupers worked in Harlem and in Philadelphia before becoming executive secretary of the National Association of Colored Graduate Nurses (NACGN) in 1934. From that position, she played a major role in desegregation of the military's nursing corps.

The armed forces claimed to be so short of nurses during WORLD WAR II that the NURSES SELECTIVE SERVICE BILL of 1945 proposed drafting women—and yet the ARMY NURSE CORPS maintained a strict quota of black nurses, while the NAVY NURSE CORPS admitted none at all. With assistance from Representative FRANCES P. BOLTON, Staupers pointed out this contradiction in countless meetings and in a well-publicized confrontation with the surgeon general. Her strategy was to force the change by generating demands from whites as well as blacks. After Staupers met with ELEANOR ROOSEVELT in November, 1944, both services announced changed policies in January. Meanwhile, the Army's WAC included black women from its beginning, while the Navy's WAVES, SPARS, and Women Marines—whose needs presumably were not as great as that of the Nurse Corps—had accepted them months earlier.

Though she resigned from the NACGN in 1946, Staupers went on to accomplish a second lifetime goal in 1948, when the giant American Nurses Association finally began admitting African-American members—though several affiliated state organizations still barred them. By 1951, she felt comfortable in taking the leadership to dissolve the NACGN because "the doors have been opened," and there was no longer any need for a separate organization. Mabel K. Staupers was honored by the NAACP that year, and in 1961, she published *No Time for Prejudice: A Story of the Integration of Negroes in the United States.*

STARR, BELLE (1848–1889) The difficulty of separating myth from reality in the life of this infamous outlaw is almost wholly due to hyperbole attached to her by adventure writers who were male. What is clear is that Belle Starr was the nineteenth century's female equivalent of Jesse James.

Like James, she grew up in the turmoil of the post-CIVIL WAR mid-South. Born Myra Belle Shirley, she dropped her first name early on, and through her brothers, became associated with the James and Younger gangs. Rationalizing their looting of neighbors as somehow caused by Yankee Reconstruction injustice, these and other gangs roamed from Texas to Minnesota, robbing banks, stealing horses, and endangering lives. Young Belle was an accessory to their crime, while she also bore two children who probably were fathered by bandit chiefs Coleman Younger and Jim Reed.

After Reed was killed in a gunfight with law enforcement in 1874, she moved to the then Indian Territory of Oklahoma and married a Cherokee named Starr. Thereafter, Belle Starr would reign in the Oklahoma hills as the "Bandit Queen." She controlled miles of rough terrain in which cattle rustlers, horse thieves, and others escaping from "Hanging" Judge Parker of Fort Smith found refuge. A federal judge, Parker's attempts to govern were continually foiled by criminals who fled to the Indian Territory across the river from the state of Arkansas. Starr's awareness of this legalism, plus her shrewd marriage to a Cherokee, is indicative of a mind superior to that of the average vandal.

In 1883, Parker finally made an indictment stick, and Starr served almost a year in a federal prison in Michigan. Incarceration did not change her ways, however, as Starr continued to plot crimes while also taking other lovers—at least one of whom was young enough to have been her child. Though arrested several more times, she never returned to prison before dying two days prior to her forty-first birthday. No one was ever punished for shooting Belle Starr in the back near her Oklahoma home. The likely assassin was not a law officer, but rather an enemy within her crime family.

Her daughter, Pearl Younger, went on to local fame as the head of a house of PROSTITUTION in Fort Smith, while her son died young in a gunfight. Like CALAMITY JANE's, Belle Starr's life served as both a romantic inspiration to unconventionality and as a warning morality play for young women. Dozens of dramatic books have been written about her, with the result that it is difficult to ascertain details beyond the clear fact that she defied all that most women of her era held holy.

STEIN, GERTRUDE (1874–1946) Gertrude Stein lived little of her life in the U.S., but she is an important example of the possibility of worldwide influence.

Born in Pennsylvania, she grew up in California, studied psychology under William James at RADCLIFFE, and spent four years in medical school at JOHNS HOPKINS before going abroad in 1902. With her brothers, Stein lived on an inheritance from a Baltimore-based clothing business developed by her German-Jewish ancestors. She remain in Europe the rest of her life, primarily in Paris, where she collected early work by Cezanne, Matisse, Picasso, and other important French painters. Within a few years, the Stein salon was a fashionable gathering place for the Parisian *avant garde.*

Stein did not wish to be known merely as an art collector, however, and began writing about 1906. She had considerable difficulty publishing, for her abstract literature, created in emulation of abstract painting, lacked popular appeal. By the outbreak of WORLD WAR I, however, she had written several books, the manuscripts for which were typed by Alice B. Toklas, an American who joined Stein in 1907 and remained as her lover and helpmate for the rest of her life. In a relationship that was openly LESBIAN, especially towards the end of their lives, Stein and Toklas achieved a new standard for acceptance and tolerance.

During the war, they drove an ambulance purchased with Stein's funds, and after the war, Stein's salon was increasingly habituated by Americans of the "Lost Generation"—a term that is attributed to her. Lectures at Cambridge and Oxford improved her academic stature, and she finally obtained a wide audience with *The Autobiography of Alice B. Toklas* (1933), a clever book written by and about herself. She chose a similarly deceptive title for the libretto of an opera with music by Virgil Thompson; called *Four Saints in Three Acts* (1936), it did not feature saints or have three acts. Other curiously titled works include *Before the Flowers of Friendship Faded Friendship Faded* (1931) and *The Geographical History of the United States* (1936), which, not surprisingly, was neither history nor geography.

Though critics and publishers often agreed that they "did not know what Miss Stein is talking about," she became an international celebrity during the depressed thirties, whose presence was sought by the literati in America as well as in Europe. Indeed, she was so well protected by her fame that, unlike most Jews, Stein not only managed to remain in France through WORLD WAR II, she even continued to publish. At the war's end, she wrote a straightforward book about the Nazi occupation, *Wars I Have Seen* (1945). Ever the hostess, she entertained American soldiers until the next year, when she died of cancer at seventy-two.

Gertrude Stein's influence on American writers, especially those who went to Europe in the twenties and thirties, was extremely important. In addition, her early art collection was indicative of Stein's uncanny ability to foresee the twentieth century's cultural future soon enough to make herself an integral—if sometimes incomprehensible—part of it. She is buried in Paris' Pere Lachaise cemetery next to her beloved Alice.

STEINEM, GLORIA (1934–   ) One of the most visible leaders of the modern women's movement, Gloria Steinem is primarily known for founding *Ms.* magazine.

Born in Toledo, Steinem graduated with a *magna cum laude* degree in government from SMITH COLLEGE in 1956. After two years in India, she settled in New York as a freelance journalist and during the 1960s was published in some of the nation's most prestigious magazines.

It was a story on her incognito experience as a Playboy bunny that brought her to national attention. Along with BETTY FRIEDAN, Steinem was a leading activist in early days of the NATIONAL ORGANIZATION FOR WOMEN, and in 1971, she co-founded Women's Political Caucus with BELLA ABZUG and SHIRLEY CHISHOLM. *Ms.* began publication the following year, and to the surprise of the journalism profession, soon became a profitable enterprise.

Gloria Steinem's biography is *Outrageous Acts and Everyday Rebellions* (1984). She remains a popular speaker and has received numerous honors.

STEWART, MARIA W. MILLER (1803–1879) Known as a PUBLIC SPEAKER when few women engaged in oratory, Maria Miller was born free in Connecticut of black parents who died when she was a child. She worked as an INDENTURED SERVANT for a family that taught her to read. Married in Boston in 1826, she became a WIDOW only three years later.

Through innate intellect and personal ambition, she continued to educate herself. The support of her black sisters also was important: decades prior to what is usually thought of as the era of the study CLUB MOVEMENT, Stewart belonged to the African-American Female Intelligence Society in Boston and, later, to the Female Literary Society in New York.

She came to public attention in the early 1830s by making at least four speeches in Boston that were reprinted in William Lloyd Garrison's ABOLITIONIST newspaper. In addition, Garrison published two tracts that Stewart wrote in 1831 and 1832. In all of these, Stewart urged blacks to greater assertiveness while reproaching whites for their prejudice. Unlike most of the era's speakers, she used little pity or pathos. Instead, she admonished African-Americans to stop their "armchair activism" and "gross neglect" of racial needs.

Apparently disenchanted with the response, Stewart made a farewell address and moved to New York in 1833. With a lowered profile, she worked as a TEACHER in the segregated public schools there for almost twenty years. As the CIVIL WAR approached, she went south to Baltimore and then Washington, where she NURSED during the war; Stewart remained in that vocation at Freedman's Hospital of HOWARD UNIVERISTY. In 1871, she opened a Sunday school after raising the necessary capital herself. Shortly before her death, she used personal funds to publish *Meditations from the Pen of Mrs. Maria Stewart* (1879).

STONE, LUCY (1818–1893) Although SUSAN ANTHONY, ELIZABETH CADY STANTON, and their supporters often treated Stone's role in the women's movement with an unfortunate degree of denigration, there is no doubt that she deserves a premier place alongside them. So vital was Lucy Stone to the advancement of women that "stoner" entered the language as a synonym for women who used their MAIDEN NAME—but she accomplished much more than that.

Born in rural Massachusetts, Lucy Stone grew up in a large family that demonstrated the different roles assigned to girls and boys. She was clearly brighter than her brothers, but was discouraged from educating herself. Like other girls, she worked as a TEACHER from age sixteen, while her brothers went on to COLLEGE. Teaching salaries reinforced her awareness of discrimination, and determined to better herself, she enrolled in 1839 at MOUNT HOLYOKE, the female SEMINARY begun by MARY LYON only two years earlier.

Lyon's innovative work-study arrangements set the pattern for Stone's true college education, for when she entered OBERLIN COLLEGE at age twenty-five, she continued to support herself by working part-time. Her father did not give her the financial aid that he could well afford until she had been self-supporting for almost a decade—unlike Anthony's father, who was emotionally, if not financially, supportive of his daughter.

Even progressive Oberlin, however, did not permit Stone to explore her interest in PUBLIC SPEAKING, and when she graduated in 1847, she turned down the "honor" of writing a commencement speech that would be read by a man. Nonetheless, her graduation with honors was a milestone for Massachusetts women, for Lucy Stone was the first female college graduate from that state—though she had to earn her degree in Ohio.

Almost thirty when she completed her education, Stone's career prospects seemed dim in this era when virtually no professions were open to women. She had come to the attention of ABOLITIONIST William Lloyd Garrison, however, while she was still at Oberlin; this, plus the intervention of ABBY KELLY FOSTER, led to Stone's hiring by the American Anti-Slavery Society—after she demonstrated her ability with her first speech, which she delivered in a church pastored by her brother. From the fall of 1847, she spoke for the abolitionist society on weekends and freelanced for women's rights during the week.

Like LYDIA MARIA CHILD, MARIA WESTON CHAPMAN, and other abolitionists, Stone was often heckled and at least once was physically attacked by a mob. Nevertheless, she proved so popular that soon she was earning far above average income for lectures that she scheduled and advanced herself. Having overcome any feminine reluctance in asking to be paid what her work was worth, she earned several thousand dollars annually. She also endured the indignity of ex-communication from her Congregationalist Church when the congregation responded to one of Stone's lecture specialties: she spoke on the inaccuracies of Greek and Latin translations that led to the Bible's apparent demeaning of women. Finally, it is important to point out that Stone's career as a controversial but profitable lecturer predated that of Anthony by a number of years, while her thoughts on the Bible predated Stanton's work in that area by decades.

In 1850—two years after the SENECA FALLS WOMEN'S RIGHTS CONVENTION—Stone led the way in convening what is known as the first national Women's Rights Convention, held in Worcester, Massachusetts. Her speech there was reprinted in the international press, where it came to the attention of English philosopher John Stuart Mill. It motivated him to collaborate with, Harriet Hardy Taylor, a married woman who later became his wife in the publication of "The Enfranchisement of Women (1851)," which predated Mill's famous *The Subjection of Women* by many years.

For five years between 1850–1855, Stone TRAVELED throughout the U.S. and Canada on the lecture circuit; she continued to attend annual women's rights conventions and presided over the seventh one. She adopted the DRESS REFORM popularized by AMELIA BLOOMER for a while, but though it doubtless drew larger lecture audiences, it also detracted from her message, and like others who briefly took up this pant-skirt, she dropped it. The fashion was ridiculed by most men, but it did not dissuade Henry Blackwell, the brother of physicians ELIZABETH and EMILY BLACKWELL. Having met Stone—who was appreciably older—through abolitionist circles, he courted her assiduously for two years before he was able to convince her that they could create an egalitarian marriage.

At his suggestion, they not only emulated the Stantons' wedding in omitting any suggestion of wifely obedience, but also incorporated into their 1855 ceremony a protest against marital law that was intended for publication—in addition to setting a new standard when Lucy Stone retained her maiden name. The year following their wedding, Henry's brother Samuel married Stone's Oberlin classmate, ANTOINETTE BROWN BLACKWELL. The Blackwells thus became the implicit first family of American feminism, and their combined influence throughout the nineteenth century was immense.

Almost thirty-seven when she married, Lucy Stone bore children at thirty-nine and forty-one. She lost the second, but her daughter ALICE STONE BLACKWELL became a comfort and source of pride to her. Alice received the parental support for education that was denied to Lucy, and she rewarded her parents by actively participating in their intellectual and political lives. At the same time, Alice remembered her childhood as somewhat lonely because Stone remained busy, especially after resuming her full-time lecture schedule when Alice was ten.

Meanwhile, Stone had set another precedent in 1858—the year between her pregnancies—when she reminded Americans of the "no taxation without representation" principle; her refusal to pay property taxes was met with the publicized impoundment and sale of household goods. She supported the LOYAL LEAGUE during the CIVIL WAR, and at its end went to Kansas to work on the referendum for suffrage there. She also served as president of the New Jersey Woman Suffrage Association and from there, helped organize the New England association, in which she would be active after the family moved to Boston in 1869. At the same time, she served on the executive committee of the AMERICAN EQUAL RIGHTS ASSOCIATION.

It was this group, formed to replace the prewar abolitionist structure so vital to the FEMINIST network, that created the bitterness between Stone and Anthony/Stanton that would afflict them—and the SUFFRAGE MOVEMENT—for the rest of their long lives. Intended to consolidate the efforts for African-Americans with those of women, the association supported the passage of the FIFTEENTH AMENDMENT, which Anthony and Stanton rejected because they feared (correctly, as it turned out) that its gender-neutral language would assure the vote only for black men. Stone, along with many women and virtually all men in the organization, was willing to accept this half-loaf measure that achieved the abolitionist portion of their goals and promised hope for women. Stanton and especially Anthony quarreled bitterly with the men over this, however, and they never forgave Stone's failure to join them.

The result was that Anthony and Stanton—in an uncharacteristically confused and conspiratorial way—formed the NATIONAL WOMAN SUFFRAGE ASSOCIATION (NWSA) in May, 1869, leaving Stone, JULIA WARD HOWE, and others to respond with the AMERICAN WOMAN SUFFRAGE ASSOCIATION (AWSA) in November. Howe was elected president, while Stone's major contribution to the AWSA was as editor of its publication, the *WOMAN'S JOURNAL*. She did an excellent job, and thus reinforced the unhappiness of the NWSA's leadership because their eccentric and debt-ridden *Revolution* compared badly. *Woman's Journal* was better capitalized and less radical, and it would make the women's movement increasingly respectable. Stone took up its editorship in 1872, after MARY LIVERMORE's initial tenure, and with Henry Blackwell and later, Alice Stone Blackwell, it was the primer publication of its type.

Lucy Stone lived to see the reunification of the suffrage associations in 1890; both her daughter and Stanton's daughter, HARRIOT STANTON BLATCH, played important roles in healing their mothers' old wounds. Stone chaired the executive committee while Stanton was president of the combined organization, but each was beyond her seventieth year and neither had much heart for continuing the struggle. Lucy Stone gave her last speech in 1893 at the COLUMBIAN EXPOSITION, and her friends commissioned sculptor Ann Whitney to make a bust of Stone that was displayed there. She sent greetings to the NATIONAL AMERICAN WOMAN SUFFRAGE ASSOCIATION'S (NAWSA) convention that year, but did not attend. A few months later, Lucy Stone was dead at seventy-five. That some of the old bitterness had at last mellowed seemed revealed in the fact that Susan Anthony kept Lucy Stone's photograph on her study wall, along with those of FRANCES WRIGHT, ERNESTINE ROSE and other beloved champions of the early days.

In requesting that she be cremated, Lucy Stone continued her tradition of innovation. Her ashes are buried in Forest Hill Cemetery in Boston, while her papers are in the Library of Congress and at RADCLIFFE COLLEGE. Alice Stone Blackwell published her mother's biography in 1930.

STOWE, HARRIET ELIZABETH BEECHER (1811–1896)

When Harriet Beecher was four, her mother died after bearing two more sons. Hattie—as she would be called by intimates

Illustrations such as this led to criticism of Harriet Beecher Stowe's Uncle Tom's Cabin *as a salacious, inflammatory work—but also increased its sales. Though the book was the nation's first bestseller and made Stowe wealthy, her motivation in writing it was to change attitudes on slavery.* LIBRARY OF CONGRESS; WOODCUT FROM DRAWING BY GEORGE CRUIKSHANK.

throughout her life—was reared by aunts, her older sister CATHARINE BEECHER, and within a few years, a new stepmother, who added still more babies. The head of this family of more than a dozen children was Reverend Lyman Beecher, who was on his ascent as one of the nineteenth century's most popular preachers—a position he held until the rise of his son Henry Ward Beecher. The Beecher family stands with the BLACKWELLS as the era's most morally influential.

At thirteen, Harriet entered Catharine Beecher's recently opened female SEMINARY in nearby Hartford, Connecticut, and at sixteen, began TEACHING there. She suffered the first of life-long bouts of depression during this period, with her uncontrollable tears probably caused both by her family's harsh Calvinism and by the contrast of her life to that of her seven brothers, all of whom went on to COLLEGE and professional lives as pastors of prominent churches.

In 1832, the family moved to Cincinnati and again Harriet taught in Catharine's school, while Lyman presided over Lane Theological Seminary. This institution changed Harriet's life, for Lane was a new school attracting a large number of liberal young men led by Theodore Weld, who later married ANGELINA GRIMKE. Though Harriet Beecher could not enroll at Lane, she did participate in its ABOLITIONIST debates and in a coeducational study club. The school also introduced her to Calvin Stowe, a thirty-four-year-old professor.

They wed on January 6, 1836. She bore five children in the next seven years (the first were twins born while her husband was in Europe) and lost a sixth to INFANT MORTALITY. Her husband's income did not match the growing family's needs, and so Stowe continued the writing that she had begun as a teacher, when she published a textbook under Catharine's name and won first prize for a story in *Western Monthly Magazine.* (The magazine, ironically, would go bankrupt in 1853, which its publisher believed was directly related to a negative review of *Uncle Tom's Cabin.*)

Stowe continued to write light magazine literature, and in 1843, a collection called *The Mayflower* was published by Harper's. Still, she saw herself as a mother and not as a writer; she had no room of her own in which to work and deemed her efforts merely "dashed off" to meet an economic need. When a servant was claimed as a runaway slave—a likely crisis in Cincinnati, where slavery was permissible across the river—she filed the experience away in her mind, but allowed her husband and brother Henry to attend to the woman's escape. Similarly, a brief trip to a nearby Kentucky plantation was stored away for future mental reference.

A major change came in 1850, when a heavily pregnant Harriet moved to Calvin's new employer, Bowdoin College in Maine. With more money and less illness in her young family, she was happier back East and even found energy to open a DAME SCHOOL in her home, where she could earn income by educating other children along with her own. Letters from her sister-in-law on the experience of Reverend Edward Beecher's congregation in aiding escapees from the Fugitive Slave Law affected Stowe deeply during this year, and despite distractions from an infant and five other children, she began the novel that marked her life.

Harriet Beecher Stowe always claimed that *Uncle Tom's Cabin* wrote itself; she said a divine power guided her as she worked late into the night by the light of her kitchen fire. It is certain that the idea for its end sprang to her mind prior to its beginning, for she finished Tom's death scene before seeking an advance to write the tale's opening. Beginning June 5, 1851 and going on to April 1, 1852, the story spun itself out in forty serialized parts in a Washington-based abolitionist newspaper. When the book came out at the tale's end, tens of thousands were waiting to purchase it. Though Stowe earned only three hundred dollars for the serialization, book sales were so good that her 10 percent royalty brought her ten thousand dollars in the first four months. At forty-one, she could afford to do such things as donate one thousand dollars to Myrtilla Miner, a white woman who recently had begun a Washington school for black teachers.

Uncle Tom's Cabin; Or, Life Among the Lowly (1852) went on to sell at least three hundred thousand copies in its first year, with estimates that include pirated copies running as high as two and a half million. Stowe's sales brought her international rank with Charles Dickens, Jane Austen, and the Bronte sisters, while no American AUTHOR of either gender had ever similarly captured public attention. In these days of poor copyright protection, a host of enterprises profited from her intellectual property: the first dramatization was done without Stowe's permission; card games and songs were based on her book; and several exhibitors even claimed to possess Uncle Tom's cabin. Because Stowe based some of her scenarios on cases she researched in abolitionist archives and on conversations with blacks (especially her Cincinnati cook), a number of people of both races plausibly presented themselves as the inspiration for favorably-drawn characters. Banned in the South, the book also served as motivation for more than two dozen novels in which slavery was positively portrayed.

Of greater importance to Stowe than profits was that her book quickly became the strongest influence on the national conscience. Fiction has emotional power far beyond facts, and *Uncle Tom's Cabin* brought sympathy for slaves and a storm of controversy unlike anything produced by thousands of earlier abolitionist speeches. Southerners denounced Stowe in abusive language, always pointing out that her experience in the South was limited to a few days in a border state. Modern critics complain that her characters were one-dimensional and the tale excessively sentimental, but her style was similar to that of acclaimed male writers of her time.

While the novel was suffused with the platitudes of nineteenth-century Christianity, at the same time there was a glimmer of FEMINISM in Stowe's work. She drew settings such as quiet kitchens in which QUAKER WOMEN provided refuge to runaways, while contrasting brutish men predominated in those scenes where mothers were separated from their children and driven to infanticide and suicide by the horror of their lives. It was men and not women, Stowe made clear, who passed and enforced the laws that permitted this great national evil.

The Brunswick, Maine house where *Uncle Tom's Cabin* was written was home to the Stowes for only two years. They moved to prestigious Andover Theological Seminary in Massachusetts in 1852 and remained there twelve years, during which she lost her oldest son to drowning. In these Andover years, Stowe published *A Key to Uncle Tom's Cabin* (1853), which was an angry refutation of the slurs cast upon her and the book, and a contrasting work the following year, *Sunny Memories of Foreign Lands* (1854), a chronicle of a triumphal European trip in which she had been welcomed by many of the era's great political and literary figures. She would take subsequent European trips, and corresponded with a number of European authors.

In 1856, Stowe wrote a follow-up novel on slavery: titled *Dred*, it predated the Supreme Court's famous Dred Scott decision. Better documented and better written than her previous novel, it sold reasonably well, but there was no protagonist with Tom's appeal. *Dred* came out at the exact midpoint between *Uncle Tom's Cabin* and the beginning of the CIVIL WAR, and Harriet Beecher Stowe wrote no more of abolitionism—nor did she actively participate in war efforts or write on the problems of the newly freed. In this, she seemingly justified both her accusers' charges of ignorance and hypocrisy, as well as her own assertions that she was merely God's messenger.

Whether it was God's voice or her own, there is no doubt of the vital role of *Uncle Tom's Cabin* in converting millions of Americans to the anti-slavery cause. Its importance can be seen in the national lore that credits Lincoln with saying to Stowe, "So, you are the little lady who started this great war." Whether or not this actually happened, however, is open to considerable doubt. Stowe left no account of meeting Lincoln, though she wrote a post-assassination sketch on him for the *Atlantic*—in which she mentioned that he did not read novels. She did go to Washington during the war, but her purpose was "to be present at a great thanksgiving dinner provided for the thousands of fugitive slaves who had flocked to the city," and because her son Fred was stationed in a nearby Army camp. Her memoirs—which were published under the name of her son Charles, who assisted with the book— neither mention meeting Lincoln nor hearing of the comment attributed to him. It seems to be only after Stowe's death that Charles told of going to the White House with his mother when he was twelve, and the documentation considered "most complete" was not published until 1934. Nonetheless, the persistence of the Lincoln–Stowe legend serves as a metaphor for the era, for Lincoln did understand and appreciate the importance of women's support in his war that freed the slaves.

During the last full year of the war, Calvin retired and Harriet clearly assumed the family's leadership. They returned to her childhood Connecticut as she supported not only her husband, but also two unmarried daughters, a middle son who submerged his wartime experience in alcohol, and her youngest, whom she educated at Harvard and abroad. Her income initially was great enough to build a palatial home in Hartford, but only five years later, it had to be sold at a loss. Like her neighbor, Mark Twain, Stowe's literary life was driven by financial worries and personal tragedy, for each writer lost adult children and each built homes they could not afford to maintain. Stowe's need for money can be seen in the fact that she wrote more than a book a year during the postwar era. None came close to replicating the power of her first, and even *Uncle Tom's Cabin* went out of print in the 1880s.

Though she never found a similarly stirring subject area, Stowe faced two other massive controversies. The tempest caused by her 1869 *Atlantic* article and its sequel, *Lady Byron Vindicated* (1870), must be understood in the context of Victorian hypocrisy, for modern mores make the outrage it generated difficult to comprehend. Essentially, Stowe was attacked because she had the temerity to speak candidly about English poet Lord Byron, who, though dead for more than forty years, enjoyed great popularity in this romantic era. The idolization of him by young people was troubling to Stowe, and she was even more distressed by a new book that she termed "an unsparing attack on Lady Byron's memory by Lord Byron's mistress." Stowe decided to reveal what Lady Byron had confided to her prior to dying: that Lord Byron had been guilty of incest.

Modern scholars know that Lady Byron's suspicions were accurate and that Lord Byron engaged in a number of scandalous liaisons, including homosexual ones—but these were subjects on which women such as Harriet Beecher Stowe were supposed to be determinedly ignorant. The literati of England and America responded furiously; the fracas seriously harmed Stowe's British sales, while some fifteen thousand mortified *Atlantic* readers cancelled their subscriptions. Stowe was condemned as both prurient and prudish, while her valid criticism of Byron's irresponsible behavior was ignored.

The other case also involved hypocrisy and double standards—but it hit much closer to home, and broke Stowe's heart. She had always shared a special bond with her brother, Reverend Henry Ward Beecher, who was closest to her in age. In the same year that Stowe published her *Atlantic* article, he was ending a secret affair with a member of his fashionable congregation. Both were married to others, but rumors of their romance spread. VICTORIA WOODHULL published the tale as part of her curious 1872 presidential campaign, and the sordid mess was replayed three years later when the woman's husband sued Reverend Beecher for alienation of affection. Stowe loyally defended her younger brother: "I taught him drawing and heard his Latin lessons," she remembered with loving maternalism, "for you know a girl becomes mature and womanly long before a boy."

The TILTON-BEECHER AFFAIR had a seriously negative effect on the SUFFRAGE MOVEMENT in the 1870s, for Beecher had served as president of the AMERICAN WOMAN SUFFRAGE ASSOCIATION, while his half-sister, Isbella Beecher Hooker, was active in the NATIONAL WOMAN SUFFRAGE ASSOCIATION. Worse, Hooker befriended several of Beecher's public critics, including the notorious Woodhull, and proclaimed her disbelief in his assertions of innocence. In return, he branded her "insane"—something to which she gave credence with bizarre seances that predicted an international matriarchy governed by herself. Despite this, however, Hooker saw male double standards for what they were, while Stowe denied reality in her brother's case.

These heartaches doubtless encouraged the Stowe family to annually escape to Florida after the 1868 purchase of a second home near Jacksonville. Stowe justified the extravagance of a winter home, which was still relatively rare at the time, as benefiting both her aging husband and her alcoholic son. The orange grove she bought to occupy him went untended, however, while she worked as energetically as ever.

Though manuscripts might be written in Florida, her best postwar books were firmly in the New England tradition. In novels that are largely forgotten, but which some critics call

her finest work, she engaged her practical Calvinistic mind in battle against the ephemeral attractions of the Gilded Age. One of the few exceptions to this somber tone was *Palmetto Leaves* (1873), a light piece celebrating the sunny relief she found in Florida; in dozens of letters, especially to Englishwoman George Eliot, she detailed her love of the tropical wilderness. Yet even there, Stowe implemented the dutiful generosity of her Christian morality and built a church for neighborhood blacks.

Always firm in the cause of African-Americans, she walked a more careful line on the question of women's liberation. Stowe positioned herself as a moderate between the conservatism of her sister Catharine, who publicly opposed the vote for women, and her brother Henry and half-sister Isbella, who agitated for it. She allowed her name to be used on lists of prominent women who favored suffrage, but was not active in the movement nor a friend of suffragist leadership in the way that Isbella Beecher Hooker was. In 1867, Calvin Stowe signed an endorsement of the suffrage referenda in Kansas, and two years later, his wife agreed to donate writing for the *Revolution*—if SUSAN ANTHONY and ELIZABETH CADY STANTON would change its name to something less inflammatory, which they refused to do. Any bitterness over this and the Tilton-Beecher affair had faded by 1883, however, for Stowe sent greetings to a Philadelphia testimonial for Anthony, while Anthony included Stowe's picture with those of other heroes on her study wall.

Calvin Stowe died in 1886, and Harriet lost her cherished brother Henry the following year. She completed her last literary effort in 1889, when she assisted her youngest son with the publication of *Life of Harriet Beecher Stowe*. She found the process of pulling together these memories "peculiar," and meeting an unfamiliar self in old letters "full of by-gone scenes and childish days" may have been a factor in the deterioration of her mind. She spent her remaining days happily working in the flower gardens that she had always preferred to housework and was lucid enough to write an occasional letter. Past eighty, her behavior was occasionally startling but never harmful, and it should not have been the source of derision that it was for Twain—who not only was younger, but also presumably enjoyed eccentricity.

Harriet Beecher Stowe died in Hartford a few days after her eighty-fifth birthday. She was buried at Andover between her husband and dearest brother and was memorialized at the annual convention of the NATIONAL AMERICAN WOMAN SUFFRAGE ASSOCIATION. Many of her papers are in RADCLIFFE COLLEGE's Schlesinger Library and in the American Women Writers Collection at the University of Wisconsin. Other manuscripts and artifacts are exhibited in Hartford. Henry Ward Beecher was elected to the HALL OF FAME in 1900; his sister—whose book was more important than any other in their mutual cause of bringing freedom to African-Americans—was added ten years later.

STRIKES, WOMEN'S It has been a repeated allegation that women cannot be counted on in strikes, commonly used as justification for the exclusion of women from organized labor. That even such a radical publication as the *Daily Worker* was capable of titles such as "Can the Woman Worker Be

Organized?" as late as 1926 shows the tenuous faith that leftist men had in the solidarity of their female colleagues. The record refutes that belief.

The strike that is commonly acknowledged as the nation's first occurred in Pawtucket, Rhode Island in 1824, when both women and men struck the TEXTILE MILLS. The very next year, however, women were the sole strikers among the United Tailoresses of New York City. The entire work force of Paterson, New Jersey struck briefly in 1828, and that same year, more than three hundred women in Dover, New Hampshire struck their local textile mill. Taunton, Massachusets women were led out on strike in 1829 by fifteen-year-old Salome Lincoln, and the pattern of regular revolts by women workers continued through the next decade.

After female shoemakers in Saugus, Masschusetts won a pay increase in 1833, for instance, their counterparts in nearby Lynn went on strike and organized a boycott until they won a similar scale. Women in the shoe manufacturing business in the Philadelphia area struck for months in 1836, while Pennsylvania cotton mill women demonstrated particular courage in 1834 and 1835 during a long period without wages. Though most of these strikes were partial victories at best, an 1834 work stoppage in Lowell, Massachusetts exhibited unusually well-defined strategy that provided the beginnings of the organization led by SARAH BAGLEY. In addition to the 1840s activism of the Lowell women, there were "turn-outs" in several textile mills in the Pittsburgh area in 1844, some of them violent.

Though the number of strikes declined because of the nation's first serious economic depression in 1837 and especially because of competition from the IMMIGRANT WOMEN and men who came to the industrial Northeast during the 1840s and 1850s, strikes nonetheless continued to erupt. When a thousand female shoemakers in Lynn, Massachusetts joined men for a demonstration in 1860—despite blizzard conditions—they led some twenty thousand who soon joined them throughout New England. In 1869, about four hundred women struck the laundries centered in Troy, New York, while eight hundred mill women in Dover, New Hampshire repeated their striking history that year.

In the next decade, female weavers in Fall River, Massachusetts separated from their male counterparts, with the women striking in response to an 1875 pay cut that the men accepted. When the Knights of Labor opened its doors to women in 1881, so many joined that 192 women's units were formed in five years. They, too, went on strike when appropriate, with walkouts of textile workers, hatmakers, and carpet weavers. The history of the Knights was short, however, and as the

Some 800 women participated in this march of striking shoemakers in Lynn, Massachusetts. Their parade took place during a snowstorm in March, 1860. LIBRARY OF CONGRESS; WOOD ENGRAVING FROM *LESLIE'S ILLUSTRATED NEWS.*

division of labor by gender rigidified in the late nineteenth century, women were largely excluded from new male unions. Most of these—along with women such as MOTHER JONES—had as their goal male wages that were high enough to enable women to remain in their proper place at home.

A few skilled women were exceptions proving the rule, with the cigar industry providing the most obvious case. Women from Bohemia who settled in the Northeast during this era led the way in cigarmaking and in unionization, and the same was true of female cigarmakers in Tampa and Key West, who went on strike repeatedly. Cuban women there not only ran the strikers' food program, but also made speeches and engaged in violent demonstrations. In the same era, German and Scandinavian women built unions in northern cities, while the influx of Jewish women in this era would be crucial to the labor movement.

An unexamined sexism is probably responsible for the fact that cigarmaking is called a skilled industry, while textile weaving and garment sewing is not. At the dawn of the twentieth century, however, there was a resurgence of strikes in those traditionally female industries where work often seemed to be defined as unskilled because women did it. As many as seventy-five thousand workers participated in textile mill strikes in the Philadelphia area in 1903, but the most famous of these actions were the great GARMENT WORKERS strike of 1909–1910 that centered in New York and Chicago and the LAWRENCE, MASSACHUSETTS TEXTILE MILLS STRIKE of 1912. In addition to these older industries, women also struck newer areas of employment: telephone operators conducted a major 1913 strike in New England, while retail clerks in Buffalo and Indiana walked out during the same era. Inflation caused by WORLD WAR I brought many strikes in 1919, including one by office scrubwomen and a major INTERNATIONAL LADIES GARMENT WORKERS strike that achieved a forty-four-hour week.

Increasing numbers of factories—especially textile and carpet mills—moved south in the early twentieth century to take advantage of cheaper labor in these states that prohibited union shops, but management soon found that Southern women did not necessarily fit stereotypes of docility. Violence was part of a 1918 strike in Columbus, Georgia, and in 1929, the Gastonia, North Carolina textile mills exploded into one of the century's most tumultuous strikes—a scenario further complicated by racism and politics. Women led the picket lines, and Ella May Wiggins, a mother of nine who was a leader in the mills, was killed when vigilantes fired at unarmed strikers.

Conditions during the Great Depression were so desperate that women's primary strike role was in an AUXILIARY status, though women continued to strike in such obscure situations as nutpickers in St. Louis. Strikes were prohibited during WORLD WAR II, but occasional exceptions occurred, including a work stoppage by Ohio telephone operators and a sitdown strike of black women who worked in North Carolina cigarette plants. As was the case with World War I, strikes erupted with the victory, including the largest by American women: 230,000 telephone operators walked off the job in 1947. In San Francisco, a 23 year old "girl" was knocked unconscious, while women in New Jersey and Chicago were arrested before the strike was successfully settled.

As service industries displaced manufacturing in the postwar era, women began to strike in areas where "professionalism" had long precluded the unladylike behavior needed for picketing and other strike action. The unrest of the 1960s and 1970s, however, brought strikes by women in such new areas as the electronics industry and in the much-publicized case of bank tellers in Wilmar, Minnesota. Calls for general strikes by women from the NATIONAL ORGANIZATION FOR WOMEN met with relatively little success, however, and the organizing of the nation's millions of female clerical workers has moved from NOW to new groups such as Nine-to-Five. Public employees in these areas of work have joined unions such as the American Federation of State, County, and Municipal Employees at a far greater rate than women in private enterprise, even though public employees are often prohibited from striking.

More attention has focused on modern strikes by women in the traditional areas of NURSING and TEACHING, in which strikes had been unknown throughout the nation's history. In 1959, thousands of workers walked out of New York City hospitals; as with factory women in the past, they endured arrests and violence, but their successful union would be emulated elsewhere. Civil rights intermingled with traditional labor issues in these medical industry strikes, as in the 1968 case of blacks who did menial hospital duty in Charleston, South Carolina. Industrial history was reversed in the service field, with its skilled workers lagging behind the unskilled: while unskilled medical workers struck in 1959, the massive 1984 strike of graduate nurses in Minnesota remains unparalleled.

Teachers have struck far more frequently—even though these strikers have been almost exclusively public employees, while many nurses work for private employers and thus have more freedom to strike. The American Federation of Teachers (AFT) led the way with New York strikes in 1967 and 1968; the Chicago AFT followed with a successful 1969 strike. The 1968 case of Florida teachers is more extraordinary: some thirty-five thousand teachers who were prohibited from striking both by state law and by their affiliation with the more conventional National Education Association (NEA) evaded the "strike" technicality by threatening to resign enmasse. Although NEA initially passed resolutions critical of the Florida action, it finally supported the teachers with funds and political lobbying. That, plus a 1972 staff strike within NEA, led the giant association into behavior that was increasingly analogous to traditional unionism. Very soon, the beginning of school each fall meant strikes of teachers in communities nationwide. Often it was women who were the elected leadership of their unions and who faced arrest and harassment. As government employees who usually operate under court injunctions banning strikes, these women accept particular risk of permanently losing their jobs.

Finally, the long history of women's participation in strikes must also include their roles in auxiliaries when no other opportunity for action existed. Nowhere is this history illustrated more clearly than in the mining industry, where women traditionally were refused jobs—but where they nonetheless actively supported strikes. In a 1913 strike in Michigan copper mines, for example, women were the users of violence rather than the victims. An aide to the governor complained, "Women continually resort to rock throwing . . . Soldiers were assaulted with brooms, which ... had been dipped with human excrement."

The LUDLOW MASSACRE is the most infamous case of violence against women and children caused by a labor dispute, but women were among those killed by militia in Baltimore and Pittsburgh during the giant strike of male railroad employees in 1877, and women, many of them Slavic, rushed to the barricades in the historic Homestead steel strike of 1892. Similar solidarity was demonstrated during the Great Depression, when women supported men in militant 1934 strikes from Minneapolis to San Francisco and in the famous 1937 "sit-down" strikes in the auto industry. Although women were denied the opportunity to work in these industries, they ran kitchens to feed strikers, did supportive secretarial work and other volunteerism for the United Auto Workers, the Teamsters, and other unions that were almost exclusively male.

Their aid was vital in these strikes—although both the industries and the unions involved excluded women from the benefits of their action. Men rarely have rallied behind women strikers with similar solidarity.

SUFFRAGE MOVEMENT Although women had greater legal rights in some colonial governments than they would enjoy later in the nation's history, women were not fully enfranchised in any colony. Some, such as New Jersey, had provisions for partial suffrage for WIDOWS and SPINSTERS who owned property, but these exceptional circumstances were more likely to be viewed as accidental legal loopholes than as an intentional grant of suffrage. Legal code rewrites after the Revolution made things worse for women instead of better, and ABIGAIL ADAMS' famous plea that the writers of the Constitution "remember the ladies" went unheeded.

It was states that decided the qualifications of electors, not the federal government, and states varied in their liberality of the franchise even without regard to the gender question. All restricted the vote to white males and most placed further requirements, such as limiting the vote to property-owners and Protestants. The elimination of such restrictions was part of the movement of Jacksonian democracy in the 1820s and 1830s.

This spread of democratic ideas among lower-class males was doubtless a factor, even if unconsciously, in the rise of demands for the vote from women, and a half-century after adoption of the Constitution, the organized effort on behalf of women's right to vote appeared. It was not the wives of the newly enfranchised Jacksonian men who claimed the right to vote, however; instead, it was the better educated, propertied women who were descended from original colonists—many of whom were understandably chagrined to see illiterate frontiersmen and recent immigrants cast ballots in exchange for a drink, while the privilege was denied to taxpaying women with a far better understanding of American history and government.

The first formal call to enfranchise women was part of the DECLARATION OF THE RIGHTS FOR WOMEN passed at the SENECA FALLS WOMAN'S RIGHTS CONVENTION in 1848. It was the most controversial item on the agenda, and ELIZABETH CADY STANTON included it over the objections of LUCRETIA MOTT and others. (Mott's reluctance may be partially explained by the fact that she was a QUAKER WOMAN, and many of the men in her faith did not exercise their right to vote.) The debate on suffrage was sharper than any other during the convention, and it passed by a close margin. Because full enfranchisement even for males was still somewhat novel, women's lack of suffrage seemed less obviously unfair; therefore this remained the most theoretical of the Seneca Falls goals. For more than a decade, the movement instead emphasized such issues as DIVORCE, GUARDIANSHIP, and MARRIED WOMEN'S PROPERTY RIGHTS.

It was the enfranchisement of black males after the CIVIL WAR that brought suffrage to the forefront. SUSAN ANTHONY was particularly angered by the priority given by the AMERICAN EQUAL RIGHTS ASSOCIATION to male ex-slaves, while educated women continued to be judged incapable of casting a ballot. After bitter confrontations with the men of the Association, she and Stanton formed the NATIONAL WOMAN SUFFRAGE ASSOCIATION (NWSA) in January, 1869. JULIA WARD HOWE, LUCY STONE, and others took up the remnants of the Equal Rights Association and regrouped as the AMERICAN WOMAN SUFFRAGE ASSOCIATION (AWSA) in November.

Especially after the ratification of the FIFTEENTH AMENDMENT a few months later, the differences were drawn for the next two decades: The AWSA remained closer to the ABOLITIONIST roots that both groups had shared, while the NWSA gave more attention to women and less to ex-slaves who, they felt, had been prioritized for several decades. Their operational styles differed also: NWSA largely excluded men and Stanton was its president during most of its existence, while the AWSA had both men and women in its leadership. Locational centers reflected ideological differences as well, for the AWSA came to be associated with literary Boston, where its *WOMAN'S JOURNAL* was published, while the NWSA established its headquarters in political Washington. Anthony (who was the NWSA's most visible leader, despite Stanton's ostensible presidency) lobbied for an amendment to the federal Constitution applicable to all states, while the AWSA adopted a strategy of state referenda on suffrage that they believed more likely to result in enfranchisement for some, if not all, women.

Victories were won in several states during this period, for the right to vote was especially likely to be granted WESTERN WOMEN in their newer state governments. Compromise suffrage situations also appeared in several states, granting women partial suffrage for municipal or school board races or on tax referenda in cases of unmarried female property owners. That these victories were not necessarily attributable to either of the large suffrage associations serves only to demonstrate the pervasiveness of the idea and the depth of the informal movement.

Indeed, for various reasons and throughout the history of the movement, many splinter groups appeared—some of which behaved as though suffrage were already obtained by calling themselves "parties." In this period, for example, VICTORIA WOODHULL organized the Equal Rights Party for her 1872 presidential campaign, while BELVA LOCKWOOD's 1884 campaign emulated this with the National Equal Rights Party. Neither was more than a skeletal organization, but such diversity helped the major associations by making them look large and respectable in comparison.

Though black women remained a distinct minority of the suffrage movement, some were involved from the beginning.

10

This 1913 suffrage parade was timed to coincide with the inauguration of President Woodrow Wilson. When marchers were physically attacked by jeering men, the police were slow to respond; the ultimate effect was to energize the suffrage movement and greatly increase membership. LIBRARY OF CONGRESS; PHOTO BY G.V. BUCK.

SOJOURNER TRUTH was present at the first national WOMEN'S RIGHTS CONVENTION in Worcester in 1850; the fact that her great "Ain't I a Woman?" speech is known today is because white women valued it enough to record it. She was featured at conventions for the rest of her life, and like her white colleagues in the movement, tested the Fifteenth Amendment by attempting to vote in Michigan in 1872. Because this was a time and place when the votes of black men were counted, it was clear that her ballot was refused because of her gender, not her race.

While it may be true that neither the AWSA nor the NWSA rushed to recruit African Americans, their original members had roots in the anti-slavery movement, and each appreciated those black women who joined. The AWSA, for example, welcomed poet FRANCES WATKINS HARPER to its leadership, while the NWSA promoted attorney CHARLOTTE RAY and featured MARY ANN SHADD CARY as a speaker. Decades later—when Reconstruction liberalism had disappeared from the rest of American society—black women such as MARY MAHONEY, NANNIE HELEN BURROUGHS, MAGGIE WALKER, and even radical IDA WELLS-BARNETT participated in the suffrage movement. MARY CHURCH TERRELL was repeatedly highlighted at conventions and made the most celebrated speech of her life before the INTERNATIONAL WOMAN SUFFRAGE ALLIANCE in 1904.

By the standards of their time, white suffragists were lead-

ers in race relations, for most organizations practiced greater segregation. Catholics and Jews also made up only a small portion of suffragist membership, but once again, cases such as ERNESTINE ROSE demonstrated a willingness to not only accept but also promote minority women who did join. Such tolerance is even more remarkable given the fact that few nineteenth century suffragists had any chance for COLLEGE education, and that most women in academia held themselves far from the middle-class housewives who formed the backbone of the movement. Even as late as 1898, for example, only two of seventy-two students in a RADCLIFFE COLLEGE class were willing to say they favored votes for women.

With such obstacles to surmount, the aging leadership of the NWSA and AWSA associations worked out a truce after two decades of destructive rivalry and reunited into the NATIONAL AMERICAN WOMAN SUFFRAGE ASSOCIATION in 1890. Tensions remained within the NAWSA for a number of years, however, in cases such as Anthony's immoderate response to the 1893 suggestion that conventions sometimes be held outside of Washington. In addition to the latent hostility between the former rivals, the NAWSA soon developed other internal factions. None was of greater significance than the tensions between Easterners and Westerners and the "wets" vs. the "drys" on the issue of PROHIBITION.

The two ran together to a large extent, for most Westerners cherished a heritage of individualism that included saloons as part of every town, whereas many Easterners associated the use of alcohol with the immigrants of their big cities—many of whom were Catholic, conservative, and anti-FEMINIST. A number of Western suffragists seriously objected to NAWSA leadership who identified themselves with the WOMAN'S CHRISTIAN TEMPERANCE UNION (WCTU) and other Prohibitionist groups, for they believed that Western men would never vote for suffrage if there was reason to think that the newly enfranchised women would then prohibit liquor. At the same time, large numbers of Eastern women—including Anthony—had an interest in temperance that predated their suffrage commitment, and they resented taking advice from women whom they saw as relative political newcomers. No case so clearly illustrates this difficulty as that of ABIGAIL SCOTT DUNIWAY, who succeeded in winning a suffrage referendum in Oregon only after disassociating from the NAWSA.

Such dissatisfaction with the progress of suffrage resulted in a profusion of turn-of-the-century groups, some of which affiliated with the NAWSA, while others did not. Among them were the college-based EQUAL SUFFRAGE LEAGUE, which was organized by MAUD WOOD PARK, and after its affiliation with the NAWSA, was presided over by M. CAREY THOMAS. The FEDERAL SUFFRAGE ASSOCIATION, founded in Chicago in 1892 by REVEREND OLYMPIA BROWN, aimed to redirect attention to the federal amendment after the NAWSA seemed to emphasize state suffrage campaigns—in a reversal of the NWSA's previous strategy. HARRIOT STANTON BLATCH, unhappy with the organization that her mother had presided over, brought some twenty thousand New York women into her Equality League; in 1910, she organized the first big suffrage parade. Variations ran from conservative suffrage groups headed by socialites to numerous working class groups in cities from San Francisco to Pittsburgh. The National Council of Women Voters was a particular point of pride, for this organization was made up of women who lived in states where they had the vote.

The movement became global with the formalization of the International Woman Suffrage Alliance in 1904; in the decade to come, even long-experienced American suffragists would learn lessons from abroad, especially from the British. This influence was extremely important, for the NAWSA had very nearly ossified by the turn of the century. Stanton died in 1902 and Anthony followed four years later; though each remained energetic until death, the organization suffered from a mellowed, static image. With its radical days seemingly behind it, some NAWSA members almost seemed to accept the inevitability of annual conventions devoted to speeches much like those of years past. Indeed, the pages of HISTORY OF WOMAN SUFFRAGE during this era are replete with commentary on floral decorations, celebrity attendance at receptions, and other details that make the NAWSA appear as much a social organization as a political one.

It was women who had worked with the British suffrage movement who challenged these attitudes. In the view of those who had gone to jail and endured the torture of hunger strikes in Britain, the NAWSA's comparable apathy was shocking: "In 1912," wrote one such critic, "the National American Woman Suffrage Association maintained a Committee [that] arranged for one formal hearing before the Senate and House Committee of each Congress . . . The Suffrage Amendment had never in the history of the country been brought to a vote in the National House of Representatives, and had only once, in 1887, been voted upon in the Senate. It had not received a favorable report from the Committee of either House since 1892 and had not received a report of any kind since 1896."

It was time for a change. With ALICE PAUL, LUCY BURNS, HARRIOT STANTON BLATCH, and MARY BEARD among their most visible leaders, younger women began working within the NAWSA, but soon they took their CONGRESSIONAL UNION (CU) in different directions. Paul's first triumph was to organize a giant parade for the inauguration of President Woodrow Wilson. On March 3, 1913, as many as eight thousand women marched from the Capitol past the White House, ending at the hall owned by the DAUGHTERS OF THE AMERICAN REVOLUTION. Because the NAWSA had never engaged in such unladylike behavior, Washington police misjudged the likely response and failed to protect the marchers from jeering men who attacked the women. The result was a swell of public sympathy; the police chief lost his job, while the suffrage cause was energized.

It was the Congressional elections of 1914, however, that demonstrated the CU's controversial new approach. Despite the fundamental differences in the structures of American and British government, Paul's group adopted the British model of pressuring the party that held the executive branch: thus, they decided to demonstrate women's strength by campaigning in the nine states (all in the West) where women had the vote. They would campaign against Democratic candidates because the president was a Democrat—regardless of whether or not the Democratic congressmen supported suffrage.

To NAWSA leadership, this was an insane strategy. They argued that to campaign against men who supported suffrage merely because they were Democrats was the least likely way to convert additional support in the majority party. They also pointed out that, unlike Britain's prime minister, an American president has no formal role in the passage of constitutional amendments. The CU women countered with arguments that can be summarized by a rhetorical question from its January newsletter: "Is it suggested that we be inactive in the only places where we possess real political power?" Thus, throughout 1914, they went across the nation with visibility techniques such as railroad cars placarded with banners—and succeeded in defeating twenty Democrats who had supported suffrage.

To many, the incongruity of defeating one's supporters only played into the hands of anti-suffragists who said that women were too irrational to vote. Moreover, neither the CU nor the NAWSA could claim much success on the suffrage referenda held in 1914; five of the seven conducted were lost, with only the additional Western states of Nevada and Montana extending the vote to women. The power of the 1914 election, however, was that it served as a profound wake-up call to the NAWSA.

At its 1915 convention, Reverend Dr. ANNA HOWARD SHAW withdrew from the presidency and was replaced by CARRIE CHAPMAN CATT. Catt had exhibited genuine political skills during her earlier presidency, when she had done such things as organize New York's various suffrage groups into a cohesive body and trained some two thousand precinct captains. Aware that effective political campaigns cost a great deal of money, she resumed the presidency in part because she knew that she could run a sophisticated campaign with the bequest of MIRIAM LESLIE. Soon after taking office, Catt formulated a "Winning Plan" that drew considerable skepticism both in and out of the suffrage movement—but only five years later, its promise would be fulfilled.

In addition to revitalizing the NAWSA, the congressional election of 1914 also got President Wilson's attention. He was up for reelection in 1916, and slowly he began to see that for political, if not constitutional, reasons he had to take a stand for suffrage. He responded favorably to Catt's careful cultivation, and his letter of June, 1916, promising to "join my fellow-Democrats in recommending to the several States that they extend the Suffrage to women" was addressed to Catt—not Alice Paul.

In the same month, Paul and her CU formally broke their long-loosened tie to the NAWSA. In June of 1916, they reconstituted as the WOMAN'S PARTY—in Chicago, during the week that the Republican and Progressive Parties were meeting there. Such astuteness indicated a continuation of its strategy of high visibility, for already in 1913, the CU had begun a Suffrage School in Washington to educate potential members, and it conducted "an uninterrupted series of indoor and outdoor meetings, numbering frequently from five to ten a day." *The Suffragist* had begun publication in November, 1913, and within three years, it replaced the venerable old *WOMAN'S JOURNAL*.

Generously funded by ALVA BELMONT, Party members worked hard against Wilson in the election of 1916, and again took little note of their defeat. When he spoke to Congress the month after reelection, they scored another coup by unfurling a banner from the House gallery—and were ready with publicity releases for "the men in the Press Gallery the instant after it happened." During the next two years, they drew tremendous attention by picketing the White House; except for Sundays, as many as a thousand pickets "of all races and religions" were there "in rain and in sleet."

Though much of their leadership had ties to Britain, the Woman's Party adamantly refused to endorse WORLD WAR I, for the war was declared only months after Wilson won reelection on the slogan of "He Kept Us Out of War." Their banners became, in the judgment of some, close to treasonous when war was declared, and after a confrontation in June, 1917, pickets were regularly arrested. Like their British mentors, they refused to pay fines, and about one hundred went to jail and endured hunger strikes—with high drama and sympathetic publicity for these brave women whose right to free speech was clearly violated.

In contrast, Catt not only supported the war, but even served on a major defense council. That strategy, however, appealed to a different segment of the public and especially to Wilson and Congress. The radicalism of the Woman's Party made the NAWSA look reasonable by comparison, and its membership soared, reaching two million by 1920. Nor did the war replace suffrage in Catt's focus, and she too had been to England and learned the methods of visibility: the NAWSA's 1917 parade particularly focused on women's contributions

to the war and included a petition signed by a million women working in the war effort.

Catt was astute in highlighting this point, for the public was deeply impressed by women's wartime roles. Women went overseas to drive ambulances and run telephone switchboards, worked in dangerous munitions plants, and even joined the military. Many who previously argued that only men should vote because only men served in war had to think again. Indeed, it may have been the war as much as any organizational strategy that finally brought the vote, for male voters demonstrated a changed view during the wartime elections.

In 1917, women won full suffrage in New York—the first Eastern state—and partial suffrage in seven other states, mostly in the Midwest. The following year, women won referenda in three of four Midwestern states, losing by a close margin only in Louisiana. The armistice was declared on November 11, 1918—a few days after the congressional elections—and the new Congress took office the following March. In May and June, the requisite two-thirds majority of the House and Senate passed the NINETEENTH AMENDMENT.

All factions of the suffrage movement worked hard to lobby it through Congress, of course, and then they continued the long struggle with ratification campaigns in thirty-six states during the remainder of 1919 and on into 1920. The final necessary vote came down to Tennessee, and after a great deal of pressure from fellow-Southerner President Wilson, its legislature ratified on August 26, 1920. The herculean labor was at last over, and women had the right to vote in all elections nationwide.

Finally, it is important to spell out the significant roles that men played in this long effort. Husbands such as James Mott, Henry Blackwell, and Henry Stanton contributed immeasurably more to the early cause than millions of women did, while William Lloyd Garrison had no peer in his dedication to women's rights. The same is true for thousands of anonymous men. In recounting efforts in 1870, for example, the *History of Woman Suffrage* remarks: "It is a noticeable fact that the movement for the enfranchisement of woman in Vermont was inaugurated wholly by men. Not a woman was on its official board, nor was there one to speak in the State. Men called the first woman's rights convention . . . ."

Decades later, one of the NAWSA's affiliates was the Men's League for Woman Suffrage, and among the first actions of the Congressional Union in 1913 was the formation of a Washington branch that was "composed largely of Congressmen." Ultimately, it is vital to remember that many women opposed suffrage, and that none would have ever received the vote had men not voted for it.

The suffrage movement was commemorated with a monument in the U.S. Capitol that was dedicated in 1921. Carved by Adelaide Johnson, it portrays the two leaders of the Seneca Falls Convention, Lucretia Mott and Elizabeth Cady Stanton, along with the indefatigable Susan Anthony.

SULLIVAN, LEONOR KRETZER (1902–1988) Elected to

Congress during what is considered a regressive era for women, Sullivan went on to author the bill that created the food stamp program and the truth-in-lending credit reform bill.

A Democrat from St. Louis, she attended Washington University there and worked in secretarial and administrative positions before and after her 1941 marriage to a congressman. He died in 1951, and two years later, she defeated the incumbent male who had been appointed to the seat. She went on to win twelve reelections, serving in Congress from 1953–1977. From 1973, she chaired the Merchant Marine and Fisheries Committee.

Representative Sullivan repeatedly introduced her bill on food stamps, but made little progress until the Kennedy-Johnson era. In 1964, President Johnson signed it, and in 1968, she was the floor manager for the Consumer Credit Protection Act. Both of these bills were important to women: the right of women to obtain loans in their own names was part of credit reform, while food stamps gave poor women greater independence than was the case with previous programs, which had prioritized the use of agricultural surpluses over the good judgment of women buying groceries for families.

Leonor K. Sullivan retired at seventy-five and died just after her eighty-sixth birthday.

SULZBERGER, I.O. (1892–1990)

The "matriarch of the *New York Times,*" Iphigene Ochs' father bought that paper when she was a child. After graduation from BARNARD COLLEGE, she married Arthur Sulzberger and bore four children, while maintaining an active presence at the newspaper. In still another example of the hidden influence of women in business, it was her husband who was named PUBLISHER when her father left the position.

Despite the lack of the most prestigious title, newsman James Reston called Sulzberger "the most remarkable woman our profession has seen in my lifetime." A longtime trustee of the *Times,* Sulzberger was active in many other causes. One of her daughters is now the publisher of the *Chattanooga Times.*

SURRATT, MARY EUGENIA JENKINS (1817–1865)

One of four people hung for their presumed involvement in the assassination of Abraham Lincoln, Mary Surratt was a WIDOW and the mother of three grown children. She operated a BOARDING HOUSE on Washington's H Street, where her son John often met with his friend actor John Wilkes Booth and other Southern sympathizers.

On April 14, 1865, Booth shot the president; at the same time, one of his associates, Lewis Powell, stabbed (but did not kill) Secretary of State William Seward, who ranked third in the presidential succession. German-born George Atzerodt, another conspirator, was assigned to kill Vice President Andrew Johnson, but failed to do so. On April 26, Union cavalry troops found Booth and another accomplice, David Herold, hiding in a Virginia barn; Herold surrendered, but Booth refused and was shot. John Surratt fled to Canada.

Meanwhile, official Washington was hysterical. Presidential assassination had never been so much as threatened during the nation's history, and the public was in a state of shock. Many, including President Johnson and the secretary of war, were convinced that the Booth plot was directly ordered by Confederate officials who aimed to win through assassination what they had lost in the war that had ended only days before.

Because the conspirators had a common thread in their association with Surratt's boarding house and because she recently had made two business trips to her former home in

The July, 1865 hanging of Mary Surratt for alleged participation in the assassination of Abraham Lincoln. Surratt is to the far left of the gallows, which were in the courtyard of Old Capitol Prison in Washington. LIBRARY OF CONGRESS.

a Southern-sympathizer area of nearby Maryland, Surratt was arrested on April 16. Taken to Old Capitol Prison, where BELLE BOYD was held earlier in the war, Mary Surratt never returned home. A military tribunal was hastily arranged, and eight were charged with conspiracy in the assassination. Of the eight, four would be sentenced to prison and the remaining four—including the only woman—were hung.

Held under military law, the trial was directed by a prosecution overly eager to convict, and seemingly uncommonly prejudiced against the lone female defendant. Important evidence, including Booth's diary, that could have cleared Surratt was withheld, while some of the men under suspicion were intimidated into falsely witnessing against her. Though the ordeal of the trial lasted from May 10 until June 29, Surratt was not allowed to testify on her own behalf, and the lawyers assigned to her learned of the guilty verdict through the newspapers.

On July 7, the three men and the (relatively older) woman climbed a scaffold in the courtyard of the Old Penitentiary Building and were executed before a somber crowd. At the last moment, Powell—the most obviously guilty of the four—again pleaded that "Mrs. Surratt is innocent and doesn't deserve to die," but the sentence was carried out.

Like ETHEL ROSENBERG almost a century later, Mary Surratt was the victim of mass paranoia. Ironically, while there was virtually no evidence that Surratt was guilty of a capital offense, women such as Belle Boyd and ROSE GREENHOW had charmed their way out of genuine acts of treason shortly before. Timing is one explanation for this seeming contradiction: Surratt had the bad fortune to be charged after the war's winner was definitely decided and her case was far more visible with its tie to a highly emotional crime that drew great public attention.

A second factor could be an unconscious resentment of successful businesswomen, for there is horrifying incongruity in the fact that she was hung while her son was not. The same ageism that beset the female victims of the SALEM WITCH TRIALS is an additional probable factor, while religion provides still another element: Surratt was Catholic during an era when there was vitriolic prejudice against Catholics, just as Rosenberg's Jewish background doubtless was a factor in her execution.

The public soon regretted its readiness to accede in Mary Surratt's hanging. Her accusers came under more thoughtful scrutiny already by 1867, when John Surratt returned from Canada and was tried in civil proceedings. He was released from prison in 1868, after prosecution was dropped when a majority of the jury voted for acquittal. The following year, Surratt's daughter received permission to give her mother's bones a proper burial. The execution of Mary Surratt stands as a shocking exception to the era's proud claims of chivalry and protection for women.

SWAIN, CLARA A. (1834–1910) An early female physician, Clara Swain practiced medicine during three decades in India.

She was born in the western New York area near SENECA FALLS that was home to many women leaders and learned her early medicine under the tutelage of her aunt, who was one class behind EMILY BLACKWELL at Western Reserve. Swain graduated from WOMAN'S MEDICAL COLLEGE OF PENNSYLVANIA, and in 1869, sailed for India under the aegis of the Woman's Foreign Missionary Society of the Methodist Episcopal Church.

In Bareilly, which is in northern India near the borders of Nepal and China, Dr. Swain treated orphanage patients, rode an elephant to remote villages, taught physiology and other medical subjects to women, and soon built a hospital that attracted thousands of women and children. While her care was aimed at the body more than the soul, she also included with each prescription a Bible verse written in three of the possible languages her patients might read.

At the same time, she was respectful to native religions and built her practice by accommodating her patients' cultural sensitivities—often at considerable inconvenience and expense for herself. In 1885, she moved into the palace of the Rajah of Rajputana after successfully treating his wife; thereafter, Dr. Swain's word on public health issues had even greater authority. She had long worked against the religious seclusion of women that limited their mobility, and she particularly spoke out against the common practice of killing baby girls.

After retirement back in New York, she lived with a niece who was also a physician and published *Glimpse of India* (1909). India's Clara Swain Hospital now treats men as well as women.

SWISSHELM, JANE GREY CANNON (1815–1884) The PUBLISHER of newspapers in three widely separated cities, Jane Swisshelm came to support of women's rights through difficult personal experience.

Largely self-educated, she was a TEACHER prior to her 1836 marriage. Afterwards, she built a corset-making business and headed a female SEMINARY, while her domineering husband's business ventures had a propensity for failure. She was particularly outraged when he attempted to sue for the dollar value of the time she spent NURSING her elderly mother—making it clear that she had no more legal right to manage her own time than a slave did.

Though he once forbade her to read, he encouraged writing when she published items in Philadelphia and Pittsburgh newspapers. He thus approved when Swisshelm began publishing the *Saturday Visiter* [sic] in Pittsburgh in 1848. She was a talented writer with a witty style, and despite the distraction of the birth of her only child in 1851, her animated editorials resulted in national circulation among ABOLITIONISTS.

After more than twenty years of unsuccessful marriage, Swisshelm left her husband in 1857 and he DIVORCED her for desertion. She sold the paper and moved with her little daughter to Minnesota, where she had family. There she began publishing the *St. Cloud Visiter,* which also was firmly antislavery. Like Elijah Lovejoy, who published a similar paper in a similar farming town in Illinois, Swisshelm's press was destroyed by political opponents. Forced to change the paper's name because of a libel suit, she called her new one the *St. Cloud Democrat*—but supported Republican Abraham Lincoln in the election of 1860 and spent the first two war years urging him to greater action.

When it was still uncommon for women to engage in PUBLIC SPEAKING, Swisshelm addressed the Minnesota House in 1860 and its Senate in 1862 on abolition and women's rights; she "was listened to with great respect." Her editorials were vivid and often amusing, laced with indignation at the injustice of handicaps on women earning an honest living. Minnesota suffragists would later honor Swisshelm as one of the state's earliest champions of legal reforms, especially for MARRIED WOMEN'S PROPERTY RIGHTS.

Like many in that place and time, however, Swisshelm was capable of great sympathy for black people while exhibiting none at all for the Native American. When the Sioux took advantage of the lack of Midwestern troops during the CIVIL WAR to attack prairie settlements, Swisshelm not only editorialized the popular local view, but went further: in lectures in several eastern cities, she argued for punishment of the Sioux greater than the hanging of thirty-eight leaders that had already taken place in Mankato, Minnesota.

Her lecture tour ended in Washington in 1863, and Swisshelm put the St. Cloud paper up for sale and remained there. She nursed in military hospitals while waiting for a promised clerkship in the War Department, and in 1865, began a newspaper in her third city. The *Reconstructionist* was intended as a voice for Lincoln's postwar plans, but his assassination and her editorial differences with the new administration soon led to bankruptcy. Washington was a difficult city for a new paper to compete in, and these were inflationary times; "a liberal sheet" called *The Wasp* that she tried in 1866 proved no more successful. Taking the advice of her friends, Mary Todd Lincoln and Secretary of War Stanton, she exercised her right to sue, obtained a share of her late husband's estate, and retreated from public life to her native Pennsylvania.

In retirement, she spoke for suffrage in Illinois and served on the NATIONAL WOMAN SUFFRAGE ASSOCIATION's finance committee in 1877—though the resolutions committee deemed Swisshelm's proposals "verbose and irrelevant." Too individualistic and wicked of tongue to work well with the protocol of the SUFFRAGE MOVEMENT, Swisshelm was critical of the NWSA in her autobiography. Her *Reminiscences of Half a Century* (1880) instead highlighted her wartime nursing experience. She died at sixty-eight and is buried in Pittsburgh.

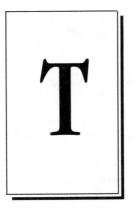

TALENT BANKS A tactic of organized women's groups during the twentieth century, talent banks are collections of data on the individual skills of women that are assembled for quick access when vacancies appear in public offices.

The BUSINESS & PROFESSIONAL WOMEN'S CLUBS especially led the development of talent banks, particularly during the Roosevelt years when there was a presumed willingness on the part of governmental leaders to appoint women to policy positions. The aim was to accumulate enough résumés so that there was always a woman available whose background was appropriate for the position, thus negating the argument of any politician who claimed to be unaware of qualified women willing to serve.

TARBELL, IDA MINERVA (1857–1944) Ida Tarbell's name ranks near the top of any list of pioneers in "muckraking" journalism. She probably would be called an investigative reporter today, and the new terminology would provide the enhanced image that she deserves, for Tarbell was a well-educated writer whose detailed publications were based on exhaustive research.

A Pennsylvanian whose family benefited from the 1859 discovery of oil there, Tarbell graduated from a local coeducational COLLEGE in 1880, when women college graduates were relatively rare. Like most educated women of her era, she worked as a TEACHER before becoming an editor of the monthly magazine of the CHAUTAUQUA MOVEMENT. After eight years in this position, she went on to study at the Sorbonne. Parisian higher education was still somewhat hostile to female students, but Tarbell was intent on her studies, especially in the history of French women. She met some of the era's outstanding thinkers, and, at the same time, began writing from Paris for the new *McClure's Magazine*.

From her 1894 return, she worked as a *McClure's* editor, while the magazine developed as a popular, progressive periodical known for its investigations into the rampant corruption of this plutocratic era. Tarbell distinguished herself from other *McClure's* writers with her series on Rockefeller's control of the oil industry, which culminated in the two-volume *History of the Standard Oil Company* (1904).

A woman who clearly understood economics, she insisted that Americans confront the difference between rhetoric and reality on the issue of competition. Her heartfelt work— motivated in part by her personal understanding of the effect of monopoly on Pennsylvania's oil fields—proved extremely influential, ultimately resulting in the enforcement of the Sherman Anti-Trust Act and the breakup of Standard Oil. She won a clear victory in a clash of power with John D. Rockefeller.

That her famous book on Standard Oil was titled "The History of . . ." was no happenstance, for while she is remembered almost entirely as a journalist, Tarbell was also a serious historian who was known for that in her lifetime. Her first book, published in 1895 shortly after her return from France, was a history of Napoleon that sold more than one hundred thousand copies. She continued to write history all of her life, including eight books on Lincoln alone. Moreover, she used the economics and business background that she developed for *Standard Oil* in other works, writing on the tariff and on the era's new "scientific management" techniques. Tarbell also did significant primary research on REVOLUTIONARY WAR WOMEN.

Tarbell left *McClure's* only two years after the oil expose, joining with a group of male colleagues to purchase *American Magazine* in 1906. She also moved to a Connecticut farm that year, which would be her home for the rest of her life. She remained politically involved, doing such things as joining other authors in a protest against the treatment of women in the GARMENT-INDUSTRY STRIKE of 1909. Tarbell worked as a coeditor of *American* until 1915 and then, at age fifty-eight, began a traveling life based on the Chautauqua lecture circuit.

She served on the Women's Committee of the Council of National Defense in WORLD WAR I and covered the postwar treaty discussions in Paris as a reporter. President Wilson recognized her economic expertise in appointing her a delegate to an international industrial conference in 1919; President Harding made her a bipartisan symbol with an appointment to a commission on unemployment in 1921. That Harding—a Republican, probusiness president—would make such an appointment is a reflection of Tarbell's increasing conservatism as she aged. Part of this conservatism was opposition to the vote for women; she spelled out her views in *The Business of Being a Woman* (1912) and *The Ways of Women* (1915).

She joined with SUFFRAGE MOVEMENT leaders, however, in the peace movement that followed World War I. She also foresaw the rise of fascism in Europe after a 1926 interview with Mussolini, and an understanding of its dangers permeated the autobiography, *All in the Day's Work* (1939), that she published in the same year WORLD WAR II began. Ida Tarbell died in the last full year of that war, forty years after publication of the book with which her name would be forever linked.

TAYLOR, SUSIE BAKER KING (1848–1912)

Like thousands of other women who volunteered as NURSES in the CIVIL WAR, Susie King Taylor probably would be forgotten today except that she wrote her memoirs.

Born into slavery on a plantation near Savannah, Susie Baker was more fortunate than most. Her mother, Hagar Ann Reed, was a favored house servant whose marriage to Raymond Baker was respected, and the family, especially on its maternal side, had an awareness of their genealogy that was unusual among slaves. Susie spent much of her childhood in Savannah with her grandmother, Deborah Reed, another slave whose intelligence earned her an uncommon degree of freedom of movement. Reed took Susie to secret schools where she learned to read in violation of Georgia law, and when she had learned all that she could in those places, Susie sought and received additional furtive tutoring from two young whites.

She was twelve years old when the Civil War began at Fort Sumter, South Carolina—only about forty miles north of Savannah. Georgia's sea islands were thus among the first objectives of the Union troops, and in the spring of 1862, Susie and part of her family escaped to St. Catherine's Island, where they placed themselves under the protection of the Federal army. They would not be proclaimed free until January of 1863 when they fell into the category of slaves freed by Lincoln's Emancipation Proclamation, but meanwhile, they

understandably did everything they could to assist the soldiers who sheltered them.

The thirty or so African-Americans were soon transferred to St. Simon's Island further south, where the commander placed young Susie in charge of TEACHING other blacks—including adults—to read. She worked at that until the fall, when they were relocated to Beaufort, South Carolina. The school was not renewed there, however, and Susie was assigned work as a laundress for the new Company E, an experimental unit of black soldiers commanded by white officers. One of these volunteers was Sergeant Edward King, whom Susie Baker married when she was probably fourteen.

As the unit began to fight, she began to nurse. Like thousands of women before her, Susie King was seen as naturally able in this "woman's work." She learned specific skills under the direction of doctors, but also probably continued as a laundress and informal teacher. The highlight of the war for her came with CLARA BARTON's visit to South Carolina in 1863; much later, she would record that "Miss Barton was always very cordial to me."

She apparently remained at Fort Beaufort for almost a year after the war was over, for she lovingly recorded the commander's farewell speech on February 9, 1866. Then the Kings returned to Savannah, where Edward worked as a stevedore while Susie taught a tuition school in her home and began preparations for motherhood. On September 16, however, Edward was killed in a work-related accident and Susie bore their son alone. Although she did manage to secure a pension based on Edward's military service, her school soon faced competition from a free school and she was forced into DOMESTIC SERVICE.

In 1873, she went with the family for whom she worked to their summer home in the north and discovered the improved status of blacks there. She took every opportunity to go north after that and ultimately settled in Boston, where she married Russell L. Taylor in 1879. He seems to have had almost no effect on her life beyond the name change, however, for her memoirs mention him only briefly and she clearly continued to make her own way in life as a laundress in Boston homes.

She helped found a chapter of the WOMEN'S RELIEF CORPS there in 1886, serving as its president in 1893. Five years later, she returned South to nurse her dying son in Louisiana. She was horrified by the abject condition of black people there, and this experience may have been her chief motivation for putting her thoughts on paper. The memoirs of Susan King Taylor were privately published as *Reminiscences of My Life in Camp* in 1902. She died a decade later and was buried in an unmarked grave in Boston's Mount Hope Cemetery. Her book probably had few readers in her lifetime, but it has recently gained a larger audience under the title of *A Black Woman's Civil War Memoirs*.

TEACHERS AND TEACHING

One of the few professions closely associated with women, teaching—in one form or another—was a part of life for almost every educated woman throughout the nation's history. Indeed, lists of famous American women probably will contain more women who taught than did not, for until recently, it was virtually an obligatory rite of passage for women intent on careers.

These two women were among many who went South to teach after slavery was abolished. Most were ostracized by other whites, and often their schools were funded by contributions they raised. Similarly ill-equipped classrooms were used by thousands of female school teachers all over the nation. LIBRARY OF CONGRESS; FROM SKETCH BY J.E. TAYLOR IN *LESLIE'S ILLUSTRATED NEWS*.

Educated or not, almost all women taught in their homes during the country's earliest years. Colonial girls learned from their mothers the basics of what would later be termed HOME ECONOMICS, as women passed on their accumulated knowledge in culinary arts, needlecraft, home NURSING, and many other indoor skills, as well as horticultural and agricultural information for the gardening, dairy, and poultry fields that also were assumed to be women's work. None of the knowledge necessary to do these tasks was innate in those born female, and all of it was in fact taught by women—whether or not they were considered teachers.

Beyond these practical arts, it was not unusual for a woman to teach the basic "three R's" to her children—and even sometimes to her husband, as in the case of ELIZA JOHNSON. Indeed, the first census that measured literacy, in 1850, found that women were as likely to be literate as men, even though the women of this era had no educated female role models because they had grown up at a time when no women were admitted to COLLEGES. Presumably many—especially isolated FRONTIER WOMEN—passed on the basics of literacy from what they had learned from their mothers and from life.

Black women were particularly likely to teach their men the fundamentals of reading and writing, for women were more likely to pick up the skills in the course of their indoor work, whereas most black men worked in the fields and thus had less opportunity for literacy. Frustrated housekeepers helped their cooks read recipes, for example, despite Southern laws against teaching slaves. SUSIE KING TAYLOR and MARY McLEOD BETHUNE are but two examples of black women taught by white women—and who, in turn, taught black men. After the end of slavery, some of these women supported themselves by running fee-based schools, often in their homes.

The precedent they followed had been set in the colonial era, when almost every northern town had its DAME SCHOOLS. Prior to the common adoption of free public education, many women supported themselves by running such schools. They charged tuition and taught both boys and girls the fundamentals of primary education. Such schools also taught domestic arts to girls, while boys were either passed on to male tutors or ended their formal educations after learning the rudiments of reading, writing, and arithmetic. These kinds of schools were prevalent enough that, when they were added to the public schools established in the Jacksonian era, a large number of jobs for women resulted. Indeed, some historians estimate that already by 1830–1860, as many as one-quarter of all native white women did "some teaching at one time or another."

Like the Dame School, another type of tuition-charging school was run by NUNS. Such schools were especially likely in the Catholic areas of Maryland and Louisiana, with those run by women aimed particularly at girls. The convent boarding school appealed even to many affluent Protestant families, for it assured parents that their daughters would be trained in devoted, pious behavior that enhanced family status.

In the South, both parochial and public schools were generally lacking outside of the big cities. Upper-class women were educated by GOVERNESSES and at FINISHING SCHOOLS, while many whites and virtually all blacks went uneducated. After the CIVIL WAR, hundreds of white women went South to teach ex-slaves, building schools intended for all ages and both genders. Some operated under the auspices of the federal Freedman's Bureau, but Congress closed that agency in 1869; many women then located their own resources in sponsorship from churches or from women's clubs back North.

Most of these teachers worked without salary and donated equipment from their own money. All of them suffered abuse from local whites, and often their experience in the South was lonely and difficult. Even though she held a low opinion of most whites, IDA WELLS-BARNETT testified to the importance of these women, saying that their students "cherish[ed] most tender memories of the northern teachers who endured ostracism, insult, and martyrdom to bring the spelling book and the Bible to educate those who had been slaves."

The end of Reconstruction that followed the Election of 1876 largely marked the end of this kind of teacher, but at the same time, thousands of educated women were heading overland in wagon trains, planning to teach in the public schools that were being established in the new towns of the Great Plains and Far West. The federal government dedicated one section of each township to education, and elected school boards used the funds from this land to build schools, recruiting teachers from back East. Though these school boards were invariably male, they usually recruited female teachers; few men were interested in making a profession of teaching when there was free land to be farmed—even though male teachers were invariably paid at least twice as much as women.

Women were expected to substitute prestige for money, and in fact, the "schoolmarm" was a respected community leader who retained this status after marriage. Most of these women did in fact marry after only a few years of teaching, and the occupation then automatically closed to them. They were replaced by other single women, who were often themselves the product of similar schools. Frequently only a few years older than their students, they passed state certification tests with little more than an elementary education.

Their work assumed their youth in other ways, too, for their low salaries were based on a system of "boarding 'round," or living a few weeks of the school term with each of the families that had children enrolled. Obviously, such teachers had little personal freedom, for parents made daily observation of their behavior. School boards often imposed onerous rules of petty detail on subjects ranging from the disposal of ashes in the school stove to the color of the teacher's clothing.

Not surprisingly, such control of the personal lives of teachers continued in parochial schools long after it disappeared from public school teaching. The one aspect of parochial schools that may have been more liberal is in the use of married teachers. This was because most parochial schools had their origins in immigrant churches, and often immigrant communities were so limited in size that they had no choice except to hire a married woman. During the early years of settlement, some immigrant communities were so eager to recruit the only woman who was capable of teaching the native language and religion that they accommodated the teacher by placing the school in or near her home.

Indeed, farm communities had long offered greater employment to female teachers than had cities. Because of the relative scarcity of educated people in rural areas, already in the mid-1700s, for example, western Massachusetts towns were hiring women teachers, while seaboard towns often limited their "public schools" to male students taught by men. The West led the East in coeducational higher education as well, which also resulted in more female teachers. Their proportion rose dramatically as the nation expanded further west: the decade between 1870 and 1880 saw an 80 percent increase in the number of female teachers. By the turn of the century, almost 75 percent of the nation's teachers were women.

A few of these women made their way into educational administration, especially in the case of WESTERN WOMEN whose men gravitated to outdoor work and left schooling to women. Already in 1883, CARRIE CHAPMAN CATT was superintendent of schools in Mason City, Iowa, while Michigan offered ALICE FREEMAN PALMER positions so attractive that she could not afford to move back East. Soon after Colorado enfranchised women, the voters elected women to the very highest educational office. Colorado suffragists proudly reported in 1920: "The office of State Superintendent of Public Instruction has been filled by a woman since 1894 and no man has been nominated for it." Wyoming elected women to the same high office during the same period—two full decades before most American women voted.

Ultimately, however, the number of women educators became a mixed blessing, as it was stereotyped as a "natural" female occupation. At the same time, even in systems that employed huge numbers of women, the male minority—who often had little actual experience—almost invariably held the top educational jobs. Like the women they supervised, these men were likely to be graduates of the "Normal Schools" that states built with the specific intention of training teachers. Though many of these institutions went on to become accredited colleges, there was more than a tinge of inferiority associated with this form of higher education.

This sense of being inferior to other (male) professions continued to be a major obstacle to the organization of teachers into professional associations and/or unions. Although Massachusetts teachers had organized such a body already in 1845, these groups, too, were long dominated by their male members. SUSAN ANTHONY, for example, was refused permission to speak at one such meeting while she was still a full-time teacher. Though founded in 1870, the National Education Association (NEA) did not elect a woman president until 1910, when Ella Flagg Young energetically campaigned and won. After women won the right to vote in 1920, NEA women directed the organization's lobbying program until women lost influence during the Great Depression, when male administrators again supplanted female teachers.

More blatant hostility between male and female teachers marked the beginnings of the American Federation of Teachers (AFT) in 1916, for even though women led radical unionization efforts in both Chicago and New York, they felt displaced by men at AFT conventions. Indeed, the Chicago Teachers Federation, which predated the AFT, maintained separate locals for men and women for decades. One bone of contention was male insistence that women pay full dues, even though school boards routinely paid women only half what men received. The AFT's affiliation with the American Federation of Labor was another constant hindrance to feminist aims, for the "family wage" ideal of blue-collar unions implicitly accepted secondary status for female wage earners.

Some brave women, however, did take on both their professional associations and their school boards. When a Chicago teacher, Mary Murphy, was fired after her 1901 marriage, she sued and won; the court ruled that "marriage was not misconduct" and thus did not fit into the board's grounds for dismissal. Most school boards ignored the decision, however, except in cases where schools needed the teacher's particular field; then married women might be retained as "substitutes" at lower salaries and without benefits.

Particularly during the Great Depression, thousands of teachers lost their jobs due solely to the fact that they were married women. Virtually all others took serious pay cuts, and systems throughout the country paid teachers in "script" that was not considered legal tender by merchants. Some school boards simply went out of existence; in Alabama, half of the schools closed and in Arkansas, a school "year" was sixty days. Major cities, especially Detroit and Chicago, did not pay teachers at all for long periods of time, asking them instead to donate their time. Doubtless such requests were based on a belief that many teachers were women, and that women worked only for "pin money." Experienced teachers were fired and replaced with less-qualified women who could be paid less—and still thousands of college graduates were never called for an interview.

WORLD WAR II and the postwar baby boom reversed all that. As millions of men were drafted and millions of women went to work in better-paid defense industries, suddenly the teacher surplus became a teacher shortage. Married women at last became acceptable as teachers, though pregnancy in the classroom remained taboo. The war was also largely responsible for the equalization of women's salaries with those men, while other court cases demanded that black teachers be paid equally with whites.

Ultimately, it was new economic conditions that changed teaching more than court decisions or even unionization. Like World War II, the revived women's movement in the late twentieth century sent millions of women into alternative fields. When women enrolled in colleges of business, medicine, science, and law rather than in colleges of education, school systems were forced to improve salaries and working conditions. Meanwhile, FEMINIST teachers continue to show leadership within their organizations; one clear symbol of change can be seen in unprecedented reelection of NEA's Mary Hatwood Futrell—a black, female president of the two million member organization.

TEASDALE, SARA (1884–1933)

A premier poet of the early twentieth century, Sara Teasdale's life resembles a romantic poem. Born in St. Louis, she grew up sheltered and shy. Her talents were reinforced by her private school teachers, and she published her first book of poetry at twenty-three. Four years later, in 1911, she issued a second.

Late in 1915, Teasdale rejected the courtship of young poet Vachael Lindsey and married a St. Louis businessman. She retained her MAIDEN NAME and they moved to New York, where she published four books in six years, including the prize-winning *Love Songs* (1917). Her work grew increasingly sophisticated, and Teasdale garnered international acclaim for fine craftsmanship of words; she was often compared with Christina Rossetti.

Dark of the Moon (1926), however, reflected her personal unhappiness, and in 1929, Teasdale divorced. She became despondent and reclusive, and when Lindsey (who was married) committed suicide late in 1931, Teasdale's depression grew profound. A trip to England brought only pneumonia, and in January of 1933—in the depths of the Great Depression—Sara Teasdale used an overdose to put herself to sleep.

Two more volumes of poetry were published posthumously; *Strange Victory* (1933) is considered her best.

TELEPHONES AND TELEPHONE OPERATORS

The 1876 invention of the telephone was fundamental to the growth of modern life, and it made a particularly profound difference in the lives of women. Though it might take several decades for telephone lines to reach rural areas, once that happened, FARM WOMEN were far less isolated. Especially in winter when roads were impassable, the phone made all the difference in relieving depression and loneliness.

City women, too, found the phone liberating, for it was faster and more cost effective than older methods of communication. Upper-class women could express their thoughts over the telephone wire instead of depending on a messenger service or servant to understand their meaning; servantless women confined to their homes by children could now speak with other adults without leaving home. Indeed, the telephone may well have been a critical factor underlying the success of the era's CLUB MOVEMENT and other forms of female organizing; participants in the great STRIKES at the turn of the century, for example, referred to the telephone in ways that make it clear that women were still learning how to use it.

At the same time, the phone system soon provided tens of thousands of new jobs for women. The Bell Telephone Company was organized in 1877, and women who had worked as telegraph operators soon learned the new technology. Although boys who had delivered telegrams were at first employed as operators, it was only a few years before management realized that women generally were more patient and courteous with customers and that well-spoken women could be hired for half the cost of comparably qualified men.

By the 1880s, women had taken over the switchboards of the first New England-based companies; by the turn of the

This 1922 telephone operator in St. Marie, Idaho, operated the switchboard out of her home. The arrangement, which enabled operators to be easily available at night, was common in small towns throughout the country until direct dialing replaced such systems at mid-century. LIBRARY OF CONGRESS.

century, over thirty-five thousand women were employed as phone operators. The word "operator" had been commonly used to mean a person who operated an assembly line machine in a factory or (especially in the case of women) a sewing machine operator in the GARMENT INDUSTRY. With the invention of the telephone, however, the usage began to change, and by the middle of the twentieth century, "operator" was generally understood to mean a telephone switchboard operator, who was assumed to be female.

Their numbers continued to grow as the numbers of phones increased. Until after WORLD WAR II, an operator was necessary to make even local calls in most communities; people picked up a phone and heard a female voice say, "Number, please." In small towns, this person was referred to as "central," and the switchboard was often in her home so that she could handle the occasional night emergency call. The onset of direct dialing brought dire forecasts of female unemployment, but increased numbers of business lines and the more frequent use of long distance calling soon proved these predictions wrong. The same was true when long distance direct dialing was implemented in the 1960s.

The International Brotherhood of Electrical Workers (IBEW) had historically represented men in the telegraph/telephone industry. The IBEW evidently placed a literal meaning on "Brotherhood," for women were not part of the union until 1909—when more than seventy-five thousand were employed as operators. Once admitted, women joined in large numbers, for they had genuine grievances. The phone business was particularly time-oriented and placed stressful demands. Operators in city systems were expected to handle two hundred and three hundred calls per hour and supervision was strict. Over the years, women supported strikes by both the IBEW and the Communications Workers of America; in some cities, strikes became violent.

In time, however, the telephone business learned to live with unionization better than many unregulated industries. If the industry had high expectations of workers, it usually also provided the background necessary to meet those expectations. Phone companies historically have been leaders in worker education; typical training for operators included classes in speech, business etiquette, and other areas that benefited women outside of the office. Even at the turn of the century, progressive systems provided well-equipped recreation rooms for breaks, and their personnel departments often led in the creation of an atmosphere that appealed to women.

Wages also were higher than women generally could expect in other work. The earliest female operators earned between eight dollars and twelve dollars weekly, at a time when most industrial women workers could expect little more than five dollars a week. Through most of the twentieth century, phone operators' pay was comparable to or better than that of NURSES and TEACHERS, even though the professional women invested money and time to earn the credentials for their work. The greatest inequity operators experienced was the sex-segregation that companies imposed by job title; until court rulings in the 1970s began to outlaw such employment patterns, women had little hope of employment in any category other than that of operator, while installation, repair, and other hands-on electronic work was done almost exclusively by men.

TEMPERANCE— *See* PROHIBITION

TERRELL, MARY ELIZA CHURCH (1863–1954) The

founding president of the NATIONAL ASSOCIATION OF COLORED WOMEN, Terrell was a mulatto who could have passed for white. Her father, who was freed by the Emancipation Proclamation just months before she was born, was the child of his Memphis master.

He had been well treated, however, and at age twenty-four, he married Louisa Ayres, another exceptionally favored slave whose master bought her a trousseau from New York for their wedding. Both Robert and Louisa Church had been taught to read in defiance of Southern law, and Louisa was a hairdresser so talented that white women were among her customers. Indeed, she not only provided the major share of their income in the first days of freedom, but even bought the family a house and carriage.

They called their baby "Mollie," and she was joined by a brother before their parents DIVORCED. Mollie's father remained an important factor in her life, however; her parents were so devoted that they took the unusual step of sending their daughter North for a proper education when she was only seven. Mollie lived with a black family in Ohio and attended the elementary school affiliated with progressive ANTIOCH COLLEGE. Her mother meanwhile had moved to New York, where she established a successful cosmetology business. Mollie visited both parents in summers before graduating from public high school in Oberlin, Ohio in 1879.

Memphis had a yellow fever epidemic that year, and real estate prices plummeted as the city's population fled. Her father bought up properties and when the economy rebounded in the next decade, he became a millionaire. By the time Mollie graduated from OBERLIN COLLEGE in 1884, he was perhaps the wealthiest black man in the South. She thus grew up far more privileged than most children, black or white, but from the beginning she chose to identify herself with poor African-Americans. Though she could have lived as a white—especially in Europe—Mary Church undertook a lifelong commitment to justice and to integration.

As one of no more than two dozen black, female COLLEGE graduates at the time, Church wanted to pursue a professional life, but her father was adamantly opposed. After a year of ornamenting his Memphis home, she took a TEACHING job at Wilberforce College in Ohio; her father was so furious that he refused to speak to her for a year. Eventually he mellowed, while his daughter moved on to teach at the Colored High School in Washington. Like many post–Civil War blacks, she made the nation's capital her home for the rest of her life—except for a European tour between 1898 and 1890, when the gifted young woman kept her diaries in the language of the country she was visiting. After earning a master's degree from Oberlin in 1888, Mary Church may have been the best-educated black woman in the world.

At age twenty-eight, Church was offered the position of registrar at Oberlin—probably the highest-ranking job then offered to a black woman at a white institution—but she turned it down to marry Robert Terrell. A Harvard graduate whose skin was even lighter than hers, he also taught at the Colored High School. After earning a law degree from HOWARD UNIVERSITY, he would go on to a successful career in education and government. His wife, like most teachers, was forced to end her career at marriage.

She lost three babies to INFANT MORTALITY before the birth of Phyllis (named for PHYLLIS WHEATLEY) in 1898; in 1905, she adopted her niece and namesake, Mary Church. Though she was understandably detailed in her supervision of these girls, Terrell did not use motherhood as an excuse for a leisurely life at the family's Newport beach home. Instead she began a thirty-year affiliation with a lecture bureau, and from 1892, developed into a national presence. She was motivated that year by the same racial violence that drove IDA WELLS-BARNETT from Memphis, for Terrell had known the victims when she lived there. She joined Frederick Douglass in what turned out to be a fruitless interview with President Benjamin Harrison for justice in this case, and then she assumed leadership in forming the Colored Women's League.

In 1896, this organization merged with others to become the NATIONAL ASSOCIATION OF COLORED WOMEN (NACW); Terrell would serve three terms before being named honorary lifetime president in 1901. The NACW took on the broad agenda of racial justice and an end to gender bias, but its goals also included such practical items as opening child nurseries for black mothers. Terrell's NACW speeches combine budgetary ambition with a strong maternal inclination, for black children were the focus of most of her fund-raising. She repeatedly spoke of them in loving terms: "how terrible is the suffering of infants of working women," she said in 1900, citing "an infant [who was] locked in a room all day, while its mother went out to wash, [who] cried itself to death." She went on to argue that if her members absolutely could not fund such projects, other approaches were possible: "No organization is so poor both in mental resources and in money that it cannot form a children's club . . ."

The NACW's presidency made her the most recognized African-American in the SUFFRAGE MOVEMENT, and she spoke before several conventions of the NATIONAL AMERICAN WOMAN SUFFRAGE ASSOCIATION (NAWSA) after 1898. Terrell made what was probably her most famous speech in 1904 at the INTERNATIONAL COUNCIL OF WOMEN in Berlin, when she delighted the audience by delivering her address in French and German, as well as English. Aging suffragist saint SUSAN ANTHONY indicated her appreciation by sending copies of her autobiography to six-year-old Phyllis. In 1908, Terrell was asked by the NAWSA to deliver two speeches during the sixtieth anniversary celebration of the SENECA FALLS WOMEN'S RIGHTS CONVENTION.

At the same time, Terrell was achieving recognition in her chosen field of education, for a year after her disappointing interview with the president, she was appointed to the School Board of the District of Columbia. She served from 1895–1911, with her priority being the enforcement of the Supreme Court's 1890 "separate but equal" ruling. While working to ensure the equal treatment of black teachers and students, Terrell also was active in the first literary and historical societies devoted to African-Americans, and she contributed articles to many periodicals.

In 1906, she again sought and received an interview with Secretary of War (and later president) William Howard Taft, when she argued for black soldiers in case of violence in Texas. The following year, she published an uncommonly candid article in the *Independent*, a progressive magazine aimed at whites, titled "What It Means to Be Colored in the Capital of the United States." Although this was indicative of her increasing impatience with the pace of progress, Terrell nonetheless served as a cofounder of Booker T. Washington's relatively moderate National Association for the Advancement of Colored People in 1909. She would, however, take W.E.B. DuBois' more radical side of conflicts within the NAACP—and began to develop a reputation for being "hard to get along with."

It was a calumny that suffragists understood, and Terrell continued to work with white women. She took the lead in the centennial celebration of the birth of HARRIET BEECHER STOWE in 1911 and regularly joined suffragists in picketing the White House. As part of women's efforts in WORLD WAR I, she took a job in the War Department, but resigned after being assigned to a segregated unit. After the war to make the world safe for democracy brought little reward for some, Terrell joined the mostly white WOMEN'S INTERNATIONAL LEAGUE FOR PEACE AND FREEDOM and was welcomed as a speaker at the group's first postwar gathering in Zurich, where she spoke frankly about the lack of freedom for people of color.

When women got the vote in 1920, Terrell probably registered at her summer home in Maryland, for the largely black population of the District of Columbia was not enfranchised. She nonetheless served as a coordinator among black women for the Republican National Committee throughout the twenties, campaigning especially hard for RUTH HANNA MCCORMICK. Though relatively few blacks dared to register to vote in this era, those that did usually thought of themselves as Republicans because that was the party of Lincoln; Terrell maintained her affiliation with the party until 1952.

This, plus her increasing age, isolated her from power during the Roosevelt years, when most blacks switched to the Democratic Party and MARY MCLEOD BETHUNE displaced Terrell as the primary national black spokeswoman. Widowed in 1925, she spent much of the thirties writing her autobiography, and H.G. Wells honored her by writing the preface to *A Colored Woman in a White World* (1940). Terrell returned to greater activism in the forties, when, sadly enough, she had

to sue the Washington chapter of the AMERICAN ASSOCIATION OF UNIVERSITY WOMEN for reinstatement of her lapsed membership; after she won, most of the women ostracized Terrell and formed another chapter.

Doubtless this was a motivation for spending less effort on women's causes and more on blacks', as during the fifties, Terrell led some of the nation's first integration actions. She developed techniques later used by the civil rights movement, particularly in the integration of eating facilities. She not only picketed, but also found a few blacks brave enough to stage a sit-in at Thompson's Restaurant; when they were refused service, she sued on the basis of Reconstruction laws that had never been repealed. At nearly ninety, Terrell testified before the Supreme Court, winning the case in 1953—when Martin Luther King was still a student.

Even more creatively, she surreptitiously bought up theater tickets and distributed them among African-Americans who turned up a few moments before curtain time, thus forcing managers to either admit them or cancel the performance. Such creativity and energy earned Terrell the respect of thoughtful people in both races, and hundreds of them honored her for her ninetieth birthday. They promised an integrated city for her one hundredth, but she died the following year—while planning another trip to Georgia on behalf of a woman and her two sons who faced the death penalty for killing a white man who assaulted her.

Mary Church Terrell's death came just weeks after the Supreme Court's seminal ruling for school integration in *Brown v. Board of Education*. It was a fitting end to life lived by her motto: "Keep on going, keep on insisting, keep on fighting injustice."

TEXTILE MILLS AND TEXTILE WORKERS The manufacturing of cloth was America's first large-scale mechanized industry, due in large part to the popularity of cotton. This cost-efficient, fiber-producing plant did not grow in the north of Europe from which most settlers came, but cotton thrived in the heat of the American South. The first factories to make cloth from it employed REVOLUTIONARY WAR WOMEN during the boycott of British goods. Especially after the introduction of the cotton gin in the 1790s, cotton displaced more expensive linen as the summer clothing staple. Samuel Slater built the first water-powered textile mill in Pawtucket, Rhode Island in 1793, but until the War of 1812, most raw cotton was shipped to England to be manufactured into cloth.

When that war demonstrated the nation's need for an independent industrial system, enterprising Boston merchants began importing cotton from the South and building factories powered by waterfalls. In Massachusetts' towns such as Fall River, Lawrence, and Lowell, local rivers were put to work generating the motion to run machines; soon mills spread into southern New Hampshire towns such as Manchester. Though some would be built further south, New England remained the heart of the textile industry throughout the nineteenth century.

In addition to water power, a second factor in the success of these mills was the availability of female labor to operate the looms. Women, of course, had spun and weaved at home for centuries, but Deborah Skinner is credited as the first woman to run a power loom in 1814. She set an important

The textile industry was the first major employer of women in manufacturing; as early as 1820, thousands of women worked in factories such as this, turning raw cotton into cloth. While women had more opportunity for independent income than was the case in an agrarian economy, these factories destroyed workers' health and offered no financial security. LIBRARY OF CONGRESS.

precedent, and when a factory opened in Waltham the following year, women were hired as the predominant work force. For the rest of the nineteenth century, women's lives would increasingly turn from HOME CONTRACT WORK to work done in an industrial setting—and importantly, work done for cash wages paid to them personally.

The possibility of such fundamental transformation, however, rarely entered the minds of New Englanders who sent their daughters to work in the mills. Their rocky, thin farmland offered only a hardscrabble living, and tens of thousands of families were more than willing for their girls to work a few years before entering the inevitable vocation of motherhood. Moreover, business advocates such as Alexander Hamilton saw women and children as ideal industrial workers, pointing out not only their exceptionally "nimble fingers," but also the advantages of keeping these people, whom they saw as society's drones, from the temptations of idleness.

Manufacturers soon responded with BOARDING HOUSES where young women could live under safe, supervised conditions,

and younger sisters worked along with older ones. For the first decades of their existence, such factories offered a reasonably pleasant life; women not only had a new opportunity to earn money and live independently from families, but companies even provided such amenities as libraries, study clubs, and literary magazines. LUCY LARCOM's famous reminiscence of this era was based in its last days, however, for Larcom worked in the mills during the 1840s, and by the end of that decade, a new type of worker began to displace these Yankee women.

In 1820—just five years from the date of the Waltham factory— approximately twelve thousand people, most of whom were women and children, worked in textile mills; the following decade, there were fifty-five thousand. A 1835 report indicates that in typical factories, more than 80 percent of the work force was women, but by 1850, when almost one hundred thousand were employed in the textile industry, increasing numbers were men. They were part of the first waves of immigration that would change New England forever, as the

Irish fled the potato famine and families from Britain and the provinces that became Germany left the Old World's 1848 political turmoil.

Most of these families did not farm in America, even if they had in Europe. The Homestead Act had not yet been passed, and few of them had the capital to begin farming. Thus, IMMIGRANT WOMEN and men began displacing native women in manufacturing. Whole families worked, combining their wages to eke out an existence, and as they acclimated to America and demanded more, they found themselves displaced by another group of new immigrants. Management sought these newcomers—especially the women—believing that they brought European habits of docility and would willingly live in substandard conditions. Moreover, their diverse languages prevented communication and reinforced attention to the machines; participants in the great LAWRENCE MASSACHUSETTS TEXTILE MILLS STRIKE of 1912, for example, spoke as many as forty-five different languages.

Workers nonetheless periodically accumulated enough grievances to overcome the barriers and STRIKE, for mill hours were long, wages were low, and living conditions deplorable. Textile mills were particularly hazardous to health: in 1912, an appalling one-third of Lawrence spinners died before they had worked a decade. They died of tuberculosis and other respiratory diseases that were caused by the inhalation of lint and machine fumes, while other workers were driven deaf by the noise.

Women not only joined men in the strikes that resulted from these conditions, but actually led in union organization, beginning already with the PAWTUCKET, RHODE ISLAND WEAVERS STRIKE in 1824 and continuing on with such activists as SARAH BAGLEY in the 1840s. In Massachusetts, Irish women struck the Holyoke mills in the 1850s; in Fall River in the 1870s, the men voted to accept a reduction in wages while the women voted to strike; and an Italian woman died in the police riot of the 1912 strike in Lawrence.

At least in part because of this unionization, manufacturers began to take their mills South. Centered in northern Georgia and the Carolinas where hilly terrain again provided water power, the industry employed over thirty-five thousand people by 1890, two-thirds of whom were women and children. Virtually all of them were white; black men might be employed as janitors, but black women were rarely hired. Again, an agrarian economy meant availability of female labor, and Southern states resisted federal attempts to pass child labor limitations throughout the 1920s. The Great Depression essentially ended child labor, and after WORLD WAR II, fewer women proved willing to work in unsafe conditions for relatively low wages. Textile mill jobs were then increasingly exported to the Third World.

TILTON-BEECHER AFFAIR The emotional triangle of Reverend Henry Ward Beecher, Theodore Tilton, and Elizabeth "Lib" Tilton made national headlines during the 1870s. Reverend Beecher, the brother of HARRIET BEECHER STOWE and CATHARINE BEECHER, was an immensely popular nineteenth-century preacher and political activist, especially as an ABOLITIONIST. Soon after the Civil War, he had a discreet affair of about two years' duration with Lib Tilton, a member of his Brooklyn congregation. Her husband, Theodore, edited a liberal maga-

zine, the *Independent,* and all three were active in the era's progressive causes. They shared friendships with leaders of the SUFFRAGE MOVEMENT; Beecher in fact had been president of the AMERICAN WOMAN SUFFRAGE ASSOCIATION, while his half-sister, Isabella Beecher Hooker, was a founder of the New England Suffrage Association.

The affair had ended when Lib Tilton told her husband of it in 1869. He initially agreed to let the matter die, but could not; as time passed, he became obsessed with hatred of Beecher and suspicion of his wife. SUSAN ANTHONY discovered the situation when she spent a night at the Tilton home in 1870; Theodore Tilton flew into a rage and ordered Anthony out of the house, while his wife feared for her life. When Anthony stood up to his anger, he acknowledged the harm that could be done to their mutual causes by gossip and promised to curb his behavior.

But neither of the Tiltons could quite let it alone. Lib sobbed out her woes to other women, including ANNA DICKINSON, for example, who wrote in 1872: "She is very lovely and quiet and beautiful, but she is insane." Meanwhile, Theodore made the mistake of confiding in his boss, who eventually used it against him. When he lost his job, Tilton sought revenge by filing suit against Reverend Beecher for adultery and alienation of affection. Courts still heard such charges, and a highly publicized trial was held in 1875—which piled yet more scandal on to the negative attention already devoted to the case in VICTORIA WOODHULL's 1872 trial for initially telling the story.

It was the nation's first case of yellow journalism on the sexuality of famous people, and the sensation was featured on the front pages of newspapers for years. Preachers and politicians used the lurid morality play to demonstrate their argument that the breakup of the family was the natural result of women's crusade for legal rights. While some accepted Beecher's vague claims that the whole thing was a fabrication—despite the testimony of servants and others—more people took the opportunity to point out that he brought these troubles on himself by associating with suffragists. When it became known the Susan Anthony had been Lib Tilton's first confidant, reporters dogged Anthony for comment that she adamantly refused to give.

One slight compensation was that some newspapers showed enough enterprise to hire female reporters in hopes of getting story details. The trial lasted six months, and according to Stowe, cost her brother $118,000. Stowe loyally defended Beecher and even wrote that his "enemies" offered a $10,000 bribe to the jury foreman. Isabella Beecher Hooker took the opposite position, siding with Lib Tilton and proclaiming her disbelief in her half-brother's claims of innocence. Not surprisingly, the male jurors seemed overwhelmed by the welter of contradictory testimony and failed to reach a decision.

When Plymouth Church excommunicated Lib Tilton but exonerated its pastor, ELIZABETH CADY STANTON was particularly outraged. She wrote fiery articles castigating the double standard and took the opportunity to attack one of her favorite targets, the hypocritical male leaders of organized religion. Published in the *Chicago Tribune,* her words on this subject may have reached a wider audience than any others she wrote, and they added more fuel to an already blazing fire.

Stanton not only took Theodore Tilton's side against Beecher publicly, but showed concern for him personally. She may have kept him from suicide when the jury (all male, of course) failed to reach a decision: "the least" he could do, she wrote him, "is to *live*."

He took her advice and exiled himself in France, while Lib Tilton ended her days in poverty and disgrace, abandoned even by some of her FEMINIST friends who thought she excessively pined her lost romance. Victoria Woodhull, of course, had gone to jail for merely telling the story, and only Reverend Beecher came through the trial relatively unscathed.

The deeper tragedy, though, was that leaders of the women's movement lost almost a decade in diversion to this emotional turmoil. While it did provide a platform for discussion of DIVORCE and other legal reform, there is a real likelihood that thousands of women who otherwise might have joined the suffrage movement in the 1870s—when key decisions were made on such things as the FIFTEENTH AMENDMENT—did not do so because they hesitated to associate themselves with the players in the Beecher-Tilton scandal.

THOMAS, M. CAREY (1857–1935) Named "Martha" and called "Minnie" in childhood, M. Carey Thomas was prominently associated with BRYN MAWR as an adult. Although she grew up influenced by the QUAKER WOMEN of her family, she nonetheless had to overcome her father's objections when she wished to enter Cornell University. After graduation in 1877, she continued to battle the educational barriers imposed on women.

Thomas went on to a frustrating year of graduate tutorials with professors at JOHNS HOPKINS UNIVERSITY, where her father was a trustee but where she was banned from classes. She then studied at German universities that the era considered essential to scholarship, but none would grant a degree to a woman. Finally she transferred to the University of Zurich, which granted her Ph.D. in 1882—the first awarded to either a woman or a non-European.

When Bryn Mawr opened in 1885, Thomas wanted to be its president, but was allowed only the deanship. Her commitment to the school was so complete, however, that she did the president's job as well as her own and was rewarded with that position in 1894. Her overriding concern was that Bryn Mawr's educational standards be as rigorous as those of male institutions. This was not an innovative idea, for other women's COLLEGES had pioneered it decades earlier, but Dr. Thomas detailed the aim by making Bryn Mawr's admissions requirements the same as Harvard's and especially by instituting the first graduate school at a major women's college.

Perhaps the most creative program introduced at Bryn Mawr was its Summer School for Women in Industry: because factory workers, especially in the GARMENT INDUSTRY, could expect to be laid off in summer, Bryn Mawr offered them facilities unused by vacationing students. The institute, however, was not opened until the last year of Thomas's presidency in 1921, and Thomas can hardly be characterized as a crusader for the lower classes. Worse, she displayed open bias against Jews, and—despite the long Quaker history on behalf of African-Americans—no black woman was admitted to Bryn Mawr under her presidency.

Dr. Thomas has a more visible presence in turn-of-the-

century feminist history than her educational achievement alone than her educational achievement alone would merit because she also was one of relatively few high-ranking academics in the leadership of the SUFFRAGE MOVEMENT. Though Thomas did not become active until late in SUSAN ANTHONY's life, Anthony and others were proud to have her involvement and elected her an officer of the NATIONAL AMERICAN WOMAN SUFFRAGE ASSOCIATION.

Thomas and her longtime companion, Mary Garrett, hosted a memorable reception at Garrett's Baltimore home during the NAWSA's 1906 convention. IDA HUSTED HARPER wrote that Anthony was moved to tears by the eloquence of Thomas' speech, and when Anthony later became ill, Garrett and Thomas personally cared for her. The reception had included some of the era's most eminent collegiate women, and it led to the founding of the EQUAL SUFFRAGE LEAGUE in 1908, with Thomas as president. At Anthony's dying request, Thomas and Garrett also raised an impressive sixty thousand dollars for the suffrage cause between February and May of 1907. Thomas supported the WOMAN'S PARTY after the vote was won, but she also spent much of that era abroad after inheriting a fortune from Garrett. A month before her death at seventy-nine, Dr. Thomas spoke at Bryn Mawr's fiftieth anniversary; the occasion was a poignant reminder of her youth, when, she said, "I had never known a woman who had gone to college nor seen anyone who had seen a woman who had gone to college."

TOMPKINS, CAPTAIN SALLY (1833–1916) Sally Tompkins was a wealthy, unmarried Virginian woman who was still in her twenties when the CIVIL WAR broke out. Immediately after the first battle of Manassas, she established a hospital in a large Richmond home, primarily at her own expense. She assumed uncommon leadership in training NURSES, and her Robertson Hospital soon established a reputation for extraordinarily good care.

When the Confederate government began placing all private hospitals under the control of the military, Tompkins insisted upon continuing as superintendent of the hospital that she had built. To avoid insulting her and yet extricate the government from this bureaucratic difficulty, Confederate President Jefferson Davis commissioned her as an army captain. She thus not only maintained her independence, but also acquired the authority to commandeer goods and services from others—though she turned down the salary that ordinarily accompanied a captain's rank.

Captain Tompkins' hospital had by far the lowest death rate of any facility in the North or South, even though physicians sent their worst cases there. Her staff of six—four of whom were black women still in slavery—treated more than thirteen hundred men during the war and lost only seventy-three. Doubtlessly this was because Captain Tompkins trained her nurses in sanitary techniques that were not yet routine with physicians. Her firm religiosity and strong administrative skills were heralded by Southern leaders, including diarist MARY CHESNUT. The hospital's record is even more impressive when considered in terms of its superintendent's youth, the slave status of most of its nurses, and its use as a facility for cases that were mostly likely to be fatal.

Captain Tompkins depleted her fortune in postwar charities

and died more than fifty years later in the Home for Confederate Women at Richmond. Her commission is displayed at the Confederate Museum there.

THOMPSON, DOROTHY (1893–1961) A brilliant

woman who deserves more recognition than she receives, Dorothy Thompson not only presaged much of modern FEMINIST thought, but also was internationally known in her time. In fact, some of her contemporaries thought of her as the second most influential woman in the world, surpassed only by ELEANOR ROOSEVELT.

Her first job after graduation from Syracuse University in 1914 was as a publicist for the New York Woman Suffrage Association; after WORLD WAR I and the passage of suffrage, she went to Europe to do publicity for the Red Cross. There she made the transition into mainstream journalism by selling exclusive stories she managed to capture. By 1924, when she was barely thirty, Thompson was Central European bureau chief for two co-owned New York and Philadelphia newspapers. From this vantage point, she watched the rise of fascism.

She interviewed Hitler in 1931 and published a warning book on him in 1932—years before the rest of the world began to take note of the ominous danger that fascism was. When the Nazis saw Thompson as enough of a threat to expel her two years later, journalists throughout the world commented on this censorship, but most Americans were deep into the Great Depression and few noticed. Hoover was still president when she wrote her book, and even later government officials paid little heed to information that she could have supplied. Thompson would never receive the recognition granted her friend ANNE O'HARE McCORMICK, whose journalistic feats in the prewar era were very similar.

She nevertheless continued to write and within a few years, over 170 newspapers published Thompson's syndicated column. She lectured widely, did political commentary on network radio and wrote a tremendous number of articles for magazines ranging from *Saturday Evening Post* to *Foreign Affairs*. In 1937, Thompson began as the featured front-piece columnist of *LADIES HOME JOURNAL*, and this became the position with which she is most strongly associated today. The Victorian-sounding name of the magazine has had an unfortunate affect in diminishing the reputation of the thoughtful pieces that she published there, for it was in this vehicle that Thompson could express not only her global expertise, but also her feminist ideas.

When the war came—making clear the accuracy of her predictions—one of Thompson's steady themes was the government's failure to utilize the skills of women. She pointed out in 1944, for example: "Sigrid Schultz, for twenty years *Chicago Tribune* correspondent in Berlin, is sitting in Westport, Connecticut. She has uncountable German and other European connections, speaks German, French, and Swedish, and why she is not in Sweden collecting data on Germany from the Germans who come and go from there is beyond me."

In addition to politics, Thompson wrote insightful pieces on the economy and especially women's place in it. She understood the long-term implications of the widespread entrance of women into the labor force, and—as had been the case with the war—she foresaw the future in a way that professional economists missed. "The trends . . . inescapably indicated," she wrote, that women "in their quiet and ladylike way, are going to produce nothing short of a social revolution . . . in the not too distant future. Employers, labor organizations, government, and social agencies should take notice."

As the war drew to an end, she increasingly wrote of the need for a postwar world without patriarchy, for she understood that without freedom in the family, it was unrealistic to expect freedom in the world. Women would never go back to life as it used to be: "There is no example . . . in which a class or group of people who have once succeeded in expanding the area of their lives is ever persuaded again to restrict it." Women, she predicted, would become involved in business and politics, and that would change everything. It was the world's best hope for an end to life as it always had been, including war.

Thompson knew whereof she spoke when she wrote of marriage and the family, for, though she retained her MAIDEN NAME, she was married virtually all of her adult life. Two of her three marriages were to Europeans; the first was from 1922 to 1927 and ended in DIVORCE, while the third, from 1943 to 1958, was a happy relationship that lasted until her husband's death. Her most famous marriage was between these two, when from 1928 to 1942, Dorothy Thompson was married to Nobel-winning novelist Sinclair Lewis.

These prewar years were the most crucial of her professional life, but far from gaining any literary benefits from her husband, she instead was diverted from her work by his alcoholism. Thompson even gave up the journalistic access that she needed in New York to buy a large home in the Vermont woods where Lewis would be less tempted to drink, but he was achingly aware that he had already written his best work: indeed, his most recognized post-Nobel book, *It Can't Happen Here* (1935), was clearly based on his wife's themes of fascism. (A few years earlier, a drunken Lewis brawled with Theodore Drieser when Lewis accused Drieser of plagiarizing from Thompson.) Even H.L. Mencken—who was Thompson's complete political opposite and no feminist—sympathized with "Mrs. Lewis" in her "heroic labors to keep his drinking within bounds." Already in 1932, she "gave him ten thousand dollars out of her own savings" to pay his debts, and in countless similar cases, she subjected her interests to his for fourteen years before finally divorcing.

The result of Thompson's personal experience with men was that her writing conveyed a deep understanding of the emotional and intellectual difficulties of combining marriage with a feminist philosophy. She also understood motherhood, for she bore a child by Lewis at age thirty-seven and became a devoted stepmother to his son—who was killed in the war that she tried so hard to prevent. All of this gave her a far more insightful perspective on women's lives than that of most of the era's writers.

The postwar period was less rewarding for her; feminism was supposed to have died with the war and her writing was less inspired as she adopted the more conservative themes of the fifties. Moreover, the area in which Thompson's opinion pieces were most original was an unpopular one in the publishing world: she concentrated on the Middle East from the

Arab point of view. Not surprisingly, more and more newspapers dropped her column. She nonetheless published a book with the telling title of *The Courage to Be Happy* in 1957 and continued with *Ladies Home Journal* until her sudden death at sixty-eight—in Lisbon, where Dorothy Thompson was still seeking a fresh angle on the world's news.

TRAVEL Limitations on female mobility contributed tremendously to women's historic lack of public participation. From the earliest days of the nation's settlement, this factor played a greater role than has generally been recognized.

The Mediterranean cultures of the Old World secluded women in the home, and the earliest expeditions from Spain and France reflected this. Ships departing from those areas were filled with soldiers and priests, but had few or no women on board. The result was that French and Spanish men either married native women or returned to the Old World. Their settlements in North America were therefore less stable than those of the English, Dutch, and other northern Europeans whose women traveled more freely. The fact that English is spoken by Americans today is thus directly related to the fact that women moved with men to establish permanent homes.

Early American women traveled reasonably freely, as is shown by SARAH WELLS BULL, SARAH KEMBLE KNIGHT, and others, including Anne Newport Royall, an AUTHOR who supported herself with ten travel books published between 1826–1831. As Americans became more affluent after the Revolution, however, women's lives were restricted. The era's "lady" served as a monument to the wealth of her family, and she was deemed too fragile to travel. Ironically, just when travel became easier with the invention of trains, it also came to be considered too risky for a woman traveling alone.

By the pre–Civil War era, a strong taboo existed against women traveling without male escort. DOROTHEA DIX, SUSAN ANTHONY, MARY LYON, and others who broke this tradition met with criticism from family and friends, as well as from strangers. Their work was further handicapped by hotel keepers who refused to rent them rooms, for it was assumed that a woman alone was likely to be of dubious moral standards. Anthony was once refused a room even when she was accompanied by another woman and a child.

It was the CIVIL WAR that changed these attitudes, for both women who worked as NURSES and others were forced to travel, especially in the turbulent battlefronts of the South. Nonetheless, restrictive attitudes on women's travel remained throughout the century among IMMIGRANT WOMEN, as legislation in both this country and abroad treated the movement of women differently from that of men. As late as 1920, the Greek government stated flatly: "the emigration of women and minors of the female sex over sixteen years of age is not allowed unless accompanied by a husband, father or mother, elder brother, son-in-law, brother-in-law or other near relation. . . .

TRIANGLE FIRE The Triangle Fire of March 25, 1911 was burned into the memories of IMMIGRANT WOMEN. The Triangle Factory was a Manhattan dress manufacturer known for shabby treatment of its predominantly female work force; in the great 1909 STRIKE against the GARMENT INDUSTRY, its manage-

ment refused to settle, and activist workers either left or were fired. Those remaining were mostly Italians or newly arrived Jews who were willing to work on Saturdays in a nonunion shop.

The tragedy began late on a Saturday afternoon when one of the few male employees apparently dropped a match near oil cans, and the flammable fabric quickly spread the fire. Those women who were not lucky enough to get to the elevators while they still functioned crowded near the windows, but the fire department's ladders stopped two stories short of the factory's floors. Survivors testified that many were pushed out by those behind them, but others jumped, for "it was jump or be burned . . . A heap of corpses lay on the sidewalk," while over fifty bodies were found piled behind locked doors.

Immediately after the fire, one of the owners rushed to deny that the doors were locked—before the charge was made. Fire regulations prohibited locked doors, but many of the era's managers routinely locked their workers in. Labor leaders did not expect these newly arrived immigrants to be brave enough to challenge the owners, so they published a list of persons to whom information could be secretly given. The district attorney soon had sufficient facts to "show that doors . . . had been kept locked."

But by December when the trial of owners Harris and Blanck was held, public outrage had dimmed. At one point the all-male JURY was evenly divided, but after two hours they issued an acquittal. One said in explanation, "I think that the girls, who undoubtedly have not as much intelligence as others might have in other walks of life, were inclined to fly into a panic."

Thus the deaths of 146 people went unavenged. "Most of them," reported the *New York Times,* "could barely speak English . . . Almost all were the main support of their hardworking families." Many had emigrated alone and had no family here; while some mourners searched the morgue in a vain attempt to determine which of over fifty unrecognizably charred bodies was their loved one, other bodies went unclaimed. Quite probably their families were in Europe, and long would be unaware of the calamity that had befallen their daughters.

Within a few days of the fire, a safety committee received over a thousand reports of dangerous conditions similar to Triangle. Eventually standards were upgraded and laws enforced—although just days after the fire, Harris and Blanck shamelessly ran an advertisement of their new location. For them it was business as usual, but the immigrant ghetto did not forget. March twenty-fifth is memorialized today by garment workers.

TROY FEMALE SEMINARY— *See* EMMA WILLARD

TRUTH, SOJOURNER (c. 1797–1883) One of the best known of nineteenth-century African-Americans, Sojourner Truth was a natural leader who used her exceptional abilities to make a legend of herself. HARRIET BEECHER STOWE—a person familiar with the idea of charisma—said of Sojourner Truth: "I do not recollect . . . anyone who had more of that . . . subtle power which we call personal presence than this woman."

Her parents may have come directly from Africa, for she was what a New York newspaper called "hideously black," and Stowe referred to her as Libyan. In any case, she was born in slavery near the end of the eighteenth century in Ulster County, New York, about fifty miles up the Hudson from New York City. Called Isabella, she was sold away from her family at about age nine and resold twice by the time she was thirteen.

This traumatic childhood was further complicated by the fact that Dutch was her native language, for the New York area in which she was born was originally New Amsterdam; when she was sold to English-speaking people, they interpreted her inability to follow orders as stupidity or stubbornness. She bore the consequences as physical scars for the rest of her life.

For almost two decades after that, Isabella was owned by a family named Dumont. She was treated better there and later spoke well of the family, especially her master. Around 1816, when she was presumably about nineteen, she bore her first child, Diana, who would live until 1904. Isabella went on to bear at least five babies, losing some to INFANT MORTALITY and seeing others sold into slavery. The children shared the same father, a slave named Thomas, but he played no role in her life after emancipation. Some have said theirs was a forced marriage aimed at producing offspring to be sold.

New York had begun a plan for gradual emancipation of its slaves in 1810, and all were to be free by 1828. Isabella nevertheless fled the Dumonts in 1827, joining a QUAKER household named Van Wagener and taking that name. Her motivation for leaving earlier than her legal freedom probably was that the Van Wageners and other Quakers supported her in filing a lawsuit on behalf of her son Peter, who had been sold South. The sale was illegal under New York law, and amazingly enough, Peter was returned from Alabama.

Feeling "tall within" from her legal victory, Isabella Van Wagnerer left for New York City about 1829. She earned a living as a DOMESTIC WORKER and spent increasing amounts of time with evangelical Christians. "I liked the Quakers," she was quoted as saying, "but they wouldn't let me sing, so I joined the Methodists." From that point on, her life would be centered on a deeply personal faith; unable to read, she scorned formal theology, saying "God Himself talks to me." She developed oratorical skills by preaching on street corners to PROSTITUTES and other derelicts in the notorious Five Points section, but remained naive about other aspects of urban life.

Handicapped by illiteracy, she was easily deceived by her increasingly wayward son; unable to read her bank account, she eventually lost her savings to religious charlatans. Her money went into a commune located in Sing Sing, where she lived in 1833. The group deteriorated into one of free sexuality and even murder accusations; although Van Wagener was not accused of sexual involvement, she did stand trial for poisoning in 1835. After acquittal, she again showed unusual assertiveness in bringing and winning a libel suit.

That she was not implicated in the sexual aspects of the scandal may be related to her uncommon appearance: in a time when most men were much shorter, she stood almost six feet tall. Extremely muscular from a lifetime of hard physical labor and possessed of a deep, powerful voice, she many times was mistaken for a man. This eased her way in the life-turning move that she made in 1843, when Isabella Van Wagener became Sojourner Truth and took to the road, earning her living as a PUBLIC SPEAKER. Saying she was directed by God, she preached first in Long Island and then went through Connecticut and up into Massachusetts, where late that year, she joined a Northampton commune.

She met her first ABOLITIONISTS there, including William Lloyd Garrison. They saw her as a tremendous asset who not only had developed oratorical skills at a time when most women did not speak in public, but who could also testify to the reality of slavery with her personal story. Sojourner Truth spoke in New England throughout the 1840s, and in 1850, headed west through Ohio to Kansas, where much abolitionist activity would be focused during the next decade.

She supported herself with the sales of *Narrative of Sojourner Truth* (1850). This autobiographical work was written ANONYMOUSLY for her by a white woman, Olive Gilbert, though Truth herself was said to have supervised its production, treating William Lloyd Garrison "like a secretary." It would be reissued in larger versions in 1875 and 1884, with these editions done by Frances Titus, a white Michigan Quaker who remained anonymous at the time. Titus also would take responsibility for Truth's business needs when she aged.

Before her 1850 departure for the West, Truth attended a women's rights convention in Worcester, Massachusetts—only two years after the first SENECA FALLS WOMEN'S RIGHTS CONVENTION. Even though the women at the meeting were markedly different from her in dress, speech, and personal experience, Sojourner Truth identified with them from the first and understood that the FEMINIST cause should not be trivialized and forced to compete with slavery. It was at her next women's rights convention, in Akron the following year, that Sojourner Truth made her most famous speech. Freed of the dialect used in the *HISTORY OF WOMAN SUFFRAGE*, its most famous part reads:

> The man over there says women need to be helped into carriages and lifted over ditches, and to have the best place everywhere. Nobody ever helps me into carriages or over puddles, or gives me the best place—and ain't I a woman?
>
> Look at my arm! I have ploughed and planted and gathered into barns, and no man could head me—and ain't I a woman? I could work as much and eat as much as a man—when I could get it—and bear the lash as well! And ain't I a woman? I have borne thirteen children, and seen most of 'em sold into slavery, and when I cried out with my mother's grief, none but Jesus heard me—and ain't I a woman?

The woman who presided over the convention had allowed this odd-appearing stranger to speak despite the protesting murmurs of the audience, but there were "roars of applause" and "streaming eyes" at the conclusion. "I have never in my life," the president wrote, "seen anything like the magical influence that subdued the snobbish spirit of the day." It was an oratorical triumph, even though Truth embellished it by substituting her mother's history for her own when she referred to thirteen children. She would make similar adjustments of the facts in the future when she believed a rhetorical license was legitimate to emphasize the central verity.

After 1851, Sojourner Truth was featured at many women's rights meetings. Somehow she managed to return from Kansas for the New York gathering in 1853; when this "mob convention" was repeatedly disrupted by gangs of jeering males, Truth admonished them: "Isn't it good for me to come and draw forth your spirit . . . ? I see that some of you have got the spirit of a goose and some of you have got the spirit of a snake." At a meeting in Silver Lake, Indiana, she shocked the audience by defiantly exposing her breast to prove wrong those skeptics who maintained that she was actually a man in disguise.

With occasional trips East, Truth lived the rest of her life in the Midwest, which was still a frontier at the time. She was physically assaulted in "Bleeding Kansas," and in the mid-1850s, settled in Battle Creek, Michigan. A house at 10 College Place became her permanent home; eventually her three daughters moved to Battle Creek and a grandson became her lifelong travel aide.

During the CIVIL WAR—when she was probably near seventy—she used her fund-raising skills to gather supplies for black soldiers. Harriet Beecher Stowe contributed greatly to her fame with a profile in one of the nation's most popular magazines in 1863, and in 1864, Sojourner Truth went to the White House to be honored by Abraham Lincoln.

She stayed in Washington through the end of the war and worked for the Freedman's Bureau. Both then and in her later visits to midwestern Freedman projects, she put a strong emphasis on cleanliness; being illiterate herself, she could do little to teach fellow ex-slaves. Recent scholarship makes a strong case that she suffered from dyslexia and, indeed, she once said of her attempts to read that "the letters all got mixed up and I couldn't straighten them out." But even though she said that "my brains is too stiff" to learn to read, Sojourner Truth understood that she had developed an equally important skill in using her magic tongue to interpret black needs to white audiences.

Her postwar years centered on two causes: the settlement of ex-slaves on free land in the West and the right of women—including black women—to vote. She visited settlements of former slaves in Kansas and encouraged their model of western settlement. In 1870, she proposed the idea in a petition personally delivered to President Grant, but the government undertook no official sponsorship and most blacks lacked the resources to make the move independently. A similar lack of success was true of suffrage during her lifetime.

Like SUSAN ANTHONY and others, Sojourner Truth tested the FIFTEENTH AMENDMENT by attempting to vote. Pointing out that she owned "a little house" and that "taxes be taxes," she tried to cast a ballot in 1872. When a Battle Creek official called her "auntie," she addressed him as "nephew," but the authorities didn't bother to arrest her as they did Anthony. She understood that it was her gender and not her race that presented the problem in this case, and her contempt for the male point of view is clear in statements such as, "It doesn't seem hard work to vote, though I have seen some men that had a hard time of it."

She attended the 1867 convention of the AMERICAN EQUAL RIGHTS ASSOCIATION and remained firmly on the side of Anthony and the other women who split from that organization over the primacy of women's rights. This renewed her rocky relationship with Frederick Douglass, an ex-slave and abolitionist like herself whom she had met in her first prewar speaking tours. Douglass was an ambitious man who adopted white ways and ultimately became very wealthy; he was regularly sponsored on the well-paid lecture circuit, while her work was itinerant and self-supporting. His resentment of her was clear: she "seemed to feel it her duty," he complained, "to ridicule my efforts to speak and act like a person of cultivation and refinement . . . She was a genuine specimen of the uncultured negro."

Though she did seem to delight in embarrassing him, theirs was a dispute of basic philosophies of life. Douglass, for example, urged rebellion against slaveowners, while Truth was shocked at his advocacy of violence: she shouted across Boston's huge Faneuil Hall, "Frederick, is God dead?" Indeed, personal faith replaced political advocacy in her life, and she viewed her speeches more nearly as sermons. In this, she was identifying with the mass of women in her era, for religiosity permeated their social reform efforts. Despite a masculine appearance, Sojourner Truth opted for women's more gentle—but nonetheless persistent—political style.

She disagreed with warnings from Douglass that women's rights would undermine black rights and, dismissing his notion of the "Negro's Hour," she concentrated more on gender than on race in her postwar life. In 1878 alone, she not only attended the annual women's rights convention in Rochester, but also spoke in thirty-six towns in her home state of Michigan. She was well over eighty at the time; that she sometimes claimed to be over one hundred does not diminish the dedication it took to build the SUFFRAGE MOVEMENT with such lifelong effort.

Her deathbed physician was Dr. John Kellogg, who later originated the idea of breakfast cereal. He was among over one thousand people who paid their respects at her funeral. They remembered Sojourner Truth in the words of LUCY STONE, as a "direct and terrible force, moving friend and foe alike."

While she is buried at Battle Creek, her birthplace has honored her with the construction of a library—dedicated to a woman who could not read. The Sojourner Truth Library at New York State University College of New Paltz contains a special collection of materials on this remarkable woman.

TUBMAN, HARRIET (c. 1820–1913) A child named
Araminta was born on MARYLAND'S Eastern Shore about 1820; she was the granddaughter of slaves brought from Africa. Later she gave herself her mother's name of Harriet, and along with about a dozen siblings, she grew up in a home more secure than that of many slave children, for both of her parents were part of her life throughout childhood.

At thirteen, however, she suffered irreparable injury when an angry overseer threw a two-pound weight at a slave boy who was running from him; the weight hit Harriet in the head, fracturing her skull. Ever after, she would be handicapped by seizures and unpredictable attacks of comalike sleep. Her recovery was slow, but eventually she was strong enough to return to physical labor; though only five feet tall and of slight build, she did a "male job" of cutting timber alongside her father. In 1844, when she was presumably about twenty-four, Harriet married John Tubman, a free black.

She remained in slavery and the union produced no children. Like a number of other black women, a husband did not become an overridingly important factor in Harriet Tubman's life.

Five years later, amid rumors that she was about to be sold, she escaped to Philadelphia. She worked in a hotel throughout 1849 and saved her money; the next year she daringly risked her freedom by returning to Baltimore to lead out her sister's family. The following year, Tubman made two more trips into Maryland, liberating her brother and his family and another group of eleven. For the rest of the 1850s, she went back again and again, making approximately nineteen dangerous trips into slave territory and rescuing as many as three hundred black people from bondage. In 1857, she had the special joy of guiding out her parents, who were in their seventies, to live their last days in freedom. She offered to bring out her husband, but he apparently was satisfied with his life and refused to take the risk.

More than any other single person of either race or gender, Harriet Tubman displayed nerves of steel and quick-witted intelligence in accomplishing these missions. Though she had the help of ABOLITIONISTS on this "Underground Railroad," there was, of course, no secret railroad: the reality was walking country roads alone in the fearful dark of night. Naturally shy, with "no pretensions" and "ordinary" in her appearance, Harriet Tubman seemingly had no special gifts to account for her extraordinary courage and skill.

Instead, she was handicapped by illiteracy and unable to read maps or signs; she operated by memorizing landmarks and developing an uncanny sense of direction. Tubman worked out codes in the Bible quotations she used in conversation and hid meanings in the songs she sang, so that what appeared to be pious passivity to whites actually delivered important information to knowing blacks. Her keen mind several times rapidly devised ruses to divert the suspicious: perhaps the most famous was when she spent precious money to buy tickets for her group on a southbound train, knowing that the man who was following them would accept this as evidence that she was a slave trusted by her master, for no free black chose to travel South in that era.

She escorted many of those that she liberated all the way to her home in St. Catherine's, Ontario, for after the Fugitive Slave Act of 1850 made it easier for slave traders to kidnap and sell them, many free African-Americans moved out of the U.S. Indeed, one of Tubman's great exploits took place in 1860 in Troy, New York, when she led a group that successfully assaulted officers who were guarding a fugitive slave, enabling him to escape to Canada. The property loss to slaveowners of such activity was so great that they unconsciously honored this small, shy woman by offering as much as forty thousand dollars in rewards for her capture.

Called Moses by other blacks because she led her people to the Promised Land, Harriet Tubman trusted prayer but nonetheless traveled with a gun. More than once she threatened to use it on quavering slaves who might have betrayed others for their personal benefit. If violence proved necessary, she would use it, and she encouraged radical abolitionist John Brown. Indeed, Brown saw her as a vital part of his planned slave revolt: he emphasized her importance in his prophetic speaking style, saying, "The first I see is General Tubman,

the second is General Tubman and the third is General Tubman." There are indications that she intended to be part of his Harper's Ferry raid in 1859 and was prevented from participation only because of illness; had she been there, her life probably would have ended prematurely as did those of other nameless ex-slaves.

It was Brown's martyrdom that was eulogized in the North, while the roles of twenty-one others who joined him were minimized. Nonetheless, Northern attitudes changed dramatically in the 1850s, and as more and more people refused to obey the Fugitive Slave Act, Tubman felt secure enough to establish a U.S. base. She bought a small farm in central New York State at a reduced price from government official and abolitionist William E. Seward, where she settled her parents and other refugees. Though she could have safely stayed there when the CIVIL WAR broke out, again Harriet Tubman headed South to assist in emancipation.

In her forties by then, Tubman continued to show physical stamina and personal bravery. With sponsorship from the governor of Massachusetts, she joined Union soldiers on the South Carolina sea islands that were the first liberated. Here General Hunter, commander of the Department of the South, provided her authorization to travel on any military transport she chose, and for the next three years, Tubman acted as a spy and scout for Union troops. She provided valuable information for the Army, for she could easily pass among black informants behind Confederate lines. Doubtless she could have done even more for the Union had officials been willing to utilize her abilities to their fullest, for her experience in covert activity surely surpassed that of virtually any intelligence officer.

But she was not only black, she was a woman, and military officials were not creative enough to make maximum use of the expertise she offered. Instead, like many women of both races, Harriet Tubman spent much of the war working as a NURSE—even though this was an area in which she was inexperienced. At the war's end, this masterfully talented woman was at Fortress Monroe, Virginia, where she supported herself by raising chickens and selling eggs, while also volunteering in a segregated hospital.

She continued to live humbly. After the war, she returned to Auburn and officially opened her little farm as the Harriet Tubman Home for Indigent Aged Negroes and began to attend the women's rights meetings that were a part of life in the SENECA FALLS area of New York where she lived. Although abolitionists and the proslavery forces who offered rewards for her capture were aware of her prewar record, it was not until five years after the war was over that the general public slowly began to learn of the extraordinary Harriet Tubman.

A white woman, Sarah Bradford, recorded the story in *Harriet Tubman: The Moses of Her People* (1869). Like the narrative that other white women wrote for SOJOURNER TRUTH, this sketch, which was expanded to a book in 1886, not only ensured the record of Tubman's contributions to freedom, but also provided her with a lifelong source of needed income. She used the profits from its sale to support her Home, for a second marriage in 1869 did not seem to change her independent status nor her need for income.

Her husband, Nelson Davis, was a former slave who had fought for the Union Army. She presumably was forty-nine when they married, and he was said to have been twenty-two years younger than she, which would make him twenty-seven when they wed. He was described as "a large man," and it may have been that this vital woman wanted a strong, young lover; those who rationalized the marriage by saying that she was nursing his alleged tuberculosis would seem to have been wrong, for he lived twenty years after they wed. He was never a prominent part of her public life, however, and she retained the Tubman name.

When Davis died, she applied for a pension as a veteran's widow, and perhaps motivated by this, she also renewed an earlier effort to be compensated for her own wartime services. Like ANNA CARROLL, Tubman's claim was ignored in the immediate postwar era. It had greater validity than Carroll's, however, and finally, in 1897, Congress granted Tubman twenty dollars a month for the services she rendered as "commander of several men as scouts during the late War of Rebellion."

Though thirty years overdue and still meager, this pension provided income for the next sixteen years. She continued to be active in old age, speaking to the NATIONAL AMERICAN WOMAN SUFFRAGE ASSOCIATION in 1896 and traveling again to the 1897 meeting, where she was honored with a reception. It was separate from the "large and brilliant" reception honoring JANE ADDAMS, however, and "Mrs. Harriet Tubman" was cryptically described in the HISTORY OF WOMAN SUFFRAGE as "the colored woman so noted in anti-slavery days for her assistance to fugitive slaves."

She lived into the twentieth century and was presumably ninety-three at death. Her burial in Auburn was with military honors; a memorial stone was dedicated by Booker T. Washington. In WORLD WAR II, a ship was christened for Harriet Tubman, and in 1978, a postage stamp in her honor was the first of the Black Heritage series.

Harriet Tubman's accomplishment in liberating hundreds of slaves is especially significant when it is remembered that she acted alone, without the comfort of a supporting organization or a military unit. Moreover, she had a number of handicaps to overcome: not only was she female, but she was physically small and lacked the intimidating presence of, for instance, Sojourner Truth. Tubman also was illiterate in a task that would have been immeasurably easier had she been able to read signs and write letters giving herself a master's permission to travel. She showed far more courage than many other literate blacks who stopped their abolitionist work short of the Confederate border. Finally, Tubman could have excused herself from danger on the valid basis of her old head injury, for at any perilous moment she might have slipped into unconsciousness.

Yet despite all of these reasons for harboring herself safely in Canada, she took trip after trip into the danger zone. No black man similarly risked his life. That fact may have motivated Frederick Douglass—who usually was sparse in his acknowledgements of women's roles—to offer praise for Tubman. "Excepting John Brown," he said in 1868, "I know of no one who has willingly encountered more perils and hardships to serve our people." Indeed, there are few others in all of American history whose records can equal Harriet Tubman's for sheer courage.

"TYPHOID MARY" In 1906, after an eight-year search, public health authorities finally tracked down the cook who worked in various places where typhoid fever epidemics later broke out. Although not ill herself, her condition as a carrier of the fatal disease could not be cured, and Typhoid Mary lived the remaining twenty-three years of her life under quarantine.

The phrase entered the language to denote a dangerous, disappearing woman.

"UNION MAID" A frequently sung anthem of the labor union movement, "Union Maid" was written by famed folksinger Woody Guthrie in 1940.

He and fellow folksinger Pete Seeger visited a small union meeting in Oklahoma, a state hit so hard by the Great Depression that it had not yet fully recovered by 1940. Anti-union men who had been hired by management to intimidate the workers attending the meeting were taken aback when they saw that women were supportive of the union along with men, and they left without breaking up the group.

Guthrie was moved to write a song praising the courage of women who took physical risks in standing up to such threats. The song's chorus makes this clear with the repetition of: "Oh, you can't scare me, I'm sticking to the union . . . til the day I die." In addition to acknowledging women's roles in labor AUXILIARIES, a verse also recognizes women who were themselves the union card holders and STRIKE participants. A playful pun on the "union made" labels attached to products made in unionized factories, the song has been popular since.

UNWED MOTHERS— *See* ILLEGITIMACY

V

VAN BUREN, ABIGAIL— *See* FRIEDMAN, PAULINE ESTHER

VAN CORTLANDT, ANNETTJE LOCKERMANS (1620?–after c. 1665) The creator of the first paved street in America, Annettje Lockermans was a young Dutch orphan who emigrated to the New Amsterdam colony in 1642. She married Captain Oloff Van Cortlandt soon after arriving; a military officer who had been in America since 1637, he was sufficiently affluent to build an imposing house for his bride.

Though young, Annetje Van Cortlandt apparently had a strong personality and keen intelligence, for soon her home was "one of the centres of the petticoat government that so often controlled the affairs of the Colony." Van Cortlandt and her aunt, ANNETTJE JANS, "overturned the best laid plans of the officials, who would have scorned to acknowledge the influence . . . of their dominant characters."

Despite this influence, Van Cortlandt was unable to get the officials of the village of Manhattan to do anything about the condition of the dirt road in front of her house. Disgusted by the mud and dust, she directed her servants in paving it with cobblestones. Thus Brower Street, a lane that ran between Whitehall and Broad Streets, was paved in 1648. "People from all the Dutch settlements came to see the 'stone street,'" which now is known by that name. Van Cortlandt bore at least three children and was the ancestor of New York notables in the Van Rensslaer and Schuyler families.

The nation's first sidewalk was also laid by a Manhattan Dutch woman. Polly Provoost, a young WIDOW and businesswoman with a large import trade, laid flagstones on both sides of her home and businesses at Broad and Marketfield streets around 1716. The novelty and convenience of clean walkways served as a profitable advertisement for her store, and thus became a model for others.

Both the sidewalk and the paved street were firsts in civil engineering that have seldom been credited to women.

VANDERBILT, AMY (1908–1974) One of the two most recognized experts on twentieth-century etiquette, Amy Vanderbilt challenged EMILY POST's dominance of this field in the era after WORLD WAR II. The two decades during which Vanderbilt wrote a syndicated column on good manners came at a time when the subject had appeal, for her beginning date of 1954 was during an era of prosperity and conservatism. While it was Vanderbilt's death that caused the column to end in 1974, that was also a time of counterculture and rejection of propriety.

In addition to her newspaper column, Vanderbilt published magazine articles and several books. She also hosted television and radio shows on etiquette in the late fifties and early sixties.

VAN KLEECK, MARY ABBY (1883–1972) A descendent of the enterprising Dutch women who settled New Amsterdam, Mary Van Kleeck grew up in the New York City area. She graduated from SMITH COLLEGE in 1904 and began her career in the relatively new field of sociology, which soon drew her into economics.

Sponsored by the RUSSELL SAGE FOUNDATION, Van Kleeck in 1908 began studying the conditions of women in several industries, and her reports had a strong effect in bringing about labor reforms. Her first book, *Artificial Flower Makers* (1913) focused on IMMIGRANT WOMEN, while diverse later studies drew a picture of the status of working women. Among the relevant titles are *Women in the Bookbinding Trade* (1913), *Wages in the Millinery Trade* (1914), *Working Girls in Evening Schools* (1914), and *A Seasonal Industry* (1917).

Van Kleeck was not content to simply publish her findings; instead she took political action on behalf of working women and—like FLORENCE KELLEY and others—she lobbied for minimum wage laws and other PROTECTIVE LEGISLATION. By WORLD WAR I, she was sufficiently well known as an expert on women's employment that she was appointed to advise the army Ordnance Department and served as a member of the War Labor Policies Board. These positions eventually resulted in the formation of the Women's Bureau of the Department of Labor, which Van Kleeck headed briefly before resigning in 1919 in favor of her assistant, MARY ANDERSON.

She returned to the Russell Sage Foundation, but continued to receive governmental appointments from the Republicans who took over the White House in 1921. She served on two presidential commissions concerned with unemployment and increasingly broadened her scope to include a wide range of international economic and social issues. In 1932, Van Kleeck presided over the International Conference of Social Work in Germany. At the same time, she also was an early advocate for black people; she chaired the National Interracial Conference in 1928 and coauthored *The Negro in American Civilization* in 1930.

By the mid-thirties, Van Kleeck had become an open Socialist—albeit a democratic Socialist who wished to avoid violence. She argued in *Creative America* (1936) for public ownership of those industries that were fundamental to production. Her *Technology and Livelihood* (1944) was a prescient analysis of the changes the labor market could expect to face when WORLD WAR II ended. She retired at sixty-five after forty years with the Russell Sage Foundation, but Van Kleeck's economic views became even more radical as she aged.

Always too far left to be part of the Roosevelt administration that employed FRANCES PERKINS and other former social workers, she made trips to the postwar Soviet Union and worked for the quixotic presidential campaign of Henry Wallace in 1948. Not surprisingly, her own candidacy for the state senate as the nominee of the American Labor Party was unsuccessful. In 1953, Van Kleeck was subpoenaed by the Senate committee headed by Joe McCarthy, which did not hesitate to question the dedication to Americanism of this seventy-year-old woman whose family lineage made her eligible for membership in the Society of Colonial Dames.

The trauma of that experience apparently left its mark, for Van Kleeck retired to Woodstock, New York and was not politically visible during the great turmoil of the sixties. She died just days before her eighty-ninth birthday.

VAN LEW, ELIZABETH (1818–1900)

Past forty when the CIVIL WAR broke out, Elizabeth Van Lew's differences with her Richmond neighbors were already well defined. Though a product of Old Virginia, she had been educated in her mother's home city of Philadelphia, where QUAKER WOMEN doubtlessly influenced the anti-slavery views that both held. During the 1850s, Elizabeth Van Lew and her WIDOWED mother gradually freed their household slaves. One slave, Mary Elizabeth Bowser, had such keen intelligence that the Van Lew women sent her to Philadelphia to be educated.

When the war began, Van Lew made her sympathies clear by visiting the prisoners who were captured in the first battles that the Union so decisively lost. She carried food and medicine to them, and despite objections from military men and society women, she continued daily visits to four Richmond internment camps throughout the war. The expectation of her presence probably was a factor in creating a more humane environment for the prisoners. More importantly, however, Van Lew soon began passing on to federal authorities the military information known to these prisoners. With careful coding in the margins of the books she lent them, they conveyed their messages about troop placements and strength, about how many weapons and how many supply wagons their rescuers might expect.

At the same time, Van Lew was building a spy ring of her own agents. With astounding aplomb, she persuaded Bowser to give up the safe haven of Philadelphia to return to Richmond, where Van Lew managed to secure a job for her in the Confederate White House itself. Bowser then acted in conspiracy with Van Lew, passing on information that she overheard at Jefferson Davis' own dining table. Even more daring, Van Lew hid escaped prisoners of war in a secret room built over the portico of her old family mansion.

As was the case with BELLE BOYD, ROSE GREENHOW, and others, Van Lew's activities were so illegal and obviously deliberate that a man in a similar situation probably would have been hung—but just as Union officials could not bring themselves to believe that Boyd and Greenhow did what they did, so also were Confederate officers unable to acknowledge that a Southern lady was indeed a spy for the North. Yet, while official action against her was limited, her Confederate neighbors nonetheless understood that Van Lew's allegiance was with the North, for she made no attempt to hide her beliefs.

They threatened her life and property, but "Miss Lizzie" ignored them except for taking the precaution of stabling her horse in her library. As the clamor against her continued, she cleverly adopted mannerisms of insanity as a way of diverting attention from her serious intent. Richmond's rebels were easily fooled by the spinster's increasingly unkempt appearance and apparently eccentric ways, and small boys soon flung mud at her carriage while jeering at "Crazy Bet." Van Lew's only response to this humiliating form of disguise was to comment in her diary that "it helps me in my work."

Early in 1863, she somehow learned—perhaps from Bowser's White House eavesdropping—that Richmond's prisoners of war were to be moved hundreds of miles into enemy territory to the southwest Georgia prison camp at Andersonville. Though the details were not yet known in the North, Andersonville was a horrifying place, with conditions comparable to the camps run by Nazis a century later. Using her code name of "Mr. Babcock," Van Lew managed to get this information to General Ben Butler. Though her note warned him not to try to free the prisoners with fewer than forty thousand men, the raid was attempted with just six thousand. They failed miserably, and the body of a war hero (the youngest colonel in the Union army) was desecrated. Later, Van Lew led her agents in digging up the mistreated corpse, disguised its appearance, and returned the body North.

While that was the most macabre exploit of "Miss Lizzie," she made her most important contribution to the Union cause in the winter of 1864, when 109 men escaped from Libby Prison through a fifty-four-foot tunnel. Though Van Lew's diary did not claim credit for herself, Richmond newspapers retrospectively held her responsible, though Confederate searches of her home turned up no evidence. By the following year, the South was so near collapse that Van Lew was able to communicate with the federal headquarters on a daily basis, and the day that Richmond fell, she hung a U.S. flag hours before the battle was over. Afterwards, she rushed to the Confederate War Department in search of papers that the Union might find valuable.

Commander in chief Ulysses S. Grant came personally to thank her for her services. When he became president in 1869, one of Grant's first appointments was that of Van Lew as postmistress of Richmond. Though her salary was high, she was shunned by all but her mother, who died the following year. When the job expired at the end of Grant's presidency, Van Lew moved to Washington, where she was an early female federal employee. Though she was of retirement age when she left government employment, some believed that she was forced out by the Cleveland administration's annoyance with her over the popular letters to the editor that she wrote and her repeated attempts to regain the Richmond post office position.

Elizabeth Van Lew returned to Richmond in the mid-1880s, where she lived with a niece in genteel poverty in the aging mansion. The death of her niece in 1889 left her without family or friends, for Richmond had never forgiven her. Her only visitor was her physician, who reported that "she was lonely but not neurotic, and she had a bright mind."

VANN, JESSE ELLEN MATTHEWS (c. 1890–1967)

The publisher of the *Pittsburgh Courier* during WORLD WAR II, her position also made her one of the era's most wealthy black women, for in 1945, the paper grossed around $2 million annually.

Vann—who contemporaries said was "so light in color that she could pass for white anywhere"—inherited the paper from her husband, Robert Lee Vann. He was similarly light-skinned, but both of them chose to associate themselves with blacks, even when given options. She was a kindergarten TEACHER and he was a law student when they met in 1908, but he joined the *Courier* a month after their 1910 wedding.

Within the decade the *Courier* had overcome many obstacles to achieve a circulation of fifty-five thousand, and it began publishing a national edition in the early 1920s. With news-gathering branches throughout the country, it soon was a primary method of communication for the nation's African-Americans; Floridian MARY MCLEOD BETHUNE, for example, was among its regional columnists for many decades.

Jesse Vann inherited the paper when Robert died in 1940. She remained its active head for the next two decades; under her leadership, the paper informed blacks of the new opportunities created by the war and participated in the postwar agitation for civil rights. With the national regression of the fifties, its fortunes understandably declined, and Vann came under attack from her board of directors. Only two years after her retirement in 1963, the board—apparently unable to do better than she—sold out to the *Chicago Defender*.

Vann died two years after the sale. For over a half-century,

she and her husband had made the *Pittsburgh Courier* a national opinion-molding organ among black people.

VAN WAGENER, ISABELLA— *See* TRUTH, SOJOURNER

VASSAR COLLEGE

Founded by Matthew Vassar in 1861 and opened for classes four years later at the end of the CIVIL WAR, the institution was the first women's COLLEGE to be located near a large northeastern city. Safely placed in the small town of Poughkeepsie, the campus was fifty miles up the Hudson River from New York.

It was Matthew Vassar's ambitious vision, however, that made the new school distinctive and controversial. Inspired by his niece, Vassar aimed for the college that he endowed not merely to tolerate women students, but to actively recruit only women and to insist upon academic quality in a strong curriculum, including math and the sciences. The idea—though vehemently resisted by establishment males and especially by medical doctors who argued that serious study would damage women's reproductive ability—proved so popular that the rest of the schools later to be known as the "SEVEN SISTERS" soon emulated Vassar.

Though the college's administrators continued to be male for decades into the future, the three hundred young women admitted to the first class were taught by a faculty that was predominately female, with astronomer MARIA MITCHELL as the most eminent. Within a decade, Vassar had graduated 183 students; they were the first American women to hold degrees that represented an education comparable to that given males.

Because Matthew Vassar's four hundred thousand dollar endowment soon was depleted by building expenses and postwar inflation, Vassar students were likely to be the daughters of America's most wealthy families. Many of these women had inherited income sufficient to provide them with comfortable lives, and therefore they did not either have to work or marry for economic security. The result was that these college-educated women became rare models of feminine independence: an 1894 survey found only 39 percent of Vassar graduates had married.

Instead, they devoted themselves to intellectual interests or to philanthropic good. Meanwhile, the atmosphere of life at Vassar became increasingly rarefied, and different from, for example, that of MOUNT HOLYOKE, where students were expected to work. Indeed, Vassar's Maria Mitchell advised against scholarships, saying bluntly that young women from poor families could not be expected to live up to the school's standards. It was thus not surprising that by 1910, Vassar had graduated only one black woman. Lucy Salmon, who introduced history to Vassar's curriculum during her long career there (1888–1926), found the college's administrators and trustees almost intolerably conservative; one example she cited was a campus prohibition against advocacy by the SUFFRAGE MOVEMENT.

Among the most notable women associated with Vassar are: AGNES ALLEN, RUTH BENEDICT, HARRIOT STANTON BLATCH, MARY BRECKINRIDGE, LUCY BURNS, MARY CALDERONE, KATHERINE GRAHAM, GRACE HOPPER, JULIA LATHROP, and MARY MCCARTHY, whose bestselling novel, *The Group* (1966), was based on the lives of Vassar women. The college library holds a number of collections related to women's rights, as well as the papers of Maria Mitchell, ELIZABETH CADY STANTON, and others. Vassar became coeducational in 1969, and its current enrollment is about twenty-three hundred.

VELAZQUEZ, LORETA JANETA (1842–?) Perhaps the most famous of Confederate women who dressed as men to fight in the CIVIL WAR, Velazquez was representative of what may have been hundreds of women who disguised themselves to become soldiers.

She initially pretended to be male so that she could accompany her husband to war, but continued to soldier long after he was killed. Velazquez had a New Orleans tailor create a wire-based chemise that concealed her waist and breasts, and when she was eventually discovered, it was because this contrivance finally came apart. Ungrateful Confederate officers responded to her enthusiasm by fining her ten dollars and sentencing her to ten days in jail.

She published her story as *The Woman in Battle: A Narrative of the Exploits, Adventures, and Travels of Madame Loreta Velazquez* (1876).

VICE COMMISSIONS As American life changed dramatically at the turn of the century, with both increased urbanization and large waves of immigration, the nation's morality also appeared to change. Some immigrant cultures had different standards of behavior that seemed morally loose to Protestant natives, while at the same time, those natives who moved from farm to city also were likely to adopt new behavior in their new setting.

The result was increased concern about illicit sexual activity. A number of widely publicized studies of moral standards—or the lack thereof—were undertaken in the Progressive era. Even though such commissions included experts in the new field of sociology, there was little pretense of objectivity in their work. They were dominated by people (usually male) who were adamant in their certainty that Christian behavior, as they defined it, was the only correct moral standard. With these preconceptions firmly in place, they called themselves "vice" commissions—making it clear that any deviant behavior was axiomatically both sinful (by the standards of Protestantism) and criminal (by the standards of the governments that they represented).

Naturally women received a great deal of attention from these vice commissions. *The Social Evil in Chicago,* for example, was the 1911 report of Chicago's Vice Commission. Though of course the Commission found no justification for the wages of sin, it was apparent that women who chose to engage in PROSTITUTION could in fact earn very good money. At a time when the minimum wage studies of FLORENCE KELLEY and others found most women earned around five dollars weekly, a streetwalker could expect at least twenty-five dollars. Popular women in houses of prostitution could earn as much as four hundred dollars a week, though they had to share part of that with the house.

Similarly thorough studies of illicit sex were conducted in other parts of the country at the same time. *Commercialized Prostitution in New York City* (1913), like other reports, found that IMMIGRANT WOMEN were not the big factor in prostitution that many natives assumed. Though moralists regretted the conclusion, it was nonetheless clear that "the foreign born are not so likely to become prostitution offenders as their

children are." The point was inescapable: the moral standards of young women deteriorated as they adopted American values of individualism and materialism.

A national report was *The Importation and Harboring of Women for Immoral Purposes* (1911) from the Immigration Commission that operated under the aegis of Congress. It, too, showed that the preconceptions of many moralists were wrong: Jews and women from the Catholic countries of eastern and southern Europe were rarely involved in prostitution. By far the majority of prostitutes who were foreign-born came from the countries of northwest Europe (England, Germany, and especially France) that were favored in immigration policy. The report, however, devoted most of its attention to nearly salacious detail on individual cases of organized rings of international WHITE SLAVERY.

These commissions routinely sought PROTECTIVE LEGISLATION for women. Among the procedures praised, for example, was the Ellis Island policy that did not allow an unaccompanied young woman to enter the country until she was either safely married to a man who accepted responsibility for her or until a social worker had investigated and approved her intended dwelling place. "Unprotected women and children are detained," wrote one woman involved in such protective work in 1905.

Like others involved with the vice commissions, her intentions were good, but the result of such attitudes was to invariably treat women as either ignorant victims or else as venal targets of suspicion. Combined with the censorship imposed by the COMSTOCK COMMISSION, these policies meant that women lost both their freedom of movement and their dignity as adults capable of making decisions about their own futures.

VILLARD, FANNY GARRISON (1844–1928) The only daughter of famous ABOLITIONIST WIlliam Lloyd Garrison, she was called Fanny despite her formal name of Helen Frances. She grew up aware of the dangers that her father's activism brought the family and developed similar courage to defy conventions in her own adulthood.

She clearly followed her father's beliefs in freedom and nonviolence when, in 1909, Villard was a founder of the National Association for the Advancement of Colored People, as well as in 1915, when she founded the Women's Peace Society. Unlike others of her suffragist friends, Villard's belief in nonviolence was so strong that she split with the Peace Society at the end of WORLD WAR I because of her support for total disarmament.

In addition, Villard was active in the consumer movement, especially for nutrition education and MILK STATIONS; she was a participant in the founding of both BARNARD and RADCLIFFE; and she donated generously to educational institutions for blacks. Though she was late to join the SUFFRAGE MOVEMENT, after 1906, Villard was simultaneously active in as many as three New York suffrage clubs, serving especially as a speaker.

Her husband, and later, her son were well known as the publishers of the New York *Evening Post* and of the liberal weekly the *Nation,* where her son promoted the career of FREDA KIRCHWEY. Villard published a book on her father, *William Lloyd Garrison and Non-Resistance* (1924) four years before her death at eighty-three.

VINDICATION OF THE RIGHTS OF WOMEN Although written by an English woman, this essay was influential in shaping American thought. Written by Mary Wollstonecraft in

1792, it was preceded by JUDITH SARGENT MURRAY's feminist writing, but Wollstonecraft's is far more famous.

Wollstonecraft's inspiration was the "natural rights" philosophy that flourished in Europe and America at the time of the American and French Revolutions. She was struck by the seemingly literal meaning of the "rights of man" language used in the Declaration of Independence and other documents, and the aim of her essay was to make explicit the exclusion of women from the practice of democracy—even if philosophers argued that their language was merely figurative.

Two centuries ahead of other thinkers, Wollstonecraft postulated that the differences between men and women were the result of education and societal expectations and, moreover, that women were capable of participating in all aspects of life along with men. Such advanced thought naturally was controversial, and when critics discovered that Wollstonecraft lived an unconventional life, that was taken as proof of the danger inherent in her views.

Nonetheless, she found an important adherent in philosopher John Stuart Mill, who took up her ideas and promoted them so successfully that her in part in developing them was soon diminished. While Mill's work was read by male college students and intellectuals in the nineteenth century, Woolstonecraft's essay seldom was acknowledged. Thus, her work was not generally known among the early FEMINISTS who would have found it a comforting affirmation of their own inchoate thought. It was not until the twentieth century that the essay was revived and widely read.

VIRGINIA A number of place names in the U.S. are in honor of Elizabeth I, who also was known as the Virgin Queen. Though Elizabeth may have had relations with several men she favored, she was careful not to repeat the mistake of her half-sister Mary, whose marriage to the king of Spain brought both personal pain and national losses. As an unmarried woman, Elizabeth was assumed to be a virgin, and she was honored with variants of "virgin."

She reigned over England's first great age of exploration, including that of the mid-Atlantic coast the English called "Virginia." When colonization was attempted in 1587, the first child born was named VIRGINIA DARE in honor of the queen. Elizabeth I died in 1603, just four years before the first permanent settlement at JAMESTOWN. Many American places that include both "Elizabeth" and "Virginia" in their names are in honor of the great queen who financed the original English explorations.

VOGUE Founded in 1893, *Vogue* magazine was one of the inheritors of the success of *GODEY'S LADIES BOOK* in developing an audience of reading women. *LADIES HOME JOURNAL*, which was founded a decade earlier than *Vogue,* also competed with the older *Godey's*.

While all three devoted many pages to fashion, *Ladies Home Journal* aimed itself more at women who were interested in public issues and civic service, while *Vogue* sought those primarily concerned with home decoration and especially clothing. Indeed, the marketing of sewing patterns soon was an important branch of *Vogue's* business. It was in DRESS REFORM, therefore, that it made its contribution to liberation: one of the first issues of *Vogue,* for example, showed a woman dressed to go hunting, daringly but sensibly clothed in high boots and a skirt several inches above her ankle.

Collections of original editions of *Vogue* are on file at Conde Nast Publications in New York.

VORSE, MARY HEATON (1874–1966) So prolific a writer was Mary Heaton Vorse that it would be difficult to do any extensive research in twentieth-century labor history and not be familiar with her name. She wrote several books and hundreds of shorter pieces on a range of issues relating to working people—even though her own life was very comfortable until she was in her thirties.

After her 1898 marriage, Vorse lived a charmed life in the seaside artist colony of Provincetown, Massachusetts, with extensive travel in Europe until her husband died suddenly in 1910, leaving her with two children to support. Since she had already published some light work, Vorse turned to writing for a living. It was her coverage of the LAWRENCE, MASSACHUSETTS TEXTILE STRIKE of 1912 that developed her social conscience and turned her into a labor specialist.

Though she remarried, she became a WIDOW once more soon after the birth of her third child and continued to write for a living. While a GOVERNESS cared for her children, Vorse covered labor stories throughout the nation. A brief third marriage and DIVORCE in the early twenties showed the wisdom of keeping her professional name, for it became closely associated with the development of twentieth-century labor issues. Few significant strikes took place without her views— always sympathetic to workers—being recorded in the nation's liberal press.

Though she wrote on labor in general, Vorse understood more than most reporters that labor included women and women's issues. Especially during the labor shortages of WORLD WAR II, Vorse interpreted the lives of working women with far more awareness than most writers on the topic. In a 1943 *Harper's* article, for example, she spelled out the problems of women recruited to work in dangerous munitions factories. Because of the very real chance of explosions, such factories were built in rural towns—which meant both social isolation and financial exploitation by greedy landlords and storekeepers in the overcrowded towns. She showed similar creativity in a 1944 article for the magazine published by the BUSINESS AND PROFESSIONAL WOMEN'S CLUBS titled "Women Don't Quit, If," which explored the reasons for absenteeism and turnover.

Her awareness of the limited welcome that women received in wartime labor unions made Vorse exceptionally perceptive in seeing the rightward trend of postwar unionism. Her work during the 1950s that exposed corruption and authoritarianism in labor organizations was indicative of the greater depth she was able to bring to any story because of her half-century of specialized writing.

A friend of FREDA KIRCHWEY, DOROTHY DAY, and other leftist women in the this era, Vorse also was capable of departing from the political and economic issues that interested her to write fiction, travel, and even humor. Indeed, it was the short story genre that put food on the family table, as Vorse published almost two hundred short stories in magazines ranging from *Woman's Home Companion* to the *New Yorker*. Women turned to magazines for entertainment in a time before television, with the result that Vorse influenced the attitudes of millions of women in this format.

Mary Heaton Vorse was honored by the United Auto Workers Union four years before her death at ninety-two.

WALD, D. LILLIAN (1867–1940) A founder of public health nursing and the SETTLEMENT HOUSE MOVEMENT, Lillian Wald grew up in a prosperous Jewish home in Rochester, New York. She was educated in FINISHING SCHOOLS, but at twenty-one, decided to seek a more viable life as a NURSE. After her 1889 graduation from New York Hospital Training school, she studied further at the Woman's Medical College in New York.

Armed with this background, she moved to the Lower East Side and offered her services as a nurse to the IMMIGRANT WOMEN who lived there. Thus, in 1893, Wald and her friend Mary Brewster opened their home to their needy neighbors—unaware of the similar, then three-year-old efforts of JANE ADDAMS in Chicago. Addams' settlement house, however, tended to emphasize employment and other legal and economic issues that plagued immigrants, while Wald began what would become, in effect, the nation's first visiting nurse association.

So great was the need and so well administered was the idea that Wald enlisted a dozen women to join her within two years, and they expanded to the Henry Street address that would become famous. Her Jewish background was certainly a factor in Wald's success, for most charities until that time were likely to dispense Protestantism along with their care and therefore were rejected by the Jews and Catholics who largely comprised the era's immigrants. Wald was careful to make her services medical and educational, with no motivations that stemmed from either religion or profit. Her nurses charged for their services based on the patient's ability to pay and were subsidized by philanthropists whom Wald recruited with her exceptional fund-raising ability.

The Henry Street women developed the concept of public health nursing by not only caring for the sick, but also by TEACHING preventative health care in classes that were especially important to immigrants from peasant cultures. Women from eastern European villages who were accustomed to fresh milk from their own cows, for instance, needed the MILK STATIONS that would be set up by public health nurses, and families that had always lived in the fresh air found these classes vital in teaching them the prevention of tuberculosis and other contagious diseases that were common to immigrant ghettos.

By 1902, Wald's efforts were so well respected that New York expanded her educational programs via its Board of Health and the public school system in what was the first school nurse program in the world. Other innovative programs that she developed included providing health care to policyholders of early insurance companies and expanding the nonemergency services of CLARA BARTON's Red Cross. Wald also was a leader in establishing New York's Bureau of Child Hygiene, which became a model for other such agencies, and she played a part in founding Columbia University's nursing school.

In 1912, Lillian Wald was elected the first president of the National Organization for Public Health Nursing. A friend of FRANCES PERKINS, FLORENCE KELLEY, and JULIA LATHROP, she was a pioneer in American social work as well as in nursing and public health. Nor was she limited to the world of charity: Wald understood the needs of the working class well enough to have been a founder of the WOMEN'S TRADE UNION LEAGUE already in 1903, and she took an active part in the STRIKE of women in the GARMENT INDUSTRY in 1909.

By the height of the Progressive Era, when WORLD WAR I began, almost a hundred nurses operated out of the Henry Street Settlement House, and Wald wrote up their history along with her own in her bestselling *The House on Henry Street* (1915). She opposed WORLD WAR I, but when the U.S. entered the conflict, she nonetheless headed a nursing committee for the National Defense Council; after the worldwide flu epidemic late in the war, she doubled the number of her nurses. The twenties, with its immigration restrictions and its regressive political leadership, naturally slowed the progress of Wald's ideas, while the Great Depression that began in the latter part of the decade placed more demands for services.

She turned sixty-six the year that her friend ELEANOR ROOSEVELT entered the White House, and Henry Street celebrated its fortieth anniversary at the same time. With four decades of hard work behind her and the promise of public adoption of social policies that she advocated, Lillian Wald retired to Connecticut. She published a second autobiography, *Windows on Henry Street* (1934) and died at age seventy-three. She was honored in the HALL OF FAME in 1970.

WALKER, MAGGIE LENA MITCHELL (1867–1934) A

financial genius among black women, Maggie Mitchell Walker is considered the first female bank president in America. She was born in Richmond two years after the CIVIL WAR ended, the daughter of ELIZABETH VAN LEW's cook and butler. She was educated by women who came South to TEACH ex-slaves, and like many other women, taught for a few years before discovering that she preferred the business world. At seventeen, she was elected an officer in the Women's Union, a local effort of black women to provide insurance for themselves, and this position led to her successful career in banking and insurance.

Mutual insurance programs have a long tradition among American minorities, for those whose existence was tenuous looked to each other in time of need. Virtually all ethnic immigrant communities in America developed mutual aid societies that were aimed at helping each other deal with sickness, death, and other catastrophes. In the usual model, members paid small weekly dues into a fund to be used when need arose. The organizations' officers then doled out the allotted benefits, which would be the only resources available to most in a time before sick leave, unemployment compensation, and other insurance that now is standard.

In the immigrant communities of the late nineteenth and early twentieth centuries, men almost always controlled these mutual aid societies, but in the African-American community, women played an important role. Despite the lack of precedent and despite their burden of poverty, black women who had been slaves created and led the institutions that protected their needy. MARY MCLEOD BETHUNE is only one example of a black woman who, despite a career in another field, nonetheless had lifelong connections with the insurance industry as both a sales agent and a corporate officer.

The insurance plan that Maggie Mitchell joined in the early 1880s had been founded by a Baltimore woman, Mary Prout, only two years after slavery ended. Named for Saint Luke, the organization reflected the religiosity of most African-Americans, and Mitchell supported those principles by beginning every business day with group prayer. At the same time, she employed highly astute business methods, including an innovative newsletter that encouraged African-Americans to make financial investments, despite limited means. She edited this newspaper each week for three decades, including in it a children's corner as well as editorials against lynchings and other injustices of the Jim Crow era. Her 1886 marriage to builder Armstead Walker changed only her name, and she continued to work while bearing three sons.

Maggie Walker's aptitude for business became clear when she was promoted to Saint Luke's executive secretary in 1899. The company was four hundred dollars in debt at the time and employed one person; at her death, it had paid out more than $3 million in benefits and its staff of fifty supervised solid assets. In 1903, Walker extended her financial background into banking. She began Saint Luke Penny Savings with about eight thousand dollars, and by 1920, could cite 645 homes "entirely paid for through our bank's help." Over the next decade, her business became so successful that when the crash of 1929 came, she absorbed most of the area's banks that served blacks into her Richmond Consolidated Bank & Trust. She paid dividends to her shareholders at a time when others went broke and gave "employment to hundreds of Negro clerks, bookkeepers, and office workers. . . ."

A generous donor, Walker was also a cofounder of several organizations, including the Council of Colored Women and other units of the CLUB MOVEMENT. Active in the SUFFRAGE MOVEMENT as well, Walker clearly understood that sexism was as real a problem as racism, saying, for example, to a 1909 audience: "If our men are so slothful and indifferent as to sleep upon their opportunities, I am here to-day to ask the women . . . to awake."

Maggie Walker suffered from diabetes that resulted in her death at sixty-eight. She left her estate to her widowed daughter-in-law, secure in the knowledge that women could successfully run major financial institutions. Her large Richmond home, which housed an extended family, is now a National Historic Landmark.

WALKER, MARY EDWARDS (1832–1919) Despite her

genuine credentials as a physician who treated Union soldiers during the CIVIL WAR, Mary Walker was also scorned by others—including FEMINISTS—as an eccentric cross-dresser.

She attended FINISHING SCHOOL in western New York and worked briefly as a TEACHER before graduating from Syracuse Medical School in 1855. Dr. Walker's medical degree was earned only six years after the famous graduation of ELIZABETH BLACKWELL and a year before that of MARIE ZAKRZEWSKA. Walker's historic achievement, however, has been discounted because of the controversial nature of her later life. Moreover—like many male doctors of the era, but unlike the Blackwells and Zakrzewska—she did not have a lifelong commitment to medicine.

After practicing briefly in Columbus, Ohio, Walker married physician Albert Miller late in 1855 and moved to his home of Rome, New York, where they practiced medicine together. Walker not only kept her career, but also retained her MAIDEN NAME at the wedding—only months after LUCY STONE's far more well known marriage. In addition, Dr. Walker joined AMELIA BLOOMER and other women in western New York State who were promoting DRESS REFORM at the time. Like them, she dropped confining corsets and billowing skirts for the pants-style bloomers that were more practical in her work.

Perhaps as a result of her unconventionality, Walker and her husband separated in 1859 after four years of marriage. DIVORCE was still extremely rare in this era, and Walker moved to the frontier state of Iowa with the hope that she could obtain a divorce in the more liberal circumstances often available to FRONTIER and WESTERN WOMEN. She practiced medicine in Iowa and studied further there—and was forced out of an all-male debating society.

When the CIVIL WAR began the following year, Walker went to Washington to volunteer. The Army officials there ignored her, and while she waited for them to realize that they needed her skills, Walker volunteered in other, slightly more acceptable areas that nonetheless were still new to women. She worked, unpaid, at the Patent Office, which offered the first civil service jobs to women and which was CLARA BARTON's route to more fulfilling work. At the same time, Walker helped organize the Women's Relief Association that aided soldiers under the aegis of the SANITARY COMMISSION.

The war dragged on much longer than any of the men involved in its beginning had expected. By 1863, field commanders understood realities that Washington officials were still unwilling to grant, and when Dr. Walker went to the battlefields of Tennessee and presented herself to General George "Pap" Thomas, he accepted her services. Men of both higher and lower rank objected, but Thomas stuck to his decision and commissioned Walker as an "assistant surgeon." She wore the uniform of a first lieutenant and was the highest-ranking woman to serve in the Civil War.

Dr. Walker worked as a surgeon through the misery of the Tennessee mountain warfare during the cold, wet winter of 1863–1864. She was away from camp rendering aid to civilians in April of 1864 when Confederate soldiers captured her. No supposed principles of Southern chivalry protected her, and this Union physician in military uniform was taken as a prisoner of war to the jails of Richmond. She spent the summer in the heat of the Confederate capital, where ELIZABETH VAN LEW tried vainly to ease the starvation of imprisoned Federals in this last desperate year of the war.

In August, Dr. Walker was included in a prisoner-of-war exchange and returned to Washington. From there, she was assigned to a Kentucky prisoner-of-war installation where the Union held Confederate women as prisoners, and then to a war-related orphanage in Tennessee. She returned to Washington near the war's end in 1865, and later in the year, Dr. Mary Walker was awarded the Congressional Medal of Honor.

It would be the zenith of her life. Like DOROTHEA DIX, CLARA BARTON, and others who pushed their abilities upon reluctant military officials, she was increasingly referred to as a "tactless" and "difficult." Her Tennessee and Kentucky subordinates complained about taking orders from a woman, and Army officials were quick to dismiss her even before the war ended. Nonetheless, her postwar popularity was sufficient to reward her with a prominent place on the lecture circuit that proved profitable for so many of the era's feminists. She not only earned a living, but also advanced her ideas with lectures throughout the nation and in England. Her home during these immediate postwar years was with BELVA LOCKWOOD in Washington.

She finally was able to formalize the end of her marriage—after a decade of legal effort—with an 1869 divorce under New York law. Afterwards, she spent increasing amounts of time in Iowa, where her family lived, and in 1872, she attempted to vote there. Like other women in the SUFFRAGE MOVEMENT, Walker believed that women were entitled to vote under the language of the FIFTEENTH AMENDMENT—but unlike most others, she held to her convictions on this so stubbornly that she refused to work for what eventually became the NINETEENTH AMENDMENT.

Moreover, Walker alienated other suffragists with the publication of her autobiographical *Hit* (1871) and *Unmasked* (1878). Their content, as well as their titles, were ahead of the times, and the latter was particularly embarrassing to the era's feminists, few of whom could tolerate Walker's discussion of sexuality and especially her apparent LESBIANISM.

Indeed, Walker not only emphasized dress reform long after others had abandoned the idea, but also increasingly masculinized her appearance. She wore men's clothing from head to toe, and by 1887, was so alienated from the established feminist movement that she was reduced to appearing in sideshows rather than on the respectable lecture circuit. Doubtless her abandonment of the practice of medicine also resulted from her unwillingness to conform to patients' expectations. Increasingly seen as bizarre, Walker entangled herself with numerous petty lawsuits in the 1890s and developed so many enemies that the damage to her reputation was irreparable.

Even the era's most tolerant feminists disassociated themselves from her. IDA HUSTED HARPER, for example, omitted any mention of Walker from her massive two-volume official biography of SUSAN ANTHONY—even though, as activists in the same long era, Anthony's path crossed Walker's more than once. Long before the turn of the twentieth century, Walker's egocentric and erratic behavior had alienated her friends, and without feminists to support her, she lost the honor that had been the high point of her life.

In 1917, when the U.S. entered WORLD WAR I and the military undertook a review of previous awards of medals to heighten the prestige of their honors, Dr. Mary Walker was included among those whose awards were withdrawn. Her Civil War contribution was genuine, and the grief and frustration she felt probably was a factor in causing the eighty-four-year-old woman to fall on the Capitol steps. Her death two years later at her rural Iowa home went largely unnoticed and unmourned.

WALKER, MADAME C.J. (SARAH BREEDLOVE WALKER) (1867–1919)

Although she would become known as the first black female millionaire, Sarah Breedlove's childhood showed anything but that promise. Born into extreme poverty in Louisiana two years after the CIVIL WAR, she was an orphan at six. She married at fourteen to escape an abusive situation, bore a daughter, and became a WIDOW at twenty. Following the model of many black women who went to urban areas for their better employment opportunities, she moved to St. Louis in the late 1880s. Having a child limited her chances for live-in DOMESTIC SERVICE, but she made a living as a washerwoman for the next two decades.

A dramatic change came to her life in 1905. As Madame

Walker later told it, her idea for a hair treatment method designed for black women came to her in a dream. Experimenting in her kitchen, she developed a shampoo and conditioner ("Wonderful Hair Grower") that, combined with the prescribed use of heated combing and curling techniques, was intended to produce healthy and stylish hair specifically for black women.

Others differ with her supernatural explanation for her invention; the preparation of hair aids for black women had a number of historical antecedents, and specifically, some charge that Walker directly plagiarized the ideas of ANNIE TURBO MALONE, who also sold these products in St. Louis in the same year. Indeed, there is evidence that Walker worked for Turbo in 1905 and that Turbo was the first to call her product "Wonderful Hair Grower."

Nonetheless, Walker developed a separate identity that eventually eclipsed her presumed mentor. After sales of her preparations met with some success in St. Louis, she moved on to Denver, where relatives lived, and quickly recruited hairdressers there into following her methods. It was in Denver that she met journalist Charles J. Walker; after their 1906 wedding, she adopted the title of Madame C.J. Walker and referred to her cosmetological approach as the Walker System.

The transformation from washerwoman to entrepreneur proceeded with such magical speed as to make her dream explanation seem credible, and Madame Walker spent her forties traveling to Southern and Eastern cities where she demonstrated her methods to astonishingly responsive audiences. Within four years, she was able to build a manufacturing plant in Indianapolis, from which she eventually built a string of beauty schools and supervised the thousands of "Walker agents" who used demonstration techniques to sell her cosmetics door-to-door. In a time when the employment opportunities of black women were extremely limited and when most women lived in lonely isolation as housewives, a "house call" by a Walker agent brought excitement—and sales.

Walker's schools and manufacturing plant clearly predated that of Annie Turbo Malone, who did not build her St. Louis complex until 1917, but the market was big enough for both of them and others. White business had ignored the possibility that there was money to be made in the development of products explicitly for African-Americans, while males of both races ignored the market that women represented. Booker T. Washington was so blind on this point that he tried to prevent Walker from speaking to the National Negro Business League in 1912. Like ROSE KNOX, however, Walker and her competitors demonstrated that women were competent, innovative managers and advertisers who could create entirely new markets capable of making them rich.

Walker's business ability is even more phenomenal when it is remembered that she had no schooling and was essentially illiterate. Within a decade, however, she had made so much money that she not only owned a townhouse in New York City but also an Italian-style villa up the Hudson. Her appreciation for education was profound, and she generously endowed many related causes, including the YOUNG WOMEN'S CHRISTIAN ASSOCIATION and even a girls' school in West Africa that she founded.

She also emphasized education of her agents, especially in cosmetological principles of safety and sanitation that were new at the time. While Walker has been criticized by some for what they see as her attempt to make her customers look white, in fact her products were primarily aimed at creating healthy, thick hair. A large part of her original motivation was based on her own thinning hair, and, in refusing to call her products hair straightener, she argued for black pride in an appearance that differed from whites.

Although her tenets included good health practices, Madame Walker was never able to control her own high blood pressure. She enjoyed only fourteen years of life after her initial success before hypertension killed her at age fifty-two. Malone, in contrast, lived a long life, but was bankrupt for most of it.

Walker left much of her estate to philanthropy, and, in the decade following her death, Madame Walker's daughter would emulate her mother's generosity with sponsorship of Harlem Renaissance artists. It was a tremendous change from her grandparents' lives as slaves on Mississippi Delta plantations.

WALKER, MARGARET ABIGAIL (1915–   )

Best known for her well researched and beautifully written CIVIL WAR novel *Jubilee* (1966), Margaret Walker is also a poet, essayist, and literary critic.

Though born black in the South, Walker managed to graduate from Northwestern University during the depression year of 1935 and later earned a Ph.D. from University of Iowa. She worked with Langston Hughes, Richard Wright, and other writers of the Harlem Renaissance and won the Yale University Younger Poets Award for poems collected as *My People* (1941). She was the first black woman to be so honored and one of the youngest blacks poets ever published.

She retained her MAIDEN NAME when she married in 1943; the marriage endured until her husband's death thirty-seven years later. While teaching and raising four children, Walker continued to write. WORLD WAR II opened American minds to the need for racial tolerance, and she responded with her autobiographical *Growing Out of the Shadows* (1943) and *How I Told My Child About Race* (1951).

After her major success with *Jubilee,* which was based on the lives of her ancestors, Walker turned to literary criticism with *How I Wrote Jubilee* (1967). An English professor at Jackson State University from 1949 to 1980, she lived through the violence of integration there, including the assassination of her neighbor, Medger Evers. The author of ten books and dozens of shorter works, she has received several honorary degrees and an award from the White House.

WALLACE, LILA BELL ACHESON (1889–1984)

Cofounder and PUBLISHER of *Reader's Digest,* Lila Bell Acheson was a Midwesterner who graduated from the University of Oregon and worked for the YOUNG WOMEN'S CHRISTIAN ASSOCIATION through WORLD WAR I. She moved to New York after the war, and in 1921, married DeWitt Wallace, a longtime friend from Minnesota. Together the two founded *Reader's Digest* in 1922.

DeWitt had recently been fired from his job, and they used borrowed money to put together the first issue of the magazine in the basement of their Greenwich Village apartment. They mailed advertising on their wedding day and returned from their honeymoon to find fifteen hundred checks from eager subscribers.

The magazine, with its unique format of condensing the best articles published in other magazines, quickly became popular. Its sales rose dramatically throughout the twenties and it continued to do well during the Great Depression, when original articles were added to the format and the magazine also began publishing in languages other than English. Condensed books were added to the publishing formula after WORLD WAR II. The magazine did not accept advertising until 1955, and even then refused ads for certain products, including liquor.

Lila Wallace had an aptitude for architecture and art as well as publishing. She personally designed the suburban offices the company moved to in 1939, where she also displayed original modern art that she collected. The Wallaces became very wealthy and were known as philanthropists. Lila Wallace received the Medal of Freedom from President Richard Nixon in 1972.

WARNER, SUSAN BOGERT (1819–1885) and ANNA BARTLETT (1827–1885)
The central character of Susan Warner's most famous book, *The Wide, Wide World* (1851), has recently been called "a feminist Huck Finn." While Mark Twain probably would disagree because of the religiosity Warner assigned to her motherless girl, it is nonetheless true that nineteenth-century audiences found Warner a joy to read. *The Wide, Wide World,* in fact, is credited with being the first American book to sell a million copies.

Warner followed it with dozens of books, averaging more than one a year for the next thirty years. For a long time, her name on the cover was enough to assure instant sales, but despite her popularity, she was never financially secure. Women were not well established as AUTHORS in this era when American literature was still separating itself from English dominance, and Warner lacked proper literary and legal representation. The lack of international copyright agreements was particularly harmful in the case of *The Wide, Wide World,* which was reprinted by almost two dozen London publishers who never paid her a dime. Indeed, Susan Warner was so popular that her classic, which is almost unknown today, outsold Charles Dickens' *David Copperfield* in mid-century England.

She lived her entire life with her sister Anna, who was also a prolific writer. Both wrote religious books, but Anna also specialized in gardening and, especially, books and verses for children. She invented a board game for children and is best remembered for the children's song, "Jesus Loves Me, This I Know." The sisters lived most of their lives in the relative isolation of an island in the Hudson River that is opposite the Army's military academy at West Point.

WARREN, MERCY OTIS (1728–1814)
Born on Cape Cod, Mercy Otis moved a few miles north to Plymouth when she married; she never saw anything beyond eastern Massachusetts—but the life of her mind was so rich that she was respected by the most cosmopolitan and politically important men of her era.

Though her brothers attended Harvard, she (like most girls in her era) got only the education that she picked up for herself. Naturally political, she involved herself from girlhood in the conversations of her father and her older brother James, a well-connected lawyer. That she waited to wed until age twenty-six showed something of her independent nature, but she married James Warren in 1754. While he developed a career in the colonial legislature, she went on to bear five sons.

When the colonies increasingly rebelled against English rule, Mercy Otis Warren became perhaps the most important of REVOLUTIONARY WAR WOMEN. Like the men of her family, she was among those ready to throw out the colonial governor. In 1772—four years before the Declaration of Independence—she ANONYMOUSLY published *The Adulateur,* a satire that cast the governor as "Rapatio," a villain intent on raping the colony. Rapatio appeared again in her second play, *The Defeat* (1773), and she published her third, *The Group* (a title she used two centuries before MARY MCCARTHY), in 1775, just as the rebellion began to be violent. All were thinly disguised attacks on specific public officials, for she unhesitatingly urged the taking of risks to achieve American independence.

Much later, at the time of the French Revolution, Warren wrote tellingly that revolutions are "permitted by Providence, to remind mankind of their natural equality." More than most of the men of her era, she saw the American Revolution as having significance beyond its apparent economic and political warfare; instead, she foresaw a deep and permanent shift of Western ideology. At a time when even most Americans still thought of democracy as an impossible notion tainted by ignorant rabble, Mercy Otis Warren understood that the natural rights philosophy inherent in the Declaration of Independence would inevitably mean democracy and egalitarianism. Indeed, so thorough a radical was Warren that she joined the minority who opposed ratification of the Constitution in the late 1780s.

The Revolution was scarcely begun before Warren began recording the history of it. During the next three decades, she worked steadily on the three volumes that were finally published—when Warren was seventy-seven—as *History of the Rise, Progress and Termination of the American Revolution* (1805). Her work not only provided an insider's view of the Revolution, but also set an important precedent for women AUTHORS. Until that time, the few who existed in America did not set out to consciously publish, but instead wrote primarily for themselves (as in the cases of ANNE BRADSTREET and PHYLLIS WHEATLEY). Warren thus became the first to publish books that marked her as a professional writer of nonfiction who—despite her upper class status—offered her work for sale.

Bitterly resentful in her old age of the restrictions imposed upon women, Warren focused particularly on educational reform. She chafed at the memory of doing needlework while her brothers were taught Latin and Greek, and she argued that such artificial limits on achievement harmed both men and women and were a violation of the natural rights philosophy espoused in the Revolution. Though it may have appeared that few understood her message at the time, the first serious educational institution for women, EMMA WILLARD'S Troy Female Seminary, appeared less than a decade after her death. Warren's thoughts on the subject may have had more influence than she knew.

Mercy Otis Warren had a clear, analytical mind that brought logic even to her poetry. *Poems, Dramatic and Miscellaneous* (1790), a collection published when she was sixty-two, was the first of her works that bore her name ("Mrs. M. Warren"), but she kept other poetry so personal that it was not published until almost two centuries after her death. Hundreds of Warren's letters to contemporaries (including Franklin, Jefferson, Hamilton, and ABIGAIL ADAMS and her husband John— with whom Warren quarreled as John Adams grew increasingly conservative) also have been published. They provide historians with interesting detail and insightful commentary on the founding of the nation by one whose gender excluded her from the direct participation that she doubtlessly would have preferred.

WAVES (WOMEN APPOINTED FOR VOLUNTARY EMERGENCY SERVICE) The Navy's unit for women who were not NURSES during WORLD WAR II, the WAVES was created as an acronym and the explanatory words behind it were seldom used. The lesson on acronyms was but one of the things that the Navy learned from the Army's earlier experience in creating a woman's unit; its thoughtless acronym of WAAC produced countless plays on "wacky."

The authorizing bill went through Congress during the first half of 1942, and the WAVES officially began on July 30, 1942. In addition to learning from the Army, the Navy had its own experience with women members during WORLD WAR I when

A member of the WAVES launching a weather balloon to check wind velocity at the Naval Air Station in Santa Ana, California, during World War II. NATIONAL ARCHIVES.

it had militarized women as YEOMAN (F) and MARINETTES. This experience had given the Navy an appreciative view of the contributions that women could make in war, and from the first, WAVES generally found their time in service to be rewarding.

Under the command of MILDRED MCAFEE, who took leave from her position as president of WELLESLEY, the WAVES recruited college-educated women. They were more likely than WAACs to train at colleges, rather than at military bases, and to serve in positions that were not menial. The Navy particularly sought women who "majored in engineering, astronomy, meteorology, electronics, physics, mathematics" and similar fields. WAVES used these backgrounds to do such jobs as charting weather patterns for planes and ships, figuring trajectories of bombs and other ammunition, and teaching male cadets various aspects of aviation. Thousands of women thus had a chance to exercise their abilities in fields that were usually closed to them; some, like GRACE HOPPER, went on to major achievement with this background.

By the end of the war, almost one hundred thousand women had joined the WAVES. By far the majority of them were white, for the WAVES' reluctance to admit black applicants (and the Navy's reluctance to accept them in general) had been a subject of NAACP protest throughout the war. The first black women were not sworn into the WAVES until late in 1944, when the conflict was almost over. A second complaint about the WAVES was that they were not allowed to go overseas as WACs were. WAVES were kept in the U.S. until 1944, when they were finally permitted to go to other parts of the Western Hemisphere—despite the Navy's experience with using women as translators and telephone operators in the European battlegrounds of World War I.

After the last class of trainees graduated in January, 1946, recruitment was suspended while the existence of women's military units was debated. The WAVES continued as a separate entity administered for and commanded by women until passage of the WOMEN'S ARMED SERVICES INTEGRATION ACT in 1948. Representative MARGARET CHASE SMITH of Maine particularly championed the WAVES in Congress, and in 1951, as the Korean War heated up, thousands of women were again sworn into the Navy.

WELD, ANGELINA GRIMKE— *See* GRIMKE, ANGELINA

WELLESLEY COLLEGE Named for the Massachusetts town in suburban Boston where it was built, Wellesley was the second of the women's COLLEGES that became known as the SEVEN SISTERS. It was founded in 1870, just five years after the end of the CIVIL WAR and the opening of VASSAR COLLEGE.

Like Vassar, Wellesley owed its existence primarily to a man, Henry Fowle Durant, who endowed its four hundred-acre, million-dollar campus. With matriculation requirements that were similar to the nearby Harvard, Wellesley provided a preparatory program for several years after its founding to assist applicants in passing its rigorous entrance examination. Nonetheless, women were so eager for higher education that there was no problem in securing the three hundred students necessary for financial stability when college-level classes finally began in 1875.

Unlike Vassar, Wellesley had women presidents from the

beginning; its second president, ALICE FREEMAN PALMER, was particularly influential on both the college and the nation. Though she was forced to resign when she married, Wellesley continued to provide an academic home for many of the nation's pioneer women in academia. One of its later presidents was MILDRED MCAFEE, who commanded the WAVES during WORLD WAR II, and other outstanding faculty included economists EDITH ABBOTT and EMILY BALCH, philosophers MARY CALKINS and SUSANNE LANGER, poet KATHERINE LEE BATES, and Pulitzer-winning biographer OLA E. WINSLOW. Famous Wellesley students include sociologist SOPHONISBA BRECKINRIDGE, astronomer ANNIE JUMP CANNON, politician MOLLY DEWSON, environmentalist MARJORIE STONE DOUGLAS, and paleontologist WINIFRED GOLDRING.

Among Wellesley's most important historical collections is work by colonial poet ANNE BRADSTREET. African-American students were accepted before 1900, and men began to be admitted in the 1970s. More than most other SEVEN SISTERS schools, however, Wellesley retains its identity as an independent women's college.

WELLS-BARNETT, IDA BELL (1862–1931)

Born into slavery in Mississippi during the first year of the CIVIL WAR, Ida Wells was orphaned by an epidemic in her early teens. She supported younger siblings while also studying at Rust College, a newly established school for ex-slaves run by TEACHERS who came South at the war's end.

In 1884, Wells moved to Memphis and continued to teach while she added to her credentials at Fisk University. At the same time, she began to write in the local news outlets for blacks. Like other women writers who veiled themselves with PSEUDONYMS, she took the pen name of Iola, but the disguise was so slight that it did not protect her from retaliation. When she not only criticized the school system's lack of support for black students, but—with amazing defiance—also sued a railroad for its segregated seating, the Memphis school board made it clear that such assertiveness was not permitted to teachers. In 1891, her contract was not renewed.

She turned to journalism as a career, for Wells had already established such a strong reputation that she had been elected an officer in the Colored Press Association at an 1887 meeting in Washington. She bought a one-third interest in Memphis' *Free Speech and Highlight* and increased its circulation by nearly 40 percent in the first year. Under this editorial banner, Wells led the charge against the loss of liberties that local blacks had under Reconstruction. As black men lost the vote that they had been accustomed to in the two decades since the Confederacy ended, it was a black woman—who never had a vote—who led the crusade against this usurpation of civil rights.

Wells would establish her primary reputation, however, for writing against lynching—another case that affected men more directly than women. When she editorialized against lynchings in small towns in the Tennessee-Arkansas-Mississippi area near Memphis, white newspapers responded with editorials charging that *Free Speech* was inciting violence. The white editors, however, assumed that the black paper's editorial voice was that of the minister whose church Wells used as her office. City officials trumped up charges against him, and he fled west—leaving the woman who was the genuine

editor behind. Thus, in 1892, Wells became half-owner and the clear power behind the paper.

Shortly thereafter, three of her friends were killed in a mob attack by racists who were jealous of the economic success of these young black men, and Wells' outraged editorials called upon Memphis blacks to resist violence with violence if that was necessary. Presaging Martin Luther King by more than a half-century, she urged blacks to boycott the city's streetcars. When thousands of the city's blacks fled to Oklahoma—the Indian Territory that had been opened to white settlement three years earlier—Wells encouraged them to go, leaving Memphis merchants without workers and customers.

The final act of the drama came in May when Wells (who had always been aware that her grandfather was white) introduced sexuality into the debate. "Nobody believes the old threadbare lies that Negro men rape white women," she wrote. The reverse was true instead—and not only did white men rape black women with impunity, but also, she added, "If Southern white men are not careful . . . a conclusion will be reached which will be very damaging to the moral reputation of their women." Memphis whites could scarcely contain their fury; Wells' office was ransacked, her life was threatened, and she left Memphis forever.

From bases with Chicago's *Conservator,* the *New York Age* and other papers, she continued to crusade against lynching in particular and discrimination against African-Americans in general. Wells first gained national prominence by writing about the exclusion of blacks from the COLUMBIAN EXPOSITION of 1893. At the same time, she organized a black woman's club in Chicago as part of the era's CLUB MOVEMENT, and she would retain the presidency of the Ida B. Wells Club for the rest of her life.

She also lectured in England that year, where her speeches drew so much favorable attention that she was invited back the following year. Newspapers portrayed Wells as having a "quiet, refined manner," and yet she also spoke candidly on sexuality; another paper quoted her explanation of lynching as tied directly to the double standard of "white men [who] constantly express an open preference for the society of black women," but who were desperately afraid of similar behavior in white women.

Her lecture tour was a tremendous success. Not only was there extensive coverage in Britain and in black newspapers in the U.S., even a white Chicago paper featured a regular column titled "Ida B. Wells Abroad." So effective a speaker was Wells that a well-funded British antilynching society was formed to influence American opinion, and Memphis newspapers were flooded with letters from British citizens threatening a boycott of cotton. In the end, the prominent *Commercial Appeal* led the city's newspapers in a pained attempt to simultaneously refute the charges while also apologizing.

Two histories of lynching based on Well's writing, *Southern Horrors* (1892) and *A Red Record* (1895), continued to publicize the cause. She married the same year the latter book was published, soon after her return from England, and afterwards was never quite as visible a leader. Age thirty-three when she wed, she bore four children in eight years, but continued to write for the newspaper owned by her journalist/politician husband. She retained her MAIDEN NAME in hyphenated form, though she sometimes is referred to as Ida B. Wells.

In 1898, she went to the White House to lobby President McKinley on lynching, but for the two decades following, Wells-Barnett concentrated primarily on her children and on mainstream organizations such as Chicago's Negro Fellowship League. Just before WORLD WAR I, she returned to more of the political action she had known before marriage, including the formation of the Alpha Suffrage Club, which marched with white women in suffrage parades. She even traveled South again to investigate lynchings.

Though she had been involved in the founding of the NATIONAL ASSOCIATION OF COLORED WOMEN and the National Association for the Advancement of Colored People, Wells-Barnett soon became scornful of the slow accommodation approach accepted by these groups. She particularly denounced Booker T. Washington and the NAACP's willingness to give leadership positions to whites. The ideas of more radical (and less popular) blacks such as Langston Hughes, Marcus Garvey and W.E.B. DuBois were more similar to her own. These men, however, seemed unwilling to share power with her, and eventually Wells-Barnett quarrelled publicly with DuBois—and, indeed, with almost all of the era's black leaders.

Many observers spoke of Wells-Barnett as a difficult personality, but few acknowledged that she was virtually unique in her time as a *woman* who espoused a radical racial philosophy. Her world appeared to be divided into two parts: those (virtually all women and most men) who concentrated on uplifting projects to improve "the Negro situation"; and a second, much smaller world of militant men who seemed to reject association with women—especially a woman who was older and more experienced than they.

The sad result for Wells-Barnett was almost inevitable frustration, anger, and loneliness—and those were the feelings that she committed to paper when she began to write her autobiography in 1928. Her isolation was demonstrated again in 1930, when she ran for the State Senate; black women clearly chose not to support her, and she was soundly defeated by the male candidates.

This apparent unpopularity also made it likely that she would be forgotten, for few among her contemporaries honored her in her final days. Indeed, her autobiography, *Crusade for Justice* (1970) was not published until almost four decades after her death—and then largely because of the efforts of her daughter. As a result, however, there has been a revival of interest in this unusual woman, including a recent Public Broadcasting video and a postage stamp issued in 1990 for Black History Month.

Ida Wells-Barnett died in 1931, at just sixty-nine. Had she lived until the next year, she would have seen the revolutionary election of 1932 and perhaps could have helped to bring about changes wrought in the era of MARY MCLEOD BETHUNE, JESSIE DANIEL AMES, and others. Even as it was, however, she doubtless saved many lives—most of them male—with her courage in speaking out during the worst of the Jim Crow days.

WELTY, EUDORA (1909–) Except for a few years at the University of Wisconsin and in New York at Columbia University, Eudora Welty spent her life in Mississippi, which is the setting of most of her literature.

She had published in ST. NICHOLAS MAGAZINE at age eleven, but came to adulthood during the Great Depression. She returned from New York to Mississippi and, like other would-be AUTHORS in that difficult time, was reduced to writing for the Works Progress Administration. In 1936, at age twenty-seven, she published her first short story, and soon her tales were appearing in increasingly prestigious magazines. Welty's first collection of stories came out in 1941, and with the return of prosperity with WORLD WAR II and her own increased reputation, she regularly published novels, plays, and especially short stories.

Her most famous work is *Ponder Heart* (1954), which one distinguished journal called "the most amusing piece of American humor since Mark Twain." She has received a tremendous number of honors, including the American Book Award, the Pulitzer Prize, and medals from the American Academy of Arts and Letters and the National Institute of Arts and Letters.

Welty never married and still lives in her family home in Jackson, Mississippi. In 1992, she won the National Book Foundation Medal for Distinguished Contribution to American Letters.

WEST, MAE (1892–1980) Reputedly the first to earn a million dollars in the movie business, Mae West was well known for her sexy style in delivering double entendres. What is less well known is that, from an early age, she wrote most of the productions in which she starred and virtually every word of her own material.

She first appeared on the stage at age seven and became a star with a play she wrote in 1926, daringly titled *Sex*. She moved from New York to Hollywood in 1932, and delivered the "come up and see me sometime" line for which she is famous in her first film. Even though she turned forty that same year, her personal fortunes continued to grow with those of the movie business. Within a few years, she was the highest salaried actor of either gender and—despite the Great Depression—starred in more than a movie a year. She performed for enthusiastic audiences through WORLD WAR II (when her name began to be used for lifejackets), and continued to be extremely popular into her sixties.

Unlike the dumb blonde image that she projected, West invested wisely in California real estate and lived well. She died at eighty-seven, leaving most of her estate to her sister.

WESTERN WOMEN When SUSAN ANTHONY died in 1906, women had full voting rights in four states—Wyoming, Utah, Colorado, and Idaho—and two nations, Australia and New Zealand. All of these areas shared the combination of an English heritage with newly settled conditions, factors that seem integral to improving the status of women.

Throughout the settlement of North America, FRONTIER WOMEN found themselves in circumstances that required independent behavior and raw courage. Women endured deprivation, pain, and death equally with men on frontiers. Their experiences included such horrors as that of the Dutch woman who was the only person to survive a 1635 ambush of her disembarking shipmates and—two centuries later—the women in the famous 1846 Donner party, who were caught in the snows of the high Sierras in starvation conditions sufficient for cannibalism.

Even without such disasters, routine settlement of frontiers

Wyoming women voting in Cheyenne in 1888. Women in several Western states voted decades prior to those in the East. LIBRARY OF CONGRESS; FROM *LESLIE'S ILLUSTRATED NEWSPAPER*.

meant lifetimes without accustomed comforts. So many women were willing to make the exchange of comfort for independence, however, that single women who went West as HOMESTEADERS were a regular feature of frontier communities. Moreover, when the accoutrements of contemporary society finally reached the frontier, the change invariably meant restrictions on women. "Civilization" meant clothing that substituted fashion for freedom, while its moral codes meant losses such as the ability to TRAVEL without an escort.

In addition to proving themselves by suffering through the same wilderness trials that men did, women on the frontier also improved their status because of their relative scarcity. Men were so eager to have women join them in remote locations that they offered economic and even political incentives unknown in urban areas. The fact that a woman could easily find another man eager to replace one who mistreated her curbed male misbehavior and liberalized legal codes, especially in DIVORCE. Women also found jobs available to them in the West that were generally reserved for men in the East.

Nowhere was this more true than in education. The schoolmaster was a rare phenomenon in the West, for men seeking free land were not interested in TEACHING; instead, thousands of women were recruited as schoolmarms and some, like CARRIE CHAPMAN CATT and ALICE FREEMAN PALMER, were promoted to principal and superintendent of large educational institutions. A 1902 update on the voting women of Wyoming in the HISTORY OF WOMAN SUFFRAGE pointed out that women served as trustees for the state university, and announced

matter-of-factly, "In many districts women serve on the school board, and nearly all of the counties elect them to the responsible position of superintendent." In addition, western women were assured of greater COLLEGE opportunity, for those states created higher education options for women decades before that was the case in the East. Indeed, the last state to provide a college for women was the long-settled Delaware, which finally made this move in 1914.

Another factor in the greater liberality of the American West (as well as of the first nations to grant women the right to vote) was an English heritage. From the Magna Carta to the VINDICATION OF THE RIGHTS OF WOMEN, the most effective of the modern world's proponents of democracy shared a common English background. In contrast, the IMMIGRANT WOMEN and men who crowded eastern cities in the latter half of the nineteenth century came mostly from continental cultures that were far less democratic—and far more restrictive of women. The theologies of the newcomers also were generally less conducive to an improved status for women, as both Catholicism and Judaism restricted women from the practice of religion in ways that Protestantism, especially the congregationalist American sects, did not. The result was that men in eastern cities were often more illiberal in their attitudes towards women than was the case with western men.

Although they have been overlooked by most historians, thousands of black women also moved West. As early as 1820, for example, there were black women who, as slaves, went to frontier Fort Snelling, Minnesota with the families of military officers stationed at the headwaters of the Mississippi. As in the South, these black women usually were DOMESTIC SERVANTS or professional cooks. Their labor apparently proved so satisfactory that recent research on Iowa blacks indicates many stayed in slavery much longer than is generally believed, with newspapers running carefully worded advertisements for black INDENTURED SERVANTS as late as the 1850s. Census figures for 1870—five years after the CIVIL WAR ended—showed more than eight thousand black females in the legendary free state of Kansas; by 1910, their numbers had increased to 26,066. Nearby Oklahoma—formerly reserved for Cherokees and other displaced natives—was understandably popular with black settlers. IDA WELLS-BARNETT reported that entire congregations of black churches moved to Oklahoma's frontier from violence-prone Memphis in 1892.

Not surprisingly, many of those women who moved West also were more likely than their stay-at-home sisters to adopt the progressive ideas of their times. For example, there were organized town clubs of women in small settlements deep in the interior already in the 1870s, while the CLUB MOVEMENT was just beginning in much larger eastern cities. At a time when East Coast women were limited to the exclusivity of SOROSIS and the New England Woman's Club, for example, there were literary clubs in such remote locations as Cedar Rapids, Iowa and Quincy, Illinois. More self-assured because of their pioneer experience, such women also were more likely to demand—and get—the vote.

In November, 1869, women in the Wyoming Territory became the first to be enfranchised, but Utah Territory women actually cast the first ballots in the election year of 1870. Although Utah was a virtual theocracy, the Mormon Church then was not the conservative bastion that it later became, and Brigham Young himself appointed Sarah M. Kimball as liaison to the national suffrage cause. Utah's Territorial Suffrage Association met annually until 1910, when, "the suffrage having been gained, it was hard to keep up the interest." Though they stopped having meetings, Utah's branch of the NATIONAL AMERICAN WOMAN SUFFRAGE ASSOCIATION still provided funds and petition signatures for other, unenfranchised women. Additional western states granted women full or partial voting rights during the 1880s and 1890s, and by the time that the NINETEENTH AMENDMENT finally came to legislative life in 1918, a map of the suffrage states would clearly reveal the advanced status of western women. Women had full voting rights in twelve states—and eleven of them were in the West.

The West was also more likely to grant women other civil rights. The constitution adopted by Wyoming Territory in 1869, for example, assured MARRIED WOMEN'S PROPERTY RIGHTS. Wyoming women not only could sue, enter into contracts, and conduct business on the same terms as men, but they also performed JURY DUTY as early as 1870—to the delight of cartoonists back East who found the idea hilarious. Moreover, an 1869 Wyoming law required EQUAL PAY for women and men in public employment, and even more strikingly, state law at the turn of the century punished males caught in a house of PROSTITUTION more severely than females guilty of the same offense.

The first female public officials also were in the West. ESTHER MORRIS became justice of the peace in 1870, just a year after her Wyoming Territory enfranchised women, and by the turn of the century, Wyoming had elected a woman, Estelle Reel, as State Superintendent of Public Instruction. Clara Clessingham, Carrie Holly, and Frances Klock were the first American women to hold legislative positions when they won election to the Colorado House of Representatives in 1894. Wyoming added Mary G. Bellemy to the statehouse in 1910, and Wyoming also is credited with having the first female governor in NELLIE TAYLOE ROSS, though Texas' MIRIAM FERGUSON also won in the same year of 1924.

The first woman in Congress, too, was from the Far West, with JEANETTE RANKIN, an unabashed pacifist and an officer in the NATIONAL AMERICAN WOMAN SUFFRAGE ASSOCIATION, elected from Montana in 1916. Finally, in 1932, the first woman elected to the U.S. Senate was HATTIE CARAWAY from Arkansas—a state that, while usually classified as Southern, is west of the Mississippi. Though the SUFFRAGE MOVEMENT was centered in the Northeast, it took those states many years to catch up with precedents set further west.

These women voters in the West were more likely to register Republican than Democratic. (To be sure, Ross, Ferguson, and Caraway were Democrats, but two of the three were from states that reflected Southern voting habits more than western.) Several factors were involved in this preference for the Republican Party, among the most important of which was its origin in the ABOLITIONIST movement and its laissez-faire and Protestant traditions, which appealed to independent-minded westerners. The Democratic Party was more likely to be supported by Southerners and, in the cities, by immigrants, Catholics, and union members; while these groups include factors that may be considered "liberal," the Democratic Party did little to reach out to women until after the turn of the century. Western women therefore were likely to vote Republican, even though many differed with easterners in their party who were PROHIBITIONISTS.

The liberals of Western Republican women, however, saw an interesting reversal between the time that they led the way to the vote in 1920 and the attempt to pass the EQUAL RIGHTS AMENDMENT in the 1970s. Although the first state to ratify was the nation's westernmost—Hawaii—many continental western states never ratified. The opposition clearly came from the headquarters of the Mormon Church in Utah, which saw the Equal Rights Amendment as a threat to the family and home—even though the Church had rejected similar arguments when they were regularly made during the long debate over women's right to vote.

Probably the factor that had changed most was not theological or political, but simply the fact that those Mormon women who were the pioneers had faded from the scene. Their daughters and granddaughters, having had no similar experience, allowed themselves to be deprived of a statement of rights that the grandmothers may well have demanded as due them for their contribution in settling the West.

WET NURSES In early America, BREASTFEEDING of infants was standard, for until the discovery of germ theory and pasteurization in the late nineteenth century, few were willing to take chances with bottlefeeding unless there was a total absence of lactating women. Thus, when a woman died in delivery and the infant survived, every effort was made to find someone capable of nursing the motherless child. The term for a woman who took on the task was "wet nurse." Used in English at least since 1620, its meaning strongly implied a paid, not a charitable, service.

Any lactating woman in a community with a motherless baby was under strong pressure to take on the extra obligation. A woman who was nursing one child simply added the needy infant, especially if her own baby was close to weaning age. Because the rate of INFANT MORTALITY was so high, however, there were frequently women available whose own babies had died and who could thus turn their tragedy into profit. Advertisements were not uncommon such as the 1776 one in the *Philadelphia Evening Post*: "Wants a place, as Wet Nurse, a young woman with a good breast of milk."

If such a woman was not available, infants in urban areas were placed in orphanages where the services of wet nurses could be obtained. Often orphanages were run in conjunction with homes for unwed mothers, and women with ILLEGITIMATE babies were required to nurse their own plus another baby as recompense for their board during pregnancy. In addition, orphanages employed appreciable numbers of women as wet nurses in foster homes: the Foundling Asylum of the Sisters of Charity in New York alone sent out more than eleven hundred such "pay babies" in 1889.

Sometimes mothers whose breastmilk seemed insufficient hired wet nurses as substitutes or supplements, but in colonial times, even wealthy women nursed their own babies. As the lives of the nation's nineteenth-century *nouveau riche* were increasingly dominated by fashionable society, however, healthy new mothers became more likely to turn their babies over to wet nurses. In the South, thousands of black women earned a living by nursing white babies.

Pasteurization, the rubber industry, and other factors at the turn of the century popularized the use of bottle-feeding among the masses. The need for wet nurses who stayed with the baby would be gone—though small numbers of women would continue to sell milk expressed from their breasts for the use of infants allergic to cow's milk and other substitutes. Thus, a form of wet nursing would remain as the only occupation for which men were axiomatically unqualified.

WHARTON, EDITH NEWBOLD JONES (1862–1937)

One of America's most outstanding novelists, Edith Wharton had a privileged childhood amid New York's first families; among her ancestors was CAROLINE SCHERMERHORN ASTOR. Taught by GOVERNESSES and by frequent European travel, she cultivated a fine mind along with her good manners, though she had no formal schooling at all.

She privately published a book of poems at sixteen and then abandoned writing for a decade, taking it up again three years after her wedding. Her 1885 marriage to a Boston banker was childless and only briefly happy. Wharton thus had little to occupy her days; she found society life shallow and was restricted from a career by the mores of her place and time. In writing, she sustained her soul.

Working first in the short story genre, she was published in several of the nation's leading magazines between 1888 and the turn of the century. Her first books, collections of unpublished stories, came out in 1899 and 1901; her first novel appeared the following year, when she was forty. Just four years later, she published one of her best novels, *The House of Mirth* (1905). Its protagonist was part of the America that Wharton knew best, a woman caught between the old world of genteel but declining fortunes and the new world of massive wealth created by the crass but clever. Neither, however, had room for a woman without money; nor were women allowed to use their abilities in either world, especially not for the purpose of earning money. Wharton's character is finally driven to suicide as the only polite alternative.

Money doubtlessly was on Wharton's mind because her husband was increasingly contentious about it. Though she had inherited wealth in addition to her earnings, he provoked endless quarrels—a matter that Wharton hid as best she could, writing only privately of her despair. She poured herself into her work to escape from his increasing irrationality. *The House of Mirth* was a popular and critical success and established Wharton's literary reputation, but, much like PEARL BUCK, she continued to write at breakneck speed, publishing seven books within the next five years.

In 1910, the Whartons sold the western Massachusetts mansion that had been their primary residence since 1899 and went to France. It would turn out to be a permanent move, for soon afterwards, her husband's mental health broke and he had to be hospitalized. During this difficult time, Wharton nonetheless managed to write the stellar *Ethan Fromme* (1911), a short novel set in circumstances seemingly very different from any that she had known. Initially published in French, *Ethan Fromme* was set in rural poverty and featured a sensitive male protagonist. Translated into English, the tale quickly became a classic that has been assigned reading for millions of students.

Wharton secured a DIVORCE in 1913, but any possible return to the U.S. was precluded by the beginning of WORLD WAR I the following year. Though she continued to write, she also busied herself with NURSING and other wartime activities, even to the extent of paying for the expenses of some six hundred war orphans. She was honored at the end of the hostilities with major medals from the governments of France and Belgium.

Her first postwar book, *The Age of Innocence* (1920), reflected Wharton's realization that the comfortable world of her youth was gone forever. Again set in late nineteenth-century New York, it won the Pulitzer Prize and became her most acclaimed novel. She returned to the U.S. in 1923 to accept an honorary doctorate from Yale but she was displeased with the increasing vulgarity of American life in the twenties. Like others of the era's artists and authors, Wharton quickly returned to France. Her writing suffered from the loss of contact with her roots, however, and though she continued to publish, she never again achieved a major success. Edith Wharton published more than fifty books, encompassing travel, criticism, and even interior decoration, as well as several genres of fiction—including ghost stories. She was elected to the National Institute of Arts and Letters in 1930 and the American Academy of Arts and Letters in 1934. Her death three years later spared her from the outbreak of WORLD WAR II, when she would have either had to return to the homeland that she visited only once after 1910 or suffer under fascism. She died at seventy-five and is buried at Versailles.

WHEATLEY PHILLIS (c. 1753–1784)

The first African-American to publish a book, Phillis Wheatley bore some other, unknown name when she came to Boston on a slave ship from Africa in 1761. Probably born in Gambia, she was about seven years old and such a fetching child that Susanna Wheatley, who had intended to buy someone older to act as her personal maid, took the thin little girl home instead. She doubtless was called Phillis because the ship on which she arrived was named that.

She grew up much more as a daughter of the Wheatley family than as a slave. Phillis ate with the family, had her own room, and—most importantly—learned to read and write while other black people did the household's work. The two teenage Wheatley children, as well as their parents, were charmed by the precocious girl, and each played a part in educating her. Only a year-and-a-half after her arrival, she not only had dropped her African language for English, but also was proficient in reading and writing it. At a time when many Americans were illiterate in their own language, Phillis Wheatley had moved on to the classics.

She soon began writing poetry, and her first piece was published in 1767, when she had been in the New World only six years. Many of her poems were elegies and most, such as "To the University of Cambridge in New England," commemorated some aspect of her Boston world, but some, such as "Africa" (1770), reflected Wheatley's unique circumstances. They were reprinted in New England newspapers, and many of the era's celebrities, including Thomas Jefferson, made a point of seeking out the accomplished African girl who was still in her early teens.

Indeed, the maturity of her work was so great that when plans were laid for the publication of her first book, a foreword was prepared that was signed by eighteen respected male friends of the Wheatley family (including John Hancock) who testified to the authenticity of the author. Thus, in 1773, when she was probably twenty, Phillis Wheatley went to England, taking along a collection of work that was soon set in print as *Poems on Various Subjects, Religious and Moral* (1773). She was accompanied by the Wheatley's son, Nathaniel, and was the guest of the Countess of Huntingdon, who probably made the publishing arrangements and to whom the book was dedicated.

Wheatley was well received by others in London, but she cut short her visit after only five weeks to return to her ailing mistress/mother. Perhaps in gratitude for her devotion and perhaps in response to pressure from English friends, John Wheatley issued Phillis's emancipation papers soon after her return. In any case, there was no doubt that Phillis Wheatley remained with the family voluntarily. When the Revolutionary War broke out, she wrote several tributes to the American Patriots, including a 1776 tribute to George Washington that he responded to with an invitation for her to visit his Cambridge encampment.

Her sheltered life began to dissolve during the war. Susanna Wheatley had died only a few months after Phillis' return from England, and daughter Mary had married and moved away in 1771. Nathaniel remained abroad when Phillis went home, and John Wheatley's fortunes suffered in the revolution. When he died in 1778, the family home broke up. Phillis Wheatley, at twenty-five, began a new life with her marriage to John Peters, a free black, in April of 1778.

Even the most sympathetic biographers of Peters say little that is positive about him beyond the fact that he was well dressed, intelligent, and proud. Evidently that pride prevented him from making the accommodations that his family needed, for he repeatedly impregnated and then deserted his wife. Phillis Wheatley Peters bore three children in the six years of her marriage, all of whom died. She worked in a BOARDING HOUSE to earn her keep—but still wrote poetry.

One of the last pieces she wrote, "Liberty and Peace," celebrated the coming end of the American Revolution; she was accumulating her poems and trying to make arrangements for publishing a second book, but her life continued instead on its downward path. The first black American author, who had been celebrated in England and America, died of malnutrition and cold in an unheated room with her third newborn in her arms. She was buried in an unmarked grave until friends discovered her fate.

Her book, which had been published only in London in her lifetime, was reissued in America in 1786 and then was largely forgotten until 1834, when a distant relative of the Wheatley family joined with other ABOLITIONISTS to revive interest with a new edition. Throughout the struggle for emancipation of slaves—when most whites believed that dark-skinned people were genetically inferior—Phillis Wheatley's words spoke from the grave to offer contrary evidence.

WHITCHER, FRANCES MIRIAM BERRY (1811–1852)

A pioneer woman in American cartooning, Miriam Berry drew sketches that gained an appreciative audience in her western New York State area. She expanded nationally after 1847, with publication in *GODEY'S LADIES BOOK*.

She continued to draw after her marriage that same year,

but never recovered her health after the birth of a child in 1849. Though she died only five years after her marriage, Whitcher retained her sense of humor to the end, and so many people enjoyed her work that a book published after her death reputedly sold one hundred thousand copies.

Whitcher's cartoons focused on women in small town situations. She enjoyed poking fun at the pretentious and was particularly adept at malaprops.

WHITMAN, NARCISSA PRENTISS (1808–1847)

One of the two white women who first crossed the Continental Divide, Whitman is remembered better than her colleague, Eliza Spaulding, partly because Whitman kept a journal describing the four-month trip and partly because her death made news throughout America.

Narcissa Prentiss was a TEACHER who probably would have been ordained a minister had she been male. Highly idealistic in her youth, she had offered herself as a missionary to the natives in the Far West, but her Presbyterian church was not interested in applications from "unmarried females." Like NANCY HASELTINE JUDSON, Prentiss found that she would have to marry and accompany a man to enter the mission field.

She had already rejected a marriage proposal from Henry Spaulding—something that would prove a long-term source of trouble when she accepted Dr. Marcus Whitman. Whitman was planning to go to the new territory of Oregon as a medical missionary, and the quickly arranged marriage was predicated on the assumption that she would go along as part of the mission team. When it turned out, however, that the Spauldings were the only other couple to go, the venture was marred by Henry Spaulding's unremitting jealousy of Marcus Whitman.

Even though Narcissa Whitman became pregnant on the journey, their trip proved less difficult than many experienced by pioneers who came later. They left Missouri in May—after finally hiring guides willing to lead a party that included women—and arrived at Fort Walla Walla on September 1. The Spauldings then settled among the Nez Pierce tribe, while the Whitmans remained near the fort among the Cayuse.

Narcissa Whitman bore a daughter in the spring, and then not only taught in the mission school but also nursed Dr. Whitman's patients. At the same time, she undertook the construction and furnishing of what became the most elaborate of the western Protestant missions—for she was very much a lady, and she cared deeply about books, intellectual conversation, and other embellishments of civilization. She was greatly disillusioned to find that the natives were less than appreciative of these things and were unenthusiastic about adopting Presbyterianism. It was Marcus Whitman's ability as a physician that was their main attraction for the natives, but even there, the Cayuse remained skeptical about this competing medicine man. They particularly rejected advice on personal hygiene, something that Narcissa Whitman found increasingly repulsive.

She was thus becoming disenchanted with the life that she had chosen when she was shattered by her daughter's drowning at age two. For four days in June of 1839, Whitman clung to her baby's body, refusing to allow a burial. Her mental state declined further when Marcus Whitman left her for almost a year—including the isolation of winter—while he returned East to settle mission disputes caused by Spaulding's continued antagonism. Dr. Whitman returned in the summer of 1843, and the following year, they adopted seven siblings who had been orphaned on the Oregon trail. The children's father had died from injuries in a buffalo stampede, while their mother died less than a month later from childbirth infection.

The children, especially the infant, brought new meaning to Narcissa Whitman's life, which had remained busy despite her depression. Every summer brought thousands of newcomers—three thousand in 1845 alone—and many of them expected the mission to provide food, housing, and medical care. Indeed, within a decade after their arrival, the Whitmans saw more white patients than Cayuse ones. All of this meant a great deal of work for Narcissa Whitman, which was made more difficult by the fact that—even though she was still in her thirties—she was going blind.

The wagon trains of 1847 brought a measles epidemic with them. Though this was a routine childhood disease that the Whitmans treated successfully in most whites, the native children who came down with the disease died in appalling numbers. Their parents did not understand the concept of immunity and became increasingly convinced that the Whitmans were poisoning their young while allowing the whites to live. On November 29, 1847, Narcissa Whitman's trials came to a tragic end: Cayuse warriors attacked the mission, killing fourteen whites, including both Whitmans and two of their adopted sons.

Narcissa Prentiss Whitman is memorialized with Whitman College and Whitman National Monument, both near Walla Walla, Washington.

WHITE ROSE HOME Founded in 1897 by a small group of African-American women in New York who had been active in the LOYAL LEAGUE, the White Rose Home served black women in much the same way that the YOUNG WOMEN'S CHRISTIAN ASSOCIATION (YWCA) served whites.

These leaders met trains and ships arriving at New York and attempted to stir young black women who were TRAVELING alone away from urban evils, especially PROSTITUTION. The Home offered temporary meals, lodging, job training, and escort service to prospective employers—usually women who were hiring DOMESTIC WORKERS. Like other institutions in the SETTLEMENT HOUSE movement, it functioned as a forerunner of today's shelters for spouse abuse victims and displaced homemakers.

More innovatively, the White Rose Home also pioneered black history and "race pride" classes. FRANCES A. KELLOR, a white social reform leader, publicized the White Rose project, and by 1910, black women received assistance from similar programs in Philadelphia, Memphis, Baltimore, and Norfolk. When the YWCA finally began to offer its services to black women, the White Rose was absorbed into the YWCA.

"WHITE SLAVERY" This American euphemism, was used primarily in the late nineteenth and early twentieth centuries as a polite term for PROSTITUTION. The phrase's reference to "white" slavery was a racist distinction from the genuine slavery that had existed legally within the memories of those who used the term, and it subliminally recalled the sexual exploitation of young black women by white men, which was common both before and after slavery.

The usage also assumed that virtually all women who sold their bodies did so only because they were forced to by male pimps or by an occasional evil madam. Young women, especially IMMIGRANT WOMEN and those from rural areas, were warned of the dangers of TRAVELING unescorted, for it was widely believed that international bands of white slavers kidnapped women who took such risks and sold them into houses of prostitution.

Though in fact most prostitutes were natives with sufficient sophistication and mercenary values to enter the trade voluntarily, enough evidence of actual force existed to give credence to the idea of white slavery. For example, a 1911 Senate investigative report, *Importation and Harboring of Women for Immoral Purposes,* printed letters that had been confiscated from pimps; the language used in them made the term appropriate, for these men spoke of buying and selling women as chattel, often at prices similar to those paid for black slaves a few decades earlier.

Indeed, while it was not as common as Americans feared, there were young women who were beguiled into friendships with pimps or madams and finally, if they did not join the trade willingly, were brutalized. A common method was to hire naive farm or immigrant girls as maids, and then, when it was difficult for them to escape, break them into prostitution. Once that happened, both the woman who was victimized and society at large usually considered her life to be beyond redemptive value.

A New York newspaper aimed at Jewish immigrants during the Progressive Era, for example, acknowledged the existence of the problem, but exhibited no sympathy for the women whose lives were ruined by it. "Letters from victims of 'white slavery' come to our attention quite often," the editor wrote complacently, "but we do not publish them. We are disgusted by this plague on society, and dislike bringing it to the attention of our readers."

It was primarily women who began speaking out on behalf of other women and advocating PROTECTIVE LEGISLATION such as the MANN ACT. This legislation was a mixed blessing, for while it did help end widespread fears of forced prostitution, it also inhibited the free movement of women.

WIDOWS From their earliest settlement, of course, American colonies had widows. Even though the older women who usually made up the class of people thought of as widows did not often emigrate, young widows soon became common in the dangers of the new land.

They were pressured to remarry quickly, for survival in the new land depended on reproduction and CELIBACY was widely disapproved. Susanna White, for example, whose wedding was the first among the PILGRIM WOMEN, had been a widow for a mere eleven weeks before her remarriage. Though pressure on young widows to remarry remained strong for most of the nation's history, greater security brought societal demands for a respectful time of mourning—which meant that there would be a period of widowhood during which a woman had to be self-supporting.

Because few occupations other than DOMESTIC SERVICE were open to women, widows—especially those with children—

almost always faced a serious financial dilemma. Even those who inherited a source of income were handicapped by a lack of education, especially in such matters as bookkeeping. It was not at all uncommon for such widows to find themselves cheated by former business associates of their late husbands, and this pattern, too, remained well into the twentieth century. Thousands of court records attest to exploitation of widows by men who took advantage of the fact that few men shared business details with their wives.

Most widows tried to eke out an existence by sewing, taking in laundry, and doing other homebound work, but often they had no choice except to seek charity. The REVOLUTIONARY WAR WOMEN who were widowed by war were among the first people to seek pensions from Congress and state legislatures, for that war created more poverty among American women than any other conflict except the CIVIL WAR. It was local government, however, that bore the brunt of routine charitable aid to widows, which could sometimes be great: in one relatively small Massachusetts seaport town, for instance, almost five hundred widows of sailors were on the pauper rolls in 1790. The efforts of more affluent women to support their widowed sisters formed the roots of much of today's institutionalized philanthropy; one of the first priorities of the meetings of QUAKER WOMEN, for example, was the care of widows in their community.

Not all widows were poor, however. Colonial legal codes assured widows of at least one-third of their late husbands' estates, and many women inherited businesses that they continued to operate alone. Widows were especially likely to run hotels, taverns, and BOARDING HOUSES as well as retail stores, especially those that dealt in the "dry goods" of cloth and clothing. This was particularly common among the enterprising Dutch women of colonial New Amsterdam; ANNETJE JANS was but one example of a woman who was widowed more than once, and thereby acquired an impressive estate in her own name. Other women who inherited land sold it to provide themselves with capital for a new business; New Yorker Margaret Hardenbrook Philipse, for example, exchanged her farmwife role for commerce, and developed the first regularly scheduled ship passages across the Atlantic.

Thus, colonial town records show that it was not uncommon for at least a few widows to be included among the most prosperous taxpayers. Indeed, the affluent widow became so prominent a feature of American society that ambitious young men often deliberately married such women instead of single women of their own age who possessed no helpful fortune. The phenomenon was already sufficiently common in 1692 that Cotton Mather cautioned widows to beware of "such a pretended lover [who] may court *hers* more than *her*." Even George Washington, "the Father of Our Country," sought out a prosperous widow for marriage and fathered no children of his own.

As the nation moved away from an agrarian economy, widows felt less pressure to remarry and were freer to support themselves. Many nineteenth century women who inherited a bit of money started female-oriented businesses such as millinery shops, and occasionally a woman demonstrated her special understanding of markets aimed at women, such as ROSE KNOX's success in the gelatin business. Very often, however, such capable women discounted their success, keeping businesses in the name of the late husband and turning them over, at least ostensibly, to sons. The result was that the public tended to see such women only as brief caretakers—even when a woman actually ran the family business for most of her life.

Indeed, though widowhood was almost always an unsought personal tragedy, it often became the pivotal liberating experience of large numbers of women who otherwise would not have been forced into individual achievement. Because writing was one of the few occupations open to educated women in need of income, this was particularly true for women AUTHORS. Except for the economic need created by their widowhood, many talented women such as HELEN HUNT JACKSON, FLORENCE FINCH KELLY, HANNAH FARNHAM LEE, and MARY HEATON VORSE otherwise probably would not have put pen to paper.

Similarly, SARAH BUELL HALE became the nineteenth century's most influential editor of women's magazines after she was forced to look for work as a widow, and although magazine publisher MIRIAM LESLIE had demonstrated her talents before being widowed, the period after her husband's death magnified her abilities. Even some of those who did not write because of economic need seemed to find widowhood important in giving them the personal freedom necessary for artistic expression; examples include GERTRUDE ATHERTON, MARY MAPES DODGE, and KATE CHOPIN.

Other affluent women who used widowhood to expand their personal development range from suffragist and architect ALVA VANDERBILT BELMONT to modern publisher KATHARINE GRAHAM. In addition, many of the earliest women elected to political office came to that role through widowhood. FLORENCE KAHN, HATTIE CARAWAY, FRANCES BOLTON, and CARDISS COLLINS are all examples of women who probably would not have had either the desire or the ability to be elected had they not been the widow of the incumbent.

Widowhood, moreover, allowed a woman a measure of indifference to public opinion that was helpful to the work of women such as unionists LEONORA LAKE and MOTHER JONES. Likewise, the spy network run by ROSE GREENHOW was far easier to do as a widow than it would have been as a wife, while the suffragist work of CARRIE CHAPMAN CATT was possible largely because of the money she inherited as a widow. Another factor in achievement was the freedom to TRAVEL that widowhood afforded—something that was crucial to the achievements of women ranging from CIVIL WAR NURSE MARY ANN BICKERDYKE to anti-lynching advocate JESSIE DANIEL AMES.

The fifty thousand widows created by WORLD WAR II did not have to fight for their pensions as had the women of the Revolution, for Congress had long since recognized a widow's right to compensatory benefits. The creation of Social Security in the 1930s likewise regularized the position of widows, acknowledging these women as entitled to an income that would allow them to maintain their independence and not be pressured to remarry out of economic need. Though far too many widows continue to live in poverty, Social Security and other entitlements for widows were expressions of the American view that a woman's life did not end when her husband's did.

WIGGIN, KATE DOUGLAS SMITH (1856–1923) A

TEACHER who pioneered kindergarten education on the West Coast, Kate Wiggin later immortalized herself as the author of *Rebecca of Sunnybrook Farm* (1903).

Like other women AUTHORS, she published in ST. NICHOLAS magazine in her youth. She taught in the 1870s and concentrated on writing after her 1881 marriage. By the time that she became a WIDOW in 1889, Wiggin had a reputation significant enough that she retained her first husband's name when she remarried in 1895. *Rebecca of Sunnybrook Farm* became one of the bestselling children's books of the twentieth century. A dramatic version ran for years both in the U.S. and abroad, while film versions starred Mary Pickford and Shirley Temple. Wiggin also wrote adult novels and an autobiography, *My Garden of Memory* (1923).

WILDER, LAURA INGALLS (1867–1957) One of the

most beloved AUTHORS of children's literature, Laura Ingalls Wilder chronicled the story of the nation's growth from a personal and family point of view. Her autobiographical tales of life amid virgin forests and prairies have become classics that profoundly influenced millions.

Her mother's life in the older and more civilized East was a constant presence in the rude cabins of the young family as they moved west during the 1870s and 1880s. Caroline Ingalls' silk dress symbolized for little Laura all that had been left behind, but the girl's heart clearly followed Charles Ingalls' adventurous spirit; while Caroline laid plans for schools and churches in the towns they helped build, Charles always saw better prospects further on. Between Laura's first years in the Wisconsin forest that she described in *Little House in the Big Woods* (1932) and her marriage, the family lived throughout the young Midwest.

From Wisconsin, they moved to the tall grass prairie of Indian Territory, where they ultimately lost their land claim and were ejected. That story was told in *Little House on the Prairie* (1935), which has proven to be Wilder's most popular book and the basis of a long-running television series. When they were forced to move, the Ingalls settled *On the Banks of Plum Creek* (1937) in southern Minnesota, where they lived in an underground dugout. All of Laura's siblings were girls, and after the birth of the fourth and last, the Ingalls moved to Dakota Territory.

These Happy Golden Years (1943) told of Laura's experience as a teenage TEACHER and of her romance with Almanzo Wilder, whom she married in 1885. She detailed the story of his home near the Canadian border of northern New York State in *Farmer Boy* (1933); published just after the successful rendering of her early girlhood, it was her second book and also has remained very popular. The Wilders had only one child, ROSE WILDER LANE, who was born late in 1886. The frequently sad story of their early struggles on a Dakota tree claim was disclosed in *The First Four Years* (1971), a manuscript hidden until long after Wilder's death.

Like her father, Laura Ingalls Wilder proved willing to take a chance on some place better. After losing their home to fire, the Wilders made a dramatic 1890 change to Westville, Florida, a pine woods area in the Florida panhandle. They hated it, however, and soon returned to South Dakota. Their final move was to the Ozark hills in 1894, where they success-

fully built an apple farm. The diary of the covered wagon trip to Missouri was posthumously published as *On The Way Home* (1962). The Wilders lived happily in Mansfield, Missouri for the rest of their long lives, with "Manly" reaching ninety-two and Laura living to ninety. A highlight of her adult life was a 1915 trip to the World's Fair in San Francisco, where Rose lived; again, the careful notes that she habitually kept on five-cent school tablets were published after her death.

Laura Ingalls Wilder was sixty-five when her first book came out during the Depression nadir of 1932. The unlikeliness of publication at that late age and in that time has led some to charge that Rose Wilder Lane essentially ghostwrote her mother's books, but others defend her independent ability. In any case, the vivid stories were her own detailed recollections of childhood experience. Even the sophisticated *New Yorker* called Wilder's work a "rich . . . record of pioneer life in the opening of the West [and of] warm-hearted human values," while the *New York Times* spoke of her tales' "authentic background, sensitive characterization, their fine integrity and spirit of sturdy independence."

Museums of Wilder lore are available in Walnut Grove, Minnesota and DeSmet, South Dakota, while her home is preserved at Mansfield, Missouri. Her popularity has extended to even a songbook and a cookbook centered on songs and foods mentioned in her series.

WILKINSON, JEMIMA (1752–1819) The founder of a

short-lived religious sect, Wilkinson was reared in Rhode Island as a QUAKER. She had a transforming experience during a 1776 illness and thereafter believed herself divinely ordained. She dropped her name, and calling herself the "Publick Universal Friend," she TRAVELED from age twenty-three proclaiming a gospel of loving kindness.

Much of her philosophy remained that of the Quakers, though she perhaps gave a stronger emphasis to the humanity of native and black Americans than most in the Society of Friends. She differed more importantly from them in her experimentation with faith healing and dream interpretation, as well as her willingness to allow herself to be portrayed as a messianic prophet. Though she advocated CELIBACY, Wilkinson did not insist upon it and her supporters generally continued to live in family groups that owned private property.

Obviously a charismatic woman, she attracted followers throughout the Northeast, some of whom even freed their slaves in response to her. In 1788, the Publick Universal Friend and nearly three hundred of her supporters moved to the frontier of western New York that was opened to settlement at the end of the American Revolution. There she made herself a friend to wilderness travelers, native and newcomer alike, and preached quietly to her faithful. Described as quite a beautiful woman, she lived unpretentiously until her death at sixty-seven. Her influence in this geographic area doubtless was a factor in the unusual number of women leaders that developed around SENECA FALLS a few decades later.

Although their timing was extraordinarily close and their philosophies strikingly similar, no evidence exists to indicate that Wilkinson knew of the similar sect imported to America by MOTHER ANN LEE in 1774—two years before Wilkinson's fateful vision. Lee's group, however, continued to grow after her death, while Wilkinson's soon evaporated. In view of

Lee's insistence on celibacy with its naturally nonrenewing membership, it was an ironic outcome.

WILLARD, EMMA HART (1787–1870) The first important female educator in America, Willard took the initial steps of moving women's education from FINISHING SCHOOLS to genuine COLLEGES.

She had not necessarily begun her life with the intention of doing so significant a task, but she did chafe at the restrictions placed upon girls as soon as she discovered how thoroughly her gender would limit her mind. Like many other successful women, Emma Hart had a father who admired her intelligence. The sixteenth of his seventeen children, little Emma grasped his attention with her ability to enjoy mathematical games. A Connecticut farmer, he paid the tuition for her to attend the local female academy, and equipped with this background, she began TEACHING while still in her teens. In 1805, Emma Hart opened a DAME SCHOOL in the family home, while also attending classes in Hartford. Two years later, at twenty-one, she left home to accept a position as preceptress of the girls school at Middlebury, Vermont. There she added to her embryonic reputation as an educator until she wed Dr. John Willard in 1809, and—as a married woman—naturally retired from teaching.

They had a child the following year, and Emma Willard also mothered her husband's four children from an earlier marriage. It was the addition of his nephew to the household, however, that made for a key change in Willard's life, for he lived with them while attending Middlebury College, and it was thus that she first got her hands on college textbooks. She made the most of the opportunity, teaching herself geometry, philosophy, and other subjects excluded from female education.

Like many other women who became famous, Willard may never have entered the pages of history except for the motivation of economic need. Physicians did not have the stable sources of income in that era that they would later, and when Dr. Willard found himself in financial trouble in 1814, his wife came to the rescue by again opening a school. This was not a particularly uncommon occurrence; what made Emma Willard's move notable was the distinctive curriculum that she intended to implement for her female students. The beginning was sufficiently rocky that Willard moved her school from Middlebury to Waterford, New York and finally to Troy, New York within the seven years between 1814 and 1821.

It was her appeal to the New York legislature in 1818 that gained lasting historical attention, despite its lack of success at the time. Decades before the better known legislative lobbying crusade mounted by DOROTHEA DIX, Willard used the technique of a written proposal accompanied by behind-the-scenes lobbying. In *An Address to the Public . . . Proposing a Plan for Improving Female Education* (1819), she argued for state taxpayer support of education for girls. Even though Willard did not advocate an equal place for women in the professions and emphasized teacher-training instead, the proposal was far too radical for her time. The majority of legislators thought her curricula contrary to God's will for women and were especially shocked by her proposal to teach anatomy. They believed that women—whose lives were far more dominated by their bodies than those of men—should remain ignorant of the accumulated scientific knowledge of bodily functions.

There were those, however, who were interested in her message. It was the industrial town of Troy, New York—across the Hudson from the capital of Albany—that responded when the elitist men in the legislature ignored Willard. The town raised taxes to endow Willard with four thousand dollars for a school, and Troy Female Seminary thus began in 1821, when Willard was thirty-four. Within a decade, it had more than three hundred students and was profitable.

Women were so eager for the opportunity to learn that classes quickly filled, despite a rigorous course that included mathematics to the level of trigonometry and sciences that were superior to those offered in many male institutions—including astronomy, chemistry, botany, physiology, and geology. At the same time, Willard continued to believe that the education of women should not be intended as vocational, and that her graduates—except for occasional teaching—would center their lives in the home. To that end, she also offered the usual classes of the FINISHING SCHOOLS and even foreshadowed the HOME ECONOMICS MOVEMENT with a class in baking.

Willard wrote some of the textbooks herself, especially in history and geography, and they proved profitable as well. Unlike MARY LYON, Willard aimed her school at the daughters of families who could afford to attend, and she eventually became quite personally wealthy and famous. Students such as ELIZABETH CADY STANTON, who graduated from Troy in 1836, would proclaim her positive influence throughout the nineteenth century.

Dr. Willard had died in 1825, only a few years after the school began, and Emma Willard continued to head it herself. In 1830, she TRAVELED to Athens, where she set up a Greek institute similar to that in the New World's Troy; she told of part of her trip in *Journal and Letters from France and Great Britain* (1833). In 1838, Willard turned her school over to her daughter-in-law and son when she remarried and moved to Boston. The marriage, however, was an unmitigated disaster, as her husband quickly demonstrated that he was after her money; when she proved difficult for him to manage, he stooped so low as to write attacks on her and her educational philosophy to the local newspapers. She left him in less than a year and again supported herself by teaching; it took until 1843, however, to finally obtain a DIVORCE from the Massachusetts legislature.

She returned to Troy the following year and spent the rest of her life as an educational advocate. Willard—who retained her first husband's name—lectured in the South and West, where public education was still beginning, and in 1854, represented the U.S. at the World's Educational Convention in London. Yet despite her lifelong advocacy of intellectual opportunity for women and despite her personal experience with women's legal difficulties in marriage and divorce, Willard remained a political conservative. She seemingly could not risk her success in one area by venturing into another; she not only opposed the SUFFRAGE MOVEMENT, but also frequently based her argument for female education in the inherent inequality that allowed taxpayers to pay less for female teachers.

She died at eighty-four, and Troy Female Seminary was

renamed the Emma Willard School on the twenty-fifth anniversary of her death. Emma Willard continues to be at the top of any list of influences on women's education, and she was among the first three women elected to the HALL OF FAME.

WILLARD, FRANCES ELIZABETH CAROLINE (1839–1898)

One of the most influential women of the nineteenth century, Frances Willard's name is inseparable from that of the WOMAN'S CHRISTIAN TEMPERANCE UNION (WCTU), but her life embodied little of the conservatism that came to be associated with the WCTU after her death.

Instead, Willard's upbringing encouraged fresh ideas. Her mother set the precedent for unconventionality, for Mary Willard had taken COLLEGE courses at OBERLIN COLLEGE when both that institution and her daughter were only a few years old. Frances' father, who was a full-time Oberlin student, tended her while his wife went to classes in the early 1840s. Both parents thus exhibited a very unusual willingness to experiment with new roles, for married men in this era seldom took care of children, while female college students of any marital status were a rarity. Indeed, Mary Thompson Willard may have been the first college student who was also a young mother.

In 1845, this intrepid young couple pioneered in Wisconsin. There Frances lived an outdoor life, joining in her brothers' activities and even referring to herself as "Frank." The children were educated largely by their mother until their father, who had become a state legislator, finally succeeded in getting a school for their area when Frances was fifteen. At seventeen, she TRAVELED to Milwaukee Female College, and the following year, went to Illinois, where she studied at North-Western Female College, from which she graduated in 1859.

Willard spent the CIVIL WAR years TEACHING in Illinois and Pennsylvania secondary schools, most of them affiliated with the Methodist Church. After a year as preceptress of a female SEMINARY in western New York near the SENECA FALLS area that spawned so many women leaders, she was able to accompany a wealthy friend on a European tour. They traveled from 1868 through 1870, going all the way to Constantinople. It was a life-changing experience for Willard; she learned the art, music, and languages that had been unavailable in the primitive schools of the Midwest, and the articles she wrote home about her travels became her first published work.

Upon her return, Willard was named president of the Evanston College for Ladies, a new school founded in 1871 with links to Northwestern, which soon absorbed it. Willard then was named dean of women at this growing university, and, with an increase in salary, became one of the first female administrators to hold a high position at a major co-educational university. Her achievement earned national recognition in 1873, when Willard was invited to be a cofounder of the ASSOCIATION FOR THE ADVANCEMENT OF WOMEN; she was elected a vice-president at the AAW's first meeting.

Despite the apparent prestige of her deanship at Northwestern, the position of women in higher education was extremely tenuous at this time. VASSAR, the first of the distinguished women's colleges, was only a few years old, and women students were still unknown on the campuses of those older eastern universities that Northwestern wished to emulate. The result was that Northwestern's leadership double-checked Willard's every move. The situation was further complicated by the fact that Willard had a brief romance in her youth with the university's president, and given his relentlessly sullen attitude towards her, she saw no hope of resolution. When another opportunity presented itself, she resigned.

After less than a year as dean of women, Willard ended her career as a college administrator in June, 1874 to begin what became her true life's work with the newly organized Woman's Christian Temperance Union. Supported by Chicago women, she organized a state association and served as a delegate to the founding conference of the national body a few months later. With the title of corresponding secretary, Willard in fact worked as an organizer during the next years, traveling and speaking in several states while also editing the WCTU's publications.

Her lectures—which were her major source of income—were particularly popular in her native Midwest, where Willard's support of the SUFFRAGE MOVEMENT did not cause the consternation that it did among eastern PROHIBITIONISTS. Indeed, Willard combined the two causes in 1879 to lead a lobbying campaign in the Illinois capital for the right of women to vote in local referenda on the sale of liquor. She gathered about 180,000 signatures in support of her petition, an effort so impressive that she gained a national reputation. When Willard was elected head of the national WCTU that same year, it was a clear indication that a majority of members had come to understand the importance of women's votes in obtaining their temperance goals.

Elected at age forty, Willard would retain the WCTU presidency for the rest of her life. Her twenty years at the head of this major organization, plus her links to the FEMINISTS who led the suffrage movement, eventually made her one of the most famous and best liked of the nineteenth century's women. She demonstrated uncommon organizational skills, including a helpful sense of humor, and an oratorical ability that enabled her to speak in every state and territory by 1883. She managed to befriend SUSAN ANTHONY while officially belonging to LUCY STONE's rival suffrage organization and networked effectively with new organizations. Among others, Willard was a participant in the INTERNATIONAL COUNCIL OF WOMEN; she was elected a vice-president of the Universal Peace Union; and she served as a cofounder of the GENERAL FEDERATION OF WOMEN'S CLUBS. By 1891, she was able to extend her own body into an international organization, becoming president of the World's WCTU at a Boston meeting.

In addition to this understanding of networking, Willard also knew the importance of political action. She presented a petition for suffrage from two hundred thousand WCTU members to Congress in 1887, and the following year, she testified to a Senate committee "as a conservative woman devoted to the idea of the ballot." More impressively, Willard went beyond such issue-oriented efforts to participate in the election of candidates who promised to further her cause.

While cloaking her feminist views in the language of "home protection," she actively worked in presidential campaigns decades before passage of the NINETEENTH AMENDMENT that gave women the right to vote. She led the way on this aspect of women's development, withstanding continual criticism from conservatives in the WCTU who wished to see themselves as above politics. Willard was a major factor in the formation of the Prohibition Party—which, in turn, captured a substantial portion of the vote in every election from 1884 through 1920—but she did not tie herself solely to that party.

Instead she formed links with the Knights of Labor, the Grange, and other agrarian/populist/labor union groups that grew out of the political turmoil of the Gilded Age. During her last years, Willard increasingly saw alcoholism as less a fault of personal behavior and more as a result of hopelessness, much of which was grounded in economic inequalities. By 1897, she was ready to predict that the "civilization we believe will be born" would be essentially socialist.

Willard went abroad the year after forming the World's WCTU and spent much of the 1890s in England. Part of her goal there was the recovery of her health, for she suffered from chronic anemia that worsened when she returned to the U.S. When she died at fifty-eight, over twenty thousand people paid their last respects. In 1905, Illinois honored her with a statue placed in the national Capitol, and in 1910, she was among the second group of women admitted to the HALL OF FAME.

She coedited with MARY LIVERMORE *A Woman of the Century* (1893), a collection of biographical sketches of the women of her era that functioned much as *Who's Who* does today. Willard also wrote a number of books devoted to temperance, but none was as popular as her autobiography, *Glimpses of Fifty Years* (1889). That story sold so well that it made Frances Willard financially secure for the last decade of her unfortunately short life.

WILLEBRANDT, MABEL WALKER (1889–1963) One of the highest-ranking women in appointed federal positions in the era after women got the vote, Mabel Willebrandt was an assistant attorney general of the U.S. from 1921 through 1929.

After a career in TEACHING, she graduated from law school at the University of Southern California in 1916. As a married woman, she worked after graduation in an unpaid position as a public defender for women charged with crimes. Like many WESTERN WOMEN, Willebrandt was a Republican, and after demonstrating still more volunteerism during WORLD WAR I, she was recommended by Californians when the Republicans won the White House in 1920. She was appointed to the Justice Department when she was only thirty-two and spent most of her career there enforcing the PROHIBITION laws then in effect.

In 1928, Willebrandt was the first woman to chair a committee at a Republican convention. She became a source of controversy, however, when the presidential campaign centered on prohibition, and felt constrained to resign the following year. She spent the rest of her life in private practice and was active in the American Bar Association. She mothered a child, befriended JACQUELINE COCHRAN and AMELIA EARHART, and learned to fly at fifty.

WINSLOW, OLA E. (1885?–1977) The winner of the Pulitzer Prize for biography in 1941, Dr. Winslow taught at WELLESLEY and RADCLIFFE. She wrote several important works on early American cultural history, especially its religious as-

pects, with her Pulitzer winner featuring eighteenth-century evangelist Jonathan Edwards. Despite this seemingly puritanical background, Winslow was a close friend of skeptic H.L. Mencken.

WINSOR, KATHLEEN (1919–   ) The author of the 1945 bestseller, *Forever Amber* (1944), Winsor's book was hidden by many of those who bought it because of the candid sexuality of her female protagonist. It was banned in Boston, and the resultant legal battles went on for years.

Much like MARGARET MITCHELL's *Gone With the Wind* a decade earlier, *Forever Amber* caught the imagination of a generation of mostly feminine readers—many of whom had time for reading because millions of husbands and lovers were gone when it was published near the end of WORLD WAR II. The novel was set in Restoration England, and it combined a sweeping plot with a memorable heroine. It sold millions of copies in this country and abroad, and more than twenty million people stood in line to see the 1947 movie version.

A 1938 graduate of the University of California, Winsor kept her MAIDEN NAME. When her husband went into the military during WORLD WAR II, she made better use of her time than most CAMP FOLLOWERS; she said that she read over 350 books on English history before writing her novel. Her first novel, however, was her only tremendous success, for none of her later books achieved similar sales.

WINTHROP, MARGARET (c. 1591–1647) For the first sixteen years of its existence, the first lady of the Massachusetts Bay Colony was Margaret Winthrop. The daughter of Sir John and Lady Tyndal of Essex County in England, she married attorney John Winthrop in 1618. Although only a few years older than she, he had already lost two wives, and Margaret Winthrop inherited his four sons and then bore eight more children, four of whom died young.

When John Winthrop established the colony that became Boston in 1630, pregnant Margaret stayed behind to bear their child and settle their estate. Lacking any other form of communication, the two arranged to use mental telepathy, for Governor Winthrop wrote in his last letter before setting sail: "Mondays and Fridays at five of the clock, we shall meet in spirit."

Almost two years passed before Margaret Winthrop could join him, and then she had to bring the news that their baby died at sea. She spent the next sixteen years in an "unpretentious" Beacon Hill house that seems to also have functioned as the governor's offices. She was a friend of ANNE BRADSTREET and shared well-water with ANNE HUTCHINSON. Though all accounts portrayed Margaret Winthrop as a dutiful wife, she may in fact have privately sympathized with Hutchinson, for during the Hutchinson trial, Winthrop wrote of herself that she felt "fierce" and "unwilling to submit."

Margaret Winthrop died after a one-day illness in June, 1647. Her husband—who seems not to have known the date of her birth, for his voluminous journals say only that she was "probably fifty-six"—took his fourth wife less than a year later.

WITCHES— *See* SALEM WITCH TRIAL

WOMAN'S BIBLE, THE— *See* ELIZABETH CADY STANTON

WOMAN'S CHRISTIAN TEMPERANCE UNION (WCTU)

From the earliest days of colonial settlement, the use of large quantities of liquor was a common habit. In Virginia in the early 1700s, for example, so much liquor was imported that the taxes on it were sufficient to run the government. In New England, rum alone provided one of the three bases of the era's well-known triangular trade. Beyond this large-scale importation, homemade liquor also was common; the College of William and Mary, for example, was not exceptional in having its own brewery to provide its students with daily beer.

Both women and men saw alcohol as fundamentally medicinal in nature and regularly used it—especially brandy, whiskey, and fruit-based wines—as a palliative for the sick and injured. Loving mothers pacified crying babies with alcohol, and regular rations of rum were supplied to teenage sailors and soldiers. Liquor was thus very much a part of daily life throughout early American history.

At the same time, the legal status of women was low, especially in regard to MARRIED WOMEN'S PROPERTY RIGHTS. Women married to alcoholics had no right to either their own earnings or their inheritance, nor any assurance of GUARDIANSHIP of the children they bore. Drunken men could—and did—beat their wives and take their property with the approbation of the legal system. Understandably, along with the effort for women's rights, there also arose a call for changed attitudes that resulted in the PROHIBITION movement.

The Woman's Christian Temperance Union was one aspect of that movement. It developed in response to a seemingly spontaneous uprising in the winter of 1873–1874, when groups of women went into the streets of several midwestern towns to pray in front of saloons. The Midwest would remain the strongest area of prohibitionist activity, and in November, 1874, the WCTU was formally organized in Cleveland.

Its first president was Annie Wittenmyer, an Iowa WIDOW who worked for the SANITARY COMMISSION during the CIVIL WAR. Her wartime experience in fund-raising and administration proved crucial in organizing amorphous and powerless women into the strong force that the WCTU soon became. In the five years of her presidency, Wittenmyer built an amazing network of more than a thousand local units with some twenty-six thousand members. She also developed a publication, *Our Union*, which was edited by FRANCES WILLARD—who, in 1879, eclipsed the more politically conservative Wittenmyer to win the presidency.

Willard would remain WCTU president for the rest of her life. Her election signaled a victory of those who supported the SUFFRAGE MOVEMENT over those WCTU members who thought that liquor laws could be changed by appeal to male voters and who wanted the organization to be solely devoted to temperance. Willard took a broader approach, and though she carefully couched her political campaigns as "Home Protection" and "Gospel Politics," she involved the WCTU with other political action.

Under her "Do Everything" banner, the WCTU worked on goals from SUFFRAGE to PROSTITUTION; other nonfeminist issues included such causes as peace, arbitration, labor law, and

prison reform. At one point, the WCTU was organized into thirty-nine different issue-oriented departments. Occasionally one met with a measurable success, as when the Social Purity Department succeeded in raising the age for consensual sex.

The Union quickly evolved from its origins as a pious, praying society into a politically sophisticated group. Annual conventions were packed with pageantry and oratory and attracted representatives from every state and territory. By 1891, when the World WCTU was formed in a Boston meeting, the organization had gathered 7 million names on their "Polyglot Petitions" that appealed to governments throughout the world to curtail narcotics as well as alcohol—for Willard also led the Union from its focus on alcohol to a broader concern with other addictive substances.

Despite these successes, tension between the suffragists and antisuffragists caused continual conflict within the WCTU—as, indeed, the issue of prohibition caused endless turmoil within the suffrage organizations. WESTERN WOMEN in particular resented the links that many suffrage leaders had with the WCTU, believing that this identification with prohibition cost women the vote in frontier states. Such women also quite reasonably argued that the Woman's Christian Temperance Union did not actually stand for "temperance" in the sense of moderate, educated use of alcohol, but rather for total prohibition.

The use of "Christian" in the organization's name also was something of a misnomer, for the WCTU was almost wholly Protestant. Indeed, Jewish women were more likely to be welcomed by the WCTU than Christians who were Catholics. Much of the membership was strongly anti-immigrant; their xenophobia ignored America's long history of alcoholic consumption to focus instead on the drinking habits of the newly arrived. Thought the WCTU included black women at conventions and even devoted an organizational department to African-Americans in the South, it rarely reached out to IMMIGRANT WOMEN.

As the numbers of immigrants increased and the nation became more cosmopolitan, the WCTU—centered as it was in small towns and farms of the Midwest—became increasingly parochial. Even before the death of Frances Willard in 1898, there were signs that her membership was on the verge of rejecting her more progressive model of leadership, and after she died, the WCTU increasingly emphasized its religious orientation, separated itself from FEMINIST networks, and concentrated on working with male-dominated organizations solely for prohibition.

WCTU members reached their goal before suffragists, and the Eighteenth Amendment that provided for prohibition was added to the Constitution in January of 1920, while the NINETEENTH AMENDMENT waited until August of that year. At the time, the WCTU had eight hundred thousand members—but success kills a single-purpose organization. Its membership steadily declined thereafter, and even the repeal of the Eighteenth Amendment in 1933 gave it only a small revival, for the union's basic goals were increasingly out-of-touch with the reality of women's lives in the twentieth century.

WCTU women still made themselves available to lecture to schoolchildren on temperance—including addictions to tobacco and caffeine as well as drugs and alcohol—but its religious orientation ultimately limited that audience, too. When substance abuse again became an educational issue in the 1970s, the union's membership was small, aged, and too sectarian to allow it to be a valid part of new coalitions. Though the WCTU continues with about twenty-five thousand members and an active publishing house today, it has long been the object of jokes and few realize that it is still extant. It gets little of the credit it deserves for the historical change it helped create in moving the nation away from a time in which drunkenness among even prominent men was excused, while women and children suffered in silence.

WOMAN'S HOME COMPANION

Originally HOME COMPANION, the magazine's name was changed in 1897 by a male editor who believed the word "lady" had been overused in the Victorian era and that women would appreciate the more realistic "woman." The name change was thus a deliberate slap at LADIES HOME JOURNAL, which would be Woman's Home Companion's chief rival throughout the twentieth century.

Especially after 1911, when the magazine began to be edited by Gertrude Battles Lane, millions of American women subscribed to Woman's Home Companion. While Lane never identified with the SUFFRAGE MOVEMENT, her thinking was feminist in other regards. She understood that the woman who read her magazine "wants to do less housework so that she will have more time for other things. She is intelligent and clearheaded . . . on the vital issues of the day."

During the next three decades, Lane increasingly dropped recipes and sewing patterns in favor of articles on women's changing roles. In addition, she aided outstanding female writers such as WILLA CATHER and ELLEN GLASGOW by publishing their work. Her editorial stance continued after Lane's 1941 death, and during WORLD WAR II, Woman's Home Companion published a number of innovative articles on subjects ranging from women in European battles to the experiences of a woman who shopped wartime black markets.

Circulation rose to 4 million by 1950—but only seven years later, the magazine collapsed. It was operating at a loss of several million dollars annually by 1957, when Crowell-Collier Publishing shut it down. Presumably the male management was less competent than Lane had been at understanding women's interests and foreseeing trends; Ladies Home Journal, which included women in its top editorial positions, continued to sell.

WOMAN'S JOURNAL

The publication of the AMERICAN WOMAN SUFFRAGE ASSOCIATION (AWSA), the first issue of the Woman's Journal appeared on January 8, 1870. The date was not coincidental, for it was the second anniversary of the Revolution, the publication of the rival NATIONAL WOMAN SUFFRAGE ASSOCIATION (NWSA), and thus caused ill feeling with SUSAN ANTHONY, ELIZABETH CADY STANTON, and other NWSA members.

From the beginning, however, the Woman's Journal aimed to be more than the Revolution was. That it was intended to be a long-lived, quality publication was clear from the planning, for the well-connected, Boston-based women of the AWSA formed a stock company to provide capital and recruited MARY LIVERMORE as its initial editor in chief. More moderate in tone, it soon drove the Revolution out of business.

From 1872 until her death in 1893, it was edited primarily by LUCY STONE, with assistance from her husband, Henry Blackwell. The Woman's Journal attracted well-known women as contributors and soon developed a large circulation. Even after the appearance of the Woman Citizen as the official publication of the unified NATIONAL AMERICAN WOMAN SUFFRAGE ASSOCIATION, the Woman's Journal continued to be considered the leading publication promoting women's suffrage.

It's editorship remained in the Stone/Blackwell family, with ALICE STONE BLACKWELL serving in this position for the next three decades until suffrage was nearly assured. In 1917—just three years before passage of the NINETEENTH AMENDMENT—the Woman's Journal merged with the Woman Citizen. It had served the women's cause for almost half a century.

WOMAN'S MEDICAL COLLEGE OF PENNSYLVANIA

Long before women were admitted to most COLLEGES, innovative Philadelphia QUAKERS rented a building at 229 Arch Street and began the Female Medical College of Pennsylvania. The school began in September of 1850—one year after ELIZABETH BLACKWELL's graduation had set the precedent for female physicians. Blackwell's crusade was a lonely one, however; the school was not a direct result of her experience, nor did her sister, EMILY BLACKWELL, enroll there.

Eight students were in the first class, with five from Pennsylvania, one each from New York and Massachusetts, and another from England. One of them, Ann Preston, would go on to assume the leadership of the college. A natural TEACHER, Preston had studied medicine prior to the college's existence; she apprenticed under a local doctor, taught health classes for Philadelphia women in the 1840s, and like Blackwell, applied without success to male medical schools. The class also included sisters-in-law Hannah and Anna Longshore, who also had studied on their own. Hannah's husband, Joseph Longshore, was a physician, and, in the Quaker tradition, he encouraged women's efforts for equality. He played a strong role in establishing the school, drafting the charter that was approved by the state legislature in 1850 and recruiting faculty to join him in teaching.

Because of their extensive prior knowledge, Hannah Longshore and Ann Preston graduated ahead of the rest of the class on the last day of 1851—at ceremonies that were threatened by disruptions from male medical students. Dr. Longshore, who was then age thirty-two and the mother of two, went on to an assistanceship at NEW ENGLAND FEMALE MEDICAL COLLEGE and then established a very successful private practice in Philadelphia. Dr. Preston's personal history became that of the college; after graduate study abroad, she returned to teach in 1853.

The school withstood an 1858 challenge from the male medical society, and in 1860, Preston organized an affiliated hospital for women and children with the assistance of a Board of LADY MANAGERS. The college faced additional problems with internal conflict between faculty members, and this was a factor in its brief closure when the CIVIL WAR began. It reopened in 1862, however, with a charter renaming it Woman's Medical College of Pennsylvania. The staff included men who had been previously associated with the institution, but also featured four women who were the school's graduates.

A NURSING school in conjunction with the medical college began in 1863, and in 1866, Dr. Preston was granted the deanship. Soon thereafter, its students gained entrance to two Philadelphia clinics that had previously excluded women.

After Preston's 1872 death, EMELINE HORTON CLEVELAND, an 1855 graduate, assumed the deanship, and during the 1870s, she set surgical precedents at the teaching hospital. Other influential early graduates were physician and environmentalist MARY PUTNAM JACOBI (1863) and India missionary CLARA SWAIN (1869). Because this school predated that of the Blackwells in New York by almost two decades, Pennsylvania women were proud of it. Their suffragists included a brief history of the institution in the second volume of *HISTORY OF WOMAN SUFFRAGE*, which was published in 1881.

Male students were first admitted in 1969, and the following year the name was changed to Medical College of Pennsylvania. It continues today at 3300 Henry Avenue in Philadelphia.

WOMAN'S NATIONAL LOYAL LEAGUE— *See* LOYAL LEAGUE

WOMAN'S PARTY

An outgrowth of the CONGRESSIONAL UNION that was formed in the WORLD WAR I era by ALICE PAUL and LUCY BURNS, the Woman's Party was a political party aimed at achieving suffrage in all states by the addition of an amendment to the Constitution. Also sometimes referred to as the National Woman's Party or the Woman National Party, it formally organized at a June, 1916 meeting in Chicago that was timed to coincide with the Republican convention.

Its immediate aim was to influence that year's election in the twelve states where women could vote for president. Woman's Party leadership showed true political science skills, as reflected in the keynote speech that spelled out the intended strategy: "These states with their four million women constitute . . . more than one-third of the votes necessary to elect a President."

The party intended to defeat President Woodrow Wilson, whom they saw as a symbol of indifference to suffrage—even though the president has no direct power in adding constitutional amendments and even though all but one of the men in Wilson's Cabinet supported suffrage. Even more controversially, the new party also encouraged the defeat of all Democratic candidates—no matter what their individual positions on suffrage—since Wilson headed the Democratic Party. Not surprisingly, this radical position was repudiated by other feminists, including the NATIONAL AMERICAN WOMAN SUFFRAGE ASSOCIATION (NAWSA).

The Woman's Party took a real risk in thus clearly defining its aims, and measured by that standard, it lost the election of 1916. Except for Illinois, there seemed to be no measurable difference between the presidential ballots cast by male and female voters. Wilson won ten of the twelve states where he had been targeted for defeat, and other Democratic candidates appeared similarly untouched. Nonetheless, the Party did influence opinion and helped moved the suffrage issue forward. More importantly, it developed leadership abilities in women and demonstrated the potential power of a bloc vote.

The following year, Woman's Party members turned to militant street action, leading demonstrations in Washington, chaining themselves to the White House fence and seeking

A manikin in a Washington window display circa 1913 advertises the availability of accessories to demonstrate support for the Congressional Union/Woman's Party.
LIBRARY OF CONGRESS; PHOTO BY HARRIS & EWING.

publicity by provoking arrest. Over two hundred women were arrested, almost half of whom served time in prison. Following the model of British women, they went on hunger strikes in jail and suffered the indignities and physical pain of force feeding.

The Woman's Party included a large number of QUAKER WOMEN who opposed all war, and when the U.S. entered WORLD WAR I—despite Wilson's campaign promise to keep the nation out of the European conflict—the Party considered this to be still another evidence of betrayal. Its position on this volatile issue, however, differed from that of many other women's groups, which saw the war as an opportunity to demonstrate that women could be patriotic citizens like men. Since men often argued that women should not vote because they were not drafted, many women considered it important to contribute to the war effort.

Though Wilson diverted himself from the war to endorse the suffrage amendment and lobby senators for it, the Woman's Party continued to denounce him during the congressional elections of 1918, even publicly burning his speeches on behalf of suffrage. All of this made the moderates of the NAWSA seem reasonable by comparison and thus eased their lobbying task. When the NINETEENTH AMENDMENT finally passed out of Congress on June 4, 1919, the Woman's Party naturally claimed that the courageous activism of its women had been the impetus for this long-delayed legislative action—while CARRIE CHAPMAN CATT and the NAWSA were equally firm in their belief that it was the result of their vigorous but reasonable lobbying.

The Party devoted 1919 to winning ratification by the necessary three-quarters of the states' legislatures—but again in a controversial way that seemed to irrationally condemn pro-suffrage Democrats, while ignoring Republicans who were anti-suffrage. The result was that the ratification victory was largely credited to Catt and the NAWSA, while the Woman's Party was increasingly seen by most of those involved in the suffrage movement as a troublesome minority.

By the time that final ratification came in August, 1920, the Party had alienated the majority of the nation's women. Few aligned themselves with it when they registered to vote, and none ran as successful candidates for office under its banner. At the same time, the NAWSA had been so single-purpose in its dedication to obtaining the vote that it had almost no postvictory agenda. Indeed, the LEAGUE OF WOMEN VOTERS that grew out of the NAWSA might well have developed as less nonpartisan and more activist had it not felt a need to distance itself from what many saw as an embarrassing Woman's Party.

The Party continued on through the twentieth century, with ratification of the EQUAL RIGHTS AMENDMENT as its primary goal, but it never moved beyond a fringe-element status and personal identification with Alice Paul. Though Paul and the Party understood important political science principles and though they had played a key role in revitalizing the suffrage movement, they alienated so many in the process that they could not follow up on their achievement. The opportunity to form a FEMINIST bloc into a genuine third party, which could have made a profound difference in voting habits of women, was never achieved.

WOMAN'S PEACE PARTY

Founded in January, 1915 by JANE ADDAMS, the party was a response to WORLD WAR I, which began in Europe in August, 1914. Among Addams' cofounders were EMILY BALCH, CARRIE CHAPMAN CATT, ALICE HAMILTON, CHARLOTTE PERKINS GILMAN, and others of the era's outstanding women.

Even though women did not yet vote in most states, these hopeful women called their organization "party" to make it clear that they intended to take political action. Moreover, they did not hesitate to jump into international action, and Addams was elected president of the INTERNATIONAL CONGRESS OF WOMEN the following April. The women of the International Congress met with governments throughout Europe in peace meditations.

They returned home to work on maintaining American neutrality, and their efforts in the election of 1916 appeared to be successful. However, when campaign promises to keep the nation out of war were overturned and war was declared in 1917, Addams and her Woman's Peace Party soon became the object of derision. Indeed, had the organization been headed by someone less famous than she, its members might well have been charged with treason, for governmental viola-

tions of civil liberties were all too frequent in this era. Some members were in fact arrested and jailed.

At the war's end, the group evolved into the WOMEN'S INTERNATIONAL LEAGUE FOR PEACE AND FREEDOM, with Addams again serving as president. Part of the reason for its name change may well have been to distinguish itself from the WOMAN'S PARTY, which arose at about the same time with a similar name but a different purpose.

WOMEN MARINES— *See* MARINES, WOMEN

WOMEN'S AIR SERVICE PILOTS (WASPs)

Long before WORLD WAR II began, there were women who urged officials to plan to utilize the abilities of the twenty-seven hundred American women who were licensed pilots in 1941. JACKIE COCHRAN, a famed aviator who held a number of international speed records in competitions that included men, had written ELEANOR ROOSEVELT in 1939 attempting to plan a place for women in the war that she foresaw. When she was ignored, Cochran became the first woman to ferry a bomber across the Atlantic, where she recruited other American women to join the British Air Transport Authority. These women proved their abilities, and by 1942, had flown one hundred twenty different types of aircraft for the British.

When the U.S. entered the war, Cochran returned home, and with the support of Air Corps General Hap Arnold, organized the Women's Air Service Pilots (WASP), based at Avenger Field in Sweetwater, Texas. She recruited women who were licensed pilots and who had managed to accumulate at least two hundred hours of flying time—at their own expense and despite a ban on civilian flying after the war began. Unlike the Army's WACs or the Navy's WAVES, however, the WASPs were not militarized; they were civilians who worked on contract with the Army Air Corps. Though they lived in military quarters and followed military orders, they had no rank, received no benefits, and were not even granted uniforms until the lack of them proved inefficient.

Despite these disincentives and a lack of publicity so severe that the very existence of the WASP was disputed, about two thousand women joined. They flew seventy-seven types of aircraft during the war and did a multiplicity of tasks. Chief among them was breaking in and delivering new planes; towing gliders for male cadets who were learning to fly; "tracking," in which WASPs flew in the glare of searchlights for artillery students who were learning to follow a plane at night; and towing targets for gunnery practice. There were also WASPs who were called "test pilots," which meant flying planes that cadets had reported as having mechanical trouble; these women deliberately put themselves through spins and other perilous maneuvers to determine if malfunctions would reappear.

By the spring of 1944, WASPs had flown more than 30 million dangerous and difficult miles. Their paramilitary status continued to be a source of endless bureaucratic problems, however, so Cochran and Arnold went to Congress to push for militarization that fall. Congress, pressured by male pilots who were envious of the WASP's jobs now that victory was in sight and their more profitable positions were disappearing, responded by ending the WASP's authorization. The first veterans of World War II, the women pilots were forced home for Christmas of 1944.

The chief reason that WASPs wished to be militarized was their lack of job benefits, particularly in insurance: since they were officially civilians, they were not entitled to military benefits, but since the work they did was dangerous, they were uninsurable privately. A monument in Sweetwater today bears witness to the thirty-eight WASPs who lost their lives in the course of their work. One of them was a professional pilot with more than twenty-five hundred hours, the sole support of her family. Other WASPs had to take up a collection to ship her body home.

Those who were still alive in 1979 finally received some benefits, primarily because of the efforts of Sen. Barry Goldwater, who had flown with WASPs during the war and who rated them "equal to or better than their male counterparts."

WOMEN'S ARMED SERVICES INTEGRATION ACT

(1948) It took almost three years after WORLD WAR II ended for the military and Congress to decide what they wanted to do about the question of servicewomen.

Part of the reason for the delay was that women were caught up in the larger controversies of the separation of the Air Force from the Army and Navy, as well as the transformation of the Department of War to the Department of Defense, but unresolved ambivalence on women's proper place also was a factor. Meanwhile, thousands of trained women who might have opted for a military career were forced out of the service because they could not afford to live with such uncertainty.

When the war first ended, almost all assumed that women would disappear from military life until the next national emergency. Original proposals called only for a skeleton organization with a few officers available for quick recall. Units of women who had been mustered out were organized in several cities; unlike male reservists, these women were volunteers, and they donated the work (especially typing) that they did for the paid male reserve units.

As women were demobilized, however, an interesting phenomenon occurred. While most military leadership agreed with the principle that women should be dismissed, every day the War Department received additional requests from individual field commanders who insisted that the female personnel in *his* headquarters were uniquely qualified and should be exceptions to the rule. The provisions for these exceptions had to be authorized by Congress, and the result eventually became the passage of legislation providing for women in the peacetime forces.

That this happened was due to the persistence of women in Congress, especially MARGARET CHASE SMITH. Military women and feminists, particularly those in the BUSINESS & PROFESSIONAL WOMEN'S CLUBS, were careful to fully support each other in lobbying for the bill, but there were many who opposed the notion of women in the peacetime military. The legislation probably would not have passed but for the intervention of generals and admirals—especially Eisenhower, Bradley, and Nimitz—who had worked closely with women during the war.

Opposition was strong enough, however, that the bill initially failed in the House and additional compromises had to

be worked out. Ignoring the fact that they had voted to draft women three years earlier with the NURSES SELECTIVE SERVICE BILL of 1945, congressmen voted against the authorizing legislation because of draft fears and because they wanted assurance that women would be barred from West Point and the other service academies.

The final bill thus was a compromise. The object of integrating women into the armed forces was achieved, with Navy women (including the Marines and Coast Guard's SPARS) entering the regular forces, while the Army and Air Force retained separate units for their WAC (WOMEN'S ARMY CORPS) and WAF (Women in the Air Force). On the other hand, women's roles were firmly limited by gender: they could hold no rank higher than lieutenant colonel (or commander in the naval branches); they could not be assigned to duties likely to result in combat situations; and their compensation was seriously decreased by provisions that disallowed benefits for their dependents.

Nonetheless, the final bill was viewed as a huge victory that could not have been foretold a few years earlier. As the years passed, the limitations would be removed by increments. Though legislation on the emotional topic of combat has not yet recognized the realities of fifty years ago, women today are increasingly fully integrated into the military.

WOMEN'S ARMY CORPS/WOMEN'S AUXILIARY ARMY CORPS (WAC/WAAC)

The six thousand women who volunteered after Pearl Harbor to staff aircraft spotting stations called attention to the need to militarize unpaid female volunteers for top efficiency. They also reminded War Department officials of studies that had gathered dust through the thirties of the thirteen thousand women who had served in the Navy and Marine Corps during WORLD WAR I.

Using British women's military units as her model (except for Britain's compulsory draft of women), Representative EDITH NOURSE ROGERS had introduced a bill to create the Women's Auxiliary Army Corps already in May of 1941. It took Pearl Harbor, however, to bring the War Department around to supporting it. Three weeks after the attack, on Christmas Eve, the secretary of war sent his approval to Congress.

Hearings were held in March and, with unanimous committee recommendation, the House passed the bill 249–83. The Senate vote two months later was much closer, but on May 15, 1942, President Roosevelt signed the bill and the precedent for women in the military in capacities other than nursing was underway. The bill had a serious flaw, however, in its half-acknowledgement of need, which gave the original WAAC its bureaucratically confusing AUXILIARY status. By the time the Army corrected that with legislation to drop "auxiliary" for the uncomplicated Women's Army Corps (WAC) in July of 1943, tens of thousands of women had joined the Army.

The first class of officers was stationed at Fort Des Moines, Iowa, and training soon expanded to Daytona Beach, Florida and Fort Oglethorpe, Georgia. Women trained much like men, focusing on parade drill, closely disciplined barrack life, and classes in military methods. By the end of the war, WACs had performed in hundreds of military occupational specialties, including cartography, computing, motor mechanics, weather forecasting, parachute packing, mail sorting, photography, air traffic control, and even dog and pigeon training. The majority, not surprisingly, ended up in clerical positions—even though their commander, OVETA CULP HOBBY, worked hard to prevent stereotypical assignments. Hobby did succeed in preventing her troops from being assigned as cooks and bakers to male units (which was the intention of many men). Those WACs who worked in kitchens served only other WACs.

Unlike the Navy's military units, WAACs were sent overseas early. Indeed, General Eisenhower was among the Army's progressives who wanted women militarized precisely because he saw them as a key to success in maintaining communications in battlefield situations with many languages. As soon as the first WAAC troops were trained, women went to North Africa as radio/telephone operators and translators. By the end of the war, there were WACs assigned to posts from Alaska to Australia and all points between. Especially large numbers of them worked in English headquarters that planned the D-day invasion of the Continent, where one of the stereotypes they dispelled was that women couldn't keep secrets. Army leadership acknowledged that fewer military secrets were leaked by women than by men.

Because Hobby was from the South, civil rights leaders were dubious about her appointment and watched closely to see that black women were accepted into the WAAC—while the Navy, in contrast, admitted none until the last year of the war. The first WAAC officers thus included black women in a percentage comparable to that of the population, but this bright beginning was not maintained. Ultimately, only about 4 percent of wartime WACs were black, but Hobby and her staff firmly believed the low number was not because of WAC prejudice, but rather because WACs were required to be high school graduates at a time when relatively few communities encouraged black students to graduate. Those black women who did join the WAC received the same training and the same overseas opportunity as white WACs, although there were complaints throughout the war about the fact that both male and female blacks lived in segregated barracks and were often assigned menial occupational specialties.

Indeed, like male soldiers, most WACs had some complaints about their experience, and a few were bitterly disillusioned. For the majority of the approximately one hundred thousand who joined, however, the experience was tremendously broadening. The Women's Army Corps gave an important boost to the self-esteem of women who had lived for more than a decade under the shadow of the Great Depression, and moreover, the work that they did was of genuine value in winning the war.

Hobby—who faced hundreds of policy-making decisions on a daily basis at the beginning—worked to the point of literal exhaustion and resigned shortly before the war was over. The Women's Army Corps dismissed most of its members during 1946, but the WOMEN'S ARMED SERVICES INTEGRATION ACT of 1948 established the WAC as part of the peacetime Army and ultimately, women were absorbed into the Army itself without a separate corps. In 1980, Congress demonstrated the change in public attitudes by extending full benefits to the sixteen thousand whose service had been during the time when women's effort was "auxiliary" by definition.

The Corps' history is preserved in the Edith Nourse Rogers WAC Museum at Fort McClellan, Alabama; other records exist in Washington and at the Gen. George C. Marshall Foundation in Lexington, Virginia.

WOMEN'S AUXILIARY FERRYING SQUADRON (WAFS)

The most short-lived of the women's military units during WORLD WAR II, the WAFS were formed by Nancy Harkness Love to ferry (or deliver) planes from aircraft factories to air bases—or any other location where a plane was needed. The factory-to-base traffic alone, however, was significant, for the nation manufactured 120,000 airplanes annually by 1944. The WAFS were intended to replace male pilots, thus making more men available for overseas duty.

A VASSAR student from 1931 to 1934, Nancy Harkness had dropped out of college to marry aviator Hubert Love, and by the beginning of WORLD WAR II, was a veteran pilot. While this nation was still neutral, she flew U.S. manufactured planes to the Canadian border, from which point Canadian pilots took them across the Atlantic. When the U.S. entered the war, her husband's position as the deputy chief of the Army's Air Transport Command helped Love find a way to translate her flying abilities into action.

At only twenty-eight, she formed the Women's Auxiliary Ferrying Squadron (WAFS) at an Army air base near Wilmington, Delaware in the summer of 1942. Love recruited forty experienced women pilots, who, supported by ten women administrators, constituted the first women pilots of the nation's military. WAFS pilots were highly qualified, with at least· five hundred hours in logged flying time and cross-country experience, but the War Department, while sanctioning their formation, remained skeptical that women could perform the work. WAFS were "experimental" and, importantly, were civilians who contracted with the Army and thus received no benefits.

Meanwhile, women with less flying experience were organized into the WOMEN'S AIR SERVICE PILOTS (WASP) under JACKIE COCHRAN. While WAFS were such capable pilots that they began work after only a short course in Army paperwork, WASPs received training that was comparable to that of male air cadets. Eventually, of course, WASPs became experienced also, and by the war's midpoint, the differences between the two programs were so negligible that General Hap Arnold, Air Corps chief, insisted that they unite. Thus, on August 5, 1943, the WAFS merged into the WASP with Cochran as commander. Love—who was younger and far less famous than Cochran—accepted the secondary position, acting as the executive liaison with the (male) Ferrying Division of the Army's Air Transport Command. Neither woman received any military rank, and the remaining history of the WASP would be bittersweet.

WOMEN'S EDUCATIONAL AND INDUSTRIAL UNION (WEIU)

A Boston program that flourished at the turn of the century, the WEIU combined the aims of settlement houses (especially the local Denison House) with those of other progressive causes. Its name was something of a misnomer, for the WEIU was neither a trade union nor primarily concerned with women who worked in industrial jobs. Unlike the New York-based WOMEN'S TRADE UNION LEAGUE that began a few years later, the WEIU focused much of its attention on women who worked in homes and on public education about the social costs of domesticity.

With leadership from such women as ELLEN RICHARDS and MOLLY DEWSON, the WEIU gathered data on a number of aspects of domestic life, such as the average wages of DOMESTIC WORKERS and their methods of seeking employment. The WEIU then used this information in an attempt to professionalize relationships between housewives and servants. Its aim was twofold: to improve the position of domestic workers and also to free housewives for other careers.

Using the new techniques of social science, the WEIU issued several reports between 1895 and 1907 on the living conditions and attitudes of domestic workers and/or IMMIGRANT WOMEN. It also ran an employment bureau and social clubs for domestic workers, as well as classes in the new field of HOME ECONOMICS. Another WEIU theme was the adoption of communal approaches to family living—such as shared meals in cooperative apartment houses—that would cut the amount of housework assigned to individual women.

The records of the Women's Educational and Industrial Union are housed in RADCLIFFE COLLEGE's Schlesinger Library. Some of its programs merged into the home economics department of Simmons College, which was founded in 1899 to provide career education to young women.

WOMEN'S HALL OF FAME

The Women's Hall of Fame is located in SENECA FALLS, the town in western New York where the first women's rights convention was held in 1848. The Hall houses memorabilia honoring women who made major contributions to the advancement of the arts, athletics, business, education, government, the humanities, philanthropy, and science. In addition to its displays, the Hall houses a library, produces traveling exhibits, sponsors an essay contest and other educational programs related to women.

The Hall of Fame was created in 1969 by the women of Seneca Falls. In 1977, a torch carried by more than one thousand runners began at Seneca Falls and went on to Houston, where the International Women's Year symposia took place. As of 1992, forty-seven distinguished American women have been admitted to the Hall, ranging alphabetically from ABIGAIL ADAMS to BABE ZAHARIAS; new nominees are taken annually.

Membership forms and further information can be obtained from the National Women's Hall of Fame; 76 Fall Street (P.O. Box 335); Seneca Falls, NY 13148.

WOMEN'S INTERNATIONAL LEAGUE FOR PEACE AND FREEDOM

Founded at the end of WORLD WAR I, the Women's International League for Peace and Freedom (WILPF) was a direct outgrowth of the INTERNATIONAL CONGRESS OF WOMEN and the WOMEN'S PEACE PARTY. JANE ADDAMS was its first president and continued in this position until her death.

EMILY BALCH, after losing her job at WELLESLEY because of her opposition to the war, became the WILPF's secretary/treasurer and spent the next three years setting up its offices in Geneva. Both Addams and Balch went on to win the Nobel Peace Prize; other founders included SOPHONISBA BRECKINRIDGE, ALICE HAMILTON, and FLORENCE KELLEY. At the group's second meeting in Zurich, MARY CHURCH TERRELL repeated the oratorical triumph she had made earlier in the century at the INTERNATIONAL COUNCIL OF WOMEN.

Throughout the twentieth century, the WILPF has continued its public education and political involvement, aiming to maintain peace while preserving freedom. Its archives are included with the Swathmore College Peace Collection in Swathmore, Pennsylvania.

WOMEN'S RELIEF CORPS

A post–CIVIL WAR phenomenon, the Women's Relief Corps worked through local chapters to relieve the sufferings of disabled veterans, war widows, and orphans. In the North, it functioned as an AUXILIARY of the Grand Army of the Republic, but in the South, where the GAR had no equivalent, there nonetheless were units of the Women's Relief Corps; Tampa, Florida, for example, was #5. Separate units run by black women on behalf of black veterans existed in the North; the Boston unit founded by SUSIE KING TAYLOR and others in 1886 was #67. In addition, some areas had similar organizations with names like Ladies Relief Society or Ladies Memorial Society.

These groups concentrated on cemetery maintenance and the erection of war memorials. The May 30 observance of Decoration Day in the South and Memorial Day in the North owed much to the organizational efforts of these women. Their era of greatest activity was in the 1880s and 1890s, when those whose lives had been shaped by the war had begun to age, and they feared that wartime sacrifices would be forgotten as the nation rushed on towards the twentieth century.

WOMEN'S RIGHTS CONVENTIONS—

See SENECA FALLS WOMEN'S RIGHTS CONVENTION

WOMEN'S TRADE UNION LEAGUE (WTUL)

The WTUL grew out of a 1903 Boston meeting of the American Federation of Labor, for the AFL put so little focus on organizing women that the need for a separate group seemed apparent to labor organizers such as MARY KENNEY O'SULLIVAN and LEONORA O'REILLY. With additional cofounders in LILLIAN WALD and the omnipresent JANE ADDAMS, the WTUL's first president was Mary Morton Kehew, a Boston philanthropist who had been working to get women into labor unions since 1892.

Kehew's philanthropic profile would set the image of the group, for the WTUL was a unique combination of the economic interests of working women with the more political aims of affluent feminists. Though it willingly accepted a subordinate position within the house of labor, the WTUL provided a very progressive model of organizing and was a rare example of women cutting across class lines to form a solid bloc. To be sure, those with money were more dedicated to the SUFFRAGE MOVEMENT, while those without money were more interested in building unions, but for a time, the two worked together in an extraordinary show of female solidarity.

This was especially true during the great STRIKES in the GARMENT INDUSTRY in 1909–1911. Led by MARY ELIZABETH DREIER in New York and her sister MARGARET DREIER ROBINS in Chicago, socialites such as ALVA BELMONT and women from the financially powerful families of Harriman, Morgan, and others boycotted clothing manufacturers who refused to settle with the INTERNATIONAL LADIES' GARMENT WORKERS UNION. Wealthy WTUL members not only provided funds for strikers, but also spoke for them with the press, helped them with picket duty, and even went to jail for them. The value of these sophisticates to the IMMIGRANT WOMEN who constituted most of the industry's work force can be seen in the report of a Russian Jew who said that when the strike began, "We hardly knew . . . what to do. But one of the American girls, who knew how to telephone, called up the Women's Trade Union League . . ."

With goals of an eight-hour day, a minimum wage, and an end to night work for women, there were branches of the WTUL by 1911 in eleven cities, ranging from Boston to Denver. The league was a factor in the LAWRENCE MASSACHUSETTS TEXTILE MILLS STRIKE and in strikes that ranged from Milwaukee breweries to corset makers in Connecticut. The WTUL was especially important in the aftermath of the TRIANGLE FIRE, when Dreier and others followed through with an exhaustive four-year study that documented unsafe conditions in New York State. As a direct result of WTUL lobbying, laws were passed that for the first time seriously restrained the power of corporations.

WORLD WAR I began as this PROTECTIVE LEGISLATION was being passed, and the WTUL would never again be so effective an organization. After the vote was won in 1920, affluent women felt less need of an alliance with workers; as they dropped out, the first woman from a working class background, Maud Swartz of the Typographers Union, rose to the presidency in 1921. She was followed by ROSE SCHNEIDERMAN in 1926, who would remain president for the rest of the organization's existence.

Meanwhile, postwar reaction brought violent repression of labor unions. The Great Depression brought additional damaging effects, and although it survived until 1950, the WTUL never returned to the power it had prior to World War I. During WORLD WAR II, management was forced to make many of the industrial changes the League advocated simply because without these improvements, they could not recruit enough women. Postwar reaction once again brought a return to class divisions, and with Schneiderman's aging, it was understandable that the WTUL disbanded just before the onset of McCarthyism.

For many years, however, to be a female union member meant to be a member of the Women's Trade Union League, for it was the only mechanism that the AFL provided for women. Labor leadership was usually indifferent and sometimes hostile to the political aspirations of women, and WTUL had a delicate task in dealing with these conservative male attitudes without jeopardizing the support of women who were more ideologically progressive. Yet the league managed to do this balancing act well for at least for two decades, and its leadership provided a model of organizing skill for countless women to come.

Records of the Women's Trade Union League are included in the New York State Department of Labor Research Library in Brooklyn.

WOODHULL, VICTORIA CLAFLIN (1838–1927) Victoria Woodhull, accompanied by her sister Tennessee and her daughter Zulu Maud, romped through the Victorian age like characters released from a raucous novel. Victoria, especially, provoked not only scandal and amusement, but also important new ideas. Her amazing life (and the widespread publicity it received) revolutionized relationships between men and women and set precedents in business and politics.

Born in Licking County, Ohio, when that area was still a frontier, Victoria grew up in a traveling medicine show operated by her one-eyed father, Buck Claflin. It featured his ten children, with one of Victoria's brothers posing as a cancer doctor while she and Tennessee practiced psychic medicine. Woodhull was adept at seances, palm reading, and other spiritualistic techniques; for the rest of her life, she would maintain that her actions were caused by powers beyond her control. Doubtless this early experience in mind manipulation provided the training that led to Woodhull's charismatic abilities as an adult, when she proved herself able to win over many of those who had been determined to dislike her.

At fifteen, she won the heart of Dr. Canning Woodhull and bore him two children, but this did not mean she settled down. They traveled as far as California before Dr. Woodhull took to alcohol and disappeared. Victoria left her mentally retarded son, and taking Zulu along, joined Tennessee at various disreputable activities throughout the Midwest. Though they were charged with PROSTITUTION, blackmail, and other criminal offenses in several places, a common solution to law enforcement problems in this era was simply to run offenders out of town, and the Woodhulls served no serious jail time—though Tennessee did have to flee from an indictment for manslaughter in Illinois when her "patient" died.

In 1866, Victoria secured a DIVORCE to marry her St. Louis lover, Colonel James Blood, but she retained the name by which she was known. Blood apparently truly believed in the "free love" that he advocated, for their marriage—if indeed they did actually wed—was an open one. He displayed nothing but support for his unconventional wife, following her to New York in 1868 when the enterprising Victoria and Tennessee (or Tennie C.) attached themselves to multimillionaire Cornelius Vanderbilt. This was the turning point in the sisters' lives, for without Vanderbilt's aid, Woodhull may well have remained a nameless petty miscreant.

Though he built a powerful railroad network and controlled vast wealth, Vanderbilt also had interests in spiritualism; his wife had recently died and the sisters had no trouble charming the old man. From there, however, they departed from standard feminine behavior. With Vanderbilt's backing, the women became serious investors, first in real estate and then in the stock market. By January of 1870, they were successful enough to open their own brokerage firm—Woodhull, Claflin & Co.—that chagrined the males of Wall Street by obviously making money. With their multitudinous family, including Colonel Blood, ensconced in a mansion, the sisters were the talk of New York.

Only month later, Victoria Woodhull declared herself a candidate for president of the U.S. She made this astounding move on April 2, 1870, when women had not yet voted in any state and before she made any contact with the SUFFRAGE MOVEMENT. Its stupefied leaders quickly divided into camps of those who admired her temerity (the initial position of SUSAN ANTHONY, ELIZABETH CADY STANTON, and others in the NATIONAL WOMAN SUFFRAGE ASSOCIATION) and those who felt that her outrageous reputation damaged the cause to which serious women had dedicated a lifetime (the position of most in the AMERICAN WOMAN SUFFRAGE ASSOCIATION).

Woodhull's announcement came almost two years before

the next presidential election, and she used the time to full effect. The *Woodhull & Claflin's Weekly* spelled out her platform, which included elimination of sexual double standards and DRESS REFORM among its directly FEMINIST planks; other newspaper features ranged from promotion of healthy diet to the first English translation of the *Communist Manifesto*. Most of the paper's material actually was written by two men—Colonel Blood and Victoria's new admirer, Stephen Pearl Andrews. A philosopher with a personal history that covered law, linguistics, medicine, and other fields, Andrews had devised a social and economic program he called "Pantarchy," which Victoria Woodhull presumably would implement as president.

Woodhull was far too intelligent to believe that she had any chance of being elected, but she used her campaign to bring attention to women's issues and, in doing so, willingly drew to herself the scorn that made other suffragists look moderate by comparison. Understanding this, Anthony accepted Woodhull's January 11, 1871 appearance before the House Judiciary Committee, where she testified for the inclusion of women in the FIFTEENTH AMENDMENT that gave voting rights to black men. Washingtonians who crowded the Capitol for a glimpse of the notorious woman were surprised to see a beautifully dressed, soft-spoken lady whose words made good sense. Many suffragists were charmed, and Woodhull later made more conquests when she addressed the NWSA membership.

Operating under the banner of her own Equal Rights Party, Woodhull chose ABOLITIONIST and ex-slave Frederick Douglass as her running mate—heedless of the fact that he did not accept. (Douglass condoned the sexist tenets of his time almost as fully as he rejected its racist beliefs. Moreover, he was closely allied with men whose wives and sisters were the leaders of the AWSA that so thoroughly disapproved of Woodhull.) Undaunted, she held a nominating convention, made fiery speeches, and using *Woodhull & Claflin's Weekly* (which never came close to weekly publication and was in bankruptcy before the election), she advocated positions that she herself, using the post–CIVIL WAR rhetoric of the era, branded as "treason" and "secession."

While she didn't persuade women to "secede" from a male world, Woodhull did cause increasing division within the women's movement. AWSA leadership, with its roots in Bostonian puritanism, continued to condemn her, but Anthony too withdrew her previous tolerance as she saw her own power in the NWSA slipping away to this untested newcomer's dreams of a third party. Anthony was outraged when Woodhull printed Anthony's name on a call for a woman's party, and by May of 1872, any friendship they once felt had evaporated. Anthony gaveled Woodhull down at the NWSA's annual meeting, and, with the platform in an uproar, adjourned the session and ordered the janitor to turn out the lights.

The worst was yet to come, however, as six months later Woodhull plunged the women's movement into the heart of one of the nineteenth century's greatest cases of yellow journalism. The scandal revolved around Reverend Henry Ward Beecher, an extremely popular New York preacher and the brother of CATHARINE BEECHER, HARRIET BEECHER STOWE, and Isabella Beecher Hooker. This highly visible family split over suffrage, with Catharine opposing it, Henry and Harriet supporting it but belonging to the relatively conservative AWSA, while Isabella was a founding officer of the NWSA and befriended Susan Anthony through countless trials.

As Victoria Woodhull rose to national prominence in 1871, Henry Beecher felt called upon to censure her, but Isbella was among those NWSA members who were enamored of her and believed her unfairly maligned. Meanwhile, a longtime friend of Anthony and Stanton, Elizabeth "Lib" Tilton, engaged in a secret affair with her pastor—the Reverend Beecher. At the same time, Dr. Woodhull wandered back into Victoria's life, and when she shared her home with both him and Colonel Blood, the era's moralists accused her of bigamy. Woodhull retaliated by telling the world of Reverend Beecher's affair—which she knew to be a fact because she not only had heard of it from Stanton, but also, and more importantly, from Tilton's husband, with whom Woodhull had a strong, quite possibly physical relationship.

To Woodhull, the exposé of the TILTON-BEECHER AFFAIR that she made in her newspaper on November 2, 1872—just days before the election—was fair play. She reasoned that a liberated woman should not allow herself to be attacked by those whom she knew to be hypocrites without revealing the truth to an otherwise gullible public. She may have even believed that the average voter, being male, would think as candidly as she did, and that this display of courage would spark her otherwise moribund presidential campaign. The effect, however, was just the opposite. Virtually all suffragists united behind Lib Tilton's right to privacy, even if that did allow Reverend Beecher to escape the consequences of his hypocrisy.

The mainstream press had refused to touch the story, something they doubtlessly regretted when the exposé sold out within a few hours and copies went for as much as forty dollars. But, because Woodhull and Claflin had revived their *Weekly* to print it, they opened themselves to charges of libel and obscenity. Young Anthony COMSTOCK began his censorship career with their arrest within hours of the mailing of the newspaper—and the presidential candidate and her sister were in jail when the election took place. The indictment was eventually dropped, but the sisters spent seven months in the Tombs, New York's notorious prison, at great stress.

In 1877, four years after their release, the sisters and Zulu left for England—amid rumors that the trip was subsidized by the chief Vanderbilt heir, who wanted them out of the country when the will was contested. Woodhull took care to first divorce Colonel Blood and to issue the last edition of the *Weekly*. She was forty-nine years old, and her life was far from over. In London, she again was a popular lecturer and returned to wealth. Both of the sisters married affluent Englishmen, with Tennie C. transforming herself into Lady Cook. With Zulu, Victoria published *Humanitarian* magazine, which had a far better publication record than her earlier periodical, lasting from 1892 to 1910. She wrote two books under her own name and a third with Tennie C., all of them confirming her unabashed radicalism. With occasional visits to her native land, Victoria Woodhull lived comfortably on a Worchestershire estate until her death at eighty-eight.

WORLD WAR I More than any other era in American history, World War I was a turning point. The five years between 1916 and 1921 made a more dramatic difference than any other similarly brief period of the world's history, and nowhere can this be seen as clearly as in the lives of women. In 1916, their roles were still largely defined by the standards of the Victorian age; by 1921, they had the vote and the FLAPPER of the Roaring Twenties symbolized their liberation.

Though little noticed at the time, a profound change occurred at the heart of the war itself: for the first time in history, women officially joined the military. The Navy, desperate for clerical workers in Washington, researched recruitment law and found no legal barrier to enlisting women. The first to join was Opha Mae Johnson, a civilian Navy employee who was sworn into the service on August 13, 1918. Some 12,500 women termed YEOMEN (F) followed her. Even though peace was declared in November, the mass of backlogged paperwork meant that they served through 1919 on the same status as male yeomen.

The Marine Corps was less enthusiastic about women, enlisting only 305—but women demonstrated their willingness to volunteer by filing thousands of applications. The "MARINETTES" who were chosen, not surprisingly, were extremely well qualified and often gave up excellent civilian jobs for what turned out to be a four-month war. Although they were entitled to veteran's benefits, doubtless many of these women had difficulty finding equivalent positions in the depressed postwar economy.

In addition, over one thousand women went overseas as civilian contract employees to the Army, where they worked as translators, telephone operators and ambulance drivers for the American Expeditionary Forces. Though they wore uniforms, subjected themselves to military discipline and shared the same hardships as men, because these women were officially civilians, they received no hospitalization or other benefits. During the Second World War, women in Congress would point to this injustice as a reason that women should be part of the regular military rather than relegated to auxiliary units.

Meanwhile, dozens of quasi-military groups emulated the RED CROSS, as organizations such as the National League for Women's Services and the Women's Committee of the Council of National Defense came into being almost overnight. Thousands of extant women's clubs switched their attention to wartime activity, rolling bandages and knitting socks for soldiers. They sold liberty bonds, organized food and clothing

Women stitching cloth to "aeroplane" wings in Buffalo, New York, during World War I. Note that they wear dresses; by the next war, women doing such work would wear pants. NATIONAL ARCHIVES; CURTISS AIRCRAFT.

drives for European refugees, and "canned a can for Uncle Sam." Women replaced men as streetcar drivers, elevator operators, and postal workers, while thousands of others obtained new jobs in dangerous munitions plants.

On the other hand, the war did not have unanimous support. Thousands of activist women spoke out against U.S. involvement, with some such as JANE ADDAMS and EMILY BALCH enduring severe harm to their careers because of their opposition. The SUFFRAGE MOVEMENT was deeply divided on the issue, but nonetheless, the obvious patriotism of women and especially their willingness to volunteer proved a crucial factor in transforming male attitudes. President Wilson, once a suffrage opponent, typified these men when he said in 1919, "Unless we enfranchise women we shall have fought to safeguard a democracy which, to that extent, we have never bothered to create."

The following year, after decades of interminable debate, the NINETEENTH AMENDMENT finally passed. Other changes occurred that were at the same time conspicuous and profoundly subtle: women shortened their skirts and bobbed their hair; they began going to movies, smoking cigarettes, driving cars, and using BIRTH CONTROL. In dozens of ways, young women's lives became more like those of men, and often these changes were motivated by a profound cynicism and a rejection of authority that was based in wartime experience. An extremely bloody war that seemingly wrought no genuine good (especially after the U.S. refused to join the League of Nations), World War I brought complex change to ordinary people and the way they lived their lives. The Western world, and especially its women, would never return to the innocence of prewar days.

WORLD WAR II Though the changes in postwar civilian life were not as dramatic as those wrought by WORLD WAR I, the Second World War began trends that were profound and lasting—even though that was not necessarily apparent in the years immediately following the war. A much greater global conflict than the first war, the second plunged many more women into far more serious achievement than the first, giving millions their first opportunity for independent action and personal self-esteem. The most obvious change was in the workplace, especially the industrial workplace.

More than any other war in history, World War II was a battle of production. The Germans and Japanese had a ten-year head start on amassing weapons, so production was essential to victory, and women, as the last labor reserve, were essential to production. When President Roosevelt asked in 1940 for fifty thousand planes a year, many thought that goal impossible—but by 1944, the U.S. was producing 120,000 planes annually. Many of these aircraft were built in plants where more than half of the employees were female, where women surprised their male supervisors with their ability to perform nontraditional tasks. The same was true in munition plants, shipyards, and hundreds of other kinds of installations.

To fulfill these production goals, industrial management had to reach out to the kind of woman who grew up in a middle-class home and who never expected to work in a factory. Her labor had to be attracted with a better offer than that given to the poor and IMMIGRANT WOMEN who historically formed the female industrial work force—and this change would eventually improve life for everyone. As middle-class women insisted on reasonable employment conditions, management discovered that the harsh disciplinary techniques they used in the past not only were unnecessary, but that production actually increased with positive incentives.

The growth of enlightened management and the permanent acceptance of middle-class women as part of the labor force were only two of the many changes World War II brought. Another was the mass migration of people, for never before had so many people moved in so many different directions in so short a time. Families went from the hills of West Virginia and North Carolina, for example, to the Atlantic's shipyards; from Missouri and Arkansas, they migrated to Los Angeles and Detroit; from small towns and farms everywhere, people uprooted themselves.

Many localities saw their population double and triple seemingly overnight. Elkton, Maryland, for instance, was a quiet farm town until a giant ammunition plant was built there and the population zoomed from six thousand to twelve thousand, with 80 percent of the growth being young women. These women were recruited from surrounding states and came to their jobs by bus, almost all of them going away from home for the first time. Factories often housed them dormitory-style, and for most, this was their first experience living outside of a patriarchal structure. Some were so unsophisticated that they had never used telephones or flush toilets—but they did important jobs that they didn't know they could do and they earned more money than they had seen in their lives, and their self-esteem soared.

In 1940, 12 million women were at work; five years later there were 19 million. While the numbers declined immediately after the war, they soon rose again, for women had discovered that they wanted the independence of earning their own income—and business had discovered that it needed women as employees, as well as customers. While veterans' preference and union seniority kept most women out of blue collar jobs after the war ended, there was a complete transformation in white collar jobs. In the Depression days before the war began, such jobs as bank tellers, retail cashiers, and office clerks were usually held by men; after the war, these became almost wholly "women's work."

Nowhere was this change more apparent than in the government, for though it was little noted, the largest and most lasting change in women's employment during the war was in having Uncle Sam as her boss. The year before Pearl Harbor saw a 43 percent annual increase in women in the executive branch of government, and that pattern continued. Thousands of young women with secretarial skills were recruited from all over the country to join Washington's massive steno pool. Again, most of them traveled for the first time in their lives, and they built independent careers that had been unimaginable to their mothers.

DOMESTIC SERVANTS, a feature of middle-class American homes for decades, largely disappeared during the war. Approximately a half-million women left domestic service during the war, many of them black women who finally found better opportunities. Some service jobs such as elevator operators, movie ushers, and messengers disappeared altogether. On the other end of the employment scale, college-educated women squeezed in past the barriers to professional employment.

Women leaving from work at a Texas shipyard during World War II. OFFICE OF WAR INFORMATION, LIBRARY OF CONGRESS, PHOTO BY JOHN VACHON.

One of the most visible was journalism, as newspaper syndicates hired their first women, and women were occasionally heard on the radio. Women lawyers found work outside of the legal secretary jobs that they had been offered during the Depression, and Congress insisted that the military commission female physicians who wanted to join the Medical Corps.

Indeed, it was the ARMY NURSE CORPS that was the first group of women to be profoundly affected by the war, as NURSES in the South Pacific withstood bombing in the days after Pearl Harbor. Some escaped, but others of them joined the approximately five hundred women whom the Japanese held as prisoners of war from 1942 until 1945. Meanwhile, all over the

globe, other Army and Navy nurses served under combat conditions in North Africa, Italy, Normandy, and other fronts. On hospital ships, a dozen nurses might work amid thousands of men packed into crowded quarters under threat from torpedoes and bombs; nurses assigned to the Air Corps worked alone on evacuation flights, often doing a doctor's duty. Meanwhile, civilian nurses found their profession revolutionized by wartime needs.

The Nurse Corps had existed since the beginning of the century, but World War II brought women's entrance into all branches of the military. The WOMEN'S AUXILIARY ARMY CORPS was authorized after Pearl Harbor, and the Navy soon emulated it with the creation of the WAVES. Almost one hundred thousand women joined each of these two corps, while smaller numbers served in the Coast Guard's SPARs and in the straightforwardly named Women MARINES. By the end of the war, these women worked in hundreds of military occupational specialties. In addition, some two thousand women performed various types of flying for the military in the WOMEN'S AIR SERVICE PILOTS and in the WOMEN'S AUXILIARY FERRYING SQUADRON. These women were not entitled to military benefits, even though thirty-eight of them lost their lives.

The war also meant significant changes even for those who lived in traditional roles. Housewives throughout the nation learned to cope with the rationing of food and other essentials. Millions of young women faced the terrible dilemma of choosing between a hasty wartime wedding or perhaps sending a sweetheart to his death without becoming his wife. Many of those who chose to wed then spent the next months or years following their husbands from camp to camp until the men shipped out. These women—often carrying their children along so that they could be with daddy a little longer—endured overcrowded trains on which soldiers had priority, overpriced housing and hostile attitudes in military towns, and almost certain unemployment amid thousands of similar wives.

Finally, about 125,000 American men became prisoners of war, while 44,000 were still missing in action a year after the war ended—which meant that the hundreds of thousands of women who were their lovers, wives, and mothers lived in a state of indefinite suspension, not knowing what had happened to the one they loved. Some fifty thousand became war widows, while about four times that many mothers lost their young sons. Hundreds of thousands of other women cared for their mentally and physically wounded men, some of whom would never recover. But while the war imposed horrible burdens on some women, for many others, it offered a first opportunity to live a life that was similar to a man's—to work, to travel, to earn, and, most satisfyingly, to contribute to ultimate peace and human freedom.

WRIGHT, FRANCES ("FANNY") (1785–1852) Frances

Wright's life would have been considered radical a century after she lived it; as it was, her liberated views and international lifestyle were far beyond the ken of her pre–CIVIL WAR contemporaries. Indeed, the effectiveness of the leadership she offered to American women may have been diminished because the independent circumstances of her life were in fact so very exceptional.

A Scot who was orphaned at two, she inherited a fortune, but spurned the indolent life she could have led for one of tireless activity. Rejecting relatives' pressures for conventionality, she studied Greek philosophy and published intellectually respectable work while in her teens. Moreover, when Wright visited the still-new U.S. at twenty-two, she was accompanied only by her younger sister Camilla—in an era when women did not TRAVEL alone.

The immediate motivation for her 1818 visit was to see the production of a play that she had written. Her lasting reputation as an author, however, would be based on *Views of Society and Manners in America* (1821). The book was the first of the American travelogue genre, predating similar works by Frenchman Alexis de Tocqueville and Englishwoman Frances Trollope by more than a decade. Wright's work was not only widely read in both Europe and America, but also has continued to be used by historians for its optimistic commentary on the early republic.

Not the least of the book's enthusiasms was the interest that American women took in public issues. This doubtless was a factor in her acceptance of an invitation from revolutionary hero LaFayette, who was moved by her book and asked her to join him in his 1824 American tour. Wright was still sufficiently concerned about gossip that she and Camilla traveled separately, but the young women did link up with the elderly man for a number of events, including visits to former Presidents Madison and Jefferson. When LaFayette returned to Europe, the Wright sisters remained, and Frances would spend the majority of her life thereafter in the new land, experimenting with new ideas.

She traveled up the Mississippi from New Orleans in 1825, when that area was still a frontier, and her observance of slave sales at river ports confirmed her abhorrence of the system. The result was another publication, with a title that again revealed a thinker far ahead of her times: *A Plan for the Gradual Abolition of Slavery in the United States Without Danger of Loss to the Citizens of the South* (1825). Moreover, Wright acted upon what she advocated: late that year, she purchased 640 acres of land to develop a self-help colony for the slaves that she bought—years before other ABOLITIONISTS offered plans for compensated emancipation.

The colony, called Nashoba, was located near Memphis. The area was still a wilderness, isolated from eastern cities by hundreds of miles of mountainous terrain or a long water route. Moreover, Nashoba's land was no developed plantation ready to be worked, but rather virgin forest that required cutting trees and digging roots before planting. Neither Frances nor Camilla Wright nor their Scottish male overseer had any applicable agricultural experience, and the blacks associated with the colony seem to have been disproportionately women and children. The fact that they managed to clear approximately one hundred acres is a testament to their willingness to work hard, but the obstacles inherent in the project were extremely difficult to overcome.

In the summer of 1827, Wright returned to Europe with Robert Dale Owen, an utopian whose colony at New Harmony, Indiana—which did not include the challenge of overcoming slavery—ultimately would be more successful. In her absence, Nashoba declined further into abject poverty; instead of building its economy, the overseer spent his time advocating "free love." The publication of his journal in an abolitionist newspaper irreparably associated the colony with scandal, and Wright was forced to abandon the project after her 1828 return. Nonetheless, she stayed after all other Nashoba whites moved on, and ultimately financed the move of approximately thirty black colonists out of the U.S., personally escorting them to Haiti in 1830.

It cost her half of her fortune. Moreover, Nashoba marked the beginning of an impossible image problem, for Fanny Wright and the loose sexuality of her colony became the target of every editor seeking to ridicule new ideas. She lost the popularity that she had when identified with her travelogue, but Wright persevered in writing and lecturing for the rest of her life and her adherents, though less numerous, were more steadfast.

Abandoning agrarian ideals, she centered herself in Cincinnati and New York, where with Robert Dale Owen, she edited the *Free Enquirer*. At the same time, she took to the lecture platform—years before SUSAN ANTHONY and others "pioneered" PUBLIC SPEAKING for women. Her 1829 tour attracted large audiences; using the Declaration of Independence as her text, Wright preached against authoritarian religion and particularly faulted it for the secondary place assigned women. She went on to advocate not only equal education for girls—an idea only then being formulated by EMMA WILLARD—but also advanced positions that would cause ELIZABETH CADY STANTON and others to be branded as radicals when they offered them decades later. Among other progressive ideas, Wright championed MARRIED WOMEN'S PROPERTY RIGHTS and DIVORCE—and, most shocking of all, BIRTH CONTROL.

Her FEMINIST ideas were part of a socialist package, and those economic ideas probably were the attraction that seems to have brought Wright more male than female supporters. She was a vital part of the formation of the Workingmen's Association in New York in 1829, and she made campaign speeches on behalf of Jacksonian Democrats throughout the 1830s. Indeed, her return trips from Europe in the late thirties may well have been motivated by a desire to participate in the 1836 and 1838 elections, for Wright spent much more time abroad after 1830.

She took her ailing sister to Paris that year, and, lonely after Camilla's death, married an older French physician in 1831—after she bore his child. The baby soon died, but, at age thirty-six, she bore another. Wright maintained her traveling life, crossing the Atlantic five times in the 1840s—which resulted in the publication of still another prescient book, an 1848 vision of global government. As might be expected, however, the extreme patriarchy of Napoleonic marital law caused endless quarrels over Wright's independent life and finances; after eleven years of marriage, she obtained a divorce in Cincinnati, surrendering the GUARDIANSHIP of her daughter.

It may have broken her heart as well as her previously strong will. Frances Wright fell on the Cincinnati ice the following year and never recovered from the complications of a broken hip. She died at fifty-seven, her remarkable foresight and experienced leadership lost to the abolitionists and feminists who could have so benefited from her presence in the difficult decades to follow.

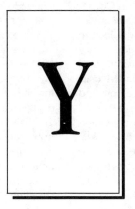

YEOMEN (F) Yeoman is the Navy's rank for petty officers who perform clerical duties, and the added "(F)" was the Navy's designation for the women it recruited during WORLD WAR I, while an "(M)" was placed behind the traditional rank to indicate a male. Sometimes these women also were referred to as "Yeomenettes" in the Navy and "MARINETTES" in the Marines.

The change was indicative of the increased importance of paperwork in the modern military and of women's rise in the business world, for the recruitment of women was a concession to the fact that women's office skills were generally superior to those of men. Especially in need of typists, the Navy's attorneys researched the law and found no specific bar to female enlistment. The Navy and Marine Corps recruited approximately thirteen thousand women who served with the same status as male yeomen. Some one thousand more uniformed women went overseas as civilians contracted with the American Expeditionary Force to serve as telephone operators and translators. When women again joined the Navy in WORLD WAR II, it was as WAVES.

YEZIERSKA, ANZIA (1880?–1970) Anzia Yezierska did not know when she was born, a fact that she made clear in *Children of Loneliness* (1923). In this autobiographical fiction, she inquired of her mother what birthdays were and why she didn't have one. The harried IMMIGRANT WOMAN, driven almost insane by poverty, harshly replied: "A birthday lays in your head? You want to be glad that you were born into the world? . . . Wouldn't it be better if you was never born already?"

A Polish Jew, Anzia came to New York when she was a child. Her father was a Talmudic scholar who depended on his wife to provide a living for his large family, and Anzia's education consisted of what she could pick up between stints in immigrant sweatshops. Her public school experience was brief and unhappy, for in clearly defining the differences between herself and more prosperous children, it led to the lifelong sense of alienation that dominated her literary work.

Night classes in SETTLEMENT HOUSES were a better alternative, and by 1900, she had sufficient self-education that she was able to enter Teachers College of Columbia University, where financial aid requirements forced her to study HOME ECONOMICS. After graduation in 1904, Yezierska became a TEACHER of home economics—though she despised all aspects of domesticity and again was bitterly unhappy.

Meanwhile, she did what she had been born to do, pouring her emotions into stories. She was still unpublished, however, when she married briefly in 1910 and, more permanently, to a second man who fathered the daughter she bore in 1912. Keeping her MAIDEN NAME and taking her toddler along, she spent a year in Los Angeles with her sister, where she saw her first story published in 1915. She severed her marriage after returning to New York and continued to write, while also studying part-time at Columbia and teaching for a living. A 1919 story won a prize as the best short story of the year and changed her life. *Hungry Hearts* (1920), a collection of short stories, was her first book—published when she probably was forty.

Yezierska thus became quite famous in the 1920s. Critics ignored her true age and her long struggle for educational

Three West Coast women enlisting in the Navy during World War I as Yeomen (Female). Uniforms for women were chronically in short supply during both world wars, so these women wear Navy tops with their civilian skirts. NATIONAL ARCHIVES.

credentials and instead praised her as a seemingly spontaneous voice of the immigrant experience. Samuel Goldwin brought her to California to work on a movie version of *Hungry Hearts* that came out in 1922, but Yezierska was not seduced by the glamour of Hollywood. Despite the offer of good money, she understood that the New York immigrant world was essential to her literary life and soon returned there. She averaged a book every other year during the twenties, including *Salome of the Tenements* (1922), *The Bread Givers* (1925), and *Arrogant Beggar* (1927), all of which centered on the poor and the alienated who were forever outsiders. *All I Could Never Be* (1932) repeated this theme with a somewhat different twist; it drew from Yezierska's romantic involvement with famous Columbia philosopher John Dewey.

When immigration virtually ended during the Great Depression, Yezierska's ideas seemed less relevant. Indeed, her popularity fell so quickly during the thirties that she was reduced to working for the federal WPA's Writers' Project. Her final book, *Red Ribbon on a White Horse* (1950), came out almost two decades later and was her best autobiographical novel. Though Yezierska never published another book, she continued to write shorter pieces for the next nineteen years, publishing her last short story just a year before her death—when she was around ninety.

YOUNG WOMEN'S CHRISTIAN ASSOCIATION (YWCA)

Both the YWCA and its male counterpart, the Young Men's Christian Association (YMCA), originated among evangelical Protestants in London; the men's group began in 1844 and the women's equivalent in 1855. In America, the male organization began in 1851, but in this—as in so many aspects of change for women—the CIVIL WAR was the impetus for women's inclusion.

A number of women's groups, including the Ladies Christian Association of New York, undertook wartime missions to meet the needs of young women who were TRAVELING for the first time. NURSES and female family members of wounded soldiers or prisoners-of-war found themselves on trains, bound for cities where they knew no one. This was a totally new phenomenon in a nation where women—especially young and unmarried women—never ventured far from home without an escort. Because unaccompanied women were assumed to be PROSTITUTES whom no respectable hotel would accommodate, these missions developed in response to women's need for safe havens amid strangers.

After the war, the YWCA was formally organized in Boston in 1866, bringing together the disparate efforts that had existed in major cities since 1855. As the nation became increasingly urbanized during the postwar period, the YWCA soon became known for the dormitories it made available to young working women. The assumption behind such housing was that women could not expect to earn enough to live in apartments or hotels, and that hotels especially could be of dubious moral reputation. YWCA housing provided a place where young women could live under close supervision, and rural parents thus could allow unmarried daughters to go to cities in search of employment, assured that the young women would be safe while they settled into a new life.

In the early part of the twentieth century, the YWCA was particularly active in work to prevent young women from falling into WHITE SLAVERY; YWCA representatives met trains that brought rural women to the big cities, and they escorted IMMIGRANT WOMEN from Ellis Island to prospective homes and jobs. During WORLD WAR I, the YWCA cooperated with the military in enforcement of the CHAMBERLAIN-KAHN ACT to prevent sexually transmitted diseases, and in WORLD WAR II, its dormitories offered safe havens for young women traveling alone. More importantly, the YWCA set up recreation centers near the defense factories that employed large numbers of lonely women who were away from home for the first time.

The YWCA took longer to reach out to black women. In the South, the first units were organized within the structures of black colleges, with Spelman having the first in 1884; about a dozen similar groups were underway by 1909. The first of the standard urban YWCA models for black women began in Dayton, Ohio in 1893; it was followed by units in Philadelphia, Baltimore, Harlem, Brooklyn, and Washington. The New York and Philadelphia units were direct outgrowths of an earlier self-help model run by African-American women called the WHITE ROSE HOME. Most of black YWCA units had little or no contact with the white YWCA in their area, and blacks would continued to be segregated through World War II.

Because its operations were run almost entirely by women, the YWCA also was important in providing employment opportunities to women. The first paid black YWCA worker was Addie Hunton, who was hired in 1907; she would be followed by other minority women, such as CRYSTAL BIRD FAUSET, who found jobs with the YWCA that otherwise seldom would be open to them. Today the YWCA is not only integrated, but also nonsectarian. With international headquarters established in Geneva in 1894, it now has about 2.5 million members throughout the world.

YOUNG WOMEN'S HEBREW ASSOCIATION (YWHA)

Originally formed in 1888 as an AUXILIARY to the Young Men's Hebrew Association, the YWHA became an independent organization in 1902. Both groups were created as a reaction to the proselytizing of Christians among New York's immigrant Jews.

Missionary efforts of the YWCA, YMCA, and other similar groups often were so insensitive to the cultural heritage of Jews that the immigrant community understandably felt the need to provide services for their youth that could compete with those available at the YWCA and YMCA. The YWHA and YMHA emulated the Christian groups in offering recreational, educational, and spiritual leadership to Hebrew youth from many nations.

The two thus became the models for broader family services, and they were eventually absorbed into Jewish Community Centers. The records of the YWHA are on file at 1395 Lexington Avenue in New York.

ZAHARIAS, "BABE" DIDRIKSON (1911?/1914–1956)

Though christened Mildred Ella, Didrikson was called Babe from childhood because of her similarity to baseball great Babe Ruth. She is generally acknowledged as one of the most talented athletes of all time; so unique was her record in a variety of sports that Associated Press journalists voted to name her the outstanding woman athlete of the century—in 1949. Despite the seeming prematurity, no other woman has seriously challenged this standing.

Her mother was an IMMIGRANT WOMAN from Norway who had been a champion ice skater, and Babe inherited her athletic ability. Like other women concerned about age discrimination, she would modify her birthdate later in life, but Babe grew up in Texas, where—despite myths about Southern women—most girls played in school sports, especially basketball. After starring as an all-American high school basketball player, Didrikson went on to play for the basketball team organized by the insurance company where she worked. When she led this semiprofessional team to a national championship, it was obvious that Didrikson belonged in sports full time.

Athletics (and other entertainment) ironically prospered during the Great Depression, and in the nadir year of 1932, Didrikson became the happy object of world attention by winning five of the eight events she entered at the Amateur Athletic Union's track tournament. In the Olympic games of the same year, she entered three contests and won a Silver Medal and two Gold Medals. She turned professional after the Olympics, playing basketball and even baseball for

money—something that very few women were able to do. She also began playing golf that year, which eventually became her most important sport.

Didrikson endured hostility from women as well as from men when she entered the exclusive atmosphere of country clubs' golf courses, but by 1935, she was winning tournaments. A mixed tournament introduced her to George Zaharias, a Greek-American sportsman, and after their 1918 marriage, he devoted himself to promoting her career. WORLD WAR II, with its limitations on travel, interrupted the tournament touring life, but she had a spectacular year in 1947, when Babe Zaharias won seventeen consecutive gold championships.

The following year, she was the paramount founder of the Ladies Professional Golf Association. The LPGA has since become the most viable mechanism for women to benefit financially from their athletic skill, and Zaharias set the precedent by earning nearly a million dollars from golf. In addition, she won prizes for tennis and diving and was an outstanding bowler.

Babe Zaharias was the top woman in the athletic world when she was stricken with cancer in 1952; she recovered sufficiently after surgery to win national golf championships in 1953 and 1954. A second surgical procedure was less successful. Aware that she was dying, she wrote her autobiography, *This Life I've Led* in 1955 and died in Texas the following year. George Zaharias retired to Tampa, Florida, where a golf course is among many memorials to the incomparable Babe.

ZAKRZEWSKA, MARIE ELIZABETH (1829–1902)

Though her name was Polish, Marie Zakrzewska was born in Germany. Her mother's work as a Berlin MIDWIFE brought Marie to the attention of a male physician who mentored her and secured a TEACHING position for her in midwifery when she was just twenty-three. He soon died, however, and when she was forced to resign, she emigrated in 1853.

Like most other IMMIGRANT WOMEN, she found her status reduced in the new land with its language and cultural barriers. Again like others, Zakrzewska did HOME CONTRACT WORK in knitting until, a year after her arrival, she met Dr. ELIZABETH BLACKWELL. Blackwell helped her gain admission to Cleveland Medical College (Western Reserve), from which her sister, EMILY BLACKWELL, had graduated a few months earlier. After completing the two-year course, Zakrzewska returned to New York and joined the Blackwells in building the hospital and medical school for women that they envisioned.

Despite her newness to America, Zakrzewska proved an adept fund-raiser and traveled to Philadelphia and Boston seeking funding for their project. On one of these trips, she met people associated with the NEW ENGLAND FEMALE MEDICAL COLLEGE in Boston, and with the New York institution well underway by 1859, Zakrzewska moved to Boston to teach at this "college," which was more nearly a school of midwifery. Soon dissatisfied with the quality of medical education offered there, she led her Board of LADY MANAGERS in founding a new teaching hospital. The New England Hospital for Women and Children opened in 1862, and, despite competing funding needs because of the CIVIL WAR, it grew so rapidly that a new building was constructed a decade later. This building, named for Zakrzewska, still exists in the Roxbury section of Boston.

None of this was accomplished without daily battles against the prejudice surrounding women in medicine. Zakrzewska was so accomplished in overcoming prejudice, however, that she even graduated the first trained black nurse, MARY ELIZABETH MAHONEY, and offered an internship to Dr. Caroline Still, a pioneer black physician. Even more than the Blackwells,

Dr. Zakrzewska was particularly successful in achieving her aim of building a medical college for women that was superior to much of what was offered to male students at the time. Indeed, her establishment was eminent enough that after 1881, she could limit her resident students to women who had already earned an M.D. At the same time, she built a strong private practice that nonetheless was always inclusive of the poor.

Dr. Zakrzewska reduced her work load in 1887, but continued to serve as a consulting physician until age seventy. Always supportive of liberal causes, she was a founding member of the New England Woman's Club, which was one of the two original study clubs that served as models in the CLUB MOVEMENT. Dr. Marie Zakrzewska's approach to life is well summarized by the fact that she wrote a scholarly paper to be read at her funeral. The New England Hospital for Women and Children published a memoir of her life the following year.

ZONTA INTERNATIONAL

Founded in Buffalo in 1919, the Zonta Clubs took their name from a Sioux word meaning trustworthy. Its 1919 founding date was indicative of its close affiliation with internationalism, for it grew out of the movement for the League of Nations in that era and was aimed at providing opportunities for women worldwide.

Now associated with the United Nations, Zonta Clubs concentrate on raising funds to improve social services and educational opportunities, especially for women and girls. Among its primary achievements has been the funding of higher education for women and the building of recreational facilities for youth. In addition, local Zonta Clubs have contributed to projects such as homes for unwed mothers and, more recently, shelters for battered women.

Headquartered in Chicago, Zonta International has more than one thousand clubs located in fifty-nine countries. Over thirty-five thousand members call themselves Zontians.